Dictionary of Literary Biography

1. *The American Renaissance in New England*, edited by Joel Myerson (1978)
2. *American Novelists Since World War II*, edited by Jeffrey Helterman and Richard Layman (1978)
3. *Antebellum Writers in New York and the South*, edited by Joel Myerson (1979)
4. *American Writers in Paris, 1920-1939*, edited by Karen Lane Rood (1980)
5. *American Poets Since World War II*, 2 parts, edited by Donald J. Greiner (1980)
6. *American Novelists Since World War II, Second Series*, edited by James E. Kibler Jr. (1980)
7. *Twentieth-Century American Dramatists*, 2 parts, edited by John MacNicholas (1981)
8. *Twentieth-Century American Science-Fiction Writers*, 2 parts, edited by David Cowart and Thomas L. Wymer (1981)
9. *American Novelists, 1910-1945*, 3 parts, edited by James J. Martine (1981)
10. *Modern British Dramatists, 1900-1945*, 2 parts, edited by Stanley Weintraub (1982)
11. *American Humorists, 1800-1950*, 2 parts, edited by Stanley Trachtenberg (1982)
12. *American Realists and Naturalists*, edited by Donald Pizer and Earl N. Harbert (1982)
13. *British Dramatists Since World War II*, 2 parts, edited by Stanley Weintraub (1982)
14. *British Novelists Since 1960*, 2 parts, edited by Jay L. Halio (1983)
15. *British Novelists, 1930-1959*, 2 parts, edited by Bernard Oldsey (1983)
16. *The Beats: Literary Bohemians in Postwar America*, 2 parts, edited by Ann Charters (1983)
17. *Twentieth-Century American Historians*, edited by Clyde N. Wilson (1983)
18. *Victorian Novelists After 1885*, edited by Ira B. Nadel and William E. Fredeman (1983)
19. *British Poets, 1880-1914*, edited by Donald E. Stanford (1983)
20. *British Poets, 1914-1945*, edited by Donald E. Stanford (1983)
21. *Victorian Novelists Before 1885*, edited by Ira B. Nadel and William E. Fredeman (1983)
22. *American Writers for Children, 1900-1960*, edited by John Cech (1983)
23. *American Newspaper Journalists, 1873-1900*, edited by Perry J. Ashley (1983)
24. *American Colonial Writers, 1606-1734*, edited by Emory Elliott (1984)
25. *American Newspaper Journalists, 1901-1925*, edited by Perry J. Ashley (1984)
26. *American Screenwriters*, edited by Robert E. Morsberger, Stephen O. Lesser, and Randall Clark (1984)
27. *Poets of Great Britain and Ireland, 1945-1960*, edited by Vincent B. Sherry Jr. (1984)
28. *Twentieth-Century American-Jewish Fiction Writers*, edited by Daniel Walden (1984)
29. *American Newspaper Journalists, 1926-1950*, edited by Perry J. Ashley (1984)
30. *American Historians, 1607-1865*, edited by Clyde N. Wilson (1984)
31. *American Colonial Writers, 1735-1781*, edited by Emory Elliott (1984)
32. *Victorian Poets Before 1850*, edited by William E. Fredeman and Ira B. Nadel (1984)
33. *Afro-American Fiction Writers After 1955*, edited by Thadious M. Davis and Trudier Harris (1984)
34. *British Novelists, 1890-1929: Traditionalists*, edited by Thomas F. Staley (1985)
35. *Victorian Poets After 1850*, edited by William E. Fredeman and Ira B. Nadel (1985)
36. *British Novelists, 1890-1929: Modernists*, edited by Thomas F. Staley (1985)
37. *American Writers of the Early Republic*, edited by Emory Elliott (1985)
38. *Afro-American Writers After 1955: Dramatists and Prose Writers*, edited by Thadious M. Davis and Trudier Harris (1985)
39. *British Novelists, 1660-1800*, 2 parts, edited by Martin C. Battestin (1985)
40. *Poets of Great Britain and Ireland Since 1960*, 2 parts, edited by Vincent B. Sherry Jr. (1985)
41. *Afro-American Poets Since 1955*, edited by Trudier Harris and Thadious M. Davis (1985)
42. *American Writers for Children Before 1900*, edited by Glenn E. Estes (1985)
43. *American Newspaper Journalists, 1690-1872*, edited by Perry J. Ashley (1986)
44. *American Screenwriters, Second Series*, edited by Randall Clark, Robert E. Morsberger, and Stephen O. Lesser (1986)
45. *American Poets, 1880-1945, First Series*, edited by Peter Quartermain (1986)
46. *American Literary Publishing Houses, 1900-1980: Trade and Paperback*, edited by Peter Dzwonkoski (1986)
47. *American Historians, 1866-1912*, edited by Clyde N. Wilson (1986)
48. *American Poets, 1880-1945, Second Series*, edited by Peter Quartermain (1986)
49. *American Literary Publishing Houses, 1638-1899*, 2 parts, edited by Peter Dzwonkoski (1986)
50. *Afro-American Writers Before the Harlem Renaissance*, edited by Trudier Harris (1986)
51. *Afro-American Writers from the Harlem Renaissance to 1940*, edited by Trudier Harris (1987)
52. *American Writers for Children Since 1960: Fiction*, edited by Glenn E. Estes (1986)
53. *Canadian Writers Since 1960, First Series*, edited by W. H. New (1986)
54. *American Poets, 1880-1945, Third Series*, 2 parts, edited by Peter Quartermain (1987)
55. *Victorian Prose Writers Before 1867*, edited by William B. Thesing (1987)
56. *German Fiction Writers, 1914-1945*, edited by James Hardin (1987)
57. *Victorian Prose Writers After 1867*, edited by William B. Thesing (1987)
58. *Jacobean and Caroline Dramatists*, edited by Fredson Bowers (1987)
59. *American Literary Critics and Scholars, 1800-1850*, edited by John W. Rathbun and Monica M. Grecu (1987)
60. *Canadian Writers Since 1960, Second Series*, edited by W. H. New (1987)
61. *American Writers for Children Since 1960: Poets, Illustrators, and Nonfiction Authors*, edited by Glenn E. Estes (1987)
62. *Elizabethan Dramatists*, edited by Fredson Bowers (1987)
63. *Modern American Critics, 1920-1955*, edited by Gregory S. Jay (1988)
64. *American Literary Critics and Scholars, 1850-1880*, edited by John W. Rathbun and Monica M. Grecu (1988)
65. *French Novelists, 1900-1930*, edited by Catharine Savage Brosman (1988)
66. *German Fiction Writers, 1885-1913*, 2 parts, edited by James Hardin (1988)
67. *Modern American Critics Since 1955*, edited by Gregory S. Jay (1988)
68. *Canadian Writers, 1920-1959, First Series*, edited by W. H. New (1988)
69. *Contemporary German Fiction Writers, First Series*, edited by Wolfgang D. Elfe and James Hardin (1988)
70. *British Mystery Writers, 1860-1919*, edited by Bernard Benstock and Thomas F. Staley (1988)

71 *American Literary Critics and Scholars, 1880–1900,* edited by John W. Rathbun and Monica M. Grecu (1988)

72 *French Novelists, 1930–1960,* edited by Catharine Savage Brosman (1988)

73 *American Magazine Journalists, 1741–1850,* edited by Sam G. Riley (1988)

74 *American Short-Story Writers Before 1880,* edited by Bobby Ellen Kimbel, with the assistance of William E. Grant (1988)

75 *Contemporary German Fiction Writers, Second Series,* edited by Wolfgang D. Elfe and James Hardin (1988)

76 *Afro-American Writers, 1940–1955,* edited by Trudier Harris (1988)

77 *British Mystery Writers, 1920–1939,* edited by Bernard Benstock and Thomas F. Staley (1988)

78 *American Short-Story Writers, 1880–1910,* edited by Bobby Ellen Kimbel, with the assistance of William E. Grant (1988)

79 *American Magazine Journalists, 1850–1900,* edited by Sam G. Riley (1988)

80 *Restoration and Eighteenth-Century Dramatists, First Series,* edited by Paula R. Backscheider (1989)

81 *Austrian Fiction Writers, 1875–1913,* edited by James Hardin and Donald G. Daviau (1989)

82 *Chicano Writers, First Series,* edited by Francisco A. Lomelí and Carl R. Shirley (1989)

83 *French Novelists Since 1960,* edited by Catharine Savage Brosman (1989)

84 *Restoration and Eighteenth-Century Dramatists, Second Series,* edited by Paula R. Backscheider (1989)

85 *Austrian Fiction Writers After 1914,* edited by James Hardin and Donald G. Daviau (1989)

86 *American Short-Story Writers, 1910–1945, First Series,* edited by Bobby Ellen Kimbel (1989)

87 *British Mystery and Thriller Writers Since 1940, First Series,* edited by Bernard Benstock and Thomas F. Staley (1989)

88 *Canadian Writers, 1920–1959, Second Series,* edited by W. H. New (1989)

89 *Restoration and Eighteenth-Century Dramatists, Third Series,* edited by Paula R. Backscheider (1989)

90 *German Writers in the Age of Goethe, 1789–1832,* edited by James Hardin and Christoph E. Schweitzer (1989)

91 *American Magazine Journalists, 1900–1960, First Series,* edited by Sam G. Riley (1990)

92 *Canadian Writers, 1890–1920,* edited by W. H. New (1990)

93 *British Romantic Poets, 1789–1832, First Series,* edited by John R. Greenfield (1990)

94 *German Writers in the Age of Goethe: Sturm und Drang to Classicism,* edited by James Hardin and Christoph E. Schweitzer (1990)

95 *Eighteenth-Century British Poets, First Series,* edited by John Sitter (1990)

96 *British Romantic Poets, 1789–1832, Second Series,* edited by John R. Greenfield (1990)

97 *German Writers from the Enlightenment to Sturm und Drang, 1720–1764,* edited by James Hardin and Christoph E. Schweitzer (1990)

98 *Modern British Essayists, First Series,* edited by Robert Beum (1990)

99 *Canadian Writers Before 1890,* edited by W. H. New (1990)

100 *Modern British Essayists, Second Series,* edited by Robert Beum (1990)

101 *British Prose Writers, 1660–1800, First Series,* edited by Donald T. Siebert (1991)

102 *American Short-Story Writers, 1910–1945, Second Series,* edited by Bobby Ellen Kimbel (1991)

103 *American Literary Biographers, First Series,* edited by Steven Serafin (1991)

104 *British Prose Writers, 1660–1800, Second Series,* edited by Donald T. Siebert (1991)

105 *American Poets Since World War II, Second Series,* edited by R. S. Gwynn (1991)

106 *British Literary Publishing Houses, 1820–1880,* edited by Patricia J. Anderson and Jonathan Rose (1991)

107 *British Romantic Prose Writers, 1789–1832, First Series,* edited by John R. Greenfield (1991)

108 *Twentieth-Century Spanish Poets, First Series,* edited by Michael L. Perna (1991)

109 *Eighteenth-Century British Poets, Second Series,* edited by John Sitter (1991)

110 *British Romantic Prose Writers, 1789–1832, Second Series,* edited by John R. Greenfield (1991)

111 *American Literary Biographers, Second Series,* edited by Steven Serafin (1991)

112 *British Literary Publishing Houses, 1881–1965,* edited by Jonathan Rose and Patricia J. Anderson (1991)

113 *Modern Latin-American Fiction Writers, First Series,* edited by William Luis (1992)

114 *Twentieth-Century Italian Poets, First Series,* edited by Giovanna Wedel De Stasio, Glauco Cambon, and Antonio Illiano (1992)

115 *Medieval Philosophers,* edited by Jeremiah Hackett (1992)

116 *British Romantic Novelists, 1789–1832,* edited by Bradford K. Mudge (1992)

117 *Twentieth-Century Caribbean and Black African Writers, First Series,* edited by Bernth Lindfors and Reinhard Sander (1992)

118 *Twentieth-Century German Dramatists, 1889–1918,* edited by Wolfgang D. Elfe and James Hardin (1992)

119 *Nineteenth-Century French Fiction Writers: Romanticism and Realism, 1800–1860,* edited by Catharine Savage Brosman (1992)

120 *American Poets Since World War II, Third Series,* edited by R. S. Gwynn (1992)

121 *Seventeenth-Century British Nondramatic Poets, First Series,* edited by M. Thomas Hester (1992)

122 *Chicano Writers, Second Series,* edited by Francisco A. Lomelí and Carl R. Shirley (1992)

123 *Nineteenth-Century French Fiction Writers: Naturalism and Beyond, 1860–1900,* edited by Catharine Savage Brosman (1992)

124 *Twentieth-Century German Dramatists, 1919–1992,* edited by Wolfgang D. Elfe and James Hardin (1992)

125 *Twentieth-Century Caribbean and Black African Writers, Second Series,* edited by Bernth Lindfors and Reinhard Sander (1993)

126 *Seventeenth-Century British Nondramatic Poets, Second Series,* edited by M. Thomas Hester (1993)

127 *American Newspaper Publishers, 1950–1990,* edited by Perry J. Ashley (1993)

128 *Twentieth-Century Italian Poets, Second Series,* edited by Giovanna Wedel De Stasio, Glauco Cambon, and Antonio Illiano (1993)

129 *Nineteenth-Century German Writers, 1841–1900,* edited by James Hardin and Siegfried Mews (1993)

130 *American Short-Story Writers Since World War II,* edited by Patrick Meanor (1993)

131 *Seventeenth-Century British Nondramatic Poets, Third Series,* edited by M. Thomas Hester (1993)

132 *Sixteenth-Century British Nondramatic Writers, First Series,* edited by David A. Richardson (1993)

133 *Nineteenth-Century German Writers to 1840,* edited by James Hardin and Siegfried Mews (1993)

134 *Twentieth-Century Spanish Poets, Second Series,* edited by Jerry Phillips Winfield (1994)

135 *British Short-Fiction Writers, 1880–1914: The Realist Tradition,* edited by William B. Thesing (1994)

136 *Sixteenth-Century British Nondramatic Writers, Second Series,* edited by David A. Richardson (1994)

137 *American Magazine Journalists, 1900–1960, Second Series,* edited by Sam G. Riley (1994)

138 *German Writers and Works of the High Middle Ages: 1170–1280,* edited by James Hardin and Will Hasty (1994)

139 *British Short-Fiction Writers, 1945–1980,* edited by Dean Baldwin (1994)

140 *American Book-Collectors and Bibliographers, First Series,* edited by Joseph Rosenblum (1994)

141 *British Children's Writers, 1880–1914,* edited by Laura M. Zaidman (1994)

142 *Eighteenth-Century British Literary Biographers,* edited by Steven Serafin (1994)

143 *American Novelists Since World War II, Third Series,* edited by James R. Giles and Wanda H. Giles (1994)

144 *Nineteenth-Century British Literary Biographers,* edited by Steven Serafin (1994)

145 *Modern Latin-American Fiction Writers, Second Series,* edited by William Luis and Ann González (1994)

146 *Old and Middle English Literature,* edited by Jeffrey Helterman and Jerome Mitchell (1994)

147 *South Slavic Writers Before World War II,* edited by Vasa D. Mihailovich (1994)

148 *German Writers and Works of the Early Middle Ages: 800–1170,* edited by Will Hasty and James Hardin (1994)

149 *Late Nineteenth- and Early Twentieth-Century British Literary Biographers,* edited by Steven Serafin (1995)

150 *Early Modern Russian Writers, Late Seventeenth and Eighteenth Centuries,* edited by Marcus C. Levitt (1995)

151 *British Prose Writers of the Early Seventeenth Century,* edited by Clayton D. Lein (1995)

152 *American Novelists Since World War II, Fourth Series,* edited by James R. Giles and Wanda H. Giles (1995)

153 *Late-Victorian and Edwardian British Novelists, First Series,* edited by George M. Johnson (1995)

154 *The British Literary Book Trade, 1700–1820,* edited by James K. Bracken and Joel Silver (1995)

155 *Twentieth-Century British Literary Biographers,* edited by Steven Serafin (1995)

156 *British Short-Fiction Writers, 1880–1914: The Romantic Tradition,* edited by William F. Naufftus (1995)

157 *Twentieth-Century Caribbean and Black African Writers, Third Series,* edited by Bernth Lindfors and Reinhard Sander (1995)

158 *British Reform Writers, 1789–1832,* edited by Gary Kelly and Edd Applegate (1995)

159 *British Short-Fiction Writers, 1800–1880,* edited by John R. Greenfield (1996)

160 *British Children's Writers, 1914–1960,* edited by Donald R. Hettinga and Gary D. Schmidt (1996)

161 *British Children's Writers Since 1960, First Series,* edited by Caroline Hunt (1996)

162 *British Short-Fiction Writers, 1915–1945,* edited by John H. Rogers (1996)

163 *British Children's Writers, 1800–1880,* edited by Meena Khorana (1996)

164 *German Baroque Writers, 1580–1660,* edited by James Hardin (1996)

165 *American Poets Since World War II, Fourth Series,* edited by Joseph Conte (1996)

166 *British Travel Writers, 1837–1875,* edited by Barbara Brothers and Julia Gergits (1996)

167 *Sixteenth-Century British Nondramatic Writers, Third Series,* edited by David A. Richardson (1996)

168 *German Baroque Writers, 1661–1730,* edited by James Hardin (1996)

169 *American Poets Since World War II, Fifth Series,* edited by Joseph Conte (1996)

170 *The British Literary Book Trade, 1475–1700,* edited by James K. Bracken and Joel Silver (1996)

171 *Twentieth-Century American Sportswriters,* edited by Richard Orodenker (1996)

172 *Sixteenth-Century British Nondramatic Writers, Fourth Series,* edited by David A. Richardson (1996)

173 *American Novelists Since World War II, Fifth Series,* edited by James R. Giles and Wanda H. Giles (1996)

174 *British Travel Writers, 1876–1909,* edited by Barbara Brothers and Julia Gergits (1997)

175 *Native American Writers of the United States,* edited by Kenneth M. Roemer (1997)

176 *Ancient Greek Authors,* edited by Ward W. Briggs (1997)

177 *Italian Novelists Since World War II, 1945–1965,* edited by Augustus Pallotta (1997)

178 *British Fantasy and Science-Fiction Writers Before World War I,* edited by Darren Harris-Fain (1997)

179 *German Writers of the Renaissance and Reformation, 1280–1580,* edited by James Hardin and Max Reinhart (1997)

180 *Japanese Fiction Writers, 1868–1945,* edited by Van C. Gessel (1997)

181 *South Slavic Writers Since World War II,* edited by Vasa D. Mihailovich (1997)

182 *Japanese Fiction Writers Since World War II,* edited by Van C. Gessel (1997)

183 *American Travel Writers, 1776–1864,* edited by James J. Schramer and Donald Ross (1997)

184 *Nineteenth-Century British Book-Collectors and Bibliographers,* edited by William Baker and Kenneth Womack (1997)

185 *American Literary Journalists, 1945–1995, First Series,* edited by Arthur J. Kaul (1998)

186 *Nineteenth-Century American Western Writers,* edited by Robert L. Gale (1998)

187 *American Book Collectors and Bibliographers, Second Series,* edited by Joseph Rosenblum (1998)

188 *American Book and Magazine Illustrators to 1920,* edited by Steven E. Smith, Catherine A. Hastedt, and Donald H. Dyal (1998)

189 *American Travel Writers, 1850–1915,* edited by Donald Ross and James J. Schramer (1998)

190 *British Reform Writers, 1832–1914,* edited by Gary Kelly and Edd Applegate (1998)

191 *British Novelists Between the Wars,* edited by George M. Johnson (1998)

192 *French Dramatists, 1789–1914,* edited by Barbara T. Cooper (1998)

193 *American Poets Since World War II, Sixth Series,* edited by Joseph Conte (1998)

194 *British Novelists Since 1960, Second Series,* edited by Merritt Moseley (1998)

195 *British Travel Writers, 1910–1939,* edited by Barbara Brothers and Julia Gergits (1998)

196 *Italian Novelists Since World War II, 1965–1995,* edited by Augustus Pallotta (1999)

197 *Late-Victorian and Edwardian British Novelists, Second Series,* edited by George M. Johnson (1999)

198 *Russian Literature in the Age of Pushkin and Gogol: Prose,* edited by Christine A. Rydel (1999)

199 *Victorian Women Poets,* edited by William B. Thesing (1999)

200 *American Women Prose Writers to 1820,* edited by Carla J. Mulford, with Angela Vietto and Amy E. Winans (1999)

201 *Twentieth-Century British Book Collectors and Bibliographers,* edited by William Baker and Kenneth Womack (1999)

202 *Nineteenth-Century American Fiction Writers,* edited by Kent P. Ljungquist (1999)

203 *Medieval Japanese Writers,* edited by Steven D. Carter (1999)

204 *British Travel Writers, 1940–1997,* edited by Barbara Brothers and Julia M. Gergits (1999)

205 *Russian Literature in the Age of Pushkin and Gogol: Poetry and Drama,* edited by Christine A. Rydel (1999)

206 *Twentieth-Century American Western Writers, First Series,* edited by Richard H. Cracroft (1999)

207 *British Novelists Since 1960, Third Series,* edited by Merritt Moseley (1999)

208 *Literature of the French and Occitan Middle Ages: Eleventh to Fifteenth Centuries,* edited by Deborah Sinnreich-Levi and Ian S. Laurie (1999)

209 *Chicano Writers, Third Series,* edited by Francisco A. Lomelí and Carl R. Shirley (1999)

210 *Ernest Hemingway: A Documentary Volume,* edited by Robert W. Trogdon (1999)

211 *Ancient Roman Writers,* edited by Ward W. Briggs (1999)

212 *Twentieth-Century American Western Writers, Second Series*, edited by Richard H. Cracroft (1999)

213 *Pre-Nineteenth-Century British Book Collectors and Bibliographers*, edited by William Baker and Kenneth Womack (1999)

214 *Twentieth-Century Danish Writers*, edited by Marianne Stecher-Hansen (1999)

215 *Twentieth-Century Eastern European Writers, First Series*, edited by Steven Serafin (1999)

216 *British Poets of the Great War: Brooke, Rosenberg, Thomas. A Documentary Volume*, edited by Patrick Quinn (2000)

217 *Nineteenth-Century French Poets*, edited by Robert Beum (2000)

218 *American Short-Story Writers Since World War II, Second Series*, edited by Patrick Meanor and Gwen Crane (2000)

219 *F. Scott Fitzgerald's* The Great Gatsby: *A Documentary Volume*, edited by Matthew J. Bruccoli (2000)

220 *Twentieth-Century Eastern European Writers, Second Series*, edited by Steven Serafin (2000)

221 *American Women Prose Writers, 1870–1920*, edited by Sharon M. Harris, with the assistance of Heidi L. M. Jacobs and Jennifer Putzi (2000)

222 *H. L. Mencken: A Documentary Volume*, edited by Richard J. Schrader (2000)

223 *The American Renaissance in New England, Second Series*, edited by Wesley T. Mott (2000)

224 *Walt Whitman: A Documentary Volume*, edited by Joel Myerson (2000)

225 *South African Writers*, edited by Paul A. Scanlon (2000)

226 *American Hard-Boiled Crime Writers*, edited by George Parker Anderson and Julie B. Anderson (2000)

227 *American Novelists Since World War II, Sixth Series*, edited by James R. Giles and Wanda H. Giles (2000)

228 *Twentieth-Century American Dramatists, Second Series*, edited by Christopher J. Wheatley (2000)

229 *Thomas Wolfe: A Documentary Volume*, edited by Ted Mitchell (2001)

230 *Australian Literature, 1788–1914*, edited by Selina Samuels (2001)

231 *British Novelists Since 1960, Fourth Series*, edited by Merritt Moseley (2001)

232 *Twentieth-Century Eastern European Writers, Third Series*, edited by Steven Serafin (2001)

233 *British and Irish Dramatists Since World War II, Second Series*, edited by John Bull (2001)

234 *American Short-Story Writers Since World War II, Third Series*, edited by Patrick Meanor and Richard E. Lee (2001)

235 *The American Renaissance in New England, Third Series*, edited by Wesley T. Mott (2001)

236 *British Rhetoricians and Logicians, 1500–1660*, edited by Edward A. Malone (2001)

237 *The Beats: A Documentary Volume*, edited by Matt Theado (2001)

238 *Russian Novelists in the Age of Tolstoy and Dostoevsky*, edited by J. Alexander Ogden and Judith E. Kalb (2001)

239 *American Women Prose Writers: 1820–1870*, edited by Amy E. Hudock and Katharine Rodier (2001)

240 *Late Nineteenth- and Early Twentieth-Century British Women Poets*, edited by William B. Thesing (2001)

241 *American Sportswriters and Writers on Sport*, edited by Richard Orodenker (2001)

242 *Twentieth-Century European Cultural Theorists, First Series*, edited by Paul Hansom (2001)

243 *The American Renaissance in New England, Fourth Series*, edited by Wesley T. Mott (2001)

244 *American Short-Story Writers Since World War II, Fourth Series*, edited by Patrick Meanor and Joseph McNicholas (2001)

245 *British and Irish Dramatists Since World War II, Third Series*, edited by John Bull (2001)

246 *Twentieth-Century American Cultural Theorists*, edited by Paul Hansom (2001)

247 *James Joyce: A Documentary Volume*, edited by A. Nicholas Fargnoli (2001)

248 *Antebellum Writers in the South, Second Series*, edited by Kent Ljungquist (2001)

249 *Twentieth-Century American Dramatists, Third Series*, edited by Christopher Wheatley (2002)

250 *Antebellum Writers in New York, Second Series*, edited by Kent Ljungquist (2002)

251 *Canadian Fantasy and Science-Fiction Writers*, edited by Douglas Ivison (2002)

252 *British Philosophers, 1500–1799*, edited by Philip B. Dematteis and Peter S. Fosl (2002)

253 *Raymond Chandler: A Documentary Volume*, edited by Robert Moss (2002)

254 *The House of Putnam, 1837–1872: A Documentary Volume*, edited by Ezra Greenspan (2002)

255 *British Fantasy and Science-Fiction Writers, 1918–1960*, edited by Darren Harris-Fain (2002)

256 *Twentieth-Century American Western Writers, Third Series*, edited by Richard H. Cracroft (2002)

257 *Twentieth-Century Swedish Writers After World War II*, edited by Ann-Charlotte Gavel Adams (2002)

258 *Modern French Poets*, edited by Jean-François Leroux (2002)

259 *Twentieth-Century Swedish Writers Before World War II*, edited by Ann-Charlotte Gavel Adams (2002)

260 *Australian Writers, 1915–1950*, edited by Selina Samuels (2002)

261 *British Fantasy and Science-Fiction Writers Since 1960*, edited by Darren Harris-Fain (2002)

262 *British Philosophers, 1800–2000*, edited by Peter S. Fosl and Leemon B. McHenry (2002)

263 *William Shakespeare: A Documentary Volume*, edited by Catherine Loomis (2002)

264 *Italian Prose Writers, 1900–1945*, edited by Luca Somigli and Rocco Capozzi (2002)

265 *American Song Lyricists, 1920–1960*, edited by Philip Furia (2002)

266 *Twentieth-Century American Dramatists, Fourth Series*, edited by Christopher J. Wheatley (2002)

267 *Twenty-First-Century British and Irish Novelists*, edited by Michael R. Molino (2002)

268 *Seventeenth-Century French Writers*, edited by Françoise Jaouën (2002)

269 *Nathaniel Hawthorne: A Documentary Volume*, edited by Benjamin Franklin V (2002)

270 *American Philosophers Before 1950*, edited by Philip B. Dematteis and Leemon B. McHenry (2002)

271 *British and Irish Novelists Since 1960*, edited by Merritt Moseley (2002)

272 *Russian Prose Writers Between the World Wars*, edited by Christine Rydel (2003)

273 *F. Scott Fitzgerald's* Tender Is the Night: *A Documentary Volume*, edited by Matthew J. Bruccoli and George Parker Anderson (2003)

274 *John Dos Passos's* U.S.A.: *A Documentary Volume*, edited by Donald Pizer (2003)

275 *Twentieth-Century American Nature Writers: Prose*, edited by Roger Thompson and J. Scott Bryson (2003)

276 *British Mystery and Thriller Writers Since 1960*, edited by Gina Macdonald (2003)

277 *Russian Literature in the Age of Realism*, edited by Alyssa Dinega Gillespie (2003)

278 *American Novelists Since World War II, Seventh Series*, edited by James R. Giles and Wanda H. Giles (2003)

279 *American Philosophers, 1950–2000*, edited by Philip B. Dematteis and Leemon B. McHenry (2003)

280 *Dashiell Hammett's* The Maltese Falcon: *A Documentary Volume*, edited by Richard Layman (2003)

281 *British Rhetoricians and Logicians, 1500–1660, Second Series*, edited by Edward A. Malone (2003)

282 *New Formalist Poets*, edited by Jonathan N. Barron and Bruce Meyer (2003)

283 *Modern Spanish American Poets, First Series*, edited by María A. Salgado (2003)

284 *The House of Holt, 1866–1946: A Documentary Volume*, edited by Ellen D. Gilbert (2003)

285 *Russian Writers Since 1980,* edited by Marina Balina and Mark Lipoyvetsky (2004)

286 *Castilian Writers, 1400–1500,* edited by Frank A. Domínguez and George D. Greenia (2004)

287 *Portuguese Writers,* edited by Monica Rector and Fred M. Clark (2004)

288 *The House of Boni & Liveright, 1917–1933: A Documentary Volume,* edited by Charles Egleston (2004)

289 *Australian Writers, 1950–1975,* edited by Selina Samuels (2004)

290 *Modern Spanish American Poets, Second Series,* edited by María A. Salgado (2004)

291 *The Hoosier House: Bobbs-Merrill and Its Predecessors, 1850–1985: A Documentary Volume,* edited by Richard J. Schrader (2004)

292 *Twenty-First-Century American Novelists,* edited by Lisa Abney and Suzanne Disheroon-Green (2004)

293 *Icelandic Writers,* edited by Patrick J. Stevens (2004)

294 *James Gould Cozzens: A Documentary Volume,* edited by Matthew J. Bruccoli (2004)

295 *Russian Writers of the Silver Age, 1890–1925,* edited by Judith E. Kalb and J. Alexander Ogden with the collaboration of I. G. Vishnevetsky (2004)

296 *Twentieth-Century European Cultural Theorists, Second Series,* edited by Paul Hansom (2004)

297 *Twentieth-Century Norwegian Writers,* edited by Tanya Thresher (2004)

298 *Henry David Thoreau: A Documentary Volume,* edited by Richard J. Schneider (2004)

299 *Holocaust Novelists,* edited by Efraim Sicher (2004)

300 *Danish Writers from the Reformation to Decadence, 1550–1900,* edited by Marianne Stecher-Hansen (2004)

301 *Gustave Flaubert: A Documentary Volume,* edited by Éric Le Calvez (2004)

302 *Russian Prose Writers After World War II,* edited by Christine Rydel (2004)

303 *American Radical and Reform Writers, First Series,* edited by Steven Rosendale (2005)

304 *Bram Stoker's* Dracula: *A Documentary Volume,* edited by Elizabeth Miller (2005)

305 *Latin American Dramatists, First Series,* edited by Adam Versényi (2005)

306 *American Mystery and Detective Writers,* edited by George Parker Anderson (2005)

307 *Brazilian Writers,* edited by Monica Rector and Fred M. Clark (2005)

308 *Ernest Hemingway's* A Farewell to Arms: *A Documentary Volume,* edited by Charles Oliver (2005)

309 *John Steinbeck: A Documentary Volume,* edited by Luchen Li (2005)

310 *British and Irish Dramatists Since World War II, Fourth Series,* edited by John Bull (2005)

311 *Arabic Literary Culture, 500–925,* edited by Michael Cooperson and Shawkat M. Toorawa (2005)

312 *Asian American Writers,* edited by Deborah L. Madsen (2005)

313 *Writers of the French Enlightenment, I,* edited by Samia I. Spencer (2005)

314 *Writers of the French Enlightenment, II,* edited by Samia I. Spencer (2005)

315 *Langston Hughes: A Documentary Volume,* edited by Christopher C. De Santis (2005)

316 *American Prose Writers of World War I: A Documentary Volume,* edited by Steven Trout (2005)

317 *Twentieth-Century Russian Émigré Writers,* edited by Maria Rubins (2005)

318 *Sixteenth-Century Spanish Writers,* edited by Gregory B. Kaplan (2006)

319 *British and Irish Short-Fiction Writers 1945–2000,* edited by Cheryl Alexander Malcolm and David Malcolm (2006)

320 *Robert Penn Warren: A Documentary Volume,* edited by James A. Grimshaw Jr. (2006)

321 *Twentieth-Century French Dramatists,* edited by Mary Anne O'Neil (2006)

322 *Twentieth-Century Spanish Fiction Writers,* edited by Marta E. Altisent and Cristina Martínez-Carazo (2006)

323 *South Asian Writers in English,* edited by Fakrul Alam (2006)

324 *John O'Hara: A Documentary Volume,* edited by Matthew J. Bruccoli (2006)

325 *Australian Writers, 1975–2000,* edited by Selina Samuels (2006)

326 *Booker Prize Novels, 1969–2005,* edited by Merritt Moseley (2006)

327 *Sixteenth-Century French Writers,* edited by Megan Conway (2006)

328 *Chinese Fiction Writers, 1900–1949,* edited by Thomas Moran (2007)

329 *Nobel Prize Laureates in Literature, Part 1: Agnon–Eucken* (2007)

330 *Nobel Prize Laureates in Literature, Part 2: Faulkner–Kipling* (2007)

331 *Nobel Prize Laureates in Literature, Part 3: Lagerkvist–Pontoppidan* (2007)

332 *Nobel Prize Laureates in Literature, Part 4: Quasimodo–Yeats* (2007)

333 *Writers in Yiddish,* edited by Joseph Sherman (2007)

334 *Twenty-First-Century Canadian Writers,* edited by Christian Riegel (2007)

335 *American Short-Story Writers Since World War II, Fifth Series,* edited by Richard E. Lee and Patrick Meanor (2007)

336 *Eighteenth-Century British Historians,* edited by Ellen J. Jenkins (2007)

337 *Castilian Writers, 1200–1400,* edited by George D. Greenia and Frank A. Domínguez (2008)

338 *Thomas Carlyle: A Documentary Volume,* edited by Frances Frame (2008)

339 *Seventeenth-Century Italian Poets and Dramatists,* edited by Albert N. Mancini and Glenn Palen Pierce (2008)

Dictionary of Literary Biography Documentary Series

1 *Sherwood Anderson, Willa Cather, John Dos Passos, Theodore Dreiser, F. Scott Fitzgerald, Ernest Hemingway, Sinclair Lewis,* edited by Margaret A. Van Antwerp (1982)

2 *James Gould Cozzens, James T. Farrell, William Faulkner, John O'Hara, John Steinbeck, Thomas Wolfe, Richard Wright,* edited by Margaret A. Van Antwerp (1982)

3 *Saul Bellow, Jack Kerouac, Norman Mailer, Vladimir Nabokov, John Updike, Kurt Vonnegut,* edited by Mary Bruccoli (1983)

4 *Tennessee Williams,* edited by Margaret A. Van Antwerp and Sally Johns (1984)

5 *American Transcendentalists,* edited by Joel Myerson (1988)

6 *Hardboiled Mystery Writers: Raymond Chandler, Dashiell Hammett, Ross Macdonald,* edited by Matthew J. Bruccoli and Richard Layman (1989)

7 *Modern American Poets: James Dickey, Robert Frost, Marianne Moore,* edited by Karen L. Rood (1989)

8 *The Black Aesthetic Movement,* edited by Jeffrey Louis Decker (1991)

9 *American Writers of the Vietnam War: W. D. Ehrhart, Larry Heinemann, Tim O'Brien, Walter McDonald, John M. Del Vecchio,* edited by Ronald Baughman (1991)

10 *The Bloomsbury Group,* edited by Edward L. Bishop (1992)

11 *American Proletarian Culture: The Twenties and The Thirties,* edited by Jon Christian Suggs (1993)

12 *Southern Women Writers: Flannery O'Connor, Katherine Anne Porter, Eudora Welty,* edited by Mary Ann Wimsatt and Karen L. Rood (1994)

13 *The House of Scribner, 1846–1904,* edited by John Delaney (1996)

14 *Four Women Writers for Children, 1868–1918,* edited by Caroline C. Hunt (1996)

15 *American Expatriate Writers: Paris in the Twenties,* edited by Matthew J. Bruccoli and Robert W. Trogdon (1997)

16 *The House of Scribner, 1905–1930,* edited by John Delaney (1997)

17 *The House of Scribner, 1931–1984,* edited by John Delaney (1998)

18 *British Poets of The Great War: Sassoon, Graves, Owen,* edited by Patrick Quinn (1999)

19 *James Dickey,* edited by Judith S. Baughman (1999)

See also DLB 210, 216, 219, 222, 224, 229, 237, 247, 253, 254, 263, 269, 273, 274, 280, 284, 288, 291, 294, 298, 301, 304, 308, 309, 315, 316, 320, 324, 338

Dictionary of Literary Biography Yearbooks

1980 edited by Karen L. Rood, Jean W. Ross, and Richard Ziegfeld (1981)

1981 edited by Karen L. Rood, Jean W. Ross, and Richard Ziegfeld (1982)

1982 edited by Richard Ziegfeld; associate editors: Jean W. Ross and Lynne C. Zeigler (1983)

1983 edited by Mary Bruccoli and Jean W. Ross; associate editor Richard Ziegfeld (1984)

1984 edited by Jean W. Ross (1985)

1985 edited by Jean W. Ross (1986)

1986 edited by J. M. Brook (1987)

1987 edited by J. M. Brook (1988)

1988 edited by J. M. Brook (1989)

1989 edited by J. M. Brook (1990)

1990 edited by James W. Hipp (1991)

1991 edited by James W. Hipp (1992)

1992 edited by James W. Hipp (1993)

1993 edited by James W. Hipp, contributing editor George Garrett (1994)

1994 edited by James W. Hipp, contributing editor George Garrett (1995)

1995 edited by James W. Hipp, contributing editor George Garrett (1996)

1996 edited by Samuel W. Bruce and L. Kay Webster, contributing editor George Garrett (1997)

1997 edited by Matthew J. Bruccoli and George Garrett, with the assistance of L. Kay Webster (1998)

1998 edited by Matthew J. Bruccoli, contributing editor George Garrett, with the assistance of D. W. Thomas (1999)

1999 edited by Matthew J. Bruccoli, contributing editor George Garrett, with the assistance of D. W. Thomas (2000)

2000 edited by Matthew J. Bruccoli, contributing editor George Garrett, with the assistance of George Parker Anderson (2001)

2001 edited by Matthew J. Bruccoli, contributing editor George Garrett, with the assistance of George Parker Anderson (2002)

2002 edited by Matthew J. Bruccoli and George Garrett; George Parker Anderson, Assistant Editor (2003)

Concise Series

Concise Dictionary of American Literary Biography, 7 volumes (1988–1999): *The New Consciousness, 1941–1968; Colonization to the American Renaissance, 1640–1865; Realism, Naturalism, and Local Color, 1865–1917; The Twenties, 1917–1929; The Age of Maturity, 1929–1941; Broadening Views, 1968–1988; Supplement: Modern Writers, 1900–1998.*

Concise Dictionary of British Literary Biography, 8 volumes (1991–1992): *Writers of the Middle Ages and Renaissance Before 1660; Writers of the Restoration and Eighteenth Century, 1660–1789; Writers of the Romantic Period, 1789–1832; Victorian Writers, 1832–1890; Late-Victorian and Edwardian Writers, 1890–1914; Modern Writers, 1914–1945; Writers After World War II, 1945–1960; Contemporary Writers, 1960 to Present.*

Concise Dictionary of World Literary Biography, 4 volumes (1999–2000): *Ancient Greek and Roman Writers; German Writers; African, Caribbean, and Latin American Writers; South Slavic and Eastern European Writers.*

Dictionary of Literary Biography® • Volume Three Hundred Thirty-Nine

Seventeenth-Century Italian Poets and Dramatists

Dictionary of Literary Biography® • Volume Three Hundred Thirty-Nine

Seventeenth-Century Italian Poets and Dramatists

Edited by
Albert N. Mancini
Ohio State University
and
Glenn Palen Pierce
University of Missouri

A Bruccoli Clark Layman Book

GALE
CENGAGE Learning

Detroit • New York • San Francisco • New Haven, Conn • Waterville, Maine • London

ST. PHILIP'S COLLEGE LIBRARY

GALE
CENGAGE Learning

Dictionary of Literary Biography, Volume 339: Seventeenth-Century Italian Poets and Dramatists
Albert N. Mancini and Glenn Palen Pierce

Advisory Board: John Baker, William Cagle, Patrick O'Connor, George Garrett, Trudier Harris, Alvin Kernan

Editorial Directors: Matthew J. Bruccoli and Richard Layman

@ 2008 Gale, Cengage Learning

ALL RIGHTS RESERVED. No part of this work covered by the copyright herein may be reproduced, transmitted, stored, or used in any form or by any means graphic, electronic, or mechanical, including but not limited to photocopying, recording, scanning, digitizing, taping, Web distribution, information networks, or information storage and retrieval systems, except as permitted under Section 107 or 108 of the 1976 United States Copyright Act, without the prior written permission of the publisher.

This publication is a creative work fully protected by all applicable copyright laws, as well as by misappropriation, trade secret, unfair competition, and other applicable laws. The authors and editors of this work have added value to the underlying factual material herein through one or more of the following: unique and original selection, coordination, expression, arrangement, and classification of the information.

For product information and technology assistance, contact us at
Gale Customer Support, 1-800-877-4253.

For permission to use material from this text or product, submit all requests online at **www.cengage.com/permissions**
Further permissions questions can be emailed to
permissionrequest@cengage.com

While every effort has been made to ensure the reliability of the information presented in this publication, Gale, a part of Cengage Learning, does not guarantee the accuracy of the data contained herein. Gale accepts no payment for listing; and inclusion in the publication of any organization, agency, institution, publication, service, or individual does not imply endorsement of the editors or publisher. Errors brought to the attention of the publisher and verified to the satisfaction of the publisher will be corrected in future editions.

EDITORIAL DATE PRIVACY POLICY. Does this publication contain information about you as an individual? If so, for more information about our editorial date privacy policies, please see our Privacy Statement at www.gale.cengage.com

---

LIBRARY OF CONGRESS CATALOGING-IN-PUBLICATION DATA

Seventeenth-century Italian poets and dramatists / edited by Albert N. Mancini and Glenn Palen Pierce.
　p. cm. — (Dictionary of literary biography ; v. 339)
"A Bruccoli Clark Layman book."
Includes bibliographical references and index.
ISBN 978-0-7876-8157-9 (hardcover)
　1. Italian literature—17th century—Dictionaries. 2. Italian literature—17th century—Bio-bibliography—Dictionaries. 3. Authors, Italian—17th century—Biography—Dictionaries. I. Mancini, Albert N. II. Pierce, Glenn Palen.

PQ4082.S484 2008
850.9'00503—dc22
[B]　　　　　　　　　　　　　　　　　　2008003051

ISBN-13: 978-0-7876-8157-9　　　ISBN-10: 0-7876-8157-1

Gale
27500 Drake Rd.
Farmington Hills, MI 48331-3535

Printed in the United States of America
1 2 3 4 5 6 7 12 11 10 09 08

Contents

Plan of the Series xiii
Introduction xv

Claudio Achillini (1574–1640) 3
   Paschal C. Viglionese

Francesco Andreini (before 1548?–1624) 9
   Francesca Savoia

Giovan Battista Andreini (1576–1654) 16
   Francesca Savoia

Isabella Andreini (1562?–1604) 28
   Francesca Savoia

Giuseppe Artale (1628–1679) 36
   Paschal C. Viglionese

Nicolò Barbieri (1576–1641) 41
   Glenn Palen Pierce

Virginia Bazzani Cavazzoni (1669–1720?) 45
   Natalia Costa-Zalessow

Guidubaldo Bonarelli (1563–1608) 50
   Nicolas J. Perella

Francesco Bracciolini (1566–1645) 55
   Laura Benedetti

Michelangelo Buonarroti *il Giovane*
  (1568–1646) 65
   Olimpia Pelosi

Gian Francesco Busenello (1598–1659) 73
   Franco Fido

Gabriello Chiabrera (1552–1638) 82
   Paolo A. Giordano

Giovanni Battista Ciampoli (1590–1643) 94
   Mauda Bregoli-Russo

Giacinto Andrea Cicognini (1606–1649) 100
   Nancy L. D'Antuono

Giulio Cesare Cortese (circa 1570–1626?) 106
   Edoardo A. Lèbano

Margherita Costa (1600/1610?–1657) 113
   Natalia Costa-Zalessow

Francesco De Lemene (1634–1704) 119
   Glenn Palen Pierce

Giovanni Delfino (1617–1699) 123
   Salvatore Bancheri

Federico Della Valle (circa 1560–1628) 128
   Laura Sanguineti White

Carlo de' Dottori (1618–1686) 135
   Laura Sanguineti White

Isabella Farnese (Suor Francesca di Gesù Maria)
  (1593–1651) 142
   Rita Cavigioli

Vincenzo da Filicaia (1642–1707) 147
   Paul Colilli

Silvio Fiorillo (1560 or 1565?–1634?) 152
   Mary Jo Muratore

Battista Guarini (1538–1612) 157
   Nicolas J. Perella

Giacomo Lubrano (1619–1692 or 1693) 169
   Elisabetta Properzi Nelsen

Carlo Maria Maggi (1630–1699) 175
   Glenn Palen Pierce

Lucrezia Marinella (1571?–1653) 182
   Laura Benedetti

Giambattista Marino (1569–1625) 191
   Francesco Guardiani

Benedetto Menzini (1646–1704) 204
   Olimpia Pelosi

Andrea Perrucci (1651–1704) 210
   Salvatore Cappelletti

Ciro di Pers (1599–1663) 216
   Paschal C. Viglionese

Girolamo Preti (1582–1626) 220
   Paschal C. Viglionese

Ottavio Rinuccini (1562–1621) 225
   Maria Galli Stampino

Contents

Giulio Rospigliosi (Pope Clement IX)
(1600–1669) 232
Maria Galli Stampino

Margherita Sarrocchi (1560–1617) 238
Natalia Costa-Zalessow

Flaminio Scala (Flavio) (1552–1624) 244
Salvatore Cappelletti

Sara Copio Sullam (circa 1592–1641) 250
Lori J. Ultsch

Alessandro Tassoni (1565–1635) 255
Laura Benedetti

Fulvio Testi (1593–1646) 264
Adrienne Ward

Francesca Turini Bufalini (1553–1641) 271
Natalia Costa-Zalessow

Appendix 1: The Arcadian Academy 279
Paul Colilli

Appendix 2: Poetry and Music
in Seventeenth-Century Italy 286
Maria Galli Stampino

Appendix 3: Theater and Spectacle 294
Glenn Palen Pierce

Checklist of Further Readings 303
Contributors 307
Cumulative Index 311

Plan of the Series

... Almost the most prodigious asset of a country, and perhaps its most precious possession, is its native literary product—when that product is fine and noble and enduring.

Mark Twain*

The advisory board, the editors, and the publisher of the *Dictionary of Literary Biography* are joined in endorsing Mark Twain's declaration. The literature of a nation provides an inexhaustible resource of permanent worth. Our purpose is to make literature and its creators better understood and more accessible to students and the reading public, while satisfying the needs of teachers and researchers.

To meet these requirements, *literary biography* has been construed in terms of the author's achievement. The most important thing about a writer is his writing. Accordingly, the entries in *DLB* are career biographies, tracing the development of the author's canon and the evolution of his reputation.

The purpose of *DLB* is not only to provide reliable information in a usable format but also to place the figures in the larger perspective of literary history and to offer appraisals of their accomplishments by qualified scholars.

The publication plan for *DLB* resulted from two years of preparation. The project was proposed to Bruccoli Clark by Frederick G. Ruffner, president of the Gale Research Company, in November 1975. After specimen entries were prepared and typeset, an advisory board was formed to refine the entry format and develop the series rationale. In meetings held during 1976, the publisher, series editors, and advisory board approved the scheme for a comprehensive biographical dictionary of persons who contributed to literature. Editorial work on the first volume began in January 1977, and it was published in 1978. In order to make *DLB* more than a dictionary and to compile volumes that individually have claim to status as literary history, it was decided to organize volumes by topic, period, or genre. Each of these freestanding volumes provides a biographical-bibliographical guide and overview for a particular area of literature. We are convinced that this organization—as opposed to a single alphabet method—constitutes a valuable innovation in the presentation of reference material. The volume plan necessarily requires many decisions for the placement and treatment of authors. Certain figures will be included in separate volumes, but with different entries emphasizing the aspect of his career appropriate to each volume. Ernest Hemingway, for example, is represented in *American Writers in Paris, 1920–1939* by an entry focusing on his expatriate apprenticeship; he is also in *American Novelists, 1910–1945* with an entry surveying his entire career, as well as in *American Short-Story Writers, 1910–1945, Second Series* with an entry concentrating on his short fiction. Each volume includes a cumulative index of the subject authors and articles.

Between 1981 and 2002 the series was augmented and updated by the *DLB Yearbooks*. There have also been nineteen *DLB Documentary Series* volumes, which provide illustrations, facsimiles, and biographical and critical source materials for figures, works, or groups judged to have particular interest for students. In 1999 the *Documentary Series* was incorporated into the *DLB* volume numbering system beginning with *DLB 210: Ernest Hemingway*.

We define literature as the *intellectual commerce of a nation:* not merely as belles lettres but as that ample and complex process by which ideas are generated, shaped, and transmitted. *DLB* entries are not limited to "creative writers" but extend to other figures who in their time and in their way influenced the mind of a people. Thus the series encompasses historians, journalists, publishers, book collectors, and screenwriters. By this means readers of *DLB* may be aided to perceive literature not as cult scripture in the keeping of intellectual high priests but firmly positioned at the center of a nation's life.

DLB includes the major writers appropriate to each volume and those standing in the ranks behind them. Scholarly and critical counsel has been sought in deciding which minor figures to include and how full their entries should be. Wherever possible, useful refer-

*From an unpublished section of Mark Twain's autobiography, copyright by the Mark Twain Company

ences are made to figures who do not warrant separate entries.

Each *DLB* volume has an expert volume editor responsible for planning the volume, selecting the figures for inclusion, and assigning the entries. Volume editors are also responsible for preparing, where appropriate, appendices surveying the major periodicals and literary and intellectual movements for their volumes, as well as lists of further readings. Work on the series as a whole is coordinated at the Bruccoli Clark Layman editorial center in Columbia, South Carolina, where the editorial staff is responsible for accuracy and utility of the published volumes.

One feature that distinguishes *DLB* is the illustration policy–its concern with the iconography of literature. Just as an author is influenced by his surroundings, so is the reader's understanding of the author enhanced by a knowledge of his environment. Therefore *DLB* volumes include not only drawings, paintings, and photographs of authors, often depicting them at various stages in their careers, but also illustrations of their families and places where they lived. Title pages are regularly reproduced in facsimile along with dust jackets for modern authors. The dust jackets are a special feature of *DLB* because they often document better than anything else the way in which an author's work was perceived in its own time. Specimens of the writers' manuscripts and letters are included when feasible.

Samuel Johnson rightly decreed that "The chief glory of every people arises from its authors." The purpose of the *Dictionary of Literary Biography* is to compile literary history in the surest way available to us–by accurate and comprehensive treatment of the lives and work of those who contributed to it.

The *DLB* Advisory Board

Introduction

This volume of the *Dictionary of Literary Biography* deals with poets and dramatists of the seicento, the seventeenth-century period in Italian literature and art. The dominant style of literature in this period is designated in Italian historiography by the term *Baroque,* rather than the broader and amorphous "early modern" that is common in Anglophone scholarship. Andrea Battistini describes the traits of the Baroque style as theatrical, spectacular, emotional, profuse, lascivious, flamboyant, and popular. In literature the Baroque movement was a challenge to the neo-Aristotelian aesthetics of the Renaissance and to notions of decorum and morality in art; it was prominent from around 1580 to 1680.

Used since the Middle Ages by jewelers to describe an irregularly shaped pearl and by Scholastic philosolphers to designate a type of specious reasoning, the word *baroque* (from the Portuguese *barrocco*) was introduced into the vocabulary of criticism by classically minded eighteenth-century art critics who used it contemptuously for whatever they considered irregular, exaggerated, or bizarre in the works of seventeenth-century Italian artists. The traditional view of the seicento held that by the middle of the sixteenth century the humanist quest to bring the classical past back to life had exhausted its vitality under the vigilance of the Roman Catholic Inquisition and the edicts of the Council of Trent of 1545 to 1563, and that Spanish domination, the contraction of international trade, and demographic decline had deprived Italy of its cultural leadership in Europe. This bleak view of a political, social, and moral decline enveloping the peninsula was asserted by eighteenth-century literary critics such as Giovan Mario Crescimbeni and Ludovico Antonio Muratori and repeated by the nationalist mid-nineteenth-century Italian literary historians Luigi Settembrini and Francesco De Sanctis. While the preeminence of seventeenth-century Italian art and music is a matter of common acceptance, the literary term *secentismo,* a derivative of *seicento,* retains pejorative connotations that reflect the negative attitude toward seventeenth-century letters. The problem with this view is that it risks ignoring one of the most intriguing periods in modern Italy's literary and cultural history. John L. Lievsay points out that the majority of English translations from Italian between 1575 and 1625 were of contemporary works rather than from the canon of "classic" Italian writers of the Renaissance.

During the first quarter of the twentieth century researchers unearthed a wealth of new material from the period, but it served mainly to uphold the presuppositions of aesthetic corruption and moral decay of the age. The 1930s and 1940s, however, brought a surge of interest in Baroque poetry, and the assumptions that had prevented scholars from approaching the subject in a receptive frame of mind gave way to a more appreciative attitude. For the historian and literary scholar Benedetto Croce, the Baroque was a period characterized by the use of certain rhetorical strategies and modes of expression and the occurrence of new contents and ideas. Giovanni Getto, one of the most influential mid-twentieth-century Italian seicento scholars, argued that the Baroque was not only an artistic and literary movement but also a way of perceiving reality that he labeled "perspective pluralism" or "multiple perspectivism." Baroque poets, Getto pointed out, broke stylistic and thematic limits in search of new ways to express allegories of the ephemeral quality of reality and the ambivalence of human knowledge.

While this phase of seicento scholarship was characterized by theoretical discussions of the origins and traits of the Baroque style and by studies of large numbers of works and authors, the second half of the twentieth century brought a disenchantment with abstract debates and stylistic readings of well-known texts. The preference for empirical research, closer investigations of individual writers, and exploration of neglected or still unexplored areas of the seventeenth-century literary corpus were the guiding forces behind the founding in 1959 of *Studi secenteschi,* the first scholarly journal devoted to Italian literature of the period. Current interest is not so much in the familiar names as in the social context they inhabited and in less-well-known writers. This perspective has yielded critical editions, bibliographies, biographies, and studies that have made seventeenth-century Italian literary culture more accessible to researchers and readers. Thanks to the labors of three generations of scholars, the seicento has come to be regarded as an essential chapter in the long annals of Italian literature, worthy of being studied rather than abused; as a literary period that had its own standards and conventions; and whose rise, spread, and decline can be traced, as it has been in several literary histories published in Italy since the 1970s. The seicento has a particular resonance in the postmodern critical climate: students of seventeenth-century Italian culture contend that the two periods share a sense of epistemological instability, a distrust of universal and absolute truths, and a search for alternative accounts of scientific knowledge. In English-speaking countries the commedia dell'arte, pastoral drama, tragicomedy, opera, the poetry of Giambattista Marino, and women writers are the areas in which literary critics are producing the most valuable work.

After the Treaty of Cateau Cambrésis in 1559, all of the Italian states except Venice and the Duchy of Savoy were under Spanish influence. Spain's direct possessions included the Duchy of Milan and the Kingdoms of Naples, Sicily, and Sardinia; Florence, the Republic of Genoa, and the Papal States had close ties with the Spanish Crown. The Duchy of Mantua, ruled by the Gonzaga dynasty, played a minor role on the international scene when Duke Carlo Emanuele I of Savoy invaded the neighboring Duchy of Monferrat, a possession of the Gonzagas, and again when the death of the last Gonzaga ruler provoked the War of the Mantuan Succession of 1627 to 1631. To protect their national interests, France, Spain, and the Holy Roman Emperor sent forces to fight in both of these regional conflicts. Venice became involved in a series of long and costly conflicts with the Ottoman Empire and was forced to yield Cyprus and its military and commercial outpost of Crete. In central Italy the papacy, which had annexed Ferrara in 1597, incorporated the Duchy of Urbino in 1631; but Pope Urban VIII's ill-advised attempt between 1641 and 1644 to acquire the small Duchy of Castro failed. The Grand Duchy of Tuscany continued under the rule of the Medicis, but Florence declined in political importance. Anti-Spanish popular uprisings in Sicily and Naples in 1647–1648 weakened Spain's military power in Italy. The Peace of Westphalia, which ended the Thirty Years' War in 1648, brought tranquility to the peninsula. In the latter part of the century, however, the northern Italian states became a battleground for the expansionist ambitions of the French Crown and the Holy Roman Empire.

The dominant political structure in Italy was the territorial state system, in which princely courts served as administrative, economic, and cultural centers. The courts were expected to provide costly entertainments for courtiers and foreign guests and to secure for that purpose the services of the best available writers, composers, artists, actors, and singers. Opera began in Florence, Rome, and Mantua as a court entertainment to commemorate special events such as royal visits and coronations. The poet Gabriello Chiabrera enjoyed the patronage of Pope Urban VIII and the dukes of Mantua and Savoy and was granted the title *Gentiluomo di Camera* (Gentleman of the Chamber) by Grand Duke Cosimo II de' Medici, who awarded him a pension that enabled him to retire to a life of writing in his native Savona. In his allegorical poem *L'elettione di Urbano Papa VIII* (1628, The Election of Pope Urban VIII) Francesco Bracciolini devotes seven cantos to the origins and merits of his patrons, the Florentine Barberini family. Marino, the most influential seicento poet, was knighted in the prestigious Order of Saints Maurice and Lazarus by Carlo Emanuele I of Savoy.

The most vital cultural institutions for the production and appreciation of literary works in the seventeenth century, however, were not the courts but the urban academies. Many such societies had been established during the Renaissance, including the Accademia degli Infiammati (Academy of the Inflamed) in Padua, the Accademia degli Svegliati (Academy of the Awakened) in Naples, the Accademia degli Intrepidi (Academy of the Fearless) in Ferrara, the Accademia dei Gelati (Academy of the Frozen) in Bologna, and the Accademia Fiorentina (Florentine Academy). Some continued into the seventeenth century under their original names, but their activities reflected the new demands of the cultural and intellectual climate of the age and the needs of a more professionally diverse membership. From a literary perspective, by far the most important of these societies was the Florentine Accademia della Crusca (Academy of the Sifters), founded in 1582, which engaged in projects for the dissemination and improvement of the Tuscan language. The major accomplishment of this prestigious linguistic society, which provided a model for similar institutions throughout western Europe, was the compilation of its *Vocabolario* (Vocabulary), first published in 1612.

The seventeenth century brought a rapid proliferation of academies: more than eight hundred were founded in more than two hundred cities. The Accademia degli Incogniti (Academy of the Unknown), founded in Venice in 1631 by the politician and patron Giovan Francesco Loredano, was dedicated principally to the promotion of the new genres of the novel and libretto and the publication of the often prohibited works of its members. Societies dedicated to scientific pursuits included the Accademia dei Lincei (Academy of the Lynx-Eyed), founded in Rome in 1603 and still active today, and the short-lived Accademia del Cimento (Cimento Academy), patronized by the Medicis of Florence and extant from 1657 to 1667.

The Accademia degli Arcadi (Arcadian Academy) was founded in 1690 to continue the activities of a group of intellectuals who had met in the Roman salon of Christina, the former queen of Sweden, after her death in 1689. The Arcadians led the reaction against what they considered the moral and aesthetic corruption of Italian letters caused by the dominant Baroque poetic style of Marino and his followers and advocated the restoration of a more sober form of literary expression. The Arcadia quickly became a national institution as branches, or "colonies," were formed in hundreds of other Italian cities. While most of the original members were poets and literary theorists, the membership eventually consisted of artists, musicians, actors, scientists, court dignitaries, and princes. This expansion was consistent with the civic program and social commitment envisioned in the rules of the academy laid down by its founding fathers, the poet and historian Crescimbeni and the poet and lawyer Gian Vincenzo Gravina. The first learned journals in Italy appeared near the end of the century: the *Giornale dei letterati* (Literati's Journal) was established in Rome in 1688, and the *Galleria di Minerva* (Minerva's Gallery), was founded in Venice in 1695.

The Neapolitan Marino is hailed as the greatest poet of the century not only in Italy but in all of Europe. Two critical directions may be discerned in scholarship on his oeuvre: one focuses on his early collection *Rime* (1602, Rhymes) and the substantial lyric corpus *Lira* (1614, Lyre); the other concentrates on his major work, the narrative poem *L'Adone* (1623; excerpts translated as *Adonis: Selections from L'Adone of Giambattista Marino*, 1967). The third part of *Lira* reveals the emergence of the highly mannered style, characterized by auditory smoothness, sensuous imagery, sustained metaphors, and lush vocabulary, that was labeled *Marinism*. In the 41,000-word *L'Adone*, written over a period of thirty years with the aim of surpassing all other poems, Marino launches an attack on the noblest of classical literary genres, the epic. Ignoring the requirements of the well-made poem of Renaissance Aristotelian literary theory—recognizable characters, expert plotting, and linear narrative—Marino brings into his "poema reale" (royal poem) chivalric and Byzantine romance, epic, the picaresque, the tale within the tale, the pastoral, and the love story. Through these clashing styles, which are often treated in a spirit of parody, and multitudinous descriptive digressions and lengthy allusions to contemporary life Marino proposes a new way of writing and reading: into an era of dogmatic certitude he introduces a universe in which everything is relative. Modern critics recognize that Marino's style is not simply ornamental but creative of a new order.

No Italian writers showed more enthusiasm for Marino's poetics than some members of the Accademia degli Incogniti. In 1624 the poet Gian Francesco Busenello wrote "La Stiglianeide" (1910), comprising a letter in praise of *L'Adone* and a collection of sonnets defending Marino against his rival Tommaso Stigliani, and Giovan Francesco Loredano published a laudatory biography of the Neapolitan poet in 1633. Immediately after its publication, *L'Adone* became the subject of a heated literary debate provoked by a favorable comparison of it with Torquato Tasso's masterpiece *Gerusalemme liberata* (1581, Jerusalem Delivered; translated as *Godfrey of Bulloigne, or The Recoverie of Hierusalem*, 1594). Though it was placed on the Catholic Church's Index of Prohibited Books in 1624, it went through at least six more editions during the seicento.

The Marinists have often been seen as mere imitators of Marino's poetics of *meraviglia* (wonder, the marvelous, and surprise); but the more-talented and ambitious ones tried to distance themselves from the master. Marino might be the only true Marinist of the Baroque Age, and even he is not one in all of his works. The common misunderstanding of the Marinists' achievements was caused in part by the circumstances of the reception of their works: twentieth-century readers were introduced to post-Renaissance poetry by such anthologies as Benedetto Croce's *Lirici marinisti* (1910, Marinist Lyrics), Carlo Calcaterra's *I lirici del Seicento e dell'Arcadia* (1936, The Lyrics of the Seicento and of Arcadia), Giuseppe Guido Ferrero's *Marino e i marinisti* (1954, Marino and the Marinists), Getto's *Opere scelte di Marino e i marinisti* (1962, Selected Works of Marino and the Marinists), and Carlo Muscetta and Pier Paolo Ferrante's *Poesia del Seicento* (1964, Poetry of the Seicento). Consequently, awareness of Marinist poetry was limited to a few texts that addressed the themes and used the devices the editors considered representative of the school. More-recent scholarship has replaced the sweeping generalizations and short selections appropriate to anthologies with more-accurate assessments of individual works, the contexts in which they were produced, and the characteristics of the poets.

In the early 1620s a group of Roman poets and literary theorists, reacting to the purported lascivious nature of the Marinistic vogue, began to promote a restoration of lyric poetry in Italian and Latin to what they maintained had been its original moral and civilizing function. The most prominent of these men were Maffeo Barberini, who became Pope Urban VIII in 1623; Giovanni Ciampoli, secretary of papal briefs from about 1620 to 1632; Virginio Cesarini, a philosopher and poet and member of the Accademia dei Lincei; and the theorist of the group, Pietro Sforza Pallavicino. Much more influential was Chiabrera, who enjoyed as much popularity in Italy as his contemporary Marino. Under the influence of the late-sixteenth-century French Pléiade poets Chiabrera turned to ancient Greek poetry, particularly the works of Anacreon and Pindar, as models for his canzonets and odes, and he never renounced the Petrarchan tradition. The Arcadians claimed him as a forerunner of their battle for a return to "good taste" in Italian poetry. Getto points out that Chiabrera adopted metrical and strophic innovations that required less risk than Marino's but, at the same time, placed greater demands on the writer's ingenuity. Chiabrera's canzonets appealed to contemporary musicians; his magniloquent Pindaric odes, many of which were written in praise of rulers and other important figures, influenced writers who at first practiced the Marinistic style but later challenged it. Notable among the latter are Fulvio Testi and Vincenzo da Filicaia, both of whom reacted to the alleged moral and aesthetic bankruptcy of Marinism by turning toward political and patriotic themes. Chiabrera bequeathed to posterity not only several influential collections of lyric poetry but also epic poems, Horatian satires, librettos, plays, an autobiography, and letters. Whether Chiabrera can accurately be characterized as a Baroque poet is an issue that still exercises scholars.

While epic poetry was welcomed and patronized by absolutist regimes throughout the seicento, the most popular long verse narratives were mock-heroic and burlesque poems that offered the authors greater freedom for innovation. The most eminent poem of the century after Marino's *L'Adone* is Alessandro Tassoni's *La secchia rapita* (1624, The Stolen Bucket; translated as *The Trophy-Bucket: A Mock-Heroic Poem, the First of the Kind*, 1710). The subject of the poem is a petty mid-thirteenth-century war between the Guelphs of Bologna and the Ghibellines of neighboring Modena caused by the theft of a wooden bucket; lowborn citizens of the two cities act in the guise of epic heroes, and the gods are degraded to the level of human beings at their least heavenly. Modern critical readings of the poem contest earlier assessments of it as an interesting but inconsequential comic invention inspired by personal pique, patriotism, or an intent to parody the outmoded literary conventions of the Renaissance epic. Instead, it is argued, the novelty of Tassoni's work lies in his treatment of materials derived from the Petrarchan lyric tradition, the satiric poets, and Tasso's and Ludovico Ariosto's epics and in his Baroque mixing of styles and languages. Tassoni was jealous of the originality of his invention and defended himself against the claim of priority of his rival, Bracciolini, who in 1618 had published the burlesque poem *Dello scherno degli dei* (The Mocking of the Gods). Tassoni's *La secchia rapita* exercised a considerable influence on the development of the mock-heroic epic throughout Europe in the seventeenth and eighteenth centuries. A noteworthy Italian contribution to the genre is Carlo de' Dottori's *L'asino* (1652, The Ass).

Satiric poetry of a classical stamp but dealing with contemporary mores and customs continued to be cultivated by conservative authors, mostly Tuscan, toward the end of the century. The most important of these authors was the Florentine Benedetto Menzini, one of the original members of the Accademia degli Arcadi, who published a treatise in verse on poetics in 1688 and wrote thirteen satires that appeared posthumously in 1718. During the early and middle seventeenth century mock epics and humorous poems were especially cultivated by poets who wrote in regional dialects, such as Giulio Cesare Cortese. In *La vaiasseide* (1612, The Servant Women) and *Micco Passaro 'nnamorato* (1619, Micco Passaro Enamored) Cortese produced mock-heroic narratives that expose local social conditions and celebrate the lowlife of his native Naples. In his best-known work, *Viaggio di Parnaso* (1621, Journey to Parnassus), Cortese defended his choice of the Neapolitan dialect instead of the standard Tuscan. Dialect literature flourished in the second half of the seventeenth century in all of the major regional centers: Naples, Rome, Bologna, Venice, Milan, and Turin. One of the most representative voices of this trend was Busenello, whose large body of Italian and Venetian dialect poems, comprising patriotic celebratory verse, satires exposing corrupt customs, and occasional poems addressed to friends, offer a realistic and lively representation of life in his native city. The critic Luigi Russo argues that the seicento was the great divide between early and modern Italian literature, as well as between standard-language "high" literature and the "popular" literature of regional dialects.

Many scholars argue that the seventeenth century represents the apex of the theater in western Europe. Civic festivities, religious rituals, fashion, manners, and speech were theatrical and dramatic, and playwrights of the period exploited the metaphors of human life as acting and of life as a dream or illusion. An inscription over the entrance to William Shakespeare's Globe Theatre in London reads *Totus mundus agit histrionem* (The whole world plays the actor). One of the most celebrated religious plays of the European Baroque repertoire is the Spanish dramatist Pedro Calderòn de la Barca's *El gran teatro del mundo* (1633, The Great Theater of the World).

To free themselves from dependence on scripted and literary comedy, Italian professional actors improvised dialogue, often adopting local dialects, with the help of *scenari* (scenarios) or *canovacci* (plot outlines). This art form, which came to be known as commedia dell'arte (comedy of the acting profession), used *lazzi* (comic verbal and physical routines); *libri generici* (formularies of typical monologues and jokes); and fixed character roles that often involved masks, such as *zanni* (scheming servants), the *Capitano* (captain; a braggart soldier), and the *Dottore* (doctor), a loquacious foil for the *Pantalone* (father). The plots usually consisted of simple love stories featuring *innamorati* (young lovers) in conflict with *vecchi* (old men or fathers). The rise of the commedia dell'arte as an established dramatic form is generally dated between 1570 and 1630. The professional acting companies enjoyed the favor of both the aristocracy and the lower classes and performed in courts, theaters, and public squares. But in the late sixteenth and early seventeenth centuries princely patronage was essential in every area of artistic and literary production, and in none more than the theater. The most prestigious acting companies of the time—the Gelosi (Jealous Ones), Accesi (Impassioned Ones), Uniti (United Ones), Confidenti (Confident Ones), and Fedeli (Faithful Ones)—obtained the support of noble families such as the Gonzagas and the Farneses. The wandering professional troupes were managed by well-educated actors who wrote the scenarios and frequently were also the principal players. Over time they began to write scripted plays, especially pastoral dramas and tragicomedies, in an attempt to win recognition from the literati as well as to defend the respectability of their profession against the hostility of the ecclesiastical authorities. For nearly two centuries the companies toured extensively not only in Italy but also in other European countries, leaving their mark on the work of dramatists such as Shakespeare, Lope de Vega, and Molière and introducing the modern system of theatrical production.

The commedia dell'arte continued to flourish in the second half of the seicento, but the performances gradually declined to the level of fixed routines, vulgar slapstick humor, and acrobatic feats that appealed to the lowest tastes of their audiences. In 1699 the poet and dramatist Andrea Perrucci published a *zibaldone* (repertory), *Dell'arte rappresentativa premeditata, ed all' improvviso* (translated as *A Treatise on Acting, from Memory and by Improvisation*, 2008), that constitutes a comprehensive manual on the staging of an improvised comedy: stock characters, masks, plot outlines, speeches, and comic routines with which the professional actor should be familiar.

The scripted neoclassical comedy, which was based on conventional themes and observed formal precepts such as the division into five acts and the dramatic unities of time, place, and subject matter, could not compete with the improvised version. It was cultivated by professional writers who adopted some of the techniques of the commedia dell'arte and was performed by amateur actors under the sponsorship of courts and academies.

The more-memorable productions of the time are associated with the Medici court in Florence. Michelangelo Buonarroti the Younger's rustic comedy *La Tancia* (1611), written mostly in verse, and *La fiera* (1619, The Fair), a spectacular sequence of five five-act comedies that portray Florentine market scenes, were intended not only as entertainment but also as vehicles for recording Tuscan popular speech for the dictionary of the Accademia della Crusca. Carlo Maria Maggi wrote comedies partly in the Milanese dialect. In Rome, groups of amateur actors linked the humanistic and learned comedy with the popular stage by using some techniques of the commedia dell'arte in performance-oriented scripted pieces called *commedie ridicolose* (laughing comedies) that were addressed primarily to a middle-class public. By midcentury, foreign influence began to be felt in theatrical production. The Spanish Golden Age comedy was adapted to the Italian stage, especially by Giacinto Andrea Cicognini, the principal exponent of the *commedia spagnoleggiante* (play written in the Spanish style).

The current neglect of the seicento literary comedy, pastoral drama, and tragedy is attributable, at least in part, to the still common view that its history is one of repetition of previous forms and themes. The prevailing critical assumption is that experimentation in pastoral drama, for example, ended with Battista Guarini's *Il pastor fido* (1590; translated as *Il pastor fido; or The Faithful Shepherd*, 1602), and modern criticism has focused on Guarini's contributions to the creation of a third dramatic genre after comedy and tragedy: the tragicomedy. In polemical writings in defense of his work Guarini argued that it was not an indiscriminate combination of tragedy and comedy but a separate dramatic form that had become necessary because the public expected dramatic entertainment that was both lofty and lively. This claim—that the tragicomedy was superior to other dramatic forms because it was spectator- and performance-oriented—representsa modern view of the social dimension of the theater. First performed in Crema in 1596 and published in its definitive edition in 1602, *Il pastor fido* represented the confluence of the pastoral drama with some standard comic features and elements of the tragedy characteristic of the time. Guidubaldo Bonarelli's *Filli di Sciro, favola pastorale* (1607; translated as *Filli di Sciro, or, Phillis of Scyros, an Excellent Pastorall*, 1655) gave rise to a heated debate over the morality of the heroine's love for two men.

The origins of opera can be traced to the 1570s, when a group of musicians, poets, and classical scholars patronized by the Florentine Bardi family and known as the Camerata began to study the extant statements on the use of music in ancient Greek tragedies and became convinced that in addition to the choruses other parts of the scripts were sung. This conclusion, which was later shown to be mistaken, inspired them to devise new forms of dramatic music. Vincenzo Galilei, the father of Galileo, urged a return to the ideals and procedures of ancient music in his *Dialogo della musica antica, e della moderna* (1581, Dialogue on Ancient and Modern Music) and conducted experiments in *recitar cantando* (singing while performing), now known as recitative—one of the essential components of opera. *Dramma per musica* (drama for music) was the term most frequently used in the seventeenth century to designate what are now called operas. The scripts for these works, somewhat contemptuously designated *libretti* (little books) because of their small size, were usually hastily published for a single performance so that the audience could read what was being sung.

Modern scholarship divides the development of early opera into three phases. The pioneering stage began in Florence in 1597 with *La Dafne,* commonly believed to be the first opera, followed in 1600 by *L'Euridice* (Eurydice); both were scored by the composer Jacopo Peri on librettos by Ottavio Rinuccini. *L'Euridice* was staged in the Pitti Palace during the celebrations for the wedding of Maria de' Medici and King Henry IV of France. The pioneering phase continued in Mantua with the first two operas composed by Claudio Monteverdi: *L'Orfeo* (1607, Orpheus) and *L'Arianna* (1608, Ariadne), on librettos by Alessandro Striggio and Rinuccini, respectively; *L'Arianna* was produced in Mantua for the wedding of Duke Francesco Gonzaga and Margherita of Savoy. This phase is characterized by dependence on mythological themes and the tragicomic pastorals of the time.

The second phase of early opera production occurred in Rome during the papacy of Urban VIII from 1623 to 1644. Urban's powerful nephews, Cardinals Antonio and Francesco Barberini, were munificent patrons of the musical theater. An influential member of the Barberini circle was Giulio Rospigliosi, one of the most prolific librettists of the midcentury. Rospigliosi's *Sant'Alessio* (St. Alexius), with music by Stefano Landi, was staged in 1631. He went on to write librettos on subjects taken from Italian literary classics such as Tasso's *Gerusalemme liberata* in 1633, Giovanni Boccaccio's *Decameron* (circa 1348–1353) in 1637, Ludovico Ariosto's *Orlando furioso* (1516; enlarged, 1532, The Frenzy of Orlando; translated as *Orlando Furioso in English Heroical Verse,* 1591) in 1642, and in the 1650s from Spanish romantic-intrigue comedies. Rospigliosi became a cardinal in 1657 and Pope Clement IX in 1667. Sophisticated mechanical stage devices and scenic designs were created for the Roman musical theater by the sculptor and architect Gian Lorenzo Bernini.

The third phase of the early development of opera was centered in Venice. The city had no princely court, but rich merchant-patrician families subsidized the building of theaters for opera productions as a financial investment and a means of gaining prestige. The first public opera house, San Casciano, opened in Venice in 1637. While opera in Florence, Mantua, and Rome mainly took the form of occasional court entertainments to commemorate important events, in Venice works were repeated many times for paying audiences. Monteverdi contributed four scores to Venetian commercial opera theaters, including his stage masterpiece, *L'incoronazione di Poppea* (1642, The Coronation of Poppea), on a libretto by Busenello. Monteverdi and the first generation of Venetian librettists clung to the Renaissance notion that gave poetry priority over music, but this idea began to break down in the midseicento. As a staged play set to music in its entirety, opera required the collaboration of writers, musicians, and singer-actors, as well as of architects for the stage effects and of theater impresarios for the promotion and management of the performances. Like the commedia dell'arte, the *dramma per musica* was an original response of the Baroque age to the increasing demands for artistic entertainment in the modern world.

The Baroque tragedy shared with the epic an elevated position among literary genres and was, therefore, far more likely than the comedy to be composed in accordance with Renaissance neo-Aristotelian rules. These plays were not, however, purely literary works intended to be read rather than performed: tragedians of the late sixteenth and early seventeenth centuries were interested in stage techniques and in developing a tragic drama that could entertain without relinquishing its moralistic and didactic functions.

The seicento boasted two major tragedians: Dottori and Federico Della Valle. Modeled on the traditional Greek tragedy, Dottori's *Aristodemo* (1657, Aristodemus) makes ample and effective use of dramatic devices such as the flight of the lovers, switching of identities, double recognition, and Senecan horror-tragedy materials. Della Valle's biblical plays *Judit* (1627, Judith) and *Esther* (1627) express his tragic vision of human destiny. His masterpiece, *La reina di Scotia* (1628, The Queen of Scotland), focuses on the last hours of the captive Mary Stuart in 1587; the confrontation between Mary and Elizabeth I and Mary's rebellion against the *ragion di stato* (reason of state) in defense of her private morality and Catholic faith dramatize then-current political and religious issues.

The militantly religious climate of the age encouraged tragedians to venture into sacred drama. The powerful Society of Jesus did not at first favor the use of the theater for the instruction of churchgoers, but Latin plays about biblical and allegorical figures and saints were approved by the order in the 1590s as aids for the study of Latin and rhetoric in its colleges. Eventually, in an effort to counter the Protestant challenge to Catholic orthodoxy and the supremacy of the papacy, Jesuit educators began to write and produce plays for their students and spectators from the larger society. The tragic hero as exemplary martyr punished for his or her religious beliefs or political ideals became a standard type in sacred plays by Jesuit dramatists. Important works based on hagiographic sources include the *Hermenegildus* (1621), written in Latin and translated into Italian, by Emanuele Tesauro, the foremost theorist of Marinism and a professor of rhetoric at the Jesuit College of Brera in Milan in the 1620s, and, on the same subject, the *Ermenegildo martire* (1644, Hermenegildus the Martyr), by the official historian of the Council of Trent, the Jesuit Pietro Sforza Pallavicino. The religious plays, constructed on neoclassical lines and combining poetry, music, and stagecraft to provoke a sense of *meraviglia*, enhanced the status of the Jesuit colleges as influential cultural centers throughout Catholic Europe.

Secular literary tragedies on historical or mythological subjects were never popular successes in Baroque Italy. Their audience was limited to the upper classes, who read or recited them or attended performances at courts or academies or in private noble homes. Comedies and mythological pageants were considered better suited than tragedies for entertainment at royal weddings or visits of foreign dignitaries. At the end of the sixteenth century the critic Angelo Ingegnieri had recognized the already irreversible decline of the "maninconosa" (gloomy) neoclassical tragedy, which was aggravated by the cost of the sets and machines necessary for its production. In the posthumously published "Dialogo sopra le tragedie" (1733, Dialogue on the Tragedy) the Venetian politician and churchman Giovanni Delfino proposed a reform of the Italian tragic stage based on his own experience as an author of tragedies. Delfino, a member of the Accademia della Crusca who died in 1699, advocated a tragedy of reflection and meditation, discursive in tone, flexible in the application of the unities of place and time, preferably based on historical subjects, and edifying in purpose. Ideas similar to Delfino's were enunciated by members of the Accademia degli Arcadi.

—*Albert N. Mancini*

Acknowledgments

This book was produced by Bruccoli Clark Layman, Inc. Philip B. Dematteis was the in-house editor.

Production manager is Philip B. Dematteis.

Administrative support was provided by Carol A. Cheschi.

Accountant is Ann-Marie Holland.

Copyediting supervisor is Sally R. Evans. The copyediting staff includes Phyllis A. Avant, Caryl Brown, and Rebecca Mayo. Freelance copyeditors are Brenda L. Cabra, Jennifer E. Cooper, and David C. King.

Pipeline manager is James F. Tidd Jr.

Editorial associates are Elizabeth Leverton and Dickson Monk.

Permissions editor is Amber L. Coker.

Office manager is Kathy Lawler Merlette.

Photography editor is Kourtnay King.

Digital photographic copy work was performed by Kourtnay King.

Systems manager is James Sellers.

Typesetting supervisor is Kathleen M. Flanagan. The typesetting staff includes Patricia M. Flanagan.

Library research was facilitated by the following librarians at the Thomas Cooper Library of the University of South Carolina: Elizabeth Sudduth and the rare-book department; Jo Cottingham, interlibrary loan department; circulation department head Tucker Taylor; reference department head Virginia W. Weathers; reference department staff Marilee Birchfield, Karen Brown, Mary Bull, Gerri Corson, Joshua Garris, Beki Gettys, Laura Ladwig, Tom Marcil, Anthony Diana McKissick, Bob Skinder, and Sharon Verba; interlibrary loan department head Marna Hostetler; and interlibrary loan staff Robert Amerson and Timothy Simmons.

Dictionary of Literary Biography® • Volume Three Hundred Thirty-Nine

Seventeenth-Century Italian Poets and Dramatists

Dictionary of Literary Biography

Claudio Achillini
(18 September 1574 – 1 October 1640)

Paschal C. Viglionese
University of Rhode Island

SELECTED BOOKS: *Mercurio e Marte: Torneo regale fatto nel superbissimo Teatro di Parma nell'arrivo della Seren. Principessa Margherita di Toscana moglie del Seren. Odoardo Farnese* (Parma: Viotti, 1628);

Teti e Flora: Prologo della gran pastorale recitata in Parma nel meraviglioso Teatro fabricato dal Sereniss. Sig. Duca Odoardo per onorar l'arrivo della Seren. Princip. Margherita di Toscana sua moglie (Parma, 1628);

Poesie di Claudio Achillini, dedicate al grande Odoardo Farnese, Duca di Parma e di Piacenza (Bologna: Clemente Ferroni, 1632);

Poesie di Clavdio Achillini (Venice & Macerata: Heirs of Saluioni & Agostino Grisei, 1633);

Rime e prose di Claudio Achillini, in questa nuova impressione accresciute di molti sonetti e altre composizioni non più stampate, con aggiunta di diverse bellissime lettere di proposta e risposta del medesimo autore (Venice: Giunti & Baba, 1650);

Rime e prose di Claudio Achillini (Venice: Giacomo Borsoli, 1656);

Poesie, edited by Angelo Colombo (Parma: Zara, 1991).

Edition in English: "On a Fair Beggar" and "A Sonnet, Writ by a Nymph in Her Own Blood," translated by Philip Ayres, in *Minor Poets of the Caroline Period*, volume 2, edited by George Saintsbury (Oxford: Clarendon Press, 1906), p. 279.

OTHER: Benedetto Croce, ed., *Lirici marinisti* (Bari: Laterza, 1910), pp. 47–54;

Giuseppe Guido Ferrero, ed., *Marino e i Marinisti* (Milan & Naples: Ricciardi, 1954), pp. 697–709;

Giovanni Getto, ed., *Lirici marinisti* (Turin: TEA, 1991), pp. 167–173.

Claudio Achillini is a chief figure of the early phase of the seventeenth-century literary trend that is known in Italy, since it took as its model the work of Giambattista Marino, as *Marinismo* (Marinism). For several hundred years he was regarded as a slavish imitator of Marino who often outdid his mentor in pomposity of style and the use of unusual and often preposterous metaphor to the detriment of substantial content. That judgment has been challenged by a reassessment of the age of Marinism that began in the 1950s with the editorial and critical work of Franco Croce.

Achillini was born into a family of writers and lawyers in Bologna on 18 September 1574. The Bolognese philosopher, physician, and pioneer anatomist Alessandro Achillini was his granduncle; the poet Giovanni Filoteo Achillini was his grandfather. He attended the University of Padua from 1594 to 1598. Throughout his life Achillini was engaged in the law, primarily as a writer on legal issues and a teacher of jurisprudence. He began teaching at the University of Bologna in 1598.

In a letter of 27 October 1601 Achillini says that he has come to Rome to see what the city is like and intends on returning home to his books as quickly as possible. Some of his friends and relatives had expectations that he would make something of himself in the ecclesiastical center; but he notes that even if he wanted to stay, there are only four ways for a young man to get ahead in Rome. The first, having a noble lineage, is not open to him, because his family is not noble enough. Neither is the second, money, since he cannot afford to spend as much as would be needed either to keep a lavish home for entertaining or to buy offices in the papal

Frontispiece for a collection of Claudio Achillini's works published in Venice in 1650 (from Battista Guarini, Opere, edited by Luigi Fassò, 1950; Thomas Cooper Library, University of South Carolina)

Curia. The third way, good fortune, is available only through papal patronage, which he does not see as likely. As for the fourth way, expending immense effort, he is not well suited to self-promotion, lobbying and begging, or conducting an intensive court career. Accordingly, Achillini returned to Bologna and began teaching at the university again, but he left in 1609 after a clash with colleagues. In 1610 he beame secretary to the archbishop of Bologna, Cardinal Allessandro Ludovisi, who was serving as papal vice-legate at the court of Savoy in Turin. While retaining that position, Achillini took a professorship at the University of Ferrara in 1612. During his time in Ferrara he was inducted into the Accademia degli Intrepidi (Academy of the Fearless).

Achillini's literary fame owes much to his friendship with and admiration for Marino, the most noted poet of the Baroque era in Italy, whom he had met during his stay in Rome between 1601 and 1606. The two poets developed a strong mutual respect. In his letters to others Marino habitually refers to Achillini's outstanding intellectual ability and good judgment and at one point called the younger man "la metà dell'anima mia" (one-half of my own soul). Whenever he sent a poem to a friend he and Achillini had in common, he would ask the recipient to be sure to get Achillini's opinion of it. In a letter of 1609 Marino thanks Achillini for the latter's concern about the attempt made on his life in Turin by Gaspare Murtola, a rival poet whom Marino had attacked in several poems. Marino praises Achillini's letter as the "parto d'arguto e vivace intelletto" (the offspring of a witty and lively intellect). In 1620 Marino prefaced his book of lyrics *La Sampogna* (The Panpipe) with a letter to Achillini in which he discusses translation, imitation, and plagiarism. This letter has become pivotal in studies of Marino's poetry and influence.

Achillini was in Rome with Ludovisi from June to November 1621, the year Ludovisi was elected to the papacy as Gregory XV. No opportunities for advancement opened up for Achillini, however, so he resumed his professorship in law at the University of Ferrara. In 1622 he was inducted into Rome's Accademia dei Lincei (Academy of the Lynx-Eyed Ones); an illustrious fellow member was Galileo Galilei.

In 1626 Achillini was invited by the duke of Parma, Odoardo Farnese, to teach at the university in that city; he remained until 1636. Achillini's students set up a plaque to honor the man they called *Lettor sopraeminente* (Most Distinguished Lector); the epithet appears on the title pages of his two works written to be set to music, which were published in Parma in 1628. One of these works was the libretto for *Mercurio e Marte* (1628, Mercury and Mars), written for the inauguration of the monumental Teatro Farnese that was built inside the Palazzo della Pilotta in 1628. The music was composed by Claudio Monteverdi, who came from Venice to test the acoustics of the new theater and found them to be rather unsatisfactory. In a 1628 letter to the marquis Alessandro Striggio in Mantua, Monteverdi says that his collaborator, "Aquilini," is quite prolific and has provided him with a "long drawn out" text of more than a thousand words, greatly increasing the amount of work the composer will have to do. The work had a magnificent production, including a naval-battle scene on the flooded stage of the huge theater, as part of the lavish celebrations of the wedding of Farnese and Margherita de' Medici. In connection with the duke's wedding Achillini also wrote *Teti e Flora* (1628, Teti and Flora), a prologue and intermezzo for a production of Torquato Tasso's pastoral drama *Aminta* (1573), with music by Monteverdi, that was performed in the Teatro Farnese. During his time in Parma he composed most of his other poems, as well, and he also became a member of the local Accademia degli Innominati (Academy of the Nameless) and the Venetian Accademia degli Incogniti (Academy of the Unknowns).

Achillini's poetry and prose reflect the Marinistic style of the time: they are filled with labored metaphors that are cleverly constructed, embellished, and usually follow one another in long sequences. In a letter written sometime prior to 1626 a description of a remarkably effective preacher who is so thin and emaciated that he is barely visible inside his robe and hood sets in motion a flow of conceits: the preacher's audience sees and hears "una lana agitata che sgrida, un mantello vocale, un capuccio che atterrisce, un fuoco che scintilla fuori delle ceneri, una nuvola bigia che tuona spaventi, una penitenza spirante, un sacco di querele che riversa adosso ai peccatori" (pulsating wool that reprimands, a vocal mantle, a hood that inspires fear, a flame that flares up from the ashes, a gray cloud that thunders out dread, a breathing penitence, a sack full of lamentations shaken out onto the sinners). Bizarre though the passage may be, Benedetto Croce says in his *Saggi sulla letteratura italiana del Seicento* (1924, Essays on Seventeenth-Century Italian Literature) that it embodies a sense of the picturesque and the colorful that is a positive aspect of the writing of the Baroque era.

A play on the various shades of meaning of a word can be seen in Achillini's five-line madrigal, "Sleal, così dicesti" (Disloyal one, here is what you said), a lover's reproach to a woman who did not keep her promise:

Sleal, così dicesti:
"Quand'è più cieco a meza notte il lume,
vien: ché ignuda t'aspetto entro le piume."
I' me ne venni, ah cruda!
ma solo ti trovai di fede ignuda.

(Disloyal one, here is what you said:
"When the light is dim at midnight,
come to me: for I'll be undressed, waiting for you in my
  bed."
I came to you, cruel one!
but only found you bare of truthfulness.)

The Marinists were fascinated with verbal artifices, with the musicality of the sound and rhythm of words, and with sensual images. In the introduction to his anthology *Lirici marinisti* (1991, Marinist Lyrics) Giovanni Getto describes the principal weakness of the Marinist poets as the depiction of sensuality and the erotic without an emotional basis in love. There are countless descriptions of the beauty of the poet's beloved lady—perhaps the most hackneyed motif in literature stemming from the poetic tradition of Petrarch. These descriptions, when presented with the Marinists' unusual and clever figures of speech, evolved into intentional distortions or permutations of the conventionalized elements of golden hair, blue eyes, and flawless

Title page for a later collection of Achillini's poetry and prose
(University of Turin)

and grotesque directions; an extreme may have been reached in sonnets by Marcello Giovanetti and Anton Giulio Brignole Sale that include descriptions of beautiful women being flogged.

Many of Achillini's poems describe scenes in nature, unusual persons and situations, and the idea or conditions of love. His focus might be on themes that are used to excess by the Marinists, such as the erotic beauty of the beloved, the fascinating beauty of a beggar woman, a woman possessed by Lucifer in a church, or the quality of embroidered lace made by the shadows cast on the ground by the newly sprouted leaves in the spring. In some poems Achillini can almost make the reader forget that he is striving to achieve the Marinists' aim of producing astonishment by the use of technical brilliance and can make the reader participate in his own wonder at the scene before him. For example, the basic conceit of "Nascita del dì d'Aprile" (Birth of an April Day) is that of the day as a newborn child nursed with maternal fervor by the flowing water of a stream that has been "sciolta pur or dalla prigion del gelo" (just now released from its prison of ice); Getto remarks that while this sonnet is shaped by an intellectually inspired search for a point of view that can startle the reader, it evokes images of a fresh and flowering nature. The sonnet "Altezza esagerata del monte Appennino" (Exaggerated Loftiness of the Apennine Mountains), while exemplifying the Marinistic tendency to "puff up reality in enormous and approximate painting," as Franco Croce puts it in *Tre momenti del barocco letterario italiano* (1966, Three Moments of Italian Literary Baroque), still includes several rather successful conceits on the spectacle of the high Apennines.

Achillini's best-known poem, the sonnet "Sudate, o fochi, a preparar metalli" (1629, Sweat, O flames, in forging metals), does not reach the level of great literature; it owes its fame, to a large degree, to chapter 28 of Alessandro Manzoni's novel *I Promessi sposi* (1830; translated as *The Betrothed*, 1844), where the first line is quoted in reference to the French incursion into northern Italy during the Thirty Years' War. This event occurred during the reign of Louis XIII, to whom the poem is addressed and whose praises make up a large part of it. Manzoni, who shared the disdain of the Neoclassicists of the eighteenth century for the ornate style of Baroque poetry, might have made the reference ironically; the opening of *I Promessi sposi*, in which the author pretends to transcribe his narrative verbatim from a dusty seventeenth-century manuscript he has found, parodies that style. But Manzoni's reference to Achillini's sonnet may also have had a serious side. The poem urges the French monarch to continue his campaign farther into Lombardy and oust the Spanish subjugators of the area; that goal would have met with the

white skin. Getto gives a typology of the subjects of such descriptions that includes the beautiful lame woman, the beautiful stutterer, the beautiful freckle-face, the beautiful dwarf, and the beautiful woman with head lice. Achillini's sonnet "Bellissima mendica" (Beautiful Beggar Woman) plays on the ironic contrast between the title figure's poverty and the abundant gold of her hair. Some of the poets went in even more bizarre

approval of the narrator of *I Promessi sposi,* who observes, somewhat sadly, that shapers of history have never paid heed to the opinions of poets.

This sonnet has drawn the most negative attention of any of Achillini's works. The pattern seems to have begun with one of the earliest critics of the Marinists, the painter-poet Salvator Rosa. In his second *Satira,* which was not published until 1719 but circulated in manuscript throughout the seventeenth century, Rosa attacks the poem for being given over to excessively bombastic tropes that are exaggerated, implausible, or ridiculous. For instance, Rosa finds it ludicrous that the speaker tells flames to "sudate . . . a preparar metalli" (sweat and toil . . . in preparing metals); Rosa's highlighting of these words suggested them to later critics, who aimed to disparage the poets of the Baroque, as a prime example of the preposterously daring metaphor. Dealing with the philosophical underpinnings of wit and metaphor in *Saggi sulla letteratura italiana del Seicento,* Benedetto Croce points out that Rosa, like most people of his time, looked at fire from the standpoint of Aristotle, who held it to be hot and dry and thus incapable of sweating, but that one could also approach the issue from the perspective of the sensualism of Bernardino Telesio, for whom fire was hot and wet. Mid- and late-twentieth-century scholars, reappraising Achillini's poem as part of the general reassessment of *Marinismo,* looked more closely at the cultural context in which it was composed and took the political associations in the text more seriously. It is now seen as endorsing the desire of the Farnese family, Achillini's patrons in Parma, to encourage the French incursion into northern Italy.

Achillini found himself in trouble because of his letter of 2 May 1629 to Louis XIII, to which "Sudate, o fochi, a preparar metalli" was appended. When the letter appeared in print, some Spaniards residing in Bologna petitioned the Holy Office to have it condemned and suppressed because, they claimed, it libeled the king of Spain: Achillini's praise of Louis and the historical parallels he used to illustrate the French king's greatness seemed to imply that the Spanish monarch's place was among heretics and infidels. On 2 June 1629 Achillini wrote to Louis's chief minister, Armand-Jean du Plessis, Cardinal Richelieu, wishing for a response from the king to the sonnet, even if it were just one line. Eleven years passed before he received a reply.

Achillini helped a young friend, Giacomo Aleandri, write a response to attacks against Marino's greatest work, *L'Adone* (1623; translated as *Adonis,* 1967), as part of a heated polemic that occupied most of the Italian literati at the time. *Difesa dell'*Adone *del Marino per risposta all'*Occhiale *del cavalier Stigliani* (1629, Defense of Marino's *Adonis* in Reply to *The Eyeglass* by the Cavalier Stigliani) appeared two years after the publication of Tommaso Stigliani's *L'Occhiale* and four years after Marino's death. Aleandri sent the manuscript to Achillini from Rome on 20 January 1629 with a letter in which he said that it would be better if Achillini's name did not appear on the work because neither of them wanted Stigliani, a former friend of Marino's who had become his principal detractor, to derive indirect glory through being attacked by "sí grande antagonista" as Achillini. Also, he said, readers would be less likely to accept criticism of Stigliani as unbiased if it came from such a good friend of Marino's as Achillini. Aleandri also called attention to the fact that he did not defend any of the strongly erotic passages of *L'Adone* that were condemned by the ecclesiastical censors but, instead, joined the censors in attacking them. This comment is a hint of the tenor of the Counter-Reformation era, with its *Index of Prohibited Books* and the Inquisition, when writers needed to cover themselves by making obvious disclaimers. (The poet Girolamo Preti's 1625 letter reporting Marino's death to Achillini mentioned Marino's will, which called for the burning of all his texts except those that are religious in theme. Achillini's reply concurred with the opinion that if the lascivious and irreverent poems were excepted, Marino's production would be truly sublime and glorious.)

In 1630 Achillini's friend Agostino Mascardi sent him an eyewitness account of the bubonic plague that was ravaging Milan. Achillini's reply, written at his family villa, "Le Torrette" (The Towers), in Il Sasso, near Bologna, earned him a place in the long line of writers of plague descriptions. He first restates what Mascardi wrote:

> Quell'essere divenute le contrade funestissimi torrenti, che altro non corron che feretri; quell'esser fatti gli umani corpi fucine di pestiferi carboni, dove su la instabile incude dell'umana pazienza si lavorano le sincopi e i dolori; quell'essersi cambiati tutti i deliziosi suburbi, già dedicati al genio e alle muse, in postriboli delle parche e in campidogli della morte; quell'essersi seminati tutti i campi della Lombardia più di cadaveri che di grani; e, per dirlo in una parola, quell'essersi spopolata la faccia e popolate le viscere della terra.

> (The countryside had become funereal torrents flowing with nothing but coffins; the bodies of men had been turned into forges of pestiferous coals for fashioning injury and pain on the changing anvil of human patience; all the delightful suburbs had been transformed from places dedicated to the genius of the Muses into bordellos of the Three Fates, into the capital cities of death; all the fields of Lombardy had been sown more with corpses than with seeds of grain; in short, [there had come about the] depopulation of the face of the earth, and the consequent overpopulation of its subterraneous viscera.)

Later in the letter he observes that the activities of men during the plague have been reduced to three: amassing worldly wealth, pursuing carnal pleasure, and carrying out organized revenge. The comment is reminiscent of Giovanni Boccaccio's claim in the *Decameron* (circa 1348–1353) that during the Black Death in 1348 people could be divided into those who believed that to be safe from infection one had to lead a life of moderation and those who gave themselves over to debauchery in an attempt to forget about the plague in excesses of pleasure.

Many saw the plague in Milan as the work of the devil; others, including Achillini, held that the pestilence was a punishment sent by God. Yet another belief, mentioned by Mascardi, was that humans in league with Satan were using hexes and other diabolical means to spread the disease. (Manzoni's *I Promessi sposi* includes an account of the same plague—which Italian literary historians frequently refer to as "the Manzonian plague"—and the *"untori"* [anointers] who were believed to be intentionally spreading the contagion; Manzoni debunks the notion.) Achillini could not believe that human beings could be so wicked; the plague, he said in his reply to Mascardi, had to be a scourge wielded by the hand of God to punish humanity. Achillini was responsible for the building of the oratory of St. Apollonia near his villa as a gesture of thanks to God for keeping him safe from the plague.

In May 1640 Achillini received a letter from Richelieu saying that he and the king held Achillini in high esteem for the poet's loyalty and for the sonnet "Sudate, o fochi, a preparar metalli" and that he could consider himself under their protection. Achillini was offered the *prima cattedra* (principal chair) at the University of Padua but declined the offer for reasons of health. Old age, he wrote in a letter shortly before his death, was intimating images of tombs, not of university chairs; it was time to listen to "le lezioni che mi fa la Morte" (the lectures Death is giving to me), rather than "far udir le mie alla gioventù di Padoa" (make the youth of Padua listen to mine). He died on 1 October 1640.

According to Franco Croce's *Tre momenti del barocco letterario italiano*, Claudio Achillini's work can be characterized as an offshoot and continuation of Marino's but displays a "hyperbolic fullness" that outdoes the Marinian model. His favorite technique is exaggeration, and he himself seems to allude to it in the title of his sonnet "Altezza esagerata del monte Appennino." A related aspect of Achillini's significance is, Croce notes, his tendency to go beyond the unusual metaphor and the *arguzia* (clever and witty turn of phrase) into "verbal violence" and "stylistic exercises," qualities that belong to the poetry of later in the century.

Letters:
"Carteggio di Claudio Achillini," in Giambattista Marino, *Epistolario: Seguito da lettere di altri scrittori del seicento,* volume 2, edited by Angelo Borzelli and Fausto Nicolini (Bari: Laterza, 1911), pp. 113–248.

References:
Angelo Colombo, *"I riposi di Pindo": Studi su Claudio Achillini (1574–1640)* (Florence: Olschki, 1988);

Colombo, "Tra 'Incogniti' e 'Lincei': Per la biografia di Claudio Achillini (1574–1640), *Studi secenteschi,* 26 (1985): 141–176;

Benedetto Croce, *Saggi sulla letteratura italiana del Seicento,* revised edition (Bari: Laterza, 1924), pp. 307–308, 373, 384–388, 407;

Franco Croce, "Nuovi compiti della critica del Marino e del marinismo," *Rassegna della letteratura italiana,* 61 (1957): 465–473; translated as "Baroque Poetry: New Tasks for the Criticism of Marino and 'Marinism,'" in *The Late Italian Renaissance 1525–1630,* edited by Eric Cochran (London: Macmillan, 1970), pp. 377–400;

Croce, *Tre momenti del barocco letterario italiano* (Florence: Sansoni, 1966), pp. 23–29, 91–92;

Battista Guarini, *Opere,* edited by Luigi Fassò (Turin: Unione Tipografico-Editrice Torinese, 1950), p. 112;

James V. Mirollo, *Marino: The Poet of the Marvelous* (New York: Columbia University Press, 1963), p. 175;

Claudio Monteverdi, *The Letters of Claudio Monteverdi,* translated by Dennis Stevens (Cambridge: Cambridge University Press, 1980), pp. 349–350, 364–365, 390;

Alois Maria Nagler, *Theatre Festivals of the Medici, 1569–1637* (New Haven: Yale University Press, 1964), pp. 143, 153;

Salvator Rosa, *Satire, Liriche, Lettere,* edited by Anton Maria Salvini and Lodovico Corio (Milan: Sonzogno, 1892);

Angelo Solerti, *Musica, ballo, e drammatica alla Corte Medicea dal 1600 al 1637* (London: Blom, 1968), pp. 193, 409–425, 481–518.

Papers:
Many of Claudio Achillini's letters and manuscripts are at the University of Bologna.

Francesco Andreini

(before 1548? – 20 August 1624)

Francesca Savoia
University of Pittsburgh

BOOKS: *Le bravure del Capitano Spavento divise in molti ragionamenti in forma di dialogo* (Venice: Giacomo Antonio Somasco, 1607); enlarged as *Nuova aggiunta alle bravure del Capitano Spavento* (Venice: Vincenzo Somasco, 1615); revised as *Le bravure del Capitano Spavento divise in molti ragionamenti* (Venice: Vincenzo Somasco, 1618); enlarged as *Le bravure del Capitano Spavento divise in molti ragionamenti* (Venice: Vincenzo Somasco, 1624);

L'ingannata Proserpina: Opera rappresentativa e scenica di Francesco Andreini da Pistoia Comico Geloso detto il Capitano Spavento (Venice: Giacomo Antonio Somasco, 1611);

L'alterezza di Narciso: Opera scenica rappresentativa di Francesco Andreini da Pistoia Comico geloso detto il Capitan Spavento (Venice: Giacomo Antonio Somasco, 1611);

Ragionamenti fantastici di Francesco Andreini, detto il Capitano Spavento: Posti in forma di dialoghi rappresentativi (Venice: Vincenzo Somasco, 1612).

Editions: *Le bravure del Capitano Spavento* (excerpts), in *La Commedia dell'Arte: Storia e testo,* volume 1, edited by Vito Pandolfi (Florence: Sansoni, 1957), pp. 359–381;

Le bravure del Capitano Spavento, edited by Roberto Tessari (Pisa: Giardini, 1987).

OTHER: *Lettere d'Isabella Andreini, comica gelosa,* edited by Andreini (Venice: M. A. Zaltieri, 1607);

Flaminio Scala, *Il teatro delle favole rappresentative, overo La ricreatione comica, boscareccia, e tragica: Divisa in cinquanta giornate,* introduction by Andreini (Venice: Giovanni Battista Pulciani, 1611);

Two sonnets and a madrigal by Francesco Andreini, in Giovan Battista Andreini, *Il Mincio ubidiente di Gio. Battista Andreini. Componimenti di pellegrini ingegni sopra l'ammirabile sostegno fatto a Governo dell'Illustre Signor Gabriel Bertacciolo,* contributions by Francesco Andreini (Venice: Bertoni, 1620);

Isabella Andreini, *Fragmenti d'alcune scritture della Signora Isabella Andreini Comica Gelosa, et accademica Intenta,*

Francesco Andreini (from Scenarios of the Commedia dell'Arte: Flaminio Scala's Il Teatro delle favole rappresentative, *edited and translated by Henry Frank Salerno, 1967; Thomas Cooper Library, University of South Carolina)*

edited by Francesco Andreini (Venice: G. B. Combi, 1620).

As actors, Francesco Andreini and his wife, Isabella, elevated the quality of the commedia dell'arte and contributed to its popularity throughout Italy and abroad. In France they were the first acclaimed representatives of their art and had an incalculable influence on the theater of the country. While Isabella's writings belong to the literary and academic traditions, Francesco wrote and published "per seguitar l'onorato grido della moglie" (to keep his wife's fame alive) and "per lasciar qualche memoria" (to leave some evidence of their work as professional actors). His works are, therefore, intimately connected with his career as a performer—in particular, with the character type of the Capitano that he helped to shape and develop.

Information about the origins of the family is scant. In the dedicatory letter to Francesco and Isabella's son Giovan Battista Andreini's poem *La Maddalena* (1610, Mary Magdalene), Giovan Battista Pietro Belli says that Francesco Andreini belonged to the noble family of the Cerracchi Del Gallo from Pistoia; he also announces that the author of the poem will explain why the family adopted the name Andreini. The explanation was never provided, and many scholars, relying on Belli's uncorroborated claim, have assumed that Andreini was a stage name. Records of Francesco's transactions at the Monte di Pietà bank in Florence and his will in the state archive of Mantua, however, identify him as the son of Antonio Andreini. Furthermore, the coat of arms that appears in some of the Andreinis' works and has been used to support the noble origin of the family has been revealed to be a fabrication by Francesco. Whether he was the illegitimate child of a nobleman of the Cerracchi family and was raised by Antonio Andreini has not been ascertained. It is known that he was born in Pistoia, probably before 1548. In *La ferza: Ragionamento secondo contra l'accuse date alla Commedia* (1625; The Lash: Second Rebuttal of the Accusations Made against the Commedia) Giovan Battista Andreini wrote that his father became a "soldato di mare" (sailor) at the age of twenty. Francesco probably joined the navy of the Grand Duchy of Tuscany and fought against the Barbary pirates; "preso dal Turco, otto anni colà dimorò" (taken prisoner by the Turk, he lived there for eight years), according to his son. Francesco refers to this experience in two of the *ragionamenti* (arguments) collected in his *Le bravure del Capitano Spavento divise in molti ragionamenti in forma di dialogo* (1607, The Bravados of Captain Spavento Divided into Many Arguments in Dialogue Form). In the seventh *ragionamento* Capitano Spavento, the stock character with whom Francesco came to be identified as a performer, tells his servant, Trappola, that his father was captured by the Turks on a voyage and ransomed ten years later. In *ragionamento* 41 the captain relates that in 1572 his fleet was surrounded and overwhelmed by the Turkish fleet and that he, his fellow officers, and the sailors were taken to Constantinople in chains.

Francesco returned to Italy from Turkey in 1575 and married thirteen-year-old Isabella Canali. Presumably soon after the birth of Giovan Battista in February 1576, they joined the Compagnia dei Gelosi (Company of the Jealous Ones), an already well-established acting troupe that, thanks to the Andreinis, went on to become the most celebrated theatrical company of its time.

The first recorded performance of the Gelosi took place during carnival in Milan in 1568. In 1571 the company, under the direction of Rinaldo Petignoni, had a highly successful tour in France; at a performance in Nogent-le-Roi, they were given the title *comédiens du roi* (king's players). In 1573 the troupe staged the first performance of Torquato Tasso's pastoral play, *Aminta,* in Ferrara. The following year the Gelosi were summoned from Milan to Venice to perform at the request of King Henry III, who was passing through on his way home to France from Poland. Flaminio Scala, the head of the company when Francesco and Isabella Andreini arrived, took it to France for a second time in 1577–1578. Under Scala's direction the Gelosi achieved even greater success and reached perhaps its highest degree of cohesion as an acting ensemble.

Francesco Andreini began his acting career as an *innamorato* (male lover), probably playing opposite his wife in love scenes, but subsequently specialized in the role of the bombastic and arrogant Capitano Spavento da Vall'Inferna (Captain Fright from the Valley of Hell). In the prologue to *Le bravure del Capitano Spavento* he writes:

> mentre ch'io vissi nella famosa compagnia de i Comici Gelosi (il cui grido non vedrà mai l'ultima notte) mi compiacqui di rappresentar nelle Comedie la parte del Milite superbo, ambizioso e vantator, facendomi chiamare il Capitan Spavento da Vall'Inferna. E talmente mi compiacqui in essa, ch'io lasciai di recitare la parte mia principale, la quale era quella dell'innamorato.
>
> (while in the famous company of the Comici Gelosi [whose fame will never see an end] I took pleasure in playing the comic role of the braggart soldier, vain and proud, assuming the name of Capitan Spavento da Vall'Inferna. And such was the pleasure I took in this part, that I stopped playing my principal role, which was that of the lover.)

Like his talented and versatile wife, Isabella, who excelled in the part of the *innamorata* (female lover) but played other roles as well, Francesco also performed as the Sicilian Doctor, the shepherd Corinto, and the necromancer Falsirone. And like Isabella, who could speak many languages and dialects—especially when performing the "mad scenes" for which she became particularly famous—Francesco made good use of his knowledge of French, Spanish, Greek, and Turkish.

Title page for the fourth edition, revised and enlarged, of The Bravados of Captain Spavento *(University of Turin)*

In *Le bravure del Capitano Spavento* Trappola asks Capitan Spavento about his former companions; in response, Spavento provides a list of the members of the Gelosi and their roles: Ludovico da Bologna played Dottor (Doctor) Gratiano; Giulio Pasquati of Padua played Pantalone; Simone da Bologna played Zanni; Gabriele da Bologna played Francatrippa; Orazio da Padova and Adriano Valerini of Verona played *innamorati* (lovers); Girolamo Salimbeni of Florence played Zanobio and Piombino; Isabella Andreini was *prima amorosa* (romantic leading lady); Prudentia da Verona was *seconda amorosa* (secondary lady in love); Silvia Roncagli of Bergamo played Franceschina; and Francesco Andreini played Capitano Spavento da Vall'Inferna. The author is unable to suppress his pride when he has Spavento compare the Gelosi to the troupes that followed: "Trappola mio, di quelle compagnie non se ne trovano più" (My good Trappola, companies such as that can no longer be found). Companies nowadays, he continues, can count on only three or four good parts, while all of the Gelosi's roles were equally special. The passage concludes with the character's proud but also sad realization that the Gelosi, at their best, represented all that commedia dell'arte could offer and thereby had set an example that was almost impossible to follow; thus, one could say that the company "fu tale che pose termine alla drammatica arte" (had put an end to dramatic art).

Spavento's list does not cover the entire period of more than thirty years during which the Gelosi toured Italy and France but is representative of the years when Francesco and his wife were in charge: probably in 1583 and 1587–1588 and certainly during their last season, 1603–1604. It does not include Vittoria Piissimi, a rival of Isabella Andreini as *innamorata,* or Giovanni Pellesini, who played Pedrolino;

their names appear in other company documents. Furthermore, players' correspondence and documents pertaining to contractual negotiations reveal that actors shuffled back and forth from one company to another (such was the case with Piissimi and Pasquati among the Gelosi) and point to occasional amalgamations of rival troupes.

In 1603 the Gelosi returned to France at the request of Queen Maria de' Medici, performing successfully at the Hôtel de Bourgogne in Paris in July and August, at Fontainebleau in October and November, and again in Paris from December to the spring of 1604. On the way back to Italy, Isabella, who was forty-two and pregnant for the tenth time, miscarried and died in Lyon on 10 June 1604. The grief-stricken Francesco released the members of the company and retired from the stage. In the prologue to *Le bravure del Capitano Spavento* he writes:

> Durò quella famosa e non abbastanza lodata compagnia de i Comici Gelosi molti e molti anni, mostrando ai Comici venturi il vero modo di componere e di recitare Comedie, Tragicomedie, Tragedie, Pastorali, Intermedii apparenti, ed altre invenzioni rappresentative, che giornalmente si veggono nell'aringo delle Scene. Finito che fu quel termine, e venuto meno il vivere d'Isabella (la quale fu lume e splendore di quella virtuosa e onorata compagnia), fui da molti amici miei consigliato a scrivere alcuna cosa e donarla alla stampa, per lasciar qualche memoria di me e per seguitare l'onorato grido della moglie mia.

> (The famous company of the Comici Gelosi, which will never be sufficiently praised, lasted for many, many years, and showed future comedians the true way of composing and performing comedies, tragicomedies, tragedies, pastoral plays, intermezzos and other dramatic inventions, as can be commonly seen today in the theatrical arena. When its time was up, and once my beloved consort Isabella [who was the brightest star of that virtuous and honorable ensemble] died, I was exhorted by many of my friends to write and publish something in order to keep some memory of me alive, and preserve the honored fame of my wife.)

This passage shows that Francesco believed that he, Isabella, and their fellow actors had attained a perfection that could not be surpassed but only preserved in memory. It also demonstrates that the traditional view of commedia dell'arte as a theater of popular origins, based on stock characters, improvisation, mimicry, and acrobatics, and often performed on impromptu stages, is—as Roberto Tessari, Siro Ferrone, and Giovanna Romei have argued—highly reductive if not totally erroneous. What emerges from Andreini's description is a picture of acting as a profession that necessitates the individual and collective acquisition, cultivation, and practice of skills to be handed down to future generations. The actors to whom Andreini refers—first and foremost, his wife and himself—were cultured people who relied on a sound literary and theoretical preparation for writing, casting, and performing a wide variety of plays. Such a repertoire appealed to a range of audiences from the popular to the aristocratic and could be performed indoors or outdoors, in courtly and public venues, and in small and large theaters. The passage also stresses the presence—revolutionary for the time—of female performers, epitomized by Isabella Andreini.

After Isabella's death and the dissolution of the Gelosi, Andreini lived in Venice for a time; he then moved to Mantua, where he was honored by the dukes Vincenzo I, Francesco, and Ferdinando and was supported by the Gonzaga court. His four daughters, who had entered two local monasteries, and his second son, Domenico, who was captain of the dukes' guards, also lived in Mantua; Giovan Battista had become *capocomico* (actor-manager) of the Compagnia dei Fedeli (Company of the Faithful); his sons Cosimo and Giacinto had entered into military careers; and his son Pietro Paolo was a monk in Pavia.

For the rest of his life Andreini engaged in intense editorial activity. He often collaborated with his friend Scala, who had become head of the Comici Confidènti (Confident Comedians) and owner of a perfumery in Venice. The first edition of his best-known work, *Le bravure del Capitano Spavento,* published in Venice in 1607 and dedicated to Amedeo di Savoia of Piedmont, comprises fifty-five *ragionamenti*. The following year six of the *ragionamenti* were published in a French translation by Jacques de Fonteny, the *contrôleur des comédiens* (inspector in charge of supervising the activities of French and foreign actors), as *Les bravacheries du Capitaine Spavente*. A second edition of *Le bravure del Capitano Spavento* appeared in 1609, followed in 1615 by an enlarged edition, *Nuova aggiunta alle bravure del Capitano Spavento* (New Addition to the Bravados of Captain Spavento), that included ten new *ragionamenti*. In 1618 the collection was republished under the original title and dedicated to Scala's patron, Don Giovanni de' Medici; it included only forty *ragionamenti,* numbers 31 to 40 being those added to the second edition. In July 1624 Andreini completed the definitive edition in two parts: the first part consisted of the original fifty-five *ragionamenti* plus the ten of the 1615 addition, numbered 56 to 65; the second part consisted of thirty new *ragionamenti*. Three *ragionamenti* from the first part were translated into German by Chim von Harrlock in 1627. One more edition of the complete *Le bravure del Capitano Spavento* was published in 1669.

To preserve his wife's memory, as he had pledged to do in the prologue to *Le bravure del Capitano Spavento,*

Andreini in costume as his character Capitano Spavento (nineteenth-century reproduction of a fresco by Bernardino Poccetti in the Basilica dell SS. Annuziata, Florence; from Allardyce Nicoll, The World of Harlequin: A Critical Study of the Commedia dell'Arte, *1963; Thomas Cooper Library, University of South Carolina)*

Andreini edited Isabella's *Lettere* (Letters) in 1607. By 1617 he had collected the materials for *Fragmenti d' alcune scritture della Signora Isabella Andreini Comica Gelosa et accademica Intenta* (Fragments of Some Writings by Mrs. Isabella Andreini, Member of the Jealous Players and of the Academy of the Intent Ones), which was published under Scala's auspices in Venice in 1620. He wrote several poems; two sonnets and a madrigal appear in Giovan Battista's *Il Mincio ubidiente* (1620, The Tamed Mincio). He also wrote two *favole boscherecce* (sylvan tales): *L'ingannata Proserpina* (Proserpine Deceived) and *L'alterezza di Narciso* (Narcissus's Arrogance); both were published in Venice in 1611, but the words "nuovamente stampata" (newly reprinted) on the frontispieces indicate the existence of previous editions of which copies have not been discovered. Finally, he contributed an introduction to Scala's *Il teatro delle favole rappresentative* (1611, The Theater of Tales for Performance), a collection of fifty *scenari* (outlines) of commedia dell'arte plays that had been successfully performed in Italy and abroad by the first generation of great professional actors, such as the Andreinis as Capitan Spavento and Isabella, Pellesini as Pedrolino, Pasquati as Pantalone, Martinelli as Arlecchino, and Scala as Flavio. In the introduction Andreini makes claims for the autonomy of the language of performance and the legitimacy of improvisational theater; since it relies on the creativity and stage expertise of professional actors and on the perfect coordination of their efforts, the commedia dell'arte is, in his view, superior to the author-centered erudite literary theater run by amateur actors.

In the years immediately following his wife's death Andreini pursued the creation of a lasting "myth" of Isabella and the Andreini family not only through the publication of his and her works but also by iconographical means. Giovan Battista relates in *La ferza* that around 1607–1608 the painter Bernardino Pocetti, who was frescoing the main cloister of the church of the Santissima Annunziata in Florence, asked Andreini to sit for him. The frescoes were to illustrate the history of the Ordine dei Servi di Maria, the order of friars in charge of the church. Pocetti inserted portraits of Francesco and Giovan Battista into a scene representing the encounter in Paris in 1270 between the vicar of the order and King Philip of France; the Andreinis are in the foreground, on the right and left of the main scene, as if to frame it. Their postures and rich clothes—probably stage costumes for Capitan Spavento and Lelio—underline the theatrical quality of the composition, in which the figure of the king occupies the vanishing point. The two actors are thus remembered for their profession and the roles in which they specialized, while at the same time being elevated to the rank of the noble dignitaries surrounding the king. Isabella is shown standing with other ladies in the background. Other effigies of Francesco Andreini appear on the frontispieces of his books and are characterized by the same solemnity and "noble" aura.

At the base of the fresco Pocetti painted, as was the tradition, the coat of arms of the noble family that had financed the work: the Usimbardi, who held important offices at the Medici court. An Andreini coat of arms also exists and can be seen in the first edition of *Le bravure del Capitano Spavento* and in engravings in several of Giovan Battista's works published between 1604 and 1610. Devised by Francesco to provide the family with proof of its distinguished position in society, it borrows at least a few elements from the Usimbardi emblem. Francesco Andreini died on 20 August 1624.

Andreini was not the inventor of the character of the Capitano, whose roots date back to the Roman comedy *Miles Gloriosus* (circa 205 B.C., Braggart Warrior) of Plautus; he was one of many actors who appropriated the type and made it famous. Some of the *lazzi* (comic routines) in *Le bravure del Capitano Spavento* have been traced by scholars to texts of the erudite comedy of the late Renaissance such as Giambattista Della Porta's *Li duo fratelli rivali* (1601, The Two Rival Brothers). The captain's abundant use of Greek mythology and his systematic personification of the calamities he claims to have encountered in his life—*il Morbo* (Disease), *la Fame* (Hunger), *la Povertà* (Poverty), and *la Morte* (Death)—had been characteristic of the role long before Andreini began to play it. Nevertheless, it is because of him that the particular traits of the character as it developed within the commedia dell'arte have been preserved for posterity in a form that tries to approximate the ephemeral, unrepeatable effects of the character's appearances onstage.

Spavento and Trappola are reminiscent of another famous duo: Miguel de Cervantes's Don Quixote and his servant, Sancho Panza. Their dialogues bear traces, if tenuous, of social satire and veiled references to the political situation in late-sixteenth-century Italy. But while this Capitano still had some ties to the realities of Andreini's time, the character soon began to live off its reputation. The original comic attraction of the character, which resided in its representation of the devastating effects of war and politics, became increasingly irrelevant. In Spavento's often phantasmagoric speeches one can already detect the pressure under which the role soon came to surpass itself in a continual game of rodomontades. Scaramuccia (Scarmouche), impersonated by Tiberio Fiorilli later in the century, was the last representative of the long series of Capitani—a character by then far removed from its archetype, with a guitar in place of a sword and no political content. Francesco Andreini thus represents the crucial moment in the development of commedia dell'arte between its full, triumphant affirmation and the beginning of its decline.

References:

Giovan Battista Pietro Belli, dedicatory letter to Giovan Battista Andreini, *La Maddalena* (Venice: Giacomo Somasco, 1610);

Paul Castagno, *The Early Commedia dell'Arte (1550–1621)* (New York: Peter Lang, 1994), pp. 102–103;

Fausto De Michele, *Guerrieri ridicoli e guerre vere nel teatro comico del '500 e del '600 (Italia, Spagna e paesi di lingua tedesca)* (Florence: Alma, 1998), pp. 95–103;

Siro Ferrone, *Attori mercanti corsari: La Commedia dell'Arte in Europa tra Cinque e Seicento* (Turin: Einaudi, 1993);

Ferruccio Marotti and Giovanna Romei, *La commedia dell'arte e la società Barocca,* volume 1 (Rome: Bulzoni, 1991), pp. 209–302;

Daniela Mauri, "Il mito di Narciso in tre testi di Isabella, Francesco e Giovan Battista Andreini," in *La Commedia dell'Arte tra Cinque e Seicento in Francia e in Europa: Atti del Convegno Internazionale di Studi, Verona-Vicenza 19–21 ottobre 1995,* edited by Elio Mosele (Fasano: Schena, 1997), pp. 207–233;

Stefano Mazzoni, "Genealogia e vicende della famiglia Andreini," in *Origini della Commedia Improvvisa o* dell'Arte, edited by Maria Chiabò and Federico Doglio (Rome: Torre d'Orfeo, 1996), pp. 107–152;

Cesare Molinari, *La Commedia dell'Arte* (Rome: Istituto Poligrafico e Zecca dello Stato, 1999), pp. 849–921;

Allardyce Nicoll, *The World of Harlequin: A Critical Study of the Commedia dell'Arte 1894–1976* (Cambridge, U.K.: Cambridge University Press, 1963), p. 102;

Vito Pandolfi, *La commedia dell'arte: Storia e testo,* 6 volumes (Florence: Sansoni, 1957–1961);

Giovanna Romei, "La professione del teatro: La commedia dell'arte e la società barocca," in *Teoria testo e scena: Studi sullo spettacolo in Italia dal Rinascimento a Pirandello,* edited by Giorgio Patrizi and Luisa Tinti (Rome: Bulzoni, 2001), pp. 177–251;

Maurice Sand, *The History of the Harlequinade,* volume 1 (London: Martin Secker, 1915), pp. 149–150.

Flaminio Scala, *Scenarios of the Commedia dell'Arte: Flaminio Scala's* Il teatro delle favole rappresentative, edited and translated by Henry Frank Salerno (New York: New York University Press, 1967);

Ferdinando Taviani and Mirella Schino, *Il segreto della Commedia dell'Arte: La memoria delle compagnie italiane del XVI, XVII e XVIII secolo* (Florence: Usher, 1982);

Roberto Tessari, "Francesco Andreini e la stagione d'oro," in *Origini della Commedia Improvvisa o dell'Arte,* pp. 85–105;

Tessari, "Sotto il segno di Giano: La Commedia dell'Arte di Isabella e di Francesco Andreini," in *The Commedia dell'Arte from the Renaissance to Dario Fo,* edited by Christopher Cairns (Lewiston, N.Y.: Edwin Mellen Press, 1989), pp. 1–33.

Giovan Battista Andreini
(9 February 1576 – 7 June 1654)

Francesca Savoia
University of Pittsburgh

BOOKS: *La Florinda: Tragedia* (Florence, 1604; corrected edition, Milan: Girolamo Bordoni, 1606);

La saggia egiziana: Dialogo spettante alla lode dell'arte scenica, di Gio. Batista Andreini Fiorentino, Comico Fedele. Con un trattato sopra la stessa arte, cavato da San Tomaso, & da altri santi (Florence: Volcmar Timan, 1604);

La divina visione, in soggetto del Beato Carlo Borromeo, cardinale di Santa Prassede & arcivescovo di Milano (Florence: Volcmar Timan, 1604);

Il pianto d'Apollo: Rime funebri in morte d'Isabella Andreini Comica Gelosa, & Accademica Intenta, detta l'Accesa, di Gio. Batista Andreini suo figliuolo, con alcune Rime piacevoli sopra uno sfortunato poeta, dello stesso Autore (Milan: Girolamo Bordoni & Pietro martire Locarni, 1606);

La Maddalena (Venice: Giacomo Somasco, 1610); revised as *La Maddalena: Sacra rappresentazione* (Mantua: Osanna, 1617); revised as *La Maddalena: Composizione sacra* (Prague: Leva, 1628); revised as *La Maddalena: Composizione rappresentativa* (Vienna: Caspar ab Rath, 1629);

La Turca: Comedia boscareccia et maritima (Casale: Pantaleone Goffi, 1611);

Lo schiavetto: Comedia (Milan: Malatesta, 1612);

Prologo in dialogo fra Momo e la Verità, spettante alla lode dell'arte comica: Da Lelio Et Florinda, Comici del Serenissimo di Mantova, in Ferrara rappresentato. Et altro Discorso più grave in favor di dett'arte (Ferrara: Vittorio Baldini, 1612);

L'Adamo: Sacra rapresentatione (Milan: Girolamo Bordoni, 1613); translated by William Cowper as *Adam*, in volume 3 of his *Cowper's Milton*, 4 volumes (Chichester, U.K.: Printed by W. Mason for J. Johnson & Co., London, 1810);

Ersilio pastore lodando Aminta seguace de' Theatri, fuggendo Amore (Mantua: Osanna, 1617);

Fama consolatrice nelle reali Nozze de' Serenissimi Sposi Ferdinando Gonzaga e Caterina Medici, nell'andata di S.A.S. a Fiorenza (Mantua: Osanna, 1617);

Composizioni funebri in morte della Serenissima Margherita Gonzaga d'Este Duchessa di Ferrara (Mantua: Osanna, 1618);

La venetiana: Comedia de sier Cocalin dei Cocalini da Torzolo, academico Vizilante, dito el Dormioto (Venice: Alessandro Polo, 1619);

Intermedio rappresentato in Mantova in honore del Sereniss.o Sign. Duca Ferdinando, nella celebrazione del real sostegno del Mincio, dall'Altezza Sua fabricato, per opera e architettura del Molt'Illustre Sig. Gabriello Bertazzolo suo meritiss.o ingegnere (Mantova: Osanna, 1620);

Lelio bandito: Tragicomedia boschereccia (Milan: Gio. Battista Bidelli, 1620);

Il Mincio ubidiente di Gio. Battista Andreini: Componimenti di pellegrini ingegni sopra l'ammirabile sostegno fatto a Governo dell'Illustre Signor Gabriel Bertacciolo (Venice: Bertoni, 1620);

La campanazza: Commedia di Giovanni Rivani da Bologna, detto il Dottor Campanaccio da Budri (Paris: Della Vigna, 1621);

La centaura: Suggetto diviso in commedia, pastorale e tragedia (Paris: Della Vigna, 1622);

La Ferinda: Commedia (Paris: Della Vigna, 1622);

Amore nello specchio: Commedia (Paris: Della Vigna, 1622);

La Sultana: Commedia (Paris: Della Vigna, 1622);

Li duo Leli simili: Commedia (Paris: Della Vigna, 1622);

Le due comedie in comedia: Suggetto stravagantissimo (Venice: Ghirardo & Iseppo Imberti, 1623);

Prologo in servizio di S.M.C. alla serenissima Madama principessa di Piemonte (Turin, 1623);

Prologo per recitare nel teatro di Luigi Giustiniano (Venice, 1623);

La Tecla vergine e martire: Poema sacro (Venice: Paolo Guerigli, 1623);

Comici martiri e penitenti (Paris: Nicolas Callemont, 1624); republished as *Teatro celeste: Nel quale si rappresenta come la Divina Bontà habbia chiamato al grado di beatitudine e di santità Comici penitenti e martiri; con un poetico esordio a' scenici professori di far l'arte virtuosamente, per lasciar in terra non solo nome famoso, ma per non chiu-*

Title page for an edition of Giovan Battista Andreini's The Young Slave, *originally published in 1612 (University of Turin)*

dersi viziosamente la via che ne conduce al Paradiso (Paris: Nicolas Callemont, 1625);

L'inchino per la novella servitù della nuova Compagnia de' Comici (Paris, 1625);

Lo specchio: Composizione sacra e poetica, nella quale si rappresenta al vivo l'imagine della Comedia, quanto vaga e deforme sia allor che da Comici virtuosi o viziosi rappresentata viene (Paris: Nicolas Callemont, 1625);

La ferza: Ragionamento secondo contra l'accuse date alla Commedia (Paris: Nicolas Callemont, 1625);

Il conflitto guerra tra bresciani e cremonesi, con la convenzione di Sant'Obicio, nobile bresciano (Brescia: Bacchi, 1630);

L'Himeneo: Nelle felicissime nozze de gl'Illustrissimi Sposi il Marchese Ottavio Ruini e Donna Maria Mattei (Bologna: Catanio, 1631);

Il penitente alla Santissima Vergine del Rosario (Bologna: Clemente Ferroni, 1631);

La Rosella: Tragicomedia boschereccia (Bologna: Clemente Ferroni, 1632);

Le cinque rose del giardino di Berico: Divoto componimento nell'apparizione della Regina de gli Angeli Maria Vergine alla contadina di Sovizzo detta Vicenza (Vicenza: Eredi Amadio, 1633);

Li duo baci: Comedia boschereccia (Bologna: Monti & Zenero, 1634);

L'Arno festeggiante a' Serenissimi Sposi Ferdinando II Gran Duca di Toscana e Vittoria della Rovere, poesia drammatica (Florence: Zanobi Pignoni, 1636);

La rosa: Commedia boschereccia (Pavia: Gio. Andrea Magri, 1638);

L'Ismena: Opera reale e pastorale (Bologna: Niccolò Tebaldini, 1639);

L'Olivastro, o vero il Poeta sfortunato: Poema fantastico (Bologna: Niccolò Tebaldini, 1642);

L'Ossequio alla Maestà Clementissima, e realissima della Regina Anna (Paris, 1643);

Le lagrime: Divoto componimento, a contemplazione della vita penitente e piangente della gran Protetrice della Francia Maria Maddalena, al Cristianissimo Luigi il Giusto Re di Francia, e di Navarra. Autore Gio. Battista Andreini, tra Comici Fedeli detto Lelio, inchinate e riverito havendo in questo viaggio a S.M.C. di Maddalena e le Reliquie e 'l luogo di sua penitenza (Paris: Charles, 1643);

Il Guerriero: Vaticinio poetico. Nell'andata al campo del Serenissimo Duca D'Anguien. General dell'Arme di sua Maestà Christianissima. In Champania. Autore lo stesso Andreini (Paris, 1644);

Il Vincente ne i novelli gloriosi conquisti del formidabil Signor Duca D'Anguien, generale di Sua Maestà Christianissima de gli eserciti di Alemagna (Paris, 1644);

Lilla piangente (Paris, 1644);

Cristo sofferente: Meditazioni in versi divotissimi sopra i punti principali della passione di Cristo (Florence: Giraffi, 1651);

La Maddalena lasciva e penitente: Azzione drammatica, e divota in Milano rappresentata (Milan: Gio. Battista & Giulio Cesare Malatesta, 1652).

Editions and Collections: *L'Adamo, sacra rappresentazione,* in Filippo Scolari, *Saggio di critica sul Paradiso Perduto, poema di Giovanni Milton, e sulle annotazioni a quello di Giuseppe Addison* (Venice: Rizzi, 1818), pp. 225–339;

L'Adamo: Sacra rappresentazione di Giovan Battista Andreini fiorentino. Pubblicato la prima volta in Milano l'anno 1617 (Lugano: Ruggia, 1834);

Adamo: Sacra rappresentazione in cinque atti e un prologo (Milan: Visay, 1860);

L'Adamo, con un saggio sull' "Adamo" e "Il paradiso perduto," edited by Ettore Allodoli (Lanciano: Carabba, 1913);

Excerpts from *La Venetiana, Lo Schiavetto, La Campanaccia, Le due comedie in commedia, La saggia egiziana, La ferza,* and *Teatro celeste,* in *La Commedia dell'Arte: Storia e testo,* 6 volumes, edited by Vito Pandolfi (Florence: Sansoni, 1957–1961), III: 134–175, 332–254;

Lo schiavetto, in *Commedie dei comici dell'arte,* edited by Laura Falavolti (Turin: Unione Tipografico-Editrice Torinese, 1982), pp. 45–213;

Le due comedie in comedia, in *Commedie dell'arte,* 2 volumes edited by Siro Ferrone (Milan: Mursia, 1986), II: 8–105;

Excerpts from *La saggia egiziana* and *La ferza,* in *Attore: Alle origini di un mestiere,* edited by Falavolti (Rome: Lavoro, 1988), pp. 41–44, 65–84, 89–99, 109–115;

Tre scene da "Il convitato di pietra," edited by Silvia Carandini and Luciano Mariti, *Teatro e Storia,* 3, no. 2 (1988): 345–362;

Excerpts from *La ferza* and *Prologo in dialogo fra Momo e la Verità,* in *La commedia dell'arte e la società barocca,* volume 2, edited by Ferruccio Marotti and Giovanna Romei (Rome: Bulzoni, 1991), pp. 473–534;

Amore nello specchio, edited by Salvatore Maira and Anna Michela Borracci (Rome: Bulzoni, 1997);

Le due comedie in comedia, in *Commedia dell'arte,* edited by Cesare Molinari and Renzo Guardenti (Rome: Istituto Poligrafico e Zecca dello Stato, 1999), pp. 663–740;

La Centaura, edited by Franco Vazzoler and Guido Davico Bonino (Genoa: Il Melangolo, 2004)–includes "Giovan Battista Andreini comico e drammaturgo," by Davico Bonino, pp. 7–16, and "Il labirinto della *Centaura*: Appunti di lettura," by Vazzoler, pp. 17–35;

La Maddalena lasciva e penitente, edited by Rossella Palmieri, introduction by Silvia Carandini (Bari: Palomar, 2006).

PLAY PRODUCTIONS: *Florinda,* Florence, Accademia degli Spensierati, late 1604;

La Maddalena, Mantua, Ducal Palace, February 1617;

Le due comedie in comedia, Venice, Giustiniani Theater, 1623;

Maddalena lasciva e penitente, Milan, 1652.

Possibly the most important Italian dramatist of the seventeenth century, Giovan Battista Andreini was the first of the nine children of the actors Francesco and Isabella Andreini and the only one to follow in his parents' footsteps. He wrote comedies, tragedies, tragicomedies, pastoral plays, mystery plays, operas, treatises on drama and performance, and poetry. While a few of his plays have long been the objects of attention of commedia dell'arte historians, only since the 1990s has the whole of Andreini's production been seriously evaluated and his contribution to European literature recognized.

Andreini was baptized in Florence on 9 February 1576. Shortly thereafter, his parents joined the acting company of the Gelosi (Jealous Ones), in which Francesco played the role of Capitano Spavento and Isabella that of first romantic lady; they ultimately assumed the direction of the troupe. To make their somewhat disreputable occupation respectable and bring prestige to it, the Andreinis endeavored to present themselves to their contemporaries as skilled professionals, cultured individuals, exemplary husband and

Title page for the first edition of Adam *(University of Turin)*

wife, and good parents who made sure that their five sons and four daughters received good educations. Domenico, Giacinto, and Cosimo joined the military, and Pietro Paolo became a monk. The daughters entered the convent: Lavinia and Caterina took the names Sister Fulvia and Sister Osanna, respectively; the other two daughters are known only by their religious names, Sister Claridiana and Sister Clarastella.

After studying in Bologna around 1594, Giovan Battista Andreini joined the Gelosi and began acting as an *innamorato* (lover) under the stage name Lelio. In 1601 he married an eighteen-year-old actress and singer, Virginia Ramponi, in Milan; shortly afterward, the couple either formed or joined another company, the Fedeli (Faithful Ones). On 10 June 1604 Isabella Andreini died suddenly in Lyon on the way home from a successful tour in France. Francesco Andreini disbanded the Gelosi and retired from the stage to dedicate himself to the publication of his and his wife's works. Toward the end of the same year Giovan Battista Andreini made his debut as an author with *La Florinda*, a tragedy set in the forests of Scotland. The play was performed by the Fedeli at the Accademia degli Spensierati (Academy of the Carefree) in Florence; Ramponi played the title role and used Florinda as her stage name for the rest of her career. Andreini ordered all copies of the poorly edited first edition of the work, which was published in Florence, to be destroyed; a corrected second edition appeared in Milan in 1606.

At the end of 1604 Andreini performed in Florence in *La pazzia di Lelio* (The Madness of Lelio), perhaps with the company of the Uniti (United Ones), and published three works: *La saggia egiziana* (The Wise Egyptian Woman), a dialogue in blank verse in defense of his art dedicated to Don Antonio de' Medici; in the same volume, "Trattato sopra l'arte comica cavato dall'opera di San Tomaso e da altri santi" (Treatise on the Art of Comedy Drawn from the Works of St. Thomas and Other Saints), which he attributed to an uncle on his father's side; and *La divina visione* (The Divine Vision), a sixty-four-stanza poem in ottava rima in praise of the archbishop of Milan, Carlo Borromeo, a steadfast censor of the theater. In *La saggia egiziana* a detractor of the theater reminds a wise old Egyptian woman that one of the Roman emperors banished all comic actors from the city. The old woman, who personifies comedy, corrects him by pointing out that only the basest and most inept comedians and street artists were exiled. She goes on to recall that the great writer and orator Cicero had immense admiration for the actor Roscio and was hesitant about delivering a public speech in Roscio's presence.

In all of his works in defense of the acting profession Andreini emphasizes the necessity of knowing how to use language both in writing and in performing. In addition to such practical and theoretical concerns he addresses moral issues, drawing a distinction between two orders of comedians whom civil and religious authorities should regard differently: on the one hand, the "comico virtuoso," a learned, God-fearing, and law-abiding professional actor who writes and performs to entertain and educate the public, and on the other hand, the disreputable actor who is apt to maintain relationships with wicked people and is only capable of performing obscenities.

Andreini often signed his letters and plays "d'Isabella figlio" (Isabella's son), and he discussed his mother's talents and virtues in many of his non-dramatic works. Her death prompted him to compose one of his earliest works of poetry, *Il pianto d'Apollo* (1606, Apollo's tears). The Muses come looking for their father, Apollo, who, disheartened by the demise of "la saggia Andreina" (the wise [Isabella] Andreini), has retreated to a dark cave, depriving the world of the light of day. Death presents itself to the young Giovan Battista, who is roaming in the darkness mourning his loss, and reminds him of the vanity of all human efforts in the face of its destructive power. Fame, however, descends from the poetic Olympus where Isabella resides, persuades Apollo to resume his duties, and invites Giovan Battista to find consolation in the thought that one day he, too, will be welcomed in that eternal celestial academy where his mother dwells. At the end of the poem Andreini tells Isabella: "il tuo zelo seguendo, mi sarai gran scala al cielo" (as I emulate your zeal, you will be my ladder to the heavens).

Like his parents, Andreini was wise in cultivating relationships with patrons. In 1605 Duke Vincenzo Gonzaga of Mantua, who had been a supporter of the Gelosi, invited the Fedeli to be his court's resident acting company; with some interruptions, the ensemble served the Gonzaga family until 1640. The Fedeli played not only in Mantua but also in other Italian courts to which the Gonzagas sent them as artistic emissaries: in 1606, for example, the troupe performed in Milan and Bologna. The Fedeli occasionally combined forces with the Accesi (Impassioned Ones), a company that was directed by Pier Maria Cecchini (Fritellino) and his wife, Orsola (Flaminia), and included Silvio Fiorillo (Capitan Matamoros) and Domenico Bruni (Fulvio). The two troupes coexisted uneasily because of the struggle for supremacy between the Andreinis and the more-renowned Cecchinis.

In the spring of 1608, while the Accesi were in France, the Fedeli gave the premiere performance of Giovan Battista Guarini's *L'idropica* (The Dropsical Damsel) and presented several of their own plays during the festivities for the wedding of Francesco IV Gonzaga and Margherita di Savoia. In the course of the celebrations Ramponi replaced the singer Caterina Martinelli, who had died of smallpox at eighteen, in the title role of *Arianna* (Ariadne) and in *Il ballo delle ingrate* (The Ball of the Ungrateful), two operas by Claudio Monteverdi with texts by Ottavio Rinuccini. As a result, when the Fedeli and the Accesi were reunited in Turin in the summer of 1609, the fame of the Andreinis equaled that of the Cecchinis.

Also in 1609 the Fedeli performed in Parma and in Milan, where Ramponi gave birth to a son, Pietro Enrico. In 1610 they appeared in Venice, where Andreini published a long poem, *La Maddalena* (Mary Magdalene). In 1611 Duke Vincenzo Gonzaga sent the company to Casale to entertain his son Francesco and daughter-in-law Margherita. There Ramponi performed successfully in the melodrama *Rapimento di Proserpina* (Abduction of Proserpine), by Giulio Cesare Monteverdi, Claudio's younger brother, and Ercole Marliani, and Andreini published his play *La Turca* (The Turkish Woman). Ramponi mentions in a letter that Pietro Enrico, whom the Andreinis had left in Mantua, was for a time in peril of dying of an illness. In 1611 the Fedeli also performed in Genoa, Rome, and Bologna. The following year they appeared in Ferrara, Milan, and Florence; Andreini's *Prologo in dialogo fra Momo e la Verità* (Prologue in the Form of a Dialogue between Momo and Truth) was published in Ferrara and dedicated to Eugenio Pio di Savoia, and his *Lo schiavetto* (The Young Slave) was published in Milan. In *Lo schiavetto* the protagonist, played by Ramponi, sang a song by Giulio Caccini. The play was dedicated to Alessan-

Illustration for Andreini's play La Venetiana *(The Venetian Woman), published in 1619 under the pseudonym Cocalin dei Cocalini (from Pierre-Louis Duchartre,* The Italian Comedy: The Improvisation, Scenarios, Lives, Attributes, Portraits, and Masks of the Illustrious Characters of the Commedia dell'Arte, *1966; Thomas Cooper Library, University of South Carolina)*

dro Striggio, one of Claudio Monteverdi's librettists and the Gonzagas' ambassador in the Lombard capital.

According to the publisher's dedication and Andreini's letter to the readers, *Lo schiavetto* earned praise wherever it was performed. The play seems to have been created to showcase the abilities of the various members of the Fedeli, including Ramponi's dancing and singing. The costumes, stage properties, scenery, and various devices described in an appendix to the text indicate that *Lo schiavetto* required an elaborate and skillful production. Three groups of characters come into contact with each other at an inn in Pesaro. Nottola, a confidence man, pretends to be a prince and surrounds himself with a pseudocourt of knaves and parasites; he actually lives off the riches he has stolen from his adoptive father, a wealthy jeweler. Florinda is a young woman disguised as a male slave to pursue her unfaithful lover, Orazio; she is accompanied by Rondone, a street performer, and Facceto, a professional actor, who reveals himself in the end to be Florinda's brother. Caught in the middle and fooled both by the swindlers and the entertainers are the Florentine innkeeper, Succiola, a practical businesswoman; the miser Alberto; his daughter, Prudenza; and Prudenza's penniless suitors, the forever pining Fulgenzio and Florinda's former lover, Orazio. A series of hoaxes and practical jokes spices up the main action of the play, which consists of Florinda's attempts to punish Orazio's unfaithfulness and ends in recognition, reconciliation, and a triple wedding: Florinda marries Orazio; Prudenza consoles herself with Fulgenzio; and Succiola accepts Nottola's father, Belisario, as her husband.

Laura Falavolti observes that Andreini contrived innovative ways to deal with the traditional material at his disposal, particularly in his creative use of language: in *Lo schiavetto* one finds the typical lofty discourse of the lovers; the colorful regional idioms of the lower-class characters; the jargon of the criminal underworld; a pastiche of Yiddish, Hebrew, and Hebrew-sounding words used by Jewish salesmen; comical gibberish; and pervasive double entendres. *Lo schiavetto* is also distinguished by Andreini's use of metatheatrical devices to allow the audience a glimpse of the inner workings of the theater: in the last act the other characters challenge Facceto, played by Andreini, to show the feats of which he is capable; he delivers a seemingly impromptu performance in which he plays a *zanni* (comic servant), Pantalone (a greedy and lecherous old man), a *dottore* (doctor), and Nespola (a female *zanni*) and speaks several dialects.

The rivalry between the Fedeli and the Accesi reached its peak when Maria de' Medici, the widow of King Henry IV of France and regent for her son, Louis XIII, entrusted the acclaimed actor Tristano Martinelli (Arlecchino) with recruiting the best Italian comedians to appear at the French court. Martinelli, who was from Mantua and had acted with the Uniti, the Confidenti (Confident Ones), the Accesi, and the Fedeli, was unable to persuade the Andreinis and the Cecchinis to perform together in France. In the end, the Fedeli signed the contract. Giovan Battista Andreini probably helped to secure their engagement by dedicating his mystery play *L'Adamo* (1613; translated as *Adam,* 1810) to the Medicis and a special reprint of *La Turca* to Louis Gonzaga, Duke of Nevers.

L'Adamo may have been the most widely known of Andreini's works between the seventeenth and the nineteenth centuries. The first edition, published in Milan, included a portrait of the author by Gerolamo Bordone and an illustration of each of the forty-two scenes by Antonio Procaccini. In *An Essay upon the Civil Wars of France: Extracted from Curious Manuscripts. And Also upon the Epick Poetry of the European Nations from Homer down to Milton* (1727) Voltaire conjectured that John Milton, traveling in Italy in 1638–1639, might have attended a performance of Andreini's play and drawn inspiration from it for his *Paradise Lost* (1667). Voltaire's hypothesis, which is supported by the existence of a Miltonian manuscript in Cambridge that features a sketchy outline of a tragedy reminiscent of *L'Adamo,* prompted a partial English translation of the play in 1796 and a complete one in 1810. The first three acts are framed by alternating choruses of devils and angels and depict the creation of Adam, his inability to resist temptation, and his fall from grace. In the fourth and fifth acts Adam and Eve, expelled from the Garden of Eden, are confronted by personifications of Hunger, Thirst, Hardship, Desperation, and Death. In the end the archangel Michael arrives as the bearer of hope for the possibility of the redemption of humankind.

The Fedeli left for Paris in the summer of 1613 under Martinelli's direction; besides Martinelli and the Andreinis, the company consisted of Giovanni Pellesini (Pedrolino), Gerolamo Garavini (Capitan Rinoceronte), Federico Ricci (Pantalone), his brother Benedetto Ricci (Leandro), Margherita Luciani (Flavia), Bartolomeo Bongiovanni (Gratiano), Lorenzo Nettuni (Fichetto), and a young actress, Virginia Rotari, who initially played the part of a maidservant but was soon promoted by Giovan Battista to the role of second romantic lady with the stage name Lidia. They performed in Paris at the Louvre, the Hôtel de Bourgogne, Fontainebleau, and Saint Germain from the fall of 1613 to the summer of 1614. When they departed for Nancy to entertain the dukes of Lorraine in July 1614, Martinelli and two or three other actors returned to Italy. Left in charge of the troupe, Giovan Battista Andreini prolonged their stay in France for a few more months. From December 1614 until the summer of 1615 the Fedeli were back in Mantua, where Andreini's father, one of his brothers, and his four sisters lived. The following year Andreini acquired Ca' di Mandraghi, an estate near the city. His letter announcing the purchase mentions a failed plan to go to Flanders with his fellow actors. In 1617 he published a reworking of *La Maddalena,* which Maria de' Medici had urged him to transform into a *sacra rappresentazione* (mystery play); it was performed that same year by the Fedeli at the festivities in celebration of Duke Ferdinando Gonzaga's marriage to Caterina de' Medici. Portions of the play were set to music by Claudio Monteverdi, Muzio Effrem, Salamone Rossi, and Alessandro Ghivizzani, all of whom were musicians in residence at the court of Mantua.

An Italian tour in 1619–1620 took Andreini and his company to Milan, Ferrara, Brescia, Venice, and back to Milan. In Venice he supervised reprintings of *Lo schiavetto* and *La Turca* and published a new play in Venetian dialect, *La venetiana* (1619, The Venetian Woman), under the pseudonym Cocalin dei Cocalini. Also in 1620 he published and played the title role in *Lelio bandito* (Lelio the Bandit), a *tragicomedia boschereccia* (pastoral tragicomedy) about the adventures of a captivating highwayman. His musical intermezzo *Il Mincio ubidiente* (The Tamed Mincio) was published and staged in Mantua in 1620 to celebrate the accomplishments of a hydraulic engineer in the service of the Gonzagas.

In their introductions to *Lo schiavetto* and *La Venetiana* the editors call the author a great actor and an accomplished writer, one of the few endowed with "facondia e saggezza" (readiness of speech and wisdom) and with "favella e dottrina" (eloquence and great learning). Some scholars have suggested that those words of praise may have been dictated by Andreini. In the preface to *La Venetiana* he asks, "se un pittore non perde la reputazione se dipinge un angelo o un satiro, perché lo scrittore è diverso?" (if a painter's reputation does not depend upon his painting an angel or a satyr, why should it be any different for a playwright?). Andreini's colleague Giovan Paolo Fabri (Flaminio) argues in the prologue to *Lelio bandito:* "Perché mai si critica il professionismo come attività remunerata quando non si contestano compensi ai medici per salvare una vita, agli avvocati per difendere un innocente, ai soldati per difendere la patria, ai maestri per educare e trasmettere il sapere?" (Why should professional performers be criticized for being paid for their activity, when nobody challenges the notion of remuneration for a doctor who saves a life, a lawyer who defends an innocent, soldiers who defend the country, teachers who educate and transmit knowledge?).

Since the summer of 1618 Louis XIII had been expressing the desire to have an Italian acting company return to his court, and the Fedeli entered into negotiations with France during their 1619–1620 tour. Fearing the unreliability of Martinelli and the competition of Pier Maria Cecchini, Andreini contacted Flaminio Scala, a former member of the Gelosi and an old friend of his father's who was then the head of the Confidenti, the company at the service of Don Giovanni de' Medici. Louis XIII's wish to have Francesco Gabrielli, the member of the Confidenti who played Scapino, at his court was well known. Furthermore, the Mantuan company was not a well-balanced ensemble at the time and could use a *zanni* such as Gabrielli, as well as an *innamorato* such as Domenico Bruni, another former member of the Gelosi who had performed with the Accesi and then defected to the Confidenti. Ercole Marliani, Mantua's secretary of state, tried to negotiate with Giovanni de' Medici a partial affiliation of his Confidenti with the Fedeli for the French engagement. The Confidenti, however, wanted to avoid breaking up the unity on which their strength was based. Therefore, de' Medici proposed that the whole Confidenti troupe go to France, along with only the best-known and most valued Mantuans, Martinelli and the Andreinis.

Before it collapsed, this plan had the effect of reviving Pier Maria Cecchini's animosity. The projected trip to France was further delayed and complicated by a rumor of a love affair between Andreini and Virginia Rotari, whose husband, Baldo, had also joined the company with his wife in 1612, though probably not as an actor. The rumor, spread mostly by Pier Maria Cec-

Title page for the first edition of The Sultana
(University of Turin)

chini, upset the spouses of the two parties and reached the Mantuan court. It seems to have been well founded, since on the death of her husband in 1633 Virginia Rotari and Andreini, by then a widower, began living together and eventually married. But when the affair was first divulged, Andreini, to keep his job and save his marriage and his company, dismissed it in a letter to the duke.

In the summer of 1620 Andreini was in Milan, ready to leave for France with his wife, Martinelli, the Cecchinis, Federico Ricci, Garavini, Virginia Rotari, and a few new members of the company. By that time Pier Maria Cecchini's tantrums and demands had increased to the point that his colleagues requested and obtained his dismissal by the duke. Just before its departure in October the company was joined by Nettuni and Benedetto Ricci; the latter died in Chambéry on the way to Paris.

The diary of the royal family's personal physician testifies to the assiduousness with which the king attended the performances of the Italian comedians in Paris between 12 January and 4 March 1621. In spite of the great success that he and his colleagues were reaping, however, and against the wishes of the French king and the Gonzagas, Martinelli abandoned the ensemble once again, leaving at the end of June. The rest of the company remained in France, still in the service of the king. In 1621–1622 Andreini staged and published six ambitious new theatrical works: three comedies in prose, *La campanazza* (1621, The Old Bell), *Amore nello specchio* (1622, Love in the Mirror), and *La Sultana* (1622, The Sultana); *La Ferinda* (1622, Ferinda), a one-act play in verse, part recited and part sung; *Li duo Leli simili* (1622, The Two Similar Lelios), an adaptation of one of his father's *scenari,* which had in turn been inspired by Plautus's *Menaechmi;* and *La centaura* (1622, The She-Centaur), dedicated to Maria de' Medici and consisting of comedy in the first act, pastoral in the second, and tragedy in the third. According to the editor's foreword to *La campanazza,* Andreini had reached his goal of having his works read and performed with great success in Italy as well as abroad: "essendo questi suoi componimenti comici di grido felicissimo, leggendosi, e 'n diverse parti rappresentandosi con applauso universale" (being that his plays are very famous, and read and performed in many places to universal applause).

In the spring of 1623 Andreini published a play that the Fedeli were performing at the Giustiniani Theater in the San Moisé district of Venice: *Le due comedie in comedia* (Two Comic Plays within a Play). In this play and in *Li duo Leli simili* the Lidia character played by Virginia Rotari takes on a more prominent position—an indication that the hierarchy of female romantic parts was being overturned in favor of the younger actress. The courtyard of the home of Rovenio becomes the stage for a competition between a group of amateur actors, the Accademia dell'Incerta Speranza (Academy of Uncertain Hope), and a professional company, the Comici Appassionati, who appear dressed in their richest stage costumes. As the two groups perform their plays, they recall acts by their host of which many of the onlookers have been victims. In the end Rovenio is forced to admit to his wrongdoings and ask for forgiveness. Although the main premise of the play appears to have been drawn from a 1618 *canovaccio* (plot outline) by Basilio Locatelli bearing a similar title, the way in which Andreini makes the characters of the actors slip back and forth from the plots of the plays within the play to the "reality" of the story that contains them was clever and original. Renzo Guardenti has compared *Le due comedie in comedia* to the works of Luigi Pirandello.

At the end of 1623 or the beginning of 1624 the Fedeli went back to Paris, along with Gabrielli and Nicolò Barbieri; they seem to have remained until October 1625. Andreini responded to a campaign against actors in the French capital by publishing three works in defense of his art: *Comici martiri e penitenti* (1624, Comedians, Martyrs, and Penitents), which was republished in 1625 under the title *Teatro celeste* (Celestial Theater) and was dedicated to the chief of Louis XIII's royal council, Armand-Jean du Plessis, Cardinal Richelieu; *Lo specchio* (1625, The Mirror), dedicated to the duke of Nevers; and *La ferza* (1625, The Lash), dedicated to the Venetian ambassador to France. In *Teatro celeste* Andreini pays homage to his mother, placing her in the heavens in the company of holy spirits; he declares that the road to eternal fame can be taken only by "professori virtuosi" (virtuous practitioners of the comic profession) such as Isabella and never by the "turba pestifera e rubella" (pernicious and unruly mob) of comedians who bring poor and filthy stories to the stage: "comici tai giù nel tartareo stanno" (such comedians belong to hell). In *La ferza,* written after the death of his father on 20 August 1624, Andreini commemorates both of his parents as shining examples of professionalism, virtue, and sobriety but dwells, once again, much more extensively on Isabella. His account of his mother's funeral, with its descriptions of the people of Lyon coming in unprecedented numbers, like pilgrims, to pay homage to Isabella and buy medallions with her effigy, transform this honest, talented, and cultured actress into a kind of saint. Maurizio Rebaudengo suggests that Andreini's glorification of Isabella should not be understood simply as a son's tribute to his mother or as the product of a typically Baroque imagination but as representing the yearning for lasting fame of an entire professional class. In *La ferza* Andreini also says that eloquence separates true comedians from charlatans and mountebanks—"Altro non è il recitatore che oratore" (An actor is but an orator)—and stresses the need for rigorous study and discipline for those who want to embrace the acting profession. The suppleness and dexterity required of the comic actor in the use of language, he explains, is not an inborn faculty but can be acquired and maintained by the continual study of ancient and modern literary classics.

The duke of Mantua, Ferdinando II, Andreini's foremost patron, died in October 1626; his successor, Vincenzo II, died the following year, and the duke of Nevers, who had supported the Fedeli since the time of their first visit to France, took over the duchy. Since war was threatening to break out over the Mantuan succession, Andreini and his fellow actors deemed it prudent to leave Italy. After a brief stay in Venice, the Fedeli were employed, thanks to Martinelli's negotiations with the imperial court, in Prague from the end of 1627 until the fall of 1628. There Andreini published a new version of his mystery play *La Maddalena*, dedicating it to the archbishop of Prague, Cardinal Ernest von Harrach, who had granted him an annual pension. The Fedeli went on to the court of Vienna, where Andreini was well received and generously compensated by Holy Roman Emperor Ferdinand II.

The company returned to Mantua in the fall of 1629 and remained there until carnival 1630, the year of the great plague. Andreini witnessed at first hand the devastation brought to the city and its territory by the war over the succession to the dukedom of Mantua, which lasted from 1628 to 1631 and in which France and Ferdinand II supported rival claimants. He described the situation in a short poem in ottava rima, *Il penitente alla Santissima Vergine del Rosario* (The Penitent to the Blessed Virgin of the Rosary), published in Bologna in January 1631:

L'uno de' mostri in minaccioso aspetto
Era la Guerra sanguinosa il manto.
La Fame l'altro horribile concetto,
Scarno, e macero il corpo in ogni canto.
Il terzo era la Peste in fier cospetto
Verminoso cadavere di pianto,
Questi in triumvirato miserando
Vanno d'horribilità vessilli alzando.

(One of the monsters of threatening appearance
Was the War, its cape all stained in blood.
Famine was the other, horrible one,
Its body thin and worn in all its parts.
The third was the Plague, a cruel and
Grievous sight of verminous corpses.
This wretched triumvirate goes on
Hoisting its hideous flags.)

Virginia Andreini died in Bologna in the summer of 1631. Shortly afterward, Andreini received news of his brother Pietro Paolo's death.

Andreini continued to publish, producing books of devotions; poetry; a comedy, *Li duo baci* (1634, The Two Kisses); a pastoral play, *La rosa* (1638, The Rose); and an opera, *L'Ismena* (1639, Ismena). Many of his late works, however, remained in manuscript. Among them were *Il convitato di pietra* (The Stone Guest) and its reworked version, *Il nuovo risarcito Convitato di pietra* (The New Revised Stone Guest), an unfinished play in five acts, fifty-two scenes, and almost eight thousand verses; and what he called a *poetica esagerazione* (poetic exaggeration), *Il litigio* (The Dispute), composed in 1640–1641 and inspired by a lawsuit brought against him in Lucca because of an unpaid loan. The suit resulted in a brief prison term for Andreini and was resolved only through the intervention of the grand duke of Tuscany,

Title page for the first edition of Two Comic Plays within a Play, *published in 1623 (University of Turin)*

Ferdinando II de' Medici, and his brother Mattias; Andreini dedicated *Il litigio* to Mattias. A further token of Andreini's gratitude to the Medicis was the dedicatory letter of *L'olivastro, o vero il Poeta sfortunato: Poema fantastico* (The Man with the Olive Complexion; or, The Unfortunate Poet: A Fantastic Poem), Andreini's longest—twenty-five cantos in ottava rima—and most powerful poem, published in Bologna in 1642.

Andreini wrote in *Il litigio* that after the experience in Lucca, he was ready to put an end to "il viaggiare di punto in punto" (the constant traveling from here to there), was "stanco alfin qui di liti e di teatri" (finally tired of controversies and theaters), and wanted to retire to his Mantuan estate, "di comico fatto agricoltore" (ceasing to be a comedian and becoming a farmer). A new call came from the French court, however, and in 1643 he went to Paris with his company once more. He returned to Italy in 1647 and continued to write and perform; his last recorded production was a successful staging in Milan of *Maddalena lasciva e penitente* (1652, Mary Magdalene Lustful and Penitent) with his second wife in the title role.

It is doubtful that, as some have claimed, Andreini spent the remaining two years of his life on his estate in Mantua. In his last known letter, addressed to Duke Carlo II Gonzaga of Nevers and dated 19 March 1652, he complained that a nobleman had been living on his property for the past four years without paying rent and asked the duke to intervene "a pro di Lelio, che 40 anni ha mantenuto commedie a' serenissimi Gonzaghi" (in favor of Lelio, who for forty years had entertained the Gozangas with comedies). Andreini signed the letter "Di Vostra Altezza serenissima / servitore invecchiato al mantovano servizio, direi senza ricompensa, ma perché la spero il taccio / Lelio Comico Fedele" (Your Most Serene Highness's / servant / aged at the service of Mantua, I would be tempted to say "without proper remuneration" but I will not, since I hope yet to receive it / Lelio, Actor of the Faithful Ones Company). Andreini was once again on the road when he died on 7 June 1654 at an inn in Reggio Emilia.

It would be difficult to name another professional performer in seventeenth-century Europe who devoted as much energy to writing, editing, and publishing as did Andreini. Andreini perhaps revealed the reason for this extraordinary effort when he wrote in *La Turca*, "per mezo di queste compositioni ch'io lascerò doppo la mia vita in vita, altri conosca quanto di buono essempio furono le cose da me portate in theatro" (thanks to these living works, which I will leave behind when I die, others shall know what good example the things I brought to the stage have set), and in *La rosa*, "Oh ben venuto sia colui, che co'l valor della sua penna ha scritto ne' libri della fama: malgrado del Tempo, e della Morte mi son fatto immortale" (Praised be the one who by the effectiveness of his pen has written in the books of fame: in spite of Time and of Death I have become immortal).

While the influence of Andreini's allegorical play *Adamo* on Milton can be—and has been—disputed, his presence in France in 1613–1614, 1620 to 1622, 1624–1625, and 1643 to 1647 and the publication of many of his works in Paris undoubtedly contributed to the development of a French taste for pastoral plays with music, opera-ballets, religious plays, and metatheatrical dramas. Critics have found elements of Andreini's work in the plays of Jean Rotrou, Pierre Corneille, Molière, and Jean-Baptiste Lulli. His reflections on comedy and his *Le due comedie in comedia* may well have inspired such famous plays-within-a-play as Corneille's *L'illusion comique* (1639; translated as *The Theatrical Illusion*, 1975) and Molière's *La critique de l'école des femmes* (1663, Critique of The School for Wives) and *L'impromptu de Versailles* (performed 1663, published 1682, The Impromptu of Versailles).

Giovan Battista Andreini demonstrated superb skill in interpreting the tastes and demands of his time. He was indefatigable in elaborating on fashionable themes, such as that of the "double" in *Li duo Leli simili*, and on classical and modern myths, such as those of Narcissus in *Amore nello specchio* and of Don Giovanni in *Il convitato di pietra;* in mixing genres as in *La Centaura*, language and dialect as in *La Venetiana*, and prose, poetry, and music as in *La Ferinda;* and in exploiting all the means of the theater, which, according to his own definition, "a guisa di trasparente cristallo, ci fa vedere le nostre azioni, come saggio e dotto volume, c'insegna molti rimedi ne' casi avversi" (like a clear lens, shows us our actions, and like a wise and learned book, teaches us many remedies in the adversities).

Letters:

Comici dell'Arte. Corrispondenze, 2 volumes, edited by Siro Ferrone, Anna Zinanni, and Claudia Buratelli (Florence: Le Lettere, 1993), I: 61–169.

References:

Enrico Bevilacqua, "Giambattista Andreini e la compagnia dei Fedeli," *Giornale storico della letteratura Italiana,* 23 (1894): 76–155; 24 (1894): 82–165;

Guido Davico Bonino, "Giovan Battista Andreini e il teatro della scrittura," in his *La commedia italiana del Cinquecento e altre note su letteratura e teatro* (Turin: Tirrenia Stampatori, 1989), pp. 183–190;

Nevia Buommino, *Lo specchio nel teatro di Giovan Battista Andreini* (Rome: Accademia dei Lincei, 1999);

Paul C. Castagno, *The Early Commedia dell'Arte (1550–1621): The Mannerist Context* (New York: Peter Lang, 1992), pp. 79–80;

Pierre-Louis Ducharte, *The Italian Comedy: The Improvisation, Scenarios, Lives, Attributes, Portraits, and Masks of the Illustrious Characters of the Commedia dell'Arte,* translated by Randolph T. Weaver (New York: Dover, 1966);

Siro Ferrone, *Attori mercanti corsari: La commedia dell'arte in Europa tra cinque e seicento* (Turin: Einaudi, 1993);

Fabrizio Fiaschini, *L' "incessabile agitazione": Giovan Battista Andreini tra professione teatrale, cultura letteraria e religione* (Pisa: Giardini, 2007);

Marco Lombardi, "L'uomo selvatico, l'egiziana, il sileno, il santo, l'attore," in his *Processo al teatro: La tragicommedia barocca e I suoi mostri* (Pisa: Pacini, 1995);

Ferruccio Marotti and Giovanna Romei, *La commedia dell'arte e la società barocca,* volume 2 (Rome: Bulzoni, 1991), pp. 467–534;

Daniela Mauri, "Il mito di Narciso in tre testi di Isabella, Francesco e Giovan Battista Andreini," in *La Commedia dell'Arte tra Cinque e Seicento in Francia e in Europa: Atti del Convegno Internazionale di Studi, Verona-Vicenza 19–21 ottobre 1995,* edited by Elio Mosele (Fasano: Schena, 1997), pp. 207–233;

Stefano Mazzoni, "Genealogia e vicende della famiglia Andreini," in *Origini della commedia improvvisa o dell'arte,* edited by Maria Chiabò and Federico Doglio (Rome: Torre d'Orfeo, 1996), pp. 107–152;

John Powell, "The Italian *pastorale* in France," in his *Music and Theatre in France 1600–1680* (Oxford: Oxford University Press, 2000), pp. 167–170;

Maurizio Rebaudengo, *Giovan Battista Andreini tra poetica e drammaturgia* (Turin: Rosenberg & Sellier, 1994);

Giovanna Romei, "La professione del teatro: La commedia dell'arte e la società barocca," in *Teoria testo e scena: Studi sullo spettacolo in Italia dal Rinascimento a Pirandello,* edited by Giorgio Patrizi and Luisa Tinti (Rome: Bulzoni, 2001), pp. 177–251;

Ferdinando Taviani, "Centaura," in *Viaggi teatrali dall'Italia a Parigi fra Cinque e Seicento* (Genoa: Costa & Nolan, 1989), pp. 200–233;

Taviani and Mirella Schino, *Il segreto della commedia dell'arte: La memoria delle compagnie italiane del XVI, XVII e XVIII secolo* (Florence: Usher, 1982);

Michael Zampelli, "Incarnating the Word: Giovan Battista Andreini, Religious Antitheatricalism, and the Redemption of a Profession," dissertation, Tufts University, 1998;

Alessandra Zazo, "*La Turca* di Giovan Battista Andreini: Un caso di editoria teatrale del seicento," in *Quaderni di teatro,* 32 (1986): 61–72.

Papers:

Extant letters of Giovan Battista Andreini are in the state archives of Mantua, Modena, and Florence. Manuscripts for *Il litigio,* dated 1641, are in the Biblioteca Nazionale in Florence and the Biblioteca Comunale in Fermo. A manuscript for *La Ferinda,* dated 1647, is in the Bibliothèque Nationale de France in Paris. Manuscripts for *Il convitato di pietra* and *Il nuovo risarcito Convitato di pietra in versi composto,* both dated 1651, are in the Archivio Cardelli in Rome and the Biblioteca Nazionale in Florence, respectively.

Isabella Andreini
(1562? - 10 June 1604)

Francesca Savoia
University of Pittsburgh

BOOKS: *Mirtilla: Pastorale d'Isabella Andreini comica gelosa* (Verona: Girolamo Discepolo, 1588); translated and edited by Julie D. Campbell as *La Mirtilla: A Pastoral* (Tempe, Ariz.: Medieval and Renaissance Texts and Studies, 2002);

Rime d'Isabella Andreini Padovana, comica gelosa & academica intenta detta l'Accesa (Milan: Girolamo Bordone & Pietromartire Locarni, 1601);

Rime d'Isabella Andreini Padovana, comica gelosa & academica intenta detta l'Accesa: Parte seconda (Milan: Girolamo Bordone & Pietromartire Locarni, 1605);

Fragmenti d'alcune scritture della Signora Isabella Andreini comica gelosa e accademica Intenta, edited by Francesco Andreini (Venice: G. B. Combi, 1627).

Editions and Collections: *Rime di diversi celebri poeti dell'età nostra nuovamente raccolte e poste in luce*, edited by Giovanni Battista Licino (Bergamo: Comino Ventura, 1587);

Componimenti poetici delle più illustri rimatrici d'ogni secolo, volume 2, edited by Luisa Bergalli (Venice: Mora, 1726), pp. 12-15;

Le scrittrici italiane dalle origini al 1800, edited by Jolanda De Blasi (Florence: Nemi, 1930), pp. 251-267;

"Fragmenti di alcune scritture della Signora Isabella Andreini Comica Gelosa, & Academica intenta," in *La commedia dell'arte: Storia e testo*, 6 volumes, edited by Vito Pandolfi (Florence: Sansoni, 1957-1961), II: 48-68;

Scrittrici italiane dal XIII al XX secolo, edited by Natalia Costa-Zalessow (Ravenna: Longo, 1982), pp. 117-122;

Le stanze ritrovate: Antologia di Scrittrici Venete dal Quattrocento al Novecento, edited by Antonia Arslan, Adriana Chemello, Gilberto Pizzamiglio, and Piermario Vescovo (Milan & Venice: Eidos, 1991), pp. 83-94;

La Mirtilla, edited by Maria Luisa Doglio (Lucca: Pacini Fazzi, 1995);

La commedia dell'arte, edited by Cesare Molinari (Rome: Istituto Poligrafico e Zecca dello Stato, 1999), pp. 957-974.

Isabella Andreini (portrait by Raphail Sadeler; from La Mirtilla: A Pastoral, *translated and edited by Julie D. Campbell, 2002; Thomas Cooper Library, University of South Carolina)*

Editions in English: "Letter on the Birth of Women"; excerpt from *Mirtilla: A Pastoral*; sonnets 1, 4, and 25; and Scherzo 1 from *Rime*, in *Women Poets of the*

Italian Renaissance, edited and translated by Anna Laura Stortoni (New York: Italica Press, 1997), pp. 227–249;

Selected Poems of Isabella Andreini, edited by Anne MacNeil, translated by James Wyatt Cook (Lanham, Md.: Scarecrow Press, 2005).

Isabella Andreini was the most celebrated actress of her time. Renowned intellectuals and great poets became her friends, correspondents, and admirers; members of the clergy and princes and monarchs in Italy and France enjoyed her company and applauded her art. Her creativity, versatility, wit and grace, and stage presence were said to be unparalleled and earned her the reverence and enthusiastic support of popular audiences and courtly spectators alike. She was extolled for her beauty as much as for her modest demeanor and reserved conduct. She was also widely recognized for her literary accomplishments. As she had ardently hoped, her writings long survived her. Her pastoral play, *Mirtilla* (1588; translated, 2002), was favorably compared to Torquato Tasso's *Aminta* (1573) and reprinted nine times between its first appearance and 1620. Her collected poems, first published in 1601, appeared in several editions throughout the seventeenth century, and her letters, published three years after her death in 1604, were republished five times in the next forty years. Her poetry was prominently featured in the second volume of Luisa Bergalli's 1726 anthology of more than 250 Italian women poets, and her work in both prose and verse has received much-deserved attention since the early 1990s.

A few French illustrations exist of the *innamorata* (young woman in love), the character Andreini played; they bear the name Isabella, but their authenticity as portraits of the actress cannot be proven. Her likeness has been preserved in two woodcuts and an engraving that appear, respectively, as the frontispieces to her play, her *Rime* (Rhymes), and her letters; a miniature oil portrait at the Museo Teatrale alla Scala in Milan; and a fresco executed after her death by Bernardino Pocelli that was discovered in 1607 or 1608 in a lunette in the main cloister of Florence's Chiesa della Santissima Annunziata (Church of the Most Holy Annunciation). The fresco presents Andreini's full figure, standing in profile, in the background, while the other pictures offer a frontal view of her perfect oval face and elegant, slender bust. Her wavy brown hair is piled high on her head, twined or braided, and adorned with flowers or small plumes. She wears earrings and one or two short strings of large pearls or a long, heavy-looking gold chain. Invariably, her neck is protected by the fashionable high collar of the late sixteenth century, either pleated or trimmed with precious lace, and her bodices appear to be richly embroidered. The image conveyed is that of an elegant, highly refined lady of stature.

Isabella Canali was born in Padua, probably of Venetian parents, almost certainly in 1562. Nothing is known of her childhood and upbringing, although her writings attest to a thorough classical education and gained her admission in 1601 to the rather exclusive Accademia degli Intenti (Academy of the Intent Ones) in Pavia, which assigned her the literary name Accesa. There is also evidence of her knowledge of French and Spanish.

Padua was important in the development of early commedia dell'arte; whether Canali was attracted to the acting profession and in pursuing it met and fell in love with Francesco Andreini, a member of the well-established Compagnia dei Gelosi (Company of the Jealous Ones) acting troupe, or whether her love for Andreini drew her to the theater, is unknown. Documents show that their first child, Giovan Battista, was born in Florence on 9 February 1576. The two had, therefore, been together at least since the spring of 1575, when Isabella was only thirteen and Francesco was twenty-seven or twenty-eight. Their marriage is traditionally believed to have taken place in 1578; Isabella's reputation as a woman of sound virtue, however, would point to an earlier date. The Andreinis had eight more children: their sons Domenico, Giacinto, and Cosimo became military officers; Pietro Paolo became a monk in Pavia; and their four daughters became nuns in two convents in Mantua. Only Giovan Battista followed his parents into a theatrical career.

By 1576 Isabella had joined Francesco and the Gelosi, who were then under the direction of Flaminio Scala, as an *innamorata*. The company had been formed eight years earlier; its name was based on the motto "Virtù, fama ed honor ne fer gelosi" (Virtue, fame and honor made us zealous). It had completed a successful round of engagements in France in 1571; the English ambassador, Thomas Sackville, Baron Buckhurst, saw them there and commended their skill. The Gelosi had also staged the first performance of Tasso's *Aminta* on the island of Belvedere in Ferrara on 31 July 1573. A year later, on his way back to France from his short-lived reign in Poland, Henry III summoned them to Venice for a command performance. Tommaso Porcacchi spoke highly of various members of the Gelosi and of their director, who at that time was Rinaldo Petignoni, in his 1574 chronicle of the king's journey. The troupe consisted of the most diverse and broadest ensemble of talents available at the time, which allowed it to produce a wide variety of works, often including song and dance, to appeal to many kinds of audiences.

Title page for the first edition of Andreini's correspondence (University of Turin)

The Gelosi were the most distinguished acting organization of their time.

Women had begun appearing onstage in commedia dell'arte, and their numbers increased as competition spurred the creation of more parts for them. The public tended to regard actresses and female dancers and singers as prostitutes, and the troupes quickly learned to exploit them for their novelty, beauty, and notoriety. The Andreinis took it upon themselves to bring respectability to actors, and Isabella, in particular, was able to create a new model of the actress. She presented herself as an exemplary wife and mother, as highly cultivated, and as an accomplished woman of letters, replacing the image of the wicked, mercenary woman with the metaphor of the actress as *diva* (literally, goddess).

At the beginning of 1577 the Gelosi, again under the direction of Scala, went back to France, where they were captured by the Huguenots on 25 January and held for ransom at Charité-sur-Loire. Eventually liberated, they performed before the king and his court at Blois and then in Paris. In the capital they also gave several public performances at the Hôtel de Bourbon and, according to the complaint of a moralistic commentator, drew much larger crowds than those who would normally gather for religious worship. The French Parliament prohibited comedies at the end of July; they resumed, by royal command, at the end of September. By the time the Gelosi returned to Italy in the spring of 1578, Andreini had become the troupe's *prima donna innamorata* (romantic leading lady). Her husband, who had begun his career as an *innamorato,* probably played opposite her many times; but he had begun specializing in the role that brought him his greatest fame: that of Capitano Spavento da Vall'Inferna, a Spanish sea captain.

Under Scala, the Gelosi had become perhaps the most unified of all the troupes of the commedia dell'arte. But the composition of any acting company and, consequently, its leadership, were subject to continual change. In the years following the Gelosi's second visit to France, Francesco and Isabella Andreini gradually took control of the ensemble and were its heads in 1583. In 1585 Tommaso Garzoni wrote an often-quoted panegyric of Isabella Andreini: "La graziosa Isabella, decoro delle scene, ornamento de' Teatri, spettacolo superbo non meno di virtù che di bellezza, ha illustrato ancor lei questa professione in modo che, mentre il mondo durarà, mentre staranno i secoli, mentre avran vita gli ordini e i tempi, ogni voce, ogni lingua, ogni grido risuonarà il celebre nome d'isabella" (The graceful Isabella, pride of the stage, ornament of the theaters, exhibition as praiseworthy for virtue as for beauty, has herself illustrated the profession in such a way that as long as the world would last, and to the end of time the famous name of Isabella will be universally held in veneration).

While the Gelosi was an independent company—a professional association that staged both courtly and public performances in all of the major Italian cities and did not depend on any one patron—individual members of the troupe, especially the most talented ones, might be befriended and supported by heads of state or other people of influence and means; a prince would sometimes manage to entice favorite comedians to remain at his court. In 1586, when the Gelosi performed in Mantua, Duke Vincenzo Gonzaga—who three years earlier had attempted to persuade Francesco Andreini to form a Mantuan company—favored Isabella with the unusual honor of standing as godfather to the Andreinis' daughter Lavina. It appears that the girl was raised at the court until the duchess arranged for her to enter a local convent.

The Andreinis were again heads of the Gelosi in 1587–1588. In 1588 Isabella published *Mirtilla;* the first pastoral play ever written by a woman, it was judged by Angelo Ingegneri, one of the foremost theorists of dramatic literature of the time, to be one of the best examples of the genre. In her choice of names for the characters Andreini pays tribute to the key works in the pastoral tradition from Virgil's *Bucolics* to the dramatic eclogues produced in Ferrara: Giambattista Giraldi Cinzio's *Egle* (1545, Egle), Agostino Beccari's *Il sacrificio* (1554, The Sacrifice), and, of course, Tasso's *Aminta*. The prologue is a dialogue between Venus and her son, Love, that weaves together references to Latin and Italian classics from Ovid to Petrarch, Angelo Poliziano, and Jacopo Sannazaro in which Andreini, expanding on the theme of Tasso's pastoral, announces not one but six stories of unreciprocated or misplaced love. The prologue promises an end to the pain and confusion that such passion brings: Love tells Venus that unhappy or impossible relationships will give way to satisfying and long-lasting ones, and such is the case in three of the stories. None of Andreini's characters has to go as far as Tasso's Aminta, who is driven to attempt suicide by false news of his beloved Silvia's death but is saved by a bush that breaks his fall from a precipice: in three of the episodes in *Mirtilla* the despondency of male lovers is quickly met with female compassion and understanding, and thoughts of the brevity of youth and life generate promises of faithful and lasting love.

Although the influence of Tasso's imagery and musical verses is evident everywhere in Andreini's play, she uses her experience as a woman and an actress to distance herself from her model. For example, in the third act the satyr Satiro, who yearns for the nymph Filli (the character Andreini apparently chose to perform herself), threatens her with violence if she does not yield to him. Filli pretends that she has concealed her love for him to test him; she promises him a kiss if he lets her tie him to a tree to prevent him from injuring her by embracing her too tightly in the heat of passion. Once Satiro is securely tied up, Filli "tortures" him by pulling his beard, making him eat the bitterest herb to cleanse his mouth before the kiss, twisting his arm, and so forth, and then leaves him. The triumph of female intelligence and shrewdness over male force is a reversal of the traditional roles and signals Isabella's departure from the pastoral tradition, as well as her rethinking of theatrical conventions: many *lazzi* (comic routines) in commedia dell'arte involved violence to women such as pulling their hair or twisting their arms. This episode is followed by a "gastronomic" monologue delivered by the goatherd Gorgo that is reminiscent of passages in mock-heroic poems by such authors as Luigi Pulci, Teofilo Folengo, and François Rabelais. This passage and the end of the play, when Gorgo spreads food on the grass to celebrate the engagements of three couples, are reminiscent of the literary tradition of the *farse rusticane* (farces that take place in peasant surroundings) and reflect a well-established stage practice of the commedia dell'arte in which food was exhibited or its presence mimed.

In addition to offers from wealthy and royal patrons, fierce competition among the companies and, within ensembles, personality conflicts and rivalries involving the status of various parts accounted for actors' moving in and out of groups. Such was particularly the case with versatile and skilled performers such

Painting of an innamorata *(young woman in love) of the Gelosi troupe, thought to be Andreini (Carnavalet Museum, Paris; from Pierre-Louis Duchartre,* The Italian Comedy: The Improvisation, Scenarios, Lives, Attributes, Portraits, and Masks of the Illustrious Characters of the Commedia dell'Arte, *1966; Thomas Cooper Library, University of South Carolina)*

as Giulio Pasquati, Vittoria Piissimi, and Giovanni Pellesini, all of whom were members of the Gelosi at one time or another. A rivalry arose between Isabella Andreini and Piissimi, who differed in their preferences for plays; each presumably wanted to perform those that would showcase her respective strengths.

Nevertheless, only two instances are recorded of Isabella appearing with companies other than the Gelosi. The first occurred in 1589, when the Compagnia de Confidenti (Company of the Confident Ones) used her name in requesting a license to perform in Parma; she was still with them when they performed in Liguria at the beginning of October of that year.

While they might give one or two of their own personality traits to the stock characters they impersonated, most commedia dell'arte actors and actresses would not give them their own names. An *innamorata* character named Isabella, always modest and dignified and speaking of tender and devoted love, existed before Andreini entered the profession and was played by the actress Vittoria degli Amorevoli. But Andreini made the character her own, enjoying tremendous success in a series of plays that featured her in the title role: *La fortunata Isabella* (Lucky Isabella), *Le burle di Isabella* (Isabella's Pranks), *La gelosa Isabella* (Jealous Isabella), *Isabella astrologa* (Isabella the Astrologer), and the most acclaimed of all, *La pazzia di Isabella* (Isabella's Madness). *La pazzia di Isabella* became her signature piece; it was staged in the Palazzo delle Cause Civili in Savona, probably in the summer of 1584, where it was seen by the poet Gabriello Chiabrera. He became a great admirer of Andreini and entered into a poetic correspondence with her. The play was one of two performed by the Gelosi in Florence in May 1589—the other was *La zingara* (The Gypsy), in which Piissimi played the title role—as part of the festivities for the marriage of Ferdinand I de' Medici and Christine of Lorraine. An account of the festivities published the same year by Giuseppe Pavoni included a highly favorable review of Andreini's performance, with a detailed description of her "mad scene."

The Gelosi spent the 1592–1593 theatrical season in the south of Italy. At the end of 1593 Andreini participated in a poetry competition in Rome held at the home of another great admirer, Cardinal Giorgio Cinzio Aldobrandini, the Pope's nephew, in which her work was judged second only to that of Tasso.

La pazzia di Isabella was performed in Rome as part of the celebrations for the Jubilee of the year 1600. The second instance of Isabella Andreini working with a company other than the Gelosi occurred in June and October 1601, when she appeared with Pellesini, and probably other members of the Gelosi, at the head of a troupe that called itself the Uniti (United Ones); it was really a group of individually selected performers summoned from Mantua to Milan and from there to Pavia for the meeting of the Prince Charles Emmanuel I of Savoy with Cardinal Aldobrandini. Also in 1601 *Rime,* a collection of more than three hundred of Andreini's poems, was published in Milan. In the proemial sonnet she warns her readers not to believe the pretended passions expressed by her verses, reminding them that she has been trained to feign emotions in the theater. Furthermore, she claims that just as onstage she has played different parts in different ways, "quanto volle insegnar Natura ed Arte" (as taught by Nature and Art), so she has been capable of ruling "con vario stil ben mille carte" (a thousand pages with varied pen).

The disturbances that followed the murders in Paris in December 1588 of Henry I de Lorraine, third Duke of Guise, and his brother, Louis II, Cardinal de Guise, as well as a decree by the French Parliament forbidding comedians to perform under penalty of severe fines and even corporal punishment, had kept the Gelosi away from France. The ban was eventually lifted, and at the end of 1602 the company was invited by Maria de' Medici, the wife of Henry IV, to perform at the French court. As was customary, negotiating the terms of the engagement took some time, but in the summer of 1603 the Gelosi, once again headed by the Andreinis, finally left for France. They enjoyed a season of sensational success in Fontainebleau and Paris during the winter and spring of 1603–1604. Flattering attempts to detain the Gelosi were made before their departure. The queen wrote a letter to her sister Eleonora de' Medici, Duchess of Mantua, in praise of Isabella's performance, and the king supplied a safe conduct for "Isabella comediante" and her company, instructing his secretary to do everything necessary to facilitate their journey home. On their departure from Paris, Isaac Du Ryer wrote the poem *Isabelle comédienne,* in which he said:

Je ne crois point qu'Isabelle
Soit femme mortelle,
C'est plutôt quelqu'un des dieux
Qui s'est déguisé en femme
Afin de nous ravir l'âme
Par l'oreille et par les yeux.

(I do not believe that Isabelle can
Be mortal woman,
It is rather one of the gods
Who has assumed woman's guise
In order to ravish away our souls
Through our ears and our eyes.)

On the way back to Italy, Andreini, who was pregnant at forty-two, miscarried and died in Lyon on 10 June 1604. Virtually the entire city attended her funeral; aldermen and magistrates sent banners and mace bearers, and representatives of the merchants' guild marched in the procession with torches. Her epitaph described her as "religiosa, pia, musis amica et artis scenicae caput" (religious, pious, friend of the Muses and a leader in the art of the stage); a bronze medallion was struck with the effigy of the actress and her name followed by the initials *C.G.* for *Comica Gelosa* (Actress of the Gelosi) on one side and the figure of Fame accompanied by the words "Aeterna fama" (eternal fame) on the other side. The historian Pierre Matthieu included Andreini's last tour and death in his 1605 account of memorable events that had occurred in the past few years in France and its provinces. He claimed that had she lived in ancient Greece, where comedy was popular and properly valued, monuments would have been erected to her as to a goddess. The Accademia degli Intenti created a posthumous impresa for her showing a rocket flying into the sky to illustrate her spectacular rise to fame, accompanied by the motto "elevat ardor" (ardor elevates).

The grief-stricken Francesco disbanded the Gelosi and retired from the stage to spend the rest of his life collecting and editing his and Isabella's writings. In 1607 he published a volume of 140 of her letters offering reflections on a variety of subjects, including women's issues. In 1627 he collected thirty-one of her dialogues, each of which features a discussion by a man and a woman of a literary or theatrical topic or a question pertaining to love relationships. Such set pieces had presumably been used by the Andreinis in their theatrical productions. They afford insights into acting and writing and the interplay between the two arts.

Title page for a collection of Andreini's writings, first published in 1627 (from History of Women, *1975; Thomas Cooper Library, University of South Carolina)*

Both in her professional and in her private life Isabella Andreini pursued her goals with great determination. In one of her letters she refers to the myth of a "golden age" and declares that she is convinced of its attainability: "Il viver fa l'età e non l'età il vivere" (The life one chooses to live determines one's time; the time in which one lives does not determine one's life).

Letters:

Lettere d'Isabella Andreini, comica gelosa, edited by Francesco Andreini (Venice: M. A. Zaltieri, 1607);

Lettere della Signora Isabella Andreini Padovana. Aggiuntovi di Nuovo li Ragionamenti piacevoli dell'istessa (Venice: G. B. Combi, 1627);

"Lettere," in *La Commedia dell'Arte,* edited by Cesare Molinari (Rome: Istituto Poligrafico e Zecca dello Stato, 1999), pp. 975–996.

Bibliography:

Nancy Dersofi, "Isabella Andreini (1562–1604)," in *Italian Women Writers: A Bibliographical Sourcebook,* edited by Rinaldina Russell (Westport, Conn.: Greenwood Press, 1994), pp. 18–25.

References:

Frances K. Barasch, "Italian Actresses in Shakespeare's World: Vittoria and Isabella," *Shakespeare Bulletin,* 3 (2001): 5–9;

Julie D. Campbell, "Love's Victory and La Mirtilla in The Canon of Renaissance Tragicomedy: An Examination of the Influence of Salon and Social Debates," *Women's Writing,* 4 (1997): 103–124;

Paul C. Castagno, *The Early Commedia dell'Arte (1550–1621)* (New York: Peter Lang, 1994), pp. 57, 61, 67, 70, 73–74, 109, 111;

Louise George Clubb, "The State of the Arts in the Andreinis' Time," in *Studies in the Italian Renaissance: Essays in Memory of Arnolfo B. Ferruolo,* edited by Gian Paolo Biasin, Albert N. Mancini, and Nicolas J. Perella (Naples: Società Editrice Napoletana, 1985), pp. 263–281;

Robert Erenstein, "A Lady of Virtue and High Renown," in *Essays on Drama and Theatre,* edited by Erica Hunningher-Schilling (Amsterdam: Mousault's Uitgeverij, 1973), pp. 37–49;

Siro Ferrone, *Attori mercanti corsari: La Commedia dell'Arte in Europa tra Cinque e Seicento* (Turin: Einaudi, 1993);

Tommaso Garzoni, "De' comici e tragedi così autori come recitatori, cioè de gli istrioni," in *La piazza universale di tutte le professioni del mondo,* volume 2, edited by Paolo Cherchi and Beatrice Collina (Turin: Einaudi, 1996), pp. 1118–1121;

History of Women [microform] (New Haven: Research Publications, 1975), reel 3, no. 19;

Angelo Ingegneri, *Della poesia rappresentativa e del modo di rappresentare le favole sceniche,* edited by Maria Luisa Doglio (Modena: Edizioni Panini, 1989), p. 4;

Anne Elisabeth MacNeil, "Music and the Life and Work of Isabella Andreini: Humanistic Attitudes towards Music, Poetry, and Theater During the

Late Sixteenth and Early Seventeenth Century," dissertation, University of Chicago, 1994;

Giovanna Malquori-Fondi, "De la 'lettre canevas' à la 'pièce de cabinet': Les *Lettere d'Isabella Andreini*, traduites par François de Grenaille," in *Contacts culturels et échanges linguistiques au XVII siècle en France*, edited by Yves Girauded (Paris: Papers on French Seventeenth Century Literature, 1997), pp. 125–145;

Ferruccio Marotti and Giovanna Romei, *La commedia dell'arte e la società barocca*, volume 2 (Rome: Bulzoni, 1991), pp. 163–208;

Daniela Mauri, "Il mito di Narciso in tre testi di Isabella, Francesco e Giovan Battista Andreini," in *La Commedia dell'Arte tra Cinque e Seicento in Francia e in Europa: Atti del Convegno Internazionale di Studi, Verona-Vicenza 19-21 ottobre 1995*, edited by Elio Mosele (Fasano: Schena, 1997), pp. 207–233;

Stefano Mazzoni, "Genealogia e vicende della famiglia Andreini," in *Origini della Commedia Improvvisa o dell'Arte*, edited by Maria Chiabò and Federico Doglio (Rome: Torre d'Orfeo, 1996), pp. 107–152;

Cesare Molinari, *La Commedia dell'Arte* (Rome: Istituto Poligrafico e Zecca dello Stato, 1999), pp. 949–996;

Daria Perocco, "Isabella Andreini ossia: Il teatro non è ianua diabuli," in *Donne a teatro: Atti del convegno Venezia, Auditorium Santa Margherita 6 ottobre 2003*, edited by Perocco (Venice: Edizioni Università Ca' Foscari, 2004), pp. 19–40;

Tommaso Porcacchi, *Le Attioni d'Arrigo Terzo Re di Francia, et Quarto di Polonia descritte in dialogo* (Venice, 1574), folio 27v;

Francesca Romana de Angelis, *La divina Isabella* (Florence: Sansoni, 1991);

Maurice Sand, *The History of the Harlequinade*, volume 2 (London: Martin Secker, 1915), pp. 135–137;

Ferdinando Taviani and Mirella Schino, *Il segreto della Commedia dell'Arte: La memoria delle compagnie italiane del XVI, XVII e XVIII secolo* (Florence: Usher, 1982);

Roberto Tessari, "O diva o 'Estable à tous chevaux': L'ultimo viaggio di Isabella Andreini," in *Viaggi teatrali dall'Italia a Parigi fra Cinque e Seicento: Atti del convegno internazionale, Torino, 6/8 aprile 1987* (Genoa: Costa & Nolan, 1989), pp. 128–142;

Tessari, "Sotto il segno di Giano: La Commedia dell'Arte di Isabella e di Francesco Andreini," in *The Commedia dell'Arte from the Renaissance to Dario Fo*, edited by Christopher Cairns (Lewiston, N.Y., Queenstown, Australia & Lampeter, U.K.: Edwin Mellen Press, 1989), pp. 1–33;

Franco Vazzoler, "Chiabrera fra dilettanti e professionisti dello spettacolo," in *La scelta della misura. Gabriello Chiabrera: L'altro fuoco del barocco italiano*, edited by Fulvio Bianchi (Genoa: Costa & Nolan, 1993), pp. 429–466;

Vazzoler, "Le pastorali dei comici dell'arte: La *Mirtilla* di Isabella Andreini," in *Sviluppi della drammaturgia pastorale nell'Europa del Cinque-Seicento*, edited by Chiabò and Doglio (Viterbo: Centro Studi sul Teatro Medievale e Rinascimentale, 1992), pp. 281–299;

Melissa Vickery-Bareford, "Reimaging 'Woman' in Early Modern Italy," dissertation, University of Missouri, 2000.

Giuseppe Artale
(1628 – 13 January 1679)

Paschal C. Viglionese
University of Rhode Island

BOOKS: *Enciclopedia poetica: Parte prima* (Perugia: Eredi del Tommaso, 1658);
Cordimarte (Venice: Storti, 1660);
Pasife overo l'impossibile fatto possibile: Melodramma, music by Daniello Castrovillari (Venice: Batti, 1661);
La bellezza alterata (Naples, 1661);
L'alloro fruttuoso (Naples: De Bonis, 1672);
Guerra tra i vivi e i morti: Tragedia di lieto fine (Naples: Bulifon, 1679).

Editions and Collections: *Enciclopedia poetica di D. Giuseppe Artale: Terza impressione* (Venice: Baba, 1664);
Enciclopedia poetica, 3 volumes (Naples: Bulifon, 1679);
Cordimarte (Naples: Bulifon, 1679);
Lirici marinisti, edited by Benedetto Croce (Bari: Laterza, 1910), pp. 449–459;
Opere scelte di Marino e dei marinisti, edited by Giovanni Getto (Turin: Unione Tipografico-Editrice Torinese, 1949), pp. 405–409;
Marino e i Marinisti, edited by Giuseppe Guido Ferrero (Milan & Naples: Ricciardi, 1954), pp. 1025–1031;
Poesia del Seicento, edited by Carlo Muscetta and Pier Paolo Ferrante (Turin: Einaudi, 1964), pp. 636–646;
Romanzieri del Seicento, edited by Martino Capucci (Turin: Unione Tipografico-Editrice Torinese, 1974), pp. 667–682;
Enciclopedia poetica, 3 volumes (Parma: Università degli studi di Parma, Facoltà di lettere e filosofia, Istituto di filologia moderna, 1990–1998)—comprises volume 1, *Guerra tra vivi e morti: Tragedia di lieto fine,* edited by Anna M. Razzoli Roio (1990); volume 2, *Il Cordimarte: Romanzo,* edited by Marzio Pieri (1990); volume 3, *Epitalami, Idilli, Epistole eroiche,* edited by Luana Salvarani, prefatory note by Pieri (1998).

OTHER: "E giungerà pur mai alla sua linea crudele?" "Cieli, stelle, Deitàdi," and "L'Astratto," in Barbara Strozzi, *Arie di Barbara Strozzi consacrate all'Altezza Serenissima di Madama Sofia Duchessa di Bransvich, e Luneburg, nata Principessa elettorale*

Giuseppe Artale (from Battista Guarini, Opere, *edited by Luigi Fassò [Turin: Unione Tipografico-Editrice Torinese, 1950]; Thomas Cooper Library, University of South Carolina)*

palatina: Opera ottava (Venice: Francesco Magni detto Gardano, 1664).

Giuseppe Artale was a member of a school of poets who flourished in Naples from 1660 to 1690 and wrote in the manner known variously as *secentismo* ("seicentism"), *concettismo* ("conceitism"), or *marinismo* (Marinism)–in essence, an imitation or continuation of the style of Giambattista Marino, Italy's most celebrated poet of the early seventeenth century. The philosopher and literary critic Benedetto Croce characterized the late-seventeenth-century Neapolitan school as an exaggerated version of the earlier movement.

Artale was born of noble lineage in Mazzarino near Caltanissetta, Sicily, in 1628. He came, as Croce put it, close to being a madman. He was devoted to chivalric tradition, adept at handling a sword, and alert for opportunities to defend his honor. He fought his first duel, which produced his first victim, when he was fifteen and boasted of being able to fight eight men at once. He went to Crete to fight against the Ottoman Turks, who were laying siege to the city of Candia; his prowess in battle led to his induction as a knight of the Constantinian Order of St. George. He returned to Italy sometime before 1654. During a sojourn in Brunswick-Lüneburg as a member of the entourage of Duke Ernst Augustus in the 1660s he acquired the nickname "The Bloodthirsty Knight" among the Germans. His ferocious nature is hinted at in his sonnet "Il teschio del Turco" (The Skull of the Turk): it describes the severed head of a Turk Artale had killed in combat, which he kept as a trophy in his home. Such accounts bring to mind another poet-swordsman of the time, the Frenchman Savinien Cyrano de Bergerac. In a prefatory note to the 1998 edition of the third volume of the *Enciclopedia poetica* (Poetic Encyclopedia), the title Artale gave to his complete works, Marzio Pieri says that not only the behaviors but also the poetic styles of the two men are similar.

The prevailing critical view has been that the work of the Marinists lacked substance and moral sense and existed only to display linguistic virtuosity. Croce, for example, saw the late version of Marinism as continuing "la disposizione frivola degli spiriti, la debole fede religiosa e politica, il superficiale interessamento filosofico" (trivial treatment of spirit, weak religious and political faith, superficial philosophical interest). Nevertheless, he thought that insufficient attention had been paid to this "stranissima letteratura" (very strange literature) and took the first step in a twentieth-century reassessment and revival of interest in the literature of Marino and the Marinists.

The Marinists made wordplay the focal point of their work, gaining the reputation of being more inclined to dabble in the language for its own sake than to pursue themes in depth. By Artale's time this mode of poetry was beginning to be considered shopworn. In *Della perfetta poesia italiana* (1821, On Perfect Italian Poetry), originally published in 1706, the rationalist historian Ludovico Antonio Muratori cites the final tercet of Artale's sonnet "A Maria Maddalena" (To Mary Magdalene), which had appeared in the 1658 edition of the *Enciclopedia poetica,* as the archetype of the Marinistic conceit: excessive, unnecessarily clever, and empty of meaning. Muratori's judgment became the standard in subsequent discussions of the poem. The sonnet likens the golden hair with which Mary dries Christ's feet to the river Tagus and her eyes to two suns. These metaphorical descriptions were commonplace; but in the elaboration of the metaphors in the final tercet, the tears from the Magdalene's eyes bathe Jesus' feet. Artale's innovation is thus the oxymoronic situation of the sun doing the wetting and a flowing river doing the drying. The depiction of the humble gesture of the ardent follower of Christ is subordinated to the rhetorical inversion of wet and dry.

W. Theodor Elwert notes the recurrent images of the flea and the head louse in Marinist poetry. In his sonnet "Pulci sulle poppe di bella donna" (1658, Fleas on a Beautiful Woman's Breast) Artale calls the flea a "picciola instabil macchia" (tiny moving spot) that, when seen against the white skin of the breast, suggests the period at the end of a sentence on a page. As Elwert interprets the poem, the period that cannot be made to stay put intimates that the poet's words of love for the lady can never come to an end. Another Marinist feature of the poem is the use of Latinisms instead of normal Italian expressions. For example, instead of the simple Italian *doppio* (double) Artale uses the learned *geminato* (geminated). He also frequently "re-Latinizes"–that is, uses a Latinism in its original sense rather than the commonly understood meaning: for example, he uses *prolisso* to signify "prolonged" or "too long," rather than "diffuse" or "prolix."

Vincenzo De Gregorio notes that the elaborate title of another sonnet in the *Enciclopedia poetica,* "Conversione di San Francesco Borgia alla veduta del cadavere della imperadrice Isabella" (Conversion of St. Francis Borgia upon Seeing the Corpse of the Empress Isabella), on the death in 1539 of the consort of Charles V, highlights a pattern that was widely used at the time: a moral lesson is taught by a morbid and macabre experience. The Baroque element of *meraviglia* (amazement) also enters in when the reader sees how one thing can lead unexpectedly to another to which it appears unrelated. De Gregorio cites another sonnet title that alludes to learning a moral lesson through an apparently trivial matter: "L'inciampo di una piccola pietra, per cui camminando armato di notte cadde precipitevolmente, gli fu cagione di ravvedimento" (Stumbling on a small pebble while walking armed at night and falling headlong led him to moral reflection).

Artale's reputation has tended to be based primarily on the sonnets that were collected in four modern anthologies: Croce's *Lirici marinisti* (1910, Marinist Lyrics), Giovanni Getto's *Opere scelte di Marino e dei marinisti* (1949, Selected Works of Marino and the Marinists), Giuseppe Guido Ferrero's *Marino e i Marinisti* (1954, Marino and the Marinists), and Carlo Muscetta and Pier Paolo Ferrante's *Poesia del Seicento* (1964, Poetry of the Seventeenth Century). But Luana Salvarani, the editor of the 1998 volume of the *Enciclopedia poetica,* asserts that dealing only with Artale's *sonettismo* (sonnet writing) fails to show how his poetry went far beyond the modalities of the late Baroque style. Salvarani's volume includes longer lyric poems—*epitalami* (epithalamia), *idilli* (idylls), and *epistole eroiche* (heroic epistles)—that display a wider variety of styles and themes than are found in the sonnets. In the *idillio* "A Bella Donna" (To a Beautiful Lady) Artale avoids direct echoes of the Petrarchan literary tradition of the poem in praise of the ideal of feminine beauty that had dominated Italian lyric.

The heroic epistle "Spinalba a Calloandro" (Spinalba to Calloandro) uses as its source one of Italy's most popular books of the seventeenth century, Giovanni Ambrosio Marini's heroic-gallant tale *Calloandro fedele* (1653, Faithful Calloandro). The letter from a seduced and abandoned woman evokes epic and chivalric tales in the tradition brought to consummation by Ludovico Ariosto and Torquato Tasso. "Spinalba a Calloandro" recalls an episode in the twenty-fifth canto of Ariosto's *Orlando furioso* (1535, Orlando Gone Mad; translated as *Orlando Furioso in English Heroical Verse,* 1591), the story of Ricciardetto, who, disguised as his sister Bradamante, becomes involved with a girl named Fiordispina. The expression in line 115, "L'empio nemico mio tiranno Amore" (My wicked and tyrannical enemy Love), shows the influence of Petrarch. The quatrains of eleven-syllable lines with alternating rhyme are unusual for continuous narrative and stand in sharp contrast to the Ariostean and Tassian chivalric epics, which were in the firmly established narrative form of the ottava rima, and to the other Italian narrative verse form, terza rima. Salvarani suggests that alternating rhymes of Artale's quatrains recall the alternation of hexameter and pentameter in the elegiac couplets of Ovid. Another of Artale's *epistole eroiche,* "Sara a Gilhair" (Sara to Gilhair), is the story of lovers martyred for their Christian beliefs in Muslim Spain. Writing to Gilhair, her Muslim consort who has converted to Christianity to marry her, Sara uses "hipostaticamente" (hypostatically), a term one would expect to find in a theological treatise, to describe the double human and divine nature of Christ.

The long poem "Il Lisonzo Trattenuto: Idillio epitalamico per musica" (The Lisonzo River Held Back: Epithalamic Idyll to Be Set to Music) was written for the marriage of Countess Silvia Della Torre and Count Antonio Lantiero. The river asks who is hindering its course; the answer is that its waters are being held back by a beautiful "torre" (tower)—a play on the bride's surname. Love changes the water to flames, and the river stops to remain near the object for which it is burning, "arso ed immoto" (scorched and immobile). Artale's epithalamium for the marriage in 1660 of King Louis XIV of France and Princess Maria Teresa of Spain is written in ottava rima to make it epic and heroic, appropriate to the occasion of such an important royal marriage.

Artale's *Cordimarte* (1660) is typical of the novels of adventure that were popular at the time: it includes feats of valor, mistaken identities, and escapes and pursuits. It also has elements of the classical and the chivalric epic, such as the narrator's "roll call" of warriors preparing for battle and descriptions of tactical formations and armament. Symmetry prevails over verisimilitude when the warriors fall in combat in the same order in which they were listed in the roll call.

The Byzantines under Cordimarte's command start to retreat after some of their leaders are killed, but Cordimarte shames them into continuing the fight; Artale describes the incident in a flowery Baroque conceit: "Così questo drappello piccolo di numero, ma Gigante di forze, cominciò col pennello della propria sperimentata gagliardìa, ad adombrare, ed a dipingere ne' petti Tartàrei e Circassi il terror della morte" (Thus, this small company, few in number but a Giant in its strength, using its clearly evident bravery as its brush, began to outline and paint the fear of death in the hearts of Tartar and Circassian). In another example of verbal showiness the enemy leader sees Cordimarte stem the flood of enemy troops by building dikes of their corpses. And Cordimarte's horse, Partifiume, is described as moving as swiftly as a shooting star, his flanks goaded by the stars on the spurs worn by his rider. Firearms lend themselves to unusual and bizarre metaphors; for instance, the firing of a gun "fa d'una canna tuonante partorire tempeste di piombo" (makes a thundering tube give birth to a tempest of lead) as it emits a flash of lightning. And a passage describing the carnage perpetrated against Circassians and Tartars by the warrior Ormauro illustrates the blend of grotesque details of the horrors of the battlefield with the Marinist poet's fascination with metaphorical combinations and contrasts. As he cuts and slashes with his sword, bones and body parts, both human and animal, rain down everywhere:

> Qui vedreste col busto d'un Tartaro il teschio d'un Circasso; là col braccio d'un nemico la mano ancor guizzante dell'altro; ivi un Cavaliere che non avendo più che sperare, spirava sotto il destriere; qui un destriero, che quasi reo de' falli della mano, o poco ardita, o meno fortunata, del suo Signore, giaceva scemo di capo, mentre ancor premealo quel piede scemo di busto.

> (In one direction you would see the trunk of a Tartar with the skull of a Circassian; in the other, with the arm of one enemy, the still twitching hand of another; over there a knight, having nothing more to hope for, giving up his soul beneath his war horse; over here, a war horse who, as though it were guilty of the wrongdoing of the less daring or less fortunate hand of its master, lay there dispossessed of its head, trampled by a foot dispossessed of its body.)

At times, plot development waits while the reader is wrapped in a swirl of words; in other cases the wordplay reflects the involutions of the plot, as when Osminda, the empress of Constantinople, disguised as a knight, meets the young Olinda, whom she does not recognize as a lady of her court because Olinda is disguised as the male page Filindo. Olinda reveals her love for Cordimarte to Osminda, not knowing that the queen is also in love with him and that she is putting herself in grave danger by communicating this truth. Mistaken identities, especially exchanges of gender, are found in many Baroque works.

Pieri says that the extraordinary entanglements of the plots in *seicento* novels leave the reader benumbed rather than enlightened. Nevertheless, he attempts to give his own outline of the plot of *Cordimarte,* even though he is sure that it will turn out badly. He begins his synopsis, "La storia del *Cordimarte* pare essere questa" (The story of *Cordimarte* seems to be this), and says at the end, "Ed è proprio la fine" (The end, really, it is).

In Venice in 1664 Artale collaborated with Barbara Strozzi, the most celebrated singer of her time and an accomplished composer of madrigals and other forms of vocal music, on three cantatas included in her *Arie di Barbara Strozzi consacrate all'Altezza Serenissima di Madama Sofia Duchessa di Bransvich, e Luneburg, nata Principessa elettorale palatina: Opera ottava* (Arias of Barbara Strozzi Dedicated to Her Most Serene Madame Sophia, Duchess of Brunswick and Luneburg, Born Princess Electress Palatine: Opus 8). Artale's contributions are "E giungerà pur mai alla linea crudele?" (Will It Ever Reach Its Cruel Limit?), a tongue-in-cheek lover's lament addressed to the composer, which uses a play on the word *barbara* (barbarous or heartless) and her given name; "Cieli, Stelle, e Deitadi" (Heavens, Stars, and Deities), a description of Princess Sophia's beauty; and "L'Astratto (The Distracted One), in which the speaker complains of the struggle required to produce poetic words and wonders at how the words manage to come out despite the difficulty.

In the final decade of Artale's life gout and syphilis inhibited his military and chivalric activities. His writing of this period is characterized by moralism, pessimism, and rejection of worldly values. His style, however, continues to exhibit what Artale scholar Franco Croce calls the "formula tonante" (thundering formula), the distinctive Marinistic flamboyance in language. Croce singles out *L'alloro fruttuoso* (1672, The Fruitful Laurel Tree) as a work with genuine moralistic substance that illustrates how the Marinists' figures of speech, when not used as an end in themselves, helped shape a vision of the world—in Artale's case, that of the world as a tragic scene of continuous ruin.

At the time of his death on 13 January 1679 Artale was finishing *Guerra tra i vivi e i morti: Tragedia di lieto fine* (War between the Living and the Dead: Tragedy with a Happy Ending). An experiment in genre, the play is not a tragicomedy, a mixture of tragic and comic characters and events, but a straight tragedy, without comic interludes, in which all turns out relatively well for the protagonists. The literary arbiters of the time censured such works because they failed to provide punishment for wrongdoing or to depict the inexorable working of fate. Artale was aware of these criticisms and reiterates in the preface to the play the widely held view of the didactic potential of tragic theater: that from the "agnizioni" (recognition [of someone or something]) will come "cognizioni virtuose" (knowledge of virtue). The plot combines the tale of Oedipus and the story of the Babylonian queen Semiramis: though wicked, Semiramis does not die at the end of the play but is punished by not being able to achieve what she wanted in love and war; Oedipus is blinded and goes into exile.

Critics place Giuseppe Artale in the late phase of Marinism, when Marino, half a century after his death, was still imitated but not as slavishly as he had been earlier. Many new elements came into Italian poetry during Artale's generation, and Artale is counted among the innovators.

References:

Benedetto Croce, *Saggi sulla letteratura del Seicento* (Bari: Laterza, 1924), pp. 397–398, 401, 403–405;

Franco Croce, "Giuseppe Artale," in *Dizionario biografico degli italiani,* volume 4, edited by Alberto M. Ghisalberti (Rome: Instituto dell'Enciclopedia Italiana, 1962), pp. 345–348;

Croce, "Tre lirici dell'ultimo barocco: I. Giuseppe Artale," *Rassegna della letteratura italiana,* 65, no. 3 (1961): 393–417;

Vincenzo De Gregorio, "Il tempo, la morte e la bellezza nella lirica barocca," *Studi secenteschi,* 12 (1971): 177–206;

W. Theodor Elwert, *La poesia italiana del Seicento: Studio sullo stile barocco* (Florence: Olschki, 1967), p. 24;

Gesualdo Interligi, *Studio su Giuseppe Artale, poeta, drammaturgo, romanziere del secolo XVII* (Catania: Muglia, 1926);

Albert N. Mancini, *Romanzi e romanzieri del Seicento* (Naples: Società Editrice Napoletana, 1981), pp. 119, 130, 259–262;

Ludovico Antonio Muratori, *Della perfetta poesia italiana spiegata e dimostrata con varie osservazioni,* volume 2 (Milan: Tipografica dei Classici Italiani, 1821), pp. 81–83;

Claudio Varese, "La lirica concettistica," in *Storia della letteratura italiana,* volume 5, edited by Emilio Cecchi and Natalino Sapegno (Milan: Garzanti, 1967), pp. 788–813.

Nicolò Barbieri
(1576 – 1641)

Glenn Palen Pierce
University of Missouri

BOOKS: *Discorso famigliare di Nicolao Barbieri detto Beltrame intorno alle comedie moderne, dou'egli dice la sua opinione* (Ferrara: Francesco Suzzi, 1628); enlarged as *La supplica: Discorso famigliare a quelli che trattano de' comici* (Venice: Marco Ginammi, 1634);
L'inavvertito, ovvero Scapino disturbato Mezzettino travagliato (Turin, 1630).

Editions: *La supplica: Discorso famigliare a quelli che trattano de' comici*, edited by Ferdinando Taviani (Milan: Polifilo, 1971);
L'Inavertito, ovvero Scappino disturbato e Mezettino travagliato, in *Commedie dell'arte*, volume 2, edited by Siro Ferrone (Milan: Mursia, 1986), pp. 107–233.

Nicolò Barbieri was a professional actor of the commedia dell'arte and the author of a significant literary treatise and a comedy. The little that is known of his life is found in a seventeenth-century collection of biographies by Giovan Domenico Ottonelli. Barbieri was born in 1576 in Vercelli, Piedmont, of uncertain parentage; he left home in 1596 to follow an acrobat known as Monferrino. In 1600 he joined the professional acting troupe Compagnia dei Gelosi (Company of the Jealous Ones), which dissolved on the death of one of its leaders, Isabella Andreini, in 1604. In 1606 he joined the Compagnia dei Fedeli (Company of the Faithful) and toured with it to Milan, Mantua, Turin, Venice, Bologna, and Ferrara. Although it is not known when or whom he married, he was widowed at thirty-one and left with young children whom he directed toward religious lives. In 1611–1612 he was a member of the Comici Confidènti (Confident Comedians). In the following years he performed in Paris, Genoa, and Venice as an independent actor.

From the middle of the sixteenth century a proliferation of characters of the *zanni* (comic servant or porter) type–or "mask," as it is traditionally called–was created by the actors of the professional companies. Among them were Pulcinella, Scapino, Buffetto, Fritellino, Flautino, Meo Patacca, and Tabarino. They were generally regional in origin; for example, Pulcinella was from Naples, Scapin from Paris. The characters were associated with the actors who created them and often died with those actors. Barbieri introduced the *zanni* Beltram in the piazzas of Milan. He strove to give his character more intelligence and astuteness than the traditional vulgar *zannis*. A descendant of the wise Comprà Zavargna, the storyteller invented by the Lombard Giovan Paolo Lomazzo, and a precursor of Meneghino, a similarly wise servant figure in the Milanese Carlo Maria Maggi's comedies at the end of the century, Beltram was, like them, associated with the popular oral poetic form of the *bosinada*, recited in the Lombard dialect. Beltram did not die with Barbieri; others portrayed the character during and after his lifetime.

In 1627 Barbieri published a manual on acting, *Trattato sopra l'arte comica, cavato dall'opere di S. Tomaso* (Treatise on the Art of Comedy, Taken from St. Thomas), followed in 1628 by *Discorso famigliare di Nicolao Barbieri detto Beltrame intorno alle comedie moderne, dou'egli dice la sua opinione* (Familiar Discourse of Nicolò Barbieri, Called Beltrame, on the Modern Comedies, in Which He Expresses His Opinion). No copies of the former are known to exist. In 1630 he wrote *L'inavvertito, ovvero Scapino disturbato Mezzettino travagliato* (Clueless; or, Scapino Disturbed and Mezzettino Travailed), a five-act comedy; it includes all the stock characters made famous by the members of the Confidenti, which Barbieri had rejoined. In this play he gives a fairly middle-class and moralistic form to Beltram and promotes *comicità* (comicalness) as opposed to *buffoneria* (buffoonery). In *L'inavvertito* the actors must memorize the script, rather than improvising on an outline of action as in the old commedia dell'arte; this practice began in the seventeenth century. The play consists of eight episodes that are generally connected to two major love plots, those of Fulvio and Celia and Cinzio and Lavinia. The fathers, Pantalone and Beltram, lack the traditional characteristics of father characters: they are neither tyrannical nor miserly but are concerned above all with the well-being and happiness of their children. Fulvio is dependent on

41

Title page for the first edition of Familiar Discourse of Nicolò Barbieri, Called Beltrame, on the Modern Comedies, in Which He Expresses His Opinion *(University of Turin)*

his intelligent, morally upright servant, Scapino, whose every plan is thwarted by the clumsiness and ineptness of his master; the traditional commedia roles are thus reversed. The script was widely copied during the rest of the century and the next, with versions adapted for Neapolitan, Venetian, and Parisian audiences. It was the principal inspiration for Molière's *l'Estourdy* (produced 1653, published 1663; translated as *The Blunderer*, 1732).

In 1634 Barbieri combined *Trattato sopra l'arte comica* and *Discorso famigliare* as *La supplica: Discorso famigliare a quelli che trattano de' comici* (The Request: A Family Discourse to Those Dealing with Actors). In this work, which was republished in 1636 and 1638, he defends the acting profession against opponents in the Catholic hierarchy such as the former archbishop of Milan, St. Carlo Borromeo, who had died in 1584 and was canonized in 1610. Opposition from the Church was not a new phenomenon; St. Bernardino da Siena had been famous for his sermons against street performers in the early fifteenth century. But in the post-Tridentine period religious authorities began to appreciate the immense impact the theater could have in promoting their vision of an ideal Christian society; if left alone as an independent secular force, they thought, it would promote worldly images in opposition to the otherworldliness of Christian imagery. The Church, therefore, tried to instill in the faithful the notion of lay theater as a source of sin and damnation.

Actors, who were often referred to as *buffoni* (buffoons) rather than *comici* (comedians), were depicted as mercenaries who took money for illegitimate reasons–the equivalent of thieves, usurers, street hawkers, and prostitutes. In 1566 Borromeo condemned the earlier, more tolerant writings on comedy of Cardinal Zaccaria Delfino of Lesina and persuaded Gabriel de la Cueva, the Spanish governor of Milan, to ban *comici* from the city. In 1567 he prohibited spectacles of any type during Lent under the penalty of interdiction. In 1573 he publicly condemned anyone who spent devotional days "in taverns in excesses, in merrymaking, in gambling, in 'profane' public spectacles, in carnality, in any dissolution whatever." In 1579 he threatened with excommunication anyone who wrote or was a spectator at comedies. In 1582 he forbade the "harboring" of actors and made it known that the archdiocese would do whatever it deemed necessary to hinder public performances that were not under the jurisdiction of the Church. Finally, in 1583 he was able to have the governor establish a "revisionary forum" of three Church members to whom all plays had to be presented for reading and revision before being performed publicly in Milan. Through long delays in its decisions this body often caused troupes such financial stress that they were forced to move on without performing in the city.

La supplica comprises fifty-seven chapters, each of which begins with a short caption summarizing its content. Barbieri's general strategy is to argue the uselessness of condemning an institution that exists, and all of its members, some of whom may admittedly not be worthy, in the name of a perfect Christian society that does not exist. He states that "intendo parlare della mia professione, difendendola come saprò, mostrando, a chi è mal informato dell'esser suo, come non è vil nè scandalosa, come tali dichiarano" (I intend to speak of my profession, defending it as I am able, by demonstrating, to whomever is not informed in the matter, how the profession is neither evil nor scandalous, as some say). Noting that the term *comico* is a recently coined word, he traces the profession of the *istrione* (actor) to ancient times: "ebbe per maestri i greci e i latini poeti, ove perciò si adornò d'onorato manto" (it had Greek and Roman poets as maestros, hence an honored beginning). *Comico* should not be used as a derogatory term, even if some individuals have not done it justice: "Le scene non fanno i mali costumi ma l'indiscretezza di chi non ha sentimento d'onore, e perciò chi non distingue da' buoni a' rei professori eclissa col mal il bene" (The stage itself does not determine bad customs as much as do those who do not have a sense of honor, and so those who do not distinguish between bad and good professionals erase the good with the bad).

After praising the plays of Giovan Battista Andreini and the acting of outstanding professionals such as Pier Maria Cecchini, Barbieri points out that the true objective of comedy, as of tragedy, pastoral drama, and melodrama, is to teach the public; therefore, the use of the word *commedia* to refer to useless farce and extravagance results from prejudice or linguistic habit on the part of the speaker and not the inherent meaning of the term.

In chapter 9, titled "Il comico è una cosa e il buffone è un'altra cosa" (The actor is one thing and the buffoon is another), Barbieri explains that the *buffone* is a ridiculous character or clown, whose actions are meant to provoke laughter. While often portrayed by the *comico*, the *buffone* is not interchangeable with him. Although a *comico* may play the part of a coarse, ridiculous, vulgar *buffone*, he does not assimilate those traits. Furthermore, the *buffone* can be found anywhere, the *comico* only in the theater. He points out that many nobles and even some Church officials have protected the *comici* and facilitated their work. Furthermore, the *comico* studies his profession by reading the classics under worthy teachers; such diligent preparation deserves praise.

Turning from the actors to the content of the works they perform, Barbieri argues that the theater provides a valuable service as a social chronicle:

> La comedia è una cronica popolare, una scrittura parlante, un caso rappresentato al vivo: e come può scrivere o rappresentare croniche senza dire la verità? Chi dicesse solamente il bene di quello di cui si tratta sarebbe lode e non vita e costume. Si raccontano nelle croniche . . . il male ed il bene; e così è cronica, e così si rappresentano i casi in commedia.

> (Comedy is a popular chronicle, writing in its spoken form, something represented live; and how is one to write or represent chronicles without speaking the truth? Whoever related only the good parts of a subject would be indulging in praise, not in the reality of life and customs. In chronicles, after all, one has to consider . . . the good and the bad; and that is what chronicle means, and that is how comedy works as well.)

The use of actresses was condemned by the Church as encouraging lust in male members of the audience. Barbieri responds: "A me pare che la modestia solamente d'una bella fanciulla sia più atta a far piaga in un cuore che il licenzioso volto o premeditato discorso d'una comica" (I think that the modesty alone of a lovely girl is more likely to cause the heart to sin than the licentious face or the premeditated soliloquy of an actress). He also points out that

Il veder un piè nudo ad una gentildonna, overo un poco di gamba, pare gran cosa, e la concupiscenza travaglia: e le lavandaie e le povere contadine mostrano e piedi e gambe, e non vi si bada, e pur tutte 'sono carni di femine, e l'onor delle donne è pur tutto ad un modo. E parché l'uno scandaliza e l'altro no?

(Seeing a nude foot of a noblewoman, or a little leg, seems like a big thing, and torments our desire: and the washerwomen and the poor country peasants show feet and legs, and nobody pays attention, and yet it is all female flesh, and the honor of the women is still intact. So why does one cause scandal and the other not?)

Barbieri concludes that anyone who might be tempted to attend a comedy for lascivious reasons would be able to satisfy those urges in much more practical ways than a public performance can provide.

Barbieri also argues for the value of theater as recreation: the relaxation it offers is good for the soul, since it prepares the body for meditation and spiritual rebuilding. Further, he suggests that just as tragedy is widely accepted as instructive for the leaders of society, comedy can teach the common people good sense and the ways in which sin might be avoided. He points out that comedy flourishes in every country in Europe; even where it needs official permission, the authorities often allow ad hoc performances in recognition of their social value in relieving the tensions and pressures of everyday life. Though there may be individual exceptions, as in any other profession, acting is a legitimate endeavor: "l'uomo ha da vivere o con le rendite o col trafico o con la virtù e con la fatica o col mendiare: l'inganno, il furto ed il tradimento sono cose infami; la comedia non è inganno nè furto nè tradimento, non prende e non uccide gli uomini, le azzioni sue non necessitano a peccato mortale, adjunque è lecita come tutti gli altri onorati ingegnamenti" (one has to live either on personal income, through commerce, through virtue or work or by begging: trickery, robbery or betrayal are disgraceful, but the comedy is neither trickery nor robbery nor betrayal; it neither imprisons nor kills men; its actions do not of necessity lead to mortal sin, and therefore it is as legitimate as all other honored work).

Barbieri notes that his travels have shown him that no city is worse off because of the presence of actors or better off because of their absence. He ends the book with a reaffirmation of the social functions of theater: it provides instruction on life without much cost to the community; it is a safe pastime, since it does not involve the use of weapons; it distracts the citizens from bad habits; it does not tire the body or confuse the soul of the spectator; and it provides happiness and thus helps to keep the citizens healthy.

There is no evidence of a written response to Barbieri's work. In part because of his exhaustive arguments, the theater came to be perceived as an art and the professional actor as an artist. In theoretical writing on the theater the issue of the morality of the profession gave way to preoccupation with practical problems such as staging. In Milan, which had a weak economy and high unemployment, the Spanish governors saw the value of dramatic performances as a safety valve for public discontent. Moreover, professional actors were garnering support from governors across the northern part of the peninsula and from the royal family of France. Finally, since the Roman papal court was also a great supporter of the theater, opposition by the clergy gradually subsided.

Nothing is known of Barbieri's activities after the publication of *La supplica* other than that in 1638 he was in Rome and Naples with the Confidenti. He died in Mantua in 1641.

Biographies:

Giovan Domenico Ottonelli, S.J., *Della Cristiana moderazione del teatro,* 3 volumes (Florence: Franceschini & Bonardi, 1646–1652);

Luigi Rasi, *I comici italiani: Biografia, bibliografia, iconografia,* volume 1 (Florence: Bacca, 1897), pp. 265–272;

Siro Ferrone, "Nota biobibliografica," in *Commedie dell'arte,* volume 2, edited by Ferrone (Milan: Mursia, 1986), pp. 109–113.

References:

Mario Apollonio, *Storia della commedia dell'arte* (Rome & Milan: Augustea, 1930), pp. 13–14, 20, 26, 39;

Federico Barbieri, *Per la storia del teatro lombardo nella seconda metà del Secolo XVI* (Pavia: Athenaeum, 1914);

Francesco Bartoli, *Notizie istoriche dei comici Italiani* (Padua: S. Lorenzo, 1781);

Claudia Buratelli, "L'Eccezione e la regola della commedia dell'arte: *L'Innavertito* di Nicolò Barbieri," *Ariel,* 2, no. 1 (1987): 461;

Siro Ferrone, "Dalle parti 'scannate' al testo scritto," *Paragone,* 34 (1983): 38–68;

Luigi Rasi, *La caricatura e I comici italiani* (Florence: A. Bemporad, 1905).

Virginia Bazzani Cavazzoni
(1669 – 1720?)

Natalia Costa-Zalessow
San Francisco State University

BOOKS: *Il beato Luigi Gonzaga* (Mantua: Osanna, 1689);

Nel felicissimo arrivo in Modena della Principessa Carlotta Felicita di Annover, Sposa di Rinaldo I, Duca di Modena (Modena: 1696);

Fantasie poetiche (Venice: Albrizzi, 1696);

Applausi poetici consacrati a Leopoldo primo Duca di Lorena (Mantua: Pazzoni, 1700);

Alla Sac. Maestà di Luigi Decimo quarto . . . Ode panegirica per l'assunzione al trono della Spagna di Filippo V (N.p., 1700);

Divertimenti poetici (Venice: Poletti, 1701);

Gl'inganni dell'ozio (Venice: Poletti, 1701);

La speranza veritiera: Nelli felicissimi sponsali della serenissima signora duchessa Susanna Enrichetta d'Elbeuf coll'altezza serenissima di Ferdinando Carlo duca di Mantova, as Virginia Bazzani de Gilles (Mantua: Pazzoni, 1704);

L'Abisai: Oratorio per musica (Mantua: Grana, n.d.).

OTHER: Telestre Ciparissiano (Giovambattista Recanati), ed., *Poesie italiane di rimatrici viventi* (Venice: Coleti, 1716), pp. 245–263;

Luisa Bergalli, ed., *Componimenti poetici delle più illustri rimatrici d'ogni secolo* (Venice: Mora, 1726), part 2, pp. 175–178, 291;

"Gemme o rime scelte di poetesse italiane," in *Parnaso italiano: Poeti italiani contemporanei maggiori e minori,* volume 2, edited by Antoine Ronna (Paris: Baudry, 1843), p. 1028;

Jolanda de Blasi, ed., *Antologia delle scrittrici italiane dalle origini al 1800* (Florence: Nemi, 1930), pp. 364–365;

Giuliana Morandini, ed., *Sospiri e palpiti: Scrittrici italiane del Seicento* (Genoa: Marietti, 2001), pp. 211–212.

Courtesy of Natalia Costa-Zalessow

Virginia Bazzani Cavazzoni produced notable poetry modeled on the best examples of the Italian Baroque period in spite of the fact that she was self-taught. The information about her in reference works is frequently incorrect. In his *Della storia e della ragione d'ogni poesia* (1741–1744, On the History and Nature of Poetry) the critic Francesco Saverio Quadro calls her a native of Mantua; the mistake was corrected by Girolamo Tiraboschi in his *Biblioteca modenese* (1781, Modenese Library) on the basis of information derived from

Title page for the first edition of Poetic Fantasies
(courtesy of Natalia Costa-Zalessow)

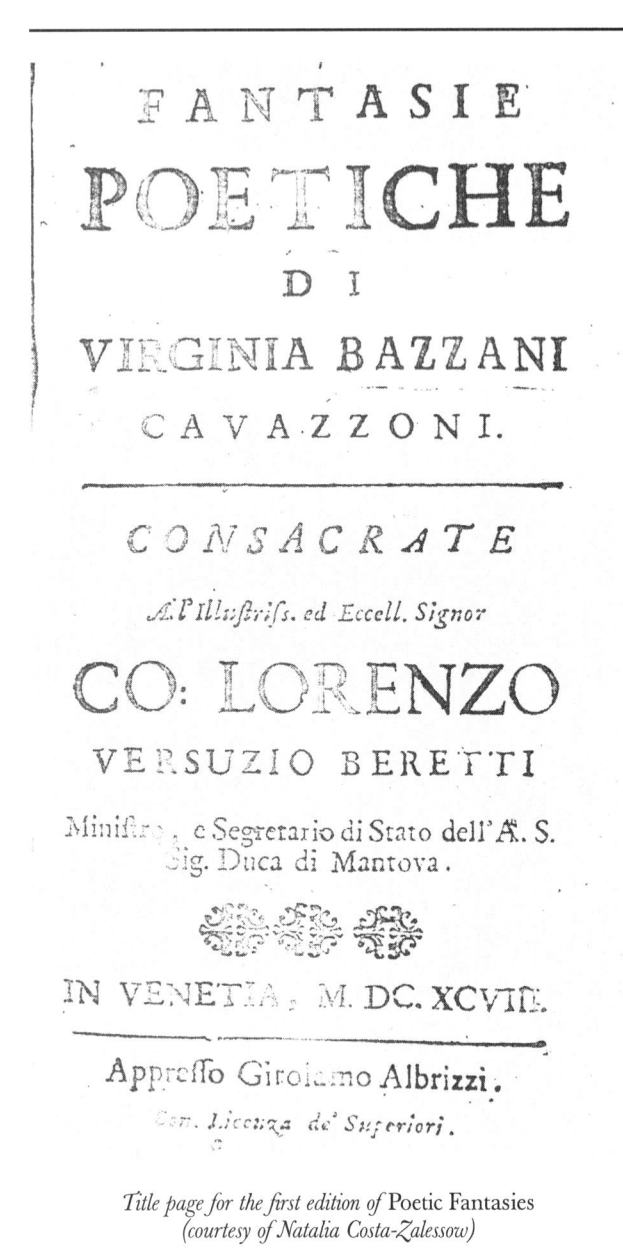

poems written in honor of Bazzani Cavazzoni by her friends, which state that she was born in Modena and moved to Mantua as a child. Bazzani Cavazzoni confirms this information in some of her poems and in the dedications of her books. (In his *Storia della letteratura italiana* [1832, History of Italian Literature] Antonio Lombardi wrongly cites Quadro as saying that Bazzani Cavazzoni was from Bologna.) Most literary dictionaries say that she was born in 1681, while in *Mantova: Le lettere* (1963, Mantua: The Letters) Emilio Faccioli gives the year as 1676. Both are mistaken: she was twenty-seven when she published her first collection of poems in 1696, which means that she must have been born around 1669. She married a gentleman in the service of Ferdinand Charles Gonzaga Nevers, the last duke of Mantua of his family line, and served as lady-in-waiting to the duke's first wife, Anna Isabella Gonzaga. She must have become a member of the Bolognese literary Accademia dei Gelati (Academy of the Frozen) in 1701, for she identifies herself as such in the second, but not the first, of her two publications of that year. Sometime later, after she remarried, she was admitted to the Roman Academy Arcadia. The year of her death has been given in various sources as 1715 and 1720; the former is certainly wrong, for she was included in Giambattista Recanati's *Poesie italiane di rimatrici viventi* (1716, Italian Poems by Women Now Living). Nothing else is known about her life.

Bazzani Cavazzoni's first literary endeavor was the text for an oratorio, *Il beato Luigi Gonzaga* (1689, St. Aloysius Gonzaga). Next she published as a pamphlet an ode to the new duchess of Modena, *Nel felicissimo arrivo in Modena della Principessa Carlotta Felicita di Annover, Sposa di Rinaldo I, Duca di Modena* (1696, On the Happy Arrival in Modena of Princess Charlotte Felicita of Hanover, Bride of Rinaldo I, Duke of Modena); it was included in her first collection of verse, *Fantasie poetiche* (1696, Poetic Fantasies), dedicated to Emperor Leopold I. In the introductory note to the reader Bazzani Cavazzoni declares that, for her, writing poetry is more whim than art, because she lacks the preparation needed to compose verse: "mi sono posta in mano una cetra lavoratami dalla natura e mi sono ingegnata con la sola scorta di qualche libro" (I took into my hands a lyre bestowed on me by nature and I did the best I could with the help of some books). Unfortunately for scholars, she does not name the books she consulted. The volume is divided into "Canzonette" (Songs), "Sonetti eroici" (Heroic Sonnets), "Sonetti amorosi" (Love Sonnets), "Sonetti morali" (Religious Sonnets), *Oratorio del Giuseppe* (Oratorio of Joseph), and "Serenata" (Serenade).

All of the pieces in "canzonette" are quatrains of eight-syllable lines; most have an alternating rhyme. Unrequited love is one of the most frequent themes; in the resulting lamentation the lover declares that he has no intention of giving up his amorous torments because they are dear to him. The insistence that love's pain is pleasurable goes back to Torquato Tasso in the sixteenth century; in the seventeenth century it was a favorite theme of Ciro di Pers. Bazzani Cavazzoni was influenced by those poets and by Giambattista Marino and some of his followers.

In the opening and closing verses of the song "Non fia più che tra catene" (No Longer in Chains) a woman boasts that she has freed herself from the chains of love and is in command of her will. The rest of the poem describes the short-lived amorous sentiments of men; their passions are pure invention, a game consisting of faked ardors and false declarations of love. The professed torments of such lovers are simulated to conquer a woman's heart. If they are declared by handsome men, beware: good looks and fidelity do not go together. Here Bazzani Cavazzoni repays in kind the poets who complain about the inconstancy of women.

Although Bazzani Cavazzoni must have felt the tremor that shook Mantua in 1693, her twenty-nine-quatrain poem on an earthquake includes no descriptions of her personal experiences but echoes a sonnet by di Pers in which the calamity is seen as a warning to sinners. She uses all the Baroque poetic techniques—alliteration, antithesis, and frequent repetition—in the composition, which ends with an invitation to repent because God's mercy is infinite.

In her song about human misery, inspired by a sonnet in Marino's *Lira* (1614, Lyre), Bazzani Cavazzoni creates an original work while elaborating on a well-known theme. She invites everyone to avoid temptation and concludes that those who are conscious of their sins but incapable of overcoming them will soon perish. The theme of life's brevity and futility, a frequently recurring one in her religious poems, is typical of the century.

Bazzani Cavazzoni's encomiastic sonnets are in good taste, never excessive. The first of her love sonnets defines the emotion in a series of antithetical metaphors to indicate its negative aspects. Her use of hyperbole in another sonnet to describe a group of dancing ladies is highly Baroque: beauty and splendor put to shame the Graces and the sun; they dance so divinely that they seem to be sorceresses tapping the floor with their feet to imprison men's hearts. Yet another sonnet takes its point of departure from a question posed by the seventeenth-century poet Antonio Bruni: whether a kiss given freely and a stolen one have the same value. Bruni does not give an answer; but Bazzani Cavazzoni does, from a woman's point of view: the thief must be punished, for pleasure can only be enjoyed if freely donated.

A common theme in the period was the pain caused by a lover's departure. Bazzani Cavazzoni used it repeatedly, but one sonnet is particularly original. The speaker contrasts his situation with that of his beloved:

Tu parti, o cara, e col partir languente
lasci la speme del mio fido amore.
Tu per poco, mio bene, sarai dolente,
io per sempre trarrò misere l'ore.
Lieve pensier io ti sarò alla mente,
tu mi sarai continua pena al core.
Per me non sentirai doglia pungente,
per te sentirò sempre immenso ardore.
Tu parti e porti teco ogni mia spene,
tu alle delizie vai, io nel martoro
resto solingo a lacrimar mie pene.

(You depart, my dear, and with your departure
you leave the hope of my faithful love to languish.
You, my love, will be sad but for a short while,
While I will always live miserable hours.
I will be but a passing thought in your mind,
you will be a constant pain in my heart.
You will not feel pungent pain for me,
I will always feel an immense ardor for you.
You are departing and taking with you all my hope;
you go toward pleasures, I in torment
remain alone to cry my pain.)

Bazzani Cavazzoni captures the trepidation of a lover that his beloved will no longer think about him by continuously opposing the reactions of the narrating "I" and those of the departing "you." The technique was used half a century later in Pietro Metastasio's famous poem "La Partenza" (1746, The Departure).

In another sonnet a gentleman tells in elaborate Baroque metaphors how his lady gave him a handkerchief to wipe away his tears:

Perch'io raccolga i liquefatti umori
che distillo da gl'occhi in larghe vene,
forse mossa a pietà de' miei dolori,
dono mi fa d'un bianco lino Irene.

(So that I may gather the liquefied secretion
that I distill from my eyes in large veins,
perhaps moved to pity by my pains,
Irene presents me a white linen.)

The "liquefied secretion" distilled from the speaker's "eyes in large veins" recalls Marino's "soave umore" (sweet secretion) and "larghe e profonde vene di pianto" (large and profound veins of tears); the latter was, in turn, based on a verse by Petrarch.

Typical of texts written for music, the oratorio is rather simple. It is divided into two parts; the action proceeds at a fast pace, presupposing the audience's familiarity with the biblical story. It depicts the attempted seduction of Joseph by Potiphar's wife, Joseph's imprisonment, and his interpretations of the dreams of a fellow prisoner and the pharaoh. The stress is on Joseph's righteousness, fear of God, and insistence that all earthly things perish rapidly. "Serenata" is a dialogue among Eternity, Virtue, Glory, and Merit.

In 1701 Bazzani Cavazzoni published the collections *Divertimenti poetici* (Poetic Pastimes) and *Gl'inganni dell'ozio* (Deceptions of Leisure). By then she was under

Scalera Stellini and in 1683 by Giuseppe Varano—begins with more than a hundred pages of encomiastic compositions, followed by "Centuria di sonetti amorosi" (One Hundred Love Sonnets). In the sonnet that begins "Ahi dolce libertà" (Oh, sweet liberty) a lover laments that he is in pain because liberty has left him; but he does not want it back, for it dwells in a place that is dear to him: his beloved. In the first quatrain of another sonnet a woman's attributes are listed according to a fixed pattern: each line starts with a noun followed by a clause introduced by the relative pronoun *che* (that)—"Bellezza, che . . ." (Beauty, that . . .), "Grazia, che . . ." (Grace, that . . .) "Virtù, che . . ." (Virtue, that . . .), "Onor, che . . ." (Honor, that . . .); the second quatrain contains nouns accompanied by adjectives, while the two tercets consist of long descriptive sentences. In "Se un martire costante" (If a constant suffering) Bazzani Cavazzoni uses *se* (if) as the first word in eleven of the obligatory fourteen lines. The sonnets are followed by ten "Dialoghi pastorali" (Pastoral Dialogues) in which two or three people—always including at least one man and one woman—discuss love. The book concludes with three long "Canzonette morali" (Religious Poems) and a "Cantata" on the theme of God's forgiveness.

Gl'inganni dell'ozio opens with seventy-eight pages of encomiastic poems. Reflecting the political connections of the duke of Mantua, many of the encomia are for French dignitaries; the book is dedicated to King Louis XIV's grandson Louis, Duke of Burgundy. Among the "Centuria di sonetti amorosi" (One Hundred Love Sonnets) that follow are many well-written though not particularly original ones. Eight "Dialoghi pastorali" (Pastoral Dialogues) and six "Canzonette amorose" (Love Songs) consist of quatrains of eight-syllable lines. The book concludes with the biblical oratorio *L'Abisai* (Abishag). Solomon, David's son by Bathsheba, is chosen by his father as heir to the throne over his older half brother, Adonijah, born to Higgith. Adonijah accepts the decision and makes peace with Solomon. But when Adonijah asks for the hand of Abishag, whom Solomon also loves, Solomon has him assassinated. Bazzani Cavazzoni interprets Abishag's love of Adonijah as directed not at him but at the throne, for she immediately transfers it to Solomon. *L'Abisai* was also published separately, without a date but probably before its inclusion in *Gl'inganni dell'ozio;* the volume was dedicated to Duchess Anna Isabella Gonzaga. It has not been determined whether either of Bazzani Cavazzoni's oratorios were set to music.

Anna Isabella died in 1703. She was loved by her subjects; Ferdinand, however, was not popular, for he ruined Mantua with excessive spending and

Title page for Virginia Bazzani Cavazzoni's Deceptions of Leisure *(University of Turin)*

the influence of the Arcadian movement, which had abandoned Baroque excess for a simple style reflecting an interest in nature and the tranquility of rustic life. The movement brought about a renewed imitation of Petrarch's sonnets, and echoes of Petrarch, Tasso, and Dante can be found in Bazzani Cavazzoni's poems. The language here is more refined than in *Fantasie poetiche,* but the content is less original and more uniform. *Divertimenti poetici*—a title also used in 1677 by Maria Antonia

imprudent policies. To obtain an heir and French protection he married Suzanne Henriette de Lorraine Elbeuf in 1704. Bazzani Cavazzoni glorified the marriage in her final publication, *La speranza veritiera: Nelli felicissimi sponsali della serenissima signora duchessa Susanna Enrichetta d'Elbeuf coll'altezza serenissima di Ferdinando Carlo duca di Mantova* (1704, True Hope: Celebrating the Happy Matrimony of the Serene Lady Duchess Susan Henrietta d'Elbeuf with His Serene Highness Ferdinand Charles, Duke of Mantua). But Ferdinand's political career was at an end. He was removed from power in 1707 by the Austrian emperor for having sided with the French, and he died in exile, without an heir, the following year.

La speranza veritiera, of which only a few copies exist, is of interest because the author's name appears as Virginia Bazzani de Gilles; the change attests to a new marriage, although it is not known when it took place or when her first husband died. The name also appears on the list of members of Arcadian Academy, in which she assumed the pastoral name Tespia Dorina.

Editors of anthologies that include Virginia Bazzani Cavazzoni's works have always selected poems from the 1701 books rather than from her first collection, even though those in *Fantasie poetiche* are more original. Her Baroque style compares favorably with that of most seventeenth-century Italian poets, who did not express emotion in their work but showcased their skills by using complex techniques of versification. The quality of her work reveals the injustice of the exclusion of women from Baroque poetry anthologies.

Biography:

Mariolina Meliadò, "Bazzani (Bazani) Cavazzoni, Virginia," in *Dizionario biografico degli Italiani,* volume 7 (Rome: Enciclopedia Treccani, 1965), p. 324.

References:

Natalia Costa-Zalessow, "*Le Fantasie poetiche* di Virginia Bazzani Cavazzoni," *Esperienze letterarie,* 2 (2002): 55–74;

Benedetto Croce, "Donne letterate nel Seicento," in his *Nuovi saggi sulla letteratura italiana del Seicento* (Bari: Laterza, 1949), p. 162;

Emilio Faccioli, ed., *Mantova: Le lettere,* volume 3 (Mantua: Istituto Carlo d'Arco, 1963), pp. 12–14, 20, 29, 39, 40, 208;

Antonio Lombardi, *Storia della letteratura italiana,* volume 5 (Venice: Andreola, 1832), p. 49;

Leonardo Mazzoldi and Giuseppe Coniglio, eds., *Mantova: La storia,* volume 3 (Mantua: Istituto Carlo d'Arco, 1963), pp. 138–192;

Francesco Saverio Quadrio, *Della storia e della ragione d'ogni poesia,* 4 volumes (Milan: Agnelli, 1741–1744), II, part 1: 337;

Girolamo Tiraboschi, *Biblioteca modenese,* volume 1 (Modena: Società Tipografica, 1781), pp. 182–183.

Guidubaldo Bonarelli

(25 December 1563 – 8 January 1608)

Nicolas J. Perella
University of California, Berkeley

BOOKS: *Orazione per l'inaugurazione dell'Accademia degli Intrepidi* (Ferrara, 1602);

Filli di Sciro, favola pastorale del C. Guidubaldo de' Bonarelli, detto l'Aggiunto (Ferrara: Vittorio Baldini, 1607); translated by J. S., Gent. [Joseph Sidnam] as *Filli di Sciro, or, Phillis of Scyros, an Excellent Pastorall* (London: Printed by J. M. for Andrew Crook, 1655);

Discorsi del Sig. Conte Guidubaldo Bonarelli, Accademico Intrepido, in difesa del doppio amore della sua Celia (Ancona: Marco Salvioni, 1612).

Collections and Editions: *Filli di Sciro, favola pastorale del C. Guidubaldo de' Bonarelli, detto l'Aggiunto, Accademico Intrepido* (Ferrara: Vittorio Baldini, 1607); republished, with an introduction, by Raffaele Manica (Rome: Vecchiarelli, 2001);

Filli di Sciro (Venice: L. Hertz, 1700)—includes "Vita del conte Guidubaldo Bonarelli della Rovere," by Apostolo Zeno;

Filli di Sciro: Discorsi e appendice, edited by Giovanni Gambarin (Bari: Laterza, 1941);

Filli di Sciro, in *Teatro del Seicento,* edited by Luigi Fassò (Milan & Naples: Ricciardi, 1956), pp. 326–461.

Edition in English: *Phyllis of Scyros,* edited and translated by Nicolas J. Perella (New York: Italica Press, 2007).

PLAY PRODUCTION: *Filli di Sciro,* Ferrara, Ducal Theater, 1607.

Written at the height of the Counter-Reformation, like its great predecessors Torquato Tasso's *Aminta* (1573; translated as *Aminta Englisht,* 1628) and Battista Guarini's *Il Pastor fido* (1602; translated as *Il pastor fido; or The Faithful Shepherd,* 1602), Guidubaldo Bonarelli's *Filli di Sciro, favola pastorale* (1607; translated as *Filli di Sciro, or, Phillis of Scyros, an Excellent Pastorall,* 1655) is today a neglected minor classic. Yet, in the first two hundred years after its publication it went through more than thirty editions and was almost as popular abroad—especially in France—as in Italy. The most immediate reason for the interest and clamor surrounding Bonarelli's pastoral tragicomedy in verse was its morally controversial portrayal of the nymph Celia's equally divided love for her two admirers, Niso and Aminta, shepherds who had saved her from being ravished by a centaur.

Bonarelli was born in Pesaro on 25 December 1563 to Count Pietro Bonarelli della Rovere and Ippolita di Montevecchio. Following the death in 1575 of his lord, Guidubaldo II della Rovere, Duke of Urbino, Pietro passed into the service of the duke's son Francesco Maria II della Rovere; but he was suspected of participating in a plot against his new lord. Dispossessed of his worldly goods and facing imprisonment, Pietro fled with his family and sought the protection of the duke of Ferrara, Alfonso II d'Este. Alfonso, however, could not risk offering hospitality to someone who had incurred the wrath of his brother-in-law, and the Bonarellis moved on to the small principality of Novellara, which was ruled by a branch of the Gonzaga family.

The first records concerning Guidubaldo Bonarelli date from 1579, when he was sent to France to study philosophy and theology. He was such a brilliant student that he is rumored to have been offered a chair in philosophy at the Sorbonne. In 1585 he was studying under the Jesuits at Pont-à-Mousson, the chief intellectual center in Lorraine. Called back to Italy by his father in 1590, who was eager to find an ecclesiastical office for him, Bonarelli stopped in Rome; from there he rejected the idea of a religious life in a 1591 letter to his father. In 1592 he went to Milan in the service of Cardinal Federico Borromeo, but before long he was at the court of Count Camillo Gonzaga in Novellara. Toward the end of 1593 the count learned that Bonarelli was carrying on a romance with Costanza, one of his nieces. This affair resulted in the banishment of the entire Bonarelli family; they again sought the protection of Alfonso II d'Este, Duke of Ferrara, and this time it was granted. The rest of the Bonarellis were allowed to establish themselves in Modena; but the duke kept Guidubaldo in Ferrara, gave him the title *maestro di camera* (chamberlain) and entrusted him with several

important diplomatic missions. Alfonso died without heirs in October 1597 and was succeeded by his cousin Cesare d'Este. Political exigencies caused Cesare to renounce his claim to Ferrara and establish a new court in Modena in January 1598. He used Bonarelli in ambassadorial missions of considerable importance, particularly those involving the papal court and France. Bonarelli was eminently successful in these endeavors, but once again he incurred the wrath of his lord. In August 1600 he seems to have secretly married Laura Coccapani, the daughter of the ducal treasurer, although the duke had other marriage plans for him. Moreover, Bonarelli involved himself in an intrigue concerning the possibility of a high-placed but secret marriage for one of his younger siblings. When his duplicity in these matters became known, the infuriated Cesare ordered him to leave the ducal lands within twenty-four hours.

Thenceforth, Bonarelli had no part in official service for any ruler. He dwelled alternately in Ferrara, Ancona, and—after being pardoned by Cesare in April 1601—in Modena. He was able to devote himself to the literary activity he had always desired but for which his courtier's life left little time. He was well received by the cultural and intellectual elite at the Ferrara court and was among the founders of the Accademia degli Intrepidi (Academy of the Fearless); he was nominated by his fellow members to deliver the academy's inaugural address on 26 August 1601.

Bonarelli wrote his masterpiece, the pastoral tragicomedy in verse *Filli di Sciro,* for the Intrepidi under the pastoral name Aggiunto; before then he seems to have written little poetry. The play was probably performed or recited in 1605 in the new ducal theater in Ferrara and was published in the city in 1607 under the auspices of the academy.

Like Guarini's *Il Pastor fido,* Bonarelli's *Filli di Sciro* has an antecedent history that is revealed in the course of the play. Born on the island of Skyros, Tirsi and Filli were among the children who were selected every fifteen years to be taken away from their parents and sent to serve in the court of the king of Thrace. Their beauty and fondness for one another so struck the king that he resolved that they would be wed when they came of age. As a pledge of this intention, he bestowed on each of them half of a specially made precious collar. But the king of Smyrna, acting on a false report of the death of the Thracian king, invaded Thrace. In the turmoil of war the young couple were abducted and taken to Smyrna. There one of the king's guardsmen disguised them as shepherds, gave them new names—Tirsi became Niso, and Filli became Clori—and separated them by placing Clori in the hands of the shepherd Melisso, who eventually made his way with Clori to Skyros. Each of the children was told that the other had died.

The play opens fifteen years after Tirsi and Filli were taken to Thrace. Oronte, the Thracian king's minister, has returned to Skyros to exact the new tribute. Fearing that the king was still searching for Clori, Melisso does his best to hide her. Meanwhile, Niso has been cast ashore on the island by a storm. Hearing cries for help, he rescues a naked nymph, Celia, from being raped by a centaur (a nearly obligatory scene in the Italian pastoral drama, usually with a satyr as the villain); he is assisted by the shepherd Aminta, who has also heard the nymph's cries. Hitherto disdainful of love, Celia finds herself invaded by tender yet passionate emotions as she cares for the wounds the shepherds suffered in their combat with the centaur; they, in turn, fall in love with her, though Aminta conceals his feelings out of friendship for Niso. Much of the play is devoted to Celia's desperate attempts to avoid contact with her two swains; to yield to either would, in her mind, entail being unfaithful to the other:

Godrò d'un sol? Non mel consente Amore.
O d'ambidue? Amor e 'l Ciel mel vieta.
Dunque morir conviensi: altro rimedio
non ha la morte mia che la mia morte.

(Enjoy but one? Love will not give me leave
To enjoy both, both Heaven and Earth forbid.
Then I must dye, for other remedy
Than death this death cannot invent [translated by Joseph Sidnam, 1655]).

Not knowing that his love is reciprocated, Niso asks the wise old nymph Nerea to plead his case to Celia and give her the half collar of gold he wears around his neck. Having already been reprimanded by Celia for speaking to her of Niso's love, Nerea asks Clori to give the half collar to Celia, with whom Clori has become close friends in the three years since her return to Skyros with Melisso. On receiving the half-collar from Nerea, Clori realizes that Niso is the presumed-dead Tirsi. Stunned at what she takes to be her betrothed's betrayal of their love, Clori decides to kill herself. But first she sends a shepherd boy to Niso with her own half of the collar joined to the half Nerea gave her. On receiving the collar, Niso realizes that Clori is his long-presumed-dead betrothed, Filli. He casts the collar, which he now regards as an ill-fated omen, into a ditch and runs off to try to find Clori before she commits suicide. The collar is retrieved by a passing Thracian soldier, who brings it to Oronte. Since an image of the king was engraved on the collar, Oronte declares the young couple guilty of lèse-majesté for throwing it to the

Title page for an English translation of Guidubaldo Bonarelli's 1607 play, Filli di Sciro *(Huntington Library)*

ground. Condemned to die, Niso and Clori try to save each other by claiming sole responsibility for the deed. But then Oronte reads the inscription on the collar, which proves to be a royal decree that not only liberates the couple but also frees Skyros from the obligation to send children to Thrace. Niso and Clori are joyfully reunited. Celia, who had unsuccessfully attempted suicide in her anguish at being unable to resolve the dilemma posed by her twofold love, discovers that Niso is her brother; thus, she is freed from what she now sees was an incestuous passion for him and can marry Aminta. It is also revealed that Aminta and Clori are brother and sister. Earlier, Oronte had recalled the Thracian king's insistence that Tirsi and Filli were to be wed because "il Cielo il vuole" (Heaven wills it); at that point the union no longer seemed possible, and Oronte had observed: "Ah che troppo alto è 'l Ciel, nè giunger puote / la mente umana a suo voler lassuso!" (Ah, Heaven is far above us, nor can the human mind attain to its lofty will). But in the happy ending the king's words are proved true. The final statement in *Filli di Sciro* is an affirmation, in the prevailing Counter-Reformation spirit, of benevolent authority in both a religious and a political sense.

The Italian pastoral drama is well known for indulging in descriptions of the sensual pleasures of love, but conspicuous by its absence from *Filli di Sciro* is anything remotely approaching the kissing episodes that Tasso and Guarini use to great effect. In the first act Celia describes to Clori her near ravishment by the beastly centaur; Bonarelli winks at his sophisticated audience through her naive misinterpretation of the centaur's intention–she thought that she was to be dismembered and eaten–and her reflexive attempt to cover her nakedness by closing her eyes. This voyeuristic indulgence gives way quickly, however, to her account of the arrival of Niso and Aminta to the rescue. The most erotic passage in the play occurs when Nerea, in enticing Aminta to love Celia, details the made-for-each-other physical charms of the nymph and the young shepherd.

The temptation to engage in cerebral wordplay was, perhaps, too great for Bonarelli, who, in addition to living in an age known for such linguistic games, had mastered the art of Scholastic subtleties in his years of study in France. Celia's obsessive wordplay continues unabated throughout the play, always on the theme of love and death.

Clori/Filli is less interesting dramatically than the erotically possessed, suppressed, and befuddled Celia, but she is the most sympathetic character in the play. Of the four young lovers, she alone has a truly human psychology and depth of character. Even she is occasionally tainted by the author's penchant for wordplay, but it does not deprive her of her humanity or of her dignity, the quality that especially distinguishes her from the other three lovers. While one hears a great deal of sophisticated and apparently passionate talk of love and death from the others, the true elegiac mode is most natural to Clori.

Over a period of three days in 1606, the year before the play was published, Bonarelli read to the academy a preemptive response to criticism of it. In 1607 he accepted an invitation to manage the household of Cardinal Alessandro d'Este in Rome. Poor health delayed his departure from Ancona; he set out near the end of the year but died en route in Fano on 8 January 1608.

Bonarelli's preemptive response was edited by his much younger brother Prospero–who earned a favorable reputation for his tragedies *Medoro innamorato* (1610, Medoro in Love) and *Il Solimano* (1619, Süleyman)–and was published in Ancona by members of the academy as *Discorsi in difesa del doppio amore della sua Celia* (1612, Discourses in Defense of Celia's Twofold Love). Though written with verve, it is weighed down by

Scholastic erudition and methodology; its deductive arguments and "proofs," piling syllogism upon syllogism and paradox upon paradox, make for difficult reading. Among the points Bonarelli makes is that the poet's imagination must have unbounded freedom if it is to produce the wonder and the "marvelous" that were the aims of Baroque poetry. Verisimilitude is to be judged on the basis of the internal coherence of a given work: what seems impossible in itself may become, in the context of a story, not only credible but necessary. He also claims for poetry the right to deal with the scabrous and embarrassing subject matter that pleases the public. Finally, he asserts that he was under no obligation to depict perfect love in Celia; his aim was to show the tumult in a heart suddenly seized by a furious passion.

Soon after his death, Bonarelli was honored in an homage volume by some of the most illustrious authors of the age. Prologues and intermezzi for *Filli di Sciro* were composed by Giambattista Marino, Fulvio Testi, and Niccolò Corradini. Marino also praised the *Discorsi in difesa del doppio amore della sua Celia* for its "nobility and purity of phrasing" and the richness of its wit and conceits. Several French translations of *Filli di Sciro,* accompanied by discussions of the play, appeared in the seventeenth century. For the most part the discussions revolved around the appropriateness or lack thereof of Bonarelli's portrayal of Celia's moral and psychological character. In the late seventeenth and eighteenth centuries French critical reaction against the supposed excessive cerebral witticisms and conceits of Italian literature included Bonarelli among the faulted authors; the major attacks were made by Adrien Baillet and Père Dominique Bouhours. In 1674 René Rapin objected that Guarini in *Il Pastor Fido* and Bonarelli in *Filli di Sciro* use distracting witticisms and ornate conceits rather than plain and natural language. In 1706 Alexander Pope insisted in a letter that "There is a certain majesty in simplicity which is far above all the quaintness of wit: insomuch that the critics have excluded it from the loftiest poetry, as well as the lowest, and forbid it to the epic no less than the pastoral. I should certainly displease all those who are charmed with *Guarini and Bonarelli,* and imitate Tasso not only in the simplicity of his thoughts, but in that of the *fable* too." The Italians were defended by their countrymen Giovan-Gioseffo Orsi and Ludovico A. Muratori.

In his magisterial history of the Italian pastoral (1909) Enrico Carrera calls attention to the erotic psychology and comic aspects of *Filli di Sciro;* though he criticizes its Baroque linguistic style, he considers it one of the most elegant and delicate works in the pastoral tradition. In 1929 the philosopher and literary critic Benedetto Croce declared that Bonarelli had a delicate painter's brush and that here and there among the ingenious conceits in the plot and style of *Filli di Sciro* one meets with true human sentiments. For Luigi Fassò the main artistic interest of the work is not the figure of Celia but the exquisite atmosphere in which Bonarelli places the other characters. Daniela Dalla Valle sees nothing comical about Celia and her twofold love, considering dignity and a tragic quality her characteristic traits. Franca Angelini Frajese refers to the skillful mixture of comic and tragic themes and the perfect flow of the action of the play. Pia Malgarotto Hollesch holds that the dominant tone of *Filli di Sciro* is a deliquescent tenderness of innocent creatures who are without malice, will, or boldness. Giovanni Gamberin argues that Celia's psychological makeup is not as unusual as it might appear at first sight. Raffaele Manica notes the playful nature of Bonarelli's treatment of Celia's twofold love and suggests that her name is meant to evoke the Italian word *celia* (joke or hoax).

Guidubaldo Bonarelli's tragicomedy *Filli di Sciro* was immensely popular in the seventeenth and eighteenth centuries, when it was invariably considered the third of the great triad of Italian pastoral dramas with Tasso's *Aminta* and Guarini's *Il Pastor fido*. Praised for the superb construction of its intricate—even labyrinthine—plot and widely translated and imitated, it was also criticized for its apparent immorality in depicting a maiden's love for two swains and for use of the Baroque conceits and witticisms in a pastoral, which ought to reflect the simplicity of language and thought of uncomplicated shepherds. Bonarelli's play was mostly ignored in the nineteenth century, but in the later years of the twentieth century it received favorable attention from Italian and French critics.

Letters:

Angelo Ingegneri, *Del buon segretario* (Rome: Guglielmo Faciotto, 1594);

Giuseppe Malagoli, "Studi, amori e lettere inedite di Guidubaldo Bonarelli," in *Giornale storico della letteratura italiana,* 17 (1891): 177–211.

Biography:

Giovanni Campori, *Commentario della vita e delle opere di Guidubaldo Bonarelli* (Modena: Vicenzi, 1887).

References:

Franca Angelini Frajese, "Bonarelli, Guidubaldo," in *Dizionario biografico degli Italiani,* volume 2 (Rome: Istituto della Enciclopedia Italiana, 1969), pp. 583–585;

Angelini Frajese, "Guidubaldo Bonarelli: La *Filli di Sciro,*" in *La letteratura italiana: Storia e testi,* edited by Carlo Muscetta, volume 5/2 (Rome & Bari: Laterza, 1974), pp. 42–52;

Adrien Baillet, *Jugemens des savans sur les principaux ouvrages des auteurs,* volume 4 (Paris: Antoine Dezallier, 1685);

Antonio Belloni, *Il Seicento* (Milan & Naples: Vallardi, 1929), pp. 395–398;

Père Dominique Bouhours, *La manière de bien penser dans les ouvrages d'esprit* (Amsterdam: Pierre Mortier, 1705);

Enrico Carrera, *La poesia pastorale* (Milan & Naples: Vallardi, 1909), pp. 370–371:

Benedetto Croce, *Storia dell'età barocca in Italia* (Bari: Laterza, 1929), pp. 335–359;

Daniela Dalla Valle, "La fortune francaise de la *Filli di Sciro* au XVIIe siècle," *Revue de la litterature comparée,* 46, no. 3 (1972): 339–359;

Luigi Fassò, ed., *Teatro del Seicento* (Milan & Naples: Ricciardi, 1956), pp. xv–xvii, 325–327;

Alain Godard, "La *Filli di Sciro* de Guidubaldo Bonarelli: précédents litteraires et nouveaux impératives idéologiques," in *Rééscritures 2: Commentaires, parodies, variations dans la littérature italienne de la Renaissance* (Paris: Université de la Sorbonne Nouvelle, 1984), pp. 141–225;

Pia Malgarotto Hollesch, "Bonarelli, Guidubaldo," in *Dizionario critico della letteratura italiana,* volume 1 (Turin: Unione Tipografico-Editrice Torinese, 1973), pp. 379–380;

Carmine Jannaco and Martino Capucci, *Il Seicento* (Padua: Piccin Nuova Libraria, 1986), pp. 391–392;

Gian Piero Maragoni, "Il carattere del genere drammatico pastorale e la *Filli di Sciro* di Guidubaldo Bonarelli," *Critica letteraria,* 8, no. 3 (1980): 559–580;

Maragoni, "Vademecum per i *Discorsi* di Guidubaldo Bonarelli," *Critica letteraria,* 10, no. 2 (1982): 352–358;

Ludovico A. Muratori, *Della perfetta poesia italiana* (Milan: Società Tipografica dei Classici Italiani, 1821), pp. 331–335;

Carlo Muscetta, ed., *Storia e testi,* volume 5/2 (Rome & Bari: Laterza, 1974), pp. 42–49, 51–52;

Giovan-Gioseffo Orsi, *Considerazione sopra il libro del P. Bouhours* (Bologna: C. Pisarri, 1703);

Bernardo Ottone, *La "Filli" di G. Bonarelli e la poetica del dramma pastorale* (Vigevano: Derelitti, 1931), pp. 5–61;

Nicolas J. Perella, *The Critical Fortune of Battista Guarini's Il Pastor Fido* (Florence: Leo S. Olschki, 1973);

Alexander Pope, *The Correspondence of Alexander Pope,* volume 1, edited by George Sherburn (Oxford: Oxford University Press, 1956), p. 19;

Renè Rapin, *Réflexions sur la Poétique d'Aristote et sur les ouvrages des poètes anciens & modernes* (Paris: F. Muguet, 1674); translated by Thomas Rymer as *Monsieur Rapin's Reflections on Aristotle's Treatise of Poesie: Containing the Necessary, Rational, and Universal Rules for Epick, Dramatick, and the Other Sorts of Poetry. With Reflections on the Works of the Ancient and Modern Poets, and Their Faults Noted* (London: Printed by T. Warren for H. Herringman, sold by Francis Saunders, 1694), pp. 59–60.

Francesco Bracciolini

(26 November 1566 – 31 August 1645)

Laura Benedetti
Georgetown University

BOOKS: *L'amoroso sdegno* (Venice: Ciotti, 1597);

Compendio della vita, morte et miracoli di San Diego (Milan: Ferioli, 1598);

Della croce racquistata (Paris: Ruelle, 1605); enlarged as *La croce racquistata* (Venice: Giunti, Ciotti, 1611; enlarged again, Florence: Giunti, 1618); translated as *The Tragedie of Alceste and Eliza as It Is Found in Italian, in La Croce Racquistata. Collected, and Translated into English, in the Same Verse, and Number, by Fr. Br. Gent. At the Request of the Right Vertuous Lady, the Lady Anne Wingfield* (London: Printed by Th. Harper for John Waterson, 1638);

L'Enea (Florence: Sermartelli, 1608);

L'Evandro (Florence: Giunti, 1612);

L'Harpalice (Florence: Giunti, 1613);

La Pentesilea (Florence: Donato, Giunti, 1614);

Dello scherno degli dei (Florence: Giunti, 1618; Venice: Guerigli, 1618; enlarged edition, Rome: Mascardi, 1626);

L'elettione di Urbano Papa VIII (Rome: Brogiotti, 1628);

Il Monserrato (Rome: Facciotti, 1629);

Ero e Leandro (Rome: Facciotti, 1630);

La Roccella espugnata (Rome: Mascardi, 1630);

Instruttione alla vita civile per li giovanetti nobili (Rome: Grignani, 1637);

La Bulgheria convertita (Rome: Mascardi, 1637);

Delle poesie liriche toscane (Rome: Grignani, 1639);

Psiche poemetto e l'ozio sepolto, l'Oresta e l'Olimpia drammi di Francesco Bracciolini dell'Api con prefazione e con saggio sull'origine delle novelle popolari, edited by Mario Menghini (Bologna: Romagnoli-Dall'Acqua, 1889).

Editions: *Amoroso sdegno* (Milan: Melchion & Eredi di Agostino Tradate, 1611);

Lo scherno degli dei (Yverdon, 1772).

OTHER: "Il Batino," in *Quattro elegantissime egloghe rusticali, ora per la prima volta poste insieme, e con ogni diligenza stampate,* edited by Daniele Farsetti (Venice: Paolo Colombani, 1760);

"Sonetti in vita e in morte della Lena Fornaia," in *Poesie di eccellenti autori toscani ora per la prima volta date in luce per far ridere le brigate* (Gelopoli [i.e., Florence], 1762);

"Ravanello alla Nenciotta," in *Poesie pastorale e rusticali,* edited by Giulio Ferrario (Milan: Società tipografica de' Classici Italiani, 1808).

A prolific and influential writer who experimented in most of the genres popular in his time, Francesco Bracciolini is remembered today as the author of *Dello scherno degli dei* (1618; enlarged, 1626, The Mocking of the Gods). This lively work, which portrays mythological deities in unusual and sometimes embarrassing situations, was at the center of a controversy between Bracciolini and Alessandro Tassoni, author of *La secchia rapita* (1621, The Stolen Bucket; translated as *The Trophy-Bucket: A Mock-Heroic Poem, the First of the Kind,* 1710), as each writer claimed priority in the invention of the mock-heroic poem.

Bracciolini was born on 26 November 1566 in Pistoia to Giuliano Bracciolini and Marietta Cellesi. His family was of noble origins but modest resources. He yielded to his father's wishes that he study law in Bologna but soon moved to Florence to pursue his literary vocation. In 1586 he joined the Accademia Fiorentina (Florentine Academy), whose members also included the scholars Francesco Patrizi and Iacopo Mazzoni, and delivered a public lecture on Cino da Pistoia's sonnet "Se 'l viso mio alla terra si china" (If my face leans toward the ground). That same year Maffeo Barberini, who later played a major role in Bracciolini's life, joined the academy, as did Giovan Battista Guarini, the author of *Il pastor fido* (1590; translated as *Il pastor fido; or The Faithful Shepherd,* 1602). The major literary debate of the time concerned the merits of Torquato Tasso's *Gerusalemme liberata* (1581, Jerusalem Delivered; translated as *Godfrey of Bulloigne, or The Recoverie of Hierusalem,* 1594); Bracciolini developed an admiration for Tasso's works that influenced his own poetry. His familiarity

Title page for a Milan edition of Francesco Bracciolini's Loving Scorn, *published the same year in Venice (University of Turin)*

with the group of intellectuals who gathered at the home of Giovan Battista Strozzi also contributed to his intellectual development.

In 1590 Bracciolini went to Rome in search of a suitable occupation but soon became discouraged and moved to Naples and then to Genoa. Angelo Grillo, the friar who had supported Tasso during his confinement in the asylum of Sant'Anna in Ferrara, and Gabriello Chiabrera aided Bracciolini's search for employment. In 1595 he became secretary to the archbishop of Milan, Federigo Borromeo.

Bracciolini's first published work, the complex pastoral comedy *L'amoroso sdegno* (1597, Loving Scorn), combines features of the two acknowledged models of the genre: Guarini's *Il pastor fido* and Tasso's *Aminta* (1573; translated as *Aminta Englisht*, 1628). In Arcadia the shepherd Acrisio is engaged to Dafne but loves Clori, a follower of the chaste goddess Diana. Clori's stern modesty makes her impervious to love, but her heart is softened when it appears for a moment that the shepherd has died to save her from being raped by a centaur. She does not surrender to love, however, until the young man fakes indignation and indifference. Bracciolini develops the theme of the power of love to conquer even the most reluctant souls in elegant passages that strive to replicate the tone of Tasso's masterpiece; for example, the nymph Urania's attempt to persuade Clori mirrors Dafne's exhortations to Silvia in *Aminta*. Urania's speech, punctuated by the refrain "Prendi, prendi partito, Clori, d'amar chi t'ama" (Make up your mind, Clori, and love the one who loves you), stresses the power of love in all living beings:

> non è fera in selva
> augello in ramo, o pecorella in gregge,
> che non asconda in sé desio d'Amore;
> I freddi, e i muti pesci ardono in mezzo all'acque;
> mira le rondinelle,
> che percotonsi il petto,
> con l'ali acute, e garrule e stridenti.
> Tutte d'amor ardenti
> chiaman gli amanti loro;
> odi quel rosignuolo,
> che canta dolcemente; e chi ti credi
> che li dia tanto spirto, e tanta voce....
> Il maestro è solo amore.
>
> (there is no wild beast in forest,
> no bird on branch, no sheep in herd,
> that does not harbor in itself desire of love.
> The cold and mute fish burn in the middle of the waters;
> look at the swallows
> that hit their chests
> with their pointed wings, garrulous and shrill.
> Burning with love,
> they all call their lovers.
> Listen to that nightingale,
> who sweetly sings. In your opinion,
> who gives him so much spirit and voice....
> Love is the only master.)

The model provided by Tasso's work is complicated by the insertion of a second love story. Silvia and Armillo had cherished each other in their early youth but were separated. Receiving false news of Silvia's death, Armillo had assumed the name Selvaggio and roamed the forest; Silvia had taken on a new identity as Dafne. They do not recognize each other when they are reunited some years later in Arcadia, but their love blossoms again. Armillo is torn between love and duty, as his beloved is soon to marry his friend, Acrisio, who really wants to marry Clori; also, Armillo has sworn eternal fidelity to the memory of Silvia and feels guilty for his attraction to the woman he knows as Dafne. Meanwhile, Silvia has been told by the nymph Echo that she will soon be reunited with Armillo and has obtained a one-year postponement of the marriage. Unable to reconcile his conflicting emotions, Armillo decides to kill himself. On his way to do so he carves on a tree a distich that discloses his true identity, and Silvia discovers it. Saved by Acrisio and Clori, Armillo is finally reunited with his beloved Silvia.

The convoluted plot defies common sense—it is particularly difficult to believe that Silvia and Armillo fail to recognize each other after having been apart for only a few years—and shows that Bracciolini is attempting to exploit all the conventions of the pastoral genre. Readers are faced with repetitions of similar incidents: Acrisio saves Clori twice, first from a wild boar, then from a centaur; Armillo tries to commit suicide twice, first with an arrow and then by throwing himself to lions; Acrisio, who runs to his rescue, is himself about to be killed by the lions when he, in turn, is rescued by Clori. The work leaves an impression of youthful exuberance, as if the author is eager to show off his technical prowess and his familiarity with the masterpieces of the genre. Its success, however, was immediate: the two thousand copies of the first edition quickly disappeared, and a second, in which the text of *L'amoroso sdegno* was accompanied by some short poems that closely follow Petrarch's model, was published in 1597.

It is unlikely that the play met with approval from Bracciolini's patron, who was greatly concerned with morality and, in particular, with the potentially detrimental effect of theater on the audience. Perhaps to reassure Borromeo, in 1598 Bracciolini composed *Compendio della vita, morte et miracoli di San Diego* (Summary of Life, Death, and Miracles of St. James) while recovering from an illness and dedicated it to his patron.

Unhappy with his position under Borromeo, Bracciolini returned to Rome and became secretary to Barberini, who was then prothonotary Apostolic. Barberini encouraged Bracciolini to complete *Della croce racquistata* (1605, Of the Cross Regained), an epic religious poem he had recently begun. Giambattista Marino's allusion to this work in progress in his *Rime* (1602, Rhymes) attests to Bracciolini's growing reputation. His activity in literary circles was intense. In Rome he was among the founders of the Accademia degli Umoristi (Academy of the Humorists), and in 1602 in Florence he entered, together with Barberini, the Accademia degli Alterati (Academy of the Altered). This period was also a time of frequent travel as Bracciolini accompanied Barberini on several delicate missions entrusted to him by Pope Clement VIII. In 1601 Barberini became an archbishop and ambassador to the court of King Henry IV of France, and Bracciolini went with him.

In 1605 Bracciolini published *Della croce racquistata* in fifteen cantos. That same year he left Barberini to

Title page for the first edition (University of Turin)

sian king Cosroe (Khosrau II); Eraclio's victory and the recovery of a fragment of the Holy Cross are interpreted as a divine miracle. Strongly influenced by Tasso's *Gerusalemme liberata,* the poem depicts the interference of infernal forces, rivalries within the Christian army, and the revelation of the Christian origins of a Persian woman warrior. The martyrdom of St. Anastasius is represented as the turning point in the war; after his sacrifice, God dispels plague and famine from the Christian encampment in preparation for the final victory. The expanded version of the poem celebrates the House of Medici, tracing its origins to the Christian heroes Batrano and Erinta.

Some characters in *La croce racquistata* have obvious counterparts in *Gerusalemme liberata:* Eraclio and Goffredo, Batrano and Rinaldo, and Erinta and Clorinda. An open tribute to Tasso, "di Goffredo il chiaro / celebrator" (Goffredo's illustrious / celebrator), opens the twentieth canto of Bracciolini's poem. The presence of many episodes that are only marginally related to the main action and the frequency of the conversions point to a tradition that predates Tasso: that of the chivalric poem that had been brought to perfection by Ludovico Ariosto.

Bracciolini wrote several tragedies between 1612 and 1614. Inspired by the episode of King Norandino in Ariosto's *Orlando furioso* (1516; revised, 1532, The Frenzy of Orlando; translated as *Orlando Furioso in English Heroical Verse,* 1591), *L'Evandro* (1612) has a complex plot involving betrayal, disguise, misunderstanding, and belated recognition. The lovers Evandro and Orontea are reunited but unaware of each other's identity; lies and deceit provoke Evandro to kill Orontea, and, in despair, he attempts to commit suicide. The title character of *L'Harpalice* (1613) dies early in the play, and her substitution by Erminia leads to misunderstanding that culminates in an act of incest. In *La Pentesilea* (1614, Penthesilea) the Amazons Penthesilea and Asbite are both in love with Achilles. Penthesilea abandons her magic weapons so as not to have an unfair advantage in battle over her rival, but her generosity proves fatal as Achilles mistakes her for Asbite and kills her. The outcome has been orchestrated from behind the scenes by cunning Ulysses, who saw Pentesilea as a major obstacle to the Greek conquest of Troy. Other plays written during Bracciolini's stay in Pistoia were published posthumously. They include *Olimpia* (1889, Olympia), inspired by episodes in works by Ovid and Ariosto and performed in 1612 in Pistoia; *Ozio sepolto* (1889, Buried Idleness); and *Oresta* (1889), which features a character from Bracciolini's *Della croce racquistata.* Still other plays, such as *Tisbe* and *Filli,* survive only as manuscripts.

Bracciolini's discontent with the critical reception of *La croce racquistata* is attested by a 1613 poem

become a parish priest in Pistoia. A long tranquil period in his hometown gave him the opportunity to devote more energy to poetry.

The definitive version of *Della croce racquistata* was published in 1611 as *La croce racquistata* (The Cross Regained; translated as *The Tragedie of Alceste and Eliza,* 1638), with a dedication to Grand Duke Cosimo II. Bracciolini had added twenty cantos to the work but had also shortened the previously published ones. The poem is set in 627–628, the last year of the war between the Byzantine emperor Eraclio (Heraclius) and the Per-in which he complains of the degraded tastes of his contemporaries. In 1618 he published a new edition of the work to which he added an explanation of its allegorical aspects. He also stresses the importance of choosing a subject neither too close nor too distant in time from the present and of avoiding superstition by allowing only those supernatural interventions that are accepted by Christian doctrine. Both precepts are derived from Tasso's *Discorsi dell'arte poetica* (1587, Discourses on the Art of Poetry). In response to criticism by Lodovico Norisio of the many digressions, Bracciolini asserts that Aristotelian precepts concerning unity of action apply to tragedy rather than to the epic and that his decision to eliminate from the poem the traditional review of the armies necessitated the introduction of certain characters in detail: "La cognizione delle persone è parte necessaria assolutamente . . . e non si è voluto calpestare il trito sentiero delle rassegne facendo pur l'istesso e conseguendo il medesimo fine per altra via" (It is absolutely necessary to know the characters . . . I did not want to travel the usual path and describe the armies. The same result has been achieved through different means). This profession of independence is unusual for Bracciolini, who insists in his letters on his respect for acknowledged authorities.

Also in 1618 Bracciolini published a fourteen-canto version of the mock-heroic poem *Dello scherno degli dei;* he may have been trying to precede the publication of Tassoni's *La secchia rapita,* which was already circulating in manuscript. In the first few stanzas Bracciolini explains his decision to explore this new literary genre:

Io che fin'or con la matita rossa,
e con la nera a disegnar mi misi
le virtù degli Eroi, l'armi e la possa,
pochi ne celebrai, molti n'uccisi,
men piacqui forse alla volgare e grossa
gente, perché severo, unqua non risi,
me ne pento, lettore, e vo' mostrarti,
che in palco io saprei far tutte le parti.
. . . .
Ed io, che al vero culto il sacro Legno
dianzi ritrassi, or la mia penna stanca
posar vorrei, ma tuttavia l'ingegno
l'impigrito desio punge e rinfranca
e dice: scrivi; alta cagion di sdegno
rimane, e questo alla bell'opra manca:
scrivi de' falsi Dei, sprezza e beffeggia,
e le favole lor danna e dileggia.

(I who with my red and black pencils have so far portrayed
the virtues, armies and force of the heroes;
I who have killed many of them, celebrated but a few;
I perhaps have not pleased vulgar and common people,
because I was too stern, and never laughed.

Oh reader, I repent, and want to show you,
that I can perform any role upon a stage.
. . . .
I, who have already rendered the Sacred wood
to the true religion, my weary pen
would like to put to rest. Nevertheless
my talent spurs and boosts my lazy desire,
and says: you must write. One glorious motif of scorn
survives, your noble deeds still are incomplete:
write about the false Gods, despise and mock,
and their false stories condemn and scorn.)

On the one hand, Bracciolini seems eager to give new proof of his versatility ("in palco saprei far tutte le parti") in an attempt to capture the attention of the portion of the public that had responded with indifference to his previous endeavors; on the other hand, he offers his work as an antidote to superstition. Critics have traditionally dismissed the latter move as mere rhetoric, since there is no evidence that classical deities posed any threat to Christianity in the author's time; but the first edition of the poem includes a preface that indicates that the target of Bracciolini's criticism was not popular superstition but a literary trend. In a conversation with Urania, the Muse of sublime poetry, Talia, the Muse of comic poetry, promises to ridicule the pagan gods so as to discourage the poets who introduce them into their works. In the text of the poem pagan gods are depicted in embarrassing predicaments. Venus and Mars are caught in a net during one of their amorous encounters by Vulcan, Venus's husband, who displays them to the other gods. Mars tries to avenge the humiliation but proves to be far less brave than expected, and Venus is distracted by maternal concerns. She spanks her son Love, guilty of throwing arrows without his blindfold, and then, overcome by remorse, follows him to Earth, where he has found refuge.

Barberini became Pope Urban VIII in 1623, making Bracciolini's decision to leave him in 1605 appear shortsighted. To regain the favor of his former patron Bracciolini rushed to Rome and immediately started writing a poem titled *L'elettione di Urbano Papa VIII* (1628, The Election of Pope Urban VIII). Tassoni promptly composed a stanza, "Ma il segretario suo, ch'era un baccello" (But his secretary, who was a fool), deriding his rival's untimely resignation, poor judgment, and desperate attempt to make up for his mistake. Bracciolini found employment with the Pope's brother, Cardinal Antonio Barberini, and followed his patron when Barberini was appointed bishop of Senigallia in early 1625. He returned to Rome as soon as he could, alleging the necessity to supervise the printing of a new poem. In a document dated 1 June 1625 the new

Pope granted Bracciolini, his brothers, and their descendants Roman citizenship and permission to include three bees, the symbol of the Barberinis, in their coat of arms and to add the suffix dell'Api (of the Bees) to their surname.

In the final version of *Dello scherno degli dei,* published in Rome in 1626 and dedicated to Cardinal Barberini, the number of cantos is increased to twenty. The addition is explained at the beginning of canto 15:

> Cugin, se tu mi preghi, io ben seguire
> l'abbandonato Scherno a te prometto,
> e sopra il suon delle sborsate lire
> ritorno allegro a maneggiar l'archetto.
> Queste fiano Ippocrene, anzi Elisire
> al semivivo mio freddo intelletto.
> Mezzo giulio ogni ottava? ecco m'accendo.
> Conta, ch'io canto, e chi m'ascolti attendo.
> Imparate, poeti, ogni fatica,
> fuorché la nostra, il guiderdone aspetta;
> se il medico, il legista s'affatica,
> se li paga il consiglio e la ricetta,
> e se il notaro i suoi contratti intrica,
> raccoglie argento ov'ei l'inchiostro getta.
> Solo il poeta, e fia quantunque buono,
> destina il ciel, che s'affatichi in dono.
>
> (Cousin, if you ask me, I promise
> to continue the interrupted Mocking,
> and at the sound of the disbursed liras,
> I happily return to handle the bow.
> The liras will be Hippocrene, or rather Elixir,
> to my half-dead, cold intellect.
> Half a *giulio* for each stanza? Here, I burn with zeal.
> Count, as I sing, and wait for an audience.
> Learn this, poets! Any enterprise,
> except for ours, claims its reward;
> if doctors, if lawyers work,
> we pay for their prescription and advice.
> If the notary his contract jumbles,
> he collects silver, whereas he loses ink.
> Only the poet, no matter how good is he,
> is destined by the heavens to work for free.)

In the added cantos some of the gods lose their immortality; Fate sends others to Earth, where they engage in a war with humans. Some crucial events, such as Mars's battles and the humans' struggle to get rid of the gods, are simply announced rather than described. The poem concludes not with a resolution but with a pause in the action as Prometheus organizes a colossal pasta feast:

> Ferve l'opera industre, e se ne fanno
> mille gran piatti a guerreggiar domani,
> e sopra tutti, oh largità infinita!
> era sparso il formaggio alto due dita.
>
> (The industrious opus goes on, and produces
> a thousand great dishes to make war tomorrow.
> And on top of them all, oh, infinite abundance!
> of grated cheese two inches tall.)

Only three years separated the publication of *Dello scherno degli dei* from that of Tassoni's *La secchia rapita,* and the two authors engaged in an acrimonious controversy in which each tried to claim priority and originality for his work. In the introduction to *La secchia rapita* Tassoni maintained that his work represented a new genre that resulted from the combination of the heroic and burlesque genres; he noted that it had been written in 1611 and publicly read in Padua, which had inspired other writers to try similar compositions. In his own introduction Bracciolini denied having imitated any living author. Modern critics assign chronological priority to Tassoni: while it is questionable that he began writing *La secchia rapita* as early as he claimed, he is commonly believed to have completed it in 1615, while Bracciolini did not begin *Dello scherno degli dei* until 1617. The two works are, however, so different that the controversy appears pointless in hindsight. Tassoni was trying new artistic forms, whereas Bracciolini set for himself the essentially moral goal of fighting against superstition; Tassoni ingeniously combines various epochs and themes, whereas Bracciolini only rarely ventures outside the mythological domain; and Tassoni's invention rests on historical fact, whereas Bracciolini gives free rein to his imagination. Bracciolini's debt to sixteenth-century burlesque poetry is clear; the supposed innovation represented by *Dello scherno degli dei* seems to be limited to its length: its ten thousand lines far exceed those of Girolamo Amelonghi's *Gigantea* (1566), its most striking precedent. Critics consider Bracciolini's stated intention of condemning the use of mythology a weak justification for such a long poem; some have suggested that his real target was the corruption of the Spanish aristocracy at a time when most of the Italian peninsula was under Spanish domination. Such an allegorical reading, however, finds little support in the text. In any case, writing in a genre that had escaped codification provided the author with a freedom of expression that produced felicitous results, and *Dello scherno degli dei* remains the most successful of Bracciolini's works. It was accompanied in various editions by shorter works in the same comic vein such as "Fillide civettina" (Fillide Flirtatious), "Batino," "Ravanello alla Nenciotta" (Ravanello to Nenciotta) and "Il piede premuto" (The Pressed Foot). Many other such poems were left unpublished.

In *L'elettione di Urbano Papa VIII* Bracciolini again claims originality for himself: "senza esempio men vo libero e solo" (I go alone and free, without models). Precedents, however, can be found: medieval litera-

Title page for the first edition (University of Turin)

ture abounds with allegorical wars similar to the one described in *L'elettione di Urbano Papa VIII*. The poem deals with a struggle provoked by the impending election of Maffeo Barberini, who promises to be a strenuous enemy of sin. While the Vices occupy the seven hills of Rome, the Virtues retire with Barberini to Castel Gandolfo. In the ensuing war Envy is vanquished by "del Barberino eroe l'alta presenza" (the imposing presence of the Hero Barberini), while Error is defeated by the Virgin Mary. The poem is clearly meant to dispel any doubts Urban VIII may have harbored about the renewed fidelity of its author, who devotes seven cantos to the origins and merits of the Barberini family.

Title page for the first edition (University of Turin)

In 1629 Bracciolini published the play *Il Monserrato* (Montserrat), inspired by Cristóbal de Virués's 1587 poem *El Monserrate* and mainly set in the Catalan mountains of Montserrat, in which the protagonists are miraculously transformed into bears, followed in 1630 by *Ero e Leandro* (Hero and Leander), written for the marriage of Taddeo Barberini and Anna Colonna. In spite of the harsh stance toward mythology he had taken in *Dello scherno degli dei,* Bracciolini makes ample use of pagan deities in this work. To disprove the opinion that he is responsible for the death of his followers, Love and his mother, Venus, decide to show that Love can bring entire populations together as he did Hero and Leander. Light and entertaining, as required by the occasion, the play is remarkable for the strong personality of Hero, who refuses to marry somebody she has not chosen. In his introduction to the first edition Ottavio Ingrillani praises the author's ability to combine the qualities of ancient and modern poets. The work is an example of "commedia con intermezzi" (comedy with intermissions), a highly popular genre that had developed since the beginning of the sixteenth century. The five acts during which the main story unfolds are separated by four intermissions featuring a secondary story about the efforts of Love and Venus to build a bridge across the Bosphorus. The two plotlines converge in the last act when a golden and silver temple becomes visible in the middle of the strait and sets the stage for the happy ending.

Bracciolini's desire to uphold his benefactor's point of view led him to abandon some of the poetic principles he had stated in the introduction to *La croce racquistata*. His epic poem *La Roccella espugnata* (1630, The Fall of La Rochelle), for example, deals with a recent event. The 1628 victory over the Huguenots was important to Urban VIII, who had baptized the French king, Louis XIII, and saw in his triumph a crucial episode in the battle against Protestantism. Bracciolini, therefore, set aside the idea that the subject of an epic poem should be distant enough in time to provide "la licenza del fingere" (the licence to invent), as Tasso had put it in the *Discorsi dell'arte poetica*. The action is limited to the last months of the siege, and Bracciolini resorts to a familiar repertoire mostly drawn from the *Gerusalemme liberata*. The work, however, includes some striking inventions, such as l'Isola del Contrasto (the Island of Contrast), where nights are bright, days are dark and gloomy, and those who enter take each person they see for their worst enemy. In spite of the author's promise to bring the poem to an end by providing five more cantos, the work was published in an incomplete fifteen-canto version.

More respectful of the rules of the epic genre than *La Roccella espugnata* is *La Bulgheria convertita* (1637, Bulgaria Converted). The poem is based on the conversion of Trebelo, the ninth-century king of the Bulgarians, an event that is remote and obscure enough to grant ample freedom to the poet's creativity. Love stories abound, developing the themes of temptation, penance, and even incest.

During the last years of his life Bracciolini worked on five poems that he left unpublished and in various stages of composition. He published a didactic treatise, *Instruttione alla vita civile per li giovanetti nobili* (1637, Advice for Civil Life for Noble Young Men), as well as his only lyrical collection, *Delle poesie liriche toscane* (1639, Tuscan Lyric Poems), which included only a small part of his poetic endeavors. The collection shows his predilection for the sonnet, and for moral rather than amorous topics. Death and repentance are recurring themes:

A morir, a morir! questa è la meta:
alziamo il ciglio ove de' gir lo strale,
sin che l'ultimo sonno non cel vieta.
Non ti muova altro oggetto egro mortale,
sgombra i desir terreni e in Dio gli acqueta,
ché la Morte ha la falce e 'l Tempo ha l'ale.

(To die, to die! This is our destination:
let's rise our eyes to where the arrow must go,
before our last sleep prevents us.
Oh poor mortal, don't let yourself be inspired by any other goal,
free yourself from earthly desire, find peace in God,
as Death has a sickle, and Time has wings.)

Urban VIII's death on 29 July 1644 brought an end to Bracciolini's Roman career. He went back to his native Pistoia, where he died on 31 August 1645. He was buried with great honors in the Church of San Francesco.

In an unpublished sonnet Bracciolini compares himself to a bird unable to soar and explains his attempt to compensate for the defects of his art through the sheer quantity of his production:

Anch'io di scriver molto ebbi vaghezza,
spesso battendo e ribattendo l'ale,
pur come augel ch'alla bramata altezza
stanco riguardi, ove poggiar non vale.

(I had the inclination to write abundantly,
flapping my wings again and again,
like a bird that, tired, looks
at the heights that it desires,
and will not succeed in reaching.)

This exceptional display of humility attests to Bracciolini's even-tempered personality and critical acumen. Critics and readers throughout the centuries have implicitly—and sometimes explicitly—subscribed to the author's fair and balanced self-assessment.

Francesco Bracciolini was highly regarded during his life, and in the century following his death *La croce racquistata* was sometimes deemed an epic masterpiece. His reputation then went into decline, and none of his poems have been republished in the twentieth or twenty-first centuries. Apart from the excerpts included by Michele Barbi in his 1897 monograph and the letters published in 1979 by Guido Baldassarri, the many manuscripts Bracciolini left behind await critical investigation. Bracciolini was a prolific writer who was remarkable for his versatility rather than for the results he achieved in any single genre. In spite of his self-proclaimed eagerness to open new paths, he was too respectful of tradition to break with literary conventions and also tended to write poems to please his patrons. Written in freedom from these concerns, *Dello scherno degli dei* remains the most readable of his poems.

Letters:

Lettere sulla poesia, edited by Guido Baldassarri (Rome: Bulzoni, 1979).

Bibliography:

Angelo Davoli, *Bibliografia storica del poema piacevole* Lo scherno degli dei *di Francesco Bracciolini pistoiese* (Reggio Emilia: Angelo D., 1930).

References:

Guido Arbizzoni, "Poesia epica, eroicomica, satira burlesca, La poesia rusticale toscana, La poesia 'figurata'" in *Storia della letteratura italiana,* volume 5: *La fine del Cinquecento e il Seicento,* edited by Enrico Malato (Rome: Salerno, 1997), pp. 727–770;

Ginetta Auzzas, "Bracciolini, Francesco," in *Dizionario critico della letteratura italiana,* volume 1, edited by Vittore Branca (Turin: Unione Tipografico-Editrice Torinese, 1973), pp. 403–406;

Michele Barbi, *Notizia della vita e delle opere di Francesco Bracciolini* (Florence: Sansoni, 1897);

Luisella Giachino, "Dalla storia al mito: *La Roccella espugnata* di Francesco Bracciolini," *Studi secenteschi,* 44 (2003): 167–195;

Marziano Guglielminetti, "La parodia dell'epica," in *Storia della civiltà letteraria italiana,* edited by Giorgio Bárberi Squarotti (Turin: Unione Tipografico-Editrice Torinese, 1990), pp. 388–396;

Carmine Jannaco and Martino Capucci, *Il Seicento* (Padua: Piccin Nuova Libraria, 1986), pp. 446–448, 536–545, 568–576, 590;

Mario Menghini, "Una poesia inedita di Francesco Bracciolini," *L'istruzione,* 3–4 (1890): 177–181;

Lovanio Rossi, "Bracciolini, Francesco," in *Dizionario biografico degli Italiani,* volume 13 (Rome: Istituto della Enciclopedia Treccani, 1971), pp. 634–636;

Mauro Sarnelli, "'Per strada non prevista': Il neo-senechismo di Francesco Bracciolini," *Studi secenteschi,* 39 (1998): 33–78;

Claudio Varese, "Teatro, prosa, poesia," in *Storia della letteratura italiana,* volume 5: *Il Seicento,* edited by Emilio Cecchi and Natalino Sapegno (Milan: Garzanti, 1967), pp. 529–928.

Papers:

Francesco Bracciolini's manuscripts are at the Biblioteca Nazionale Centrale, the Biblioteca Barberini, and the Biblioteca Vaticana in Rome; the Biblioteca Nazionale and the Biblioteca Riccardiana in Florence; the Biblioteca Comunale Forteguerriana in Pistoia; and the Biblioteca Marciana in Venice.

Michelangelo Buonarroti *il Giovane*
(1568 – 11 January 1646)

Olimpia Pelosi
State University of New York at Albany

SELECTED BOOKS: *Descrizione delle felicissime nozze della Cristianissima Maestà di Madama Maria de' Medici, regina di Francia e di Navarra* (Florence: Marescotti, 1600);

Il Natal d'Ercole (Florence: Giunti, 1605);

Il giudizio di Paride (Florence: Sermartelli, 1608);

La Tancia, anonymous (Florence: Giunti, 1612);

Il balletto della cortesia (Florence: Marescotti, 1613 [i.e., 1614]);

Delle lodi del Gran Duca di Toscana Cosimo II.: Orazione di Michelangelo Buonarroti. Recitata dà lui nell'Accademia Fiorentina il dì 21. di dicembre 1621 (Florence: Pietro Cecconcelli, 1622);

L'Avinavolio (Florence: Filippo Papini, 1643);

La fiera: Terza redazione (Florence: Tartini & Franchi, 1726);

Satire di Michelangelo Buonarroti il Giovane, date ora in luce per la prima volta, edited by Luigi Carrer (Venice: Alvisopoli, 1845).

Editions and Collections: *La Tancia,* edited by Anton Maria Salvini (Florence: Tartini & Franchi, 1726);

La fiera e La Tancia, edited by Pietro Fanfani (Florence: Lemonnier, 1860);

Opere varie in versi e in prosa di Michelangelo Buonarroti il Giovane, edited by Fanfani (Florence: Lemonnier, 1863);

Gli esercizi emendati (Florence: Tipografia Calasanziana, 1881);

Il passatempo, Il balletto della cortesia, and *Siringa,* in *Musica, ballo e drammatica alla Corte Medicea dal 1600 al 1637,* edited by Angelo Solerti (Florence: Bemporad, 1905), pp. 281–339, 519–588;

"Sopra i pianeti Medicei," in *Galileo Galilei nella poesia del suo secolo: Raccolta di poesie edite e inedite scritte da' contemporanei in lode di Galileo, pubblicate in occasione del 3. centenario delle sue scoperte celesti,* edited by Nunzio Vaccaluzzo (Milan: Sandron, 1910), pp. 55–56;

Uberto Limentani, "I *capitoli* di Michelangelo Buonarroti *il Giovane* a Niccolò Arrighetti," *Studi secenteschi,* 16 (1975): 3–42;

Limentani, "Tre satire inedite di Michelangelo Buonarroti *il Giovane,*" *Studi secenteschi,* 17 (1976): 3–31;

La fiera: Redazione originaria, edited by Limentani (Florence: Olschki, 1984);

La fiera: Seconda redazione, edited by Olimpia Pelosi (Naples: Liguori, 2003).

Edition in English: *Selected Poems from Michelangelo Buonarroti, with Translations from Various Sources,* edited by Ednah D. Cheney (Boston: Lee & Shepard / New York: Charles T. Dillingham, 1885).

PLAY PRODUCTIONS: *Il Natal d'Ercole,* Florence, mansion of Antonio de' Medici, 22 October 1605;

Il giudizio di Paride, Florence, Medici court, 19 October 1608;

La Tancia, Tuscany, country house of Antonio de' Medici, 25 May 1611;

Il passatempo, Florence, Palazzo Pitti, 1614;

La fiera, Florence, Uffizi Gallery, 11 February 1619;

Siringa, Florence, Palazzo Vecchio, 1634.

OTHER: *Rime di Michelangelo Buonarroti il Vecchio,* edited by Buonarroti (Florence: Giunti, 1623).

Michelangelo Buonarroti *il Giovane* (the Younger) was one of the most versatile writers of his time. He was a man of letters, an inventor, a choreographer and director of *feste* (festivals) and plays at court, and a fair draftsman and musician. These qualities combined to make him one of the most refined Italian court poets of the seventeenth century. The grandnephew of the artist Michelangelo Buonarroti, he was born in Florence in 1568 to Leonardo Buonarroti, a merchant, and Cassandra Ridolfi; he was baptized on 4 November. He had two older brothers, Buonarroto and Lodovico, and a younger one, Francesco. Among his playmates was Maffeo Barberini, the future Pope Urban VIII; the two became lifelong friends. Buonarroti started writing poetry at an early age: one of his manuscripts bears the notation "Le prime poesie che io facessi mai a' miei dí,

Title page for Michelangelo Buonarroti il Giovane's *play*
Paris's Choice *(University of Turin)*

di età di sedici anni" (Here are the first poems which I ever wrote, at the age of sixteen). Buonarroti and Barberini were roommates at the University of Pisa and became friends of the scientist Galileo Galilei, who was a professor there.

In 1585 Buonarroti joined the Accademia Fiorentina (Florentine Academy). In 1589 he joined the Accademia della Crusca (Academy of the Sifters) with the academic nickname "Impastato" (kneaded or made into a paste). Among his many early works was "Madrigali" (Madrigals), presented to the Accademia della Crusca in 1591; the pieces are strongly influenced by the poetry of Francesco Redi. He also wrote verses dedicated to several women, including four sonnets to a Melena in 1592. In 1596 he became *arciconsolo* (president) of the Accademia della Crusca.

In 1599 or 1600 Buonarroti joined the Accademia dei Pastori Antellesi (Academy of the Antellesi Shepherds), where he took the untranslatable nickname "Alfesibeo." He held an important office in the Accademia degli Elevati (Academy of the Dignified). Around 1600 he wrote *L'Avinavolio* in collaboration with his friend Pier de' Bardi during meetings of the Accademia dei Pastori Antellesi. Their aim was to rewrite in a farcical fashion the story of the paladins Avino, Avolio, Ottone, and Berlinghieri from Ludovico Ariosto's *Orlando furioso* (1516, Orlando Gone Mad; translated as *Orlando Furioso in English Heroical Verse,* 1591). Cantos 1, 3, and 5 were by Bardi, cantos 2, 4, and 6–the last of which remained unfinished–by Buonarroti. *L'Avinavolio* was published in 1643.

In 1600 Buonarroti was hired by the Medicis as a court poet. At the court he enjoyed the protection of Grand Duchess Cristina and led a brilliant social life. Among the several noblewomen with whom he had affairs, only Francesca (Cecchina) Caccini was able to induce him into a long relationship. The daughter of the composer and court musician Giulio Caccini, she was a singer and composer and wrote Italian and Latin poetry. Francesca set some of Buonarroti's verses to music and taught him to refine his poetry with musical nuances.

In 1600 Buonarroti published *Descrizione delle felicissime nozze della Cristianissima Maestà di Madama Maria de' Medici, regina di Francia e di Navarra* (Description of the Happy Marriage of the Very Christian Majesty Madam Maria Medici, Queen of France and Navarre). Scholars have found in this work valuable descriptions of the choreography of the Italian Baroque theater.

In 1601 Buonarroti wrote "Favola di Antilla e Mompello" (The Tale of Antilla and Mompello), a short pastoral poem in two cantos about the legendary origin of the river Antella and the hill of Montepilli in Tuscany. The shepherd's daughter Antilla and the shepherd Mompello are in love but are ordered to separate by her father, Esone. Antilla goes to Mompello's dwelling and dies at his feet of a broken heart. She is changed into a spring that gives birth to the river, and he undergoes a metamorphosis into the hill. The tale closes with Buonarroti's exhortation to the members of the Accademia dei Pastori Antellesi to enjoy life and avoid the sorrows caused by love. The main merit of the work is Buonarroti's description of the beauty of the Tuscan landscape.

Il Natal d'Ercole (1605, The Birth of Hercules), Buonarroti's first *favola musicale* (tale to be set to music), was written for the visit of Alfonso III d'Este, prince of Modena and Reggio Emilia, and his brother Luigi to Florence in October 1605. The tale is divided into five episodes without a connecting plot; the style is lively and harmonious. *Il giudizio di Paride* (1608, Paris's Choice) is a *favola musicale* that was presented in honor of the marriage on 19 October 1608 of Cosimo II de' Medici and Maria Maddalena of Austria; it was performed a second time when the duke of Mantua, Vincenzo Gonzaga, visited Florence on 19 November. In 1610 Buonarroti wrote "Sopra i pianeti Medicei" (On the Medici Planets), an ode to his friend Galileo.

La Tancia (Tancia), a five-act pastoral play in hendecasyllables, was performed on 25 May 1611 at the country house of Antonio de' Medici with Grand Duke Cosimo II and members of his court in the audience; it was published in 1612. The wealthy Pietro, who lives in the city, falls in love with the country girl Tancia. Her avaricious father, Giovanni, approves of the relationship, while Pietro's relatives try to persuade him not to marry Tancia but to take her as a lover:

> Perch'ella è contadina, e mal consuona
> Al grado tuo che tu la sposi mai.
> S'ella ti piace, tu puoi vagheggiarla,
> Seguirla, e sol per tuo trastullo amarla.

> (She is a peasant, and you are not allowed
> to marry her because of your higher social condition.
> If you like her so much, therefore, you can court her
> and make love with her for your pleasure.)

Buonarroti masters the vivacious jargon of the Tuscan countryside and transfers it to the page with elegance and ease. Memorable characters in the work include the peasants Giovanni, Cecco, Ciapino, Tina, and Giannino; Mona (Lady) Antonia; and Pancia (Tummy), Pietro's uncle's servant. Musical intermezzi and beautiful ballades helped to make *La Tancia* Buonarroti's most successful play with both critics and the public.

Buonarroti completed *L'Ebreo* (The Jew) in 1613, but it was never performed or published. Buonarroti wrote *Il passatempo* (The Pastime) for Carnival in 1614; it was performed in the Palazzo Pitti before an audience of noble Florentines. It includes the allegorical characters Pastime, Laughter, and Solace and stock types such as the stingy old man, the reckless youth, and the crafty servant. The comedy *La dote* (The Dowry) was written after 1615. Buonarroti also wrote two sacred plays: *Il Ginnesio*, about the conversion to Christianity and martyrdom of St. Genesius of Rome during the reign of the emperor Diocletian, and *Il velo di Sant'Agata* (St. Agathe's Veil), based on the legend of the saint whose relic saved the city of Catania from the lava flowing down from Mt. Etna the year after her martyrdom in 251.

The play to which Buonarroti devoted the greatest amount of effort was the comedy *La fiera* (The Fair), commissioned by the grand duke and presented at Carnival in 1619. Never satisfied with the play, Buonarroti worked on it throughout his life and created three versions. The original version was 3,642 verses in length, the second almost 15,000 verses, and the third nearly 32,000. In five *giornate* (days), or acts, Buonarroti seeks to present as realistically as possible the daily life of a crowded city that is at first unnamed and is later identified as Pandora; references to monuments, roads, and other sites indicate that Pandora is Florence. The *podestà* (mayor) has moved into a mansion outside the walls of the city to avoid possible riots; the jail, the hospital, and a tavern are nearby. *Il coro di Soldati* (the Soldiers' chorus) opens the play with a song. L'Arte (Art) then enters on a chariot decorated with trophies and festoons and escorted by other allegorical characters: Labor, Commerce, Poverty, Skills, and Parsimony. Interest and Hypocrisy cause trouble at the fair. The Lie is a pivotal character, indispensable to the prosperity of the merchants of Pandora. Buonarroti wants to convey to his audience the paradoxical message that an "honest" lie, when used for a good purpose, is the equivalent of the truth:

Tu non se' la Bugia; nome sì fatto
Ti viene imposto a torto.
Tu se' la Poesia: ti riconosco
Agli artifici tuoi grati e salubri.
Tu se' la Poesia che 'n forma nuova,
Con gli scaltri argomenti hai persuasa
Costei d'averti seco.
Tu i trionfi, tu i gesti,
E le grandi opre degli eroi subblimi
Su cetera ingemmata
Fai risonare.
Ma in questo, o in caso tal non pur non sei
Qual ti di', la Bugia;
Ma né la poesia fia chi ti crederà.
Tu se' la stietta e mera Verità.

(Thou art not the Lie; such a name
Has been given to you wrongfully.
You are indeed Poetry: I am able to ascertain that
Because of your pleasurable and salubrious artifices.
Your indisputable and convincing reasons
Have persuaded Poetry
to have you as a companion,
But with a new role.
You play on a lyre adorned with gems
All the triumphs, the great deeds
And noble enterprises of the lofty gods.
But, even though you aren't the Lie, as you define yourself,
No one will ever believe that you are Poetry.
In fact, there is a better definition for you.
You are the pure, simple, and plain Truth.)

At the climax of the play all of the separate scenes mingle into a gigantic one set in the typical Baroque wide square of the fair: noisy, swarming with people and goods, a place where daily reality takes shape as an immense, changing, and mobile theater symbolizing every facet of society. The play ends with a ball at the *podestà*'s mansion.

Beneath its façade of balance and common sense the work conceals a profound sense of the grotesque. In spite of his classical education, Buonarroti is fascinated by the restless and fragmented vision of the *anima in barocco* (Baroque soul): this attraction is shown in the closing verses of the third version of *La fiera*:

Tutte le cose stan sulle cannucce,
Gli uomin sotto 'l mantel tutti han le grucce.
E così far si dee d'ogn'altra cosa,
Che 'n questo mondo sia desiderabile:
E chi dentro un tal fin non si riposa,
La sua vita fia sempre miserabile,
Dura, austera, trista, penuriosa,
Abborrita, fuggita, detestabile.
Se di quel ch'uom può aver non si contenta,
Sempre un verme ha nel sen che lo tormenta.

(Everything looks quite unstable,
Under their cloaks all men carry their crutches.
We should try to enjoy everything
That we desire:
Everyone who does not want to pursue the goal of happiness
Will forever have a miserable,
Harsh, austere, sad, penurious,
Execrable life.
If human beings are not satisfied with their own life and with things they can afford,
They will forever have a worm gnawing at their hearts.)

In 1623 Buonarroti published the *Rime* (Rhymes) of his famous granduncle, dedicating the volume to Cardinal Barberini. He selected from the variants of the poems the ones he thought best and discarded the other versions, which would have been of interest to modern scholars. That same year Maffeo Barberini was elected Pope Urban VIII. Buonarroti went to Rome, hoping for an office or a pension, but was disappointed and returned to Tuscany. On the second anniversary of Urban's papacy Buonarroti praised him in a short poem, "Nella creazione dopo Urbano VIII" (Creation after Urban VIII), inspired by Petrarch and Torquato Tasso. The unpublished poem includes references to the wretched condition of Italy, ravaged by conflict and disease during the Thirty Years War.

By 1626 Buonarroti's relationship with Francesca Caccini was deteriorating, perhaps because he had fallen in love with another woman. Caccini complained in letters to him of her loneliness and the seclusion in which she lived after her husband's death, but Buonarroti did not answer the letters. In 1629 he traveled to Rome as the guest of Carlo Barberini, the Pope's brother. He soon moved to the Pope's court, where he became acquainted with such eminent writers as Gabriello Chiabrera, Giovanni Ciampoli, and Francesco Bracciolini. In exchange for his protection, the Pope asked Buonarroti to listen to his own Latin compositions for hours at a time. Eventually, Buonarroti was granted a pension of one hundred *scudi* a year by the papal court. After the Pope's brother died in 1630, Buonarroti wrote "Canzone per la morte di Carlo Barberini" (Canzone for the Death of Carlo Barberini). The poem depicts Carlo's soul in Paradise, begging God to grant peace to Italy.

In 1630 Buonarroti returned to Florence but not to the Medici court. Because of the difficult social and economic situation in Italy, Grand Duke Ferdinand II was less inclined to sponsor lavish parties than his father, Cosimo II, had been. Buonarroti also feared a negative reaction from Ferdinand to his friendship with the Barberinis, who were hostile to the Medici regime. The response of the court to Buonarroti's absence was cold: no one asked him to return. Being away from the court gave Buonarroti the time to research the genealogies of ancient Florentine families. He also restored his mansion in Settignano, the Villa Scopeto, which had been bought by his ancestors, the Simoni family, in the second half of the fourteenth century, and his home on the Via Ghibellina in Florence. He wrote to famous artists and painters, many of whom were friends of his, asking for portraits to add to the collection in the *galleria* (gallery) of the Florence house.

When the plague reached its peak in Florence, Buonarroti took refuge at the Villa Montedomini, the home of his friend Niccolò Arrighetti. There he gave vent to his frustration and melancholy by writing satires in which he criticized the hostility between the Pope and the grand duke and attacked Ferdinand II and all other Italian statesmen who bowed before France and Spain. Buonarroti had never before worked in the satiric genre; he explains in one of the poems that his younger friend, the poet Jacopo Soldani, encouraged him to do so:

Tu mi facesti insuperbire altero,
E m'inducesti a salir l'alte scale,
E parvemi a salirle esser leggero.

(You made me become confident [about writing satires], and [I became] almost too proud of myself;
You enticed me to climb the uneasy stairs [of the satiric genre],
And with your support those stairs seemed to me very easy to climb.)

Buonarroti was aware of his weakness as a satiric poet; he often praised Soldani's satires while confessing that he considered his own verses superficial and improvised. But he made up for his lack of depth with stylistic elegance and wit. In his first satire, addressed to Arrighetti in 1632, he exalts the carefree rural life and the beauty of the trees—in particular, olive trees—and then inveighs against the evils that are vexing Italy and several events that occurred between 1629 and 1631: the war against Poland started by Gustav Adolf of Sweden, the surrender of Mantua, and the conquest of Magonza. In the second satire, also written in 1632, Buonarroti suggests that Soldani leave the city to escape the plague and dedicate himself to poetry in the countryside. In the third satire, written in 1632 or 1633 and addressed to the astronomer Mario Guiducci, Buonarroti complains about the falseness and opportunism of people who are reverent to those who are rich and powerful but rapidly forsake them when their wealth vanishes. The fourth satire, composed at the same time and also dedicated to Guiducci, deals with ingratitude and the cynicism of powerful people. He speaks in generic terms, but his bitterness is clearly directed at the Medici family and the entire grand ducal court:

Noi siamo appresso ai grandi come i cani,
Del pari esposti alle lusinghe e a' calci,
E a salir monti e a tombolar ne' piani.

(We courtiers follow our powerful masters as if we were dogs,
We are exposed both to their false benevolence and to their abuse,
And we are forced by them to climb mountains and to roll over through the plains.)

In his fifth satire, probably written before 1633 and sent to Jacopo Giraldi, a member of the Accademia della Crusca and the Academia Fiorentina, Buonarroti reflects on the brevity of life and the significance of his experiences. He also gives his thoughts on the moral function of satire: the satirist should calmly observe and report vices and defects with a light, though sharp, irony.

In 1633 Buonarroti wrote an emotional letter to Cardinal Barberini, the chairman of the committee of the Inquisition that had called Galileo to be interrogated about his support for the Copernican model of the solar system. Arguing that Galileo's health was failing and that the scientist would not be able to undertake such a long journey while the peninsula was ravaged by the plague, he asked the cardinal to call off the meeting. The request was denied; Galileo pleaded guilty to holding heretical opinions, recanted them, and was placed under house arrest for the rest of his life.

In 1634 Buonarroti's pastoral play *Siringa* (Syrinx) was presented at the Palazzo Vecchio in Florence to honor the arrival of Prince Alexander of Poland. The god Pan pursues the nymph Siringa into a river; Siringa calls on the other gods for help and is transformed into a reed. Pan cuts the reed into pieces of unequal length and fashions them into the panpipe so that he can give vent to his sorrow in music.

Buonarroti's sixth satire, undated and dedicated to his friend Tommaso Segni, focuses on the arrogance and vanity of the noblemen of his time who are irrationally attracted to foreign fashions. The seventh satire, composed between 1642 and 1645, is addressed to his close friend Niccolò Panciatichi and complains about the rapid onset of old age:

Veggola in su la soglia dell'uscita,
Voltomi addietro a riguardar suoi passi,
Sì della scesa e sì della salita.

(I am looking back at my life, standing now on the exit threshold;
I remember the most important moments of my existence,
Both the unfortunate and the fortunate ones.)

Title page for the first edition (University of Turin)

In 1644 Buonarroti wrote the play *Le Mascherate* (The Costume Balls). It is set at the home of a Florentine nobleman during Carnival and features *Gioco del Giulé* (the Game of Giulé), a card game that was popular at the time. The play includes mythological characters. *Le Mascherate* has been criticized as overly long, tedious, redundant, and lacking a clear plot.

Buonarroti's eighth satire, composed on his seventy-seventh birthday and addressed to Segni, complains about old age and poor health. In 1645 Buonarroti wrote a letter to his friend Francesco Rondinelli in which he warned against the careless performance of dishonorable jobs and praised beauty, simplicity, rectitude, and moderation. The letter concluded: "Il fine, insomma, o Rondinelli, è Dio" (The final goal, my dear Rondinelli, is God).

Buonarroti's ninth satire, addressed to Segni, is a kind of spiritual last will and testament. Written during the two months before his death, it gives vent to his sadness at being lonely and ill. The nine satires were published in Venice in 1845. Three more satires were published by Uberto Limentani in 1976. The first of these satires, dedicated to Vieri de' Cerchi, a powerful noble and banker at the Medici court, condemns the greed and corruption of judges. The second is dedicated to his friend Luigi Arrigucci, a prominent architect. Buonarroti states that he has no aptitude for being a courtier and is disgusted by people who display a servile attitude. The third satire expresses indignation at cardinals who wish for the Pope's death in hopes of sitting on the throne themselves. In addition to the twelve formal satires, Buonarroti's satirical canon includes four works published for the first time in 1975 by Limentani. Written in terza rima in a familiar style modeled on Horace's epistles, they are designated by the author as "capitoli" (chapters). Dedicated to Arrighetti, they recall the stay of Buonarroti and his family at his friend's Villa Montedomini in the Tuscan countryside during the plague. Buonarroti died on 11 January 1646.

Michelangelo Buonarroti the Younger was a writer of many literary interests, from pastoral drama to comedy and from lyrical poetry to satire. Much of his massive and eclectic production remains to be transcribed from his manuscripts and studied. Several modern scholars have shown a renewed interest in his work for its linguistic and historical relevance, originality, poetic quality, and use of stylistic and rhetorical devices.

Bibliography:
Danilo Romei, *Bibliografia "aperta" di Michelangelo Buonarroti il Giovane*, Banca Dati Telematica "Nuovo Rinascimento" <http://www.unifi.it/istituzioni/nrin/bibliogr/html/romei/buonarrg/nota.htm> (accessed 5 October 2007).

References:
Franca Angelini, "La commedia letteraria: Michelangelo Buonarroti *il Giovane*," in *La letteratura italiana: Storia e testi*, volume 5, edited by Carlo Muscetta (Rome & Bari: Laterza, 1974), pp. 225–233;

Mario Apollonio, *Storia del teatro italiano*, volume 2 (Florence: Sansoni, 1981), pp. 294–314;

Guido Arbizzoni, "Poesia epica, eroicomica, satirica, burlesca: La poesia rusticale in Toscana. La 'poesia figurata,'" in *Storia della letteratura italiana*, volume 5, edited by Enrico Malato (Rome: Salerno, 1997), pp. 7–127;

Alberto Asor Rosa, "Satirici, ditirambici, didascalici," in *La letteratura italiana*, volume 5, pp. 529–564;

Antonio Belloni, *Il Seicento* (Milan: Vallardi, 1929), pp. 291–293, 361–363, 870–871;

Enrico Carrara, *La poesia pastorale* (Milan: Vallardi, 1909), p. 236;

Vittorio Cian, *La satira*, volume 2, second edition (Milan: Vallardi, 1945), pp. 79–95, 225–231;

Carmine Jannaco and Martino Capucci, *Il Seicento* (Padua: Piccin Nuova Libraria, 1986), pp. 423–433, 477, 550–551;

Title page for a nineteenth-century collection of Buonarroti's works (University of Turin)

Uberto Limentani, "Quattro capitoli inediti di Michelangelo Buonarroti *il Giovane*," in *Essays in Honour of John Humphreys Whitfield: Presented to Him on His Retirement from the Serena Chair of Italian at the University of Birmingham*, edited by Harry Clayton Davis (London: St. Georges Press for the Department of Italian, University of Birmingham, 1975), pp. 204–208;

Limentani, *La satira nel Seicento* (Milan & Naples: Ricciardi, 1961), pp. 66–84;

Maria Giovanna Masera, *Michelangelo Buonarroti il Giovane* (Turin: Fondo Studi Parini-Chirio, 1941);

Severina Parodi, ed., *Accademia della Crusca: Gli Atti del primo Vocabolario* (Florence: Sansoni, 1974);

Olimpia Pelosi, *"La fiera" come gran teatro del mondo: Michelangelo Buonarroti il Giovane fra tradizione accademica e prospettiva barocca* (Salerno: Palladio, 1983);

Gian Francesco Busenello
(24 September 1598 – 27 October 1659)

Franco Fido
Harvard University

BOOKS: *Scenario dell'opera reggia intitolata la Coronatione di Poppea* (Venice, 1643);
Il Nerone overo l'incoronatione di Poppea (Naples: R. Mollo, 1651);
Lettera panegirica alla gloria immortale di D. Diego Michiel Colomera (Venice: G. P. Pinelli, 1653);
La Statira principessa di Persia, dramma per musica, impiego di hore otiose (Venice: A. Giuliani, 1655);
La prospettiva del navale trionfo riportato dalla Repubblica serenissima contro il turco: Al signor cavalier Pietro Liberi, pittore insigne e famoso (Venice: G. P. Pinelli, 1656); translated by Thomas Higgons as *A Prospective of the Naval Triumph of the Venetians over the Turk* (London: H. Herringham, 1658);
Delle ore ociose: Parte prima (Venice: A. Giuliani, 1656);
Panegirico all'illustrissimo et eccellentissimo sig. Lazaro Mocenigo (Venice: G. P. Pinelli, 1657);
Sonetti morali ed amorosi, critical edition, edited by Arthur Livingston (Venice: G. Fabbris, 1911).

Editions: *L'incoronazione di Poppea*, note by Piero Nardi (Venice: Neri Pozza, 1949);
Opere scelte di G. B. Marino e dei Marinisti, edited by Giovanni Getto, volume 2: *I Marinisti* (Turin: Unione Tipografica-Editrice Torinese, 1954; revised, 1962), pp. 492–494;
Il fiore della lirica veneziana, volume 2: *Seicento e Settecento*, edited by Manlio Dazzi (Venice: Neri Pozza, 1956), pp. 43–72;
Poesia del Seicento, volume 2, edited by Carlo Muscetta and Pier Paolo Ferrante, translation from Venetian dialect to Italian by Ludovico Zorzi (Turin: Einaudi, 1964), pp. 1278–1323;
Poesia italiana del Seicento, edited by Lucio Felici (Milan: Garzanti, 1978), pp. 400–408;
L'incoronazione di Poppea, in *Il Barocco, Marino e la poesia del Seicento*, edited by Marzio Pieri (Rome: Istituto Poligrafico e Zecca dello Stato, 1995), pp. 777–824;
L'incoronazione di Poppea, in *Libretti d'opera italiana dal Seicento al Novecento*, edited by Giovanna Gronda and Paolo Fabbri (Milan: Mondadori, 1997), pp. 49–105.

PLAY PRODUCTIONS: *Gli amori di Apollo e Dafne*, music by Pier Francesco Cavalli, Venice, Teatro di San Casciano, 1640;
La Didone, music by Cavalli, Venice, Teatro di San Casciano, 1641;
L'incoronazione di Poppea, music by Claudio Monteverdi, Venice, Teatro Grimano, 1642; as *Il Nerone overo l'incoronatione di Poppea*, Naples, Giuoco della palla, 1651;
La prosperità infelice di Giulio Cesare dittatore, music by Cavalli, Venice, Teatro Novissimo, 1646;
La Statira principessa di Persia, music by Cavalli, Venice, Teatro dei SS. Giovanni e Paolo, 1655.

OTHER: *Quella maga d'amor bella e canora . . .* , in *Teatro delle glorie della signora Adriana Basile* (Venice: Deuchino, 1623);
"Veduto ho i bronzi . . . ," in *Venezia edificata*, by Giulio Strozzi (Venice: A. Pinelli, 1624);
"Signor le stelle il giorno han destinato . . ." and "A gara Giove e Giuno," in *Imeneo di Pindo nelle nobilissime nozze del sig. Annibale Marescotti e d. Barbara Rangona* (Bologna: G. Monti, 1630);
"Regia donzella già da l'onde uscita," in *Le glorie delle armi venete celebrate nell'accademia de' signori Imperfetti* (Venice: G. P. Pinelli, 1651);
"Santa eccelsa sublime . . . ," in *Applausi poetici al valore emerito del sig. Giacomo da Riva* (Venice: P. Pinelli, 1652);
"A venerar sanguinolento nume . . . ," in *Lagrime della Fama nella morte della marchesa Lucrezia Orologio degli Obizzi* (Padua: Frambotto, 1655).

SELECTED PERIODICAL PUBLICATION–
UNCOLLECTED: "La Stiglianeide," in Arthur Livingston, "G. F. Busenello e la polemica Stiglini-Marino," *Ateneo veneto* (July–August 1910).

Gian Francesco Busenello was a lawyer and a member of the renowned Accademia degli Incogniti (Academy of the Unknowns). Among his works are a

A PROSPECTIVE Of the Naval Triumph Of the VENETIANS over the TURK.

To Signor PIETRO LIBERI That Renowned, and famous Painter.

By GIO: FRANCESCO BVSENELLO.

LONDON,
Printed for *Henry Herringman*, and are to be sold at his shop at the signe of the Anchor, in the lower walke in the *New-Exchange*. 1658.

Title page for the English translation of Gian Francesco Busenello's La prospettiva del navale trionfo riportato dalla Repubblica serenissima contro il turco, *published in 1656 (Yale University Libraries)*

large body of Italian and Venetian-dialect poetry and several opera librettos. In his lifetime he was appreciated mostly as a poet, while today his best-known work is the libretto for Claudio Monteverdi's *L'incoronazione di Poppea* (1642, The Coronation of Poppaea).

Busenello was born in Venice on 24 September 1598 to Alessandro Busenello and Laura Muscorno. On his father's side he belonged to a wealthy old family of *cittadini originari* (original citizens), an upper middle class that was entitled to exercise important administrative and bureaucratic functions; they were excluded from the actual government of the city, which was reserved to the patricians. Probably of Milanese origin, the Busenellos had been active in public life since the fourteenth century. Alessandro Busenello was a notary to the doge and, in 1618, secretary of the Senate; Gian Francesco Busenello's elder brother, Marcantonio, held high diplomatic and political offices.

In Venice, Busenello attended the lessons of the historian Paolo Sarpi; later, at the University of Padua, he attended those of the Aristotelian philosopher Cesare Cremonini. In 1620 he became dean of the Scuola grande della Misericordia (Great School of the Misericord), a Venetian institution devoted to religious and charitable purposes. That same year he married Barbara Bianchi; they had at least five children, one of whom, Alessandro, became secretary of the powerful executive Council of the Ten. In 1623 Busenello began to apply himself seriously to the practice of law. According to documents concerning some of his trials, he was given to a florid eloquence rich in erudite quotations. He was financially successful: his estate grew to include several houses in Venice and in the countryside, among them a villa in the resort of Legnaro, near Padua. In 1630 he became vicar of the Scuola grande della Misericordia. He may have traveled in France and Spain–in some of his sonnets he speaks of Madrid; a trip to Dubrovnik, Croatia, seems more probable. He spent most of his time in Venice, and his poems are a lively mirror of the daily life of the city.

Busenello was an avid reader of the works of Statius, Apuleius, Lucian, and, above all, Lucretius, and he participated in literary discussions and epistolary exchanges in prose and in verse with such leading intellectuals, painters, and singers as Carlo Assonica, Claudio Achillini, Angelico Aprosio, Carlo de' Dottori, Ciro di Pers, Francesco Pona, Giovanni Ciampoli, Tommaso and Zuanne Garzoni, Gian Francesco Loredan, Ascanio and Dario Varotari, Jacopo Palma the Younger, Adriana Basile, and Margherita Confaloniera. Especially significant was his encounter with the poetry of Giambattista Marino. From a youthful and belated Petrarchian taste attested by some of the pieces collected by Arthur Livingston in 1911 as *Sonetti morali ed amorosi* (Moral and Love Sonnets), Busenello was converted in 1623, the year of publication of Marino's *L'Adone* (excerpts translated as *Adonis,* 1967) in Paris, to a poetry filled with sensual images, Baroque conceits, quibbles, and long metaphorical variations. In 1624 Busenello wrote a letter and collection of sonnets, "La Stiglianeide" (1910), defending Marino against Tommaso Stigliani, a fierce rival of the Neapolitan poet.

The plague of 1630 killed several of Busenello's relatives and friends and led him to write some of his most thoughtful verses. In 1646 *cittadini originari* were given the opportunity to be inducted into the nobility through the payment of one hundred thousand ducats; Busenello either refused or could not afford to pay the sum. Between 1631 and 1656 his father, his mother, and his wife died. Ailing with gout and probably with syphilis, he spent increasingly long periods at his villa in Legnaro but did not cease his literary activities. Busenello's writings include patriotic compositions in Italian and in dialect to celebrate Venice, particularly its victories over the Turks; satires of contemporary customs; novels; dramas; and poems in dialect addressed to his friends, from the austere Niccolò Crasso to partners in debauchery such as Giacomo Badoer, a former schoolmate in Padua and the author of the libretto for Monteverdi's *Il ritorno di Ulisse in patria* (1642, Ulysses' Homecoming). Only a small portion of his work was published during his life, mostly in encomiastic or occasional *raccolte* (collections). In 1656 he published, in Italian, *La prospettiva del navale trionfo riportato dalla Repubblica serenissima contro il turco;* through Thomas Higgons's translation, *A Prospective of the Naval Triumph of the Venetians over the Turk* (1658), it became a model for English poets such as Edmund Waller. Busenello died on 27 October 1659.

Busenello's Venetian rhymes comprise the major portion of his writings; they were never collected in book form by the author but are found in codices in public libraries in Venice, Padua, Milan, Florence, Rome, Verona, Vicenza, Treviso, Rovigo, Rouen, and London. In these codices, which are not in Busenello's hand, the same texts often recur in different versions. The only plausible criterion for dating the poems–the author's increasing pessimism, shown in regrets about the past and forebodings of death–leads one to assign to the 1650s darker compositions such as "Compare, passa el tempo, e se vien vecchi. / La morte aspetta con la falce in man" (Friend, time is passing, and we are getting old. / Death is waiting, holding her scythe), "Questo è 'l mio mal, compare, e l'è 'l più forte; / Per non aver remedi che ghe sia; / Sì che decider mai no saveria / Che cossa sia pezzor: vecchiezza o morte" (This is my trouble, friend, and it is all the stronger; / Because there is no cure for it; / So that I could never decide which is worse: old age or death), and "Voga voga, compare, al fin son zonto" (Rowing, rowing, friend, I have reached the end).

Common to both Busenello's Italian and dialect verse is the pride of the old Venetian aware of the honors bestowed on his family and of the myth of Venice as the heir of Rome, queen of the Adriatic Sea, and bulwark of Christian civilization against the Turks. In "L'uso del mondo al Badoer" (The Ways of the World to Badoer) comparison of the present with the glorious past of the Republic and the virtues of his ancestors leads to condemnation of the present, with its extravagant and scandalous fashions and its corruption of customs and justice:

> Se sassina se amazza e se scongiura
> se fa mille sporchezzi e infamità;
> questa è la più trista e grama età
> che ghe sia stà daspò ch'el mondo dura.

> (They assassinate, they murder, they swear,
> they do lots of filthy infamous things;
> this is the meanest and saddest age
> there ever was since the world began.)

Not even an ancient family or nobility of birth can hold back the present immorality:

> No distingue dal Mondo l'operar
> nascita granda o nobiltà preclara.
> Le bone action no fa la fama chiara
> né fa le brutte la gloria isporcar.

(A great birth or famous nobility
is no distinction in the world.
Good deeds don't make fame glisten,
Nor do ugly ones stain one's glory.)

This situation suggests to him some curious professions of "democracy":

No amiro nò chi porta dai parenti
grandezze nobiltà sangue real;
né biasmo quello che porta el nadal
da ignota stirpe e scuri descendenti.

(I don't admire those who carry from their parents
greatness, nobility, royal blood;
nor do I blame one who has received his birth
from unknown race and dark descent.)

But the inability to tell great and small people apart does not depend on an egalitarian spirit: rather, it is the effect of a chaotic situation in which traditional standards of judgment are out of circulation.

Praise of times past and outrage at moral decadence do not lead to austerity; on the contrary, they push Busenello to seek the only satisfactions that his "sentimental materialism" enables him to enjoy. A large part of his verse deals with sensual pleasures; the joys of carnal love; distinguishing among the delightful favors of common girls, the sophisticated ones of ladies, and the mercenary and despicable ministrations of whores; food and wine; hunting and fishing; and the *filò* (evening parties spent in chatting and sipping must). The simple contentments and dalliances of the countryside, seen from the point of view of a city dweller and as a return to nature, are among the most typical motives of Venetian dialect poetry from Andrea Calmo in the sixteenth century to Pietro Buratti in the nineteenth; but in Busenello's works they constitute a vein especially rich in images and flavors—a minute and charming chronicle of meals and drinks in company and of hunting parties that turn into amusing anecdotes, such as that of a capon killed by a dog and duly paid for in "I spassi della villa" (The Country's Amusements):

Criar no val, che fuora d'un cason
un caponato in bocca l'ha portao:
vero xe ben che l'havemo pagao
al pover homo che giera paron.

(Shouting was of no avail, as from a barn
he brought a capon in his mouth:
It is true that we reimbursed it
to the owner, poor man.)

As in Calmo's poems, the celebration of rustic pleasures is symmetrically completed by the "trattamenti di chi vive in Venetia" (entertainments of Venetians)—above all, fishing in the lagoon—with an abundance of details. Thanks to an elaborate manneristic analogy between fishing and making love, Busenello is able to pass in the same composition to the other major theme of his dialect verse: women and sex. This facet of his work earned him a reputation as an erotic—even obscene—writer. The bawdy character, verging on pornography, of some of Busenello's and his friends' poems must be placed within an open-minded Venetian tradition that extends from Pietro Aretino in the sixteenth century to Giorgio Baffo in the eighteenth and a cultural climate marked by the tendency to materialism of the Padua faculty, which was a far cry from the prudery that was the rule in Duke Cosimo I de' Medici's Florence. At the same time, along with the celebration of physical love and other sensual pleasures one finds in Busenello's writings anathemas against the indecent customs of his time.

Busenello was also capable of expressing love, as in the long sequences of quatrains of "Le fantasie amorose" (The Amorous Fancies) and "Le consolation amorose" (The Amorous Consolations):

Benedetto però quel zorno e l'hora
che seguitando amor el tempo ho speso.

(Blessed be the day and the hour
when I spent my time in following love.)

Felicità ch'ogni tristezza in bando
che fa felicitar ogni infelice
e fatto felicissimo el felice
felicissimo va felicitando.

(Happiness banishing all sadness,
that makes happy any unhappy one,
and makes the happy even happier,
and keeps filling him with happiness.)

Parallel to the vein of fulfilled and triumphant eros is that of disappointment and sorrow at the end of love, especially in presumably later poems such as "Le fantasie amorose":

Sospiri de passion, che sotto el manto
d'una falsa delitia, el fiel tien sconto;
sospiri eterni che ne tira al ponto
de viver sempre e de morir col pianto.

(Sighs of passion, that under the cloak
of false delight keep gall concealed;
eternal sighs that drag us to the point
of living and dying ever in tears.)

Frustrated desire and betrayed love are depicted as manifestations of an ineluctable process by which every happiness vanishes, with little hope of compensation in the other world; Busenello writes in "Il mondo alla moda" (The Faddish World):

> Corre a scavezzacollo el tempo e passa
> I zorni e le ore che a pena se vede.
> E 'l mondo che no ha più leze né fede
> ride de drio de mi ch'el se sganazza.
>
> (Time runs at breakneck speed, and so fast
> days and hours pass that you hardly see them.
> And the world that no more has law or faith
> behind me splits its sides with laughter.)

Artistic creation should provide some form of survival, Busenello says in "Do brazzolari in man ha la natura" (Two Yardsticks Has Nature in Her Hand): "Ho sui quadri mio nono e mio bisnono: / Più dell'original la copia dura" (I have in likenesses my grand- and great-grandfather: / more than the original the copy lasts). But he notes in "Vita nostra e morte al signor Niccolò Crasso" (Our Life and Death, to Mr. Niccolò Crasso) that the comfort of art turns to illusion in the face of death:

> L'omo co 'l nasse el paga al mondo tristo
> la bona intrada con sospiri e guai,
> e quand'el mor el paga de contai
> de cinque pie de terra el gramo acquisto.
>
> (As soon as he comes into the world
> man pays his entrance fee with sighs and whines
> and when he dies he pays in cash
> for the paltry purchase of five feet of ground.)

Busenello's meditation on the vanity of life and impotence of memory in "Quatrine italiane" (Italian Quatrains) is reminiscent of Torquato Tasso's stanza "Muoiono le città, muoiono i regni" (Cities Die, Kingdoms Die) in *Gerusalemme liberata* (1581, Jerusalem Delivered; translated as *Godfrey of Bulloigne, or The Recoverie of Hierusalem*, 1594):

> Restan li scritti di memoria privi
> anco l'oblivion s'estingue e muore.
> Si perdono l'idiomi e la figura
> delle provincie: il mar vorace cangia
> l'antichità e l'abisso assorbe e mangia
> le rimembranze, i tempi e la natura.
>
> (Writings remain devoid of memory,
> oblivion too comes to an end and dies.
> Tongues and shapes of provinces
> are lost: the hungry ocean changes
> antiquity, and the abyss absorbs and swallows
> recollections, times and nature.)

Thus, even the literary fame that he had tenaciously pursued and that envious slanderers had tried to take from him turns out to be a lure and a mere shadow. In "Le stravaganze della fortuna" (The Oddities of Fortune) he finds the same deceitful character in the sciences: "Altri ha lassà la pelle in specular / L'essenzia e proprietà de sta natura" (Others lost their life in speculating / On the essence and properties of nature). The lament on the vanity of existence is a frequent theme in the seventeenth-century poetry; Busenello's verse also displays other Baroque commonplaces such as biblical sonnets, sonnets on odd objects, misogynist or even scatological poems, bawdy tales, and—in the tercets of "El gondolier ruffian" (The Pimping Gondolier; titled in some codices "Il forastier et il gondolier al Buso" [The Stranger and the Gondolier of the El Buso Ferry]) puns alluding to the danger of venereal diseases: *patti . . . petta . . . putta . . . potta* (pacts . . . sticks . . . wench . . . cunt).

The contradictory nature of human beings and doubts about one's identity were among the most widespread subjects of seventeenth-century poetry and can be found in Busenello's "L'uso del Mondo" (The Ways of the World):

> . . . in mezzo d'un mondo alla roversa
> me catto trasformao via de mi stesso
> e col viver contrario che xe adesso
> trovo ogni mia rason cascada e persa.
>
> (. . . amid a topsy-turvy world
> I feel transformed and taken away from myself
> and in the perverted ways of life of nowadays
> I find all my reason fallen down and gone.)

Busenello's representation of Venetian life in its glorious and absurd aspects has led scholars to compare him to another sharp critic of Venetian society: the satirical poet from Brescia, Bartolomeo Dotti. A wealth of lively and curious details can be drawn from texts such as "Compare dov'è andae le bone usanze" (Friend, where have the good ways gone), "Le braghesse alla moda" (The Fashionable Breeches), "I successi carnevaleschi" (What Happens in Carnival), "Contro i critici maldicenti" (Against Disparaging Critics), "Contro certi avocati moderni" (Against Some Modern Lawyers), "Xe pur fenii quei chiassi e quei morbini" (That Hubbub and Merrymaking Are Really Over), "Che niole in ciel seren che all'improvviso" (What Clouds in the Clear Sky That Suddenly), and "El mondo alla roversa" (The Topsy-Turvy World). These quatrains—and, more rarely, tercets—compose a striking description of society: priests, fops, hypocrites, false witnesses, pimps, prostitutes, cardsharpers, lewd old people, nymphomaniac patricians, maids, and country girls; they are full of gossip and verbal inventions, as in "La gondola a 23 ore" (The Gondola at Dusk):

> Adesso I porta al cul certe braghesse
> ch'alle vergogne ghe fa perolotto:
> tutto sta descoverto e panza e petto,
> tanto sarave che no I ghe ne havesse:
> Braghesse no le xe: le xe un estratto
> un vapor de braghesse rarefatto.
>
> (Now they wear on their ass some breeches
> that show the small mound of their genitals:
> everything is exposed, belly and breast,
> it would be tantamount to having none.
> Breeches they are not: they are an extract,
> a rarefied mist of breeches.)

Language accounts for both the merits and the limits of the satire in these compositions. The liveliness of Busenello's Venetian world is enhanced by the use of dialect, a vernacular rich in synonymic variants, terms hinting at the most minute details of everyday life, and surprising metaphors, but the satirical effect is weakened by digressions and repetitions and by long anaphoric series that often become the "spiritosi concetti e versi sgionfi" (witty conceits and swollen lines) that the author had declared in "Il Conflitto navale . . . l'anno 1656" (The Naval Battle . . . of the Year 1656) that he wanted to avoid.

No less prolix are Busenello's Italian novels, the unfinished and unpublished "Fileno" and "Floridiana," found in two nonautographic codices at the Museo Correr in Venice. Rather than in Venetian life, the inspiration for these works is to be sought in popular seventeenth-century novels and in the genre practiced by his fellow Incogniti, the *novella galante* (love tale). Stylized characters dwell in a fabulous geographical setting imitated from the great epic poems of the sixteenth century. Exotic kings, unhappy princesses, spellbound knights, and treacherous damsels travel through a pagan world that worships the Greek gods or Fortune, looking for each other and talking endlessly. In "Floridiana" the amatory and political arguments are more interesting than the complicated plot, and the canzoni inserted in "Fileno" prove that the author was more at ease in verse than in prose.

Busenello wrote librettos for six operas. Pier Francesco Cavalli's *Gli amori di Apollo e Dafne* (1640, The Love of Apollo and Daphne), *La Didone* (1641, Dido), *La prosperità infelice di Giulio Cesare dittatore* (1646, The Unhappy Prosperity of Julius Caesar, Dictator), and *La Statira principessa di Persia* (1655, Statyra, Princess of Persia), and Monteverdi's *L'incoronazione di Poppea* are printed in reworked versions in his collected works, *Delle ore ociose* (1656, The Idle Hours). The sixth libretto, never published and presumably never performed, is titled *La discesa* (The Descent) in some codices and *Il viaggio d'Enea all'inferno* (Aeneas's Journey to Hell) in others. In the introductions to the librettos in *Delle ore ociose* Busenello claims the right to "scrivere come li piace" (write as he pleases): to be free from tradition—for instance, in *La Didone* the heroine does not kill herself but marries Iarbas "per schiffare il fine tragico" (to avoid a tragic ending); to neglect the rules of unity of space and time; and to use a multiple plot, a device legitimized by Giovan Battista Guarini in *Il Pastor fido* (1590; translated as *Il pastor fido; or The Faithful Shepherd*, 1602). Busenello's innovations also include frequent comic insertions and the historical rather than mythological content of *L'incoronazione di Poppea* and *La prosperità infelice di Giulio Cesare dittatore*.

In *Gli amori di Apollo e Dafne* Apollo has exposed Venus to the sneers of the other gods when he found her naked in the arms of Mars. To avenge his mother's humiliation, Love makes the solar god fall in love with Daphne; but the nymph's father, the river god Peneus, transforms her into a tree to keep her from being subjected to his desires. In this libretto Busenello invents a spoken language for the opera with an interplay of meters and tones, as in act 1, scene 5, where Filena says:

> Quel tesor del labbro bello,
> che vezzoso coralleggia,
> quel loquace spiritello
> che tra perle rubineggia,
> quel purpureo serpentello
> che dolcissimo lingueggia.
>
> (That treasure of beautiful lips
> that graciously turns coral,
> that loquacious little spirit
> that among pearls shows ruby,
> that vermillion little snake
> that so sweetly darts about.)

The same scene includes an expression of the carpe diem motif; as Filena says:

> Una volta si nasce,
> una volta si more,
> lo spazio della vita
> è una carriera sola.
> Godiam la luce in fin che dura il giorno,
> Ché l'andata mortal non fa ritorno.
>
> (Once we were born, once we die,
> the space of life is just one progress.
> Let us enjoy the light while the day lasts,
> because the mortal advance has no return.)

In act 1, scene 1 epigrammatic witticisms directed against the old and impotent Tithonus function as a counterpoint to the florid lyric language of the two amorous couples, Daphne and Apollo and Aurora and Cephalus: "Credi alle rughe tue, credi allo specchio, / Compendio d'ogni noia è l'esser vecchio" (Believe your wrinkles, believe the mirror, / Epitome of all troubles is being old). As in Busenello's poetry, but at a faster pace because of the obligatory meter of the melodramatic form, sensual touches and puns follow one another closely as Apollo speaks in act 2, scene 4:

Mentre d'amor l'acuto stral mi tocca
tu puoi di un vivo Dio baciar la bocca. . . .
Ma s'è pur mio svantaggio
l'esser nume celeste
io mi disimmortalo,
diseterno me stesso, e in dolce sorte
per goderti cor mio soccombo a morte.

(While I am wounded by the sharp arrow of love
you can kiss the mouth of a living God. . . .
But if it is my disadvantage
to be a celestial deity,
I'll desimmortalize,
I'll deseternalize myself, and it will be sweet
to be subject to death in order to enjoy you, my darling.)

La Didone begins with a slow-paced first act, in which Creusa dies and her shade appears to Aeneas; he cries, "O sparita speranza, / O spirata mia luce" (Oh my disappeared hope, / Oh my vanished light). The story then moves on to Carthage and takes on a swifter and semicomical course as Iarbas goes insane from jealousy but recovers his wits in time to marry the African queen after Aeneas's departure. The latter's perpetual wavering and submissiveness to the orders of the gods make him a precursor of the "soft" Aeneas in the opera *Didone abbandonata* (1724, Dido Abandoned), by Metastasio (Pietro Trapassi).

La prosperità infelice di Giulio Cesare dittatore, based on Seneca's tragedies and the histories of Tacitus and Plutarch, unfolds through a series of detached tableaux with a systematic breaking away from the unities of space and time. Defeated at Pharsalus by Julius Caesar, Pompey the Great takes refuge in Egypt; but Ptolemy has him killed and gives his head to Caesar, who mourns his rival's death. After returning to Rome, Caesar fails to heed a prophecy of his death and is murdered by Brutus and Cassius. A happy ending is provided by the wedding of Pompey's youngest son, Sextus, and Brutus's fictional daughter Maximilla and by the announcement, sung by Freedom and Neptune, that Venice will inherit and perpetuate the greatness of Rome.

The exotic plot of *Statira* thickens with a rapid succession of disguises and recognitions and is resolved by the generous Usimano, who renounces Statira, the daughter of King Dario, so that she will be able to wed the Arab prince Cloridaspe; Usimano will marry Cloridaspe's sister Floralba. A comic thread involves the black servant Vaffrino, who laments that "Nella commedia del commercio umano / Già fei l'innamorato, hor fo il ruffiano" (In the comedy of human intercourse / I used to be the lover, now I am the pimp), and a pair of old preceptors who expound with farcical gravity on the overbearing ways of princes and comment on their masters' amorous whims and exchanges of fiancées.

L'incoronazione di Poppea, Monteverdi's last opera, was performed in the fall of 1642 at the Grimani family's SS. Giovanni e Paolo Theater in Venice. On that occasion only the scenario–a scene-by-scene summary–was published. After another staging in Venice in 1646, the opera was presented in Naples in 1651; this time the full libretto was published with the title *Il Nerone, overo l'incoronatione di Poppea* (Nero; or, The Coronation of Poppaea). Busenello recast the work when he collected it in *Delle ore ociose;* this version was republished in 1949 (it is his only opera to appear in a modern edition). Thus, by comparing the 1642 scenario, the extant manuscripts of the score, the 1651 Neapolitan edition, and the 1656 collection, scholars are able to trace the process by which, from an early close collaboration between librettist and composer adhering to musical and performance criteria, Busenello revised his work in accordance with the literary image he wanted to leave of himself.

The "historicity" of the drama is enhanced by an allusion to recent events that Monteverdi had witnessed: the dissolution of the marriage of Margherita Farnese and the duke of Mantua, Vincenzo Gonzaga, and the duke's remarriage to Leonora de' Medici. Using Tacitus's account as a starting point, Busenello imagines that the emperor Nero is induced by his mistress, Poppaea, to have Seneca killed because he condemns their love, while the outraged empress, Octavia, orders Otho to murder Poppaea, his former wife. To approach Poppaea, Otho borrows the clothes of her confidante Drusilla; but the crime is prevented by the god Love. To exculpate Otho, whom she loves, Drusilla claims that it was she who attempted to kill Poppaea; but Otho confesses and denounces Octavia as the instigator. Nero is so happy to be able to repudiate Octavia and marry Poppaea that he limits himself to exiling Otho and Drusilla. *L'incoronatione di Poppea* is not a moral work, as the conclusion grants happiness to two tainted individuals; but what mattered to the authors was the free expression of love and joy and the representation of the complexity of the characters. For example, in act 1, scene 3, Poppaea's feelings for Nero are dictated by ambition and calculation; but–with the help of the music–they sound like sincere passion:

Deh non dir
di partir
ché di voce sì amara a un solo accento
ahi perir, ahi spirar quest'alma sento . . .
Tornerai?

(Alas! don't speak
of leaving.
Ah, at just the sound of such a bitter word
I already feel my soul perishing and failing . . .
Will you come back?)

In act 1, scene 5, Octavia addresses the absent Nero:

In braccio di Poppea
tu dimori felice, e godi, e in tanto
il frequente cader de' pianti miei
pur va quasi formando
un diluvio di specchi, in cui tu miri
dentro alle tue delitie i miei martiri.

(In the arms of Poppaea
you find joy and happiness
while my ceaseless weeping, my tears
almost make a deluge of mirrors
for you to see my anguish
in the midst of your pleasure.)

As in the other operas, comic moments follow pathetic scenes. For instance, Seneca faces his death with a Socratic serenity in act 2, scene 3:

Breve angoscia è la morte;
un sospir peregrino esce dal core,
ov'è stato molt'anni
quasi in hospitio, come forastiero,
e sen vola all'Olimpo
della felicità soggiorno vero.

(Death is but a brief moment of anguish.
A pilgrim sigh escapes from the heart,
where, like the stranger at an inn,
it has dwelt for many years,
and it soars up to Olympus,
the true abode of happiness.)

Two scenes later occurs a mischievous duet between Page and Maidservant in which the boy's first amorous flutter is encouraged by the more expert girl.

In *L'incoronazione di Poppea* the lyrical effusions of the serious parts, the funny counterpoint, and the common sense of the subordinate stock characters are tied together in a new realistic melodramatic style that lasted until the reform of Apostolo Zeno and Metastasio in the eighteenth century. Zeno and Metastasio insisted on the primacy of words over music, of which *L'incoronazione di Poppea* is the first clear illustration, in the sense–agreed on by Monteverdi–that the score must translate into notes the emotional charge of the text.

The first and third acts of the unpublished *La discesa* or *Il viaggio d'Enea all'inferno* take place in Latium–at Aeneas's camp and at King Latinus's court, respectively–with the usual situation of various young people in love. The descent of the hero, accompanied by the Sybil, to the kingdom of Pluto occupies most of the second act and is freely adapted from the sixth book of Virgil's *Aeneid*. Busenello brings onto the stage various mythical characters: Tisiphone; Charon; Cerberus; Orpheus and Eurydice on the threshold of hell; Tityus, Tantalus; Pallas, recently arrived after being killed by Turnus; Dido, still desperate and angry at Aeneas ("Fosti cagion delle mie colpe al mondo / Vuoi farmi peccatrice anche all'inferno?" [You were the cause of my faults in the world, / do you want to make me sin even in hell?]); and Dido's betrayed husband, Sychaeus ("Patisco in questa tenebrosa sera / Due tormenti, l'inferno e la mogliera" [I suffer in this dark evening / Two torments, hell and my wife]). In a happy conclusion Aeneas kills Turnus and marries Lavinia, while the Neapolitan princess Lindadori, formerly smitten with Pallas, is content to marry Coralbo.

With the exception of Livingston's 1911 volume–which, with its many lengthy citations and often inexact transcriptions, has been the source of all subsequent readings–little has been written on Gian Francesco Busenello, and not until the second half of the twentieth century were some of his poems included in anthologies of seventeenth-century poetry. Firsthand knowledge of Busenello's work has been hindered by the dispersal of his verse in codices and by the scant attention that literary critics have paid to librettos other than *L'incoronazione di Poppea*.

Letters:

G. G. Nicolini, *Ombre del pennello glorioso del Molt'Illustre sig. Pietro Bellotti* (Venice: Valvasense, 1639), pp. 17-19, 104-105, 109;

Claudio Achillini, *Rime e prose* (Venice: Conzatti, 1662), pp. 294-299;

Arthur Livingston, "Una scappatella di Polo Vendramin e un sonetto di G. F. Busenello," *Fanfulla della domenica* (Rome), 24 September 1911;

Giambattista Marino, *Epistolario, seguito da lettere di altri scrittori del Seicento,* volume 2, edited by Angelo Borzelli and Fausto Nicolini (Bari: Laterza, 1912), pp. 100-104, 108-109.

References:

Franca Angelini, "Il teatro pubblico a Venezia: Gian Francesco Busenello," in her *Il teatro barocco* (Bari: Laterza, 1975), pp. 117-128;

Emanuele Cicogna, *Delle iscrizioni veneziane,* 6 volumes (Venice: G. Orlandelli, 1824-1853), IV: 167, 179, 230, 683; VI: 34, 537;

Manlio Dazzi, *Il fiore della lirica veneziana,* volume 2: *Seicento e Settecento* (Venice: Neri Pozza, 1956), pp. 43–54;

Giovanni Getto, "Esperienze poetiche della civiltà veneziana nell'età barocca," *Barocco in prosa e in poesia* (Milan: Rizzoli, 1969), pp. 287–318;

Arthur Livingston, "Gian Francesco Busenello, cittadino originario veneziano," *Modern Language Notes* 23 (May 1908);

Livingston, "Una poesia di Gian Francesco Busenello in Inghilterra," *Ateneo veneto* (July–August 1908);

Livingston, *La vita veneziana nelle opere di Gian Francesco Busenello* (Venice: V. Callegari, 1913);

Pompeo Molmenti, *La storia di Venezia nella vita privata,* sixth edition, volume 3 (Bergamo: Istituto italiano d'arti grafiche, 1926), pp. 26n, 72, 75, 88, 161n, 172n, 175n, 183n, 219, 358n;

Salvatore S. Nigro, "Dalla lingua al dialetto: La letteratura popolaresca," in *I poeti giocosi dell'età barocca,* by Nigro and Alberto Asor Rosa (Bari: Laterza, 1975), pp. 126–135;

R. L. Stuart, "Busenello's Libretto to Monteverdi's *L'incoronazione di Poppea*," *Musical Times* (October 1927);

Emilio Zanette, *Suor Arcangela monaca del Seicento veneziano* (Venice & Rome: Istituto per la collaborazione culturale, 1960), pp. 334–338.

Papers:

Unpublished papers of Gian Francesco Busenello are in the Marciana Library, the Museo Correr, the Querini Stampalia, and the Seminario in Venice; the Museo Civico and the Biblioteca Universitaria in Padua; the Biblioteca Ambrosiana in Milan; the Biblioteca Marucelliana and the Magliabechiana in Florence; the Biblioteca Vaticana in Rome; the Biblioteca Bertolinana in Vicenza; the Biblioteca Comunale in Verona; the Museo Civico in Treviso; the Accademia dei Concordi in Rovigo the Bibliothèque Municipale in Rouen; and the British Museum in London.

Gabriello Chiabrera
(18 June 1552 - 14 October 1638)

Paolo A. Giordano
University of Central Florida

BOOKS: *Delle guerre dei Goti* (Venice: Gioacchino Brugnolo, 1582);

Delle Canzoni, 3 volumes (Genoa: Girolamo Bartoli, 1586-1588);

Canzonette (Genoa: Girolamo Bartoli, 1591);

Le maniere dei versi toscani (Genoa: Giuseppe Pavoni, 1599);

Scherzi e canzonette morali (Genoa: Giuseppe Pavoni, 1599);

Rime (Genoa: Giuseppe Pavoni, 1599);

Il rapimento di Cefalo: Rappresentato nelle nozze della cristianissima Maria Medici Regina di Francia è di Navarra, music by Giulio Caccini (Florence: Giorgio Marescotti, 1600);

Narrazione della morte di s. Gio. Batista (Florence: Giunti, 1602);

Herodiate (Florence: Giunti, 1602);

Alcuni scherzi (Mondovì: De Rossi, 1603);

Rime sacre (Genoa: Francesco Bolzeta, 1604);

Gelopea (Mondovì: De Rossi, 1604);

Rime (Venice: Sebastiano Combi, 1605)–includes "Le vendemmie di Parnaso" and *Erminia;*

Poesie, 3 volumes (Genoa: Giuseppe Pavoni, 1605-1606);

Egloghe (Florence: Giorgio Antonio Caneo, 1608);

Meganira (Florence: Giorgio Antonio Caneo, 1608);

Alcippo: Favola boschereccia (Genoa: Giuseppe Pavoni, 1614);

Alcune canzoni composte per la corte di Toscana (Florence: Giorgio Antonio Caneo, 1615);

Favolette da rappresentarsi cantando (Florence: Pignoni, 1615);

Il pianto di Orfeo (Florence: Pignoni, 1615);

Angelica in Ebuda (Florence: Pignoni, 1615);

Il Firenze (Florence: Pignoni, 1615; enlarged edition, Florence: Ciotti, 1628; revised, 1637);

Vegghia delle Grazie (Florence: Caneo, 1616);

Poesie, 3 volumes (Florence: Pignoni, 1618);

Il presagio dei giorni (Florence: Pignoni, 1618);

Versi, Meteore (Florence: Cecconcelli, 1618);

Gabriello Chiabrera (portrait by an unknown early-sixteenth-century artist; from Canzonette, rime varie, dialoghi di Gabriello Chiabrera, *edited by Luigi Negri, 1952; Thomas Cooper Library, University of South Carolina)*

Il vivaio dei Boboli (Genoa: Giuseppe Pavoni, 1620);

Per San Carlo Borromeo (Genoa: Giuseppe Pavoni, 1620);

Amedeide (Genoa: Giuseppe Pavoni, 1620; revised edition, Naples, 1635);

Galatea o le grotte di Fassolo (Genoa: Giuseppe Pavoni, 1623);

Il Forzano (Alessandria: G. Soto, 1626);

Poesie, 4 volumes (Florence: Ciotti, 1628);

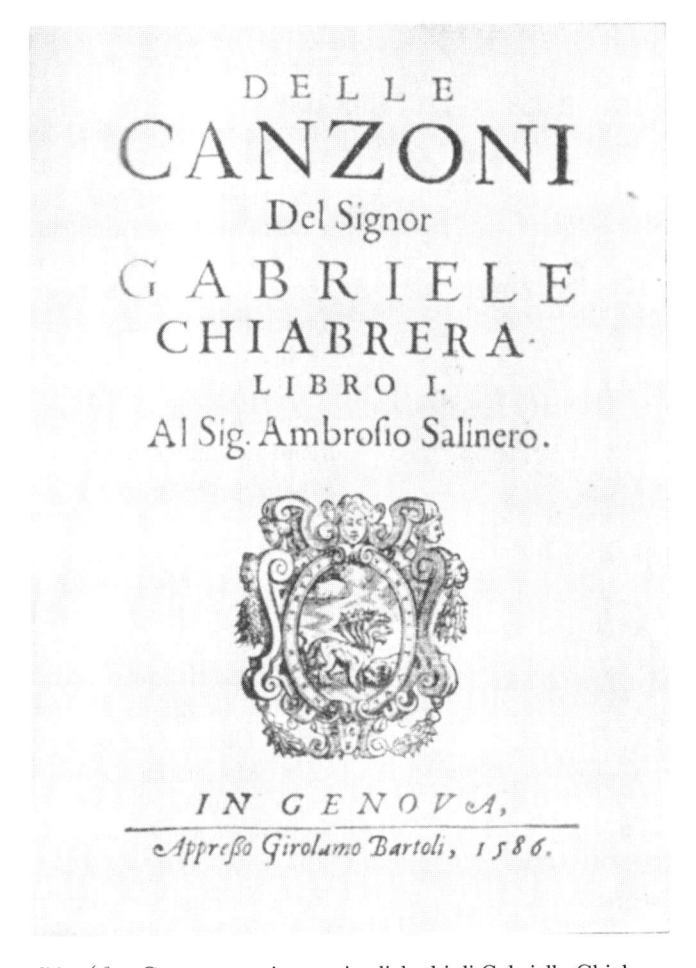

Title page for the first edition (from Canzonette, rime varie, dialoghi di Gabriello Chiabrera, *edited by Luigi Negri, 1952; Thomas Cooper Library, University of South Carolina)*

Foresto (Genoa: Guasco, 1653);

Ruggiero (Genoa: Guasco, 1653);

Discorsi fatti da Gabriello Chiabrera nell'Academia degli Addormentuti in Genova, edited by Alessandro Dego (Genoa: Franchello, 1670);

Rime, edited by G. Paolucci (Rome: Salvioni, 1718)–includes "Vita scritta da lui medesimo" and "Sermoni";

Alcune poesie di Gabriele Chiabrera non mai prima d'ora pubblicate, edited by Olimpio Fenicio (Genoa: Caffarelli, 1794);

Canzonette, rime varie, dialoghi di Gabriello Chiabrera, edited by Luigi Negri (Turin: Einaudi, 1952).

Editions and Collections: *Sermoni . . . aggiiunte le osservazioni di Clementino Vannetti* (Genoa, 1830);

Il rapimento di Cefalo, in *Gli Albori del melodramma,* volume 3 by A. Solerti (Milan, Palermo & Naples: Sandron, 1904);

I lirici del Seicento e dell'Arcadia, edited by Carlo Calcaterra (Milan: Rizzoli, 1936);

Poesia del Seicento, volume 1, edited by Carlo Muscetta and Pier Paolo Ferrante (Turin: Einaudi, 1964), pp. 690–734;

Opere di Gabriello Chiabrera e lirici del classicismo barocco, edited by Marcello Turchi (Turin: Unione Tipografico-Editrice Torinese, 1984), pp. 523–616;

Gelopea: Favola boschereccia, edited by Franco Vazzoler (Genoa: Marietti, 1988).

Edition in English: *From Marino to Marinetti: An Anthology of Forty Italian Poets,* translated by Joseph Tusiani (New York: Baroque Press, 1974), pp. 15–23.

PLAY PRODUCTION: *Il rapimento di Cefalo,* music by Giulio Caccini, Florence, 1600.

Benedetto Croce opened a new chapter in Italian Baroque criticism in 1929 by pointing to the common aspects of the poetics of Giambattista Marino and Gabriello Chiabrera, who are generally considered the

Title page for The Style of Tuscan Verses (from Canzonette, rime varie, dialoghi di Gabriello Chiabrera, edited by Luigi Negri, 1952; Thomas Cooper Library, University of South Carolina)

most important poets of the period. Although quite different in their approaches, Croce argued, both writers were in search of a style that would produce in readers a reaction of startled amazement. Like many Baroque writers, they took their inspiration from an understanding of reality that was profoundly different from that of the sixteenth century. This new worldview was created by the Council of Trent, the emergence of new science, and the discovery of the New World.

Chiabrera was equally at home in composing heroic poems, poems about everyday life, love poems, occasional poems, popular poems, and poems on sublime topics. This wide range of interests goes far to explain his long-lasting fame, which did not wane until the twentieth century. He was a friend of such luminaries as Ansaldo Cebà and Pier Giuseppe Giustiniani, both of whom were members of the Genoese Accademia degli Addormentati (Academy of the Sleepyheads); a close friend and collaborator of the Florentine writers Roberto Titi and Gian Battista Strozzi and the renowned librettist Ottavio Rinuccini; and acquainted with the poets Fulvio Testi, Carlo de'Dottori, and Francesco Redi and the satirist Benedetto Menzini. He is considered, along with Alessandro Guidi and Francesco De Lemene, a precursor of the eighteenth-century Arcadian literary movement.

Chiabrera was born in Savona on 18 June 1552. His father, Gabriello, died before he was born, and his mother, Geronima Murassana, remarried soon afterward. Chiabrera's paternal uncle Giovanni and his wife, Margherita, assumed responsibility for Chiabrera's upbringing and brought him to live with them in Rome when he was nine. He was educated by private tutors and then at the Jesuit Collegio Romano. In Rome he came into contact with many prominent cultural figures but was especially influenced by Paolo Manunzio, a renowned philologist and classical scholar who lived next door to his uncle; Marc Antoine Muret, a friend of the French poet Pierre de Ronsard and a translator of Ronsard's works; and, above all, the critic, dramatist, and philosopher Sperone Speroni. Chiabrera met Torquato Tasso, the author of the epic poem *Gerusalemme liberata* (1581, Jerusalem Delivered; translated as *Godfrey of Bulloigne, or The Recouerie of Hierusalem*, 1594) at Speroni's home in December 1575.

After his uncle's death in 1572, Chiabrera entered the service of Cardinal Luigi Cornaro, but he had to leave Rome and return to Savona in 1579 because of a violent controversy with a Roman nobleman. His combative personality caused him further problems in Savona. Between 1579 and 1581 and again in 1583 he was forced to leave that city to avoid incarceration and bodily harm. He returned to Savona in 1585 and lived there in relative tranquility for the rest of his life.

Chiabrera embarked on his writing career with the heroic poem *Delle guerre dei Goti* (The War of the Goths), which was published in Venice in 1582 and dedicated to Carlo Emanuele I, Duke of Savoy. In fifteen eight-line cantos it deals with the last two months of the war in which the Greeks and Italians defeated the Ostrogoths in 553 and sings the praises of Vitiello, the

Roman knight entrusted by heaven with the victory. After their king, Teia, is killed, the Goths surrender their arms and are allowed to live in peace under their own laws. The subtext of the poem is the contemporary conflict between the Roman Catholic Church and the northern Reformers.

During his long life Chiabrera produced a vast quantity of lyrical, epic, tragic, pastoral, and satirical verse, but his reputation as one of the two best poets of the Italian literary Baroque is mainly based on his lyrical compositions: three volumes of *Canzoni* (1586–1588, Canzones), *Canzonette* (1591, Canzonets), *Le maniere dei versi toscani* (1599, The Style of Tuscan Verses), *Scherzi e canzonette morali* (1599, Scherzi and Moral Canzonets), and "Le vendemmie di Parnaso" (1605, Harvests in Parnassus). Like that of Marino, Chiabrera's poetry is innovative and creates a sense of *meraviglia* (wonder) in the reader. But unlike Marino and the Marinists, who create this sense through an abundance of extravagant metaphors and witty conceits, Chiabrera shifts the emphasis from imagery to form by using classical Greek and Latin metric schemes. Although he read widely and was well versed in the classical canon, his major influences were Pindar, Anacreon, Horace, and Catullus. His understanding of classical literature was filtered through his reading of Ronsard, the preeminent poet of the avant-garde Pléiade movement. The Pléiade aimed to create a new poetry that would make a decisive break from the moribund medieval tradition, enrich French by composing verse in that language instead of in Latin, and equal or surpass works of the classical period and the Italian Renaissance. The more than 180 canzones in Chiabrera's 1586–1588 and 1599 volumes can be divided into four thematic groups: 95 praise the exploits of heroes; 16 are mournful or funereal and are dedicated to fallen heroes; 44 impart a moral lesson and deprecate vice and error; and 20 are *canzoni sacre* (sacred compositions) honoring Christian saints and martyrs.

Chiabrera's heroic verses consecrate the election of popes, sing the praises of winners of athletic contests, and celebrate the victories of Christian knights over "infidels." He had great confidence in his poetic talent and referred to himself as the Italian Pindar; his canzones use classical topoi and have constant recourse to myth. Among the laudatory canzones are odes in celebration of Emanuele Filiberto, Duke of Savoy, reformer of the Savoyard state and winner of the Battle of San Quentin in Picardy in 1556; Christopher Columbus; and Enrico Dandolo, doge of Venice from 1192 to 1205, who led the Fourth Crusade and the conquest of Constantinople and was regarded by many as the true founder of the Venetian empire.

EGLOGHE
DI GABRIELLO
CHIABRERA
Nelle quali sotto nome di Tirsi
Canta del Sig; Iacopo
Corsi.

*Donate da lui al M. Illust. Sig. il S.
Ricardo Ricardi.*

Title page for Chiabrera's Eclogues, *1608 (University of Turin)*

Chiabrera's myths are not simply ornaments to display the poet's erudition but are necessary structural components of the odes and a means of amplifying the praise of the heroes. Well-known tales from the Homeric repertory and of the labors of Hercules appear alongside less familiar stories of metamorphoses and magic. Chiabrera's champions are immersed in the classical world of heroes and heroines, gods and demigods, Achilles and Jason, and the *Odyssey* and the *Iliad:* his subjects and the heroes of classical antiquity become one and the same; the exploits and virtues of his champions become the exploits and virtues of their classical counterparts. Where the subject matter does not allow for the use of classical pagan mythology, as in the compositions in praise of popes, Chiabrera substitutes grandiose and marvelous episodes from the Bible.

First page of Chiabrera's pastoral drama, published in 1608 (University of Turin)

Poetry and the poet are also celebrated in Chiabrera's canzones. For example, the canzone on Emanuele Filiberto opens with a brief reference to locality and landscape, after which Chiabrera describes his duty as a poet, expresses confidence in his skill, and extols his role as a writer of encomiastic poetry that is destined to astonish the reader in the same way as the exploits it depicts: "io meco ho strali avuti / che sanno altrui ferir di maraviglia" (I have with me sharp darts / that can wound others with the wondrous).

The canzones also include war songs that celebrate the naval victories of the Tuscan galleys over the "infidels." Representative is the canzone dedicated to the battle of Bona (today Annaba) on the coast of Algeria (called Libya in the text), in which Florentine ships had taken part:

Con qual dunque corona
bella Flora, nel sen delle tue mura
farassi onore eterno al dì presente,
in cui l'orribil Bona
dentro nembo di pianto il ciglio oscura
per gli assalti di tua nobil gente?
Certo di dedalei marmi
Déi scolpir di sì bell'armi.

(Then, with what crown
beautiful Flora, within the womb of your walls
will you today bestow eternal honor,
now that terrible Bona
darkens the sky with clouds of its tears
for the fierce attacks of your noble people?
Certainly in Daedalean marble
You must sculpt so great a fleet.)

Chiabrera goes on to praise the commander of the fleet, Grand Duke Cosimo I de' Medici:

E se feroce in guerra
Cosmo ara il mare, ed orgogliosi liti
fa tremare il suo nome in strani modi.

(If fiercely as in war
Cosimo sails the sea, proud shores
will tremble at the sound of his name.)

He compares Cosimo to Jason, who sailed with the Argonauts in search of the Golden Fleece to reclaim the throne of Iolkos from the usurper Pelia.

In another poem Chiabrera praises Columbus for persisting against all odds, not being deterred by his detractors, and ardently believing in the truth of his ideas:

L'ocean corse, e i turbini sostenne
vinse le crude immagini di morte;
poscia dell'ampio mar spenta la guerra,
scorse dianzi favolosa terra.

Allor del cavo Pin scende veloce,
e di gran orma il nuovo mondo imprime;
né men ratto per l'aria erge sublime,
segno del Ciel, l'insuperabil Croce.

(He sailed the oceans and withstood storms
He overcame crude images of death;
After he won the war against an expansive sea,
he saw the fabled land in front of him.

From his ship he quickly descends
and with historical footprints he marked the New World;
and as quickly he erects a sublime sign
of heaven, the unexcelled Cross.)

Columbus's well-earned triumph is that of a heroic devout Christian who conquers the ocean and discovers a new world not for himself but for his country and all of humanity.

In the canzones Chiabrera employs a learned vocabulary, Hellenisms, rhetorical figures, anaphoras, parallelisms, antitheses, and iterations to create a vigorous but solemn language capable of transmitting a wide variety of feelings from the most exalted to the desperate cries of the afflicted and downtrodden. The latter can be found in his intense and dramatic apostrophe to a personified Italy:

Ma tu qual trarrai pianto
e quali Italia gemiti infiniti
misera madre degli eroi traditi?

(But you, what tears, what infinite wails
will you draw, oh Italy,
wretched mother of betrayed heroes?)

Three of Chiabrera's *canzoni sacre* are dedicated to the martyred Sicilian St. Lucy, to whom he also alludes in other writings.

In 1590 Chiabrera composed the tragedy *Ippodamia*, which was posthumously published in 1794. It is based on the episode in Homer's *Iliad* in which Priam's daughter, Polyxena, lures Achilles into an ambush by Paris.

During the last two decades of the century Chiabrera largely devoted himself to the composition of canzonets, his first collection of which was published in 1591. In his autobiography, "Vita scritta da lui medesimo" (1718, Life Written by Himself), and in the dialogue "Il Geri: Della tessitura delle canzoni" (1952, Geri: On the Composition of Canzones) he states that his main sources of inspiration for the canzonets were Anacreon and Ronsard. His principal motivation for turning to the genre was his desire to have his poetry set to music; short verses are easier to sing:

Dolcissimo ben mio
io ben come desio
ognor posso adorarti
ma non posso lodarti
ognor come desio,
dolcissimo ben mio.

(Sweet love of mine
I fully desire thee
every hour I adore thee
but I cannot praise thee
every hour as I wish,
Sweet love of mine.)

He also wanted to attract the new reading public of young men and women who had no taste for the serious and solemn songs of Dante and Petrarch. In poems such as the celebrated "Belle rose porporine" (Beautiful

Engraving by Pompeo Caccini (from Canzonette, rime varie, dialoghi di Gabriello Chiabrera, *edited by Luigi Negri, 1952; Thomas Cooper Library, University of South Carolina)*

Vermillion Roses) he creates a blend of images and sounds that intoxicate the senses:

> Se bel rio se bell'auretta
> tra lerbetta
> sul mattin mormorando erra;
> se di fiori un praticello
> si fa bello
> noi diciam: ride la terra.

> (If a clear stream, if a soft breeze
> through the grass
> in the morning wanders murmuring;
> if a meadow with flowers
> makes itself beautiful
> we say: the earth laughs.)

In the canzonet "Sono da schivarsi gli affanni" (Worries Are to Be Avoided) Chiabrera exhorts the painter Il Bronzino (Angelo Allori) to enjoy and immerse himself in the present; worrying about what he cannot control will not solve the problems that beset the world or change the course of history. "O da ricrearsi nelle stagioni noiose" (One Must Amuse Oneself during the Midday Hours) creates a vivid scene of recreational delights such as floating lazily on a boat and fishing for octopus with a trident to while away the hot, humid afternoon hours. The pain that love brings is described in "Dissuade amore" (Deters from Loving), as well as in "Non vuole più amare la sua donna" (He No Longer Wants to Love His Lady):

> In van lusinghimi
> in van minaccimi,
> figlio di venere:
> quel giogo impostomi
> dolce o spiacevole
> i più nol vo'.

> (In vain you deceive me
> in vain you threaten me,
> son of Venus:
> the game you impose on me
> sweet or unpleasant
> I do not seek anymore.)

In *Scherzi e canzonette morali,* dedicated to the Florentine playwright Iacopo Cicognini, Chiabrera expresses the desire to spend the rest of his days in healthy idleness, far from the pomp and splendor of the Roman curia. He praises the quiet pastoral life and condemns courtly rituals:

> Io solitario, e fin dagli anni acerbi
> uso alle selve, odio palagi alteri,
> né soffro onda di duci in su destrieri,
> e grandi in toga pareggiar superbi.

> (In solitude, from my earliest years
> I loved the countryside, and hated haughty palaces,
> Nor can I suffer waves of dukes on their steeds,
> nor great men in togas in arrogant competition.)

Chiabrera is content in his solitude and feels close to nature; but his longing for recognition as a great poet who celebrates great men is still alive.

The canzonets received critical praise from the Arcadian poets and from critics and scholars of the eighteenth and nineteenth centuries. Francesco De Sanctis, who was generally harsh in his judgment of Chiabrera's works, regarded the canzonets as the only poems by Chiabrera that were worth reading.

In 1600 Chiabrera was invited to Florence to participate in the wedding festivities of Maria de' Medici and King Henry IV of France. The celebrations were crowned with a presentation of his *Il rapimento di Cefalo* (The Abduction of Cephalus), set to music by Giulio Caccini. By the beginning of the seventeenth century

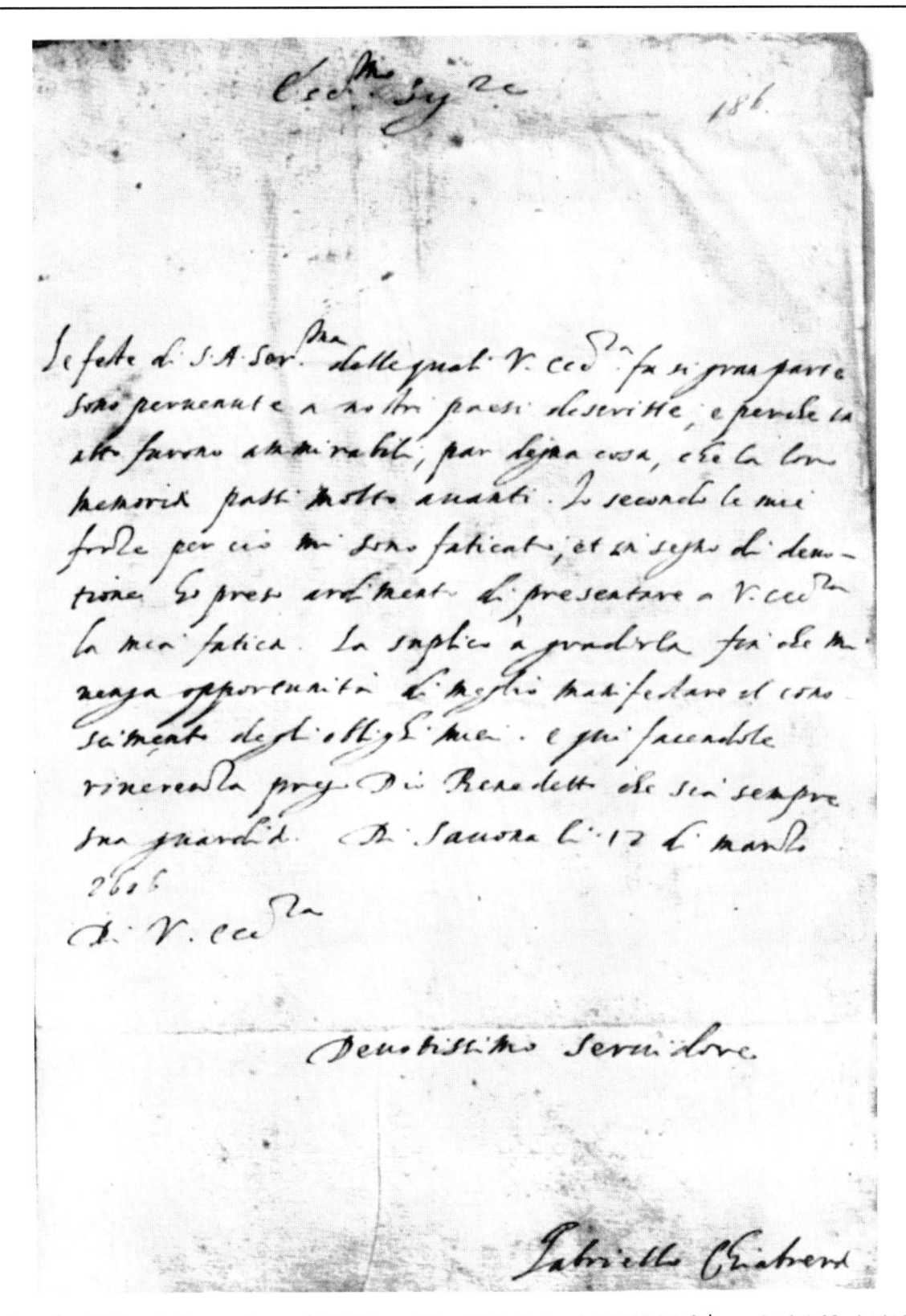

Letter from Chiabrera in Savona to Lorenzo de' Medici, son of Grand Duke Ferdinando I de' Medici of Tuscany, dated 17 March 1616 (from Canzonette, rime varie, dialoghi di Gabriello Chiabrera, *edited by Luigi Negri, 1952; Thomas Cooper Library, University of South Carolina)*

Chiabrera's literary accomplishments began to be recognized and rewarded. He received honors from the dukes of Savoy, Mantua, and Florence; Pope Urban VIII; the Republic of Genoa; and Grand Duke Ferdinando I de' Medici of Tuscany, who in 1600 conferred on him the title *Gentiluomo del Granduca* (Gentleman of the Grand Duke) and a monthly stipend that required little work on Chiabrera's part. From 1600 until his death he also held various minor civil appointments in Florence.

Chiabrera's pastoral drama *Gelopea* (1604) is modeled on Battista Guarini's *Il Pastor fido* (1590; translated as *Il pastor fido; or The Faithful Shepherd*, 1602). The rivalry between Filebo, a poor shepherd boy, and Berillo, a farm laborer, for the hand of Gelopea, the daughter of a rich and powerful shepherd, is an allusion to the conflict between the wealthy merchants and the impoverished Genoese nobility. With the marriage of Filebo and Gelopea, Chiabrera proposes a solution based on tolerance, love, and reconciliation.

Chiabrera's *Rime* (1605, Rhymes) includes "Vendemmie in Parnaso," fifty-three bacchic odes of 7 to 132 verses in which the speaker invites his friends to drink in the refined atmosphere of an aristocratic country villa: "Beviam, a diansi al vento / i torbidi pensieri. . . . Beviam, che non è ria / ogni gentil follia" (Let's drink, and abandon to the wind / our troubled thoughts. . . . Let's drink, gentle folly / is not a wicked thing). Modeled on classical Greek poetry, Chiabrera's bacchic poems replace the themes of youthful and playful love in the canzonets with a celebration of the enjoyment of fine wines that is more consonant with the tranquility of middle age. Referring to the mourning of Venus for the death of Adonis, a popular myth of tragic love, Chiabrera writes, "A Si detto fatto / alla mia man ricorda / che per canto d'amor non tocchi corda" (This well-known event / reminds my hand / not to touch the strings of love's song). Wine is the remedy for the pain of unhappy love: "Sciocchezze! Con buon vin cangia la donna / Bevi gagliardo fin che il ciglio assonna" (Foolishness! Good wine changes the woman / Drink, brave man, until sleep's onset). In poem 48, "Aure serene e chiare" (Calm and Clear Breezes), set in the countryside, the speaker offers a woman a precious cup adorned with images:

Sulla sponda romita
lungo il bel rio di questa riva erbosa,
o Filli, a bere invita
ostro vivo di fragola odorosa.

Fra mie tazze pij care
reca la più diletta
quella dove saetta
Amor sopra un delfin gli dei del mare.

(On the solitary mound
along the grassy shore of this beautiful river,
oh Filli, the clear purple of strawberry wine
invites us to drink.

Among my most precious goblets
I brought the most beloved
the one where Love on a dolphin
darts across the sea.)

The poems include references to regional wines, caves that serve as natural wine cellars, guests, hunts, greyhounds, and the hills surrounding Chiabrera's native Savona.

Chiabrera believed that the theater should be made accessible to as wide an audience as possible by drawing on popular literary works. Accordingly, his second tragedy, *Erminia,* also included in *Rime,* is adapted from Tasso's *Gerusalemme liberata* and completes the story of the Saracen princess Erminia, who commits suicide after the Christian knight Tancredi rejects her love.

Meganira (1608), the least known and least successful of Chiabrera's three pastoral dramas, draws from Tasso's *Aminta* (1573; translated, 1591) the motif of the false death of the protagonist. His third pastoral play, *Alcippo* (1614), uses the stock situation of the shepherd dressed in women's clothes. In the guise of Megilla, Alcippo enters the community of nymphs to try to persuade the huntress Clori to abandon her way of life and consider marriage. Alcippo's true identity is discovered; the law requires the intruder to be put to death; Clori's compromised honor will have to be vindicated; and her right to live the life she has chosen must be restored. A tragic resolution is avoided by the recognition of Alcippo as the long-believed-dead son of the elder Tirsi. Clori, who was born to humble parents, consents to the marriage to Alcippo proposed by Tirsi and the high priest Montano out of gratitude to those who brought her up and protected her. But the happy ending is marred by Clori's lack of enthusiasm: resigned to her fate, she accepts the restrictions imposed by a patriarchal society that condemns women to live a life chosen for them: "che più dirvi degg'io? / Sia nelle vostre mani, e voi reggete il freno / di ciascun mio desio" (What more can I say to you? / I am in your hands / and you hold the reins / to all my desires). The plots of *Gelopea, Meganira,* and *Alcippo* reflect the conservative rural setting where the Genoese aristocracy spent its leisure time.

Chiabrera's final tragedy, *Angelica in Ebuda* (1615), is adapted from Ludovico Ariosto's chivalric poem *Orlando furioso* (1516, Orlando Enraged; translated as *Orlando Furioso in English Heroical Verse,* 1591). It dramatizes the capture of the pagan princess Angelica by the monstrous Orc and her rescue by the African knight Ruggiero and a flying horse. Chiabrera's tragedies were not as well received as his pastoral dramas; his attempt to write dramas based on popular literature to attract a wider public was premature. Reform of the Italian tragic theater in this direction was accomplished by the Arcadian Metastasio (Pietro Trapassi) with his sentimental melodramas of the early eighteenth century.

Chiabrera had conceived the idea of an epic poem in honor of the House of Savoy in 1582 and had begun writing it in 1590. He submitted the manuscript for the first version to his patron, Carlo Emanuele I, in 1607. Three years later he presented the duke a revised version of the poem, expanded to twelve cantos. He gave the duke another revised and enlarged version in 1617. In 1629 he revised it a third time, enlarged it to 1,335 octaves in twenty-three cantos, and published it as the *Amedeide*. The hero of the *Amedeide* is Count Amedeo V, who, according to legend, defended the island of Rhodes from the Turks in the early fourteenth century. In the final battle, described in great detail in cantos 19 through 21, Amedeo kills the Turkish king Ottoman. In the final canto St. John the Baptist predicts the future glories of Dukes Emanuele Filiberto and Carlo Emanuele I. Chiabrera's most ambitious and complex work, the *Amedeide* was reduced to ten cantos in a fourth revision, published in 1635.

Chiabrera's other major contribution to the epic genre, *Il Firenze* (Florence), was published in octaves in ten cantos in 1615 and dedicated to Cosimo II de' Medici, Grand Duke of Tuscany. He expanded it to fifteen cantos and recast it in unrhymed eleven-syllable lines for the second edition, dedicated to Ferdinand II de' Medici, in 1628 and reduced it to ten cantos for the third edition in 1637. The poem celebrates the coming to power of the Medici dynasty in the mid ninth century. The pious Christian hero, Cosmo, liberates Florence from submission to the neighboring city of Fiesole, ruled by the godless and dissolute King Feralmo.

Two other epic poems—*Foresto*, three cantos in octaves on Attila the Hun, and *Ruggiero*, ten cantos in unrhymed verse on the character from *Orlando furioso*—were published posthumously in 1653. Chiabrera also composed at least thirty-two *poemetti* (much shorter heroic poems with less intricate plots) on both sacred and profane topics. He participated in one of the most important literary debates of his time, the reform of the epic genre, in his dialogue "Vecchietti: Intorno al verso eroico volgare" (1952, Vecchietti: On the Vernacular Heroic Verse) and in many letters. He advocated the adoption of the classical precept of unity of action and the use of hendecasyllabic blank verse.

In the last twenty years of his life Chiabrera seldom left Savona except for pleasure trips and occasional

Title page for the enlarged second edition of Chiabrera's epic poem, Florence, originally published in 1615 (University of Turin)

visits to the courts of princes who summoned him. In 1625 he wrote the short autobiography "Vita scritta da lui medesimo," which was published posthumously in 1718. Referring to himself in the third person, he offers an idealized account of his life.

Between 1624 and 1632 Chiabrera composed thirty satirical poems that were collected in 1718 as "Sermoni" (Sermons). While most of his predecessors identified satire with the self-righteous invective of the Roman writer Juvenal, Chiabrera's satires are in the familiar and whimsical vein of Horace and Ariosto;

some take the form of letters addressed to real-life friends. Expressing a mature wisdom that is only rarely tainted by acrimony, Chiabrera condemns the pursuit of fame and wealth, praises the simple country life, laments the corruption of the judicial system, and deplores the ravages of modern warfare. The "Sermoni" are composed in unrhymed eleven-syllable lines rather than terza rima, the traditional meter of Italian satirical poetry. Chiabrera's satires were much admired by later Italian practitioners of the genre such as Giuseppe Parini and Giacomo Leopardi. Chiabrera died on 14 October 1638.

In his autobiography Gabriello Chiabrera wrote that he tried to follow Columbus in discovering a "new world" of poetry in reaction to the tired and lackluster Petrarchism of his time and what he considered its degenerate poetic style, and his lyrics paved the way for the Arcadian reform of Italian poetry and drama. While he declared himself opposed to the use of traditional fixed-rhyme structures and wrote some of his longer poems in blank verse, he introduced metrical and strophic innovations adopted from classical literatures that had a long-lasting influence on Italian poetry. The grave and solemn style of his heroic and moral poems and the light, musical style of the canzonet brought him accolades during his lifetime and assured him a place in the annals of seventeenth-century Italian literature alongside Marino.

Letters:
Lettere di Gabriello Chiabrera, edited by Giacomo Filippo Porrata (Bologna: Printed by Lelio dalla Volpe for the Istituto delle Scienze, 1672);
Ottavio Varaldo, "Rime e lettere inedite di Gabriello Chiabrera," *Atti e memorie della società storica savonese,* 1 (1888): 281–349; 2 (1889–1890): 395–424;
Lettere (1585–1638), edited by Simona Morando (Florence: Olschki, 2003).

Bibliographies:
Ottavio Varaldo, "Bibliografia delle opere a stampa di Gabriello Chiabrera," *Giornale ligustico di archeologia, storia e letteratura,* 13 (1886): 280–423;
Varaldo, "Bibliografia chiabreresca: Supplemento," *Giornale ligustico di archeologia, storia e letteratura,* 14 (1887): 406–425;
Severino Ferrari, *Gabriello Chiabrera e le raccolte di rime da lui medesino ordinate: Studio bibliografico* (Faenza: Conti, 1888);
Varaldo, "Bibliografia delle opere a stampa di Gabriello Chiabrera," *Atti e memorie della società storica savonese,* 2 (1889–1890): 425–457;
Gustavo Costa, "Gli autografi del Chiabrera presso la Biblioteca Vaticana (appunti critico-bibliografici con alcuni inediti," *Studi Secenteschi,* 8 (1967): 43–71;
Franco Vazzoler, "Lettere inedite di Gabriello Chiabrera," *La rassegna della letteratura italiana,* 73 (1969): 27–36.

Biography:
Nicola Merola, "Gabriello Chiabrera," in *Dizionario biografico degli italiani,* volume 24, edited by Alberto M. Ghisalberti (Rome: Istituto dell'Enciclopedia Italiana, 1980), pp. 465–475.

References:
Antonio Belloni, *Gli epigoni della* Gerusalemme liberata (Padua: Angelo Draghi, 1893), pp. 32–46, 149–173;
Belloni, *Il Seicento,* second edition (Milan: Vallardi, 1955), pp. 200–202, 394–395;
Giorgio Bertone, *Per una ricerca metricologica su Chiabrera* (Genoa: Marietti, 1991);
Bertone, *Per una ricerca su Chiabrera* (Genoa: Marietti, 1988);
Fulvio Bianchi, "Gabriello Chiabrera," in *La letteratura ligure: La repubblica aristocratica (1528–1797),* by Bianchi, Franco Arato, Franco Vazzoler, and others (Genoa: Costa & Nolan, 1988), pp. 149–215;
Bianchi, "Per una definizione critica del Chiabrera: Riflessioni su una questione ancora aperta," in *Studi di filologia e letteratura offerti a Franco Croce* (Florence: Bulzoni, 1997), pp. 213–229;
Bianchi and Paolo Rossi, eds., *La scelta della misura: Gabriello Chiabrera. L'altro fuoco del barocco italiano. Atti del Convegno di studi su Gabriello Chiabrera nel 350° anniversario della morte: Savona, 3–6 novembre 1988* (Genoa: Costa & Nolan, 1993);
Carlo Calcaterra, *Poesia e canto: Studi sulla poesia melica italiana e sulla favola per musica* (Bologna: Zanichelli, 1951);
Vittorio Cian, *La satira dall'Ariosto al Chiabrera,* volume 2, second edition (Milan: Vallardi, 1945);
Marco Corradini, *Genova e il barocco: Studi su Angelo Grillo, Ansaldo Cebà, Anton Giulio Brignole Sale* (Milan: Vita e Pensiero, 1994), pp. 21–22, 25, 27–28, 56–66, 125, 132–133, 146, 238–239;
Benedetto Croce, *Storia dell'età barocca* (Bari: Laterza, 1929), pp. 281–284, 426–427;
Francesco De Sanctis, *Storia della letteratura italiana,* edited by Croce (Bari: Laterza, 1958), pp. 199–202;
Giovanni Getto, "Gabriello Chiabrera poeta barocco," in his *Barocco in prosa e in poesia* (Milan: Rizzoli, 1969), pp. 123–162;
Enzo Noé Girardi, *Esperienza e poesia di Gabriello Chiabrera* (Milan: Vita e Pensiero, 1950);

Girardi, "Gabriello Chiabrera," in *Letteratura italiana: I minori,* volume 2 (Milan: Marzorati, 1961), pp. 1427–1447;

Carmine Iannaco and Martino Capucci, *Il Seicento* (Padua: Piccin Nuova Libraria, 1986), pp. 228–251, 566–567;

Giacomo Jori, "Poesia lirica 'marinista e anti marinista': Fra classicismo e barocco," in *Storia della letteratura italiana,* volume 5, edited by Enrico Malato (Rome: Salerno Editore, 1997);

Albert N. Mancini, "Writing the Self: Forms of Autobiography in the Late Italian Renaissance," *Canadian Journal of Italian Studies,* 14 (1991): 11–22;

Francesco Luigi Mannucci, *La lirica di Gabriello Chiabrera: Storia e caratteri* (Naples, Genoa & Città di Castello: Francesco Perella, 1925);

Gian Piero Maragoni, "Gabriel in villa: Coup d'essay sul Chiabrera bucolico," *Dismisura,* 12 (1983): 63–66;

Quinto Marini, "Orazio e i *Sermoni* di Gabriello Chiabrera," in *Orazio e la letteratura italiana: Contributi alla storia della fortuna del poeta latino. Atti del convegno svoltosi a Licenza dal 19 al 23 aprile 1993 nell'ambito delle celebrazioni del bimillenario della morte di Quinto Orazio Flacco* (Rome: Istituto poligrafico e Zecca dello Stato, Libreria dello Stato, 1994), pp. 241–276;

Ferdinando Neri, *Chiabrera e la Pléiade francese* (Turin: Bocca, 1920);

Marzia Pieri, "Vanità e onesti diletti: Il teatro di Gabriello Chiabrera," *Rassegna della letteratura italiana,* 95 (1991): 5–20;

Franco Vazzoler, "Letteratura e ideologia aristocratica a Genova nel primo seicento," in *La letteratura ligure,* pp. 230–244.

Giovanni Battista Ciampoli

(1590 – 8 September 1643)

Mauda Bregoli-Russo
University of Illinois at Chicago

BOOKS: *Poesia in lode dell'inchiostro: Dedicata al signor Georgio Coneo gentilhuomo scozzese* (Rome: Giacomo Mascardi, 1626);

Poesie sacre, edited by Carlo Alessandro Sarti (Bologna: Carlo Zenero, 1648);

Rime, edited by Sforza Pallavicino (Rome: Heredi del Corbelletti, 1648);

Prose di monsignor Giovanni Ciampoli, edited by Pallavicino (Rome: Printed by Manelfo Manelfi for Giovanni Casoni, 1649);

Poesie funebri e morali di Monsignor Gio. Ciampoli: Dedicate Al Sig. Cavagliere Giacomo Danioli (Bologna: G. B. Ferroni, 1653);

Dei frammenti dell'opere postume di monsignor Giovanni Ciampoli (Bologna: G. B. Ferroni, 1654);

Poesie sacre di monsignor Giovanni Ciampoli (Venice: Zaccaria Conzatti, 1662);

Rime scelte di monsignor Giovanni Ciampoli fra le qvali, contengonsi alcune di quelle, che men correttamente furono impresse in diverse stampe dopo il primo volume vscitone in Roma; ed altre non più divulgate: divise in sacre, eroiche, laudatiue, morali, varie, e facete (Rome: Fabio di Falco, 1666);

Prose di monsignor Giovanni Ciampoli: Zoroastro; Difesa d'Innocenzo II; Istoria della Polonia; Discorso sopra l'umiltà (Rome: Fabio di Falco, 1667);

Inediti di Giovanni Ciampoli, edited by Mario Costanzo, Critica e poetica del primo Seicento, volume 1 (Rome: Bulzoni, 1969).

Editions and Collections: *Scelta di poesie italiane non mai per l'addietro stampate de' più nobili autori del nostro secolo* (Venice: Paolo Baglioni, 1686);

Opere di Gabriello Chiabrera e lirici non marinisti, edited by Marcello Turchi (Turin: Unione Tipografico Editrice Torinese, 1973), pp. 779–798.

OTHER: *Componimenti poetici di vari autori*, contributions by Ciampoli (Rome: Camerale, 1629).

SELECTED PERIODICAL PUBLICATION– UNCOLLECTED: Marziano Guglielminetti and Mariarosa Masoero, "Lettere e poesie inedite (o parzialmente inedite) di Giovanni Ciampoli," *Studi secenteschi*, 19 (1978): 131–237.

Giovanni Battista Ciampoli was one of the most prominent members of a circle of writers, philosophers, and scientists associated with the papal court in the first three decades of the seventeenth century. The poets and literary theorists of the group promoted a revival of classical poetry in strong opposition to the lasciviousness of contemporary verse and set about to restore Italian poetry, both in Latin and in the vernacular, to its original moral and civilizing function. Ciampoli was also an advocate of the new science and a member of the first scientific society of lasting importance, the Accademia dei Lincei (Academy of the Lynxes) in Rome; his long-standing friendship with Galileo Galilei and his support for the scientist in the latter's trial by the Roman Inquisition brought his brilliant career in the Vatican bureaucracy to an end.

Ciampoli was born in Florence in 1590 into an ancient and noble Florentine family from Greve. His parents were Lodovico and Francesca Ciampoli, née Cavoni. His education began, as was customary, with the study of grammar, rhetoric, and logic at Jesuit and Dominican religious schools. Perceiving in the fourteen-year-old a disposition for philosophy and poetry, the scholar Gian Battista Strozzi took Ciampoli under his wing. Because of his prodigious ability to compose verse, Ciampoli was in great demand in local literary circles and at the court of Ferdinand I de' Medici, Grand Duke of Tuscany; he became a close friend of the duke's sons, particularly Prince Cosimo. His eloquence was often utilized at the court on occasions such as weddings and visits by dignitaries.

Ciampoli met Galileo at the grand duke's villa in the summer of 1608; the encounter determined his critical attitude toward the philosophy of Aristotle, which was dominant in the schools, and strengthened his conviction that mathematics was the foundation of scientific investigation. In 1610 Galileo moved to Florence from Padua, where he had taught since 1592; he and

Frontispiece and title page for the first edition of Giovanni Battista Ciampoli's Sacred Poems *(University of Turin)*

Ciampoli resumed their acquaintance, and Ciampoli became privy to some of the scientist's astronomical discoveries: for example, he was the first person after Galileo to observe the moons of Jupiter, which Galileo had named "the Medicean stars" in honor of the Medici family.

At the end of 1610 Ciampoli enrolled at the University of Padua to study law. There he became acquainted with some of Strozzi's friends, including Giangiorgio, Ippolito, and Aldobrandino Aldobrandini, the nephews of the late Pope Clement VIII. In 1612 he traveled to Milan to visit Cardinal Federico Borromeo, whom he had met in Rome on the occasion of the beatification of the cardinal's cousin, Carlo Borromeo. Cardinal Borromeo became one of Ciampoli's most assiduous correspondents and an appreciative reader of his moral and sacred poems. When Ciampoli returned to Florence, Cardinal Maffeo Barberini, a distinguished poet both in Latin and the vernacular and a patron of intellectuals and artists, offered him lodgings in Bologna so that he could continue his studies there. He completed his doctorate in *utroque iure* (civil and canon law) at the University of Pisa in 1614.

Ciampoli's growing reputation prompted an invitation to the court of the duke of Urbino, Francesco Maria II della Rovere, but Strozzi persuaded him to settle in Rome and provided him with substantial financial help. For the same reason, Ciampoli declined an invitation to return to his native Florence that was extended to him by his childhood playmate, Cosimo, who had become grand duke of Tuscany in 1609. In 1614 Ciampoli entered the priesthood, a prerequisite for a career in the Curia. In a well-known letter of 28 February 1615 Ciampoli advised Galileo to be prudent and recommended that he leave the interpretation of the Scriptures to the church. That same year Galileo introduced him to Prince Federico Cesi, who had founded the Accademia dei Lincei in 1603.

During this period Ciampoli was writing poetry in a variety of lyrical forms, including canzones, canzonets, sonnets, madrigals, and dithyrambs. He sought out the company of other poets in Rome; in addition to Cardinal Barberini, he had especially close relationships with the cardinal's nephew, Federico Barberini, and the philosopher-poet Virginio Cesarini. The literary theorist of the group was Sforza Pallavicino, who became the editor of some of Ciampoli's posthumously published works.

In 1618 Cesi had Ciampoli formally admitted to the Accademia dei Lincei. The following year he urged Ciampoli to become involved in a controversy between the Jesuit scientist Orazio Grassi and Galileo's student Mario Guiducci over Guiducci's *Discorso delle comete* (1619, Discourse on the Comets), which appeared to be an attack on the scientists of the Jesuit College. Ciampoli assumed a conciliatory stance and suggested that Galileo prepare a formal response.

Meanwhile, Ciampoli pursued his career in the Curia. In the early seventeenth century ecclesiastical advancement depended on the favor of powerful cardinals, their relatives, and the functionaries who served them; Ciampoli had the support of prominent families connected with Vatican politics such as the Borromeos, Capponis, and Ubaldinis. When the uncle of his friend Cardinal Ludovico Ludovisi was elected Pope Gregory XV in 1621, Ciampoli began a rapid rise in the church. Beginning as Ludovisi's secretary of Latin letters, he became, through Cardinal Barberini's intercession, papal secretary of secret briefs and *canonico di San Pietro* (canon of the cathedral of St. Peter). His familiarity with Gregory XV enabled him to show favor to some of his own friends; for example, Virginio Cesarini, in whose home he lodged for a time, was hired as secret chamberlain and later became master of the papal chamber. Immediately after being elected Pope Urban VIII in 1623, Barberini appointed Ciampoli his confidential secretary. In that capacity Ciampoli was charged with drawing up reports on the relations of the church with Spain and England.

In 1623 Ciampoli sent Galileo the first printed pages of *Il saggiatore* (The Assayer), the scientist's response to the controversy over Guiducci's *Discorso delle comete,* with the Curia's imprimatur and informed him of the favorable reception of the work by Urban VIII. The Accademia dei Lincei published the book and dedicated it to the new Pope. In 1624 Galileo visited Rome and had six friendly audiences with the Pope, after which he believed that he had obtained permission to write a book discussing the merits of the heliocentric theory. Ciampoli and other influential members of the Pope's entourage shared Galileo's optimism.

In 1626 Ciampoli published *Poesia in lode dell'inchiostro* (Poetry in Praise of Ink). The work celebrates the moral and civic functions of poetry, particularly in conferring lasting fame on meritorious figures.

Galileo's new book took the form of a dialogue between supporters of the old and new cosmologies; it was a subtle but strong indictment of Ptolemaic geocentrism and a clear endorsement of the Copernican theory. When the manuscript was completed in January 1630, Ciampoli suggested that Galileo come to Rome to obtain authorization to publish it from the Congregation of the Index. The head of the congregation, Father Niccolò Riccardi, thought that Galileo had already secured the Pope's permission and granted the authorization subject to changes aimed at stressing that the heliocentric theory was a mere mathematical hypothesis. At the last minute Galileo was instructed to change the original title, "Dialogo del flusso e deflusso della marea" (Dialogue of the Ebb and Flow of the Sea), because it would stress a physical argument for the movement of the earth. Retitled *Dialogo sopra i due massimi sistemi* (Dialogue Concerning the Two Chief World Systems), the work was printed in Florence in February 1632.

Soon afterward, Galileo's relationship with the Pope soured. Urban VIII had never committed himself publicly to a radical change of church policy with regard to Copernicanism, and it was clear that Galileo had not complied with the demands that the heliocentric theory be treated as a mere hypothesis and that the discussion of the tides be omitted. Alarmed by the growing hostility among church leaders between the conservatives and the more-liberal supporters of the new science and modern culture, the Pope asked the Roman Inquisition to review the work. The Florentine Inquisition impounded the *Dialogo sopra i due massimi sistemi,* and Galileo was summoned to Rome to be interrogated. In April 1633 he was forced to abjure the heliocentric theory, and in June he was sentenced to an indefinite term of house arrest at his home in Arcetri.

Urban VIII accused Ciampoli of misinterpreting the suggestions for corrections to be made to the *Dialogo sopra i due massimi sistemi* as an authorization to publish and denounced him as a friend of the "New Philosophy." Other possible reasons for Ciampoli's fall from favor with the Pope and the papal court were his alleged ingratitude in having had contacts with the Pope's political rival, Cardinal Gaspare Borgia, and having voiced reservations about a papal brief. At the end of 1632 Ciampoli was appointed governor of Montalto; later he was transferred to various small cities in the Marche and Umbria regions of the Papal States: Norcia in 1636, Sanseverino in 1637, Fabriano in 1640, and Iesi in 1642. Administrative duties did not exhaust his energies: in addition to writing, he carried out a program of scientific studies on the structure of matter. He maintained close ties with members of Galileo's school, especially the mathematician Benedetto Castelli. Between 1636 and 1641 his secretary was Evangelista Torricelli, the inventor of the barometer and a frequent guest at Arcetri during the last months before Galileo's death on 8 January 1642. Ciampoli died in Iesi on 8 September 1643.

Ciampoli left his manuscripts to the king of Poland, Władysław IV, whom he had known in Rome and of whom he had promised to write a laudatory biography. After careful scrutiny by the censors of the Curia, Ciampoli's papers were sent to Warsaw. His scientific manuscripts were lost and probably deliberately destroyed; some of his poems and prose writings were published posthumously from 1649 and 1667, mainly through the efforts of his friend Pallavicino, who had become a priest and had worked at the Curia from 1630 until he accepted an assignment as governor of Iesi in 1632.

Ciampoli's literary reputation rests primarily on his lyric poetry. Circulated first in manuscript and often addressed to patrons and friends, they were published after his death as *Rime* (1648, Rhymes), *Poesie sacre* (1648, Sacred Poems), *Poesie funebri e morali* (1653, Mournful and Moral Poems), and *Rime scelte* (1666, Selected Rhymes). In his poetry Ciampoli leaned toward the classical style of Gabriello Chiabrera but was influenced by the modernity of Giambattista Marino and Marino's followers. His work is rich in encomiastic verses for figures such as Cesarini; Cosimo II de' Medici; Duke Ferdinando II of Mantua; King Philip II of Spain; Cristiana of Lorraine, grand duchess of Tuscany; and Cardinals Federico Borromeo and Francesco Barberini. He also wrote poems celebrating occasions such as the *ferragosto,* a mid-August holiday. The predominant themes of his moral poems are typical of Baroque satire: the court's intrigue and corruption, courtiers' envy and flattery, and disloyal and slanderous friends at court. Ciampoli presents himself as persecuted but uncorrupted, a lover of justice, incapable of pretense, and forgiving of his enemies. His satirical verve is often replaced by a pensive melancholy. His religious poems are often inspired by current events such as the coronation of Urban VIII or the admission of a friend to a monastic order, but "Madrigale contro gli empi" (Madrigal against the Blasphemous) is a diatribe directed at the enemies of Christ:

Cangia in fulmini i chiodi
Tonante Crucifisso!
Fassi il mondo un abisso
Di strupi e stragi, fra rapine e frodi.
La barbarie felice
Trionfa ardita, e dice
Che tu sei statua e i nostri guai non odi.
Veggia la mentitrice
Che, ad estirpar delitti,
Tu sei Dio vivo e non hai pie' confitti.

(Change your nails into thunderbolts
Thundering Crucifix!
The world becomes an abyss
Of rape and slaughter, robbery and fraud.
Happy barbarism
Is bold and triumphant, and says
That you are a statue and you don't hear our troubles.
May the liar see
That you, by extirpating crimes
Are alive, God, and that your feet are no longer nailed.)

Ciampoli also wrote love poems such as "Rosa donata ma secca" (Rose Given but Withered):

Amante: Per mantenere in vita
La tua fragil beltade,
Dagli occhi miei non ti mancar rugiade,
O rosa inaridita.
Ed or come ci mostri
Della tua gioventù pallidi gli ostri!

Rosa: Mi mancò l'oriente
Di quegli occhi sì belli,
Che in un orto ridente
Fan sempre germogliar fiori novelli.
Con sì soavi note
La bella rosa al mio parlar rispose.

(Lover: To keep alive
Your fragile beauty,
And not to cause the dew from my eyes to be lacking
O withered rose
And how will you, now pale, show us
The purple of your youth?

Rose: I missed the sun
Of those beautiful eyes
Which in a pretty garden
Always make new flowers bloom.
With such sweet notes
The beautiful rose responded to my words.)

The most successful of Ciampoli's poems in this light vein are adapted from Greek models, such as "Le nozze di Bacco e della neve" (The Nuptials of Bacchus and the Snow), "La Mascherata di Parnaso" (The Masquerade of Parnassus), and "Le vendemmie di Castelgandolfo" (The Grape Harvests of Castelgandolfo), the last of which describes the revelry of bacchantes, satyrs, the Cynic philosopher Diogenes, and the commedia dell'arte stock character Capitano Spavento.

Some contemporary critics found Pallavicino's introduction to his 1648 collection of Ciampoli's poems overly flattering. According to Pallavicino, Ciampoli was recognized for the vigor of his style, his ability to maintain a high rhetorical level, and the noble content of his poems. The Baroque aspiration to a modern poetry seemed to Pallavicino to have found a satisfying model in his friend's work: a poetry of "expressive and pompous" figures that reconciled the styles of Chiabrera and Marino. Pallavicino, however, recognized that Ciampoli's verse could be blemished by confusion, hardness, and obscurity, defects that could be attributed to his daring attempt to achieve grandeur. His friend's poems, he noted, could be compared to beef bones that can damage weak teeth without showing their flavor, while those with stronger teeth would find in them food of special pleasure and substance.

Since Ciampoli's scientific manuscripts are lost, his merits as a scientist must be judged from his letters and from the prose writings composed for the most part during his ten years of forced exile and published between 1649 and 1667. In the introduction to his edition of Ciampoli's *Prose* (1649) Pallavicino says that he "ordinò e aggiustò" (arranged and mended) the pile of papers left in preliminary drafts and out of order by his friend. Ciampoli's fragment "Della filosofia naturale" (About Natural Philosophy) may have been intended as an introduction to a collection of his scientific papers. As a follower of Galileo, he takes the empiricist position that all knowledge is based on sense experience; the human intellect should not engage in metaphysical speculation but should concentrate on applying the principles of mathematics to natural phenomena.

Ciampoli's chief preoccupation in his extant prose writings is moral philosophy. In the papers collected in *Dei frammenti dell'opere postume* (1654, Fragments of Posthumous Works) he discusses prejudice, the language to be used in practical matters, the origin of virtue, the power of the public, and property. In considering religion he evidences a dislike of doctrinal disquisitions and theological dogmatism; his main concerns are with church government and the relationship between religion and the new science. For Ciampoli, as for Galileo, scientific discoveries and theology were distinct and autonomous spheres of knowledge.

Ciampoli's "Discorso sopra la Corte di Roma" (Discourse on the Roman Court), published in its entirety only in 1978, is considered the most revealing document of the author's period of forced exile. A polemical work written in an ironic vein tainted by a sense of bitterness and disappointment, it is a pseudo-confession of the errors committed by a member of the papal court who has been punished for being unable to accept the precepts required of modern courtiers. The main burden of Ciampoli's polemic is the impossibility of speaking one's mind in the post-Tridentine Curia, which is dominated by despotic and capricious rulers and filled with envious, slanderous, unscrupulous, and evil-minded courtiers.

Seventeenth-century writers often caricature Ciampoli as a haughty and arrogant man, perpetually immersed in his dreams of glory. Other observers, however, found Ciampoli's ambition an indication of a strong and assertive personality. Chiabrera depicts him at age thirty-five as the secretary of the papal briefs who displayed the Pope's will to ruling princes and gave orders in all the royal palaces of Europe with strength and forcefulness but was also able to answer royal ambassadors' questions in a thundering voice and with such eloquence that all were shaken—not by fear but in great astonishment.

Giovanni Battista Ciampoli was a man of modern culture whose ideas on the problems of the relationship between faith and science and between authority and reason are still relevant. Like his master and friend Galileo, Ciampoli accepted modernity, knowing full well that he was exposing himself to the persecution of theologians and censors. He combined the interests of the scientist with those of the moralist who had experience of political realities and the complexities of human relations.

Letters:

Lettere di monsignor Giovanni Ciampoli . . . : Accresciute di ventinove lettere del medesimo auttore, & in questa terza impressione d'altre ventitre (Venice: Giovanni Giacomo Hertz, 1661);

Lettere (Macerata: Eredi Grisei & Piccini, 1666);

Lettere (Venice: Menafoglio, 1676);

Lettere (Venice: Pezzana, 1676);

Lettere (Venice: Paolo Baglioni, 1676);

Lettere (Venice: Prodecimo, 1683).

Biography:

Augusto De Ferrari, "Giovanni Battista Ciampoli," in *Dizionario biografico degli italiani*, volume 25 (Rome: Istituto della Enciclopedia Italiana, 1981), pp. 147–152.

References:

Martino Capucci, "La poesia fra classicismo e concettismo," in *Il Seicento,* edited by Capucci and Carmine Iannaco (Padua: Piccin, 1986), pp. 265–268, 740–741;

Gabriello Chiabrera, *Dialoghi dell'arte poetica* (Venice: Alvisopoli, 1830), p. 165;

Domenico Ciampoli, *Nuovi studi letterari e bibliografici: Un amico del Galilei, monsignor Giovanni Ciampoli* (Rocca San Casciano: Licinio Cappelli, 1900);

Raffaele Colapietra, "Stile e scienza nei discepoli di Galileo," *Convivium,* 23 (1955): 533–556;

Giovanni Maria Crescimbeni, *Dell'istoria della volgar poesia,* volume 4 (Venice: L. Basegio, 1730), p. 190;

Franco Croce, *Tre momenti del barocco letterario italiano* (Florence: Sansoni, 1966), pp. 190–216;

Stillman Drake, *Galileo* (New York: Hill & Wang, 1980), pp. 73–79;

Sforza Pallavicino, *Vindicationes Societatis Jesu* (Rome: Eredi di F. Corbelletti, 1649);

Vittorio Ragazzini, "Evangelista Torricelli e Giovanni Ciampoli," *Convivium,* 27 (1959): 51–55;

Ezio Raimondi, "Avventure del mercato editoriale," in his *Anatomie secentesche* (Pisa: Nistri-Lischi, 1966), pp. 114–117;

Raimondi, *Letteratura barocca: Studi sul Seicento italiano* (Florence: Leo S. Olschki, 1961), pp. 327–356;

Mario Scotti, ed., *Storia del Concilio di Trento ed altri scritti di Sforza Pallavicino* (Turin: Unione Tipografico Editrice Torinese, 1968), pp. 19–21, 34;

Franco Vazzoler, "Un'inedita parafrasi pindarica di Giovanni Ciampoli," in *Studi di filologia e letteratura 2–3, Dedicati a Vincenzo Pernicone* (Genoa: Università di Genova, Istituto di Letteratura Italiana, 1975), pp. 259–280.

Giacinto Andrea Cicognini
(13 November 1606 – 21 November 1649)

Nancy L. D'Antuono
Saint Mary's College

BOOKS: *Descrizione del corso al palio dei villani trasformati in civettoni* (Florence: Pietro Cecconcelli, 1619);

Il Celio (Florence: F. Franceschini & A. Logi, 1646);

Il Giasone (Venice: G. Batti, 1649); republished as *Contezza del Giasone* (Palermo: N. Bua, 1655); republished as *Giasone* (Piacenza: G. Bazachi, 1655); republished as *Il novello Giasone* (Rome: Mascardi, 1671);

L'Orontea (Venice: G. Batti, 1649);

Gl'amori di Alessandro Magno e di Rossane (Venice: G. P. Pinelli, 1651); republished as *La Rosane con gli amori di Alessandro Magno* (Venice [i.e., Rome]: B. Lupardi, 1663); republished as *Amicitia riconosciuta* (Venice: Bartoli, 1665); republished as *L'Alessandro amante* (Venice: F. Nicolini & S. Curti, 1667); republished as *Le glorie e gli amori di Alessandro Magno e di Rossane* (Bologna: G. Longhi, 1678);

La forza del fato ovvero Il matrimonio nella morte (Florence: F. Onofri, 1652);

La Mariene ovvero Il maggior mostro del mondo, adapted from Pedro Calderón de la Barca's *El mayor monstruo los celos* (Perugia: Zecchini, 1656);

La moglie di quattro mariti (Perugia: S. Zecchini, 1656);

L'Adamira ovvero La statua dell'honore (Perugia: Sebastiano Zecchini, 1657);

Il don Gastone di Moncada, adapted from Calderón's *Gustos y disgustos no son más que imaginación* (Venice: Batti, 1658); republished as *Il gran tradimento contra più constante delle maritate overo L'amico traditore fedele* (Perugia: S. Zecchini, 1658); republished as *Il don Gastone di Moncada* (Bologna: D. Barbieri, 1660); republished as *Il D. Gastone overo La più constante tra le maritate* (Rome: Moneta, 1664);

La forza dell'amicizia ovvero L'onorato ruffiano di sua moglie (Venice: N. Pezzana, 1658); republished as *L'amicitia riconosciuta* (Venice: Camillo Bortoli, 1665); republished as *La più resoluta fra le donne* (Bologna: Antonio Pisarri, 1665);

La conversione di Santa Maria Egiziaca (Todi: Ciccolini, 1659); republished as *Santa Maria Egiziaca* (Venice: Batti, 1660); republished as *La Maria Egiziaca* (Bologna: G. Monti, 1663); republished as *Maria Egiziaca, azione sacra* (Bologna: G. Monti, 1687);

La donna più sagace fra le altre (Venice: N. Pezzana, 1660);

Il marito delle due moglie (Venice: G. Batti, 1660);

La forza dell'innocenza ne' successi di Papirio (Perugia: S. Zecchini, 1660);

La caduta del gran capitan Belisario sotto la condanna di Giustiniano imperatore, adapted from Mira de Améscua's *Belisario* (Bologna: A. Pisarri, 1661);

Il Pietro Celestino (Rome: Moneta, 1662);

L'innocenza calunniata ovvero La regina di Portogallo Elisabetta la santa (Viterbo: Lupardi, 1663);

L'amorose furie d'Orlando (Bologna: G. Monti, 1663); republished as *L'Orlando furioso ovvero L'amorose furie di Orlando* (Rome: G. Zenobi, 1717);

Il Cipriano convertito, adapted from Calderón's *El mágico prodigioso* (Bologna: G. Monti, 1663); republished as *Lo schiavo del demonio per gli amori di S. Cipriano con S. Giustina* (Bracciano: Giacomo Fei, 1664);

La disposizione e forza del destino (Bologna: Peri, 1663); republished as *La forza del destino* (Rome: Moneta, 1667);

I due prodigi ammirati ovvero il privato per favorito per forza e il prencipe infaticabile in sostenerlo, adapted from Tirso de Molina's *Privar contra su gusto* (Perugia: S. Zecchini, 1663);

Il maritarsi per vendetta, adapted from Francisco de Rojas Zorilla's *Casarse por vengarse* (Bologna: C. A. Peri, 1663);

La vita è un sogno, adapted from Calderón's *La vida es sueño* (Bologna: C. A. Peri, 1663);

L'innocente giustificato o Il sognator fortunato (Bracciano: Iacomo Fei, 1664);

Nella bugia si trova la verità, adapted from Juan de Villegas's *El marido de su hermana* (Bracciano: G. Dei, 1664);

Il principe giardiniero (Bologna: G. Monti, 1664);

L'amor vuol suoi pari (Bologna: Sarti, 1665);

L'amicitia riconosciuta (Venice: Bortoli, 1665); republished as *La più resoluta fra le donne* (Bologna: Antonio Pisarri, 1665);

Il convitato di pietra, adapted from Tirso de Molina's *Burlador de Sevilla y convidado de piedra* (Venice: F. Lupardi, before 1666); *L'innocenza difesa nel castigo dell'empio* (Bologna: A. Pisarri, 1668);

Il segreto in pubblico, adapted from Calderón's *El secreto a voces* (Rome: Moneta, 1669);

Le gelosie fortunate del prencipe Rodrigo (Milan: Cardi & Marelli, n.d.).

Giacinto Andrea Cicognini was renowned throughout the seventeenth century as the greatest dramatist of his age. He was also the most prolific and successful exponent of the *commedie spagnoleggianti* (plays in the Spanish mode), works either adapted directly from Spanish golden age drama or written in the Spanish style. The authorship of many of the plays credited to Cicognini, however, was challenged within decades of his death. Of the thirty-three plays that have been determined to be his in modern studies, 270 editions had been printed by 1700. The most popular were *Il Giasone,* which appeared in 47 editions between 1649 and 1684, and *L'Orontea,* published in 27 editions between 1649 and 1686. Little is known about the order in which his plays were written, since, with one exception, they were all published after his death.

Cicognini was born in Florence on 13 November 1606 to the playwright Jacopo Cicognini and Isabella di Domenico Berti. He was baptized on 16 November in the Florence Cathedral with Cristina of Lorraine, Grand Duchess of Tuscany, as his godmother. The grand duchess brought him to the Medici court as a page at age seven. At thirteen Cicognini caught the public's eye with his prose work *Descrizione del corso al palio dei villani trasformati in civettoni* (1619, Description of the Course of the Race of the Villagers Transformed into Large Owls). In 1622 he performed in a hagiographic play, *Sant'Agata* (St. Agatha), written by his father for presentation by the Accademia degli Infiammati (Academy of the Inflamed). After completing his undergraduate courses at the Collegio Ferdinando in Pisa, Cicognini went on study law there while continuing to perform regularly with his father in Florence. He earned his degree in 1627 but soon abandoned the practice of law and became an active participant in the theatrical offerings of the Florentine academies. In 1632 he adapted Tirso de Molina's *Burlador de Sevilla y convidado de piedra* (The Trickster of Seville and The Stone Guest) as *Il convitato di pietra* (The Stone Guest); it was performed in Florence and in Pisa and was a huge success in both cities.

As the godson of the grand duchess of Tuscany, Cicognini enjoyed the protection of the Florentine court. In 1646, however, he moved to Venice, where he remained until his death. Several hypotheses have been advanced regarding his sudden departure from Florence. One is that some high-ranking ladies and their husbands were offended by certain allusions in his writings. Another is that the academies that produced his plays may have had proprietary rights to the texts that prohibited their publication. Finally, Venice offered broader professional freedoms and was a leading publishing center. Of the three plays whose editions Cicognini supervised and for which he wrote the dedicatory letters, only *Il Celio* (1646) was published in Florence; *L'Orontea* and *Il Giasone* were published in Venice the year he died.

Cicognini quickly gained a reputation as a writer of highly successful plays. Much of his work circulated widely in manuscript among performers, stage designers, singers, musicians, and noble patrons, who freely altered the texts as the need arose. The Roman impresario Filippo Accaiuoli, the poet Giovan Filippo Apolloni, and the composer Alessandro Stradella had no qualms about reshaping Cicognini's *Il novello Giasone* (1671, The New Giasone) to their own requirements when they presented it at the newly inaugurated Teatro Tordinona in Rome on 17 January 1671. These adaptations account not only for the variations among the editions of many of Cicognini's plays but also for plays with almost identical titles that may have been inspired by Cicognini's work but are, in fact, totally different creations.

The issue of authenticity is complicated further by the fact that publishers and booksellers were not above listing Cicognini as the author of a play to increase sales. Prior to the 2001 bibliography by Silvia Castelli and Flavia Cancedda, Cicognini's first play was supposed, on the basis of the phrase "il primo parto della mia penna" (the first-born of my pen) in the foreword, to have been *Il figlio ribelle overo il David dolente* (1667, The Rebellious Son or the Anguished David); Castelli and Cancedda established that it was actually written by Bartolomeo Banichi. At the end of an edition of Cicognini's *I due prodigi ammirati ovvero il privato per favorito per forza e il principe infaticabile in sostenerlo* (1663, The Two Admired Prodigies; or, The *Privato* by Obligation and the Prince Determined to Sustain Him) the Roman editor and bookseller Bartolomeo Lupardi lists twenty-five plays by Cicognini that are available in his shop; he also appended the list to a 1664 edition of *Il Celio*. In the foreword to his comedy *Amore opera a caso* (1668, Love as Chance) the marquis Mattias Maria Bartolommei objected to the large number of plays attributed to Cicognini by unscrupulous publishers and listed eighteen works as the total output of the Florentine dramatist. Of the thirty-five plays credited to Cicognini by Castelli and Cancedda, eleven have been traced to Spanish sources; four of these pieces are clearly derived

LA FORZA
DELL'AMICITIA,
Ouero
L'HONORATO RVFFIANO
Di sua Moglie.
OPERA SCENICA
Del Dottor
GIACINTO ANDREA
CICOGNINI

IN MILANO
Per Gio. Pietro Cardi, &
Gioseffo Marelli. 1660

LA DONNA
PIV SAGACE
FRA L'ALTRE.

Opera del D.
GIACINTO ANDREA
CICOGNINI
Fiorentino.

IN MILANO MDCLXI
Per Gio. Pietro Cardi, & Gioseffo
Marelli
Al segno della Fortuna

LE
GELOSIE
FORTVNATE
DEL PRENCIPE
RODRIGO.
OPERA
DI GIACINTO ANDREA
CICOGNINI.
FIORENTINO

IN BOLOGNA, M.DC.LXXXV.
Per Gioseffo Longhi. Con Lic. de' Sup.

Title pages for later editions of three works by Giacinto Andrea Cicognini (University of Turin)

from the plays of Pedro Calderón de la Barca, while others have been traced to dramas by Tirso de Molina, Lope de Vega, and Francisco de Rojas. Since all but one of Cicognini's plays were published after his death, information about changes in the original texts to accommodate a particular singer, the needs of an orchestra, or the demands of an impresario or patron must be gathered from ambassadorial dispatches, newsletters, personal letters, rental receipts for properties, and payments to actors from municipal coffers or charitable organizations.

The evolution of Cicognini's plays was conditioned by two main factors: the rise of opera and the *dramma per musica* (melodrama), with the attendant technological advances in staging in which Italy was the undisputed leader; and the unflagging popularity of the commedia dell'arte. The former catered to the spectators' taste for plots centering on the excessive passions of bigger-than-life protagonists, accompanied by spectacular theatrical effects such as floods and erupting volcanoes and complemented by musical and vocal experimentation, while the offerings of the actors of the commedia dell'arte appealed to audiences' penchant for raucous, bawdy physical humor, action-driven plots, and witty wordplay. Cicognini met both demands, although his plays did not always achieve as successful a melding of the sublime with the ridiculous as the Spanish originals had.

Although Cicognini's comedies and dramas were performed regularly and republished until the end of the *Seicento*, post-seventeenth-century critics generally took a dim view of his accomplishments. Despite objecting to the works on neoclassical grounds, however, Carlo Goldoni, Italy's greatest eighteenth-century playwright and reformer of the Italian comic theater, paid homage to Cicognini in his memoirs and recalled the immense pleasure he derived from reading the plays as a youth.

Until the 1970s critics approached Cicognini's plays exclusively as literary works. Since then scholars have reevaluated the pieces as theatrical phenomena, oriented to the spectators and dependent for their success on the musical components and on the spectacular scenery. Cicognini repeated the same formulas over and over, much to the delight of Italian theatergoers. Thus, his plays were often found wanting as literature, but as theater they could not be matched.

Cicognini's preference for the theater of Calderón stems from Calderón's reputation among seventeenth-century Italian dramatists and critics as the best of the Spanish playwrights. The Cicognini dramas traceable to works by Calderón are *La Mariene ovvero Il maggior mostro del mondo* (1656, Mariene; or, The Worst Monster in the World), adapted from *El mayor monstruo los celos* (translated as *Jealousy, the Greatest Monster*, 1990); *Il Cipriano convertito* (1663, Ciprian's Conversion), republished as *Lo schiavo del demonio per gli amori di S. Cipriano con S. Giustina* (1664, The Slave of the Devil for the Love of S. Ciprian and St. Justina), from *El mágico prodigioso* (1637; translated as *The Mighty Magician*, 1853); *La vita è un sogno* (1663, Life Is a Dream), from *La vida es sueño* (1635; translated as *Life, a Dream*, 1830); and *Il segreto in pubblico* (1669, The Public Secret), adapted from *El secreto a voces* (1653; translated as *The Secret in Words*, 1853).

La Mariene ovvero Il maggior mostro del mondo was republished ten times, the last edition appearing in Bologna in 1670. It reproduces the main plot of its source: the obsessive jealousy of Herodes (Herod the Great), Tetrarch of Jerusalem, of his wife, Mariene (Mariamne), set against the backdrop of the struggle between Mark Antony and Octavian for control of Egypt and Jerusalem. It also preserves the intense passions; the multitude of personages, including the Roman and Jewish soldiers, musicians, servants, ladies-in-waiting, and Jewish citizens; and the elaborate palace scenes that lent themselves to the contemporary view of drama as lavish and grandiose spectacle. But whereas Calderón limits his setting to Jafa (Haifa), Nenfis, and Jerusalem, locales within a reasonable distance of one another, Cicognini moves from Jerusalem to Rome and back. He also recasts the servants Filipo and Polidoro as Ruzzante and Trivellino, comic personages easily recognized by contemporary spectators; the confusion of Trivellino with Mariene's brother, Aristobolo (Aristobolus), results in a beating–the customary stage violence of the commedia dell'arte. The "letter" scene in act 2 constitutes a playlet or intermezzo in its own right. Finally, whereas irrevocable fate is at the center of Calderón's plot, Mariene takes center stage in the Italian rendering. Stronger and more independent than her Spanish counterpart, she speaks firmly–not as a victim but as a royal equal–when she asks Octavian to spare the tetrarch's life. Later, her response to the tetrarch's plan to have her killed is equally forceful and direct: Mariene challenges Herodes to perform the deed himself; when he refuses, she rejects him, preferring voluntary confinement. One night Octavian comes to her apartment to offer her protection; Herodes arrives to kill the intruder, whom he does not recognize. In the ensuing struggle Herodes accidentally stabs Mariene, fatally wounding her. Cicognini underlines the tetrarch's perversity by presenting Mariene as a martyr to love; she loves unconditionally and forgives Herodes with her dying breath.

Cicognini's *La vita è un sogno* was the most popular seventeenth-century recasting of Calderón's *La vida es sueño;* it was republished eight times after its first appearance in 1663. In Calderón's play Prince Segismundo of Poland has been imprisoned since birth by his father, King Basilio, to prevent the fulfillment of a prediction by court astrologers that he would overthrow his father and be a cruel and unjust king. At the king's request Segismundo is drugged by a potion and brought back to court; his ensuing barbaric behavior appears to confirm the forebodings. Drugged again and reimprisoned, Segismundo is told when he awakes that the previous day's events were only a dream. Nevertheless, he recognizes the need to rise above his baser instincts. The citizens prefer Segismundo to his cousin Astolfo, Duke of Muscovy, as their future ruler; they revolt, providing the prince the opportunity to manifest his newfound self-control. Interwoven into the main plot are the political aspirations of Astolfo and Princess Estrella and a love triangle involving Astolfo, Estrella, and Lady Rosaura.

Cicognini retains but Italianizes the names of most of the characters; the only major changes are the substitution of Alfonso for Astolfo, Re di Polonia (King of Poland) for Basilio, and Piccariglio for the servant Clarín. He makes the Alfonso/Stella/Rosaura triangle the main focus of act 2; Segismondo's appearance in court is reduced to a brief episode sufficient to confirm his propensity for cruelty. Cicognini reduces the intensity of the prince's violence as depicted by Calderón and further undermines the tension of the scene by inserting a comic interlude featuring Piccariglio. Calderón's long verse monologues, with their elaborate reasoning, are reduced, with few exceptions, to succinct prose summaries. Segismundo's philosophical soliloquy at the end of Calderón's act 2 becomes a dialogue between Segismondo and his guardian and mentor, Grottardo, that alludes to the theme of the original—the relationship of life and dream—but focuses on the need "chi ben opra" (to perform well). Holding to the spirit of the original, if not the subtleties, Cicognini reproduces Calderón's views on astral influences and on the individual's ultimate responsibility for his or her behavior.

Italian audiences preferred plays with happy endings that resulted in one or more marriages; they were not especially attracted to religious works. Thus, in Cicognini's recasting of Calderón's *El mágico prodigioso* as *Il Cipriano convertito* the theological aspects take second place to the cape-and-sword elements. The dedicatory letter to the 1663 Bologna edition states that the play was performed by the Accademici de Ringioveniti della Sua Religione (Academicians of Those Rejuvenated by Their Faith) in Bologna and was well received. Lupardi's dedication to the 1664 Bracciano edition, retitled *Lo schiavo del demonio per gli amori di S. Cipriano con S. Giustina*, offers no performance data. The Bologna edition includes a soliloquy by Giustina in act 3 that is omitted from the Bracciano edition; the Bracciano edition includes an allegorical prologue featuring a *Spirito* (Ghost) whose words are spoken, rather than summarized for the audience as in the earlier edition. Cicognini may have revised his adaptation at the request of an acting troupe. Calderón's play is a variation of the Faust theme in which Ciprian makes a pact with the devil for the conquest of Justina but undergoes a conversion and is martyred with her: the "wonder-working magician"—the devil—is undone by the only force more powerful than his. Cicognini renames the devil Aladino and adds two new characters: Ermellina, who is disguised as Brandigi, Giustina's betrothed, until act 3, and Pasquella, the infant Cipriano's wet nurse, whom Aladino courts to achieve his ends.

Il segreto in pubblico is a fairly faithful adaptation of Calderón's *El secreto a voces*. Federico devises a scheme to permit him and his beloved, Laura, to converse secretly in the presence of Laura's mistress, Duchess Flérida: a wave of Laura's handkerchief will signal her desire to communicate, and the first word of each verse will form the message. Flérida, who is secretly in love with Federico, knows that he is involved in an affair and is determined to thwart it, though she does not yet know the identity of the other woman. Flérida eventually comes to her senses and accepts a marriage proposal from Enrique, who, unbeknownst to her, is the duke of Mantua, and Federico and Laura wed. Cicognini shifts the locale from Parma to Amalfi and nearby Salerno. He also modifies the lovers' mode of communication: in the Spanish version Federico summarizes the secret content of Laura's messages in asides to the audience; Cicognini's heroine raises the handkerchief to her lips to signal each word of her message. Further, Cicognini eliminates the short stories told by Calderón's servant, Fabio, since they were tied to the original Spanish milieu; he substitutes for the stories several comic sequences featuring the servant, whose name he changes to Piccariglio. Finally, the ending is fleshed out to include Laura's explanation of the secret code, and she, rather than Calderón's *gracioso* (clown), brings the play to a close by referring to "il nostro secreto a voce" (our secret aloud).

Cicognini's comedies were popular in Italy and abroad well into the next century. In the eighteenth century, however, theatrical tastes changed under the influence of neoclassicism: adherence to the unities of action, time, and place became the standard against which all drama was judged. Rigid adherence to this stance led to the heaping of abuse on Spanish golden-age drama and its seventeenth-century Italian imitators, particularly Cicognini.

In fact, Italian dramatists had never abandoned the classical precepts as theoretical guides; but once theater became a commercial enterprise, the rules were ignored or interpreted loosely in practice. The proponents of neoclassicism were committed to theater as an abstract academic exercise, not as the passionate engagement of playwright and actors in creating works to stir the emotions of the public. A man of consummate theatrical experience, Giacinto Andrea Cicognini was a dramatist with the soul of a performer whose plays touched his public deeply. Faced with the alternatives of writing drama to be read as literature or to be performed, Cicognini opted for performance. This choice garnered him fame and success for almost a century; if interest in and appreciation for his work waned after the first quarter of the eighteenth century, the cause is to be sought not in any defect in the Italian's mastery of his craft but in shifting sensibilities in regard to the form and content of drama.

Bibliographies:

Anna Maria Crinò, "Documenti inediti sulla vita e l'opera di Iacopo e Giacinto Andrea Cicognini," *Studi secenteschi*, 2 (1961): 255–286;

Saverio Franchi, *Le impressioni sceniche: Dizionario bio-bibliografico degli editori e stampatori romani e laziali di testi dramatici di libretti per musica (1579–1800)* (Rome: Storia e Letteratura, 1994), pp. 18–19, 46, 66, 210, 239–240, 278, 352–358, 360–366, 369, 371, 373, 375, 402, 409, 457, 459, 464, 565–566, 831;

Silvia Castelli and Flavia Cancedda, *Per una bibliografia di Giacinto Andrea Cicognini* (Florence: Alinea, 2001).

Biography:

Ludwig Grashey, *G. A. Cicognini Leben und Werke* (Leipzig: A. Diechert, 1909).

References:

Leone Allacci, *Drammaturgia* (Rome: Mascardi, 1666);

Antonio Belloni, "Per la storia del teatro italo-spagnolo nel secolo XVII," *La Biblioteca delle scuole italiane*, 10, no. 5 (1904): 1–3;

A. Cantella, *Calderón de la Barca in Italia nel secolo XVII* (Rome: Audonia, 1923);

Silvia Castelli, "Drammaturgia spagnola nella Firenze Secentesca," in *Otro Lope no ha de haber: Atti del Convegno internazionale su Lope de Vega, 10–13 febbraio 1999*, volume 3, edited by Maria Grazia Profeti (Florence: Alinea, 2000), pp. 225–238;

Castelli, *Manoscritti teatrali della Biblioteca Riccardiana di Firenze* (Florence: Polistampa, 1998), pp. 108–116;

Nancy L. D'Antuono, "The *Commedia alla spagnolesca*: Theatrical Success; Literary Failure," in *Italiana: Selected Papers from the Proceedings of the Third Annual Conference of the American Association of Teachers of Italian, December 27–28, 1986, New York, N.Y.*, edited by Albert N. Mancini, Paolo Giordano, and Pier Raimondo Baldini (River Forest, Ill.: Rosary College, 1988), pp. 185–197;

Martin Franzbach, *El teatro de Calderón en Europa* (Madrid: Fundación Universitaria Española, 1982);

G. Gobbi, "Le fonti spagnole del teatro drammatico di G. A. Cicognini," *La Biblioteca delle scuole italiane*, 11 (30 November 1905): 218–221;

Alberto Lisoni, *Gli imitatori del teatro spagnolo in Italia* (Parma: Ferrari & Pellegrini, 1895), pp. 44–60;

Carmen Marchante Moralejo, "Calderón en Italia, traducciones, adaptaciones, falsas atribuciones y 'scenari,'" in *Tradurre, riscrivere, mettere in scena*, edited by Profeti (Florence: Alinea, 2000), pp. 17–64;

Ireneo Sanesi, *La commedia: Storia dei generi letterari italiani*, second edition (Milan: Vallardi, 1954), pp. 692–723;

Claudio Sartori, *I libretti a stampa dalle origini al 1800*, 7 volumes (Milan: Bertola & Locatelli, 1990-1993), I: 21–22, 132, 184, 193; II: 102, 222–224, 391; III: 218. 272, 310–313, 455; IV: 333–336; VI: 68, 148;

D. Simini, "Alcune opere'spagnole' di Giacinto Andrea Cicognini fra traduzione, adattamento e creazione," in *Teatro, Scena, Rappresentazione dal Quattrocento al Settecento: Atti del Convegno (Lecce, 15–17 maggio 1997)*, edited by Paolo Andrioli Nemola and others (Galatina: Congedo, 2000);

Henry W. Sullivan, *Calderón in the German Lands and the Low Countries* (Cambridge: Cambridge University Press, 1983), pp. 2, 73, 81, 123, 295, 418, 424–425, 427;

Rosario Verde, *G. A. Cicognini*, Studi sull'imitazione spagnuola nel teatro italiano del Seicento, volume 1 (Catania: Nicolò Giannotta, 1912).

Papers:

Manuscripts and letters of Giacinto Andrea Cicognini are in the Archivio di Stato, the Biblioteca Riccardiana, the Biblioteca Nazionale, and the Biblioteca Laurenziana, all in Florence; the Biblioteca Nazionale Marciana in Venice; and the Vatican Library in Rome.

Giulio Cesare Cortese
(circa 1570 – 1626?)

Edoardo A. Lèbano
Indiana University

BOOKS: *La vaiasseide* (Naples: Tarquinio Longo, 1612); enlarged as *La vaiasseide: Poema di Giulio Cesare Cortese. Il Pastor Sebeto: A compiuta perfettione ridotta. Con gli Argomenti, et alcune prose di Gian Alesio Abactutis. Dedicata al Potentiss. Re de' Venti. Con privilegio* (Naples: Tarquinio Longo, 1615);

Li travagliuse ammure di Ciullo e Perna (Naples: Scorriggio, 1614);

Micco Passaro 'nnammorato (Naples: Nicolò Longo, 1619);

Viaggio di Parnaso (Venice: Misserini, 1621);

La Rosa (Naples: Ferrante Maccarano, 1621);

Opere burlesche in lingua napoletana (Naples: Domenico di Ferrante Cammarano, 1621);

Lo Cerriglio 'ncantato (Messina: Brea, 1628);

De la Tiorba a taccone de Felippo Sgruttendio de Scafato, attributed to Cortese (Naples: Camillo Cavallo, 1646).

Editions and Collections: *Opere di Giulio Cesare Cortese in lingua napoletana: In questa XV. impressione purgate con somma accuratezza da infiniti errori, che la rendeuano mancheuoli, e difettose, e ridotte alla vera perfettione dell'autore* (Naples: Printed by Novello de Bonis for Adriano Scultore, 1666);

Viaggio di Parnaso, edited by Malato (Naples: Fausto Fiorentino Editore, 1963);

Poesia del Seicento, edited by Carlo Muscetta and Pier Paolo Ferrante (Turin: Einaudi, 1964), pp. xxx–xxxi, 1397–1450;

Opere poetiche, edited by Enrico Malato (Rome: Dell'Ateneo, 1967);

Prose, edited by Maurice Slawinski (Turin: RES, 2000).

Giulio Cesare Cortese's significance rests on his contributions to the birth of the modern mock-heroic poem and the establishment of a distinct Neapolitan literary dialect. While most other dialect writers of the seventeenth century wrote both in the standard language and in a regional dialect, Cortese—except for some encomiastic and occasional verse in Tuscan—wrote exclusively in the Neapolitan idiom. As a result, in addition to their intrinsic interest his works are valuable as a source of Neapolitan cultural history.

Cortese was born in Naples around 1570 to Fabio and Giuditta Cortese, née Borrello. His father was a public official responsible for wheat provisions. He had two sisters: Isabella, who married a man named Vollaro, and Vittoria, who became a Clarisse nun. He fathered an illegitimate daughter, Giuditta, who married in 1626.

In 1594, while a student of law at the University of Naples, Cortese went to Spain and was presented at the court of King Philip III. He earned his doctorate in jurisprudence in 1597 and returned to Spain in 1599 as a member of the Florentine delegation sent to Madrid by Ferdinand de' Medici, Grand Duke of Tuscany, for the wedding of Philip III to Margaret of Austria. Toward the end of that year Fernandez de Castro, Count of Lemos and Viceroy of Naples, appointed him city assessor of Trani in Puglia. He remained in the position for a year.

Cortese made his third trip to Spain in 1601–1602, probably as a member of the retinue of Fernandez and Francisco de Castro. His time in Spain gave him the opportunity to become familiar with contemporary Spanish literature—particularly with the picaresque narrative, which is believed to have exerted an influence on his own literary production. In 1602 Cortese was a guest and protégé of the grand duke of Tuscany, but he departed abruptly in 1603 after a noblewoman of the Florentine court rejected his advances. In 1606 he was dispatched to Lucania as governor of Lagonegro. He returned to Naples in 1610.

Cortese's first creative work was *La vaiasseide* (The Servant Women), a poem of five cantos in ottava rima in the Neapolitan dialect; the first known edition is dated 1612. The poem tells the stories of several Neapolitan *vaiasse* (maidservants) who are treated harshly and kept in a condition of semi-slavery by their masters. All of the women want to marry and raise families, but only Renza succeeds in obtaining her master's consent to wed. She marries Menechiello and bears a beautiful daughter. Envious of Renza's good fortune, all but two of the other *vaiasse* run away with their lovers. They are eventually abandoned by the men and, unable to earn an honest living, become prostitutes and die of syphilis. Two *vaiasse,* Preziosa and Carmosina, locked in their masters' cellars and unable to run away, escape the tragic ending of their friends. Preziosa is finally allowed to marry Cienzo, but the marriage of Carmosina and Ciullo cannot be consummated because of a spell that was cast on the young man. The late appearance of a new character, Micco Passaro, the future protagonist of Cortese's mock-heroic poem *Micco Passaro 'nnammorato* (1619, Micco Passaro Enamored), brings about a happy ending by undoing the spell.

Cortese's attitude toward the lower classes in *La Vaiasseide* is a benevolent, though somewhat detached, paternalism; his social realism is free of any reformist intention. The colorful Neapolitan dialect is the main tool he uses in creating a vivid description of the world of the *vaiasse* and contributes to the overall comic effect of the work. Various aspects of Neapolitan life are rendered through realistic descriptions of weddings, births, banquets, religious practices, popular customs, common prejudices, and superstitions. For example, Renza gives birth to her daughter, "Y che vessica parea chiena de viento, / e sùbeto che scijo fece la cacca" (Who seemed like a bag full of wind, / and as soon as she came out, she defecated). Menechiello happily salutes the birth of his child: "Ànna a tata, figlia de na vacca, / ca chilloch'have bella reda a fare / bisogna de na squacquara 'ncignare" (Come to your daddy, daughter of a cow, / because the one who is to inherit much / must begin with a great defecation).

The publication of *La Vaiasseide* generated considerable debate among Cortese's contemporaries. While some accused the poet of lack of respect for the Aristotelian rules, others praised his originality and his artistic rewriting of the dialect of Naples. He followed the work in 1614 with a novel, *Li travagliuse ammure di Ciullo e Perna* (The Troublesome Loves of Ciullo and Perna), about the vicissitudes of two young lovers set against a background of pirates. Cortese added to the 1615 edition of *La Vaiasseide* a sonnet addressed "Alle Damme Sciorentine" (To the Florentine Ladies), leading some critics to propose an allegorical and satirical reading of the poem: in writing about the Neapolitan *vaiasse* he was actually alluding to the ladies of the Medici court and avenging the humiliation inflicted on him by the noble lady who scorned his love.

Promises of remunerative employment made by Fernandez de Castro never materialized. When de Castro left Italy for Spain in 1616, Cortese, also abandoned by Francisco de Castro, who succeeded his brother as viceroy, could no longer count on support

Internal title page for Cortese's The Servant Women, *in the 1666 collection of his works (University of Turin)*

from the rulers of Naples. He earned a modest living from some rental property and by lending out small sums of money at interest.

In 1619 Cortese published *Micco Passaro 'nnammorato,* a mock-heroic poem of 351 stanzas in ten cantos that became one of his most widely read works. It is set in the last decade of the sixteenth century, when the viceroy of Naples was engaged in a struggle against bandits from the mountains of the Abruzzi

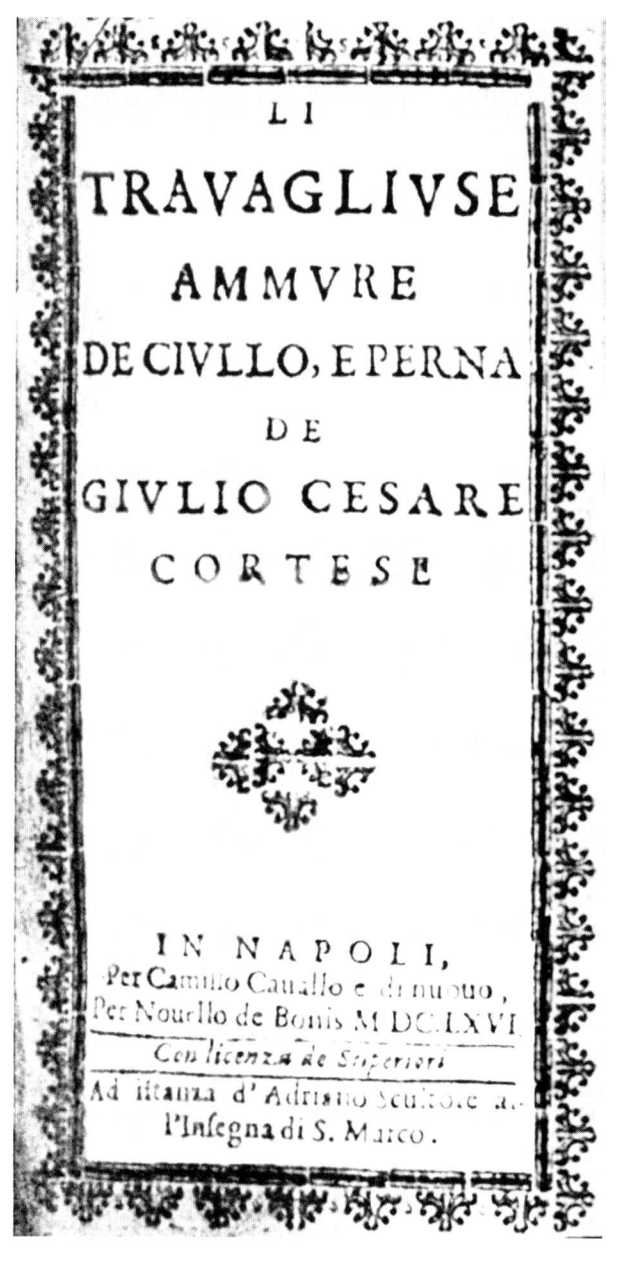

Internal title page in a collection of Cortese's works for his The Troublesome Loves of Ciullo and Perna, *originally published in 1614 (University of Turin)*

region. Micco Passaro is based on a well-known Neapolitan *guappo* (street thief) and low-class miles gloriosus who died in 1605. Cortese's Micco has enrolled as a volunteer in the viceroy's expeditionary force but is less interested in fighting the bandits than in pursuing Grannizia, a not-so-young Neapolitan *vaiassa* who is in love with a man much younger than she. Micco tells Grannizia's master that she has reduced his heart to ashes and made his chest as fragile as glass; his soul will soon leave his body if he does not marry the woman he loves, whom he is willing to take as his wife with only the clothes she has on her back. But Nora, Micco's betrothed, is not willing to give him up and succeeds, through a series of shrewd if conventional ploys, in reclaiming his love and bringing him to the altar.

Cortese's most significant and celebrated work, *Viaggio di Parnaso* (Journey to Parnassus), a poem in seven cantos in ottava rima, was published in Venice in 1621. At the beginning of the poem Cortese reaches the castle of Apollo atop Mount Helicon and is warmly welcomed by the god of poetry, who resides there with the Muses. Some poets, several of them Tuscan, who live on Parnassus as Apollo's guests loudly object to Cortese's arrival, declaring that he comes from one of Naples's most ill-famed districts. Cortese asserts his right as a poet to be present and defends his use of the Neapolitan dialect:

> Co lecienzia d'Apollo a sto paise
> pò vevere chi vóle allegramente,
> o Spagnuolo, o Todisco, o sia Franzese,
> vasta che sia de miereto e balente;
> ca lo sommiero ch'a fare se mese
> chest'acqua, de vertù tant'azzellente,
> pe tutte voze fare la fontana,
> no' schitto pe la Grezia e pe Toscana.
>
> Le Muse vanno dove so' chiammate,
> ca no' stanno co buie co lo strommiento,
> e quanta vote a me se so' 'nzeccate
> cose hanno fatto lustre comm'argiento;
> le parole de Napole 'mpastate
> non songo, frate mio, d'oro pommiento,
> ma de zuccaro e mèle: e famma vola
> se fanno a tutte lengue cannavòla.
>
> Ma, ca non fosse niente quanto dico,
> mentre che Apollo non l'have pe male
> ed have gusto, e sta buono co mmico,
> perché facite vuie de lo fiscale?
> Co le chellete vostre io no me 'ntrico
> né nce aggio che spartire manco sale:
> io scrivo commo parlo, e la fortuna
> po' portare a me puro fi' a la luna.
>
> (With Apollo's permission in this place
> anyone who wishes can happily drink,
> be he Spanish, German or French,
> provided that he be worthy and capable;
> because the ass Pegasus
> that gave such excellent power to this water,
> did make this spring flow for everyone,
> not only for Greeks and Tuscans.
>
> The Muses go everywhere they are called,
> because they are not bound to anyone by a contract,
> and whenever they approached me
> they always did things as shining as silver;
> the words of Naples, my brother, are not mixed
> with fake gold, but with sugar and honey:
> and their reputation spreads to attract all tongues.
>
> Even if what I say is of no importance,
> and Apollo is not upset,
> but is rather pleased and feels good about me,
> why do you behave like tax collectors?
> I do not meddle in your business
> nor do I have salt to share with you:
> I write as I speak and fortune
> can take me even to the moon.)

Internal title page in a collection of Cortese's works for his mock-heroic poem Micco Passaro Enamored, *originally published in 1619 (University of Turin)*

Cortese's words not only please Apollo but also favorably impress the Tuscan satirist Francesco Berni, who declares himself in agreement with his Neapolitan colleague: "Egli ha raggion quest'omiccino" (This little man is right). Cortese goes on to describe in a lively and amusing fashion marvelous gardens, Apollo's por-

Internal title page in a collection of Cortese's works for his most celebrated poem, Journey to Parnassus, *originally published in 1621 (University of Turin)*

trait gallery, and debates on a variety of semiserious topics such as an ironically funny discussion of whether or not it is shameful to be a *cornuto* (cuckold).

Apollo gives a banquet at which the food is prepared by Poetry and served by one hundred pages. A salad of lyric poetry, with zucchini flowers and borage, is served first; it has too much vinegar and not enough oil. Then comes a large dish of epic poetry roasted with pepper and vinegar; it is too dry, salty, and lean. Next are the appetizers, of which a great quantity is consumed: they consist of eclogues, farces, and pastoral dramas. The guests lick their fingers with Battista Guarini's character Mirtillo, Guidobaldo Filli, and Torquato Tasso's Aminta, which is for upper-class people. The remaining offerings are left for the servants.

After reporting the high honor bestowed on his friend Giovan Battista Basile, who had been named *Conte Palatino* (Count of the Palace) and *gentiluomo* (gentleman) by the duke of Mantua, Cortese is overcome by a desire to return home. As a parting gift Apollo gives him a magic napkin that can provide him with the most delicious food and exquisite wines:

Perzò songo contento che sbignare
craie tu puozze alle belle toie Serene;
ma perché a li poete li denare
songo nnemmice, ed io te voglio bene,
piglia sto stoiavucco, e se magnare
tu vuoie, stiennelo 'n terra, e bì che bene!

(I am happy that you will sneak off
tomorrow so that you can return to your beautiful Sirens;
and because money is the enemy
of poets and I wish you well,
take this napkin and, when you want to eat,
spread it on the ground and you shall see what good
   things you receive.)

On the way home Cortese encounters a young man who shows him a magic knife that will transform itself into a beautiful castle when one stabs it into the ground and utters the word "auciello" (bird). Cortese exchanges the napkin for the knife. At the end of the poem Cortese, famished and unable to find a piece of land on which to build his dream castle, curses the knife and blames himself for being a foolish and coarse man.

The genre of imaginary voyages to Mount Parnassus was fashionable among European men of letters of Cortese's time; the Spanish writer Miguel de Cervantes Saavedra wrote *Viaje del Parnaso* (1614; translated as *A Voyage to Parnassus*, 1870), which the cultural historian Benedetto Croce considered inferior to Cortese's work. According to Enrico Malato, Cortese's originality lies in his rejection of the conventional mythology used in similar works; he infuses new life into Apollo, who appears not only as the god of poetry but also as a benevolent wizard.

In 1621 Cortese also published *La Rosa* (Rosa); it is a pastoral drama in five acts, each ending with a brief sententious chorus. The work, written entirely in the Neapolitan dialect, concerns the tragicomic amorous adventures of two couples. During the time that he believed that his lover, Rosa, was dead, Mase fell in love with Lella. But Lella, whose real name is Rita, is revealed to be Mase's sister. Mase marries Rosa, and Rita marries Mase's friend Fonzo.

A charter member of the Neapolitan Accademia dei Sileni (Academy of the Followers of Silenus) and a member of the prestigious Florentine Accademia della Crusca (Academy of the Sifters), Cortese spent most of his life in Naples. The date of his death is something of a mystery: legal documents indicate that he was alive in 1640, leading some scholars to believe that the reports of his death in 1626 originated with the poet himself. If so, Cortese was responsible for the creation of a myth that was perpetuated by his friend Basile, who is best known for *Lo Cunto de li Cunti* (1634–1636, The Story of Stories). Basile states in the introduction to ode 12 of his

Internal title page in a collection of Cortese's works for his Enchanted Cerriglio, *originally published in 1628 (University of Turin)*

Madrigali e Ode (1609, Madrigals and Odes) that Cortese "mostrò la grandezza dell'ingegno nella piccolezza del corpo, la ricchezza della virtù nella povertà della fortuna" (always showed the greatness of his mind in the smallness of his body, the richness of virtue in the poverty of fortune).

Cortese's *Lo Cerriglio 'ncantato* (Enchanted Cerriglio), a mock-heroic poem in 258 stanzas, appeared in

1628; if Cortese did die in 1626, it is a posthumously published work. It takes its title from the most celebrated tavern in Naples of the time and is a parody of the etiological poem, a narrative designated to celebrate the noble origin of a city or dynasty. Generally considered Cortese's least interesting work linguistically or stylistically, it relates the deeds of a group of young Neapolitan braggarts led by Cola Sarchiapone who wage war on the fictitious kingdom of Cerriglio, conquer it, and transform it into a huge tavern.

The last work attributed, though with reservations, to Cortese is a collection of satirical sonnets, *De la Tiorba a taccone de Felippo Sgruttendio de Scafato* (On the Theorbo and Pick of Felippo Sgruttendio de Scafato), published in Naples in 1646. The theorbo was a two-necked musical instrument similar to a lute with eight or ten strings; it was played with a leather pick called a *taccone* (patch). The oddly named Felippo Sgruttendio de Scafato is the owner and player of the theorbo. The sonnets make fun of the *canzonieri d'amore* (collections of love verse) that flourished in the late sixteenth and early seventeen centuries. The book is divided into ten *corde* (sections) addressing a variety of topics; most of the poems discuss love and women. The woman most frequently mentioned is Cecca, who is characterized by an uncontainable sexuality. When Felippo Sgruttendio finds himself in the presence of the woman he loves, he is possessed by an overwhelming amorous passion that he expresses in desecrating and comically obscene language: "Io moro, io crepo, io spasemo ed abbotto / so' fatto giallo come na scarola!" (I die, I croak, I yearn and I swell / I become as yellow as an endive." Seeing Cecca's "facce de recotta" (face of ricotta cheese) and "chillo fronte traslucente / Tutto me caco da paura sotta" (that translucent forehead, / overcome with fear, I shit in my pants). Cecca's demise is announced in the fifth *corda,* and, with a parodic reference to Petrarch's Laura, the speaker addresses the laments in the final five *corde* to her.

Cortese's use of the dialect of his native city in his anti-academic poetic narratives was much imitated for several decades after his disappearance from the Neapolitan literary scene. But while Cortese's aim was to give the people of Naples and their language a place in the country's literary tradition, his imitators failed to follow his example. Malato writes in "La scoperta di un poeta: Giulio Cesare Cortese" (1977, The Discovery of a Poet: Giulio Cesare Cortese) that after Cortese's death, "Neapolitan dialect literature, which in the following centuries experienced a very rich flourishing, at times enlisting writers of noteworthy literary talent, basically remained as a local curiosity, or divertissement of bright minds–or comic or semi-serious literature– totally deprived of the cultural reasons that had inspired its founder."

The subversive choice of the Neapolitan dialect enabled Giulio Cesare Cortese to distance himself from the aristocratic neoclassical epic and identify with the readership to which his mock-heroic narratives were addressed. The defense of the Neapolitan dialect in the *Viaggio di Parnaso* has allowed deeper insights in Cortese's poetics and ideological intentions. His works suggest a preference for personal merit over social rank, resentment of social injustice, and sympathy for the low-lifes of his native Naples.

References:

Giovan Battista Basile, *Madrigali e Ode* (Naples, 1609);

Benedetto Croce, *Saggi di letteratura italiana del Seicento* (Bari: Laterza, 1962), pp. 28–36, 119–122, 133–136;

Pino Fasano, "Gli incunabili della letteratura dialettale napoletana" in *Letteratura e critica: Studi in onore di Natalino Sapegno,* volume 2, edited by Walter Binni and others (Rome: Bulzoni, 1975), pp. 443–488;

Fasano, "La questione *Sgruttendio*," *Giornale storico della letteratura italiana,* 88, fascicle 46 (1971): 49–91;

Giorgio Fulco, "La letteratura dialettale napoletana: Giulio Cesare Cortese e Giovan Battista Basile; Pompeo Sarnelli," in *Storia della letteratura italiana: Cinquecento e Seicento,* volume 5, edited by Enrico Malato (Rome: Salerno, 1995), pp. 813–867;

Carmine Jannaco and Martino Capucci, "I napoletani: Giulio Cesare Cortese," in their *Il Seicento,* revised and enlarged edition, Storia letteraria d'Italia, volume 8 (Milan: F. Vallardi, 1986), pp. 312–325;

Enrico Malato, *La poesia dialettale napoletana: Testi e note,* 2 volumes (Naples: Esi, 1959);

Malato, "La scoperta di un poeta: Giulio Cesare Cortese," *Filologia e critica,* 2 (1977): 35–117;

Ferdinando D. Maurino, "Cervantes, Cortese, Caporali and Their Journeys to Parnassus," *Modern Language Quarterly,* 19 (1958): 43–46;

Salvatore Nigro, "Dalla lingua al dialetto: La letteratura popolaresca," in *Letteratura italiana: Storia e testi,* volume 5, part 2: *Il Seicento,* edited by Carlo Muscetta (Bari: Laterza, 1974), pp. 451–474;

Nigro, "'Vaiasse' e smargiassi nel 'romanzo' napoletano di un poeta postumo a se stesso," in *Storia generale della letteratura italiana,* volume 6: *Il secolo barocco: Arte e scienza nel Seicento,* edited by Nino Borsellino and Walter Pedullà (Milan: Motta, 1999), pp. 271–277;

Franco Vazzoler, "Il carnevale alla rovescia," *L'immagine riflessa,* 3 (1979): 321–336.

Margherita Costa
(1600/1610? – after 4 May 1657)

Natalia Costa-Zalessow
San Francisco State University

BOOKS: *Istoria del viaggio d'Alemagna del serenissimo Gran Duca di Toscana Ferdinando Secondo* (Venice, circa 1630);

La chitarra (Francfort [i.e., Italy]: Daniel Wastch, 1638);

Il violino (Francfort [i.e., Italy]: Daniel Wastch, 1638);

Ottave per l'incendio dei Pitti (Florence: Massi & Landi, 1638);

Lo stipo (Venice, 1639);

Lettere amorose (Venice, 1639);

Flora feconda: Poema (Florence: Massi & Landi, 1640);

La selva di cipressi: Opera lugubre (Florence: Massi & Landi, 1640);

La Flora feconda (Florence: Massi & Landi, 1640);

Li buffoni (Florence: Massi & Landi, 1641);

Cecilia martire: Poema sacro (Rome: Mascardi, 1644);

La selva di Diana (Paris: Craimoisy, 1647);

La tromba di Parnaso (Paris: Craimoisy, 1647);

Festa reale per balletto a cavallo (Paris: Craimoisy, 1647);

Gli amori della Luna (Venice: Giuliani, 1654);

Al serenissimo Ferdinando II, Gran Duca di Toscana, per la festa di San Giov. Battista (Venice, n.d.);

Al serenissimo principe Gio. Carlo di Toscana, per la carica di generaliss. del mare conferitagli dalla M. Cattolica (Florence: Massi & Landi, n.d.).

Editions: "Lettere amorose," in *Scielta di lettere amorose* (Venice: Bartoli, 1656);

Luisa Bergalli, *Componimenti poetici delle più illustri rimatrici d'ogni secolo* (Venice: Mora, 1726), pp. 149–154;

"Gemme o rime di poetesse italiane," in *Parnaso italiano: Poeti italiani contemporanei maggiori e minori,* volume 2, edited by Antoine Ronna (Paris: Baudry, 1843), pp. 1025–1027;

Jolanda de Blasi, ed., *Antologia delle scrittrici italiane dalle origini al 1800* (Florence: "Nemi," 1930), pp. 334–341;

Natalia Costa-Zalessow, ed., *Scrittrici italiane dal XIII al XX secolo: Testi e critica* (Ravenna: Longo, 1982), pp. 146–152;

Li buffoni, in *Commedie dell'Arte,* volume 2, edited by Siro Ferrone (Milan: Mursia, 1986), pp. 233–359;

Margherita Costa (from La chitarra, *1638; Bancroft Library, University of California, Berkeley)*

Giuliana Morandini, ed., *Sospiri e palpiti: Scrittrici italiane del Seicento* (Genoa: Marietti, 2001), pp. 114–124.

Margherita Costa is the most "Baroque" of seventeenth-century Italian women writers. She published two books of prose, six volumes of poetry, three plays, two narrative poems, and an allegorical pageant for knights on horseback. She was one of the few Italian women poets to use humor: many of her poems start out as lamentations and come to amusing conclusions, and

Title page for the first edition of Costa's The Buffoons
(University of Turin)

she creates double entendres that border on indecency in her comedy *Li buffoni* (1641, The Buffoons). She was also something of a feminist, criticizing men for their infidelity and urging women to repay them in kind.

Costa was born into a poor family in Rome in the early seventeenth century. Her father and brother, whose names are not known, had unsavory reputations–the former for guiding Costa and her sister Anna Francesca, toward singing careers, which were associated with courtesans (another sister became a nun), the latter for being involved in a brawl and a murder. Costa was sometimes called a courtesan and even a common prostitute; nonetheless, she was invited to perform for ladies of the high nobility. The five-act opera *La catena d'Adone* (1626, The Chain of Adonis), by the composer Domenico Mazzocchi with libretto by Ottavio Tronsarelli, was originally written for a singing competition between Costa, who was protected by Prince Giovanni Giorgio Aldobrandini, and her rival Cecca (Francesca) del Padule, protected by another roman nobleman, Giandomenico Lupini. Based on cantos 12 and 13 of Giambattista Marino's poem *L'Adone* (1623; excerpts translated as *Adonis,* 1967), the work is important for such innovations as the use of more arias, longer parts for the choir, ballet sections performed to singing, and a complex setting of enchanted gardens with mysterious grottoes. The contest never took place, because Aldobrandini's mother, Olimpia, did not want the family name associated with a competition between two women of ill repute.

Costa moved to Florence in 1628 in hopes of finding protection at the Medici court. At some point she married and had children; her husband was probably the actor and court jester Bernardino Ricci ("Tedeschino"), who was in the service of the grand duke of Tuscany, Ferdinand II de' Medici. "Ronaca" is sometimes added to her name by historians but has never been explained. She published almost all of her work under the name Margherita Costa, usually adding *romana* (from Rome). But her final publication, *Gli amori della Luna* (1654, The Loves of the Moon Goddess), has Maria Margherita Costa on the title page and as the signature on the dedication.

Costa wrote most of her works during the sixteen years she lived in Florence. Her first book, *Istoria del viaggio d'Alemagna del serenissimo Gran Duca di Toscana Ferdinando Secondo* (1630, A History of the Trip to Germany Undertaken by Ferdinand II, Grand Duke of Tuscany), carries no date of publication but probably appeared in 1630. Ferdinand de' Medici had succeeded his father, Cosimo II, as grand duke in 1621, when he was ten; he made the journey in 1627 to honor Holy Roman Emperor Ferdinand II in Prague before assuming his duties when he came of age at eighteen. Costa explains at the beginning of the book that her text is based on notes kept by Benedetto Guerrini, who had accompanied Ferdinand on the trip and later became his secretary. Ferdinand departed from Florence on 23 February and made a diplomatic detour to Rome to see Pope Urban VIII; in addition to the Pope, he made courtesy calls on several Roman princesses, including the Pope's sister-in-law. He left Rome on 18 March, visited several Italian cities, crossed the Alps, and stopped in Innsbruck and Munich on the way to Prague. He returned to Florence on 14 July 1628, his eighteenth birthday. Costa's work consists mainly of dates of arrivals and departures, names of towns in which the party stayed, weather conditions, formalities, and ceremonies. While it makes for monotonous reading, it documents the splendors and hardships of travel by the high nobility in the seventeenth century. The prose style is so good—short, precise sentences without needless embellishment—that Costa was accused of not having written it herself.

In 1638–1639 Costa published three volumes of poetry: *La chitarra* (1638, The Guitar), *Il violino* (1638, The Violin), and *Lo stipo* (1639, The Cabinet). In the dedication to the first she notes that the guitar, a common instrument played by the poor, is a worthy symbol of lowly verses; the violin is one step above the guitar. In *Lo stipo* the poems are grouped into seven "cassettini" (drawers) named after precious stones and metals: "Carbunculi e diamanti" (Carbuncles and Diamonds), "Smeraldi e rubini" (Emeralds and Rubies), "Oro e perli" (Gold and Pearls), and so forth. Costa makes no effort to eliminate stylistic imperfections from her poems; she adhered to the musical tradition, which permitted greater flexibility in poetry. Many of the pieces are laudatory poems about people of rank of both sexes from whom she hoped to gain favors and protection. In these collections, as in all of her publications, she hyperbolically stresses her ignorance in dedications and notes to the reader. In *La chitarra*, for example, she declares that her thoughts corresponded for a while with the Muses; but the thoughts were devoid of talent, so that a deformed monster was born who is comparable to a crippled and ill-formed dwarf. Critics interpreted such declarations as evidence of insecurity rather than as a Baroque exaggeration of the tradition, which had become a norm, of Italian Renaissance women poets minimizing their ability when comparing themselves to male writers.

The 573-page *La chitarra,* which Costa calls "un piccolo volume" (a little volume), consists of sonnets, canzonets, and poems written in tercets and in the eight-line stanzas traditionally used in narrative verse. The pieces betray a knowledge of the major Italian authors Dante Alighieri, Petrarch, Ludovico Ariosto, and Torquato Tasso, as well as of such seventeenth-century poets as Marino, Ottavio Rinuccini, Pier Francesco Paoli, and Gabriello Chiabrera. Costa frequently uses the technique of speaking through a *bella donna* (beautiful woman): the persona is autobiographical in some cases, as when the speaker complains of being far from her native city or deplores her difficult past and praises the happier present. Such statements are only hints or allusions, not detailed descriptions of her life. A preferred theme is a lamentation by a man or women over a lover's departure or long absence, but the most frequent is that of a woman complaining about her lover's infidelity and shortcomings and consoling herself with another man; thus, the tension built up in the complaint dissolves in humor. Similarly, what starts out as a tragic poem about a lady killed by a scorned lover ends with tongue-in-cheek advice to women to kiss men whenever they are asked to do so, unless they want to part with their lives. In another poem, which she labels a joke, she tells women that they must never love only one man at a time; if they do, they will lose their liberty to possessive men. In a composition popular with anthologists she complains of having suffered all the tortures of love, only to realize that love is blind; therefore, she has stopped loving and now limits herself to spinning, women's true calling:

> Alle donne è dato in sorte,
> fin dal cielo e dalle stelle,
> di vestir abito imbelle
> e filar fino alla morte;
> e chi sdegna l'ago e il fuso
> della donna perde ogn'uso;
> ond'io lascio ogn'altro affare,
> e solo bramo di filare.

> (Destiny imposed on women,
> from Heaven and the stars,
> to be timid

and to spin till death;
and she who refuses needle and spindle,
loses all womanly traits,
therefore I am dropping everything
and long only to spin.)

She humorously advises other women to do the same, poking fun at the belief that a woman's place is in the home.

The critic Martino Capucci considered the idyll "Violamento di Lilla" (The Rape of Lilla) in *Il violino* a reflection of the author's immoral life; he seems not to have noticed that she was imitating, with a feminist twist, an erotic poem by Marino. In another idyll Costa competes with Marino's followers, who sometimes picked absurd subjects to create antitheses and metaphors never used before, by relating the praise bestowed on an ugly old woman by her lover: he is happy with her even though she is as tall as a cypress, stupid, and inexperienced and has silver hair, damaged skin, black teeth, a wide neck, a flat chest, rough hands, and colorless, sullen, and threatening eyes. In a surrealistic poem a desperate mother lists the difficulties her baby girl will face in life; the child is suddenly changed into a boy, who will be loved by everyone. Yet, there are also many examples of seriously treated themes, such as the grief of a woman whose lover has died in "È morto, ahi lassa, è morto" (He Is Dead, Poor Me, He Is Dead) and a mother imploring God to restore the health and beauty of her sick daughter in "Pargoletta amorosa" (Beloved Little One).

Of particular note in *Lo stipo* is an autobiographical poem in which the speaker declares that she was ill-treated in Rome, where others were jealous of her ability to conquer hearts, but has found protection and fortune in Tuscany; the name Costa appears in the concluding verse. The hint at the author's love life is elaborated in a poem in which the speaker admits to having frequent affairs but ascribes her weakness to the destiny imposed on her by the stars. In a fifteen-page poem the speaker, lamenting the loss of her beauty to the ravages of time, observes that women are taught to cultivate their appearance, not their intelligence; as a result, they lead frivolous lives filled with envy of each other. The speaker, however, has thrown away all of her makeup, for among the poets of Parnassus a painted face does not count.

In *Lettere amorose* (1639, Love Letters) Costa essays the epistolary genre that had been popular since the Renaissance. Some of the letters are serious, others humorous; several were chosen for the collection *Scielta di lettere amorose* (1656, Selected Love Letters), which also included pieces by authors such as Ferrante Pallavicino, Luca Assarino, and Girolamo Parabosco and was reprinted in 1662, 1671, 1675, and 1683.

In 1640 Costa published three books; according to the dates of her dedications, *Flora feconda* (Fertile Flora) appeared first, followed by *La selva di cipressi: Opera lugubre* (Cypress Grove: A Mournful Work) and *La Flora feconda* (The Fertile Flora). The first work is a mythological narrative poem; the last is a play adapted from it. Flora and Zephyr, eager to have children, undertake a trip to consult Jupiter's oracle. On their return a son is born to them, but Jupiter decides to keep the baby and promises the couple that they will have other children. The story is an allegory of the birth and death of the firstborn of Grand Duke Ferdinand II and his wife, Vittoria della Rovere; references to the oak, which was the emblem of the della Rovere family, and prophecies glorifying the Medicis are inserted into the plot. The poem consists of ten cantos: one for each of the nine months of pregnancy, with the tenth added at the last moment, as the author explains in her dedication to the duke, to acknowledge the death of the infant. Reflecting the Medicis' preference for grandiose entertainment based on mythological themes, the play, in five acts of eight to eleven scenes each, calls for elaborate sets, music, singing, and dancing.

La selva di cipressi consists of lamentations; most are on the deaths of great men, but in "Le lagrime dell'Alpi" (Tears of the Alps) Italy mourns the miserable condition of her states, especially the dukedom of Savoy. In the final piece, "Elisa infelice" (Unfortunate Elisa), Costa complains about her life and the lack of appreciation of her literary efforts. She ascends Parnassus to appeal to the gods and is consoled by Apollo, who reminds her of the miseries of others and points out that laurel leaves are bitter and that poets must learn to suffer.

Published in 1641, the comedy *Li buffoni* is dedicated to Costa's probable husband, Ricci. It is a Baroque extravaganza—a potpourri of stupidities, trivialities, and crude double entendres, with an exotic Moroccan setting and characters the author describes in "Al lettore" (To the Reader) as "pazzi, buffoni e nani" (crazies, buffoons and dwarfs), including a hunchback she calls "scherzo di natura" (nature's joke). At the end the betrayed wife gets revenge on her rival.

Costa left Florence in 1644, perhaps because Ricci had died. She returned to Rome in the company of the former bandit Fra Paolo, who had served in Grand Duke Ferdinand II's military forces in Tuscany and was traveling to the city as a penitent under the protection of the Barberini family. In Rome, Costa sought the protection of Cardinal Francesco Barberini; her brother was employed by the cardinal and might have served as an intermediary.

Costa dedicated *Cecilia martire: Poema sacro* (1644, The Martyr Cecilia: A Sacred Poem) to Cardinal Barberini. The patron saint of church music, Cecilia is thought to have been martyred in Rome in the late second or early third century. According to legend, she was first condemned to be suffocated by fire in the bath of her home; when she remained unharmed, she was ordered to be decapitated. Three blows of the executioner's sword wounded her but failed to separate her head from her body. She lived for three days, during which she arranged for her house to be consecrated as a church after her death. She enjoyed renewed veneration after her sarcophagus in the Roman catacombs was identified and opened in 1599, inspiring Stefano Maderno to create his marble statue of her for the Church of Santa Cecilia. She was the subject of the nun Cherubina Venturelli's mystery play *Santa Cecilia Vergine e martire* (St. Cecilia, Virgin and Martyr), which appeared in four editions between 1612 and 1685.

Costa's poem is preceded by brief explanations of the allegorical meanings of the four cantos, which are titled "Il bagno" (The Bath), "Il martirio" (The Martyrdom), "Il tempio" (The Temple), and "Il sepolcro" (The Sepulcher). The flames of the bath represent lasciviousness, the art of the devil, who acts through human beings such as Cecilia's persecutor; the saint's failed beheading symbolizes the immortality of the soul; Cecilia's house is a temple, because the soul of a virgin is heaven's temple; and the sepulcher stands for the eternal peace of the just. Costa inserts into the poem a glorification of Maffeo Barberini, who had become Pope Urban VIII in 1623 and died on 29 July 1644, in the form of a prophecy tied to the name of Pope Urban I, who consoles Cecilia in her last hour. The chaos created by the infernal forces in the bath scene are a Baroque bravura of descriptions of heat and flames. The eulogy of Cecilia pronounced by her husband includes an allusion to Maderno's statue: he calls the saint's neck, which had been struck three times by the sword, whiter than Parthian marble. He concludes with the theme, dear to Baroque poets, that all must end; nothing lasts, not even for powerful men, because

> tutto è un'ombra di mortal pensiero,
> un inganno, ch' ai cor danni produce.
> Passa ogni sol più chiaro in dì più nero,
> e la felicità miserie adduce. . . .
>
> (everything is but a shadow of mortal thought,
> a deception, that causes damage to the hearts.
> The brightest of suns yields to the darkest of days,
> and happiness leads to misery. . . .)

Costa obtained a temporary position as a singer at the court of Duchess Christine of Savoy in Turin in early 1645; she was back in Rome by August. In 1646 she was invited to Paris with a group of musicians in the service of Cardinal Antonio Barberini. There she obtained the protection of the prime minister, Cardinal Jules Mazarin, who helped her to publish three books in 1647: two volumes of poems, *La selva di Diana* (Diana's Forest) and *La tromba di Parnaso* (The Trumpet of Parnassus), and *Festa reale per balletto a cavallo* (Royal Pageantry, Ballet on Horseback), a complex allegorical pageant in which Discord yields to Peace against the background of three teams of ten knights on horseback accompanied by their standard-bearers. Although the published version was dedicated to Mazarin in the vain hope of having the pageant performed in Paris, it was originally intended for the Tuscan court: a manuscript preserved in Florence includes a dedication to Ferdinand II de' Medici dated 27 January 1640.

La selva di Diana, dedicated to Christine of Savoy, recalls Costa's stay in Turin in the poem "L'Alpi" (The Alps). That piece is followed by a series of poems praising ten ladies of the Roman nobility for whom Costa had given a recital. A sonnet describes the raindrops on a desolate day as tears to accompany those of a woman. A group of seven sonnets, one for each day of the week, expresses amorous passion. A sonnet addressed to a person who claimed that Costa did not write her own works replies that her century is one of laziness and vice, in which exceptions to the rule are not recognized. Her stay in Paris is recorded in stanzas about the honors she received for her singing from Louis XIII's widow, Queen Anne. The volume concludes with a lament about her 1647 departure from Rome.

La tromba di Parnaso consists of laudatory verses about Queen Anne, other members of the French court, visiting foreign noblemen, singers, and the composer Luigi Rossi, whose opera *L'Orfeo* (Orpheus) was performed in Paris in 1647. Costa sang the part of Juno, while her sister, Anna Francesca, was acclaimed as Eurydice.

Not much is known about Costa's life after 1647. Her three-act play in verse, *Gli amori della Luna* (1654, The Loves of the Moon Goddess), attests to a stay in Germany: it is dedicated to the dukes of Brunswick-Lüneburg, and Costa says that she has not written in Italian for four years, while living under a foreign sky. In the play Cupid makes the moon goddess Diana fall in love with the youth Endymion; but Endymion is conquered by Cupid's rival, Somnus, the god of sleep. Sense and Reason comment on the tension between the two opposing forces of love and sleep. In the end love triumphs, for Endymion's resistance to Cupid falls at daybreak. Although the story of Endymion had appeared in poetry during the Renaissance, Costa seems to have been the first Italian writer to use it in a play.

The last known document concerning Costa is a 4 May 1657 letter in which she implores Cardinal Mario Chigi, Pope Alexander VII's brother, for assistance. She describes herself as a widow in great need who is supporting two daughters; one is married to a Flemish captain who is fighting in a war on the island of Crete, and the other is single. The date of Costa's death is unknown.

While much of Margherita Costa's literary production holds only historical value as documentation of seventeenth-century taste and as a source of information about her contemporaries, some of her compositions deserve to be studied for their Baroque peculiarities, originality, and humor. The critic, literary historian, and poet Giovanni Mario Crescimbeni, who did not like the Baroque period, praised her in his *Dell'istoria della volgar poesia e Comentarj intorno alla medesima* (1702–1711, On the History of Vulgar Poetry and Comments on the Same) and said that her talent surpassed that of some of her contemporaries. Most critics, however, were more interested in her personal life than in her work, which they condemned for her self-deprecating dedications and sycophantic laudatory poems; they failed to see these defects as shortcomings of the literature of the time. In 1925 Dante Bianchi published the most detailed study of Costa, in which he reconstructs her life as far as possible and examines all of the autobiographical references in her poems; but he makes no effort to understand her literary production, dismissing it with a few negative remarks. A comprehensive analysis of Costa's style and themes in relation to those of her contemporaries has yet to be made.

References:

Alessandro Ademollo, *I primi fasti della musica italiana a Parigi (1645–1662)* (Milan: Ricordi, 1884), pp. 36–39;

Ademollo, *I teatri di Roma nel secolo decimosettimo* (Rome: Pasqualucci, 1888), pp. 9, 150;

Roberto Alonge, "Tensione tematica e tensione formale in alcune commedie del Seicento," *Studi secenteschi,* 12 (1971): 86–87;

Dante Bianchi, "Una cortigiana rimatrice del Seicento: Margherita Costa," *Rassegna critica della letteratura italiana,* 29 (1924): 1–31, 187–203; 30 (1925): 158–211;

Martino Capucci, "Costa, Margherita," in *Dizionario biografico degli Italiani,* volume 30, edited by Alberto M. Ghisalberti (Rome: Istituto della Enciclopedia italiana, 1984), pp. 232–234;

Giovanni Mario Crescimbeni, *Dell'istoria della volgar poesia e Comentarj intorno alla medesima,* volume 3 (Venice: Besegio, 1730), p. 202;

Benedetto Croce, *Nuovi saggi sulla letteratura italiana del Seicento* (Bori: Laterza, 1931), pp. 161;

Norman Demuth, *French Opera: Its Development to the Revolution* (Horsham, U.K.: Artemis Press, 1963), pp. 64–69;

Giacinto Gigli, *Diario romano (1608–1670),* edited by Giuseppe Ricciotti (Rome: Tumminelli, 1958), p. 242;

Letizia Panizza and Sharon Wood, eds., *A History of Women's Writing in Italy* (Cambridge: Cambridge University Press, 2000), pp. 49–50, 53, 139;

Marcella Sului, "'Il solito è sempre quello, l'insolito è più nuovo': *Li buffoni* e le prostitute di Margherita Costa fra tradizione e innovazione," *Forum Italicum,* 38, no. 2 (2004): 376–399.

Papers:

Manuscripts for Margherita Costa's *Cecilia martire, La tromba di Parnaso,* and some poems, as well as the letter to Cardinal Mario Chigi, are in the Vatican Library in Rome. A manuscript for her *Festa reale per balletto a cavallo* is in the National Library in Florence.

Francesco De Lemene

(19 February 1634 - 24 July 1704)

Glenn Palen Pierce
University of Missouri

BOOKS: *Della discendenza e nobiltà dei Maccaroni* (Modena, 1654);
Il giudizio di Paride (Lodi, 1666);
Il Narciso (Lodi, 1667);
La ninfa Apollo (Lodi, 1667);
L'Endimione (Lodi, 1668);
Dio: Sonetti e Hinni consagrati al vicedio Innocenzo undecimo, pontefice ottimo massimo (Milan: G. dall'Oglio & I. Rosati, 1684);
Rosario di Maria Vergine: Meditationi poetiche (Milan: Giuseppe Marelli, 1691);
Poesie diverse (Milan: Carlo G. Quinto, 1692)–includes *Dialogo pastorale;*
Giacobbe al fonte (Lodi, 1700);
La sposa Francesca (Lodi: Carlo Giuseppe Astorino Sevesi, 1709);
Sofronia e Olindo: Episodio della Gerusalemme liberata, edited by Cesare Vignati (Milan: C. Wilmant, 1852).

Editions and Collections: *La sposa Francesca: Commedia del Conte Francesco Lemene* (Lodi: Giovanni Pallavicini, 1818);
"Parnaso Italiano," in *Poesia del Seicento,* volume 7, edited by Carlo Muscetta and Pier Paolo Ferrante (Turin: Einaudi, 1964), pp. 905–913;
Opere di Gabriello Chiabrera e lirici del classicismo barocco, edited by Marcello Turchi (Turin: Unione Tipografico-Editrice Torinese, 1974), pp. 839–850;
La sposa Francesca, edited by Dante Isella (Turin: Einaudi, 1979);
Scherzi e favole per musica, edited by Maria Grazia Accorsi (Modena: Mucchi, 1992).

Francesco De Lemene has received critical attention primarily as a regional playwright from Lombardy who helped pave the way for theater reform in the eighteenth century. He was also a poet and practiced that profession long before he wrote the play for which he is most noted. He enjoyed the esteem of his contemporaries for a mock-heroic poem, pastoral dialogues, lyric and religious poetry, and librettos for musical plays.

De Lemene was born in Lodi on 19 February 1634 to Antonio De Lemene, a lawyer, and Apollonia De Lemene, née Garati. Both parents were members of the lower Lombard nobility. As a child he was instructed by the local literary figures Francesco Bovio and Gian Battista Scopa. Influenced by these mentors, at age twelve De Lemene wrote a poetic version of the romance *Guerin Meschino* (1473, Wretched Guerrino), by Andrea da Barberino (pseudonym of Andrea de' Mangiabotti), followed by an epic poem, "Lodi riedificata" (Lodi Rebuilt). Later, he studied rhetoric with the Jesuits in Novara and philosophy and theology with the Barnabite Brothers in Lodi. He considered becoming a priest but instead studied law at the University of Pavia in 1652–1653 and the University of Bologna in 1654–1655. While in Bologna he composed a mock-epic poem, *Della discendenza e nobiltà dei Maccaroni* (1654, On the Origin and Nobility of the Maccaroni), about a Bergamasc and a Neapolitan who duel with forks over the country of Maccaroni. This effort earned him a mention in Francesco Redi's dithyramb *Bacco in Toscana* (1685, Bacchus in Tuscany):

> Io dico lui, che giovanetto scrisse
> Nella scorza de' faggi e degli allori
> Del paladino Macaron le risse.
>
> (I speak of the one who, as a youth wrote
> On beech and laurel bark
> Of the disputes of the Knight of Maccaroni.)

Also at this time De Lemene freely rendered in mock-heroic style and the Lodigiano dialect the Olindo and Sophronia episode of book 2 of Torquato Tasso's classic, *Gerusalemme liberata* (1581, Jerusalem Delivered; translated as *Godfrey of Bulloigne, or The Recoverie of Hierusalem,* 1594); it was not published until 1852.

De Lemene received his doctorate in civil and canon law from the University of Pavia in the autumn of 1655 and returned to Lodi, where he enjoyed the patronage of the duke of Mantua, Ferdinando Carlo IV Gonzaga-Nevers, who granted him the title of count.

He was a leader of Lodi's Accademia dei Coraggiosi (Academy of the Courageous). He organized concerts, balls, and theatrical performances at his palace; in the latter he served as playwright, director, and amateur actor. In 1664 he received an appointment as *decurione* (city councillor). He served as the official host at the court of Milan in Lodi. In 1665 he was chosen to recite the funeral oration of King Philip IV of Spain; the following year he was sent to Madrid to represent Lodi at the marriage of the sister of Philip's son, King Charles II, to Holy Roman Emperor Leopold I.

Much of De Lemene's early poetry is ponderous and employs themes inspired by more-talented poets such as Giambattista Marino, but it is also imbued with an elegant sensuality that can be seen in the sonnet "Lidia morsicata da l'api" (Lydia Stung by the Bees):

> Entra Lidia ne l'orto. Ite, volate
> a quell labbro, a quel seno, api ingegnose.
> Per fabbricar dolcezze, ite, svenate
> di quel seno, di quel labbro, e gigli e rose.
> Da le rose del labbro ite, succiate
> Le porpore umidette e preziose.

> (Lydia enters the garden. Go, fly
> to that lip, to that breast, you clever bees.
> In order to fabricate your sweets, go, drain
> from that breast, from that lip, lilies and roses.
> From the roses of the lip go, suck
> the moist and precious blush.)

De Lemene wrote four libretti that were set to music by local composers: a drama for music, *Il giudizio di Paride* (1666, The Judgment of Paris), and the pastoral fables *Il Narciso* (1667, The Narcissus), *La ninfa Apollo* (1667, The Nymph Apollo), and *L'Endimione* (1668, Endymion). He also composed an opera, *Eliata,* on a Spanish historical subject in 1661 that was never published; *Baccanale,* a short dithyramb in honor of the former Queen Christina of Sweden to be sung at her academy in Rome during carnival; and *Dialogo pastorale* (Pastoral Dialogue), written for a garden festival of dance and published in 1692. In these pieces De Lemene moves away from the Baroque poetic style toward the more sober neoclassical style later promoted by the Arcadian Academy. As Walter Binni points out, while works of this kind have light themes and simple forms and can become repetitive and overly sweet, they have value as a poetry of detail, of small truths, and of a certain kind of life. In *Il Narciso,* for example, De Lemene introduces a Lombard character, Tulipano, as a comic alter ego of Narcissus. The final scene, in which the two nymphs who had been in love with Narcissus return to the men who love them, reveals a practical Lombard attitude to love.

In 1672 De Lemene moved to Milan, where Count Bartolomeo Arese had secured a two-year appointment for him as *oratore* (orator) for the city of Lodi the Milanese senate. He resigned from the position in 1673 and returned to the family palace in Lodi to dedicate himself to writing.

In 1680 De Lemene suffered a severe illness. For some years thereafter he composed only religious poetry. In 1684 he published *Dio: Sonetti e Hinni consagrati al vicedio Innocenzo undecimo, pontefice ottimo massimo* (God: Sonnets and Hymns Dedicated to the Vicar of Jesus Innocent XI, Supreme Pontiff), an attempt to put St. Thomas Aquinas's *Summa Theologica* (1265 or 1266–1273, Summary of Theology) into verse. When Charles II's wife, Maria Luisa, died in 1689, De Lemene was chosen to compose and deliver her eulogy. The Arcadian Academy was founded in Rome in 1690; De Lemene joined it, adopting the pastoral name Arezio Galeate. His *Rosario di Maria Vergine: Meditationi poetiche* (1691, Rosary of the Virgin Mary: Poetic Meditations) is a collection of canzonets, sonnets, and madrigals in which he recounts events of the Virgin's life and shows their enduring significance in the rituals of the church.

De Lemene wrote his final sacred cantata, *Giacobbe al fonte* (1700, Jacob at the Well), in 1694. That year his older brother, Alfonso, died; De Lemene was forced to resign from his post as *decuriore* of the city of Lodi and take over the administration of the family estate.

De Lemene helped to edit the final works of his friend Carlo Maria Maggi, which were written in the four years before the latter's death in 1699. The enterprise had a strong and immediate artistic effect on De Lemene: several episodes in his comedy in Lodigiano dialect, *La sposa Francesca* (The Wife Francesca), seem to have been inspired by Maggi's Milanese-dialect comedies. But De Lemene's play is a masterpiece, superior on all levels to Maggi's works; Dante Isella calls it "one of the most wonderful comedies of all Italian theater." Written at the end of the seventeenth century or the beginning of the eighteenth and published in 1709, it can be seen as a precursor of the plays of Carlo Goldoni in the eighteenth century; it is depicted, along with Maggi's comedies, among the books in Goldoni's library in the frontispiece to the first edition of Goldoni's comedies (1770). Well before the most famous historical novel in Italian literature, Alessandro Manzoni's *I Promessi Sposi* (1825–1827, The Betrothed; translated as *The Betrothed Lovers: A Milanese Tale of the XVIIth Century,* 1828), De Lemene, a member of the nobility with close ties to the Spanish court, gave the world a view of a Lombard peasantry made desperately poor by the misguided Spanish economic policies that had driven the formerly healthy silk and weaving industry to ruin. The plot is pure social realism; all of the action takes place in the streets and the piazza of Lodi and seems totally authentic. There are no stock characters; the peasants and aristocrats are believable as real individuals living in a rural Lombard town.

Francesca is the town busybody, aggressively determined to survive; her husband, missé Steven, is a perennially unemployed and abusive drunkard. They want to marry off their only child, Catelina, to Cecco, the not overly bright son of Madonna Lucia and missé Bassan, until the local nobleman Giulio pays attention to Catelina as a way to approach her childhood friend Chiara, a young noblewoman. Mistakenly believing that he is in love with Catelina, Francesca makes a series of excuses to postpone the official engagement of Catelina to Cecco.

The realism of the play is reinforced by the contrast between the Italian speech of the two noble characters, Giulio and Chiara, which is laced with mythological references and linguistic conceits, and the unadorned, gritty Lodigiano dialect of Cecco and Catelina:

Catelina: O Cecco, ho da parlat.
Cecco: Vegni da in piazza.
Catelina: Cosè m'het crompat?
Cecco: I ho crompat des nos,
Spartimele mò in du,
Cinq per mì, cinq per vu.
Catelina: Te me regali ben!
Cossa vot mò che fazza de cinq nos?

(Catelina: Oh Cecco, I must speak.
Cecco: I've just been in the piazza.
Catelina: What did you buy me?
Cecco: I bought some nuts,
Let's eat them between us,
Five for me, five for you.
Catelina: Some gift!
What am I supposed to do with five nuts?)

The economic disparity between the classes is made clear when this exchange is compared to a later one between Chiara and Giulio in which Chiara is unable to decide between one expensive cloth and another for her wedding gown. It is further underlined when Francesca tries to persuade Giulio to marry Catelina by listing the expenses of a traditional aristocratic wedding that he would thereby avoid: Dutch horses to pull the carriage, large staff to serve the guests, expensive clothes that will have to be imported for the countless changes of dress for both bride and groom, and jewels for the bride. That she describes these extravagances in dialect emphasizes the vast socio-economic chasm between the classes she and Giulio represent.

Further emphasizing the impossibility of someone in Francesca's situation ever experiencing the world she describes to Giulio is the final scene of act 2, in which she displays Catelina's pitifully scant dowry to Lucia, her daughter's prospective mother-in-law. Lucia reacts sarcastically to the squalid items in Catelina's hope chest, which Francesca is about to send off for appraisal:

Francesca: Guardè chì in prima.
Questi chì ien du paier de ninzoi.
Lucia: Du paier de ninzoi de fassa sgreza,
Longhi trì brazzi e de do fette e mezza.
Francesca: Che I cressen o che i calen,
I s'arran da stimà per quel che I valen.
Todì se trè fodrette.
Lucia: Ma parchè trè? Despaiere e desgiuste,
E ne metteghei giuste?
Francesca: Tal qual I ho crompe an mì ghe I ho mettude.
E mì i ho crompe al Mont in trè mettude.

Francesca: Look here first.
Here are two pairs of sheets.
Lucia: Two pairs in rough cloth,
Short and narrow.
Francesca: Big or little,
They'll be appraised for their worth.
Here, take these three pillowcases.
Lucia: But why three? Unmatched and in different colors,
Why not buy them identical?
Francesca: I bought them just as you see them there
In three trips to the pawnshop.)

Francesca becomes so angry at Lucia's belittling that she insults Lucia's family; Lucia returns the insult, calling Francesca's family a bunch of failed silkworm weavers, and the scene ends in a brawl between the two that dispels any remaining possibility of a marriage between Catelina and Cecco. His parents break off the engagement and marry him to a servant girl, Bernardina, who possesses a better dowry. Finally, missé Steven, on his way to have the objects in Catelina's hope chest appraised, instead sells them for money to buy a round of drinks for a few of his friends, leaving the family in even more abject poverty than before.

Francesco De Lemene died in Milan on 24 July 1704. A wealthy provincial nobleman who enjoyed both a vast network of literary connections and proximity to a peasant class that he carefully observed, he is a representative of a new and more diverse literary class that was emerging across Europe. He and many others like him deserve to be considered in their own right rather than as marginal offshoots of a primarily urban literary activity.

Letters:

Cesare Vignati, "Francesco De Lemene e il suo epistolario inedito," *Archivio storico lombardo,* 19 (1892).

Biographies:

Tommaso Ceva, *Memorie d'alcune virtù del Signor Conte Francesco De Lemene: Con alcune riflessioni sulle sue poesie* (Milan: Domenico Bellagatta, 1718);

Ludovico Antonio Muratori, "La vita di Francesco De Lemene," in *Raccolta delle opere minori di Ludovico Antonio Muratori,* 21 volumes, edited by Giuseppe Ponzelli (Naples: G. Ponzelli, 1757–1764), XVIII.

References:

Walter Binni, "La letteratura nell'epoca arcadico-razionalistica," in *Storia della letteratura italiana,* volume 6, edited by Emilio Cecchi and Natalino Sapegno (Milan: Garzanti, 1968), pp. 341–343, 350–351;

Franco Brevini, ed., *La poesia in dialetto,* volume 2 (Milan: Mondadori, 1999), pp. 1818–1835;

Carmine Jannaco and Martino Capucci, "La poesia melica e religiosa del Lemene" and "La sposa Francesca," in their *Storia letteraria d'Italia,* volume 5: *Il Seicento* (Milan: Vallardi, 1986), pp. 368–371;

Bruno Maier, "Francesco de Lemene," in *Dizionario critico della letteratura italiana,* volume 2 (Turin: Unione Tipografico-Editrice Torinese, 1986), pp. 553–556;

A. Ruschioni, "Francesco de Lemene, Poesie e teatro," *Archivio storico lodigiano,* 101, no. 43 (1982): 67;

Vittorio Saulino, *Francesco de Lemene nella vita e nelle opere* (Palermo: Emanuele Priulla, 1921).

Giovanni Delfino
(22 April 1617 - 19 July 1699)

Salvatore Bancheri
University of Toronto

BOOKS: *Parnaso: Contiene le due tragedie Cleopatra e Lucrezia* (Utrecht: Guglielmo Croon, 1730);

Le tragedie di Giovanni Delfino: Cioè La Cleopatra, La Lucrezia, Il Creso, Il Medoro; ora la prima volta alla sua vera lezione ridotte; e illustrate col Dialogo apologetico dell'autore, non più stampato (Padua: Giuseppe Comino, 1733);

Della terra, edited by F. Anselmo (Messina: Peloritana, 1964);

Rime scelte, edited by Mario Costanzo, introduction by Rocco Paternostro (Rome: Bulzoni, 1995);

Nuove rime scelte, edited by Paternostro and Mauro Sarnelli (Rome: Bulzoni, 1999).

Editions and Collections: *Tragedie del Cardinale Giovanni Delfino: Con Dialogo sopra di esse* (Rome: Giuseppe Maria Salvioni, 1733);

Cleopatra, in *La tragedia classica dalle origini al Maffei,* edited by Giammaria Gasparini (Turin: Unione Tipografico-Editrice Torinese, 1976), pp. 741–786;

La Cleopatra, edited by Mauro Sarnelli (Rome: Quid, 1994).

OTHER: *La Cleopatra del Cardinal Delfino non più stampata,* in *Teatro italiano; o sia, Scelta di tragedie per uso della scena: Premessa un'istoria del teatro, e difesa di esso,* volume 3, edited by Scipione Maffei (Verona: J. Vallarsi, 1725), pp. 291–376;

"Della creazione," "Dell'anima," "Degli atomi," "Dell'astronomia," "Delle meteore," and "Della chimica," in *Miscellanea di varie operette,* volume 1 (Venice: G. M. Lazzaroni, 1740), pp. 4–160.

As a writer of tragedies Cardinal Giovanni Delfino holds a place in histories of Italian literature of the seicento alongside the better-known Carlo de' Dottori and Federico Della Valle. His tragedies, with their noble and sententious tone and their heartfelt pessimism, contributed to the demise of the lightheartedness inherited from sixteenth-century theater. Delfino also wrote poetry and philosophical and scientific dialogues.

Delfino was born in Venice on 22 April 1617 to Nicolò di Piero Delfino, a high-ranking military officer, and Elisabetta di Angelo Delfino, née Priuli. His parents were members of two of the wealthiest and most powerful families of Venice. In 1619 they took him to Rome to live with his great-uncle and namesake Cardinal Giovanni Delfino, who promised him to the priesthood to assure him of an ecclesiastical pension. In 1621 he returned to Venice, where he received a classical and scientific education with a solid preparation in Greek and Latin. While a student at the University of Padua he wrote love poems in the style of Gabriello Chiabrera. After receiving his doctorate in *utroque iure* (civil and canon law), he decided against an ecclesiastical career so that he could care for his younger brothers and the family estate during his father's long absences on military missions.

In 1638 Delfino killed his rival in love, a distant cousin named Bernardo Delfino, in self-defense. He was tried before the Consiglio dei Dieci (Council of the Ten) and declared innocent as a result of the intervention of the victim's brother, the powerful Lorenzo Delfino.

In 1640, after reading the poet Fulvio Testi's tragedy *L'isola di Alcina* (1636, The Island of Alcina), which was based on Ludovico Ariosto's *Orlando furioso* (1516, The Frenzy of Orlando; translated as *Orlando Furioso in English Heroical Verse,* 1591), Delfino decided to experiment with drama and chose the story of Medoro from Ariosto's poem. In 1642 he became a senator and had to renounce his ecclesiastical pension. He completed *Il Medoro,* a pastoral fable in three acts, in 1645. He was made senator for life in 1650 and was considered as a candidate for doge. In 1651 he declined an appointment as ambassador to France because he believed that he could serve his family better by remaining at home: his father was in debt, and two of his brothers were serving in the war against the Turks.

In 1656 Delfino abandoned his political career to become a bishop and coadjutor to the patriarch of Aquileia, Girolamo Gardenico. At that time, as he

123

wrote to his cousin, the poet Ciro di Pers, he destroyed the love poems he had composed during his university years in Padua. What is left of Delfino's poetic output are his later poems, comprising sixty-two heroic odes, six of them in quatrains; six sonnets; one short poem; and a chorus. Delfino refused to publish his poems, but he allowed them to be read in manuscript form in the major European courts and prepared bound volumes for writers and intellectuals who requested them. Delfino documents this practice in a poem addressed to Pers: what motivates him to write poetry, he says, is not "brama di gloria o van desio di lode" (longing for fame or a vain desire of glory) but a wish to fight idleness. For many years, he continues, he filled his papers with rhymes only for his own pleasure; later he shared them with a few friends, after swearing them to silence, and he does not know how one of his humble poems found its way to the kingdom of Austria.

In December 1657 Delfino succeeded Gardenico as patriarch. In 1659 he reworked *Il Medoro* as a tragedy in which, in compliance with Counter-Reformation poetics, he respects moral as well as social decorum by having Angelica admit to being in love with Medoro only after she learns that he has royal blood. One of the main themes is the common post-Tridentine conflict between reason of state and love or personal ethics; in act 3, scene 1 the shepherd Nicandro addresses the transience of earthly power:

Quei che paion' a voi ricchi diletti,
Sono pompose pene,
Affanni maestosi,
Che turbano i riposi.
Gioja dell'alma è l'alma; ella a se stessa
Può formar scettri, e stabilir corone.

(What you take as delightful pleasures,
Are but pompous torments,
Majestic worries,
That trouble sleep.
Joy of the soul is the soul itself; it
Can craft for itself scepters and crowns.)

The same theme is expressed in the shepherds' chorus in act 4:

Un giorno, un'ora rende
L'infelice contento;
Che il mondo nostro vacillante, e infermo
Non ha stabil fortuna, o stato fermo.

(One day, one hour renders
The unhappy merry;
Our dithering and ailing world
Has not unwavering fortune nor a state of stability.)

After reading *Il Medoro*, Pers realized that Delfino had a talent for tragedy and encouraged him to continue to apply himself to the genre but to use historical subjects. He also suggested that Delfino not use rhyme. Delfino followed Pers's advice in his other three tragedies: *La Lucrezia, La Cleopatra,* and *Il Creso* (Croesus). Delfino's tragedies, like most such works at the beginning of the seventeenth century, were written mainly to be read, not to be performed.

La Lucrezia praises the honor and virtue of the Roman heroine Lucrezia, who killed herself after being violated by Sextus, the son of the tyrant Tarquinius Superbus. In his "Dialogo sopra le tragedie" (1733, Dialogue on Tragedies) Delfino says that he chose the topic in part because it gave him the opportunity to refer to the martyrdom of Lucrezia Dondi, the wife of the marquis Pio Enea degli Obizzi, who was killed near Padua in 1654 because she refused to dishonor the conjugal bed. In act 1, scene 2 the *nutrice* (nurse) suggests that she and Lucrezia play a debating game in which she will defend love and Lucrezia will defend honor. Honor is the clear winner as Lucrezia points out that beauty and love will fade as a flower but that the soul has its own beauties, which are stable and not ephemeral.

In act 1, scene 5, Tarquinius Superbus summarizes the art of governing for his adviser, Curzio:

È giusto ciò che giova,
È ingiusto ciò che nuoce:
Ed è virtù regnare;
Nè van distinti i mezzi;
Che l'opre loda il fine.

(What is useful is just,
What is harmful is unjust;
It is a virtue to reign;
And one cannot be concerned about means;
Because the end justifies the means.)

In act 4, scene 1, one finds the typical Baroque metaphor of the world as a theater as Lucrezia says:

Teatro è il basso mondo,
E di tragici eventi è tutto carco,
E nelle scene sue crudeli, e orrende
Gli uomini son gli attori.

(The mortal world is a theater,
Brimful of tragic events;
And in its cruel and horrendous scenes,
Human beings are the actors.)

The tragedy ends with the fall of the Tarquin dynasty.

Many critics consider *La Cleopatra* the best of Delfino's tragedies; it was certainly his most successful one. The main theme of the play is the conflict between

Title page for a collection of Giovanni Delfino's plays (University of Turin)

love and "reason of state." Augustus is in love with Cleopatra and wants to make her his queen, but reason of state dictates that he not marry her but bring her to Rome as a prisoner. He writes a letter to the Roman Senate stating that he had to promise Cleopatra "speranze per catene" ([false] hope [of marriage] in order to [bring her to Rome] in chains). By chance, Cleopatra reads the letter, believes that she has been deceived, and commits suicide. As she dies, she says that her death is a just punishment for being unfaithful to Marc Antony. In contrast to other dramatic representations of the main characters, Delfino's Cleopatra is not a cunning and frivolous woman who uses her beauty and feminine flattery to save her kingdom and her position. Instead, she is faithful to the concept of the perfect queen even at the cost of her life, while Augustus is a magnanimous sovereign who always keeps in mind the duties of his office. The plot of *La Cleopatra* is simple and linear, but Emilio Bertana notes that the play could be considered a "tragedia implessa" (complex tragedy) because of the complicated psychological makeup of Cleopatra and Augustus.

La Cleopatra includes many philosophical digressions. For example, in act 1, scene 1 the ghost of Aeneas predicts the future of the Roman people; in act 2, scene 6 Acoreo explains the religion and philosophy of the Egyptians to Agrippa; and in act 3, scene 3 he describes death as a passage from one form of life to another: "la morte altro non è, che mutar vita" (death is just a change of life). Throughout these digressions runs the sense that destiny toys with the human mind, making people believe that they, not it, are to blame for the evil surrounding them and for their own unhappiness.

Destiny is the main theme of *Il Creso*, Delfino's favorite tragedy. The play recounts the story of Croesus, the legendarily wealthy king of Lydia, who is about to lose his kingdom to the Persian king, Cyrus. Like *La Cleopatra, Il Creso* presents many digressions. In act 4, scene 1 the sage Solon, close to death, speculates that the soul is composed of air, water, and fire but is primarily made of light. In the following scene, as the Persians ransack the city of Sardi, he consoles Queen Jade with the thought that blind Fortune can take away only what belongs to her; she cannot take away the queen's virtue. Delfino's digressions are not intrusions but are integral to what he conceived of as the exhortative function of tragedy.

In the "Dialogo sopra le tragedie" three men of letters–Pers, Niccolò Sagredo, and Bartolomeo Varisano Grimaldi–meet in a garden to discuss Delfino's four tragedies. They agree that tragedies based on historical accounts are preferable to purely invented plots but that it is acceptable to invent, as in *La Cleopatra,* as long as history is not violated. Unity of place is strictly observed in *La Cleopatra* but not in the other tragedies. Unity of time is essential but should not be so rigorously adhered to that an excellent story is distorted. Blank verse maintains the gravity required by tragedy better than rhymed verse does; Delfino uses unrhymed hendecasyllables and septenaries (verses of seven metrical feet) in his tragedies. A playwright should not be afraid to introduce scientific and philosophical disquisitions into a tragedy, as long as they blend in naturally and the subject matter is singular and noble. Agnition (an important acknowledgment or recognition by a character) is an essential element of a tragedy because it promotes introspection and imparts a moral lesson; such incidents occur twice in *Il Creso*. The most important characteristic of tragedies is their moral value. Thus, *La Lucrezia* does not end, as one would expect, with the death of the protagonist but with the fall of the Tarquins, showing that God punishes tyranny and that destiny is the enemy of the conceited. Similarly, Delfino's introduction in *Il Medoro* of Artabano's order to kill the infant Medoro is morally justified because it shows the unhappiness and pain caused by wickedness. An author who does not want to be useful to living and future generations deserves punishment. Grimaldi says that *Il Creso* is equal to Delfino's other tragedies as far as "costume" (propriety) and "sentenza" (style) are concerned but is "superiore, e non poco, essendo una tessitura di più fila che si congiungono insieme in modo, che la diversità delle azioni non può essere ragionevolmente opposta" (superior, and by far, because it comprises many threads that are so closely linked that one cannot justly say that the actions are different). The presence of more than one plot, Sagredo explains, is acceptable as long as the subplots are logically and appropriately tied to the main story and respect the unity of time, and "quel poeta che saprà inserire propriamente in una stessa Tragedia più azioni, meriterà più lode" (the poet who is able to appropriately use in the same tragedy more than one action will deserve more praise).

In addition to the "Dialogo sopra le tragedie," Delfino wrote sixteen dialogues on philosophical and scientific topics. "Della creazione" (On Creation), "Dell'anima" (On the Soul), "Degli atomi" (On Atoms), "Dell'astronomia" (On Astronomy), "Delle meteore" (On Meteors), and "Della chimica" (On Chemistry) are in verse, in hendecasyllables and septenaries; "Delle sette dei filosofi" (On the Sects of Philosophers), "Del mondo in universale" (On the World in General), "Dei principii" (On Principles), "Della generazione" (On Generation), "Dell'anima," "Dei sensi" (On the Senses), "Della terra" (On the Earth), "Delle meteore," "Dell'astronomia," and "Di Dio e della provvidènza" (Of God and Providence) are in prose. Because of these dialogues, at the end of the eighteenth century Carlo Gastone della Torre di Rezzonico named Delfino as one of the few writers who were able to give a poetic voice to the authority of science.

Delfino became a cardinal in 1667; the appointment ended his literary pursuits, as he deemed creative activity inconsistent with his new role as prince of the church. Shortly thereafter, he was elected a member of the prestigious Florentine philological institution, the Accademia della Crusca (Academy of the Sifters). In 1674 he sent a copy of *Il Medoro* to Pierre Corneille at the French playwright's request. In 1691 he participated in his fifth conclave for the election of a new pope and was among the *papabili* (cardinals considered worthy of being pope). He died in Venice on 19 July 1699.

In his day Giovanni Delfino was known primarily as a tragedian; one of the main reasons for the success of his tragedies was their didactic aspect. According to Benedetto Croce, Delfino's tragedies have a different tone than the Baroque sensual literature of the time; *La Cleopatra,* in particular, is filled with "figurazioni piene di nobiltà" (concepts full of nobility) and "alti pensièri" (noble thoughts). Giovanni Getto considers him the best of the minor writers of tragedies of the seventeenth century. According to Claudio Varese, in his tragedies Delfino explored the moral and political issues of his time in clear and logical discussions conducted in a classic language.

Letters:

Mauro Sarnelli, "Meravigliosa chiarezza,' 'raccomandazioni,' e 'mal di pietra': Il carteggio Delfino-Pers," *Studi secenteschi,* 37 (1996): 225–315.

Biography:

Gino Benzoni, "Dolfin, Giovanni," in *Dizionario biografico degli Italiani,* volume 40 (Rome: Istituto della Enciclopedia Italiana, 1991), pp. 532–542.

References:

Franca Angelini, "Poesia e letteratura tragica," in *La letteratura italiana storia e testi,* volume 5/2: *Il Seicento: La nuova scienza e la crisi del Barocco,* edited by Carlo Muscetta (Rome & Bari: Laterza, 1974), pp. 137–222;

Guido Baldassarri, "'Acutezza' e 'Ingegno': Teoria e pratica del gusto barocco," in *Storia della cultura veneta,* volume 4/1: *Il Seicento,* edited by Girolamo Arnaldi and Manlio Pastore Stocchi (Vicenza: Neri Pozza, 1983), pp. 223–247;

Antonio Belloni, *Il Seicento* (Milan: Vallardi, 1929), pp. 381–382, 386–387;

Emilio Bertana, *La tragedia* (Milan: Vallardi, 1905), pp. 152–156;

Benedetto Croce, *Storia dell'età barocca in Italia* (Rome & Bari: Laterza, 1967), pp. 84–85, 369, 373–377;

Franco Croce, "Giovanni Delfino," *La rassegna della letteratura italiana,* 67, no. 2 (1963): 262–270;

Giammaria Gasparini, Introduction to *La tragedia classica dalle origini al Maffei,* edited by Gasparini (Turin: Unione Tipografico-Editrice Torinese, 1976), pp. 741–786;

Giovanni Getto, *Barocco in prosa e poesia* (Milan: Rizzoli, 1969), pp. 309–312;

Gianvincenzo Gravina, *Scritti critici e teorici,* edited by Amedeo Quondam (Rome & Bari: Laterza, 1973), pp. 192–193, 636–639;

Carmine Jannaco and Martino Capucci, *Il Seicento* (Milan: Vallardi, 1966), pp. 342, 380;

Nicola Mangini, "La tragedia e la commedia," in *Storia della cultura veneta,* pp. 297–326;

Pier Jacopo Martello, *Scritti critici e satirici,* edited by Hannibal S. Noce (Rome & Bari: Laterza, 1963), p. 172;

Francesco Tateo, "La letteratura della Controriforma," in *Storia della letteratura Italiana,* volume 5, edited by Enrico Malato (Rome: Salerno, 1997), pp. 111–224;

Carlo Castone della Torre di Rezzonico, *Ragionamento su la volgar poesia* in *Opere poetiche,* edited by Elvio Guagnini (Ravenna: Longo, 1977), pp 331–410;

Claudio Varese, "Teatro," in *Storia della letteratura italiana,* volume 5: *Il Seicento,* edited by Emilio Cecchi and Natalino Sapegno (Milan: Garzanti, 1970), pp. 521–618.

Papers:

Manuscripts for Giovanni Delfino's *La Cleopatra* and *Il Creso* are at the University of Chicago Library. Manuscripts for his poems are at the Biblioteca Arcivescovile in Udine. Many of his letters are at the Biblioteca Comunale Vincenzo Joppi in Udine.

Federico Della Valle
(circa 1560 – 1628)

Laura Sanguineti White
Rutgers University

BOOKS: *Orazione nelle esequie di Filippo terzo re potentissimo di Spagna* (Milan, 1621);

Orazione di Federico Della Valle nelle esequie della eccellentissima Signora Duchessa di Feria all'Eccellentissimo Signore Don Gonzalo di Cordova, Luogotenente generale di Sua Maestà nel governo di Milano (Milan, 1623);

Judit et Esther (Milan: Heredi di Melchior Malatesta, 1627);

La reina di Scotia (Milan: Heredi di Melchior Malatesta, 1628);

Adelonda di Frigia (Turin: Cavalleris, 1629);

Tragedie, edited by Carlo Filosa (Bari: Laterza, 1939);

Tutte le opere, edited by Pietro Cazzani (Milan: Mondadori, 1955).

Editions and Collections: *La reina di Scotia,* edited by Benedetto Croce (Bologna: Zanichelli, 1930);

Teatro del Seicento, edited by Luigi Fassò (Milan & Naples: Ricciardi, 1956);

Teatro tragico italiano, edited by Federico Doglio (Bologna: Guanda, 1960);

Judit, edited by Gigi Livio (Turin: Einaudi, 1963);

Judit, edited by Andrea Gareffi (Rome: Bulzoni, 1978);

Tragedie, edited by Gareffi (Milan: Mursia, 1988);

Opere, edited by Maria Gabriella Stassi (Turin: Unione Tipografico-Editrice Torinese, 1995);

Opere, 2 volumes, edited by Matteo Durante (Messina: Sicania, 2000, 2005).

PLAY PRODUCTION: *Adelonda di Frigia,* music by Pietro Veccoli, Turin, 25 November 1595.

OTHER: "Epitalamio per la venuta dell' Infanta Caterina Sposa di Carlo Emanuele," in *Scelta di Rime di diversi moderni autori non più stampate* (Genoa: Gerolamo Bartoli, 1591).

Federico Della Valle is the author of three important tragedies, a tragicomedy, and minor works occasioned by his service at the court of Savoy during the late sixteenth and early seventeenth centuries, a time of great religious turmoil and political change in western Europe. After the rediscovery of Della Valle's tragic theater in 1929, a new phase of scholarship began with the appearance of modern critical editions of the texts, whose original editions had been reduced to a few copies, and the inclusion of selections from them in standard anthologies of Italian dramatic literature. Evidence of the continuing interest in his relatively small corpus is a vast output of critical studies. Della Valle's tragedies have come to be recognized as high-quality poetic expressions of a tragic vision of the human condition, as well as of an unwavering belief in divine justice and God's goodness.

Della Valle was born in Asti around 1560. His literary activity seems to have begun with the composition of an epithalamium and a madrigal to celebrate the arrival in Turin in 1585 of the infanta Caterina, the daughter of King Philip II of Spain and bride of Duke Carlo Emanuele I of Savoy. In 1586 he entered Caterina's service as *furiere maggiore della cavallerizza* (administrator of cavalry), a position of great responsibility and little remuneration that he held until the duchess's death in 1597.

In 1593 Della Valle composed "Ragionamento fatto nella raunanza degli stati della Francia per l'elezione di un Re" (Debate Held at the Gathering of the States of France for the Election of a King), in which he supported, albeit cautiously, the duke's candidacy for the French throne after the violent death of Henry III, the last descendant of the Valois. But the text goes beyond the dutiful support of a prince by a courtier: it also expresses a deeply felt pacifism and compassion for those who suffer from war, and it stresses the responsibilities of rulers. These concerns became central themes in his major works. During the last decade of the sixteenth century Della Valle also composed a divertimento, "Ordine de la mascarata de li quattro elementi" (Order of the Pageant of the Four Elements), in honor of Carlo Emanuele; the text consisted of poems recited by allegorical characters. The only manuscript was lost in a fire at the National University Library in Turin in 1904.

After a failed attempt at an epic poem on Amedeo VI, a fourteenth-century count of Savoy, Della Valle wrote a tragicomedy, *Adelonda di Frigia* (1629), that was commissioned by Carlo Emanuele I for the visit to Turin of Archduke Albert of Austria. Influences on the tragicomedy that have been identified include Euripides' *Iphigenia in Tauris* (circa 414 B.C.), Torquato Tasso's *Aminta* (1573; translated as *Aminta Englisht,* 1628), Giovanni Botero's *Ragion di Stato* (1589, Reason of State; translated as "Practical Politics," 1949), and Battista Guarini's *Il pastor fido* (1590; translated as *Il pastor fido; or The Faithful Shepherd,* 1602).

Adelonda, the daughter of the king of Frigia, was promised in marriage to the prince of Pontus, Mirmirano. While voyaging to join him, she is shipwrecked on the island of the Amazons. There she is made priestess of the temple of the idol to whom all men who venture onto the island are to be sacrificed. Searching for Adelonda, Mirmirano arrives at the island; he is captured and handed over to Adelonda to be sacrificed. She recognizes him, and the two escape. As they race to Mirmirano's ship on the shore, Antiope, the Amazon queen, is prevented from ordering their capture by the idol itself, which tells the queen to let Adelonda and Mirmirano go on their way. The idol also demands that the queen repeal the law requiring human sacrifice and open her heart to love, in accordance with the teaching of Nature. The play was staged, with intermezzi by the author and music by Pietro Veccoli, on 25 November 1595. It was well received but was never polished for publication by the author; it was published posthumously in 1629 by Della Valle's nephew, Federico Parona. Only four copies of this edition are known to exist: in the Centro Alfieriano in Asti, the Braidense Library in Milan, the Ambrosiana Library in Milan, and the National Library in Turin.

Della Valle's three tragedies were composed between 1591 and 1600. Only the first, *La reina di Scotia* (1628, The Queen of Scotland), can be precisely dated: a manuscript in Bergamo is dated January 1591 and dedicated to the marchioness Vittoria Solara, who apparently encouraged the composition. Another manuscript, in Naples, is dated January 1595 and dedicated to Ranuccio Farnes, the duke of Parma and Piacenza. Most scholars agree that *Esther* was the second play, with *Judit* (Judith), the most stylistically and structurally mature of the three, coming last.

Della Valle's tragedies are best understood against the literary and cultural background of his time. Tragic works at the end of the sixteenth century and in the seventeenth century were composed in the classical style of Sophocles and Euripides, which included division into five acts, the presence of a chorus, and observation of the unities of space, time, and action; the sense of horror and gloom in the themes and atmosphere was based on the works of Seneca. The tragedies were written for an audience of readers rather than of spectators and were characterized by a moralistic spirit and a religious outlook. The themes were taken from classical history, mythology, and the Bible but also from contemporary political events and religious controversies.

La reina di Scotia portrays the execution in 1587 of Mary Queen of Scots, an event that shocked all of Europe, especially the Catholics, and generated several literary works. In the dedication to his text Della Valle expresses the conviction that he has composed an original work on a subject not yet dealt with in Italy; he calls his tragedy a "poema singolarissimo" (most unique poem). Possible sources are Adam Blackwood's *Martyre de Marie Stuart* (1587, Martyrdom of Mary Stuart) and Antonio de Herrera's *Historia de lo sucedido en Escocia en los cuarenta y cuatro anos que vivió Maria Estuarda* (1589, History of the Events that Took Place in Scotland during the Forty-four Years of the Life of Mary Stuart); but since the details of Mary's last hours in those works do not correspond to those in Della Valle's text, Luigi Fassò suggests in the introduction to his *Teatro del Seicento* (1956, Theater of the Seicento) that other reports that were circulating in large numbers among Catholics could also have been sources for the dramatist.

Presented as a martyr for her Catholic faith and a victim of tyrannical power, the once beautiful and triumphant Mary Stuart is aged and weakened by twenty years of imprisonment and humiliation. For Della Valle, Mary embodies the legitimate government in opposition to Elizabeth—called Isabella in the play—who never appears but is represented by her arrogant ministers or by the harsh descriptions of her by other characters. Mary is surrounded by a loyal little court, consisting of her *cameriera* (maid), *maggiordomo* (majordomo), and *damigelle* (maids-in-waiting). The prologue is delivered by the *ombra* (ghost) of her first husband, Francis II, the king of France, who expresses sorrow for her suffering. Mary despairs of ever being freed and finds her only solace in prayer, but the *cameriera* encourages her to hope for a better future. A servant informs the prisoner that an emissary from Isabella has come to talk to her, perhaps bearing good news. The servant later relates his encounter with Mary to the *damigelle,* describing with admiration her piety, generosity, and gracious demeanor. The queen joins her female companions in hoping for freedom and reinstatement in their kingdom, but disappointment follows because of the conditions imposed by Isabella's emissary, Beel: Mary must renounce her title, abdicate in favor of her son, reject Catholicism, and introduce the Lutheran faith into Scotland. After the queen proudly rejects the demands,

Beel reveals that whatever her answer might have been, her destiny was already decided: Isabella's ministers bear the letter ordering her immediate execution. Mary bids farewell to her *cameriera* and *damigelle*:

> O figlie, a Dio,
> A rivederci altrove,
> In più libera stanza e più serena!
> A rivederci in Cielo!
>
> (O my daughters, adieu,
> We will meet again somewhere else
> In a freer and more serene place!
> I will see you again in heaven!)

In the last two acts the queen gradually acquires the dimensions of quasi sainthood. In an analogy to Christ's ascent to Golgotha, Della Valle describes her death as a journey to martyrdom as she becomes progressively detached from earthly passions and rises to a more intense spirituality. Escorted by the *maggiordomo* and with a crucifix held tightly to her chest, she accepts her execution in a spirit of forgiveness. The decapitation is described in realistic detail by the chorus.

The protagonists of Della Valle's other two tragedies are strong but sensuous women who save their people from great danger. The title character of *Esther* is the Jewish wife of the Persian king Assuero (Xerxes). The play begins with a prologue by a *nube* (cloud) who announces that two connected events are to take place: the liberation of an entire population and the punishment of an individual. The first act opens with the lamentations of the chorus of Jews and their spiritual leader, Mardocheo (Mordecai), and their plea to Esther for help. The Jews are being persecuted by the arrogant and ambitious minister Aman (Haman), who has acquired enormous power at court. Aman, in turn, is pressured, on the one hand, by his even more ambitious wife, Zares (Zeresh), and, on the other hand, warned by his wise friend Dagan of the inconstancy of kings' favors. Esther risks death by appearing unsummoned before her husband, but her beauty and tears win over the king's heart. She invites Assuero and Aman to a banquet, at which she plans to plead the Jews' cause. Aman interprets the invitation as a sign of additional favor and becomes even more arrogant; he is convinced of his ability to dominate the monarch: "Egli è la ruota; io sono / la mano che l'aggira" (He is the wheel; I am / the hand that turns it). But just as he thinks he has reached the peak of his power, the predictions of his friend Dagan prove true. Asked by Assuero to devise a way to honor a faithful subject, Aman, convinced that he is the one to be honored, suggests that the person be dressed in regal attire, crowned, escorted, and paraded on the king's horse. To his bitter surprise, Aman discovers that Mardocheo, whom he considers his worst enemy, is the one to be honored, while Aman will be the escort chanting the Jew's praises. After this humiliation, at the banquet Esther informs the king of Aman's plotting against the Jews and reveals herself as one of them. Aman claims ignorance of the fact and begs for mercy; but Assuero condemns him, and Aman dies of the same torture he had planned for Mardocheo. In the midst of the exultation following the escape of her people from mortal danger, Esther shows pity and pleads for Aman's body to be returned to his family; this detail is a significant departure from the biblical source. The tragedy ends with a lament by Zares, who has been condemned to exile with her children, and a reminder by the chorus of the mutability of the human condition and the consequent need for humility.

Judit begins with a prologue by an angel, after which a chorus of Assyrian soldiers comments on the reality of war as experienced by those who fight it and suffer from it:

> O guerra, guerra . . .
> Porti indistinti i tempi
> a le vigilie, ai sonni
> sonni rotti, tremanti,
> vigilie piene di ferite e piaghe.
> Vegghiando, fiera morte hai sempre avanti,
> e se dormi, ti cova in su le spalle.
>
> (O war, o war . . .
> you do not distinguish
> the waking from the sleeping time,
> broken, fearful sleep,
> vigils full of wounds and pains.
> Fearful death is always before you while awake,
> And hovers behind you while asleep.)

Judit and her servant, Abra, leave the city of Betulia (Bethulia), which is being besieged by the Assyrian general Holofernes. Judit asks the Assyrian captain for protection and finds shelter in the camp of the besiegers. Holofernes is strongly attracted by her beauty and royal demeanor, and his servant and adviser Vagao further incites his passion by evoking sensuous images of the Jewish noblewoman. Ignoring the advice of his chief commander and longtime companion in arms, Arimaspe, to remain focused on the siege of Betulia, Holofernes invites his captains to a sumptuous banquet as a prelude to an amorous encounter with Judit. In a scene that is not enacted onstage but is related with sarcasm by a servant, Judit intoxicates Holofernes with passion and wine; the two of them retire to his tent, where she beheads him. In the ensuing scene, the drunken captains return to their tent, staggering and disoriented, after the banquet. Judit and Abra take Holofernes's head to Betulia; the inhabitants of the city, galvanized by the sight, attack their besiegers. The Assyrian camp has been abandoned by the soldiers, who have gone to the spring to quench their thirst after seeing their captains quenching theirs with wine. The military structure and discipline of the besiegers are quickly undone: an immensely powerful army is defeated and in flight and a besieged, weakened population is victorious. The chorus of fleeing soldiers comments bitterly on the insecurity of life, the reversal of fortunes, and the suffering of all, including the innocent.

The three tragedies, in hendecasyllables and septenaries (verses of seven metrical feet), follow the classical model of the genre established in the Renaissance. At the same time, their morality and religiosity are typical of the Counter-Reformation spirit. The prologue of each text is presented by an evanescent nonhuman figure—a ghost, a cloud, and an angel—metaphors of the frailty of life and the comforting presence of the supernatural dimension. On the other hand, the structures of the tragedies present marked differences. For instance, in *La reina di Scotia* the tragic dialectic between two opposite forces is nonexistent: Mary is the absolute protagonist, at the center of the dramatic action, and her psychological features are analyzed in depth; the antagonist, Isabella, does not appear onstage but is merely evoked as the representative of an absolute oppressive power. In the other two tragedies protagonist and antagonist are both at the center of the action, and their natures and personalities are scrutinized equally. Paralleling this development, as Della Valle's understanding of courts and rulers became deeper, is an increasing pessimism about the possibility of a political system based on justice and aimed at the welfare of the subjects. The moral decline of the minister/courtier exemplifies this deepening pessimism: from the first tragedy to the third the character undergoes a transformation from an official with a certain political stature to an egotistically ambitious courtier and, finally, a procurer who actually holds the power and molds the desires of his ruler. These characters embody the consequences of political absolutism and the corrupting influence of power. Nevertheless, Della Valle has compassion for their human weaknesses: he condemns evil but humanizes the "villain," opening the possibility of redemption. In the biblical tragedies the female protagonists triumph, but the plays conclude with loss and defeat that also affect the innocent. Della Valle also depicts the universal fascination with beauty, the most elusive and frail of human possessions. This pessimistic existential vision is accepted with classical stoicism and Christian resignation. Tragedy, for Della Valle, is embedded in the human condition, and sudden reversals of fortune make life precarious. The only certainty lies in the supernatural world.

Title page for the first edition of two of Federico Della Valle's plays (University of Turin)

Della Valle's pictorial style and multiperspectival point of view is rooted in the portraiture tradition begun by Leonardo da Vinci. He uses the figurative and evocative power of language to create three-dimensional images and to convey chromatic and luminescent effects. His attention to physiognomy reflects the interest of his time in the discipline that can be seen in treatises such as Giovan Paolo Lomazzo's *Trattato dell'arte della pittura, scultura et architettura* (1584; translated as *A Tracte Containing the Arts of Curious Paintings, Carvings and Buildings,* 1598) and Giovan Battista Della Porta's *De Humana Physiognomonia* (1586, On Human Physiognomy). Andreina Griseri points to parallels between Della Valle and the contemporary art scene in Turin, especially the work of Francesco del Cairo.

Della Valle's presence in Turin is documented as late as 1601. His departure from the Piedmont capital took place before 1608; according to Cesare Greppi, he left in 1604. Judging from the identities of the people for whom his later funeral orations were written, Luigi

Firpo and Carlo Filosa suggest that he spent time in Spain before going to Milan. The first sign of his literary activity in Milan is *Orazione nelle esequie di Filippo terzo re potentissimo di Spagna* (1621, Funeral Oration for the Most Powerful Philip III King of Spain). Two years later he published *Orazione di Federico Della Valle nelle esequie della eccellentissima Signora Duchessa di Feria all'Eccellentissimo Signore Don Gonzalo di Cordova, Luogotenente generale di Sua Maestà nel governo di Milano* (Funeral Oration by Federico Della Valle for the Most Excellent Lady the Duchess of Feria Offered to the Most Excellent Don Gonzalo of Cordova, Lord Lieutenant General of His Majesty in the Government of Milan). He appears to have held some official position in Milan, since he delivered the two orations himself.

Della Valle extensively revised *La reina di Scotia* before publishing all three tragedies in two volumes. The first volume, dated 1627, comprises *Judit* and *Esther*; the second, dated 1628 and dedicated to the Virgin Mary and Pope Urban VIII, consists of *La reina di Scotia*. Only three copies of the first volume are known to exist: one is in the Vatican Library, the second in Turin's National Library, and the third in the University Library of Bologna. Only two copies of the second volume are known to exist, both at the Vatican Library. A fourth copy of the first volume and a third copy of the second were at the Ambrosiana Library in Milan; they were destroyed during the bombing of the city in 1943. This edition does not divide the texts into acts and scenes as in the manuscripts; Pietro Cazzani suggests that by the time of publication Della Valle no longer considered any staging of the tragedies possible. The partition into acts and scenes was reinstated by modern editors. The original manuscript for *Judit* was burned in the 1904 fire at the National Library in Turin. Della Valle died in Milan in 1628.

Della Valle was barely known by his contemporaries, merely mentioned in catalogues and histories of poetry in the seventeenth and eighteenth centuries, and then ignored until he was rediscovered in 1929 by Benedetto Croce, who stressed the lyrical quality and the religious and political inspiration of his dramas. In 1934 Attilio Momigliano considered the deep melancholy and somber meditative quality of his writing and the evasive atmosphere that especially permeates *Judit*, his most mature tragedy. Croce and Momigliano, however, saw Della Valle's work as tainted by Baroque taste, which they viewed as artificial and bizarre. Nevertheless, the comments of the two authoritative critics helped spark a revival of interest in the author. In 1948 Giuseppe Giacalone identified deep religiosity as the main characteristic of Della Valle's tragedies; he compared the dark and disturbing atmosphere of the banquet scene in *Judit* with the classical theater of Aeschylus. In 1950 Gaetano Trombatore drew comparisons with Tasso's poetry and stressed Della Valle's dramatic perception of life and fatalistic view of religion.

In the second half of the twentieth century scholarly concern with the definition of such styles as Mannerism and the Baroque in art and literature caused interest in Della Valle's work to reach an apex. Like Croce, Bruno Baldis (1952), Ferruccio Ulivi (1952), and Mario Terzera (1954) stressed religious inspiration as the nucleus of Della Valle's theater. Fassò (1956) considered *Esther* and *Judit* Della Valle's most "performable" plays, while *La reina di Scotia* is more "readable." In 1954 Cazzani published the first complete edition of Della Valle's works, with an introduction that offered biographical data and critical analyses of the texts. He drew linguistic and metric parallels between Della Valle and Tasso and between Della Valle and Giacomo Leopardi; he also described two performances of *La reina di Scotia*, one of them directed by Cazzani himself. Concluding that Della Valle's vision of politics and human life was rooted in "darkness and sorrow," Cazzani viewed him as a representative figure of the Counter-Reformation rather than of the seicento. On the other hand, Giovanni Getto (1958) saw Della Valle's theater as deeply rooted in the Baroque and considered Judit the character who best exemplifies the coexistence of opposites and the mutability of the human condition. Giorgio Pullini (1958) stressed the modernity of Della Valle's ideology and his skill in molding the characters and presenting their psychological conflicts; for Pullini, the best reference point for Della Valle is William Shakespeare rather than Aeschylus. Marcello Fabiani (1960) called Della Valle "poeta di un'età di transizione" (poet of an age of transition). Federico Doglio (1960) considered the tragedies the highest achievements of the Catholic tragic theater of the time, a trilogy illustrating the concepts of regality and political power. This idea was developed in Franco Croce's 1965 monograph examining Della Valle's works in their historical context. Sergio Raffaelli (1973 and 1974) centered his analysis on the dramatist's language and style. Franca Angelini (1974 and 2001) examined Della Valle's rhetorical techniques and the function of the "happy ending" in *Esther* and *Judit* and, in the latter work, the theme of beauty's power of seduction. Laura Sanguineti White (1992) examined the dramatic structure and pictorial quality of the language of the tragedies. Monica Bilotta (1999) focused on the representation of political power in the plays.

In spite of the paucity of biographical data and of surviving manuscripts and copies of original editions, interest in Federico Della Valle has been growing steadily since 1929. The Piedmontese poet is now seen as one of the most important and sensitive spokesmen of post-Tridentine Catholic religiosity. It is generally acknowledged that his verse dramas reflect the anguished apprehensions of the Baroque period, an age of religious dissent, political absolutism, and intense longing for the spiritual peace provided by a sincere religious faith. Della Valle's status as a major figure in the history of Italian tragic theater has been established.

Biography:
Carlo Filosa, "Contributo allo studio della biografia di Federico Della Valle," *Giornale storico della letteratura italiana*, 113 (1938): 161–210.

References:
Franca Angelini, *Il Seicento*, volume 5, part 2 of *La letteratura italiana: Storia e testi*, edited by Carlo Muscetta (Rome & Bari: Laterza, 1974), pp. 146–180;

Angelini, "Variazioni su Giuditta," in *I luoghi dell'immaginario barocco: Atti del convegno di Siena, 21–23 ottobre 1999*, edited by Lucia Strappini (Naples: Liguori, 2001), pp. 135–145;

Luisa Anglois, *Il teatro alla corte di Carlo Emanuele I* (Turin: Arti Grafiche Bairati, 1930);

Mario Apollonio, *Storia del teatro italiano*, volume 2 (Milan: Rizzoli, 2003), pp. 275–286;

Bruno Baldis, "Di una nuova redazione manoscritta della tragedia *La Reina di Scotia* di Federico Della Valle," *Aevum*, 4, no. 26 (1952);

Carla Bella, "Le dieu châtieur: La *Judit* di Federico Della Valle," in her *Eros e censura nella tragedia dal '500 al '700* (Florence: Nuove Edizioni Vallecchi, 1981), pp. 221–237;

Alessandro Bianchi, "Il dolore che uccide e la femminilità pericolosa nell'*Adelonda di Frigia* di Federico Della Valle," *Lettere italiane*, 54, no. 2 (2002): 242–261;

Monica Bilotta, "Federico Della Valle e le tragedie del potere," dissertation, Università degli Studi di Pisa, 1999;

Pietro Cazzani, "Questioni dellavalliane," in *Dai dettatori al Novecento*, special issue of *Convivium* (1953): 135–164;

Gregorio Cianflone, *L'opera tragica di Federico Della Valle* (Naples: Treves, 1961);

Benedetto Croce, "Ancora della *Reina di Scotia*," *Critica*, 34 (1936): 389–393;

Croce, *Nuovi saggi sulla letteratura italiana del Seicento* (Bari: Laterza, 1931), pp. 46–74;

Croce, *Storia dell'età barocca in Italia* (Bari: Laterza, 1929), pp. 360–363;

Croce, "La tragedia di Federico Della Valle," *Critica*, 27 (1929): 377–379;

Franco Croce, *Federico Della Valle* (Florence: La Nuova Italia, 1965);

Matteo Durante, "La prima redazione de *La Reina di Scotia*," *Siculorum Gymnasium*, 34 (1981): 1–50;

Marcello Fabiani, "Elegia e dramma in Federico Della Valle, poeta di un'età di transizione," *Studi secenteschi*, 1 (1960): 89–104;

Fabiani, "Note sull'*Adelonda* e sugli sviluppi del teatro dellavalliano," *Studi secenteschi*, 4 (1963): 31–42;

Fabiani, "Sullo stile e il linguaggio poetico di Federico Della Valle," *Convivium*, 26 (1958): 148–153;

Luigi Fassò, "Gli intermedi dell'*Adelonda* di Federico Della Valle," *Rendiconti dell'Istituto Lombardo di Scienze e Lettere*, 88 (1955);

Francesco Flora, *Storia della letteratura italiana*, volume 3, part 2 (Milan: Mondadori, 1942), pp. 385–388;

Andrea Gareffi, "L'età dell'oro della pastorale: Ancora sull'*Adelonda di Frigia*," in *I luoghi dell'immaginario barocco*, pp. 31–42;

Mary D. Garrard, *Artemisia Gentileschi: The Image of the Female Hero in Italian Baroque Art* (Princeton: Princeton University Press, 1989);

Gabriele E. Gerato, "Un'anima traviata: *La Reina di Scotia* di Federico Della Valle," *Neuphilologische Mitteilungen*, 1 (1980);

Giovanni Getto, "Il teatro barocco di Federico Della Valle," *Il Verri*, 2 (1958): 14–52; republished in his *Barocco in prosa e poesia* (Milan: Rizzoli, 1969), pp. 217–259;

Giuseppe Giacalone, "Federico della Valle," *Convivium*, 6 (1948): 831–847;

Marcella Gorra, "Conobbe il Manzoni il teatro di Federico Della Valle?" *Belfagor*, 11 (1956);

Gorra, "Lineamenti e sviluppi della critica dellavalliana," *La critica stilistica e il Barocco letterario: Atti del 2 Congresso internazionale di studi italiani* (Florence: Le Monnier, 1958), pp. 302–315;

Cesare Greppi, "Un documento per la biografia di Federico Della Valle," *Lettere italiane*, 32 (1980);

Andreina Griseri, *Le metamorfosi del Barocco* (Turin: Einaudi, 1967);

Helmut A. Hatzfeld, *Literature through Art* (Chapel Hill: University of North Carolina Press, 1969);

Carmine Jannaco and Martino Capucci, *Il Seicento: Storia della letteratura d'Italia* (Padua: Piccin Nuova Libraria, 1986), pp. 449–464, 478–490;

Norbert Jonard, "Le thème du temps dans la poésie baroque," *Studi secenteschi*, 7 (1966): 20–33;

Claudio Magris, "La *Judit* di Della Valle: Una storia barocca dal retrogusto erotico," *Corriere della sera* (Milan), 9 September 2001, p. 31;

Roberto Mercuri, "*La Reina di Scotia* di Federico Della Valle e la forma della tragedia gesuitica," *Calibano*, 4 (1979): 142–161;

Attilio Momigliano, *Storia della letteratura italiana,* volume 2 (Messina: Principato, 1934), pp. 63–69;

Lawry Nelson, *Baroque Lyric Poetry* (New York: Octagon, 1979);

Carlo Ossola, *Autunno del Rinascimento* (Florence: Olschki, 1971);

Ossola, "Fare del movimento un segno e di un segno movenza," *Lettere Italiane,* 43, no. 1 (1991): 81–85;

Antonio Pigler, *Barockthemen* (Budapest: Académiai Kiadó, 1974);

Giorgio Pullini, "Consistenza drammatica della tragedia del Seicento," in *La critica stilistica e il Barocco letterario,* pp. 302–315;

Mario Puppo, *Teatro tragico italiano: Dal Barocco al Romanticismo* (Turin: ERI Edizioni RAI, 1964);

Sergio Raffaelli, *Aspetti della lingua e dello stile di Federico Della Valle* (Rome: Bulzoni, 1974);

Raffaelli, *Semantica tragica di Federico Della Valle* (Padua: Liviana, 1973);

Ezio Raimondi, *Anatomie secentesche* (Pisa: Nistri-Lischi, 1966);

Marcel Raymond, *Baroque & Renaissance poétique* (Paris: Corti, 1955);

Paul Renucci, "Federico Della Valle," in *Dizionario critico della letteratura italiana,* volume 2, second edition, edited by Vittore Branca (Turin: Unione Tipografico-Editrice Torinese, 1989), pp. 137–140;

Renucci, "Une tragedié de la 'raison de Dieu': La *Judit* de Federico Della Valle," *Revue des études italiennes,* 24 (1978): 174–194;

Jean Rousset, *La Littérature de l'âge Baroque en France* (Paris: Librairie Corti, 1953);

Laura Sanguineti White, *Dal detto alla figura: Le tragedie di Federico Della Valle* (Florence: Olschki, 1992);

Sanguineti White, "Federico Della Valle e la critica: Rassegna," *Lettere italiane,* 42, no. 1 (1990): 136–145;

Natalino Sapegno, *Compendio di storia della letteratura italiana,* volume 2 (Florence: La Nuova Italia, 1949), pp. 353–354;

Benedetto Soldati, *Il Collegio Mamertino e le origini del teatro gesuitico* (Turin: Einaudi, 1908);

Lucia Strappini, "Il valore dell'esempio nella drammaturgia barocca," in *I luoghi dell'immaginario barocco,* pp. 81–93;

Mario Terzera, "La scoperta di Federico Della Valle," *Saggi di Umanesimo cristiano* (1954);

Roberto Tessari, "La *Judit* di Della Valle: Pitture di 'sperati diletti,'" in *Teatri barocchi: Tragedie, commedie, pastorali nella drammaturgia europea tra '500 e '600,* edited by Silvia Carandini (Rome: Bulzoni, 2000), pp. 109–124;

Gaetano Trombatore, "Le tragedie di Federico Della Valle," in his *Saggi critici* (Florence: La Nuova Italia, 1950), pp. 167–192;

Pasquale Tuscano, "Federico Della Valle," *Cultura e scuola,* 11, no. 42 (1972): 5–23;

Ferruccio Ulivi, "Prima dell'Arcadia," *Paragone,* 28 (1952).

Papers:

Manuscripts for Federico Della Valle's *La reina di Scotia* are in Bergamo and Naples.

Carlo de' Dottori

(9 October 1618 – 23 July 1686)

Laura Sanguineti White
Rutgers University

BOOKS: *Poesie liriche* (Padua: Paolo Frambotto, 1643);

L'Alfenore del Signor Carlo de' Dottori donato alle dame della sua patria (Padua: Frambotto, 1644);

Le ode di Carlo de' Dottori: Prima e seconda parte (Padua: Crivellari, 1647; enlarged edition, Padua: Printed by Camerale for Andrea Baruzzi, 1651);

Canzoni (Padua: Printed by G. B. Pasquati for Andrea Baruzzi, 1650);

L'asino: Poema eroicomico, as Iroldo Crotta (Venice: Combi, 1652);

Aristodemo (Padua: Matteo Cadorino, 1657);

Lettere famigliari (Padua: G. B. Pasquati, 1658);

Le ode sacre e morali (Padua: Matteo Cadorino, 1659);

Zenobia di Radamisto, music by Antonio Bertali (Vienna: Cosmerovio, 1662);

Bianca, as Eleuterio Duralete (Padua: Pietro Maria Frambotto, 1671);

Ode e sonetti aggiunti con l'Aristodemo (Padua: Pietro Maria Frambotto, 1680);

Zenobia di Radamisto (Venice: Francesco Valvasense, 1686);

Ippolita: Drama per musica (Padua: Pietro Maria Frambotto, 1695);

Opere (Padua: Pietro Maria Frambotto, 1695);

Confessioni, as Duralete (Padua: Sebastiano Spera in Dio, 1696);

Il Parnaso, edited by Carlo L. Golino (Berkeley: University of California Press, 1957);

Galatea: Poemetto in 5 canti inediti, edited by Antonio Daniele (Bologna: Commissione per i testi di lingua, 1977).

Editions: *Aristodemo,* in *Teatro italiano ossia scelta di tragedie per l'uso della scena,* volume 3, edited by Scipione Maffei (Verona: Vallarsi, 1725);

L'asino: Poema eroicomico (Padua: P. Brandolese, 1796);

L'asino (Venice, 1843);

L'asino (Lanciano: Carabba, 1919);

Aristodemo, edited by Benedetto Croce (Florence: Le Monnier, 1948);

Carlo de' Dottori (from Aristodemo, *edited by Benedetto Croce, 1948; Thomas Cooper Library, University of South Carolina)*

Aristodemo, in *Teatro italiano del Seicento,* edited by Luigi Fassò (Milan & Naples: Ricciardi, 1956);

Aristodemo, in *Il teatro tragico italiano,* edited by Federico Doglio (Bologna: Guanda, 1960);

La prigione, edited by Carlo L. Golino, *Studi secenteschi,* 2 (1961): 147–253;

Lettere a Domenico Federici, edited by Giorgio Cerboni Baiardi (Urbino: Argalia, 1971);

Zenobia di Radamisto [libretto], in *Carlo de' Dottori: Lingua, cultura, e aneddoti,* edited by Antonio Daniele (Padua: Antenore, 1986);

L'asino, edited by Daniele (Rome & Bari: Laterza, 1987);

Confessioni di Eleuterio Duralete, introduction by Daniele (Padua: Antenore, 1987).

PLAY PRODUCTIONS: *Aristodemo,* Padua, 1657;
Ippolita, Vienna, 1662;
Zenobia di Radamisto, music by Antonio Bertali, Vienna, 1662;
Bianca, Padua, home of Girolamo Gradenigo, 1671.

The poet and dramatist Carlo de' Dottori is one of Italy's most noteworthy and provocative writers of the second half of the seventeenth century. His prolific and eclectic literary production includes lyric poetry, mythological and mock-heroic narrative poem, love and adventure novel, social satire, tragicomedy, tragedy, drama for music, and autobiography. The critical rediscovery in 1929 of his dramatic masterpiece *Aristodemo* (1657), which deals with the popular Baroque themes of power and "reason of state," has led to serious consideration of Baroque Italian tragic dramaturgy. *Aristodemo* is a complex text that reflects but also transcends its time: the issues the author raises are still relevant today.

Dottori was born in Padua on 9 October 1618; he was the second of five sons of Antonio Maria and Nicolosa de' Dottori, née Mussato. The Dottori family was aristocratic and distinguished in letters, arms, and politics. Part of the Republic of Venice since 1404, Padua was still an important cultural center during Dottori's lifetime but, like other Italian cities in the seventeenth century, it had grown somewhat provincial. The local aristocracy was declining in prestige and divided into rancorous factions, and the climate of restlessness was intensified by the presence of a large transient body of university students who were often involved in brawls and controversies and of refugees from neighboring city-states, such as Mantua, which were in a condition of turbulence and decadence.

A Giovanni Rossi from Ravenna, about whom little else is known, was apparently Dottori's early instructor in grammar and rhetoric; Dottori dedicated the ode "Su l'inospito verno" (About the Inhospitable Winter) to him and mentions him in *Il Parnaso* (1957, Parnassus). Dottori's biographer, Natale Busetto, says that he was self-taught and pursued a multiplicity of interests without a systematic plan of study. He was incarcerated in Venice from March to July 1641 as a consequence of a mordant pamphlet written with his friends Alessandro Zacco and Ciro Anselmi that was judged defamatory of Paduan ladies.

Dottori and some literary friends formed the Fraglia dei Padrani (Corporation of the Fathers [*fraglia* was the ancient Venetian term for a corporation of artisans; *Padrani* was probably derived from the Latin *patres*]), a fraternity that gathered for merriment and poetry reading in seclusion and away from the city quarrels. Dottori had a long-lasting friendship with Leopoldo de' Medici, to whom he dedicated his *Ode* (1647, Odes). One of his closest friends was the Friulian poet Ciro di Pers, to whom he sent his writings for evaluation and with whom maintained a lifelong correspondence.

The poems in Dottori's first collection, *Poesie liriche* (1643, Lyric Poems) are modeled on those of Fulvio Testi. Testi had merged classical taste with seventeenth-century style to create a poetry of high decorum and elegance that Dottori imitated enthusiastically. The Testian inspiration is also pervasive in the solemn *Ode* of 1647, the *Canzoni* (Songs) of 1650, the *Ode sacre e morali* (Sacred and Moral Odes) of 1659, the *Ode e sonetti aggiunti con l'Aristodemo* (Odes and Sonnets with the Addition of *Aristodemus*) of 1680, but the influence of Giambattista Marino is also traceable in these works. Furthermore, Dottori was increasingly influenced by the poetry of Pers: his pessimistic moralism and the gloomy and lugubrious tones of some of his descriptions are reminiscent of his friend's "Italia calamitosa" (probably 1629, Calamitous Italy). Another recurrent motif in Pers's work, the clock as a symbol of the conflict between time and eternity, is present in Dottori's "Orologio da sole in un crocefisso" (Sundial in a Crucifix). Other themes typical of the Baroque sensibility are the relics and vestiges of antiquity in "Venezia supplicante generosa" (Venice Generous Supplicant) and landscapes of precipices and horrifying beauty that convey an exemplary teaching in "L'Apennino" (The Apennines).

In 1643 Dottori composed *La prigione* (The Prison), a long poem inspired by his incarceration in 1641. Not published until 1961, the work was probably influenced by Marino's narration of his own imprisonment in 1611–1612. *La prigione* is a humorous and satirical poem apparently intended for an intimate circle of friends; it begins with an amusing fresco of the litigious Paduan society and goes on to recount Dottori's experience in prison and other episodes from his early life. Like Marino, Dottori describes his imprisonment in playful and detached tones and, in keeping with the taste for caricature and the desire to arouse *meraviglia* (amazement) that were dear to the Baroque poetics, emphasizes its most grotesque aspects.

In 1644 Dottori published a novel, *L'Alfenore,* a mixture of intrigue, adventure, and situations of love and honor "donato alle dame della sua patria" (presented to the ladies of his homeland). That same year he married Lodovica Botton. They had two sons and two daughters; three of the children predeceased their father. In 1645 Dottori became a member of the Accademia dei Ricovrati (Academy of Patients).

Between 1647 and 1651 Dottori wrote the narrative poem *Il Parnaso*. Apollo sends a mission to heal Padua of the many evils it is suffering, which Dottori describes extensively and in humorous tones. He particularly singles out the disturbances and violence caused by the many "bravoes" (hired ruffians) in the city and expresses outrage at seeing individual freedom infringed upon by senseless violence.

Dottori published the ten-canto *L'asino: Poema eroicomico* (1652, The Ass: A Mock-Heroic Poem) under the pseudonym Iroldo Crotta, an anagram for his real name. Modeled on Alessandro Tassoni's *Secchia rapita* (1621, The Stolen Bucket), the poem begins with the Paduans' seizing of the Vicentine banner with its emblem of a donkey. When the ambassadors from Vicenza come to demand its return, they are greeted by a bray from a spectator that is picked up by the crowd filling the square and a long war between the two city-states ensues. The plot is animated by vivacious caricatures and swift, humorous portraits of some of the author's contemporaries. Into the mock-heroic plot Dottori inserts the sorrowful episode in which Desmanina, the repudiated wife of Lord Ezzelino da Romano, faces her husband in a duel to defend her honor from accusations of adultery and is killed. Critics have noted the influence on this passage of the Tancredi and Clorinda episode from Torquato Tasso's *Gerusalemme liberata* (1581, Jerusalem Delivered; translated as *Godfrey of Bulloigne, or The Recoverie of Hierusalem*, 1594). Maria Luisa Doglio points out that the inclusion of the story is characteristic of the Baroque alternation of laughter and tears.

In 1650 Dottori went to Rome as the secretary of Cardinal Rinaldo d'Este. He received protection from Eleonora Gonzaga Nevers, the sister of the duke of Mantua, Carlo II, who married the Holy Roman Emperor Ferdinand III in 1651. The poet maintained a regular exchange of letters with the empress for many years. The cardinal assigned him the task of collecting lyrics written by leading poets in honor of former queen Christina of Sweden, who settled in Rome after her abdication in 1654 and became another of Dottori's protectors.

In the early 1650s Dottori composed a tragicomedy, *Zenobia di Radamisto*, based on Tacitus's *Annals;* it was published posthumously in Venice in 1686. In the years 30–31 Zenobia and her husband, Radamisto, the king of the Armenians, are separated while fleeing from the Romans and endure many dramatic vicissitudes before being reunited. The complex plot involves exchanges of identities, romantic entanglements, and an alternation of tragic and comic episodes.

Dottori completed the first draft of *Aristodemo* in 1654 and sent the manuscript to some of his most trusted friends for their opinions. On 16 March he wrote to Pers that the work had had a "lunga gravidanza" (long pregnancy) but a "parto precipitoso" (precipitous delivery). Pers criticized the drama for being based on a little-known historical event, violating Aristotle's rule that the plot of a tragedy must be widely recognizable; he also thought that the number of vicissitudes depicted was excessive. Dottori ignored those strictures; but the published version of the play, which appeared in 1657, appears to reflect some stylistic revisions made in response to critical remarks by Leopoldo de' Medici and, perhaps, some modifications prompted by the staging of the tragedy.

The subject of the play is taken from "Messenia," the fourth book of Pausanias's second-century *Periegesis* (Description of Greece), but incidents from other periods of the history of Messenia are included. In a letter to Pers, Dottori revealed that his literary sources were Seneca, Euripides' *Iphigenia* (circa 414 B.C.), and, for the chorus, Sophocles.

Messenia and Sparta are at war. To appease the gods, who have been enraged by acts of desecration carried out by two Messenian warriors, the oracle has asked for the sacrifice of a young virgin. The names of Merope, the daughter of Aristodemo, and Arena, the daughter of Licisco, were placed in an urn. The play opens with rejoicing by Aristodemo; his wife, Amfia; Merope's *nutrice* (nurse); and Policare, Merope's fiancé, because Arena's name has been drawn. But when Merope enters, she does not share the general mood; her narrow escape from death has left her melancholy:

Ma non so già se porti
dallo scorso periglio
qualche men grata impression la vita,
che bella non m'appar com'io sperai,
e men lieta, e men avida, l'incontro.

(But I do not know if
from the past danger
a less agreeable impression marked my life
which does not appear as beautiful as hoped for
and less cheerful, and less eager I face it.)

The situation is suddenly reversed by the announcement that Licisco has fled with his daughter, whose paternity he denies, and a small retinue. Aristodemo and some soldiers pursue them, but they find sanctuary in the Spartan camp. The first act ends with a prayer to the Dioscuri by the chorus that reflects the darkening mood after Arena's flight puts Merope's life in danger again.

A new Messenian king must be elected, and Aristodemo is the favorite. In the second act, after a troubled soliloquy modeled on Seneca's *Thyestes* in which he expresses his internal conflict between paternal love and political ambition, Aristodemo announces that he is offering Merope to be sacrificed for the survival of his country:

> Merope dono a Dite.
> Crudel, ma generoso
> sí; redimer mi piace
> con parte del mio sangue un regno intero.
>
> (Merope I give to Dis.
> Cruel yet generous
> I like to ransom
> with part of my blood an entire kingdom.)

Amfia and Policare condemn Aristodemo's ambition and the "reason of state" that he uses to justify his action. The second act concludes with an invocation by the chorus of a reality ruled by hostile forces.

In act 3 the lovers meet for the last time. Merope claims the right to die to give life to her beloved and her homeland and orders Policare not to follow her in death but to live on as the custodian of her memory. For the moment she holds the conviction that she is the architect of her own destiny. Like her father, she desires fame; but unlike Aristodemo, she is innocent and generous. In response to her comment, "Io mi credea che 'l meno / che ti piacesse in me fosse il mio volto" (I believe what least / you liked in me was my visage), Policare cries out in sorrow and passion:

> Il tuo corpo mi piacque
> sede d'una bell'anima, e fin tanto
> ch'io son uomo, e non ombra
> piango le cose umanamente amate.
>
> (I liked your body
> vessel of your beautiful soul, and as long as
> I am a man, and not a shadow
> I long for things humanly loved.)

Up to this point Merope's dialogue has taken the form of simple statements, while Policare's has been a series of questions and exclamations that revealed his tumultuous emotions. But when the archers arrive to take the young woman to the sacrificial hall, the two modes of discourse are reversed. Faced with the unexpected display of force that limits her freedom to be a voluntary victim, Merope voices her fear and rebellion in a series of pressing questions, while Policare expresses his grief in an elegiac lament: "Dove n'andrai, crudele, senza di me?" (Where will you go, cruel one, without me?). The act ends with the description by the chorus of the voyage of the dead modeled on Seneca's *Hercules furens* (The Madness of Hercules): a multitude of lonely "ombre ignude" (naked shadows) incessantly flows in a dark, misty space; they are equalized by the democracy of death and distinguished by virtue: "Passa indistinto il re dal servo, e sola / virtù distinta passa" (Passes the king undistinguished from the servant, and / virtue alone passes distinguished). The chorus expresses a mournful entreaty to "beauty," so prized and fleeting, and to life, so frail and transient.

In an attempt to save Merope's life Policare, Amfia, and the *nutrice* plot a "compassionate" intrigue in act 4 that will turn, in the end, into a "nefasto inganno" (ill-fated deception). Policare tells Aristodemo that Merope is pregnant and, therefore, not eligible for a sacrifice that requires a virgin. Aristodemo pretends to accept the situation. Meanwhile, Merope serenely tells the high priest who wants to prepare her to meet her demise that death has been with her since her name was placed in the urn. The act ends with a monologue by the ambitious Aristodemo, who wants revenge, followed by an invective by the chorus against arms and wars and a short but intense lament by the Messenian women.

At the beginning of the fifth act the *nutrice* narrates the horrendous deed that has been perpetrated by Aristodemo. Alliterations, enjambments, and past perfects give the verses a broken rhythm, rendering the convulsive movement of the avenging father who penetrated the sacred seclusion where Merope awaited death and pierced his daughter's womb with a sword in search of proof of her guilt. Merope is described as silent in front of the unexpected executioner, her gentle hand raised to cover her face in order not to see him. After ascertaining her innocence and attempting unsuccessfully to take his own life, Aristodemo tries to exploit his crime by presenting it as a sacrifice to save the homeland. He also incites the people against Policare, and they stone the young man to death. At this point the raving Aristodemo faces the final revelation. Licinio returns and relates Arena's death from an arrow shot by Aristodemo during their flight. He goes on to say that after years of barren marriage, he and his wife secretly received the infant Arena from the priestess Erasitea. Erasitea interrupts to declare that Arena was the fruit of "furtivi antichi amori" (furtive ancient love) with Aristodemo, who was unaware of his double paternity and who now realizes that he is guilty of a double filicide. When the oracle reveals that the gods have refused to accept the deaths of the two young virgins as sacrifice, the tragedy moves to its inevitable close. Aristodemo's suicide, narrated by a soldier, takes place in the same hall where Merope died:

Frontispiece (Biblioteca Marciana, Venice; from Louise George Clubb, Italian Drama in Shakespeare's Time, *1989; Thomas Cooper Library, University of South Carolina) and title page (University of Turin) for the first edition*

S'abbandonò su quella stessa spada,
con che fu dianzi Merope trafitta;
non parlò, non gemé. . . .

(He abandoned himself on that same sword
by which shortly before Merope was pierced;
he uttered no words, no groans. . . .)

The fifth act diverges from the pattern of the first four as the wise man Tisi, rather than the chorus, concludes the tragedy. Left alone on the stage, he expresses the horror of human deeds and fearfully anticipates the inevitable wrath of the gods.

In this tragedy Dottori reflects some of the major issues of his troubled era. He criticizes political absolutism, the "reason of state" that crushes the individual. He also attacks the objectification of human beings: for instance, Merope's name is constantly coupled with a possessive adjective, and she is often identified by the term *dono* (gift) as if she were a thing that could be given away or exchanged. Moreover, Dottori condemns the excessive ambition that destroys the humanity in a person. His pessimism stems from his perception of human existence as precarious and lonely and from the insight that in the end one's attainments are frequently the opposite of one's intentions. The language of the play is solemn and decorous, in accordance with Baroque taste; at the same time, it is vibrant and passionate with lyrical moments of extraordinary intensity. The changes from the draft to the final version, especially in the last four acts, mostly concern the language and reveal a movement toward a clearer and less excessive oratory as Dottori eliminates unusual words in favor of a homogeneous and compact vocabulary.

The tragedy was presented successfully by twelve Paduan gentlemen on three consecutive nights; Pers traveled from his castle in remote Friuli for the occasion. Only brief, though generally positive, references to the work appeared during the following two centuries. Interest intensified around the end of the nineteenth century and the beginning of the twentieth; the play was then forgotten until 1929, when it was rediscovered by Benedetto Croce. Croce focused his analysis on the psychology of Merope, whom he identified as the real protagonist of the play. Natalino Sapegno (1941) and Francesco Flora (1942) echoed Croce's positive evaluation of the work. Giuseppe Italo Lopriore (1950) described *Aristodemo* as a political tragedy and the title character as a victim of the Baroque theory of the reason of state. This opinion was shared by Luigi Fassò (1956), who also pointed to Aristodemo's dark, turbulent nature. Franco Croce (1957 and 1959) examined Dottori's cultural and historical background, life, and canon; analyzed the characters in *Aristodemo* in relation to one another; and studied the differences between the 1654 manuscript and the 1657 edition of the play. Giorgio Pullini (1959) named Dottori and Federico Della Valle the two most original seventeenth-century Italian dramatists. Giovanni Getto (1959) described the major themes of the play as grandeur, death, and affection; he also analyzed the psychological features of the characters. In the introduction to his 1960 edition of the play Federico Doglio viewed death as the central theme. Marco Ariani (1972) concentrated on Dottori's literary style in the tragedy. Drawing a parallel between *Aristodemo* and French and Elizabethan tragedy, Franca Angelini (1974) saw the conclusion of the play as a complete overturning of the initial premises. In the introduction to his edition of *Galatea* (1977) Antonio Daniele noted the presence in *Aristodemo* of a "sensualismo tragico" (tragic sensuality). Carmine Jannaco and Martino Capucci (1986) stressed the influence of the contemporary culture and poetics on the pessimism that permeates the tragedy. Giovanni Calendoli (1987) called attention to the originality of the structure of the play, particularly the progressive "disvelamento" (unveiling) of Aristodemo by the other characters that leads to the final tragic epiphany. Laura Sanguineti White (1988) discussed *Aristodemo* as a tragedy of spiritual imprisonment and deprivation of individual freedom. Louise George Clubb (1989) viewed the text as a "pagan tragedy made radically Christian." Marco Zanardi (1989) focused on the language and style of *Aristodemo*, specifically on the *figure armoniche* (harmonic figures) defined by Emanuele Tesauro in his *Cannocchiale aristotelico* (1654, Aristotelian Spyglass) as those that are aimed at flattering the sense of hearing. Alessandro Bianchi (2000) identified the human relationship with God as a fundamental theme of the tragedy and held that Aristodemo becomes more humane through his "terribile autocoscienza" (dreadful self-awareness).

Dottori's wife died in childbirth in 1657. In 1658 the new Holy Roman Emperor, Leopold I, invited him to the imperial court in Vienna, where many of the poets and musicians, the orchestra conductor, and the director of theatrical performances were also Italians. In 1662 Dottori composed the musical melodrama *Ippolita* at the request of Empress Eleonora to celebrate the emperor's birthday. That same year Antonio Bertali's opera *Zenobia di Radamisto* was staged in celebration of Empress Eleonora's birthday; Dottori wrote the libretto, which he based on his tragicomedy of the same title.

In 1671 Dottori published the prose tragedy *Bianca* under the pseudonym Eleuterio Duralete. An historical drama about local events, it was staged at the home of Girolamo Gradenigo, the captain of Padua; later, its performance was forbidden by Cardinal Gregorio Barbarigo. Dottori used the same pseudonym for his autobiography, *Confessioni* (Confessions), which was written in the late 1670s but published posthumously in 1696. Modeled on the *Confessions* (circa 400) of St. Augustine, the text is permeated by devout humility and is characterized by the rejection of seventeenth-century ideals such as dueling, gallantry, intrigue, and pomp; according to Franco Croce, it establishes "un continuo nesso tra le esperienze di vita e i problemi etici" (a continuous connection between life experiences and ethical problems). Dottori died in Padua on 23 July 1686.

During his lifetime Carlo de' Dottori enjoyed notable success as a lyric poet in Italian literary circles and at the Austrian court, but his fame had waned by the middle of the eighteenth century. The critical rediscovery of his tragedy *Aristodemo* has stimulated the production of modern editions of his other works, especially the satirical texts in which he attacks the social and cultural myths of his age. After centuries of quasi-oblivion, Dottori is now recognized as one of the most interesting cultural figures of the late seventeenth century, and *Aristodemo* is regarded not only as a masterpiece of Baroque dramaturgy but also as a major work of Italian tragic theater.

Biography:

Natale Busetto, *Carlo de' Dottori letterato padovano del secolo XVII* (Città di Castello: S. Lapi, 1902).

References:

Franca Angelini, *La letteratura italiana: Storia e testi*, volume 5, part 2: *Il Seicento* (Rome & Bari: Laterza, 1974), pp. 180–197;

Marco Ariani, "Note sullo stile tragico dell'*Aristodemo* di Carlo de' Dottori," *Studi secenteschi,* 13 (1972): 163-179;

Girolamo Arnaldi and Manlio Pastore Stocchi, eds., *Storia della cultura veneta,* volume 4/1: *Il Seicento* (Vicenza: Neri Pozza, 1983);

Carla Bella, "Le dieu caché: L'*Aristodemo* di Carlo de' Dottori," *Paragone,* no. 340 (1978): 23-53;

Emilio Bertana, *La tragedia* (Milan: Vallardi, 1905), pp. 156-161;

Alessandro Bianchi, "L'*Aristodemo* di Carlo de' Dottori: Civiltà di colpa e ambiguità tragica. I furori necessari," *Italianistica,* 29, no. 2 (2000): 209-227;

Carlo Calcaterra, *Il Parnaso in rivolta* (Milan: Mondadori, 1940);

Louise George Clubb, *Italian Drama in Shakespeare's Time* (New Haven & London: Yale University Press, 1989), pp. 231-247;

Benedetto Croce, *Storia dell'eta' barocca in Italia* (Bari: Laterza, 1929), pp. 248-253;

Franco Croce, *Carlo de' Dottori* (Florence: La Nuova Italia, 1957);

Croce, "L'*Aristodemo* del Dottori e il Barocco," in *La critica stilistica e il Barocco letterario: Atti del 2 Congresso internazionale di studi italiani* (Florence: Le Monnier, 1959), pp. 177-199;

Antonio Daniele, *Carlo de' Dottori: Lingua, cultura e aneddoti* (Padua: Antenore, 1986)—the appendix contains the text of the libretto *Zenobia di Radamisto;*

Daniele, "Note sull'*Aristodemo* di Carlo de' Dottori," in *Studi di filologia romanza e italiana offerti a Gianfranco Folena* (Modena: S.T.E.M.-Mucchi, 1980);

Daniele, ed., *Carlo de' Dottori e la cultura padovana del Seicento: Atti del convegno di studi, Padova, 26-27 novembre 1987* (Padua: Accademia Patavina di Scienze e Lettere ed Arti, Università degli Studi di Padova, 1990)—includes Giovanni Calendoli, "L'*Aristodemo* e l'originalità della sua struttura drammatica";

Giovanni da Pozzo, "Rassegna di studi dottoriani," *Giornale storico della letteratura italiana,* 169 (1992): 95-127;

Guido di Pino, "In margine all'*Aristodemo,*" in his *Linguaggio della tragedia alfieriana e altri studi* (Florence: La Nuova Italia, 1952);

Maria Luisa Doglio, "Carlo de' Dottori," in *Dizionario critico della letteratura italiana,* volume 2, edited by Vittore Branca, second edition (Turin: Unione Tipografico-Editrice Torinese, 1989), pp. 180-183;

Luigi Fassò, Introduction to *Teatro del Seicento,* edited by Fassò (Milan & Naples: Ricciardi, 1956), pp. xxvi-xxix;

Francesco Flora, *Storia della letteratura italiana* (Milan: Mondadori, 1942), pp. 781-785;

Giovanni Getto, "L'*Aristodemo* capolavoro del Barocco," *Nuova Antologia,* no. 475 (1959): 445-472; republished in his *Barocco in prosa e poesia* (Milan: Rizzoli, 1969), pp. 261-286;

Carlo L. Golino, "De' Dottori and the Italian Baroque," *Italica,* 39, no. 1 (1962): 31-43;

Carmine Jannaco and Martino Capucci, *Il Seicento: Storia letteraria d'Italia* (Padua: Piccin Nuova Libraria, 1986), pp. 351-355, 464-470, 480-481, 555-558;

Giuseppe Italo Lopriore, *Saggio sull'Aristodemo di Carlo de' Dottori* (Pisa: Arti Grafiche Tornar, 1950);

Annalisa Marin, "Sul testo dell'*Aristodemo* di Carlo de' Dottori," in *Annali della facoltà di Lettere e Filosofia dell'Università di Padova,* volume 2 (Florence: Olschki, 1978), pp. 187-232;

Attilio Momigliano, *Storia della letteratura italiana* (Messina: G. Principato, 1936), p. 315;

Giorgio Pullini, "Consistenza drammatica delle tragedie del Seicento," in *La critica stilistica e il Barocco letterario,* pp. 302-315;

Mario Puppo, *Teatro tragico italiano: Dal barocco al romanticismo* (Turin: RAI, 1964);

Ezio Raimondi, "Paesaggi e rovine nella poesia di un virtuoso," in his *Anatomie secentesche* (Pisa: Nistri-Lischi, 1966), pp. 42-72;

Luigi Russo, "La tragedia nel Cinque e nel Seicento," *Belfagor,* 14 (1959): 14-22;

Laura Sanguineti White, "*Aristodemo,* tragedia della libertà," *Studi secenteschi,* 19 (1988): 95-121;

Natalino Sapegno, *Compendio della letteratura italiana* (Florence: La Nuova Italia, 1941), pp. 280-281;

Roberto Senardi, "*Aristodemo* di Carlo de' Dottori: L'aristocrazia secentesca nello specchio del Classicismo," in his *Studi sul teatro tragico italiano tra Manierismo ed età dell'Arcadia* (Rome: Ateneo, 1982);

Vincenzo Trombatore, *La concezione tragica dell'Aristodemo di Carlo de' Dottori* (Palermo: Lao, 1903);

Marco Zanardi, "La *figure armoniche* e l'elocuzione barocca di Carlo de' Dottori," *Studi secenteschi,* 30 (1989): 131-168.

Isabella Farnese
(Suor Francesca di Gesù Maria)
(6 January 1593 – 17 October 1651)

Rita Cavigioli
University of Missouri

BOOKS: *Costituzioni delle monache delli monasterii di S. Maria delle Grazie di Farnese, della Concezione di Albano e di S. Chiara in Palestrina* (Rome: Stamparia delle Reverenda Camera Apostolica, 1640);

Lettera spirituale ed esortatoria (Rome: Moneta, 1642);

Pie e divote poesie composte dalla ven. madre suor Francesca di Giesù Maria, fondatrice delli monasterii di S. Maria delle Gratie di Farnese, della SS. Concettione di Albano e di Roma e riformatrice di quello della Madonna degli Angeli di Palestrina, per eccitare le sue Religiose al maggiore Amor di Dio e disprezzo del Mondo (Rome: Angelo Bernabò, 1654);

Poesie sacre composte dalla molto Rev. Madre suor Francesca Farnese di Giesù Maria, Fondatrice delli Monasterii di Santa Maria delle Gratie di Farnese e della Santiss. Concettione di Albano e di Roma, e Riformatrice del Monasterio di Santa Maria degli Angioli di Palestrina con altre composte da Religiose del suo instituto (Rome: Francesco Cavalli, 1657).

OTHER: Andrea Nicoletti, *Vita delle venerabile madre suor Francesca Farnese detta di Giesù Maria dell'ordine di Santa Chiara, fondatrice delli Monasterii di Santa Maria delle Gratie di Farnese e della SS. Concettione di Albano e di Roma e riformatrice del Monasterio di Santa Maria degli Angeli di Palestrina* (Rome: Giacomo Dragondelli, 1660; enlarged, 1678)–includes selections from Farnese's works.

SELECTED PERIODICAL PUBLICATIONS–
UNCOLLECTED: Severino Gori, "Esortazioni e ricordi della Ven. Fr. Farnese alle anime consacrate a Dio," *Santa Chiara*, 1 (1967): 20–25; 1 (1968): 11–13;

Giovanni Baffioni, "Liriche sacre inedite di Francesca Farnese," *Atti e memorie dell'Arcadia*, third series, 6, no. 2 (1973): 91–197.

Isabella Farnese was a poet, convent founder and reformer, author of monastic constitutions, and spiritual director. Her reputation in Roman religious circles was so great by the time of her death that an exemplary biography was commissioned by Cardinal Francesco Barberini to honor her contribution and pave the way for her sanctification. Andrea Nicoletti's *Vita delle venerabile madre suor Francesca Farnese detta di Giesù Maria dell'ordine di Santa Chiara, fondatrice delli Monasterii di Santa Maria delle Gratie di Farnese e della SS. Concettione di Albano e di Roma e riformatrice del Monasterio di Santa Maria degli Angeli di Palestrina* (1660, Life of the Venerable Mother Sister Francesca Farnese Called of Jesus Mary of the Order of St. Clare, Founder of the Monasteries of St. Mary of the Graces of Farnese and of the Very Holy Conception of Albano and Rome and Reformer of the Monastery of St. Mary of the Angels of Palestrina), includes autobiographical fragments, letters, and testimonies collected in the monasteries where she lived and worked.

Farnese was born in Parma on 6 January 1593 into a lesser branch of the noble family that governed the Parma dukedom. Her father, Mario Farnese, lord of Farnese and Latera, small fiefs near Viterbo, had purchased a palace in Parma with the generous dowry of his wife, Camilla Meli Lupi. Through canny political and financial strategies he secured for his lineage a prestige that lasted several decades and the connections with Roman civil and ecclesiastic power that later promoted his daughter's religious career.

Under the tutelage of her grandmother, Marquise Isabella Pallavicino of Cortemaggiore, who was intent on preparing her for a prestigious marriage, Farnese received a typical late-Renaissance education in a milieu in which the appreciation of profane literature had not yet been censored by Counter-Reformation pedagogy. She studied Latin, recited pastoral dramas, and learned to appreciate music and chivalric literature. But she contracted smallpox and, shortly afterward, fell over a brazier. Her facial disfigurement caused her grandmother to lose interest in her, and she returned to her parents.

In 1602 Mario Farnese became general lieutenant of the papal army and moved his family into a sumptuous residence in the Via Giulia in Rome. He boarded Isabella at the Convent of San Lorenzo in Panisperna and placed her under the guidance of her aunt, Sister Francesca Farnese. After her aunt's death two years later, Isabella lost interest in spiritual matters and resumed her reading of profane literature.

At the beginning of 1607 Farnese returned to her parents' home, where she spent a year studying music, learning to play the organ, and reading classical and chivalric literature and St. Teresa of Avila's spiritual exercises. With her smallpox scars partly healed and some of her beauty restored, she took part in her sister Giulia's wedding. On 7 December 1607 she reentered San Lorenzo in Panisperna as a novice. She became a nun on 8 January 1609; taking the name of her late aunt, she became known as Sister Francesca di Gesù Maria. During the first seven years of her cloistered life she vacillated between religious fervor and profane pursuits and between depression and impatience. She organized the other young nuns in reciting comedies and pastoral dramas, continued her study of the organ and the harpsichord, and hired a singing master to instruct her in *canto figurato* (polyphony). She also composed spiritual verses in the vernacular. In 1611 her sister Vittoria entered the same convent, taking the name Sister Isabella. Farnese oversaw the education of her sister, who became her lifelong companion.

At twenty-three, impressed by the exemplary biographies of Franciscan nuns in Marcus of Lisbon's *Croniche di San Francesco* (1583–1586, St. Francis's Chronicles), Farnese underwent a spiritual conversion. She decided to devote her soul entirely to God and detach herself from worldly concerns, following the examples of early Christian anchoritism and of St. Francis's and St. Clare's asceticism. She had her vernacular poetry and profane books burned and gave up her valuables and her yearly revenue. Sister Isabella saved some of the autobiographical notes and verses that Farnese had ordered to be burned; they were preserved in the monastery of Albano until its destruction in 1944.

Farnese's harsh penitential practices undermined her health and her sister's and antagonized the abbess, who saw them as a violation of convent rules. To resolve the conflict and find a place where she could cultivate her longing for mortification, rigor, and solitude, she asked her father to help her set up a new religious community. In 1617 Mario Farnese obtained Pope Paul V's consent to entrust Farnese with the establishment of a Poor Clare community at the monastery of S. Maria delle Grazie in Farnese. Farnese and Sister Isabella entered the monastery on 9 May 1618; because of their youth, two aunts were summoned from another convent to direct the community. Farnese was appointed novice mistress. A few years later, in spite of the custom that four or more members of the same family rarely lived in one monastery, Farnese arranged for the entry of two more of her birth sisters into the convent. Her extreme rigor challenged orthodox notions of appropriate female devotional behavior and aroused criticism both from novices' families and from religious authorities.

Farnese waged a seven-year battle to win the right to draft the constitutions for her convent. Women were seldom allowed to carry out this duty; the only exception had been St. Teresa of Avila, whose constitutions for the Carmelites inspired Farnese. She also found inspiration in St. Carlo Borromeo's recommendations for the reform of Milanese monasteries. In 1625, following a letter of approval from the Sacred Congregation of Bishops and Nuns, Bishop Alessandro Carissimi of Castro, the chief town of the dukedom, authorized her to regulate devotional practice and convent organization.

Farnese's constitutions define the Farnesian Poor Clare as a spiritual aristocrat who takes a vow of poverty, obedience, contemplation, and total detachment from her family and the world. Reminding her community that "in questa elettione consiste tutta la lor pace e quiete" (their inner peace is to be found entirely in this choice), she warns nuns from noble families to resist the allurements of their rank: "Non si lascino movere per rispetti humani, né si metta mai fra loro quella pestifera usanza di far che l'Abbadessa, anzi il suo offitio, sia hereditario nella casata più nobile del monasterio, ma quella che avanzarà tutte l'altre nelle virtù, quella sia eletta e questo intieramente s'osservi" (Let them be unaffected by human reverence, and never introduced to that pernicious custom of making the Abbess's office hereditary in the noblest family of the monastery; let the one who will surpass all the others in virtue be elected, and this be entirely observed). Farnesian Poor Clares were to despise their bodies and to view their physical surroundings, which were restricted to guarantee spiritual isolation, as a temporary prison. Farnese told her nuns to make it known to the world that even in the seventeenth century there were "anime che se non nei deserti d'Egitto e della Scithia, almeno nella sepoltura di quattro mura, vivano talmente fuori d'esso e così lontane da tutto quanto egli cerca e stima, che chiuse ancora nel corpo terreno di carne, hanno di lui intieramente trionfato e se lo tengono sotto i piedi" (souls that, if not in the deserts of Egypt and of Scythia, at least buried inside four walls, live so removed from the world and from what the world seeks and values that, although still locked in their earthly bodies, have triumphed over it entirely and keep it under their feet).

Most of Farnese's poems appear to have been written between 1618 and 1630; the majority were intended for cloistral singing. Although not highly inspired, her poems reveal a command of technique and a versatile use of the metrics of her time; her knowledge of Latin is displayed in her employment of anagrams and epigrams. Stefano Andretta comments on her poetic technique in his *La venerabile superbia: Ortodossia e trasgressione nella vita di suor Francesca Farnese (1593–1651)* (1994, Venerable Pride: Orthodoxy and Transgression in the Life of Sister Francesca Farnese [1593–1651]):

> Banditi i sonetti, tipici del petrarchismo da cui appare quasi del tutto affrancata, poco utilizzati i moduli tradizionali della lauda umbra, apparivano ottave, quartine, terzine, distici monorimi con settenari ed endecasillabi con uso di versi sdruccioli e tronchi, quinari, senari, ottonari trocaici e persino la canzonetta anacreontica che ricondurrebbe a una conoscenza non superficiale di Chiabrera. Insomma, un bagaglio tecnico imprevedibile di una versificazione varia e confezionata con naturalezza in cui, al di là del non eccelso spessore dell'ispirazione, era possibile constatare un uso immaginifico e sensuale della sensibilità poetica barocca.
>
> (As she had banned sonnets, typical of a Petrarchism from which she seemed to have emancipated herself, and seldom employed the traditional forms of the Umbrian laud, there appeared octaves, quatrains, and tercets, monorhyme couplets with seven-syllable lines and hendecasyllables with the use of trisyllabic and apocopated rhymes, pentasyllables, six-syllable lines, trochaic octosyllabic verses, and even the anacreontic canzonet, which would document a nonsuperficial knowledge of [Gabriello] Chiabrera. In conclusion, she displayed an unexpected technical mastery of varied and confidently used verse patterns, in which, in spite of her far from lofty inspiration, one can detect a highly imaginative and sensual use of Baroque poetic sensibility.)

The poetic voice is that of a woman whose Christ-centered spirituality reveals a special devotion to the Virgin Mary. In keeping with the Franciscan focus on the humanity of Christ, most of Farnese's poems deal with his infancy or his Passion. Her references to objects and ornaments evoke a feminine religious world in which devotion is often portrayed as a spiritual wedding or as intoxication with divine love. Music and singing play an important role in the poet's imagination. Her central theme, the joy resulting from the detachment from worldly matters, is expressed in her praise of the cloistered condition and its components–the cell, the convent wall, isolation, and mortification–and the longing for death as release from the body. The constituent elements and nature of cloistered bliss and empowerment are exemplified by stanzas from her "Allegrezza di due monache" (Two Nuns' Happiness), a song for two voices:

> Le mie veste e gl'ornamenti
> Le mie gemme e i miei pendenti
> Son sì ricche e sì pregiate,
> Son sì rare e sì stimate,
> Ch'infinito è il lor valore,
> Ch'abbarbaglia il lor splendore.
>
> . . . .
>
> Quando miro in Cielo o in Terra
> Ciò ch'il mondo in sé riserra
> Tutto a me serv' e ubidisce,
> A mie voglie s'esibisce,
> Sendo sposa al lor Fattore
> Perché servo al lor Signore.
>
> Serve a me l'argento e l'oro
> Scherno fò d'ogni thesoro,
> I piaceri e 'l mondo sprezzo,
> Niente qua giù in Terra apprezzo,
> Né ho pensier di robb' o honore,
> Sciolt' e liber' ho 'l mio core.
>
> Passo lieta i giorni e gl'anni
> Vivo quieta e senz'affanni
> Nella mia Celletta amata,
> Fra 'sti chiostri ritirata,
> Solo il mio Giesù bramando
> Al mio Dio sempre aspirando.
>
> Se nel mondo è fame e guerra
> Se v'è pest' o affann' in terra
> Se va a mal robba e havere
> Se si secca ogni Podere,
> Poc' o nulla io di ciò sento,
> Non si turba il mio contento.
>
> Se al morir penso tal' hora,
> Se contemplo l'ultim' hora,
> Cresce all'hora il mio contento,
> D'allegrezza empir mi sento
> Perché andrò dal Sposo mio,
> Perché vederò il mio Dio. . . .
>
> (My clothes and ornaments
> My gems and my pendants
> Are so rich and precious,
> Are so rare and esteemed,
> That their value is infinite,
> And their splendor dazzling.
>
> . . . .
>
> What I see in Heaven and Earth
> Whatever the world holds inside
> All serves me and obeys me,

And offers itself to my will,
Because I am their Maker's bride,
Because I serve their Lord.

Silver and gold are at my service
I scorn all treasures,
I despise the world and its pleasures,
There is nothing I value on this Earth,
Nor do I have concerns about property or honor,
Loose and free is my heart.

I spend my days and years merrily
Peaceful and carefree is my life
In my beloved little Cell,
Secluded in these cloisters,
Only yearning for my Jesus,
Always aspiring to my God.

If there is hunger and war in the world
If there is plague or trouble
If things and possessions rot
If every Holding withers,
This hardly affects me,
Or spoils my contentment.

If I sometimes think about death,
If I contemplate the last hour,
My contentment grows,
I am filled with joy
Because I will go to my Bridegroom,
Because I will see my God. . . .)

Following the model set by St. Teresa of combining the ideal of solitude with a commitment to active life and monastic reform, Farnese pursued funds and protection among the Roman nobility by establishing connections with pious and enterprising noblewomen, such as her distant relative Princess Caterina Savelli of Albano and Costanza Magalotti Barberini, who supported the reorganization of Franciscan institutions in the area with the aim of making them more austere. Under Savelli's patronage Farnese entered the monastery of Albano on 16 March 1631 as abbess and novice mistress; she was charged with reforming the community and supervising the establishment of a strict new convent of Poor Clares, the Convent of the Immaculate Conception. Barberini introduced Farnese to Pope Urban VIII and his nephew, Cardinal Francesco Barberini; the latter became the official protector of the Farnesian Poor Clares convents in 1638. The protection of pious institutions was one of the cornerstones of the Barberinis' politics, and Farnese's public image as a rigorous reformer counterbalanced the Barberinis' worldly unscrupulousness and arrogance.

In 1638 Farnese and Sister Isabella left Albano for a Poor Clare convent in the nearby town of Palestrina; Isabella was named abbess. They reformed the convent according to the constitutions Farnese had written for the monastery of Santa Maria delle Grazie in Farnese. The constitutions were legitimized by a papal decree of Urban VIII in 1638 and published in Rome in 1640 under the title *Costituzioni delle monache dei monasteri di S. Maria delle Grazie di Farnese, della Concezione di Albano e di S. Chiara in Palestrina* (Constitutions of the Nuns of the Monasteries of St. Mary of Mercy in Farnese, of the Conception in Albano and of St. Clare in Palestrina). Farnese's *Lettera spirituale ed esortatoria* (Spiritual and Exhortatory Letter), addressed to the nuns of the Farnese, Albano, and Palestrina monasteries, was published in Rome in 1642. Farnese and Isabella also supervised the three-year construction of a second convent in Palestrina, the Convent of Santa Maria degli Angeli, a project funded by Taddeo Barberini. The convent and its church were inaugurated on 21 November 1642.

Farnese's final ambitious project was the construction of a large convent in the Rione Monti in Rome. Dedicated, like the convent in Albano, to the Immaculate Conception, it was completed in 1643 and became the mother house of the reformed congregation. It hosted the nuns from the Farnese monastery, which had been abandoned in 1640. The decline of that monastery after Farnese's departure for Albano in 1631 was related to the decline of the Farnese family and to the war between the dukedom of Castro and the Vatican State, which ended with the destruction of the city in 1649. Once again, the Barberini family contributed support and funds, as did the Rondinini and Peretti families. Farnese spent the last eight years of her life governing the convent. During this time the myth of her holiness and perfection grew.

Farnese's fame in Roman religious circles outlasted her death on 17 October 1651. Until the 1680s the Farnesian Poor Clares were viewed as devotional models: by challenging, with its rigor, the passive role assigned to women in post-Tridentine religious practice, the order fascinated female aristocrats and had a prominent place in the complex realm of Baroque spirituality. The reputation of the order was enhanced by the favor that Farnese had enjoyed with the Barberini Pope, Urban VIII, and his successors: Innocent X, who opposed the Barberini family, and Alexander VII.

A collection of approximately eighty of Farnese's poems was published by Angelo Bernabò in 1654; a 1657 edition by Francesco Cavalli added twenty compositions by other nuns of the Farnesian Poor Clares, most of them by Sister Isabella. Cavalli attributes only forty of the poems with absolute certainty to Farnese. The Cavalli edition was reprinted in 1659. Nicoletti's edifying biography was published in 1660; the autobiography that Farnese had written by order of her confessors is preserved only in the fairly extensive excerpts in the *Vita,* which also includes twelve of her letters and her spiritual will. In 1661, to promote Farnese's beatification, Nicoletti drafted a manuscript appendix devoted to her miracles during her lifetime and after her death. A second edition of her collected poems was published by Bernabò in 1666; Urban VIII had one hundred copies of this edition bound at his expense. The biography was republished in 1678. To this edition Nicoletti added "Ricordi di Suor Francesca alle religiose" (Sister Francesca's Mementos to Her Nuns), fourteen spiritual sermons addressed to the novices; "Meditazioni per le domeniche d'avvento e feste dei santi" (Meditations for Advent Sundays and Saints' Days); "Meditazioni del SS. Sacramento" (Meditations on the Holy Sacrament); "Offizio particolare della Beata Vergine" (Special Office for the Blessed Virgin); "Orazioni particolari per tutte le azioni del giorno" (Special Prayers for All Daily Deeds); "Meditazioni sopra il Pater Noster" (Meditations on the Paternoster); a treatise for the instruction of novices; and a selection of her sacred poems.

Farnese's poems were read in the salons of pious noblewomen and were included in the libraries of most monastic orders; but after the death of Cardinal Barberini in 1679, her fame dramatically declined. The last edition of her poems was printed by Giacomo Hertz in Venice that same year. Among the reasons for the fading of her name and message were the suspicion that the Farnesian monasteries were affected by deviant quietist devotional practices and the impracticability of her rigorous rule. She has been largely neglected by the Roman Catholic Church; in his 1971 visit to the Immaculate Conception monastery in Albano, Pope Paul VI incorrectly identified its founder's name and dates.

If Farnese fell into oblivion as an historical figure in the Catholic Church, her poetry received constant, although limited, attention. In the eighteenth century she was mentioned in Ginevra Canonici Fachini's bibliography of Italian women of letters, and in the twentieth century Benedetto Croce counted her and her sister among Baroque women poets. Severino Gori discovered a manuscript of spiritual instruction for novices attributed to Farnese at the monastery of Santa Maria delle Grazie in Farnese and published part of it in 1967 as "Esortazioni e ricordi della Ven. Fr. Farnese alle anime consacrate a Dio" (Venerable Farnese's Exhortations and Mementos to the Souls Consecrated to God). A nonautobiographical poetry notebook attributed to Farnese was discovered in the archive of the same monastery by Giovanni Baffioni, who published it in 1973.

Isabella Farnese's devotional poems, autobiographical fragments, and spiritual treatises outline the inner struggles of one of the most significant religious personalities of the Roman Baroque period in her search for perfection. Two well-documented studies testify to the authority and originality of her reform design, aimed at promoting a new devotional style that would make women's cloistered state more meaningful. The first is Nicoletti's seventeenth-century commemorative biography; the second is the 1994 monograph by Andretta, which discusses her role in political, religious, and women's devotional history. Combining the power derived from family status and from her leadership in religious institutions, Farnese partook of a climate of intense mysticism in which women challenged, in obstinately tortuous ways, post-Tridentine models of female devotional passivity. As Farnese had well understood since the days of her novitiate and had confided in her spiritual autobiography, "poiché per esser donna né con armi, né con lettere potevo farmi famosa concludevo in somma che bisognava esser santa" (since as a woman I could not become famous either through arms or through letters, I thereby concluded that I needed to be a saint).

Bibliography:

Ginevra Canonici Fachini, *Prospetto biografico delle donne italiane rinomate in letteratura dal secolo decimoquarto fino a'giorni nostri di Ginevra Canonici Fachini con una risposta a Lady Morgan risguardante alcune accuse da lei date alle donne italiane nella sua opera l'Italie* (Venice: Tipografia di Alvisopoli, 1824).

Biographies:

Andrea Nicoletti, *Vita delle venerabile madre suor Francesca Farnese detta di Giesù Maria dell'ordine di Santa Chiara, fondatrice delli Monasterii di Santa Maria delle Gratie di Farnese e della SS. Concettione di Albano e di Roma e riformatrice del Monasterio di Santa Maria degli Angeli di Palestrina* (Rome: Giacomo Dragondelli, 1660);

Stefano Andretta, "Francesca Farnese," in *Dizionario biografico degli Italiani,* volume 45 (Rome: Istituto dell'Enciclopedia Italiana, 1995), pp. 87–90.

References:

Stefano Andretta, *La venerabile superbia: Ortodossia e trasgressione nella vita di suor Francesca Farnese (1593–1651)* (Turin: Rosenberg & Sellier, 1994);

Benedetto Croce, "Donne letterate nel Seicento," in his *Nuovi saggi sulla letteratura italiana del Seicento* (Bari: Laterza, 1931), pp. 154–171;

Luigi Fiorani, "Monache e monasteri romani nell'età del quietismo," *Ricerche per la storia religiosa di Roma,* 1 (1977): 63–111;

Severino Gori, "La venerabile Francesca Farnese (1593–1651) riformatrice delle Clarisse a Roma," *Frate Francesco,* 32 (1965): 69–77, 129–136;

Mario Rosa, "The Nun," in *Baroque Personae,* edited by Rosario Villari, translated by Lydia G. Cochrane (Chicago: University of Chicago Press, 1995), pp. 195–238.

Vincenzo da Filicaia

(30 December 1642 – 24 September 1707)

Paul Colilli
Laurentian University

BOOKS: *Canzoni in occasione dell'assedio e liberazione di Vienna* (Florence: Piero Matini, 1684);

In lode della beata Umiliana: Canzone (Florence: Guiducci, 1694);

Poesie toscane, edited by Scipione Filicaia (Florence: Piero Matini, 1707);

Poesie toscane (Florence & Pistoia: Stefano Gatti, 1708);

Poesie toscane di Vincenzo da Filicaia senatore fiorentino e accademico della Crusca, coll'aggiunta della vita dell'autore in questa nuova edizione (Venice: Lorenzo Baseggio, 1771);

Poesie toscane di Vincenzo da Filicaia patrizio fiorentino, 2 volumes (London & Leghorn: G. T. Masi, 1781);

Opere del senatore Vincenzo da Filicaja, 2 volumes (Venice: Lorenzo Baseggio, 1787);

Poesie toscane del senatore Vincenzo da Filicaia con nuove aggiunte (Florence: Gregorio Chiari, 1823).

Editions and Collections: *Poesia del Seicento,* volume 1, edited by Carlo Muscetta and P. P. Ferrante (Turin: Einaudi, 1964), pp. 261–981;

Chiabrera e i lirici del classicismo barocco, edited by Marcello Turchi (Turin: Unione Tipografico-Editrice Torinese, 1974), pp. 863–881.

Edition in English: Joseph Tusiani: "Verse Translations of Seicento Poets," *Seicento Revisited,* special issue of *Forum Italicum,* edited by Albert N. Mancini, 7 (1973): 370–371.

OTHER: Tommaso Bonaventuri, ed., *Carmina illustrium poetarum Italorum* (Florence: Stamperia Reale, 1719), pp. 321–350.

Vincenzo da Filicaia (from <http://www.liberliber.it/biblioteca/f/filicaia/index.htm>)

Intended as a reaction against the purported lascivious nature of Baroque verse, Vincenzo da Filicaia's lyric poetry marks a decisive turn in the history of Italian literature. The poet Ugo Foscolo said that Filicaia was "tra i primi che ritrassero dall'ampollosa barbarie del Seicento la poesia italiana" (among the first to have pulled Italian poetry out of the pompous barbarity of the seventeenth century). Along with strong moral and rationalist veins, Filicaia's poetry includes features of the cinquecento "classical" lyric. The result is a form of poetic expression that moves in the direction of the "balanced" poetics of the Arcadian movement. His work also displays a political engagement that prefigures Romanticism. Filicaia thus stands at the end of the Baroque period and on the threshold of the Arcadian age. Filicaia enjoyed fame for his poetry in continental

Europe and was similarly appreciated in England, where George Gordon, Lord Byron translated his sonnet "Italia, Italia, o tu, cui feo la sorte" ("Italia, O Italia, on whom / The fatal gift of beauty was bestowed") in stanzas 42 and 43 of the fourth canto of *Childe Harold* (1813).

Filicaia was born in Florence on 30 December 1642 to Senator Braccio da Filicaia and Caterina di Cristofano Spini. He was named for his paternal grandfather, who was also a senator. The Filicaia family was distinguished both for its ancient origins and for its visibility in the civic affairs of Florence. Filicaia writes about his ancestors in the poem "Ai suoi figliuoli" (To His Children). Filicaia's mother died when he was about two; he had a brother, Vincenzo Maria Cappuccino da Filicaia, to whom he addressed some sonnets and a Latin poem.

Filicaia's father, who had been a member of the Accademia della Crusca (Academy of the Sifters) since 1627, was greatly involved in the education of his children. Typical of the aristocratic youth of the age, Filicaia spent a few years at the Jesuit college in Florence; he then moved to the University of Pisa, where he studied law, philosophy, and theology for five years.

Following his university studies, Filicaia practiced law in the office of G. Federighi, a friend of the family. He was also a skillful singer and violinist who gave public performances. He entered the Accademia della Crusca on 8 November 1664 and was its censor in 1667, 1690, 1702, and 1705. In 1673 he married Anna Capponi. They had two sons, Braccio and Scipione; in a series of Latin poems included in the anthology *Carmina illustrium poetarum Italorum* (1719) Filicaia refers to a daughter who died young. The former Queen Christina of Sweden, who had converted to Catholicism, abdicated her throne in 1654, and moved to Rome in 1655, financed the education of his children and provided him with a regular stipend until her death in 1689.

The Turkish siege of Vienna from 17 July to 12 September 1683 ended in the defeat of the Turks by a combined force led by King John III Sobieski of Poland. Filicaia's correspondence with his friends Francesco Redi and Benedetto Gori, whom he had met in Pisa, indicates that he saw the victory of the Christian army as a moment that favored the rebirth of poetry as an instrument for expressing lofty political and religious themes. To monumentalize the event he composed six long poems that were published in 1684 by the printer Piero Matini of Florence as *Canzoni in occasione dell'assedio e liberazione di Vienna* (Canzones on the Occasion of the Siege and Liberation of Vienna). Three of the poems are prefaced by dedicatory letters in Latin to the heroes of the liberation of Vienna: Holy Roman Emperor Leopold I; John III Sobieski, the most important figure in the battle; and Duke Charles of Lorraine. In these poems, as in most of his other lyrics, Filicaia seeks to transform the ludic and apolitical quality of Baroque verse into poetry that is characterized by civic and ethical themes. Foscolo observed that in Filicaia's political poems "una scintilla di quel sentimento patriottico che aveva infiammato le anime di Dante e del Petrarca parve ridestarsi in lui, e per mezzo di lui, ne' suoi lettori" (a spark of that patriotic sentiment that had inflamed the souls of Dante and of Petrarch seems to have reawakened in him, and through him, in his readers).

While Filicaia's initial renown derived from the theme of martial conflict, his poetry is heavily imbued with religious thought. His acquaintances remembered him as a "poeta-theologus" (poet-theologian), in part because of the many biblical allusions that permeate his verse. Commenting on Filicaia's poems on the liberation of Vienna, which he had read in manuscript, in a letter dated 26 September 1683, Redi wrote that "se uno de' più nobili profeti del Vecchio Testamento avesse oggi dovuto parlare con Dio per un affare simile a quello dell'assedio di Vienna non avrebbe potuto farlo né più maestosamente, né con più decorosa e santa umiltà" (if one of the most noble prophets of the Old Testament had to speak today with God about an affair similar to the siege of Vienna he would not have been able to do so neither more majestically nor with more decorous and holy humility). Filicaia was convinced that God's intervention enabled one to discover the sublime and to express it through appropriate stylistic and linguistic means. In an 11 October 1683 letter to Redi he said of his plan to write a poem in honor of the king of Poland, "Dio che mi vede il cuore sa che io non lo fo per vanità, ma per vero zelo di glorificare in questo gran Re la divina misericordia" (God who sees my heart knows that I do it not for vanity, but for the true zeal of glorifying the divine mercy in the great King).

Filicaia's son Braccio became a page in the Medici court in 1691. That same year Filicaia became a member of the Accademia degli Arcadia (Arcadian Academy), which had been founded in Rome in 1690, taking the pseudonym "Polibo Emonio." The Arcadians sought to make an epistemological and aesthetic break from the purportedly shocking and tasteless poetry of the Baroque and to revive the sort of balanced and measured lyric that had been cultivated during the Renaissance. Filicaia played an important role in this effort, because he infused his poetry with an ethical ideology that is central to Arcadian poetics. For him, only when the poet is sincere in what is written is a balance between art and morality achieved; in "Ai suoi figli" (To His Children) he writes: "Rado, o non mai s'oppone / A i costumi la penna, e non si scrive, / Se non co' sensi, onde si parla e vive" (Rarely, or never / does the pen oppose the customs and does not write, / if not without the meanings for which one speaks and lives).

Filicaia alludes to his intention to cultivate a new poetics that will move beyond "lascivi amori" (lustful loves) in the direction of noble themes in the poem "La poesia" (Poetry), dedicated to Christina:

Nel più alto silenzio, allor che amico
sonno, col dolce ventilar dell'ale,
gli occhi al mondo affaticato serra,
grave in vista, e di stirpe alta immortale
donna m'apparve di sembiante antico.

(In the loftiest silence, when friendly
sleep, with the sweet batting of the wings,
closes my eyes to the tired world,
grave in sight, and of lofty immortal origin
a woman of ancient semblance appeared to me.)

Maria Pia Paoli has demonstrated that Filicaia's poetry is a blend of humanism and spirituality that is typical of the Florentine environment of the time. A fusing of elements of the Neoplatonic and Petrarchan traditions is apparent in Filicaia's "Forza dell'amor celeste" (The Power of Celestial Love), which presents harmony as a symphony of discordant notes: "Come da occulta simpatia di corde / e di voci diverse un sol concento / esce" (As from a hidden sympathy of strings / and of diverse voices one harmony / arises). Another motif is pessimism: "Deh, perché a vita sì crudel si nasce? / Perché son padre? / e perché voi miei figli?" (Why is one born into such a cruel life? / Why am I a father? / And why are you my children?). This outburst of despair is, however, tempered by the sense of hope that is inherent in the theological culture of which Filicaia was a part; it is not a naive hope but is coupled with the realization that one must do battle against the cruelty of the world.

Carmine DiBiase notes a confessional tone in Filicaia's poetry. It is not the passionate outpouring of emotion that was later typical of the Romantics but a controlled and rational articulation of profound introspection. Filicaia states in the poem "Nel riaprimento dell'Accademia della Crusca" (On the Reopening of the Academy of the Sifters) that he composes poetry to fathom the depths of his soul: "Canto a me stesso, e sol che meco io viva. / Io stesso m'udirò, s'altri non m'ode" (I sing to myself, and only so that I live with myself. / I myself will hear myself, if others do not hear me). These verses convey a mood of total detachment and absolute independence that is found elsewhere in Filicaia's poetry and is highly reminiscent of the Petrarchan sense of isolation from the world. Filicaia is seeking to rediscover the inner solitude that the founders of the Arcadian Academy believed the Baroque had misplaced.

Filicaia's resolve to descend to the depths of his soul is remarkable. He is interested both in representing and in understanding himself. The point of departure for such a quest can vary from an episode in history to images from the natural world to banal particulars from everyday life. "Riflessi morali alludenti all'Alluvione" (Moral Reflections Alluding to the Flood) presents an image of a powerful wave that destroys the architecture of the poet's conscience; the ravaging flow of water expresses the hardship of existence that overpowers the poet. In "Raccoglimento in se stesso" (Recollection in Oneself) Filicaia remembers his past life in a way that is analogous to the confessional lament in Petrarch's "Voi ch'ascoltate in rime sparse il suono" (You who hear in scattered rhymes the sound). This poem and others by Filicaia point to a Petrarchan past and an Arcadian future. Filicaia wants to find the linguistic register that will allow him to express the new artistic measure to which the Arcadian ideal will aspire: one that is based on moral rectitude and clothed in the garb of clear and unencumbered expression. His experimentation with the Petrarchan model garnered much praise at first; according to Ludovico A. Muratori, Filicaia's poetry was the continuation of the best that the Petrarchan tradition produced.

Filicaia's biographer Tommaso Bonaventuri relates that the poet spent a considerable amount of time in Figline, in the countryside far from Florence, leading a life of solitude spent in the "contemplazione dell'altissime meraviglie della natura e di Dio" (contemplation of the highest marvels of nature and of God). Filicaia's love of his native Florence is expressed in "Nel tornare dalla Villa di Figline a Firenze" (On Returning from the Figline Villa to Florence), Florence is home to the beauty of nature and art. But Florence is also the "Donna dell'Arno" (Woman of the Arno) who is witness to his pain and suffering.

The poet's spiritual closeness to nature is evident in sonnets such as "Villeggiatura di Primavera" (Spring Vacation). Filicaia often establishes a relationship of personal union with nature, as in "Nel camminar lungo l'Elsa" (On Walking along the Elsa River). In "In occasione di uno stranissimo temporale" (On the Occasion of a Strangest Storm) the fleetingness of the natural world is expressed in colorless images and a meter that evokes a sensation of weariness. Filicaia seeks to capture the moment of transformation in the natural order in "In occasione delle Nevi" (On the Occasion of the

Snow). In "In morte di Vicenzo Viviani" (On the Death of Vincenzo Viviani) he uses language typical of the scientific literature of the period and the evocation of Galileo to show how human valor, one of the highest expressions of nature, is reborn from one generation to the next.

Filicaia's poetry shows traces of the Baroque style, but there is always an attempt to dismantle the uneven distribution of weight between idea or image and language. Filicaia's is a search for rational equilibrium with the aim of building a poetic image that is at once solemn, sublime, and appropriately measured. Filicaia strives for narrative consistency within the context of lyric intimacy and interiority, an approach that discards the hyperbole of the Baroque but appropriates its sense of the sublime.

After his son Braccio's death in 1695, Filicaia became gravely ill. When he recovered from the ailment he became a senator—not, as he told his friend Lorenzo Magalotti, out of ambition but out of financial need. He was appointed commissioner of Volterra by the grand duke of Tuscany, Cosimo III de' Medici, and between 1699 and 1701 he held the same post in Pisa. In 1701 he became *Secretario delle Tratte* (Secretary of Trade) and fell seriously ill again. Filicaia died in Florence on 24 September 1707. His son Scipione, with the patronage of the Accademia della Crusca, published his lyrics—except for the Latin poems, most of which remain unpublished—that same year.

The transitional characteristic of Filicaia's poetry has stimulated both the esteem and the ire of literary critics. At first he was perceived as one of the most important figures in the history of Italian and European literature. Girolamo Tiraboschi refers to Filicaia as one who, together with Benedetto Menzini, rediscovered the beauty and elegance of the Italian poetic tradition, but whose lyrics are characterized by an unparalleled expression of the sublime. Foscolo saw in Filicaia's poetry an example of the "desiderio nascente del vero" (burgeoning desire of truth) that took place between the seventeenth and eighteenth centuries and was to be contrasted with the "deliri dei Secentisti" (deliriousness of the seventeenth-century poets). Vittorio Alfieri judged the heroic and historical poems of Filicaia "bellissime e nobili" (most beautiful and noble) and used them as a model for his *L'America libera: Odi* (1784; translated as *Alfieri's Ode to America's Independence*, 1976).

But scathing criticism eventually surfaced. Luigi Settembrini believed that Filicaia's Italy "is outside of the poet" and that his Baroque side is empty and superficial as a consequence of the style as well as the "weakness of the spirit." This negative judgment is echoed by Francesco de Sanctis, according to whom the poems for the liberation of Vienna are deceptively prophetic, appearing to be driven by a sacred furor but giving way to a "pomposa rhetorica nella quale si scopre la simulazione della vita" (pompous rhetoric in which one finds the simulation of life). Benedetto Croce terms Filicaia's poetry devoid of any emotion or persuasion and says that his name should disappear from the pages of literary history. More recently, a more benign assessment of Filicaia has prevailed. Scholars such as Walter Binni credit Filicaia with appropriating the sublime from the Baroque and tempering it with tasteful art. In Binni's mind, Vincenzo da Filicaia's high profile in the Arcadian Academy and during all of the eighteenth century is attributable to the fact that his poetics was seen as having the characteristics of nobility, clarity, linearity, lofty solemnity, vast and noble concepts, and an organic and orderly development of verse.

Letters:

Lettere inedite a Lorenzo Magalotti, edited by Ferruccio Ferrari (Pisa: T. Nistri, 1885).

Biographies:

Ugolino Verino, *De illustratione urbis Florentiae,* volume 3 (Paris, 1633), p. 28;

L. Fabbri, *Orazione in morte del senatore Vincenzo da Filicaia detta nell'Accademia degli Apatisti* (Florence, 1709);

Tommaso Bonaventuri, "Vita di Vincenzo da Filicaia Senatore Fiorentino detto Polibo Emonio," in *Le Vite degli arcadi illustri,* volume 2 (Rome: Antonio de' Rossi, 1710), pp. 61-82;

Bonaventuri, "Lodi del Senatore Vincenzo da Filicaia," in *Prose e Rime inedite del Sen. Vincenzo da Filicaia, d'Anton Maria Salvini e d'altri,* edited by Domenico Moreni (Florence: Magheri, 1821);

Moreni, ed., *Sonetti di Angiolo Allori detto il Bronzino ed altre rime inedite di più insigni poeti* (Florence: Magheri, 1823), pp. 169-178;

Demostene Turibilli Giuliani, *Sommario storico delle famiglie celebri della Toscana,* volume 1 (Florence, 1862), p. 40;

Gustavo Caponi, *Vincenzo da Filicaia e le sue opere* (Prato: Giachetti, 1901);

Maria Pia Paoli, "Vincenzo da Filicaia," in *Dizionario biografico degli italiani,* volume 47 (Rome: Istituto della Enciclopedia Italiana, 1997), pp. 658-660.

References:

Vittorio Alfieri, *Vita,* volume 1, edited by Luigi Fassò (Asti: Casa dell'Alfieri, 1951), p. 227;

Walter Binni, *L'Arcadia e il Metastasio* (Florence: La Nuova Italia, 1963), pp. 39-44;

Benedetto Croce, "Intorno a un giudizio del Macaulay su Vincenzo da Filicaia," in his *Nuovi saggi sulla letteratura del Seicento* (Bari: Laterza, 1949), pp. 318–325;

Francesco De Sanctis, *Storia della letteratura italiana,* volume 2, edited by Croce (Bari: Laterza, 1954), pp. 202–203;

Carmine DiBiase, *Arcadia edificante* (Naples: Edizioni Scientifiche Italiane, 1969), pp. 141–262;

Ugo Foscolo, *Saggi di critica storico-letteraria,* volume 10 of his *Opere edite e postume,* edited by F. S. Orlandini and Enrico Mayer (Florence: Le Monnier, 1923), pp. 345–360;

Maria Pia Paoli, "Esperienze religiose e poesia nella Firenze del '600," *Rivista di storia e letteratura religiosa,* 29 (1993): 35–78;

Luigi Settembrini, *Lezioni di letteratura italiana,* volume 2 (Naples: Morano, 1872), pp. 321–322;

Girolamo Tiraboschi, *Storia della letteratura italiana,* volume 8, part 1 (Florence: Molini, Landi, 1802), pp. 469–471.

Papers:

Manuscripts for many of Vincenzo da Filicaia's unpublished works and many of his letters are held by the Archivio Geddes Filicaia in Montaione, near Florence.

Silvio Fiorillo

(1560 or 1565? – 1634?)

Mary Jo Muratore
University of Missouri

BOOKS: *La ghirlanda: Egloga in napoletana e toscana lingua* (Naples: Longo, 1602);

L'amor giusto: Egloga pastorale in napoletana e toscana lingua (Naples: Stigliola, 1604);

Li tre capitani vanagloriosi: Capricciosa rappresentazione di strani amorosi avvenimenti (Naples: D. F. Maccarano, 1621);

La cortesia di Leone e di Ruggiero, con la morte di Rodomonte suggetto cavato dall'Ariosto, e ridotto in stile rappresentativo (Milan: Malatesta, 1624);

Il mondo conquistato (Milan: Malatesta, 1627);

L'Ariodante tradito, e morte di Polinesso da Rinaldo Paladino (Pavia: Rossi, 1627);

La Lucilla costante con le ridicolose disfide e prodezze di Policinella (Milan: Malatesta, 1632).

Editions: *La Lucinda cortese*, in *Commedie dei comici dell'arte*, edited by Laura Falavolti (Turin: Unione Tipografico-Editrice Torinese, 1982);

La Lucilla costante, edited by Monica Brindicci (Naples: Bellini, 1995);

La cortesia di Leone e di Ruggiero con la morte di Rodomonte suggetto cavato dall'Ariosto e ridotto in stile rappresentativo, edited by Francesca Savoia (Pisa: Pacini Fazzi, 1996).

Silvio Fiorillo was a popular and highly respected actor of the commedia dell'arte; he was also a talented playwright whose works reflect his belief that a drama must satisfy the dual demands of theater as performance and as literature. He is best known for the roles of the braggart Spanish soldier Capitan Matamoros and of Pulcinella ("Little Chick"), a character many scholars credit him with inventing. Fiorillo's published writings include comedies in the commedia dell'arte tradition that capture the spirit of his stage improvisations, monologues that could be performed spontaneously with minimal preparation, and pastoral eclogues in the Neapolitan and Tuscan dialects. His plays are characterized by a mixture of erudite and popular comic techniques. For example, he gives classical names to stock commedia dell'arte characters: Pantalone is sometimes called

Silvio Fiorillo as Capitan Matamoros in the frontispiece for his La Lucilla costante con le ridicolose disfide e prodezze di Policinella *(Constant Lucilla with the Ridiculous Challenges and Feats of Policinella), published in 1632 (from Benedetto Croce,* Saggi sulla letteratura italiana dei seicento, *1962; Thomas Cooper Library, University of South Carolina)*

Andolfo or Alberto, and the lovers are not Orsola, Valeria, or Lelio but Lucrezia, Lucilla, or Cosimo. Another feature of his works is an absence of stage directions that is attributed to two possible motivations. First, there is no evidence that Fiorillo was head of a troupe when he published his plays, and he may have thought that stage directions were more appropriately the domain of the director than the writer; to provide specific stage directions would limit the creativity of the director and the actors. Second, because he performed with so many troupes, he may not have wanted any of his plays to be too closely associated with one particular company; the more rigidly controlled the performance, the more it would be linked to the troupe that performed it most regularly. Thus, the sketchy directions would allow the troupe with which he was performing the maximum in flexibility.

Of Neapolitan descent, Fiorillo is thought to have been born in Capua around 1560 or 1565. He may have been a cavalry captain before taking up the theater. He is known to have had two sons, who were also actors: Giovan Battista, who performed under the name Trappolino and was known as the Neapolitan Scaramouche; and Girolamo, about whom little is known. He reportedly had a daughter and may have had a third son. Giovan Battista's wife, Beatrice Vitali, was also an actress; she and her husband were regularly invited to perform with her father-in-law or with any company with which he was affiliated, if Fiorillo so requested.

Fiorillo's first documented appearance as an actor occurred in 1589 at the hospital Santa Maria del Popolo degli Incurabili (St. Mary of the People for the Incurables) in Naples, where he played Capitan Matamoros with the Fedeli (Faithful Ones) troupe. The hospital received half of the revenues generated by the performance.

Based on the ancient Roman figure of the miles gloriosus (braggart soldier), Fiorillo's Capitan Matamoros is endowed not only with farcical but also with human traits; the combination provides this usually one-sided character with additional depth and complexity and makes Matamoros a bit more engaging than the typical braggart soldier. The traditional figure is notorious for verbal heroism and behavioral cowardice; Fiorillo puts less emphasis on the character's cowardice than on the noble and classical vice of pride that leads to his boastful exaggerations. In the prologue to *Li tre capitani vanagloriosi* (1621, The Three Vainglorious Captains), which features two Spanish captains, Matamoros and Don Corta Rincones, and one Italian, Capitano Tempesta, Fiorillo states: "Non lascerò ancora di dirvi de quanto valore e potenza hoggi frà noi mortali li vanagloria sia" (I never get tired of pointing out how important vanity is, how strong its power over mankind).

Matamoros's uniform consisted of a wide-brimmed hat with feathers, a military jacket, and a cape. He usually sported a long sword at his side; but sometimes the weapon was replaced with a *corno* (horn), indicating that the captain was not only a braggart but also a cuckold. He generally had a prominent nose and typically did not wear a mask.

As an actor Fiorillo was noted for his sense of timing and gift for wordplay. His Capitan Matamoros, while generally based on the miles gloriosus, is more specifically patterned after the Spanish military men of the time, and Fiorillo generally spoke Spanish when playing the role. Fiorillo's captain provided Italians with a means to vent anti-Spanish sentiments caused by the presence of Spanish mercenary soldiers in Italy during the cinquecento; for this reason, the braggart soldier was a much-beloved figure in Italy but fell out of favor in the early seventeenth century, when performances outside Italy increased and hostility toward Spain decreased. Some of the captain's characteristics evolved into the character of Scaramucia. Nevertheless, records indicate that Fiorillo continued to play the role of the captain at least until 1628. Other famous captains include Francesco Andreini's Capitano Spavento della Valle Infernal, Fabrizio de Fornaris's Capitano Cocodrillo, Girolamo Garavini's Capitano Rinoceronte, Giuseppe Bianchi's Capitano Spezzafer, and Diego Ancatoni's Capitano Sangue y Fuego.

The next record of Fiorillo is in 1594, when a revamped and enlarged Uniti (United Ones) troupe arrived in Milan: the roster of actors lists a Silvio who is believed to be Fiorillo. The duke of Mantua, Vincenzo I Gonzaga, saw Fiorillo perform in the role of the captain sometime in 1599. A letter from Fiorillo to the duke indicates that he was living in Naples and for family reasons could not work for the Gonzaga troupe during the 1599–1600 season, as he was contracted to do. He went to Mantua in 1600 and met the duke as the guest of Tristano Martinelli, superintendent of all actors of the Mantuan state. He remained in the duke's service for one year. In 1601 he was with the Accesi (Impassioned Ones) in France. In 1604 he published the pastoral eclogue *L'amor giusto* (Proper Love). The eclogue is written partly in the Neapolitan dialect and partly in Tuscan, and the prologue includes a rather daring partisan affirmation: "Ca vàle chiù na scarpa cacata da no Napoletano (con reverentia de 'se faccie voste) che quante toscanicchie se trovano pe lo munno" (Because a shoe shat upon by a Neapolitan is worth more [with all due respect to those present] than all the little Tuscans in the world). In *L'amor giusto* the Neapolitan Cola mixes freely with mythological deities such as Diana and Cupid, and he is dressed not in the local manner but in the rags of a shepherd.

Fiorillo performed with the Accesi in Turin in 1605 and in France in 1608. In the latter year he rejoined the Fedeli. Some scholars believe that he performed in the role of Pulcinella for the first time in

1609, perhaps because the role of the captain was losing favor. An often-quoted anecdote states that when the duke of Mantua was preparing to send the Fideli troupe to France with Fiorillo playing Matamoros, the other actors revolted, claiming that Fiorillo's talents were on the wane. It is fairly certain that Fiorillo introduced Pulcinella into the comedia dell'arte, although some aspects of the character may have existed in outline long before Fiorillo was born. Pulcinella reflects the characteristics of the peasants of Acerra and may have been patterned after a Neapolitan peasant turned actor, Puccio D'Aniello. It is more likely that he is simply a conglomeration of characteristics of peasants in the region near Naples. He is an oafish figure, awkward in appearance and vulgar in manner, and a fundamentally sensual being whose quest to satisfy his many appetites seems endless. His speech is sprinkled with words that mimic popular Neapolitan dialect and is often garbled, incoherent, and incomprehensible. Pulcinella is slow-witted but believes himself to be quite shrewd, and he is the hapless victim of misfortunes of all kinds. He is traditionally dressed in a big peaked hat with feathers; a black half mask with a prominent nose resembling the beak of a chick; a long, white, loose and belted blouse; white baggy pants; and slippers with rosettes on the toes. He carries a stick. He is hunchbacked and has a fat stomach that results from his love of food, especially gnocchi. Variations of the character include Andrea Calcese's Ciuccio, Polichenelle in France, and Punch in England.

During the 1609–1610 season Fiorillo toured the provinces with the actress Flaminia Tosetta, who was playing the role of Silvia. The two were reportedly lovers, and it is speculated that the celebrated actor Tiberio Fiorillo, whose performances in the role of Scaramouche were so heralded that he came to be known by that name alone, was their son; the theory has never been substantiated.

Fiorillo was with the Fideli in Naples in 1611 and with the Accesi in Milan in 1612. In 1613 he was on his way to Mantua to visit Duke Fernando I and decided to stop in Florence, where the Fedeli troupe was playing. Perhaps jealous of Fiorillo's increasing celebrity status, one of the players wrote a negative assessment of his acting talents to the duke. Fiorillo performed with the company of Ottavio and Vittoria Bernardini in Mantua in 1613. In 1614 he was in Florence and Genoa with the Uniti and in the same cities with the Accesi. He appeared with the Uniti in Naples and with the Accesi in Florence in 1615.

In 1616 Fiorillo went into voluntary exile from Naples for five years. He was with the Confidenti (Confident Ones) in Mantua in 1619 and with the Accesi in the area around Modena in 1620. In the latter year he and Giovan Battista were in Bologna with the Castiglioni company. During the same season he played the roles of Pulcinella and Matamoros with the Cecchini troupe and returned with them to Naples in 1621 for the inauguration of the San Bartolomeo theater. That same year he published *Li tre capitani vanagloriosi*, which he dedicated to Marino Caracciolo, prince of Santobuono. He was in Venice in 1622 and with the Accesi in Florence in 1623. In 1624 he published *La cortesia di Leone e Ruggiero* (1624, The Kindness of Leone and Ruggiero), a play based on an episode from Ludovico Ariosto's *Orlando Furioso* (1516, The Frenzy of Orlando; translated as *Orlando Furioso in English Heroical Verse*, 1591), in Milan. The work is a mixture of ancient and popular elements, and Fiorillo's subtle focus on the moral consequences of behavior lends it an elevated tone. Fiorillo is one of the few playwrights who managed fully to exploit the many facets of Ariosto's masterpiece.

Fiorillo was with the Accesi in Venice in 1624–1625. In 1627 his work in verse, *L'Ariodante tradito, e morte di Polinesso da Rinaldo Paladino*, was published in Pavia; his *Il mondo conquistato* (The World Conquered) was published in Milan the same year.

Fiorillo was still with the Accesi in 1632, when he published *La Lucilla costante con le ridicolose disfide e prodezze di Policinella* (Constant Lucilla with the Ridiculous Challenges and Feats of Policinella), which is considered his masterwork. He had written it in Milan for the actress Lucilla Trenta. The comedy is dedicated to a real Spanish captain, Gómez Suárez de Figueroa, governor of the state of Milan in 1624. Two captains are featured in the play: the Italian Squarcialeone (Lionripper) and the Spanish Matamoros, played by Fiorillo.

A leitmotif that runs throughout Fiorillo's works, constancy in love, evolved over time: in his early plays fidelity is highly prized, while in the later ones it is unattainable. This transition can be seen in *La Lucilla costante*, in which the ideal of constancy and the reality of infidelity come into conflict on both the linguistic and the moral levels. For the aging Fiorillo, unflinching fidelity is nothing more than an impractical ideal; it can be found in literature but not in real life. Fidelity may be routine for heroes of chivalric romances or those of the courtly-love tradition such as Ruggiero, Orlando, and Leone, but for most mortals total constancy in love is an unrealistic goal, perhaps even an unnatural one. Life for Fiorillo is carnal, sensual, exciting, unpredictable, and ever changing—the very things that make it worthwhile.

An example of the Italian attitude toward the Spanish can be seen in *La Lucilla costante* when Matamoros's peacemaking initiatives provoke a piece of less than friendly advice from his servant:

Matamoros: Nunca jamas se harán, se yo ne me resuelvo un dia de irme a España a tratallass y a concluillas con la mayestad del rey mi seōr, y despues luego passarme por la buelta de Francia y desde alli con un salto en Alemana.
Alberto: E perché no lo fate, signore? Vi raccomando il mondo.

(Matamoros: They [the peace treaties] will never, ever be made, if I do not resolve one day to go to Spain to negotiate them and conclude them with the authority of the king, my lord, and then go over to France, and from there, hop over to Germany.
Alberto: And why don't you do it, Sir? I recommend the world to you [that is, get out, and also "beware of the world"]).

The captain generally boasts of his amazing exploits, both military and sexual, usually to a servant whose more reality-based perspective contradicts or refutes the captain's boasts. A typical example of this banter is the exchange between Squarcialeone and Scaramuzza in *La Lucilla costante*:

Squarcialeone: E se tanti e tanti famosissimi poeti, con sonoro ed eroico stile, celebrano e cantano le mie generose azioni, la bravura, i risoluti assalti, le tremende scaramuzze, le distruzioni, le morti, le vittorie e i mie fatti egreggi....
Scaramuzza: E le foiute e le ritirate.

(Squarcialeone: And if so many most famous poets, with resonant and heroic style, celebrate my magnanimous deeds, the skill, the resolute assaults, the horrific skirmishes, the destructions, the deaths, the victories and my outstanding feats....
Scaramuzza: And the flights and the retreats.)

At the end of the play, instead of the duel between braggart captains that usually occurs in such works, Matamoros is pitted against his servant Pulcinella. The formal language of the braggart soldier is juxtaposed with the pedestrian speech of the valet:

Fulgensio (legge la lettera di Cap. Mamtamoros): Yo, el gran capitan Matamoros ganavanderas, horrible, terrible, incredible, tremendo, estupendo, horrendo, animoso, valeroso, espanto de Marte y de la Muerte, sobrino de Belona, nieto de la fortuna, naçido y criado dentro del gran baratro enfernal, entres los diabolicos gritos de Pluton, Mijera, Tersifone y Eletto, notrido y sustendado de sangre humano, arcecavalleraço de España, destruydor de camos enemigos rompedor de exercitos, deribador de castillos, conquistador de reynos, temor de imperios, vencedor de battallas, parientes del Soffi, señor de Eteopia, tributado dal turquo, dal persiano y dal grandissimo Lucifero, sostancia y braveza de la guerra y plus ultra, mas allá de todo el mundo, sessenta mil milliones de leguas, desafio el noble Pulcinella a pelear con migo, armado de la manera que a el fuera de gusto, antes que el claro sol se vaia dentrol del oceano y todo lo hago por mantenerle que lo que de mi ha dicho es muy gran mentira.

La risposta de Pulcinella: Io lo gran nobele e illustrissimo signore Policinella de Gamaro de Tamaro cocumaro de Napole, nasciuto a Pontaselece, figio de Marco Sfila e de Madama Sbignapriesto, pe mangiare no cacavo de macarune, mangiatore de galline, picciune, fasane, pernice, pastice, sausiccie, migliacie e capune, squarciatore de cosse de porcelle, accedtore de puorce sarvatece, sgareatore de galle d'Innia, e deluviatore d'ogni genere musicorum de vidanne squisite, smafaratore de vuote de grieco, lagrema, guarnacia, marvasia, leateco, mangia guerra, scolatore de fiasche, polizatore de scotelle, così de iurno comme de notte, co lumme e senza lumme, dintro e fora coreggia, azzeto la desfida de lo capitanio Matamora re e monarca de li pultrune, arcefanfaro delli castrate.

(Filgensio [reads Captain Matamoros's letter]: I, the great Captain Matamoros, flag conqueror, horrible, terrible, incredible, tremendous, marvelous, horrific, brave, valiant, the fear of Mars and of Death, nephew of Belona, grandson of Fortune, born and raised inside the great infernal abyss, amid the diabolical screams of Pluto, Mijera, Tersifone and Eletto, nourished and sustained by human blood, rowdy arch-knight of Spain, destroyer of enemy camps, smasher of armies, demolisher of castles, conqueror of kingdoms, the dread of empires, winner of battles, relative of Soffi, Lord of Ethiopia, receiver of tributes from the Turk, the Persian and from the most great Lucifer, essence and fury of war and much further, far beyond the whole world, sixty-six thousand million leagues, I challenge the noble Pulcinella to fight with me, armed in the manner that suits him, before the bright sun disappears into the ocean, and all of this I do to demonstrate to him that what he said about me is a very big lie.

Pulcinella's reply: I, the great and most illustrious Signor Pulcinella de Gamaro de Tamoro [*gamaro* means "clever" but also "drunkard"; *tamoro* means "rough" or "uncouth"], fool of Naples, born in Pontaselece, son of Marco Sfila, and of Lady Sbignapriesto, for being able to guzzle much macaroni, eater of chickens, pigeons, pheasants, partridges, pies, sausages, black puddings and capons, slasher of pork chops, killer of wild boars, gobbler of turkeys, scourge of every kind of table delicacy, of exquisite dishes, guzzler of emptied containers of Greek, Lagrema, Guarnacia, Marvasia, Letreco wines, war eater, swigger of flasks, scourger of bowls, in daytime as in night, with lamp or without, within and without the belt, accept the challenge of Captain Matamoros and king of the loafers, arch-braggart of the castrated.)

The duel between Matamoros and Pulcinella is an exception to Fiorillo's reluctance to provide stage directions: here he provides the actors with detailed guidance. While the captain fights with traditional weapons in pursuit of glory and honor, Pulcinella wields cooking utensils and fights for something to eat. With the help of some other servants, Pulcinella wins the battle, but they allow Matamoros to believe it was all a joke.

When the Affezionati put on *Il creduto principe* (The Supposed Prince) in 1632 in Venice, Silvio Fiorillo may have doubled as Matamoros and the jailer, Puccannello. The Pulcinella character assumes its official literary form in this comedy. Fiorillo refers to himself in this play as an impassioned, affectionate, and resolute actor, playing on the names of some of the many acting troupes with which he was affiliated. His last known performance was with the Affezionati during Carnival in Bologna in 1634. He is presumed to have died shortly thereafter; the place and date of his death are unknown.

Letters:

Giovanna Checchi, *Due lettere inedite di Silvio Fiorillo* in "Quaderni di teatro," 24 (1984): 73–79;

Claudia Burattelli, Domenica Landolfi, and Anna Zinanni, eds., *Comici dell'arte: Corrispondenze* (Florence: Le Lettere, 1993).

Bibliography:

Thomas F. Heck, *Commedia dell'Arte: A Guide to the Primary and Secondary Literature* (New York: Garland, 1988).

Biography:

Giovanna Checchi, "Fiorillo, Silvio," in *Dizionario biografico degli Italiani*, volume 48 (Rome: Istituto dell'Enciclopedia Italiana, 1997), pp. 189–191.

References:

Anton Bragaglia, *Pulcinella* (Rome: Casinis, 1953);

Monica Brindicci, "La Commedia dell'arte a Napoli nella prima metà del XVII secolo: Silvio Fiorillo e altre esperienze," in *Origini della commedia improvisa o dell'arte*, edited by Maria Chiabò and Federico Doglio (Rome: Torre d'Orfeo, 1996), pp. 187–203;

Silvia Carandini, *Teatro e spettacolo nel Seicento* (Rome: Laterza, 1990);

Paul C. Castagno, *The Early Commedia dell'arte* (New York: Peter Lang, 1994), pp. 102–103;

Giovanna Checchi, *Silvio Fiorilli in arte Capitan Matamoros* (Capua: Capuanova, 1986);

Benedetto Croce, *Pulcinella e il personaggio del napoletano in commedia: Ricerche ed osservazioni* (Rome: Loescha, 1899);

Croce, "Pulcinella e le relazioni della commedia dell'arte con la commedia popolare romana," *Archivio storico per le provincie napoletane*, 23 (1898): 605–608;

Croce, *Saggi sulla letteratura italiana dei Seicento* (Bari: Laterza, 1962), p. 199;

Fausto De Michele, *Guerrieri ridicoli e guerre vere nel teatro comico del '500 e del '600 (Italia, Spagna e paesi di lingua tedesca)* (Florence: Alma, 1998), pp. 88–95;

Pier Luis Duchartre, *La Comédie italienne: L'improvisation, les canevas, vies, caractères, portraits, masques des illustres personnages de la commedia dell'arte* (Paris: Librairie de France, 1924);

Laura Falavolti, "Nota al testo," in her *Commedie dei comici dell'arte* (Turin: Unione Tipografico-Editrice Torinese, 1982);

S. Ferrone, *Commedie dell'Arte*, 2 volumes (Milan: Mursia, 1985, 1986);

Romei Giovana, "La Commedia dell'Arte e la favola pastorale," in *Sviluppi della drammaturgia pastorale nell'Europa del Cinque-Seicento: Convegno di studi, Roma 23–26 maggio 1990*, edited by Maria Chiabò and Federico Doglio (Viterbo: Centro studi sul teatro medioevale e rinascimentale, 1992), pp. 181–199;

U. Prota Giurleo, *I teatri de Napoli nel '600: La commedia e le maschere* (Naples: Fiorentino, 1962), pp. 9, 15;

Kathleen Marguerite Lea, *Italian Popular Comedy: A Study in the Commedia dell'arte, 1560–1630, with Special Reference to the English Stage* (Oxford: Clarendon Press, 1934);

Allardyce Nicoll, *Masks, Mimes and Miracles: Studies in Popular Theatre* (New York: Harcourt Brace, 1931);

Nicoll, *World of Harlequin* (Cambridge: Cambridge University Press, 1963);

John Rudlin, *Commedia dell'Arte: An Actor's Handbook* (London & New York: Routledge, 1994);

Ferdinando Tavianai and Mirella Schino, *Il segreto della commedia dell'arte: La memoria delle compagnie teatrali del XVI, XVII e XVII secolo* (Florence: Usher, 1982).

Battista Guarini
(10 December 1538 – 7 October 1612)

Nicolas J. Perella
University of California, Berkeley

BOOKS: *Il Verrato ovvero difesa di quanto ha scritto Messer Giason Denores contra le tragicomedie e le pastorali, in un suo discorso di poesie* (Ferrara: Printed by Vincenzo Galdura for Alfonso Caraffa, 1588);

Il pastor fido: Tragicomedia pastorale (Venice: Giovanni Battista Bonfadino, 1590; Ferrara: Benedetto Mamarello, 1590); enlarged as *Il pastor fido: Tragicomedia pastorale. Ora in questa XX. impressione di curiose, & dotte annotationi arricchito, & di bellissime figure in rame ornato. Con vn compendio di poesia tratto da i duo verati, con la giunta d'altre cose notabili per opera del medesimo s. caua* (Venice: Giovanni Battista Ciotti, 1602); translated by Edward Dymock as *Il pastor fido; or The Faithful Shepherd* (London: Simon Waterson, 1602);

Il Verato [sic] secondo ovvero replica dell'Attizzato accademico ferrarese in difesa del Pastorfido: Contra la seconda scrittura di Messer Giason de Nores intitolata Apologia (Florence: Filippo Giunti, 1593);

Il segretario: Dialogo di Battista Guarini nel qual non sol si tratta dell' ufficio del segretario, et del modo del compor lettere ma sono sparsi in finiti concetti alla retorica, alla loica & alla morali pertinenti (Venice: Ruberto Megietti, 1594;

Rime del molto illustre Signor caualiere Battista Guarini (Venice: Giovanni Battista Ciotti, 1598);

Compendio della poesia tragicomica tratto dai duo Verati (Venice: Giovanni Battista Ciotti, 1601);

La idropica (Venice: Giovanni Battista Ciotti, 1613);

Trattato della politica libertà, edited by Gaetano A. Ruggieri (Venice: Andreola, 1818).

Editions and Collections: *Il pastor fido e le Rime: Aggiuntoui di nuouo le Rime de [sic] diuersi nobili ingegni in morte dl. autore* (Venice: Giovanni Battista Ciotti, 1621);

Delle opere del Cavaliere Battista Guarini, 4 volumes, edited by Giovanni Andrea Barotti and Apostolo Zeno (Verona: Tumermani, 1737–1738);

Il Pastor Fido e il Compendio della poesia tragicomica, edited by Gioachino Brognoligo (Bari: Laterza, 1914);

Battista Guarini (from Opere, *edited by Luigi Fassò, 1950; Thomas Cooper Library, University of South Carolina)*

Opere di Battista Guarini, edited by Luigi Fassò (Turin: Unione Tipografico-Editrice Torinese, 1950);

Il Pastor Fido, edited by Fassò, in *Teatro del Seicento* (Milan & Naples: Ricciardi, 1956), pp. 91–323;

Opere di Battista Guarini, edited by Marziano Guglielminetti (Turin: Unione Tipografico-Editrice Torinese, 1971);

La questione del "Pastor fido," introduction by Andrea Gareffi (Manziana: Vecchiarelli, 1997)–comprises Guarini's "Annotazioni" and Faustino Summo's "Due discorsi";

Il Pastor Fido, edited by Elisabetta Selmi, introduction by Guido Baldassari (Venice: Marsilio, 1999).

Editions in English: *Il Pastor, Fido the Faithfull Shepherd: a Pastorall,* translated by Richard Fanshawe (London: Printed by R. Raworth, 1647);

The Faithful Shepherd: a Dramatic Pastoral, Translated into English from the Pastor Fido of the Cav. Guarini. Attempted in the Manner of the Original, translated by William Grove (London: Printed by Francis Blyth, sold by G. Robinson, G. Mitchell, and M. Davis, 1782);

Il pastor fido, or, The faithful shepherd a pastoral tragi-comedy: attempted in English blank verse, translated by William Clapperton (Edinburgh: Printed by C. Stewart for the translator; sold by A. Black, Manners & Miller, Constable & Co., Brown & Crombie, J. & J. Robertson, W. Arnot & Co.; & Longman, Hurst, Rees & Orme, London, 1809);

"Compendium," translated by Allan H. Gilbert, in his *Literary Criticism: Plato to Dryden* (New York & Cincinnati: American Book Company, 1940), pp. 504–533;

A Critical Edition of Sir Richard Fanshawe's 1647 Translation of Giovanni Battista Guarini's Il Pastor Fido, edited by Walter F. Staton Jr. and William E. Simeone (Oxford: Clarendon Press, 1964);

Il Pastor Fido: The Faithful Shepherd (1647), translated by Fanshawe, edited by J. H. Whitfield (Austin: University of Texas Press, 1976);

The Faithful Shepherd: A Translation of Battista Guarini's Il Pastor Fido, translated by Thomas Sheridan, edited and completed by Robert Hogan and Edward A. Nickerson (Newark: University of Delaware Press, 1989);

Pastor Fido, in *Three Renaissance Pastorals: Tasso–Guarini–Daniel,* edited by Elizabeth Story Donno (Binghamton, N.Y.: Medieval and Renaissance Texts and Studies, 1993), pp. 56–172.

PLAY PRODUCTIONS: *Il pastor fido,* Crema, 1596; *La Idropica,* Mantua, 1608.

Throughout the seventeenth and eighteenth centuries Battista Guarini's *Il pastor fido* (1590; translated as *Il pastor fido; or The Faithful Shepherd,* 1602) was the most widely read and extravagantly praised and condemned text of secular literature in Europe. Most opinions were highly favorable; blame was leveled primarily on moral and secondarily on stylistic grounds. When interest in Guarini's pastoral tragicomedy was on the wane at the beginning of the nineteenth century, the literary critics August and Friedrich Schlegel revived it by hailing the play as one of the supreme achievements of modern European literature, equal to the best of ancient Greek tragedy, a work in which the Romantic spirit is fused with a classical form. Though Friedrich had reservations, he nonetheless declared it the only Italian literary masterpiece since those of Dante, Petrarch, Giovanni Boccaccio, and Ludovico Ariosto. This judgment did not result in renewed general praise for Guarini's pastoral, but it provoked the leader of modern Italian literary criticism, Francesco De Sanctis, to discuss it at length. According to De Sanctis, *Il pastor fido* perfectly illustrated a period of ethical and literary decadence in Italy's spiritual life. De Sanctis's opinion became the ground on which most subsequent criticism was based until 1958, when Nicolas J. Perella rejected the prevailing view that the value of *Il pastor fido* lay not in its plot or dramatic structure but in the poet's lyrico-rhetorical and musical bent. Perella undertook a careful scrutiny of the action of the play and the interrelationships among the characters, bringing to light the persistence of several themes and a "tale" that reveal Guarini to be a writer with a fascinating turn of mind that belongs as much to the Baroque as to the neoclassical side of the Renaissance. The new critical approach was buttressed by the work of Louise George Clubb, and further studies by Perella and Clubb have changed critical perceptions of Guarini both in Italy and abroad. Meanwhile, Anglo-American scholars have pursued a comparative inquiry into the relationship between Guarini's theoretical writings and his pastoral, on the one hand, and English Renaissance drama–above all, William Shakespeare's late plays–on the other hand.

Guarini was born in Ferrara on 10 December 1538 into the illustrious Veronese family that had produced the great humanist Guarino de' Guarini in 1374. He was guided in his early education by his uncle Alessandro; he then studied at the University of Padua, where at nineteen he was made professor of rhetoric and poetry. In 1557 he moved to the University of Ferrara to teach the same subjects. Around 1560 he married Taddea di Niccolò Bendidio; she was the sister of the singer Lucrezia Bendidio, whose praises were sung by Torquato Tasso and the reigning poet at the Ferrara court, Giambattista Pigna. They had eight children.

In 1564, at the invitation of the influential patron of letters Scipione Gonzaga, Guarini went to Padua, where he became a member and soon secretary of the newly founded Accademia degli Eterei (Academy of the Ethereals) and contributed to its volumes of verse. The academy disbanded with Gonzaga's departure from Padua in 1567.

Guarini returned to Ferrara to begin a long period of political and diplomatic service to Duke Alfonso II d'Este. His missions took him to Turin,

Rome, and Venice, and twice to Poland. The duke soon conferred on him the title *Cavaliere* (Knight). At court he enjoyed friendships with scholars, scientists, and poets, including Tasso. Following the death of Pigna in 1575, Guarini became the court's dominant literary figure. He wrote many sonnets; for the most part they are erotic gallantry or other occasional poems, some on religious themes. As the author of some two hundred madrigals, Guarini occupies a significant place in the history of the Italian lyric in the last decades of the seventeenth century both for the euphonic quality of his verses and for his collaboration with the composers at the Ferrarese court, especially Luzzasco Luzzaschi. Beginning with the third book of his *Madrigali a cinque voci* (1582, Madrigals for Five Voices), Luzzaschi emphasized Guarini's texts above those of other poets; Guarini's poems also occupy the most prominent places in Luzzaschi's collections *Lauro secco* (1582, Dry Laurel) and *Lauro verde* (1583, Green Laurel). The Luzzaschi-Guarini madrigal is characterized by epigrammatic concision, "Petrarchan" antitheses and oxymorons, witty brevity, and lightness rather than gravitas. Thematically, the madrigals are chiefly of an amatory nature; but some are encomiastic, and a few express religious sentiments. Among the longer madrigals, "Tirsi morir voleva" (Tirsi Wished to Die) was enormously popular for its double-entendre character.

During intervals in his diplomatic travels Guarini preferred to stay at his villa in San Bellino, near Padua, rather than at the court in Ferrara, since his relationship with Alfonso was tense at times. *Il pastor fido* was mostly written during a lull in his ambassadorial duties between 1580 and 1585. In this same period Guarini composed a comedy, *La idropica* (The Dropsical Damsel). In a prologue written for the published version (1613) Guarini criticizes the degenerate state of Italian comedy and the commedia dell'arte of his day, especially on moral grounds, and claims that his aim in *La idropica* is to give his era a reformed and respectable, though zesty, comedy.

Cassandra, the daughter of Bernardo Cattari of Ragusa, was put in the care of her nurse, Maddalena, in Venice, where she was raised with Maddalena's daughter, Gostanza. On arriving in Venice, Bernardo sends Cassandra to his sister in Padua to be cured of "dropsy"; the condition is, in fact, pregnancy brought on by her affair with Flavio. Bernardo, however, has promised Cassandra to Patrizio, a Paduan nobleman who intends to have her marry his son, Pistofilo. But Pistofilo and Gostanza are in love with each other. Maddalena dies, and Gostanza is brought to Padua by her stepfather, Lurco the pimp, who is seeking to sell her for two hundred ducats. Cassandra's servants Nica and Grillo, with the help of Pistofilo's servant, Moschetta,

Title page for Guarini's reply to an essay by Giasone De Nores that attacked the notion of pastoral tragicomedy as "monstrous and ill-conceived" (University of Turin)

concoct a scheme to get the two hundred ducats from the pedant Zenobio for Gostanza's favors. The servants take Gostanza to Pistofilo and find a whore, Loretta, to take Gostanza's place in Zenobio's bed. Going along with the scheme, Pistofilo pretends to be willing to marry Cassandra, who, sick with the "dropsy," is to be carried in a litter to Patrizio's house. On the way Nica claims that Cassandra is having an attack and has the litter stop at Lurco's house, where Gostanza takes Cassandra's place and is carried to Pistofilo. Patrizio does not notice that the exchange has been made, but Bernardo comes upon the scene and discovers the trickery. Patrizio is furious, as is Lurco, who arrives complaining that the two hundred ducats given him by Zenobio were counterfeit. But Cassandra confesses to Bernardo

Letter from Guarini in Mantua to a Florentine gentleman, dated 24 December 1591 (State Archives, Florence; from Opere, *edited by Luigi Fassò, 1950; Thomas Cooper Library, University of South Carolina)*

Title page for the enlarged version of Guarini's best-known work, originally published in 1590 (from Opere, *edited by Luigi Fassò, 1950; Thomas Cooper Library, University of South Carolina)*

that Gostanza is his true daughter; she herself is the daughter of Lurco and the late Maddalena, who had sent her to Ragusa in place of Bernardo's real daughter, Gostanza, to make her rich. Maddalena's will confirms Cassandra's statements. All ends happily: Pistofilo, it turns out, is in love with the woman his father had assigned to him; Cassandra will wed Flavio, who has appeared in the guise of a fake doctor; Bernardo appeases Lurco by giving him two hundred real ducats; and Zenobio is reimbursed the money Moschetta has wrested from the greedy Loretta. While the play shows the author's dexterity in harnessing a complicated comedy of intrigue, it does not rise above the "erudite" comedy then in vogue. It even has elements of the commedia dell'arte against which Guarini fulminated–particularly the many double entendres, a mannerism in which Guarini was prone to indulge.

In December 1585 Alfonso recalled Guarini to Ferrara to be ducal secretary. Guarini left the post in 1588 and returned to his villa in San Bellino. From there he traveled frequently to Padua and Venice, where he participated in the literary milieu of the courts. By this time he was a lionized author–especially as the author of *Il pastor fido,* which, though not published until December 1589 (but bearing the date 1590), had circulated widely in manuscript form for three or four years and had already become a cause célèbre. The polemics surrounding the play echoed throughout Europe down to the twentieth century, but the basic terms were set by the earliest of the work's detractors, Giasone De Nores, and by Guarini himself. In 1587 De Nores, professor of moral philosophy at the University of Padua, published an essay proclaiming a moral and utilitarian view of art in general and particularly of comedy, tragedy, and the epic. De Nores attacked the notion of "pastoral tragicomedy" as an outrageous anomaly on formalistic and moral grounds. As a genre, he said, tragicomedy is a "mostruoso e disproporzionato componimento" (monstrous and ill-conceived composition) because of its indiscriminate mixing of tragic and comic elements; moreover, pastoral has no redeeming civil or moral value. Hence, the coupling of a pastoral mode with tragicomedy necessarily results in a literary absurdity of the most useless kind. De Nores was intent on demolishing a hedonistic concept of literature; his conventional definition of poetry joins Aristotelian literary theory and the Counter-Reformation's demands for the inculcation of virtues with a view to the well-being of the state.

Though De Nores did not refer to *Il pastor fido* by name, it was the only work then circulating under the label of a *tragicomedia pastorale,* and in 1588 Guarini replied in an essay written under the pseudonym of a famous actor, Verrato. Guarini claims that nowhere does "the philosopher" (Aristotle) speak of the moralizing function of poetry, nor does he exclude the possibility of new genres such as tragicomedy. Poetry, Guarini asserts, whether in the heroic or the tragic mode, teaches nothing. He protests that his own play is not a mere injudicious mixing of elements from tragedy and comedy but the creation of a third legitimate dramaturgical genre having its own perfection and laws. Tragicomedy takes from tragedy "le persone grandi, non l'azione, la favola verisimile, ma non vera, gli affeti mossi, ma rintuzzati, il diletto, non la mestizia, il pericolo, ma non la morte" (great characters but not great actions, a plot that is verisimilar without being true, strong but tempered emotions, delight and not sadness, danger but not death); and from comedy it takes "il riso non dissoluto, le piacevolezze modeste, il modo finto, il rivolgimento felice e soprattuto l'ordine comic" (a laughter that is not dissoluto but mild pleasantry, a fictitious story, a happy turn of events, and above all a comic mode or structure). Such is Guarini's theory; but in his play itself, not yet in print at the time of publication of the polemical tract under Verrato's name, great or heroic action and mode are not eschewed.

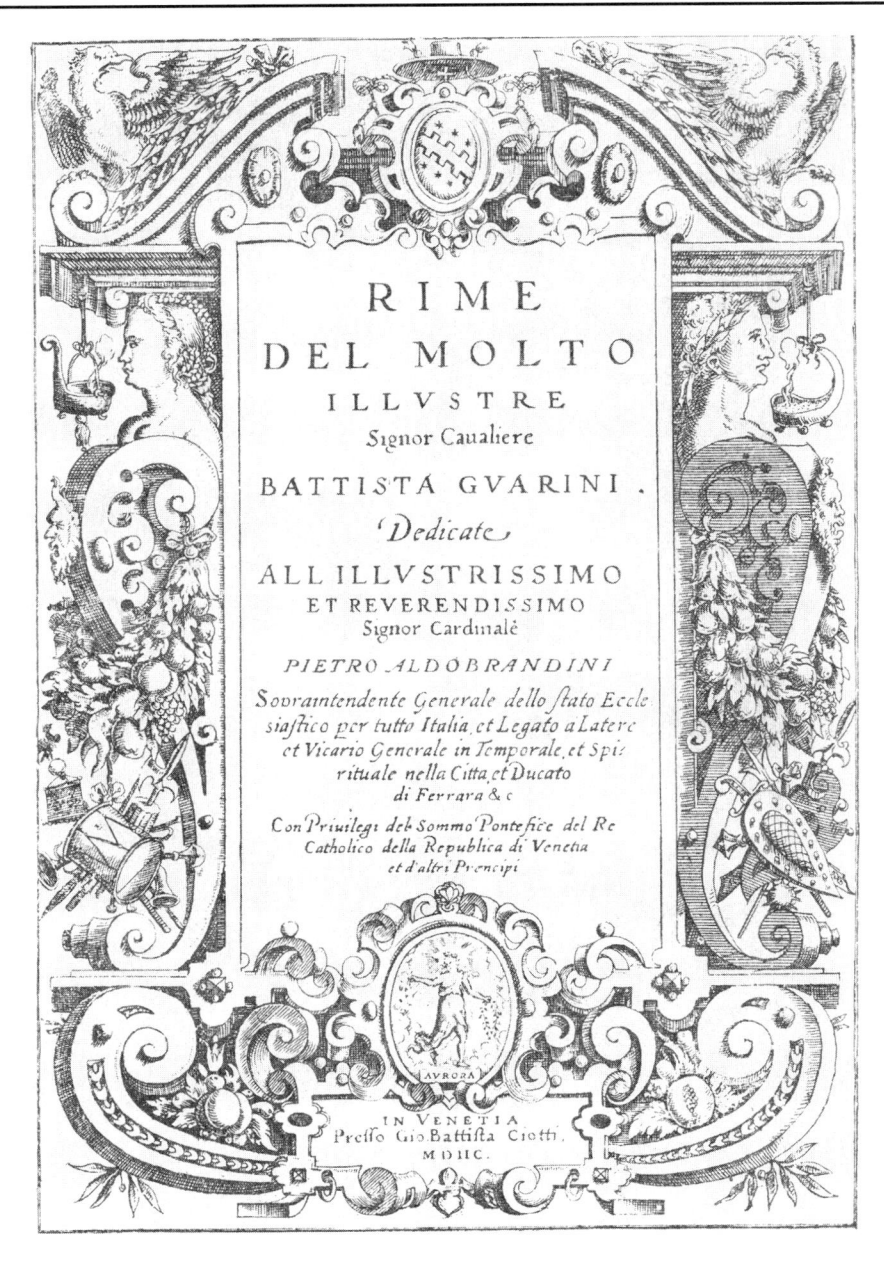

Title page for the first edition of Guarini's Poems (from Opere, edited by Luigi Fassò, 1950; Thomas Cooper Library, University of South Carolina)

Though written in emulation of Tasso's *Aminta* (1573; translated as *Aminta Englisht*, 1628) and evocative at times of the elegiacally sensual atmosphere of that work, *Il pastor fido* is far from a mere imitation of its predecessor's classically structured pastoral drama. It has its own story to tell, a highly complicated one that is three times as long—some six thousand verses—as Tasso's and includes three interlocking plots. Furthermore, the content and pluralistic poetic style are indicative of the Baroque spirit. Guarini considered his play a "corrective" to the nostalgia for a pagan concept of love in *Aminta*, but *Il pastor fido* betrays a certain equivocation on the point.

For many years Arcadia has been threatened with a pestilence by Diana, the goddess of chastity and of hunting, whose wrath was aroused when the Arcadian nymph Lucrina was callously unfaithful to her betrothed. The pestilence can be held at bay only by an annual sacrifice of a maiden to the goddess. Moreover, any nymph found guilty of breaking her troth must be put to death, although her place may be taken by a male or female volunteer. The oracle has told the Arca-

Illustration from the 1602 edition of Il pastor fido *(Folger Shakespeare Library; from Louise George Clubb,* Italian Drama in Shakespeare's Time, *1989; Thomas Cooper Library, University of South Carolina)*

dians that the calamity will not end until two conditions are met. First, two Arcadian descendants of the gods must be joined in wedlock, and only now have suitable candidates emerged: Silvio, a descendant of Hercules, and Amarilli, descended from Pan, are of marriageable age. Accordingly, the high priest Montano betroths his son, Silvio, to Amarilli, the daughter of his friend Titiro. The second condition—atonement for the "antico errore" (ancient sin) by means of the "l'alta pietà" (the noble compassion) of a faithful shepherd—is obscure, but the Arcadians hope that it will be fulfilled by the marriage of Silvio and Amarilli. But Silvio and Amarilli do not love one another and do not want to marry. Silvio, who is loved by the nymph Dorinda, is dedicated only to hunting—that is, to Diana—and has only scorn when love is mentioned. Meanwhile, a stranger, Mirtillo, has arrived in the city, and he and Amarilli have fallen in love; but they must conceal their feelings for the sake of the community.

Through the machinations of the wily and treacherous city nymph Corisca, who desires Mirtillo for herself, the lovers are entrapped in a compromising situation. Amarilli is thought to have been unfaithful to Silvio and is sentenced to die as required by Diana's law. But in keeping with the law, Mirtillo volunteers to take her place. Peripeteia follows peripeteia until, in a recognition scene inspired by Sophocles' *Oedipus Tyrannus* (circa 420 B.C., Oedipus the King), it is revealed that

Mirtillo is Montano's first-born son and that his real name is Silvio. Losing his son as a child and thinking him dead, the high priest had revived the name for his second son. The blind seer, Tirenio, announces that Mirtillo, in offering himself for immolation in Amarilli's stead, has proved to be the faithful shepherd prophesied by the oracle. Atonement is granted without the shedding of blood, Mirtillo's sincere intent being sufficient for the occasion; the marriage of Mirtillo and Amarilli will satisfy the first condition for Arcadia's redemption. Earlier, Silvio, the hunter, after unintentionally wounding Dorinda with an arrow, had cast his weapons away and yielded to Dorinda's embrace. To complete the happy ending, Corisca repents her former devious ways and is forgiven.

Perella considers Corisca the most intriguing figure in the play. In an attempt to gain her own ends she goes beyond her role of licentious and unscrupulous purveyor of a doctrine of free love and becomes the chief manipulator of events. Everything about the wily Corisca is false; she personifies the illusions to which humans fall victim in life. Seized by a raging satyr seeking revenge for having been scorned by her, she eludes her captor by leaving him holding a wig of blond tresses. But the illusions she creates somehow lead to the truth or to what Fate intended all the while. Yet, Corisca, too, is as much *ingannata* (deceived or tricked) as she is an *ingannatrice* (deceiver)—a blind instrument of mysterious but ultimately beneficent Fate.

Finally, Guarini integrates the heroic into the pastoral mode. Tasso's *Aminta* had put shepherds in love on an equal footing with heroes in the matter of refined sentiments and speech; Guarini goes one step further and merges *pastori* (the idyllic) and *eroi* (the heroic) in creating a new type of pastoral hero and heroine. Amarilli is no less heroic than her suitor.

Luzzaschi set to music the highly praised dance scene "Giuoco della cieca" (blindman's buff) in act 3, scene 2 of *Il pastor fido*. Among the other composers who set Guarini's texts to music, including "madrigalesque" passages from *Il pastor fido,* Claudio Monteverdi is the best known. Guarini's pastoral tragicomedy formed the basis of George Frideric Handel's opera *Il pastor fido* (1712). Six sonatas for flute, oboe or violin, and basso continuo titled *Il pastor fido* were published in 1737 under Antonio Vivaldi's name but are believed to have been composed by Nicolas Chédeville.

Guarini's wife died in 1590. That same year De Nores published *Apologia contra l'auttor del* Verato *[sic]* (Apologia contra the Author of the *Verrato*); it was mainly concerned with defending his good name, which he thought had been sullied in *Il Verrato*. In 1592 Guarini entered the service of Vincenzo I

Title page for an early English translation of Guarini's play (from Walter F. Stanton Jr. and William E. Simeone, eds., A Critical Edition of Sir Richard Fanshawe's 1647 Translation of Giovanni Battista Guarini's Il Pastor Fido, *1964; Thomas Cooper Library, University of South Carolina)*

Gonzaga, Duke of Mantua, who sent him to Innsbruck on a diplomatic mission to the Archduke Ferdinand of Austria; but under the pressure of Alfonso II, Guarini was obliged to leave Mantua in June 1593. Also in 1593 he replied to De Nores's *Apologia* in *Il verato secondo* (The Second Verato); it is even more vitriolic than his response to De Nores's first essay had been, and his claims for the independence of poetry from strict morality and for the legitimacy of the new genre of tragicomedy are even more forceful. In 1594 he published *Il Segretario* (The Secretary), in which he discusses the culture required of a secretary to an overlord, the duties inherent to the office, and the art of writing letters.

Title page for the first edition of Guarini's The Dropsical Damsel *(from* Opere, *edited by Luigi Fassò, 1950; Thomas Cooper Library, University of South Carolina)*

A reconciliation of sorts with Alfonso occurred in 1595, but Guarini left Ferrara and moved to Padua. In 1599, at the invitation of Grand Duke Ferdinand I de' Medici, he went to Florence, where he was made archconsul of the prestigious Accademia della Crusca (Academy of the Sifters). His *Trattato della politica libertà* (Treatise on Political Liberty), written in Florence in 1599, is an unabashed panegyric to Ferdinand in the form of an argument in favor of absolutism under "a good ruler" as opposed to a republican government; the latter, in Guarini's view, leads not to liberty but to chaos and license. First published in 1818, it was greeted with ire and scorn by Italian patriots.

In October 1601 Guarini went to Venice to oversee the definitive edition of *Il pastor fido;* accompanied by his "Compendio della poesia tragicomica" (Compendium of Tragicomic Poetry; excerpts translated as "Compendium," 1940), drawn from the two critical tracts he had written to defend his play as a new genre, and "Annotazioni" (Annotations), an allegorical commentary in a moralizing key on *Il pastor fido*. The work was printed by Giovanni Battista Ciotti at the beginning of 1602.

From Venice, Guarini went to Urbino, where he served Duke Francesco Maria della Rovere until 1604. Returning to Ferrara, he was sent to Rome to pay homage to the new Pope, Paul V. It was his last diplomatic mission. The remaining years of his life were marked by ever-increasing fame as a poet but also by deep bitterness in his personal life. An ambitious and cantankerous man, he was embroiled in quarrels and litigation with his own children, the city of Venice, and Marfisa d'Este, the wife of Alfonso d'Este, Marquis of Montecchio. He was suddenly taken ill, and he died in Venice on 7 October 1612.

The name Battista Guarini has come down to the present almost exclusively as the author of *Il pastor fido*. His pastoral tragicomedy won the admiration of countless readers, served as a textbook for learning Italian beyond Italy's borders, and spawned hundreds of pastoral dramas across Europe. Two examples indicate the extraordinary praise it elicited. First, in Ben Jonson's play *Volpone* (1606) a garrulous lady who has read all the Italian poets opines:

> Petrarch? Or Tasso? Or Dante?
> Guerrini [sic]? Ariosto? Aretine?
> Cieco di Hadria? . . .
> Here's *Pastor fido*. . . .
> All our English writers
> I mean such, as are happy in th'Italian,
> Will deigne to steale out of this author, mainly.

Second, the French philosopher Voltaire observes in his *Essai sur l'histoire générale et sur les moeurs et l'esprit des nations, depuis Charlemagne jusqu'à nos jours* (1756; translated as *The Universal History and State of All Nations from the Time of Charlemain to Lewis XIV*, 1758): "Why are entire scenes of the *Pastor Fido* known by heart today in Stockholm and Petersburg and why has no passage from Shakespeare been able to cross the sea? It's because the good is sought by all nations." Finally, the tracts in which Guarini defended and expounded a then-daring theory of the new literary genre of tragicomedy have enjoyed a revival. His "Compendio della poesia tragicomica," along with his play, has been used as a touchstone for tracing the concept of tragicomedy in European plays from *Il pastor fido* down to and including the twentieth century.

Letters:
Lettere del signor cavaliere Battista Guarini nobile ferrarese, edited by Agostino Michele (Venice: Giovanni Battista Ciotti, 1598).

Biography:
Elisabetta Selmi, "Guarini Battista," in *Dizionario biografico degli Italiani*, volume 60 (Rome: Istituto della Enciclopedia Italiana, 2003), pp. 345–352.

References:
Franca Angelini, "Il *Pastor Fido* di Battista Guarini," in *Letteratura italiana: Le opere*, volume 2: *Dal Cinquecento al Settecento*, edited by Alberto Asor Rosa (Turin: Einaudi, 1993), pp. 705–724;

Louise George Clubb, *Italian Drama in Shakespeare's Time* (New Haven & London: Yale University Press, 1989), pp. 97–123, 128–140, 156–187;

Clubb, "The Moralist in Arcadia," *Romance Philology*, 19 (1965): 340–352;

Clubb, "The Pastoral Play: Conflations of Country, Court and City," in *Il teatro italiano del Rinascimento*, edited by Maristella de Panizza Lorch (Milan: Edizioni di Comunità, 1980), pp. 65–73;

Daniela Dalla Valle, "L'eroe pastorale barocco," *Studi francesi*, 15 (1971): 36–56;

Dalla Valle, "Il mito dell'età dell'oro e la concezione dell'amore dall'*Aminta* alla pastorale barocca francese," in her *La frattura: Studi sul barocco letterario francese* (Ravenna: Longo, 1970), pp. 29–38, 75–81;

Giasone De Nores, *Apologia contra l'auttor del* Verato *di Iason de Nores, di quanto ha egli detto in un suo discorso delle tragicomedie, & delle pastorali* (Padua: Paulo Meietti, 1590);

De Nores, *Discorso di Iason de Nores intorno à que principii, cause, et accrescimenti, che la comedia, la tragedia, et el poema heroico ricevono dalla philosophia morale, & civile, & da' governatori delle republiche* (Padua: Paulo Meieto, 1587);

Gianfranco Folena, "La mistione tragicomica e la metamorfosi dello stile nella poetica del Guarini," in *La critica stilistica e il Barocco letterario: Atti del secondo congresso internazionale di studi italiani* (Florence, 1957), pp. 344–349;

Robert Henke, *Pastoral Transformations: Italian Tragicomedy and Shakespeare's Late Plays* (Newark: University of Delaware Press & London Associated University Presses, 1997), pp. 72–77, 88–94, 120–132, 166–172;

Marvin T. Herrick, *Tragicomedy: Its Origin and Development in Italy, France and England* (Urbana: University of Illinois Press, 1955) pp. 135–142;

David L. Hirst, *Tragicomedy* (London & New York: Methuen, 1984);

Norbert Jonard, "Le baroquisme du *Pastor Fido*," *Studi secenteschi*, 10 (1969): 3–18;

Joseph Loewenstein, "Guarini and the Presence of Genre," in *Renaissance Tragicomedy: Explorations in*

Genre and Politics, edited by Nancy Klein Maguire (New York: AMS Press, 1987), pp. 33–55;

Nicolas J. Perella, "Amarilli's Dilemma: The *Pastor Fido* and Some English Authors," *Comparative Literature,* 12 (Fall 1960): 348–359;

Perella, "The Autonomy of Poetry in Battista Guarini's Polemical Tracts," in "Seicento Revisited," special issue of *Forum Italicum,* edited by Albert N. Mancini, 7 (1973): 338–352;

Perella, *The Critical Fortune of Battista Guarini's* Il Pastor Fido (Florence: Leo S. Olschki, 1973);

Perella, "Fate, Blindness and Illusion in the *Pastor Fido,*" *Romanic Review,* 49 (December 1958): 252–268;

Perella, "Heroic Virtue and Love in the *Pastor Fido,*" *Atti dell'Istituto Veneto di Scienze, Lettere ed Arti,* 132 (1973-1974): 658–706;

Perella, "The *Pastor Fido:* of Heroic Virtue and Love," in *Medusa's Gaze: Essays on Gender, Literature, and Aesthetics in the Italian Renaissance, in Honor of Robert J. Rodini,* edited by Paul A. Ferrara and others, Italiana, volume 9 (Lafayette, Ind.: Bordighera Press, 2004), pp. 157–179;

Marzia Pieri, *La scena boschereccia nel Rinascimento italiano* (Padua: Liviana, 1983), pp. 151–180;

Claudio Scarpati, "Poetica e retorica in Battista Guarini," in his *Studi sul Cinquecento italiano* (Milan: Vita e Pensiero, 1985), pp. 201–238;

Scarpati, *Tasso, i Classici e i Moderni* (Padua: Antenore, 1995), pp. 96–104;

Elisabetta Selmi, *Classici e moderni nell'officina del Pastor Fido* (Alessandria: Orso, 2001);

Bernard Weinberg, *A History of Literary Criticism in the Italian Renaissance,* 2 volumes (Chicago: University of Chicago Press, 1961), I: 26–30, 672–684; II: 1074–1106.

Giacomo Lubrano
(1619 – 1692 or 1693)

Elisabetta Properzi Nelsen
San Francisco State University

BOOKS: *Geminatus Fortunae triumphus: Oratio R. P. Jacobi Lubrani Societatis Jesu in parentalibus reverendissimi P. Mag. F. Nicolai Rodulphi Ord. Praed.* (Naples: Secundini Roncalioli, 1651);

Il tempio della memoria: Panegirico in lode dell'illustrissimo Sig. Don Diego di Chiroga y Faxardo, Cavaliere dell'Ordine di Calatrava e Capitan generale dell'Artiglieri nel Regno di Napoli (L'Aquila: Gregorio Gobbi, 1653);

L'anfiteatro della Costanza vittoriosa: Orazione funerale del P. Giacomo Lubrani della Compagnia di Giesù. Detta nel duomo di Palermo per le solenni esequie celebrate alla Cattolica Maestà di Filippo IV il Grande, re delle Spagne e di Sicilia (Palermo: Andrea Colicchi, 1666);

Scintille poetiche o poesie sacre e morali di Paolo Brinacio Napoletano, introduction by Silvestro di Fusco (Naples: Domenico Antonio Parrino & Michele Luigi Muzi, 1690);

Suaviludia Musarum ad Sebethi Ripam: Epigrammaton Libri X Jacobi Lubrani e Societate Jesu Neapolitani (Naples: Jacobi Raillard, 1690);

Il cielo domenicano, col primo Mobile della Predicazione, con piu' pianeti di Santità: Panegirici sacri del P. Giacomo Lubrani della Compagnia di Giesù, 2 volumes (Naples: Giacomo Raillard, 1691, 1693);

Prediche quaresimali postume del P. Giacomo Lubrani della Compagnia di Giesù (Naples: Raillard & Muzi, 1702).

Editions and Collections: *Scintille poetiche* (Padua, 1703);

Il Solstizio della Gloria Divina nel Nome santissimo di Giesù, predicato in due mondi da' Santi e Beati della sua Compagnia: Panegirici (Venice: Andrea Poletti, 1703);

Il fuoco sacro della Divinità nel Nome santissimo di Giesù, predicato in due mondi da' Santi e beati della sua Compagnia: Panegirici (Venice: Andrea Poletti, 1703);

Raccolta di varii sagri discorsi del P. Giacomo Lubrani della Compagnia di Giesù (Naples: Giovanni Roselli, 1727);

I Marinisti, edited by Giovanni Getto (Turin: Unione Tipografico-Editrice Torinese, 1954), pp. 410–422;

Poesia del Seicento, volume 1, edited by Carlo Muscetta and Pier Paolo Ferrante (Turin: Einaudi, 1964), pp. 653–659;

Piero E. Pieretti, "Testi inediti di Giacomo Lubrano," *Studi secenteschi*, 10 (1969): 289–299;

Scintille poetiche, edited by Marzio Pieri (Ravenna: Longo Editore, 1982);

"Scintille poetiche," in *Il Barocco: Marino e la poesia barocca*, edited by Pieri (Rome: Istituto Poligrafico e Zecca dello Stato, 1995), pp. 851–879;

Scintille Poetiche, o, Poesie sacre, e morali: Aggiunta La mutolezza eloquente e una scelta di poesie sparse, edited by Pieri with a note by Luana Salvarani (Trento: La Finestra, 2002)–includes CD-ROM of *Prediche quaresimali*;

In tante trasparenze: Il verme setaiolo e altre scintille poetiche, edited by Giancarlo Alfano and Gabriele Frasca (Naples: Cronopio, 2002).

OTHER: "Ode alcaica," preface to Placido Carrafa, *Prediche* (Venice: Baglioni, 1632);

Acta Dioecesanae Hydruntinae Synodi sub Caietano Cosso Archiepiscopo anno a nativitate Domini MDXXLI, edited by Lubrano (Lecce: Pietro Michell, 1641);

"Elogium," in *Le egloghe symboliche*, edited by Ascanio Grandi (Lecce: Pietro Micheli, 1642), n.pag.;

Cristoforo Ivanovich, *Minerva al tavolino: Lettere diverse di proposta e risposta a varii personaggi, sparse d'alcuni componimenti in prosa e in verso* (Venice: Niccolò Pezzana, 1681), pp. 241–333.

Giacomo Lubrano is one of the most representative authors of Italian Baroque religious poetry and prose. His sonnets, sermons, and panegyrics show the typical literary characteristics of the Counter-Reformation age: they are imbued with a sense of the limits of human life, an obsession with the morbid aspects of existence, a tormented feeling of the passing of time and the vanity of hope, and a sense of cosmic insignificance and disorientation in a vast space. Often, Lubrano's observations focus on changes of form and the dissolving of balance and a natural world that appears absurd and unreal.

Lubrano was born in 1619, either in Naples or, according to the philosopher Giambattista Vico, on the island of Procida off the Neapolitan coast. Nothing is known of his family background. In 1632 he wrote "Ode alcaica" (Alcaic Ode) as the preface to Placido Carrafa's *Prediche* (Sermons). He entered the Jesuit order on 30 April 1635. In 1641 he collected and published *Acta Dioecesanae Hydruntinae Synodi sub Caietano Cosso Archiepiscopo* (Proceedings of the Bishops' Synods under the Supervision of Archbishop Gaetano Cosso). The following year he contributed "Elogium" (Eulogy) to Ascanio Grandi's *Le egloghe symboliche* (The Symbolic Eclogues). He began preaching in 1649 or 1650 and soon became well known in that capacity. In 1651 his funeral oration *Geminatus Fortunae triumphus* (The Dual Triumph of Fortune) was published in Naples, followed in 1653 by his panegyric *Il tempio della memoria* (The Temple of Memory) for Don Diego of Chiroga, captain of artillery of the Kingdom of Naples.

Lubrano began living in the Jesuit House in Naples in 1660 but traveled widely, mainly in southern Italy, to deliver his Lenten sermons. He also went to Venice and Modena in northern Italy, where his hyperbolic and metaphorical style of preaching was criticized. Between 1680 and 1690 Lubrano suffered from a disease that caused his tongue to tremble and resulted in stuttering. He did not quit preaching, however, but developed a mouth exercise that helped with his pronunciation. In his autobiography (1725) Vico describes an incident that occurred when, as a young man, he met the old Jesuit and submitted a poem on the rose for Lubrano's comments. Lubrano loved the poem and recited one of his own works on the same topic in spite of his affliction.

Lubrano preached before popes, kings, and other authorities at important secular and religious events; among the latter was the canonization of St. Francis Borgia in the Church of Jesus in Rome in 1670. Notwithstanding the criticism of his overblown style, his poetry was always acknowledged to be theologically orthodox.

Lubrano published his *Scintille poetiche o poesie sacre e morali* (Poetic Sparks or Moral and Sacred Poems) in 1690; it was printed with the permission of his superiors and received the imprimatur of the archbishop of Naples; nevertheless, he published it under the pseudonym Paolo Brinacio, an anagram of his real name. *Scintille poetiche* is a collection of primarily religious sonnets and odes. Some poems express theological concepts; others are inspired by historical events and natural disasters such as earthquakes, floods, and epidemics; still others deal with the lives of saints. All of the pieces in *Scintille poetiche* are aimed at instructing readers on moral and religious issues. The work includes an introduction by Lubrano's fellow Jesuit Silvestro di Fusco, who writes that one of Lubrano's singular merits is to have balanced "la penna, che stilla a pari l'inchiostro, e lo spirito" (his writing ability with spiritual meaning).

Lubrano's interpretation of the religious ideas of the Counter-Reformation reflects a series of changes that had a deep impact on the epistemological foundations of his culture. The enthusiasm of the philosopher Giordano Bruno for the idea of an infinite universe in his *Dell'infinito universo e mondi* (1584, Of the Infinite Universe and Worlds) was replaced during the seventeenth century by a frightening perception: the notion of infinity no longer implied endless human possibilities but oppressed the mind. The thoughts of the French mathematician and philosopher Blaise Pascal reflect the recognition of the human being lost in a hidden corner of the universe, unaware of his origins and purpose in life and confounded by the mystery of death. Acquisition of knowledge only brings sorrow and desperation. Lubrano's message is that the gap between the misery of life and the perfection of divinity must be filled by Jesus Christ.

In five sonnets in the *Scintille poetiche* God speaks in the first person; for example, in sonnet 73: "Io do le fughe al Tempo, a i Cieli il giro / la vita al Niente, ed a la vita il fiato" (I give speed to Time and movement to the Celestial Spheres, / life to Nothing and breath to Life). In sonnet 76 Lubrano affirms that the universe is nothing if it is not sustained by God. In other sonnets he uses sophisticated theological oxymora to emphasize such mysteries as the Trinity and the omniscience and omnipresence of God.

There are lyrical and melancholic tones in Lubrano's poetry, such as the exclamations of resignation in which he attests to a human condition of inevitable diminution:

O come il punto de la terra è breve
A chi dal Cielo il mira!
Atomo che s'aggira
Su le ruote del caso, incerto, e lieve
Perduto si riceve.
Ove fra 'l Riso e 'l Lutto
Sfuma in nebbia la luce, in nulla il tutto.

(How the dot of the Earth is short
If someone looks at it from the Sky!
'Tis an atom that goes around
On the wheels of chance, uncertain, and light,

When it finds itself it is already lost.
Where between Laughter and Mourning,
Light dissolves into fog, and everything dissolves into nothing.)

In Lubrano's poetry the notion of time blends with a sense of unstable and ephemeral life. This conception of the passing of time derives from the humanistic contemplation of life as transient. Humanists were committed to savoring experience through the pleasures of art and knowledge. Usually associated with the notion of carpe diem, Lorenzo de' Medici's line "Di doman non c'è certezza" (There is no certainty about tomorrow) in *Il trionfo di Bacco e Arianna* (1490, The Triumph of Bacchus and Ariadne) took on a different meaning during the Baroque age. Lubrano presents time as subdivided into brief instants that pass away before being lived; it is a shattered perception of time in which each moment is buried in the past and threatened by the imminent future. The topos Lubrano chooses for meditation on time is the clock. Hourglasses, wax clocks, and water clocks provide varying interpretations of the passing of time. In poem 33, "Oriuolo di cere intrecciate" (Wax Clock), he declares:

> O breve Eternità di nostra vita,
> che ti scateni in fluidi momenti:
> questa di molli Cere urna fiorita
> le tue corte misure apre a le Genti.
> . . . .
> Deh cessa di sognar gli anni futuri:
> come le Cere sol vivono estinte,
> così nel viver tuo morendo duri.
>
> (Brief Eternity of our life,
> you who break out in fluid moments
> this flowery urn of soft waxes,
> opens to the People your short figures of time
> . . . .
> Alas, stop dreaming the years to come:
> just as Wax lives only while extinct,
> so you last in your life only by dying.)

In poem 34, "Oriuolo ad acqua" (Water Clock), he asks:

> A che sognar con temerarii vanti
> secoli ne l'Età mezzo sparita,
> se bastan sole ad annegar la vita
> minutissime gocciole d'istanti?
> . . . .
> Quanto è, quanto sarà s'imprime in acque,
> cifra di fughe: e in fluido feretro
> naufraga seppellito il "Fu" che piacque.
>
> (Why boast with recklessness centuries
> of half-disappeared Ages
> if tiny drops of instants
> are enough to drown life?
> . . . .
> What is, what will be remains impressed in waters,
> figures of escapes and the "was" that pleased us
> fails buried in a fluid coffin.)

Water and wax offer the pretext for the tragic sense of the passing of life. Life is metaphorically suffocated by drowning from tiny drops of water; at the same time, wax becomes cold and hardens as it flows farther from the fire that melted it. The equivalence of life and movement is pictured by the ebb and flow of water; the metaphor of wax signifies death's solidifying effect.

Lubrano also recognizes water as a liquid mirror, offering and taking away the reflected image; his Baroque poetics focuses on what is fleeting, transient, and elusive in descriptions of fountains and minimalist images of tears, crystals, pearls, glasses, and stalactites. The link among these elements is whiteness and transparency. All of them lend themselves to a kind of cosmic narcissism, as though nature wishes to see itself and can do so only through water.

The motif of death in Lubrano's poetry is consistent with the Counter-Reformation's religious atmosphere and the confessional activism of the time. Morbid symbols such as tombs, skulls, and corpses are adopted as means of salvation, following the Catholic mystical tradition. The tombstone, the decomposing body, the skeleton, and dust are tormenting images in Lubrano's fantasy. His poetic expressions of death evoke smoke, vapors, ashes, and the ignis fatuus or "will-o'-the-wisp," forming a vision of a decomposing world. Through these images Lubrano intends to provoke a feeling of inexorability and inevitability and a consciousness of a fatal destiny.

Another literary theme connected with death is that of sleep. Classic and Renaissance literature personified sleep as a young deity who descends on weary human beings to relieve physical and spiritual fatigue. The poet Giovanni Della Casa, for example, depicted Sleep as the placid son of the shady Night and the comfort of tormented mortals. In contrast, in Lubrano's poetry sleep is another metaphor for death.

Yet, Lubrano presents acceptance of death as the means to eternal life in heaven made possible by Jesus Christ's death and resurrection. Lubrano explains the mystery of resurrection by observing some common living objects that show a rhythm of death and rebirth. Silkworms appear prominently in his poetry: thirty sonnets are included in the section of *Scintille poetiche* titled "Moralità tratte dalla considerazione del verme setaiuolo" (Moral Teachings Extracted from Observations of the Silkworm). In one of Lubrano's metaphors of resurrection the cocoon gives birth to the butterfly, which makes its nest in the grave of the caterpillar. Lubrano extends the metaphor: the silkworm becomes the dying Daedalus, who allows Icarus, the new butterfly, to fly. According to Ezio Raimondi, nature is for Lubrano a "well-learned teacher and a witty poet." His poetry is filled with unusual beings, particularly insects, that were alien to the poetic world of the Renaissance. Mosquitoes, fireflies, and moths are fascinating to Lubrano because they are marvelous and difficult to describe. In the autobiographical sonnet "Alla Zanzara che disturbava l'Autore negli studi letterari" (To the Mosquito That Bothered the Author Intent on His Literary Studies) this insect is called "istrice minutissimo" (tiny porcupine) and "punto sol divisibile in punture" (dot only divisible in stings). A crescendo of metaphors describes the animal without mentioning the word *zanzara* (mosquito) excerpt in the title.

The firefly is a typical Baroque motif explored by other Marinist poets such as Guido Casoni, Girolamo Fontanella, and Tommaso Stigliani. In Lubrano's work fireflies are often metaphors for the stars. He defines them as "faville alate" (winged sparks), "vivi baleni" (live lightnings), and "pennuti rubini" (heathered rubies).

Lubrano's sonnets 68 and 69, respectively, present images of the moth that consumes paper and of the paper that is eaten. The moth is depicted as a tiny object with the tiresome and ruinous function of destroying–in this case, the culture of the past. As a consequence, discussion will be provoked among literary and historical scholars, since the documents have been confused and damaged by the moth's gnawing. The metaphors that identify the moth show Lubrano's virtuosity in pairing nouns and adjectives: the moth is the "arpiuccia de' libri" (book's tiny harpy) and an "animuccia vile" (vile little soul). Many meanings are included in the expression "book's tiny harpy," among them the notions of consumption, thievery, greed, rapacity, and ugliness. Lubrano also uses opposites to intensify the distressing action of the moth that "morde chi la produsse e la nutrisce" (gnaws at what has produced and nourished it)–that is, the paper–and, "nata aborre la luce" (after being born, abhors light).

In Lubrano's poetics there are also traces of a new representation of women in which sensuality merges with a consciousness of the progressive decay of female beauty. Until Giambattista Marino, feminine beauty was fixed in the Petrarchan stereotypical metaphors of the eyes as suns, hair as gold, and teeth as pearls. Marino, however, described his beloved as "pallidetto mio sole" (my little pale sun), forging a link between the sun and pallor to create a sense of languor and sensuality. Lubrano's lyrical poetry develops this theme by including the vanity of beauty in the process of passing and corruption. Woman is portrayed in her youth and simultaneously projected in the future of her impending senility and death. The canzone "Rosa caduca" (Frail Rose), written in honor of the duchess of Marigliano, Giulia Albertini, is structured around the popular Baroque motif of the rose that symbolizes beauty in its flowering and withering. Baroque poetry tends to insist on three crucial moments in the lives of flowers in general and the rose in particular. The first moment is the flower's blooming; the second is the withering that takes place when the flower is picked, trampled on, or stricken by cold or lack of water; the third moment occurs when the flower blooms again. In "Rosa caduca" the woman is portrayed as a red rose, bright in the snow, the first signal of spring in the last days of winter. Lovers, compared to bees, court her as she gains pleasure from the realization that her suitors thirst for her attractive appearance. But soon this idyllic situation is shattered: the rose is only a phantom of spring, just as beauty is a phantom of youth.

The long title of ode 12 of *Scintille poetiche* points out the moralistic and pedagogical aim of the poem: "Una povera donzella nell'inondazione di Palermo, sorpresa nel letto ignuda dalla piena delle acque, volle più tosto interizire a pericolo della vita, che fuggire a danno dell'Onestà" (A Poor Gentle Young Woman During the Flood of Palermo, Caught Naked in Bed by Water, Rather Preferred to Freeze to Death than Escape, in Order to Preserve Her Honor). The girl is likened to a martyr who is ready to die in the name of faith. The young woman is pale, as in Marino's representation, but her pallor is contrasted with the blush of her shame.

In sonnet 33 Lubrano realistically portrays a woman dressed in the fashion of the day, then points out that her fine clothes and jewels are merely a prelude to her funeral. Lubrano despises vanity in regard to the human body while exalting the mystical experiences of saints; inner beauty is synonymous with purity of heart and candor of soul. The sonnet "Pioggia improvvisa nell'esequie d'una bella e divota donna" (Sudden Rain During the Funeral of a Beautiful and Pious Noblewoman) includes a play on words between the real sun and the woman as sun: as the latter is buried in the ground, the former is buried in the clouds.

Besides female beauty, Lubrano is also attracted by the natural environment. Baroque landscape description does not follow the classic pattern of harmony and rationality dominant during the Renaissance but instead appears in extravagant forms and hallucinatory visions. In the sonnet "Cedri fantastici variamente figurati negli orti reggitani" (Fabulous Citron Trees in Different Forms in the Orchards of Reggio Calabria) tree branches transform themselves into various shapes. The citron trees are "guerrieri e adulteri di Pomona" (warriors and adulterers of Pomona) because they deceive the goddess of gardens by taking on forms unknown to her. The trees also evoke wandering ghosts of the ancient Roman culture and exotic images of far-away countries.

Lubrano's most original ode is, perhaps, "La Fata Morgana nel Faro Siciliano cioè varie apparenze riverberanti in aria per un misto di ombre e di luci" (The Fata Morgana, or the Mirage Formed by the Sicilian Lighthouse, in Various Appearances Reverberating in the Air, in a Mixture of Shadow and Light.) The ode is dedicated to Cardinal Giulio Rospigliosi, who became Pope Clement IX in 1667; Clement was a playwright and one of the first scholars to research the origins of melodrama. The mirage to which the poem refers was a well-known phenomenon visible in the Strait of Messina. The ode is long and is difficult to interpret because of the richness of its metaphors, but the mirage represents the political mistakes that result in the impermanence of history:

> Maëstro di più moti
> il pennel di natura in varie tinte
> abbozza lontananze
> di provincie indistinte
> . . . .
> Non è di Roma antica il circo insano
> quel selciato di nembi aereo piano?
>
> Teacher of many movements,
> the brush of Nature sketches in various colors
> distances of undistinguished provinces.
> . . . .
> Is not that aerial flat pavement of clouds
> the insane Circus of ancient Rome?)

Scintille poetiche was Lubrano's main contribution to Italian literature. The rest of his works were written in his role as a preacher. In 1690 he published a collection of Latin epigrams, *Suaviludia Musarum* (Sweet Poems of the Muses). Some of the epigrams refer to events in his preaching career, such as his address to the congregation in the church of the Gerolamini in Naples on 27 October 1686, regarding the conquest of the city of Buda by the Hapsburg empire after a long period of Turkish rule. Others address some of the same themes found in *Scintille poetiche,* such as the frailty of beauty and the reproach of female vanity.

In 1691 Lubrano published the first volume of *Il cielo domenicano* (The Dominican Sky); the second volume appeared in 1693. Both are subtitled *Panegirici sacri* (Sacred Panegyrics). The pieces are praises of Dominican saints such as St. Dominic, St. Thomas Aquinas, St. Raymond of Pignafort, and St. Vincent Ferrer. While they are in prose, Lubrano uses some of the stylistic devices of *Scintille poetiche,* including antithesis, analogy, metaphor, and imagery of flowers, mosquitoes, water, and sleep.

Some biographers say that Lubrano died in 1692; others give 1693 as the year. In his *Giornali di Napoli* (1679–1701, Chronicles of Naples) for 23 October 1693 Domenico Confuorto writes, "È morto il padre Lubrano gesuvita nel Collegio di San Giuseppe a Chiaia, soggetto degno nella sua Religione per dottrina ed erudizione, e particolarmente famoso nell'arte oratoria, nelle prediche e panegirici" (The Jesuit father Lubrano has died in the College of St. Joseph's at Chiaia, a man worthy in his Religion for his doctrine and erudition, and particularly famous in the art of oratory, in sermons and panegyrics).

Lubrano's *Prediche quaresimali* (Sermons for Lent), published posthumously in 1702, belongs to the Counter-Reformation trend requiring adherence to religious practice and submission to ecclesiastical authority. Lubrano describes God as "Arbitro di tutto il possibile, Direttore di tutto il fortuito, Artefice di tutto il prodigioso . . . Potenza di tutti gli atti, Attualità di tutte le potenze, Vitalità di tutte le vite, Idea di tutte le creature" (Arbiter of all possibilities, Manager of all fortuitous events, Artifex of miracles . . . Power of all actions, Vitality of all lives and Idea of all creatures). The sermons, written for the Lenten time of penance, often confront the theme of death, and their length allows Lubrano to use elaborate examples to frighten listeners into reflecting on their mortality. Earthquakes, volcanic eruptions, epidemics, droughts, and wars are vividly described to juxtapose sumptuous and libertine life with ever-threatening death, which is depicted as a deep abyss, an "ignoto vacuo" (unknown vacuum) that consumes each aspect of life. Lubrano's overstated antitheses organized in parallel sentences correspond to the excessive decoration of Baroque figurative arts.

In the introduction to *Scintille poetiche* di Fusco explains that Giacomo Lubrano is not simply a poet "colla Cetera al collo" (with a lyre strapped around his neck) but an orator: an author whose goal is to demonstrate that it is possible to write poetry without being lascivious. Lubrano is always consistent in his religious convictions; his poetry is characterized by rigorous moral teachings expressed in a style marked by his versatility in employing metaphorical language. He is one of the most engaging and representative writers of the late seventeenth century and is worthy of further study.

Biography:

Claudio Sensi, "Giacomo Lubrano: Contributi per una biografia," *Italianistica*, 5, no. 2 (1976): 238–259.

References:

Giancarlo Alfano, ed., *Tre catastrofi: Eruzioni, rivolta e peste nella poesia del Seicento napoletano* (Naples: Cronopio, 2000);

Domenico Confuorto, *Giornali di Napoli dal MDCLXXIX al MDCIC,* volume 1, edited by Nicola Nicolini (Naples: Luigi Lubrano, 1930);

Giuseppe Conte, *La metafora barocca* (Milan: Mursia, 1972);

Benedetto Croce, *Saggi sulla letteratura italiana del Seicento* (Bari: Laterza, 1948), pp. 399, 401, 404–407;

Franco Croce, *Tre momenti del Barocco letterario italiano* (Florence: Sansoni, 1966), pp. 10, 13, 25, 29, 227, 268–322, 330, 338, 363, 381–383, 391–392;

Giovanni Getto, *Barocco in prosa e poesia* (Milan: Rizzoli, 1962);

Denzil Kelly, "The Apex of the Poetics of Confidence and Orthodoxy: Heroes of the Church in the Odes and Sonnets of Giacomo Lubrano," in *Altro Polo: Italian Studies in Memory of Frederick May,* edited by Suzanne Kiernan (Sydney: Frederick May Foundation for Italian Studies, University of Sydney, 1996), pp. 125–143;

Riccardo Massano, "Sulla tecnica e sul linguaggio dei lirici maristi," in *La critica stilistica e il barocco letterario: Atti del 2 Congresso internazionale di studi italiani* (Florence: Le Monnier, 1957), pp. 283–301;

Giovanni Pozzi, *La rosa in mano al professore* (Freiburg: University Editions, 1974);

Ezio Raimondi, *Letteratura barocca* (Florence: L. S. Olschki, 1961);

Jean Rousset, "Quelches reflexion en marge d'une anthologie mariniste," *Lettere italiane,* 6, no. 3 (1954): 291–295;

Alessandra Ruffino, "Nebbie edificate in mondi: Note su Iacopo Lubrano," *Airesis: Lubrano–Scintille Poetiche* <http://www.airesis.net/recensioni/lubrano_scintille.htm> (accessed 16 November 2007);

Claudio Sensi, *L' "arcimondo" della parola: Saggi su Giacomo Lubrano* (Padua: Liviana, 1983);

Sensi, "Cultura barocca tra consenso e polemica: Gli epigrammi latini di Giacomo Lubrano," *Esperienze letterarie,* 3, no. 2 (1978): 31–54;

Sensi, "La retorica dell'apoteosi," *Studi seicenteschi,* 24 (1983): 69–152;

Sensi, *La tralucenza dell'antico* (Parma: Zara, 1984);

Giambattista Vico, *Autobiografia, Carteggio e Poesie varie,* edited by Benedetto Croce and Fausto Nicolini (Bari: Laterza, 1929), pp. 8–9.

Carlo Maria Maggi
(3 May 1630 – 22 April 1699)

Glenn Palen Pierce
University of Missouri

SELECTED BOOKS: *Rime varie* (Florence: S.A.S., 1688);

Rime varie, 4 volumes, edited by Lodovico Antonio Muratori (Milan: Giuseppe Pandolfo Malatesta, 1700);

Commedie, e rime in lingua milanese, 2 volumes (Milan: Giuseppe Pandolfo Malatesta, 1701);

Scelta di poesie edite ed inedite di Carlo Maria Maggi nel secondo centenario della sua morte, edited by Antonio Cipollini (Milan: U. Hoepli, 1900).

Editions and Collections: *Il teatro milanese,* 2 volumes, edited by Dante Isella (Turin: Einaudi, 1964);

"Rime milanesi," edited by Isella, *Studi secenteschi,* 6 (1965): 67–264;

I consigli di Meneghino, edited by Isella (Turin: Einaudi, 1965);

"Otto poesie inedite in lingua di Carlo Maria Maggi," edited by Emilia Foglio, *Studi secenteschi,* 17 (1976): 161–170;

"Sonetti religiosi inediti di Carlo Maria Maggi," edited by Foglio, *Rivista di storia e letteratura religiosa,* 3 (1977): 495–533.

Edition in English: *The Beauties of Carlo-Maria Maggi, Paraphrased, to Which Are Added, Sonnets,* translated by Mariana Starke (Exeter, U.K.: Printed for the author by S. Woolmer and sold by Longman, Hurst, Rees & Orme, London; by Upham, and also by Barratt, Bath, 1811).

OTHER: François Guilloré, *Ritiramento per le dame con gli esercizii da farsi in esso,* translated by Maggi (Ferrara: Bernardino Pomatelli, 1687).

The poet and playwright Carlo Maria Maggi, who was also a professor of classics and secretary of the Milanese Senate, was one of the most prolific authors of the second half of the seventeenth century. During his youth he concentrated on writing encomiastic and occasional verse. From 1666 to 1675 he was a court poet, writing melodramas and tragedies with a distinct Milanese flavor. While Maggi was renowned for these theatrical works, which were filled with music and spectacle, today he is recognized primarily for his pre-Arcadian comedies in the Milanese dialect that feature local settings and middle-class themes. He is considered an important playwright who set a precedent for the establishment of a distinct Lombard regional literary culture.

Maggi was born into a wealthy mercantile family in Milan on 3 May 1630; his parents were Giovanni Battista and Angela Maggi, née Riva. The year of his birth was that of the great plague described in Alessandro Manzoni's novel *I Promessi Sposi* (1825–1827, The Betrothed; translated as *The Betrothed Lovers: A Milanese Tale of the XVIIth Century,* 1828). The family escaped the epidemic by moving to a villa they owned in Lesmo in the province of Brianza. After they returned to Milan, Maggi began his education at the Jesuit school in the Brera district of the city. In 1647 he went to the University of Bologna to study civil and canon law. Though not enthusiastic about these subjects, Maggi applied himself to them and received his degree in 1649. While in Bologna he spent much of his time in the company of writers. After leaving Bologna, he traveled throughout Italy and spent long periods in Rome, Naples, Venice, and the Friuli region. He returned to Milan in 1656. That same year he married Anna Maria Monticelli, with whom he had eleven children. For the rest of their lives the couple remained close to Milan, leaving the city only for short trips to the Lago Maggiore retreat of Maggi's friend Count Vitaliano Borromeo or to family holdings in Brianza and Abbiategrasso.

Maggi cultivated friendships with some of the leading literary, social, and political figures of Milan, such as Vitaliano Borromeo, Count Bartolomeo Arese, and the playwright Tommaso Santagostino. He was a member of the Accademia della Crusca (Academy of the Sifters) in Florence; the Accademia dei Faticosi (Academy of the Toilsome) in Milan; the Accademia degli Arcadi (Arcadian Academy) in Rome, where he acquired the nom de plume, Nicio Meneladio, that he used in his earlier writings; the Accademia dei Concordati (Academy of the Agreements) of Ravenna; and the

Accademia dei Olimpici (Academy of the Olympians) of Vicenza.

Maggi was popular among the literary, intellectual, socially prominent, and politically dominant figures of his time, and his plays were performed in the homes of such prominent families as the Areses and the Borromeos. Bartolomeo Arese, president of the Milanese senate, often invited Maggi to his villa at Casano Maderno; many of his verses in Italian and Latin still adorn the paintings there. A patron of the arts, Vitaliano Borromeo courted Maggi's friendship at his home in Milan and at Isola Bella, his island retreat on Lake Maggiore. Maggi sometimes stayed at Isola Bella for weeks and amused the guests with readings of his poems and plays. The plays were often performed by the guests.

Among his professional relationships Maggi most probably valued that with the Tuscan poet, scientist, and satirist Francesco Redi. A voluminous correspondence exists in which they exchanged views on each other's works, the use of certain words and phrases, and other stylistic points. Redi mentions Maggi in his dithyramb *Bacco in Toscana* (1685; translated as *Bacchus in Tuscany*, 1825) in words that reveal both warm feelings for the man and esteem for the poet:

> Se per sorte avverrà che un dí lo assaggi
> dentro a' Lombardi suoi grassi cenacoli,
> colla ciotola in man farà miracoli
> lo splendor di Milano, il saggio Maggi.

> (If one day you are fortunate enough to taste
> the wine of Lombardy during one of the great feasts,
> with his glass in hand the splendor of Milan,
> the sage Maggi, will work miracles.)

Title page for the first edition of Carlo Maria Maggi's Various Rhymes *(University of Turin)*

Redi conveyed to Maggi the wish of Cosimo II de' Medici, Grand Duke of Tuscany, to have a portrait of the poet. Maggi responded by sending a sonnet to the duke that included a humorous description of himself as tall and lean, with long hair, a melancholy eye, and an ugly, pock-marked face marked with lines caused by never getting anything done while worrying about everything. After much cajoling, Maggi did have a painting done and sent to the grand duke. The episode underscores the fame he enjoyed in literary circles far from Milan and points to his modesty, his simple tastes, and the typical Lombard humor and common sense he incorporated into his comedies in dialect.

In 1661, thanks to his friendship with Arese, Maggi obtained the office of secretary of the Milanese Senate. Four years later he was called to the Palatine Schools, where he taught Latin and Greek when his duties in the senate permitted him to do so. In 1671 he became superintendent of the University of Pavia; he seems to have maintained his position in the senate for the next five years without pay, with others standing in for him until he returned and took over himself. He held the office until his death. During his tenure he compiled nearly four hundred legal briefs and reports, most in Latin but some in Spanish and Italian; all were destroyed during the bombardments of World War II.

Many of Maggi's librettos were commissioned for official celebrations of the arrivals of potentates. *La Lucrina* (Lucrina), a pastoral fable for music, was presented at Arese's villa at Casano Maderno for Margherita of Austria, the wife of Holy Roman Emperor Leopold I, in 1666. *L'Ippolita regina delle Amazzoni* (Hyppolita, Queen of the Amazons) was written for the arrival from Madrid in 1670 of Gaspar Téllez-Girón, fifth Duke of Osuna, to become governor of the duchy of Milan. For the duke's second marriage in 1672 Maggi wrote *Il trionfo d'Augusto in Egitto* (The Triumph of Augustus in Egypt). He composed *La gratitudine umana*

Opening page of Maggi's play The Baron of Roguery *in the first volume of* Commedie, e rime in lingua milanese *(University of Turin)*

over *Affari e amore* (Human Gratitude; or; Affairs and Love) in honor of the new Spanish regent, Claude Lamoral, third Prince of Ligne, in 1675. These elegant, socially unengaged pieces lack any real dramatic force; they are *commedie spagnoleggianti* (reflections of the taste of the time for Spanish culture), inferior imitations of the Spanish comedies of Lope de Vega and Tirso de Molina written to please the Spanish occupiers. In all of these works he pays great attention to scene changes, arias, and duets; love themes dominate. A typical example is *Amor tra l'armi overo Corbulone in Armenia* (1673, Love and Arms; or, Corbulone in Armenia), which is little more than a traditional *opera di occasione* (occasional dramatic work for music), with repeated asides and inserts referring to the couple for whom it was composed. Characters fly about the stage and disappear at the whim of a sorceress, and the scene changes back and forth between the camps of battling armies, towers, and forests. In the tradition of the commedia dell'arte, the servants are depicted as buffoons; whipped by one of the princesses in the play to force them to pull a coach, they drag it into a pond. *Amor tra l'armi* was Maggi's final libretto. He wrote two plays, *Il ritorno d'Asoto, ossia Rappresentazione sacra del figliuolo prodigo* (1676, The Return of Asoto; or, Sacred Drama of the Prodigal Son) and *Il Teopiste* (1677, The Theosophist) for presentation by the students at the Jesuit school he had attended.

Maggi eventually disavowed some of these works, but they are of interest to scholars in showing the Milanese taste for local culture and the distancing of Milanese opera from the Venetian models that dominated the times. Maggi's main objection to Venetian opera was its ribaldry. In the introduction to *La Bianca in Castiglia* (1669, Bianca of Castile), which is dedicated to women, he deplores "I motti men che onesti" (the shocking language) of the melodramas of the Venetian vogue, which he claims that he has always avoided. In his introduction to *Affari ed amori* (1675, Political Affairs and Love), also dedicated to women, Maggi complains that the public could exhibit more critical acumen than is apparent in its willingness to see the same themes and stories continually repeated in the theater. He says that he will try to implement a wider range of themes in his own works and suggests that if women, in particular, show appreciation for his modest attempts, others more gifted than he will respond; women might thus be credited with restoring to the theater the prestige it has lost. This special attention to women foreshadows the importance Maggi gives the female characters in his later dialect plays. Maggi's complaints in these introductions reveal his dissatisfaction with the court audience for which he was writing, and *Affari ed amori* includes a subplot of a melodrama being developed for the court. Codreno, an artisan, asks Lotario, the court musician, when the new drama for which Lotario wrote the music will be performed. Lotario replies that he has had so many problems that he doubts that it will ever appear. The women want him to add arias, and right in the middle of everything people will start talking, and the *Signora* will laugh about the writer's supposed love affairs. The obnoxious atmosphere in the court theater caused by a talkative and unappreciative audience is discussed in *Il concorso de' Meneghini* (1698, The Audition for Meneghinos) years later, indicating that the problem had still not been resolved. Maggi also refers in these court melodramas to dealing with scheming impresarios and the egos and idiosyncracies of pampered singers. All of these comments indicate that he was disillusioned by the fame he had achieved by pleasing the court.

In 1688 Maggi published *Rime varie* (Various Rhymes), a collection of 149 sonnets and canzones mostly on moral and devotional themes. He omitted much of his early occasional lyric poetry from the volume and revised many of the poems with the assistance of Redi and the famed Jesuit preacher Paolo Segneri.

One of the major plot elements of the plays in dialect that Maggi began writing in 1695 is the marriage game, in which a monied bourgeois class marries off its daughters to an impoverished aristocracy. The dialect works also feature servants who good-naturedly observe the customs of the middle class. The main servant figures in Maggi's works in dialect are Meneghino and his female counterpart, Beltramina, both of whom are characterized by folk wisdom and good sense, and Tarlesca (elsewhere named Cricca), the funny, not-too-bright convent servant. Beltramina comments on the moral messages of the plays in the prologues and intermezzi, monologues in which she expounds in a comical way on current issues that may or may not be involved in the action of the play, such as the custom of putting daughters in convents to avoid having to pay dowries, ambition, moral and social hypocrisy, materialism, and laziness. While Tarlesca's stupidity contrasts with the wisdom of Meneghino and Beltramina, she is an effective vehicle for satirizing the moral corruption of the convents, and her simplicity throws into relief the pompous affectation of the nobility that surrounds her. In the dialect plays only the servants speak in the Milanese dialect; the rest of the characters speak either standard Italian, other regional dialects, or *parlar corrent* (commonly accepted language), a dialect that contains quite a bit of standard Italian and is spoken by uneducated upper-class women and by lower-class female characters who are trying to emulate them.

The "type" embodied by Meneghino is different from the traditional "mask" of the commedia dell'arte, which is aimed at instant recognition by the audience; the spectators at Maggi's dialect plays had to associate the "type" with the reality of everyday life. Maggi never offers a description of Meneghino; although subsequent authors and actors gave him physical attributes, and he became known as the "mask" of Milan, for his original Milanese audiences he represented a typical servant of a bourgeois family, speaking dialect to remind the middle class of its origins among the common people.

In Maggi's first dialect comedy, *Il manco male* (The Lesser Evil), the young widow Pandora has three suitors: the bully Trasone, the litigious Fileride, and the ambitious nobleman Don Filotimo. Her financial adviser, the manipulative Panurgo, mediates for all three hopefuls for reasons of his own. In the end, all, including the frustrated trickster, fail in their aims but avoid the worst evil, public exposure; Pandora will retire into the *collegio delle vedove* (college for widows), a recently established institution in Milan. Making do with the lesser evil and being satisfied that things are not worse is the highest good that human beings can

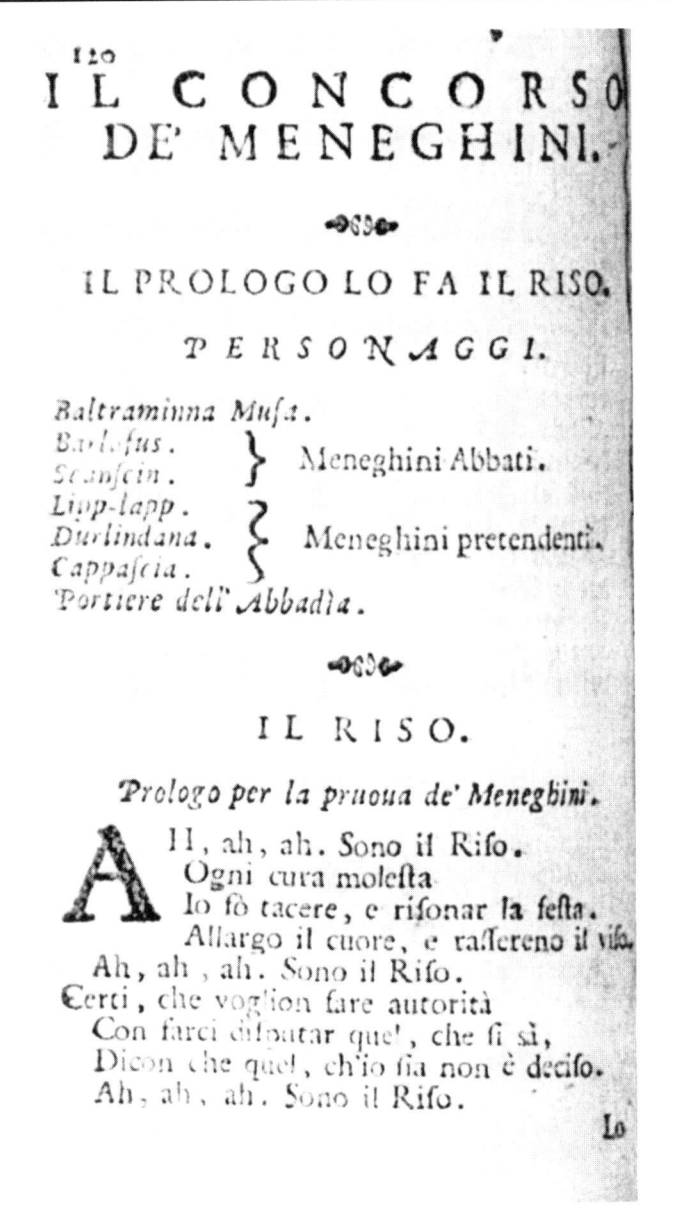

Opening page of Maggi's play The Audition of Meneghinos *in the second volume of* Comedie, e rime in lingua milanese
(University of Turin)

achieve. Maggi is distancing himself from the happy ending of the classical comedy.

The second dialect play, *Il barene di birbanza* (1696, The Baron of Roguery), deals with the theme of marriages arranged for money, a common practice in Milanese high society at the time. The false baron plans to make a fortune by deceiving the competitors for the supposed large dowry of his unattractive daughter. The honest servant Meneghino defeats the scheme; believing that he will have to leave his beloved city to escape the protagonist's vengeance, he bids farewell to his favorite eating and drinking places by name, as well as to the Verziere, Milan's produce market, the Parnassus of the Milanese populace. For Maggi the theater should be accessible to all levels of society.

I consigli di Meneghino (1697, Meneghino's Counsels) is the best-known, and the best, of Maggi's four dialect plays. The plot is cohesive, devoid of confusing subplots and burlesque *lazzi* (jokes); the character development and insights into Milanese life surpass all of Maggi's other works in richness and variety. In this play Meneghino assumes a primary role for the first time: while in the previous two plays he was temporary help, now he is a permanent fixture in the family and more of a father to his master, Fabio, than is Fabio's real father, the hardworking merchant Don Anselmo, who is trying to arrange a marriage between the hapless Fabio and an aristocrat's daughter. Although Meneghino does not enter directly into the action of the play, he constantly gives advice to Fabio regarding all aspects of the plot, and Fabio takes his counsels seriously. Other main characters are Beltramina, who makes moral observations in the prologues and intermezzi, and Tarlesca. In the second of the two short prologues Beltramina symbolically dismisses from the stage both tragedy and commedia dell'arte, the latter because it has nothing to do with Milanese reality and because of the obscenities for which it was notorious. The major issues in the play are arranged marriages between wealthy middle-class individuals and impoverished, parasitic aristocrats; dueling; and the worldly atmosphere of convents overflowing with girls who are waiting for a good marriage and forced to become nuns if that option is not realized.

Maggi's last work in dialect was *Il concorso de' Meneghini,* a one-act play in which three characters audition for the role of Meneghino. A prologue in standard Italian by the personification of laughter expresses the conviction that satire should target institutions and customs, not individuals, and that it should be delivered in a good-natured manner if the didactic value of the work is to be widely appreciated. This philosophy is taken up in dialect by Beltramina in the opening lines of the first act:

Giacchè la Poesia d'I Meneghin
Dal Tiater comeza a sopportass,
Mi Baltraminna Musa, che bescanta
Su I rivv della Vecchiabbia,
Sont andàe strolegand, par sostentà
Sta nosta Poesia, cossa 's pò fà.

(Since the poetry of the Meneghini
Is becoming accepted in the theater
I, Beltramina, the Muse who sings
On the banks of the Vettabbia [the main transportation canal linking Milan with the countryside],
Am trying to figure out a way
Of keeping this poetry going and preserving it.)

The first candidate, Lipp-Lapp, insists that theater must be made attractive to the growing commercial bourgeoisie:

El mestè d'I comedij
l'è co'I parsonn rappresentad on fagg
De gent de mezza tacca.

(The art of the comedy is to represent,
With fictitious figures, stories of
People of middle rank.)

To reflect this ascending middle class, he says, plays should include simple and comprehensible plots; ample use of dialect; and a representation of the everyday Milanese social atmosphere. Lipp-Lapp ends his monologue with one of Maggi's best-known lines:

Art, che no iutta al ben,
O che 'l màe no corresg,
L'è perdiment de temp, se no l'è pegg.

(Art, that doesn't do good,
Or correct an evil,
Is a waste of time, if not worse.)

The words have an eighteenth-century ring and are often quoted to prove Maggi's social engagement. The next contestant, Durlindana, describes a disastrous evening in one of the many private theaters in Milan. Durlindana is followed by Cappascia, who, confusing the words *impegno* (responsibility) and *in pegno* (in hock), delivers a comical but scathing satire of aristocrats and aspiring aristocrats: thanks to the Spanish equation of ostentation with success and fulfillment, these groups fall into financial ruin by trying to maintain the obligatory social facades. For their keen observations, their self-knowledge, and their ability to convey what they see and understand in a popular tone and in a way understandable to all, all three candidates are promoted to Meneghino. Beltramina's closing remarks urge the three to do all they can to support the Milanese dialect in its contest with Tuscan and Latin, underlining its value as symbolic of the older traditions and thus as a rein on the new commercially oriented social reality. Everyone in every class, she says, will be able to understand a message couched in the "essempij, panzanegh, e proverbij" (examples, folktales, and proverbs) of the city's language.

Carlo Maria Maggi died in Milan on 22 April 1699 and was buried in the Basilica of San Nazzaro. A four-volume collection of his poetry was published the following year by the historian and librarian Lodovico Antonio Muratori. In a time when operas were usually set in exotic climes, Maggi's insistence on keeping the action of his plays in a locale recognizable to those watching them made his comedies extremely successful. Dialect theater remained popular in Milan until the economic boom of the 1950s and 1960s swelled the city with a nonnative population that was unable to follow the language; since then, not only dialect theater but also the Milanese dialect itself have virtually disappeared.

Bibliography:

Dante Isella, *Bibliografia delle opere a stampa della letteratura in lingua milanese* (Milan: Biblioteca Nazionale Braidense, 1999).

Biographies:

Antonio Ludovico Muratori, *Vita di Carlo Maria Maggi* (Milan: Malatesta, 1700);

Emanuela Bufacchi, "Carlo Maria Maggi," in *Dictionario biografico degli Italiani,* volume 67 (Rome: Istituto della Enciclopedia Italiana, 2006), pp. 328–331.

References:

Mario Apollonio, "Carlo Maria Maggi ed il moralismo lombardo," *Civiltà moderna,* 1 (1932): 55–67;

Federico Barbieri, *Per la storia del teatro lombardo nella seconda metà del Secolo XVII* (Pavia: Athenaeum, 1914);

Walter Binni, "La commedia del Maggi," in his *L'Arcadia e il Metastasio* (Florence: La Nuova Italia, 1984), pp. 169–175;

Martino Capucci, "Lettura del Maggi lirico," *Studi secenteschi,* 3 (1962): 65–87;

Jackson I. Cope, "*Il manco male:* Maggi's Meneghino in Milan," in his *Secret Sharers in Italian Comedy: From Machiavelli to Goldoni* (Durham, N.C.: Duke University Press, 1986), pp. 117–135;

Emilio De Marchi, *Carlo Maria Maggi: Saggio critico* (Milan: Vallardi, 1930);

Pietro Gibellini, "Carlo Maria Maggi," in *Dizionario critico della letteratura italiana,* volume 3 (Turin: Unione Tipografico-Editrice Torinese, 1986), pp. 17–20;

Marcella Gorio, *Una poeta milanese del '600: Carlo Maria Maggi* (Parma: Donati, 1922);

Dante Isella, "Le rime milanesi di Carlo Maria Maggi," *Studi secenteschi,* 6 (1965): 65–262;

Carmine Jannaco and Martino Capucci, *Il Seicento* (Padua: Piccin Nuova Libraria, 1986), pp. 336–339, 371–375, 435–437, 477–478;

Domenico Manzella and Emilio Pozzi, *I teatri di Milano* (Milan: Mursia, 1971);

Glenn Palen Pierce, *The* Caratterista *and Comic Reform from Maggi to Goldoni* (Naples: Società Editrice Napoletana, 1986);

Pierce, "Carlo Maria Maggi and the *bosinada,*" *Forum italicum,* 13 (1979): 480–495;

Pierce, "Evidence and Transition in the Early Works of Carlo Maria Maggi," *Canadian Journal of Italian Studies,* 3 (1980): 193–222.

Lucrezia Marinella

(1571? – 9 October 1653)

Laura Benedetti
Georgetown University

BOOKS: *La colomba sacra* (Venice: Ciotti, 1595);

Vita del Serafico e Glorioso San Francesco, descritta in ottava rima, con un discorso del rivolgimento amoroso verso la Somma Bellezza (Venice: Pietro Maria Bertano e Fratelli, 1597);

Amore innamorato e impazzato (Venice, 1598);

Le nobiltà et eccellenze delle donne et i diffetti, e mancamenti degli huomini (Venice: Ciotti, 1600); revised and enlarged as *La nobiltà et l'eccellenza delle donne co' diffetti et mancamenti de gli huomini* (Venice: Ciotti, 1601); abridged and translated by Anne Dunhill as *The Nobility and Excellence of Women and the Defects and Vices of Men*, introduction by Letizia Panizza (Chicago & London: University of Chicago Press, 1999);

Vita di Maria Vergine, Imperatrice dell'universo, descritta in prosa e in ottava rima (Venice: Barezzo Barezzi, 1602);

Rime sacre (Venice: Collosini, 1603);

L'Arcadia felice (Venice: Ciotti, 1605);

Vita di Santa Giustina, in ottava rima (Florence, 1606); revised as *Olocausto d'amore della vergine Santa Giustina* (Venice: Matteo Leni, 1648);

De' Gesti heroici, e della vita maravigliosa della Serafica Santa Caterina da Siena (Venice: Barezzo Barezzi, 1624);

L'Enrico, ovvero Bisanzio acquistato (Venice: Ghirardo Imberti, 1635); republished as *L'Enrico, overo Costantinopoli acquistato* (Venice: Ghirardo Imberti, 1641); edited and translated by Maria Galli Stampino as *L'Enrico, or Byzantium Conquered* (Chicago & London: University of Chicago Press, 2008);

Essortationi alle donne et a gl'altri se a loro saranno a grado (Venice: Francesco Valvasense, 1645).

Editions: *Rime delle signore Lucrezia Marinella, Veronica Gambara, ed Isabella della Morra, con giunta di quelle fin'ora raccolte dalla Signora Maria Selvaggia Borghini*, edited by Antonio Bulifon (Naples: Antonio Bulifon, 1693);

L'Enrico, ovvero Bisanzio acquistato (Venice: Antonelli, 1844);

Arcadia felice, edited by Françoise Lavocat (Florence: Olschki, 1998).

OTHER: "Argomenti e allegorie," in *Le lagrime di San Pietro,* by Luigi Tansillo (Venice: Barezzo Barezzi, 1606).

The most productive and versatile early modern Italian woman writer, Lucrezia Marinella experimented in genres from the pastoral comedy to the epic poem but devoted the bulk of her work to religious topics. Virtually forgotten by the end of the seventeenth century, she was rediscovered when women writers of the past became the focus of sustained scholarly attention in the last quarter of the twentieth century. The literary value and cultural significance of Marinella's *Le nobiltà et eccellenze delle donne et i diffetti, e mancamenti degli huomini* (1600; revised and enlarged as *La nobiltà et l'eccellenza delle donne co' diffetti et mancamenti degli huomini,* 1601; abridged and translated as *The Nobility and Excellence of Women and the Defects and Vices of Men,* 1999) have been widely acknowledged. The only early modern treatise in praise of women written by an Italian woman, *Le nobiltà et eccellenze delle donne et i diffetti, e mancamenti degli huomini* documents its author's self-confidence, erudition, and skill in argumentation.

Most scholars accept Girolamo Tiraboschi's claim that Marinella was born in 1571. But in the dedication of *Vita di Maria Vergine, Imperatrice dell'universo, descritta in prosa e in ottava rima* (1602, Life of the Virgin Mary, Empress of the Universe, Described in Prose and in Ottava Rima) to the doge and senate of Venice, Marinella asks that her audacity be excused in light of her young age—a statement that would be almost unthinkable for a thirty-one-year-old woman to make at that time. Furthermore, Marinella died in 1653; if she was born in 1571, she would have reached the remarkable, though not impossible, age for the period of eighty-two. It is possible, then, that the year of her birth

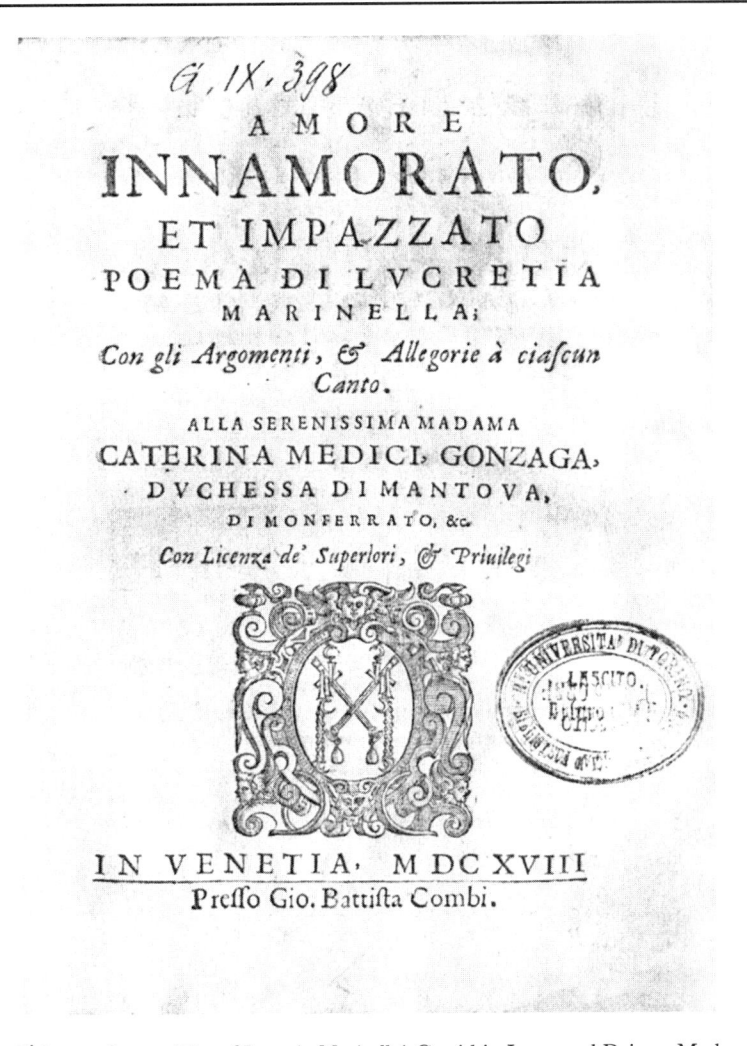

Title page for an edition of Lucrezia Marinella's Cupid in Love and Driven Mad, *originally published in 1598 (University of Turin)*

was closer to the end of the century than is commonly believed.

Although Marinella, like many women writers of her time, was Venetian by birth, she felt strong ties to her father's home city of Modena; in a letter written to accompany a copy of *Vita di Maria Vergine* she declared herself a "serva e suddita" (servant and subject) of the duchess of Mantua. Nothing is known of her mother, but her father, Giovanni Marinelli, was a renowned physician as well as the author of a tract on rhetoric, *La copia delle parole* (1562, The Abundance of Words); a manual on cosmetics, *Gli ornamenti delle donne* (1562, Women's Ornaments); and a highly successful treatise on gynecology, *Le medicine partenenti alle infermità delle donne* (1563, Medicines Pertaining to Women's Illnesses). According to archival documents uncovered by Susan Haskins, Marinella had a sister, Diamantina, who was married in 1594, and two brothers: Curzio became a physician and a writer, and Antonio became a Servite monk at the monastery of S. Giacomo della Giudecca and took the name Fra Angelico. Lucrezia was probably the youngest in the family. The 1591 census reported her as living–presumably after her father's death and before her marriage–with Curzio in Campiello dei Squelini.

While this stimulating family environment might have had a positive effect on Marinella's intellectual development, it remains unclear how she acquired the education and the confidence that allowed her to publish her first poem, *La colomba sacra* (The Holy Dove), in 1595. Written in octaves, the work combines a devotional topic, the martyrdom of St. Colomba, with themes and images of the epic tradition as revised by Torquato Tasso.

Marinella probably referred to the popular *Legendario delle Santissime Vergini* (1532, Legends of the Holy Virgins) and combined the scant information in that source with a careful reading of Tasso's *Gerusalemme liberata* (1581, Jerusalem Delivered; translated as *Godfrey of Bulloigne, or The Recoverie of Hierusalem,* 1594). The relationship of Colomba and the Roman emperor Aurelian, who ordered her execution in what is now Sens, France, is clearly modeled on that of Sofronia and Aladino in canto 2 of Tasso's poem. Marinella describes Aurelian's reaction on first seeing Colomba:

> Al folgorar de le sue rare, e sante
> bellezze, amor placò l'irato aspetto;
> placò quel cor l'angelico sembiante
> scemò lo sdegno rio nel regio petto;
> quel piú che marmo, o rigido diamante
> or prende in mirar lei pace, e diletto:
> diletto, pace prende, e meraviglia
> de l'aureo crin, de le stellante ciglia.

> (When that rare and saintly beauty shone,
> love calmed the angered expression;
> that angelic apparition calmed that heart,
> diminished the impious rage in the royal soul;
> he who was sterner than marble or hard diamond
> now finds peace and pleasure in looking at her;
> he finds pleasure, peace, and wonder
> before the golden hair, the shining eyes.)

But pleasure, peace, and wonder are dispelled from the emperor's soul when he is confronted by Colomba's unshakable faith. The real conflict the young woman faces in Marinella's poem is, however, not with Aurelian but with her own attachment to life. The struggle takes place within the character's psyche and finds its resolution in Colomba's fervent prayer in the final canto. After a vision in which she is called by Christ to his kingdom, Colomba is able to face martyrdom not just with resignation but even with glee: "E lieta aspetta il colpo, che le doni / morte, e ch'in Ciel poi viva la coroni" (She happily waits for the blow that will give / her death and then crown her, alive, in heaven). Two years later Marinella published *Vita del Serafico e Glorioso San Francesco* (Life of the Seraphic and Glorious St. Francis), followed in 1598 by *Amore innamorato e impazzato* (Cupid in Love and Driven Mad).

In 1600 appeared the work that has guaranteed Marinella a place in the history of Italian literature, *Le nobiltà et eccellenze delle donne et i diffetti, e mancamenti degli huomini*. It was written in response to Giuseppe Passi's *I donneschi difetti* (Women's Defects), published in Venice the previous year, which cites religious and classical authorities to describe women's shortcomings. Marinella goes beyond refuting Passi's arguments for female inferiority to demonstrate the superiority of women to men. To support her opinion Marinella relies heavily on Plato, especially his dialogue *The Republic*.

The first part of Marinella's book, devoted to women's virtues, shows the influence not only of Plato but also of Henricus Cornelius Agrippa's *De nobilitate et praecellentia foeminei sexus* (1529, On the Nobility and Preeminence of the Female Sex; translated as *The Glory of Women; or, A Treatise Declaring the Excellency and Preeminence of Women above Men, Which Is Proved Both by Scripture, Law, Reason, and Authority, Divine, and Humane,* 1652). After examining the etymologies of various words for "woman"—*donna, femina,* and *mulier*—Marinella moves on to the Scriptures and, following a line of reasoning popular at the time, demonstrates Eve's superiority over Adam. First, better material was used in her creation: Adam's rib, as opposed to mud. She was created in a better place: the earthly Paradise. Finally, among individuals of the same species, those who are created last are better than those created earlier. In the fourth chapter Marinella challenges the opinions of those who do not believe that women can excel in war and scholarship. These beliefs would easily be proven wrong, Marinella maintains, by an experiment that allowed girls to study and exercise as much as boys:

> O Dio volesse, che a questi nostri tempi fosse lecito alle donne l'essercitarsi nelle armi, et nelle lettere, che si vederebbono cose meravigliose, et non piú udite nel conservare i regni, e nell'ampliarli. . . . Se non si adoprano, questo avviene perché non si essercitano, essendo ciò a loro dagli homini vietato, spinti da una loro ostinata ignoranza persuadendosi che le donne non sieno buone da imparare quelle cose che imparano i maschi. Io vorrei, che questi tali facessero una esperienza tale, che essercitassero un putto, et una fanciulla d'una medesima età, ambiduoi di buona natura et ingegno nelle lettere, et nelle armi che vederebbono in quanto minor tempo piú peritamente sarebbe instrutta la fanciulla del fanciullo.

> (If God would but grant that in our times women be permitted to exercise in arms and letters! We would witness wonderful things we have never heard of, in the conservation as well as in the expansion of the state. . . . If they do not try, it is because men prevent them from training, as their stubborn ignorance has convinced them that women are unable to learn the things they do. I would like these men to try the experiment of training a good-natured boy and girl of about the same age and intelligence in letters and arms. They would then see how quickly the girl would surpass the boy.)

She then puts forth an impressive list of women who have actually excelled in the arts, the sciences, and war. The first part of the book concludes with a rebuttal of negative opinions about women expressed by various authors, particularly Aristotle. Many of Marinella's definitions of vices and virtues are derived from Aristotle, but this dependence does not prevent her from challenging the philosopher's views on women:

> Varie furno le cagioni che spinsero e sforzorno alcuni uomini sapienti e dotti a biasmar, e vituperar le donne. . . . Onde si potrebbe dire che quando Aristotile, o alcuno altro biasmò le donne, che o sdegno, o invidia, o troppo amor di lor medesimi ne sia stata la cagione.
>
> (There are several reasons that inspired and forced some learned and cultivated men to blame and insult women. . . . One could say that when Aristotle, or somebody else, criticized women, they did it out of contempt, envy, or excessive love for themselves.)

On the other hand, Plato, "quel grande uomo, in vero giustissimo" (that great and truly just man), provides arguments to correct women's denigrators. For example, Passi considers female beauty a source "di superbia e d'altri mali" (of pride and other evils); Marinella uses the Platonic notion that external beauty is a sign of internal nobility to argue that women's appearance can become a means of spiritual elevation for the men who love them, as Beatrice did for Dante and Laura for Petrarch. Marinella also cites Plato's plea in *The Republic* and *The Laws* for women's participation in social and political life.

The second part of the work, dealing with men's shortcomings, presents a gallery of greedy, envious, wrathful, and fickle men. It would be pointless to search for originality in Marinella's arguments or in most other tracts of this kind, including Passi's. Treatises that upheld women's equality or superiority were common throughout the sixteenth century; showing a thorough understanding of the conventions of the genre, Marinella intermingles history and legend, classical and Renaissance epic poems, and the lyrical tradition. Although many of her examples derive from Giovanni Boccaccio's *De mulieribus claris* (1361-1632; translated as *Concerning Famous Women,* 1963), Marinella also displays an amazing familiarity with vernacular literature: she refers to a wide variety of Italian authors, including Dante, Petrarch, Tasso, Ludovico Ariosto, Luigi Tansillo, and Moderata Fonte.

A revised edition of the work came out a year later. The considerable changes and many additions in the revision support Marinella's claim that the first version was sent out in haste to provide a timely rebuttal to Passi's work. At the end of the first part she added four short chapters rejecting the opinions of Ercole Tasso and Arrigo of Namur, Sperone Speroni, Torquato Tasso, and Boccaccio. Here Marinella displays not only erudition but also courage and critical acumen. Her critique of Tasso is particularly noteworthy. In 1580, during his confinement in the Sant'Anna asylum, Tasso wrote and dedicated to Duchess Eleonora Gonzaga of Mantua a brief discourse, *De la virtú feminile e donnesca* (On Feminine and Womanly Virtue), in which he tries to reconcile his Aristotelian premises with his desire to please his addressee. The result is an ambiguous piece in which he struggles to define a new kind of "virtú donnesca" (womanly virtue) that is the exclusive prerogative of princesses, whereas the rest of the female sex should practice traditional "virtú femminili" (feminine virtues) such as obedience and chastity. In her rebuttal Marinella criticizes Tasso for his uncritical acceptance of Aristotle's authority, describes with sarcasm his "novella invenzione" (novel invention) of dividing women's virtues into two kinds, and demands the same rights and consideration for all women, regardless of their social status. Chief among her concerns is that women have access to education. Polemical fervor thus leads Marinella to formulate principles that are striking in their boldness and modernity. She greatly expanded the second part of the work by inserting many more examples and adding ten new chapters; along with the four chapters added to the first part, this expansion brings the total number to thirty-five–the same number of chapters as Passi's *I donneschi difetti.*

In 1602 Marinella returned to devotional literature with *Vita di Maria Vergine, imperatrice dell'universo.* Dedicated to the Venetian authorities, the volume is an unusual attempt to present one topic in two formats: prose and ottava rima. Marinelli's main concern in her address to the readers is to justify her prose, which is rich in rhetorical techniques such as repetition and hyperbole that are more commonly found in poetry:

> Le azioni che hanno del grande, del magnifico e del divino, e che trapassano le operazioni umane, ricercano un modo di dire grande e mirabile, molto diverso da quello che si usa nel raccontar quelle azioni, che picciole, umili e basse sono. Et più si ricerca lo stile diverso, quando che tali azioni dipendono da persone che eccedono per l'eccellenza della lor natura gli uomini e gli eroi. Ritrovandosi adunque tutte queste condizioni nel mio ragionamento, cioè azioni trapassanti il sommo d'ogn'altra azione, e persone che contengono in sé ciò che di maraviglioso vien pertecipato da tutte le altre creature, delle quali il mondo adornato si vede, ho eletto questo modo di parlar poetico.
>
> (Great, magnificent and divine actions, that overcome human activity, demand a great and admirable style, very different from the one used to describe small, humble and low-key actions. Such a style is even more necessary when individuals whose excellent nature is

superior to that of men and heroes perform such actions. Since my work contained all the above characteristics, such as actions that overcome all other actions, and people who embody all the wonders that are usually divided among all the other creatures that embellish the world, I chose this way of poetic speech.)

This explanation of the reasons behind the adoption of such a grandiloquent style is followed by a citation of the religious authorities Marinella used as sources for the life of Mary. Judging from the number of editions—it was republished in 1604, 1610, and 1617—*Vita di Maria Vergine* seems to have been Marinella's most popular work. That success was met with insinuations that she was not the real author of the book. The charge, which was often brought against women writers, was emphatically denied by her publisher, Giovan Battista Ciotti, in the introduction to her *L'Arcadia felice* (1605, Happy Arcadia).

In 1603 Marinella published her only collection of poems, *Rime sacre* (Sacred Rhymes). Mostly sonnets and madrigals, the pieces comprise poems on religious themes interspersed with others in which the speaker repents her sins, condemns her insufficient piety and her impatience, and vows to renounce the world and its vanities.

In 1605 Marinella published her only pastoral romance, *L'Arcadia felice,* which she dedicated to Leonora Gonzaga. The protagonist is the Roman emperor Diocletian, who abdicated in 305 and retired to Dalmatia. Marinella glosses over the emperor's persecution of Christians, which was stressed by most authors of her time, to emphasize his noble decision to turn away from worldly pursuits:

> Non solamente avea il magnanimo Diocleziano con la sua prudenza retto molti e molti anni il grande e 'l glorioso Impero Romano, ma . . . avea raccolto sotto l'ali dell'Aquila Romana le ribellate Provincie ed i ribellati Regni; abbassate quelle lancie e rintuzzato il furore di quelle spade che si erano mosse contra il petto di lei; e l'avea fatta formidabile a tutte le nazioni, arricchita di trionfi, ornata di vittorie, e veduta (mercè del suo valore) giunta al colmo della tranquillità della pace. Quando egli divisò tra se stesso fuggendo le grandezze degli onori e delle pompe imperiali transferirsi al giusto, al quieto ed al leale delle rozze ville.

(Not only had magnanimous Diocletian with his prudence governed for many years the great and glorious Roman empire, but . . . he had reunited under the wings of the Roman eagle the rebel provinces and kingdoms; he had driven back the wrath of swords and spears that had moved against its heart; he had made it formidable among all nations, enriched by its triumphs, embellished by its victories. He could see that, thanks to his valor, Rome had reached the summit of its tranquillity and peace. At that point, he decided to escape the grandeur of imperial honor and pomp, and to move to the just, calm and loyal atmosphere of the rustic countryside.)

Most of the work deals with the emperor's arrival in the countryside and the celebrations held in his honor, but this main theme is interrupted by various secondary stories. Marinella's departure from the model of Jacopo Sannazaro's *Arcadia* (1502) is apparent in this tendency toward plot development, as well as in a drastic reduction of the sections in verse. Equally original is her introduction of two female characters, Ersilia and Canente, who excel in athletic and poetic endeavors, respectively.

Marinella's works seem to have enjoyed the favor of the Accademia Veneziana (Venetian Academy), to which, as a woman, she could not be admitted. Boncio Leone, president of the academy, contributed a sonnet in praise of the author to the introduction to *La colomba sacra,* and Marinella dedicated *Le nobiltà et eccellenze delle donne et i diffetti, e mancamenti degli huomini* to the physician Lucio Scarano, the academy's secretary. Marinella contributed allegorical explanations and *argomenti* (summaries of the cantos) to a 1606 edition of Tansillo's *Lagrime di San Pietro* (1585, St. Peter's Tears). That same year she published *Vita di Santa Giustina, in ottava rima* (Life of St. Justine, in Ottava Rima).

Following her 1607 marriage to Girolamo Vacca, a physician twelve years her senior, Marinella retreated into a long silence that can probably be attributed to her raising their children, Antonio and Paulina. In 1624 *De' Gesti heroici, e della vita maravigliosa della Serafica Santa Caterina da Siena* (The Heroic Deeds and Wonderful Life of the Seraphic St. Catherine of Siena) marked her comeback to the literary scene.

Marinella's greatest accomplishment during the last forty-seven years of her life was the epic poem *L'Enrico, ovvero Bisanzio acquistato* (1635; translated as *L'Enrico, or Byzantium Conquered,* 2008). This lengthy work deals with what is now known as the Fourth Crusade, which lasted from 1202 to 1204. Unique among the Crusades in that the Christian army never confronted the Muslims, the military expedition that culminated in the fall of Byzantium was dear to Venetian pride; its celebration can be interpreted as Marinella's attempt to gain favor in her home city after her earlier tributes to Modena and the Gonzagas. Praise for Venice abounds, especially in Erina's historical overview and prophecy to Pietro Venier in canto 7.

The preface shows concerns that seem to belong to the sixteenth century: Marinella promises to follow Aristotle's precepts, in particular those concerning the unity of action. She also attributes to

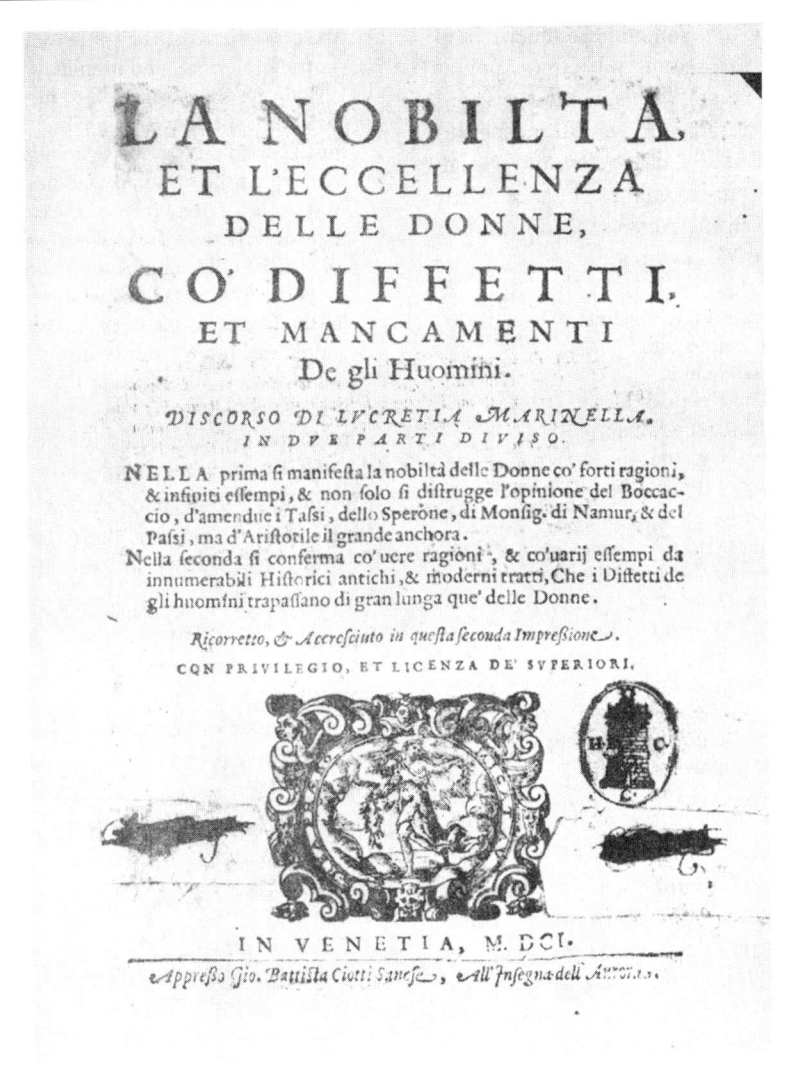

Title page for the revised and enlarged edition of On the Nobility and Excellence of Women and the Defects and Vices of Men *(courtesy of Laura Benedetti)*

Aristotle narrative principles that seem to have been extrapolated from Tasso's *Discorsi dell'arte poetica* (1587; translated as "Discourses on the Art of Poetry," 1993): "Gli episodi ed altre digressioni pur, come piace allo stesso filosofo, ho procurato che sieno così unite colla principale azione, che non si potese facilmente levarne una parte senza confondere il tutto" (I arranged for the episodes and the other digressions, as recommended by the same philosopher, to be so tightly connected with the main plot, that it would be impossible to omit one part without ruining the whole). The poem focuses on the capture of Byzantium; digressions are rigidly controlled, even at the expense of internal coherence. This incoherence becomes apparent in the only love story that is allowed a certain development: that between Giacinto and Idilia. The two are called to perform deeds that in Tasso's *Gerusalemme liberata* are distributed among several characters: like Tasso's Tancredi, Giacinto fights a duel against an enemy warrior; like Vafrino, he is sent as a spy into the enemy camp and, like Clorinda, he saves a virgin who is about to be burned at the stake; like Sofronia, Idilia is rescued by Giacinto but is soon taken away and ends up in a pastoral setting, where she, like Tasso's Erminia, carves her story and the name of her beloved on the trees. Surprisingly, their story lacks a conclusion: whereas Giacinto appears again and again in episodes that stress his prowess and devotion to the Christian cause, Idilia is only mentioned as one of the illusions that serve as obstacles to progress toward Byzantium.

Marinella's octaves are sometimes generic and formulaic, particularly in their use of adjectives such as "aspra e fera" (harsh and fierce), "bella, vezzosa e vaga" (beautiful, graceful and attractive), "estinte e spente" (extinguished and dead), and "alto e sovrano" (high and sovereign). But she seems to gain confidence as the poem progresses. In the central cantos reflection on the defeated combines horror with sympathy:

> Chi dir potrebbe in quanti modi e 'n quante
> maniere a' stuoli il Greco estinto cada;
> come la morte in orrido sembiante
> movendo l'altrui braccio opri la spada;
> chi tronco ha 'l capo, e l'altre membra infrante
> orrenda strage copre campo e strada,
> quivi le pompe sue dispiega e mostra
> l'alta miseria de la vita nostra.

> (Who could say in how many ways, in how many
>   manners
> entire groups of Greeks fall to their deaths;
> how death, in horrendous guise,
> maneuvers its sword by using others' arms;
> one has his head severed, his bones broken;
> a horrendous massacre covers fields and streets,
> here its pomp reveals and displays
> the high misery of our life.)

Far from playing the traditional role of diverting heroes from their goal, women are portrayed as active participants on both sides. Particularly noteworthy are the many women warriors, such as Emilia, Claudia, and Meandra. Emilia combines the attributes of Venus and Diana and performs many heroic deeds—most notably, the killing of Venier—before returning to the forest and turning into a goddess. Claudia's first appearance in the poem is particularly striking:

> L'ultima è Claudia altera, che discese
> dal gran sangue latin, progenie augusta;
> costei ne' suoi primi anni avid'apprese
> de' prischi eroi l'alta virtú vetusta;
> e 'n cheta pace, e 'n militari offese
> si mostrò ognor magnanima e venusta;
> mostra che l'uso e non natura ha messo
> timor ne l'un, valor ne l'altro sesso.
> E quando d'ozio alquanto mai concede
> il sovran duce a le gradite squadre;
> qua e là con gli altri esercitar si vede
> ne l'opre di Bellona alte e leggiadre.
> Dopo tai scherzi move audace il piede
> a le selve, a le grotte oscure ed adre,
> cacciatrice guerriera a dar spavento
> a' boschi, ed avanzar col corso il vento.

> (Last comes proud Claudia, who descended,
> noble offspring, from great Latin blood.
> In her first years she zealously learned
> the great virtue of ancient heroes.
> In tranquil peace, and in military strikes
> she always showed herself to be generous and
>   beautiful; she shows that habit, not nature,
> instilled timidity in one sex, valor in the other.
> And when the supreme captain grants some
> rest to the grateful troops, she can be seen
> here and there as she practices with the
> others the noble and beautiful arts of
> Bellona. After these games she bravely moves
> to the forests, to the dark and obscure
> caves; she, the warrior huntress who frightens
> the woods, and runs faster than the winds.)

A comparison of Claudia with other women warriors in the Italian literary tradition shows the novelty of Marinella's approach. Ariosto, Tasso, and Matteo Maria Boiardo present their female fighters as isolated wonders, exceptions to the rule of women's frailty. Marinella, on the contrary, uses Claudia to show that the flaws attributed to women are not intrinsic to their nature but the result of social customs and their upbringing.

Women's excellence in battle, however, does not come at the expense of other aspects of the female personality. The speech given by the queen of Argo to her son, who is leaving to go on the Crusade, is striking for its combination of maternal concerns and bellicose pride:

> S'io fossi ne l'età che oppressi e vinsi
> i vincitori, e i forti re fei servi;
> ch'alte mura abbattei, che i fiumi spinsi
> di sangue al mar vincendo i cor protervi,
> ch'io stetti contra un campo intiero, e 'l strinsi
> fuggir, come da i can timidi cervi,
> e di mille trofei, di mille spoglie
> fregiando me, posi i nemici in doglie.
> Se non l'etade, verdi almen le posse
> fossero in me, ch'ancor ti seguirei;
> ogni brando, ch'a te drizzato fosse,
> te difendendo, sopra me torrei.
> Da nemici, da ferri e da percosse
> salvo e vittorioso ti trarrei;
> ma, poi che gli anni e la mutata scorza
> me 'l contraddice, mi sto lenta a forza.

> (If I were at the age when I defeated and triumphed over
> the winners, and made strong kings become servants;
> when I destroyed high walls, when I pushed toward the
>   ocean
> rivers of blood as I defeated arrogant souls;
> when I faced an entire army, and forced it to flee,
> like fearful deer flee from dogs;
> and with innumerable prizes, innumerable trophies
> I adorned myself, and made the enemies mourn.
> If my strength were young, since my years are not,
> I would still follow you.
> Any sword aimed at you, to protect you,

I would direct towards myself.
I would rescue you, safe and victorious,
from enemies, swords and blows.
But since my years and my changed body
prevent me, I am forced to stay behind.)

Certain passages seem to be inspired by a desire to provide alternative endings to corresponding episodes of *Gerusalemme liberata*. Emilia kills Alfeo immediately after he falls in love with her, as if to avoid dying like Clorinda does in canto 12 of Tasso's poem. And whereas Tasso prevented Gildippe and Clorinda from fighting each other, reserving them for stronger enemies–Solimano and Tancredi, respectively–Marinella has Claudia and Meandra die at each other's hand, as if to imply that there cannot be a better match.

The lukewarm reception of *L'Enrico* may have influenced Marinella's last published volume, *Essortationi alle donne et a gli'altri se a loro saranno a grado* (1645, Exhortations to Women and to Others if They Please). The first impression one receives is that it is a palinode of the opinions expressed in *La nobiltà et l'eccellenza delle donne co' diffetti et mancamenti de gli huomini* and reasserted in *L'Enrico*. The writer who had proudly sung the glory of her sex against its detractors no longer sees women's subordination to men as a result of social constraints but as the manifestation of natural order and even of divine will. Profound bitterness permeates the text as Marinella gives the reader a glimpse of what may have been her own experiences. The life of a learned woman, according to Marinella, can only be a series of disappointments. Scorned by her family for her passion for knowledge, she is destined to be the object of men's jealousy and women's contempt. Rewards are rare, as rulers are inclined to favor equally or even less talented men, and her works are often suspected of having been written by someone else.

The publication of *Essortationi alle donne et a gl'altri se a loro saranno a grado* coincided with the drafting of Marinella's will. While she designated her son, Antonio, as her main heir, she left small legacies to her daughter, Paulina, and the children of her sister, Diamantina. An addendum dated three years later is the only extant indication of the existence of a granddaughter: Angioletta, Paulina's daughter, is designated to receive a small sum at Marinella's death.

Marinella died on 9 October 1653. Praised by contemporaries such as Francesco Sansovino, Francesco Agostino Della Chiesa, and Cristofero Bronzino for her poetic and musical talent and for her knowledge of philosophy, she was soon forgotten, and most of her works were not republished after the seventeenth century. One exception is *L'Enrico,* which appeared in 1844. In the introduction the editor, "F.Z.," says that the work deserves attention for its subject rather than for the poetic talent of the author, who is representative of the degraded tastes of her century. This opinion, already expressed by Tiraboschi, was echoed by all nineteenth-century scholars who dealt with Marinella and was subscribed to in the twentieth century by Benedetto Croce. Only in the last quarter of the twentieth century did this erudite and prolific artist begin to receive the critical attention she deserves.

Lucrezia Marinella's oeuvre is striking for its combination of conformism and originality. It mainly consists of devotional works that are examples of the Counter-Reformation practice of promoting orthodoxy through literature. *La nobiltà et l'eccellenza delle donne co' diffetti et mancamenti de gli huomini,* on the contrary, reveals an independent and almost rebellious spirit, unafraid of questioning even the most established authorities. The pastoral work *L'Arcadia felice* and the epic poem *L'Enrico* complete the picture of an artist always willing to experiment with new genres. The link among such diverse works is the representation of women–whether saints or amazons–as proud, complete individuals, capable of excelling in all domains of the human spirit.

References:

Prudence Allen and Filippo Salvatore, "Lucrezia Marinella and Woman's Identity in Late Italian Renaissance," *Renaissance and Reformation / Renaissance et Réforme,* 4 (1992): 5–39;

Laura Benedetti, "Le *Essortationi* di Lucrezia Marinella: L'ultimo messaggio di una misteriosa veneziana," *Italica* (forthcoming);

Benedetti, "Saintes et guerrières: L'héroïsme féminin dans l'œuvre de Lucrezia Marinella," in *Les femmes et l'écriture: L'amour profane et l'amour sacré,* edited by Claude Cazalé Bérard (Paris: Presses Universitaires de Paris X, 2005), pp. 93–109;

Benedetti, "Virtù femminile o virtù donnesca? Torquato Tasso, Lucrezia Marinella ed una polemica rinascimentale," in *Torquato Tasso e la cultura estense,* edited by Gianni Venturi (Florence: Olschki, 1999), pp. 449–456;

Cristoforo Bronzini, *Della dignità e nobiltà delle donne* (Florence: Zanobi Pignoni, 1624), Settimana I, Giorno IV, p. 112;

Adriana Chemello, "La donna, il modello, l'immaginario: Moderata Fonte e Lucrezia Marinella," in *Nel cerchio della luna: Figure di donna in alcuni testi del XVI secolo,* edited by Marina Zancan (Venice: Marsilio, 1983), pp. 95–170;

Chemello, "Lucrezia Marinella," in *Le stanze ritrovate: Antologia di scrittrici venete dal Quattrocento al Novecento,* edited by Chemello, Antonia Arslan, and Gilberto Pizzamiglio (Venice: Eidos, 1991), pp. 96–108;

Ginevra Conti Odorisio, *Donna e società nel Seicento* (Rome: Bulzoni, 1979), pp. 47–73, 113–157;

Virginia Cox, "The Single Self: Feminist Thought and the Marriage Market in Early Modern Venice," *Renaissance Quarterly,* 3 (1995): 513–581;

Cox, "Women as Readers and Writers of Chivalric Poetry in Early Modern Italy," in *Sguardi sull'Italia: Miscellanea dedicata a Francesco Villari,* edited by Gino Bedani and others (Leeds, U.K.: Society for Italian Studies, 1997), pp 134–145;

Benedetto Croce, *Barocco in prosa e in poesia* (Milan: Rizzoli, 1969), p. 291;

Francesco Agostino Della Chiesa, *Theatro delle donne letterate con un breve discorso della preminenza e perfettione del sesso donnesco* (Mondoví: Gislandi & Rossi, 1620), p. 224;

Susan Haskins, "Vexatious Litigant, or the Case of Lucrezia Marinella? New Documents Concerning Her Life (Part One)," *Nouvelles de la République des Lettres,* 1 (2006): 80–128;

Stephen Kolski, "Moderata Fonte, Lucrezia Marinella, Giuseppe Passi: An Early Seventeenth-Century Feminist Controversy," *Modern Language Review,* 4 (2001): 972–989;

Claire Lesage, "Femmes de lettres à Venise aux XVIe et XVIIe siècles: Moderata Fonte, Lucrezia Marinella, Arcangela Tarabotti," *Clio: Histoire, Femmes et Sociétés,* 13 (2001): 135–144;

Paola Malprezzi Price, "Lucrezia Marinella," in *Italian Women Writers: A Bio-Bibliographical Sourcebook,* edited by Rinaldina Russel (Westport, Conn.: Greenwood Press, 1994), pp. 234–242;

Malpezzi Price, "Moderata Fonte, Lucrezia Marinella and Their 'Feminist' Work," *Italian Studies,* 12 (1994): 201–214;

Girolamo Tiraboschi, *Biblioteca modenese,* volume 3 (Modena: Società Tipografica, 1783), pp. 158–163.

Giambattista Marino
(14 October 1569 – 25 March 1625)

Francesco Guardiani
University of Toronto

BOOKS: *Rime* (Venice: Ciotti, 1602);

Il ritratto del Serenissimo don Carlo Emmanuello duca di Savoia, panegirico del Marino al Figino (Turin, 1608);

Lira (Venice: Ciotti, 1614);

Dicerie sacre del cavalier Marino divise in tre: Cioè pittura, musica et cielo (Turin: Luigi Pizzamiglio, 1614);

Il tempio: Panegirico (Lyon: Nicolo Jullieron, 1615);

Gli epitalami del Cav. Marino (Paris: Tussan du Bray, 1616);

La Murtoleide, fischiate del cavalier Marino, con La Marineide, risate del Murtola (Norinbergh: Joseph Stamphier, 1619);

La galeria del cav. Marino, distinta in pitture, e sculture (Venice: Ciotti, 1620);

La Sampogna, del cavalier Marino, divisa in idilii favolosi, & pastorali (Paris: Abraham Pacard, 1620);

L'Adone (Paris: Oliviero di Varano, 1623); excerpts translated by Harold Martin Priest as *Adonis: Selections from L'Adone of Giambattista Marino* (Ithaca, N.Y.: Cornell University Press, 1967);

Il Tebro festante, panegirico. Del Cavalier Marino. Con idillij, e canzoni non più stampate del detto Autore. Et alcune poesie in lode dell'istesso. Quarta parte de gl'Epitalami (Venice: Ciotti, 1624);

La sferza invettiva contro i quattro ministri della iniquità (Paris: Tussan du Bray, 1625);

Il settimo canto della Gierusalemme distrutta, poema eroico del sig. cavalier Gio. Battista Marino: Aggiuntoui alcune altre composizioni del medesimo. Con La ciabattina pudica, e La bella gialla, canzoni d'incerto (Venice: Girolamo Piuti, 1626);

La strage de gl'innocenti (Naples: Beltrano, 1632); translated by T.R. as *The Slaughter of the Innocents by Herod* (London: Printed by Andrew Clark for Samuel Mearne, 1675).

Editions and Collections: *Poesie varie,* edited by Benedetto Croce (Bari: Laterza, 1913);

L'Adone, edited by Gustavo Balsamo-Crivelli (Turin: Paravia, 1922);

La galeria, del cavalier Marino (Lanciano: G. Carabba, 1926);

Giambattista Marino; seventeenth-century painting by an unknown artist; Uffizi Gallery, Florence (from Scelte di Giovan Battista Marino e dei marinisti, *edited by Giovanni Getto, 1970; Thomas Cooper Library, University of South Carolina)*

Poesie e prose varie, edited by Carlo Culcasi (Milan: Sonzogno, 1930);

Marino e i marinisti, edited by Giuseppe Guido Ferrero (Milan & Naples: Ricciardi, 1954);

Dicerie sacre e La strage degli Innocenti, edited by Giovanni Pozzi (Turin: Einaudi, 1960);

Opere: Dalle lettere e dedicatorie, dalla Lira, dalla Galeria, dalla Sampogna, dagli Epitalami, dall'Adone, dalle Dicerie sacre, dalla Strage de gli Innocenti, dai versi satirici e giocosi Giambattista Marino, edited by Alberto Asor Rosa (Milan: Rizzoli, 1967);

Scelte di Giovan Battista Marino e dei marinisti, edited by Giovanni Getto (Turin: Unione Tipografico-Editrice Torinese, 1970);

L'Adone, 2 volumes, edited by Marzio Pieri (Bari: Laterza, 1975, 1977);

L'Adone, edited by Pozzi (Milan: Mondadori, 1976);

Galeria, edited by Pieri (Padua: Liviana, 1979);

Amori, edited by Alessandro Martini (Milan: Rizzoli, 1982);

Gierusalemme distrutta e altri teatri di guerra, edited by Pieri (Parma: La Pilotta, 1985);

Rime amorose, edited by Martini and Ottavio Besomi (Modena: Panini, 1987);

Rime maritime, edited by Besomi, Martini, and Costanzo Marchi (Modena: Panini, 1988);

Rime boscherecce, edited by Janina Hauser-Jakubowic (Modena: Panini, 1991);

La sampogna, edited by Vania De Maldé (Parma: Guanda, 1993);

La sferza e *Il tempio,* edited by Gian Piero Maragoni (Rome: Beniamino Vignola, 1995);

Rime lugubri, edited by Vincenzo Guercio (Modena: Panini, 1999);

La canzone dei baci ed altre poesie: Giambattista Marino. Con uno scritto di Guglielmo Felice Damiani, edited by Davide Dei (Florence: Le Càriti, 1999);

Rime eroiche, edited by Besomi, Martini, and Maria Cristina Newlin-Gianini (Modena: Panini, 2002).

Editions in English: "Forsaken Lydia," in *Salmacis, Lyrian & Sylvia, Forsaken Lydia, the Rape of Helen, a Comment Thereon, with Severall Other Poems and Translations,* translated by Sir Edward Sherburne (London: Printed by W. Hunt for Thomas Dring, 1651);

Cynthia and Daphne: Translated from the Italian of Il Cavalier Marino. With a Dedication in Blank Verse, to the Duke of York, translated by N. Masterson (London: printed for the author, sold by J. Almon & W. Nicoll, 1766);

The Suspicion of Herod, Being the First Book of The Murder of the Innocents, translated by Richard Crashaw (London: Bournes, 1834).

Since the work in the 1970s of the critic Giovanni Pozzi, Giambattista Marino (sometimes spelled Marini) has been recognized as the most important poet of the Italian Baroque and as one of the greatest in the wider European milieu that includes contemporary figures such as William Shakespeare, Francisco Lope de Vega Carpio, and Luis de Góngora y Argote. Pozzi edited three of Marino's works, fostering an objective and modern rereading of them, and his commentaries confirmed the highly representative character of Marino's poetry in the Baroque environment.

The first of seven children, Marino was born in Naples on 14 October 1569 into a family of petit bourgeoisie. His father, Gian Francesco Marino, wanted him to become a lawyer. Marino's first teacher, the grammarian and humanist Don Alfonso Galeota, predicted a great future for him. Marino studied law at the University of Naples from 1583 to 1586 and obtained a license to practice without earning his doctorate. Around 1588 he gave the first public readings of his poetry, and his father, realizing that he would never become a lawyer, disowned him. Marino then became a *famiglio* (servant without particular duties or regular salary) for the noble Pignatelli family; he later served the Manso and Guevara families and became a close friend of the marquis Giovan Battista Manso, to whom he wrote several letters requesting loans that he was unable to repay.

Between 1588 and 1592 Marino edited a collection of lyric poetry for the Accademia degli Svegliati (Academy of the Awakened) that was never published. His fiercest critic, Tommaso Stigliani, later charged that Marino pillaged the Svegliati anthology for material for his own poetry. During the same period Marino also edited a collection of lyric poetry for Manso; it, too, remained unpublished. From 1592 to 1600 he was secretary to Matteo di Capua, *Principe di Conca e Grande Ammiraglio del Regno* (Prince of Conca and Great Admiral of the Kingdom of Naples). A 1593 letter from Camillo Pellegrino to Alessandro Pera mentions that Marino is at work on a poem about the myth of Adonis. Marino's *L'Adone* (excerpts translated as *Adonis: Selections from L'Adone of Giambattista Marino,* 1967) was not published until 1623; the poem to which Pellegrino refers was probably one of the many idylls Marino was writing at the time. He earned immediate fame for the sensual "Canzone dei baci" (Canzone of the Kiss), which was set to music by the Sienese composer Tommaso Pecci and translated into several languages even before it was published in Venice in 1602.

During his youth Marino was jailed twice. Reliable documentation regarding the first incarceration, in April 1598, is unavailable, but two persistent rumors surround the incident. The first, that Marino was arrested for sodomy, is probably an untruth perpetrated by the more malicious of his critics. The second scenario is far more likely. According to a contemporary source, he impregnated Antonella Testa, the daughter of a wealthy merchant from Sicily who opposed her marriage to a penniless poet; Testa died of a botched abortion in her sixth month of pregnancy. Marino was released after a few days through the influence of his powerful patrons. Those patrons did not act as promptly at the time of his second arrest some months

Letter from Marino in Paris to Ottavio Magnanini, dated 2 August 1619 (from Scelte di Giovan Battista Marino e dei marinisti, *edited by Giovanni Getto, 1970; Thomas Cooper Library, University of South Carolina)*

Title page for the first edition of Marino's The Gallery *(from* Scelte di Giovan Battista Marino e dei marinisti, *edited by Giovanni Getto, 1970; Thomas Cooper Library, University of South Carolina)*

later. This time he was accused of falsifying a public document to save the life of his friend Marc Antonio d'Alessandro, who had been condemned to death for assaulting an official of the royal treasury. D'Alessandro lost the offending hand and then was decapitated, and Marino would have shared the latter fate had not the prince of Conca provided a sizable bribe for the prison guards. Marino fled to Rome.

Marino arrived in Rome in 1600. The fame of the "Canzone dei baci," which had preceded him, together with letters of recommendation from his influential Neapolitan patrons, allowed him to find a safe haven in the home of the wealthy Melchiorre Crescenzio, *Chierico di Camera* and *Coadiutore del Camerlengo Pontifico* (Clerk of the Treasury and Coadjutor of the Papal Chamberlain). Marino had brought with him manuscripts for several of his unpublished works, which were greatly appreciated in Rome. The witty rhymes that closed his madrigals, similar to the final rhyming couplet of a Shakespearean sonnet, were especially popular. He gave private readings for the elite of Roman society and offered suggestions and encouragement to aspiring poets who were in awe of his skill. He also wrote several poems dedicated to specific individuals and events. His fame grew enormously, and he had not yet published a single book.

With funding from Crescenzio, Marino traveled to Venice with stopovers in Siena and Florence; in both cities he was admired as a new poet of authentic greatness. In Venice he oversaw the publication of his first book, *Rime* (1602, Rhymes), in the printing shop of Giovan Battista Ciotti. The collection is divided into two parts and comprises 750 lyric poems. The first part includes only sonnets and is divided into eight sections: "Rime Amorose" (Love Rhymes), "Rime Marittime" (Maritime Rhymes), "Rime Boscherecce" (Sylvan Rhymes), "Rime Heroiche" (Heroic Rhymes), "Rime Lugubri" (Mournful Rhymes), "Rime Morali" (Moral Rhymes), "Rime Sacre" (Sacred Rhymes), and "Rime Varie" (Varied Rhymes). The first part ends with a series of sonnets in which thirty-five *nobili ingegni* (noble intelligences) wish Marino luck–a large number of such messages even by the ample standards of the time. To avoid *ambizione delle precedenze* (wrangling over precedence) the sonnets were arranged in alphabetical order by the names of the authors, who included Francesco Bracciolini, Orsatto Giustiniani, Battista Guarini, Celio Magno, Camillo Pellegrini, Alessandro Pera, Margherita Sarrocchi, Giovan Battista Strozzi, and Torquato Tasso. The second part, "Madrigali e canzoni" (Madrigals and Canzones) includes compositions devoted to love, the visual arts, and religious topics.

Marino's return to Rome was triumphant, and the Crescenzios presented him with a golden collar. They also passed the patronage of Marino to Cardinal Pietro Aldobrandini, the nephew of Pope Clement VIII (Ippolito Aldobrandini) and one of the most powerful men in Rome. The cardinal delighted in surrounding himself with artists and writers not only for his personal pleasure but also to compete with the Pope's other nephew, his cousin Cardinal Cinzio Aldobrandini, the celebrated patron of Tasso. Pietro Aldobrandini was a shrewd diplomat, esteemed in all the courts of Europe, and his protection opened all doors to Marino; his compositions were set to music and discussed in the academies. Aldobrandini built a villa in Frascati, near Rome, that all of the major artists of the time participated in decorating. Marino praised Cavaliere d'Arpino (Giuseppe Cesari), the artist responsible for most of the frescoes, in a song he offered to the cardinal to mark the opening of the villa. Among the artists Marino met in Rome was Caravaggio (Michelangelo Merisi); he describes a painting titled *Susanna e i Vecchioni* (Susanna and the Elders) that he received from Caravaggio and placed in his private collection, but no trace of such a work has ever been found. The Genoese painter and engraver Bernardo Castello helped Marino to establish connections with several patrons and writers in Genoa: Scipione della Cella, Giacomo Doria, and Gian Vincenzo Imperiali. Marino attended meetings of the Accademia degli Ordinati (Academy of the Trim) and the more gifted Accademia degli Umoristi (Academy of the Humorists); among the members of the latter were Bracciolini, Guarini, Alessandro Tassoni, and Gabriello Chiabrera. He became involved with the Neapolitan poet Sarrocchi, who was about ten years older than he; but competition for public attention soon ended their relationship, and the woman Marino had called a "sirena" (siren) and a "phoenix" became a "noiosa pica" (annoying magpie) in *L'Adone*.

After Clement VIII died on 5 March 1605, the papal throne remained vacant for a month. The Aldobrandinis were at risk of losing their power and prestige; but the new Pope, who assumed the name Leo XI, was their close friend Cardinal Ottaviano de' Medici. Marino participated in the Aldobrandinis' celebration of their escape from danger with a panegyric poem of twenty-eight stanzas, "Il Tebro festante" (The Festive Tiber). But the seventy-year-old Pope died twenty-seven days after his election and was succeeded by Cardinal Camillo Borghese, a personal enemy of the Medicis and the Aldobrandinis, as Pope Paul V. Pietro Aldobrandini lost all of his state commissions and was forced to leave Rome for Ravenna, of which he was bishop. Marino accompanied his patron, but his feelings about his new home were made clear in a February 1605 letter to his friend Simon Carlo Rondinelli: "Questa è una città, anzi un deserto, che non l'abiterebbono i zingari. Aria pestifera. Penuria di vitto. Vini pessimi. Acque calde ed infami. Gente poca e selvatica. . . . O bella Roma, io ti sospiro" (This is a city, I mean a desert, that the gypsies would not live in. The air is pestilent. There is not much food. The wines are the worst. The water is warm and dreadful. People are few and feral. . . . Oh beautiful Rome, I sigh thinking of you).

From the day he arrived in Ravenna, Marino thought only of leaving. Given the impossibility of returning to Rome because of his association with his patron, he turned his sights to the north. He spent short sojourns in Venice, Rimini, Modena, Parma, and Bologna; he was received enthusiastically everywhere and made many useful alliances. In Bologna he became friendly with the members of the Accademia dei Gelati (Academy of the Frozen), particularly Girolamo Preti and Claudio Achillini, who became his most fervent supporters. In Parma he was admitted to the Accademia degli Innominati (Academy of the Unnamed), headed by Pomponio Torelli. He wrote sonnets to be

Title page for the first edition of Marino's The Panpipe *(from* Scelte di Giovan Battista Marino e dei marinisti, *edited by Giovanni Getto, 1970; Thomas Cooper Library, University of South Carolina)*

included in other poets' books and compositions for weddings and other occasions, worked on *L'Adone,* and began another ambitious epic poem, *Gierusalemme distrutta* (Jerusalem Destroyed). He also devoted himself to the study of sacred texts, out of which the prose of *Dicerie sacre* (Sacred Sayings) was born in 1614.

Near the end of 1607 Marino and his patron participated in the celebrations of the double wedding of the daughters of Carlo Emanuele, Duke of Savoy: Donna Margherita married Don Francesco Gonzaga, Prince of Mantua, and Donna Isabella married Don Alfonso d'Este, Prince of Modena. Marino composed two epithalamiums and a monumental poetic portrait of the father of the brides. The latter, 1,428 lines in six-line stanzas, left no doubt as to Marino's desire to move to Turin under a new patron. The duke, an amateur poet and patron of the arts, showed his appreciation by appointing Marino *Cavaliere dei Santi Maurizio e Lazzaro*

(Knight of Sts. Maurice and Lazarus) on 16 March 1609.

Marino's knighthood aroused the jealousy of Carlo Emanuele's personal secretary, the Genoese poet Gasparo Murtola. He appears to have initiated some anonymous gossip against Marino, who reacted by composing satirical sonnets, called "Fischiate" (Whistles), against his rival. Murtola responded with a clumsy set of *risate* (laughs) that began by accusing Marino of being an inferior poet and went on to engage in vitriolic personal attacks. But Marino was the more skillful poet and had more-powerful friends. Murtola shot Marino point-blank in the street, but Marino survived the attempt on his life; he later claimed that the bullet was blocked by the thick prayer book he always carried in his breast pocket. Murtola was condemned to death but was pardoned. At the beginning of 1610 the duke hired Marino to replace Murtola as his secretary.

In April 1611 Marino was incarcerated for fourteen months for writing satirical poems about the duke. Marino denied the charge, but the duke did not believe him. Marino's friends and supporters across Europe wrote letters asking for his release, and the English ambassador finally obtained his freedom. Marino engaged in a dispute in 1612 with Ferrante Carli, a minor contemporary writer who had caught a mistaken mythological reference in one of Marino's poems.

With an elaborate dedication to Pope Paul V that has been called a rhetorical masterpiece in itself, Marino's *Dicerie sacre* was published in Turin in the spring of 1614. The title is meant to indicate the author's humility in entering the realm of theological disquisitions—the work is not a treatise, a summa, or a declaration, just a simple series of sayings. *Dicerie sacre* is, however, more about rhetoric than theology. It consists of three extensive prose pieces: "La pittura. Diceria prima. Sopra la sacra Sindone" (On Painting. First Saying. On the Holy Shroud), "La musica. Diceria seconda. Sopra le sette parole dette da Cristo in croce" (On Music. Second Saying. On the Seven Words Said by Christ on the Cross), and "Il cielo. Diceria terza" (On Heaven. Third Saying). Marino declares in the introduction that his style in each section is based on the metaphor of the title of that section.

Also in 1614 Marino published *Lira* (Lyre), which includes more than a thousand compositions. The introductory letter, signed "Onorato Claretti" but written by Marino, includes a long, detailed list of new works soon to be published: epic poems, epithalamiums, panegyrics, dramas, heroic epistles, and what would today be called a "multimedia" work, "La Galeria" (The Gallery), consisting of drawings by the great artists of the time with poetic commentary by Marino; few of these projects came to fruition. *Lira* is divided into three parts. The first two are identical to the two parts of *Rime;* the new third part consists of four sections: "Amori" (Loves), "Lodi" (Praises), "Divotioni" (Devotions), and "Capricci" (Whims).

With the help of some powerful allies Marino approached Maria de' Medici, the widow of the assassinated French king Henry IV and regent for her son, Louis XIII. The queen spoke Italian in her court, and her staff—from the chefs, who created modern French cuisine, to the administrators into whose hands she put the running of the state—consisted of Florentines. Her most trusted advisers were Concino Concini and his wife, Leonora Galigaï. Marino impressed the court with a technically accomplished poem, *Il tempio* (1615, The Temple), written in the same six-line-stanza style as the one he had composed for the duke of Savoy. He moved to Paris, far from the envy of his Italian enemies, in 1615. The following year he published *Gli epitalami* (The Epithalamiums), a collection of nuptial songs in honor of various patrons that he had presented at their weddings or those of their children.

On 24 April 1617 the captain of the royal guards assassinated Concini, and his body was dismembered by a mob; Galigaï was arrested and beheaded soon afterward; and Maria de' Medici was sent into retirement in Blois. Finding himself in a dangerous situation, Marino submitted to Louis XIII's secretary of state, Armand-Jean du Plessis, duc de Richelieu, the manuscript for a short, hastily composed prose piece, *La sferza invettiva contro i quattro ministri della iniquità* (The Invective Whip against the Four Ministers of Iniquity), demonstrating the ignorance and insolence of the four most prominent Huguenots. Richelieu admired the work, and Marino retained his position as court poet. *La sferza invettiva contro i quattro ministri della iniquità* was not published until 1625.

The years that followed were a period of intense work. The protection of Louis and Richelieu, handsome subsidies, and exemption from court duties allowed Marino to immerse himself in his art. A biographer wrote of his habit of keeping his drapes closed for several days at a time to allow him to concentrate. In 1620 *La galeria* was finally published in Venice, but without the images mentioned in the introduction to *Lira*. It is divided into two parts, "Pitture" (Paintings) and "Sculture" (Sculptures), each with its own frontispiece; each part is in turn divided into "Favole," (Fables), "Historie" (Stories), and "Ritratti" (Portraits), which lead to subcategories and further partitions. The majority of the poems are madrigals, but there are several sonnets and a few poems of other forms. The "Pitture" section comprises 542 poems, while 82 make up "Sculture"; the imbalance reflects the passion for painting that is amply documented in Marino's correspondence. Many of the madrigals in "Pitture" had first appeared, with minor differences, in part 2 of *Rime*. The edition was rife with typographical errors, and Marino complained bitterly to Ciotti. He wrote that he would destroy every copy he could find to avoid the embarrassment of looking at it; he also declared that he would never send another work to Ciotti.

Marino kept his word: *La Sampogna* (1620, The Panpipe) was printed in Paris by Abraham Pacard. The first part, "Idilli favolosi" (Mythological Idylls), comprises "Orfeo" (Orpheus), "Atteone" (Acteon), "Arianna" (Ariadne), "Europa" (Europa), "Proserpina" (Proserpina), "Dafni" (Daphne), "Siringa" (Syrinx), and "Piramo e Tisbe" (Pyramus and Thisbe). Part 2, "Idilli pastorali" (Pastoral Idylls), consists of "La bruna pastorella" (The Dark-Haired Shepherdess), "La ninfa avara" (The Avaricious Nymph), "La disputa amorosa" (The Amorous Dispute), and "I sospiri d'Ergasto" (The Sighs of Ergasto).

After *La Sampogna* appeared, Marino devoted himself to *L'Adone*. The poem was published in the spring of 1623 in *folio grande* (large folio) at the expense of Louis XIII, to whom it is officially dedicated; in the proemial letter, however, Marino also gives the queen mother, Maria de' Medici, the honor of the royal patronage. In a laudatory introduction Jean Chapelain, a young critic, calls the work a *poème de paix* (poem of peace); the phrase was often used in later criticism of the work. The five thousand stanzas of the poem total forty-two thousand lines; they are divided into twenty cantos—the same number as Tasso's *Gerusalemme liberata* (1581, Jerusalem Delivered; translated as *Godfrey of Bulloigne, or The Recoverie of Hierusalem,* 1594), which is less than one-third the length of *L'Adone*. Each canto has a title and is introduced by an *argomento* (topic description) and an *allegoria* (unveiling of the symbolic meaning of the canto); the *argomentos* and *allegorias* were written by two of Marino's most trusted friends, Count Fortuniano Sanvitale and Don Lorenzo Scoto, respectively.

In canto 1, "La Fortuna" (Fortune), Cupid, seeking revenge against his mother, Venus, who chastised him for his impertinence in making Jupiter fall in love again, decides to make her fall in love with Adonis. Adonis is sailing in the ocean in Fortuna's boat and is swept away by a tempest. He is shipwrecked on Cyprus, where he is rescued by a shepherd, Clizio (identified in the *allegoria* as the Genoese poet Gianvincenzo Imperiale). The title of canto 2, "Il palagio d'Amore" (The Palace of Love), refers to the residence of Venus and Cupid on Cyprus. In front of the main entrance is a tree that bears golden apples. Clizio, the first of Adonis's many tutors in the poem, explains that the tree was planted to commemorate Venus's triumph over Minerva and Juno in a beauty contest. In canto 3, "L'innamoramento" (The Falling in Love), Venus comes upon Adonis sleeping in a secluded meadow and is hit by an arrow shot by Cupid, who thus obtains the vengeance announced in canto 1. When Adonis wakes up, he is frightened, then surprised, and finally pleased by Venus's attentions, and he reciprocates her love.

In canto 4, "La novelletta" (The Little Story), Adonis is admitted to the Palace of Love, where Cupid recounts the story of his own love affair with Psyche, a mortal. Canto 5, "La tragedia" (The Tragedy), describes a lavish theatrical performance organized by Mercury in honor of Adonis. The play is the story of Acteon, the deer hunter who accidentally saw Diana, the goddess of hunting, bathing naked; she turned him into a stag, and he was killed by his own dogs. This classical myth and others recalled in the canto point to the tragic outcome of a union between a god or a goddess and a human being. In canto 6, "Il giardino del piacere" (The Garden of Pleasure), Venus guides Adonis through the gardens of Sight and Smell; in canto 7, "Le delizie" (The Delights), they visit the gardens of Hearing and Taste and then are the guests of honor at a magnificent banquet, at the end of which Momus entertains the diners by narrating the adulterous affair of Venus and Mars. The canto concludes with a hymn to love performed by Thalia, the Muse of love poetry.

In canto 8, "I trastulli" (The Playful Games), the lovers enter the garden of Touch, the most important sense. Here Mercury officiates at the wedding of Venus and Adonis, who consummate their union in the *cameretta* (wedding chamber) in the center of the palace and also in a cave, thus indicating both the civilized and the natural aspects of love. In canto 9, "La fontana di Apollo" (The Fountain of Apollo), the newlyweds visit the island of poetry, where Fileno, the alter ego of Marino, narrates his own life story. The canto includes a review of Italian and French patrons of poetry, followed by a series of portraits of Greek, Latin, and Italian poets. In canto 10, "Le meraviglie" (The Wonders), Mercury guides the couple to the moon; the voyage gives Marino the opportunity to praise Galileo. On the moon are "la Grotta della Natura" (the Grotto of Nature) and "L'isola dei sogni" (the Island of Dreams). The exploration of space continues with a visit to the sphere of Mercury, where Venus and Adonis visit "il Palazzo delle Arti" (the Palace of the Arts), "il Museo degli Inventori" (the Museum of the Inventors), "la Biblioteca Universale" (the Universal Library), and "la sala del Mappamondo" (the Globe Room), where future wars are prophesied. In canto 11, "Le bellezze" (The Beauties), Adonis is admitted to the third heaven, Venus's own sphere. Marino presents a review of the most beautiful women on Earth; Venus becomes jealous and abruptly brings the journey to an end.

Frontispiece and title page for the first edition of Adonis *(frontispiece from* Adonis: Selections from L'Adone of Giambattista Marino, *translated by Harold Martin Priest, 1967; title page from James V. Mirollo,* The Poet of the Marvellous: Giambattista Marino, *1963; Thomas Cooper Library, University of South Carolina)*

In canto 12, "La fuga" (The Flight), jealousy brings Mars to Cyprus. To avoid a confrontation, Venus sends Adonis away with a magic ring to help him resist charms and temptations. Adonis is soon captured by enchantress Falsirena, who tries, in vain, to seduce him. In canto 13, "La prigione" (The Prison), Mercury visits the incarcerated Adonis and warns him of impending danger. Falsirena, eager to try a new love potion on Adonis, mistakenly gives him an elixir that transforms him into a parrot. He flies to the Palace of Love, where he sees Venus and Mars copulating in the Garden of Touch. He cries in a human voice and is caught. Mercury tells him to return to Falsirena's grotto and describes a procedure that will enable him to regain his human form; Adonis complies. In canto 14, "Gli errori" (The Errors), Adonis escapes from Falsirena's prison dressed as a woman and undergoes several adventures, narrated as episodes from chivalric literature, in which he is pursued by men who think he is a girl.

In canto 15, "Il ritorno" (The Return), Adonis, in male attire once more, meets a beautiful gypsy girl, Filomanta of Melfi, who reads his palm. She reveals herself to be Venus, and they return to their life of love and entertainment. In a chess game that he wins by cheating, Adonis receives the kingdom of Cyprus. But in canto 16, "La corona" (The Crown), a formal competition is held for the election of the king: the crown will be given to the handsomest aspiring monarch. Adonis wins but renounces the kingship to return to his life with Venus. In canto 17, "La dipartita" (The Departure), Venus must go to Cythera for the annual celebration in her honor. Adonis complains that she does not care about him and obtains permission to hunt in the Forbidden Garden that only Diana has the right to enter.

In canto 18, "La morte" (Death), a gigantic boar, urged on by Mars, attacks the young hunter. Adonis hits the animal with an arrow that he stole from Cupid; the wound makes the boar fall in love with Adonis, and in an amorous fury he penetrates and kills the youth with his symbolically single *corno* (tusk). In canto 19, "La sepoltura" (The Burial), Apollo, Tethis, Bacchus, and Ceres console Venus by telling her of their own young lovers who died violently and received the gift of immortality from their divine partners. Venus makes Adonis immortal as a flower, the anemone, that will return every spring. Canto 20, "Gli spettacoli" (The Spectacles), the longest canto (515 stanzas), describes three days of games honoring the memory of Adonis. Venus invites mortals and immortals from all over the world and from heaven and hell, and all of them come. The goddess of love becomes the goddess of peace as she praises and offers rich prizes to winners and losers alike. At the end of the third day, and of the poem, the poet Fileno reappears and promises to tell the story of the deceased young man in his new poem, *L'Adone*.

Marino returned to Italy in May 1623, taking with him copies of the freshly printed *L'Adone*, the gold he had earned as court poet, and his personal art collection. He was warmly received in Turin, enjoying even the lavish praise of the duke who had had him imprisoned eleven years previously. In Rome the noblest families fought to have him as their guest; he chose the home of Crescenzio, showing his loyalty to the patron who had taken him in as a fugitive from Naples twenty-three years before. The Umoristi honored him with extraordinary sessions of the academy.

Pope Gregory XV died on 8 July 1623, and Maffeo Barberini was elected as Pope Urban VIII on 6 August. Marino naively exulted in the change in August in a letter to Castello: "Lodato Iddio, dopo tante turbolenze di sedia vacante abbiamo un papa poeta, vistuoso e nostro amicissimo" (God be blessed! After so many turbulent times with a vacant seat, we finally have a pope who is also a poet, who is virtuous, and who is our friend). Marino's enthusiasm was short-lived: Urban VIII ordered the Inquisition to examine *L'Adone* for obscenity, and Marino began work on a sanitized version of the poem. But the new Pope did not like Marino, and his attitude was encouraged by the poet's enemies. Defections took place among the most loyal of his allies; the most traumatic to Marino was that of Preti. Immediately after the appearance of *L'Adone* in Italy in 1623, Agatio di Somma, a cleric with literary ambitions in the service of Francesco Barberini, the new Pope's nephew, said in a letter to Fabrizio Ricci that he had not read the work but, judging by the parts he had heard Marino recite at the Accademia degli Umoristi in Rome, he could declare it superior to Tasso's *Gerusalemme liberata*. Somma claimed that Preti shared his opinion. Preti angrily denied that he had declared *L'Adone* superior to *Gerusalemme liberata* and insisted that he did not think that it was. The loss of Preti's friendship had a deleterious effect on Marino's health, which had already begun to fail.

In April 1624 Marino returned to Naples, the city of his birth. Manso, his old patron, met him in Capua with a coterie of Neapolitan nobles and poets and escorted him into the city. In Naples the Accademia degli Infuriati (Academy of the Furious) and the Accademia degli Oziosi (Academy of the Idlers) vied for Marino's membership; he joined the latter out of loyalty to Manso, its founder and main supporter. The academy required the presentation of a new academic discourse every Wednesday by one of its most prestigious members, and Marino was constantly pressed to perform; he was brilliant in this genre, to judge by the only surviving text : "Discorso accademico del cavaliere Marino" (Academic Discourse of the Cavalier Marino), included in *La strage de gl'innocenti* (1663; translated as The Slaughter of the Innocents by Herod, 1675).

Marino's health grew steadily worse; his kidneys were failing, and the attacks of strangury to which he was prone all his life became more severe and frequent. The stress of the ecclesiastical examination of *L'Adone* and grief over the loss of several friends took their toll on Marino, who lacked the energy to perfect the final draft of his last major poem, *La strage de gl'innocenti*, which was published after his death on 25 March 1625. The Inquisition placed *L'Adone* in the *Index librorum prohibitorum* (Index of Prohibited Books) in 1627.

Giambattista Marino continued to dominate the Italian cultural scene after his death because of a long and bitter dispute over the literary merit of *L'Adone*. In 1627 Stigliani published *Dello occhiale* (The Eyeglass), an extremely harsh critique of Marino's poem. The work prompted a flood of defenses of Marino from all over Italy. The first and most systematic response to *L'Occhiale* came from Girolamo Aleandri in Bologna; he was encouraged to write *Difesa dell'Adone, poema del cav. Marini* (1629, Defense of the *Adonis*, Poem by the Cavalier Marino) by Achillini, Marino's staunchest supporter. Two more defenses were published that same year: *L'Occhiale appannato: Dialogo, nel quale si difende* L'Adone *del cavalier Gio. Battista Marino, contra l'Occhiale del cavalier fra Tomaso Stigliano* (The Foggy Eyeglass Dialogue in Which the Cavalier Gio. Battista Marino's *Adonis* Is Defended against the *Eyeglass* of the Cavalier Brother Tommaso Stigliani), by Scipione Errico, and "Le strigliate a Tomaso Stigliani" (The Rebuking of Tommaso Stigliani), by Robusto Pogommega (pseudonym of Andrea Barbazza). The dispute was between Stigliani on one side and Marino's followers, the Marinists, on the other. Stigliani was soon isolated and abandoned even by his anti-Marinist Roman friends, but the dispute continued for another thirty years. Among the participants was Niccola Villani. In *L'uccellatura di Vincenzo Foresi all'*Occhiale *del cavaliere fra Tomaso Stigliani contro* l'Adone *del cavalier Gio: Battista Marini, e alla difesa di Girolamo Aleandro* (1630, Bird-Catching of Vincenzo Foresi in the *Eyeglass* of Tommaso Stigliani against the *Adonis* of the Cavalier Gio. Battista Marini, and in Defense of Girolamo Aleandro) and *Consideratoni di messer Fagiano sopra la seconda parte dell'*Occhiale *del cavaliere Stigliano, contro alo Adone del cavalier Marino, e sopra la seconda difesa di Girolamo Aleandro* (1631, Considerations of Sir Pheasant on the Second Part of the *Eyeglass* of the Cavalier Stigliano against the *Adonis* of the Cavalier Marino, and on the Second Defense of Girolamo Aleandro) he maintained, in a condescending tone and ironic style, that Stigliani was right but too extreme in condemning Marino and that Aleandro's attack on Stigliani was too severe. The truth, he concluded, lay in his own books, in which a leisurely rereading of all of the works involved allowed him to identify everyone else's technical faults and ideological biases. Perhaps the most enthusiastic defender of *L'Adone* was Angelico Aprosio, who published the pseudonymous *L'occhiale stritolato di Scipio Glareano: Per risposta al Sig. Cavalier Tommaso [sic] Stigliani* (1641, The Crushed Eyeglass of Scipio Glareano: In Response to Mr. Cavalier Tommaso Stigliani) and *La sferza poetica di Sapricio Saprici, lo Scantonato accademico heteroclito: Per risposta alla prima censura dell'*Adone *del cavalier Marino, fatta del cavalier Tommaso Stiglian [sic]* (1643, The Poetic Whip of Sapricio Saprici, the Slipped-off Heteroclite Academic: In Response to the First Censorship of the *Adonis* by the Cavalier Marino, Made by the Cavalier Tommaso Stigliani)." For more than two centuries thereafter no books were published on *L'Adone* or Marino, but the poet and his masterpiece were repeatedly quoted and referred to as the perfect example—positive or negative, depending on the critic—of the Italian Baroque. The critical rediscovery of Marino in the last quarter of the twentieth century stimulated the production of new editions and studies, none of which significantly challenged Pozzi's assessment that what had been regarded as frivolous and trivial in Marino's melodious stanzas must be read as pure expressions of human creativity, since for him the verbal construct is more important than any reference to reality.

Letters:

Lettere: Gravi, argute, e familiari, facete, e piacevoli, dedicatorie (Venice: Francesco Baba, 1627);

Epistolario: Seguito da lettere di altri scrittori del seicento, 2 volumes, edited by Angelo Borzelli and Fausto Nicolini (Bari: Laterza, 1911, 1912);

Lettere, edited by Marziano Guglielminetti (Turin: Einaudi, 1966);

Girolamo De Miranda, "Giambattista Marino, Virginio Orsini e Tommaso Melchiorri in materiali epistolari inediti e dimenticati," *Quaderni d'italianistica*, 14, no. 1 (1993): 17–32.

Bibliography:

Francesco Giambonini, *Bibliografia delle opere a stampa di Giambattista Marino* (Florence: Olschki, 2000).

Biographies:

Giovan Battista Baiacca, *Vita del Cavalier Marino* (Venice: Sarzina, 1625);

Giovan Francesco Loredano, *Vita del Cavalier Marino* (Venice: Sarzina, 1633);

Angelo Borzelli, *Il Cavalier Giovan Battista Marino* (Naples: Artigianelli, 1898).

References:

Maria Grazia Accorsi, "*La Sampogna* di Marino tra narrazione e teatro. Commento a un'edizione," *Studi e problemi di critica testuale*, 52 (1996): 153–176;

Girolamo Aleandro, *Difesa dell'Adone, poema del cav. Marini*, 2 volumes (Venice: G. Scaglia, 1629, 1630);

Angelico Aprosio, *L'occhiale stritolato di Scipio Glareano: Per risposta al signor cavalier Tommaso Stigliani* (Venice: T. Pavoni, 1641);

Aprosio, *La sferza poetica di Sapricio Saprici, lo Scantonato accademico heteroclito: Per risposta alla prima censura dell'*Adone *del cavalier Marino, fatta del cavalier Tommaso Stiglian [sic]* (Venice: Stamparia Guerigliana, 1643);

Aprosio, *Del veratro: Apologia di Sapricio Saprici per risposta alla seconda censura dell'*Adone *del cavalier Marino, fatta dal cavalier Tommaso Stigliani*, 2 volumes (Venice: M. Leni, 1645, 1647);

Ignazio Baldelli, "Elementi lontani dalla tradizione nel lessico dell'*Adone*," in *La critica stilistica e il barocco letterario: Atti del secondo congresso internazionale di studi italiani*, edited by Ettore Caccia (Florence: Le Monnier, 1958), pp. 146–153;

Giorgio Bárberi Squarotti, "Il tragico negato: *Adone* XIX," *Critica letteraria*, 2-3 (2000): 441–452;

Ottavio Besomi, *Esplorazioni secentesche* (Padua: Antenore, 1975), pp. 7–52;

Lorenzo Bianconi, "G. B. Marino e la poesia per musica," in *Storia della musica*, volume 4: *Il Seicento*, edited by the Società Italiana di Musicologia (Turin: E.D.T., 1982), pp. 9–15;

Angelo Borzelli, *Il Cavalier Marino con gli artisti e la Galeria* (Naples: Cosmi, 1891);

Françoise Bouthier, "L'educazione secondo il cavalier Marino: Mercurio e Venere maestri di Adone," *Studi italiani*, 1 (2000): 47–58;

Enrico Canevari, *Lo stile del Marino nell'*Adone *ossia analisi del Secentismo* (Pavia: Frattini, 1901);

Javier Gutiérrez Carou, "Alliterazione e segno linguistico: il mito di Narciso nell'*Adone*," *Cuadernos de filología italiana*, 6 (2000): 375–383;

Carlo Caruso, "Saggio di commento alla *Galeria* di G. B. Marino: 1 (esordio) e 624 (epilogo)," *Aprosiana*, 9 (2001): 71–89;

Marzia Cerrai, "A proposito del XVII canto dell'*Adone*: Il poema del Marino e le descrizioni fiorentine delle feste per Maria de' Medici," *Studi secenteschi*, 44 (2003): 197–218;

Paolo Cherchi, "Il re *Adone*," in *The Sense of Marino: Literature, Fine Art, and Music of the Italian Baroque*, edited by Francesco Guardiani (Ottawa: Legas, 1994), pp. 9–33;

Cherchi, "Tessere mariniane," *Quaderni d'italianistica*, 3, no. 2 (1982): 202–218;

Carmela Colombo, *Cultura e tradizione nell'*Adone *del Marino* (Padua: Antenore, 1967);

Davide Conrieri, "Postille all'*Adone*," *Studi secenteschi*, 44 (2003): 318–322;

Guglielmo Felice Damiani, *Sopra la poesia del Cavalier Marino* (Turin: Clausen, 1899);

Vania De Maldé, "Sull'ortografia del Seicento: Il caso Marino," *Studi di grammatica italiana*, 12 (1983): 107–166;

Carlo Del Corno, "Rassegna mariniana (1969–1974)," *Lettere italiane*, 27, no. 1 (1975): 91–109:

Agazio Di Somma, *I primi due canti dell'America* (Rome: Heirs of Bartolomeo Zannetti, 1624);

Scipione Errico, *L'occhiale appannato: Dialogo, nel quale si difende l'*Adone *del cavalier Gio. Battista Marino, contra l'*Occhiale *del cavalier fra Tomaso Stigliano* (Messina: G. F. Bianco, 1629);

Pierantonio Frare, "Marino al Cannocchiale," *Aprosiana*, 9 (2001): 97–107:

Frare, "Marino post-moderno? (A proposito di due recenti studi mariniani)," *Italianistica*, 20, no. 1 (1991): 139–140;

Giorgio Fulco, "Giovan Battista Marino," in *Storia della letteratura italiana*, volume 5: *La fine del Cinquecento e il Seicento,* edited by Enrico Malato (Rome: Salerno, 1997), pp. 597–647;

Fulco, "Notizia di novità mariniane in Trivulziana," *Filologia e critica*, 15, nos. 2–3 (1990): 551–582;

Luisella Giachino, "'Dispensiera di lampi al cieco mondo': La poesia di Cesare Rinaldi," *Studi secenteschi*, 42 (2001): 85–124;

Roberto Gigliucci, "Contro la luna: Appunti sul motivo antilunare nella lirica d'amore da Serafino Aquilano al Marino," *Italique*, 4 (2001): 19–29;

Francesco Guardiani, "Descrizioni liriche di temi teatrali nel poema epico del Marino," in *Theatre and the Visual Arts,* edited by Giuliana Sanguinetti Katz, Vera Golini, and Domenico Pietropaolo (Ottawa: Legas, 2001), pp. 99–110;

Guardiani, "Dieci pezzi sacri del Marino: Per un edizione della *Lira* II," in *"Feconde venner le carte": Studi in onore di Ottavio Besomi,* edited by Tatiana Crivelli (Bellinzona: Casagrande, 1997), pp. 348–370;

Guardiani, "L'idea dell'immagine nella *Galeria* di G. B. Marino," in *Letteratura italiana e arti figurative: Atti del XII Convegno dell'Associazione Internazionale per gli Studi di Lingua e Letteratura Italiana (AISLLI), Toronto–Hamilton–Montréal, 6–10 maggio 1985,* 3 volumes, edited by Antonio Franceschetti (Florence: Olschki, 1988), II: 647–654;

Guardiani, *La meravigliosa retorica dell'*Adone *di G. B. Marino* (Florence: Olschki, 1989);

Guardiani, "Marino lirico: L'apertura di *Madrigali e canzoni*," *Aprosiana*, 9 (2001): 51–76;

Guardiani, "Oscula mariniana," *Quaderni d'italianistica*, 16, no. 2 (1995): 197–243;

Guardiani, ed., *Lectura Marini:* L'Adone *letto e commentato da Guido Baldassarri et alii* (Ottawa: Dovehouse, 1989);

Guardiani, ed., *The Sense of Marino: Literature, Fine Art, and Music of the Italian Baroque* (Ottawa: Legas, 1994);

Guardiani and Antonio Rossini, "Un'apologia del Marino ex cathedra: L'orazione di Paganino Gaudenzi (1595–1649)," *Quaderni d'italianistica*, 19, no. 1 (1998): 101–133;

Vincenzo Guercio, "Ancora sui 'Baci di carta': Marino, Guarini, Fenaruolo," *Studi italiani*, 2 (2000): 5–47;

Guercio, "Postille ai 'Baci di carta' (*Rime*, II, 13–31) di G. B. Marino," *Studi secenteschi*, 44 (2003): 315–318;

Gian Piero Maragoni, "Foscolo, Leopardi e qualche loro antica fonte," *Aprosiana*, 9 (2001): 85–95;

Alessandro Martini, "Giovan Battista Marino: Opere," in *Dizionario delle opere della letteratura italiana,* edited by Giorgio Inglese and Angela Asor Rosa (Turin: Einaudi, 1998);

James V. Mirollo, *The Poet of the Marvellous: Giambattista Marino* (New York: Columbia University Press, 1963);

Gavriel Moses, "*Care gemelle d'un parto nate:* Marino's *picta poesis*," *Modern Language Notes*, 100, no. 1 (1985): 82–110;

A. Paudice, "Un giudizio 'parziale' svelato: Agazio Di Somma e il primato dell'Adone," *Filologia e critica,* 3, no. 1 (1978): 95–116;

Susan N. Peters, "The Anatomical Machine: a Representation of the Microcosm in the *Adone* of G. B. Marino," *Modern Language Notes,* 88, no. 1 (1973): 95–110;

Peters, "Metaphor and Meraviglia: Tradition and Innovation in the *Adone* of G. B. Marino," *Lingua e stile,* 7, no. 2 (1972): 321–341;

Peters, "A Mirror of the World: The Use of Image of the World Theatre in the *Adone,*" *Barroco,* 2 (1970): 19–36;

Marzio Pieri, "Eros e manierismo nel Marino," *Convivium,* 36, no. 4 (1968): 543–481;

Robusto Pogommega (i.e., Andrea Barbazza), "Le Strigliate a Tomaso Stigliano," in *La Murtoleide: Fischiate* (Spira: Henrico Starckio, 1629), pp. 85–118;

Bruno Porcelli, *Le misure della fabbrica: Studi sull'*Adone *del Marino e sulla* Fiera *del Buonarroti* (Milan: Marzorati, 1980);

Giovanni Pozzi, *La rosa in mano al professore* (Fribourg: Edizioni Universitarie, 1974);

Renato Reichlin and Giovanni Sopranzi, *Pastori barocchi fra Marino e Imperiali* (Fribourg: Edizioni Universitarie, 1988);

Guido Sacchi, "Letterato laico e savio cristiano: Daniello Bartoli e Giambattista Marino," *Studi secenteschi,* 43 (2002): 75–117;

Sacchi, "Schede mariniane," *Studi secenteschi,* 43 (2002): 313–329;

Fernando Salsano, *Marino e marinismo* (Rome: Elia, 1977);

Claes Schaar, *Marino and Crashaw: Sospetto d'Herode. A Commentary* (Lund: Gleerup, 1971);

Riccardo Scrivano, "Le meraviglie del sapere nell' universo mariniano," *Esperienze letterarie,* 17, no. 4 (1992): 3–18;

Maurice Slawinski, "Poesia e commercio librario nel primo Seicento: Su alcune edizioni mariniane ignote o poco note," *Filologia e critica,* 2-3 (2000): 316–334;

Slawinski, "The Poet's Senses: G. B. Marino's Epic Poem *L'Adone* and the New Science," *Comparative Criticism,* 13 (1991): 51–81;

Tommaso Stigliani, *Dello Occhiale: Opera difensiva del Cavalier Fr. Tomaso Stigliani. Scritta in risposta al Cavalier Gio: Battista Marini* (Venice: Pietro Carampello, 1627);

Edoardo Taddeo, *Studi sul Marino* (Florence: Sandron, 1971);

Gary Tomlinson, "Music and the Claims of Text: Monteverdi, Rinuccini and Marino," *Critical Inquiry,* 7 (1982): 565–589;

Emilio Torchio, "Marino amante ovidiano," *Studi secenteschi,* 41 (2000): 89–121;

Niccola Villani, *Consideratroni di messer Fagiano sopra la seconda parte dell'*Occhiale *del cavaliere Stigliano, contro alo* Adone *del cavalier Marino, e sopra la seconda difesa di Girolamo Aleandro* (Venice: G. P. Pinelli, 1631);

Villani, *L'uccellatura di Vincenzo Foresi all'*Occhiale *del cavaliere fra Tomaso Stigliani contro l'*Adone *del cavalier Gio: Battista Marini, e alla difesa di Girolamo Aleandro* (Venice: A. Pinelli, 1630);

Gianni Ernesto Viola, *Tre tesi sulla poetica di G. B. Marino* (Rome: Cadmo, 1978).

Benedetto Menzini

(1646 – 7 September 1704)

Olimpia Pelosi
State University of New York at Albany

BOOKS: *Per S. Filippo Benizi: Canzone* (Florence: Condotta, 1674);

De literatorum hominum invidia: Liber ad nobilem & verè doctum virum Franciscvm Redi. Nunc primùm prodüt (Florence: Printed by Antonio de Bonardi & Luca de Luti, 1675);

Della costruzione irregolare della lingua toscana (Florence: Carlieri, 1679);

Poesie liriche toscane, as Benedetto Fiorentino (Florence, 1680);

Opere di Benedetto Fiorentino (Florence: Condotta, 1680);

Dell'arte poetica di Benedetto Menzini, accademico della real maestà di Cristina regina di Svezia: Libri cinque (Florence: Piero Manini, 1688);

Dell'opera di Benedetto Menzini (Rome: G. B. Molo, 1690);

Del terrestre Paradiso (Rome: G. B. Molo, 1691);

Sonetti di Benedetto Menzini (Rome: G. B. Molo, 1692);

Elegie (Rome: G. B. Molo, 1697);

Lamentazioni di Geremia espresse nei loro dolenti affetti (Rome: Zenobii, 1704);

Accademia Tusculana di Benedetto Menzini, edited by Francesco Del Teglia (Rome: Antonio de' Rossi, 1705);

Satire di Benedetto Menzini (Amsterdam [i.e., Lucca]: Con Licenza de' Superiori, 1718);

Opere di Benedetto Menzini Fiorentino, 4 volumes (Florence: Tartini & Franchi, 1731–1732);

Operum Benedicti Menzini complectens quae tum soluta oratione tum versibus latine scripta sunt (Venice, 1750);

Poetica e satire di Benedetto Menzini, edited by Giuseppe Paolucci (Milan: Società Tipografica de' classici italiani, 1808);

Prose di Benedetto Menzini (Venice: Alvisopoli, 1828).

Editions and Collections: *Della costruzione irregolare della lingua toscana* (Venice: Costantini, 1710);

Rime degli Arcadi, edited by Giovanni Mario Crescimbeni, volume 2 (Rome: A. de' Rossi, 1716);

Dell'opera di Benedetto Menzini (Florence: All'insegna del Leon d'oro, 1728);

Lamentazioni di Geremia espresse nei loro dolenti affetti, edited by Anton Maria Salvini (Florence: Paperini, 1728);

Rime di Benedetto Menzini, 4 volumes, edited by Francesco Moücke (Florence: Nestenus & Moücke, 1730–1734);

Lamentazioni di Geremia espresse nei loro dolenti affetti (Florence: Piacentini, 1736);

Satire di Benedetto Menzini, edited by Anton Maria Salvini, Anton Maria Biscioni, Giorgio Van-der-Broodt, and others (Leiden [i.e., Lucca]: Van-Eet, 1759);

Le satire di Benedetto Menzini, edited by Pier Casimiro Romolini, Giorgio Van-der-Broodt, Anton Maria Biscioni, and Anton Maria Salvini (Bern, 1782);

Poesie di Benedetto Menzini, Fiorentino (Nice: Società Tipografica, 1782);

Raccolta de' satirici (London: Sold in Leghorn by T. Masi, 1788);

L'arte poetica italiana in cinque canti (London: T. Becket, 1804);

Satire di Benedetto Menzini, edited by Salvini (London: G. Masi, 1820);

Arte poetica (Florence: Pagani, 1824);

Saggio di Rime, prose e iscrizioni (Bologna: Gamberini & Parmeggiani, 1825);

Della costruzione irregolare della lingua toscana, edited by Silvestro Camerini (Florence: Passigli, 1837);

Satire, rime e lettere scelte di Benedetto Menzini, edited by Giosuè Carducci (Florence: Barbera, 1874);

Satire di Lodovico Ariosto, Salvator Rosa, Benedetto Menzini, Vittorio Alfieri, edited by Francesco Costèro (Milan: Sonzogno, 1879).

Edition in English: "Arcadia Returned to Arcadia," in *Italy in the Baroque: Selected Readings,* edited and translated by Brendan Dooley (New York: Garland, 1995), pp. 608–617.

One of the most innovative and openly anti-Baroque men of letters of the second half of the seventeenth century, Benedetto Menzini is also one of the most important Italian literary theorists and writers of his time because of the clarity of his ideas and the elegance of his style. He was born in 1646 into one of the poorest families of Florence in a cabin built on the Rubaconte Bridge (now the Ponte alle Grazie). The marquis Giovan Vincenzo Salviati assisted him financially with his education. He was privately tutored in rhetoric by a priest, Filippo Migliorucci; among his other teachers was Francesco Redi, who became his lifelong friend, counselor, and protector. He learned Greek, Latin, French, and the basics of Hebrew and joined the Accademia degli Apatisti (Academy of the Apathetics).

A talented orator, Menzini performed successfully as *ottimo dicitore* (foremost speaker) on several important official occasions; in one instance he replaced Migliorucci as *pubblico lettore di retorica* (public reader of rhetoric). He was also a gifted preacher and was asked to substitute for Paolo Segneri in giving a sermon to the Order of San Benedetto Bianco. His acquaintances included some of the most prominent writers and scientists of the time, such as Anton Maria Salvini, Carlo Roberto Dati, Lorenzo Panciatichi, Lorenzo Bellini, Giovan Mario Crescimbeni, and Lorenzo Magalotti.

An alcoholic, a gambler, and a briber, Menzini profoundly resented the low social status into which he was born and praised himself at every opportunity in a presumptuous and exaggerated fashion; in one of his satires he calls himself "onor della Toscana lira" (the honor of Tuscan lyric poetry). He flattered the powerful people who sponsored and supported him and was arrogant toward everyone else, and his self-centeredness gained him a considerable number of enemies. After becoming a priest, he taught elocution in several Tuscan cities. Harsh competition and a growing number of detractors led to the loss of his position at the University of Prato in 1677.

In 1680 Menzini published *Poesie liriche toscane* (Tuscan Lyrical Poems) under the pen name Benedetto Fiorentino. The collection was enthusiastically received, and critics acclaimed the author as the savior of Tuscan poetry. The lyrics show Menzini's tendency to experiment and his desire to combine the best of the pre-Baroque poetic tradition with Baroque classicism. Menzini creates charming landscapes by imitating ancient Greek lyrical poets such as Pindar and Anacreon:

> Aure lievi, odorate,
> Figlie dell'alba amate,
> Che al ventolar dell'ali
> Lusingate i mortali.
> . . . .
> Il volo, aure, volgete
> Colà dove vedete
> Quella barchetta, quella
> Spalmata navicella

> Che come il vello d'oro
> Sen porta il mio tesoro.
> . . . .
> Voi d'intorno alla prora,
> Quai d'intorno all'Aurora,
> Aure lievi, odorate,
> A suo favor spirate.

> (Sweet, gentle, scented breezes,
> beloved daughters of Dawn;
> you, who flatter the humans
> by the waving of your wings.
> . . . .
> Please, breezes, turn your flight over there,
> where you can see
> that gracious little boat,
> that glossy little ship,
> which is carrying my beloved
> as if she were the golden fleece.
> . . . .
> You, gentle scented breezes,
> who surround the bows
> in the same
> way in which you surround Dawn,
> please blow for it a favorable wind.)

Menzini was denied positions at the University of Pisa in 1681 and at the University of Padua in 1682. In 1685, with the support of the grand duchess of Tuscany, Vittoria della Rovere, he moved to Rome. There he was introduced to Christina, the former queen of Sweden; Christina was impressed by Menzini's writing and granted him a large stipend and the title *letterato trattenuto* (full-time scholar). In 1688 Menzini published *Dell'arte poetica* (On the Art of Poetry), a treatise in terza rima divided into five books. Critics consider it one of the first convincing attempts to react to Baroque literary taste and to propose new linguistic and stylistic guidelines. After Christina's death in 1689, Menzini entered the service of Cardinal Augustyn Michal Stefan Radziejowski but refused to accompany him when he was recalled to Poland. In 1691 Menzini was received in the Arcadian Academy with the nickname Euganio Libade. That same year he wrote *Del terrestre Paradiso* (On the Earthly Paradise), a poem in octaves divided into three books about the sin of Adam and Eve and their expulsion from the Garden of Eden. The poem is not patterned after John Milton's *Paradise Lost* (1667) but appears to be an attempt to imitate Torquato Tasso's *Gerusalemme liberata* (1581, Jerusalem Delivered; translated as *Godfrey of Bulloigne, or The Recoverie of Hierusalem,* 1594); the meter and images remind one of the works of the poet Gabriello Chiabrera. In 1692 Menzini published *Sonetti* (Sonnets); the poems are crafted on the model of Greek lyrics and, according to the critic Francesco Flora, anticipate the poetic landscapes of Giacomo Leopardi and Giacomo Zanella:

> Sento in quel fondo gracidar la rana,
> Indizio certo di futura piova.
> Canta il corvo importuno, e si riprova
> La foliga a tuffarsi alla fontana.
> La vaccherella in quella falda piana
> Gode di respirar dell'aria nuova:
> Le nari allarga in alto, e sì le giova
> Aspettar l'acqua che non par lontana.
> Veggio le lievi paglie andar volando:
> E veggio come obliquo turbo spira
> E va la polve qual paleo, rotando.
>
> (I hear the frog croaking in that pond,
> A certain sign of imminent rain.
> The tiresome crow is singing, and the coot
> Tries once more to dive into the fountain.
> The young cow grazing on the plain slope
> Enjoys breathing the fresh air:
> She widens her nostrils, and points them toward the sky,
> Waiting for the rain that will not be long in coming.
> I watch the light straws flying about:
> And the turbulent wind blowing sideways
> And how the dust turns around like a spinning wheel.)

Menzini had connections with some of the most important Roman notables: Paolo and Alessandro Falconieri granted him their protection; cardinals of the highest rank, such as Pietro Ottoboni and Neri Corsini, sponsored him; he even received the benevolent attention of two Popes, Innocent XII and Clement XI. In 1695 he declined the offer of a position at the University of Padua and became *cameriere segreto* or *bussolante* (personal aid) to Innocent XII and curate of the parish of Sant'Angelo in Peschiera. The seventeen poems in Menzini's *Elegie* (1697, Elegies) are rich in natural descriptions and include autobiographical references. In 1699 Menzini joined the Accademia Fiorentina (Florentine Academy); in 1701 he was named coadjutor to Cardinal Michele Brugueres at the University of Rome "La Sapienza"; the following year he became a member of the Accademia della Crusca (Academy of the Sifters).

In 1702, while recovering from an illness at the Abbey of San Paolo Albano on the Tuscolo hill near Rome, Menzini began to write a series of books in verse titled "Della Etopedia ovvero instituzione morale" (On Ethopedia or Moral Institution); he had envisioned a total of nine books but was able to complete only four before he died. Menzini states that prudence is the source of eloquence and that the ideal man of letters always has to be aware and proud of his own dignity and use balanced judgment; he also makes negative remarks about courts and courtiers. In 1704 he published *Lamentazioni di Geremia espresse nei loro dolenti affetti* (Lamentations of Jeremiah Expressed with Sorrowful Emotions), a paraphrase in verse of the Book of Lamentations from the Old Testament dedicated to Clement XI. The Pope greatly enjoyed the poems; on Holy Thursday of 1704 he had copies of the work distributed to the College of Cardinals.

Menzini died of dropsy on 7 September 1704. His unfinished *Accademia Tusculana* (Tusculan Academy) was published the following year; it is inspired by Jacopo Sannazaro's *Arcadia* (1502; translated, 1966) and alternates prose and poetry. Some scholars consider it lacking in originality, but others find it noteworthy for the descriptions of natural landscapes and the elegance of the verse.

Menzini is mainly remembered for his *Satire* (Satires), published in 1718. A letter to his friend Father Giuseppe Semenzi dated 23 June 1682 indicates that Menzini had already written seven of the satires, and it is the unanimous opinion of scholars that he must have written the other five in Florence between 1682 and 1685. Menzini wrote the satirical poems separately, without a precise plan or sequence, following waves of anger. In addition, he allowed his friends to make handwritten copies of the manuscripts and to pass them around, and some of the originals were never returned. Three additional satires have been attributed to Menzini on the basis of a 10 August 1697 letter from the librarian Benedetto Bresciani, a friend of Menzini's, to the marquis Ferdinando de' Bartolommei in which Bresciani praises the marquis for having purchased a handwritten volume of Menzini's fifteen satires; such a volume has never been found, and the majority of modern scholars do not recognize the three additional satires as having been written by Menzini. Two of them, "Pasquino zelante al Conclave" (The Zealous Pasquino at the Conclave) and "Il secondo Pasquino zelante" (The Second Zealous Pasquino), have never been published; the manuscripts are in the fifth section of Codex Palatinus 258 in the Biblioteca Nazionale (National Library) in Florence. The third was found in a manuscript in the library of the former Collegio Romano (Roman College) and was published by Costantino Arlía in the periodical *Il Borghini* in 1876.

Menzini aimed in his satires to emulate the Latin satirists Horace, Persius, and Juvenal and Italian writers such as Dante, Ludovico Ariosto, and Francesco Berni. Merits of the satires include Menzini's vivacious style, command of Tuscan language, and effective use of images. The satires were greatly admired by his contemporaries, but in the view of modern critics the lack of impersonality and the verbal violence—which reach a peak in "Satira III"—render Menzini's poems inferior to their models.

In "Satira I" Menzini expresses indignation at the papal court, where the Jesuits vex the men of science with their narrow-mindedness, and criticizes the magnates of the Florence court, who raise the mediocre poets who flatter them to the highest ranks and neglect Menzini and other poets who are truly worthy of praise. Beneath the general accusation lies an indirect critique of Cosimo III de' Medici, Grand Duke of Tuscany. The first part of the work consists of tedious personal outbursts, which are somewhat softened by classical and other erudite references. The satire achieves a degree of originality and sincerity, however, when Menzini discusses Galileo as an example of a genius treated unfairly, tormented, and cast out by the Roman religious hierarchy and the bigoted Florentine court. "Satira II" is based mainly on *Jupiter Tragoedus* (Jupiter in Tragedy), one of Lucian of Samosata's dialogues, and attacks powerful statesmen who give undeserved honors to their servants and even grant them titles of nobility. "Satira III" focuses, using scurrilous language and violent images, on the physician Giovan Andrea Moniglia, a lecturer in medicine, author of melodramas, and influential courtier to Cosimo III who had plotted against Menzini when he applied for a position at the University of Pisa. Menzini gives him the nickname "Curculione," an insect with powerful mandibles; the name is taken from the Roman playwright Plautus's comedy *Curculio* (Sting). Menzini calls Moniglia "minus habens" (ignorant) and says that he merited neither his degree nor his academic titles:

> La laurea no; meglio era dargli un sasso
> nel capo, o una pedata arcisolenne
> in quel corpaccio sbraculato e grasso.

> (No one should have granted a degree to him; indeed, it
>   was better to hit him on the head
> with a stone, or to give him a solemn kick
> in that flabby and fat body of his.)

The attack extends to Moniglia's family: they pass by in their carriage,

> ove siede colui, che ha corna e cozza,
> e la moglie bagascia, e infame il figlio
> e coscienza scellerata e sozza.

> (where is seated that despicable, cuckolded man who has
>   horns for butting,
> a prostitute for a wife, an infamous son,
> and a dirty and wicked conscience.)

"Satira IV" is the most impersonal and most anti-Baroque piece in the collection. Menzini ridicules the mediocre followers of Pindar, Marino's imitators, and the crowd of amateurs who gather in the public streets

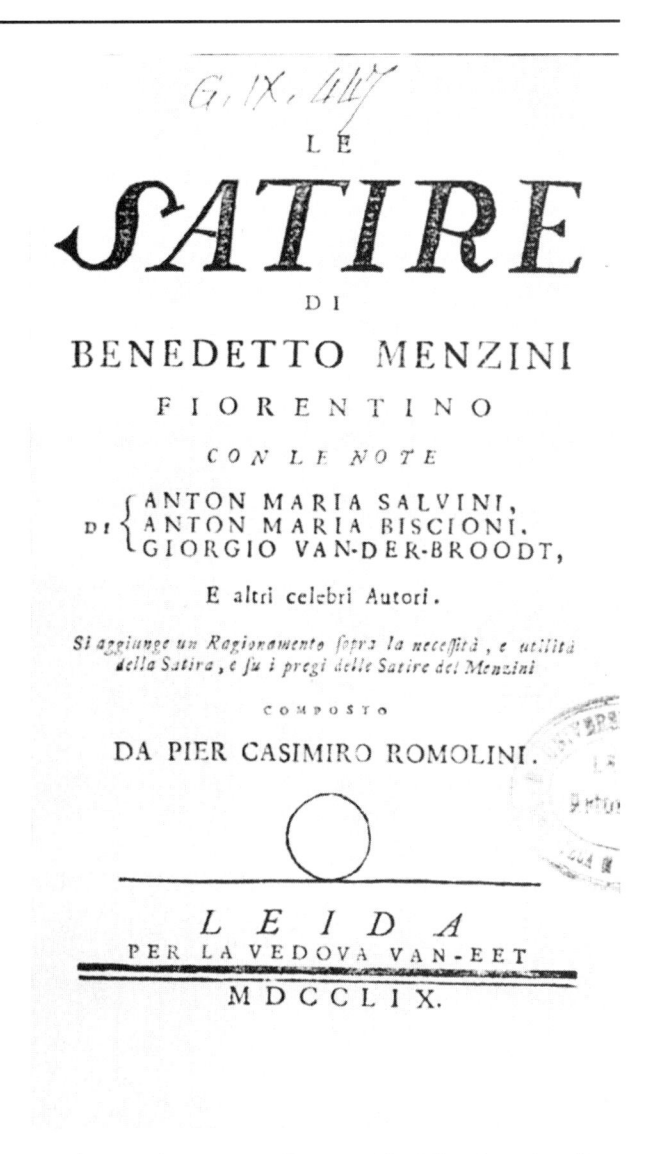

Title page for an edition of Benedetto Menzini's satires, originally published in 1718 (University of Turin)

and squares and degrade poetry with their bizarre and grotesque artifices:

> Donde imparaste mai sì vaghe, e belle
> maniere? E voi mi dite: è pindaresco
> lo stile . . . ?
>
> Che tracotanza, e che superbia è questa,
> con un parlar spropositato e matto
> con Pindaro voler alzar la cresta?
> . . . .
> Ma voi, cervelli terricurvi e corti
> . . . .
> ma voi bevete le stemprate aurore,
> polverizzate stelle e liquefatti
> i Cieli che d'ambrosia hanno il sapore. . . .

O boia, un giorno il canapale addoppia,
ed appicca costoro a un travicello,
de' traditori della patria in coppia.

(Where did you ever learn such beautiful and attractive
 ways of writing? And you are telling me that you have
   taken your style
from Pindar . . . ?

How dare you compare yourselves with Pindar
when you are using
such a crazy and exaggerated style?
. . . .
But you, whose small brains are bending low toward the
   ground,
. . . .
you who drink the diluted sunrises,
you who create horrible figures
of speech, stardust and liquefied Heavens that taste like
   ambrosia. . . .
Please, hangman, one of these days make a slip-knot with
   your rope and hang them all to a beam,
along with the traitors to their country.)

Critics point to similarities between this satire and Salvatore Rosa's satire "La poesia" (1719, Poetry) but note that while Rosa focuses on the need for a moral renewal in poetry, Menzini is more concerned with the recovery of simplicity and beauty in poetic style and in opposing convoluted Baroque metaphors.

"Satira V" is aimed at the false followers of Stoicism, who go into the streets dressed in rags and with humble faces but are in reality mean and arrogant people. Menzini includes Moniglia among these individuals and once again ferociously denigrates him. "Satira VI" is more original and less tedious than the preceding satires. Taking his model from Juvenal, Menzini abstains from personal references and attacks. The work is a misogynistic piece in which Menzini criticizes bad wives, especially those of the upper class, who represent the worst examples of corruption and moral degradation. He accuses rich, married noblewomen of being frivolous, promiscuous, unfaithful, capable of poisoning their husbands and killing their newborns, and of giving birth to bastards. The satire is most effective when Menzini attacks the custom of *monacazioni forzate* (forced taking the veil). The sincerity and strength of the piece are comparable, in the eyes of critics, to the work of the Venetian writer Arcangela Tarabotti:

O povere ragazze, io non vi zombo
per questo no, che contro alla natura
matto è ben quei, che fa schiamazzo e rombo.
E veggio ancor perché Buda, e Musura
vuol, che la figlia imbavagliata il mento
del secol faccia una solenne abiura.
Perché ha egli a dar mille, se con cento
se la toglie di casa? Un bianco velo
val men che di broccato un paramento.

(O poor girls, I do not condemn you,
because he who tries to repress and constrain women in an
   unnatural way
is an unbalanced person.
And I understand why Buda and Musura
want his daughter, with her chin gagged by the wimple,
to make a solemn abjuration of the world.
Why should the parent indeed give away one thousand
   scudi of dowry
when he can send her away from home with one hundred?
   A white nun's veil
costs less than a brocade bridal outfit.)

Juvenal is also the inspiration for "Satira VII," which stigmatizes the opulence and ostentatious habits of both the old nobility and wealthy parvenus, and "Satira VIII," on the moral degradation of the Florentine court of Cosimo III. In the latter work Menzini criticizes courtiers' greed for honors; his rage is particularly directed against the erudite Antonio Magliabechi, who was entrusted by the grand duke with the direction of the Florentine Biblioteca Palatina (Palatine Library). In Menzini's view, Magliabechi is a frivolous, arrogant pseudoscholar and plagiarist. He also ridicules the courtier Giuseppe Bonaventura Del Teglia as a hypocrite and a bigot.

"Satira IX" has been judged one of the most accomplished of the twelve because of its objective tone and balanced structure. Directed at the avarice, greed, and ignorance of the clergy, it includes images and descriptions that are reminiscent of the Bible and of Dante's *Divina Commedia* (circa 1308–1321, Divine Comedy; translated as *The Divina Comedia of Dante Alighieri*, 1802). In "Satira X" Menzini deals with lack of religious conviction among priests and attacks some specific Florentine clergymen. He is intransigent with this category of sinners, rejoices when he sees them condemned and imprisoned by the Inquisition, and favors their being burned at the stake and hanged in the public square. "Satira XI" returns to the court in Florence, depicting it as a sink of corruption and vice. Menzini again violently criticizes the greedy and hypocritical courtiers Moniglia and Magliabechi and adds Senator Ferrante Capponi to his targets. "Satire XII" is inspired by Persius, Juvenal, and Horace in its central theme of the vanity of all human desire and ambition. Menzini's invective is focused on the uselessness of impossible desires, dishonest prayers, and foolish vows made to God. According to critics, Menzini's satire does not achieve the poise or elegance of its models.

Scholars agree that Benedetto Menzini's satires are inferior to the works of the more-famous satirists of his time: they are less strong and vivacious than those of Rosa and less structured and balanced than those of Michelangelo Buonarroti the Younger and Jacopo Soldani. But these critics concede that the satires show a command of both the formal and vernacular Tuscan languages. They also point to his commitment to combating Baroque excesses by proposing a new model of clarity of style and realistic content, combined with a measured and prudent imitation of classic authors. Uberto Limentani has said that *Satire* contains "il fermento di un'epoca nuova" (the ferment of a new age). It has also been claimed that Menzini's multifaceted oeuvre is crucial to understanding the evolution of Italian literature at the end of the Seicento.

Letters:

Lettere di Benedetto Menzini e del Senatore Vincenzo da Filicaia a Francesco Redi, edited by Domenico Moreni (Florence: Magheri, 1828).

Biographies:

Giuseppe Paolucci da Spello, "Vita di Benedetto Menzini Fiorentino, detto Euganio Libade," in *Le vite degli Arcadi illustri,* volume 1, edited by Giovan Mario Crescimbeni (Rome: De' Rossi, 1708), pp. 169–188;

Paolucci da Spello, "Vita di Benedetto Menzini," in *Opere di Benedetto Menzini,* volume 4 (Florence: Tartini & Franchi, 1732), pp. 1–40;

Mario Saccenti, "Benedetto Menzini," in *Dizionario critico della letteratura italiana,* volume 3, edited by Vittore Branca (Turin: Unione Tipografico-Editrice Torinese, 1986), pp. 156–159.

References:

Costantino Arlía, "Quante satire scrisse il Menzini?" *Il Bibliofilo,* 1 (1866): 5–6;

Antonio Belloni, *Il Seicento* (Milan: Vallardi, 1943), pp. 304–310;

Walter Binni, "La formazione della poetica arcadica e la letteratura fiorentina di fine Seicento," in his *L'Arcadia e il Metastasio* (Florence: La Nuova Italia, 1968), pp. 18–37;

Carlo Calcaterra, *I lirici del Seicento e dell'Arcadia* (Milan & Rome: Rizzoli, 1936), pp. 28–29, 885;

Vittorio Cian, *La satira,* volume 2 (Milan: Vallardi, 1945), pp. 231–271;

Benedetto Croce, *Saggi sulla letteratura italiana del Seicento* (Bari: Laterza, 1964), pp. 73, 336, 338;

Carla De Bellis, "Le arti nello specchio della poesia: Sei sonetti di Benedetto Menzini," in *La lotta contro Proteo: Metamorfosi del testo e testualità della critica. Atti del XVI Congresso AISLLI, Associazione internazionale per gli studi di lingua e letteratura italiana, University of California, Los Angeles, UCLA, 6–9 ottobre 1997,* edited by Luigi Ballerini, Gay Bardin, and Massimo Ciavolella (Fiesole: Cadmo, 2000), pp. 525–547;

Carmine Di Biase, *Arcadia edificante* (Naples: Edizioni scientifiche italiane, 1969), pp. 25–128, 615–632;

Francesco Flora, *Storia della letteratura italiana,* volume 3 (Milan: Mondadori, 1964), pp. 460–463;

Carmine Jannaco, "Tradizione e rinnovamento nelle poetiche dell'età barocca," *Convivium,* 6 (1959): pp. 658–672;

Jannaco and Martino Capucci, *Il Seicento* (Padua: Piccin Nuova Libraria, 1986), pp. 79–84, 229, 349, 362–364, 374, 499, 504–510, 514–515, 560, 889;

Giacomo Jori, "Poesia lirica 'marinista' e 'antimarinista,' tra Classicismo e Barocco," in *Storia della letteratura italiana,* volume 5, edited by Enrico Malato (Rome: Salerno, 1997), pp. 653–726;

Luca Lamperini, "Sui sonetti di Benedetto Menzini," *Dialoghi,* 17 (1969): pp. 35–47;

Uberto Limentani, *La satira nel Seicento* (Milan & Naples: Ricciardi, 1961), pp. 283–338;

G. Magrini, *Studio critico su Benedetto Menzini* (Naples: La Cava, 1885);

Guido Mazzoni, *Del* Monte Oliveto *e del* Mondo creato *di Torquato Tasso* (Bologna: Zanichelli, 1891), pp. 63–66;

Salvatore Rago, *Benedetto Menzini e le sue satire* (Naples: Morano, 1901).

Andrea Perrucci
(1 June 1651 – 6 May 1704)

Salvatore Cappelletti
Providence College

BOOKS: *Difendere l'offensore overo La Stellidaura vendicata* (Naples: Porsile, 1674); revised as *La Stellidaura vendicante* (Naples: Porsile, 1678);

Chi tal nasce tal vive overo L'Alessandro Bala (Naples: Cavallo, 1677);

L'Agnano zeffonato co La malatia d'Apollo, as Andrea Perruccio (Naples: Paci, 1678);

Il convitato di pietra, as Enrico Preudarca (Naples: Mollo, 1678);

L'eresia discacciata dal secolo dal suolo di Partenope dalla fede di S. Gaetano (Naples: Mutio, 1679);

Le fatiche d'Ercole per Deianira (Naples: Porsile, 1679);

Gli amori di Cinthia con Endimione (Naples: Castaldo, 1679);

Il figlio del Serafino di S. Pietro D'Alcantara (Venice: Zini, 1684);

Il Sansone (Naples: Porsile, 1686);

La Susanna (Naples: Porsile, 1686);

La fede trionfante su le rovine di Buda (Naples: Monaco, 1687);

La vera armonia per S. Cecilia (Palermo: Epiro, 1687);

Serenata (Naples: Cavallo, 1689; Naples: Mutium, 1689);

Il devoto della Vergine Maria Immacolata (Rome: Mascardo, 1691);

Il Zelo animato dal gran proffeta Elia (Naples: Paci, 1691);

La sirena consolata (Naples: Parrino & Mutio, 1692);

Elogio a S. Rosalia vergine palermitana (Naples: Parrino & Mutio, 1693);

La Biageide o vero Il secondo D. Ciccio (Naples, 1693);

Costanza nelle sventure (Naples & Venice: Troise, 1694);

Unione d'amore, realtà, e grazia (Naples: Mutio, 1694);

La fragilità costante nel martirio dei SS. Vito, Modesto e Crescenzo (Naples: Troise & Pietroboni, 1695);

Idee delle Muse (Naples: Parrino & Mutio, 1695);

Nel complire con la sua obbligazione (Naples: Porpora & Troise, 1697);

Colloandro o vero L'infedele fedele (Naples, 1698);

Il Vero Lume tra l'ombre, overo La Spelonca arricchita, per la nascita del Verbo Umanato, as Dottor Casimiro Ruggiero Ogone (Naples: Paci, 1698); translated by Mimi and Nello D'Aponte as *Shepherds' Song: La cantata dei pastori* (Madrid: Turanzas, 1982);

Dell'arte rappresentativa premeditata ed all'improvviso, 2 volumes (Naples: Mutio, 1699); translated and edited by Francesco Cotticelli, Anne Goodrich Heck, and Thomas F. Heck as *A Treatise on Acting, from Memory and by Improvisation (1699)* (Lanham, Md.: Scarecrow Press, 2008);

Il roveto di Mosè (Naples: Mutio, 1700);

Il Gedeone (Naples: Pittante, 1701);

Oscurarsi per risplendere (Naples: Parrino, 1701);

From Giacinto Gimma, Elogi accademici della Società degli Spensierati di Rossano *(1703); Biblioteca Nazionale Universitaria, Turin*

Sodissimi fondamenti (Naples, 1701);

L'arca del testamento di Gerico ed il laccio purporeo di Rab (Naples: Troise, 1702);

Il desio di Napoli (Naples: Parrino, 1702);

Distinto diario dell'operato della Maestà Cattolica di Filippo V Re delle Spagne, Napoli e Sicilia (Naples: Parrino & Mutio, 1702);

La verga, la manna, e la legge (Naples: Pittante, 1703);

Amore mal corrisposto o vero La verità celata (Viterbo, 1718);

Chi non ha cuore non ha pietà o vero La Rosaura (Naples: Mutio, 1719).

Editions and Collections: "Andrea Perrucci," in *Lirici marinisti*, edited by Benedetto Croce (Bari: Laterza, 1916), pp. 517–521, 540;

"Dell'arte rappresentativa premeditata ed all'improvviso," part 2, in *La commedia dell'arte: Storia, tecnica, scenari*, edited by Enzo Petraccone, preface by Croce (Naples: Ricciardi, 1927), pp. 67–201;

"Andrea Perrucci," in *La poesia dialettale napoletana*, edited by Enrico Malato (Naples: Edizioni Scientifiche Italiane, 1960), pp. xxvii, 227–241;

Dell'arte rappresentativa premeditata ed all'improvviso, edited by Anton Giulio Bragaglia (Florence: Sansoni, 1961);

"Andrea Perrucci," in *Poeti napoletani dal Seicento ad oggi*, edited by Enrico De Mura (Naples: Marotta, 1963), pp. 37–43;

"Andrea Perrucci," in *Le origini della commedia dell'arte*, by Achille Mango and Rosaria M. Lombardi (Salerno: Libreria Internazionale Editrice, circa 1970), pp. 125–167;

Le opere napoletane: "L'Agnano zeffonnato" e "La malatia d'Apollo," edited by Laura Facecchia (Rome: Benincasa, 1986);

Il convitato di pietra, edited by Roberto De Simone (Turin: Einaudi, 1998);

"Andrea Perrucci," in *La commedia dell'arte: Scelta e introduzione*, edited by Cesare Molinari (Rome: Istituto Poligrafico e Zecca dello Stato, 1999), pp. iii–xxvii, 1201–1234;

La cantata dei pastori, edited by De Simone (Turin: Einaudi, 2000).

Editions in English: "Directions as to the Preparation of a Performance from a Scenario," translated by Edward Gordon Craig, *Mask*, 4 (October 1911): 113–115;

"Introduction to Impromptu Acting," translated by Joseph M. Bernstein, in *Actors on Acting: The Theories, Techniques, and Practices of the World's Great Actors, Told in Their Own Words*, edited by Toby Cole and Helen Krich Chinoy (New York: Crown, 1954), pp. 55–57;

Giacomo Oreglia, *The Commedia dell'Arte* (New York: Hill & Wang, 1968), pp. 82–83, 106, 119–122;

Kenneth Richards and Laura Richards, *La Commedia dell'Arte: A Documentary History* (Oxford & Cambridge, Mass.: Blackwell, 1990), pp. 178–182, 201–203, 205–209;

"Andrea Perrucci: The Art of Representation," in *Italy in the Baroque: Selected Readings*, edited and translated by Brendan Dooley (New York & London: Garland, 1995), pp. 495–517.

PLAY PRODUCTIONS: *Il schiavo di sua moglie*, music by Francesco Provenzale, Naples, San Bartolomeo Theater, Fall 1671;

Difendere l'offensore overo La Stellidaura vendicata, music by Provenzale, Naples, Palace of Prince Giambattista Cicinelli Cursi, 2 September 1674;

Chi tal nasce tal vive, overo L'Alessandro Bala, Naples, San Bartolomeo Theater, 20 December 1677;

La Zenobia, Naples, San Bartolomeo Theater, Fall(?) 1678;

Le fatiche d'Ercole per Deianira, Naples, San Bartolomeo Theater, Fall(?) 1678;

Gli amori di Cinthia con Endimione, Naples, Palazzo Reale Theater, 21 December 1679;

Mitilene, regina delle Amazzoni, Naples, Palazzo Reale Theater, 6 November 1681;

L'Epaminonda, Naples, Palazzo Reale Theater, 21 December 1684.

Andrea Perrucci was the major theorist of drama of the seventeenth century; a pioneering librettist; a significant contributor to the development of theatrical dance; a renowned stage director; an occasional actor; a poet who wrote in Latin, Italian, Sicilian, Neapolitan, Calabrian, and Spanish; a prolific writer of secular and sacred plays; and the author of many oratorios, intermezzos, prologues, serenades, and popular songs. He states in his theoretical treatise, *Dell'arte rappresentativa premeditata ed all'improvviso* (1699, On the Premeditated and Impromptu Art of Acting; translated as *A Treatise on Acting, from Memory and by Improvisation*, 2008), that he did not translate foreign plays but adapted several, particularly works by Lope de Vega, to accord with Italian tastes.

According to his friend and first biographer, Giacinto Gimma, Perrucci was born in Palermo at 1:00 P.M., Thursday, 1 June 1651. His parents were Francesco Perrucci, a naval officer, and Anna Perrucci, née Fardella; both were aristocrats from Trapani, Sicily. The family moved to Naples when Perrucci was eight. He completed his secondary education in literary studies with the Jesuits; the Dominicans trained him in philosophy and theology. Around 1665 he enrolled at the University of Naples. An active member of several societies for the propagation of Catholicism, he became secretary of the Sacred Cross Congregation in 1668; although some sources refer to him as "Abbot Perrucci," he was not a clergyman. In 1670 he received doctorates in letters and in civil and canonical law. Shortly thereafter, he returned to Palermo to recover his family's estate; when he was unable to do so, he vowed never to go back to his ungrateful "patria" (country). He traveled extensively on the Italian mainland, where he learned the various dialects that he used in his works. He practiced law, but only occasionally and out of financial necessity; literature—especially the theater—was his main occupation. He was elected to the Oziosi Academy in Naples, the Pellegrini Academy in Rome, and the Pigri Academy in Bari; he was secretary of the Raccesi in Palermo and the Rozzi in Naples and salaried promoter general of the Spensierati of Rossano.

The opera *Il schiavo di sua moglie* (1671, The Slave of His Wife), with libretto by Perrucci and score by Francesco Provenzale, was written for Giulia De Caro; known as "Ciulla," De Caro was the leading female singer and impresario of the San Bartolomeo Theater in Naples. The Greek warriors Timante, Theseo (Theseus), and Ercole (Hercules) have been captured by the Amazon queen Ippolita (Hippolyta) and her sister, Menalippa. Ercole loves Menalippa, but Menalippa loves Theseo, whose love for Ippolita seems to be unrequited. Timante is actually Menalippa's husband, Leucippe, who is thought to be dead; to find out whether Menalippa still loves him, he tells her that he is her husband's twin brother. When he learns of Menalippa's love for Theseo, he disguises himself as a Turkish slave in service to his wife. One day Menalippa wakes up in a garden and recognizes Leucippe; but, believing him to be a ghost, she flees. Leucippe feels rejected and wants to commit suicide, but revelations and a happy ending soon follow: husband and wife are reunited, Ippolita and Theseo declare their love for each other, and Ercole rejoices in the happiness of the others.

Provenzale's best-known opera, *Difendere l'offensore overo La Stellidaura vendicata* (Defending the Offender; or, Stellidaura Vindicated), premiered on 2 September 1674 with De Caro in the leading role. Orismondo is in love with Stellidaura, but she loves his friend Armidoro. Orismondo disguises himself and tries to murder Armidoro, and Stellidaura, disguised as a man, tries to kill Orismondo but is stopped by Armidoro. Stellidaura refuses to reveal her identity and is condemned to be buried alive. Armidoro finds out about her disguise and volunteers to die with her in the crypt. Meanwhile, Orismondo discovers that Stellidaura is his long-lost sister. The opera ends happily with the marriage of Stellidaura and Armidoro.

Perrucci and Provenzale collaborated again on *Chi tal nasce tal vive, overo L'Alessandro Bala* (Those Who Are Born One Way, Live as Such; or, Alexander Balas), which premiered at the San Bartolomeo Theater on 20 December 1677. The following year Perrucci published *L'Agnano zeffonato co La malatia d'Apollo* (The Sunken Agnano with The Malady of Apollo); the two mythological poems in Neapolitan dialect are preceded by eight poems in praise of the author by other poets. In the preface to "L'Agnano zeffonato" Perrucci says that he fell asleep by Lake Agnano, which, according to legend, was formed when the city of Agnano sank. He was awakened by a frog leaping out of the water. The frog, who had lived in the lake since it was formed, assured him that the legend was true. As the frog recounted the tale, the poet, in a dreamy state, wrote it down. The queen of Agnano was the sister of the king of Naples; she was murdered by her husband, who thought that she had committed adultery, and a rivalry between Naples and Agnano ensued. Finally, Jupiter, tired of the feuding, caused rain to fall on Agnano until it sank; he also changed its citizens into waterfowl. The description of life in the former city is a satire of the social and moral corruption prevalent in Perrucci's time: virtue does not exist; politicians are corrupt; jewelers are thieves; physicians, in collusion with pharmacists, write unintelligibly to hide what they are prescribing; and lawyers thrive on money and gifts from clients, with the result that "lo tristo nn'esce, e 'mpiso è lo 'nnozente" (the wicked one goes free, and the innocent one is hanged). "La malatia d'Apollo" is a satirical idyll directed at contemporary poetasters: the works of atrocious poets, replete with images and sounds of donkeys, owls, and werewolves, give Apollo, the god of poetry, a hernia.

In 1678 Perrucci published *Il convitato di pietra* (The Guest of Stone) under the pseudonym "Enrico Preudarca," an anagram of his name. It is based on the myth of Don Juan or Don Giovanni, which was handed down in a long oral tradition from the Middle Ages by minstrels, puppeteers, and itinerant actors. The story was popular in Italy and had been dramatized earlier in the seventeenth century in the anonymous *L'ateista fulminato* (date unknown, The Atheist Struck down by Lightning), Bartolomeo Bocchini's *Le pazzie dei savi, ovvero Il Lambertaccio* (1641, The Sages' Follies; or, Lambert the Vile), Giovanni Battista Andreini's *Il convitato di pietra* (1651), and Pippo (Filippo) Acciaiuoli's *L'empio punito* (1669, The Rake Punished). Perrucci's main source was Tirso de Molina's *El burlador de Sevilla y convidado de piedra* (1630, The Trickster of Seville and the Guest of Stone), which was translated into Italian in 1640 by Giacinto Andrea Cicognini and in 1652 by Onofrio Giliberto di Solofra; Perrucci is probably referring to these versions when he notes in his preface that his play is not a translation.

Perrucci's *Il convitato di pietra* is distinguished by its multilingualism: the *innamorati* (lovers) and aristocrats speak standard Italian; the Dottore (Doctor) is from Bologna and speaks Bolognese, but his daughter, Pimpinella, was brought up in Naples and speaks Neapolitan; Neapolitan is also used by the *zanni* (comic servants) Pollicinella, Rosetta, and Coviello. The play includes contemporary and traditional Neapolitan songs, as well as the tarantella, which is danced by Pollicinella and Pimpinella. In act 2 Don Giovanni says to his servant, Coviello: "Che mi vai raccontando tu di Cielo, sciocco? Che cosa è questo Cielo, altro che un composto di materia come noi? Anzi, s'egli erra, essendo di me più nobile, come non posso errare io, che sono fragile?" (Fool, what are you telling me about heaven? What is this heaven, other than a mixture of matter like us? In fact, being nobler than I, if it errs, how can I not err, being fragile?). Heaven should correct its own faults, he goes on: it has a sun that suffers eclipses, a silly moon that plays hide-and-seek, and wanton planets that travel erratically across the sky; moreover, heaven is too remote to be offended by the "diletto" (delight) he seeks in life. In the closing lines of the play, however, Don Giovanni, in hell, admonishes the audience that ruthless love and "pensieri sensuali" (sensuous thoughts) lead to eternal damnation. Perrucci's *Il convitato di pietra* was the main source for Giovanni Bertati and Giuseppe Gazzaniga's 1787 opera *Don Giovanni;* that work, in turn, served as the basis for Wolfgang Amadeus Mozart and Lorenzo Da Ponte's famous opera of the same title, produced later that same year.

In 1678 Perrucci was appointed resident poet, librettist, and director at the San Bartolomeo Theater; he held the position for about seven years, during which he also directed performances at the Palazzo Reale and the Fiorentini Theaters in Naples. His *Mitilene, regina delle Amazzoni* (Mytilene, Queen of the Amazons), set to music by Giovanni Bonaventura Viviani, was performed at the Palazzo Reale on 6 November 1681 and shortly afterward at the Fiorentini; his melodrama *L'Epaminonda* (Epaminondas), with music by Severo de Luca, was performed at the Palazzo Reale on 21 December 1684.

In 1693 Perrucci published an oratorio, *Elogio a S. Rosalia vergine palermitana* (Eulogy to St. Rosalia the Palermitan Virgin), about the patron saint of Palermo, and *La Biageide o vero Il secondo D. Ciccio* (Pertaining to Biagio; or, The Second Don Ciccio), consisting of two hundred burlesque sonnets directed at a critic named Biagio who had been mocking him. Two years later, he published *Idee delle Muse* (Ideas of the Muses), a huge collection of poems that abounds in dramatic landscape descriptions.

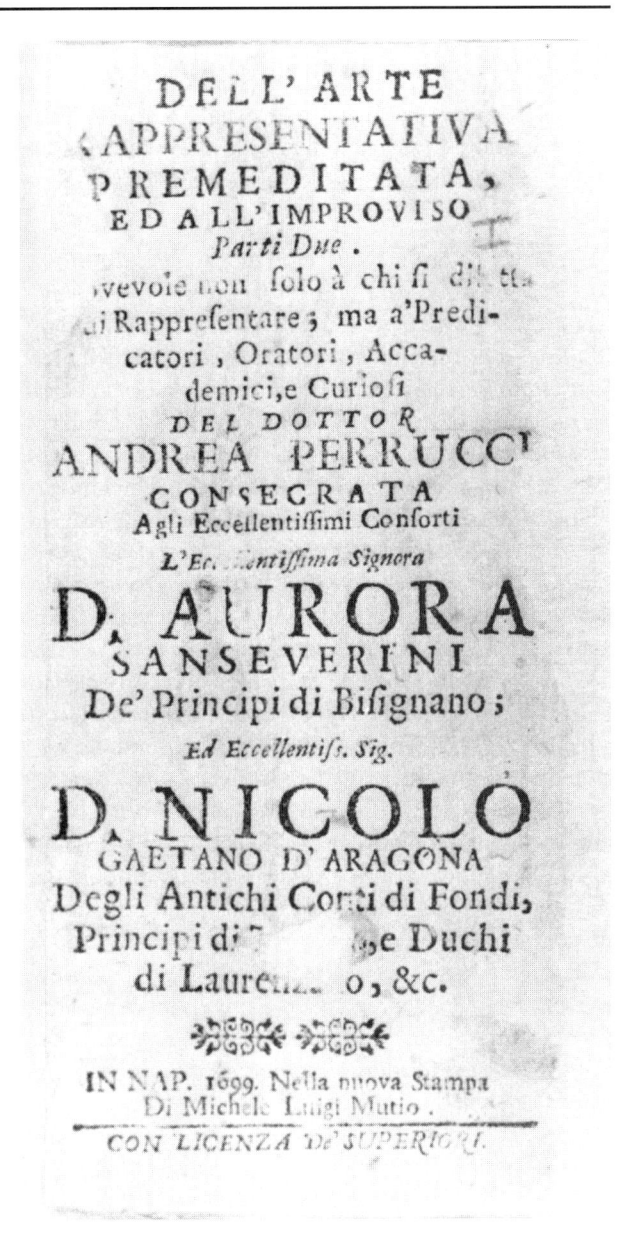

Title page for the first edition of On the Premeditated and Impromptu Art of Acting, Part Two *(Biblioteca Nazionale Marciana, Venice)*

Perrucci published his play *Il Vero Lume tra l'ombre, overo La Spelonca arricchita, per la nascita del Verbo Umanato* (1698, The True Light among the Shadows; or, The Enriched Hovel for the Birth of the Human Word; translated as *Shepherds' Song: La cantata dei pastori*, 1982), also known as *La cantata dei pastori* (Shepherds' Song), under the pseudonym Dottor Casimiro Ruggiero Ogone. In conformity with the didactic and moralizing objectives of Jesuit theater, it was part of an effort to eradicate the 25 December pagan celebration associated with the birth of the sun god Mithras. The play, in which demons try to prevent Mary and Joseph from traveling to Bethlehem, combines commedia dell'arte with sacred and pastoral drama; Italian is spoken by all of the characters except Razullo, who speaks Neapolitan. It is still performed annually in Italy between 24 December and 6 January, with radio and television productions since the 1950s.

A year after the publication of *La cantata dei pastori,* Perrucci brought out his best-known work, *Dell'arte rappresentativa premeditata ed all'improvviso.* It was preceded by other treatises on similar topics, such as Leone Hebreo de' Sommi's *Quattro dialoghi in materia di rappresentazioni sceniche* (circa 1575–1588, Four Dialogues on the Subject of Stage Performances), Tommaso Garzoni's *La piazza universale di tutte le professioni del mondo* (1586, The Universal Plaza of all the Professions of the World), Angelo Ingegneri's *Della poesia rappresentativa e del modo di rappresentare le favole sceniche* (1598, On Dramatic Declamation and the Manner of Staging Plays), Pier Maria Cecchini's *Frutti delle moderne commedie e avisi a chi le recita* (1625, Fruits of Modern Comedies and Advices to Those Playing Them), Nicolò Barbieri's *Trattato sopra l'arte comica* (1627, Treatise on Comic Art) and *La supplica: Discorso famigliare a quelli che scriuendo o parlando trattano de' comici trascurando i meriti delle azzioni uirtuose* (1634, The Appeal: Friendly Remarks to Those Who in Writing or Speaking Deal with Players but Overlook the Merits of Virtuous Theatrical Actions), and the anonymous *Il corago, o vero, alcune osservazioni per metter bene in scena le composizioni drammatiche* (circa 1630, The Choragus; or, Some Observations on Properly Staging Dramatic Compositions). *Dell'arte rappresentativa premeditata ed all'improvviso* includes original scenarios; detailed analyses of the stock commedia dell'arte roles; advice on gestures, diction, and portraying various emotions; the role of music and singing; and the writing of stage directions. He is particularly concerned with the language to be used by various character types: he recommends Italian for the *innamorati,* local dialects for the *zanni* and *zagne* (male and female servants), a mixture of Bolognese or Tuscanized Bolognese and Latin for the Dottore, Venetian for Pantalone (the avaricious old man), and a mixture of Spanish and an Italian dialect for the Spanish captain. He also provides examples of lines in Italian and various dialects. Perrucci holds that the use of multilingualism is both a realistic reflection of the dialects spoken in Italy and also a source of the misunderstandings, equivocations, and plays on words that audiences find entertaining. He advises actors to change their intonation according to feelings and circumstances but to keep it attuned to the role being played. Perrucci offers several chapters on dance, with descriptions of dances and suggestions on how to use them; he corroborates his observations with Greek and Latin sources.

Around 1700 Perrucci was appointed chief law officer of Naples by the viceroy. In 1701 he published *Il Gedeone* (Gideon), an oratorio about the biblical judge of Israel with music by Nicolò Porpora, and *Sodissimi fondamenti* (Very Sound Grounds), a biography of St. Rosalia in which he argues that, contrary to popular belief, she was not a nun. In 1702 he published his last oratorio, *L'arca del testamento di Gerico ed il laccio purporeo di Rab* (The Ark of the Testament of Jericho and the Purple Rope of Rahab), set to music by Francesco Mancini, in which the servant character Tufalo sings in Neapolitan, and *Il desio di Napoli* (Longing for Naples), a collection of sonnets commemorating the arrival of the Spanish viceroy Emmanuel Fernandes Pacheco. That same year Perrucci produced *Distinto diario dell'operato della Maestà Cattolica di Filippo V Re delle Spagne, Napoli e Sicilia* (Distinguished Diary of the Deeds of the Catholic Majesty, Philip V, King of the Spains, Naples and Sicily), a detailed chronicle of the Spanish king's trip to Italy from his departure from Barcelona and through his stay in the vicinity of Naples. Perrucci died from a severe fever on 6 May 1704.

Andrea Perrucci's literary reputation continues to be high. He is remembered for his innovative contributions to opera, dance, and, above all, to dramaturgy, for which he is acknowledged in *Histoire des spectacles* (1965, History of Spectacles) as "le plus grand théoricien de l'arte" (the greatest theorist of the commedia dell'arte).

Bibliographies:

Franca Angelini, "Perrucci, Andrea," in *Enciclopedia dello spettacolo,* volume 8 (Rome: Le Maschere, 1961), pp. 18–19;

Anton Giulio Bragaglia, *Dell'arte rappresentativa premeditata ed all'improvviso,* by Andrea Perrucci (Florence: Sansoni, 1961), pp. 35–48;

Achille Mango and Rosaria M. Lombardi, *Le origini della commedia dell'arte* (Salerno: Libreria Internazionale Editrice, 1970), pp. 165–167;

Pietro Martorana, "Andrea Perrucci," in *Notizie biografiche e bibliografiche degli scrittori del dialetto napoletano* (Bologna: Forni, 1972), pp. 323–327;

Annibale Ruccello, *Il sole e la maschera: Una lettura antropologica della "Cantata dei pastori"* (Naples: Guida, 1978), pp. 44–46.

Biographies:

Giacinto Gimma, *Elogi accademici della Società degli Spensierati di Rossano,* volume 2 (Naples: Troise, 1703), pp. xxxiii, 47–62;

Michele Scherillo, "Andrea Perrucci," in his *L'opera buffa napoletana durante il settecento: Storia letteraria* (Naples: Sandron, 1917), pp. 35–41;

Carmelo Musumarra, *La sacra rappresentazione della Natività nella tradizione italiana* (Florence: Olschki, 1967), pp. 19–20;

Vittorio Viviani, "Andrea Perrucci," in his *Storia del teatro napoletano* (Naples: Guida, 1969), pp. 175–223;

Annibale Ruccello, *Il sole e la maschera: Una lettura antropologica della "Cantata dei pastori"* (Naples: Guida, 1978), pp. 37–44;

Mario Apollonio, *Storia del teatro italiano*, volume 2 (Florence: Sansoni, 1981), pp. 100–105.

References:

Irene Alm, "Humanism and Theatrical Dance in Early Opera," *Musica Disciplina*, 49 (1995): 79–93;

Lucia Balbi and Roberto De Simone, *Demoni e santi: Teatro e teatralità barocca a Napoli* (Naples: Electa, 1984);

Salvatore Cappelletti, "Questioni tecnico-artistiche: L'educazione del nuovo attore e la riscoperta del volto umano," in his *Luigi Riccoboni e la riforma del teatro: Dalla commedia dell'arte alla commedia borghese* (Ravenna: Longo, 1986), pp. 63–97;

Silvia Carandini and Enrica Cancelliere, eds., *Meraviglie e orrori dell'aldilà: Intrecci mitologici e favole cristiane nel teatro barocco* (Rome: Bulzoni, 1995);

Maria Chiabò and Federico Doglio, *I Gesuiti e i primordi del teatro barocco* (Rome: Torre D'Orfeo, 1995);

Gianrenzo Clivio, "The Language of the Commedia dell'Arte," in *The Science of Buffoonery: Theory and History of the Commedia dell'Arte*, edited by Domenico Pietropaolo (Ottawa: Dovehouse, 1989), pp. 209–237;

Mariateresa Colotti, ed., *L'opera buffa napoletana* (Rome: Benincasa, 1999);

Andrea della Corte and Guido Pannain, *Storia della musica: Dal Medioevo al Seicento*, volume 1 (Turin: Unione Tipografico-Editrice Torinese, 1952), pp. 499–506;

Benedetto Croce, *Saggi sulla letteratura italiana del Seicento* (Bari: Laterza, 1962), pp. 198–231, 290;

Croce, *I teatri di Napoli: Dal Rinascimento alla fine del secolo decimottavo* (Bari: Laterza, 1916), pp. 88–121;

Sandro D'Amico, "La commedia dell'arte," in *Histoire des spectacles*, edited by Guy Dumur, Enciclopédie de la Plèiade, volume 19 (Tours: Gallimard, 1965), pp. 636–645;

Roberto De Simone, "Il mito del Convitato di pietra nella tradizione napoletana," in *Il convitato di pietra*, by Andrea Perrucci, edited by De Simone (Turin: Einaudi, 1998), pp. v–xvii;

Giovanni Dotoli, "La rivoluzione della commedia dell'arte," in *La commedia dell'arte tra Cinquecento e Seicento in Francia e in Europa,* edited by Elio Mosele (Fasano di Brindisi: Schena, 1977), pp. 19–47;

Hans Ulrich Ganz, *Carlo Goldoni e Andrea Perrucci* (Florence: Sansoni, 1963);

Rosalba Gasparro, "Maschere italiane in Europa tra teoria e pratica teatrale," in *La commedia dell'arte tra Cinquecento e Seicento in Francia e Europa*, pp. 87–110;

Mimi Gisolfi-D'Aponte, "*La cantata dei pastori*: A Neapolitan Nativity Play of Mixed Genre," *Educational Theatre Journal*, 23 (1973): 456–462;

Franco Carmelo Greco, "Andrea Perrucci e l'istituzione del teatro," in *Origini della commedia improvvisa o dell'arte*, edited by Maria Chiabò and Federico Doglio (Rome: Torre D'Orfeo, 1996), pp. 205–229;

Irene Mamczarz, "La commedia dell'arte e la musica: La commedia madrigalesca di Orazio Vecchi e Adriano Banchieri," in *La commedia dell'arte tra Cinquecento e Seicento in Francia e in Europa*, pp. 119–120;

Carmelo Musumarra, "Il *Gelindo*, la *Cantata dei pastori*, la *Nascita di Gesù Bambino*," in *La sacra rappresentazione della Natività nella tradizione*, by Musumarra and Giuseppe Maria Musmeci Catalano (Florence: Olschki, 1957), pp. 17–28;

Allardyce Nicoll, *The World of Harlequin: A Critical Study of the Commedia dell'Arte* (New York & Cambridge: Cambridge University Press, 1986), pp. 33–39, 65–67, 137, 149–151, 225–232;

Roger Parker, ed., *The Oxford Illustrated History of Opera* (New York: Oxford University Press, 1994), p. 173;

Ulisse Prota-Giurleo, *I teatri di Napoli nel '600: La commedia e le maschere* (Naples: Fausto Fiorentino, 1962);

Amedeo Quondam, "Dal Barocco all'Arcadia," *Storia di Napoli*, 6 (1970): 809–1094;

Jean Rousset, *Le mythe de Don Juan* (Paris: Colin, 1978), pp. 26, 48, 151, 202–203, 244;

Ireneo Sanesi, *Storia dei generi letterari italiani: La commedia*, volume 2 (Florence: Sansoni, 1951), pp. 86–87, 91, 98–99, 100, 102, 104;

Pietro Spezzani, "*L'Arte rappresentativa* di Andrea Perrucci e la lingua della commedia dell'arte," in his *Dalla commedia dell'arte a Goldoni: Studi linguistici* (Padua: Esedera, 1997), pp. 121–216;

Roberto Tessari, *La commedia dell'arte nel Seicento: Industria e arte giocosa della civiltà barocca* (Florence: Olschki, 1969), pp. 4–8, 23, 38, 42, 67–68, 89–109, 115–118, 136–157, 176–196, 225–280.

Papers:

Manuscripts for Andrea Perrucci's *Il convitato di pietra* and for his unpublished "Embrioni Aganippes" are in the Biblioteca Nazionale in Naples.

Ciro di Pers

(17 April 1599 – 7 April 1663)

Paschal C. Viglionese
University of Rhode Island

BOOKS: *Il giardino* (Udine: Schiratti, 1633);

L'umiltà esaltata ovvero Ester Regina (Bassano: Remondini & Rossi, 1664);

Poesie del Cavalier frà Ciro di Pers (Vicenza: Giacomo Amadio, 1666);

Relazione sulla Patria del Friuli (Venice, 1676).

Editions and Collections: *Poesie del Cavalier frà Ciro di Pers: Dedicate alla sacra cesarea maestà di Leopoldo Imperatore Augusto Pio Pannonico* (Venice: Andrea Poletti, 1689);

Lirici marinisti, edited by Benedetto Croce (Bari: Laterza, 1910), pp. 361–406;

Marino e i marinisti, edited by Giuseppe Guido Ferrero (Milan & Naples: Ricciardi, 1954), pp. 927–966;

Lirici marinisti, edited by Giovanni Getto (Turin: TEA, 1962), pp. 499–528;

Poesia del Seicento, volume 1, edited by Carlo Muscetta and Pier Paolo Ferrante (Turin: Einaudi, 1964), pp. 924–950;

Poesie, edited by Michele Rak (Turin: Einaudi, 1978).

Ciro di Pers is generally considered a Marinist; this characterization is largely accurate, for most seventeenth-century Italian poets were participants to varying degrees in a rebellion that originated in the poetry of Torquato Tasso and was brought to a peak by Giambattista Marino. The rebellion was against certain traditional modes of composing poetry. Petrarchism, which came to its greatest flowering in the early sixteenth century among the followers of Cardinal Pietro Bembo, was the principal model that the Marinists wished to discard. They also rejected elements of the *dolce stil nuovo* (sweet new style) of Dante and Guido Cavalcanti. Despite the poets' desire to rebel, however, much of the lyric of the Seicento is linked to the earlier tradition.

Benedetto Croce suggested that Pers, though remembered as a full-fledged member of the school of Marinism, went somewhat against the grain of the

From Giovanni Getto, ed., Opere scelte di Giovan Battista Marino e dei Marinisti, *1962; Thomas Cooper Library, University of South Carolina*

times. For example, he was one of the few who did not emphasize the physical and the sensual in writing about love. The beloved woman in Pers's poetry, Croce maintains, has the beauty of God in her, and the love expressed in some of Pers's lyrics contrasts markedly with the voluptuous kind generally found in the poems of other Marinists. Croce's estimation seems to be supported by Pers's sonnet "Bella per nome Chiarastella" (Beautiful Woman Named Chiarastella), which was published posthumously, as was most of his poetry, in 1666. Starting with the woman's name, which means "bright star," and going on to the notion of a star or heavenly entity found on Earth, the poem recalls the Petrarchan tradition, while the *dolce stil nuovo* seems to have influenced the description of the beloved as an angelic creature sent by God. In the end, however, Chiarastella is not depicted as having been sent by God; after various suggestions as to who she may be—Sirius, or the constellation of the Great Bear—it is proposed that she is the goddess Venus and is in charge of the third heaven in the Ptolemaic system of the universe. The sonnet ends with a prayer that at least one beam of her light may guide the smitten heart through a sea of tears into a safe haven. Pers concludes the sonnet with a Marinist *concetto* (concept)—a witty metaphor, often a paradox or antithesis—as he describes the bright star/woman emitting a beam of light that has the power to burn but, at the same time, to bless.

Pers was born on 17 April 1599 into the noble family of Pers at its castle in San Daniele, near Udine in the northern Italian region of Friuli. His parents were Giulio Antonio dei Signori di Pers and Ginevra dei Signori di Colloredo. While studying literature and philosophy at the University of Bologna, he met many notable men of science and letters, possibly including Nicolaus Copernicus. He associated with and learned much from the poets Claudio Achillini and Girolamo Preti, and he met poets from other parts of Europe, including the Spaniards Francisco de Quevedo, Luis de Góngora, and Lope de Vega (on the occasion of whose death in 1635 Pers wrote two commemorative sonnets).

Pers published infrequently: usually poem by poem rather than in collections, often in manuscript form, in response to some specific occasion. He thought of himself as an amateur not worthy of serious attention from critics. One of his earliest publications was the autobiographical ode "Fileno racconsolato" (Fileno Consoled)—Fileno is the name he uses for himself in the poem. He recited the ode before a meeting of the Accademia dei Disuniti (Academy of the Disunited) in Pisa in 1627; it was published in his *Poesie* (Poesy) in 1666.

In 1620 Pers had fallen in love with his cousin, the noblewoman Taddea di Colloredo, but her parents would not permit them to marry. Pers decided to enter monastic life, joining the Knights of Malta in 1627. Colloredo became the beloved woman of his love poetry, in which she is always referred to by the classical name Nicea.

Pers spent his years with the Knights of Malta on galleys in the eastern Mediterranean, fighting the Ottoman Turks. He describes his experiences in an ode he wrote at the time, "A Iola: Racconta l'auttore i viaggi fatti sopra le galere di Malta" (To Iola: The Author Recounts His Voyages on the Galleys of Malta). The poem tells of sailing on the open sea and visiting various regions surrounding the Mediterranean—particularly ancient cities in ruins, which stimulate reflection on one of his favorite subjects: the rapid passage of earthly glory. Of such once-proud cities "sasso a pena / v'è ch'a sasso sovrasta" (hardly a stone / remains that rests on another stone). Immediately afterward the description becomes repetitive in the typical Marinist manner. The poem does, however, include many effective passages. For example, the sudden appearance of the Turkish fleet on the horizon at Alexandria is pictured with images such as "di torreggianti pini / la vasta forma" (the vast mass / of towering pines), referring to the masts, and the "tremolar le tracie lune" (crescent moons quivering) on the sterns. After the battle, he arrives at the island of Cyprus, the legendary home of Aphrodite, and exclaims, "Anco qui regna Amore" (Here, too, Love rules). This phrase is one of the many instances in his poetry of language that evokes Petrarch—intentionally, it appears in this case, as shown by the addition of "anco" (too) to the original words, "Here Love rules," in Petrarch's canzone "Chiare fresche e dolci acque" (Clear, fresh and dulcet streams). Much of the imagery is Marinistic: for instance, in describing Sicily he makes Mount Etna, with its fiery crater surrounded by snow, an oxymoronic emblem. The description seems poetically fanciful; it is, however, an accurate picture of the summit of the volcano.

Pers left the Knights of Malta in 1629 and returned to his birthplace, the castle in San Daniele. He remained there for the rest of his life, physically isolated but in touch with the literary community through correspondence with his many friends. Among them was Carlo de' Dottori, a playwright who was also a friend of the Tuscan poet, physician, and experimental scientist Francesco Redi. Pers thereby kept abreast of what was happening in the great centers of culture such as Venice, Florence, Turin, Rome, Genoa, and Pisa. He also continued to compose texts of various kinds, including poems.

Much of Pers's poetry is deeply pessimistic. In one of the two sonnets he wrote about the hourglass he says: "sol di travagli nel morir mi privo, / finirà con la vita il mio martoro" (in dying I give up nothing but my suffering; / my martyrdom will end with the end of my life). The mournful ode "Della miseria e vanità umana" (On Human Wretchedness and Vanity) is a series of vignettes describing a person defeated and rendered helpless by life. In the first vignette a lengthy sequence of metaphorical images—fog suddenly dispersed, a flash of lightning, flowers that bloom and quickly fade or are consumed or destroyed in various ways—illustrate how mortal life is an empty shadow. The sequence is followed by a description of a solitary farmer bending over and working the soil; the land had promised abundant sustenance, but drought has left it barren.

Pers's best-known works are his poems about devices for telling time: hourglasses, sundials, and clocks. The seventeenth century regarded the measurement of time as of fundamental importance to the development of science. Pers's "clock poems" address the ineluctable passage of time and the fleetingness of human life, themes that were dominant in Petrarch's lyrics in the fourteenth century; they also recall poems by Quevedo. The affinities between Quevedo and Pers probably reflect the influence of the Spaniard on the Italian. Pers uses many of the same titles as Quevedo and correspondences also can be observed in the content: in phrases such as the Spanish *reloj molesto* (irksome clock), which is echoed by the Italian *orologio molesto,* and in concepts such as the glass in the hourglass representing the living human body and the sand symbolizing the dust to which the body reverts at death. In the sonnet that begins "Mobile ordigno di dentate rote" (A mobile device of toothed wheels) Pers describes the mechanism of the clock as it

> lacera il giorno e lo divide in ore
> ed ha scritto di fuor con fosche note
> a chi legger le sa: *Sempre si more.*

> (lacerates the day, dividing it into hours,
> and has, inscribed on its face in melancholy notes
> for those who know how to read them: *We die continually.*)

The poem is witty, but the cleverness does not detract from the seriousness of the theme. The final tercets read:

> Perch'io non speri mai riposo o pace
> questo che sembra in un timpano e tromba
> mi sfida ogn'or contro a l'età vorace
> e con que' colpi onde 'l metal rimbomba
> affretta il corso al secolo fugace
> e, perché s'apra, ogn'or picchia a la tomba.

> (Since I may never hope for rest or peace,
> this clock, that seems both drum and trumpet,
> impels me to face voracious time.
> And with such tolling, which makes metal resound,
> it speeds up the course of the fleeting world
> and now knocks at the door of the tomb to make it open.)

Critics have discussed whether Marinist poetry conveys genuinely felt emotion or merely reflects a fascination with the technical features of the writing itself. Petrarch used some of the same technical devices as the Marinisti but is universally admired, while poets of the age of Marino have received harsh criticism. A certain amount of clever rhetoric is deemed acceptable, but the repetitive use of many witty figures in a short span of text is thought to show a lack of imagination and to produce indifference in the reader. In Pers's sonnet "Sopra l'archibugiar in valle" (On the Harquebus Fired in the Valley) a hunter waits through the night for his prey; at dawn he fires one shot and kills a thousand birds. Instead of dealing with the moral issues that arise when a thousand deaths are brought about, the poem ends with a type of conceit that was used repeatedly by the Marinists: the pun created by the similarity between the words *piombo* (lead) and *piombare* (to fall). With the motion of one finger the hunter is able to "Far il piombo volar, piombar il volo" (cause lead to fly, and flying things to fall like lead).

In 1652 Pers was invited by Dottori to write a sonnet for a commemorative collection of poems in honor of Queen Christina of Sweden. He replied that he was firmly resolved to write no more poetry, especially on command; even so, he sent a sonnet, referring to it as "parto più della mia obbidienza che del mio ingegno" (born of my obedience rather than my wit). In 1654 the duke of Modena, Francesco I d'Este, asked Pers to become tutor to his son Almerigo. Pers declined the offer, explaining to a friend that he preferred to stay in his castle and enjoy the freedom of not having to adhere to schedules or respond to the wishes of other people. When the Este family repeated the invitation, he replied that he was not suited for life among courtiers because it had become impossible for him to relearn the courtly skills of "come si celino i sentimenti che si hanno, e come si palesino quelli che non si hanno" (how to hide the feelings you have, and show those you do not have). Nevertheless, he received visits from prominent people and even appeared briefly at court at times; once he did so at the request of Holy Roman Emperor Leopold I, who was staying at nearby Gorizia.

During the last years of his life Pers studied the classical tragedies of Sophocles and Seneca and wrote a tragedy of his own: *L'umiltà esaltata ovvero Ester Regina* (1664, Humility Praised; or, Queen Esther). It is based on the Old Testament Book of Esther, in which Queen Esther saves the Hebrews from annihilation by the Persians.

Pers was often in unbearable pain from kidney and bladder stones but wrote about them humorously. "Travagliato l'autore da mal di pietra" (The Author Afflicted by the Malady of Stones) is a rhetorical game of clever conceits based on antitheses such as "servono i sassi a fabricar, ma questi / per distrugger la fabrica son nati" (stones are used to build, but these / in my body are born to destroy the building) and on witty metaphors such as "ben posso chiamar mia sorte dura / s'ell'è di pietra" (my fate is truly hard, / it's made of stone) and "Ha preso a lapidarmi / da le parti di dentro la natura" (nature has begun to stone me / from the inside). Some critics have condemned the poem for its excessive number of variations on the same theme, concluding that Pers missed an opportunity to offer a profound contemplation of the imminence of death. Others, however, claim that there is an unavoidable poignancy in this ironic contemplation of the exasperating and unfair afflictions of age. Pers died on 7 April 1663.

Nearly twenty editions of Pers's poetry appeared between 1666 and 1689. For the next two centuries publication of his poems was limited to the occasional appearance of one or more of about twenty sonnets that came to be favored by compilers of anthologies of lyric poetry of the Italian Baroque such as Croce, Giuseppe Guido Ferrero, Giovanni Getto, Carlo Muscetta, and Pier Paolo Ferrante. The first complete edition of Pers's poems since the seventeenth century was edited in 1978 by Michele Rak.

Critics have begun to take a more careful look at Ciro di Pers and to try to make a precise assessment of the roles played by Marinism and anti-Marinism in shaping his poetry. Quinto Marini suggests that it may even be possible to reverse the prevailing view of Pers as a Marinist poet and to locate him among the anti-Marinists of his day. Positive critical judgments of Pers are frequently made, and his important place in the history of Italian poetry is indicated by assertions of the influence he may have had on the eighteenth- and nineteenth-century pre-Romantic trend, on some sonnets of Vittorio Alfieri, and on Italy's greatest nineteenth-century poet, Giacomo Leopardi.

Letters:
Natale Busetto, *Carlo de' Dottori, letterato padovano del secolo decimosettimo* (Città di Castello: Lapi, 1902), pp. 289-305.

Bibliography:
Lorenzo Carpané, *La tradizione manoscritta e a stampa delle poesie di Ciro di Pers* (Milan: Guerini, 1997).

Biography:
Ginetta Auzzas, "Pers, Ciro di (1599-1663)," in *Dizionario critico della letteratura italiana,* volume 3, edited by Vittore Branca (Turin: Unione Tipografico-Editrice Torinese, 1986), pp. 417-419.

References:
Vitaniello Bonito, "Intertestualità barocche: Quevedo e Ciro di Pers," *Rivista di letterature moderne e comparate,* 45, no. 3 (1992): 231-244;

Bonito, "Il nodo dell'antitesi: Da Góngora a Ciro di Pers," *Lingua e stile,* 23, no. 3 (1988): 427-444;

Bonito, *L'occhio del tempo: L'orologio barocco tra letteratura, scienza ed emblematica* (Bologna: Clueb, 1995), p. 138;

Natale Busetto, *Carlo de' Dottori, letterato padovano del secolo decimosettimo* (Città di Castello: Lapi, 1902), pp. 104-105;

Ciro di Pers, 1599-1999: Atti del Convegno Nazionale "4 secoli di Ciro di Pers" (San Daniele del Friuli: Grafiche Tielle, 2000);

Benedetto Croce, *Saggi sulla letteratura del Seicento* (Bari: Laterza, 1924), pp. 359, 389;

Giovanni Getto, ed., *Opere scelte di Giovan Battista Marino e dei Marinisti* (Turin: Unione Tipografico-Editrice Torinese, 1962);

Carmine Jannaco and Martino Capucci, *Il Seicento* (Padua: Piccin Nuova Libraria, 1986), pp. 282, 299-304;

Quinto Marini, "'Chiare fresche e dolci acque': Ciro di Pers, *Poesie,* edited by Michele Rak," *Rassegna della letteratura italiana,* 83 (1979): 417-420;

Domenico Pancini, *Ciro di Vermo-Pers: Memorie biografiche letterarie* (Udine: Patronato, 1883);

Olimpia Pelosi, "The Ellipse and the Circle: An Analysis of Some Lyrics by Ciro di Pers between *Anima in Barocco* and Neoplatonism," in *The Image of the Baroque,* edited by Aldo Scaglione and Gianni Eugenio Viola (New York: Peter Lang, 1995), pp. 93-107;

Mario Pinna, "Quevedo e Ciro di Pers," *Filologia moderna,* 4 (1965): 211-221.

Papers:
Manuscripts and letters of Ciro di Pers are at the Biblioteca Comunale of San Daniele del Friuli and the Biblioteca Comunale of Udine.

Girolamo Preti
(1582 – 6 April 1626)

Paschal C. Viglionese
University of Rhode Island

SELECTED BOOKS: *La Salmace, idilio del signor Girolamo Preti bolognese, dedicato al molto illustre signore, il sig. Gio. Battista Visconti* (Bologna: Rossi, 1608); translated as "Salmacis," in *Poems and Translations, Amorous, Lusory, Morall, Divine*, edited and translated by Edward Sherburne (London: Printed by W. Hunt for Thomas Dring, 1651);

Rime di Girolamo Preti al serenissimo signor d. Alfonso d'Este prencipe di Modana (Bologna: B. Cocchi, 1618)–includes "Oronta di Cipro," translated by Thomas Stanley as "Oronta," in his *Poems* (London, 1651).

Editions and Collections: *Gl'Idillii di diversi ingegni illustri del secol nostro novamente raccolti da Gio. Batt. Bidelli; insieme aggiontovi alcuni non più veduti* (Milan: Bidelli, 1618);

Lirici marinisti, edited by Benedetto Croce (Bari: Laterza, 1911), pp. 55–62;

Marino e i marinisti, edited by Giuseppe Guido Ferrero (Milan & Naples: Ricciardi, 1954), pp. 711–719;

Lirici marinisti, edited by Giovanni Getto, volume 2 (Turin: TEA, 1962), pp. 115–117, 174–178;

La Salmace e altri idilli barocchi: Preti–Argoli–Busenelli, edited by Marzio Pieri (Verona: Fiorini, 1987);

Poesie, edited by Domenico Chiodo (San Mauro Torinese: RES, 1991);

Poesie, edited by Stefano Barelli, *Scrittori italiani commentati*, no. 14 (Rome: Antenore, 2006).

Edition in English: "From Girolamo Preti, out of Italian, on a Race-Horse," "On the Death of Cynthia's Horse: A Sonnet," and "Love's Garden: Translated from Girolamo Preti," translated by Philip Ayres, in his *Lyric Poems, Made in Imitation of the Italians, of Which Many Are Translations from Other Languages* (London: Printed by J. M. for Jos. Knight and F. Saunders, 1687), pp. 273, 275, 278.

OTHER: "Discorso intorno all'onestà della poesia," preface to *Le lagrime di Maria Vergine*, by Ridolfo Campeggi (Bologna: B. Ciocchi, 1618);

Several sonnets in Lodovico Antonio Muratori, *Della perfetta poesia italiana spiegata, e dimostrata con varie osservazioni*, volume 1 (Modena: B. Soliani, 1706).

Although Girolamo Preti has long been identified as a slavish follower of Giambattista Marino, the most important seventeenth-century Italian poet, his work actually reveals decidedly anti-Marinist tendencies. Domenico Chiodo, the editor of a 1991 edition of Preti's works, maintains that the most serious of Preti's many misfortunes was the mistaken reputation he acquired. That reputation was created by Preti's own avowals, as in his sonnet "Alla penna del Cavalier Marino" (1618, To the Pen of Cavalier Marino), that he was a loyal follower of the master, and it was solidified in the centuries following his death as a result of the limited number of his works that were available: beginning in the eighteenth century the tendency in literary circles was to neglect the writers of the age of Marino. Thus, it was taken for granted that Preti was no more than an imitator of the leader of the prevailing seventeenth-century Italian school; in fact, he was one of the strongest anti-Marinist poets of the time.

Preti was born into an aristocratic family in Bologna in 1582. He studied law at the University of Bologna in the first decade of the seventeenth century; the poet Claudio Achillini was a member of the law faculty, and the two became close friends. Preti spent nearly all his life as a page, *maestro di camera* (chamber master), or secretary in the service of various princes and influential ecclesiastics. In addition to Bologna, he lived in Modena, Genoa, Turin, and Rome.

Preti's first work, *La Salmace* (1608; translated as "Salmacis," 1651), is an *idillio* (idyll) recounting the story from Ovid's *Metamorphoses* of the naiad Salmacis and Hermaphrodite, the son of Hermes and Aphrodite. The differences between *La Salmace* and the *idilli favolosi* (fabulous idylls) and *idilli pastorali* (pastoral idylls) in Marino's *La Sampogna* (1620, The Panpipe) are striking. The latter work offers many examples of the excesses typical of Marinistic poetry; for instance, when the trees and animals of the forest gather to listen to the beautiful music made by Orpheus, each is named and is described, usually by means of a conceit: the cypress is the "piramide dei boschi, arbor gigante, / emulator degli obelischi alteri" (Pyramid of the forest, giant tree, / emulator of lofty obelisks). This mass of detail contrasts with Preti's use of a minimum of descriptive elements. For example, in *La Salmace* he writes of a lake with small fish that have black backs and silver undersides; Chiodo selects the passage to highlight Preti's masterful descriptions of nature as a dominant feature of his poems:

> Ma, come il sol per lucido cristallo,
> Così 'l guardo per l'onde
> Penetrando s'interna, e scorge in quelle
> Di coloriti sassi
> Dipinto il suolo e miniato il fondo,
> E mirando distingue
> I muti nuotatori a cento a cento,
> Ch'hanno d'ebano il dorso, il sen d'argento.
>
> (Like the sun
> Penetrating lucid glass
> Your gaze enters within the waves,
> And sees in them
> The soil of the bottom
> Painted with colored pebbles,
> And as it observes it makes out silent swimmers by the hundreds,
> With backs of ebony, breasts of silver.)

Petrarchan echoes in *La Salmace* show that Preti maintained links with tradition when the prevailing sentiment among the Marinisti was to emphasize the gap between the modern and the old and largely to reject the latter. Petrarch's sonnet "Solo e pensoso i più deserti campi" (Alone and Lost in Thought in the Most Forsaken Fields) includes the phrase "stampa l'arena" (sets foot on the ground); in *La Salmace* Preti writes:

> Ma la ninfa gentile,
> D'altri studi seguace,
> Del bel fiorito loco altera Donna,
> Fuor del romito suo noto confine
> Sdegna con l'orme sue stampar l'arena.
>
> (But the gentle nymph,
> Learned in other fields of study,
> The haughty ruler of the flowery place,
> Does not deign to set foot on the ground
> Outside her familiar rustic confines.)

The immediately following lines are another of the many echoes of Petrarchan wording: "Quivi a le belle membra / Porge il lago vicino" (Here near her lovely form / The lake is placed) recalls "Ove porse le belle membra / colei che sola a me par donna" (Where she who alone seems a woman to me / placed her lovely form) from Petrarch's famous canzone of the *locus amoenus* (pleasant place), "Chiare, fresche, e dolci acque" (Clear, Cool, and Fresh Waters). The links with his great predecessor are strengthened when Preti writes of Salmacis:

> Or s'arretra, or s'inoltra,
> Or sembra audace, or agghiaccia, e in un momento
> Cangia speme, pensier, voglia e spavento.
>
> (Now she stops, and then moves forward,
> Now she seems brave, at other times frozen with fear, and in one and the same instant
> Switches hope, thought, will and fear.)

The parallel with Petrarch's canzone "Di pensier in pensier" (From Thought to Thought) can easily be seen:

> Ivi s'acqueta l'alma sbigottita;
> et come Amor l'envita,
> or ride, or piange, or teme, or s'assecura;
> e 'l volto che lei segue ov'ella il mena
> si turba et rasserena,
> et in un esser picciol tempo dura.
>
> (Here my troubled soul is calmed;
> and as love dictates
> now laughs, now weeps, now fears, now is reassured;
> and my appearance, which follows wherever the soul takes it,
> grows troubled, then serene,
> and stays one way but briefly.)

La Salmace was Preti's most widely read work both in Italy and abroad.

Preti published an authorized collection of his poetry in Bologna in 1618. He explains in the dedication to the duke of Modena, Cesare d'Este, that he has seen many of his poems that were not ready for publication circulating in manuscript form or stolen by printers for their own financial gain. How curious, he muses, to see compositions having better fortune than their composer. He tells Alfonso that "Cominciai a peregrinar per lo mondo . . . per tutto 'l corso dell'età mia, cangiando diversi paesi, impiegandomi in diversi studi, applicandomi a diverse professioni, aggirato da diversi travagli, in tanta varietà di vita trovai sempre uniformità di fortuna" (I began to wander through the world . . . for the entire course of my life, changing to different countries, engaging in different kinds of study, practicing different professions, surrounded by different travails, I always found uniformity of fortune). He laments that he was never able to spend all his time composing poetry; he envies those who were able to write poetry as recre-

Frontispiece and title page for a volume that includes the English translation of Girolamo Preti's La Salmace *(Huntington Library)*

ation and "per ischerzo acquistarsi l'immortalità" (achieve immortality while at play). He says that his one bit of good luck was the protection he received from the House of Este, which enabled him to begin the study of literature. (His protection by the Este family had begun during his early childhood, during the reign of Duke Alfonso II of Ferrara and Modena, and continued under Alfonso's cousin, Cesare, who succeeded Alfonso in 1597. In 1598 the fief of Ferrara had been returned to the Papal States, and Cesare had moved his court from Ferrara to Modena.) Later, however, he lost the tranquillity necessary for fruitful literary studies; a life of constant turmoil is not conducive to devotion to the Muses. If he had a moment or two of respite from his misfortunes, he says, he would use it for other kinds of study that, while not more serious or important than poetry, could be materially rewarding with less effort than poetry requires.

The 1618 collection includes the sonnet "Un pastor descrive un luogo dove la sua ninfa stava sollazzandosi" (A Shepherd Describes a Place Where His Nymph Once Stayed to Refresh Herself). The title is suggestive of Petrarch's canzone of the *locus amoenus,* "Chiare, fresche, e dolci acque." The mild eroticism of Preti's work is exemplified in the first tercet of the sonnet:

Mira, o Tirsi, colà, come lasciva
or bagna il suo bel viso ed or le piante
ne l'onda cristallina e fuggitiva.

(Behold, Tirsi, over there, how she first bathes
her beautiful face and then her feet
in the fleeting, crystalline wave.)

Benedetto Croce cites the final tercet of the sonnet as an effective description of a "tacito paesaggio alpestre" (quiet mountain landscape):

> I' giurerei che quella rupe amante
> è di lei fatta; e quella fonte viva
> è di pianto amoroso onda stillante.
>
> (I would swear that the rock
> has become her lover; and that the spring
> is now a gushing wave of tears of love.)

The collection also includes "Oronta di Cipro" (Oronta of Cyprus; translated as "Oronta," 1651), an epic written in the standard ottava rima of Italian narrative verse. The young heroine is among the Cypriots being taken to Byzantium as slaves after the Ottoman conquest of Cyprus in 1571. When the prisoners' prayer for a storm to sink the ship is not answered, Oronta ignites the gunpowder stored in the hold; the entire Turkish fleet catches fire and is destroyed. Chiodo observes that the tale is told masterfully and that its description of a storm at sea is reminiscent of a passage in Virgil's *Aeneid*.

Also in 1618 Preti contributed the preface to his friend Ridolfo Campeggi's *Le lagrime di Maria Vergine* (The Tears of the Virgin Mary): "Discorso intorno all'onestà della poesia" (Discourse on the Propriety of Poetry). The preface is unusual in that it is an essay on poetic theory rather than the usual praise of the author, the work, or the patron to whom the book is dedicated, and it is also significant for its anti-Marinism. Preti condemns the emphasis in the poetry of his day on the sexual and physical aspects of love at the expense of the sentimental attributes and expresses gratitude that Campeggi's poem "non vaneggiasse fra le lascivie e fra gli amori" (did not stray among lasciviousness and loves). In the first few sentences Preti restates the ancient idea of the social utility of poetry: before one can judge a poem to be worthy of applause, one must find in it the neoclassicist pair "l'utile" (the useful) and "lo diletto" (the enjoyable). Campeggi's poem, he notes, avoids excesses of "impudicizia" (licentiousness) and combines the useful and the pleasurable. Poetry, like all art, must justify its existence by serving the ends of the well-being and the betterment of humanity. Poets who neglect to exploit the power of their art to influence for good but include instead the licentious and the lascivious are inspired by Satan. He also affirms the value of the formal decorum of poetry, which seems to have been superseded by uninhibited embellishment of language: he condemns flamboyance for its own sake, which was typical of poets who had fallen under the spell of Marino, to the detriment of the rules of good poetic composition. The poetry of his day, Preti observes, is contaminated by the presence not only of elements that are of no practical use—embellishment—but also of dangerous ones: licentious subject matter. Preti does not exempt himself from the accusations he makes, referring at one point to "miei pochi e deboli componimenti" (my few and weak compositions) in which he was guilty of straying from moral and pious thoughts into libidinous ones. Examples of the sensuality and carnality of the age can be found in Preti's poetry; but in general his eroticism is rather subdued, and there is a great deal of admonishment to keep love on a spiritual level. His poems are also largely free of *arguzia* (verbal wit or cleverness), the mainstay of the Marinist poets. Only occasionally does Preti show an inclination of his own toward using poetic conceits—as he does, for example, at the end of the "Discorso intorno all'onestà della poesia" itself, where he calls for "una poetica teologia, e una teologica poesia" (a poetical theology, and a theological poetry).

Immediately after Marino's lengthy narrative poem *L'Adone* (excerpts translated as *Adonis: Selections from* L'Adone *of Giambattista Marino,* 1967) was published in Paris in 1623, Agazio di Somma, a cleric who was a friend of both Marino's and Preti's, claimed in a talk delivered before the Accademia degli Umoristi (Academy of the Humorists) in Rome that it was the equal of, or even better than, Torquato Tasso's *Gerusalemme liberata* (1581, Jerusalem Delivered; translated as *Godfrey of Bulloigne, or The Recoverie of Hierusalem,* 1594) and that Preti agreed with this assessment. Four years earlier Preti had written Marino from Bologna that he judged Marino to have surpassed all other poets in all ages not only in lyric but also in heroic and epic verse and had referred to the anxious wait of all Italy for the soon-to-be-published *L'Adone*. Nevertheless, he publicly announced that he did not agree with Somma about the superiority of *L'Adone* to *Gerusalemme liberata*. Marino wrote Preti from Naples in the summer of 1624 to express dismay at his comments. The following year Preti wrote to Achillini, giving an account of Marino's death on 25 March 1625 and recalling with regret that his response to Somma had led the master to consider him disloyal.

Preti's letter to Achillini was written from Rome, where he served as *maestro di camera* to Cardinal Antonio Barberini and then as secretary to Cardinal Francesco Barberini; both men were nephews of Maffeo Barberini, who became Pope Urban VIII in 1623. In 1626 Francesco Barberini took Preti with him on a mission to King Philip III of Spain. Preti became gravely ill on the voyage and died on 6 April, shortly after landing in Barcelona.

Lodovico Antonio Muratori, one of the leaders of the Arcadian Academy and of the rationalist, neoclassicist age of *Illuminismo* (Enlightenment) in Italy, included several sonnets by Preti in his *Della perfetta poesia italiana spiegata, e dimostrata con varie osservazioni* (1706, On Perfect Italian Poetry Displayed, and Demonstrated with Various Observations). But most Arcadians found little of value in Preti's work. Preti's reputation as a strict follower of Marino is based on a limited selection of his short lyric poems; little attention has been paid to his longer pieces, even though *La Salmace* was his most widely read work in its time and, in the opinion of many, is his best and historically most important one. Critics such as Franco Croce and Marzio Pieri believe that had he lived longer, Girolamo Preti might have displaced Gabriello Chiabrera as the generally recognized leader of the trend away from Marinism.

Letters:

Giambattista Marino, *Epistolario,* volume 2, edited by Angelo Borzelli and Fausto Nicolini (Bari: Laterza, 1911), pp. 52–55, 61, 97–98, 149–152, 162–164, 168–169, 175–178, 243–248;

Marino, *Lettere,* edited by Marziano Guglielminetti (Turin: Einaudi, 1966), pp. 239–240, 394–401.

References:

Domenico Chiodo, "Introduzione al 'Discorso intorno all'onestà della poesia' di Girolamo Preti," *Stracciafoglio,* 1, no. 1 (2000) <http://www.edres.it/num1.html> (accessed 19 December 2007);

Chiodo, "Note sull'opera di Girolamo Preti," *Giornale storico della letteratura italiana,* 169 (1992): 253–277;

Chiodo, "Preti, Tassoni e la paternità della dedicatoria al Barberini," *Critica letteraria,* 81 (1993): 781–788;

Jackson I. Cope, "Preti's Aesthetic Allegory: A Marinistic Poem on Violence in Love and Art," *Modern Language Notes,* 72 (1962): 92–94;

Benedetto Croce, *Saggi sulla letteratura del Seicento* (Bari: Laterza, 1924), p. 373;

Franco Croce, *Tre momenti del barocco letterario italiano* (Florence: Sansoni, 1966), pp. 6–92;

James V. Mirollo, *The Poet of the Marvelous: Giambattista Marino* (New York: Columbia University Press, 1963), pp. 258–259;

Francesco Saverio Quadrio, *Della storia e della ragione di ogni poeta,* volume 2 (Bologna & Milan: Pisani & Agnelli, 1752), p. 297;

Mario Rosa, "The 'World's Theatre': The Court of Rome and Politics in the First Half of the Seventeenth Century," in *Court and Politics in Papal Rome, 1492–1700,* edited by Gianvittorio Signorotto and Maria Antonietta Visceglia (Cambridge: Cambridge University Press, 2002), p. 85.

Gerolamo Tiraboschi, *Storia della letteratura italiana,* volume 4 (Milan: Bettoni, 1833), p. 552;

Claudio Varese, "La lirica concettistica," in *Storia della letteratura italiana,* volume 5, edited by Emilio Cecchi and Natalino Sapegno (Milan: Garzanti, 1967), pp. 788–813.

Ottavio Rinuccini

(20 January 1562 – 28 March 1621)

Maria Galli Stampino
University of Miami

BOOKS: *Maschereata di bergiere* (Florence: Giorgio Marescotti, 1590);

La Dafne (Florence: Giorgio Marescotti, 1600);

L'Euridice (Florence: Cosimo Giunti, 1600);

L'Arianna (Mantua: Osanna, 1608);

Mascherata dell'ingrate (Mantua: Osanna, 1608);

Mascherata di ninfe di Senna (Florence: Marescotti's heirs, 1613);

Comparsa d'eroi celesti (Florence: Marescotti's heirs, 1613);

Mascherata di selvaggi (Florence: Marescotti's heirs, 1613);

Versi sacri cantati nella Cappella della Serenissima Arciduchessa d'Austria, G. Duchessa di Toscana (Florence: Zanobi Pignoni, 1619);

Poesie del Sig. Ottavio Rinuccini (Florence: Giunti, 1622);

Il Narciso, edited by Luigi Maria Rezzi (Rome: Vincenzo Poggiali, 1829);

Gli albori del melodramma, volume 2: *Ottavio Rinuccini,* edited by Angelo Solerti (Milan: Sandron, 1904).

PLAY PRODUCTIONS: *Maschere d'amazzoni,* Florence, Pitti Palace, 1579;

Rinaldo e il Tasso, Florence, 6 February 1586;

Intermezzo about the contest between the Muses and Pierides, music by Luca Marenzio, Florence, Uffizi Theater, 2 May 1589;

Intermezzo about Apollo's fight with Python, music by Marenzio, Florence, Uffizi Theater, 2 May 1589;

Intermezzo about Arion's Song, music by Cristofano Malvezzi and Emilio de' Cavalieri, Florence, Uffizi Theater, 2 May 1589;

Intermezzo about Apollo and Bacchus's descent to earth from heaven with Rhythm and Harmony, music by Malvezzi, Florence, Uffizi Theater, 2 May 1589;

Mascherata di bergiere, Florence, 1590;

Mascherata degli accecati, music by Pietro Strozzi, Florence, Pitti Palace, 25 February 1596;

Mascherata di stelle, Florence, Pitti Palace, 27 February 1596;

La Dafne, music by Jacopo Peri, Florence, home of Jacopo Corsi, 1597;

L'Euridice, music by Peri, Florence, Pitti Palace, 6 October 1600;

L'Arianna, music by Claudio Monteverdi, Mantua, 28 May 1608;

Balletto dell'ingrate, music by Monteverdi, Mantua, Ducal Theater, 4 June 1608;

Mascherata di ninfe di Senna, Florence, Pitti Palace, 14 February 1613;

Comparsa d'eroi celesti, Florence, 17 February 1613;

Mascherata di selvaggi, Florence, Strozzi Palace, 5 February 1614;

Versi sacri, Florence, Pitti Palace Chapel, 2 April 1619;

L'annunciazione, Florence, Pitti Palace Chapel, 25 February 1620.

As the author of *La Dafne* (Daphne), set to music by Jacopo Peri and first performed in 1597, Ottavio Rinuccini is often called "the earliest librettist," and his choice of verse forms influenced poems that were written to be set to music for centuries. Nevertheless, his poetry has attracted little critical attention, and a modern edition of the part of his production that was not set to music is still lacking.

Rinuccini was born on 20 January 1562 into a noble Florentine family that had distinguished itself in cultural and diplomatic affairs for three centuries. His poetry indicates that he was educated as a young nobleman would have been in the Florentine intellectual circles of his time: he would have learned Latin and Greek, and through readings and exercises he would have acquired rich rhetorical and poetic skills.

For the 1579 wedding of Francesco I de' Medici, Grand Duke of Tuscany, and Bianca Cappello, Rinuccini composed *Maschere d'amazzoni* (Masks of the Amazons), which is extant only in manuscript. It consists of six octaves, spoken or sung–it is unclear whether it was ever set to music–by Amazons who praise their warring life and despise the lives of other women. The message to the bride is that she, like the Amazons, must stay

Title page for the first edition of Ottavio Rinuccini's Daphne, *generally considered the first opera (University of Turin)*

away from "dov'arde d'amor lascivo foco" (the place where the lusty fire of love burns).

From a metrical standpoint *Maschere d'amazzoni* established the model for all of the short pieces that Rinuccini subsequently composed for dancing. His second courtly work, also extant only in manuscript, was *Rinaldo e il Tasso* (Rinaldo and Tasso), a masked ball performed during a joust in honor of the wedding of Cesare d'Este and Virginia de' Medici on 6 February 1586. The work consists of two parts of five octaves each. In the first part Rinaldo calls on his opponents to fight him; in the second part Rinaldo, directed by Torquato Tasso, battles infernal demons, as he does in Tasso's epic poem *Gerusalemme liberata* (1581, Jerusalem Delivered; translated as *Godfrey of Bulloigne, or The Recoverie of Hierusalem,* 1594). On 4 September 1586 Rinuccini was inducted into the Accademia degli Alterati (Academy of the Altered), of which his older brother, Alessandro, was already a member. He took the name "Sonnacchioso" (The Sleepy One).

For the monthlong celebration in 1589 of the wedding of the grand duke of Tuscany, Ferdinando I de' Medici, and Christine of Lorraine six intermezzi were staged three times each at the Uffizi Theater in Florence: on 2 May before, between the acts of, and after Girolamo Bargagli's *La pellegrina* (The Female Pilgrim) by the Sienese Intronati (Stunned) troupe; on 6 May before, between the acts of, and after *La zingara* (The Gypsy Woman) by the Gelosi (Zealous) troupe; and on 13 May before, between the acts of, and after *La pazzia d'Isabella* (The Madness of Isabella) by the Gelosi. Rinuccini wrote all of the lyrics for the second intermezzo, about the contest between the Muses and Pierides; for the third intermezzo, about Apollo's fight with the dragon Python; and for the sixth intermezzo, about Apollo and Bacchus's descent to earth from heaven with Rhythm and Harmony. He wrote most of the lyrics for the fifth intermezzo, Arion's song (one madrigal was by Giovanni de' Bardi). The second and third intermezzi were set to music by Luca Marenzio, the fifth by Cristofano Malvezzi, and the sixth by Malvezzi and Emilio de' Cavalieri. These pieces mark Rinuccini's shift to freer verse forms: they are madrigals in *settenari* (seven-syllable lines) and *endecasillabi* (eleven-syllable lines), occasionally arranged according to a rhyme scheme.

During the following seven years Rinuccini wrote three *mascherate* (masquerades) for the Florentine court; the first, the *Mascherata di bergiere* (1590, Masquerade of Shepherdesses), was his earliest printed work. Dedicated to Christine of Lorraine and consisting of eleven octaves, it is a narrative piece about a group of shepherdesses who leave France to join their queen in Florence; it was sung by Lucia Caccini, the wife of the composer and singer Giulio Caccini. The *Mascherata degli accecati* (Masquerade of the Men Blinded by Love) and the *Mascherata di stelle* (Masquerade of Stars) were performed during carnival season of 1596, on 25 and 27 February, respectively. Neither was published at the time; they first appeared in print in 1904. Set to music by Pietro Strozzi, the *Mascherata degli accecati* comprises five six-line stanzas rhyming ABABCC; the first line in each stanza is a *settenario,* and the rest are *endecasillabi.* The theme and vocabulary draw heavily from the Petrarchan tradition of describing the features of the beloved's face, especially her eyes. The *Mascherata di stelle* is a two-octave piece dedicated to Christine of Lorraine. The dancers, the "Donna real" (Royal Lady) observes, "Donne non son, ma de 'l ciel lumi e stelle" (Are not women, but stars that light up the sky) and "muovon danzando il piè per tuo diletto" (move their feet in dance for your enjoyment). Marie de' Medici, the daughter of Francesco and niece of Ferdinando, appeared in the production. The *mascherata* celebrates both its dedicatee and its performers but is virtually unintelligible without the dedicatory letter in which

Rinuccini specifies the dancers' fictional identities. He endowed the characters in his works with as many identifying features as possible, but misidentifications occurred even on the part of audience members who were well versed in classical mythology.

Rinuccini's next work was *La Dafne;* a play set to music in its entirety, it is generally considered the first opera. It was first performed semiprivately in the home of Jacopo Corsi in Florence in 1597. The prologue is sung by Ovid, whose *Metamorphoses* provides the subject matter; the six scenes are written in alternating *settenari* and *endecasillabi,* except for the choruses. The first scene celebrates Apollo's victory over Python, the subject of the third intermezzo of 1589. The chorus ends the scene with four six-verse stanzas rhyming ABCABC that use the rare *ottonario* (eight-syllable verse). In the second scene Apollo encounters Venus and Love and recognizes that he is inferior to them, despite his courage and his skill as an archer; the concluding chorus of five seven-*ottonario* stanzas, rhyming ABBAACC, comments on the pain generated by Love. In the third scene Apollo meets Daphne and falls in love with her, but she rejects him. In the fourth scene Love and Venus discuss Love's intervention in human affairs; the chorus, comprising seven stanzas alternating *settenari* and *endecasillabi* and rhyming AABCDEFF, with the last rhyme always *core* (heart) and *amore* (love), underscores the power of Love. In the fifth scene a *nunzio* (announcer) tells of Daphne's metamorphosis into a laurel. In the sixth scene Apollo mourns the loss of his beloved; his song includes ten lines in terza rima. In eight six-line stanzas of *ottonari* and *quadrisillabi* (four-syllable lines) rhyming AABCCB the chorus points out that the laurel shows that the power of poetry surpasses even the power of Love.

Rinuccini's *L'Euridice* (Eurydice), with music by Peri, was performed at the Pitti Palace in Florence on 6 October 1600 during the celebration of the wedding of Marie de' Medici and the French king Henry IV; it was published the same year. Tragedy sings the prologue, seven four-*endecasillabo* stanzas rhyming ABBA. She announces that "Ecco i mesti coturni e i foschi panni / Cangio, e desto ne i cor più dolci affetti" (I replace the sad shoes and mournful clothes / Of Greek tragedy, and I awaken sweeter feelings in the audience's hearts), honors Marie and her wedding, and urges the audience to pay attention to what is to follow: "del Tracio Orfeo date l'orecchia al canto" (bestow your ears on the Thracian Orpheus's song).

Like *Dafne, L'Euridice* is divided into six scenes and mainly alternates *settenari* and *endecasillabi* linked by occasional rhymes. The first scene connects the events depicted onstage with the occasion for which the opera was written: a chorus of nymphs and shepherds joyfully sings about Orpheus and Eurydice's wedding, and the bride expresses her happiness. The closing chorus comprises three stanzas and one refrain, alternating seven- and eleven-syllable verses and rhyming ABBA. The second scene opens with Orpheus telling his companions Tirsi and Arcetro that he wishes that night would come sooner, so that he could enjoy his bride; the conversation is sustained far longer than anything Rinuccini had written previously and provides a detailed description of the hero's feelings. Daphne enters and sings a thirty-two-line aria in which she recounts Eurydice's death after being bitten by a snake. The closing chorus—six stanzas and a refrain, each of four *ottonari* rhyming ABAB–laments the power of death over human beings. In the third scene Arcetro sings of Orpheus's desperation and the help he has received from a "Donna . . . celeste" (heavenly . . . lady). Structurally, this scene is unusual because the chorus does not conclude it: the three six-*ottonario* stanzas, rhyming ABCABC, are followed by the shepherds' decision to go to a temple to sacrifice to the gods. In the fourth scene Orpheus, in hell, successively pleads his cause with Venus, Pluto, Proserpine, Rhadamanthus, and Charon. So convincing are his words that Pluto relents: "Trionfi oggi pietà ne' campi inferni, / E sia la Gloria e 'l vanto / De le lagrime tue, del tuo bel canto" (May pity triumph today in hell; / And may this be a sign of glory and a reason / To boast for your tears and your song). The chorus of "Ombre e Deità d'Inferno" (Infernal Shadows and Divinities) points out in five six-*settenario* stanzas rhyming ABABCC that no human being has ever before crossed into hell before his or her death. In the fifth scene Arcetro notes the progress of the sun across the sky to underscore the length of Orpheus's absence. Aminta arrives and shares his good news: Eurydice is "Più che mai bella e viva" (More beautiful and alive than ever). A five-line passage by the chorus, rhyming ABBCC, comments on time passing and happiness regained. The sixth scene, which opens with Orpheus and Eurydice's entrance, largely celebrates the power of music: "De l'alto don fu degno / Mio dolce canto e 'l suon di questa cetra" (My sweet song and the music of this cithara / deserved such a great gift); "Modi or soavi, or mesti, / Fervidi preghi e flebili sospiri, / Temprai sì dolce, ch'io / Ne l'implacabil cor destai pietate" (I elicited such sweet and sad moods, / Passionate prayers and somber sighs / From my instrument / That I awoke pity in an implacable heart). The closing chorus, comprising eight six-line stanzas alternating eight and four syllables and rhyming AABCCB, celebrates the triumph of love.

Peri published his score for *L'Euridice* in February 1601. His competitor Giulio Caccini also wrote music for Rinuccini's text; his score was published in Decem-

Title page for the first edition of Eurydice *(University of Turin)*

ber 1601. According to the Medici court diarist Cesare Tinghi, Caccini's version was performed at the Pitti Palace on 5 December 1602. Tinghi also mentions a performance of *Dafne* at the palace on 26 October 1604 for the visit of Ranuccio I Farnese, fourth Duke of Parma, to the Medici court. The occasion was momentous enough that the printer of the 1600 libretto, Giorgio Marescotti, distributed the leftover copies with a new title page.

Rinuccini's importance at the Medici court seems to have declined after the marriage of Henry IV and Marie de' Medici. Between December 1600 and July 1607 he appears to have gone to France three times. The poet Francesco Cini expressed a harsh judgment of Rinuccini in a letter to Ferdinando Gonzaga on 29 September 1607: "in materia di Poesie egli è tal hora troppo partiale di se medesimo e si lascia talvolta . . . trasportare dall'interesse" (he is very partial when it comes to poetry, and . . . lets himself be carried away with self-interest).

During the 1608 carnival season *Dafne* was staged with a new score by Marco da Gagliano. Rinuccini's opera *L'Arianna* (Ariadne) was performed on 28 May and his *Balletto dell'ingrate* (Ballet of the Ungrateful Women) on 4 June of that year, both for the wedding of Francesco IV Gonzaga and Margherita di Savoia. The singer Caterina Martinelli, who was to play the title role in *L'Arianna,* had died on 26 February and had to be replaced quickly by the well-known commedia dell'arte performer Virginia Andreini.

L'Arianna–whose score, by Claudio Monteverdi, is lost except for the famous "Lamento" (Lament) in scene 6–opens with a prologue sung by Apollo; it consists of six stanzas of four *endecasillabi,* rhyming ABBA, addressed to the bride and extolling the power of music and the rebirth of ancient theater: "forse avverrà che de la scena argiva / L'antico onor ne' novi canti ammiri" (it will perhaps occur that you admire / The ancient honor of the Greek stage in these new songs). The opera is divided into eight scenes, consisting mainly of seven- and eleven-syllable lines. In the first scene Venus tells Love about Ariadne's plight; the information is for the audience's benefit, for as Love says, "Tutto m'è noto, e tutto / Opra è del mio valor quanto a dir prendi" (I am aware of all you are about to tell, / As I accomplished it with my might). In the second scene Theseus arrives in Athens, accompanied by a chorus, and addresses his soldiers. Ariadne provides a counterpoint to his militaristic rhetoric: she misses her homeland, which is never named, but is happy to make the sacrifice to be with her beloved. Two groups of fishermen praise Ariadne's eyes by likening them to the sun, which is setting. The closing chorus, four stanzas of *settenari* and *endecasillabi* rhyming AABCCB, is addressed to the stars. The third scene introduces a device that became customary both in opera and in tragedy: Theseus discusses his options with a *consigliero* (counselor). He decides to leave the island; after the fishermen invoke the rising sun, the chorus summons dawn with a four-line refrain of eight-syllable lines rhyming ABBA and three stanzas, each comprising eight eight-syllable lines rhyming ABBAABBC, where C is the same word in all stanzas and coincides with the first rhyme of the refrain. In the fourth scene Ariadne awakens filled with dread and has to persuade her servant, Dorilla, that her feelings are warranted. The fishermen tell the two women that Theseus and his ships have left; the concluding chorus– four stanzas of six alternating *settenari* and *endecasillabi* rhyming ABBACC–criticizes him for abandoning this beautiful, loving woman. The fifth scene is a rather static description of Ariadne's appearance and feelings by a *nunzio* and the fishermen; it ends with three lines that bring Ariadne back onstage. Her lament, occasionally interrupted by the chorus commenting on her plight, takes up almost the entire sixth scene. Dorilla enters and announces that the sounds "di voci e squille" (of voices and trumpets) have been heard; perhaps Theseus's fleet has returned. The concluding chorus of five six-*settenario* stanzas rhyming ABBACC recalls Orpheus's trip to the netherworld to rescue Eurydice and praises the power of love. In the seventh scene another *nunzio* tells the chorus that Bacchus, not Theseus, has arrived; he and Ariadne have fallen in love and are about to be married. Instead of closing with a chorus, the scene ends with the *nunzio* singing "amici, amici / Ecco gli sposi, ecco i reali amanti" (friends, friends, / Behold the newlyweds, the royal lovers)—words that refer to Bacchus and Ariadne onstage and also to Francesco and Margherita. The eighth scene, which includes some eight- and four-syllable lines, is a short celebration of the newlywed deities that ends with Jupiter's appearance in the sky and Bacchus's words to Ariadne, who is about to become immortal.

The *Balletto dell'ingrate* was also set to music by Monteverdi and danced by Duke Ferdinando and Francesco Gonzaga with six knights and eight ladies of the court. Venus and Love are at the entrance to hell; they want to talk to the ladies who have been sent there because they did not reciprocate their lovers' affection. They remind Pluto of his love for Proserpine, and he has to recognize that their power exceeds his. He calls forth the ungrateful dead women, and as they dance he addresses the audience, especially the newlywed Margherita, in eight four-*endecasillabo* stanzas rhyming ABBA: he is showing them his charges "Perché cangiando omai voglie e consiglio / Non piangessi ancor voi ne 'l Negro chiostro" (So that you change your mind / And I do not have to cry for you in Hell). The moral of the ballet is repeated by one of the lost souls, sung by Andreini, in two eight-line stanzas alternating seven- and eleven-syllable lines rhyming ABAACCDD.

Rinuccini's libretto *Il Narciso* (1829, Narcissus) was composed for the wedding in 1608 of Cosimo II de' Medici, Grand Duke of Tuscany, and Maria Maddalena von Hapsburg, but it was not staged then. He gave the text to the singer and composer Loreto Vittori in 1610, to no avail; Monteverdi looked at it in 1627, six years after Rinuccini's death, but he did not set it to music, either. The prologue, which is independent of the plot and wholly linked to the occasion for which the work was written, was to be sung by Giulio Caccini, also known as Giulio Romano, as himself. *Il Narciso* is Rinuccini's only opera that is divided into acts; the end of each act is denoted by the chorus. Finally, *Il Narciso* includes Rinuccini's first comic scene: the first scene in the second act, in which the nymph Lydia rejects the old shepherd Elpino.

Written largely in *settenari* and *endecasillabi* occasionally linked by rhymes, *Il Narciso* opens with a conversation between the nymphs Phyllis and Echo in which Echo explains that she is in love with Narcissus but lacks the courage to reveal her feelings to him. A chorus of nymphs enters; all of them are also in love with Narcissus, despite their vows of chastity to Diana, the goddess of hunting. The act concludes with the chorus extolling the power of the god Love in five seven-*settenari* stanzas rhyming ABABBCC. Act 2 opens with a chorus of hunters who sing that people in love have only themselves to blame, not luck or the god Love. One of them, Elpino, is in love with a nymph, but she, like her companions, longs only for Narcissus. Narcissus declares that he cares for nothing but hunting; he scorns love and those who are in love. The chorus of nymphs tries to change his mind, to no avail. Narcissus invites Echo to hunt with him, and she happily accepts. He accedes to the nymphs' request that he remain with them until dawn; at daybreak several nymphs bemoan his harshness. Diana appears and reminds the nymphs that love brings only suffering; the nymph chorus agrees, rejecting Love and vowing revenge on him in three ten-*settenari* stanzas rhyming ABBAABCCDD. In act 3 a distraught Echo tells Phyllis that she disclosed her love to Narcissus and was rejected; pain will be her only companion from now on. Phyllis vows to follow her, and the nymph chorus wishes solace for her. A shepherd *nunzio* tells the nymphs how Echo revealed her love to Narcissus and how he cruelly cast her aside. In six six-line stanzas alternating *settenari* and *endecasillibi* and rhyming AABCCB the chorus praises Love for his sweetness and condemns him for his unkindness.

In act 4 the nymphs ask Narcissus why he rejected Echo so harshly; he replies that he wants to be left alone to hunt. Phyllis enters, confused by what she saw and heard in her pursuit of Echo: "S'a queste orecchio credo, è viva ancora; / Ma s'agli occhi do fe', di vita è priva" (If I believe my ears, she's alive; / But if I trust my eyes, she is deprived of life). Phyllis recounts to Narcissus and the nymphs Echo's metamorphosis into a voice that repeats her interlocutor's words. Diana and Love appear; the goddess says that Echo's fate should be a warning to all lovers, and the god vows to quell "D'un pastorel l'orgoglio" (A mere shepherd's pride). The nymphs bring the act to a close with a song comprising a refrain of four *ottonari* rhyming ABBA and three eight-*ottonari* stanzas rhyming ABBAACCD in which they implore Diana to protect them and dispel feelings of love from their hearts. In act 5 it is night, and the hunters, who have searched for Narcissus all day, ask the nymphs if they know where he is; they suggest

Title page for the first edition of Ariadne *(University of Turin)*

that he might be looking for Echo. Love enters and boasts of his power; the hunters and nymphs criticize his harshness and vow to resist him, and he promises to ravage their hearts and make them an example for the entire world. A *nunzio* named Tirsi weeps over Narcissus's fate: the young man, he says, has been transformed into a beautiful white flower. The chorus ends the play by equating love with torment; therefore, "tra pudichi pensier, tra caste voglie / Averà gioia 'l core e ver contento" (in pure thoughts, and chaste desires / Will the heart find joy and true happiness). The message is reminiscent of that in the *Maschere d'amazzoni,* also written for a wedding celebration.

Rinuccini wrote two untitled *mascherate* that may or may not have been staged for the Medici-Hapsburg wedding; they were first published in 1904. One is six octaves in length, sung by an unnamed character, and filled with references to Austria, Florence, and the wedding. The other is four octaves long, sung by Apollo and Paris, and retells the story of Jupiter's bestowing of the golden apple on Paris so that the latter can give it to the goddess he deems the most beautiful.

Rinuccini's *Mascherata di ninfe di Senna* (Masquerade of the Nymphs of the Seine) was performed twice at the Pitti Palace in 1613: on 14 February for carnival and on 5 May for the wedding of Mario Sforza, Count of Santa Fiora, and Arnea of Lorraine; the prologue was changed for each performance. It is divided into two parts with an intermezzo midway through the second part. The work praises the beauty of a nymph from the Seine, understood to represent Arnea of Lorraine, and the power of Tuscan rulers. In both instances noblemen and noblewomen of the Florentine court–including Cosimo II and Maria Maddalena during the February staging–danced to the music of the *mascherata.*

For the 1613 carnival season Rinuccini also wrote *Comparsa d'eroi celesti* (Appearance of the Celestial Heroes), the sixth part of a nine-part tournament. It opens with a chorus of gods singing six eight-syllable four-line stanzas rhyming ABBA; moves on to a duet alternating seven- and eleven-syllable lines sung by Pallas and Alcides, in which the former spurs the latter to pick up his weapons against Love; and closes with Pallas and Alcides' visit to Vulcan, armorer of the gods, who avows that he no longer loves Venus and asks who Love's opponents in the tournament will be. The piece cannot be understood outside the context of the larger work of which it forms a part.

On 5 February of the following carnival season Rinuccini's *Mascherata di selvaggi* (Mask of the Savages) was performed by young Florentine men at the Strozzi Palace with the grand duke and duchess in attendance. The piece alternates the usual *settenari* and *endecasillabi,* often rhyming. Love explains that he is about to free a royal lady from captivity. The queen calls on the "glorïoso figlio / Del gran Fernando, o sole / Della Medicea prole" (the great Fernando's / Glorious son, sun / Of the Medici progeny) to help her gain her freedom. Finally, one of the wild men who is holding the queen acknowledges his cowardliness and frees her.

In 1616 Rinuccini and Peri traveled to Bologna, where *L'Euridice* was staged for four cardinals, and to Mantua, where it was performed for the Gonzaga court. On 2 April 1619, during Easter week, the widowed Maria Maddalena and the French ambassador, François Annibal d'Estrées, marquis of Coeuvre, heard professional singers perform Rinuccini's *Versi sacri* (Sacred Verses) for compline. Six saints, a blessed man, and a blessed woman identify themselves through their saintly works. Eleven-syllable lines dominate, except for St. Cecilia's part: as the patron saint of music, she has the longest and most elaborate set of verses, comprising a four-line refrain of *ottonari* rhyming ABAB and five eight-line stanzas, the first of *endecasillabi* rhyming ABABABCC and the rest of *ottonari* rhyming ABABBCCB. On the following two days, Maundy Thursday and Good Friday, another untitled piece was performed by a singer representing an anonymous saint. In alternating seven- and eleven-syllable lines he prays to Jesus on the cross that the faithful might suffer with him.

On 25 February–Annunciation Day in the Catholic calendar–and 2 April 1620 Rinuccini's *L'annunciazione* (The Annunciation) was performed at the Medici court; it is his last piece known to be staged. A castrato sang the archangel Gabriel's part, alternating with a chorus of angels. Stage machinery, including a cloud that carries Gabriel down from heaven, was devised by the court architect, Giulio Parigi. Gabriel does not identify himself when he enters but explains what he is about to do. The chorus praises Mary in five stanzas of eight-syllable lines, foresees her future in two long stanzas alternating seven- and eleven-syllable lines, and finally asks Gabriel, in five terza rima stanzas and a quatrain, to explain what took place. The work ends with a long aria sung by Gabriel in which he narrates the Annunciation. The change in subject matter in these late works is usually attributed to the more pious atmosphere that prevailed at the Medici court after Cosimo II's death.

Ottavio Rinuccini died in Florence on 28 March 1621. His life deserves further scrutiny, and his oeuvre should be assessed outside the category of "occasional verses" that is usually imposed on it.

References:

Lorenzo Bianconi, *Music in the Seventeenth Century* (Cambridge: Cambridge University Press, 1987), pp. 161–180, 210–226;

Carlo Calcaterra, *Poesie e canto: Studi sulla poesia melica italiana e sulla favola per musica* (Bologna: Zanichelli, 1951), pp. 35–39, 128–142, 191–194, 202–212, 223–238;

Amelia Civita, *Ottavio Rinuccini e il sorgere del melodramma in Italia* (Mantua: Aldo Manuzio, 1900);

Robert Donington, *The Rise of Opera* (New York: Scribners, 1981), pp. 103–205;

Iain Fenlon, "The Origins of the Seventeenth-Century Staged *Ballo*," in *Con che soavità: Studies in Italian Opera, Song, and Dance, 1580–1740,* edited by Fenlon and Tim Carter (Oxford: Clarendon Press, 1995), pp. 13–40;

Barbara Russano Hanning, "Music in Italy on the Brink of the Baroque," *Renaissance Quarterly,* 32, no. 1 (1984): 7–9, 12, 15;

Hanning, *Of Poetry and Music's Power: Humanism and the Creation of Opera* (Ann Arbor: UMI Research Press, 1980), pp. 1–19, 43–180;

Warren Kirkendale, *The Court Musicians in Florence during the Principate of the Medici* (Florence: Olschki, 1993), pp. 146–150, 194–210, 217–221, 237–240, 338–339;

Claude Palisca, "The Alterati of Florence, Pioneers in the Theory of Dramatic Music," in *New Looks at Italian Opera,* edited by William W. Austin (Ithaca, N.Y.: Cornell University Press, 1968), pp. 9–39;

Palisca, *Baroque Music* (Englewood Cliffs, N.J.: Prentice Hall, 1991), pp. 32–33, 36, 39–41;

Francesco Raccamadoro-Ramelli, *Ottavio Rinuccini: Studio biografico e critico* (Fabriano: Gentile, 1900);

James M. Saslow, *The Medici Wedding of 1589: Florentine Festival as* Theatrum Mundi (New Haven: Yale University Press, 1996), pp. 28, 39–40, 182;

Angelo Solerti, *Gli albori del melodramma,* volume 2: *Ottavio Rinuccini* (Milan: Sandron, 1904);

Solerti, *Musica ballo e drammatica alla Corte Medicea dal 1600 al 1637: Notizie tratte da un diario, con appendice di testi inediti e rari* (Florence: R. Bemporad, 1905), pp. 9–26, 70–72, 76–77, 144–145;

Frederick William Sternfeld, *The Birth of Opera* (Oxford: Clarendon Press, 1993), pp. 117–126;

Gary Tomlinson, *Monteverdi and the End of the Renaissance* (Berkeley: University of California Press, 1987).

Papers:

Manuscripts of Ottavio Rinuccini are at the Biblioteca Trivulziana in Milan and the Biblioteca Nazionale in Florence.

Giulio Rospigliosi
(Pope Clement IX)
(27 or 28 January 1600 – 9 December 1669)

Maria Galli Stampino
University of Miami

WORKS: *Poesie di Ecc[ellentissi]mi autori in lode della famosissima Cappella del Sig. Guido Nolfi eretta nel Duomo di Fano* (Rome: Guglielmo Facciotti, 1625);

"Discorso del Sig. Giulio Rospigliosi sopra l'*Elettione di Urbano VIII* poema del Sig. Francesco Bracciolini Dell'Api," in *L'Elettione di Urbano VIII di Francesco Bracciolini Dell'Api* (Rome: Brogiotti, 1628);

"Su l'auree foglie," in *Componimenti poetici di vari autori nelle nozze delli Eccellentissimi Signori D. Taddeo Barberini e D. Anna Colonna* (Rome: Camerale, 1629), p. 90;

Applausi poetici alle glorie della Signora Leonora Baroni (Bracciano: G. B. Cavatta, 1639);

Sant'Alessio, in *Drammi per musica dal Rinuccini allo Zeno,* 2 volumes, edited by Andrea della Corte (Turin: Unione Tipografico-Editrice Torinese, 1958), I: 195–265;

Melodrammi profani, edited by Danilo Romei (Florence: Studio Editoriale Fiorentino, 1998)—comprises *Erminia sul Giordano, L'Egisto,* and *Dal male il bene;*

Melodrammi sacri, edited by Romei (Florence: Studio editoriale fiorentino, 1999)—comprises *Santi Didimo e Teodora, L'innocenza difesa nella Rappresentazione di san Bonifacio,* and *La comica del Cielo, ovvero, La Baldassara.*

Giulio Rospigliosi, Pope Clement IX (artist unknown; from <http://www.hotelrospigliosi.com/history.html>)

PLAY PRODUCTIONS: *Sant'Alessio,* music by Stefano Landi, Rome, Palazzo Barberini ai Giubbonari, 8 March 1631;

Erminia sul Giordano, music by Michelangelo Rossi, Rome, Palazzo Barberini alle Quattro Fontane, carnival 1633;

Santi Didimo e Teodora, music by Landi or Virgilio Mazzocchi, Rome, Palazzo Barberini alle Quattro Fontane, carnival 1635;

Egisto, o Chi soffre speri, music by Mazzocchi and Marco Marazzoli, Rome, Palazzo Barberini alle Quattro Fontane, carnival 1637;

L'innocenza difesa nella Rappresentazione di san Bonifacio, music by Mazzocchi, Rome, Palazzo della Cancelleria, carnival 1638;

Prologue and intermezzi for Seneca's *Troades,* music by Mazzocchi, Rome, Palazzo Rusticucci-Campeggi, carnival 1640;

La Genoinda, o L'innocenza difesa, music by Mazzocchi (?), Rome, Palazzo della Cancelleria, January 1641;

Il palazzo incantato, music by Luigi Rossi, Rome, Palazzo Barberini alle Quattro Fontane, 22 February 1642;

Sant'Eustachio, music by Mazzocchi, Rome, Palazzo Rusticucci-Campeggi, carnival 1643;

Dal male il bene, music by Antonio Maria Abbatini and Marazzoli, Rome, Palazzo Barberini alle Quattro Fontane, carnival 1654;

Le armi e gli amori, music by Marazzoli, Rome, 1656;

La vita humana o Il trionfo della pietà, music by Marazzoli, Rome, Palazzo Barberini alle Quattro Fontane, carnival 1656;

La comica del Cielo ovvero La Baldassara, music by Abbatini, Rome, Palazzo Rospigliosi, 1669.

Giulio Rospigliosi has often been criticized for lack of originality: the plots of most of his librettos are derived from preexisting sources. Nevertheless, his work was crucial for the development of the so-called Roman opera. Rospigliosi was central to the promotion of sung entertainment at the papal court: first in his capacity as official librettist of the Barberini family and later when, as Pope Clement IX, he made the first permanent theater in Rome possible. His work and career reflect the unique theatrical situation in Rome: the papacy was alternately in favor of and against staged entertainment but was the only institution with the power and resources to bring librettos to life onstage.

Rospigliosi belongs to the second generation of opera librettists: he was born in Pistoia to Girolamo and Maria Caterina Rospigliosi on 27 or 28 January 1600, the year the first courtly opera performance, Ottavio Rinuccini and Jacopo Peri's *L'Euridice* (Eurydice), was staged for the wedding of Maria de' Medici and King Henry IV of France. Rospigliosi had a brother, Camillo.

Pistoia is twenty miles from Florence, to which it had been politically subordinate since 1401. The Rospigliosi family had acquired prominence under the Medicis as a provider of military leaders, but Giulio was pointed toward an ecclesiastical career. In 1609 or 1610 he received minor orders from Bishop Alessandro Del Caccia. On 16 March 1614 he left for Rome, where he studied under the classicists Famiano Strada and Bernardino Castelli and the writer Bernardino Stefonio at the Jesuit Seminario Romano. In 1618 or 1619 he moved to the University of Pisa to study theology, philosophy, and law. He was named lecturer in philosophy there in 1623; the following year he received a degree in canon and civil law and returned to Rome, where he entered the service of Cardinal Antonio Barberini Sr., the nephew of Maffeo Barberini, who had become Pope Urban VIII in 1623. In 1624 another nephew of the Pope, Cardinal Francesco Barberini, started the Accademia dei Virtuosi (Academy of the Followers of Virtue) in his palace on the Quirinale; Rospigliosi delivered the second lecture at the first meeting. In 1625 he went to France with Francesco Barberini, who had been named papal legate to the country; that same year two of his sonnets appeared in a collection of poems in honor of the Nolfi chapel in Fano. In 1626 he accompanied the cardinal to Spain. In 1628 a learned disquisition on the power of poetry by Rospigliosi was appended to a poem by Francesco Bracciolini celebrating Urban VIII's election as Pope. Rospigliosi states his opposition to the Baroque exaggerations of Giambattista Marino's poetry and advocates a more classical and moralistic verse. Rospigliosi's position coincided with that of the Barberini family.

Poetry and music began to be intertwined in Rospigliosi's work in 1629: he contributed to a collection in honor of the marriage of Taddeo Barberini and Anna Colonna two sonnets, an ode, and a canzonet of ten stanzas of eight five- and eleven-syllable lines, rhyming AABCDDBC, suitable for a musical score. In 1630 he reportedly wrote a Christmas dialogue that was set to music by Johann Hieronimus Kapsberger; it has been lost.

Rospigliosi became secretary to the Congregation of Rites in 1631. On 8 March of that year his first opera, *Sant'Alessio* (St. Alexius), set to music by Stefano Landi, was staged at the Palazzo Barberini ai Giubbonari. All of Rospigliosi's operas were written as carnival entertainment for the Barberini family; all are in three acts, are largely written in *settenari* (seven-syllable lines) and *endecasillabi* (eleven-syllable lines), and deliver a moral message. None appeared in print at the time; an *Argomento* (Argument) distributed at each performance provided audience members with a scene-by-scene plot summary but not with the names of the librettist or the composer. Alexius is a noble Roman who has converted to Christianity in Syria and come back incognito to his family home, where he lives as a mendicant and endures the scorn of his father's servants. Steadfast in his faith, he resists the devil's temptations; but when he overhears his mother and wife planning to leave Rome to look for him, he vacillates in his decision to keep his identity a secret. This scene offers comic relief in the characters of the servants, who mock their masters. At the end of the opera Alexius is found dead on his family's doorstep; his identity and tribulations are revealed in a letter discovered on his body. Angels appear and persuade his family that his life and death are a cause for rejoicing, not for mourning. *Sant'Alessio* alternates recitatives in seven- and eleven-syllable lines with arias in four-, five-, and eight-syllable lines.

In addition to its moral teachings, *Sant'Alessio* offers a political message. Preceded onto the stage by a chorus of slaves, Rome sings the prologue: the city identifies herself as "Quella . . . / che già calcai col piede / de' miei famosi eroi / i campi Mauritani, e i lidi Eoi" (The one . . . / who conquered Africa / and the Mediterranean / through the famous heroes who issued from me); yet, "molti han compiuto / vie più chiare imprese / dietro all'orme di Cristo / per di più stabil Regno / eterno acquisto" (many carried out / glorious feats in Christ's name, / to achieve an eternal gift / in a more permanent kingdom). *Roma* (Rome) is also the last word of the opera. The continuity between the Roman Empire and the Catholic faith is thus underscored, and the papacy's worldwide relevance is asserted. *Sant'Alessio* was restaged on 18 January and 17 February 1632 at the Palazzo Barberini alle Quattro Fontane. That year Rospigliosi became referendary (reporting member) of the Segnatura (church court) and received a benefice at Cardinal Antonio Barberini's basilica of Santa Maria Maggiore.

In 1633 Rospigliosi declined the governorship of Fermo and Loreto so that he could remain at the papal court. His *Erminia sul Giordano* (Erminia on the Jordan) was staged during carnival that year at the Palazzo Barberini alle Quattro Fontane, sponsored by Cardinal Taddeo Barberini. Based on an episode in canto 7 of Torquato Tasso's epic poem *Gerusalemme liberata* (1581, Jerusalem Delivered; translated as *Godfrey of Bulloigne, or The Recoverie of Hierusalem,* 1594) and scored by Michelangelo Rossi, *Erminia sul Giordano* used many stage effects designed by Francesco Guitti of Ferrara. The prologue, for example, is sung on the river Jordan in the presence of nymphs and naiads. Rospigliosi modified the ending of the episode from Tasso's version so that the love of Princess Erminia of Antioch for the Christian knight Tancredi is requited; the mood of the work is romantic and pastoral, rather than war-like and sacrificial as in the original. It has many linguistic and narrative similarities to Tasso's pastoral play *Aminta* (1573; translated as *Aminta Englisht,* 1628). *Sant'Alessio* was reworked and staged seven times in January and February 1634.

In 1635 Monsignor Giovanni Ciampoli fell from papal grace following Galileo's trial, and Rospigliosi acquired his post as the Pope's secretary of letters to princes. That year his *Santi Didimo e Teodora* (Sts. Didymus and Theodora) was performed at least six times during carnival at the Palazzo Barberini alle Quattro Fontane, sponsored by Francesco Barberini. The score, which was composed by Landi or Virgilio Mazzocchi, is lost. Set in Alexandria in 304, the work recounts the travails of the Christian Theodora under the harsh rule of the Roman prefect Eustratius Proculus: both are strong willed and convinced of the rightness of their calling. Theodora has taken a vow of celibacy; when she refuses to marry, Eustratius has her placed in a brothel. Her first client is Didymus, a Christian soldier who has actually come to rescue her. They exchange clothes; Theodora escapes, and Didymus remains in the brothel. When the deception is discovered, Didymus is sentenced to be beheaded; Theodora refuses to allow him to die alone and joins him in martyrdom. The libretto makes use of many of the stock elements of Baroque spectacle: Didymus reads a letter that he believes to be from Theodora but might have miraculously appeared, and a divine echo reassures him in his despair; Eustratius announces a tournament to decide who will marry Theodora, the knights enter and utter their challenge, and the audience is led to believe that a combat-based intermezzo is about to take place, but a dispatch arrives asserting Theodora's refusal of the marriage; and Eustratius is torn apart by the Furies, a physical manifestation of his inner torment. *Santi Didimo e Teodora* was performed again during the following carnival season.

In 1637 carnival coincided with the visit to Rome of Frederick, Landgrave of Hesse, and Francesco Barberini had Rospigliosi's *Egisto, o Chi soffre speri* (Egisto; or, He Who Suffers May Hope) performed at the Palazzo Barberini alle Quattro Fontane. *Egisto* was set to music by Mazzocchi and Marco Marazzoli; the plot is taken from the story of Federigo degli Alberighi in day 5, tale 9 of Giovanni Boccaccio's *Decameron* (circa 1348–1353). Far more narrative in style than Rospigliosi's previous librettos, *Egisto* is devoid of stage effects but is enriched by the presence of four commedia dell'arte stock characters: the servants Zanni from Bergamo and Coviello from Naples and their sons Frittellino and Colello. The various languages spoken onstage–Florentine, *bergamasco*, and Neapolitan–generate clashes and allow Rospigliosi to meet new poetic challenges, such as the comic scene 6 in act 1 where the same canzone, composed in *settenari* and *endecasillabi*, is sung in two dialects. *Egisto* is often called the first comic opera; Giacinto Cornacchioli's *La Diana schernita* (Diana Mocked) had been published in 1629 with a dedication to Taddeo Barberini but may never have been performed.

For the 1638 carnival season Francesco Barberini had Rospigliosi's *L'innocenza difesa nella Rappresentazione di san Bonifacio* (Innocence Defended in the Representation of St. Boniface) performed six times at the Palazzo della Cancelleria. Set to music by Mazzocchi, the opera used no stage machinery, had intermezzi set to music, and was sung by boy sopranos. Boniface is asked by his fiancée, Aglae, to go to Tarsus to fight for the Christians for a year. While he is away, Aglae has to repel the advances of a Roman captain and withstand her family's criticism. When Boniface is captured by the Romans, he chooses martyrdom. The opera ends with Aglae learning of Boniface's death and praising her beloved, while the Church Militant and the Church Triumphant sing joyfully of their victory over sin. *L'innocenza difesa nella Rappresentazione di san Bonifacio* includes few arias and juxtaposes comic and serious scenes somewhat mechanically, but it was highly successful: it was repeated in Palestrina in August 1638; again in Rome on 25 November 1638 at the Palazzo della Cancelleria for Johann Eggenberg, Duke of Krumau and imperial ambassador; four times at the Cancelleria; and four more at the Palazzo alle Quattro Fontane for the 1639 carnival. *Egisto* was performed during a banquet for the Auditori di Rota (judges of the Sacra Rota, a court of appeals of the Holy See for cases heard at the diocese level) and expanded with a lively intermezzo on the fair at Farfa in the Roman *campagna* (countryside). Also in 1639 Rospigliosi contributed a sonnet to the collection *Applausi poetici alle glorie della Signora Leonora Baroni* (Poetic Commendations of the Glories of Signora Leonora Baroni) in which he describes and praises a portrait of Baroni by a painter identified only as Don Fabio.

The 1640 carnival festivities did not include an opera, but Rospigliosi contributed a prologue and intermezzi to Seneca's tragedy *Troades* (The Trojan Women) that were set to music by Mazzocchi. The two apparently collaborated again the following year on *La Genoinda, o L'innocenza difesa* (Genoinda; or, The Defense of Innocence), but the score has been lost. It was staged at the Palazzo della Cancelleria under the sponsorship of Francesco Barberini in honor of Isabella Gioieni Colonna, Anna Colonna Barberini's sister-in-law, and more than one hundred other noblewomen. Set in a castle and a forest near the Rhine, the opera recounts the tribulations of Duchess Genoinda: while her husband is away on a Crusade, she resists the advances of one of his most trusted men. When the duke returns, he discovers that Genoinda was killed for being faithful to him; but an announcer delivers the news that she is alive, and on her return to court she forgives her unwanted suitor. The moral message is unmistakable: Genoinda embodies the ideal of the submissive woman to which Roman ladies of the time were expected to aspire.

On 29 April 1641 Rospigliosi became house prelate to the Pope; on 4 January 1642 he was made canonic consultant to the Penitenzieria Apostolica (Apostolic Penitentiary), a tribunal that deals with the forgiveness of sins. On 22 February his *Il palazzo incantato* (The Enchanted Palace) opened at the theater in the Palazzo alle Quattro Fontane. Rospigliosi's verses were set to music by Luigi Rossi, and the staging was devised by Andrea Sacchi. Sponsored by Antonio Barberini, the opera depicts the episode of Ruggiero's liberation from Atlas's castle by Bradamante from canto 4 of Ludovico Ariosto's *Orlando furioso* (1516; enlarged, 1532, The Frenzy of Orlando; translated as *Orlando Furioso in English Heroical Verse,* 1591). It was eight hours long, and the stage machinery malfunctioned; nevertheless, seats were in high demand, perhaps because the plot could be read as a clue to the politics of the Pope and his relatives: according to Frederick Hammond, Atlas could refer to Urban VIII, Ruggiero to his nephew Antonio, and the castle to the Barberini palace. *Il palazzo incantato* was repeated in March 1642 in honor of Cardinal Ippolito d'Este's visit to the Pope.

For the 1643 carnival Francesco Barberini sponsored a Latin drama performed by boys from the Seminario di S. Pietro; Rospigliosi and Mazzocchi's *Sant'Eustachio* (St. Eustachius) was presented as an intermezzo to that play. Eustachius, a successful Roman general, is a Christian who has been secretly practicing his faith with his family. When he proclaims his belief to Emperor Hadrian, he is imprisoned and then martyred along with his children. A static libretto–in many scenes a narrator tells the characters and audience about events that have occurred offstage–it depicts Eustachius's progression from military to spiritual victory and thus presents the audience with yet another inspiring and rousing character.

On 27 July 1643 Rospigliosi was named *sigillatore* (keeper of the seal) of the Penitenzieria Apostolica. On 29 March 1644 he was made titular bishop of Tarsus and papal nuncio to Spain. He left Rome by ship in late April and was presented to King Philip IV on 2 July. Urban VIII died on 29 July; Rospigliosi remained nuncio under Urban's successor, Innocent X, until September 1652. His eight-year sojourn at the Madrid court put him in contact with the Spanish *siglo de oro* (golden age) theater, which was then in full bloom. Three of his four later librettos have Spanish sources and differ from his previous works in tone and subject matter.

Rospigliosi left Madrid in early January 1653; he spent some time in Pistoia and arrived in Rome in the early summer. In 1654 his *Dal male il bene* (From Evil Comes Good), set to music by Marazzoli and Antonio Maria Abbatini, was staged at the Palazzo Barberini alle Quattro Fontane in honor of Taddeo Barberini's son and heir, Maffeo, and Maffeo's bride, Olimpia Giustiniani, the Pope's grandniece. The plot is derived from a 1652 Spanish play by Antonio Sigler de Huerta: the love of two noble couples in seventeenth-century Madrid goes unrequited because each is ignorant of a key element of his or her beloved's identity; for example, a sister is believed to be a lover. Two comic servants help to clear up the various mistaken identities. *Dal male il bene* is plot driven and character centered and less overtly moralizing than Rospigliosi's earlier works.

This period seems to have been difficult for Rospigliosi economically, and he apparently pondered retiring to private life in Tuscany. After Innocent X's death on 7 January 1655, however, he was named governor of Rome by the Camerlengo, the administraor of the property and revenues of the Holy See. Fabio Chigi was elected Pope Alexander VII on 7 April 1655 and immediately made Rospigliosi his secretary of state.

Dal male il bene was repeated during the 1656 carnival celebrations in honor of the recently converted Queen Christina, who had abdicated the Swedish throne and moved to Rome in 1653, at the Palazzo Barberini alle Quattro Fontane and the Palazzo Farnese. Rospigliosi's new operas, *Le armi e gli amori* (The Arms and Loves) and *La vita humana o Il trionfo della pietà* (Human Life; or, The Triumph of Piety) were also performed at this time. Derived from Pedro Calderón de la Barca's *Los empeños de un acaso* (1651, The Obligations of Chance) and set to music by Marazzoli, *Le armi e gli amori* is essentially a variation on the themes and plot of *Dal male il bene:* it involves four noble families and their servants in seventeenth-century Madrid and centers on the discrepancy between appearance and reality and between honor and the possibility of scandal for noblemen and noblewomen in love. *La vita humana* was set to music by Marazzoli, with sets by Giovan Francesco Grimaldi and choreography by Luca Cherubini. Like the allegorical Spanish *autos sacramentales* (sacramental plays), the opera depicts abstract figures: the main characters are Innocenza (Innocence) and Colpa (Guilt.)

Rospigliosi was among the first group of cardinals created by Alexander on 9 April 1657. Alexander died on 22 May 1667, and Rospigliosi was elected Pope on 20 June; on his consecration six days later, he took the name Clement IX. His papacy largely followed the direction set by Alexander VII. His first notable act was to reorganize the Congregation for the State of the Regulars on 11 April 1668. The thorniest issues he faced during his papacy were Jansenism and the fate of the Cretan port city Candia (now Iraklion).

Jansenism was an anti-Jesuit Catholic reform movement based on the propredestination teachings of the Flemish bishop Cornelius Otto Jansen, especially his posthumously published *Augustinus* (1640). Urban VIII had forbidden the reading of the *Augustinus* in 1642, and five propositions of Jansenism had been condemned by Innocent X in 1653 and by Alexander VII in 1656, but the doctrine flourished among the nuns at the abbey of Port-Royal-des-Champs in France. Louis XIV regarded the conflict between the Jesuits and the Jansenists as a threat to the unity of the country; Clement defused the situation temporarily through a compromise known as the *Pax Clementina* (Clementine Peace), concluded on 2 February 1669. The agreement was well received in France, but most European courts saw it as a sign of the Pope's weakness.

Candia was a Venetian colony that Clement believed to be crucial for the protection of Christianity from political, economic, and religious influences from the eastern Mediterranean. He supported the Venetian defense of the city with expeditions in 1668 and 1669 under the command of his nephew Giacomo but failed to secure military aid from France; after a twenty-year siege, the city fell to Ottoman troops on 5 September 1669.

On 17 June 1669 Rospigliosi promulgated a bull dealing with the duties and privileges of missionaries, till then largely abused, especially from the commercial standpoint. On 6 July his *motu proprio* (a papal rescript including the phrase *motu proprio* [of his own accord]) *In ipsis pontificatus nostri primordiis* (At the Very Beginning of Our Papacy) established the Congregation for Indulgences and Relics.

Rospigliosi's last work to be staged was *La comica del Cielo ovvero La Baldassara* (The Comic Actress of Heaven; or, Baldassara); it was performed at Palazzo Rospigliosi, constructed in the late sixteenth century by the Pope's ancestors, during the 1669 carnival season with a score by Abbatini and sets by Gian Lorenzo Bernini. Tradition holds that Clement, hidden from the audience's view, watched the production. The plot is taken from the Spanish play *La Baltasara* (1652), by Luis Vélez de Guevara, Antonio Coello, and Francisco de Rojas. Alessandro Ademollo cites a source claiming that Rospigliosi wrote it while serving as nuncio in Madrid. Baldassara is a professional actress who yearns for a more fulfilling life. The work is highly self-referential: Baldassara's troupe performs a play based on the story of Clorinda from Tasso's *Gerusalemme liberata,* the poem that served as the source of Rospigliosi's *Erminia sul Giordano;* Baldassara enters on the wrong cue, and her onstage confusion parallels that which she feels in her life. Further, the real audience is confronted with the reactions of the audience within the play. In the end, Baldassara dies a saintly death as an anchorite.

Clement suffered a stroke on the night of 25–26 October 1669; he had largely recovered by 29 November, when he had another stroke. He died on 9 December. Giulio Rospigliosi left behind a few poems and the plays *Gioseffo, Isacco,* and *La Sofronia,* and possibly *Adrasto,* on whose attribution scholars disagree; the plays are undated and were perhaps never staged. His librettos, however, tied opera's Florentine beginnings to the courtly ambience that prevailed in Rome, contributed to the professionalization of stage singing, and influenced the Accademia dell'Arcadia (Arcadian Academy) that flourished in the late seventeenth and eighteenth centuries. Metrically, his works largely follow Rinuccini's model by using *settenari* and *endecasillabi* lines; but his arias include lines of four, five, and eight syllables. More significantly, he took advantage of the multiplicity of stresses of Italian words by exploiting *rime tronche* (words whose stress falls on the last syllable) and *rime parossitone* (words whose stress falls on the third-to-last syllable) in his arias. Finally, during his papacy Clement approved the construction of Rome's first public opera theater, the Teatro Tordinona, which opened in 1671 under Christina of Sweden's auspices. Opera in Rome thereby ceased to be solely a courtly pastime and also acquired a permanence that could transcend the papacy's unpredictable position on staged entertainment–at least to a certain extent: under subsequent popes the theater was closed, reopened, torn down, and rebuilt.

Bibliographies:

Galliano Ciliberti, *Antonio Maria Abbatini e la musica del suo tempo (1595-1679): Documenti per una ricostruzione bio-bibliografica* (Perugia: Gestias, 1986), pp. 263-330, 505-547;

Saverio Franchi and Orietta Sartori, *Drammaturgia romana: Repertorio bibliografico cronologico dei testi drammatici pubblicati a Roma e nel Lazio, secolo XVII* (Rome: Edizioni di storia e letteratura, 1988), pp. 201-202, 208, 216-217, 223-224, 232-233, 243-244, 248-249, 251-252, 308, 776.

References:

Alessandro Ademollo, *I teatri di Roma nel secolo decimosettimo* (Rome: Pasqualucci, 1888), pp. 7-24, 28-31, 63-88, 98-105, 114-118;

Lorenzo Bianconi, *Il teatro d'opera in Italia: Geografia, caratteri, storia* (Bologna: Il Mulino, 1993), pp. 17-40, 50;

Chiara D'Afflitto and Danilo Romei, eds., *I teatri del Paradiso: La personalità, l'opera, il mecenatismo di Giulio Rospigliosi (papa Clemente IX)* (Pistoia: Maschietto & Musolino, 2000);

Paolo Fabbri, *Il secolo cantante: Per una storia del libretto d'opera nel Seicento* (Bologna: Il Mulino, 1990);

Frederick Hammond, *Music and Spectacle in Baroque Rome: Barberini Patronage under Urban VIII* (New Haven: Yale University Press, 1994), pp. 103-104, 199-254;

Margaret Murata, *Operas for the Papal Court 1631-1668* (Ann Arbor: UMI Research Press, 1981), pp. 2-80, 178-188;

Gianvittorio Signorotto and Maria Antonietta Visceglia, eds., *Court and Politics in Papal Rome 1492-1700* (Cambridge: Cambridge University Press, 2002), pp. 150-153, 196-197, 200-202, 206-208;

Leopold Silke, "Rome: Sacred and Secular," in *The Early Baroque Era from the Late 16th Century to the 1660s*, edited by Curtis Price (Englewood Cliffs, N.J.: Prentice Hall, 1993), pp. 49-74.

Papers:

Giulio Rospigliosi's manuscripts and the bulk of his correspondence are at the Vatican Library and the Archivo Segreto Vaticano, both in Rome.

Margherita Sarrocchi

(1560 – 29 October 1617)

Natalia Costa-Zalessow
San Francisco State University

BOOK: *La Scanderbeide: Poema heroico* (Rome: Lepido Facij, 1606; revised and enlarged edition, Rome: Andrea Fei, 1623); edited and translated by Rinaldina Russell as *Scanderbeide: The Heroic Deeds of George Scanderbeg, King of Epirus* (Chicago: University of Chicago Press, 2006).

Editions: *La Scanderbeide: Poema eroico* (Naples: Antonio Bulifon, 1701);

Luisa Bergalli, *Componimenti poetici delle più illustri rimatrici d'ogni secolo* (Venice: Antonio Mora, 1726), part 2, pp. 111–112;

Jolanda de Blasi, ed., *Antologia delle scrittrici italiane dalle origini al 1800* (Florence: Nemi, 1930), pp. 286–296;

Natalia Costa-Zalessow, *Scrittrici italiane dal XIII al XX secolo: Testi e critica* (Ravenna: Longo, 1982), pp. 131–134;

Giuliana Morandini, *Sospiri e palpiti: Scrittrici italiane del Seicento* (Genoa: Marietti, 2001), pp. 39–50.

Margherita Sarrocchi is remembered for *La Scanderbeide: Poema heroico* (The Poem of Skanderbeg: A Heroic Poem; translated as *Scanderbeide: The Heroic Deeds of George Scanderbeg, King of Epirus,* 2006), published in incomplete form in 1606 and posthumously in a longer version in 1623. The work is an original contribution to the heroic-epic genre made popular in Italy in the late sixteenth century by Torquato Tasso and cultivated by many writers in the seventeenth century.

Sarrocchi was born in Naples in 1560. After the death of her father, Giovanni, her education was supervised by his friend Guglielmo Sirleto. Sirleto took her to Rome in 1565, the year he was made a cardinal. A scholar of Greek who became director of the Vatican Library in 1570, Sirleto placed Scarocchi in the school of the Convent of Santa Cecilia and later provided her with private tutors. She studied poetry, Latin, Greek, philosophy, theology, arithmetic, and geometry; among her teachers were the humanist and poet Rinaldo Corso and the mathematician Luca Valerio.

While still quite young, Sarrocchi began her literary career by commenting on the poems of Petrarch and the Renaissance poet Giovanni della Casa; she also translated Musaeus's epic poem *Hero and Leander* from Greek into Italian, elaborated on some of Euclid's theorems, and wrote a treatise in Latin on predestination. All of these works have been lost, although two letters written in Latin were published in a 1990 article by Nadia Verdile. Sarrocchi also composed poems that received praise; Tasso wrote sonnets to her in response to two of hers. Her talent attracted the attention of Roman high society as well as some learned men, several of whom became her correspondents. Only a few of the poems have survived. When she was fifteen, Muzio Manfredi asked her to contribute a sonnet to a book he was editing titled *Componimenti raccolti da diversi per Dame Romane* (1575, Poems by Various Authors for Roman Ladies). One of the ladies to whom the volume was dedicated was Felice Orsini Colonna, the wife of Marcantonio Colonna, the hero of the Battle of Lepanto in 1571. Sarrocchi traveled with the Colonnas and was their guest in Naples; she enjoyed the protection of Marcantonio Colonna until his death in 1584.

In 1588 Sarocchi married Carlo Biraghi (or Birago), a Piedmontese military man. She held a literary salon—almost an academy—in their home that was frequented by scientists as well as men of letters. She met the poet Giambattista Marino during his stay in Rome from 1600 to 1605; they exchanged complimentary poems that, according to gossip, led to a love affair. But the relationship soon soured. Sarrocchi became an ardent enemy of Marino and his Baroque style, and Marino attacked her in his sonnets and his poem *L'Adone* (excerpts translated as *Adonis: Selections from L'Adone of Giambattista Marino,* 1967): alluding to *La Scanderbeide,* in canto 9 of *L'Adone* he calls her "loquacissima pica" (a loquacious magpie) that "con strilli importuni in rozzi carmi / dassi anch'ella a gracchiar d'amori e d'armi" (croaks of love and arms, with pestering, rustic rhymes). He spoke of her in vulgar terms that scandalized his friend-turned-adversary Ferrante Carli, who characterized her (in a document published in 1975 by Carlo Delcorno) as "una donna di valor singolare nelle più belle e nelle migliori lettere" (a women of unusual merit in the most beautiful and best of letters). Sarrocchi had other detractors who accused her of being overly proud, incapable of accepting criticism, and prone to quarreling with those who disagreed with her.

La Scanderbeide was published in Rome in 1606 under Sarrocchi's name but, according to the title page, "senza saputa di lei" (without her knowledge), by "Arrotato Academico Raffrontato" (The Sharp One, Member of the Academy of the Well Experienced); the claim was most likely a stratagem to avoid criticism should the work not be well received. It was dedicated to Marcantonio and Felice Colonna's daughter, Costanza Colonna Sforza, marchioness of Caravaggio. The introduction states that the work was rushed to publication in incomplete form to avoid its subject being used by other poets who were familiar with Sarrocchi's poem. It consists of nine cantos, a short prose summary of the material that would have appeared in cantos 10 and 11, canto 12, a prose summary of canto 13, and stanzas 62 through 108 of canto 14. While heroic poems normally dealt with ancient Rome or the Middle Ages, Sarrocchi chose an era much closer to her own time. Modeled on Tasso's masterpiece *Gerusalemme liberata* (1581, Jerusalem Delivered; translated as *Godfrey of Bulloigne, or The Recoverie of Hierusalem,* 1594), it glorifies the struggle of the Albanian national hero George Kastrioti, known as Skanderbeg or Iskander Bey, against the Ottoman Turks. Kastrioti was a Christian who was taken hostage as a boy and brought up in the Muslim faith at the court of Sultan Murad II, who made him a bey, or provincial governor. In 1443 he abjured Islam and led his countrymen in a revolt against the Turks. The Albanians were supported at various times by the king of Naples, the Venetian Republic, and the Pope, but they became increasingly isolated. They repulsed thirteen Turkish invasions, but the Albanian resistance collapsed with Kastrioti's death in 1468. Sarrocchi's choice of subject reflects the contemporary preoccupation with the renewed Turkish push on eastern Europe that continued until the defeat of their siege of Vienna in 1683. *La Scanderbeide* was widely praised, but Sarrocchi continued to work on it for several years.

In 1608 some of Sarrocchi's followers protested the Baroque style favored by the Accademia degli Umoristi (Academy of the Humorists) by leaving it and forming the Accademia degli Ordinati (Academy of the Orderly Ones). The new academy was organized by Cardinal Battista Deti, in whose residence it met, and

Title page for the first edition of Margherita Sarrocchi's book (Biblioteca Nazionale Marciana, Venice)

Giulio Strozzi; but Sarrocchi received all the blame for the split and was involved in a dispute with Ottavio Tronsarelli regarding the emblems of the two academies.

Sarrocchi had been put in touch with Galileo by Valerio, who had met the scientist in Pisa in the late 1580s. She met Galileo during his visit to Rome in 1611 and began a correspondence with him. In a 26 August 1611 letter to Guido Bettoli, a professor at the University of Perugia who had requested information from her about Galileo's much-talked-about new discovery, she states that she has seen the satellites of Jupiter through Galileo's telescope and goes on to elaborate on some of the scientific particulars. This letter and others from her to Galileo were printed for the first time in an article by Antonio Favaro in 1894.

With the death of her husband in 1613, Sarrocchi found herself in financial difficulty. She was assisted by Valerio, who had become a professor of mathematics and moral philosophy at La Sapienza, the University of Rome; he even did some of her

*Title page for the revised and enlarged edition
(Vatican Library)*

shopping. Some of their contemporaries considered Valerio's attachment to Sarrocchi a senile infatuation, but to some modern critics a stanza in canto 9 of the 1606 edition of *La Scanderbeide* appears to depict the true nature of their relationship:

> Natura avvince con tenace nodo
> d'amor, di carità sovente un core;
> ma con più saldo e più soave modo
> fa di santa amistà possente amore
> due anime, che lontan d'inganno e frodo
> seguan chiara virtù, verace onore
> simili di costumi e pari d'anni
> conformi ne le gioie e negli affanni.

> (Nature ties with a tenacious knot,
> of love, of charity, a heart;
> but with more lasting and in a gentler way
> ties, with mighty love of holy friendship
> two souls, that, far from treachery and fraud,
> follow noble virtue, true honor,
> alike in habits and of equal age,
> similar in joy as well as in pain.)

Sarrocchi sent a copy of the manuscript for the enlarged version of *La Scanderbeide* to Galileo with a request that he make corrections—especially of the language, which she wanted to be as Tuscan as possible. Galileo was at first too busy to respond, then became ill; in any case, he preferred Ludovico Ariosto to Tasso, her model. Later, she wrote to him that she had made more changes and asked him to return her manuscript so that she could send him the new version. She may have become offended when he did not oblige, or perhaps he made negative comments to others. Sarrocchi claimed that her poem was ready for publication in 1614, but it did not appear at that time. Some scholars blame Sarrocchi for Valerio's rift with Galileo, who had asked Valerio to intercede on his behalf with the Inquisition through Valerio's protector, Cardinal Pietro Aldobrandini. In fact, however, Valerio was afraid of losing his professorship: he stated in his letter of resignation to the Accademia dei Lincei (Academy of the Lynx-Eyed) in 1616 that he could not accept the academy's support of Galileo's ideas because they had been censured by the Church.

Sarrocchi died of a fever on 29 October 1617. Many men of letters and members of various Roman academies attended her funeral; as she had requested in her will, she was buried in the Church of Santa Maria sopra Minerva. Her heir was Giovanni Latini, whom she had raised; all that is known about him is that he was from Fermo and was a member of the Accademia degli Umoristi. He wrote an epitaph for Sarrocchi in which he called himself "sororis filius, ed heres (son of her sister, and heir), to whom she had been "sibi mater, sibi magistra" (a mother and a teacher). Nothing is known about Sarrocchi having a sister. Valerio signed his will two days before his death on 16 January 1618, and he, too, designated Latini as his heir. A contemporary, Girolamo Baruffaldi, claimed in a letter that Valerio left his belongings to the illegitimate son of his landlady, a woman poet—an obvious allusion to Sarrocchi. It is still undetermined whether Latini was Sarrocchi's son or nephew, or the mysterious boy alluded to in the will written by Beatrice Cenci three days before Cenci was beheaded in 1599. Cenci, her stepmother, and her brothers had been condemned for the murder of her father, a violent man who had mistreated his children. She bequeathed to Sarrocchi and Caterina De Sanctis, a widow who lived in Sarrocchi's home, the interest on a sum of money set aside as an inheritance for a "poor boy" she had previously recommended to the two women. Some scholars believe that the boy was an illegitimate child of Cenci's, but no proof exists.

The revised version of *La Scanderbeide*, in twenty-three cantos, was published by Latini in 1623. Both structural and stylistic differences exist between the 1606 and 1623 versions: some episodes appear in different cantos in the two editions, while others are modified or dropped in the later one; some names have been changed; a few character descriptions have been retouched; new material has been added; and the language has been refined.

Led by Skanderbeg, an exemplary warrior, and aided by God and their superior military strategies, the Christians achieve victory over an enemy that greatly outnumbers them in a final battle that concludes the poem and ends with Sultan Murad's death. The descriptions of battles, skirmishes, personal duels, intrigues, betrayals, and religious differences between Christians and Muslims are interwoven with love episodes.

Sarrocchi describes her characters with precision and an eye for detail. She realistically depicts the horror and carnage of combat on plains, mountains, marshes, rivers, and the sea. She says that the ways of death are many, and she seems to include all of them: characters perish by sword, lance, club, knife, arrow, fire, water, hunger, and plague; they are trampled to death by horses and crushed when the animals fall on them. She also depicts in a masterly fashion the various emotions of lovers. Her description—found only in the 1606 edition—of the married Calidora's torment when she falls in love with Serano is frequently anthologized. Even better known is the episode, which occurs in different cantos in the two editions, of Pallante and Flora, who believe that they are brother and sister: Sarrocchi depicts their first signs of love, the increasing attraction they feel for each other, and their unspoken anguish—and then their joy, followed by their impatiently awaited love embrace, when they discover that they are not related. Their story is a psychological study of a budding love that turns into an ardent passion. Quite different is the relationship of Ariodeno and the intellectual Sofia: his long-endured desire for her is countered by her insistence that their love can only exist on a noble, platonic plane. The sultan's warrior daughter, Rosmonda (named Rosana in the 1606 edition), captures and imprisons the Christian champion Vaconte. They gradually fall in love without daring to confess it, until she must turn against her father to save Vaconte from death. In the end she marries him and becomes a Christian. Another daughter of the sultan, Glicera, is reputed to be so beautiful that Erifilio, the son of the Persian king, falls in love with her sight unseen; he writes to her and, at her invitation, becomes her servant. Their story ends tragically when Erifilio's mother arrives and identifies him in front of the sultan.

The important role played by women in *La Scanderbeide* is not restricted to the love episodes. In canto 1 Murad orders Dori (Donica in the 1606 edition) kidnapped for his harem, triggering Skanderbeg's rebellion. The widow Filena's demand for vengeance from the sultan provides Sarrocchi with the opportunity to describe Turkish customs (canto 4 in the 1606 edition, canto 3 in the 1623 edition). In canto 5 of the 1623 edition Amilla accompanies her husband, Varadino, to the Turkish camp dressed as his squire, only to be killed in his bed during a surprise attack—a notable difference from canto 7 of the earlier version, in which Varadino is in bed with a boy. The huntress Silveria (Clori in the 1606 edition) was abandoned by her father in a forest and nursed by a bear until she was found by a hunter. She joins Rosmonda's soldiers and distinguishes herself in battle, arousing the envy of the Turkish knights. She challenges three of them and defeats them all, thereby earning their hatred. She is converted to Christianity along with Rosmonda but is crushed to death by the corpse of a maddened elephant she has just killed. Another notable character is Vaconte's mother, Dianora, a perfect Christian woman who had borne arms in her youth.

Dust jacket for the English translation of Sarrocchi's poem (Library of Congress)

A 1701 Naples edition of *La Scanderbeide* was based on the 1606 version, probably because the publisher, Antonio Bulifon, was not aware of the 1623 revision. In the early eighteenth century the critic Giovanni Mario Crescimbeni considered the work a great contribution to Italian poetry and praised the author for courageously opposing Marino's excesses. But as interest in heroic poems faded, Sarrocchi was forgotten. The nineteenth-century critic Tommaso Vallauri found a manuscript of part of *La Scanderbeide* in the library of the University of Turin, misidentified the author as Piedmontese, and lamented that so little of her work had been preserved. He admired her images, her precise language, and the harmoniousness of her verses and quoted two stanzas from canto 13, the episode of Rosmonda and Vaconte. The two stanzas differ from those in the final version of 1623, where a better choice of words appears; the manuscript must be an intermediate draft that came between the two published versions. In 1904 Bernardinus Peyron described the Turin manuscript as consisting of thirty sheets of paper containing an incomplete canto of a heroic poem by Sarrocchi, beginning with "La magnanima donna i lumi gira" (The noble woman turned her eyes); the verse refers to Rosmonda just before she sees Vaconte surrounded by her soldiers. According to Verdile, only a few sections of the manuscript, consisting of parts of cantos 13 and 14, are still legible; the rest has been badly burned. In the late nineteenth century Antonio Belloni placed Sarrocchi among the imitators of Tasso. He pointed to her refined style and poetic intuition, which he held to be derived from her reading of masters such as Ariosto, Dante, and Angelo Poliziano. He also praised her ability to describe nascent passion and its evolution. He illustrated these characteristics with examples, all of which are taken from the 1606 edition.

In the twentieth century Benedetto Croce briefly mentioned Sarrocchi as a "scrittrice corretta e di buona tradizione" (correct writer and of a good literary tradition), meaning that she avoided the excesses of Baroque style. Yet, she was not immune to its influence: *La Scanderbeide* makes extensive use of similes and metaphors and includes many playful constructions based on the Baroque technique of repeating the same or similar words in short sequences.

The first critic to examine Margherita Sarrocchi seriously and to reconstruct her life was Angelo Borzelli in 1927. Studies of her life and that of Valerio were published in the early 1990s by Verdile and by Ugo Baldini and Pier Daniele Napolitani. Verdile constructed aspects of Sarrocchi's life and literary career through published and unpublished poems, letters, and other documents written by Sarrocchi and by her admirers and detractors, while Baldini and Napolitani provided Italian translations of Latin texts referring to Sarrocchi. The renewed interest in women writers has called attention to *La Scanderbeide* both for its merit as a heroic poem and as a work in which strong women play an important part. In 2005 Serena Pezzini argued that Sarrocchi's heroines are different from those in earlier heroic poems because they are seen from a woman's point of view. In 2006 Rinaldina Russell published a translation of *La Scanderbeide* into English prose with an introduction dealing with Italian heroic poetry and Skanderberg's wars. A modern Italian edition is still lacking.

Biographies:

Nadia Verdile, "Contributi alla biografia di Margherita Sarrocchi," *Rendiconti della Accademia di Archeologia Lettere e Belle Arti,* new series, 62 (1990): 165–206;

Ugo Baldini and Pier Daniele Napolitani, "Per una biografia di Luca Valerio: Fonti edite e inedite per una ricostruzione della sua carriera scientifica," *Bollettino di storia delle scienze matematiche,* 11, no. 2 (1991): 3–157.

References:

Antonio Belloni, *Gli epigoni della Gerusalemme Liberata* (Padua: Draghi, 1893), pp. 133–140, 497–498;

Angelo Borzelli, *Note intorno a Margherita Sarrocchi ed al suo poema La Scanderbeide* (Naples: Artigianelli, 1935);

Borzelli, *Storia della vita e delle opere di Giovan Battista Marino* (Naples: Artigianelli, 1927), pp. 84–87;

Maria Cristina Cabani, *Gli amici amanti: Coppie eroiche e sortite notturne nell'epica italiana* (Naples: Liguori, 1995), p. 56;

Virginia Cox, "Women as Readers and Writers of Chivalric Poetry," in *Sguardi sull'Italia: Miscellanea dedicata a Francesco Villari dalla Society for Italian Studies,* edited by Gino Bedani (Exeter, U.K.: Society for Italian Studies, 1997), pp. 134–145;

Giovanni Mario Crescimbeni, *Dell'istoria della volgar poesia e Comentarj intorno alla medesima,* 6 volumes (Venice: L. Basegio, 1730–1731), III: 146–147;

Benedetto Croce, *Nuovi saggi sulla letteratura italiana del Seicento* (Bari: Laterza, 1931), pp. 162–163;

Carlo Delcorno, "Un avversario del Marino: Ferrante Carli," *Studi secenteschi,* 16 (1975): 69–155;

Antonio Favaro, "Amici e corrispondenti di Galileo Galilei," *Atti del Reale Istituto Veneto di Scienze, Lettere ed Arti,* series 7, 5 (1894): 552–580;

Michele Maylender, *Storia delle accademie d'Italia,* 5 volumes (Bologna: Forni, 1976–1981), IV: 140–141; V: 370–381;

Letizia Panizza and Sharon Wood, eds., *A History of Women's Writing in Italy* (Cambridge: Cambridge University Press, 2000), pp. 50, 58, 60–61, 329;

Bernardinus Peyron, *Codices Italici manu exarati qui in Bibliotheca Taurinensis Athenaei ante diem XXVI ianuarii MCMIV asservabantur* (Turin: Clausen, 1904), p. 166;

Serena Pezzini, "Ideologia della conquista, ideologia dell'accoglienza: *La Scanderbeide* di Margherita Sarrocchi (1623)," *Modern Language Notes,* 120, no. 1 (2005): 190–222;

Tommaso Vallauri, *Storia della poesia in Piemonte,* volume 1 (Turin: Chirio & Mina, 1841), pp. 400–401.

Flaminio Scala
(Flavio)
(27 September 1552 – 9 December 1624)

Salvatore Cappelletti
Providence College

BOOKS: *Il Postumio, comedia del signor I. S. posta in luce per Flaminio Scala detto Flavio, Comico Acceso,* as I. S. (Lyon: Roussin, 1601);

La schiava, comedia nuova e ridicolosa: Nuovamente posta in luce, ad instantia d'ogni spirito gentile, anonymous, attributed to Scala (Pavia: Pietro Bartoli, 1602); act 1 translated by Edward Gordon Craig, as G. B. Ambrose, in his "Real Acting. Or, Can the Actor Create?" *Mask,* 9 (1923): 12–14;

Il teatro delle favole rappresentative, overo La ricreatione comica, boscareccia, e tragica: Divisa in cinquanta giornate, composte da Flaminio Scala detto Flavio Comico del Sereniss. Sig. Duca di Mantova (Venice: Giovanni Battista Pulciani, 1611);

Il finto marito (Venice: Andrea Baba, 1618).

Editions and Collections: *Il marito, Il ritratto, Li tappeti alessandrini, L'Alvida,* and *La forsennata principessa,* in *La commedia dell'arte: Storia, tecnica, scenari,* edited by Enzo Petraccone, preface by Benedetto Croce (Naples: Ricciardi, 1927), pp. 302–349;

Il marito, in *Commedia italiana: Raccolta di commedie da Cielo D'Alcamo a Goldoni,* edited by Mario Apollonio (Rome, Florence & Milan: Bompiani, 1947), pp. 553–565;

Li duo vecchi gemelli, La fortuna di Flavio, La fortunata Isabella, Le burle d'Isabella, Flavio tradito, Li tragici successi, La gelosa Isabella, and *Isabella astrologa,* with a sonnet and a preface by Francesco Andreini, in *La commedia dell'arte: Storia e testo,* volume 2, edited by Vito Pandolfi (Florence: Sansoni, 1957), pp. 166–243;

"Prologo della comedia del *Finto marito*" and "Prologo per recitare," in Carmine Jannaco, "Stesura e tendenza letteraria della commedia improvvisa in due prologhi di Flaminio Scala," *Studi secenteschi,* 1 (1960): 195–207;

Il teatro delle favole rappresentative, 2 volumes, edited by Ferruccio Marotti (Milan: Il Polifilo, 1976);

La schiava, in *Il teatro delle favole rappresentative,* volume 1, edited by Marotti (Milan: Il Polifilo, 1976), pp. xci–c;

"La poetica di Flaminio Scala: Prologo a *Il finto marito,*" in *Commedia dell'arte: La maschera e l'ombra,* edited by Roberto Tessari (Milan: Mursia, 1981), pp. 120–123;

Il finto marito, in *Commedie dei comici dell'arte,* edited by Laura Falavolti (Turin: Unione Tipografico-Editrice Torinese, 1982), pp. 215–365;

"Prologo della comedia del *Finto marito,*" in *La commedia dell'arte e la società barocca: La professione del teatro,* edited by Marotti and Giovanna Romei (Rome: Bulzoni, 1991), pp. 58–62;

La pazzia d'Isabella: Scrittura scenica e drammatica, introduction by Ezio Maria Caserta (Rome: Torre d'Orfeo, 1997);

La fortuna di Flavio, La fortunata Isabella, Le burle d'Isabella, Il vecchio geloso, La finta pazza, Il marito, Il dottor disperato, Il pellegrino fido amante, La travagliata Isabella, Lo specchio, Li duo capitani simili, La gelosa Isabella, Li tappeti alessandrini, Flavio finto negromante, Il fido amico, La caccia, La pazzia d'Isabella, Il ritratto, Rosalba incantatrice, L'arbore incantato, and *La fortuna di Foresta principessa di Moscovia,* in *La commedia dell'arte: Scelta e introduzione,* edited by Cesare Molinari (Rome: Istituto Poligrafico e Zecca dello Stato, 1999), pp. 65–211.

Editions in English: *The Faithful Friend: "Il fido amico" of Flaminio Scala,* in *The Drama,* volume 5 (London: Smart & Stanley, 1903), pp. 237–244;

Li tragici successi, in Winifred Smith, "A Comic Version of Romeo and Juliette," *Modern Philology,* 7 (October 1909): 217–220;

The Portrait: Plays for the College Theater, edited by Garrett Hasty Leverton (New York: S. French, 1932);

The Portrait, translated by Ethel van der Meer, in *World Drama,* volume 2, edited by Barrett Harper Clark (New York: Dover, 1933), pp. 10–14;

Scenarios of the Commedia dell'Arte: Flaminio Scala's "Il teatro delle favole rappresentative," translated by Henry F. Salerno, foreword by Kenneth McKee (New York: New York University Press, 1967);

Il finto marito, excerpts in *La Commedia dell'Arte: A Documentary History,* by Kenneth Richards and Laura Richards (Oxford & Cambridge, Mass.: Blackwell, 1990), pp. 197–200.

OTHER: *Fragmenti di alcune scritture della Signora Isabella Andreini Comica Gelosa, et Academica Intenta,* edited by Scala (Venice: Giovanni Battista Combi, 1616);

"Lettere di Flaminio Scala," edited by Domenica Landolfi, in *Comici dell'arte: Corrispondenze. G. B. Andreini, N. Barbieri, P. M. Cecchini, S. Fiorillo, T. Martinelli, F. Scala,* volume 1, edited by Landolfi, Claudia Burattelli, and Anna Zinanni; introduction by Siro Ferrone (Florence: Le Lettere, 1993), pp. 437–587.

Flaminio Scala is one of the greatest figures in the history of theater: scenario writer, playwright, actor (with the stage names Flavio, the lover, and Claudione, an Italianate Frenchman), director, producer, manager, agent, and editor. He is most famous for publishing the first collection of scenarios: *Il teatro delle favole rappresentative, overo La ricreatione comica, boscareccia, e tragica: Divisa in cinquanta giornate, composte da Flaminio Scala detto Flavio Comico del Sereniss. Sig. Duca di Mantova* (1611, The Theater of Tales for Performance, or for Comic, Rustic, and Tragic Recreation, Divided into Fifty Days, and Composed by Flaminio Scala, Named Flavio, Comedian of the Most Serene Lord Duke of Mantua). His scenarios were a source of inspiration to playwrights such as Lope de Vega, William Shakespeare, Ben Jonson, and Molière.

Domenica Landolfi has established that Scala was born in Rome on 27 September 1552; prior to her findings, little was known about his date and place of birth. Little is still known about his aristocratic family, except that his father's name was Giacomo.

Scala is thought to have played the role of the *innamorato* (lover) in the Gelosi (Jealous) troupe in Florence before 1577. It is also believed that he brought Isabella Andreini, the sixteen-year-old wife of the actor Francesco Andreini (whose stage name was Capitan Spavento), into the Gelosi; she went on to become a celebrated actress and poet. From 1579 through 1596 he was associated as an actor and occasionally as an agent with the Accesi (Stimulated Ones), Desiosi, (Desired Ones), and Uniti (United Ones). In 1597 he submitted a request to the Senate of Genoa for permission for the Desiosi to perform in that city for three months; the following year he made a similar request on behalf of the Uniti. Both requests were granted. From 1600 to 1602 he performed in France and Flanders as a member of the Accesi, who had been invited by the French king and queen, Henry IV and Maria de' Medici; the troupe also included Pier Maria Cecchini, Silvio Fiorillo, Tristano Martinelli, and Diana Ponti. During this period he probably met the military leader and architect Don Giovanni de' Medici, the illegitimate son of Cosimo I de' Medici, Grand Duke of Tuscany. Giovanni de' Medici became a close friend and was later the patron of Scala's Confidenti (Confident Ones) company.

In 1601 Scala published *Il Postumio, comedia del signor I. S. posta in luce per Flaminio Scala detto Flavio, Comico Acceso* (Postumius, Comedy by Mr. I. S., Published by Flaminio Scala Named Flavio, Comedian of the Stimulated Ones) in Lyon; it was his first fully scripted play, as opposed to a scenario. Scala's stage name Flavio appears for the first time on the frontispiece of this book. The play is prefaced with verses by Ponti, who was also the first woman director of a professional theater troupe: the Desiosi, also known as the Diana Company.

In 1602 the first complete scenario was published: *La schiava, comedia nuova e ridicolosa: Nuovamente posta in luce, ad instantia d'ogni spirito gentile* (The Slave Girl, a New and Amusing Comedy: Recently Published at the Instance of Every Noble Spirit). Ferruccio Marotti argues convincingly for Scala's authorship. The comedy was discovered around 1923 in Florence by the British actor, producer, director, set designer, and theater theorist Edward Gordon Craig. In 1923 Craig reproduced and translated the first act in his article "Real Acting. Or, Can the Actor Create?" to show that actors can "invent" and "weave their own dialogue" from scenarios, as was the practice of commedia dell'arte players, and that their ability to respond promptly to impromptu lines and actions by other players makes each performance unique. Craig advises actors not to let "a name, even a great one, drive them to refuge under extinguishing modesty" and stop them from writing plays, "for the actors [Francesco] Andreini and Scala were better playwrights–though not better play-writers–than Shakespeare." The original scenario seems to have been lost when the Craig Collection was transferred from Florence to the Bibliothèque Nationale in Paris in 1957.

Craig's distinction between "playwrights" and "play-writers" is subtle but perceptive: Scala was a master of stagecraft, skilled in composing scenarios out of plots and dialogue from other sources and in producing them onstage. His scenarios were based on specific performances in which actors created their own dialogue; accordingly, as Tim Fitzpatrick points out in "Flaminio Scala's Prototypal Scenarios: Segmenting the Text/

Performance" (1989), "to speak of 'Scala's scenarios' is a necessary oversimplification, the collective nature of the enterprise precluding any attribution to Scala of the sole responsibility for the dramaturgical solutions implicit in the scenarios which he published; as such, the schematic form of the scenarios is a device to guide actors through the segmentation of the performance process, as it develops diachronically through the time sequencing of its elements, and synchronically, concerning the technique through which the same elements are combined at any one time."

In his preface to Scala's *Il teatro delle favole rappresentative* Francesco Andreini formulates a theoretical definition of the commedia dell'arte:

> Avrebbe potuto il detto Signor Flavio . . . distender l'opere sue, e scriverle da verbo a verbo, come s'usa da fare; ma perché oggidì non si vede altro che Comedie stampate con modi diversi di dire, e molto strepitosi nelle buone regole, ha voluto con questa sua nuova invenzione mettere fuori le sue Comedie solamente con lo Scenario, lasciando a i bellissimi ingegni (nati solo all'eccellenza del dire) il farvi sopra le parole.
>
> (Mr. Flavio . . . could have written out his plays in full, and set them down word for word, as it is usually done; but because nowadays we see nothing else but plays printed with different forms of speech, and very flamboyant in the accepted norms, he decided, with this new creation of his, to offer only the scenario of his plays, leaving it up to great minds [born exclusively to be exceptional in speech] to fill in the words.)

Andreini points out that the plays were written with no other goal than to please; he adds that "Avrebbe potuto l'istesso Signor Flavio descrivere ancora gli apparati tanto comici, quanto tragici, e boscarecci" (Mister Flavio himself could have described the stage settings for comedies, tragedies, and pastorals) but decided to let experts in stagecraft create their own sets for the performances.

The *Teatro delle favole rappresentative* comprises fifty three-act scenarios: forty popular comedies, a tragedy, a pastoral, a heroic comedy, an opera, and six royal comedies, three of which form a trilogy. Each scenario is preceded by an *argomento* (argument), a list of characters, and a list of props. Unlike the prologue in the literary comedy, which is an integral part of the performance, the *argomento* is addressed to the reader and functions as a summary of the plot. As Roberto Tessari notes in his *Commedia dell'arte: La maschera e l'ombra* (1981, Commedia dell'arte: The Mask and the Shadow), Scala succinctly describes the psychological aspects of the characters, thus providing behavioristic definitions of them. Fitzpatrick notes Scala's technique of grouping actors in pairs, a binary patterning that is also found in Shakespeare's *A Midsummer Night's Dream* (circa 1595–1596) and *Twelfth Night* (circa 1601). Within the scenarios scene changes, entrances, and exits are clearly indicated. For Konstantin Miklashevskii the scenarios "distinguish themselves for their variety, wealth of creativity, and are written with perfect knowledge of the stage and audiences' tastes." In her *La Commedia dell'Arte* (1964) Winifred Smith credits Scala and his Confidenti with showing the "true method of composing and performing plays." Kathleen Margaret Lea holds that the scenarios were written for an ideal troupe "with such an all-star cast as the Duke of Mantua and the King of France had dreamed but rarely achieved."

The *Teatro delle favole rappresentative* includes some of the scenarios that made Isabella Andreini famous: *La fortunata Isabella* (Fortunate Isabella), *La gelosa Isabella* (Jealous Isabella), *La pazzia d'Isabella* (The Madness of Isabella), and *La finta pazza* (The Fake Madwoman). Molière's *Le mèdecin malgré lui* (1666, The Physician in Spite of Himself) echoes several elements of *La finta pazza*. Louis (Luigi) Riccoboni, the author of the first history of the Italian theater, analyzed Scala's scenarios; he staged *La finta pazza* in 1717 as part of his first repertoire as leader of the New Comédie-Italienne in Paris.

With the exception of courtesans in ancient Roman theater, women first appeared onstage in the commedia dell'arte; some of them gained important positions as performers and directors. The first professional actress was Donna Lucrezia, known as the Senese (Sienese); she and six other players signed a contract in her home in Rome on 10 October 1564. Nothing else, including her surname, is known about Donna Lucrezia. The inclusion of actresses in commedia dell'arte troupes brought about the writing of many scenarios in which madness was used as an expedient for having an actress tear off her clothes, which was one of the reasons for the Church's condemnation of the commedia dell'arte. For instance, in *La pazzia d'Isabella* Isabella, hearing that her lover, Oratio, has been murdered, "diventa pazza affatto, si straccia tutte le vestimenta d'attorno, e come forsennata se ne corre per strada" (becomes quite mad, tears off all clothes from her body, and runs through the street like a woman out of her wits).

Scala directed and managed the Confidenti company from 1614 through 1621; he often funded its productions, thereby becoming the first professional theatrical producer. Don Giovanni de' Medici's patronage, though devoid of financial support, bestowed social approval on the company, protected it from opponents, and facilitated the gaining of permission for performances at home and abroad. Scala was de' Medici's confidant and a close friend of his second wife, Livia Vernazza, whom he often escorted on journeys to join her husband.

Isabella Andreini had died in childbirth in France in 1604. In 1616, at Francesco Andreini's request, Scala edited *Fragmenti di alcune scritture della Signora Isabella Andreini Comica Gelosa, et Academica Intenta* (Fragments of Some Writings by Lady Isabella Andreini, Comedian of the Gelosi, and Academician of the Intenti). It was the first edition of Andreini's love dialogues.

In the prologue to his play *Il finto marito* (1618, The Fake Husband), which is based on the scenario *Il marito* (The Husband) in the 1611 collection, Scala advances what Kenneth and Laura Richards describe as "a reasoned and coherent aesthetic for actor-devised drama . . . giving more importance to movement and gestures than to language." In the "Prologo per recitare" (Prologue for Acting) in the same play Scala holds that comedy is "lo specchio della vita umana" (the mirror of human life) and "non è biasimevole né lodevole per sé stessa" (neither blameworthy nor praiseworthy in itself); considering that "onde avendo ella per sé il fine di giovare con l'esempio, il difetto non può mai esser suo, ma sì bene di chi mal se ne serve" (its end is to be of use by means of example, the fault can never be its, but that of those who make bad use of it).

Since the eighteenth century, scholars have linked Scala's plays and scenarios to the works of other dramatists. For example, several scenes in Jonson's *Volpone* (1606) and the plot of Molière's *Tartuffe* (1669) are closely connected to Scala's *Il pedante* (The Pedant); other scenes in *Volpone* are drawn from Scala's *La fortuna di Flavio* (Flavio's Fortune). In 1909 Smith published a translation of Scala's *Li tragici successi* (The Tragic Events) in *Modern Philology,* calling it a comic version of *Romeo and Juliet* (circa 1595–1596); the article inspired other scholars to find links between Scala and Shakespeare. Scala's *Alvida,* for example, is the source of Shakespeare's *Cymbeline* (1609), while his *L'arbore incantato* (The Enchanted Tree) is the main source of *The Tempest* (1611); parallels have been found between Scala's scenario *I duo vecchi gemelli* (The Two Old Twins) and Shakespeare's *The Comedy of Errors* (circa 1592–1594) and between *La fortuna di Foresta prencipessa di Moscovia* (The Fortune of Foresta, Princess of Muscovy) and *The Winter's Tale* (1611). In addition to *Romeo and Juliet, Li tragici successi* also has many points of resemblance to Lope de Vega's tragicomedy *Castelvines y Montesses* (1647, The Castelvines and the Monteses).

Scala left the largest body of correspondence of any commedia dell'arte actor or director; of the 112 letters, which are dated between 1615 and 1624, 91 are addressed to Giovanni de' Medici and 1 to Livia de' Medici. Most concern performances, financial matters, management, and disputes among the Confidenti players; Cecchini seems to have been a particular source of disharmony. On 10 November 1618 Scala wrote to Gio-

Title page for Flaminio Scala's The Theater of Tales for Performance, or for Comic, Rustic, and Tragic Recreation, Divided into Fifty Days, *the first collection of commedia dell'arte scenarios (Library of Congress)*

vanni de' Medici: "Insomma tutte questi accidenti son per tribulare maggiormente il povero Flavio, perché io non penso in altro che in tenerli uniti; se la mi si vedesse, la darebbe parerli vedere Moisé mantenere in speranza il popolo ebreo" (In conclusion, all these accidents are for tormenting even more the poor Flavio, since I think of nothing else but to keep them united; if you saw me, it would give you the impression of seeing Moses keeping the Hebrew people hopeful). The letters also reveal that Scala owned a perfume shop named Fama, located by the Rialto in Venice. Several read like intelligence reports in which Scala informs de' Medici about political matters in states and cities where the Confidenti were performing: he relates information about the duke of Mantua, disputes between the kings of France and Spain, the latter's itinerary for a trip to Portugal and plans for wars, and the execution of Rodrigo Calderón, Count of Oliva.

In 1624 Scala sold the perfume shop to his manager, Pietro Baldanzini, and moved to Mantua to open a new shop and serve as personal perfumer to Ferdinando Gonzaga, sixth Duke of Mantua, and Ferdinando's consort, Caterina de' Medici, Don Giovanni's niece. He died shortly after his arrival, on 9 December; he was seventy-two, not seventy-four or seventy-seven, as stated in many sources.

Flaminio Scala is important for having published the first and best collection of commedia dell'arte scenarios, many of which have been a source of inspiration to other playwrights. Since improvisation is an important element of commedia dell'arte, the scenarios fostered creativity in acting; actors felt free to vary the ways they played their roles, making each performance unique.

Bibliographies:

Bruno Brunelli, "Scala, Flaminio," in *Enciclopedia dello spettacolo,* volume 8 (Rome: Le Maschere, 1961), pp. 1552–1553;

Laura Falavolti, "Flaminio Scala: *Il finto marito,*" in *Commedie dei comici dell'arte,* edited by Falavolti (Turin: Unione Tipografico-Editrice Torinese, 1982), p. 221;

Thomas F. Heck, *Commedia dell'Arte: A Guide to the Primary and Secondary Literature* (New York & London: Garland, 1988), pp. 8, 10, 35–37, 54, 133, 150, 177, 199;

Domenica Landolfi, "Flaminio Scala," in *Comici del'arte: Corrispondenze. G. B. Andreini, N. Barbieri, P. M. Cecchini, S. Fiorillo, T. Martinelli, F. Scala,* edited by Landolfi, Claudia Burattelli, and Anna Zinanni (Florence: Le Lettere, 1993), p. 449.

Biographies:

Luigi Rasi, "Flaminio Scala," in his *I comici italiani: biografia, bibliografia, iconografia,* volume 3 (Florence: Francesco Lumachi, 1905), pp. 512–520;

Francesco Bartoli, "Scala Flaminio," in his *Notizie istoriche de' comici italiani,* volume 2 (Bologna: Arnoldo Forni, 1978), pp. 155–163;

Ferruccio Marotti, "La figura di Flaminio Scala," in *Alle origini del teatro moderno: La commedia dell'arte,* edited by Luciano Mariti (Rome: Bulzoni, 1980), pp. 21–43;

Renzo Guardenti, "Flaminio Scala," in *La commedia dell'arte: scelta e introduzione,* edited by Cesare Molinari (Rome: Istituto Poligrafico e Zecca dello Stato, 1999), pp. 65–71.

References:

G. B. Ambrose (Edward Gordon Craig), "Real Acting. Or, Can the Actor Create?" *Mask,* 9 (1923): 12–14;

Richard Andrews, *Scripts and Scenarios: The Performance of Comedy in Renaissance Italy* (Cambridge: Cambridge University Press, 1993), pp. 173, 195–199, 255, 267;

Franca Angelini, "La pazzia di Isabella," in *Letteratura italiana: Teatro, musica, tradizione dei classici,* volume 6, edited by Alberto Asor Rosa (Turin: Einaudi, 1986), pp. 112–113;

Mario Apollonio, "Flaminio Scala," in "Prelezioni sulla commedia dell'arte," in *Contributi dell'Istituto di Filologia Moderna: Serie Storia del Teatro,* volume 1 (Milan: Vita e Pensiero, 1968), pp. 151, 156–161, 189;

Apollonio, *Storia della commedia dell'arte* (Rome: Augustea, 1930), pp. 21, 84, 103, 107, 119, 132, 140, 141, 154–156, 161, 163, 183, 196, 219, 316;

Mario Ariani, "Flaminio Scala: *Il finto marito,*" in *Il teatro: Repertorio dalle origini a oggi,* edited by Cesare Molinari (Milan: Mondadori, 1982), pp. 351–352;

Daniel C. Boughner, *The Braggart in Renaissance Comedy: A Study of Comparative Drama from Aristophanes to Shakespeare* (Minneapolis: University of Minnesota Press, 1954), pp. 105–108, 315;

Christopher Cairns, "La commedia dell'arte in Inghilterra: Il gran rifiuto, mito o realtà?" in *Origini della commedia improvvisa o dell'arte: Convegno di studi, Roma, 12–14 ottobre 1995, Anagni, 15 ottobre 1995,* edited by Maria Chiabò and Federico Doglio (Rome: Torre d'Orfeo, 1996), pp. 291–301;

Paul Castagno, *The Early Commedia dell'Arte, 1550–1621: The Mannerist Context* (New York: Peter Lang, 1994), pp. 56–57, 75, 80–81, 93, 107, 130;

Luise George Clubb, *Italian Drama in Shakespeare's Time* (New Haven & London: Yale University Press, 1989), pp. 19–21, 185, 250–256, 265, 270;

Siro Ferrone, *Attori mercanti corsari: La commedia dell'arte in Europa tra Cinque e Seicento* (Turin: Einaudi, 1993), pp. xix, xxi, 9, 19, 24, 29, 36, 40, 42, 49, 53, 66, 113, 115, 118–123, 125, 127, 133, 136, 142, 149–164, 166, 168, 172–178, 180, 182, 192, 193, 195, 197, 200, 201, 212, 215, 217, 223, 225, 230, 265, 274, 282, 284, 287, 289–292, 297, 299, 302, 306–308, 310, 315, 317, 319, 320, 335, 337;

Ferrone, "La compagnia dei comici 'Confidenti' al servizio di don Giovanni dei Medici (1613–1621)," *Quaderni di teatro,* 7 (1984): 135–156;

Tim Fitzpatrick, *Commedia dell'Arte and Performance: The Scenarios of Flaminio Scala* (Warwick, U.K.: Graduate School of Renaissance Studies, 1985);

Fitzpatrick, "Flaminio Scala's Prototypal Scenarios: Segmenting the Text/Performance," in *The Science of Buffoonery: Theory and History of the Commedia dell'Arte,* edited by Domenico Pietropaolo (Toronto: Dovehouse, 1989), pp. 177–198;

David George, "Shakespeare and the Actors of the Commedia dell'Arte," in *Studies in the Commedia dell'Arte,* edited by David J. George and Christopher J. Gossip (Cardiff: University of Wales Press, 1993), pp. 13-47;

Renzo Guardenti, "Flaminio Scala," in *La commedia dell'arte: Scelta e introduzione,* edited by Molinari (Rome: Istituto Poligrafico e Zecca dello Stato, 1999), pp. 571-576;

Robert Henke, *Performance and Literature in the Commedia dell'arte* (Cambridge: Cambridge University Press, 2002), pp. 13-15, 18, 22-24, 26-27, 46, 100-102, 109, 120, 125-126, 129, 130-131, 147, 149, 183-196;

Carmine Jannaco, "Stesura e tendenza letteraria della commedia improvvisa in due prologhi di Flaminio Scala," *Studi secenteschi,* 1 (1960): 195-207;

Steen Jansen, "Cos'è, nella fattispecie, il canovaccio? Appunti sul *Teatro delle favole rappresentative* di Flaminio Scala," *Revue Romane,* 25 (October 1997): 323-342;

Jansen, "On the Clauses in a Scenario of Flaminio Scala," *Quaderni d'italianistica,* 2, no. 2 (1990): 175-196;

Jansen, "Sur la segmentation du texte dramatique et sur quelques scénarios de Flaminio Scala," in *The Science of Buffoonery: Theory and History of the Commedia dell'Arte,* edited by Pietropaolo (Toronto: Dovehouse, 1989), pp. 149-165;

Joseph Spencer Kennard, *Masks and Marionettes* (New York: Macmillan, 1935), pp. 4, 7, 17, 24, 66-68;

Rosalind Kerr, "The Actress as Androgyne in the Commedia dell'Arte Scenarios of Flaminio Scala," dissertation, University of Toronto, 1993;

Kerr, "Transgressive Transvestism in Three Scala Scenarios," in *Gendered Contexts: New Perspectives in Italian Cultural Studies,* edited by Laura Benedetti, Julia L. Hairston, and Silvia M. Ross (New York: Peter Lang, 1996), pp. 109-120;

Kathleen Margaret Lea, *Italian Popular Comedy: A Study in the Commedia dell'Arte, 1560-1620, with Special Reference to the English Stage,* volume 1 (Oxford: Clarendon Press, 1934), pp. 4, 52, 67, 72, 104, 131-133, 146, 149, 200-203, 212, 213, 267, 277-278, 292-301, 306-308, 316, 331, 335;

Richard Lester, "An Alternative Theory of the Oxford Cover-Up," *Elizabethan Review,* 7 (Spring 1999): 33-45;

Ferruccio Marotti, "*Il teatro delle favole rappresentative:* Un progetto utopico," *Biblioteca, teatrale,* 15-16 (1976): 191-215;

Konstantin Miklashevskii, *La commedia dell'arte, o il teatro dei comici italiani nei secoli XVI, XVII e XVIII* (Venice: Marsilio, 1981), pp. 66-87;

Cesare Molinari, "Actors-Authors of the Commedia dell'Arte: The Dramatic Writings of Flaminio Scala and Giambattista Andreini," translated by M. A. Katritzky, *Bibliotèque d'Humanisme et Renaissance: Travaux et documents,* 23 (Summer 1998): 142-151;

Allardyce Nicoll, *The World of Harlequin* (New York & London: Cambridge University Press, 1986), pp. 1-2, 24, 39-55, 60, 70, 89, 101, 115-118, 126-136, 141, 148, 151, 154, 159, 166, 177, 180, 217-218, 223, 224, 229;

Louis (Luigi) Riccoboni, *Histoire du théâtre italien,* volume 1 (Paris: Pierre Delormel, 1728), pp. 39-42, 49-50, 154;

Kenneth Richards and Laura Richards, *The Commedia dell'Arte: A Documentary History* (Oxford: Blackwell, 1990), pp. 7, 58, 64-67, 76, 82, 92, 120, 123, 141-150, 185-187, 191-200, 211, 225-227, 238, 243, 287;

Giovanna Romei, "La professione del teatro: la commedia dell'arte e la società barocca," in her *Teoria testo e scena: Studi sullo spettacolo in Italia dal Rinascimento a Pirandello,* edited by Giorgio Patrizi and Luisa Tinti (Rome: Bulzoni, 2001), pp. 177-180, 190, 194-196, 204, 207-209, 211, 214, 215, 218, 220, 228-230, 231, 233, 234, 237;

John Rudlin and Olly Crick, *Commedia dell'Arte: A Handbook for Troupes* (New York & London: Routledge, 2001), pp. 20, 30, 36, 38-40, 58, 73, 87, 97, 108, 128, 194, 196;

Winifred Smith, *La Commedia dell'Arte* (New York: Benjamin Blom, 1964), pp. 98-99, 111, 125, 128, 135, 163-164, 194-195, 200, 211, 214-216, 240-241;

Roberto Tessari, *Commedia dell'arte: La maschera e l'ombra* (Milan: Mursia, 1981), pp. 7, 19, 50-56, 60, 67-68, 71, 85, 94, 96, 120, 123, 150, 169;

Tessari, "Lo sperimentalismo di Flaminio Scala," in his *La commedia dell'arte nel Seicento: "Industria" e "arte giocosa" della civiltà barocca* (Florence: Olschki, 1969), pp. 109-135;

Jane Tylus, "Women at the Windows: Commedia dell'Arte and Theatrical Practice in Early Modern Italy," *Theatre Journal,* 49 (October 1997): 323-342;

Ludovico Zorzi, "La raccolta degli scenari italiani della commedia dell'arte," in *Alle origini del teatro moderno: La commedia dell'arte,* edited by Luciano Mariti (Rome: Bulzoni, 1980), pp. 104-115.

Papers:

Flaminio Scala's papers are in the State Archives in Florence.

Sara Copio Sullam
(circa 1592 – 1641)

Lori J. Ultsch
Hofstra University

BOOKS: *Manifesto di Sarra Copia Sulam hebrea nel quale è da lei riprovate, e detestata l'opinione negante l'immortalità dell'anima, falsemente attribuitale da Sig. Baldassare Bonifaccio* (Venice: Alberti, 1621);
Sonetti editi ed inediti raccolti e pubblicati insieme ad alquanti cenni biografici, edited by Leonello Modona (Bologna: Società Tipografica già Compositori, 1887).

OTHER: "La bella Hebrea che con devoti accenti," "Signor, pianto non merta il gran Lanfranco," "Se mover a pietà Stige ed Averno," and "L'imago è questa di colei che al core," in *Lettere d'Ansaldo Cebà scritte a Sarra Copia e dedicate a Marc'Antonio Doria* (Genoa: Giuseppe Pavoni, 1623);
"Amai, Zinan, qui il ben d'ogni ben mio," in *Rime diverse,* edited by Gabriele Zinano (Venice: Deuchino, 1627).

Sara Copio Sullam resided in the Venetian Jewish ghetto during the first half of the seventeenth century. She wrote Petrarchan poetry and published one prose work, the pamphlet *Manifesto di Sarra Copia Sulam hebrea nel quale è da lei riprovate, e detestata l'opinione negante l'immortalità dell'anima, falsemente attribuitale da Sig. Baldassare Bonifaccio* (1621, The Manifesto of Sarra Copia Sulam, a Jewish Woman, in Which She Refutes and Disavows the Opinion Denying the Immortality of the Soul, Falsely Attributed to Her by Signor Baldassare Bonifaccio). Contemporaries such as the Talmudic scholar Rabbi Leon Modena praised her as a learned woman with admirable talents in poetic improvisation and music. In the dedication of his 1619 tragedy *Ester* to Sullam, Modena recalled conversations in which she had expressed admiration for Ansaldo Cebà's heroic poem *La reina Esther* (1615, Queen Esther). Sullam considered herself a poet but, as a Jew, was repeatedly forced to participate in theological debates. Her extant poems comprise fourteen sonnets; they were scattered among three books and a manuscript until they were collected in Leonello Modona's 1887 edition. In most of the sonnets, which combine elements of neo-Platonism and Petrarchism, the poet represents herself figuratively as a suffering and distant lover enchained by her overpowering emotions. As a Jew and a female intellectual, Sullam at first used her poetry to participate in a dialogue with her male peers and later to defend herself from charges that resulted from her entrance into an arena dominated by Christian men. The sonnets that depart from the Petrarchan model and display a mordant and incisive manner are autobiographical ones in which Sullam addresses attacks on her character by male acquaintances and would-be proselytizers. Her one prose work was written in response to an allegation that she had publicly argued against the immortality of the soul. Sullam and Deborah Ascarelli, who translated hymns and prayers, are rare examples of Jewish women authors in Italy in the early modern period.

Little record of Sullam's life has survived. What is known about her largely revolves around three literary controversies that occurred in the period from 1618 to 1626. Contemporary sources that addressed these controversies provide information on her literary career, reputation, and poetry; without these male-authored works, Sullam's poetry would most likely have remained unpublished. In her manifesto she claims to have no desire to have her works published; addressing Baldassare Bonifaccio, she writes: "Ancorchè mi provocaste di nuovo con mille ingiurie, non sarò più per contrapporvi alcuna replica, per non consumare inutilmente il tempo, massime essendo io tanta nemica do sottopormi agli occhi del mondo nelle stampe" (Even if you were to provoke me again with a thousand insults, I will not reply again, in order to not consume my time uselessly, especially since I am so averse to exposing myself to the eyes of the world in print).

The exact date of Sara Copio's birth is not known, but the majority of sources place it around 1592. Her parents, Simon and Rebecca (Ricca) Copio, raised Copio and her younger sister, Stella, in the Venice ghetto. The family's wealth allowed Sara to study literature, astrology, Jewish history, languages, and theology; she was also gifted musically. Her father may have provided a tutor for her; it is not known whether she was ever formally a student of Modena, who was a friend of the family. Simon Copio established an informal salon in their home over which Sara presided as hostess. Her reputation, poetic skills, and fashionable conversation attracted both Venetians and foreigners.

In 1613 Copio married Giacobbe Sullam. Shortly afterward she hired Numidio Paluzzi, a Roman poet and prose writer, as her tutor in literature. A generous employer, she found Paluzzi lodgings in Venice and financed his treatments with sulfur for advanced syphilis. Sullam also occasionally employed Paluzzi's friend Alessandro Berardelli, a painter and poet from Rome.

In 1618 Sullam wrote to Cebà, an elderly nobleman, statesman, and poet in the Republic of Genoa who became a monk when his fiancée entered a convent, to compliment him on *La reina Ester*: she was impressed that the Catholic poet had chosen an Old Testament figure for his heroine. She included a sonnet, "La bella Hebrea che con devoti accenti" (The beautiful Jewish woman who in devout tones). On 19 May 1618 Cebà responded with a sonnet and a letter in which he said: "Nuova cosa m'è paruta, ch'una giovane donna si sia talmente invaghita d'un Poema, che ragiona di cose grandi, che non habbia potuto temperarsi di procurar la conoscenza di chi l'ha scritto: ond'io mi paio obligato a far di voi altro giudicio, che non si suole ordinariamente fare del vostro sesso" (It seems to me a singular thing that a young woman should be so enamored of a Poem, that speaks of great things, that she could not restrain herself from making the acquaintance of he who wrote it; thus, I feel obliged to make a judgment of you different than that which one ordinarily makes of your sex).

What began as an invitation from Sullam to converse about poetry and exchange poems quickly became, on the Catholic nobleman's part, a crusade: for the next four years Cebà tried ceaselessly to persuade Sullam of the falsity of her faith. On 30 March 1619 he wrote: "dogliomi, che chi possiede tanta parte dell'anima mia si serva del lume dell'intelletto per profondarsi nelle tenebre della perditione" (it pains me that she who possesses so much of my soul should make use of the light of reason to sink into the darkness of eternal damnation). Sullam resisted these efforts with grace and wit and continued to attempt to engage Cebà as an equal in a formal Petrarchan sonnet exchange.

In addition to poetry, Sullam's interests included theology, philosophy, astrology, Hebrew literature and history, music, and the Italian, Hebrew, Latin, Greek, and Spanish languages. Topics from these fields were often discussed in the literary circle that gathered in her home. In 1621 Bonifaccio, a member of the circle, who later became bishop of Capodistria (today Koper), published *Dell'immortalità dell'anima: Discorso* (On the Immortality of the Soul: Discourse), in which he accused Sullam of having argued against the doctrine of immortality. Sullam responded immediately with her manifesto, which methodically addresses each of Bonifaccio's points. The work is dedicated to the memory of her father:

> A te mio svisceratissimo Genitore . . . ho voluto fare questo picciolo dono. Primieramente perchè possi accrescere le tue gioie con quel poco di acquisto di fama che nel mio nome forse vedrai, per la qual cagione penso non ti sarà men caro haver prodotto una donna, per conservazione del tuo nome al mondo, di quel che ti sarebbe stato l'haver prodotto un huomo, come in questa vita mostravi estremo desiderio.
>
> (To you, my doting Father . . . I want to give this gift. Above all, so that it can make your joy grow with that small addition of fame that perhaps you will see in my name; for this reason I think that having produced a woman to preserve your name in this world rather than a man—for which you showed such great longing during your life—will seem no less dear to you.)

The dedication is followed by two sonnets in which Sullam invokes God's aid in defending herself from Bonifaccio's calumny. She attributes Bonifaccio's accusation to envy and characterizes her detractor as vain, slanderous, arrogant, avid for fame, simpleminded, boastful, and cowardly. She goes on to critique his presentation of his arguments, pointing to evidence of poorly understood terminology and premises, distorted and faulty syntax, invalid syllogisms, strange transitions, unmotivated citations from unrelated sources, and errors in language usage. Critics have suggested that the inexorable sarcasm of the manifesto indicates some guidance by Modena.

The manifesto closes with two more sonnets. The first answers one written by Bonifaccio and included in his *Discorso*. Bonifaccio compares Sullam's beauty to a tomb that conceals sin and a corrupt soul. Sullam responds that salvation of her soul is the only fame that she seeks. Sullam's second sonnet, "All'anima umana" (To the Human Soul), is a neo-Platonic reflection on the soul and its relationship to the divine:

> O di vita mortal forma divina
> E dell'opre di Dio meta sublime,
> In cui se stesso, e 'l suo potere esprime,
> E di quanto ei creò ti fe' Reina.
>
> Mente che l'huomo informi, in cui confina
> L'immortal col mortale, e tra le prime
> Essenze, hai fede nel volar da l'ime
> Parti, là dove il Cielo a te s'inchina.
>
> Stupido pur d'investigarti hor cessi
> Pensier che versa tra caduchi oggetti,

Che sol ti scopri allhor ch'a Dio t'appressi.
E per far paghi qui gl'Humani petti,
Basti saper che son gl'Angeli stessi
A custodirti, et a servirti eletti.

(Oh divine form of mortal life,
Sublime goal of God's works,
In which he expresses himself and his power.
Of everything created he made you Queen.

Mind that informs man, in which
The mortal and immortal meet, and among
The highest beings, you have faith in flying from the lowest
Parts, to where the Sky bows to meet you.

Amazed to examine yourself, let there now end
All thought that reflects upon transient objects,
Since you discover yourself only when you draw near to God.

And to content the human breast,
Let it be enough to know that it is the very Angels,
The chosen ones, who watch over and serve you.)

Bonifaccio answered Sullam with *Risposta al manifesto della signora Sara Copia* (Response to the Manifesto of Signora Sara Copia), also published in 1621, in which he once again argued for his views. The *Risposta* also includes the sole extant letter by Sullam, dated 10 January 1619. Sullam did not respond to this work.

Sullam and Cebà never met. No records exist that Sullam ever traveled out of Venice; she was gravely ill in 1618 after a miscarriage and alludes in the manifesto to another illness in 1621. Cebà's letters often refer to the infirmities of age that make travel impossible for him. Cebà, however, took advantage of a friend's trip to Venice to get a firsthand opinion of Sullam's reputed beauty and poise.

On 29 August 1620 Cebà had confessed to Sullam that he had been keeping copies of their letters to each other because he considered them a novelty that merited a careful record. He broke off the correspondence in 1622. The following year he published a collection of his letters to Sullam, the poems he had sent to her, and four sonnets that she had sent to him; he did not include any of her letters. In his preface Cebà alludes to forty letters written by Sullam and provides a brief summary of their content. Perhaps Cebà opted not to publish Sullam's letters to avoid the risk of his work being censored. In his last letter, in which he definitively breaks off their correspondence–previous letters allude to this intention–he clarifies his position regarding Sullam's religious beliefs and intellectual aspirations. He denounces her as a vain woman, intent on procuring worldly fame for herself through her studies and writings.

The four sonnets by Sullam included in Cebà's book are "La bella Hebrea che con devoti accenti," "Signor, pianto non merta il gran Lanfranco"(Sir, the great Lanfranco does not merit tears), "Se mover a pietà Stige ed Averno" (If Styx and Hades can be moved to compassion) and "L'imago è questa di colei, che al core" (The image of her, who in her heart). The first sonnet praises Cebà for the skill with which he represents the Old Testament heroine Esther in his *La reina Esther* and compares him to Apollo. The second expresses Sullam's concept of salvation and the afterlife on the occasion of the death of Cebà's brother, Lanfranco, in Malta. The third sonnet constructs an extended metaphor based on a comparison of Cebà with Orpheus. The final sonnet presumably accompanied a portrait of herself that Sullam had sent to Cebà:

L'imago è questa di colei, ch'al core
Porta l'imago tua sola scolpita,
Che con la mano al seno al mondo addita,
Qui porto l'Idol mio ciascun l'adore.

Sostien con la sinistra arme d'amore
Che fur tuoi carmi, il loco ov'è ferita
La destra accenna, e pallida, e smarrita
Dice, Ansaldo, il mio cor per te si more.

(The image is of her, who in her heart
Carries only your image sculpted,
And who with hand to her breast indicates to the world,
Here I carry my idol, adored by all.

She holds in her left hand weapons of love
Which were your poems; the place where she was wounded
She indicates with her right, and pale and lost
She says, Ansaldo, my heart dies for you.)

No definitive portrait of Sullam has surfaced, but in a 1986 article Carla Boccato analyzes a picture that may well be the one in question.

Cebà died in 1624. His book survives as a seventeenth-century testament to a failed attempt at proselytizing and as an indictment of a woman of letters. The sonnets constitute a gallant dialogue about religion discussed with the lexicon, themes, and topoi of Petrarchan models. The dialogue develops an extended literary conceit in which the lover attempts to woo his beloved to embrace not him but Christianity.

Between 1618 and 1624 Sullam's tutor Paluzzi, in league with his friend Berardelli, a washerwoman named Paola and her family, and a servant of Sullam's referred to as "La Mora" (The Black Woman) took advantage of Sullam's naiveté and belief in supernatural phenomena to steal from her. They led

Sullam to believe that the servant possessed magical powers such as levitation and the ability to communicate with spirits; the spirits, the swindlers maintained, were responsible for the disappearance of various objects in the Sullam household, including food, jewelry, and money. The fraud culminated in their inducing Sullam to commission Berardelli to paint an expensive portrait of herself that, they explained, an aerial spirit had requested on behalf of a French nobleman who had met Sullam in her home and become enamored of her. Alerted by an outsider to the series of crimes that had been perpetrated against her, in 1624 Sullam fired Paluzzi and denounced Berardelli to the Signori di Notte al Criminal, the state authorities responsible for investigating complaints of criminal activity in Venice. No record of the denunciation survives in the State Archives in Venice.

Paluzzi died in 1625; the following year Berardelli published an edition of his friend's poetry that included the accusation that Paluzzi, not Sullam, was the author of the sonnet "All'anima umana." This claim resulted in a collaborative effort to defend Sullam that is known as the codex of Giulia Soliga. The codex was once the property of the Venetian historian and bibliophile Emmanuele Antonio Cicogna, who published a brief biographical study and annotated bibliography of Sullam in 1864; he donated the manuscript of the codex to the Correr Library in Venice. The identity of Soliga, and whether she was a contributor to the miscellany or merely the amanuensis, remain a mystery. The work is a valuable example of the Baroque literary convention of the *ragguaglio* (report), which is most famously represented by the *Ragguagli di Parnaso* (1612–1613, Reports from Parnassus) of Traiano Boccalini. The codex describes the imaginary prosecution on Mt. Parnassus of the spirit of Paluzzi. Sullam's defenders believed that Paluzzi had taken part in defaming the character of his student-patron by co-authoring with Berardelli a satiric pamphlet, *Le satire Sarreidi* (The Sara Satires). The pamphlet no longer exists, but the codex discusses its origin, content, and dissemination.

The codex consists of three long prose sections—a dedicatory letter focusing on the crime of ingratitude; background events leading up to the trial; and the trial itself—separated by many compositions in verse. A veritable pantheon of authors is present at the trial: Pietro Aretino is the prosecutor; Cino da Pistoia is the defense attorney; Isabella Andreini is the interrogator; Vittoria Colonna, Veronica Gambara, and Sappho are jurors; and Boccalini, Baldassare Castiglione, Poliziano (pseudonym of Angelo Ambrogini), Garcilaso de la Vega, and Giovanni Boccaccio are onlookers. Members of the courtroom audience often interrupt the trial, disagree loudly, challenge each other to duels, and ultimately make peace by exchanging sonnets. The jury ultimately vindicates Sullam of the charges of plagiarism and sexual misconduct and sentences Paluzzi to the pillory, while Berardelli's effigy is dragged through the streets of Parnassus behind a team of horses. The codex concludes with a selection of poems in imitation of Torquato Tasso and Petrarch and a series of satiric compositions in Venetian dialect.

The codex includes five sonnets by Sullam in reply to those written by her defenders; in each sonnet Sullam replicates the rhymes of the one to which she is responding. With abundant references to Greek tragedy, mythology, and the themes of fame, reputation, honor, and the democratization of knowledge; comparisons to the animal world; use of assonance and consonance; and a style that with its realistic detail is at times reminiscent of Francesco Berni's sixteenth-century satires, Sullam represents herself in these sonnets as the wronged, innocent victim of Paluzzi and Berardelli. Sullam calls her enemies swine and oxen and compares her victory over them to Hercules slaying the Hydra and Ulysses resisting the Sirens. Sullam's final sonnet alludes to the passage of much time between the events described in the codex and the composition of the sonnet.

Sara Copio Sullam is remembered in eighteenth- and nineteenth-century literary histories as one of the outstanding female poets of her time. Her fourteen sonnets, culled from Cebà, the manifesto, the Soliga codex, and a 1627 anthology edited by Gabriele Zinano, were first brought together in Modona's 1887 edition. Boccato's archival investigations in the 1980s into Sullam and the seventeenth-century Venetian ghetto paved the way for criticism by Corinna Da Fonseca-Wollheim (1999) and Lori J. Ultsch (2000) that focuses on the backlash against Sullam as a Jew and a female intellectual.

References:

Carla Boccato, "Una disputa secentesca sull'immortalità dell'anima: Contributi d'archivo," *La Rassegna mensile di Israel,* 44, no. 3 (1988): 594–606;

Boccato, "Il presunto ritratto di Sara Copio Sullam," *La Rassegna mensile di Israel,* 52, no. 3 (1986): 191–204;

Boccato, "Sara Copio Sullam, la poetessa del ghetto di Venezia: Episodi della sua vita in un manoscritto del secolo XVII," *Italia: Studi e ricerche sulla storia, la cultura e la letteratura degli ebrei d'Italia,* 6, nos. 1–2 (1987): 104–218;

Baldassare Bonifaccio, *Dell'immortalità dell'anima: Discorso* (Venice: A. Pinelli, 1621);

Bonifaccio, *Risposta al manifesto della signora Sara Copia* (Venice: A. Pinelli, 1621);

Emmanuele Antonio Cicogna, "Notizie intorno a Sara Copia Sulam, coltissima ebrea veneziana del secolo XVII," *Memorie dell'Istituto Veneto di Scienze, Lettere ed Arti,* 12 (1864): 227–246;

Corinna Da Fonseca-Wollheim, "Acque di Parnaso, acque di Battesimo: Fede e fama nell'opera di Sara Copio Sullam," in *Le donne delle minoranze: Le ebree e le protestanti d'Italia,* edited by Claire Honess and Verina Jones, *Nostro Tempo,* no. 64 (Turin: Claudiana, 1999), pp. 159–170;

Umberto Fortis, *La "Bella Ebrea": Sara Copio Sullam, poetessa nel ghetto di Venezia del '600* (Turin: Zamorani, 2003);

Bartolommeo Gamba, *Lettere di donne italiane del secolo decimosesto* (Venice: Alvisopoli, 1832), pp. 253–265;

Numidio Paluzzi, *Rime del sig. Numidio Paluzzi,* edited by Alessandro Berardelli (Venice: Ciotti, 1626);

Lori J. Ultsch, "Sara Copio Sullam: A Jewish Woman of Letters in 17th-Century Venice," *Italian Culture,* 18, no. 2 (2000): 73–86.

Alessandro Tassoni
(29 September 1565 – 25 April 1635)

Laura Benedetti
Georgetown University

BOOKS: *Parte dei quisiti* (Modena: Cassiani, 1608); revised and enlarged as *Varietà di pensieri* (Modena: Verdi, 1612); revised and enlarged again as *Dieci libri di pensieri diversi* (Venice: Brogiollo, 1620; revised and enlarged, 1627; revised, 1636);

Considerazioni sopra le Rime del Petrarca (Modena: Cassiani, 1609);

Avvertimenti di Crescenzio Pepe (Modena: Cassiani, 1611);

La tenda rossa: Risposta di Girolamo Nomisenti a i dialoghi di Falcidio Melampodio (Frankfurt [i.e., Modena], 1613);

Le filippiche, anonymous (N.p., 1615);

Risposta alla scrittura del Signor N.N. (Rome, 1617);

La secchia, as Androvinci Melisone (Paris: Du Bray, 1622 [i.e., 1621]); revised and enlarged as *La secchia rapita* (Ronciglione [i.e., Rome]: Brogiotti, 1624); revised as *La secchia rapita, con le dichiarazioni del Sig. Gasparo Salviani e il primo canto dell'Oceano* (Venice: Giacomo Scaglia, 1630); translated by John Ozell as *The Trophy-Bucket: A Mock-Heroic Poem, the First of the Kind* (London: Printed by J.D. for Egbert Sanger, 1710);

Postille scelte alla Divina Commedia (Reggio: Pietro Fiaccadori, 1826);

Manifesto di Alessandro Tassoni intorno le relazioni passate tra esso e i principi di Savoia (Florence: Viesseux, 1849);

Ragionamento intorno ad alcune cose notate nel duodecimo dell'Inferno di Dante (Modena: Vincenzi, 1867);

I Testamenti (Florence: Gazzetta d'Italia, 1877);

Rime di Alessandro Tassoni raccolte su i codici e le stampe, edited by Tommaso Casini (Bologna G. Romagnoli, 1880);

Difesa di Alessandro Macedone (Leghorn: Giusti, 1904);

Conclave in cui fu eletto Papa Gregorio XV, in *Raccolta di scritti originali per onorare la memoria di Monsignor Maria Ceriani* (Milan: Hoepli, 1910);

Scritti inediti, edited by Pietro Puliatti (Modena: Aedes Muratoriana, 1966);

Scritti inediti, edited by Puliatti (Modena: Aedes Muratoriana, 1975);

Prose politiche e morali: Pensieri diversi, 2 volumes, edited by Puliatti (Bari: Laterza, 1977);

Pensieri e scritti preparatori, edited by Puliatti (Modena: Panini, 1986).

Editions: *La secchia rapita,* edited by Pietro Puliatti (Modena: Panini, 1989);

La secchia rapita: Prima redazione, edited by Ottavio Besomi (Padua: Antenore, 1989);

La secchia rapita: Redazione definitiva, edited by Besomi (Padua: Antenore, 1990).

Edition in English: *La secchia rapita; or, The Rape of the Bucket: An Heroicomical Poem in 12 Cantos,* translated by James Atkinson (London: J. M. Richardson, 1825).

Alessandro Tassoni was an unconventional writer who challenged established authorities and actively participated in the intellectual life of his times. His varied and often controversial production earned him a reputation among his contemporaries as a philosopher, a linguist, and a political thinker. He is known today, however, chiefly for *La secchia rapita* (1624, The Stolen Bucket; translated as *The Trophy-Bucket: A Mock-Heroic Poem, the First of the Kind,* 1710), which is considered the first modern heroicomic poem.

Tassoni was born on 29 September 1565 into a noble Modenese family. His parents, Bernardino and Sigismonda Tassoni, née Pellicciari, died during his early childhood. His youth was marked by various misdeeds and by a tendency to resort to violence as a means of resolving conflicts.

After studying Latin and eloquence in Modena, Tassoni developed and refined his literary interests at the University of Pisa. At eighteen he wrote his first work, the tragedy *Enrico.* Odoardo, the king of England, courts Apocritea, unaware that she is his son Enrico's mistress. Enrico kills his unknown rival, only to learn he has slain his father; his secretary then reveals that Apocritea is Odoardo's long-lost daughter and, therefore, Enrico's sister. Apocritea's suicide is followed by the chorus's final tribute to a bloodthirsty Fortune.

Title page for Alessandro Tassoni's Observations on Petrarch's Rhymes, *which provoked a critical attack by Giuseppe degli Aromatari (University of Turin)*

Enrico reveals the influence of Seneca, Torquato Tasso, and Giovambattista Giraldi Cinzio. Tassoni soon turned away from tragedy and did not pursue the publication of *Enrico*, which did not appear in print until 1975.

Tassoni received a degree in canon and civil law at the University of Ferrara when he was twenty. He soon lost interest in the law, but the study of philosophy, which he began in Ferrara under the guidance of Cesare Cremonini, had a long-lasting effect on him. In 1591 he was found guilty of beating a painter who had helped a weaver obtain permission to use her loom at home, against Tassoni's wishes. Around this time he fathered a son, Marzio, with Lucia Mezzadri; he legally recognized the child as his but disinherited him in 1609.

In 1597 Tassoni moved to Rome in search of an occupation. He joined the Accademia della Crusca (Academy of the Sifters) in 1598. The following year he became secretary to Cardinal Ascanio Colonna. Tassoni accompanied the cardinal when the latter moved to Spain in 1600; he returned to Rome in 1602 as the cardinal's envoy to Pope Clement VIII, and again in 1603, when he was assigned the delicate task of administering the cardinal's finances. This demonstration of trust was soon followed by dismissal for reasons that have never been clearly explained.

Between 1604 and 1606 Tassoni joined the Accademia degli Umoristi (Academy of the Humorists). In 1606 he went to work for Cardinal Bartolomeo Cesi and began to pursue his literary and philosophical interests. In 1608 he published *Parte dei quisiti* (Part of the Questions), a series of 150 reflections on diverse topics. He revised and added to the work throughout the rest of his life. In the second edition, published in 1612 as *Varietà di pensieri* (Variety of Thoughts), the number of entries grew to 232, divided into nine books. As the title indicates, a tenth book was added in the 1620 edition, *Dieci libri di pensieri diversi* (Ten Books of Various Thoughts), which comprised 268 entries; a 1627 revision with the same title brought the number of entries down to 249. Substantial revisions can even be found in the posthumous 1636 edition, although it is impossible to determine whether they should be attributed to the author or to the editor.

The work constituted a sort of depository for Tassoni's developing interests. Some of the observations originated as academic exercises, and two of the most controversial—one directed against literary studies and the other praising executioners—were expansions of speeches he had delivered at meetings of the Accademia degli Umoristi. The topics range from astronomy to military science and from zoology to ethics. The tone oscillates from solemn to frivolous in essays such as "Se occupar la libertà della patria possa essere sotto pretesto alcuno cosa lodevole e onorata" (Whether Usurping the Freedom of the Fatherland May Be Considered, under Any Pretext, an Honorable and Praiseworthy Action), "Se le lettere e le dottrine siano necessarie alle repubbliche" (Whether Literature and Learning Are Necessary to Nations), and "Se i capelli ricciuti siano (come è in proverbio) argomento di poco senno" (Whether Curly Hair Is [as Maintained in the Proverb] Proof of Little Intellect). Widely debated by Tassoni's contemporaries, the *Pensieri* is a ponderous document of the tendency to encyclopedic erudition that characterized the author and his times.

The 1612 edition of the *Pensieri* gave Tassoni the opportunity to voice his reservations about the first *Vocabolario degli Accademici della Crusca* (Dictionary of the Academy of the Sifters), published a few months earlier. He was harshly critical of the solution to the *questione della lingua* (debate over the language) put forth in the *Vocabolario*. In particular, he challenged the idea, at the core of the Accademia's linguistic philosophy, that fourteenth-century Florentine or Tuscan—Tassoni used the terms interchangeably—should be taken as a model. Quisito 15, "Se trecento anni sono meglio si scrivesse in volgare italiano o nell'età presente" (Whether Written Italian Was Better Three Hundred Years Ago or in the Present Day), conveys his faith in the perfectability of human inventions and in the progress that time inevitably brings forth:

> Le lingue, come gli uomini stessi, nascono rozze, e tanto piú rozza è da credere, che questa nostra nascesse, quanto ch'ella ebbe origine dalla corruzione della latina e d'altre varie straniere e barbare, che si meschiarono insieme nelle miserie d'Italia. . . . È ben vero, che i nominati autori con miglior giudicio degli altri cercaron di fare scelta delle frasi e voci, che loro parver piú belle; ma si non la seppero, né potero eglino far perfetta, che i moderni non abbiano trovato che riprendere, aggiugnere, moderare e lasciare, seguitando, oltre la ragione, anche l'uso, che è il vero giudice e padron delle lingue.

> (Languages, like men themselves, are born unrefined, which is all the more true for our language, which originated from the corruption of Latin and other barbarian and foreign languages, that were mixed together in the misery of Italy. . . . It is true that the authors quoted [in the *Vocabolario*], more than the others, tried to choose phrases and terms they considered more beautiful. But they could not make a perfect language. Modern authors thus found it necessary to criticize, add, moderate, and drop, following not only reason but also custom, which is the real judge and master of languages.)

The language used by the fourteenth-century Florentine historian Giovanni Villani seemed to Tassoni less elegant and precise than that of Francesco Guicciardini in the sixteenth century, while Giovanni Boccaccio's style, in his view, could only be imitated by creative writers, not by secretaries or authors of philosophical or political treatises. Throughout the discussion Tassoni is firm in his refusal of an archaic and strictly literary solution to the *questione della lingua*.

A similiar attitude inspires "Incognito da Modana contro ad alcune voci del Vocabolario della Crusca" (1975, Unknown from Modena versus Some Words in the Dictionary of the Sifters), which was addressed to the Accademia della Crusca and not intended for public circulation. Tassoni's tone is more sarcastic here than in the *Pensieri*, both in the introduction, where the *Vocabolario della Crusca* is called "grandemente pernizioso alla gioventù e a' forestieri" (highly dangerous for youth and foreigners), and in the annotations to individual *Vocabolario della Crusca* entries. For example, the *Vocabolario della Crusca* defines *padre* (father) as "il maschio di qualunque animale che fa figliuoli" (the male of any animal that begets its young); Tassoni objects that "con questa definizione i figliuoli del primo marito avranno il secondo per padre" (on the basis of this definition, the first husband's children will have the second husband as father). Cleverness gives way to irreverence in the annotation to *culo* (ass), prudishly defined in the *Vocabolario della Crusca* as "parte del corpo con la quale si siede" (part of the body with which one sits). Tassoni comments: "nel mio paese si caca col culo e si siede con le natiche. Non so a Firenze" (where I come from, we use the ass to shit and the buttocks to sit. I don't know about Florence). Tassoni resented the extensive inclusion of obsolete terms in the *Vocabolario della Crusca:* far from representing the inclination of the academy as a whole, the archaisms were, in his view, the result of the "mero capriccio d'alcuni particolari" (mere whim of some individuals).

The same reluctance to grant traditional authorities unconditional power over modern creativity can be found in Tassoni's *Considerazioni sopra le Rime del Petrarca* (1609, Observations on Petrarch's Rhymes), which includes some remarks on Petrarch's *Trionfi* (Triumphs). Probably inspired by literary conversations hosted by Paolo Teggia, the work was written during Tassoni's trip to Spain in the winter of 1602–1603 and intersperses textual commentary with descriptions of the adventurous journey. Consideration of the sonnet "Ite caldi sospiri al freddo cuore" (Go, Warm Sighs, to Her Cold Heart), for instance, is coupled with remarks on the extreme temperatures that had forced Tassoni to stop at Les Martigues: "Ma viemmi da ridere, che mentre sto qui scrivendo . . . s'è gelata tutta questa marina, e tutto questo stagno di Martega di sorte, ch'egli ci vorrà altro, che sospiri a rompere il ghiaccio per uscirne" (And I almost laugh when I notice that, while I am busy writing, the shores and the pond of Les Martigues have frozen so hard that we will need more than sighs to break the ice and get out).

The target of Tassoni's criticism is not Petrarch, who is hailed as a genius but also criticized for his unrealistic stance and stylistic obscurity, as much as it is his followers, the *Petrarchisti,* who strove to restrict poetry to strict imitation of the model of their master. Tassoni's protest against classicism and call for artistic freedom led him to attack the Renaissance as a dark age of limitations, blind deference to tradition, and absurd rules.

The work provoked outrage, especially in Paduan cultural circles. A medical student, Giuseppe degli Aromatari, wrote *Risposte di Gioseffe degli Aromatari alle Considerationi del sig. Alessandro Tassoni, sopra le Rime del Petrarca* (1611, Answers of Giuseppe degli Aromatari to the Considerations of Mr. Alessandro Tassoni on Petrarch's Rhymes), criticizing Tassoni's book on the basis of Aristotelian principles. Although Tassoni was eager to attack tradition, he resented any questioning of his own authority. In his rushed response, *Avvertimenti di Crescenzio Pepe* (1611, Warnings of Crescenzio Pepe); Aromatari's *Dialoghi di Falcidio Melampodio in risposta à gli Avvertimenti dati sotto nome di Crescentio Pepe à Gioseffe degli Aromatari, intorno alle Risposte fatte da lui alle Considerationi del Sig. Alessandro Tassoni sopra le Rime del Petrarca* (1613, Dialogues of Falcidio Melampodio in Answer to Warnings Given under the Name of Crescenzio Pepe to Giuseppe degli Aromatari, about the Answers Made by Him to the Considerations of Mr. Alessandro Tassoni on Petrarch's Rhymes); and Tassoni's *La tenda rossa: Risposta di Girolamo Nomisenti a i dialoghi di Falcidio Melampodio* (1613, The Red Tent: Response of Girolamo Nomisenti to the Dialogues of Falcidio Melampodio) the debate descends to the level of personal insults and veiled threats. The decline is reflected in the editorial history of *La tenda rossa:* although the cover indicated that the work had been printed in Frankfurt, it had actually been published, without official permission, in Modena. Linked to this controversy is the appearance of some anonymous defamatory writings about Tassoni. Tassoni suspected that they had been written by the father and son Paolo and Alessandro Brusantini, against whom he began to harbor a relentless acrimony that found its artistic transfiguration in the creation of the count of Culagna in *La secchia rapita.*

In the meantime, Tassoni had established solid links with the Savoy embassy in Rome. In the years that followed the Monferrato War of Succession of 1613 to 1615, Duke Carlo Emanuele I of Savoy, who had opposed Spanish supremacy, seemed to many to be the prince who could rally Italian forces and lead them in the fight against foreign domination. In this climate Tassoni wrote *Le filippiche* (The Philippics), two speeches that were published clandestinely and anonymously in 1615. The work is an exhortation to the Italian rulers to unite in support of Carlo Emanuele in his effort to resist Spanish domination and liberate Italy. Tassoni's attack on Spain, which he describes as an elephant with the soul of a chick, is accompanied by heartfelt considerations of Italy's oppression:

> Tutte l'altre nazioni, quante n'ha il mondo, non hanno cosa piú cara della lor patria, scordandosi l'odio e l'inimicizie che regnano fra loro, per unirsi a difenderla contro gl'insulti stranieri; anzi i cani, i lupi, i leoni dell'istessa contrada, del medesimo bosco, della foresta medesima, si congiungono insieme per la difesa comune; e noi soli italiani, diversi da tutti gli altri uomini, da tutti gli altri animali, abbandoniamo il vicino, abbandoniamo l'amico, abbandoniamo la patria, per unirci con gli stranieri nemici nostri! Fatale infelicità d'Italia, che dopo aver perduto l'imperio, abbiamo parimenti perduto il viver politico; e senza riguardo di legge umana o divina, abbiamo in costume di abbandonare i nostri e aderire all'armi straniere per seguitar la fortuna del piú potente.

> (All the other nations in the world hold nothing as dear as the fatherland. They forget internal hatred and animosity, in order to unite and defend the fatherland against foreign attacks. Even dogs, wolves, lions of the

same neighborhood, the same wood, the same forest, unite for the common defense. Only we Italians, unlike all other men and animals, forsake our neighbor, our friend, the fatherland, to unite with our foreign enemies! This is Italy's fateful unhappiness, that after losing our power, we have lost our political life as well, and that without any consideration towards human and divine laws, we have the custom of abandoning our own people to join foreign forces and follow the destiny of the strongest.)

The popularity of *Le filippiche* is attested not only by its wide circulation but also by its inclusion in several compilations of political writings, such as *La quinta essenza della ragion di stato* (1615, The Fifth Essence of the Reason of State). Of course, Tassoni's stance also elicited criticism. An author known only as Soccino published in Milan the *Discorso nel quale si dimostra la giustezza dell'imperio delli Spagnuoli in Italia* (Discourse in Which Is Demonstrated the Justness of the Empire of the Spanish in Italy). Tassoni's detailed and sarcastic *Risposta alla scrittura del Signor N.N.* (1617, Rebuttal to the Writing of Mr. N.N.), commonly referred to as "Risposta al Soccino" (Rebuttal to Soccino), concludes by urging his rival not to write anymore, since he has no talent. Tassoni's role as a staunch advocate of the Savoy cause was recognized in 1619, when he became the secretary of Cardinal Maurice of Savoy and moved to Turin.

This period of intense political activity coincided with Tassoni's artistic maturity, which found expression in the work that granted him a place in the history of Italian literature. Like *I Pensieri*, *La secchia rapita* had a rather tormented history: a first version in ten cantos was written between 1614 and 1616; two more cantos were added in 1617–1618. Artistic scruples and ecclesiastical censorship inspired many revisions, and complex negotiations delayed publication while the work circulated in manuscript. Hiding behind the pseudonym Androvinci Melisone, Tassoni finally published the work as *La secchia* (The Bucket) in Paris in 1621, although the title page bears the date 1622. A revised edition, titled *La secchia rapita,* appeared in Rome in 1624; the definitive 1630 Venetian edition includes "Dichiarazioni" (Pronouncements), written under the pseudonym Gasparo Salviani.

The introductory notes to the reader reveal the author's awareness of the novelty of his experiment. The creation of a new kind of poem is inspired, he maintains, by a desire to satisfy modern taste:

E oggidí è chiaro che le azioni di molti dilettano piú che quele d'un solo, e che è piú curiosa da vedere una battaglia campale di qualsivoglia duello. Perciochè il diletto de la poesia epica non nasce dal vedere operare un uomo solo, ma dal sentir rappresentare verisimilmente azioni maravigliose: le quali quanto sono piú, tanto piú dilettano.

(Today, it is clear that the actions of many people are more pleasing than those of a single man, and that it is more intriguing to see a critical battle than any duel. This is because the pleasure of epic poetry does not derive from seeing a man operate alone, but from the verisimilar representation of wonderful deeds. The more these deeds are, the more they produce pleasure.)

For this reason Tassoni finds Ludovico Ariosto "diletta molto più" (is much more pleasing) than Homer. He proceeds to present his poem as an experiment aimed at reaching a wider public:

quando l'autore compose questo poema (che fu una state ne la sua gioventú) non fu per acquistar fama in poesia, ma per passatempo e per curiosità di vedere come riuscivano questi due stili mischiati insieme, grave e burlesco; imaginando che se ambidue dilettavano separati, avrebbono eziandio dilettato congiunti e misti: se la mistura fosse stata temperata con artificio tale che da la loro scambievole varietà tanto i dotti quanto gl'idioti avessero potuto cavarne gusto.

(when the author composed this poem [during a summer of his youth], he did not do it to gain glory as a poet, but to pass his time and out of curiosity to see the results of the combination of two styles, the grave and the burlesque. He figured that if they were enjoyable separately, they could be all the more pleasing when united and mixed, provided that their combination be obtained so skillfully that both learned and common people could find it to their taste.)

Since the first draft of *La secchia* was not written before 1614, this description of the poem as a youthful interlude is merely rhetorical. The claim indicates, however, that for Tassoni poetry constituted an activity of lesser importance than philosophy, science, and politics. He expressed this disdain for poetry in several letters, while insisting at the same time on the originality of his attempt and jealously defending his invention of the genre of the *poema eroicomico* (heroicomic poem) against competitors, chief among them Francesco Bracciolini.

The historical context of the poem is the wars between the Modenese and the Bolognese in the thirteenth and fourteenth centuries. The work centers on a marginal episode in the conflict: the Modenese theft of a bucket from the Bolognese in 1325. Tassoni's choice of this incident reveals his intention of rewriting the central themes of the epic tradition in a comic register: "vedrai, s'al cantar mio porgi l'orecchia, / Elena trasformarsi in una secchia" (If you lend your ear to my singing, / you will see Helen turn into a bucket). Heroic elements that undergo comic treatment include the

Title page for Tassoni's The Red Tent: Response of Girolamo Nomisenti to the Dialogues of Falcidio Melampodio, *part of his literary debate with Aromatari. Both men were writing under pseudonyms (University of Turin).*

council of the gods; the love triangle of Venus, Bacchus, and Vulcan; the review of the armies; and the invocation of the Muse. References abound to Ariosto's *Orlando furioso* (1516; revised, 1532, The Frenzy of Orlando; translated as *Orlando Furioso in English Heroical Verse*, 1591) and Tasso's *Gerusalemme liberata* (1581, Jerusalem Delivered; translated as *Godfrey of Bulloigne, or The Recoverie of Hierusalem*, 1594) both in quick comparisons to elucidate a character's features, such as the count of Culagna as Martano and Foresto's horse as Frontino, and in more-complex rewriting of episodes, such as Renoppia's deeds as an archer that are modeled on those of Clorinda in *Gerusalemme liberata*.

While gods and mortals fight over a bucket, the count of Culagna tries to poison his wife so that he will be free to pursue the warrior woman Renoppia. He ends up a victim of his own machinations, and his wife finds a more appreciative lover. The count's adventures receive ample treatment only in the final twelve-canto version, where they constitute a long parenthesis in cantos 10 and 11. The invention of the character stemmed from Tassoni's scorn for Brusantini: in 1608 Cesare of Este had assigned Alessandro's father, Paolo, a fief that included the territory of Culagna with the privilege of passing it on to his descendants. Tassoni makes his hero a relative of "quel Don Chisotto in armi sì sovrano, / principe de gli erranti e de gli eroi" (that Don Quixote, master of arms, / prince of heroes and wandering knights). Through this allusion Don Quixote entered the Italian literary scene for the first time. Tassoni, however, misses the complexity of Miguel de Cervantes's hero, using this superficial comparison as an easy means of further degrading the count of Culagna by attributing Spanish origins to him.

The poem served as a testing ground for Tassoni's linguistic theories and provided him with an artistic venue to express his disagreement with the Accademia della Crusca's rigid codification. In particular, the use of dialect highlights the contrast between the supposed solemnity of a given situation and its provincial context to produce a comic effect, as in the juxtaposition of Ugo Machella's rhetorical and flawlessly Florentine speech and the spontaneous reaction of his improvised troops expressed in the Bolognese dialect:

> Ugo Machella a quel parlar sorrise
> e disse rivoltato a quei prudenti:
> –Se chiudiamo le strade in queste guise,
> Dov'entreranno poi le nostre genti?
> Prendiamo l'armi: il Ciel sovente arrise
> a le piú audaci e risolute menti.–
> Qui s'alzar tutti, e gridar senza tema:
> –A la fé che l'è vera, andema, andema.–

> (Ugo Machella smiled at these words,
> And turned to those cautious souls, exclaimed:
> –If we close in this way every street,
> how are our own people to get in?
> Let us take arms: Heaven often favored
> the most brave and resolute hearts.–
> At this, they all rose, and cried without fear:
> –In faith, that's true! Onward, onward!–)

Sometimes Tassoni interjects his own ironic metalinguistic comments. For example, he follows the description of "trecento incavallati" (three hundred saddled men) with a sarcastic note on *incavallati* (saddled): "vocabol fiorentino antico e bello" (an antique and beautiful Florentine word). Later, Culagna "s'affaticava in trovar voci elette, / di quelle che i Toscan chiamano prette" (was struggling to find noble words, / of the kind the Tuscans call pristine). He also tends to compose the first six lines of an octave in an epic register that is made incongruous by a comic twist introduced in the final distich. Tassoni seems less interested in developing a coherent plot than in surprising the reader over and over with skillful variations in tone and unpredictable clashes of situations, terms, and languages.

In spite of acknowledging the importance of Ariosto's example, Tassoni drastically limits the territory covered by his protagonists. While the adventures of *Orlando furioso* span three continents, those of the *La secchia rapita* are restricted to a municipal landscape. Not even the reviews of the armies, which could have provided an easy means of expanding the geography of the narration, are exceptions to this rule. Rather than endowing his heroes with exotic origins, Tassoni exalts their provincial roots: "Lugo, Bagnacavallo, Argenta e Massa, / Cotognola e Barbian madri d'eroi" (Lugo, Bagnacavallo, Argenta and Massa, Cotognola and Barbian, mothers of heroes). On the other hand, it is impossible to find any coherence in the time of the action: literature, history, and legend are inextricably confused so that the reader finds side by side historical figures belonging to different times, such as Emperor Frederick II and Antonio Querenghi; classical gods; and characters from Roman history, such as Lucretia.

Tassoni was a fierce defender of the originality of his invention. His main rival was Bracciolini, who in 1618 had published *Lo scherno degli dei* (Mockery of the Gods). In several introductions to *La secchia rapita* written under various pseudonyms Tassoni claims that his poem was completed in October 1611 and hails it as a "perfetto poema grave e burlesco . . . un drappo cangiante, in cui mirabilmente risplendono ambidue i colori del burlesco e del grave" (a perfect epic and comic poem . . . an iridescent drape, in which both epic and comic colors wonderfully shine). But Bracciolini's answer to the crisis of the epic model was so different that the issue of the priority of one poem over the other seems irrelevant. *Lo scherno degli dei* closely follows the model of Renaissance burlesque poems such as Girolamo Amelonghi's *Gigantea* (1566, The War of the Giants). In *La secchia rapita,* on the other hand, parody coexists with respect for established epic rules such as the choice of an historical topic and unity of action. Occasionally, Tassoni's ironical interpretation of the canon gives way to tribute to tradition. In these episodes, such as Venus's journey to Naples and the love of Endymion and the Moon, comic and realistic tones are replaced by idyllic and lyrical ones. That Tassoni's attempt to infuse new life into the moribund epic tradition was timely and successful is attested by the many writers who followed in his footsteps throughout the seventeenth century, such as Giovan Battista Lalli and Carlo de' Dottori.

Tassoni's thorough familiarity with epic conventions is confirmed by the unfinished "L'Oceano," the opening canto of which is included in the first edition of *La secchia rapita*. In the "Lettera ad un amico" (Letter to a friend) that precedes "L'Oceano" Tassoni discusses the inspiration exerted by the discovery of the New World on authors such as Tommaso Stigliani. The model for a poem such as Stigliani's *Il mondo nuovo* (1617, The New World), Tassoni argues, should be Homer's *Odyssey,* rather than Virgil's *Aeneid* or Tasso's *Gerusalemme liberata*. In particular, Christopher Columbus should not be depicted as a military leader, as Stigliani had done in *Il mondo nuovo,* but as an adventurous explorer. "L'Oceano" illustrates the principles laid down in the letter. Columbus is presented as the epitome of human dignity and thirst for knowledge, and his speech to his companions as they leave the pillars of Hercules behind elaborates on concepts expressed by Dante's Ulysses in *The Divine Comedy:*

Oggi, compagni, è il punto,
che 'l nostro sole a l'oriente è giunto.
Oscura abbiamo neghittosa vita
fin qui dormito, or s'incomincia l'ora
che fuor de la vulgar nebbia infinita
usciamo al di' lucente; ecco l'aurora.
Questa via, ch'altri mai non ha più trita,
vi conduco a solcar del mondo fuora,
a ciò che fuor de la comune schiera
usciate meco a fama eterna e vera.

(Friends, today our sun is rising.
We have heretofore slept and led a lazy life.
Now begins the time
when we exit the vulgar infinite fog
to go toward a bright day. Here is the dawn.
I lead you outside the world, to take the path
that none have ever known,
So that you may come with me,
outside the common crowd,
to eternal and true fame.)

Unlike Dante's Ulysses, however, Tassoni's Columbus has God on his side; such a powerful ally is necessary to defeat the devil, who has tied the winds in an attempt to prevent the hero's journey. The 1630 edition of *La secchia rapita* adds to the first canto of "L'Oceano" the first stanza of the second; no more was ever written.

Pope Paul V died at the beginning of 1621, and Tassoni was sent to Rome to assist Cardinal Maurice in the negotiations for the election of a new pope. When he reached Siena, however, he was informed of the election on 9 February of Alessandro Ludovisi as Pope Gregory XV. Tassoni's relationship with Maurice of Savoy deteriorated, culminating in his dismissal in 1623. He describes these events in the *Manifesto di Alessandro Tassoni intorno le relazioni passate tra esso e i principi di Savoia* (1849, Alessandro Tassoni's Manifesto on His

Relations with the Princes of Savoy); he does not resort to his usual biting sarcasm but employs a meditative and philosophical tone, perhaps because he is dealing with highly influential people. Nevertheless, the work was not published for more than two centuries after the author's death. His relationship with the Savoy court is reconstructed in detail and documented by the inclusion of several letters. Tassoni presents the work as an attempt to save his reputation and as a warning to other courtiers:

> Questi furono i primi guiderdoni e successi della mia servitú con la casa serenissima di Savoia, dai quali, oltre la curiosità, ne potranno anco, cred'io, i cortigiani cavare qualche utile; imperoché l'arte della corte è come quella della chirurgia, che s'impara dalle ferite altrui.

> (These were my first rewards and successes in service of the excellent House of Savoy. Besides satisfying their curiosity, courtiers may, I believe, draw something useful from them, since the art of courtly life, like surgery, is learned from other people's wounds.)

In 1626 Tassoni entered the service of the Pope's nephew, Cardinal Ludovico Ludovisi, in Bologna. After the cardinal's death in 1632, Tassoni yielded to the entreaties of his Modenese friends and accepted a position with Francesco I d'Este, Duke of Modena and Reggio. He spent his last few years in relative tranquility in his native town, where he died on 25 April 1635.

Tassoni's lyrical poems were not collected in a single volume until Tommaso Casini published *Rime di Alessandro Tassoni raccolte su i codice e le stampe* (Rhymes of Alessandro Tassoni Gathered from His Manuscripts and Publications) in 1880. The book allows the reader to follow Tassoni's poetic development from the youthful love poetry of the years 1585 to 1590 to the satirical, realistic, and often vulgar poems in which he attacks his personal enemies, such as Bracciolini in "Ma il segretario suo, ch'era un baccello" (But his secretary, who was a fool); expresses his hatred of Spain in "Ritratto di Madrid" (Portrayal of Madrid) and "Bellezze di Valladolid" (Beauties of Valladolid); and voices his disappointment at the Italians' passivity and resignation in "Italia madre ai principi suoi figli" (Mother Italy to Her Sons the Princes).

Following a custom of the time, Tassoni devoted considerable care to the preparation of a collection of his correspondence. This corpus includes more than a thousand letters by important personalities of the period such as Antonio Querenghi and Ottaviano degli Ubaldini, as well as those by Tassoni himself, some of them written on behalf of his patrons. After surviving in manuscript for more than two centuries, the letters began to be published in the nineteenth century in an effort of preservation and analysis that culminated in the two volumes edited by Giorgio Rossi at the beginning of the twentieth century.

Alessandro Tassoni's desire to break free of literary conventions; his disregard for the most celebrated authorities, including Homer, Aristotle, and Petrarch; and his proclivity for paradox and scandal were objects of intense debate and, in some cases, reprobation by his contemporaries. While eighteenth-century critics tended to focus on *La secchia rapita,* in the nineteenth century Ugo Foscolo started the celebration of Tassoni as a political thinker whose *Le filippiche* rallied the Italian rulers to war against the Spanish invader. Other critics followed suit, portraying Tassoni as something close to a Romantic hero whose ideals anticipated the Risorgimento. This point of view, in turn, led to a new interpretation of *La secchia rapita* as a criticism of the domestic disputes that pitted Italians against each other and diverted energies that would have been better spent in the fight against a common enemy. This interpretation coexisted with a less idealistic one according to which the poem was primarily inspired by Tassoni's desire to denigrate his enemies, in particular Brusantini. Toward the end of the century, documents uncovered by positivistic scholars led to an unflattering portrayal of the author as sarcastic, greedy, vengeful, misogynistic, prone to attack everything and everybody but unwilling to accept criticism, and incapable of engaging in a civil exchange of opinions. In the twentieth century Tassoni was regarded first and foremost as the author of *La secchia rapita,* while his political and philosophical works were relegated to the background. Benedetto Croce saw the poem as a meaningless exercise and an example of the futility of dividing literature into genres such as the "heroicomic poem." Most critics, however, expressed a more appreciative opinion. While some criticized the poem for its lack of focus, others, such as Giorgio Barberi-Squarotti, pointed out that this variety of perspectives makes the poem a prime example of Baroque sensibility.

Letters:

Lettere di Alessandro Tassoni: Ora nella maggior parte pubblicate per la prima volta, edited by Bartolommeo Gamba (Venice: Alvisopopoli, 1827);

La lettere di Alessandro Tassoni, 2 volumes, edited by Giorgio Rossi (Bologna: Romagnoli dell'Acqua, 1901, 1910).

Bibliography:

Pietro Puliatti, *Bibliografia di Alessandro Tassoni,* 2 volumes (Florence: Sansoni, 1969, 1970).

References:

Guido Arbizzoni, "Poesia epica, eroicomica, satirica, burlesca: La poesia rusticale toscana. La 'poesia figurata,'" in *Storia della Letteratura Italiana,* volume 5, edited by Enrico Malato (Rome: Salerno, 1997), pp. 720–770;

Bruno A. Arcudi, "The Author of the *Secchia* Does Battle with Pietro Bembo's School," *Italica,* 44 (1962): 291–313;

Arcudi, "Some Seicento Doubts about Homer," in *Seicento Revisited,* edited by Albert N. Mancini, special issue of *Forum italicum,* 7, no. 2 (1973): 163–176;

Giuseppe degli Aromatari, *Dialoghi di Falcidio Melampodio in risposta à gli Avvertimenti dati sotto nome di Crescentio Pepe à Gioseffe degli Aromatari, intorno alle Risposte fatte da lui alle Consideratoni del Sig. Alessandro Tassoni sopra le Rime del Petrarca* (Venice: E. Deuchino, 1613);

Aromatari, *Risposte di Gioseffe degli Aromatari alle Considerationi del sig. Alessandro Tassoni, sopra le Rime del Petrarca* (Padua: Orlando Iadra, 1611);

Clotilde Bertoni, *Percorsi europei dell'eroicomico* (Pisa: Nistri-Lischi, 1997);

Benedetto Croce, *Estetica come scienza dell'espressiine e linguistica generale: Teoria e storia* (Milan, Palermo & Naples: Sandron, 1902), p. 40;

Paul B. Diffley, "Tassoni's Linguistic Writings," *Studi secenteschi,* 33 (1992): 68–92;

Luigi Fassò, "Alessandro Tassoni," in *Enciclopedia italiana di scienze, lettere ed arti* (Rome: Istituto Poligrafico dello Stato, 1950), pp. 317–319;

Ugo Foscolo, "Narrative and Romantic Poems of the Italians," *Quarterly Review,* 21 (1819): 486–566;

Carmine Jannaco and Martino Capucci, *Storia letteraria d'Italia: Il Seicento* (Padua: Piccin Nuova Libraria, 1986), pp. 38–42, 263–264, 522–536, 588–590, 778–780;

Albert N. Mancini, "Alessandro Tassoni," in *Dictionary of Italian Literature,* revised and enlarged edition, edited by Peter Bondanella, Julia Conaway, and Jody Robin Shiffman (Westport, Conn.: Greenwood Press, 1996), pp. 572–575;

Mancini, "Alessandro Tassoni: Between the Renaissance and the Baroque," *Italian Quarterly,* 14 (Fall 1970): 113–120;

Pietro Puliatti, "Il Tassoni e l'epica," *Studi secenteschi,* 25 (1994): 3–52;

Studi tassoniani: Atti e memorie del convegno nazionale di studi per il IV centenario di Alessandro Tassoni, Modena, 6–7 novembre 1965 (Modena: Aedes Muratoriana, 1966)—includes Giorgio Barberi-Squarotti, "La struttura della *Secchia rapita*," pp. 39–62;

Claudio Varese, "Teatro, prosa, poesia: Storia," in *Storia della letteratura italiana,* volume 5, edited by Emilio Cecchi and Natalino Sapegno (Milan: Garzanti, 1967), pp. 854–861.

Fulvio Testi

(23 August 1593 - 28 August 1646)

Adrienne Ward
University of Virginia

SELECTED BOOKS: *Rime di Fulvio Testi* (Venice: Ciotti, 1613; revised edition, Modena: Cassiani, 1617);

L'Italia a Carlo Emanuello Duca di Savoia (Modena?, 1617?);

Poesie liriche del Cav. Don Fulvio Testi all'Altezza Serenissima del Principe Alfonso d'Este (Modena: Cassiani, 1627);

L'isola d'Alcina: Tragedia (Modena: Totti, 1636);

Delle poesie liriche, 2 volumes (Modena: Cassiani, 1645);

La terza parte delle Poesie del Sig. Conte Don Fulvio Testi Commendatore dell'Inoiosa stampate questa prima volta dopo la morte dell'Autore (Modena: Cassiani, 1646);

L'Arsinda; overo, La descendenza de' serenissimi prencipi d'Este: Dramma tragicomico, by Testi and Girolamo Spolverini (Modena: B. Soliani, 1652);

Opere scelte del Conte D. Fulvio Testi (Modena: Società tipografica, 1817);

Il Conte Fulvio Testi alla corte di Torino negli anni 1628 e 1635, edited by Domenico Perrero (Milan: G. Daelli, 1865); revised and enlarged as *Il Conte Fulvio Testi alla corte di Torino negli anni 1628 e 1635: Documenti inediti* (Bologna: A. Forni, 1975).

Editions and Collections: *Raccolta generale delle poesie del signor commendator dell'Inoiosa il Co: D. Fulvio Testi, divisa in tre parte* (Modana [i.e. Modena]: B. Soliani, 1648);

Raccolta generale delle poesie del Conte Testi (Modena: Sogliani, 1653);

Poesie liriche, con le aggiunte delle poesie liriche dell'abbate Francesco Dini, applaudite per l'eccellenza del linguaggio toscano, e copia d'inventioni (Venice: D. Louisa, 1701);

Opere di Gabriello Chiabrera e di Fulvio Testi (Milan: N. Bettoni, 1834).

OTHER: *Scritti inediti di Daniello Bartoli, Fulvio Testi, Alberto Lollio, ora per la prima volta pubblicati* (Ferrara: Negri alla Pace, 1838);

I lirici del Seicento e dell'Arcadia, edited by Carlo Calcaterra (Milan: Rizzoli, 1936), pp. 877–878, 305–342;

Liriche secentesche in lode della carta, edited by Andrea Francesco Gasparinetti (Milan: Edizioni Culturali della rivista *L'industria della carta,* 1953), n.pag.;

Poesia del Seicento, volume 1, edited by Carlo Muscetta and Pier Paolo Ferrante (Turin: Einaudi, 1964), pp. 951–960;

Opere di Gabriello Chiabrera e lirici del classicismo barocco, edited by Marcello Turchi (Turin: Unione Tipografico-Editrice Torinese, 1974), pp. 625–732;

Poesia italiana del Seicento, edited by Lucio Felici (Milan: Garzanti, 1978), pp. 276–282.

Edition in English: "To Count Raimondo Montecuccoli," in *From Marino to Marinetti,* translated by Joseph Tusiani (New York: Baroque Press, 1974), pp. 26–29.

Fulvio Testi combined the vocations of poet and statesman to become one of the leading cultural lights in seventeenth-century Italy. His extensive diplomatic assignments on behalf of the Este court in Modena put him in contact with major literary, artistic, and political figures across the peninsula, as well as in Spain and Austria. Friendships with personages such as Gabriello Chiabrera, Alessandro Tassoni, Giambattista Marino, Gian Lorenzo Bernini, Pope Urban VIII, and Duke Charles Emanuel of Savoy contributed to Testi's fame both as a political strategist and as a poet. In the midst of performing his official duties for the Modenese dukes he produced several volumes of lyric poetry, the works for which he is most renowned. His prolific correspondence—more than 2,100 letters over the course of thirty years—is an invaluable historical artifact as well as an exemplar of contemporary prose stylistics. His minor works include two theatrical pieces and three uncompleted epic poems.

Fulvio Lodovico Testi was born in Ferrara on 23 August 1593, one of the three sons of Giulio Testi, a druggist, and Margherita Calmoni. In early 1598 Testi's father raised the family's status by entering into the service of Duke Cesare d'Este as *maestro del conto* (supervisor of accounts). Testi received a Jesuit education and attended the Universities of Bologna and Ferrara. At eighteen he joined his father in the duke's employ as a copyist. He had already begun composing poems, many of which were circulated and received highly positive reviews from the court literati. In 1613 he published *Rime* (Rhymes) in Venice; most of the sonnets, madrigals, epigrams, and canzones of which the volume consists were written, Testi claims in his dedication, when he was only sixteen. Lyrics such as "Bella donna invecchiata" (Beautiful Aged Woman), "La bella vedova" (The Beautiful Widow), and "La gelosia" (Jealousy) exhibit many of the canonical themes and rhetorical sleights intrinsic to Baroque poetics. Using conceits and juxtapositions designed to produce *meraviglia* (shock and wonder), Testi elaborates traditional Baroque topoi of feminine beauty, sleep, death, and the ephemerality of love and time.

Testi went to Rome in December 1613 to study and write poetry; there he met and formed a lasting friendship with Tassoni. On a visit to Naples he met Marino, the most celebrated poet of the day. In 1614 he married Anna Leni in Modena; they had at least five children—four sons and a daughter.

Dissatisfied with what he considered the immaturity of *Rime* and annoyed by the plethora of typographical errors in the volume, Testi published a second edition in Modena in 1617. He dedicated it to Duke Charles Emanuel I of Savoy, to whom he may have looked for inspiration to liberate Italy from its Spanish shackles. Testi's vitriol toward Spain was familiar to readers from his patriotic forty-three-stanza canzone *L'Italia a Carlo Emanuello Duca di Savoia* (Italy to Charles Emanuel, Duke of Savoy), familiarly known as "Pianto d'Italia" (The Suffering of Italy), which had been circulating for two years. In Testi's most famous poem Italy speaks bitterly to the poet about her oppressor:

Grand'ella è sì, ma tanto alpestra e dura
Che l'Erimaspe in paragon vi perde.
Sterili i campi sono, e la natura
Ciò che altrove dispensa, ivi disperde.
Colà non giunge April, nè s' assicura
Que' diserti giammai vestir di verde;
E i monti di spezzati e nudi sassi
Stancano gli occhi altrui, non men che i passi.

Da regione sì inospita e sì fiera
Per satollar la non mai satia fame
Del sangue mio, scese la gente Ibera
Pronta a furti, a rapine, a frondi, a trame:
Turba tanto più vil, quanto più altera;
Scellerate reliquie, avanzo infame
Di quanti mai con barbari furori
Predar l'Italia o Saracini, o Mori.

(She is great, yes, but so rocky and harsh
That Erimaspe diminishes in comparison.
Her fields are barren, and what nature
Generously bestows elsewhere, there is lost.
April does not arrive there, nor do those deserts
Ever promise to bloom green;
And the mountains of broken, bare stones
Exhaust the eyes no less than one's steps.

From this inhospitable and savage region
To satisfy their insatiable hunger
For my blood, the Iberian people descended,
Wild for thievery, ravishment, revolts, plots:
Upheaval as cowardly as it was frenzied;
Wreaking atrocious havoc, abominable waste,
As great as any that the Saracens or Moors,
With their barbarous violence, ever unleashed upon Italy.)

The poems in Testi's 1617 collection revealed still more anti-Spanish sentiment. As a result, the Modenese court authorities imprisoned the printer, sequestered all copies, and accused Testi of contumacy. Testi fled to nearby lands his father managed and remained in exile for nine months. Owing at least in part to the poem "La Supplica al Serenissimo Signor Principe Alfonso d'Este" (Appeal to the Most Serene Lord, Prince Alfonso d'Este), in which he begged for forgiveness and retracted his slights against Spain, Cesare's son, Alfonso III, pardoned Testi, welcomed him back to court, and appointed him to organize a literary academy. During the next two years Charles Emanuel awarded Testi the Croce dell'Ordine dei SS. Maurizio e Lazzaro (Cross of the Order of Sts. Maurice and Lazarus), and Duke Cesare named him *virtuoso di camera* (court poet virtuoso), put him in charge of the court library, and finally appointed him ducal secretary. He was inducted into several literary academies, among them the Intrepidi (Intrepid Ones) in Ferrara, the Gelati (Frozen Ones) in Bologna, and the Fantastici (Fantastic Ones) in Rome. Testi frequently considered transferring his skills to the Savoy court or to Rome; at other times he leaned toward abandoning the complicated machinations of the nobility altogether. Poems such as "Che i poeti deono fuggir la corte, e che labile è la grazia de' Principi" (Poets must flee the court, the favor of rulers is fleeting), "Che presso a Signori grandi i suggetti più meritevoli più sono sottoposti alle persecuzioni dell'invidia" (In the service of great noblemen those who are most deserving are most persecuted by envy), and "Che instabili sono le grandezze della Corte, e che la vita privata è piena di felicità" (The court's favors are unstable, private life brings great contentment) reveal his mixed feelings about courtly life. His aspiration to a more morally rigorous existence emerges in verses such as "Che la virtù s'invigorisce ne' travagli, e che non s'arriva alla gloria, se non per la via della fatica" (Virtue is invigorated by trials, one does not achieve glory except by struggle), "Che l'età presente è corrotta dall'Ozio" (The present age is corrupted by Idleness), and "Che l'Invidia non dee temersi, e che la Poesia è sollevamento dell'avverse fortune" (One must not fear envy, Poetry uplifts in the face of adverse fortune).

These three canzones appeared in Testi's *Poesie liriche* (Lyric Poems), published in Modena in 1627. In the preface he repudiates his early works even more passionately than he had in the 1617 edition, and the volume includes none of the amorous Marinist sonnets of *Rime*. Testi concentrates exclusively on the canzone form, whose classic restraint and lofty, moralizing capacity better suited his desire to imitate the achievement of the ancient poets. Modeling his work on the handling of the Pindaric style by Chiabrera, Testi also tried to re-create the more accessible, "natural" eloquence of Horatian lyric.

These new compositions enjoyed resounding success because of the increasing critical disapproval of the undignified subjects and stylistic contortions of Marinist verse. The thirty-four canzones of *Poesie liriche* comprise sober political orations, uplifting encomia, epithalamia, and funereal verse. Poems such as "In lode della carta" (In praise of paper), "Che la virtù più che la Nobiltà fa l'uomo riguardevole" (Virtue more than Nobility makes a man esteemed), and "Che gli anni volano, ma che dall'eccellenza de' suoi poetici componimenti egli dee sperare l'immortalità" (The years fly, but he may expect immortality from the excellence of his poetry), dedicated to a fellow courtier, sought not to shock but to educate and inspire. Even when treating mundane subjects, as in a poem thanking a friend, "Per un regalo di Carciofi, e Cavolfiori fatto di Dicembre all'Autore" (For a gift of artichokes and cauliflower, given to me in December), Testi maintains a solemn eloquence that reflects his belief in strong ethical and intellectual foundations. Martino Capucci observes that Testi's new poetry reveals his pained awareness of the schism between humankind's moral potential, on the one hand, and historical events, on the other hand: "Se gli uomini hanno poco credito in patria, se sono fallaci le speranza e instabili le grandezze della Corte, se l'età presente è corrotta dall'ozio e dalle soverchie delizie, il Testi indica la via d'uscita nella solitudine, nell'amore di una realtà semplice e spoglia, nel culto severo della virtù" (If men count for little in their fatherland, if hopes are false and the majesty of the Court is unstable, if the present age is degraded by idleness and excessive luxury, Testi points to solitude as the way out, to the love of a simple, spare existence, based on the strict cult of virtue). *Poesie liriche* was republished in many cities throughout Italy, including Rome, Venice, Naples, and Bologna.

Cesare d'Este died in 1628; he was succeeded by Alfonso III, who appointed Testi personal secretary to his son, Prince Francesco, and secretary of state. After only a few months as duke, Alfonso abdicated to enter the Capuchin order, leaving nineteen-year-old Francesco I as head of the Este line. Francesco designated Testi resident of the court in 1630 and sent him on ambassadorial missions to Rome, Venice, Mantua, Parma, Turin, and Milan, and to Vienna in 1632. In 1633 Testi was appointed the duke's resident minister in Rome, where he forged a friendship with Pope Urban VIII. In 1635, following successful embassies to Venice and Turin, Francesco made Testi count of Busanella and Gualtieri. That same year he named Testi extraordinary ambassador to the Spanish court; one result was the winning of Correggio for the Este court. In Spain in 1636 and again in 1638 Testi received accolades in Madrid and Barcelona; in 1638 he was awarded the Commenda di Sant'Iago (Commendation of the Order of St. Iago). Like most of his previous honors, this recognition was accompanied by a munificent monetary award.

In 1636, during Testi's first sojourn in Spain, his tragedy *L'isola d'Alcina* (The Island of Alcina) was published in Modena. Testi had written the work ten years earlier to commemorate an Este marriage, but the death of Prince Alfonso's wife had canceled the performance. Based on an episode in Ludovico Ariosto's *Orlando furioso* (1516, Orlando Gone Mad; translated as *Orlando Furioso in English Heroical Verse,* 1591), the play recounts Ruggiero's reawakening to his heroic mission and subsequent escape from the island garden of his evil seductress. Critics generally judge *L'Isola d'Alcina* competent but unimpressive, although Carlo Ossola remarks on the effective influence of Torquato Tasso's character psychology in Alcina's passionate monologues.

Testi also began a tragicomic drama treating the Roman origins of the Este house; its date of composition is not known, though Girolamo Tiraboschi and Antonio Belloni postulate 1623–1624. *L'Arsinda; overo, La descendenza de' serenissimi princìpi d'Este* (Arsinda; or, The Origins of the Most Serene Estense Princes) remained unfinished after four acts. The play was completed by Count Girolamo Spolverini and published in 1652. Its performance met a lukewarm reception: Pier Jacopo Martello commented on its lack of naturalness and annoying length. Testi's only other theatrical works consist of minor dramatic compositions for court festivals and ballets.

Testi's return from Spain to Modena in 1639 marked the beginning of a cooling in his relations with the Este court. In 1640 he requested and was granted the governorship of Garfagnana. His letters from this outpost epitomize the ambivalence he felt toward the court milieu and the busy life of poet-ambassador: on the one hand, he relished the solitude and the distance from dynastic intrigues and travails; on the other hand, he resented the unappreciative provincial rulers with whom he had to deal and struggled with his own appetite for power and glory. As Tiraboschi notes, Testi both detested the court and yearned for it.

During his exile Testi began an epic poem, "Costantino" (Constantine), but left it incomplete at one canto. At some point he began another epic, "L'India conquistata" (India Conquered), which he also abandoned after a single canto. Both attempts mirror Tassian motifs and characters, but they do not come close to the sixteenth-century master's achievement and are generally regarded as lesser examples of Testi's poetic talent. Two cantos exist of a third epic, "Amori in Pantea" (Loves in Panthea), based on ancient Greek material; it has shared the same critical fate as its counterparts.

In the early 1640s tensions over contested lands erupted between Odoardo Farnese, Duke of Parma, with whom Francesco I had joined forces, and Pope Urban VIII. Testi acted quickly to take advantage of the situation, offering Francesco not only his services but also generous material and financial aid. He was reinstated at the court as the duke's *segretario e consigliere di stato* (secretary and state counselor) in 1642 and in that capacity traveled to Milan to assist in treaty negotiations between France and Spain. Also in 1642 the War of Castro broke out between the duke of Parma and the Papal States; Testi was a key participant in the treaty congress that ended the war in March 1644. In 1645 he published a two-volume collection of verse, *Delle poesie liriche;* it was reprinted immediately in Bologna, Venice, and Naples. Testi's son-in-law, Count Francesco Ottonelli, the minister of the Modenese court, arranged for the Naples publication.

In January 1646 Testi was arrested and imprisoned in the Modena fortress. The reasons are not entirely clear, but Tiraboschi concludes that official papers that should have been delivered to Testi fell into the duke's hands and revealed the poet's correspondence with the French prime minister, Cardinal Jules Mazarin, through whom he hoped to enter the service of the French court in Rome. Such a move would not have entailed a betrayal of the Este regime: Duke Francesco, increasingly frustrated with the Spanish, had himself initiated an alliance with the French Crown and intended to place his brother, Cardinal Rinaldo d'Este, in Rome as *protettore della Francia* (Protector of France); Testi hoped to become the cardinal's secretary, thereby remaining faithful to the Este family and simultaneously disentangling himself from its vicissitudes in Modena. But he fell ill and died on 28 August 1646, just as the mollified Francesco was preparing his release from prison.

Shortly after his death, Testi's children added another group of compositions to *Poesie liriche* under the title *La terza parte delle Poesie del Sig. Conte Don Fulvio Testi Commendatore dell'Inoiosa stampate questa prima volta dopo la morte dell'Autore* (1646, Part Three of the Poems of Count Don Fulvio Testi, Knight Commander of the Inoiosa, Printed for the First Time after the Death of the Author). The complete collection, republished as *Poesie liriche* and as *Raccolta generale delle poesie del signor commendator dell'Inoiosa il Co: D. Fulvio Testi, divisa in tre parte* (1648, General Collection of the Knight-Commander of the Inoiosa the Count Don Fulvio Testi, Divided into Three Parts) is generally considered Testi's definitive poetic work.

Testi left behind a massive body of correspondence that itself constitutes a formidable literary achievement. Capucci states that Testi's letters amount to "una nitida radiografia del costume del secolo" (an X-ray of seventeenth-century customs). Maria Louisa Doglio points to the insights the letters offer into the expressive modes, rhetorical strategies, and aesthetic and psychological contexts of the period. The letters reveal what the poetry does not, according to Capucci, who notes the many instances of ironic genius contained in the poet-statesman's correspondence. Naturally, the court is a ubiquitous presence in Testi's missives, whether that of Modena, Rome, Madrid, or others he visited. Detailed coverage of his activities expose the functions and minute ceremonies associated with courtly life, while the author's literary judgments shed light on contemporary aesthetic sensibilities. Testi's correspondence also provides miniature word portraits of the pivotal players and leaders of his age. For example, he notes that "le natiche del marchese Bevilacqua, trovando angusta la sedia di Sassuolo, vorrebbono dilatarsi per la spaziosità dell'Appennino" (the buttocks of the Marquis Bevilacqua find the "chair" of Sassuolo far too restrictive, and wish to spread across the immense space of the Appenines). Elsewhere he says that he is convinced that the ailing Pope Urban VIII wears makeup to camouflage his degraded complexion. Testi's so-called Roman letters are especially compelling for the insider's view they give of the church hierarchy, papal court operations, Urban VIII's personality, and Testi's diplomatic cunning. Recounting to the duke of Modena a private meeting he had with the Pope, he writes:

Dopo i discorsi narrati a V. Altezza nell'altra mia, il Papa levatosi da sedere s'è messo a passeggiare per la Camera, e con viso ridente m'ha dimandato che facciano le mie muse. Io colla moltiplicità delle occupazioni ho procurato di scusare la mia negligenza; ma Sua Santità ripigliandomi ha soggiunto: E Noi pure habbiamo qualche negozio; e con tutto ciò per nostra ricreazione facciamo alle volte qualche componimento. Ci sono ultimamente usciti dalla penna alcuni versi latini, e vogliamo che V. S. li senta; e così tirandosi nell'altra Camera, dove dorme, ha dato di piglio a un foglio, e m'ha letta un oda fatta a imitazione d'Orazio, che veramente è bellissima. Io l'ho lodata, e esaltata fino alle stelle, perchè certo nei componimenti latini il Papa ha pochi, o nissun che l'agguagli. È tornata S. Santità a sedere, e diffendendoci amendue, cioè il Papa nel compiacimento delle lodi, e io nell'ingrandimento degli encomi, è tornato un'altra volta a levarsi in piedi, e menandomi nella stessa camera m'ha fatta vedere un'altr'oda pur latina contra gli ippocriti, graziosa in vero, e bella al paragone dell'altra. Messosi poi a passeggiare per la camera, m'ha detto d'havere molte composizioni toscane fatte da poco tempo in quà, e di volere, ch'io le vegga una per una.

(After the conversations which I reported to your Highness in my previous letter, the Pope rose from his seat and began to walk the room. Smiling, he asked me how my muses inspire me. I excused my negligence, citing my many tasks and occupations, but his Saintliness scolded me, saying, We, too, have duties, and yet we nonetheless write a poem from time to time, as a recreation. I've just recently penned some Latin verses, and would like you to hear them. Retreating into the room where he sleeps, he took out a sheet and read me an ode written in the manner of Horace, which was truly beautiful. I praised and exalted it to the stars, because where Latin poetry is concerned, the Pope has few, if any, equals. His Saintliness sat down again and as we both regaled the other with praises, he stood once more. Taking me to the other room, he showed me another Latin ode, against hypocrites, truly graceful and as beautiful as the preceding one. Walking about the room, he told me he had just completed many Tuscan poems, and that he wanted me to see them one at a time.)

Testi then relates the "grandissima bugia" (great lie) he told to humor the Pope: that the duke keeps a book of the Pope's verses on his desk and knows some of them by heart. After describing the Pope's happiness on hearing this report, Testi advises the duke to be sure to place a copy of the book on his desk so that intimates of the Pope who visit the court will see it. This "bagatella può giovar infinitamente" (trifle may be of infinite use), Testi notes.

Other prevalent themes include travel, the complicated procedures of diplomacy, Testi's evolving understanding of poetry and his personal poetics, intellectual exchanges with friends, and private family matters and affections. As in his lyrics, a strong moralizing tendency invigorates Testi's correspondence, together with a resolute faith in the virtues of modernity over blind obsequiousness to the past. Advising the duke on the proper education for his son, Testi encourages study of modern vernaculars rather than the "dead languages" Greek and Latin. He suggests that the prince take a practical approach, learning languages through conversation and reading rather than through traditional grammar-based methodologies. The prince should also study the sciences, especially mathematics, for their great utility in contemporary governing. As regards the practice of poetry, however, Testi is much less optimistic:

la poetica è una professione oziosa, di molto gusto, ma di poco profitto, da lodar in altri più che da desiderare in sè: difficilissima da praticarsi, perchè in tutte l'altre arti s'ammette la mediocrità, in questa totalmente s'esclude, essendo degno di riso e di fischiate quel poeta che nel suo genere non arriva all'eccellenza. . . . Bisogna consumare tutta intiera l'età d'un uomo in rivolgere i libri de' Greci e de' Latini, e spesse volte non basta. Ella è poi una maliarda che incanta gli animi di chiunque comincia a professarla, e gli fa mettere in dimenticanza ogn'altro affare. . . .

(poetry writing is an indolent profession, very enjoyable, but of little profit, something to praise in others more than to desire in oneself. It is extremely difficult to practice, because in all the other arts mediocrity is accepted, while in this one it is totally disallowed, as the poet who does not achieve excellence in his genre earns laughter and boos. . . . One must consume an entire lifetime attending to the works of the Greeks and Latins, and often that is not enough. Poetry is a vamp who enchants the mind of whoever begins to practice it, and makes him forget every other task. . . .)

In other letters, however, Testi affirms poetry's value as a diplomatic tool:

Ho fatta una canzonetta in lode delle bellissime *Storie* del signor cardinal Bentivoglio. Il mio fine è stato più tosto politico che poetico, avendo creduto che per questa strada non mi sia difficile il guadagnarmi l'animo di Sua Eminenza e di rendermelo più amorevole per tutto quello che possa occorrere in servigio di V. A.

(I wrote a canzonet in praise of Cardinal Bentivoglio's wonderful *Histories*. My aim was more political than poetic, believing that by this route it would not be difficult to win over His Eminence and to make myself more pleasing in his eyes for all that might be needed in serving Your Highness.)

Inevitably, the correspondence returns often to its author's mixed relations with the court. A passage emblematic of many of Testi's letters demonstrates the dance of self-defense in which he was continually engaged, together with the ambivalence that incited him to seek asylum from his courtier duties and simultaneously aspire to a more visible and rewarding public life:

È bugia ch'io avessi intenzione di violentare la liberalità di S. A. in farmi regali e donativi. . . .

È menzogna, ch'io sia sospettoso e mi rompa facilmente con gli amici. L'essere stato infinite volte ingannato, tradito, venduto da i più cari, più confidenti, più obbligati, m'ha insegnato d'essere cauto, e circonspetto. . . .

È falsità ch'io sia instabile e inquieto. Ha 19 anni che servo questo Serenissima Casa, e nella carica di Segretario di Stato la mia assiduità di giorno e di notte, al caldo, al freddo, senza sonno, e senza cibo, ha stancati i medesimi Padroni, ammazzati i Cancellieri, rovinata la mia per altro robustissima complessione: e questa si chiama instabilità? Sono stato chiamato al servigio del già gloriosissimo Carlo Emanuello Duca di Savoia, mediante il Co: Agliè, e l'Abate Broglia; a quello del Gran Duca Padre del presente . . . ; a quello della Serenissima Repubblica di Venezia . . . , a quello dell'odierno Pontefice con istanze vivissime del Marchese Pallavicino, e di Monsignor Ciampoli, . . . e frescamente a quello d'una Testa Coronata con uffici gagliardissimi di Personaggio grande Y e tutti gli ho rinunciati per servire a' miei Principi: e questa s'addimanda inquietudine? Potrei dire mille concetti un dietro all'altro, ma per non parer superbo, me li seppellisco nel cuore. Amo la quiete, desidero la quiete, sospiro la quiete, e se questa non mi sarà conceduta dagli huomini, non mi sarà forse negata da Dio.

(It is a lie that I intended to abuse Your Highness's generosity by arranging gifts and perquisites to come my way. . . .

It is a lie that I am suspicious of others and break easily with friends. Having been deceived, betrayed, and sold out an infinite number of times by my dearest, closest, most indebted confidantes has taught me to become cautious and circumspect. . . .

It is a falsehood that I am unstable and restless. I have served this House for 19 years, and my determination, as Secretary of State, day and night, in the heat, in the cold, without sleep, without food, has wearied my very patrons, exhausted the Chancellors, and ruined my otherwise robust complexion; and this is called instability? Through the offices of Count Agliè and Abbott Broglia I have been called to serve the former most glorious Charles Emanuel, duke of Savoy; . . . I have been called to serve the Great Duke, father of the present duke; . . . I have been called to serve the Serene Republic of Venice, as well as the current Pope, thanks to the urging of Marquis Pallavicino and Monsignor Ciampoli; . . . most recently, through the most earnest offices of an Extremely Important Person, I have been called to serve a Crowned Head . . . and I have renounced them all to serve my Princes—and this is labeled restlessness? I could cite a thousand arguments, one after the other, but so as not to seem arrogant, I bury them in my heart. I love peace and quiet, I desire peace and quiet, I yearn for peace and quiet, and if it won't be given to me by man, perhaps it won't be denied me by God.)

Critics have consistently included Fulvio Testi in the triumvirate of eminent seventeenth-century Italian poets whose other members are Marino and Chiabrera. Giacomo Leopardi considered him the greatest poet of the seicento because of his fervent classicism and moral integrity. While many scholars recognize Testi's particular achievement in the anti-Baroque poetics of his solemn odes and canzones, some also prize his early lyrics for their adept and original elaboration of the aesthetics of *meraviglia*. Testi's French imitators—François Maynard, Urbain Chevreau, and Gilles Ménage, for example—especially revered his Baroque verse. Giovanni Getto identifies Baroque sensibilities throughout Testi's corpus and particularly admires his capacity to marry a lofty, majestic register with arresting images of light and gloom. These recurring chiaroscuro motifs not only enrich the moral imperative of Testian verse but also demonstrate the capacity of Italy's most respected seventeenth-century civil poet to convey his period's acute awareness of the contrast between an elusive golden age and an impending sense of corruption and death.

Letters:
Frammenti di una corrispondenza poetica del secolo XVII (Modena: G. Cavazzuti, 1910);
Lettere, 3 volumes, edited by Maria Luisa Doglio (Bari: Laterza, 1967);
Luisa Varini, "Lettere inedite di Fulvio Testi a Ottavio Bolognesi (1630–1645)," *Studi secenteschi,* 12 (1971): 367–442; 13 (1972): 293–358;
Miscellanea di lettere del Conte D. Fulvio Testi (N.p., n.d.).

Bibliography:
Giorgio Boccolari, "Fulvio Testi: Bibliografia critica," in *Atti e Memorie dei Deputati di storia patria per le antiche provincie modenesi,* series 8, no. 6 (Modena: Artioli, 1954), pp. 1–19.

Biographies:
Girolamo Tiraboschi, *Vita del conte D. Fulvio Testi* (Modena: Società Tipografica, 1780);
Tiraboschi, *Vita del conte D. Fulvio Testi accresciuta* (Venice, 1795);
Giovanni de Castro, *Fulvio Testi e le corti italiane nella prima metà del XVII secolo* (Milan: N. Battezzati, 1875);

Elina Massano, *La vita di Fulvio Testi* (Florence: G. Civelli, 1900);

Armando Zamboni, *Fulvio Testi (1593-1646)* (Turin: G. B. Paravia, 1939);

Monica Cristina Storini, "Testi, Fulvio," in *Letteratura italiana: Gli autori. Dizionario bio-bibliografico e Indici,* volume 2, edited by Alberto Asor Rosa (Turin: Einaudi, 1982), p. 1714.

References:

Francesco Bartoli della Rossa, *Fulvio Testi: Autore di prose e poesie politiche e delle Filippiche* (Città di Castello: S. Lapi, 1900);

Antonio Belloni, *Il Seicento* (Milan: Vallardi, 1929), pp. 124-141;

Martino Capucci, "Fulvio Testi," in *Il Seicento,* edited by Capucci and Carmine Jannaco (Padua: Piccin Nuova Libraria, 1986), pp. 251-261, 385-387;

Marina Castagnetti, "L'epistolario di Fulvio Testi," *Studi secenteschi,* 14 (1973): 13-50;

Maria Luisa Doglio, "Intorno alle lettere edite e inedite di F. Testi," *Lettere italiane,* 4 (1964): 425-444;

Giovanni Getto, "Irrequietezza di Fulvio Testi," in *Barocco in prosa e in poesia* (Milan: Rizzoli, 1969), pp. 163-198;

Giacomo Jori, "Poesia lirica 'marinista' e 'antimarinista,' tra classicismo e barocco: Gabriello Chiabrera," in *Storia della letteratura italiana,* volume 5: *La fine del Cinquecento e il Seicento,* edited by Enrico Malato (Rome: Salerno, 1997), pp. 673-679;

Toby Osborne, *Dynasty and Diplomacy in the Court of Savoy: Political Culture and the Thirty Years' War* (Cambridge: Cambridge University Press, 2002), pp. 77-78, 227, 239, 255;

Carlo Ossola, *L'anima in Barocco* (Turin: Scriptorium, 1995), pp. 176-180;

Giuseppe Ottone, "Sullo stile epistolare di Fulvio Testi," *Aevum,* 44 (1970): 486-493;

Ezio Raimondi, "Alla ricerca del classicismo," in his *Anatomie secentesche* (Pisa: Nistri-Lischi, 1966), pp. 27-41;

Cecilia Rizza, "Sulla fortuna di Fulvio Testi nella Francia del secolo XVII," *Lettere italiane,* 9 (1957): 145-167;

Mario Saccenti, "Un cortigiano pellegrino," in his *Libri e maschere del Seicento italiano* (Florence: Le Monnier, 1972), pp. 117-170;

Claudio Varese, "Teatro, prosa, poesia," in *Storia della letteratura italiana,* volume 5: *Il Seicento,* edited by Emilio Cecchi and Natalino Sapegno (Milan: Garzanti, 1988), pp. 852-859, 986-987.

Francesca Turini Bufalini

(23 July 1553 – 25 April 1641)

Natalia Costa-Zalessow
San Francisco State University

BOOKS: *Rime spirituali sopra i Misteri del Santissimo Rosario* (Rome: Gigliotti, 1595);

Rime (Città di Castello: Santi Molinelli, 1627; enlarged, 1628).

Editions and Collections: Giacomo Guaccimani, ed., *Raccolta di sonetti d'autori diversi et eccellenti dell'età nostra* (Ravenna: Pietro de' Paoli & Giovanni Battista Giovannelli, 1623), pp. 48–51;

Saggio di sonetti sacri e profani di Francesca Turina all'illustre suo discendente Sig. Marchese Filippo Bufalini di Città di Castello, nel giorno 29 agosto 1846, in cui si sposa con la Signora Contessa Virginia Orlandi di Firenze, già Principessa Pallavicini (Città di Castello, 1846);

Daniele Ponchiroli, ed., *Lirici del Cinquecento* (Turin: Unione Tipografico-Editrice Torinese, 1958), p. 525;

Pasquale Tuscano, ed., *Umbria* (Brescia: "La Scuola," 1988), pp. 118–122;

Alma Forlani and Marta Savini, eds., *Scrittrici d'Italia: Le voci femminili più rappresentative della nostra letteratura raccolte in una straordinaria antologia di prose e di versi* (Rome: Newton Compton, 1991), pp. 77–80;

"Rime spirituali sopra i Misteri del Santissimo Rosario," edited by Paolo Bà, *Letteratura Italiana Antica*, 6 (2005): 147–223.

OTHER: Giovanni Battista Marzi, *Ottavia furiosa* (Florence: Filippo Giunti, 1589), p. 7;

Giulio Segni, ed., *Tiempo: All'illustrissimo et reverendissimo signor Cinthio Aldobrandini, Cardinale S. Giorgio* (Bologna: Rossi, 1600), pp. 291–292;

Scipione Francucci, *Il trinfo celeste: Panegirico per la morte di Antonio Corvini* (Viterbo: Pietro & Agostino Discepoli, 1616), p. A4;

"Offerendo Maria l'Agnel celeste" and "Rinchiudete le l'agrime, serbate," in *Componimenti poetici delle più illustri rimatrici d'ogni secolo,* edited by Luisa Bergalli (Venice: Mora, 1726), part 2, pp. 77–78;

Vittorio Corbucci, *Una poetessa umbra: Francesca Turina Bufalini, Contessa di Stupinigi, 1544–1641* (Città di Castello: S. Lapi, 1901), pp. 51–56.

Francesca Turini Bufalini wrote most of her poetry in the traditional style of the Italian Renaissance that was still cultivated by some writers in the seventeenth century, but she was not immune to Baroque influences. Her best poems are unique for their time in their autobiographical content: they are a detailed description of her life and emotions from childhood to old age. No previous Italian woman poet or any of her contemporaries recorded their lives with such precision. Moreover, she is the first Italian poet to write about the joys of motherhood with exuberance. These characteristics make her seem closer to the Romantic tendency of personal confession than to her own age, which was in search of marvelous new techniques to be applied to impersonal subjects.

Francesca Porzia Turini was born on 23 July 1553 in Sansepolcro, Tuscany, the youngest child of the three sons and three daughters of the professional soldier Giovanni Turini and Camilla Turini, née Carpegna. Her father had distinguished himself in the service of the French king, Francis I, by whom he was made marshal and count of Stupinigi and Villafranca in Piedmont; her mother was the daughter of Count Francesco Carpegna and had been raised in the refined atmosphere of the court of the dukes of Urbino. Giovanni Turini died in Corsica in 1554; his widow died soon afterward, and Francesca was brought up by her uncle, Count Pietro Carpegna, in his castle, Gattara, on the border of Tuscany and Montefeltro.

In 1574 Turini married Count Giulio Bufalini, a military officer in the service of the Pope, and moved to his castle at San Giustino, near Città di Castello, Umbria. Forty-seven years her senior, he was twice widowed and had had ten children with his previous wives; only five daughters were still alive, in addition to an illegitimate, though legally recognized, son from an earlier relationship. He was frequently away for long periods and left the management of his financially troubled estate to Francesca. On 15 November 1580 she had to

Title page for the enlarged edition of Francesca Turini Bufalini's Poems *(Biblioteca Nazionale, Rome)*

prepare an armed defense of the castle when it was surrounded by General Vincenzo Vitelli's men in a dispute over bricks ordered from a nearby furnace. Peace was restored by the governor of Città di Castello before any injuries or damage occurred. After her husband's death in Rome on 5 February 1583, Turini Bufalini was left with three young children of her own–Giulio, Camilla, and Ottavio–in addition to her stepdaughters. She also had to try to save the financially precarious estate entrusted to her by testament but destined for her son Giulio. She repeatedly went to Rome and finally succeeded in securing the family property.

During one of her Roman stays Turini Bufalini published her first book, *Rime spirituali sopra i Misteri del Santissimo Rosario* (1595, Spiritual Verses on the Mysteries of the Holy Rosary), which she dedicated to Pope Clement VIII. The religious subject matter reflects a trend that began in the Renaissance and was greatly cultivated in the Baroque period. On the title page she used the feminine form of her maiden name, Turina, together with Bufalini. The book is divided into sections called "misteri" (mysteries). The first mystery, "Gaudioso" (Joyous), consists of fifty sonnets. The second mystery, "Doloroso" (Sorrowful), comprises a madrigal, thirty-seven sonnets, and the twenty-octave "Pianto della Madonna" (Lament of the Madonna). The third mystery, "Glorioso" (Glorious), consists of a madrigal, forty sonnets, and "Ottave della Gloria del Paradiso" (Octaves on the Glory of Paradise), a poem of twenty-five octaves. The poems treat the major events of the New Testament from Christ's birth through the death and ascension of the Madonna and culminates with Mary's coronation in heaven. While the poetry is not always refined or original, Turini Bufalini's religious fervor is simple and genuine. Twenty-three sonnets and a madrigal on the death of Turini Bufalini's husband conclude the volume; they are stylistically of better quality than the preceding pieces.

Turini Bufalini managed the family possessions well, but in 1614 her sons, who constantly quarreled with each other but united against her, forced her to yield the administration of the property to them. She moved to Rome, where she became a lady-in-waiting to Lucrezia Tomacelli Colonna, the wife of Constable Filippo Colonna, Duke of Paliano, and the teacher of their two daughters. When Lucrezia died in 1622, Turini Bufalini moved into a palace her husband had built in Città di Castello. In 1623 her widowed son, Ottavio, was mortally wounded trying to break up a brawl. After his death, she led a secluded life and devoted herself to raising her orphaned grandson.

In 1627 Turini Bufalini published the 144-page collection of sonnets titled *Rime* (Poems); an enlarged edition of 313 pages appeared the following year. In the dedication to Filippo and Lucrezia Colonna's daughter Anna, Turini Bufalini declares that she wrote the sonnets to alleviate the sufferings of her youth and of her maturity and that she had found a refuge from her domestic troubles in the Colonna household. The first group of poems consists of encomiastic sonnets dedicated to Anna, to other members of the Colonna family, and to their friends. The next section comprises a series of autobiographical poems, followed by poems on themes such as the passing of time, death, and religious topics. The book concludes with additional encomiastic sonnets.

The autobiographical poems are arranged in a loose chronological order. Turini Bufalini says that her suffering began soon after she was born–"Quando, misera, apersi in questo infido / mondo, gli occhi a le lacrime, al dolore" (When, wretched me, I opened onto this treacherous / world my eyes to tears, to pain)—because her father died when she was a baby. Her mother had to abandon their home:

> Né qui fermò, che la mia sorte ingrata
> nel maggior uopo, ancor mi tolse lei,
> onde fui in tutto de' parenti orbata.
>
> (Nor did it stop here, for my cruel destiny,
> with greater harm, took her also away,
> so that I was orphaned of both parents.)

Rime includes two particularly remarkable sonnets. One is addressed to the "Cara, fida, secreta cameretta" (Dear, faithful, secret little room) in which she passed her youth, crying night and day, giving wings to her thoughts, and writing poetry while neglecting household duties. The other is addressed to her "Letto, porto fedel de' miei lamenti" (Bed, faithful port of my lamentations), the only witness to her tears and to the pain that made her wish for death until sleep brought oblivion and peace. This sort of intimacy with inanimate objects as witnesses of a poet's pain is frequently found in the Romantic period, but not in Turini Bufalini's day.

Francesca was taken in by her maternal uncle: "pianse pietoso, sol per pianger nata" (he, compassionate, cried, I, born only to cry). The verse exemplifies the Baroque technique of using similar-sounding words, and the repeated *p* sound gives the poem a harsh ending, as if to reinforce the cruelty of fate.

Francesca's years with her uncle were a happy time, however. Turini Bufalini calls his rustic castle "libero Catai" (free Cathay), as though it were a mythical, exotic, faraway country. Francesca roamed freely through fields and forests in the company of village girls, tending sheep, making baskets, picking flowers, and singing and dancing. She won footraces against the other girls, mastered the bow and arrow not only for target shooting but also for hunting, and imagined herself to be a second Camilla, the warrior maiden of Virgil's *Aeneid*. She learned to ride a horse, and a sonnet on her reckless gallops close to precipices is the only one of its kind by an Italian woman poet.

Francesca's freedom was interrupted by a stay in a convent school, where she was taught to use a needle and a spindle. After a few years she returned to her beloved mountains, whose rugged landscape Turini Bufalini describes with a vividness and simplicity that is largely free of the artificiality of the academic writing that was popular in her day.

When "Sposo d'alto valor, d'alto intelletto" (A groom of valor, of great intellect) asked for Francesca's hand, she eagerly accepted. In two sonnets Turini Bufalini describes taking leave of her beloved mountains and her friends, the shepherdesses, whom she promised never to forget. She recounts their arrival at her husband's castle, San Giustino, accompanied by a retinue of gentlemen and ladies. One sonnet is devoted to a description of the castle. She writes that she was lonely when his military duties called him away; during one of his long absences she almost died from a miscarriage, but the desire to see him again kept her alive. His return restored her health and her happiness. She dedicates several poems to him that clearly render her emotions, including her impatient wait for the conjugal embrace. Nowhere in the poems is there a complaint about their age difference.

Three sonnets commemorate the births of Turini Bufalini's sons, but none that of her daughter. The second of the two devoted to her firstborn is the most intimate:

> Viscere del mio sen, cara pupilla
> degli occhi miei, vezzoso pargoletto,
> quanto di gioia il cor arde e sfavilla
> qualor ti bacio e mi ti stringo al petto.
> Oh, con che dolce e che materno affetto
> non madre pur, ma ti son fatta ancella,
> or ti vezzeggio, o a dormir ti alletto
> cantando, e meno in ciò vita tranquilla.
> Fra l'animate rose la mamella
> talor ti porgo e il latte in un col core
> ti dono, e 'l prendi tu con gran diletto.
>
> (Fruit of my womb, dear apple
> of my eye, charming little one,
> how full of joy burns and shines my heart,
> when I kiss you and press you to my heart.
> Oh, with what sweet and maternal love,
> not just your mother, but your servant I've become.
> Now I caress you, now, with singing, I invite you to sleep,
> and thus I lead a tranquil life.
> Among animated roses my breast
> I offer you, and with my milk my heart
> I give to you. You take it with great joy.)

The death of Turini Bufalini's husband is the subject of several poems. Turini Bufalini writes that she was sorry that her youth did not prolong his life—the only allusion in the volume to the disparity in their ages. She could see no relief from the pain of widowhood. Her beautiful home and blooming garden were no consolation; she longed only to be buried one day next to him, although in her dreams she heard his familiar voice whispering encouragement to her. She turned to God, and only her responsibility for her children deterred her from seeking peace in a convent. But she was forced to flee from her home when her sons turned against her. She frequently thought that death would be better for her. Yet, with time she realized that she must try to forget her lost happiness:

> Vaneggiante pensier ch'errando vai
> la notte e 'l dì senza aver mai quiete,
> quanto più volgi in te gli andati guai
> tanto entri più ne la terrena rete.
>
> (Ravaging thoughts, that wander about
> at night and day, without repose,
> the more you ponder about troubles of the past,
> the more in earthly nets you get enmeshed.)

She hoped to find consolation by composing poetry, which was for her a refuge from the ills of life:

> Deh, cessa omai; tornin tranquille e liete
> le Muse, e rasserena i mesti rai,
> e tutti caggian ne l'oblio di Lete
> i duri affanni e non risorgan mai.
>
> (Oh cease, by now; let the Muses return,
> calm and happy, and let my sad eyes brighten,
> let all severe anguish fall into oblivion and never rise again.)

Of a more optimistic tone are the sonnets Turini Bufalini composed to glorify the successes of her grandsons, Giulio's sons Nicolò and Giovanni, in their first jousts.

Turini Bufalini found a personal way to deal with traditional themes such as the inexorable passing of time: she looks at herself in a mirror and sees graying hair that used to be blond and a gap where a tooth has been lost. A sonnet on human misery is influenced by a famous one on the subject written by the master of Baroque poetry, Giambattista Marino; yet, Turini Bufalini gives her version a unique touch by seeing the prenatal state as a tomb:

> O miserabil uom,
> . . . .
> Tu fra l'ombre e gli orror del sen materno,
> quasi morto e sepolto, anzi che nato
> hai tomba anzi la cuna, e, vomitato,
> esci poi quindi a soffrir caldo e verno.
> Prima che latte altrui, lasso, ti pasce
> il proprio pianto, e l'altrui man t'avvezza
> ai lacci e a le catene, entro le fasce.
> Come fior passa via tua giovinezza
> tra le cure, e avvien che 'l viver lasce
> pria che venghino i dì della vecchiezza.
>
> (Oh pitiable man,
> . . . .
> in the darkness and horrors of your mother's womb,
> almost dead and buried before being born,
> you have a tomb before you have a cradle, and, vomited forth,
> you come out to suffer heat and cold.
> Oh wretched one, before the taste of milk,
> your own tears feed you, and someone else's hand
> accustoms you, in swaddling clothes, to snares and chains.
> Like a flower your youth fades
> among cares, and it can happen that your life departs
> before the days of old age arrive.)

Other Baroque influences are evident in her sonnets on death—especially in one addressed to a skull, a symbol of death frequently depicted by painters and sculptors of the seventeenth century. Her spiritual compositions attest to her profound religious belief and express the desire to see the Church return to its original state of purity and poverty.

In a letter to the reader at the beginning of *Rime* the publisher, Santi Molinelli, refers to a narrative poem titled "Il Florio" (Florio); he calls it Turini Bufalini's major work and says that it is almost complete. According to Vittorio Corbucci, Turini Bufalini continued to work on it until 1640; she then sent the manuscript to her relative Cardinal Ulderico di Carpegna and asked for his opinion. His favorable reply is dated 18 January 1641; Turini Bufalini died on 25 April, and the work remained unpublished. According to Giuseppe Milani, the poem, which he found among the Bufalini family papers in the 1990s, consists of thirty-nine cantos. Based on Giovanni Boccaccio's prose romance *Il Filocolo* (circa 1336; translated, 1985), it deals with the love of Florio and Biancofiore. Turini Bufalini also left behind a series of unpublished sonnets on great Italian poets of the past and on minor contemporary writers; these compositions, some of which were published in Corbucci's book, reveal her understanding of literary trends. For example, she calls Marino the most harmonious poet of all time, a greater charmer than Orpheus or the Sirens, and one who is capable of moving the wildest beast to pity with his laments. Her many letters, all unpublished, to her husband, children, and friends are valuable documents of her times.

Turini Bufalini was known and respected for her literary endeavors by her contemporaries, but only within a limited circle. She probably became a member of the academy of the Accinti (Prepared) in Città di Castello, as well as the highly regarded academy of the Insensati (Foolish) of Perugia. Giovanni Mario Crescimbeni briefly mentions her publications in his *Dell'istoria della volgar poesie e Comentarj intorno alla medesimia* (1730, On the History of Vulgar Poetry and Commentary on

All of the Same), as does Francesco Saverio Quadrio in *Della storia e della ragione d'ogni poesia* (1739–1749, On the History and Reason of All Poetry). Luisa Bergalli included only two poems by Turini Bufalini, both religious, in her 1726 anthology. The autobiographical poems remained unnoticed until 1901, when Corbucci analyzed some of them and praised their quality. Corbucci also provided information on the Turini family and on Giulio Bufalini and his wives and children but was unable to trace Turini Bufalini's date of birth. At the end of the book he included a selection of her unpublished poems: sonnets on the poets Marino, Petrarch, Ludovico Ariosto, Torquato Tasso, and Battista Guarini; two sonnets on her own "Il Florio"; a madrigal; and some stanzas in which Venus describes her son, Cupid, and the havoc he creates. The sonnets on "Il Florio" relate Turini Bufalini's escape into creative writing: she says that she longed for nighttime and the solitude and privacy of her bed, where she was free to immortalize Florio in her verses. She addresses her creation directly, a highly unusual technique at that time:

> Florio mio, tu sei quel ch' 'n tanti affanni
> Infino ad or m'hai mantenuto in vita,
> ché dal sen fatto avria l'alma partita
> per le pene e i martir ch'apportan gli anni.

> (My Florio, you are the one who, in so many afflictions,
> has kept me alive up to now,
> for my soul would have departed from me
> because of the pain and sufferings that the years bring on.)

Corbucci also provided a list of fifty-seven of Turini Bufalini's unpublished poems that he had seen in the G. Margherini-Graziani Archive, which has since been dispersed. But six are, in fact, by other authors, and two of Turini Bufalini's poems had already been published. Of the remaining forty-nine, Corbucci published seven in his book.

In "La lirica cinquecentesca" (1930, The Lyrical Poetry of the Sixteenth Century) Benedetto Croce praised Turini Bufalini's religious and autobiographical poems for their simplicity and candor and cited "Cara, fida, secreta cameretta" as an example. But he considered her a sixteenth-century poet, a Renaissance noblewoman like Vittoria Colonna and Veronica Gambara: well read, morally strong, and with profound feelings–qualities he did not find typical of the Baroque period, as he subsequently stated in his essay "Donne letterate nel Seicento" (1931, Literary Women of the Seicento). As a result, "Cara, fida, secreta cameretta" was included in Daniele Ponchiroli's anthology *Lirici del Cinquecento* (1958, Lyric Poets of the Sixteenth Century) and quoted by Ettore Bonora in *Storia della letteratura italiana: Il Cinquecento* (1966, History of Italian Literature: The Sixteenth Century). Ponchiroli and Bonora ignored the fact that most of Turini Bufalini's poems were published in 1627 and 1628. They also failed to examine Corbucci's work and an article by Igea Torrioli that had appeared in 1940. Torrioli reconstructs the cultural ambience of Città di Castello, one of the Renaissance centers of Umbria, where painters as well as writers were active. She also provides information on the Turini and Bufalini families and the friendships Turini Bufalini cultivated with other poets. Discussing *Rime,* Torrioli observes that no one before Turini Bufalini had described the memories of childhood emotions in such detail; she also mentions Turini Bufalini's joyful, tender expression of the theme of motherly love. In 1991 Alma Forlani and Marta Savini anthologized five sonnets by Turini Bufamili, and in 1998 Milani, who had discovered the manuscript for "Il Florio" in the family archives, added information about the author's children and stepchildren and their descendants. Paolo Bà contributed the concluding chapter to Milani's book; there, and in several later articles, he analyzes Turini Bufalini's themes, poetic techniques, and language. He also published an edition of her *Rime spirituali sopra i misteri del Santissimo Rosario* in 2005 and commented on it in 2007.

Francesca Turini Bufalini deserves a place among the poets of the early seventeenth century. Her poems are well written and offer a realistic and detailed description of the life of an Italian noblewoman of the late sixteenth and early seventeenth centuries.

References:

Paolo Bà, "Due valli viste da una poetessa: Francesca Turina Bufalini già nota come Francesca Turrini," *Pagine altotiberine,* 11 (2000): 75–88;

Bà, "Francesca Turina sposa Giulio I. Bufalini," *Pagine altotiberine,* 14 (2001): 113–130;

Bà, "Il mondo di Francesca Turina Bufalini e le sue *Rime spirituali,*" *Letteratura Italiana Antica,* 8 (2007);

Bà, "Pene ed entusiasmi giovanili di Francesca Turina Bufalini," *Pagine altotiberine,* 13 (2001): 45–60;

Daniele Barni, "Alla ricerca dei manoscritti perduti di Vittorio Corbucci," *Pagine altotiberine,* 21 (2003): 75–82;

Ettore Bonora, "Il Classicismo dal Bembo al Guarini," in *Storia della letteratura italiana: Il Cinquecento,* edited by Emilio Cecchi and Natalino Sapegno (Milan: Garzanti, 1966), pp. 247–248;

Vittorio Corbucci, *Una poetessa umbra: Francesca Turina Bufalini* (Città di Castello: Lapi, 1901);

Giovanni Mario Crescimbeni, *Dell'istoria della volgar poesia e Commentarj intorno alla medesimia,* volume 4 (Venice: Besegio, 1730), p. 119;

Benedetto Croce, "Donne letterate nel Seicento," in his *Nuovi saggi sulla letteratura italiana del Seicento* (Bari: Laterza, 1931), pp. 154–171;

Croce, "La lirica cinquecentesca," in his *Poesia popolare e poesia d'arte* (Bari: Laterza, 1930), pp. 339–438;

Enrico Mercati and Laura Giangamboni, *L'archivio e la biblioteca della famiglia Bufalini di San Giustino* (Città di Castello: Petruzzi, 2001);

Giuseppe Milani and Paolo Bà, *I Bufalini di San Giustino: Origine e ascesa di una casata–Francesca Turina Bufalini, poetessa 1553–1641. Una donna che ha dato lustro a una famiglia* (San Giustino: Tipografia "Tiber," 1998);

Francesco Saverio Quadrio, *Della storia e della ragione d'ogni poesia,* 4 volumes (Milan: Agnelli, 1739–1749), II: 278;

Igea Torrioli, "Francesca Turina Bufalini e la società colta tifernate nel sec. XVI," *L'alta valle del Tevere,* 8 (1940): 1–36.

Papers:

Some of Francesca Turini Bufalini's manuscripts are in the Bufalini archives in the Castello di San Giustino, which is now public property and includes a library; copies of manuscripts that were in the now-dispersed G. Margherini-Graziani Archive are in the Biblioteca Comunale in Città di Castello.

Appendix 1: The Arcadian Academy

Appendix 2: Poetry and Music in Seventeenth-Century Italy

Appendix 3: Theater and Spectacle

Appendix 1: The Arcadian Academy

Paul Colilli
Laurentian University

During the second half of the seventeenth century poetic theory reacted against what were considered the aesthetic deformations of the literature of the Baroque period, and a movement back toward the Renaissance ideal of literary creation began. It was believed, as Giuseppe Parini put it in the next century, that Italy had to reawaken "dalla sua vertigine" (from its dizziness) and return to "gustare il vero e ad esprimerlo co' suoi propri colori" (taste the truth and express it with its own colors). This development culminated in the founding of the Accademia dell'Arcadia (Arcadian Academy) in Rome in 1690. As Anna Laura Bellina and Carlo Caruso have demonstrated, the founding of the academy signaled the birth of a new literary consciousness imbued with the rationalist philosophy that characterized the eighteenth-century Enlightenment. The emphasis was on the potential of reason to investigate the phenomena of the world; equally important was the need to articulate the results of any investigation in a clear language that could be understood by all. Much importance was placed on the search for and verification of "il vero" (the truth) and on the ideal of "buon gusto" (good taste). One of the theorists of this ideal was Lodovico Antonio Muratori: in his *Delle riflessioni sopra il buon gusto nelle scienze e nelle arti* (1715, Reflections on Good Taste in the Sciences and the Arts) Muratori is concerned with establishing methodologies that encourage sound and balanced critical judgments, and "buon gusto" finds its genesis in the principles of reason and in the information that philological inquiry is able to provide. Rationalism emphasized logical order, linear thinking, measurable limits, and a form of expression that was coherent, simple, and clear. Verisimilitude was highly prized but did not necessarily imply realism; the central features of verisimilitude were naturalness, simplicity, and beauty.

The Arcadian reaction against the Baroque style is evident in Giovanni Mario Crescimbeni's preface to the first volume of the *Rime degli Arcadi* (1716–1720, Rhymes of the Arcadians): "Per lo total risorgimento del buon gusto nelle belle lettere cotanto in Italia nel passato secolo deteriorato, fu istituita, ha ventisei anni in Roma la Ragunanza degli Arcadi" (For the total resurgence of good taste in letters that deteriorated so much in Italy during the last century, the Gathering of the Arcadians was instituted twenty-six years ago). The beginnings of the Arcadia, however, give evidence of a continuity of certain sixteenth-century features. Giosuè Carducci observes that

> La riazione necessariamente comincia su i limiti e con le forze dell'azione stessa contro la quale si volge. Quindi il primo elemento dell'Arcadia è l'arte del Seicento nelle due forme: la raffinata e arguta, epigrammatica e madrigalesca: la solenne e concitata e pomposa, lirica e ... se non che la riazione importa anche, in gran parte, ristaurazione. E la ristaurazione fu delle forme del Cinquecento.

> (The reaction necessarily begins with the limits and the strengths of the same action against which one is turning. Thus, the first element of the Arcadia is the art of the seicento: the refined and the witty, the epigrammatic and the madrigal-like: the solemn and the excited and pompous lyric ... but the reaction also entails, in great measure, a restoration. And the restoration was of the forms of the cinquecento.)

Carlo Calcaterra went on to illustrate extent to which the Arcadian movement retained key Baroque features—especially the musical genres.

The reaction against the Baroque style led to critical investigation into the metrical and rhetorical models that the Italian tradition had to offer. This historical and philological research resulted in the work that is considered the first modern history of Italian literature, Crescimbeni's *L'istoria della volgar poesia* (1698, The History of Vernacular Poetry). Roberto Tissoni notes that the techniques of philological exegesis devised by the Arcadians were highly influential in subsequent centuries.

In 1687 a French cleric, Dominique Bouhours, published *De la manière de bien penser dans les ouvrages d'esprit* (On the Manner of Proper Thinking in the Works of the Spirit; translated as *The Art of Criticism: or, The Method of Making a Right Judgment upon Subjects of Wit and Learning*, 1705). Citing as his examples sixteenth-century poets such as Torquato Tasso and seventeenth-century poets including Giambattista Marino, Bouhours criticized what he considered the major shortcomings of the Italian poetic tradition: a lack of serious content and an exaggerated emphasis on rhetorical embellishment. Bouhours's attack was answered by Giovanni Giuseppe Orsi in *Considerazioni sopra un famoso libro francese intitolato La manière de bien penser dans les ouvrages d'esprit* (1703, Considerations on a Famous French Book Titled The Manner of Proper Thinking in the Works of the Spirit). Orsi's response reflected the outlook of the Arcadian Academy. First, he asserted that the attack on the cinquecento and the epic poem made no sense and betrayed Bouhours's lack of understanding of the Italian literary tradition. Second, he rejected the idea of "national" poetic tastes, which was contrary to the humanist idea of the universality of poetic expression. Nevertheless, Bouhours's claim that Italian letters went astray in the seventeenth century was endorsed by most critics.

The Orsi-Bouhours debate stimulated theoretical discussions of poetry and poetics. In *Della perfetta poesia italiana* (1706, On the Perfect Italian Poetry) Muratori argued for the rediscovery of the Italian poetic tradition and contended that poetry should serve civic, moral, and pedagogical ends. He also held that poetic creation should be a function of the imagination and not proceed according to rigorous rules of composition. This notion was echoed by Tommaso Leva in *Memorie d'alcune virtù del Signor Conte Francesco de Lemene, con alcune riflessioni su le sue poesie* (1706, Memoirs of Some Virtues of Count Francesco De Lemene, with Some Reflections on His Poems).

The most philosophically informed exposition of the new poetics was provided by Gianvincenzo Gravina. In "Discorso sopra l'*Endimione*" (1692, Remarks on the *Endymion*), which dealt with Alessandro Guidi's pastoral drama of the same year, Gravina argued that poetry has an indispensable social and civic function, but that to sustain such a role it had to have the true and the natural as its central point of reference. In 1696 Gravina published *Delle antiche favole* (On Ancient Fables), in which he argued that the ancient past can be understood through Greek and Roman myths. In *Della ragion poetica: Libri due* (1708, On Poetic Reason: Two Books) Gravina cited Homer as the greatest poet of all: "Ma l'intero campo [del rappresentabile] fu largamente occupato da Omero" (But the entire field [of the representable] was largely occupied by Homer) and said that the poets of the cinquecento were models for recovering and imitating the ancients and thus ensuring the purity of language and style. In *Della tragedia: Libro uno* (1715, On the Tragedy: One Book) he contended that literature must be created in a symbiotic connection between philosophy and poetry.

Before the founding of the Arcadian Academy, but during the final days of the Baroque period, there existed a literary trend scholars call pre-Arcadian. Two geographic areas were particularly represented by pre-Arcadian poetry: Florence and northern Italy. The Florentine group undertook linguistic and literary experiments to counter the Baroque style, and they established innovative contacts among scientists, linguists, and literati who wanted to rediscover the literary tradition by employing a language that was rooted in tradition but vital and living, as well. There was much interest in translating the works of classical authors such as Anacreon and Lucretius; the former, in particular, played an influential role in the development of Arcadian poetics. The ancient texts served as instruments in the search for a language that was at once classical and current.

The principal Florentine pre-Arcadians include Lorenzo Bellini, Alessandro Marchetti, and Lorenzo Magalotti. The best idea of Florentine pre-Arcadian poetics, however, can be gleaned from certain writings of Francesco Redi, Benedetto Menzini, and Vincenzo Filicaia.

In Redi's letters one finds sustained emphasis on the idea that literary art must be guided by "evidenza e chiarezza" (evidence and clarity), an ideal that can be put into practice by using "singole parole" (single words). This minimalist approach runs counter to the rhetorical and lexical opulence and abstraction of the Baroque style. Viewing literature through a scientist's eyes, Redi has a penchant for words and images that reflect verifiable experiences. He encourages clarity and just measure and eschews the use of puns, hyberbole, paradoxes, oxymorons, and exaggerated metaphors. Redi's poems written in the Anacreontic style anticipate Arcadian poetics:

> Io vidi un giorno quel crudel d'Amore
> per la foresta affaticato e stanco,
> con l'arco in mano e la faretra al fianco
> in abito legger di cacciatore. . . .
> . . . .
> Io pietoso gli offersi il pianto mio.
>
> (One day I saw that cruel god of Love
> in the forest fatigued and tired,
> with bow in hand and quiver by his side
> in hunter's light garb. . . .
> . . . .
> I, compassionate, offered him my tears.)

In 1688 Menzini published *Dell'arte poetica* (On the Art of Poetry) "per fine di opporsi alla corruttela del secolo" (to counter the corruption of the century). Menzini had great disdain for Baroque poetry and sought to overcome its deficiencies by turning to a more ancient and noble tradition. Reacting against the "lascivia" (lasciviousness) of Baroque poetry, he called for moral values to be the cornerstones of a more civil literary tradition. The objective was to create a poetics characterized by a balance of ethics, literature, erudition, and culture. In "Discorso nel quale si prova che le lettere deon essere congiunte alle morali discipline" (Oration in Which It Is Proven That Letters Must Be Connected with the Moral Disciplines) Menzini wrote: "Vorrebbesi dunque far sí che l'acquisto delle belle arti servisse non alla superbia, ma alla carità, non all'inquietudine, ma alla tranquillità, non ad una folle jattanza, ma all'uso" (It is sought that the acquisition of the fine arts serve not haughtiness, but charity, not preoccupation, but tranquility, not an insane boastfulness, but use). A key element of Menzini's poetics was "prudenza" (prudence), on which any attempt to make sound and informed judgments must be based. In a 3 December 1690 letter to Francesco del Teglia, Menzini encouraged a form of poetry that is "non servile, ma gentilissima" (not servile, but very gentle), a style that, in being an evenly measured combination of modern and ancient, becomes a "terza specie di stile" (a third kind of style). In book 5 of the *Dell'arte poetica* Menzini described poetic inspiration as a "gentil foco" (gentle fire), a restrained enthusiasm that adheres to the laws of sound judgment:

> E sì soavemente egli s'interna
> nell'intelletto, che ubbidir conviene
> a lui, che l'alme a suo piacer governa.
> Ma con l'entusiasmo ancor sen viene pur da natura il buon
>   giudizio: oh quanto,
> quanto è l'imperio, ch'ei in Parnaso tiene!
>
> (And so gently it [the gentle fire] enters deeply
> into the intellect, who had better
> obey him, as he rules over the souls as he pleases.
> But with enthusiasm good judgment comes from nature:
>   oh, how much,
> how much is the empire he holds in Parnassus.)

In Menzini's poetics, Petrarch provides the sublime model of "buona poesia" (good poetry), which combines "perspicuitade" (perspicuity), "vaghezza e nobiltade" (longing and nobility), and "nobiltà e chiarezza" (nobility and clarity). In the first book of *Dell'arte poetica* Petrarch is presented as the creator and savior of Italian poetry:

> Dolce d'ambrosia e d'eloquenza un fiume
> scorrer vedrai dell'umil Sorga in riva
> per quei, ch'è dei poeti onore e lume.
> Né chieder devi ond'egli eterno viva;
> perché 'l viver eterno a quel si debbe
> stil puro e terso che per lui fioriva.
>
> (You will see a river
> sweet with ambrosia and eloquence
> flow from the humble Sorgue to the shore
> through him, who is the honor and light of poets.
> Nor do you need to ask where he lives in eternity;
> because eternal life is owed to him
> pure and terse style that flourished through him.)

While northern Italy did not have openly anti-Baroque centers such as Florence, poets such as Carlo Maria Maggi and Francesco De Lemene were developing a poetics that transcended the "charlatanism" of the seicento. A professor of classics and secretary of the Milan Senate, Maggi had strong religious and moral principles and reacted against the "lascivia" of Marino and his followers. Like Menzini, Maggi attempted to employ Petrarchism as a means of breaking away from Baroque poetics. In poems such as "Gode in pensare alla mutazione di se stesso" (He Takes Pleasure in Thinking about the Change in Himself) the reader is confronted with a quest for lyrical simplicity and clarity, together with a sense of moral reawakening that is modeled on the Renaissance Petrarchists:

> Dove sono i sospir, che al giovinetto
> mio cor porger solean vano alimento,
> . . . .
> Riconosco ognor pij, quanto più 'vecchio,
> che le speranze mie furon di vetro,
> e di quel vetro all'avvenir fo specchio.
>
> (Where are the sighs that used to
> give my youthful heart vain nourishment,
> . . . .
> I recognize all the more, as I get older,
> that my hopes were made of glass,
> and in the future I made that glass a mirror.)

Religious themes are particularly evident in poems such as "Desiderio di sapere se i peccati sian perdonati, in desolazione di spirito" (The Desire to Know If the Sins Are Forgiven, in the Desolation of the Spirit):

> Dite, dov'è il mio Dio?
> Egli era nel cuor mio,
> Ma non v'è più.
> Ahi, sdegnerà tornar,
> Che nol seppi guardar
> Quando vi fu.

(Pray tell, where is my God?
He was in my heart
But he is no longer there.
Ah, he will be too offended to return,
As I did not know how to look at him
When he was there.)

Maggi's attempt to cultivate a new "sound" poetics was acknowledged by Muratori, who said that Maggi made a balanced and controlled use of style, images, and rhetorical figures and achieved a sense of majestic graveness that was natural and incorporated the "true." Scipione Maffei praised Maggi for reacting against Baroque poetry and for writing beautiful sonnets but considered his expression of his ideas "prosaico e invenusto" (prosaic and graceless), sententious, and overelaborate.

De Lemene received more praise from the founders of the Arcadian Academy than did Maggi. According to Walter Binni, there were two main reasons for the difference: De Lemene's insistence on religious and theological themes, as in his collection *Dio: Sonetti e Hinni consagrati al vicedio Innocenzo undecimo, pontefice ottimo massimo* (1684, God: Sonnets and Hymns Dedicated to the Vicar of Jesus Innocent XI, Supreme Pontiff), which articulates Thomistic philosophy in verse form; and the Arcadian predilection for melodic lyric, which De Lemene purged of any lascivious Baroque residue. Muratori said that De Lemene's literary career hinged on finding a point of convergence between the musical possibilities of poetry and religious themes.

The pre-Arcadian poet who was seen by the Arcadians as the most audacious and as best reflecting the characteristics of Arcadian poetry was Guidi. In dialogue 10 of *La bellezza della volgar poesia* (1700, The Beauty of Vernacular Poetry) Crescimbeni singled Guidi out as a highly original poet who made every word an image; at the same time, however, Crescimbeni suspected Guidi of being sympathetic to the poetry of the seicento because his poetry was "tutta d'immagine" (all imagery). Nevertheless, Guidi received much praise in Arcadian circles; according to Gravina, he was the only true contemporary poet.

One finds in Guidi's poetry a strong presence of moral and heroic themes. For example, in his *Rime* (1704, Rhymes) one reads:

Da le moderne e da l'antiche tombe
polverose reliquie in Pindo chiama.
E de gli eroi a suscitar la fama
di guerrieri concerti arma le trombe.
. . . .
Da le tombe famose aura vitale
porge invitto fomento a nobil core,
le prisch'orme calcando alto valore.

(From the modern and from the ancient tombs
dusty relics Pindo calls.
And for the heroes who will bring fame
warriors in concert the trumpet sounds.
. . . .
From the famous tombs a vital aura
offers unconquered instigation to a noble heart
ancient traces following the footsteps of high valor.)

The Arcadian Academy was a successor to the Accademia Reale (Royal Academy) of Sweden, founded by Queen Christina in 1653. In 1654 Christina converted to Catholicism and abdicated her throne; she obtained protection from Pope Alexander VII and arrived in Rome on 23 December 1655. In January 1656 she chaired the first Italian meeting of the Accademia Reale in the Farnese Palace. Among those who attended were Filicaia, Guidi, Redi, Menzini, and Paolo Coardi. Several articles of the constitution of the Italian Accademia Reale prefigured those of the Arcadian Academy, including the promotion of Latin and Italian in article 5, the emphasis on the musicality of poetry in article 9, the involvement of learned individuals from all of Italy in article 17, the rejection of satiric works in article 28, and the importance placed on collegial decision making. The constitution provides directives as to the linguistic and literary models the members must seek out:

> In quest'Accademia si studi la purità, la gravità, e la maestà della lingua Toscana. S'imitino per quanto si può i maestri della vera eloquenza de' secoli d'Augusto e di Leone X, poiche' negli autori di quei tempi, si trova l'idea d'una perfetta e nobil eloquenza e percio' si dia il bando allo stile moderno, turgido e ampolloso, ai traslati, metafore, figure, etc.
>
> (In this Academy the purity, the gravity, and the majesty of the Tuscan language are to be studied. The masters of the true eloquence of the centuries of Augustus and of Leo X are to be imitated as much as is possible, in that in the authors of those times one finds the idea of a perfect and noble eloquence and for this the bombastic and pompous modern style, figurative speech, metaphors, figures, etc., are to be banished.)

The constitution also specifies how the meetings of the academy were conducted, foreshadowing what took place during meetings of the Arcadian Academy:

> Ogn'Accademia comincerà con una sinfonia, dopo la quale si canterà la prima parte del componimento musicale, destinato per l'Accademia di quel giorno. Finita questa prima parte, si farà la lezione Accademica, dopo la quale si canterà la seconda parte della composizione, e cosi finirà con la musica, come principio.

(Each [meeting of the] Academy will begin with a symphony, after which the first part of the musical composition, planned for the meeting of that day, will be sung. Once this part is finished, there will be the reading, after which the second part of the musical composition will be sung, and so it will end with music like the beginning.)

A constitution drafted in 1680 added several regulations, including article 27, which prescribed that members must submit compositions to the secretary of the academy for approval before publication.

Christina died on 9 April 1689. The traditional account of the founding of the Arcadian Academy is that at a subsequent meeting of the Accademia Reale, held at the Prati di Castelli, one of those present proclaimed that "Egli mi sembra che noi abbiamo oggi rinovata l'Arcadia" (It appears to me that today we have renewed Arcadia), the region of Greece where pastoral poetry was born. According to proceedings of the academy, however, the name was selected because the Venetian Republic won back the Peloponnese, in which Arcadia is located, from the Turks in 1690. The name was ratified on 5 October 1690 by fourteen individuals who met in the Gardens of San Pietro in Montorio on the Janiculum Hill: Crescimbeni, Gravina, Coardi, Leonio, Giuseppe Paolucci, Silvio Stampiglia, Giovan Battista Felice Zappi, Carlo Tommaso Maillard di Tournon, Pompeo Figari, Paolo Antonio del Negro, Melchiorre Maggi, Jacopo Vicinelli, Paolo Antonio Viti, and Agostino Maria Taja.

Crescimbeni, who had been active in organizing the activities of the Accademia Reale, was elected the first *custode generale* (general custodian) of the Arcadian Academy; he held the post until his death in 1728. Although he did not enjoy the intellectual authority of his cofounder and rival Gravina, Crescimbeni had important connections with church authorities and became a member of the Jesuit order about two months before he died. His *L'Arcadia* (1711), inspired by Jacopo Sannazaro's 1502 work of the same title, relates in mythological garb the figures and the events that led to the founding of the Arcadian Academy. In addition to *L'istoria della volgar poesia* and *La bellezza della volgar poesia,* Crescimbeni composed the *Comentarj intorno alla sua istoria della volgar poesia* (1702–1711, Commentaries on His History of Vernacular Poetry). Crescimbeni was the key figure in the publication projects of the Arcadian Academy, as evidenced by his editing of the eight-volume *Rime degli Arcadi,* and was, as well, an historian of the academy in writings such as the four-volume *Le vite degli Arcadi illustri* (1708–1727, The Lives of Illustrious Arcadians) and the three-volume *Notizie istoriche degli Arcadi morti* (1720–1721, Historical Notices of Deceased Arcadians).

The Arcadian Academy was the first Italian literary academy to include representatives from all across Italy: Crescimbeni was from Macerata, Gravina from Cosenza, Coardi from Turin, Leonio from Spoleto, Paolucci from Spello, Stampiglia from Lanuvio, Zappi from Imola, Maillard di Tournon from Nice, Figari and Negro from Genoa, Maggi from Florence, Vicinelli from Rome, Viti from Orvieto, and Taja from Siena. Each member selected a pseudonym composed of a first name taken from the tradition of pastoral poetry and a surname that referred to a real or imaginary place made famous in literature. For example, Gravina chose the pseudonym "Opico Erimanteo" from the wise Opicus in Sannazaro's *L'Arcadia* and the Erimanto forest from which Hercules expelled the wild boar. The meeting place of the academy was called the Bosco Parrasio (Parrhasian Grove), after a forest in Arcadia that was dear to Apollo. The symbol of the Arcadian Academy was a *siringa* (syrinx) crowned with laurels and pine above the word *Arcades* or *Arcadi*.

The Arcadian Academy was organized on the basis of *collegi* (colleges), each of which elected a *custode generale* and *vice-custode*. In 1696 Gravina wrote the academy's constitution, the *Leges Arcadum* (Arcadian Laws), in archaic Latin. While the Arcadian Academy relied on the generosity of benefactors—for example, King John V of Portugal made possible the construction of a headquarters on the Janiculum—and while its ideas were in consonance with Catholic ideology, it was autonomous and immune to external influence. "Colonies" of the Arcadian Academy opened throughout Italy; one of the best known was the Colonia Renia of Bologna.

In his "Lettera sul Romanticismo" (1871, Letter on Romanticism) Alessandro Manzoni made a comment that led to a serious misunderstanding of the Arcadian Academy: "Avvenne una mattina che tutti i poeti italiani . . . si trasformarono . . . in tanti pastori, abitanti in una regione del Peloponeso" (It happened one morning that all the Italian poets transformed themselves into many shepherds, inhabitants of a region of the Peloponnese). Manzoni's assessment gives the impression that the Arcadians were concerned primarily, if not exclusively, with pastoral poetry; their custom of reciting poetry in pastoral garb opened the Arcadians up to ridicule, but their challenge to Baroque culture owed as much to contemporary philosophical and philological theories and practices as it did to classical and Renaissance poetic and linguistic forms.

Manzoni's negative assessment of the Arcadian movement was echoed by generations of Italian scholars until Benedetto Croce put forward a more balanced view in the twentieth century. Croce's positive reevaluation focused on three key points: the Arcadia was a reflection of the rationalist Enlightenment spirit that dominated Europe during the 1700s; it stressed the pedagogical and ethical elements of "il buon gusto," which is essential for the good life; and it promoted the ideal of a civic and national culture. Amedeo Quondam argues further that the Arcadian Academy aimed to establish a hegemony of intellectuals to combat the cultural developments that had brought about the corruption of Italian letters during the Baroque period.

References:

Maria Teresa Acquaro Graziosi, *L'Arcadia: Trecento anni di storia* (Rome: Palombari, 1991);

Adunanza tenuta dagli Arcadi in Arcadia, il ritratto Della Sacra Real Maestà di Stanislao I. Re di Polonia, Duca di Lorena, di Bar &c. Fra gli arcadi acclamati Eutimio Alifireo (Rome: Antonio de' Rossi, 1753);

Anna Laura Bellina and Carlo Caruso, "Oltre il barocco: La fondazione dell'Arcadia. Zeno e Metastasio: La riforma del melodramma," in *Storia delle letteratura italiana,* volume 6, edited by Enrico Malato (Rome: Salerno, 1998), pp. 239-312;

Walter Binni, *L'Arcadia e Metastasio* (Florence: La Nuova Italia, 1968);

Dominique Bouhours, *De la manière de bien penser dans les ouvrages d'esprit* (Paris: Widow of Sebastien Mabre-Cramoisy, 1687); translated as *The Art of Criticism: Or, The Method of Making a Right Judgment upon Subjects of Wit and Learning* (London: Printed for D. Brown and A. Roper, 1705);

Carlo Calcaterra, *Il barocco in Arcadia e altri scritti sul Settecento* (Bologna: Zanichelli, 1950);

Giosuè Carducci, "Il Parini principiante," in *Studi su Giuseppe Parini: Il Parini minore,* volume 13 of his *Opere* (Bologna: Zanichelli, 1903);

Isidoro Carini, *L'Arcadia dal 1690 al 1890* (Rome: Cuggiani, 1891);

Giovanni Mario Crescimbeni, *L'Arcadia* (Rome: Antonio de' Rossi, 1711);

Crescimbeni, *La bellezza della volgar poesia* (Rome: Giovanni Francesco Buagni, 1700);

Crescimbeni, *Comentarj intorno alla sua istoria della volgar poesia,* 5 volumes (Rome: Antonio de' Rossi, 1702-1711);

Crescimbeni, *L'istoria della volgar poesia* (Rome: Chracas, 1698; revised and enlarged edition, Venice: Basegio, 1730);

Crescimbeni, *Notizie istoriche degli Arcadi morti,* 3 volumes (Rome: Antonio de' Rossi, 1720-1721);

Crescimbeni, *Le vite degli Arcadi illustri,* 4 volumes (Rome: Antonio de' Rossi, 1708-1727);

Crescimbeni, ed., *Rime degli Arcadi,* 8 volumes (Rome: Antonio de' Rossi, 1716-1720);

Benedetto Croce, "L'Arcadia e la poesia del Settecento," in his *La letteratura italiana del Settecento* (Bari: Laterza, 1949), pp. 1-14;

Francesco De Lemene, *Dio: Sonetti e Hinni consagrati al vicedio Innocenzo undecimo, pontefice ottimo massimo* (Milan: G. dall'Oglio & I. Rosati, 1684);

Anna Maria Giorgetti Vichi, *Gli Arcadi dal 1690 al 1800: Onomasticon* (Rome: Arcadia, Accademia Letterarie Italiana, 1977);

Gianvincenzo Gravina, *Delle antiche favole* (Rome: Printed by Antonio de' Rossi for S. Silvestro, 1696);

Gravina, *Della ragion poetica: Libri due* (Rome: Francesca Gonzaga, 1708);

Gravina, *Della tragedia: Libro uno* (Naples: Nicolò Naso, 1715);

Gravina, "Discorso sopra l'*Endimione*," "Della ragion poetica libri due," and "Della tragedia libro uno," in his *Opere letterarie,* volume 1: *Scritti critici e teorici,* edited by Amedeo Quondam (Bari: Laterza, 1973), pp. 49-73, 195-327, 503-589;

Alessandro Guidi, *Rime* (Rome: Gio. Giacomo Komarek, 1704);

Tommaso Leva, *Memorie d'alcune virtù del Signor Conte Francesco de Lemene, con alcune riflessioni su le sue poesie* (Milan: Malatesta, 1706);

Scipione Maffei, *Nella prima radunanza della colonia arcadica di Verona* in *Rime e prose* (Venice: Sebastiano Coleti, 1719);

Francesco Maria Mancurti, *Vita di Gio. Mario Crescimbeni, arciprete della Basilica di S. Maria in Cosmedin di Roma, e custode generale d'Arcadia: Col racconto de' fatti più memorabili della ragunanza degli Arcadi* (Rome: Antonio de' Rossi, 1729);

Alessandro Manzoni, "Lettera sul Romanticismo," in his *Tutte le opere,* volume 5/3, edited by Carla Ricciardi and Biancamaria Travi (Milan: Mondadori, 1991);

Michele Mayenlender, *Storia delle Accademie d'Italia* (Bologna: Forni, 1988);

Benedetto Menzini, *Dell'arte poetica di Benedetto Menzini, accademico della real maestà di Cristina regina di Svezia: Libri cinque* (Florence: Piero Manini, 1688);

Menzini, "Discorso nel quale si prova che le lettere deon essere congiunte alle morali discipline," in his *Opere: Accresciute, & riordinate e divise in quattro tomi,* volume 3: *Contenente le prose volgari* (Florence: Tartini & Santi, 1731);

Michel Giuseppe Morei, *Memorie istoriche dell'Adunanza degli Arcadi* (Rome: Antonio de' Rossi, 1761);

Lodovico Antonio Muratori, *Della perfetta poesia italiana* (Modena: Soliani, 1706);

Muratori, *Delle riflessioni sopra il buon gusto nelle scienze e nelle arti* (Cologne: B. M. Renaud, 1715);

Giovanni Giuseppe Orsi, *Considerazioni sopra un famoso libro francese intitolato* La manière de bien penser dans les ouvrages d'esprit (Bologna: Pisarri, 1703);

Giuseppe Parini, "Discorso di belle lettere," in his *Prose,* volume 2, edited by Egidio Bellorini (Bari: Laterza, 1915);

Amedeo Quondam, "L'istituzione Arcadia: Sociologia e ideologia," *Quaderni storici,* 30 (1973): 369–438;

Francesco Redi, *Lettere di Francesco Redi gentiluomo aretino dedicate all'Illustrissimo Signore Antonio Vallisnieri* (Florence: Giuseppe Manni, 1724);

Mario Saccenti and Maria Grazia Accorsi, eds., *La colonia Renia: Profilo documentario e critico dell'Arcadia bolognese. 1. Documenti bio-bibliografici. 2. Momenti e problemi* (Modena: Mucchi, 1988);

Roberto Tissoni, "Il commento ai classici italiani nel Sette e nell'Ottocento (Dante e Petrarca)," in *Il Commento ai testi: Atti del Seminario di Ascona, 2–9 ottobre 1989,* edited by Ottavio Besomi and Carlo Caruso (Basel: Birkhäuser, 1992), pp. 433–652.

Appendix 2: Poetry and Music in Seventeenth-Century Italy

Maria Galli Stampino
University of Miami

The traditional view of the Renaissance holds that by the second half of the sixteenth century the humanist quest to bring the classical past back to life had extended to the field of music. Theoretical works such as Girolamo Mei's *De modis musicis antiquorum* (1567–1673, On the Musical Modes of the Ancients) and Vincenzo Galilei's *Dialogo della musica antica e della moderna* (1581; translated as *Dialogue on Ancient and Modern Music,* 2003) are cited to support this interpretation. These treatises do attempt to reconstruct the music played in classical antiquity, whether by itself or as an accompaniment to tragedies or comedies. Nevertheless, critics today generally agree that scholars such as Mei and Galilei were not interested in re-creating Greek tragedy in the late sixteenth century but in gaining knowledge of how music was used in classical antiquity.

In other circles, however, the relationship between texts and music elicited practical as well as theoretical interests. When Vicenza's Accademia Olimpica (Olympic Academy) bestowed on Angelo Ingegneri the responsibility of bringing to the stage Orsatto Giustiniani's 1585 adaptation of Sophocles' *Oedipus Tyrannus,* he opted to have only the chorus sung, without accompaniment; Andrea Gabrieli, *maestro di cappella* (chapel master [choir conductor]) of St. Mark's Basilica in Venice, set those parts to music. Additionally, courtly entertainments made extensive use of sung words in *intermezzi apparenti* (staged interludes), as well as in *concerti di donne* (ladies' vocal concertos). The latter consisted of three sopranos singing in virtuoso style and were a tradition of the ruling Este family of Ferrara that was soon emulated in the courts of Mantua and Florence.

Intermezzi apparenti are especially helpful in dispelling the misconception that music burst onto the Italian cultural scene only at the end of the sixteenth century. These works were so called to differentiate them from *intermezzi non apparenti,* which consisted of instrumental music marking the separation between the acts of a play. While *intermezzi apparenti* were also performed between the acts of a comedy or tragicomedy, they were sung and availed themselves of rich stage sets and the accompaniment of varying numbers and types of instruments. Their earliest documented use occurred in Florence in 1526 in a repeat performance of Niccolò Machiavelli's comedy *Mandragola.* By the 1550s many drama theoreticians and practitioners were complaining that the intermezzi had become more important than the plays—indeed, that the plays had become mere excuses for staging intermezzi. In the early seventeenth century this complaint became a critical cliché, so persistent and recurrent that later scholars took it to signify the novelty of the genre, rather than the pervasiveness of it. Despite the many complaints about the frequent and lavish exploitation of *intermezzi apparenti,* Anna Laura Bellina and Thomas Walker contend that this type of musical interlude influenced the Italian tradition of "teatro per musica" in one fundamental way: all of the texts are in verse, none in prose. This feature is but one element in the complex relationship between intermezzi and other forms of sung entertainment, a relationship that has so far elicited little critical attention. Intermezzi continued to be performed after 1600, the canonical year of the "birth" of opera; in fact, the acts of some operas were separated by sung intermezzi.

While a rich tradition of instrumental and sung music for the stage was already in existence, the first years of the seventeenth century were unusually fertile in musical innovations. This trend is not just evident from the standpoint of later observers but elicited comment from music theoreticians and practitioners of the time. In 1597 Ottavio Rinuccini's *La Dafne* (Daphne) was staged in Florence with a score by Jacopo Peri. In October 1600 Rinuccini's *L'Euridice* (Eurydice) was performed, also in Florence and also with a score by Peri. That winter separate scores for *L'Euridice* by Peri and by Giulio Caccini were printed. Also in 1600 Emilio de' Cavalieri's *Rappresentazione di Anima, et di Corpo* (Representation of the Soul, and of the Body) was performed and printed in Rome. Finally, in 1602 Caccini's *Le nuove musiche* (The New Music) for vocal solo and Ludovico da Viadana's *Cento concerti ecclesiastici* (One Hundred Ecclesiastical Concerti) were published; the latter, though instrumental only, offers the first printed example of continuo (also known as figured bass or thoroughbass), a bass line that runs through the piece and was a crucial element of sung entertainment because it provided the essential melodic scaffolding on which other instruments and voices could build.

This flourishing of musical experiments had repercussions on the ties between music and lyrics. As Gary Tomlinson observes, sung performances of the early modern period in Italy "involve not one text but two: a preexistent poetic text, with its own meanings . . . , and a musical text, constructed to reflect in various ways the meaning of the poetry it sets yet not without its own, more-or-less independent levels of meaning." Consequently, one should not consider the poetic aspect from the musical or vice versa. To further complicate matters, Gavriel Moses points out that "many of the texts chosen for musical setting tended to be unstable in their self-definition as texts of one kind [genre] or another."

The madrigal was the poetic genre most frequently set to music in the late sixteenth and seventeenth centuries. The poetic madrigal of that period did not correspond to the fourteenth-century form used by Petrarch, which consisted of two or three three-line stanzas followed by a refrain; it was a one-stanza, seven- and eleven-syllable poem, usually comprising twelve lines, with no set verse order or rhyme scheme. Musical madrigals made use of poetic madrigals as well as of other poetic forms, including canzones, sonnets, and ballads. According to Lorenzo Bianconi, the musical madrigal was the premier polyphonic genre; poems by various authors were gathered in printed collections, and composers turned to those volumes to find texts to set to music.

Both poetic and musical madrigals are usually short pieces and thus are unable to articulate complex ideas. Composers concentrated on the images in the poems, rather than try to translate the metric or rhetorical structure into music. Lyrical pieces by some poets were more suited to the musicians' needs than those by others. In his analysis of the frequency with which texts by various poets were set to music, Bianconi has determined that Torquato Tasso's *Rime* (1581, Rhymes) prevailed among composers until the publication of collections of the same title by Giovan Battista Guarini in 1598 and by Giambattista Marino in 1602. Alessandro Martini has shown that Marino's madrigals were eminently suitable for musical setting because they were limited to thirteen lines and always ended with a rhyming couplet but provided variation in line length as well as in rhyme number and position. Bellina and Walker note that Gabriello Chiabrera introduced the *canzonetta pindarica* (Pindaric canzonet) and the *ode anacreontica* (Anacreontic ode) to musicians in Florence, where courtly circumstances were particularly favorable for the joint exploitation of poetry and music. While these four canonical writers provided many texts to be set to music, some of which were used multiple times by various musicians, the majority of poems set to musical madrigals are anonymous and have defied all attempts to identify the authors.

The theme of love predominates in the poetry that composers such as Caccini and Claudio Monteverdi set to music. Guarini's and Marino's lyrics follow the Petrarchan tradition of describing the beloved's features but concentrate on one or two details such as the eyes or the lips. This practice had musical ramifications: Diane Kelsey McColley notes that "Italian madrigalists liked to set 'occhi,' eyes, on pairs of whole notes, miming the lovers' long gaze, so that a pair of eyes seems to gaze at the singer from the page. Since in Renaissance notation notes are commonly lozenge or diamond-shaped, the Petrarchism of eyes like diamonds is literalized."

Musical madrigals are through-composed: that is, series of notes are rarely repeated. In this respect, too, musical structure corresponds to the poetic one, as Petrarchan forms eschew "popular" compositions built around refrains. In the seventeenth century madrigals were composed in cities with music-promoting courts such as those in Rome, Modena, Mantua, and Turin.

Cantatas are generally much longer than madrigals; include sections for solos, duets, and trios; and lack counterpoint. They were usually composed for a patron or a particular singer and for a specific occasion. Rome was the principal center for the composition and performance of these pieces–though their publication, when it took place at all, occurred in Venice, Italy's printing capital–because it was home to many wealthy families who could act as patrons for the musicians, singers, organists, and harpsichordists who came there to be trained or to try to secure a post at a church or private chapel. These wealthy patrons were, however, barred by the government of the Republic of Venice from building or sponsoring their own theaters; thus, cantatas were typically performed as vocal chamber music at gatherings in private palaces. The audiences were highly selected and included experts on music–or people who considered themselves such; cantatas, therefore, underscored technical skills on the part of the composer and the singers. The lyrics were also highly erudite to appeal to an educated audience. Unlike intermezzi, which were also occasional pieces, cantatas were not written to celebrate important events. For this reason they circulated mostly in manuscript, as gifts from the master of the palace to his guests. Since they were rarely committed to print, many cantatas have no doubt been lost.

Singers depended on the patronage of noble families and courts for support and public recognition. Caccini was employed at the Medici court in Florence, where he served as singer and composer of musical entertainment for the wedding celebration of Ferdinando I de' Medici, Grand Duke of Tuscany, and Christine of Lorraine in 1589 and for that of King Henry IV of France and Maria de' Medici in 1600. His elder daughter, Francesca, was already famous in 1600, at thirteen, for singing in Rinuccini and Peri's *L'Euridice* and in *Rapimento di Cefalo* (The Abduction of Cephalus), with libretto by Chiabrera and score by her father. During the family's sojourn at the French court in 1604–1605 she was offered a salaried position and a substantial dowry by Maria de' Medici, but the grand duke refused to give her father permission to accept on her behalf. Francesca was on the Medici payroll from 1607 to 1627 as a singer, composer, and teacher; in the 1620s she was the highest-paid musician employed by the Florentine ruling family. Her sister Settimia was recruited by Duke Ferdinando Gonzaga of Mantua in 1613 and was one of the highest-paid musicians at that court at the time of her departure in 1620.

Adriana Basile sang at the Mantua court from 1610 to 1626. She traveled extensively in the service of the Gonzagas, performing in operas as well as singing madrigals and cantatas. After her release from Mantua she lived and sang in Naples and, from 1633, in Rome. Her daughter Eleonora (or Leonora) Baroni was born at the Gonzaga court in 1611 and named after the late duchess. Refined in her manners and endowed with a widely admired voice, Eleonora wrote both poetry and music. She was highly successful in Naples in 1627, and soon after her family's arrival in Rome in 1633 she was proclaimed the best chamber singer of the age. In 1644–1645 she lived and sang in Paris, having been invited there by the queen regent, Anne of Austria. Her career in Rome continued until her death in 1670, prospering especially during the papacy of Clement IX from 1667 to 1669; before becoming Pope, Giulio Rospigliosi had been an opera librettist. Because most of Eleonora's career took place in Rome, where women were barred from singing onstage, she is not known to have ever sung in an opera.

Courts also played a crucial role in promoting composers and their contributions, using them both for in-house events such as *concerti di donne* and for more-lavish celebrations. Rinuccini's texts, for example, were conceived for specific household celebrations: *L'Euridice* was performed at Florence's Pitti Palace for the wedding of Henry IV and Maria de' Medici; *L'Arianna* was staged in Mantua with Monteverdi's music for the marriage of Duke Francesco Gonzaga and Margherita of Savoy in 1608; and *Mascherata di ninfe di Senna* (Masque of the Nymph of the Seine) was produced at the Pitti Palace in May 1613 for the nuptials of Count Mario Sforza and Arnea of Lorraine.

Until the 1980s critics emphasized the role played by courts in the emergence of new musical genres. Since then, awareness has become widespread that the genre that emerged in the Florentine court between 1597 and 1600 and is usually referred to as "opera" is quite different from opera in Venice after 1637; Bianconi argues that the two genres share a name but little else. Like the intermezzo, courtly opera was designed to dazzle its audience in a one-time performance; the cost of production was high, and the benefits were political and cultural. Public opera, conversely, was a risky business endeavor staged by impresarios in theaters built specifically for the purpose; it had to attract many spectators to sustain a run long enough to repay the initial investment. Furthermore, since anyone with the money for a ticket could gain entrance, the audiences were more varied than the ones invited to courtly performances. Finally, memories of courtly opera performances were passed on to posterity in lavish semiofficial or official books called *descrizioni* (descriptions); commercial opera is far less documented but established its own traditions through what Bianconi calls "the habits and customs of its faithful supporters." When "a company of musicians rented the Teatro S. Cassiano (traditionally used for performances of the *commedia dell'arte*)" in Venice to stage Benedetto Ferrari and Francesco Manelli's *Andromeda* for the 1637 carnival season, the institutionalization of opera as it is known today had begun.

One composer was able to make the transition between courtly and commercial opera: Monteverdi. In addition to nine books of madrigals and many other compositions, he scored Alessandro Striggio's *Orfeo* (Orpheus), performed in Mantua in 1607 under the patronage of Francesco Gonzaga, the duke's elder son, and for Rinuccini's *L'Arianna*. He also worked with commercial impresarios, as evidenced by his score for Giacomo Badoaro's *Il ritorno d'Ulisse in patria* (The Return of Ulysses to His Homeland), produced at the Teatro San Cassiano during carnival of 1639–1640; the anonymous and now-lost *Le nozze d'Enea in Lavinia* (The Marriage of Aeneas in Lavinia), staged at the Teatro Santi Giovanni e Paolo for carnival of 1640–1641; and Giovan Francesco Busenello's *L'incoronazione di Poppea* (The Coronation of Poppea), performed at the Teatro Santi Giovanni e Paolo during carnival of 1642–1643.

Monteverdi's work as a composer went side by side with theoretical pronouncements on the relationship between lyrics and music. Bianconi points out that after the publication of his fourth book of madrigals in 1603, Monteverdi was attacked by the Bologna theorist Giovan Maria Artusi "on the grounds of the unlawfulness of certain dissonant contrapuntal procedures." These procedures constituted a significant innovation: Monteverdi had introduced a new musical form, akin to "the declamatory articulation of the musical 'speech'" and "based on the principles of correspondence, antiphrasis, repetition, alternation and the recapitulation of musically recognizable sections"–all derived from the rhetorical tradition. Monteverdi replied to Artusi's attacks in the preface to his *Quinto libro de' Madrigali a cinque voci* (1605, Fifth Book of Madrigals for Five Voices). Two years later, Monteverdi's brother, Giulio Cesare, expanded, commented on, and explained this short preface in the "Dichiarazione" (Declaration) that opened his own *Scherzi musicali a tre voci* (Musical Scherzos for Three Voices). In these texts the Monterverdis assert the emergence of a *seconda pratica* (second practice) that is replacing an older *prima pratica* (first practice). The latter, according to Giulio Cesare, "intende che sia quella che versa attorno alla perfetione del armonia; cioè che considera l'armonia non comandata, ma comandante, e non serva ma signora del'orazione" (is concerned with the perfection of harmony; that is, it considers harmony not as led by, but as leader of, oration, not its servant but its lord). *Seconda pratica* originated with Cipriano da Rore in the sixteenth century and was taken up by composers such as Peri and Caccini.

One element of affinity between poetry and music during the period derives from the pervasive presence of classical rhetoric in the intellectual milieu of the time. Important links exist between late-sixteenth- and early-seventeenth-century stances on the relationship of words and music, on the one hand, and Platonic, Aristotelian, and Horatian ideas on music, poetry, and theater, on the other hand. In his *Republic*, Plato pointed out that certain musical tonalities provoke specific reactions in the hearers; for example, as McColley notes, he recommended that musicians "avoid 'slack' modes associated with 'drunkenness, effeminacy, and inactivity' when training warriors." Aristotle argued that poets are superior to philosophers and historians, since they deal with events not as they are but as they should be and thus can influence the actions of their audiences through examples. Finally, Horace's *Ars poetica* (Art of Poetry), according to Bernard Weinberg, "considers above all the dramatic forms, in relation both to nature and to their capacity to please and to instruct an audience of a given kind that would see them in a given age under given circumstances." Horace's remarks were commonly extended to nondramatic poetic forms but were directly applicable to a staged genre such as opera. In sum, these classical authorities shared a belief in the power of words and music over audiences, and early modern poets and musicians found this notion reinforced, Bianconi notes, by "the psychological theory of affections, legacy of the natural magic of the sixteenth century, in particular, of the *musicae vis mirifica* (wondrous power of music), itself based on a supposed harmony and affinity between numerical proportion in music and the passion of the human heart." In addition to these general considerations, each musical instrument was believed to characterize and elicit specific emotions and was used in particular circumstances. Music reinforced the emotional power of words to spur people to action; therefore, according to Tomlinson, the musician had a responsibility to recognize "the passions as dynamic forces directing human thought and action, and . . . to control and exploit." Barbara Russano Hanning argues that the earliest humanist-educated musicians' belief in "the power of the solo voice to move their listeners by conveying the worlds clearly" led them to write their compositions down, rather than improvise them.

Mythological sources–above all, the myth of Orpheus–were prevalent in Venetian opera at least until 1630: according to Bianconi, "It is as though the foundation of the new musical and theatrical genre–based on a musical language that was capable of representing and moving the affections . . . was destined to take place less under the banner of the tragic catharsis of heroic and tragic mythology . . . than on the fertile–indeed, enchanted–terrain of a mythology of metamorphoses and origins." Mythology provided the source for public as well as courtly operas; Maiolino Bisaccioni and Giovanni Rovetta's *Ercole in Lidia* (Hercules in Lydia), first performed in Venice in 1645, provides a prime example. Francesco Cavalli was one of the most prolific composers for the Venice opera houses, and his works also treat mythological subjects. His first score, for Orazio Persiani's *Le nozze di Teti e di Peleo* (The Marriage of Thetis and Peleus), sung in 1639 at the Venice Teatro San Cassiano, and his score for Giovanni Faustini's *Calisto* (1651) both use mythology as an excuse for complex plots that derive many elements from romances, commedia dell'arte and other plays, and collections of short stories.

Another essential plot source for Venetian opera was ancient history; as Albert N. Mancini points out, opera's sudden and dazzling success made it a popular vehicle for bringing competing conceptions of power to the stage, and it replaced tragedy in this role. The best-known example is Busenello and Monteverdi's *L'incoronazione di Poppea*: Nero rules by following his baser instincts, but at the end of the opera he has solidified his hold on power. The image of the just monarch is thus turned upside down. Less-celebrated works include Bisaccioni's *Semiramide in India* (Semiramis in India), which was probably set to music by Francesco Sacrati and was performed in Venice in 1648, and Niccolò Minato's *Scipione africano* (1664, Scipio Africanus), *Muzio Scevola* (1665, Mucius Scaevola), and *Pompeo Magno* (1666, Pompey the Great). Paolo Getrevi points out that Bisaccioni's text is similar to Busenello's in that both portray strong-willed, power-driven women clashing with their faithful, chaste, and sentimental opposites. Conversely, Minato's librettos can be seen as inviting Venetian citizens to revel in their city-state's power over an extended geographical domain at a time when that was endangered: despite the efforts of Pope Clement IX, in 1669 Venice lost its important military and commercial outpost in Crete, the port city Candia (now Iráklion).

In Rome all musical entertainment was courtly in nature until the city's first public theater, the Tordinona, opened in 1671. Papal patronage of Roman opera waxed and waned, depending on the individual Pope. For example, Urban VIII (Maffeo Barberini), Pope from 1623 to 1644, and his nephews, Cardinals Francesco and Antonio Barberini, were staunch patrons of sung musical entertainments; but Urban's successor, Innocent X (Giovanni Battista Pamphilj), had little interest in art, and musical performance in Rome retreated from the papal court to private noble households. The Catholic Church's prohibition against women performing onstage had a profound effect on opera in Rome that spread to Italy and Europe as a whole: female parts were sung by castrati—men whose testicles had been removed before puberty to preserve their high-pitched voices. When this operation was successful, it produced voices that were not only pliable but also, because of the lung capacity and physical bulk of the singers' adult bodies, powerful and resounding.

As the librettos written by Rospigliosi before he became Pope attest, classical mythology found no place on the Roman operatic stage. Most plots concerned a Christian saint or other holy person and were explicitly inspirational. Ancient history, however, played a considerable role as a source of examples of heroic and holy behavior in the face of religious and political obstacles. Works such as Rospigliosi's *San Bonifacio* (1638, St. Boniface) depict ancient Rome as the center of a despotic pagan empire, implicitly contrasting it with seventeenth-century Rome as the capital of an equally large but spiritually sound domain.

Another genre often performed in Rome was the oratorio. From the Latin *orare* (to pray), the term at first referred to a place in which prayers were held and later to the prayers themselves. In its musicological use, *oratorio* refers to a specific genre of sung melodies: according to Howard E. Smither, it "is nearly always a sacred, unstaged work with a text that is either dramatic or narrative dramatic. In the dramatic type of text, the plot unfolds entirely through dialogue among the personages; in the narrative-dramatic type, the plot is revealed partially by a narrator . . . and partially through dramatic dialogue."

Throughout Italy, beginning in the 1550s, impulses to reform Catholic worship were opposed by the official Counter-Reformation effort to instill renewed respect for Catholic doctrine and hierarchy. The Society of Jesus, or Jesuits, a religious order established by the Spaniard St. Ignatius of Loyola in 1534, used theatrical stagings in its *collegi* (boardinghouses) to offer their pupils vivid examples of virtuous actions to imitate or of immoral behavior to eschew. Smither points out that "although the dramas were largely spoken, inserted musical numbers were essential to the genre." Florentine *compagnie* (companies), originally conceived, according to John Walter Hill, for "the religious education of adolescent boys not destined for the clergy," also introduced singing into their devotional practices at the end of the sixteenth century.

In Rome, the capital of the genre in Italy, oratorios were almost exclusively linked to the spiritual exercises of the Congregazione dell'Oratorio, founded in 1548 by St. Philip Neri. Born in Florence in 1515 to a devout father who had been an admirer of the reformer Girolamo Savonarola, Neri was undoubtedly exposed to the local tradition of polyphonic singing during religious services. He began gathering groups of six to eight laymen to conduct informal daily discussions of religious texts and to pray. Attendance increased after he was ordained in 1551, and a space had to be set aside for these gatherings: the first oratorio. Neri used music to attract even more people to his devotional practices.

From approximately 1630 to 1660 Romans and visitors to the city could opt to hear oratorios in Italian or in Latin: *oratorio volgare* (vernacular oratorio) or *oratorio latino*. The two types of oratorio are indistinguishable musically, but the librettos differ not only in language but also in that the *oratorio volgare* was in verse and the *oratorio latino* in prose. Smither says that "librettos of the *oratorio volgare* in this period were intended to communicate to a wide audience and thereby to assist in attracting people of every station of life into the oratory." They shared topics with Roman opera, and in 1625, Smither notes, tensions emerged "between Oratorians interested in elaborate music and those who wished to retain the former modesty in the devotional exercises." *Oratorio volgare* consisted of one- or two-part compositions; the former lasted between twenty and thirty minutes and the latter between forty-five minutes and an hour. The librettos consisted of seven- and eleven-syllable lines for the recitative and four-, six- and eight-syllable lines for the arias and choruses. Topics were generally drawn from the Bible and hagiography, but some oratorios dealt with spiritual and moral topics in a freer manner. Each character was sung by one singer, although the narrator's part was occasionally performed by an ensemble. Instruments included those performing the continuo—harpsichords, lutes, harps, theorbos, cellos, bass viols, and others capable of playing in the bass register—and violins; they rarely accompanied a solo voice but served to introduce the piece and to support refrains and choruses.

The audience for *oratorio latino* was better educated than that for *oratorio volgare*. *Oratorio latino* was performed at the Oratorio del Santissimo Sacramento, which had been founded in 1526 by a group of Roman noblemen, near the San Marcello church. The predominant form of *oratorio latino* between 1630 and 1660 is in one part; is both narrative and dramatic in structure (no purely dramatic text is extant for Latin oratorios); and draws its topics only from the Bible. The texts for the pieces set to music by the most prominent composer of this subgenre, Giacomo Carissimi, are anonymous.

The composition and performance of oratorios increased from around 1660 to the end of the century. The genre came to be perceived as an alternative to opera during the Lenten season, when theaters were closed and noble families could not entertain at home. As the two genres became more closely related in style, the oratorio threatened to turn the prayer hall into a place of entertainment. In 1690 the oratorio *Il martirio di Sant'Eustachio* (The Martyrdom of St. Eustachius), with lyrics by Crateo Pradalini and music by an anonymous composer, was staged as an opera, with costumes, acting, and set changes. As Smither notes, "no longer used primarily as a means of drawing a crowd into an oratory to attend a spiritual exercise, no longer an integral part of an essentially devotional and didactic experience in a place of prayer, the oratorio became the central and often the only feature of an evening's program." In the 1660s librettos for oratorios began to be printed for the use of those in attendance. This practice also began to be used in Rome for operas; it had been common for opera performances outside Rome in the first half of the century.

From the 1660s to the end of the century oratorios were usually structured in two parts; they continued to mix drama and narrative and to draw topics from the Bible—though increasingly from the Old Testament at the expense of the New—and from hagiography. Allegorical figures representing Christian virtues also appeared. Musically, compositions became less flexible: recitatives and arias alternated in standardized ways; three to five solo voices were required; and ensembles were formed by combining the soloists—choral groups were almost never used. In terms of instrumentation, only those performing the continuo and two violins were needed; occasionally a viola was called for, but large orchestras were not used before the 1680s and then only rarely. Oratorios were composed and sung in both Italian and Latin throughout the seventeenth century.

In early modern literature *Italian* is a shorthand expression for the written literary language based on the Florentine dialect used by Dante, Petrarch, and Giovanni Boccaccio and progressively adopted and codified by later writers and scholars. Operas, madrigals, cantatas, oratorios, and other sung pieces were usually written in this language, which constituted a literary lingua franca. A few texts set to music are written in a regional dialect or a combination of several dialects. The most notable examples are works by the Sienese Orazio Vecchi. In 1595 he published *Amfiparnaso,* a "comedia harmonica" (play set to music) consisting of fourteen pieces in which various commedia dell'arte characters sing in their stereotypical regional languages. His madrigal collection *Veglie di Siena . . . a 3, a 4, a 5 et a 6 voci* (1604, Sienese Evening Entertainments . . . for Three, Four, Five, and Six Voices) includes a game consisting of imitations of Sicilian, German, Spanish, Venetian, Hebrew, and other languages. The scarcity of texts of this kind could be attributed to the fact that highbrow genres such as the opera, madrigal intermezzo, oratorio, and cantata, were alien to "popular" writers and musicians and to pastiches such as Vecchi's. Conversely, texts in regional languages might not have been printed as often, or considered as worthy of preservation and collection, as those in Italian.

Opera and other types of musical entertainment in Italian became successful throughout Europe. One reason for this success, pointed out by Bianconi, is that "Venetian music publishers were actively present on the German market (in particular, at the Frankfurt book fairs) with their vast array of madrigal collections." Between 1596 and 1664 "the Italian polyphonic madrigal was to become a kind of refined musical language of trans-European, 'supernational' significance." Pierre Béhar and Helen Watanabe-O'Kelly note that Italian soon became the language of choice for most learned musical genres in Europe, and that situation remained unchanged—though not unchallenged—well into the eighteenth century. Italian musicians were in great demand in European courts and cities, and the tradition began of European musicians spending several years in Italy as apprentices. In the 1620s a tradition of ballet sung in Italian emerged at the Innsbruck imperial court, and the Viennese imperial court routinely employed

Italian choreographers, composers, librettists, and set designers—for example, for the spectacle *La contesa dell'aria e dell'acqua* (The Quarrel between the Air and the Water), with libretto by Francesco Sbarra and score by Marc'Antonio Cesti, staged in honor of the wedding of Emperor Leopold I and the Spanish infanta Margarita Teresa in 1667. Even religious pieces such as oratorios were performed in Italian. Béhar and Watanabe-O'Kelly point out that Italian was the language of choice for courtly opera after the Thirty Years' War as far north as Denmark and that in the 1710s and 1720s opera in the Holy Roman Empire included "recitative in German, arias mainly in Italian." Printed programs handed to courtly audiences were bilingual or offered a translation of the plot for those who could not understand Italian; examples remain in German beginning in 1662 and in Polish beginning in 1637.

Musical forms traveled throughout Europe and were modified as they came into contact with local traditions. The most extensively studied case is that of France: Italian troupes were called to the country in 1647 by the Italian-born prime minister, Jules Cardinal Mazarin (originally Giulio Mazarini), but were later rejected in favor of French opera, the brainchild of the Italian-born composer Jean-Baptiste Lully (originally Giovanni Battista Lulli). Even then, the Italian example was firmly ensconced as a paradigm, albeit a negative one. More research is needed into how Italian cultural influences were adapted, modified, rejected, or adopted in Europe. Yet, it is already evident that in regard to language and, more importantly, to form, Italian experiments concerning the relationship of poetry and music had a profound and long-lasting impact on Western culture.

References:

Nello Anfuso, "La vocalità al tempo di Monteverdi," in his *Monteverdi al quale ognuno deve cedere* (Parma, 1993), pp. 21–36;

Pierre Béhar and Helen Watanabe-O'Kelly, eds., *Spectaculum Europæum: Theatre and Spectacle in Europe (1580–1750) / Histoire du Spectacle en Europe (1580–1750)* (Wiesbaden: Harassowitz, 1999);

Anna Laura Bellina and Thomas Walker, "Il teatro per musica," in *Manuale di letteratura italiana: Storia per generi e problemi*, edited by Franco Brioschi and Costanzo Di Girolamo (Turin: Bollati Boringhieri, 1994), pp. 849–869;

Lorenzo Bianconi, "Il Cinquecento e il Seicento," in *Letteratura italiana*, volume 6: *Teatro, musica, tradizione dei classici*, edited by Alberto Asor Rosa (Turin: Einaudi, 1986), pp. 319–363;

Bianconi, "I Fasti musicali del Tasso, nei secoli XVI e XVII," in *Torquato Tasso tra letteratura, musica, teatro e arti figurative*, edited by Andrea Buzzoni (Bologna: Nuova Alfa, 1985), pp. 143–150;

Bianconi, *Music in the Seventeenth Century* (Cambridge: Cambridge University Press, 1987);

Fernand Braudel, "L'Italia fuori d'Italia," in *Storia d'Italia*, volume 2: *Dalla caduta dell'impero romano al secolo XVIII*, edited by Ruggiero Romano and Corrado Vivanti (Turin: Einaudi, 1974), pp. 2089–2248;

Beatrice M. Corrigan, "All Happy Endings: Libretti of the Late Seicento," *Seicento Revisited*, special issue of *Forum Italicum*, edited by Albert N. Mancini, 7 (Summer 1973): 250–267;

Benedetto Croce, *I teatri di Napoli* (Milan: Adelphi, 1992);

Edward Doughtie, "Madrigal," in *The New Princeton Encyclopedia of Poetry and Poetics*, edited by Alex Preminger and T. V. F. Brogan (Princeton: Princeton University Press, 1993), pp. 730–731;

Alberto Gallo, *La prima rappresentazione al teatro Olimpico* (Milan: Il Polifilo, 1973);

Paolo Getrevi, *Labbra barocche: Il libretto d'opera da Busenello a Goldoni* (Verona: Essedue, 1987);

Barbara Russano Hanning, "Images of Monody in the Age of Marino," in *The Sense of Marino*, edited by Francesco Guardiani (Toronto: Legas, 1994), pp. 465–486;

John Walter Hill, "Oratory Music in Florence, I: *Recitar Cantando*, 1583–1655," *Acta musicologica*, 51 (1979): 108–136;

Robert M. Isherwood, *Music in the Service of the King: France in the Seventeenth Century* (Ithaca, N.Y.: Cornell University Press, 1973);

Anthony Lewis and Nigel Fortune, eds., *Opera and Church Music* (London: Oxford University Press, 1975);

G. Francesco Malipiero, *Claudio Monteverdi* (Milan: Treves, 1929);

Albert N. Mancini, "Retorica e spettacolo del potere in alcuni libretti d'opera del medio Seicento veneziano," *Rivista di studi italiani*, 15 (December 1997): 93–120;

Alessandro Martini, "Marino e il madrigale attorno al 1602," in *The Sense of Marino*, pp. 361–393;

Diane Kelsey McColley, *Poetry and Music in Seventeenth-Century England* (Cambridge: Cambridge University Press, 1997), pp. 7–52;

James V. Mirollo, *Mannerism and Renaissance Poetry: Concept, Mode, Inner Design* (New Haven: Yale University Press, 1984);

Gavriel Moses, "Tasso to Monteverdi: Intertextual Poetics," in *Studies in the Italian Renaissance: Essays in Memory of Arnolfo B. Ferruolo*, edited by Gian Paolo Biasin, Albert N. Mancini, and Nicolas J. Perella

(Naples: Società Editrice Napoletana, 1985), pp. 245–261;

David Nutter, "Intermedio," in *New Grove Dictionary of Music and Musicians,* volume 12, second edition, edited by Stanley Sadie (London: Macmillan, 2001), pp. 476–488;

Claude V. Palisca, *Baroque Music,* third edition (Englewood Cliffs, N.J.: Prentice Hall, 1991), pp. 8–176, 221–248;

James M. Saslow, *The Medici Wedding of 1589: Florentine Festival as* Theatrum Mundi (New Haven: Yale University Press, 1996);

Ulrich Schulz-Buschhaus, *Das Madrigal: Zur Stilgeschichte der italienischen Lyrik zwischen Renaissance und Barock* (Bad Homburg: Gehlen, 1969);

Howard E. Smither, *A History of the Oratorio,* volume 1: *The Oratorio in the Baroque Era, Italy, Vienna, Paris* (Chapel Hill: University of North Carolina Press, 1977);

Angelo Solerti, *Musica ballo e drammatica alla corte medicea dal 1600 al 1637* (Florence: Bemporad, 1905);

Maria Galli Stampino, "Classical Antecedents and Teleological Narratives: On the Contamination of Opera and Courtly Sung Entertainment in the Early Seventeenth Century," *Italica,* 77 (Autumn 2000): 331–356;

F. W. Sternfeld, *The Birth of Opera* (Oxford: Clarendon Press, 1993);

Gary Tomlinson, *Monteverdi and the End of the Renaissance* (Berkeley: University of California Press, 1987);

Bernard Weinberg, *A History of Literary Criticism in the Italian Renaissance,* 2 volumes (Chicago: University of Chicago Press, 1961);

Elisabeth Wright, "Marino and Music: A Marriage of Expressive Rhetorical Gesture," in *The Sense of Marino,* pp. 505–550.

Appendix 3: Theater and Spectacle

Glenn Palen Pierce
University of Missouri

The expression *theatrum mundi* (the theater of the world), often used to characterize the late cinquecento and the seicento, refers to a societal expectation of theatricality and festivity that first became prevalent in the court-dominated cities of Italy but quickly spread throughout the peninsula. From religious events and celebrations of court marriages to baptisms and birthdays, city life became a scene of constant spectacle. Triumphal entries of important personages and other occasions of civic pageantry were choreographed to impress the citizens who beheld them, as well as the guests being honored. Huge triumphal arches resembling stage proscenia were erected in Milan and Rome, and a large, beautifully appointed galley, the *Bucentaur*, was used to welcome foreign dignitaries to Venice. Civic festivities such as fairs and equestrian races took on a theatrical flair and were frequently accompanied by instrumental music, song, and dance. Huge portable theatrical machines were brought out for such occasions to produce special effects of all kinds, from fireworks to scene changes. Anything—official ceremonies, entertainment, food and drink, or mode of dress—could be considered a performance to be witnessed by a specified or unspecified audience. Thus, "theater"—in the sense of spectacle, staging, illusion, and metaphor—permeated all aspects of seventeenth-century Italian society.

Impressive court theaters capable of elaborate stage settings and performances had been built at the end of the previous century, replacing improvised stages in the ballrooms and courtyards of private homes and palaces. Andrea Palladio and Vincenzo Scamozzi's Teatro Olimpico was completed in Vicenza in 1585. Bernardo Buontalenti built a theater at the Uffizi Palace in Florence for the marriage of Virginia de' Medici and Cesare d'Este; the Teatro degli Uffizi was used for the rest of the century and throughout the seicento for ornate theatrical presentations. Scamozzi's Teatro all'Antica in Sabbioneta, near Mantua, was completed in 1590. In 1598 an impressive court theater was built in the Ducal Palace in Milan, using a previously constructed porticoed side of the palace. Measuring 140 feet by 87 feet, it was used for tournaments and other spectacles in the beginning; but its elaborate sets and machines indicate that it was ultimately used primarily for operas. A smaller theater, the Teatrino, was built a few years later exclusively for the staging of dramas; in addition to boxes for the aristocrats, it had benches where a limited number of paying members of the public were allowed to sit at the discretion of the Order of Spanish Virgins, which was granted financial management of those spaces by the Spanish governor.

Mantua, Florence, and Ferrara had theaters supported by their dukes and managed by standing groups of technical professionals in the fields of staging, lighting, and so on. In Bologna and Modena the medieval communal palaces of the *podestà* (mayors) were converted into civic theaters. Several literary academies, including the Intronati (Stunned) and the Rozzi (Rough Ones) in Siena and the Faticosi (Toilsome) in Milan, were involved in the study of drama and began offering performances of highly professional quality on a regular basis for their members and friends.

Giovanni Battista Aleotti, known as l'Argenta and trained in the Palladian school, built the Teatro della Sala Grande in Ferrara in 1612; it has been destroyed, but Aleotti went on to construct the most important court theater of the first half of the century: the Teatro Farnese in the Palazzo della Pilotta in Parma. Designed in 1618 and completed in 1628, it is 285 feet long with a stage 131 feet deep and a large U-shaped space in front of the stage that was used for equestrian tournaments and flooded for naval events. Along one side, huge windows look out onto the city; on the opposite side and at the end facing the stage, arches support loggias covering tiers that serve as seats. With its ability to accommodate all the spectacles of the period, the symbolism of the windows overlooking the city, and the "outside" activities painted on its ceilings and decorations, the Teatro Farnese has been called the paradigm of Italian Baroque theater buildings and an example of the dialogue between modern accomplishment and classical tradition. A visit to it was a must for dignitaries

Stage of Andrea Palladio and Vincenzo Scamozzi's Teatro Olimpico in Vicenza (photograph by Alimari; from Pierre-Louis Duchartre, The Italian Comedy: The Improvisation, Scenarios, Lives, Attributes, Portraits, and Masks of the Illustrious Characters of the Commedia dell'Arte, *1966; Thomas Cooper Library, University of South Carolina)*

and architects interested in constructing other theaters. Thus, the Teatro Farnese became a bible for the physical shape public theaters took in the second half of the century, especially in its emphasis on vertical seating.

A key term for understanding the secular and religious obsession with spectacle in Baroque Italy is *meraviglia* (awe), which refers to the reaction the spectacle was intended to produce in the beholder. An appeal in the first instance to the senses, *meraviglia* was intended ultimately to engage the human intellect in new perspectives. It was not a new term in Italian literature: Dante had used it in *Il convivio* (circa 1304–1307, The Banquet) as a synonym for "miracle" in reference to the human capacity for understanding the divine intellectually. By the time he wrote the *Divina Commedia* (circa 1308–1321, Divine Comedy), Dante was using the term to designate visible signs and worldly wonders. It retained this denotation in the epic and travel literature of the Renaissance.

During the seicento Giambattista Marino held that the object of poetry is to "rompere le regole a tempo e luogo" (break the rules whenever necessary) to produce *meraviglia*, which for him denoted "surprise." The theater was an ideal vehicle for creating awe with the lavish productions made possible by new technical advances, the decoration of theater buildings, and the use of intermezzi with dance and music that most often had nothing to do with the plot of the major presentation. The public's love of spectacle encouraged the development of theatrical hybrid genres, such as the melodrama, *tragicommedia* (tragicomedy), *tragicommedia boscareccia* (pastoral tragicomedy), and *tragedia spirituale* (spiritual tragedy), aimed at satisfying the whims of the audiences.

But *meraviglia* in the sense in which Dante had used it in *Il convivio*—appealing to the intellect by means of the senses—was best understood in the seventeenth century by the Roman Catholic Church. In the second

Gian Lorenzo Bernini; self-portrait at the Borghese Gallery in Rome (<www.artelibre.net>)

half of the previous century the archbishop of Milan, Carlo Borromeo, realizing the power that profane spectacle could have on the public, had dedicated much of his energy to opposing it in all of its forms. His efforts, however, led to the construction of private indoor theaters where professional companies performed. By the seicento the church had assimilated the theater as a rhetorical ally: theatrical style permeated religious ceremonies and church sculpture, architecture, painting, and music. The celebration of Holy Week was a spectacle, with floats, elaborate costumes, sets, and opera music–the last of which was used for the first time in Florence in 1620. The Jesuits were the dominating force in religious theater. The order had long recognized the educational value of religious dramas and staged them regularly in their schools; the Collegio de' Nobili in Milan gave two sophisticated presentations a year, including Giovan Battista Andreini's *Maddalena lasciva e penitente* (1652, Mary Magdalene Lustful and Penitent) in 1612. During Federico Borromeo's term as archbishop of Milan from 1595 to 1631, all official celebrations were entrusted to the order. The celebration of their centenary lasted a full year in Rome and was celebrated all over the peninsula with spectacles ranging from drama to processions, dances, and pyrotechnics.

The Barberini Palace in Rome, completed in 1632, had a theater that is said to have been capable of holding more than three thousand people. It was not a public theater, however, since no one paid: admission was at the discretion of the hosts. The first public theater was inaugurated in Venice in 1637 when a group of artists rented the dilapidated San Cassiano theater, which was owned by the Tron family, to present Francesco Manelli's opera *Andromeda*. The public was allowed to purchase tickets, with the best seats reserved for the upper classes. The following year another group rented the theater for Manelli's opera *La maga fulminata* (The Raging Sorceress). Both productions, which used orchestras, lavish costumes, dances, and the latest machinery for set changes, boasted quality equal to that of the court spectacles, and both realized a profit. The noble Grimani family of Venice soon opened its own modern, sumptuous public theater for opera. Similar initiatives on the part of families and then of entrepreneurial individuals quickly followed. Nine new theaters opened in the city before the middle of the century. In the process the roles of producer and impresario and the problem of financing theaters were born.

Venice was a mercantile and aristocratic city rather than a court; it had its own artistic traditions and was not involved in the politics of the Counter-Reformation. Whereas artistic creativity in Rome tended to reflect the outlook of the church, in Venice it was rooted in city life. Accordingly, stage design was less spectacle oriented in Venice than in Rome; instead, it was inspired by everyday life: operas were set in homes or on the street, where everyday citizens could recognize their daily living space. Venetian libretti were grounded in mundane and heroic history rather than in mythological or religious themes, which were almost always relegated to intermezzi. Mundane matters were not relegated to the position of comic counterpoint to tragic plots but were the main themes, or, if not, at least found their way into the concerns of the protagonists. The playwright Gian Francesco Busenello, for instance, whose opera *L'incoronazione di Poppea* (1642, The Coronation of Poppaea) was set to music by Claudio Monteverdi, was also a lawyer and a businessman, wrote poetry in Italian and in dialect, and was in close touch with the daily reality of his audiences. His characters, although involved in tragic enterprises, are always preoccupied with the tasks and vicissitudes of everyday living. Busenello eschewed mythology, and his historical plots were thinly disguised portrayals of his contemporary society.

In the second half of the seventeenth century at least fifteen commercial theaters were always in opera-

Celebrations in honor of the former queen Christina of Sweden in the courtyard of the Barberini Palace in Rome, 28 February 1656; seventeenth-century painting by Filippo Gagliardi and Filippo Lauri (Musea di Roma: <http://museodiroma.comune.roma.it>)

tion in Venice. The public's avid support of theater helped to lay the groundwork for the Venetian dramatist Carlo Goldoni's reforms in the next century. Goldoni's struggle to bring theater back under the control of social-minded directors with a message to convey could only have been aided by a public who wanted to see itself realistically reflected and who would pay to do so.

Fabrizio Carini Motta was given the title of court architect when he entered the service of the ruling Gonzaga family of Mantua in 1650. His *Trattato sopra la struttura de' theatri e scene* (1676, Treatise on the Structure of Theaters and Scenes) is the first study to treat the theater auditorium as a separate edifice. In 1688 he published *Costruzione de teatri e machine teatrali* (Construction of Theaters and Theatrical Machines); it includes material on the duties of stagehands and thus gives evidence of the existence of a professional workforce in that field. Also in 1688 Motta rebuilt the Mantua court theater, which had originally been constructed in 1608.

Italian stage design made enormous progress during the seventeenth century. With the development of techniques in perspective, the three-dimensional set was replaced by the deceptively painted flat surface. Aleotti was the first to employ this flat-wing system, in Ferrara in 1606, and he introduced it to the Teatro Farnese in Parma for the 1618–1619 season. The first description of the flat wing in writing was Giulio Troili's *Paradossi per pratticare la prospettiva* (1672, Paradoxes of the Practice of Perspective). Andrea Pozzo's two-volume *Prospettiva de' pittori e architetti* (1693, 1700, Perspective of Painters and Architects) incorporated Troili's work.

Born in 1598, Gian Lorenzo Bernini moved to Rome from Naples in 1606 with his sculptor father, Pietro. Bernini owed to his father not only his early training in marble but also his introduction to powerful families of patrons, the Borgheses and the Barberinis. His series of life-size and amazingly life-like statues *Aeneas, Anchises, and Ascanius Fleeing Troy* (1618–1619),

Statues of David by Bernini, at the Borghese Gallery in Rome, and by Michelangelo, at the Galleria dell'Accademia in Florence (<www.wga.hu/index.html>)

The Rape of Proserpine (1621–1622), *David* (1623), and *Apollo and Daphne* (1622–1625) for Cardinal Scipione Borghese established his prominence in Rome. After being elected Pope Urban VIII in 1623, Maffeo Barberini chose him to design the Barberini Palace. Bernini became the principal artist in the papal court and in Rome and was recognized as one of the greatest sculptors of the seventeenth century. With the death of Carlo Maderno in 1629, he also became Rome's foremost architect and transformed it into the "theatrical" city it remains today: buildings no longer hid their beauties inside but began to appeal outwardly to the citizen and visitor; buildings, parks, and fountains were carefully incorporated into a larger theatrical concept aimed at creating *meraviglia* in the beholder.

Bernini was also acclaimed as a painter, playwright, and stage designer. The only text he is known to have written that survives today is an untitled work called by its modern editor (1963) *La Fontana di Trevi* (The Trevi Fountain; translated as *The Impresario,* 1985), which is not a script but a detailed commedia dell'arte farcical scenario. Bernini directs the audience's attention not to the lovers and their actions but to the professional activity surrounding the production: the impresario Graziano, the carpenters and scene painter, and the courtier and would-be producer Cinzio. Contrary to all commedia dell'arte tradition, the subject of the plot is the staging of a play in which the same characters and plot occur in a mirror image, leading to a curious monologue between Graziano and "Graziano," the character in the play within the play:

"Gratiano": . . . che el, chi el quel Gratian chè inamorà de quela serva, chi el?

Gratiano: Chi el? Liè la favola de sta Comedia, liè!

Sculptures of cardinals in Bernini's Cornaro Chapel of Santa Maria della Vittoria in Rome (<http://www.usc.edu/schools/annenberg/asc/projects/comm544/library/images/029bg.jpg>)

"Gratiano": Sigur, sel mond non lè altr ch'una Comedia, Gratian lè la favola del mond. Puh, vergogna, el piè nte la fossa, el cor nte le sensualità. Non lè ancora satio quel tripponazz; n'hà fatt porghe. Non morirà, non morirà cosi prest, nò, quest pezz de carnaccia ranzida perche 'l ziel non permett che i tristi possin metter in essecution i lor sporchi pensieri.

("Graziano": Who is this Graziano who's in love with his maid? Who is he?

Graziano [as he writes the part of "Graziano"]: Who is he? He's the fool of this play, that's who he is.

"Graziano": I see. And if the world's nothing but a play, then Graziano's the biggest fool in the world. Poh, shame on him, one foot in the grave and lechery in his heart. Hasn't he had enough, the hog? That old piece of rancid meat isn't about to die, because heaven isn't about to grant dismal dodderers the realization of their dirty dreams.)

Since the exchange is made in front of Rosetta, the object of Graziano's lust, the monologue is a ploy to seduce her. The rest of the action primarily concerns the building of sets and the methods Graziano employs in doing so, as well as the attempts of a jealous rival to learn how he does it.

Written testimonies exist of Bernini's court spectacle of 1638, *L'inondazione del Tevere* (The Flood of the Tiber). A long canal-like basin filled with water that extended the width of the stage represented the river. Engineers used beams and planks in an attempt to keep the water from overflowing its banks, as the actual Tiber had done the year before. At a certain point the beams appeared to give way; the bank collapsed; and the water ran out of the basin toward the spectators, disappearing in a drain at the last moment before drenching the audience. In a later scene a faked fire from a torch being rubbed against a backdrop by an actor "unaware" of what was happening seemed to spread out of control. The audience panicked and had to be reassured by Bernini himself, speaking from a box seat, that all was well and the fire only simulated. *L'inondazione del Tevere* ended with a scene, referred to by critics as "I due teatri" (The Two Theaters), "Le due

Stage set designed by Giacomo Torelli for the prologue of the opera Bellerofonte *(Bellerophon), with libretto by Vincenzo Nolfi and Francesco Sacrati, performed at the Teatro Novissimo in Venice in 1642 (engraving by Giovanni Giorgi; from Ellen Rosand,* Opera in Seventeenth-Century Venice: The Creation of a Genre, *1990 <http://www.cdlib.org/>)*

rappresentazioni" (The Two Presentations), "I due prologhi" (The Two Prologues), or "I due Covielli" (The Two Coviellos), that invited the audience to reflect more calmly on its own participation in the theatrical experience–to contemplate where life leaves off and theater begins. As the character Coviello began to address the audience a curtain behind him fell to reveal an identically dressed actor facing in the opposite direction and addressing another audience. The second audience was made up partly of real people and, behind them, people painted on a backdrop; the second audience was laughing at what the other "Coviello" was saying. The curtain was then pulled up to block this view and dropped again to show a reproduction of the square in front of the theater where the piece was being presented: the audience saw itself departing in horse-drawn carriages under torchlight and a moonlit sky.

Other works to which Bernini is known, through the comments of his contemporaries, to have contributed include two operas produced under the patronage of the Pope's nephew Cardinal Francesco Barberini: the first comic opera, *Egisto, o Chi soffre speri* (1639, Egisto; or, He Who Suffers May Hope), with libretto by Giulio Rospigliosi and score by Virgilio Mazzocchi and Marco Marazzoli, for which Bernini staged the *Fiera di Farsa* (Farfa Fair) intermezzo with live barnyard and sunset sequences; and *L'innocenza difesa nella Rappresentazione di san Bonifacio* (1641, Innocence Defended in the Representation of St. Boniface), with libretto by Rospigliosi and score by Mazzocchi, for which he repeated the sunset effects to the amazement of those present. In these works his primary contribution was as stage designer. The English diarist John Evelyn noted that in 1644 Bernini produced a public opera for which he painted the scenes, sculpted the statues, invented the stage machinery, composed the music, wrote the libretto, and even built the theater.

The link between Bernini's work in sculpture and theater can perhaps be appreciated by comparing his *David* with that of Michelangelo, created more than a hundred years earlier during the Renaissance. Bernini's life-size David is portrayed in the action of hurling the stone at Goliath; the viewer must completely circle the statue to understand its dynamics and comes away with a sense of drama and involvement. Michelangelo's David, on the other hand, giant in size and standing in a relaxed pose, is completely understandable from a stationary frontal observance. Its "action" is internal and intellectual, reflected in the furrowed brow and the scouring eyes.

If one attempts to create a parallel between Michelangelo's statue and Renaissance theater, one would imagine a seated audience, perhaps at Palladio's Teatro Olimpico in Vicenza, passively awaiting the action that will take place on the stage before fixed stock scenery portraying an ideal Renaissance city or palace in perfect perspective. It is difficult to conjure up any theatrical space of the period to parallel Bernini's *David*. His statue makes one think of movement and action and, above all, of the necessity of spectator involvement, for which no theater of the time had been conceived—unless it was another work by Bernini: the Cornaro Chapel of Santa Maria della Vittoria. Constructed between 1644 and 1652, the chapel is generally considered to epitomize Bernini's style by combining sculpture, architecture, and painting into an illusionistic theatrical whole that is virtually a self-contained *dramma sacro* (religious drama). The main altarpiece situates sculptures of the ecstasy of St. Theresa in a proscenium-like temple lighted by gilded wooden rays sent from above; the Cornaro cardinals are framed in their "boxes" on either side of the main altar. The cardinals' expressions show that they are emotional participants in the spectacle they behold, which includes not only St. Theresa's martyrdom before them but also heaven above and—suggestively represented by the skeletons gazing upward from a round, black background on the floor of the chapel—hell below. The effect on the viewer is one of the play-within-a-play technique that was popular during the century. As the spectator, looking to one side and then to the other, sees the reaction of the cardinals, he or she is led to think about the cause of that reaction: St. Theresa and her ecstatic state. Thus, the spectator feels directly involved in what is happening and becomes an "actor," conscious of being an active participant in what is happening. A seventeenth-century viewer, seeing the cardinals in the boxes usually occupied by members of the aristocracy, would be led to appreciate their position of power and authority. Pulling away from the scene, the viewer becomes aware that someone has created his or her response, just as the spectators witnessing the presentation of Bernini's theatrical sketches had to give him credit for creating a situation in which they were involved.

Records exist from as early as 1628 of Franco Guitti in Rome using a system of grooves, carriages, and a winch with counterweights to operate wings, backdrops, and borders. By midcentury the set designer, architect, and mathematician Giacomo Torelli was doing the same in Venice. Employing the expertise he had garnered as a naval engineer at the Venice city arsenal, Torelli was the moving spirit behind the founding, on property of the Dominican Fathers, of the most sumptuous and technically advanced theater in Venice, the Teatro Novissimo, in 1641. The Novissimo was the most famous institution of the "academic" phase of Baroque theater in Italy, and its advanced set techniques were the harbinger of the "industrial" phase at the close of the century, when theater building became virtually a business. From the "great wheel" capable of changing sixteen wings simultaneously with the twist of a wrist to the lavish printed programs he distributed, Torelli's initiative signaled the grand scale of opera in the next century. His innovations were, however, too expensive for any single theater; when the Novissimo failed in 1645, he accepted an invitation to be sent by the duke of Parma to the French court as an exponent of Italian set design. He returned to Italy in 1661 and designed and built the Teatro della Fortuna in Fano in 1665.

Thanks to Torelli, entire scenes could be changed in an instant by turning a central drum beneath the stage. Other specialized machines made clouds appear to grow or shrink, and the re-creation of seaports, gardens, wild landscapes, piazzas, palaces, sea monsters, and battle scenes with charging chariots were all possible. Creating *meraviglia* in the spectators became the goal of every architect engaged in developing such machinery, and technicians copied each other's methods of achieving that goal. Less spectacular, but equally important, techniques of simulating marble, oak, and other "courtly" materials, as well as the enhancement of lighting, were also developed. By the end of the century, most of the technical advances that are taken for granted in modern-day theater had been invented in Italy.

References:

Franca Angelini, *Il Teatro Barocco* (Rome & Bari: Laterza, 1975);

Paol Anrioli Nemola, ed., *Teatro, Scena, Rappresentazione dal Quattrocento al Settecento: Atti del Convegno Internazionale di Studi, Lecce, 15–17 maggio 1997* (Galantina [i.e., Lecce]: Congedo, 2000);

Maria Grazia Bernardini and Maurizio Fagiolo Dell'Arco, eds., *Gian Lorenzo Bernini: Regista del Barocco* (Milan: Skira, 1999);

Gian Lorenzo Bernini, *Fontana di Trevi: Commedia inedita*, edited by Cesare D'Onofrio (Rome: Staderini Editore, 1963); edited and translated by Massimo Ciavolella and Donald Beecher as *The Impresario (Untitled)* (Ottawa: Published for the Carleton University Centre for Renaissance Studies and Research by Dovehouse Editions, 1985); Italian version edited by Ciavolella as *L'impresario* (Rome: Salerno, 1992);

Emilio Bertana, *La tragedia: Storia dei generi letterari italiani* (Milan: Vallardi, 1946);

Silvia Carandini, *Teatro e spettacolo nel Seicento* (Bari & Rome: Laterza, 1990);

Maria Chiabò and Federico Doglio, eds., *I Gesuiti e i primordi del teatro barocco in Europa: Convegno di studi, Roma 26–29 ottobre 1994, Anagni 30 ottobre 1994* (Rome: Torre d'Orfeo, 1995);

Mario Costanzo, *Il "Gran Teatro del Mondo": Schede per lo studio dell'iconografia letteraria nell'età del Manierismo* (Milan: Scheiwiller, 1964);

Maurizio Dell'Arco and Marcello Fagiolo Dell'Arco, *Bernini: Una introduzione al "Gran Teatro" del Barocco* (Rome: Bulzoni, 1967);

Carlo De Stefano, *La censura teatrale in Italia* (Bologna: Cappelli, 1964);

Luigi Dossi, S.J., "I Gesuiti a Milano," *Giovinezza,* 9 (1966): n.pag.;

John Evelyn, *Memoirs, Illustrative of the Life and Writings of John Evelyn, Esq., F.R.S.: Comprising His Diary, from the Year 1641 to 1705–6 and a Selection of His Familiar Letters,* 2 volumes, edited by William Bray (London: Printed for Henry Colburn, 1818);

Irving Lavin, *Bernini and the Unity of the Visual Arts,* 2 volumes (New York & London: Pierpont Morgan Library/Oxford University Press, 1960);

Albert N. Mancini, "Retorica e spettacolo del potere in alcuni libretti d'opera del medio Seicento veneziano," *Rivista di studi italiani,* 15, no. 2 (1997): 93–120;

Franco Mancini, *Scenografia italiana: Dal Rinascimento all'età romantica* (Milan: Fabbri, 1966);

Fabrizio Carini Motta, *Theatrical Writings,* edited and translated by Orville K. Larson (Carbondale & Edwardsville: Southern Illinois University Press, 1987);

Dunbar H. Ogden, ed. and trans., *The Italian Baroque Stage: Documents* (Berkeley: University of California Press, 1978);

Louis J. Oldani and Victor R. Yaniteiu, "Jesuit Theater in Italy: Its Entrances and Exit," *Italica,* 76 (Spring 1999): 18–32;

Nicola Sabbattini, *Scene e macchine teatrali,* edited by Alberto Perrini (Rome: Associati, 1989);

Attilio Simioni, "Per la Storia del Teatro Gesuitico in Italia," *Rassegna critica della letteratura italiana,* 12 (1907): 145–162;

Carlo Antonio Vianello, *Teatri, spettacoli, musiche a Milano nei secoli scorsi* (Milan: Literia Lombarda, 1941).

Checklist of Further Readings

Andrews, Richard. *Scripts and Scenarios: The Performance of Comedy in Renaissance Italy.* Cambridge: Cambridge University Press, 1993.

Asor Rosa, Alberto. "La Nuova Scienza: Il Barocco e la crisi," in *Il Seicento: La nuova scienza e la crisi del barocco,* La Letteratura italiana: Storia e testi, volume 5, part 1, edited by Carlo Muscetta. Bari: Laterza, 1974, pp. 3–50.

Asor Rosa, ed. *Letteratura italiana: Gli autori. Dizionario bio-bibliografico,* 2 volumes. Turin: Einaudi, 1990, 1991.

Battistini, Andrea. "La cultura del Barocco," in *Storia della letteratura italiana,* volume 5, edited by Enrico Malato. Rome: Salerno, 1997, pp. 463–559.

Bondanella, Peter, and Julia Conaway Bondanella. *Dictionary of Italian Literature,* revised, expanded edition. Westport, Conn.: Greenwood Press, 1996.

Branca, Vittore, ed. *Dizionario critico della letteratura italiana,* second edition, 4 volumes. Turin: Unione Tipografico-Editrice Torinese, 1986.

Brand, Peter, and Lino Pertile, eds. *The Cambridge History of Italian Literature.* Cambridge: Cambridge University Press, 1996.

Braudel, Fernand. *Out of Italy: 1440–1650,* translated by Sian Reynolds. Paris: Flammarion, 1991.

Burke, Peter. *The Historical Anthropology of Early Modern Italy.* Cambridge: Cambridge University Press, 1977.

Cairns, Christopher, ed. *The Commedia dell'Arte from the Renaissance to Dario Fo.* Lewiston, N.Y.: Edwin Mellen Press, 1989.

Calabrese, Omar. *Neo Baroque: A Sign of the Times,* translated by Charles Lambert. Foreword by Umberto Eco. Princeton: Princeton University Press, 1992.

Calcaterra, Carlo. *Il Parnaso in rivolta: Barocco e Antibarocco nella poesia italiana.* Milan: Mondadori, 1940.

I capricci di Proteo: Percorsi e linguaggi del Barocco. Atti del convegno di Lecce, 23–26 ottobre 2000. Rome: Salerno, 2002.

Carandini, Silvia. *Teatro e spettacolo nel Seicento.* Rome & Bari: Laterza, 1990.

Chiabò, Maria, and Federico Doglio, eds. *I Gesuiti e i primordi del teatro barocco in Europa.* Rome: Torre d'Orfeo, 1995.

Ciavolella, Massimo, and Patrick Coleman, eds. *Culture and Authority in the Baroque.* Toronto: University of Toronto Press, 2005.

Clubb, Louise George. *Italian Drama in Shakespeare's Time.* Princeton: Princeton University Press, 1989.

Cochrane, Eric. *Italy 1530–1630,* edited by Julius Kirshner. London & New York: Longman, 1988.

Checklist of Further Readings

Croce, Benedetto. *Storia dell' età barocca in Italia.* Bari: Laterza, 1929.

Croce, Franco. *Tre momenti del Barocco letterario italiano.* Florence: Sansoni, 1966.

De Sanctis, Francesco. *History of Italian Literature,* volume 2, translated by Joan Redfern. New York: Barnes & Noble, 1968.

Dombroski, Robert S. *Gadda e il Barocco.* Turin: Bollati Boringhieri, 2002.

Dooley, Brendan, ed. *Italy in the Baroque: Selected Readings.* New York: Garland, 1995.

Ferrone, Siro. "Il teatro," in *Storia della letteratura italiana,* volume 5, edited by Enrico Malato. Rome: Salerno, 1997, pp. 1057–1109.

Ferrone and Annamaria Testaverde. "Vitalità del teatro italiano," in *Storia della letteratura italiana,* volume 12, edited by Enrico Malato. Rome: Salerno, 2002, pp. 483–527.

Fumaroli, Marc. "L'Italia tridentina: Una civiltà dell'otium," in *Storia generale della letteratura italiana,* volume 6, edited by Nino Borsellino and Walter Pedullà. Milan: Federico Motta, 1999, pp. 549–575.

Getto, Giovanni. *Barocco in prosa e poesia.* Milan: Rizzoli, 1969.

Guglielminetti, Marziano. *Manierismo e Barocco: Storia della civiltà letteraria italiana,* volume 3, edited by Giorgio Bàrberi Squarotti. Turin: Unione Tipografico-Editrice Torinese, 1990.

Guglielminetti. "Marino e i Marinisti," in *Storia generale della letteratura italiana,* volume 6, edited by Nino Borsellino and Walter Pedullà. Milan: Federico Motta, 1999, pp. 127–198.

Hanlon, Gregory. *Early Modern Italy, 1550–1800: Three Seasons in European History.* New York: St. Martin's Press, 2000.

Hendrix, Harald. "Persistenza del prestigio nell'età della crisi," in *Storia della letteratura italiana,* volume 12, edited by Enrico Malato. Rome: Salerno, 2002, pp. 437–482.

Henke, Robert. *Performance and Literature in the Commedia dell'Arte.* Cambridge: Cambridge University Press, 2002.

Holmes, George, ed. *The Oxford History of Italy.* Oxford: Oxford University Press, 1997, pp. 113–176.

Iannaco, Carmine, and Martino Capucci. *Storia letteraria d'Italia: Il Seicento,* third edition. Padua: Piccin Nuova Libraria, 1983.

Ingegnieri, Andrea. *Della poesia rappresentativa e del modo di rappresentare le favole sceniche,* edited by Maria Luisa Doglio. Modena: Panini, 1989.

Lievsay, John L. *The Englishman's Italian Books, 1550–1700.* Philadelphia: University of Pennsylvania Press, 1969.

Maravall, José Antonio. *Culture of the Baroque: Analysis of a Historical Structure,* translated by Terry Cochran. Minneapolis: University of Minnesota Press, 1986.

Marini, Quinto. "La critica nell'età barocca," in *Storia della letteratura italiana,* volume 11, edited by Enrico Malato. Rome: Salerno, 2003, pp. 451–484.

Marino, John A., ed. *Early Modern Italy 1550–1796.* Oxford: Oxford University Press, 2002.

Mirollo, James V. *Mannerism and Renaissance Poetry: Concept, Mode, Inner Design.* New Haven: Yale University Press, 1984.

Morandini, Giuliana, ed. *Sospiri e palpiti: Scrittrici italiane del Seicento.* Genoa: Marietti, 2002.

Muscetta, Carlo, and Pier Paolo Ferrante. *Poesia del Seicento,* 2 volumes. Turin: Einaudi, 1964.

Ors, Eugenio d'. *Du baroque.* Paris: Gallimard, 1935. Translated into Italian by Luciano Anceschi as *Del barocco.* Milan: Rosa & Ballo, 1945.

Ossola, Carlo. *L'anima in Barocco: Testi del Seicento italiano.* Turin: Scriptorium, 1995.

Panizza, Letizia, ed. *Women in Italian Renaissance Culture and Society.* Oxford: European Humanities Research Center, 2000.

Panizza and Sharon Wood, eds. *A History of Women's Writing in Italy.* Cambridge: Cambridge University Press, 2000.

Pieri, Marzio, ed. *Il Barocco, Marino e la poesia del Seicento.* Rome: Istituto Poligrafico e Zecca dello Stato, 1995.

Raimondi, Ezio. *Letteratura barocca: Studi sul Seicento italiano.* Florence: Olschki, 1961.

Richards, Kenneth, and Laura Richards. "Commedia dell'Arte," in *A History of Italian Theatre,* edited by Joseph Farrell and Paolo Puppo. Cambridge: Cambridge University Press, 2006, pp. 102–123.

Rosand, Ellen. *Opera in Seventeenth-Century Venice.* Berkeley & Los Angeles: University of California Press, 1991.

Russell, Rinaldina, ed. *Italian Women Writers: A Bio-Bibliographical Sourcebook.* Westport, Conn.: Greenwood Press, 1994.

Russo, Luigi. "La letteratura seicentesca e I dialetti," in *Ritrattti e disegni storici,* series 2. Florence: Sansoni, 1961, pp. 291–302.

Santangelo, Giorgio. *Il Secentismo.* Palermo: Palumbo, 1958.

Scaglione, Aldo, and Gianni Eugenio Viola, eds. *The Image of the Baroque.* New York: Peter Lang, 1995.

Segre, Carlo, and Carlo Ossola, eds. *Antologia della poesia italiana: Seicento.* Turin: Einaudi-Gallimard, 2001.

Sella, Domenico. *Italy in the Seventeenth Century.* London: Longman, 1988.

Settembrini, Luigi. *Lezioni di letteratura italiana,* volume 2. Naples: Antonio Morano, 1875, pp. 668–711.

Slawinski, Maurice. "The Seventeenth-Century Stage," in *A History of the Italian Theatre,* edited by Joseph Farrell and Paolo Puppa. Cambridge: Cambridge University Press, 2006, pp. 127–142.

Strappini, Lucia, ed. *I luoghi dell 'immaginario barocco: Atti del convegno di Siena, 21–13 ottobre, 1999.* Naples: Liguori, 2001.

Taviani, Ferdinando, and Mirella Schino. *Il segreto della Commedia dell'Arte: La memoria delle compagnie italiane del XVI, XVII, e XVIII secolo,* second edition. Florence: La Casa Usher, 1986.

Viglionese, Paschal C., ed. and trans. *Italian Writers of the Seventeenth and Eighteenth Centuries: A Selection of the Best Literature.* Jefferson, N.C.: McFarland, 1988.

Villari, Rosario, ed. *Baroque Personae,* translated by Lydia G. Cochrane. Chicago: University of Chicago Press, 1995.

Warnke, Frank J. *Versions of Baroque: European Literature in the Seventeenth Century.* New Haven: Yale University Press, 1972.

Weaver, Elissa B. *Convent Theatre in Early Modern Italy: Spiritual Fun and Learning for Women.* Cambridge: Cambridge University Press, 2004.

Wölfflin, Heinrich. *Renaissance und Barock: Eine Untersuchung über Wesen und Entstehung des Barockstils in Italien.* Munich: T. Ackermann, 1888. Translated by Kathrin Simon as *Renaissance and Baroque.* Ithaca, N.Y.: Cornell University Press, 1966.

Zorzi, Ludovico. *L'attore, la commedia, il drammaturgo.* Turin: Einaudi, 1990.

Contributors

Salvatore Bancheri . . . .*University of Toronto*
Laura Benedetti . . . . *Georgetown University*
Mauda Bregoli-Russo . . . . *University of Illinois at Chicago*
Salvatore Cappelletti . . . . *Providence College*
Rita Cavigioli . . . .*University of Missouri*
Paul Colilli . . . .*Laurentian University*
Natalia Costa-Zalessow . . . . *San Francisco State University*
Nancy L. D'Antuono . . . .*Saint Mary's College*
Franco Fido . . . . *Harvard University*
Paolo A. Giordano . . . . *University of Central Florida*
Francesco Guardiani . . . .*University of Toronto*
Edoardo A. Lèbano . . . . *Indiana University*
Mary Jo Muratore . . . .*University of Missouri*
Olimpia Pelosi . . . .*State University of New York at Albany*
Nicolas J. Perella . . . . *University of California, Berkeley*
Glenn Palen Pierce . . . .*University of Missouri*
Elisabetta Properzi Nelsen . . . . *San Francisco State University*
Francesca Savoia . . . .*University of Pittsburgh*
Maria Galli Stampino . . . . *University of Miami*
Lori J. Ultsch . . . . *Hofstra University*
Paschal C. Viglionese . . . .*University of Rhode Island*
Adrienne Ward . . . . *University of Virginia*
Laura Sanguineti White . . . . *Rutgers University*

Cumulative Index

Dictionary of Literary Biography, Volumes 1-339
Dictionary of Literary Biography Yearbook, 1980-2002
Dictionary of Literary Biography Documentary Series, Volumes 1-19
Concise Dictionary of American Literary Biography, Volumes 1-7
Concise Dictionary of British Literary Biography, Volumes 1-8
Concise Dictionary of World Literary Biography, Volumes 1-4

Cumulative Index

DLB before number: *Dictionary of Literary Biography,* Volumes 1-339
Y before number: *Dictionary of Literary Biography Yearbook,* 1980-2002
DS before number: *Dictionary of Literary Biography Documentary Series,* Volumes 1-19
CDALB before number: *Concise Dictionary of American Literary Biography,* Volumes 1-7
CDBLB before number: *Concise Dictionary of British Literary Biography,* Volumes 1-8
CDWLB before number: *Concise Dictionary of World Literary Biography,* Volumes 1-4

A

Aakjær, Jeppe 1866-1930 . . . . DLB-214
Aarestrup, Emil 1800-1856 . . . . DLB-300
Abbey, Edward 1927-1989 . . . . DLB-256, 275
Abbey, Edwin Austin 1852-1911 . . . . DLB-188
Abbey, Maj. J. R. 1894-1969 . . . . DLB-201
Abbey Press DLB-49
The Abbey Theatre and Irish Drama,
 1900-1945 . . . . DLB-10
Abbot, Willis J. 1863-1934 . . . . DLB-29
Abbott, Edwin A. 1838-1926 . . . . DLB-178
Abbott, Jacob 1803-1879 . . . . DLB-1, 42, 243
Abbott, Lee K. 1947- DLB-130
Abbott, Lyman 1835-1922 . . . . DLB-79
Abbott, Robert S. 1868-1940 . . . . DLB-29, 91
'Abd al-Hamid al-Katib
 circa 689-750 . . . . DLB-311
Abe Kōbō 1924-1993 . . . . DLB-182
Abelaira, Augusto 1926- DLB-287
Abelard, Peter circa 1079-1142? DLB-115, 208
Abelard-Schuman DLB-46
Abell, Arunah S. 1806-1888 . . . . DLB-43
Abell, Kjeld 1901-1961 . . . . DLB-214
Abercrombie, Lascelles 1881-1938 . . . . DLB-19
 The Friends of the Dymock Poets Y-00
Aberdeen University Press Limited DLB-106
Abish, Walter 1931- DLB-130, 227
Ablesimov, Aleksandr Onisimovich
 1742-1783 . . . . DLB-150
Abraham à Sancta Clara 1644-1709 . . . . . . DLB-168
Abrahams, Peter
 1919- DLB-117, 225; CDWLB-3
Abramov, Fedor Aleksandrovich
 1920-1983 . . . . DLB-302
Abrams, M. H. 1912- DLB-67
Abramson, Jesse 1904-1979 . . . . DLB-241
Abrogans circa 790-800 . . . . DLB-148
Abschatz, Hans Aßmann von
 1646-1699 . . . . DLB-168

Abse, Dannie 1923- DLB-27, 245
Abu al-'Atahiyah 748-825? DLB-311
Abu Nuwas circa 757-814 or 815 . . . . DLB-311
Abu Tammam circa 805-845 . . . . DLB-311
Abutsu-ni 1221-1283 . . . . DLB-203
Academy Chicago Publishers DLB-46
Accius circa 170 B.C.-circa 80 B.C. DLB-211
"An account of the death of the Chevalier de La
 Barre," Voltaire DLB-314
Accrocca, Elio Filippo 1923-1996 . . . . DLB-128
Ace Books DLB-46
Achebe, Chinua 1930- DLB-117; CDWLB-3
Achillini, Claudio 1574-1640 . . . . DLB-339
Achtenberg, Herbert 1938- DLB-124
Ackerman, Diane 1948- DLB-120
Ackroyd, Peter 1949- DLB-155, 231
Acorn, Milton 1923-1986 . . . . DLB-53
Acosta, José de 1540-1600 . . . . DLB-318
Acosta, Oscar Zeta 1935?-1974? DLB-82
Acosta Torres, José 1925- DLB-209
Actors Theatre of Louisville DLB-7
Adair, Gilbert 1944- DLB-194
Adair, James 1709?-1783? DLB-30
Aðalsteinn Kristmundsson (see Steinn Steinarr)
Adam, Graeme Mercer 1839-1912 . . . . DLB-99
Adam, Robert Borthwick, II
 1863-1940 . . . . DLB-187
Adame, Leonard 1947- DLB-82
Adameşteanu, Gabriel 1942- DLB-232
Adamic, Louis 1898-1951 . . . . DLB-9
Adamov, Arthur Surenovitch
 1908-1970 . . . . DLB-321
Adamovich, Georgii 1894-1972 . . . . DLB-317
Adams, Abigail 1744-1818 . . . . DLB-183, 200
Adams, Alice 1926-1999 . . . . DLB-234; Y-86
Adams, Bertha Leith (Mrs. Leith Adams,
 Mrs. R. S. de Courcy Laffan)
 1837?-1912 . . . . DLB-240
Adams, Brooks 1848-1927 . . . . DLB-47

Adams, Charles Francis, Jr. 1835-1915 . . . . DLB-47
Adams, Douglas 1952-2001 . . . . DLB-261; Y-83
Adams, Franklin P. 1881-1960 . . . . DLB-29
Adams, Glenda 1939- DLB-325
Adams, Hannah 1755-1832 . . . . DLB-200
Adams, Henry 1838-1918 . . . . DLB-12, 47, 189
Adams, Herbert Baxter 1850-1901 . . . . DLB-47
Adams, James Truslow
 1878-1949 . . . . DLB-17; DS-17
Adams, John 1735-1826 . . . . DLB-31, 183
Adams, John Quincy 1767-1848 . . . . DLB-37
Adams, Léonie 1899-1988 . . . . DLB-48
Adams, Levi 1802-1832 . . . . DLB-99
Adams, Richard 1920- DLB-261
Adams, Samuel 1722-1803 . . . . DLB-31, 43
Adams, Sarah Fuller Flower
 1805-1848 . . . . DLB-199
Adams, Thomas 1582/1583-1652 . . . . DLB-151
Adams, William Taylor 1822-1897 . . . . DLB-42
J. S. and C. Adams [publishing house] DLB-49
Adamson, Harold 1906-1980 . . . . DLB-265
Adamson, Sir John 1867-1950 . . . . DLB-98
Adamson, Robert 1943- DLB-289
Adcock, Arthur St. John
 1864-1930 . . . . DLB-135
Adcock, Betty 1938- DLB-105
 "Certain Gifts" DLB-105
 Tribute to James Dickey Y-97
Adcock, Fleur 1934- DLB-40
Addams, Jane 1860-1935 . . . . DLB-303
Addison, Joseph
 1672-1719 . . . . DLB-101; CDBLB-2
Ade, George 1866-1944 . . . . DLB-11, 25
Adeler, Max (see Clark, Charles Heber)
Adlard, Mark 1932- DLB-261
Adler, Richard 1921- DLB-265
Adonias Filho
 (Adonias Aguiar Filho)
 1915-1990 . . . . DLB-145, 307
Adorno, Theodor W. 1903-1969 . . . . DLB-242

311

Cumulative Index

Adoum, Jorge Enrique 1926- DLB-283

Advance Publishing Company DLB-49

Ady, Endre 1877-1919...... DLB-215; CDWLB-4

AE 1867-1935 .... DLB-19; CDBLB-5

Ælfric circa 955-circa 1010 .... DLB-146

Aeschines circa 390 B.C.-circa 320 B.C. DLB-176

Aeschylus 525-524 B.C.-456-455 B.C.
................DLB-176; CDWLB-1

Aesthetic Papers DLB-1

Aesthetics
   Eighteenth-Century Aesthetic
     Theories DLB-31

African Literature
   Letter from Khartoum............. Y-90

African American
   Afro-American Literary Critics:
     An Introduction............... DLB-33
   The Black Aesthetic: Background DS-8
   The Black Arts Movement,
     by Larry Neal DLB-38
   Black Theaters and Theater Organizations
     in America, 1961-1982:
     A Research List DLB-38
   Black Theatre: A Forum [excerpts] ... DLB-38
   Callaloo [journal].................... Y-87
   Community and Commentators:
     Black Theatre and Its Critics..... DLB-38
   The Emergence of Black
     Women Writers DS-8
   The Hatch-Billops Collection........ DLB-76
   A Look at the Contemporary Black
     Theatre Movement DLB-38
   The Moorland-Spingarn Research
     Center DLB-76
   "The Negro as a Writer," by
     G. M. McClellan DLB-50
   "Negro Poets and Their Poetry," by
     Wallace Thurman DLB-50
   Olaudah Equiano and Unfinished Journeys:
     The Slave-Narrative Tradition and
     Twentieth-Century Continuities, by
     Paul Edwards and Pauline T.
     Wangman DLB-117
   PHYLON (Fourth Quarter, 1950),
     The Negro in Literature:
     The Current Scene DLB-76
   The Schomburg Center for Research
     in Black Culture DLB-76
   Three Documents [poets], by John
     Edward Bruce DLB-50

After Dinner Opera Company Y-92

Agassiz, Elizabeth Cary 1822-1907...... DLB-189

Agassiz, Louis 1807-1873 .... DLB-1, 235

Agee, James
   1909-1955 .... DLB-2, 26, 152; CDALB-1
   The Agee Legacy: A Conference at
     the University of Tennessee
     at Knoxville................... Y-89

Agnon, Shmuel Yosef 1887-1970 .... DLB-329

Aguilera Malta, Demetrio 1909-1981 .... DLB-145

Aguirre, Isidora 1919- DLB-305

Agustini, Delmira 1886-1914 .... DLB-290

Ahlin, Lars 1915-1997 .... DLB-257

Ai 1947- DLB-120

Ai Wu 1904-1992................... DLB-328

Aichinger, Ilse 1921- DLB-85, 299

Aickman, Robert 1914-1981........... DLB-261

Aidoo, Ama Ata 1942- DLB-117; CDWLB-3

Aiken, Conrad
   1889-1973........ DLB-9, 45, 102; CDALB-5

Aiken, Joan 1924-2004 .... DLB-161

Aikin, John 1747-1822............... DLB-336

Aikin, Lucy 1781-1864 .... DLB-144, 163

Ainsworth, William Harrison
   1805-1882 .... DLB-21

Aïssé, Charlotte-Elizabeth 1694?-1733 ... DLB-313

Aistis, Jonas 1904-1973 ..... DLB-220; CDWLB-4

Aitken, Adam 1960- DLB-325

Aitken, George A. 1860-1917 .... DLB-149

Robert Aitken [publishing house]........ DLB-49

Aitmatov, Chingiz 1928- DLB-302

Akenside, Mark 1721-1770 .... DLB-109

Akhmatova, Anna Andreevna
   1889-1966 .... DLB-295

Akins, Zoë 1886-1958............... DLB-26

Aksakov, Ivan Sergeevich 1823-1826.....DLB-277

Aksakov, Sergei Timofeevich
   1791-1859 .... DLB-198

Aksyonov, Vassily 1932- DLB-302

Akunin, Boris (Grigorii Shalvovich Chkhartishvili)
   1956- DLB-285

Akutagawa Ryūnosuke 1892-1927....... DLB-180

Alabaster, William 1568-1640.......... DLB-132

Alain de Lille circa 1116-1202/1203 .... DLB-208

Alain-Fournier 1886-1914............. DLB-65

Alanus de Insulis (see Alain de Lille)

Alarcón, Francisco X. 1954- DLB-122

Alarcón, Justo S. 1930- DLB-209

Alba, Nanina 1915-1968............... DLB-41

Albee, Edward 1928- ... DLB-7, 266; CDALB-1

Albert, Octavia 1853-ca. 1889 .... DLB-221

Albert the Great circa 1200-1280 .... DLB-115

Alberti, Rafael 1902-1999............. DLB-108

Albertinus, Aegidius circa 1560-1620.... DLB-164

Alcaeus born circa 620 B.C. DLB-176

Alcoforado, Mariana, the Portuguese Nun
   1640-1723..................... DLB-287

Alcott, Amos Bronson
   1799-1888................ DLB-1, 223; DS-5

Alcott, Louisa May 1832-1888
   ... DLB-1, 42, 79, 223, 239; DS-14; CDALB-3

Alcott, William Andrus 1798-1859 .... DLB-1, 243

Alcuin circa 732-804................. DLB-148

Aldana, Francisco de 1537-1578 .... DLB-318

Aldanov, Mark (Mark Landau)
   1886-1957 ....DLB-317

Alden, Henry Mills 1836-1919.......... DLB-79

Alden, Isabella 1841-1930 .... DLB-42

John B. Alden [publishing house] DLB-49

Alden, Beardsley, and Company DLB-49

Aldington, Richard
   1892-1962 ....DLB-20, 36, 100, 149

Aldis, Dorothy 1896-1966 .... DLB-22

Aldis, H. G. 1863-1919............... DLB-184

Aldiss, Brian W. 1925- DLB-14, 261, 271

Aldrich, Thomas Bailey
   1836-1907 ....DLB-42, 71, 74, 79

Alegría, Ciro 1909-1967 .... DLB-113

Alegría, Claribel 1924- DLB-145, 283

Aleixandre, Vicente 1898-1984...... DLB-108, 329

Aleksandravičius, Jonas (see Aistis, Jonas)

Aleksandrov, Aleksandr Andreevich
   (see Durova, Nadezhda Andreevna)

Alekseeva, Marina Anatol'evna
   (see Marinina, Aleksandra)

d'Alembert, Jean Le Rond 1717-1783 .... DLB-313

Alencar, José de 1829-1877 .... DLB-307

Aleramo, Sibilla (Rena Pierangeli Faccio)
   1876-1960.................. DLB-114, 264

Aleshkovsky, Petr Markovich 1957- ... DLB-285

Aleshkovsky, Yuz 1929- DLB-317

Alexander, Cecil Frances 1818-1895..... DLB-199

Alexander, Charles 1868-1923 .... DLB-91

Charles Wesley Alexander
   [publishing house] DLB-49

Alexander, James 1691-1756............ DLB-24

Alexander, Lloyd 1924- DLB-52

Alexander, Meena 1951- DLB-323

Alexander, Sir William, Earl of Stirling
   1577?-1640.................... DLB-121

Alexie, Sherman 1966- DLB-175, 206, 278

Alexis, Willibald 1798-1871 .... DLB-133

Alf laylah wa laylah
   ninth century onward DLB-311

Alfonso X 1221-1284................. DLB-337

Alfonsine Legal Codes DLB-337

Alfred, King 849-899 .... DLB-146

Alger, Horatio, Jr. 1832-1899 .... DLB-42

Algonquin Books of Chapel Hill DLB-46

Algren, Nelson
   1909-1981 ....DLB-9; Y-81, 82; CDALB-1
   Nelson Algren: An International
     Symposium Y-00

Ali, Agha Shahid 1949-2001........... DLB-323

Ali, Ahmed 1908-1994 .... DLB-323

Ali, Monica 1967- DLB-323

'Ali ibn Abi Talib circa 600-661 .... DLB-311

Aljamiado Literature................. DLB-286

Allan, Andrew 1907-1974 ....DLB-88	The Library of America.................DLB-46	*Amsterdam,* 1998 Booker Prize winner, Ian McEwan DLB-326
Allan, Ted 1916-1995..................DLB-68	The Library of America: An Assessment After Two Decades Y-02	Amyot, Jacques 1513-1593.............DLB-327
Allbeury, Ted 1917-2005 ....DLB-87	*America: or, A Poem on the Settlement of the British Colonies,* by Timothy Dwight DLB-37	Anand, Mulk Raj 1905-2004 ....DLB-323
Alldritt, Keith 1935- DLB-14		Anania, Michael 1939- DLB-193
Allen, Dick 1939- DLB-282		Anaya, Rudolfo A. 1937- DLB-82, 206, 278
Allen, Ethan 1738-1789 ....DLB-31	American Bible Society Department of Library, Archives, and Institutional Research Y-97	*Ancrene Riwle* circa 1200-1225 ....DLB-146
Allen, Frederick Lewis 1890-1954 ....DLB-137		Andersch, Alfred 1914-1980 ....DLB-69
Allen, Gay Wilson 1903-1995 ..... DLB-103; Y-95	American Conservatory Theatre..........DLB-7	Andersen, Benny 1929- DLB-214
Allen, George 1808-1876 ....DLB-59	American Culture American Proletarian Culture: The Twenties and Thirties DS-11	Andersen, Hans Christian 1805-1875 ....DLB-300
Allen, Grant 1848-1899 .... DLB-70, 92, 178		Anderson, Alexander 1775-1870 ....DLB-188
Allen, Henry W. 1912-1991.................Y-85	Studies in American Jewish Literature........Y-02	Anderson, David 1929- DLB-241
Allen, Hervey 1889-1949..........DLB-9, 45, 316	The American Library in Paris Y-93	Anderson, Frederick Irving 1877-1947......................DLB-202
Allen, James 1739-1808 ....DLB-31	American Literature The Literary Scene and Situation and . . . (Who Besides Oprah) Really Runs American Literature? Y-99	
Allen, James Lane 1849-1925............DLB-71		Anderson, Jessica 1916- DLB-325
Allen, Jay Presson 1922- DLB-26		Anderson, Margaret 1886-1973 ....DLB-4, 91
John Allen and Company DLB-49	Who Owns American Literature, by Henry Taylor Y-94	Anderson, Maxwell 1888-1959 .... DLB-7, 228
Allen, Paula Gunn 1939- DLB-175		Anderson, Patrick 1915-1979.............DLB-68
Allen, Samuel W. 1917- DLB-41	Who Runs American Literature? Y-94	Anderson, Paul Y. 1893-1938 ....DLB-29
Allen, Woody 1935- DLB-44	American News Company..............DLB-49	Anderson, Poul 1926-2001 ....DLB-8
George Allen [publishing house] DLB-106	A Century of Poetry, a Lifetime of Collecting: J. M. Edelstein's Collection of Twentieth-Century American Poetry...........Y-02	Tribute to Isaac Asimov Y-92
George Allen and Unwin Limited DLB-112		Anderson, Robert 1750-1830..........DLB-142
Allende, Isabel 1942- DLB-145; CDWLB-3	The American Poets' Corner: The First Three Years (1983-1986) Y-86	Anderson, Robert 1917- DLB-7
Alline, Henry 1748-1784 ....DLB-99		Anderson, Sherwood 1876-1941 ....DLB-4, 9, 86; DS-1; CDALB-4
Allingham, Margery 1904-1966..........DLB-77	American Publishing Company..........DLB-49	
The Margery Allingham Society Y-98	*American Spectator* [Editorial] Rationale From the Initial Issue of the American Spectator (November 1932)................DLB-137	Andrade, Jorge (Aluísio Jorge Andrade Franco) 1922-1984 ....DLB-307
Allingham, William 1824-1889 ....DLB-35		Andrade, Mario de 1893-1945...........DLB-307
W. L. Allison [publishing house] DLB-49		Andrade, Oswald de (José Oswald de Sousa Andrade) 1890-1954................DLB-307
The *Alliterative Morte Arthure and the Stanzaic Morte Arthur* circa 1350-1400 ....DLB-146	American Stationers' Company..........DLB-49	
	The American Studies Association of Norway.........................Y-00	Andreae, Johann Valentin 1586-1654 ....DLB-164
Allott, Kenneth 1912-1973 ....DLB-20		Andreas Capellanus fl. circa 1185 ....DLB-208
Allston, Washington 1779-1843 ......DLB-1, 235	American Sunday-School Union DLB-49	Andreas-Salomé, Lou 1861-1937 ....DLB-66
Almeida, Manuel Antônio de 1831-1861 ....DLB-307	American Temperance Union DLB-49	Andreev, Leonid Nikolaevich 1871-1919 ....DLB-295
	American Tract Society................DLB-49	
John Almon [publishing house] DLB-154	The American Trust for the British Library ...Y-96	Andres, Stefan 1906-1970 ....DLB-69
Alonzo, Dámaso 1898-1990............DLB-108	American Writers' Congress 25-27 April 1935 ....DLB-303	Andresen, Sophia de Mello Breyner 1919- DLB-287
Alsop, George 1636-post 1673 ....DLB-24		
Alsop, Richard 1761-1815 ....DLB-37	American Writers Congress The American Writers Congress (9-12 October 1981) Y-81	Andreu, Blanca 1959- DLB-134
Henry Altemus and Company...........DLB-49		Andrewes, Lancelot 1555-1626 ..... DLB-151, 172
Altenberg, Peter 1885-1919 ....DLB-81		Andrews, Charles M. 1863-1943.........DLB-17
Althusser, Louis 1918-1990 ....DLB-242	The American Writers Congress: A Report on Continuing Business Y-81	Andrews, Miles Peter ?-1814 ....DLB-89
Altolaguirre, Manuel 1905-1959 ....DLB-108		Andrews, Stephen Pearl 1812-1886 ......DLB-250
Aluko, T. M. 1918- DLB-117	Ames, Fisher 1758-1808................DLB-37	Andrian, Leopold von 1875-1951 ....DLB-81
Alurista 1947- DLB-82	Ames, Mary Clemmer 1831-1884 ....DLB-23	Andrić, Ivo 1892-1975 .. DLB-147, 329; CDWLB-4
Alvarez, A. 1929- DLB-14, 40	Ames, William 1576-1633 ....DLB-281	Andreini, Francesco before 1548?-1624................DLB-339
Alvarez, Julia 1950- DLB-282	Amfiteatrov, Aleksandr 1862-1938 ......DLB-317	
Alvaro, Corrado 1895-1956............DLB-264	Amiel, Henri-Frédéric 1821-1881........DLB-217	Andreini, Giovan Battista 1576-1654.....DLB-339
Alver, Betti 1906-1989 ......DLB-220; CDWLB-4	Amini, Johari M. 1935- DLB-41	Andreini, Isabella 1562-1604............DLB-339
Amadi, Elechi 1934- DLB-117	Amis, Kingsley 1922-1995 ...DLB-15, 27, 100, 139, 326; Y-96; CDBLB-7	
Amado, Jorge 1912-2001 ....DLB-113		Andrieux, Louis (see Aragon, Louis)
Amalrik, Andrei 1938-1980 ....DLB-302	Amis, Martin 1949- DLB-14, 194	Andrus, Silas, and Son................DLB-49
Ambler, Eric 1909-1998................DLB-77	Ammianus Marcellinus circa A.D. 330-A.D. 395 ....DLB-211	Andrzejewski, Jerzy 1909-1983 ....DLB-215
	Ammons, A. R. 1926-2001 ....DLB-5, 165	Angell, James Burrill 1829-1916 ....DLB-64
	Amory, Thomas 1691?-1788 ....DLB-39	

Cumulative Index

Angell, Roger 1920- DLB-171, 185
Angelou, Maya 1928- DLB-38; CDALB-7
    Tribute to Julian Mayfield Y-84
Anger, Jane fl. 1589................. DLB-136
Angers, Félicité (see Conan, Laure)
The Anglo-Saxon Chronicle
    circa 890-1154 .... DLB-146
Angus and Robertson (UK) Limited DLB-112
Anhalt, Edward 1914-2000............. DLB-26
Anissimov, Myriam 1943- DLB-299
Anker, Nini Roll 1873-1942 .... DLB-297
Annenkov, Pavel Vasil'evich
    1813?-1887.....................DLB-277
Annensky, Innokentii Fedorovich
    1855-1909 .... DLB-295
Henry F. Anners [publishing house]...... DLB-49
Annolied between 1077 and 1081 .... DLB-148
Anouilh, Jean 1910-1987............. DLB-321
Anscombe, G. E. M. 1919-2001 .... DLB-262
Anselm of Canterbury 1033-1109....... DLB-115
Ansky, S. (Sh. An-Ski; Solomon Zainwil [Shloyme-Zanvl] Rapoport) 1863-1920 .... DLB-333
Anstey, F. 1856-1934 ....DLB-141, 178
'Antarah ('Antar ibn Shaddad al-'Absi)
    ?-early seventh century?........... DLB-311
Anthologizing New Formalism DLB-282
Anthony, Michael 1932- DLB-125
Anthony, Piers 1934- DLB-8
Anthony, Susanna 1726-1791 .... DLB-200
Antin, David 1932- DLB-169
Antin, Mary 1881-1949 ....DLB-221; Y-84
Anton Ulrich, Duke of Brunswick-Lüneburg
    1633-1714.................... DLB-168
Antschel, Paul (see Celan, Paul)
Antunes, António Lobo 1942- DLB-287
Anyidoho, Kofi 1947- DLB-157
Anzaldúa, Gloria 1942- DLB-122
Anzengruber, Ludwig 1839-1889 ...... DLB-129
Apess, William 1798-1839..........DLB-175, 243
Apodaca, Rudy S. 1939- DLB-82
Apollinaire, Guillaume
    1880-1918................. DLB-258, 321
Apollonius Rhodius third century B.C..... DLB-176
Apple, Max 1941- DLB-130
Appelfeld, Aharon 1932- DLB-299
D. Appleton and Company DLB-49
Appleton-Century-Crofts DLB-46
Applewhite, James 1935- DLB-105
    Tribute to James Dickey.............. Y-97
Apple-wood Books DLB-46
April, Jean-Pierre 1948- DLB-251

Apukhtin, Aleksei Nikolaevich
    1840-1893 ....DLB-277
Apuleius circa A.D. 125-post A.D. 164
    .... DLB-211; CDWLB-1
Aquin, Hubert 1929-1977............. DLB-53
Aquinas, Thomas 1224/1225-1274...... DLB-115
Aragon, Louis 1897-1982 .... DLB-72, 258
Aragon, Vernacular Translations in the
    Crowns of Castile and 1352-1515 ... DLB-286
Aralica, Ivan 1930- DLB-181
Aratus of Soli
    circa 315 B.C.-circa 239 B.C. DLB-176
Arbasino, Alberto 1930- DLB-196
Arbor House Publishing Company DLB-46
Arbuthnot, John 1667-1735........... DLB-101
Arcadia House DLB-46
Arce, Julio G. (see Ulica, Jorge)
Archer, William 1856-1924............ DLB-10
Archilochhus
    mid seventh century B.C.E..........DLB-176
The Archpoet circa 1130?-? DLB-148
Archpriest Avvakum (Petrovich)
    1620?-1682..................... DLB-150
Arden, John 1930- DLB-13, 245
Arden of Faversham DLB-62
Ardis Publishers Y-89
Ardizzone, Edward 1900-1979 .... DLB-160
Arellano, Juan Estevan 1947- DLB-122
The Arena Publishing Company DLB-49
Arena Stage......................... DLB-7
Arenas, Reinaldo 1943-1990.......... DLB-145
Arendt, Hannah 1906-1975 .... DLB-242
Arensberg, Ann 1937- Y-82
Arghezi, Tudor 1880-1967 ... DLB-220; CDWLB-4
Arguedas, José María 1911-1969 ...... DLB-113
Argüelles, Hugo 1932-2003 .... DLB-305
Argueta, Manlio 1936- DLB-145
'Arib al-Ma'muniyah 797-890 .... DLB-311
Arias, Ron 1941- DLB-82
Arishima Takeo 1878-1923........... DLB-180
Aristophanes circa 446 B.C.-circa 386 B.C.
    .... DLB-176; CDWLB-1
Aristotle 384 B.C.-322 B.C.
    ....DLB-176; CDWLB-1
Ariyoshi Sawako 1931-1984 .... DLB-182
Arland, Marcel 1899-1986 .... DLB-72
Arlen, Michael 1895-1956 ......DLB-36, 77, 162
Arlt, Roberto 1900-1942............. DLB-305
Armah, Ayi Kwei 1939- ...DLB-117; CDWLB-3
Armantrout, Rae 1947- DLB-193
Der arme Hartmann ?-after 1150 ...... DLB-148
Armed Services Editions............. DLB-46
Armitage, G. E. (Robert Edric) 1956- .. DLB-267

Armstrong, Jeanette 1948- DLB-334
Armstrong, Martin Donisthorpe
    1882-1974......................DLB-197
Armstrong, Richard 1903-1986 .... DLB-160
Armstrong, Terence Ian Fytton (see Gawsworth, John)
Arnauld, Antoine 1612-1694 ....DLB-268
Arndt, Ernst Moritz 1769-1860.......... DLB-90
Arnim, Achim von 1781-1831 .... DLB-90
Arnim, Bettina von 1785-1859 .... DLB-90
Arnim, Elizabeth von (Countess Mary Annette
    Beauchamp Russell) 1866-1941 .....DLB-197
Arno Press DLB-46
Arnold, Edwin 1832-1904 .... DLB-35
Arnold, Edwin L. 1857-1935 ....DLB-178
Arnold, Matthew
    1822-1888 .... DLB-32, 57; CDBLB-4
    Preface to *Poems* (1853) DLB-32
Arnold, Thomas 1795-1842 .... DLB-55
Edward Arnold [publishing house]...... DLB-112
Arnott, Peter 1962- DLB-233
Arnow, Harriette Simpson 1908-1986 ..... DLB-6
Arp, Bill (see Smith, Charles Henry)
Arpino, Giovanni 1927-1987............DLB-177
Arrabal, Fernando 1932- DLB-321
Arrebo, Anders 1587-1637 .... DLB-300
Arreola, Juan José 1918-2001 .... DLB-113
Arrian circa 89-circa 155................DLB-176
J. W. Arrowsmith [publishing house] DLB-106
Arrufat, Antón 1935- DLB-305
Art
    John Dos Passos: Artist Y-99
    The First Post-Impressionist
    Exhibition......................DS-5
    The Omega Workshops............. DS-10
    The Second Post-Impressionist
    Exhibition......................DS-5
Artale, Giuseppi 1628-1679 .... DLB-339
Artaud, Antonin 1896-1948 ...... DLB-258, 321
Artel, Jorge 1909-1994 .... DLB-283
Arthur, Timothy Shay
    1809-1885 ....DLB-3, 42, 79, 250; DS-13
Artmann, H. C. 1921-2000............ DLB-85
Artsybashev, Mikhail Petrovich
    1878-1927...................... DLB-295
Arvin, Newton 1900-1963 .... DLB-103
Asch, Nathan 1902-1964 .... DLB-4, 28
    Nathan Asch Remembers Ford Madox
    Ford, Sam Roth, and Hart Crane Y-02
Asch, Sholem 1880-1957 .... DLB-333
Ascham, Roger 1515/1516-1568........ DLB-236
Aseev, Nikolai Nikolaevich
    1889-1963 .... DLB-295
Ash, John 1948- DLB-40
Ashbery, John 1927- DLB-5, 165; Y-81

314

Ashbridge, Elizabeth 1713-1755 ....DLB-200

Ashburnham, Bertram Lord
  1797-1878.....................DLB-184

Ashendene Press DLB-112

Asher, Sandy 1942- Y-83

Ashton, Winifred (see Dane, Clemence)

Asimov, Isaac 1920-1992 ....DLB-8; Y-92

  Tribute to John Ciardi................Y-86

Askew, Anne circa 1521-1546 ....DLB-136

Aspazija 1865-1943 ....DLB-220; CDWLB-4

Asselin, Olivar 1874-1937 ....DLB-92

The Association of American Publishers......Y-99

The Association for Documentary Editing....Y-00

The Association for the Study of
  Literature and Environment (ASLE)......Y-99

Astell, Mary 1666-1731 ....DLB-252, 336

Astley, Thea 1925- DLB-289

Astley, William (see Warung, Price)

Asturias, Miguel Ángel 1899-1974
  ....DLB-113, 290, 329; CDWLB-3

Atava, S. (see Terpigorev, Sergei Nikolaevich)

Atheneum Publishers...................DLB-46

Atherton, Gertrude 1857-1948.....DLB-9, 78, 186

Athlone Press.......................DLB-112

Atkins, Josiah circa 1755-1781 ....DLB-31

Atkins, Russell 1926- DLB-41

Atkinson, Kate 1951- DLB-267

Atkinson, Louisa 1834-1872..........DLB-230

The Atlantic Monthly Press............DLB-46

Attaway, William 1911-1986 ....DLB-76

Atwood, Margaret 1939- DLB-53, 251, 326

Aubert, Alvin 1930- DLB-41

Aub, Max 1903-1972 ....DLB-322

Aubert de Gaspé, Phillipe-Ignace-François
  1814-1841.....................DLB-99

Aubert de Gaspé, Phillipe-Joseph
  1786-1871.....................DLB-99

Aubigné, Théodore Agrippa d'
  1552-1630.....................DLB-327

Aubin, Napoléon 1812-1890 ....DLB-99

Aubin, Penelope
  1685-circa 1731 ....DLB-39

  Preface to The Life of Charlotta
    du Pont (1723)...................DLB-39

Aubrey-Fletcher, Henry Lancelot (see Wade, Henry)

Auchincloss, Louis 1917- DLB-2, 244; Y-80

Auden, W. H.
  1907-1973...........DLB-10, 20; CDBLB-6

Audiberti, Jacques 1899-1965 ....DLB-321

Audio Art in America: A Personal Memoir....Y-85

Audubon, John James 1785-1851........DLB-248

Audubon, John Woodhouse
  1812-1862.....................DLB-183

Auerbach, Berthold 1812-1882 ....DLB-133

Auernheimer, Raoul 1876-1948 ....DLB-81

Augier, Emile 1820-1889 ....DLB-192

Augustine 354-430..................DLB-115

Aulnoy, Marie-Catherine Le Jumel
  de Barneville, comtesse d'
  1650/1651-1705..................DLB-268

Aulus Gellius
  circa A.D. 125-circa A.D. 180?........DLB-211

Austen, Jane 1775-1817 ......DLB-116; CDBLB-3

Auster, Paul 1947- DLB-227

Austin, Alfred 1835-1913...............DLB-35

Austin, J. L. 1911-1960 ....DLB-262

Austin, Jane Goodwin 1831-1894 ....DLB-202

Austin, John 1790-1859 ....DLB-262

Austin, Mary Hunter
  1868-1934 ....DLB-9, 78, 206, 221, 275

Austin, William 1778-1841..............DLB-74

Australie (Emily Manning) 1845-1890....DLB-230

Authors and Newspapers Association DLB-46

Authors' Publishing Company............DLB-49

Avallone, Michael 1924-1999 .....DLB-306; Y-99

  Tribute to John D. MacDonald..........Y-86

  Tribute to Kenneth Millar..............Y-83

  Tribute to Raymond Chandler Y-88

Avalon Books DLB-46

Avancini, Nicolaus 1611-1686..........DLB-164

Avendaño, Fausto 1941- DLB-82

Averroës 1126-1198..................DLB-115

Avery, Gillian 1926- DLB-161

Avicenna 980-1037 ....DLB-115

Ávila Jiménez, Antonio 1898-1965 ......DLB-283

Avison, Margaret 1918-1987 ....DLB-53

Avon Books DLB-46

Avyžius, Jonas 1922-1999 ....DLB-220

Awdry, Wilbert Vere 1911-1997 ....DLB-160

Awoonor, Kofi 1935- DLB-117

Ayala, Francisco 1906- DLB-322

Ayckbourn, Alan 1939- DLB-13, 245

Ayer, A. J. 1910-1989.................DLB-262

Aymé, Marcel 1902-1967..............DLB-72

Aytoun, Sir Robert 1570-1638 ....DLB-121

Aytoun, William Edmondstoune
  1813-1865...................DLB-32, 159

Azevedo, Aluísio 1857-1913 ....DLB-307

Azevedo, Manuel Antônio Álvares de
  1831-1852.....................DLB-307

Azorín (José Martínez Ruiz)
  1873-1967 ....DLB-322

B

B.V. (see Thomson, James)

Ba Jin 1904-2005 ....DLB-328

Babbitt, Irving 1865-1933 ....DLB-63

Babbitt, Natalie 1932- DLB-52

John Babcock [publishing house].........DLB-49

Babel, Isaak Emmanuilovich
  1894-1940.....................DLB-272

Babits, Mihály 1883-1941 ...DLB-215; CDWLB-4

Babrius circa 150-200..................DLB-176

Babson, Marian 1929- DLB-276

Baca, Jimmy Santiago 1952- DLB-122

Bacchelli, Riccardo 1891-1985..........DLB-264

Bache, Benjamin Franklin 1769-1798......DLB-43

Bachelard, Gaston 1884-1962 ....DLB-296

Bacheller, Irving 1859-1950...........DLB-202

Bachmann, Ingeborg 1926-1973 ....DLB-85

Bačinskaitė-Bučienė, Salomėja (see Nėris, Salomėja)

Bacon, Delia 1811-1859..............DLB-1, 243

Bacon, Francis
  1561-1626 .....DLB-151, 236, 252; CDBLB-1

Bacon, Sir Nicholas circa 1510-1579 .....DLB-132

Bacon, Roger circa 1214/1220-1292 .....DLB-115

Bacon, Thomas circa 1700-1768.........DLB-31

Bacovia, George
  1881-1957 ....DLB-220; CDWLB-4

Richard G. Badger and Company........DLB-49

Bagaduce Music Lending Library Y-00

Bage, Robert 1728-1801................DLB-39

Bagehot, Walter 1826-1877 ....DLB-55

Baggesen, Jens 1764-1826 ....DLB-300

Bagley, Desmond 1923-1983 ....DLB-87

Bagley, Sarah G. 1806-1848?...........DLB-239

Bagnold, Enid
  1889-1981 ....DLB-13, 160, 191, 245

Bagryana, Elisaveta
  1893-1991 ....DLB-147; CDWLB-4

Bahr, Hermann 1863-1934 ....DLB-81, 118

Baïf, Jean-Antoine de 1532-1589 ....DLB-327

Bail, Murray 1941- DLB-325

Bailey, Abigail Abbot 1746-1815.........DLB-200

Bailey, Alfred Goldsworthy 1905-1997 ....DLB-68

Bailey, H. C. 1878-1961 ....DLB-77

Bailey, Jacob 1731-1808 ....DLB-99

Bailey, Paul 1937- DLB-14, 271

Bailey, Philip James 1816-1902 ....DLB-32

Francis Bailey [publishing house].........DLB-49

Baillargeon, Pierre 1916-1967 ....DLB-88

Baillie, Hugh 1890-1966 ....DLB-29

Baillie, Joanna 1762-1851................DLB-93

Bailyn, Bernard 1922- DLB-17

Bain, Alexander
  English Composition and Rhetoric (1866)
  [excerpt].....................DLB-57

Bainbridge, Beryl 1933- DLB-14, 231

Baird, Irene 1901-1981 ....DLB-68

Baker, Alison 1953- DLB-335

Cumulative Index

Baker, Augustine 1575-1641 . . . . DLB-151

Baker, Carlos 1909-1987 . . . . DLB-103

Baker, David 1954- DLB-120

Baker, George Pierce 1866-1935 . . . . DLB-266

Baker, Herschel C. 1914-1990 . . . . DLB-111

Baker, Houston A., Jr. 1943- DLB-67

Baker, Howard
    Tribute to Caroline Gordon Y-81
    Tribute to Katherine Anne Porter Y-80

Baker, Nicholson 1957- DLB-227; Y-00
    Review of Nicholson Baker's *Double Fold:*
    Libraries and the Assault on Paper Y-00

Baker, Samuel White 1821-1893 . . . . DLB-166

Baker, Thomas 1656-1740 . . . . DLB-213

Walter H. Baker Company
    ("Baker's Plays") DLB-49

The Baker and Taylor Company DLB-49

Bakhtin, Mikhail Mikhailovich
    1895-1975 . . . . DLB-242

Bakunin, Mikhail Aleksandrovich
    1814-1876 . . . . DLB-277

Balaban, John 1943- DLB-120

Bald, Wambly 1902-1990 . . . . DLB-4

Balde, Jacob 1604-1668 . . . . DLB-164

Balderston, John 1889-1954 . . . . DLB-26

Baldwin, James 1924-1987
    . . . . . . DLB-2, 7, 33, 249, 278; Y-87; CDALB-1

Baldwin, Joseph Glover
    1815-1864 . . . . DLB-3, 11, 248

Baldwin, Louisa (Mrs. Alfred Baldwin)
    1845-1925 . . . . DLB-240

Baldwin, William circa 1515-1563 . . . . . . DLB-132

Richard and Anne Baldwin
    [publishing house] DLB-170

Bale, John 1495-1563 . . . . DLB-132

Balestrini, Nanni 1935- DLB-128, 196

Balfour, Sir Andrew 1630-1694 . . . . DLB-213

Balfour, Arthur James 1848-1930 . . . . DLB-190

Balfour, Sir James 1600-1657 . . . . DLB-213

Ballantine Books DLB-46

Ballantyne, R. M. 1825-1894 . . . . DLB-163

Ballard, J. G. 1930- DLB-14, 207, 261, 319

Ballard, Martha Moore 1735-1812 . . . . . . DLB-200

Ballerini, Luigi 1940- DLB-128

Ballou, Maturin Murray (Lieutenant Murray)
    1820-1895 . . . . DLB-79, 189

Robert O. Ballou [publishing house] DLB-46

Bal'mont, Konstantin Dmitrievich
    1867-1942 . . . . DLB-295

Balzac, Guez de 1597?-1654 . . . . DLB-268

Balzac, Honoré de 1799-1855 . . . . DLB-119

Bambara, Toni Cade
    1939-1995 . . . . DLB-38, 218; CDALB-7

Bamford, Samuel 1788-1872 . . . . DLB-190

A. L. Bancroft and Company DLB-49

Bancroft, George 1800-1891 . . . DLB-1, 30, 59, 243

Bancroft, Hubert Howe 1832-1918 . . . . DLB-47, 140

Bandeira, Manuel 1886-1968 . . . . DLB-307

Bandelier, Adolph F. 1840-1914 . . . . DLB-186

Bang, Herman 1857-1912 . . . . DLB-300

Bangs, John Kendrick 1862-1922 . . . . . DLB-11, 79

Banim, John 1798-1842 . . . . DLB-116, 158, 159

Banim, Michael 1796-1874 . . . . DLB-158, 159

Banks, Iain (M.) 1954- DLB-194, 261

Banks, John circa 1653-1706 . . . . DLB-80

Banks, Russell 1940- DLB-130, 278

Bannerman, Helen 1862-1946 . . . . DLB-141

Bantam Books DLB-46

Banti, Anna 1895-1985 . . . . DLB-177

Banville, John 1945- DLB-14, 271, 326

Banville, Théodore de 1823-1891 . . . . DLB-217

Bao Tianxiao 1876-1973 . . . . DLB-328

Baraka, Amiri
    1934- DLB-5, 7, 16, 38; DS-8; CDALB-1

Barańczak, Stanisław 1946- DLB-232

Baranskaia, Natal'ia Vladimirovna
    1908- DLB-302

Baratynsky, Evgenii Abramovich
    1800-1844 . . . . DLB-205

Barba-Jacob, Porfirio 1883-1942 . . . . DLB-283

Barbauld, Anna Laetitia
    1743-1825 . . . . . . DLB-107, 109, 142, 158, 336

Barbeau, Marius 1883-1969 . . . . DLB-92

Barber, John Warner 1798-1885 . . . . DLB-30

Bàrberi Squarotti, Giorgio 1929- DLB-128

Barbey d'Aurevilly, Jules-Amédée
    1808-1889 . . . . DLB-119

Barbier, Auguste 1805-1882 . . . . DLB-217

Barbieri, Nicolò 1576-1641 . . . . DLB-339

Barbilian, Dan (see Barbu, Ion)

Barbour, Douglas 1940- DLB-334

Barbour, John circa 1316-1395 . . . . DLB-146

Barbour, Ralph Henry 1870-1944 . . . . DLB-22

Barbu, Ion 1895-1961 . . . . . . DLB-220; CDWLB-4

Barbusse, Henri 1873-1935 . . . . DLB-65

Barclay, Alexander circa 1475-1552 . . . . . DLB-132

E. E. Barclay and Company DLB-49

C. W. Bardeen [publishing house] DLB-49

Barham, Richard Harris 1788-1845 . . . . . DLB-159

Barich, Bill 1943- DLB-185

Baring, Maurice 1874-1945 . . . . DLB-34

Baring-Gould, Sabine 1834-1924 . . . DLB-156, 190

Barker, A. L. 1918-2002 . . . . DLB-14, 139

Barker, Clive 1952- DLB-261

Barker, Dudley (see Black, Lionel)

Barker, George 1913-1991 . . . . DLB-20

Barker, Harley Granville 1877-1946 . . . . . . DLB-10

Barker, Howard 1946- DLB-13, 233

Barker, James Nelson 1784-1858 . . . . DLB-37

Barker, Jane 1652-1727 . . . . DLB-39, 131

Barker, Lady Mary Anne 1831-1911 . . . . DLB-166

Barker, Pat 1943- DLB-271, 326

Barker, William circa 1520-after 1576 . . . . DLB-132

Arthur Barker Limited DLB-112

Barkov, Ivan Semenovich 1732-1768 . . . . . DLB-150

Barks, Coleman 1937- DLB-5

Barlach, Ernst 1870-1938 . . . . DLB-56, 118

Barlow, Joel 1754-1812 . . . . DLB-37
    The Prospect of Peace (1778) DLB-37

Barnard, John 1681-1770 . . . . DLB-24

Barnard, Marjorie (M. Barnard Eldershaw)
    1897-1987 . . . . DLB-260

Barnard, Robert 1936- DLB-276

Barne, Kitty (Mary Catherine Barne)
    1883-1957 . . . . DLB-160

Barnes, Barnabe 1571-1609 . . . . DLB-132

Barnes, Djuna 1892-1982 . . . . DLB-4, 9, 45; DS-15

Barnes, Jim 1933- DLB-175

Barnes, Julian 1946- DLB-194; Y-93
    Notes for a Checklist of Publications Y-01

Barnes, Margaret Ayer 1886-1967 . . . . DLB-9

Barnes, Peter 1931- DLB-13, 233

Barnes, William 1801-1886 . . . . DLB-32

A. S. Barnes and Company DLB-49

Barnes and Noble Books DLB-46

Barnet, Miguel 1940- DLB-145

Barney, Natalie 1876-1972 . . . . DLB-4; DS-15

Barnfield, Richard 1574-1627 . . . . DLB-172

Baroja, Pío 1872-1956 . . . . DLB-322

Richard W. Baron [publishing house] DLB-46

Barr, Amelia Edith Huddleston
    1831-1919 . . . . DLB-202, 221

Barr, Robert 1850-1912 . . . . DLB-70, 92

Barral, Carlos 1928-1989 . . . . DLB-134

Barrax, Gerald William 1933- DLB-41, 120

Barreno, Maria Isabel (see The Three Marias:
    A Landmark Case in Portuguese
    Literary History)

Barrès, Maurice 1862-1923 . . . . DLB-123

Barrett, Andrea 1954- DLB-335

Barrett, Eaton Stannard 1786-1820 . . . . . . DLB-116

Barrie, J. M.
    1860-1937 . . . . . DLB-10, 141, 156; CDBLB-5

Barrie and Jenkins DLB-112

Barrio, Raymond 1921- DLB-82

Barrios, Gregg 1945- DLB-122

Barry, Philip 1896-1949 . . . . DLB-7, 228

Barry, Robertine (see Françoise)

Barry, Sebastian 1955- DLB-245

Barse and Hopkins....................DLB-46	Baxter, Charles 1947- DLB-130	Beckett, Mary 1926- DLB-319
Barstow, Stan 1928- DLB-14, 139, 207	Bayer, Eleanor (see Perry, Eleanor)	Beckett, Samuel 1906-1989 .... DLB-13, 15, 233, 319, 321, 329; Y-90; CDBLB-7
Tribute to John Braine................Y-86	Bayer, Konrad 1932-1964 ....DLB-85	Beckford, William 1760-1844........DLB-39, 213
Barth, John 1930- DLB-2, 227	Bayle, Pierre 1647-1706............DLB-268, 313	Beckham, Barry 1944- DLB-33
Barthelme, Donald 1931-1989 .... DLB-2, 234; Y-80, 89	Bayley, Barrington J. 1937- DLB-261	Bećković, Matija 1939- DLB-181
Barthelme, Frederick 1943- DLB-244; Y-85	Baynes, Pauline 1922- DLB-160	Becon, Thomas circa 1512-1567 ....DLB-136
Barthes, Roland 1915-1980 ....DLB-296	Baynton, Barbara 1857-1929 ....DLB-230	Becque, Henry 1837-1899 ....DLB-192
Bartholomew, Frank 1898-1985.........DLB-127	Bazin, Hervé (Jean Pierre Marie Hervé-Bazin) 1911-1996 ....DLB-83	Beddoes, Thomas 1760-1808...........DLB-158
Bartlett, John 1820-1905 ....DLB-1, 235	Bazzani Cavazzoni, Virginia 1669-1720? DLB-339	Beddoes, Thomas Lovell 1803-1849 ......DLB-96
Bartol, Cyrus Augustus 1813-1900 ....DLB-1, 235	The BBC Four Samuel Johnson Prize for Non-fiction......................Y-02	Bede circa 673-735....................DLB-146
Barton, Bernard 1784-1849 ....DLB-96	Beach, Sylvia 1887-1962.........DLB-4; DS-15	Bedford-Jones, H. 1887-1949 ....DLB-251
Barton, John ca. 1610-1675 ....DLB-236	Beacon Press DLB-49	Bedregal, Yolanda 1913-1999...........DLB-283
Barton, Thomas Pennant 1803-1869.....DLB-140	Beadle and Adams...................DLB-49	Beebe, William 1877-1962 ....DLB-275
Bartram, John 1699-1777 ....DLB-31	Beagle, Peter S. 1939- Y-80	Beecher, Catharine Esther 1800-1878 ....DLB-1, 243
Bartram, William 1739-1823 ....DLB-37	Beal, M. F. 1937- Y-81	Beecher, Henry Ward 1813-1887 ....DLB-3, 43, 250
Barykova, Anna Pavlovna 1839-1893 ....DLB-277	Beale, Howard K. 1899-1959............DLB-17	Beer, George L. 1872-1920..............DLB-47
Bashshar ibn Burd circa 714-circa 784 ....DLB-311	Beard, Charles A. 1874-1948 ....DLB-17	Beer, Johann 1655-1700 ....DLB-168
Basic Books DLB-46	Beat Generation (Beats) As I See It, by Carolyn Cassady DLB-16	Beer, Patricia 1919-1999 ....DLB-40
Basille, Theodore (see Becon, Thomas)	A Beat Chronology: The First Twenty-five Years, 1944-1969................DLB-16	Beerbohm, Max 1872-1956 ....DLB-34, 100
Bass, Rick 1958- DLB-212, 275	The Commercialization of the Image of Revolt, by Kenneth Rexroth....DLB-16	Beer-Hofmann, Richard 1866-1945.......DLB-81
Bass, T. J. 1932- Y-81	Four Essays on the Beat Generation ...DLB-16	Beers, Henry A. 1847-1926 ....DLB-71
Bassani, Giorgio 1916-2000 .... DLB-128, 177, 299	in New York City DLB-237	S. O. Beeton [publishing house].........DLB-106
Basse, William circa 1583-1653 ....DLB-121	in the West DLB-237	Begley, Louis 1933- DLB-299
Bassett, John Spencer 1867-1928 ....DLB-17	Outlaw Days DLB-16	Bégon, Elisabeth 1696-1755.............DLB-99
Bassler, Thomas Joseph (see Bass, T. J.)	Periodicals of DLB-16	Behan, Brendan 1923-1964 ....DLB-13, 233; CDBLB-7
Bate, Walter Jackson 1918-1999...... DLB-67, 103	Beattie, Ann 1947- DLB-218, 278; Y-82	Behn, Aphra 1640?-1689........ DLB-39, 80, 131
Bateman, Stephen circa 1510-1584.......DLB-136	Beattie, James 1735-1803 ....DLB-109	Behn, Harry 1898-1973 ....DLB-61
Christopher Bateman [publishing house] DLB-170	Beatty, Chester 1875-1968 ....DLB-201	Behrman, S. N. 1893-1973 .... DLB-7, 44
Bates, H. E. 1905-1974............DLB-162, 191	Beauchemin, Nérée 1850-1931 ....DLB-92	Beklemishev, Iurii Solomonvich (see Krymov, Iurii Solomonovich)
Bates, Katharine Lee 1859-1929 ....DLB-71	Beauchemin, Yves 1941- DLB-60	Belaney, Archibald Stansfeld (see Grey Owl)
Batiushkov, Konstantin Nikolaevich 1787-1855......................DLB-205	Beaugrand, Honoré 1848-1906 ....DLB-99	Belasco, David 1853-1931 ....DLB-7
B. T. Batsford [publishing house]........DLB-106	Beaulieu, Victor-Lévy 1945- DLB-53	Clarke Belford and Company DLB-49
Batteux, Charles 1713-1780 ....DLB-313	Beaumarchais, Pierre-Augustin Caron de 1732-1799 ....DLB-313	Belgian Luxembourg American Studies Association Y-01
Battiscombe, Georgina 1905- DLB-155	Beaumer, Mme de ?-1766..............DLB-313	Belinsky, Vissarion Grigor'evich 1811-1848 ....DLB-198
The Battle of Maldon circa 1000 ....DLB-146	Beaumont, Francis circa 1584-1616 and Fletcher, John 1579-1625 ....DLB-58; CDBLB-1	Belitt, Ben 1911-2003...................DLB-5
Baudelaire, Charles 1821-1867 ....DLB-217	Beaumont, Sir John 1583?-1627........DLB-121	Belknap, Jeremy 1744-1798 ....DLB-30, 37
Baudrillard, Jean 1929- DLB-296	Beaumont, Joseph 1616-1699...........DLB-126	Bell, Adrian 1901 1980 ....DLB-191
Bauer, Bruno 1809-1882 ....DLB-133	Beauvoir, Simone de 1908-1986..... DLB-72; Y-86	Bell, Clive 1881-1964.................... DS-10
Bauer, Wolfgang 1941- DLB-124	Personal Tribute to Simone de Beauvoir Y-86	Bell, Daniel 1919- DLB-246
Baum, L. Frank 1856-1919 ....DLB-22	Beaver, Bruce 1928- DLB-289	Bell, Gertrude Margaret Lowthian 1868-1926 ....DLB-174
Baum, Vicki 1888-1960 ....DLB-85	Becher, Ulrich 1910-1990...............DLB-69	Bell, James Madison 1826-1902..........DLB-50
Baumbach, Jonathan 1933- Y-80	Beck, Warren 1896-1986 ....DLB-335	Bell, Madison Smartt 1957- DLB-218, 278
Bausch, Richard 1945- DLB-130	Becker, Carl 1873-1945 ....DLB-17	Tribute to Andrew Nelson Lytle Y-95
Tribute to James Dickey Y-97	Becker, Jurek 1937-1997 ....DLB-75, 299	Tribute to Peter Taylor Y-94
Tribute to Peter Taylor Y-94	Becker, Jurgen 1932- DLB-75	Bell, Marvin 1937- DLB-5
Bausch, Robert 1945- DLB-218		
Bawden, Nina 1925- DLB-14, 161, 207		
Bax, Clifford 1886-1962............DLB-10, 100		

Bell, Millicent 1919- DLB-111	Benn Brothers Limited DLB-106	A Statement by Thomas Berger......... Y-80
Bell, Quentin 1910-1996.............. DLB-155	Bennett, Alan 1934- DLB-310	Bergman, Hjalmar 1883-1931 .... DLB-259
Bell, Vanessa 1879-1961 ....DS-10	Bennett, Arnold 1867-1931.... DLB-10, 34, 98, 135; CDBLB-5	Bergman, Ingmar 1918- DLB-257
George Bell and Sons DLB-106		Bergson, Henri 1859-1941 .... DLB-329
Robert Bell [publishing house] DLB-49	The Arnold Bennett Society........... Y-98	Berkeley, Anthony 1893-1971.......... DLB-77
Bellamy, Edward 1850-1898............ DLB-12	Bennett, Charles 1899-1995 .... DLB-44	Berkeley, George 1685-1753.....DLB-31, 101, 252
Bellamy, Joseph 1719-1790 .... DLB-31	Bennett, Emerson 1822-1905 .... DLB-202	The Berkley Publishing Corporation DLB-46
John Bellamy [publishing house].........DLB-170	Bennett, Gwendolyn 1902-1981 .... DLB-51	Berkman, Alexander 1870-1936 .... DLB-303
La Belle Assemblée 1806-1837 .... DLB-110	Bennett, Hal 1930- DLB-33	Berlin, Irving 1888-1989.............. DLB-265
Bellezza, Dario 1944-1996 .... DLB-128	Bennett, James Gordon 1795-1872 .... DLB-43	Berlin, Lucia 1936- DLB-130
Belli, Carlos Germán 1927- DLB-290	Bennett, James Gordon, Jr. 1841-1918 .... DLB-23	Berman, Marshall 1940- DLB-246
Belli, Gioconda 1948- DLB-290	Bennett, John 1865-1956 .... DLB-42	Berman, Sabina 1955- DLB-305
Belloc, Hilaire 1870-1953 .... DLB-19, 100, 141, 174	Bennett, Louise 1919- DLB-117; CDWLB-3	Bernal, Vicente J. 1888-1915 .... DLB-82
Belloc, Madame (see Parkes, Bessie Rayner)	Benni, Stefano 1947- DLB-196	Bernanos, Georges 1888-1948 .... DLB-72
Bellonci, Maria 1902-1986 .... DLB-196	Benoist, Françoise-Albine Puzin de La Martinière 1731-1809 .... DLB-313	Bernard, Catherine 1663?-1712 ....DLB-268
Bellow, Saul 1915-2005 .... DLB-2, 28, 299, 329; Y-82; DS-3; CDALB-1		Bernard, Harry 1898-1979 .... DLB-92
	Benoit, Jacques 1941- DLB-60	Bernard, John 1756-1828 .... DLB-37
Tribute to Isaac Bashevis Singer......... Y-91	Benson, A. C. 1862-1925 .... DLB-98	Bernard of Chartres circa 1060-1124? ... DLB-115
Belmont Productions DLB-46	Benson, E. F. 1867-1940 .... DLB-135, 153	Bernard of Clairvaux 1090-1153 .... DLB-208
	The E. F. Benson Society............. Y-98	Bernard, Richard 1568-1641/1642 ...... DLB-281
Belov, Vasilii Ivanovich 1932- DLB-302	The Tilling Society.................. Y-98	Bernard Silvestris fl. circa 1130-1160 .... DLB-208
Bels, Alberts 1938- DLB-232	Benson, Jackson J. 1930- DLB-111	
Belševica, Vizma 1931- DLB-232; CDWLB-4	Benson, Robert Hugh 1871-1914 .... DLB-153	Bernardin de Saint-Pierre 1737-1814..... DLB-313
Bely, Andrei 1880-1934 .... DLB-295	Benson, Stella 1892-1933 .... DLB-36, 162	Bernari, Carlo 1909-1992..............DLB-177
Bemelmans, Ludwig 1898-1962 .... DLB-22	Bent, James Theodore 1852-1897........DLB-174	Bernhard, Thomas 1931-1989 ....DLB-85, 124; CDWLB-2
Bemis, Samuel Flagg 1891-1973 .... DLB-17	Bent, Mabel Virginia Anna ?-?..........DLB-174	
William Bemrose [publishing house] DLB-106	Bentham, Jeremy 1748-1832 .... DLB-107, 158, 252	Berniéres, Louis de 1954- DLB-271
Ben no Naishi 1228?-1271?............. DLB-203	Bentley, E. C. 1875-1956............... DLB-70	Bernstein, Charles 1950- DLB-169
Benavente, Jacinto 1866-1954.......... DLB-329	Bentley, Phyllis 1894-1977 .... DLB-191	Béroalde de Verville, François 1556-1626 .... DLB-327
Benchley, Robert 1889-1945............ DLB-11	Bentley, Richard 1662-1742 .... DLB-252	
Bencúr, Matej (see Kukučin, Martin)	Richard Bentley [publishing house] DLB-106	Berriault, Gina 1926-1999 .... DLB-130
Benedetti, Mario 1920- DLB-113	Benton, Robert 1932- DLB-44	Berrigan, Daniel 1921- DLB-5
Benedict, Pinckney 1964- DLB-244	Benziger Brothers DLB-49	Berrigan, Ted 1934-1983 .... DLB-5, 169
Benedict, Ruth 1887-1948............. DLB-246	*Beowulf* circa 900-1000 or 790-825 .... DLB-146; CDBLB-1	Berry, Wendell 1934- DLB-5, 6, 234, 275
Benedictus, David 1938- DLB-14		Berryman, John 1914-1972.... DLB-48; CDALB-1
Benedikt Gröndal 1826-1907 .... DLB-293	Berberova, Nina 1901-1993 .... DLB-317	Bersianik, Louky 1930- DLB-60
Benedikt, Michael 1935- DLB-5	Berent, Wacław 1873-1940 .... DLB-215	Berssenbrugge, Mei-mei 1947- DLB-312
Benediktov, Vladimir Grigor'evich 1807-1873 .... DLB-205	Beresford, Anne 1929- DLB-40	Thomas Berthelet [publishing house].....DLB-170
	Beresford, John Davys 1873-1947............... DLB-162, 178, 197	Berto, Giuseppe 1914-1978.............DLB-177
Benét, Stephen Vincent 1898-1943 .... DLB-4, 48, 102, 249		Bertocci, Peter Anthony 1910-1989 ......DLB-279
	"Experiment in the Novel" (1929) [excerpt]..................... DLB-36	Bertolucci, Attilio 1911-2000 .... DLB-128
Stephen Vincent Benét Centenary Y-97		Berton, Pierre 1920-2004 .... DLB-68
Benét, William Rose 1886-1950 .... DLB-45	Beresford-Howe, Constance 1922- DLB-88	Bertrand, Louis "Aloysius" 1807-1841 ....DLB-217
Benford, Gregory 1941- Y-82	R. G. Berford Company............... DLB-49	Besant, Sir Walter 1836-1901 ...... DLB-135, 190
Benítez, Sandra 1941- DLB-292	Berg, Elizabeth 1948- DLB-292	Bessa-Luís, Agustina 1922- DLB-287
Benjamin, Park 1809-1864 .... DLB-3, 59, 73, 250	Berg, Stephen 1934- DLB-5	Bessette, Gerard 1920- DLB-53
Benjamin, Peter (see Cunningham, Peter)	Bergelson, David (Dovid Bergelson) 1884-1952 .... DLB-333	Bessie, Alvah 1904-1985............... DLB-26
Benjamin, S. G. W. 1837-1914 .... DLB-189		Bester, Alfred 1913-1987............... DLB-8
Benjamin, Walter 1892-1940 .... DLB-242	Bergengruen, Werner 1892-1964 .... DLB-56	Besterman, Theodore 1904-1976 .... DLB-201
Benlowes, Edward 1602-1676 .... DLB-126	Berger, John 1926- DLB-14, 207, 319, 326	Beston, Henry (Henry Beston Sheahan) 1888-1968 ....DLB-275
Benn, Gottfried 1886-1956............ DLB-56	Berger, Meyer 1898-1959 .... DLB-29	
	Berger, Thomas 1924- DLB-2; Y-80	

Best-Seller Lists
   An Assessment Y-84

   What's Really Wrong With
      Bestseller Lists Y-84

Bestuzhev, Aleksandr Aleksandrovich
   (Marlinsky) 1797-1837 .... DLB-198

Bestuzhev, Nikolai Aleksandrovich
   1791-1855 .... DLB-198

Betham-Edwards, Matilda Barbara
   (see Edwards, Matilda Barbara Betham-)

Betjeman, John
   1906-1984 .... DLB-20; Y-84; CDBLB-7

Betocchi, Carlo 1899-1986............. DLB-128

Bettarini, Mariella 1942- DLB-128

Betts, Doris 1932- DLB-218; Y-82

Beveridge, Albert J. 1862-1927........... DLB-17

Beveridge, Judith 1956- DLB-325

Beverley, Robert circa 1673-1722...... DLB-24, 30

Bevilacqua, Alberto 1934- DLB-196

Bevington, Louisa Sarah 1845-1895 ..... DLB-199

Beyle, Marie-Henri (see Stendhal)

Bèze, Théodore de (Theodore Beza)
   1519-1605 .... DLB-327

Bhatt, Sujata 1956- DLB-323

Białoszewski, Miron 1922-1983 .... DLB-232

Bianco, Margery Williams 1881-1944 .... DLB-160

Bibaud, Adèle 1854-1941............... DLB-92

Bibaud, Michel 1782-1857 .... DLB-99

Bibliography
   Bibliographical and Textual Scholarship
      Since World War II............... Y-89

   Center for Bibliographical Studies and
      Research at the University of
      California, Riverside............... Y-91

   The Great Bibliographers Series Y-93

   Primary Bibliography: A Retrospective.... Y-95

Bichsel, Peter 1935- DLB-75

Bickerstaff, Isaac John 1733-circa 1808 .... DLB-89

Drexel Biddle [publishing house] DLB-49

Bidermann, Jacob
   1577 or 1578-1639 .... DLB-164

Bidwell, Walter Hilliard 1798-1881 .... DLB-79

Biehl, Charlotta Dorothea 1731-1788..... DLB-300

Bienek, Horst 1930-1990................ DLB-75

Bierbaum, Otto Julius 1865-1910......... DLB-66

Bierce, Ambrose 1842 1914?
   ...... DLB-11, 12, 23, 71, 74, 186; CDALB-3

Bigelow, William F. 1879-1966........... DLB-91

Biggers, Earl Derr 1884-1933 .... DLB-306

Biggle, Lloyd, Jr. 1923-2002............... DLB-8

Bigiaretti, Libero 1905-1993 .... DLB-177

Bigland, Eileen 1898-1970............... DLB-195

Biglow, Hosea (see Lowell, James Russell)

Bigongiari, Piero 1914-1997 .... DLB-128

Bilac, Olavo 1865-1918 .... DLB-307

Bilenchi, Romano 1909-1989........... DLB-264

Billinger, Richard 1890-1965 .... DLB-124

Billings, Hammatt 1818-1874........... DLB-188

Billings, John Shaw 1898-1975 .... DLB-137

Billings, Josh (see Shaw, Henry Wheeler)

Binchy, Maeve 1940- DLB-319

Binding, Rudolf G. 1867-1938 .... DLB-66

Bing Xin 1900-1999.................. DLB-328

Bingay, Malcolm 1884-1953 .... DLB-241

Bingham, Caleb 1757-1817............. DLB-42

Bingham, George Barry 1906-1988...... DLB-127

Bingham, Sallie 1937- DLB-234

William Bingley [publishing house]...... DLB-154

Binyon, Laurence 1869-1943 .... DLB-19

Biographia Brittanica.................. DLB-142

Biography
   Biographical Documents............ Y-84, 85

   A Celebration of Literary Biography Y-98

   Conference on Modern Biography Y-85

   The Cult of Biography
      Excerpts from the Second Folio Debate:
      "Biographies are generally a disease of
      English Literature" Y-86

   New Approaches to Biography: Challenges
      from Critical Theory, USC Conference
      on Literary Studies, 1990 .... Y-90

   "The New Biography," by Virginia Woolf,
      New York Herald Tribune,
      30 October 1927............... DLB-149

   "The Practice of Biography," in *The English
      Sense of Humour and Other Essays*, by
      Harold Nicolson DLB-149

   "Principles of Biography," in *Elizabethan
      and Other Essays*, by Sidney Lee ... DLB-149

   Remarks at the Opening of "The Biographical
      Part of Literature" Exhibition, by
      William R. Cagle Y-98

   Survey of Literary Biographies Y-00

   A Transit of Poets and Others: American
      Biography in 1982 .... Y-82

   The Year in Literary
      Biography.................... Y-83–01

Biography, The Practice of:
   An Interview with B. L. Reid Y-83

   An Interview with David Herbert Donald... Y-87

   An Interview with Humphrey Carpenter.... Y-84

   An Interview with Joan Mellen Y-94

   An Interview with John Caldwell Guilds Y-92

   An Interview with William Manchester ... Y-85

John Bioren [publishing house] DLB-49

Bioy Casares, Adolfo 1914-1999 .... DLB-113

Birch, Thomas 1705-1766 .... DLB-336

Bird, Isabella Lucy 1831-1904 .... DLB-166

Bird, Robert Montgomery 1806-1854.... DLB-202

Bird, William 1888-1963 .... DLB-4; DS-15

   The Cost of the *Cantos*: William Bird
      to Ezra Pound Y-01

Birdsell, Sandra 1942- DLB-334

Birken, Sigmund von 1626-1681 .... DLB-164

Birney, Earle 1904-1995................. DLB-88

Birrell, Augustine 1850-1933 .... DLB-98

Bisher, Furman 1918- DLB-171

Bishop, Elizabeth
   1911-1979 .... DLB-5, 169; CDALB-6

   The Elizabeth Bishop Society Y-01

Bishop, John Peale 1892-1944 .... DLB-4, 9, 45

Bismarck, Otto von 1815-1898 .... DLB-129

Bisset, Robert 1759-1805 .... DLB-142

Bissett, Bill 1939- DLB-53

Bitov, Andrei Georgievich 1937- DLB-302

Bitzius, Albert (see Gotthelf, Jeremias)

Bjørnboe, Jens 1920-1976............. DLB-297

Bjørnson, Bjørnstjerne 1832-1910 ...... DLB-329

Bjørnvig, Thorkild 1918- DLB-214

Black, David (D. M.) 1941- DLB-40

Black, Gavin (Oswald Morris Wynd)
   1913-1998 .... DLB-276

Black, Lionel (Dudley Barker)
   1910-1980 .... DLB-276

Black, Winifred 1863-1936 .... DLB-25

Walter J. Black [publishing house]........ DLB-46

Blackamore, Arthur 1679-? DLB-24, 39

Blackburn, Alexander L. 1929- Y-85

Blackburn, John 1923-1993 .... DLB-261

Blackburn, Paul 1926-1971 .... DLB-16; Y-81

Blackburn, Thomas 1916-1977 .... DLB-27

Blacker, Terence 1948- DLB-271

Blackmore, R. D. 1825-1900 .... DLB-18

Blackmore, Sir Richard 1654-1729....... DLB-131

Blackmur, R. P. 1904-1965 .... DLB-63

Blackwell, Alice Stone 1857-1950........ DLB-303

Basil Blackwell, Publisher DLB-106

Blackstone, William 1723-1780 .... DLB-336

Blackwood, Algernon Henry
   1869-1951 .... DLB-153, 156, 178

Blackwood, Caroline 1931-1996 ..... DLB-14, 207

William Blackwood and Sons, Ltd........ DLB-154

Blackwood's Edinburgh Magazine
   1817-1980 .... DLB-110

Blades, William 1824-1890 .... DLB-184

Blaga, Lucian 1895-1961 .... DLB-220

Blagden, Isabella 1817?-1873 .... DLB-199

Blair, Eric Arthur (see Orwell, George)

Blair, Francis Preston 1791-1876.......... DLB-43

Blair, Hugh
   Lectures on Rhetoric and Belles Lettres (1783),
   [excerpts] DLB-31

Blair, James circa 1655-1743 .... DLB-24

Blair, John Durburrow 1759-1823 .... DLB-37

Blais, Marie-Claire 1939- DLB-53

Blaise, Clark 1940- DLB-53

Cumulative Index

Blake, George 1893-1961 . . . . DLB-191

Blake, Lillie Devereux 1833-1913 . . . . DLB-202, 221

Blake, Nicholas (C. Day Lewis)
1904-1972. . . . . DLB-77

Blake, William
1757-1827 . . . . . . DLB-93, 154, 163; CDBLB-3

The Blakiston Company. DLB-49

Blanchard, Stephen 1950- DLB-267

Blanchot, Maurice 1907-2003 . . . . DLB-72, 296

Blanckenburg, Christian Friedrich von
1744-1796 . . . . DLB-94

Blandiana, Ana 1942- DLB-232; CDWLB-4

Blanshard, Brand 1892-1987. . . . . .DLB-279

Blasco Ibáñez, Vicente 1867-1928 . . . . DLB-322

Blaser, Robin 1925- DLB-165

Blaumanis, Rudolfs 1863-1908 . . . . DLB-220

Bleasdale, Alan 1946- DLB-245

Bledsoe, Albert Taylor
1809-1877 . . . . DLB-3, 79, 248

Bleecker, Ann Eliza 1752-1783 . . . . DLB-200

Blelock and Company DLB-49

Blennerhassett, Margaret Agnew
1773-1842 . . . . DLB-99

Geoffrey Bles [publishing house] DLB-112

Blessington, Marguerite, Countess of
1789-1849 . . . . DLB-166

Blew, Mary Clearman 1939- DLB-256

Blicher, Steen Steensen 1782-1848 . . . . . . DLB-300

The Blickling Homilies circa 971 . . . . DLB-146

Blind, Mathilde 1841-1896 . . . . DLB-199

The Blind Assassin, 2000 Booker Prize winner,
Margaret Atwood. DLB-326

Blish, James 1921-1975 . . . . DLB-8

E. Bliss and E. White
[publishing house] DLB-49

Bliven, Bruce 1889-1977 . . . . DLB-137

Blixen, Karen 1885-1962 . . . . DLB-214

Bloch, Ernst 1885-1977. . . . . DLB-296

Bloch, Robert 1917-1994 . . . . DLB-44

Tribute to John D. MacDonald Y-86

Block, Lawrence 1938- DLB-226

Block, Rudolph (see Lessing, Bruno)

Blok, Aleksandr Aleksandrovich
1880-1921 . . . . DLB-295

Blondal, Patricia 1926-1959 . . . . DLB-88

Bloom, Harold 1930- DLB-67

Bloomer, Amelia 1818-1894 . . . . DLB-79

Bloomfield, Robert 1766-1823 . . . . DLB-93

Bloomsbury Group. DS-10

The *Dreadnought* Hoax DS-10

Bloor, Ella Reeve 1862-1951. . . . . DLB-303

Blotner, Joseph 1923- DLB-111

Blount, Thomas 1618?-1679 . . . . DLB-236

Bloy, Léon 1846-1917 . . . . DLB-123

Blume, Judy 1938- DLB-52

Tribute to Theodor Seuss Geisel Y-91

Blunck, Hans Friedrich 1888-1961 . . . . DLB-66

Blunden, Edmund 1896-1974 . . . . DLB-20, 100, 155

Blundeville, Thomas 1522?-1606 . . . . DLB-236

Blunt, Lady Anne Isabella Noel
1837-1917 .DLB-174

Blunt, Wilfrid Scawen 1840-1922 . . . . . DLB-19, 174

Bly, Carol 1930- DLB-335

Bly, Nellie (see Cochrane, Elizabeth)

Bly, Robert 1926- DLB-5

Blyton, Enid 1897-1968 . . . . DLB-160

Boaden, James 1762-1839 . . . . DLB-89

Boal, Augusto 1931- DLB-307

Boas, Frederick S. 1862-1957 . . . . DLB-149

The Bobbs-Merrill Company DLB-46, 291

The Bobbs-Merrill Archive at the
Lilly Library, Indiana University. Y-90

Boborykin, Petr Dmitrievich
1836-1921 . . . . DLB-238

Bobrov, Semen Sergeevich
1763?-1810 . . . . DLB-150

Bobrowski, Johannes 1917-1965 . . . . DLB-75

Bocage, Manuel Maria Barbosa du
1765-1805. DLB-287

Bodenheim, Maxwell 1892-1954 . . . . . DLB-9, 45

Bodenstedt, Friedrich von 1819-1892 . . . . DLB-129

Bodini, Vittorio 1914-1970 . . . . DLB-128

Bodkin, M. McDonnell 1850-1933 . . . . DLB-70

Bodley, Sir Thomas 1545-1613 . . . . DLB-213

Bodley Head DLB-112

Bodmer, Johann Jakob 1698-1783 . . . . DLB-97

Bodmershof, Imma von 1895-1982 . . . . . . DLB-85

Bodsworth, Fred 1918- DLB-68

Böðvar Guðmundsson 1939- DLB-293

Boehm, Sydney 1908-1990 . . . . DLB-44

Boer, Charles 1939- DLB-5

Boethius circa 480-circa 524 . . . . DLB-115

Boethius of Dacia circa 1240-? DLB-115

Bogan, Louise 1897-1970 . . . . DLB-45, 169

Bogarde, Dirk 1921-1999 . . . . DLB-14

Bogdanov, Aleksandr Aleksandrovich
1873-1928. DLB-295

Bogdanovich, Ippolit Fedorovich
circa 1743-1803 . . . . DLB-150

David Bogue [publishing house] DLB-106

Bohjalian, Chris 1960- DLB-292

Böhme, Jakob 1575-1624 . . . . DLB-164

H. G. Bohn [publishing house] DLB-106

Bohse, August 1661-1742 . . . . DLB-168

Boie, Heinrich Christian 1744-1806 . . . . . . DLB-94

Boileau-Despréaux, Nicolas 1636-1711 . . . .DLB-268

Bojunga, Lygia 1932- DLB-307

Bok, Edward W. 1863-1930 . . . . . . DLB-91; DS-16

Boland, Eavan 1944- DLB-40

Boldrewood, Rolf (Thomas Alexander Browne)
1826?-1915. . . . . DLB-230

Bolingbroke, Henry St. John, Viscount
1678-1751 . . . . DLB-101, 336

Böll, Heinrich
1917-1985 . . . . . DLB-69, 329; Y-85; CDWLB-2

Bolling, Robert 1738-1775 . . . . DLB-31

Bolotov, Andrei Timofeevich
1738-1833. DLB-150

Bolt, Carol 1941- DLB-60

Bolt, Robert 1924-1995 . . . . DLB-13, 233

Bolton, Herbert E. 1870-1953. . . . . .DLB-17

Bonarelli, Guidubaldo 1563-1608 . . . . DLB-339

Bonaventura DLB-90

Bonaventure circa 1217-1274 . . . . DLB-115

Bonaviri, Giuseppe 1924- DLB-177

Bond, Edward 1934- DLB-13, 310

Bond, Michael 1926- DLB-161

Bondarev, Iurii Vasil'evich 1924- DLB-302

The Bone People, 1985 Booker Prize winner,
Keri Hulme DLB-326

Albert and Charles Boni
[publishing house] DLB-46

Boni and Liveright DLB-46

Bonnefoy, Yves 1923- DLB-258

Bonner, Marita 1899-1971 . . . . DLB-228

Bonner, Paul Hyde 1893-1968 . . . . DS-17

Bonner, Sherwood (see McDowell, Katharine
Sherwood Bonner)

Robert Bonner's Sons. DLB-49

Bonnin, Gertrude Simmons (see Zitkala-Ša)

Bonsanti, Alessandro 1904-1984 . . . . .DLB-177

Bontempelli, Massimo 1878-1960 . . . . DLB-264

Bontemps, Arna 1902-1973 . . . . DLB-48, 51

The Book Buyer (1867-1880, 1884-1918,
1935-1938. . . . . DS-13

The Book League of America. DLB-46

Book Reviewing
The American Book Review: A Sketch . . . Y-92

Book Reviewing and the
Literary Scene Y-96, 97

Book Reviewing in America Y-87–94

Book Reviewing in America and the
Literary Scene Y-95

Book Reviewing in Texas. Y-94

Book Reviews in Glossy Magazines. Y-95

Do They or Don't They?
Writers Reading Book Reviews. Y-01

The Most Powerful Book Review
in America [*New York Times
Book Review*] Y-82

Some Surprises and Universal Truths Y-92

The Year in Book Reviewing and the
    Literary Situation Y-98

Book Supply Company DLB-49

The Book Trade History Group Y-93

The Booker Prize. Y-96–98
    Address by Anthony Thwaite,
        Chairman of the Booker Prize Judges
        Comments from Former Booker
        Prize Winners Y-86

Boorde, Andrew circa 1490-1549. . . . . . . DLB-136

Boorstin, Daniel J. 1914- DLB-17
    Tribute to Archibald MacLeish Y-82
    Tribute to Charles Scribner Jr. Y-95

Booth, Franklin 1874-1948. . . . . DLB-188

Booth, Mary L. 1831-1889 . . . . DLB-79

Booth, Philip 1925- Y-82

Booth, Wayne C. 1921- DLB-67

Booth, William 1829-1912. . . . . DLB-190

Bor, Josef 1906-1979. . . . . DLB-299

Borchardt, Rudolf 1877-1945 . . . . DLB-66

Borchert, Wolfgang 1921-1947. . . . . . . DLB-69, 124

Bording, Anders 1619-1677 . . . . DLB-300

Borel, Pétrus 1809-1859. . . . . DLB-119

Borgen, Johan 1902-1979. . . . . DLB-297

Borges, Jorge Luis
    1899-1986 . . . DLB-113, 283; Y-86; CDWLB-3
    The Poetry of Jorge Luis Borges Y-86
    A Personal Tribute Y-86

Borgese, Giuseppe Antonio 1882-1952 . . . DLB-264

Börne, Ludwig 1786-1837 . . . . DLB-90

Bornstein, Miriam 1950- DLB-209

Borowski, Tadeusz
    1922-1951 . . . . DLB-215; CDWLB-4

Borrow, George 1803-1881 . . . . . . DLB-21, 55, 166

Bosanquet, Bernard 1848-1923 . . . . DLB-262

Boscán, Juan circa 1490-1542 . . . . DLB-318

Bosch, Juan 1909-2001. . . . . DLB-145

Bosco, Henri 1888-1976. . . . . DLB-72

Bosco, Monique 1927- DLB-53

Bosman, Herman Charles 1905-1951 . . . . DLB-225

Bossuet, Jacques-Bénigne 1627-1704 . . . . . . DLB-268

Bostic, Joe 1908-1988. . . . . DLB-241

Boston, Lucy M. 1892-1990 . . . . DLB-161

Boston Quarterly Review DLB-1

Boston University
    Editorial Institute at Boston University. . . . Y-00
    Special Collections at Boston University. . . Y-99

Boswell, James
    1740-1795. . . . . DLB-104, 142; CDBLB-2

Boswell, Robert 1953- DLB-234

Bosworth, David Y-82
    Excerpt from "Excerpts from a Report
        of the Commission," in *The Death
        of Descartes* Y-82

Bote, Hermann circa 1460-circa 1520. . . . DLB-179

Botev, Khristo 1847-1876 . . . . DLB-147

Botkin, Vasilii Petrovich 1811-1869 . . . . . . DLB-277

Botta, Anne C. Lynch 1815-1891 . . . . . DLB-3, 250

Botto, Ján (see Krasko, Ivan)

Bottome, Phyllis 1882-1963. . . . . DLB-197

Bottomley, Gordon 1874-1948. . . . . DLB-10

Bottoms, David 1949- DLB-120; Y-83
    Tribute to James Dickey Y-97

Bottrall, Ronald 1906-1959 . . . . DLB-20

Bouchardy, Joseph 1810-1870 . . . . DLB-192

Boucher, Anthony 1911-1968 . . . . DLB-8

Boucher, Jonathan 1738-1804 . . . . DLB-31

Boucher de Boucherville, Georges
    1814-1894 . . . . DLB-99

Boudreau, Daniel (see Coste, Donat)

Bouhours, Dominique 1628-1702 . . . . DLB-268

Bourassa, Napoléon 1827-1916 . . . . DLB-99

Bourget, Paul 1852-1935 . . . . DLB-123

Bourinot, John George 1837-1902 . . . . DLB-99

Bourjaily, Vance 1922- DLB-2, 143

Bourne, Edward Gaylord 1860-1908. . . . . . DLB-47

Bourne, Randolph 1886-1918 . . . . DLB-63

Bousoño, Carlos 1923- DLB-108

Bousquet, Joë 1897-1950 . . . . DLB-72

Bova, Ben 1932- Y-81

Bovard, Oliver K. 1872-1945 . . . . DLB-25

Bove, Emmanuel 1898-1945 . . . . DLB-72

Bowen, Elizabeth
    1899-1973 . . . . DLB-15, 162; CDBLB-7

Bowen, Francis 1811-1890 . . . . DLB-1, 59, 235

Bowen, John 1924- DLB-13

Bowen, Marjorie 1886-1952. . . . . DLB-153

Bowen-Merrill Company DLB-49

Bowering, George 1935- DLB-53

Bowering, Marilyn 1949- DLB-334

Bowers, Bathsheba 1671-1718 . . . . DLB-200

Bowers, Claude G. 1878-1958 . . . . DLB-17

Bowers, Edgar 1924-2000 . . . . DLB-5

Bowers, Fredson Thayer
    1905-1991 . . . . DLB-140; Y-91
    The Editorial Style of Fredson Bowers Y-91
    Fredson Bowers and
        Studies in Bibliography. Y-91
    Fredson Bowers and the Cambridge
        Beaumont and Fletcher. Y-91
    Fredson Bowers as Critic of Renaissance
        Dramatic Literature Y-91
    Fredson Bowers as Music Critic Y-91
    Fredson Bowers, Master Teacher Y-91
    An Interview [on Nabokov] Y-80
    Working with Fredson Bowers Y-91

Bowles, Paul 1910-1999. . . . . . DLB-5, 6, 218; Y-99

Bowles, Samuel, III 1826-1878 . . . . DLB-43

Bowles, William Lisle 1762-1850 . . . . DLB-93

Bowling, Tim 1964- DLB-334

Bowman, Louise Morey 1882-1944. . . . . . . DLB-68

Bowne, Borden Parker 1847-1919 . . . . DLB-270

Boyd, James 1888-1944 . . . . DLB-9; DS-16

Boyd, John 1912-2002. . . . . DLB-310

Boyd, John 1919- DLB-8

Boyd, Martin 1893-1972 . . . . DLB-260

Boyd, Thomas 1898-1935 . . . . . DLB-9, 316; DS-16

Boyd, William 1952- DLB-231

Boye, Karin 1900-1941 . . . . DLB-259

Boyesen, Hjalmar Hjorth
    1848-1895 . . . . DLB-12, 71; DS-13

Boylan, Clare 1948- DLB-267

Boyle, Kay 1902-1992
     . . . . DLB-4, 9, 48, 86; DS-15; Y-93

Boyle, Roger, Earl of Orrery 1621-1679 . . . DLB-80

Boyle, T. Coraghessan
    1948- DLB-218, 278; Y-86

Božić, Mirko 1919- DLB-181

Bracciolini, Francesco 1566-1645. . . . . DLB-339

Brackenbury, Alison 1953- DLB-40

Brackenridge, Hugh Henry
    1748-1816 . . . . DLB-11, 37
    The Rising Glory of America DLB-37

Brackett, Charles 1892-1969 . . . . DLB-26

Brackett, Leigh 1915-1978 . . . . DLB-8, 26

John Bradburn [publishing house] DLB-49

Bradbury, Malcolm 1932-2000 . . . . . . DLB-14, 207

Bradbury, Ray 1920- DLB-2, 8; CDALB-6

Bradbury and Evans DLB-106

Braddon, Mary Elizabeth
    1835-1915 . . . . DLB-18, 70, 156

Bradford, Andrew 1686-1742. . . . . DLB-43, 73

Bradford, Gamaliel 1863-1932. . . . . DLB-17

Bradford, John 1749-1830 . . . . DLB-43

Bradford, Roark 1896-1948. . . . . DLB-86

Bradford, William 1590-1657 . . . . DLB-24, 30

Bradford, William, III 1719-1791. . . . . . DLB-43, 73

Bradlaugh, Charles 1833-1891 . . . . DLB-57

Bradley, David 1950- DLB-33

Bradley, F. H. 1846-1924. . . . . DLB-262

Bradley, Katherine Harris (see Field, Michael)

Bradley, Marion Zimmer 1930-1999 . . . . . . DLB-8

Bradley, William Aspenwall 1878-1939 . . . . DLB-4

Ira Bradley and Company DLB-49

J. W. Bradley and Company DLB-49

Bradshaw, Henry 1831-1886 . . . . DLB-184

Bradstreet, Anne
    1612 or 1613-1672. . . . . . . DLB-24; CDALB-2

Bradūnas, Kazys 1917- DLB-220

Cumulative Index

Bradwardine, Thomas circa 1295-1349 .. DLB-115

Brady, Frank 1924-1986.............. DLB-111

Frederic A. Brady [publishing house]..... DLB-49

Braga, Rubem 1913-1990............ DLB-307

Bragg, Melvyn 1939- DLB-14, 271

Brahe, Tycho 1546-1601.............. DLB-300

Charles H. Brainard [publishing house] ... DLB-49

Braine, John 1922-1986 . DLB-15; Y-86; CDBLB-7

Braithwait, Richard 1588-1673 .... DLB-151

Braithwaite, William Stanley
  1878-1962................... DLB-50, 54

Bräker, Ulrich 1735-1798 .... DLB-94

Bramah, Ernest 1868-1942............. DLB-70

Branagan, Thomas 1774-1843 .... DLB-37

Brancati, Vitaliano 1907-1954.......... DLB-264

Branch, William Blackwell 1927- DLB-76

Brand, Christianna 1907-1988 ....DLB-276

Brand, Dionne 1953- DLB-334

Brand, Max (see Faust, Frederick Schiller)

Brandão, Raul 1867-1930 .... DLB-287

Branden Press.................... DLB-46

Brandes, Georg 1842-1927 .... DLB-300

Branner, H.C. 1903-1966 .... DLB-214

Brant, Sebastian 1457-1521 ....DLB-179

Brantôme (Pierre de Bourdeille)
  1540?-1614................... DLB-327

Brassey, Lady Annie (Allnutt)
  1839-1887................... DLB-166

Brathwaite, Edward Kamau
  1930- DLB-125; CDWLB-3

Brault, Jacques 1933- DLB-53

Braun, Matt 1932- DLB-212

Braun, Volker 1939- DLB-75, 124

Brautigan, Richard
  1935-1984 ....DLB-2, 5, 206; Y-80, 84

Braverman, Kate 1950- DLB-335

Braxton, Joanne M. 1950- DLB-41

Bray, Anne Eliza 1790-1883 .... DLB-116

Bray, Thomas 1656-1730 .... DLB-24

Brazdžionis, Bernardas 1907-2002 ...... DLB-220

George Braziller [publishing house] DLB-46

The Bread Loaf Writers' Conference 1983.... Y-84

Breasted, James Henry 1865-1935 .... DLB-47

Brecht, Bertolt
  1898-1956 .... DLB-56, 124; CDWLB-2

Bredel, Willi 1901-1964 .... DLB-56

Bregendahl, Marie 1867-1940.......... DLB-214

Breitinger, Johann Jakob 1701-1776....... DLB-97

Brekke, Paal 1923-1993 .... DLB-297

Bremser, Bonnie 1939- DLB-16

Bremser, Ray 1934-1998 .... DLB-16

Brennan, Christopher 1870-1932 .... DLB-230

Brentano, Bernard von 1901-1964 .... DLB-56

Brentano, Clemens 1778-1842 .... DLB-90

Brentano, Franz 1838-1917............ DLB-296

Brentano's...................... DLB-49

Brenton, Howard 1942- DLB-13

Breslin, Jimmy 1929-1996............ DLB-185

Breton, André 1896-1966.......... DLB-65, 258

Breton, Nicholas circa 1555-circa 1626... DLB-136

The Breton Lays
  1300-early fifteenth century DLB-146

Brett, Lily 1946- DLB-325

Brett, Simon 1945- DLB-276

Brewer, Gil 1922-1983 .... DLB-306

Brewer, Luther A. 1858-1933 .... DLB-187

Brewer, Warren and Putnam DLB-46

Brewster, Elizabeth 1922- DLB-60

Breytenbach, Breyten 1939- DLB-225

Bridge, Ann (Lady Mary Dolling Sanders O'Malley)
  1889-1974.................... DLB-191

Bridge, Horatio 1806-1893 .... DLB-183

Bridgers, Sue Ellen 1942- DLB-52

Bridges, Robert
  1844-1930 .... DLB-19, 98; CDBLB-5

The Bridgewater Library DLB-213

Bridie, James 1888-1951 .... DLB-10

Brieux, Eugene 1858-1932 .... DLB-192

Brigadere, Anna
  1861-1933 .... DLB-220; CDWLB-4

Briggs, Charles Frederick
  1804-1877 .... DLB-3, 250

Brighouse, Harold 1882-1958.......... DLB-10

Bright, Mary Chavelita Dunne
  (see Egerton, George)

Brightman, Edgar Sheffield 1884-1953....DLB-270

B. J. Brimmer Company............... DLB-46

Brines, Francisco 1932- DLB-134

Brink, André 1935- DLB-225

Brinley, George, Jr. 1817-1875.......... DLB-140

Brinnin, John Malcolm 1916-1998 ...... DLB-48

Brisbane, Albert 1809-1890 .... DLB-3, 250

Brisbane, Arthur 1864-1936 .... DLB-25

British Academy.................... DLB-112

The British Critic 1793-1843 .... DLB-110

British Library
  The American Trust for the
    British Library.................. Y-96
  The British Library and the Regular
    Readers' Group.................. Y-91
  Building the New British Library
    at St Pancras Y-94

British Literary Prizes............DLB-207; Y-98

British Literature
  The "Angry Young Men"........... DLB-15
  Author-Printers, 1476-1599 .... DLB-167

The Comic Tradition Continued..... DLB-15

Documents on Sixteenth-Century
  Literature................. DLB-167, 172

Eikon Basilike 1649 .... DLB-151

Letter from London.................. Y-96

A Mirror for Magistrates DLB-167

"Modern English Prose" (1876),
  by George Saintsbury DLB-57

Sex, Class, Politics, and Religion [in the
  British Novel, 1930-1959]........ DLB-15

Victorians on Rhetoric and Prose
  Style........................ DLB-57

The Year in British Fiction Y-99–01

"You've Never Had It So Good," Gusted
  by "Winds of Change": British
  Fiction in the 1950s, 1960s,
  and After.................... DLB-14

British Literature, Old and Middle English
  Anglo-Norman Literature in the
    Development of Middle English
    Literature................... DLB-146

  The *Alliterative Morte Arthure* and the
    Stanzaic Morte Arthur
    circa 1350-1400................ DLB-146

  Ancrene Riwle circa 1200-1225 .... DLB-146

  The *Anglo-Saxon Chronicle* circa
    890-1154 .... DLB-146

  The *Battle of Maldon* circa 1000 ..... DLB-146

  Beowulf circa 900-1000 or
    790-825 .... DLB-146; CDBLB-1

  The Blickling Homilies circa 971 .... DLB-146

  The Breton Lays
    1300-early fifteenth century..... DLB-146

  The *Castle of Perseverance*
    circa 1400-1425 .... DLB-146

  The Celtic Background to Medieval
    English Literature DLB-146

  The Chester Plays circa 1505-1532;
    revisions until 1575 .... DLB-146

  Cursor Mundi circa 1300 .... DLB-146

  The English Language: 410
    to 1500 .... DLB-146

  The Germanic Epic and Old English
    Heroic Poetry: *Widsith, Waldere,*
    and *The Fight at Finnsburg*....... DLB-146

  Judith circa 930 .... DLB-146

  The Matter of England 1240-1400... DLB-146

  The Matter of Rome early twelfth to
    late fifteenth centuries DLB-146

  Middle English Literature:
    An Introduction.............. DLB-146

  The Middle English Lyric DLB-146

  Morality Plays: *Mankind* circa 1450-1500
    and *Everyman* circa 1500........ DLB-146

  N-Town Plays circa 1468 to early
    sixteenth century............. DLB-146

  Old English Literature:
    An Introduction.............. DLB-146

  Old English Riddles
    eighth to tenth centuries DLB-146

  The Owl and the Nightingale
    circa 1189-1199 .... DLB-146

  The Paston Letters 1422-1509 .... DLB-146

The Seafarer circa 970 . . . . DLB-146

The *South English Legendary* circa
  thirteenth to fifteenth centuries DLB-146

*The British Review and London Critical
  Journal* 1811-1825 . . . . DLB-110

Brito, Aristeo 1942- DLB-122

Brittain, Vera 1893-1970. . . . . DLB-191

Briusov, Valerii Iakovlevich
  1873-1924 . . . . DLB-295

Brizeux, Auguste 1803-1858 . . . . DLB-217

Broadway Publishing Company DLB-46

Broch, Hermann
  1886-1951 . . . . DLB-85, 124; CDWLB-2

Brochu, André 1942- DLB-53

Brock, Edwin 1927-1997 . . . . DLB-40

Brockes, Barthold Heinrich
  1680-1747 . . . . DLB-168

Brod, Max 1884-1968 . . . . DLB-81

Brodber, Erna 1940- DLB-157

Brodhead, John R. 1814-1873 . . . . DLB-30

Brodkey, Harold 1930-1996. . . . . DLB-130

Brodsky, Joseph (Iosif Aleksandrovich Brodsky)
  1940-1996 . . . . DLB-285, 329; Y-87

  Nobel Lecture 1987. . . . . .Y-87

Brodsky, Michael 1948- DLB-244

Brocg, Bob 1918- DLB-171

Brøgger, Suzanne 1944- DLB-214

Brome, Richard circa 1590-1652 . . . . DLB-58

Brome, Vincent 1910-2004 . . . . DLB-155

Bromfield, Louis 1896-1956. . . . . . . DLB-4, 9, 86

Bromige, David 1933- DLB-193

Broner, E. M. 1930- DLB-28

  Tribute to Bernard Malamud Y-86

Bronk, William 1918-1999. . . . . DLB-165

Bronnen, Arnolt 1895-1959 . . . . DLB-124

Brontë, Anne 1820-1849 . . . . DLB-21, 199

Brontë, Charlotte
  1816-1855 . . . . . . DLB-21, 159, 199; CDBLB-4

Brontë, Emily
  1818-1848 . . . . . . DLB-21, 32, 199; CDBLB-4

The Brontë Society Y-98

Brook, Stephen 1947- DLB-204

Brook Farm 1841-1847 . . . . DLB-1; 223; DS-5

Brooke, Frances 1724-1789. . . . . DLB-39, 99

Brooke, Henry 1703?-1783. . . . . DLB-39

Brooke, L. Leslie 1862-1940 . . . . DLB-141

Brooke, Margaret, Ranee of Sarawak
  1849-1936 . . . . DLB-174

Brooke, Rupert
  1887-1915 . . . . DLB-19, 216; CDBLB-6

  The Friends of the Dymock Poets. Y-00

Brooker, Bertram 1888-1955 . . . . DLB-88

Brooke-Rose, Christine 1923- DLB-14, 231

Brookner, Anita 1928- DLB-194, 326; Y-87

Brooks, Charles Timothy 1813-1883. . . DLB-1, 243

Brooks, Cleanth 1906-1994 . . . . DLB-63; Y-94

  Tribute to Katherine Anne Porter Y-80

  Tribute to Walker Percy Y-90

Brooks, Gwendolyn
  1917-2000 . . . . DLB-5, 76, 165; CDALB-1

  Tribute to Julian Mayfield Y-84

Brooks, Jeremy 1926-1994. . . . . DLB-14

Brooks, Mel 1926- DLB-26

Brooks, Noah 1830-1903 . . . . DLB-42; DS-13

Brooks, Richard 1912-1992 . . . . DLB-44

Brooks, Van Wyck 1886-1963 . . . . DLB-45, 63, 103

Brophy, Brigid 1929-1995 . . . . DLB-14, 70, 271

Brophy, John 1899-1965 . . . . DLB-191

Brorson, Hans Adolph 1694-1764 . . . . DLB-300

Brossard, Chandler 1922-1993 . . . . DLB-16

Brossard, Nicole 1943- DLB-53

Broster, Dorothy Kathleen 1877-1950 . . . . DLB-160

Brother Antoninus (see Everson, William)

Brotherton, Lord 1856-1930 . . . . DLB-184

Brougham, John 1810-1880 . . . . DLB-11

Brougham and Vaux, Henry Peter
  Brougham, Baron 1778-1868. . . . DLB-110, 158

Broughton, James 1913-1999. . . . . DLB-5

Broughton, Rhoda 1840-1920 . . . . DLB-18

Broun, Heywood 1888-1939 . . . . DLB-29, 171

Browder, Earl 1891-1973 . . . . DLB-303

Brown, Alice 1856-1948. . . . . DLB-78

Brown, Bob 1886-1959 . . . . DLB-4, 45; DS-15

Brown, Cecil 1943- DLB-33

Brown, Charles Brockden
  1771-1810 . . . . DLB-37, 59, 73; CDALB-2

Brown, Christy 1932-1981 . . . . DLB-14

Brown, Dee 1908-2002 . . . . .Y-80

Brown, Frank London 1927-1962 . . . . DLB-76

Brown, Fredric 1906-1972 . . . . DLB-8

Brown, George Mackay
  1921-1996 . . . . DLB-14, 27, 139, 271

Brown, Harry 1917-1986 . . . . DLB-26

Brown, Ian 1945- DLB-310

Brown, Larry 1951- DLB-234, 292

Brown, Lew 1893-1958 . . . . DLB-265

Brown, Marcia 1918- DLB-61

Brown, Margaret Wise 1910-1952 . . . . DLB-22

Brown, Morna Doris (see Ferrars, Elizabeth)

Brown, Oliver Madox 1855-1874. . . . . DLB-21

Brown, Sterling 1901-1989 . . . . DLB-48, 51, 63

Brown, T. E. 1830-1897 . . . . DLB-35

Brown, Thomas Alexander (see Boldrewood, Rolf)

Brown, Warren 1894-1978 . . . . DLB-241

Brown, William Hill 1765-1793 . . . . DLB-37

Brown, William Wells
  1815-1884 . . . . DLB-3, 50, 183, 248

Brown University
  The Festival of Vanguard Narrative. Y-93

Browne, Charles Farrar 1834-1867 . . . . DLB-11

Browne, Frances 1816-1879 . . . . DLB-199

Browne, Francis Fisher 1843-1913. . . . . . . DLB-79

Browne, Howard 1908-1999 . . . . DLB-226

Browne, J. Ross 1821-1875 . . . . DLB-202

Browne, Michael Dennis 1940- DLB-40

Browne, Sir Thomas 1605-1682 . . . . DLB-151

Browne, William, of Tavistock
  1590-1645 . . . . DLB-121

Browne, Wynyard 1911-1964 . . . . DLB-13, 233

Browne and Nolan. DLB-106

Brownell, W. C. 1851-1928 . . . . DLB-71

Browning, Elizabeth Barrett
  1806-1861 . . . . DLB-32, 199; CDBLB-4

Browning, Robert
  1812-1889 . . . . DLB-32, 163; CDBLB-4

  Essay on Chatterton DLB-32

  Introductory Essay: *Letters of Percy
    Bysshe Shelley* (1852) DLB-32

  "The Novel in [Robert Browning's]
    'The Ring and the Book'" (1912),
    by Henry James DLB-32

Brownjohn, Allan 1931- DLB-40

  Tribute to John Betjeman Y-84

Brownson, Orestes Augustus
  1803-1876 . . . . DLB-1, 59, 73, 243; DS-5

Bruccoli, Matthew J. 1931- DLB-103

  Joseph [Heller] and George [V. Higgins] . . .Y-99

  Response [to Busch on Fitzgerald]. Y-96

  Tribute to Albert Erskine Y-93

  Tribute to Charles E. Feinberg Y-88

  Working with Fredson Bowers Y-91

Bruce, Charles 1906-1971 . . . . DLB-68

Bruce, John Edward 1856-1924

  Three Documents [African American
    poets] DLB-50

Bruce, Leo 1903-1979 . . . . DLB-77

Bruce, Mary Grant 1878-1958. . . . . DLB-230

Bruce, Philip Alexander 1856-1933 . . . . DLB-47

Bruce-Novoa, Juan 1944- DLB-82

Bruckman, Clyde 1894-1955. . . . . DLB-26

Bruckner, Ferdinand 1891-1958. . . . . DLB-118

Brundage, John Herbert (see Herbert, John)

Brunner, John 1934-1995. . . . . DLB-261

  Tribute to Theodore Sturgeon Y-85

Brutus, Dennis
  1924- DLB-117, 225; CDWLB-3

Bryan, C. D. B. 1936- DLB-185

Bryan, William Jennings 1860-1925 . . . . . DLB-303

Bryant, Arthur 1899-1985 . . . . DLB-149

Cumulative Index

Bryant, William Cullen 1794-1878 .... DLB-3, 43, 59, 189, 250; CDALB-2

Bryce, James 1838-1922 .... DLB-166, 190

Bryce Echenique, Alfredo 1939- DLB-145; CDWLB-3

Bryden, Bill 1942- DLB-233

Brydges, Sir Samuel Egerton 1762-1837 .... DLB-107, 142

Bryskett, Lodowick 1546?-1612 .... DLB-167

Buchan, John 1875-1940 .... DLB-34, 70, 156

Buchanan, George 1506-1582 .... DLB-132

Buchanan, Robert 1841-1901 .... DLB-18, 35

"The Fleshly School of Poetry and Other Phenomena of the Day" (1872) DLB-35

"The Fleshly School of Poetry: Mr. D. G. Rossetti" (1871), by Thomas Maitland DLB-35

Buchler, Justus 1914-1991 .... DLB-279

Buchman, Sidney 1902-1975 .... DLB-26

Buchner, Augustus 1591-1661 .... DLB-164

Büchner, Georg 1813-1837 .... DLB-133; CDWLB-2

Bucholtz, Andreas Heinrich 1607-1671 .... DLB-168

Buck, Pearl S. 1892-1973 ...... DLB-9, 102, 329; CDALB-7

Bucke, Charles 1781-1846 .... DLB-110

Bucke, Richard Maurice 1837-1902 ...... DLB-99

Buckingham, Edwin 1810-1833 .... DLB-73

Buckingham, Joseph Tinker 1779-1861.... DLB-73

Buckler, Ernest 1908-1984 .... DLB-68

Buckley, Vincent 1925-1988 .... DLB-289

Buckley, William F., Jr. 1925- DLB-137; Y-80

Publisher's Statement From the Initial Issue of *National Review* (19 November 1955) DLB-137

Buckminster, Joseph Stevens 1784-1812 .... DLB-37

Buckner, Robert 1906-1989 .... DLB-26

Budd, Thomas ?-1698 .... DLB-24

Budé, Guillaume 1468-1540 .... DLB-327

Budrys, A. J. 1931- DLB-8

Buechner, Frederick 1926- Y-80

Buell, John 1927- DLB-53

Buenaventura, Enrique 1925-2003 ...... DLB-305

Bufalino, Gesualdo 1920-1996 .... DLB-196

Buffon, Georges-Louis Leclerc de 1707-1788 .... DLB-313

"Le Discours sur le style" DLB-314

Job Buffum [publishing house]......... DLB-49

Bugnet, Georges 1879-1981 .... DLB-92

al-Buhturi 821-897 .... DLB-311

Buies, Arthur 1840-1901 .... DLB-99

Bukiet, Melvin Jules 1953- DLB-299

Bukowski, Charles 1920-1994 ... DLB-5, 130, 169

Bulatović, Miodrag 1930-1991 .... DLB-181; CDWLB-4

Bulgakov, Mikhail Afanas'evich 1891-1940 .... DLB-272

Bulgarin, Faddei Venediktovich 1789-1859 .... DLB-198

Bulger, Bozeman 1877-1932 .... DLB-171

Bull, Olaf 1883-1933................. DLB-297

Bullein, William between 1520 and 1530-1576....... DLB-167

Bullins, Ed 1935- DLB-7, 38, 249

Bulosan, Carlos 1911-1956........... DLB-312

Bulwer, John 1606-1656 .... DLB-236

Bulwer-Lytton, Edward (also Edward Bulwer) 1803-1873 .... DLB-21

"On Art in Fiction "(1838).......... DLB-21

Bumpus, Jerry 1937- Y-81

Bunce and Brother DLB-49

Bunin, Ivan 1870-1953 .... DLB-317, 329

Bunner, H. C. 1855-1896 .... DLB-78, 79

Bunting, Basil 1900-1985 .... DLB-20

Buntline, Ned (Edward Zane Carroll Judson) 1821-1886................ DLB-186

Bunyan, John 1628-1688 ..... DLB-39; CDBLB-2

The Author's Apology for His Book DLB-39

Buonarroti il Giovane, Michelangelo 1568-1646 .... DLB-339

Burch, Robert 1925- DLB-52

Burciaga, José Antonio 1940- DLB-82

Burdekin, Katharine (Murray Constantine) 1896-1963 .... DLB-255

Bürger, Gottfried August 1747-1794 ...... DLB-94

Burgess, Anthony (John Anthony Burgess Wilson) 1917-1993 ...... DLB-14, 194, 261; CDBLB-8

The Anthony Burgess Archive at the Harry Ransom Humanities Research Center Y-98

Anthony Burgess's *99 Novels*: An Opinion Poll Y-84

Burgess, Gelett 1866-1951 .... DLB-11

Burgess, John W. 1844-1931........... DLB-47

Burgess, Thornton W. 1874-1965....... DLB-22

Burgess, Stringer and Company......... DLB-49

Burgos, Julia de 1914-1953............ DLB-290

Burick, Si 1909-1986................. DLB-171

Burk, John Daly circa 1772-1808 .... DLB-37

Burk, Ronnie 1955- DLB-209

Burke, Edmund 1729?-1797 ... DLB-104, 252, 336

Burke, James Lee 1936- DLB-226

Burke, Johnny 1908-1964 .... DLB-265

Burke, Kenneth 1897-1993 ...... DLB-45, 63

Burke, Thomas 1886-1945 .... DLB-197

Burley, Dan 1907-1962 .... DLB-241

Burley, W. J. 1914- DLB-276

Burlingame, Edward Livermore 1848-1922 .... DLB-79

Burliuk, David 1882-1967 .... DLB-317

Burman, Carina 1960- DLB-257

Burnard, Bonnie 1945- DLB-334

Burnet, Gilbert 1643-1715 .... DLB-101

Burnett, Frances Hodgson 1849-1924 .... DLB-42, 141; DS-13, 14

Burnett, W. R. 1899-1982........... DLB-9, 226

Burnett, Whit 1899-1973 .... DLB-137

Burney, Charles 1726-1814............ DLB-336

Burney, Fanny 1752-1840............. DLB-39

Dedication, *The Wanderer* (1814)...... DLB-39

Preface to *Evelina* (1778) DLB-39

Burns, Alan 1929- DLB-14, 194

Burns, Joanne 1945- DLB-289

Burns, John Horne 1916-1953 .... Y-85

Burns, Robert 1759-1796 .... DLB-109; CDBLB-3

Burns and Oates.................... DLB-106

Burnshaw, Stanley 1906- DLB-48; Y-97

James Dickey and Stanley Burnshaw Correspondence Y-02

Review of Stanley Burnshaw: The Collected Poems and Selected Prose Y-02

Tribute to Robert Penn Warren......... Y-89

Burr, C. Chauncey 1815?-1883 .... DLB-79

Burr, Esther Edwards 1732-1758....... DLB-200

Burroughs, Edgar Rice 1875-1950 .... DLB-8

The Burroughs Bibliophiles............ Y-98

Burroughs, John 1837-1921 ....DLB-64, 275

Burroughs, Margaret T. G. 1917- DLB-41

Burroughs, William S., Jr. 1947-1981 ..... DLB-16

Burroughs, William Seward 1914-1997 .... DLB-2, 8, 16, 152, 237; Y-81, 97

Burroway, Janet 1936- DLB-6

Burt, Maxwell Struthers 1882-1954 .... DLB-86; DS-16

A. L. Burt and Company DLB-49

Burton, Hester 1913-2000 .... DLB-161

Burton, Isabel Arundell 1831-1896 ..... DLB-166

Burton, Miles (see Rhode, John)

Burton, Richard Francis 1821-1890 .... DLB-55, 166, 184

Burton, Robert 1577-1640............. DLB-151

Burton, Virginia Lee 1909-1968 .... DLB-22

Burton, William Evans 1804-1860 .... DLB-73

Burwell, Adam Hood 1790-1849 .... DLB-99

Bury, Lady Charlotte 1775-1861........ DLB-116

Busch, Frederick 1941-2006 .... DLB-6, 218

Excerpts from Frederick Busch's USC Remarks [on F. Scott Fitzgerald] Y-96

Tribute to James Laughlin Y-97

Tribute to Raymond Carver Y-88

Busch, Niven 1903-1991 . . . . DLB-44

Busenello, Gian Francesco 1598-1659 . . . . DLB-339

Bushnell, Horace 1802-1876 . . . . DS-13

Business & Literature
　The Claims of Business and Literature:
　　An Undergraduate Essay by
　　Maxwell Perkins Y-01

Bussières, Arthur de 1877-1913 . . . . DLB-92

Butler, Charles circa 1560-1647 . . . . DLB-236

Butler, Guy 1918- DLB-225

Butler, Joseph 1692-1752 . . . . DLB-252

Butler, Josephine Elizabeth 1828-1906 . . . . DLB-190

Butler, Juan 1942-1981 . . . . DLB-53

Butler, Judith 1956- DLB-246

Butler, Octavia E. 1947-2006 . . . . DLB-33

Butler, Pierce 1884-1953 . . . . DLB-187

Butler, Robert Olen 1945- DLB-173, 335

Butler, Samuel 1613-1680 . . . . DLB-101, 126

Butler, Samuel
　1835-1902 . . . . DLB-18, 57, 174; CDBLB-5

Butler, William Francis 1838-1910 . . . . DLB-166

E. H. Butler and Company DLB-49

Butor, Michel 1926- DLB-83

Nathaniel Butter
　[publishing house] DLB-170

Butterworth, Hezekiah 1839-1905 . . . . DLB-42

Buttitta, Ignazio 1899-1997 . . . . DLB-114

Butts, Mary 1890-1937 . . . . DLB-240

Buzo, Alex 1944- DLB-289

Buzzati, Dino 1906-1972 . . . . DLB-177

Byars, Betsy 1928- DLB-52

Byatt, A. S. 1936- DLB-14, 194, 319, 326

Byles, Mather 1707-1788 . . . . DLB-24

Henry Bynneman
　[publishing house] DLB-170

Bynner, Witter 1881-1968 . . . . DLB-54

Byrd, William circa 1543-1623 . . . . DLB-172

Byrd, William, II 1674-1744 . . . . DLB-24, 140

Byrne, John Keyes (see Leonard, Hugh)

Byron, George Gordon, Lord
　1788-1824 . . . . DLB-96, 110; CDBLB-3

　The Byron Society of America Y-00

Byron, Robert 1905-1941 . . . . DLB-195

Byzantine Novel, The Spanish DLB-318

C

Caballero Bonald, José Manuel
　1926- DLB-108

Cabañero, Eladio 1930- DLB-134

Cabell, James Branch 1879-1958 . . . . DLB-9, 78

Cabeza de Baca, Manuel 1853-1915 . . . . . DLB-122

Cabeza de Baca Gilbert, Fabiola
　1898-1993 . . . . DLB-122

Cable, George Washington
　1844-1925 . . . . DLB-12, 74; DS-13

Cable, Mildred 1878-1952 . . . . DLB-195

Cabral, Manuel del 1907-1999 . . . . DLB-283

Cabral de Melo Neto, João
　1920-1999 . . . . DLB-307

Cabrera, Lydia 1900-1991 . . . . DLB-145

Cabrera Infante, Guillermo
　1929- DLB-113; CDWLB-3

Cabrujas, José Ignacio 1937-1995 . . . . DLB-305

Cadell [publishing house] DLB-154

Cady, Edwin H. 1917- DLB-103

Caedmon fl. 658-680 . . . . DLB-146

Caedmon School circa 660-899 . . . . DLB-146

Caesar, Irving 1895-1996 . . . . DLB-265

Cafés, Brasseries, and Bistros DS-15

Cage, John 1912-1992 . . . . DLB-193

Cahan, Abraham 1860-1951 . . . . DLB-9, 25, 28

Cahn, Sammy 1913-1993 . . . . DLB-265

Cain, George 1943- DLB-33

Cain, James M. 1892-1977 . . . . DLB-226

Cain, Paul (Peter Ruric, George Sims)
　1902-1966 . . . . DLB-306

Caird, Edward 1835-1908 . . . . DLB-262

Caird, Mona 1854-1932 . . . . DLB-197

Čaks, Aleksandrs
　1901-1950 . . . . DLB-220; CDWLB-4

Caldecott, Randolph 1846-1886 . . . . DLB-163

John Calder Limited
　[Publishing house] DLB-112

Calderón de la Barca, Fanny
　1804-1882 . . . . DLB-183

Caldwell, Ben 1937- DLB-38

Caldwell, Erskine 1903-1987 . . . . DLB-9, 86

H. M. Caldwell Company DLB-49

Caldwell, Taylor 1900-1985 . . . . DS-17

Calhoun, John C. 1782-1850 . . . . DLB-3, 248

Călinescu, George 1899-1965 . . . . DLB-220

Calisher, Hortense 1911- DLB-2, 218

Calkins, Mary Whiton 1863-1930 . . . . DLB-270

Callaghan, Mary Rose 1944- DLB-207

Callaghan, Morley 1903-1990 . . . . . DLB-68; DS-15

Callahan, S. Alice 1868-1894 . . . . DLB-175, 221

Callaloo [journal] Y-87

Callimachus circa 305 B.C.-240 B.C. DLB-176

Calmer, Edgar 1907-1986 . . . . DLB-4

Calverley, C. S. 1831-1884 . . . . DLB-35

Calvert, George Henry
　1803-1889 . . . . DLB-1, 64, 248

Calverton, V. F. (George Goetz)
　1900-1940 . . . . DLB-303

Calvin, Jean 1509-1564 . . . . DLB-327

Calvino, Italo 1923-1985 . . . . DLB-196

Cambridge, Ada 1844-1926 . . . . DLB-230

Cambridge Press DLB-49

Cambridge Songs (Carmina Cantabrigensia)
　circa 1050 . . . . DLB-148

Cambridge University
　Cambridge and the Apostles DS-5

Cambridge University Press DLB-170

Camden, William 1551-1623 . . . . DLB-172

Camden House: An Interview with
　James Hardin Y-92

Cameron, Eleanor 1912-2000 . . . . DLB-52

Cameron, George Frederick
　1854-1885 . . . . DLB-99

Cameron, Lucy Lyttelton 1781-1858 . . . . . DLB-163

Cameron, Peter 1959- DLB-234

Cameron, William Bleasdell 1862-1951 . . . . DLB-99

Camm, John 1718-1778 . . . . DLB-31

Camões, Luís de 1524-1580 . . . . DLB-287

Camon, Ferdinando 1935- DLB-196

Camp, Walter 1859-1925 . . . . DLB-241

Campana, Dino 1885-1932 . . . . DLB-114

Campbell, Bebe Moore 1950-2006 . . . . . . DLB-227

Campbell, David 1915-1979 . . . . DLB-260

Campbell, Gabrielle Margaret Vere
　(see Shearing, Joseph, and Bowen, Marjorie)

Campbell, James Dykes 1838-1895 . . . . . . DLB-144

Campbell, James Edwin 1867-1896 . . . . . . DLB-50

Campbell, John 1653-1728 . . . . DLB-43

Campbell, John W., Jr. 1910-1971 . . . . DLB-8

Campbell, Ramsey 1946- DLB-261

Campbell, Robert 1927-2000 . . . . DLB-306

Campbell, Roy 1901-1957 . . . . DLB-20, 225

Campbell, Thomas 1777-1844 . . . . DLB-93, 144

Campbell, William Edward (see March, William)

Campbell, William Wilfred 1858-1918 . . . . DLB-92

Campion, Edmund 1539-1581 . . . . DLB-167

Campion, Thomas
　1567-1620 . . . . DLB-58, 172; CDBLB-1

Campo, Rafael 1964- DLB-282

Campton, David 1924- DLB-245

Camus, Albert 1913-1960 . . . . . . DLB-72, 321, 329

Camus, Jean-Pierre 1584-1652 . . . . DLB-268

The Canadian Publishers' Records Database . . . Y-96

Canby, Henry Seidel 1878-1961 . . . . DLB-91

Cancioneros DLB-286

Candelaria, Cordelia 1943- DLB-82

Candelaria, Nash 1928- DLB-82

Candide, Voltaire DLB-314

Canetti, Elias
　1905-1994 . . . . . DLB-85, 124, 329; CDWLB-2

Canham, Erwin Dain 1904-1982 . . . . DLB-127

Canin, Ethan 1960- DLB-335

Cumulative Index

Canitz, Friedrich Rudolph Ludwig von
   1654-1699 . . . . DLB-168

Cankar, Ivan 1876-1918 . . . . . DLB-147; CDWLB-4

Cannan, Gilbert 1884-1955 . . . . DLB-10, 197

Cannan, Joanna 1896-1961 . . . . DLB-191

Cannell, Kathleen 1891-1974 . . . . DLB-4

Cannell, Skipwith 1887-1957. . . . . DLB-45

Canning, George 1770-1827 . . . . DLB-158

Cannon, Jimmy 1910-1973 . . . . DLB-171

Cano, Daniel 1947- DLB-209

   Old Dogs / New Tricks? New
   Technologies, the Canon, and the
   Structure of the Profession. Y-02

Cantar de mio Cid circa 1200 . . . . DLB-337

Cantigas in the Galician-Portuguese
   Cancioneiros. DLB-337

Cantú, Norma Elia 1947- DLB-209

Cantwell, Robert 1908-1978 . . . . DLB-9

Jonathan Cape and Harrison Smith
   [publishing house] DLB-46

Jonathan Cape Limited. DLB-112

Čapek, Karel 1890-1938 . . . . DLB-215; CDWLB-4

Capen, Joseph 1658-1725 . . . . DLB-24

Capes, Bernard 1854-1918 . . . . DLB-156

Caponegro, Mary 1956- DLB-335

Capote, Truman 1924-1984
   . . . . DLB-2, 185, 227; Y-80, 84; CDALB-1

Capps, Benjamin 1922- DLB-256

Caproni, Giorgio 1912-1990. . . . . DLB-128

Caragiale, Mateiu Ioan 1885-1936 . . . . . . DLB-220

Carballido, Emilio 1925- DLB-305

Cardarelli, Vincenzo 1887-1959 . . . . DLB-114

Cardenal, Ernesto 1925- DLB-290

Cárdenas, Reyes 1948- DLB-122

Cardinal, Marie 1929-2001. . . . . DLB-83

Cardoza y Aragón, Luis 1901-1992 . . . . . DLB-290

Carducci, Giosuè 1835-1907. . . . . DLB-329

Carew, Jan 1920- DLB-157

Carew, Thomas 1594 or 1595-1640 . . . . DLB-126

Carey, Henry circa 1687-1689-1743 . . . . . . DLB-84

Carey, Mathew 1760-1839 . . . . DLB-37, 73

M. Carey and Company. DLB-49

Carey, Peter 1943- DLB-289, 326

Carey and Hart. DLB-49

Carlell, Lodowick 1602-1675 . . . . DLB-58

Carleton, William 1794-1869 . . . . DLB-159

G. W. Carleton [publishing house] DLB-49

Carlile, Richard 1790-1843 . . . . . . DLB-110, 158

Carlson, Ron 1947- DLB-244

Carlyle, Jane Welsh 1801-1866. . . . . DLB-55

Carlyle, Thomas
   1795-1881. . . . . . DLB-55, 144, 338; CDBLB-3

"The Hero as Man of Letters:
   Johnson, Rousseau, Burns"
   (1841) [excerpt] DLB-57

The Hero as Poet. Dante; Shakspeare
   (1841) DLB-32

Carman, Bliss 1861-1929 . . . . DLB-92

Carmina Burana circa 1230 . . . . DLB-138

Carnap, Rudolf 1891-1970 . . . . DLB-270

Carnero, Guillermo 1947- DLB-108

Carossa, Hans 1878-1956 . . . . DLB-66

Carpenter, Humphrey
   1946-2005 . . . . DLB-155; Y-84, 99

Carpenter, Stephen Cullen ?-1820? DLB-73

Carpentier, Alejo
   1904-1980 . . . . DLB-113; CDWLB-3

Carr, Emily 1871-1945 . . . . DLB-68

Carr, John Dickson 1906-1977 . . . . DLB-306

Carr, Marina 1964- DLB-245

Carr, Virginia Spencer 1929- DLB-111; Y-00

Carrera Andrade, Jorge 1903-1978 . . . . . DLB-283

Carrier, Roch 1937- DLB-53

Carrillo, Adolfo 1855-1926. . . . . DLB-122

Carroll, Gladys Hasty 1904-1999 . . . . DLB-9

Carroll, John 1735-1815 . . . . DLB-37

Carroll, John 1809-1884 . . . . DLB-99

Carroll, Lewis
   1832-1898 . . . . . . DLB-18, 163, 178; CDBLB-4

The Lewis Carroll Centenary Y-98

The Lewis Carroll Society
   of North America Y-00

Carroll, Paul 1927-1996 . . . . DLB-16

Carroll, Paul Vincent 1900-1968 . . . . DLB-10

Carroll and Graf Publishers DLB-46

Carruth, Hayden 1921- DLB-5, 165

Tribute to James Dickey. Y-97

Tribute to Raymond Carver Y-88

Carryl, Charles E. 1841-1920. . . . . DLB-42

Carson, Anne 1950- DLB-193

Carson, Rachel 1907-1964 . . . . DLB-275

Carswell, Catherine 1879-1946. . . . . DLB-36

Cartagena, Alfonso de circa 1384-1456 . . DLB-286

Cartagena, Teresa de 1425?-? DLB-286

Cărtărescu, Mirea 1956- DLB-232

Carte, Thomas 1686-1754 . . . . DLB-336

Carter, Angela
   1940-1992 . . . . DLB-14, 207, 261, 319

Carter, Elizabeth 1717-1806. . . . . DLB-109

Carter, Henry (see Leslie, Frank)

Carter, Hodding, Jr. 1907-1972 . . . . DLB-127

Carter, Jared 1939- DLB-282

Carter, John 1905-1975 . . . . DLB-201

Carter, Landon 1710-1778 . . . . DLB-31

Carter, Lin 1930-1988 . . . . Y-81

Carter, Martin 1927-1997 . . . . DLB-117; CDWLB-3

Carter, Robert, and Brothers DLB-49

Carter and Hendee. DLB-49

Cartwright, Jim 1958- DLB-245

Cartwright, John 1740-1824 . . . . DLB-158

Cartwright, William circa 1611-1643 . . . . DLB-126

Caruthers, William Alexander
   1802-1846 . . . . DLB-3, 248

Carver, Jonathan 1710-1780 . . . . DLB-31

Carver, Raymond 1938-1988 . . . DLB-130; Y-83, 88

First Strauss "Livings" Awarded to Cynthia
   Ozick and Raymond Carver
   An Interview with Raymond Carver. . . . Y-83

Carvic, Heron 1917?-1980 . . . . DLB-276

Cary, Alice 1820-1871. . . . . DLB-202

Cary, Joyce 1888-1957 . . . DLB-15, 100; CDBLB-6

Cary, Patrick 1623?-1657 . . . . DLB-131

Casal, Julián del 1863-1893 . . . . DLB-283

Case, John 1540-1600. . . . . DLB-281

Casey, Gavin 1907-1964 . . . . DLB-260

Casey, Juanita 1925- DLB-14

Casey, Michael 1947- DLB-5

Cassady, Carolyn 1923- DLB-16

"As I See It" DLB-16

Cassady, Neal 1926-1968 . . . . DLB-16, 237

Cassell and Company. DLB-106

Cassell Publishing Company DLB-49

Cassill, R. V. 1919-2002 . . . . DLB-6, 218; Y-02

Tribute to James Dickey. Y-97

Cassity, Turner 1929- DLB-105; Y-02

Cassius Dio circa 155/164-post 229 . . . . . DLB-176

Cassola, Carlo 1917-1987 . . . . DLB-177

Castellano, Olivia 1944- DLB-122

Castellanos, Rosario
   1925-1974. . . . . DLB-113, 290; CDWLB-3

Castelo Branco, Camilo 1825-1890 . . . . . DLB-287

Castile, Protest Poetry in DLB-286

Castile and Aragon, Vernacular Translations
   in Crowns of 1352-1515. . . . . DLB-286

Castillejo, Cristóbal de 1490?-1550 . . . . . DLB-318

Castillo, Ana 1953- DLB-122, 227

Castillo, Rafael C. 1950- DLB-209

The Castle of Perseverance
   circa 1400-1425 . . . . DLB-146

Castlemon, Harry (see Fosdick, Charles Austin)

Castro, Brian 1950- DLB-325

Castro, Consuelo de 1946- DLB-307

Castro Alves, Antônio de 1847-1871 . . . . . DLB-307

Čašule, Kole 1921- DLB-181

Caswall, Edward 1814-1878 . . . . DLB-32

Catacalos, Rosemary 1944- DLB-122

Cather, Willa 1873-1947
   . . . . DLB-9, 54, 78, 256; DS-1; CDALB-3

The Willa Cather Pioneer Memorial
and Education Foundation Y-00
Catherine II (Ekaterina Alekseevna), "The Great,"
Empress of Russia 1729-1796 . . . . . DLB-150
Catherwood, Mary Hartwell 1847-1902 . . . DLB-78
Catledge, Turner 1901-1983 . . . . DLB-127
Catlin, George 1796-1872 . . . . DLB-186, 189
Cato the Elder 234 B.C.-149 B.C. DLB-211
Cattafi, Bartolo 1922-1979 . . . . DLB-128
Catton, Bruce 1899-1978 . . . . DLB-17
Catullus circa 84 B.C.-54 B.C.
. . . . DLB-211; CDWLB-1
Causley, Charles 1917-2003 . . . . DLB-27
Caute, David 1936- DLB-14, 231
Cavendish, Duchess of Newcastle,
Margaret Lucas
1623?-1673 . . . . DLB-131, 252, 281
Cawein, Madison 1865-1914 . . . . DLB-54
William Caxton [publishing house] DLB-170
The Caxton Printers, Limited DLB-46
Caylor, O. P. 1849-1897 . . . . DLB-241
Caylus, Marthe-Marguerite de
1671-1729 . . . . DLB-313
Cayrol, Jean 1911-2005 . . . . DLB-83
Cecil, Lord David 1902-1986 . . . . DLB-155
Cela, Camilo José
1916-2002 . . . . DLB-322, 329; Y-89
Nobel Lecture 1989 . . . . Y-89
Celan, Paul 1920-1970 . . . . DLB-69; CDWLB-2
Celati, Gianni 1937- DLB-196
Celaya, Gabriel 1911-1991 . . . . DLB-108
Céline, Louis-Ferdinand 1894-1961 . . . . DLB-72
Celtis, Conrad 1459-1508 . . . . DLB-179
Cendrars, Blaise 1887-1961 . . . . DLB-258
The Steinbeck Centennial Y-02
Censorship
The Island Trees Case: A Symposium on
School Library Censorship Y-82
Center for Bibliographical Studies and
Research at the University of
California, Riverside Y-91
Center for Book Research Y-84
The Center for the Book in the Library
of Congress Y-93
A New Voice: The Center for the
Book's First Five Years Y-83
Centlivre, Susanna 1669?-1723 . . . . DLB-84
The Centre for Writing, Publishing and
Printing History at the University
of Reading Y-00
The Century Company DLB-49
A Century of Poetry, a Lifetime of Collecting:
J. M. Edelstein's Collection of
Twentieth-Century American Poetry Y-02
Cernuda, Luis 1902-1963 . . . . DLB-134
Cerruto, Oscar 1912-1981 . . . . DLB-283
Cervantes, Lorna Dee 1954- DLB-82

Césaire, Aimé 1913- DLB-321
de Céspedes, Alba 1911-1997 . . . . DLB-264
Cetina, Gutierre de 1514-17?-1556 . . . . . . DLB-318
Ch., T. (see Marchenko, Anastasiia Iakovlevna)
Cha, Theresa Hak Kyung 1951-1982 . . . . DLB-312
Chaadaev, Petr Iakovlevich
1794-1856 . . . . DLB-198
Chabon, Michael 1963- DLB-278
Chacel, Rosa 1898-1994 . . . . DLB-134, 322
Chacón, Eusebio 1869-1948 . . . . DLB-82
Chacón, Felipe Maximiliano 1873-? DLB-82
Chadwick, Henry 1824-1908 . . . . DLB-241
Chadwyck-Healey's Full-Text Literary Databases:
Editing Commercial Databases of
Primary Literary Texts Y-95
Challans, Eileen Mary (see Renault, Mary)
Chalmers, George 1742-1825 . . . . DLB-30
Chaloner, Sir Thomas 1520-1565 . . . . DLB-167
Chamberlain, Samuel S. 1851-1916 . . . . DLB-25
Chamberland, Paul 1939- DLB-60
Chamberlin, William Henry 1897-1969 . . . DLB-29
Chambers, Charles Haddon 1860-1921 . . . DLB-10
Chambers, María Cristina (see Mena, María Cristina)
Chambers, Robert W. 1865-1933 . . . . DLB-202
W. and R. Chambers
[publishing house] DLB-106
Chambers, Whittaker 1901-1961 . . . . DLB-303
Chamfort, Sébastien-Roch Nicolas de
1740?-1794 . . . . DLB-313
Chamisso, Adelbert von 1781-1838 . . . . DLB-90
Champfleury 1821-1889 . . . . DLB-119
Champier, Symphorien 1472?-1539? DLB-327
Chan, Jeffery Paul 1942- DLB-312
Chandler, Harry 1864-1944 . . . . DLB-29
Chandler, Norman 1899-1973 . . . . DLB-127
Chandler, Otis 1927-2006 . . . . DLB-127
Chandler, Raymond
1888-1959 . . . . DLB-226, 253; DS-6; CDALB-5
Raymond Chandler Centenary Y-88
Chang, Diana 1934- DLB-312
Channing, Edward 1856-1931 . . . . DLB-17
Channing, Edward Tyrrell
1790-1856 . . . . DLB-1, 59, 235
Channing, William Ellery
1780-1842 . . . . DLB-1, 59, 235
Channing, William Ellery, II
1817-1901 . . . . DLB-1, 223
Channing, William Henry
1810-1884 . . . . DLB-1, 59, 243
Chapelain, Jean 1595-1674 . . . . DLB-268
Chaplin, Charlie 1889-1977 . . . . DLB-44
Chapman, George
1559 or 1560-1634 . . . . DLB-62, 121
Chapman, Olive Murray 1892-1977 . . . . . DLB-195

Chapman, R. W. 1881-1960 . . . . DLB-201
Chapman, William 1850-1917 . . . . DLB-99
John Chapman [publishing house] DLB-106
Chapman and Hall [publishing house] . . . DLB-106
Chappell, Fred 1936- DLB-6, 105
"A Detail in a Poem" DLB-105
Tribute to Peter Taylor Y-94
Chappell, William 1582-1649 . . . . DLB-236
Char, René 1907-1988 . . . . DLB-258
Charbonneau, Jean 1875-1960 . . . . DLB-92
Charbonneau, Robert 1911-1967 . . . . DLB-68
Charles, Gerda 1914-1996 . . . . DLB-14
William Charles [publishing house] DLB-49
Charles d'Orléans 1394-1465 . . . . DLB-208
Charley (see Mann, Charles)
Charrière, Isabelle de 1740-1805 . . . . DLB-313
Charskaia, Lidiia 1875-1937 . . . . DLB-295
Charteris, Leslie 1907-1993 . . . . DLB-77
Chartier, Alain circa 1385-1430 . . . . DLB-208
Charyn, Jerome 1937- Y-83
Chase, Borden 1900-1971 . . . . DLB-26
Chase, Edna Woolman 1877-1957 . . . . DLB-91
Chase, James Hadley (René Raymond)
1906-1985 . . . . DLB-276
Chase, Mary Coyle 1907-1981 . . . . DLB-228
Chase-Riboud, Barbara 1936- DLB-33
Chateaubriand, François-René de
1768-1848 . . . . DLB-119
Châtelet, Gabrielle-Emilie Du
1706-1749 . . . . DLB-313
Chatterjee, Upamanyu 1959- DLB-323
Chatterton, Thomas 1752-1770 . . . . DLB-109
Essay on Chatterton (1842), by
Robert Browning DLB-32
Chatto and Windus DLB-106
Chatwin, Bruce 1940-1989 . . . . DLB-194, 204
Chaucer, Geoffrey
1340?-1400 . . . . DLB-146; CDBLB-1
New Chaucer Society Y-00
Chaudhuri, Amit 1962- DLB-267, 323
Chaudhuri, Nirad C. 1897-1999 . . . . DLB-323
Chauncy, Charles 1705-1787 . . . . DLB-24
Chauveau, Pierre-Joseph-Olivier
1820-1890 . . . . DLB-99
Chávez, Denise 1948- DLB-122
Chávez, Fray Angélico 1910-1996 . . . . DLB-82
Chayefsky, Paddy 1923-1981 . . . . . DLB-7, 44; Y-81
Cheesman, Evelyn 1881-1969 . . . . DLB-195
Cheever, Ezekiel 1615-1708 . . . . DLB-24
Cheever, George Barrell 1807-1890 . . . . . . DLB-59
Cheever, John 1912-1982
. . . . DLB-2, 102, 227; Y-80, 82; CDALB-1
Cheever, Susan 1943- Y-82

Cheke, Sir John 1514-1557 . . . . DLB-132	Children's Book Illustration in the Twentieth Century DLB-61	Church, Peggy Pond 1903-1986 . . . . DLB-212
Chekhov, Anton Pavlovich 1860-1904 . . . . DLB-277	Children's Illustrators, 1800-1880 . . . DLB-163	Church, Richard 1893-1972 . . . . DLB-191
Chelsea House DLB-46	The Harry Potter Phenomenon Y-99	Church, William Conant 1836-1917 . . . . . DLB-79
Chênedollé, Charles de 1769-1833 . . . . . . DLB-217	Pony Stories, Omnibus Essay on DLB-160	Churchill, Caryl 1938- DLB-13, 310
Cheney, Brainard Tribute to Caroline Gordon Y-81	The Reality of One Woman's Dream: The de Grummond Children's	Churchill, Charles 1731-1764 . . . . DLB-109
Cheney, Ednah Dow 1824-1904 . . . . . . DLB-1, 223	Literature Collection Y-99	Churchill, Winston 1871-1947 . . . . DLB-202
Cheney, Harriet Vaughan 1796-1889 . . . . . DLB-99	School Stories, 1914-1960 . . . . DLB-160	Churchill, Sir Winston 1874-1965. . . DLB-100, 329; DS-16; CDBLB-5
Chénier, Marie-Joseph 1764-1811 . . . . DLB-192	The Year in Children's Books Y-92–96, 98–01	Churchyard, Thomas 1520?-1604 . . . . . . DLB-132
Cheng Xiaoqing 1893-1976 . . . . DLB-328	The Year in Children's Literature Y-97	E. Churton and Company DLB-106
Cherny, Sasha 1880-1932 . . . . DLB-317	Childress, Alice 1916-1994 . . . . .DLB-7, 38, 249	Chute, Marchette 1909-1994 . . . . DLB-103
Chernyshevsky, Nikolai Gavrilovich 1828-1889 . . . . DLB-238	Childress, Mark 1957- DLB-292	Ciampoli, Giovanni Battista 1590-1643 . . . . DLB-339
Cherry, Kelly 1940 . . . . .DLB-335; Y-83	Childs, George W. 1829-1894 . . . . DLB-23	Ciardi, John 1916-1986. . . . . .DLB-5; Y-86
Cherryh, C. J. 1942- DLB-335; Y-80	Chilton Book Company DLB-46	Cibber, Colley 1671-1757 . . . . DLB-84
Chesebro', Caroline 1825-1873 . . . . DLB-202	Chin, Frank 1940- DLB-206, 312	Cicero 106 B.C.-43 B.C. DLB-211, CDWLB-1
Chesney, Sir George Tomkyns 1830-1895 . . . . DLB-190	Chin, Justin 1969- DLB-312	Cicognini, Giacinto Andrea 1606-1649 . . . . DLB-339
Chesnut, Mary Boykin 1823-1886 . . . . . . DLB-239	Chin, Marilyn 1955- DLB-312	Cima, Annalisa 1941- DLB-128
Chesnutt, Charles Waddell 1858-1932 . . . . .DLB-12, 50, 78	Chinweizu 1943- DLB-157	Čingo, Živko 1935-1987. . . . . DLB-181
Chesson, Mrs. Nora (see Hopper, Nora)	Chinnov, Igor' 1909-1996. . . . . DLB-317	Cioran, E. M. 1911-1995 . . . . DLB-220
Chester, Alfred 1928-1971. . . . . DLB-130	Chitham, Edward 1932- DLB-155	Čipkus, Alfonsas (see Nyka-Niliūnas, Alfonsas)
Chester, George Randolph 1869-1924. . . . DLB-78	Chittenden, Hiram Martin 1858-1917 . . . . DLB-47	Cirese, Eugenio 1884-1955. . . . . DLB-114
The Chester Plays circa 1505-1532; revisions until 1575 . . . . DLB-146	Chivers, Thomas Holley 1809-1858. . . DLB-3, 248	Cīrulis, Jānis (see Bels, Alberts)
Chesterfield, Philip Dormer Stanhope, Fourth Earl of 1694-1773 . . . . DLB-104	Chkhartishvili, Grigorii Shalvovich (see Akunin, Boris)	Cisneros, Antonio 1942- DLB-290
Chesterton, G. K. 1874-1936 . . . DLB-10, 19, 34, 70, 98, 149, 178; CDBLB-6	Chocano, José Santos 1875-1934 . . . . DLB-290	Cisneros, Sandra 1954- DLB-122, 152
"The Ethics of Elfland" (1908) DLB-178	Cholmondeley, Mary 1859-1925 . . . . DLB-197	City Lights Books. DLB-46
Chettle, Henry circa 1560-circa 1607 . . . . DLB-136	Chomsky, Noam 1928- DLB-246	Civil War (1861–1865) Battles and Leaders of the Civil War . . . DLB-47
Cheuse, Alan 1940- DLB-244	Chopin, Kate 1850-1904. . . DLB-12, 78; CDALB-3	Official Records of the Rebellion DLB-47
Chew, Ada Nield 1870-1945 . . . . DLB-135	Chopin, René 1885-1953 . . . . DLB-92	Recording the Civil War DLB-47
Cheyney, Edward P. 1861-1947 . . . . DLB-47	Choquette, Adrienne 1915-1973 . . . . DLB-68	Cixous, Hélène 1937- DLB-83, 242
Chiabrera, Gabriello 1552-1638 . . . . DLB-339	Choquette, Robert 1905-1991 . . . . DLB-68	Claire d'Albe, Sophie Cottin DLB-314
Chiang Yee 1903-1977 . . . . DLB-312	Choyce, Lesley 1951- DLB-251	Clampitt, Amy 1920-1994 . . . . DLB-105
Chiara, Piero 1913-1986 . . . . .DLB-177	Chrétien de Troyes circa 1140-circa 1190 . . . . DLB-208	Tribute to Alfred A. Knopf Y-84
Chicanos Chicano History DLB-82	Christensen, Inger 1935- DLB-214	Clancy, Tom 1947- DLB-227
Chicano Language DLB-82	Christensen, Lars Saabye 1953- DLB-297	Clapper, Raymond 1892-1944 . . . . DLB-29
Chicano Literature: A Bibliography . . .DLB-209	The Christian Examiner DLB-1	Clare, John 1793-1864 . . . . DLB-55, 96
A Contemporary Flourescence of Chicano Literature Y-84	The Christian Publishing Company DLB-49	Clarendon, Edward Hyde, Earl of 1609-1674 . . . . DLB-101
Literatura Chicanesca: The View From Without DLB-82	Christie, Agatha 1890-1976 . . . . .DLB-13, 77, 245; CDBLB-6	Clark, Alfred Alexander Gordon (see Hare, Cyril)
Child, Francis James 1825-1896 . . . DLB-1, 64, 235	Christine de Pizan circa 1365-circa 1431 . . . . DLB-208	Clark, Ann Nolan 1896-1995 . . . . DLB-52
Child, Lydia Maria 1802-1880 . . . . DLB-1, 74, 243	Christopher, John (Sam Youd) 1922- . . DLB-255	Clark, C. E. Frazer, Jr. 1925-2001 . . .DLB-187; Y-01
Child, Philip 1898-1978 . . . . DLB-68	Christus und die Samariterin circa 950 . . . . . . DLB-148	C. E. Frazer Clark Jr. and Hawthorne Bibliography DLB-269
Childers, Erskine 1870-1922 . . . . DLB-70	Christy, Howard Chandler 1873-1952 . . . DLB-188	The Publications of C. E. Frazer Clark Jr. DLB-269
Children's Literature Afterword: Propaganda, Namby-Pamby, and Some Books of Distinction . . . DLB-52	Chu, Louis 1915-1970. . . . . DLB-312	Clark, Catherine Anthony 1892-1977 . . . . . DLB-68
	Chukovskaia, Lidiia 1907-1996 . . . . DLB-302	Clark, Charles Heber 1841-1915 . . . . DLB-11
	Chulkov, Mikhail Dmitrievich 1743?-1792 . . . . DLB-150	Clark, Davis Wasgatt 1812-1871 . . . . DLB-79
	Church, Benjamin 1734-1778 . . . . DLB-31	Clark, Douglas 1919-1993 . . . . .DLB-276
Children's Book Awards and Prizes . . . DLB-61	Church, Francis Pharcellus 1839-1906 . . . . DLB-79	Clark, Eleanor 1913-1996 . . . . DLB-6

Clark, J. P. 1935- DLB-117; CDWLB-3

Clark, Lewis Gaylord
1808-1873 .... DLB-3, 64, 73, 250

Clark, Mary Higgins 1929- DLB-306

Clark, Walter Van Tilburg
1909-1971 .... DLB-9, 206

Clark, William 1770-1838 .... DLB-183, 186

Clark, William Andrews, Jr.
1877-1934 .... DLB-187

C. M. Clark Publishing Company DLB-46

Clarke, Sir Arthur C. 1917- DLB-261

    Tribute to Theodore Sturgeon........... Y-85

Clarke, Austin 1896-1974............ DLB-10, 20

Clarke, Austin C. 1934- DLB-53, 125

Clarke, George Elliott 1960- DLB-334

Clarke, Gillian 1937- DLB-40

Clarke, James Freeman
1810-1888 .... DLB-1, 59, 235; DS-5

Clarke, John circa 1596-1658 .... DLB-281

Clarke, Lindsay 1939- DLB-231

Clarke, Marcus 1846-1881............ DLB-230

Clarke, Pauline 1921- DLB-161

Clarke, Rebecca Sophia 1833-1906 .... DLB-42

Clarke, Samuel 1675-1729 .... DLB-252

Robert Clarke and Company DLB-49

Clarkson, Thomas 1760-1846 .... DLB-158

Claudel, Paul 1868-1955 ...... DLB-192, 258, 321

Claudius, Matthias 1740-1815 .... DLB-97

Clausen, Andy 1943- DLB-16

Claussen, Sophus 1865-1931 .... DLB-300

Clawson, John L. 1865-1933 .... DLB-187

Claxton, Remsen and Haffelfinger DLB-49

Clay, Cassius Marcellus 1810-1903 .... DLB-43

Clayton, Richard (see Haggard, William)

Cleage, Pearl 1948- DLB-228

Cleary, Beverly 1916- DLB-52

Cleary, Kate McPhelim 1863-1905 ..... DLB-221

Cleaver, Vera 1919-1992 and
Cleaver, Bill 1920-1981 .... DLB-52

Cleeve, Brian 1921-2003 .... DLB-276

Cleland, John 1710-1789.............. DLB-39

Clemens, Samuel Langhorne (Mark Twain)
1835-1910 .... DLB-11, 12, 23, 64, 74,
186, 189; CDALB-3

    Comments From Authors and Scholars on
their First Reading of *Huck Finn*....... Y-85

    Huck at 100: How Old Is
Huckleberry Finn?................. Y-85

    Mark Twain on Perpetual Copyright Y-92

    A New Edition of *Huck Finn* Y-85

Clement, Hal 1922-2003 ....DLB-8

Clemo, Jack 1916-1994 .... DLB-27

Clephane, Elizabeth Cecilia 1830-1869 ... DLB-199

Cleveland, John 1613-1658 ....DLB-126

Cliff, Michelle 1946- DLB-157; CDWLB-3

Clifford, Lady Anne 1590-1676......... DLB-151

Clifford, James L. 1901-1978 .... DLB-103

Clifford, Lucy 1853?-1929..... DLB-135, 141, 197

Clift, Charmian 1923-1969 .... DLB-260

Clifton, Lucille 1936- DLB-5, 41

Clines, Francis X. 1938- DLB-185

Clive, Caroline (V) 1801-1873.......... DLB-199

Edward J. Clode [publishing house]....... DLB-46

Clough, Arthur Hugh 1819-1861 .... DLB-32

Cloutier, Cécile 1930- DLB-60

Clouts, Sidney 1926-1982 .... DLB-225

Clutton-Brock, Arthur 1868-1924 .... DLB-98

Coates, Robert M.
1897-1973............ DLB-4, 9, 102; DS-15

Coatsworth, Elizabeth 1893-1986 .... DLB-22

Cobb, Charles E., Jr. 1943- DLB-41

Cobb, Frank I. 1869-1923 .... DLB-25

Cobb, Irvin S. 1876-1944........ DLB-11, 25, 86

Cobbe, Frances Power 1822-1904 .... DLB-190

Cobbett, William 1763-1835 .... DLB-43, 107, 158

Cobbledick, Gordon 1898-1969 .... DLB-171

Cochran, Thomas C. 1902-1999......... DLB-17

Cochrane, Elizabeth 1867-1922 ...... DLB-25, 189

Cockerell, Sir Sydney 1867-1962 .... DLB-201

Cockerill, John A. 1845-1896............ DLB-23

Cocteau, Jean 1889-1963....... DLB-65, 258, 321

Coderre, Emile (see Jean Narrache)

Cody, Liza 1944- DLB-276

Coe, Jonathan 1961- DLB-231

Coetzee, J. M. 1940- DLB-225, 326, 329

Coffee, Lenore J. 1900?-1984............ DLB-44

Coffin, Robert P. Tristram 1892-1955..... DLB-45

Coghill, Mrs. Harry (see Walker, Anna Louisa)

Cogswell, Fred 1917- DLB-60

Cogswell, Mason Fitch 1761-1830 .... DLB-37

Cohan, George M. 1878-1942 .... DLB-249

Cohen, Arthur A. 1928-1986............ DLB-28

Cohen, Leonard 1934- DLB-53

Cohen, Matt 1942- DLB-53

Cohen, Morris Raphael 1880-1947 ..... DLB-270

Colasanti, Marina 1937- DLB-307

Colbeck, Norman 1903-1987............ DLB-201

Colden, Cadwallader 1688-1776 .. DLB-24, 30, 270

Colden, Jane 1724-1766 .... DLB-200

Cole, Barry 1936- DLB-14

Cole, George Watson 1850-1939........ DLB-140

Colegate, Isabel 1931- DLB-14, 231

Coleman, Emily Holmes 1899-1974 .... DLB-4

Coleman, Wanda 1946- DLB-130

Coleridge, Hartley 1796-1849 .... DLB-96

Coleridge, Mary 1861-1907............DLB-19, 98

Coleridge, Samuel Taylor
1772-1834 .... DLB-93, 107; CDBLB-3

Coleridge, Sara 1802-1852.............DLB-199

Colet, John 1467-1519 .... DLB-132

Colette 1873-1954 .... DLB-65

Colette, Sidonie Gabrielle (see Colette)

Colinas, Antonio 1946- DLB-134

Coll, Joseph Clement 1881-1921 .... DLB-188

A Century of Poetry, a Lifetime of Collecting:
J. M. Edelstein's Collection of
Twentieth-Century American Poetry Y-02

Collier, John 1901-1980............ DLB-77, 255

Collier, John Payne 1789-1883.......... DLB-184

Collier, Mary 1690-1762 .... DLB-95

Collier, Robert J. 1876-1918............ DLB-91

P. F. Collier [publishing house] DLB-49

Collin and Small DLB-49

Collingwood, R. G. 1889-1943 .... DLB-262

Collingwood, W. G. 1854-1932.......... DLB-149

Collins, An floruit circa 1653........... DLB-131

Collins, Anthony 1676-1729 .... DLB-252, 336

Collins, Arthur 1681?-1762 .... DLB-336

Collins, Merle 1950- DLB-157

Collins, Michael 1964- DLB-267

Collins, Michael (see Lynds, Dennis)

Collins, Mortimer 1827-1876 .... DLB-21, 35

Collins, Tom (see Furphy, Joseph)

Collins, Wilkie
1824-1889 .... DLB-18, 70, 159; CDBLB-4

    "The Unknown Public" (1858)
[excerpt] DLB-57

    The Wilkie Collins Society Y-98

Collins, William 1721-1759 .... DLB-109

Isaac Collins [publishing house].......... DLB-49

William Collins, Sons and Company..... DLB-154

Collis, Maurice 1889-1973............. DLB-195

Collyer, Mary 1716?-1763? DLB-39

Colman, Benjamin 1673-1747 .... DLB-24

Colman, George, the Elder 1732-1794..... DLB-89

Colman, George, the Younger
1762-1836 .... DLB-89

S. Colman [publishing house] DLB-49

Colombo, John Robert 1936- DLB-53

Colonial Literature DLB-307

Colquhoun, Patrick 1745-1820 .... DLB-158

Colter, Cyrus 1910-2002 .... DLB-33

Colum, Padraic 1881-1972............. DLB-19

The Columbia History of the American Novel
A Symposium on..................... Y-92

Columbus, Christopher 1451-1506...... DLB-318

Columella fl. first century A.D........... DLB-211

Colvin, Sir Sidney 1845-1927 .... DLB-149

Colwin, Laurie 1944-1992 .... DLB-218; Y-80

Comden, Betty 1915- and
    Green, Adolph 1918-2002 ...... DLB-44, 265

Comi, Girolamo 1890-1968 .... DLB-114

Comisso, Giovanni 1895-1969 .... DLB-264

Commager, Henry Steele 1902-1998 ..... DLB-17

Commynes, Philippe de
    circa 1447-1511 .... DLB-208

Compton, D. G. 1930- DLB-261

Compton-Burnett, Ivy 1884?-1969 .... DLB-36

Conan, Laure (Félicité Angers)
    1845-1924 .... DLB-99

Concord, Massachusetts
    Concord History and Life DLB-223

    Concord: Literary History
      of a Town................... DLB-223

    The Old Manse, by Hawthorne..... DLB-223

    The Thoreauvian Pilgrimage: The
      Structure of an American Cult... DLB-223

Concrete Poetry DLB-307

Conde, Carmen 1901-1996 .... DLB-108

Condillac, Etienne Bonnot de
    1714-1780 .... DLB-313

Condorcet, Marie-Jean-Antoine-Nicolas Caritat,
    marquis de 1743-1794............. DLB-313

    "The Tenth Stage" DLB-314

Congreve, William
    1670-1729 .... DLB-39, 84; CDBLB-2

    Preface to *Incognita* (1692) DLB-39

W. B. Conkey Company DLB-49

Conlon, Evelyn 1952- DLB-319

Conn, Stewart 1936- DLB-233

Connell, Evan S., Jr. 1924- DLB-2, 335; Y-81

Connelly, Marc 1890-1980 .... DLB-7; Y-80

Connolly, Cyril 1903-1974 .... DLB-98

Connolly, James B. 1868-1957 .... DLB-78

Connor, Ralph (Charles William Gordon)
    1860-1937...................... DLB-92

Connor, Tony 1930- DLB-40

Conquest, Robert 1917- DLB-27

Conrad, Joseph
    1857-1924.... DLB-10, 34, 98, 156; CDBLB-5

John Conrad and Company DLB-49

Conroy, Jack 1899-1990 .... Y-81

    A Tribute [to Nelson Algren] Y-81

Conroy, Pat 1945- DLB-6

The Conservationist, 1974 Booker Prize winner,
    Nadine Gordimer................ DLB-326

Considine, Bob 1906-1975 .... DLB-241

Consolo, Vincenzo 1933- DLB-196

Constable, Henry 1562-1613 .... DLB-136

Archibald Constable and Company DLB-154

Constable and Company Limited....... DLB-112

Constant, Benjamin 1767-1830 .... DLB-119

Constant de Rebecque, Henri-Benjamin de
    (see Constant, Benjamin)

Constantine, David 1944- DLB-40

Constantine, Murray (see Burdekin, Katharine)

Constantin-Weyer, Maurice 1881-1964.... DLB-92

Contempo (magazine)
    Contempo Caravan:
      Kites in a Windstorm Y-85

The Continental Publishing Company.... DLB-49

A Conversation between William Riggan
    and Janette Turner Hospital............ Y-02

Conversations with Editors Y-95

Conway, Anne 1631-1679............. DLB-252

Conway, Moncure Daniel
    1832-1907.................... DLB-1, 223

Cook, Ebenezer circa 1667-circa 1732..... DLB-24

Cook, Edward Tyas 1857-1919......... DLB-149

Cook, Eliza 1818-1889 .... DLB-199

Cook, George Cram 1873-1924 .... DLB-266

Cook, Michael 1933-1994 .... DLB-53

David C. Cook Publishing Company..... DLB-49

Cooke, George Willis 1848-1923 .... DLB-71

Cooke, John Esten 1830-1886 .... DLB-3, 248

Cooke, Philip Pendleton
    1816-1850 .... DLB-3, 59, 248

Cooke, Rose Terry 1827-1892 ....DLB-12, 74

Increase Cooke and Company DLB-49

Cook-Lynn, Elizabeth 1930- DLB-175

Coolbrith, Ina 1841-1928 .... DLB-54, 186

Cooley, Dennis 1944- DLB-334

Cooley, Peter 1940- DLB-105

    "Into the Mirror"................ DLB-105

Coolidge, Clark 1939- DLB-193

Coolidge, Susan
    (see Woolsey, Sarah Chauncy)

George Coolidge [publishing house]...... DLB-49

Coomaraswamy, Ananda 1877-1947..... DLB-323

Cooper, Anna Julia 1858-1964 .... DLB-221

Cooper, Edith Emma 1862-1913 .... DLB-240

Cooper, Giles 1918-1966 .... DLB-13

Cooper, J. California 19??- DLB-212

Cooper, James Fenimore
    1789-1851....... DLB-3, 183, 250; CDALB-2

    The Bicentennial of James Fenimore Cooper:
      An International Celebration........ Y-89

    The James Fenimore Cooper Society..... Y-01

Cooper, Kent 1880-1965................ DLB-29

Cooper, Susan 1935- DLB-161, 261

Cooper, Susan Fenimore 1813-1894..... DLB-239

William Cooper [publishing house] DLB-170

J. Coote [publishing house]............ DLB-154

Coover, Robert 1932- DLB-2, 227; Y-81

    Tribute to Donald Barthelme........... Y-89

    Tribute to Theodor Seuss Geisel Y-91

Copeland and Day DLB-49

Ćopić, Branko 1915-1984.............. DLB-181

Copland, Robert 1470?-1548 .... DLB-136

Coppard, A. E. 1878-1957 .... DLB-162

Coppée, François 1842-1908 ....DLB-217

Coppel, Alfred 1921-2004 .... Y-83

    Tribute to Jessamyn West.............. Y-84

Coppola, Francis Ford 1939- DLB-44

Copway, George (Kah-ge-ga-gah-bowh)
    1818-1869 ....DLB-175, 183

Copyright
    The Development of the Author's
      Copyright in Britain DLB-154

    The Digital Millennium Copyright Act:
      Expanding Copyright Protection in
      Cyberspace and Beyond Y-98

    Editorial: The Extension of Copyright ... Y-02

    Mark Twain on Perpetual Copyright Y-92

    Public Domain and the Violation
      of Texts Y-97

    The Question of American Copyright
      in the Nineteenth Century
      Preface, by George Haven Putnam
      The Evolution of Copyright, by
        Brander Matthews
      Summary of Copyright Legislation in
        the United States, by R. R. Bowker
      Analysis of the Provisions of the
        Copyright Law of 1891, by
        George Haven Putnam
      The Contest for International Copyright,
        by George Haven Putnam
      Cheap Books and Good Books,
        by Brander Matthews DLB-49

    Writers and Their Copyright Holders:
      the WATCH Project Y-94

Corazzini, Sergio 1886-1907........... DLB-114

Corbett, Richard 1582-1635............ DLB-121

Corbière, Tristan 1845-1875 ....DLB-217

Corcoran, Barbara 1911- DLB-52

Cordelli, Franco 1943- DLB-196

Corelli, Marie 1855-1924 .... DLB-34, 156

Corle, Edwin 1906-1956................. Y-85

Corman, Cid 1924-2004............ DLB-5, 193

Cormier, Robert 1925-2000 ... DLB-52; CDALB-6

    Tribute to Theodor Seuss Geisel Y-91

Corn, Alfred 1943- DLB-120, 282; Y-80

Corneille, Pierre 1606-1684 ....DLB-268

Cornford, Frances 1886-1960.......... DLB-240

Cornish, Sam 1935- DLB-41

Cornish, William
    circa 1465-circa 1524 .... DLB-132

Cornwall, Barry (see Procter, Bryan Waller)

Cornwallis, Sir William, the Younger
    circa 1579-1614 .... DLB-151

Cornwell, David John Moore (see le Carré, John)

Cornwell, Patricia 1956- DLB-306

Coronel Urtecho, José 1906-1994 ...... DLB-290

Corpi, Lucha 1945- DLB-82

Corrington, John William 1932-1988 ... DLB-6, 244

Corriveau, Monique 1927-1976 ... DLB-251

Corrothers, James D. 1869-1917 ... DLB-50

Corso, Gregory 1930-2001 ... DLB-5, 16, 237

Cortázar, Julio 1914-1984 ... DLB-113; CDWLB-3

Cortese, Giulio Cesare circa 1570-1626? ... DLB-339

Cortéz, Carlos 1923-2005 ... DLB-209

Cortez, Jayne 1936- ... DLB-41

Corvinus, Gottlieb Siegmund 1677-1746 ... DLB-168

Corvo, Baron (see Rolfe, Frederick William)

Cory, Annie Sophie (see Cross, Victoria)

Cory, Desmond (Shaun Lloyd McCarthy) 1928- ... DLB-276

Cory, William Johnson 1823-1892 ... DLB-35

Coryate, Thomas 1577?-1617 ... DLB-151, 172

Ćosić, Dobrica 1921- ... DLB-181; CDWLB-4

Cosin, John 1595-1672 ... DLB-151, 213

Cosmopolitan Book Corporation ... DLB-46

Cossa, Roberto 1934- ... DLB-305

Costa, Margherita 1600/1610?-1657 ... DLB-339

Costa, Maria Velho da (see The Three Marias: A Landmark Case in Portuguese Literary History)

Costain, Thomas B. 1885-1965 ... DLB-9

Coste, Donat (Daniel Boudreau) 1912-1957 ... DLB-88

Costello, Louisa Stuart 1799-1870 ... DLB-166

Cota-Cárdenas, Margarita 1941- ... DLB-122

Côté, Denis 1954- ... DLB-251

Cotten, Bruce 1873-1954 ... DLB-187

Cotter, Joseph Seamon, Jr. 1895-1919 ... DLB-50

Cotter, Joseph Seamon, Sr. 1861-1949 ... DLB-50

Cottin, Sophie 1770-1807 ... DLB-313

Claire d'Albe ... DLB-314

Joseph Cottle [publishing house] ... DLB-154

Cotton, Charles 1630-1687 ... DLB-131

Cotton, John 1584-1652 ... DLB-24

Cotton, Sir Robert Bruce 1571-1631 ... DLB-213

Couani, Anna 1948- ... DLB-325

Coulter, John 1888-1980 ... DLB-68\

Coupland, Douglas 1961- ... DLB-334

Cournos, John 1881-1966 ... DLB-54

Courteline, Georges 1858-1929 ... DLB-192

Cousins, Margaret 1905-1996 ... DLB-137

Cousins, Norman 1915-1990 ... DLB-137

Couvreur, Jessie (see Tasma)

Coventry, Francis 1725-1754 ... DLB-39

Dedication, *The History of Pompey the Little* (1751) ... DLB-39

Coverdale, Miles 1487 or 1488-1569 ... DLB-167

N. Coverly [publishing house] ... DLB-49

Covici-Friede ... DLB-46

Cowan, Peter 1914-2002 ... DLB-260

Coward, Noel 1899-1973 ... DLB-10, 245; CDBLB-6

Coward, McCann and Geoghegan ... DLB-46

Cowles, Gardner 1861-1946 ... DLB-29

Cowles, Gardner "Mike", Jr. 1903-1985 ... DLB-127, 137

Cowley, Abraham 1618-1667 ... DLB-131, 151

Cowley, Hannah 1743-1809 ... DLB-89

Cowley, Malcolm 1898-1989 ... DLB-4, 48; DS-15; Y-81, 89

Cowper, Richard (John Middleton Murry Jr.) 1926-2002 ... DLB-261

Cowper, William 1731-1800 ... DLB-104, 109

Cox, A. B. (see Berkeley, Anthony)

Cox, James McMahon 1903-1974 ... DLB-127

Cox, James Middleton 1870-1957 ... DLB-127

Cox, Leonard circa 1495-circa 1550 ... DLB-281

Cox, Palmer 1840-1924 ... DLB-42

Coxe, Louis 1918-1993 ... DLB-5

Coxe, Tench 1755-1824 ... DLB-37

Cozzens, Frederick S. 1818-1869 ... DLB-202

Cozzens, James Gould 1903-1978 ... DLB-9, 294; Y-84; DS-2; CDALB-1

Cozzens's *Michael Scarlett* ... Y-97

Ernest Hemingway's Reaction to James Gould Cozzens ... Y-98

James Gould Cozzens—A View from Afar ... Y-97

James Gould Cozzens: How to Read Him ... Y-97

James Gould Cozzens Symposium and Exhibition at the University of South Carolina, Columbia ... Y-00

Mens Rea (or Something) ... Y-97

Novels for Grown-Ups ... Y-97

Crabbe, George 1754-1832 ... DLB-93

Crace, Jim 1946- ... DLB-231

Crackanthorpe, Hubert 1870-1896 ... DLB-135

Craddock, Charles Egbert (see Murfree, Mary N.)

Cradock, Thomas 1718-1770 ... DLB-31

Craig, Daniel H. 1811-1895 ... DLB-43

Craik, Dinah Maria 1826-1887 ... DLB-35, 163

Cramer, Richard Ben 1950- ... DLB-185

Cranch, Christopher Pearse 1813-1892 ... DLB-1, 42, 243; DS-5

Crane, Hart 1899-1932 ... DLB-4, 48; CDALB-4

Nathan Asch Remembers Ford Madox Ford, Sam Roth, and Hart Crane ... Y-02

Crane, R. S. 1886-1967 ... DLB-63

Crane, Stephen 1871-1900 ... DLB-12, 54, 78; CDALB-3

Stephen Crane: A Revaluation, Virginia Tech Conference, 1989 ... Y-89

The Stephen Crane Society ... Y-98, 01

Crane, Walter 1845-1915 ... DLB-163

Cranmer, Thomas 1489-1556 ... DLB-132, 213

Crapsey, Adelaide 1878-1914 ... DLB-54

Crashaw, Richard 1612/1613-1649 ... DLB-126

Crate, Joan 1953- ... DLB-334

Craven, Avery 1885-1980 ... DLB-17

Crawford, Charles 1752-circa 1815 ... DLB-31

Crawford, F. Marion 1854-1909 ... DLB-71

Crawford, Isabel Valancy 1850-1887 ... DLB-92

Crawley, Alan 1887-1975 ... DLB-68

Crayon, Geoffrey (see Irving, Washington)

Crayon, Porte (see Strother, David Hunter)

Creamer, Robert W. 1922- ... DLB-171

Creasey, John 1908-1973 ... DLB-77

Creative Age Press ... DLB-46

Creative Nonfiction ... Y-02

Crébillon, Claude-Prosper Jolyot de *fils* 1707-1777 ... DLB-313

Crébillon, Claude-Prosper Jolyot de *père* 1674-1762 ... DLB-313

William Creech [publishing house] ... DLB-154

Thomas Creede [publishing house] ... DLB-170

Creel, George 1876-1953 ... DLB-25

Creeley, Robert 1926-2005 ... DLB-5, 16, 169; DS-17

Creelman, James 1859-1915 ... DLB-23

Cregan, David 1931- ... DLB-13

Creighton, Donald 1902-1979 ... DLB-88

Crémazie, Octave 1827-1879 ... DLB-99

Crémer, Victoriano 1909?- ... DLB-108

Crenne, Helisenne de (Marguerite de Briet) 1510?-1560? ... DLB-327

Crescas, Hasdai circa 1340-1412? ... DLB-115

Crespo, Angel 1926-1995 ... DLB-134

Cresset Press ... DLB-112

Cresswell, Helen 1934- ... DLB-161

Crèvecoeur, Michel Guillaume Jean de 1735-1813 ... DLB-37

Crewe, Candida 1964- ... DLB-207

Crews, Harry 1935- ... DLB-6, 143, 185

Crichton, Michael (John Lange, Jeffrey Hudson, Michael Douglas) 1942- ... DLB-292; Y-81

Crispin, Edmund (Robert Bruce Montgomery) 1921-1978 ... DLB-87

Cristofer, Michael 1946- ... DLB-7

Criticism

Afro-American Literary Critics: An Introduction ... DLB-33

The Consolidation of Opinion: Critical Responses to the Modernists ... DLB-36

"Criticism in Relation to Novels" (1863), by G. H. Lewes ... DLB-21

The Limits of Pluralism ... DLB-67

Cumulative Index

Modern Critical Terms, Schools, and
   Movements DLB-67

"Panic Among the Philistines":
   A Postscript, An Interview
   with Bryan Griffin................ Y-81

The Recovery of Literature: Criticism
   in the 1990s: A Symposium......... Y-91

The Stealthy School of Criticism (1871),
   by Dante Gabriel Rossetti DLB-35

Crnjanski, Miloš
   1893-1977............. DLB-147; CDWLB-4

Crocker, Hannah Mather 1752-1829 .... DLB-200

Crockett, David (Davy)
   1786-1836............. DLB-3, 11, 183, 248

Croft-Cooke, Rupert (see Bruce, Leo)

Crofts, Freeman Wills 1879-1957 .... DLB-77

Croker, John Wilson 1780-1857 .... DLB-110

Croly, George 1780-1860 .... DLB-159

Croly, Herbert 1869-1930............. DLB-91

Croly, Jane Cunningham 1829-1901 ..... DLB-23

Crompton, Richmal 1890-1969 .... DLB-160

Cronin, A. J. 1896-1981 .... DLB-191

Cros, Charles 1842-1888 .... DLB-217

Crosby, Caresse 1892-1970 and
   Crosby, Harry 1898-1929 and ...DLB-4; DS-15

Crosby, Harry 1898-1929 .... DLB-48

Crosland, Camilla Toulmin (Mrs. Newton
   Crosland) 1812-1895 .... DLB-240

Cross, Amanda (Carolyn G. Heilbrun)
   1926-2003 .... DLB-306

Cross, Gillian 1945- DLB-161

Cross, Victoria 1868-1952 ....DLB-135, 197

Crossley-Holland, Kevin 1941- DLB-40, 161

Crothers, Rachel 1870-1958 ....DLB-7, 266

Thomas Y. Crowell Company DLB-49

Crowley, John 1942- Y-82

Crowley, Mart 1935- DLB-7, 266

Crown Publishers DLB-46

Crowne, John 1641-1712 .... DLB-80

Crowninshield, Edward Augustus
   1817-1859..................... DLB-140

Crowninshield, Frank 1872-1947 .... DLB-91

Croy, Homer 1883-1965............... DLB-4

Crumley, James 1939- DLB-226; Y-84

Cruse, Mary Anne 1825?-1910......... DLB-239

Cruz, Migdalia 1958- DLB-249

Cruz, Sor Juana Inés de la 1651-1695.... DLB-305

Cruz, Victor Hernández 1949- DLB-41

Cruz e Sousa, João 1861-1898 .... DLB-307

Csokor, Franz Theodor 1885-1969....... DLB-81

Csoóri, Sándor 1930- DLB-232; CDWLB-4

Cuadra, Pablo Antonio 1912-2002 ..... DLB-290

Cuala Press DLB-112

Cudworth, Ralph 1617-1688.......... DLB-252

Cueva, Juan de la 1543-1612 .... DLB-318

Cugoano, Quobna Ottabah 1797-? Y-02

Cullen, Countee
   1903-1946 .... DLB-4, 48, 51; CDALB-4

Culler, Jonathan D. 1944- DLB-67, 246

Cullinan, Elizabeth 1933- DLB-234

Culverwel, Nathaniel 1619?-1651?..... DLB-252

Cumberland, Richard 1732-1811 .... DLB-89

Cummings, Constance Gordon
   1837-1924......................DLB-174

Cummings, E. E.
   1894-1962 .... DLB-4, 48; CDALB-5

The E. E. Cummings Society.......... Y-01

Cummings, Ray 1887-1957............. DLB-8

Cummings and Hilliard DLB-49

Cummins, Maria Susanna 1827-1866..... DLB-42

Cumpián, Carlos 1953- DLB-209

Cunard, Nancy 1896-1965 .... DLB-240

Joseph Cundall [publishing house] DLB-106

Cuney, Waring 1906-1976 .... DLB-51

Cuney-Hare, Maude 1874-1936 .... DLB-52

Cunha, Euclides da 1866-1909......... DLB-307

Cunningham, Allan 1784-1842 .... DLB-116, 144

Cunningham, J. V. 1911-1985 .... DLB-5

Cunningham, Michael 1952- DLB-292

Cunningham, Peter (Peter Lauder, Peter
   Benjamin) 1947- DLB-267

Peter F. Cunningham
   [publishing house] DLB-49

Cunqueiro, Alvaro 1911-1981 .... DLB-134

Cuomo, George 1929- Y-80

Cupples, Upham and Company......... DLB-49

Cupples and Leon DLB-46

Cuppy, Will 1884-1949................. DLB-11

Curiel, Barbara Brinson 1956- DLB-209

Curley, Daniel 1918-1988 .... DLB-335

Edmund Curll [publishing house]........ DLB-154

Currie, James 1756-1805.............. DLB-142

Currie, Mary Montgomerie Lamb Singleton,
   Lady Currie (see Fane, Violet)

Currie, Sheldon 1934- DLB-334

Cursor Mundi circa 1300 .... DLB-146

Curti, Merle E. 1897-1996 .... DLB-17

Curtis, Anthony 1926- DLB-155

Curtis, Cyrus H. K. 1850-1933 .... DLB-91

Curtis, George William
   1824-1892 .... DLB-1, 43, 223

Curzon, Robert 1810-1873 .... DLB-166

Curzon, Sarah Anne 1833-1898 .... DLB-99

Cusack, Dymphna 1902-1981 .... DLB-260

Cushing, Eliza Lanesford 1794-1886 ..... DLB-99

Cushing, Harvey 1869-1939.......... DLB-187

Custance, Olive (Lady Alfred Douglas)
   1874-1944..................... DLB-240

Cynewulf circa 770-840 .... DLB-146

Cyrano de Bergerac, Savinien de
   1619-1655 ....DLB-268

Czepko, Daniel 1605-1660............ DLB-164

Czerniawski, Adam 1934- DLB-232

D

Dabit, Eugène 1898-1936............. DLB-65

Daborne, Robert circa 1580-1628 .... DLB-58

Dąbrowska, Maria
   1889-1965 .... DLB-215; CDWLB-4

Dacey, Philip 1939- DLB-105

"Eyes Across Centuries:
   Contemporary Poetry and 'That
   Vision Thing,'" DLB-105

Dach, Simon 1605-1659 .... DLB-164

Dacier, Anne Le Fèvre 1647-1720....... DLB-313

Dagerman, Stig 1923-1954 .... DLB-259

Daggett, Rollin M. 1831-1901 .... DLB-79

D'Aguiar, Fred 1960- DLB-157

Dahl, Roald 1916-1990.......... DLB-139, 255

Tribute to Alfred A. Knopf Y-84

Dahlberg, Edward 1900-1977 .... DLB-48

Dahn, Felix 1834-1912 .... DLB-129

The Daily Worker DLB-303

Dal', Vladimir Ivanovich (Kazak Vladimir
   Lugansky) 1801-1872............. DLB-198

Dale, Peter 1938- DLB-40

Daley, Arthur 1904-1974 ....DLB-171

Dall, Caroline Healey 1822-1912 ..... DLB-1, 235

Dallas, E. S. 1828-1879................ DLB-55

The Gay Science [excerpt](1866) DLB-21

The Dallas Theater Center.............. DLB-7

D'Alton, Louis 1900-1951............. DLB-10

Dalton, Roque 1935-1975............. DLB-283

Daly, Carroll John 1889-1958......... DLB-226

Daly, T. A. 1871-1948................. DLB-11

Damon, S. Foster 1893-1971............ DLB-45

William S. Damrell [publishing house] DLB-49

Dana, Charles A. 1819-1897...... DLB-3, 23, 250

Dana, Richard Henry, Jr.
   1815-1882 .... DLB-1, 183, 235

Dandridge, Ray Garfield 1882-1930...... DLB-51

Dane, Clemence 1887-1965 ....DLB-10, 197

Danforth, John 1660-1730 .... DLB-24

Danforth, Samuel, I 1626-1674.......... DLB-24

Danforth, Samuel, II 1666-1727 .... DLB-24

Dangerous Acquaintances, Pierre-Ambroise-François
   Choderlos de Laclos DLB-314

Daniel, John M. 1825-1865 .... DLB-43

Daniel, Samuel 1562 or 1563-1619....... DLB-62

Daniel Press DLB-106	Davíð Stefánsson frá Fagraskógi 1895-1964 . . . . DLB-293	Day, Frank Parker 1881-1950 . . . . DLB-92
Daniel', Iulii 1925-1988 . . . . DLB-302	Davie, Donald 1922-1995 . . . . DLB-27	Day, John circa 1574-circa 1640 . . . . DLB-62
Daniells, Roy 1902-1979 . . . . DLB-68	Davie, Elspeth 1919-1995 . . . . DLB-139	Day, Marele 1947- DLB-325
Daniels, Jim 1956- DLB-120	Davies, Sir John 1569-1626 . . . . DLB-172	Day, Thomas 1748-1789 . . . . DLB-39
Daniels, Jonathan 1902-1981 . . . . DLB-127	Davies, John, of Hereford 1565?-1618 . . . . DLB-121	John Day [publishing house] DLB-170
Daniels, Josephus 1862-1948 . . . . DLB-29	Davies, Rhys 1901-1978 . . . . DLB-139, 191	The John Day Company DLB-46
Daniels, Sarah 1957- DLB-245	Davies, Robertson 1913-1995 . . . . DLB-68	Mahlon Day [publishing house] DLB-49
Danilevsky, Grigorii Petrovich 1829-1890 . . . . DLB-238	Davies, Samuel 1723-1761 . . . . DLB-31	Day Lewis, C. (see Blake, Nicholas)
Dannay, Frederic 1905-1982 . . . . DLB-137	Davies, Thomas 1712?-1785 . . . . DLB-142, 154	Dazai Osamu 1909-1948 . . . . DLB-182
Danner, Margaret Esse 1915- DLB-41	Davies, W. H. 1871-1940 . . . . DLB-19, 174	Deacon, William Arthur 1890-1977 . . . . . . DLB-68
John Danter [publishing house] DLB-170	Peter Davies Limited DLB-112	Deal, Borden 1922-1985 . . . . DLB-6
Dantin, Louis (Eugene Seers) 1865-1945 . . . . DLB-92	Davin, Nicholas Flood 1840?-1901 . . . . DLB-99	de Angeli, Marguerite 1889-1987 . . . . DLB-22
Danto, Arthur C. 1924- DLB-279	Daviot, Gordon 1896?-1952 . . . . DLB-10 (see also Tey, Josephine)	De Angelis, Milo 1951- DLB-128
Danzig, Allison 1898-1987 . . . . DLB-171	Davis, Arthur Hoey (see Rudd, Steele)	Debord, Guy 1931-1994 . . . . DLB-296
D'Arcy, Ella circa 1857-1937 . . . . DLB-135	Davis, Benjamin J. 1903-1964 . . . . DLB-303	De Bow, J. D. B. 1820-1867 . . . . DLB-3, 79, 248
Darío, Rubén 1867-1916 . . . . DLB-290	Davis, Charles A. (Major J. Downing) 1795-1867 . . . . DLB-11	Debs, Eugene V. 1855-1926 . . . . DLB-303
Dark, Eleanor 1901-1985 . . . . DLB-260	Davis, Clyde Brion 1894-1962 . . . . DLB-9	de Bruyn, Günter 1926- DLB-75
Darke, Nick 1948- DLB-233	Davis, Dick 1945- DLB-40, 282	de Camp, L. Sprague 1907-2000 . . . . DLB-8
Darley, Felix Octavious Carr 1822-1888 . . . . DLB-188	Davis, Frank Marshall 1905-1987 . . . . DLB-51	De Carlo, Andrea 1952- DLB-196
Darley, George 1795-1846 . . . . DLB-96	Davis, H. L. 1894-1960 . . . . DLB-9, 206	De Casas, Celso A. 1944- DLB-209
Darmesteter, Madame James (see Robinson, A. Mary F.)	Davis, Jack 1917-2000 . . . . DLB-325	Dechert, Robert 1895-1975 . . . . DLB-187
Darrow, Clarence 1857-1938 . . . . DLB-303	Davis, John 1774-1854 . . . . DLB-37	Declaration of the Rights of Man and of the Citizen DLB-314
Darwin, Charles 1809-1882 . . . . DLB-57, 166	Davis, Lydia 1947- DLB-130	Declaration of the Rights of Woman, Olympe de Gouges DLB-314
Darwin, Erasmus 1731-1802 . . . . DLB-93	Davis, Margaret Thomson 1926- DLB-14	Dedications, Inscriptions, and Annotations Y-01–02
Daryush, Elizabeth 1887-1977 . . . . DLB-20	Davis, Ossie 1917-2005 . . . . DLB-7, 38, 249	De' Dottori, Carlo 1618-1686 . . . . DLB-339
Das, Kamala 1934- DLB-323	Davis, Owen 1874-1956 . . . . DLB-249	Dee, John 1527-1608 or 1609 . . . . DLB-136, 213
Dashkova, Ekaterina Romanovna (née Vorontsova) 1743-1810 . . . . DLB-150	Davis, Paxton 1925-1994 . . . . Y-89	Deeping, George Warwick 1877-1950 . . . . DLB-153
Dashwood, Edmée Elizabeth Monica de la Pasture (see Delafield, E. M.)	Davis, Rebecca Harding 1831-1910 . . . . DLB-74, 239	Deffand, Marie de Vichy-Chamrond, marquise Du 1696-1780 . . . . DLB-313
Dattani, Mahesh 1958- DLB-323	Davis, Richard Harding 1864-1916 . . . . DLB-12, 23, 78, 79, 189; DS-13	Defoe, Daniel 1660-1731 . . . DLB-39, 95, 101, 336; CDBLB-2
Daudet, Alphonse 1840-1897 . . . . DLB-123	Davis, Samuel Cole 1764-1809 . . . . DLB-37	Preface to Colonel Jack (1722) DLB-39
d'Aulaire, Edgar Parin 1898-1986 and d'Aulaire, Ingri 1904-1980 . . . . DLB-22	Davis, Samuel Post 1850-1918 . . . . DLB-202	Preface to The Farther Adventures of Robinson Crusoe (1719) DLB-39
Davenant, Sir William 1606-1668 . . . . DLB-58, 126	Davison, Frank Dalby 1893-1970 . . . . DLB-260	Preface to Moll Flanders (1722) DLB-39
Davenport, Guy 1927-2005 . . . . DLB-130	Davison, Peter 1928- DLB-5	Preface to Robinson Crusoe (1719) DLB-39
Tribute to John Gardner Y-82	Davydov, Denis Vasil'evich 1784-1839 . . . . DLB-205	Preface to Roxana (1724) DLB-39
Davenport, Marcia 1903-1996 . . . . DS-17	Davys, Mary 1674-1732 . . . . DLB-39	de Fontaine, Felix Gregory 1834-1896 . . . . . DLB-43
Davenport, Robert circa 17th century DLB-58	Preface to The Works of Mrs. Davys (1725) DLB-39	De Forest, John William 1826-1906 . . . . DLB-12, 189
Daves, Delmer 1904-1977 . . . . DLB-26	DAW Books DLB-46	DeFrees, Madeline 1919- DLB-105
Davey, Frank 1940- DLB-53	Dawe, Bruce 1930- DLB-289	"The Poet's Kaleidoscope: The Element of Surprise in the Making of the Poem" DLB-105
Davidson, Avram 1923-1993 . . . . DLB-8	Dawson, Ernest 1882-1947 . . . . DLB-140; Y-02	
Davidson, Donald 1893-1968 . . . . DLB-45	Dawson, Fielding 1930- DLB-130	DeGolyer, Everette Lee 1886-1956 . . . . . . DLB-187
Davidson, Donald 1917-2003 . . . . DLB-279	Dawson, Sarah Morgan 1842-1909 . . . . . . DLB-239	de Graff, Robert 1895-1981 . . . . Y-81
Davidson, John 1857-1909 . . . . DLB-19	Dawson, William 1704-1752 . . . . DLB-31	de Graft, Joe 1924-1978 . . . . DLB-117
Davidson, Lionel 1922- DLB-14, 276	Day, Angel fl. 1583-1599 . . . . DLB-167, 236	De Groen, Alma 1941- DLB-325
Davidson, Robyn 1950- DLB-204	Day, Benjamin Henry 1810-1889 . . . . DLB-43	De Heinrico circa 980? DLB-148
Davidson, Sara 1943- DLB-185	Day, Clarence 1874-1935 . . . . DLB-11	Deighton, Len 1929- DLB-87; CDBLB-8
	Day, Dorothy 1897-1980 . . . . DLB-29	DeJong, Meindert 1906-1991 . . . . DLB-52

Cumulative Index

Dekker, Thomas circa 1572-1632 ..... DLB-62, 172; CDBLB-1

Delacorte, George T., Jr. 1894-1991 ...... DLB-91

Delafield, E. M. 1890-1943 .... DLB-34

Delahaye, Guy (Guillaume Lahaise) 1888-1969 .... DLB-92

de la Mare, Walter 1873-1956 .... DLB-19, 153, 162, 255; CDBLB-6

Deland, Margaret 1857-1945 .... DLB-78

Delaney, Shelagh 1939- DLB-13; CDBLB-8

Delano, Amasa 1763-1823 .... DLB-183

Delany, Martin Robinson 1812-1885 ..... DLB-50

Delany, Samuel R. 1942- DLB-8, 33

de la Roche, Mazo 1879-1961 .... DLB-68

Delavigne, Jean François Casimir 1793-1843 .... DLB-192

Delbanco, Nicholas 1942- DLB-6, 234

Delblanc, Sven 1931-1992 .... DLB-257

Del Castillo, Ramón 1949- DLB-209

Deledda, Grazia 1871-1936 .... DLB-264, 329

De Lemene, Francesco 1634-1704 .... DLB-339

De León, Nephtal 1945- DLB-82

Deleuze, Gilles 1925-1995 .... DLB-296

Delfini, Antonio 1907-1963 .... DLB-264

Delfino, Giovanni 1617-1699 .... DLB-339

Delgado, Abelardo Barrientos 1931- DLB-82

Del Giudice, Daniele 1949- DLB-196

De Libero, Libero 1906-1981 .... DLB-114

Delibes, Miguel 1920- DLB-322

Delicado, Francisco circa 1475-circa 1540? DLB-318

DeLillo, Don 1936- DLB-6, 173

de Lint, Charles 1951- DLB-251

de Lisser H. G. 1878-1944 .... DLB-117

Dell, Floyd 1887-1969 .... DLB-9

Dell Publishing Company DLB-46

Della Valle, Federico circa 1560-1628 .... DLB-339

delle Grazie, Marie Eugene 1864-1931 .... DLB-81

Deloney, Thomas died 1600 .... DLB-167

Deloria, Ella C. 1889-1971 .... DLB-175

Deloria, Vine, Jr. 1933- DLB-175

del Rey, Lester 1915-1993 .... DLB-8

Del Vecchio, John M. 1947- DS-9

Del'vig, Anton Antonovich 1798-1831 ... DLB-205

de Man, Paul 1919-1983 .... DLB-67

DeMarinis, Rick 1934- DLB-218

Demby, William 1922- DLB-33

De Mille, James 1833-1880 .... DLB-99, 251

de Mille, William 1878-1955 .... DLB-266

Deming, Philander 1829-1915 .... DLB-74

Deml, Jakub 1878-1961 .... DLB-215

Demorest, William Jennings 1822-1895 ... DLB-79

De Morgan, William 1839-1917 .... DLB-153

Demosthenes 384 B.C.-322 B.C. DLB-176

Henry Denham [publishing house] DLB-170

Denham, Sir John 1615-1669 .... DLB-58, 126

Denison, Merrill 1893-1975 .... DLB-92

T. S. Denison and Company DLB-49

Dennery, Adolphe Philippe 1811-1899 .... DLB-192

Dennie, Joseph 1768-1812 ...... DLB-37, 43, 59, 73

Dennis, C. J. 1876-1938 .... DLB-260

Dennis, John 1658-1734 .... DLB-101

Dennis, Nigel 1912-1989 .... DLB-13, 15, 233

Denslow, W. W. 1856-1915 .... DLB-188

Dent, J. M., and Sons DLB-112

Dent, Lester 1904-1959 .... DLB-306

Dent, Tom 1932-1998 .... DLB-38

Denton, Daniel circa 1626-1703 .... DLB-24

DePaola, Tomie 1934- DLB-61

De Quille, Dan 1829-1898 .... DLB-186

De Quincey, Thomas 1785-1859 .... DLB-110, 144; CDBLB-3

"Rhetoric" (1828; revised, 1859) [excerpt] DLB-57

"Style" (1840; revised, 1859) [excerpt] DLB-57

Derby, George Horatio 1823-1861 .... DLB-11

J. C. Derby and Company DLB-49

Derby and Miller DLB-49

De Ricci, Seymour 1881-1942 .... DLB-201

Derleth, August 1909-1971 .... DLB-9; DS-17

Derrida, Jacques 1930-2004 .... DLB-242

The Derrydale Press DLB-46

Derzhavin, Gavriil Romanovich 1743-1816 .... DLB-150

Desai, Anita 1937- DLB-271, 323

Desani, G. V. 1909-2000 .... DLB-323

Desaulniers, Gonzalve 1863-1934 .... DLB-92

Desbordes-Valmore, Marceline 1786-1859 .... DLB-217

Descartes, René 1596-1650 .... DLB-268

Deschamps, Emile 1791-1871 .... DLB-217

Deschamps, Eustache 1340?-1404 ...... DLB-208

Desbiens, Jean-Paul 1927- DLB-53

des Forêts, Louis-Rene 1918-2001 .... DLB-83

Deshpande, Shashi 1938- DLB-323

Desiato, Luca 1941- DLB-196

Desjardins, Marie-Catherine (see Villedieu, Madame de)

Desnica, Vladan 1905-1967 .... DLB-181

Desnos, Robert 1900-1945 .... DLB-258

Des Périers, Bonaventure 1510?-1543? DLB-327

Desportes, Philippe 1546-1606 .... DLB-327

DesRochers, Alfred 1901-1978 .... DLB-68

Des Roches, Madeleine 1520?-1587? and Catherine des Roches 1542-1587? DLB-327

Des Roches, Madeleine 1520?-1587? DLB-327

Desrosiers, Léo-Paul 1896-1967 .... DLB-68

Dessaulles, Louis-Antoine 1819-1895 ..... DLB-99

Dessì, Giuseppe 1909-1977 .... DLB-177

Destouches, Louis-Ferdinand (see Céline, Louis-Ferdinand)

Desvignes, Lucette 1926- DLB-321

DeSylva, Buddy 1895-1950 .... DLB-265

De Tabley, Lord 1835-1895 .... DLB-35

Deutsch, Babette 1895-1982 .... DLB-45

Deutsch, Niklaus Manuel (see Manuel, Niklaus)

André Deutsch Limited DLB-112

Devanny, Jean 1894-1962 .... DLB-260

Deveaux, Alexis 1948- DLB-38

De Vere, Aubrey 1814-1902 .... DLB-35

Devereux, second Earl of Essex, Robert 1565-1601 .... DLB-136

The Devin-Adair Company DLB-46

De Vinne, Theodore Low 1828-1914 ..... DLB-187

Devlin, Anne 1951- DLB-245

DeVoto, Bernard 1897-1955 .... DLB-9, 256

De Vries, Peter 1910-1993 .... DLB-6; Y-82

Tribute to Albert Erskine Y-93

Dewart, Edward Hartley 1828-1903 ..... DLB-99

Dewdney, Christopher 1951- DLB-60

Dewdney, Selwyn 1909-1979 .... DLB-68

Dewey, John 1859-1952 .... DLB-246, 270

Dewey, Orville 1794-1882 .... DLB-243

Dewey, Thomas B. 1915-1981 .... DLB-226

DeWitt, Robert M., Publisher DLB-49

DeWolfe, Fiske and Company DLB-49

Dexter, Colin 1930- DLB-87

de Young, M. H. 1849-1925 .... DLB-25

Dhlomo, H. I. E. 1903-1956 .... DLB-157, 225

Dhu al-Rummah (Abu al-Harith Ghaylan ibn 'Uqbah) circa 696-circa 735 .... DLB-311

Dhuoda circa 803-after 843 .... DLB-148

The Dial 1840-1844 .... DLB-223

The Dial Press DLB-46

"Dialogue entre un prêtre et un moribond," Marquis de Sade DLB-314

Diamond, I. A. L. 1920-1988 .... DLB-26

Dias Gomes, Alfredo 1922-1999 .... DLB-307

Díaz del Castillo, Bernal circa 1496-1584 .... DLB-318

Dibble, L. Grace 1902-1998 .... DLB-204

Dibdin, Thomas Frognall 1776-1847 .... DLB-184

Di Cicco, Pier Giorgio 1949- DLB-60

Dick, Philip K. 1928-1982 ....DLB-8

Dick and Fitzgerald DLB-49

Dickens, Charles 1812-1870
...DLB-21, 55, 70, 159, 166; DS-5; CDBLB-4

Dickey, Eric Jerome 1961- DLB-292

Dickey, James 1923-1997 .... DLB-5, 193;
Y-82, 93, 96, 97; DS-7, 19; CDALB-6

    James Dickey and Stanley Burnshaw
        Correspondence Y-02

    James Dickey at Seventy–A Tribute Y-93

    James Dickey, American Poet Y-96

    The James Dickey Society..............Y-99

    The Life of James Dickey: A Lecture to
        the Friends of the Emory Libraries,
        by Henry Hart Y-98

    Tribute to Archibald MacLeish Y-82

    Tribute to Malcolm Cowley Y-89

    Tribute to Truman Capote Y-84

    Tributes [to Dickey]..................Y-97

Dickey, William 1928-1994 ....DLB-5

Dickinson, Emily
1830-1886 ....DLB-1, 243; CDALB-3

Dickinson, John 1732-1808 ....DLB-31

Dickinson, Jonathan 1688-1747 ....DLB-24

Dickinson, Patric 1914-1994 ....DLB-27

Dickinson, Peter 1927- DLB-87, 161, 276

John Dicks [publishing house] DLB-106

Dickson, Gordon R. 1923-2001...........DLB-8

Dictionary of Literary Biography
Annual Awards for Dictionary of
Literary Biography Editors and
Contributors....................Y-98–02

Dictionary of Literary Biography
Yearbook Awards Y-92–93, 97–02

The Dictionary of National Biography DLB-144

Diderot, Denis 1713-1784..............DLB-313

    "The Encyclopedia" DLB-314

Didion, Joan 1934-
.... DLB-2, 173, 185; Y-81, 86; CDALB-6

Di Donato, Pietro 1911-1992.............DLB-9

Die Fürstliche Bibliothek Corvey...........Y-96

Diego, Gerardo 1896-1987...........DLB-134

Dietz, Howard 1896-1983.............DLB-265

Díez, Luis Mateo 1942- DLB-322

Digby, Everard 1550?-1605 ....DLB-281

Digges, Thomas circa 1546-1595........DLB-136

The Digital Millennium Copyright Act:
Expanding Copyright Protection in
Cyberspace and Beyond.............Y-98

Diktonius, Elmer 1896-1961 ....DLB-259

Dillard, Annie 1945- DLB-275, 278; Y-80

Dillard, R. H. W. 1937- DLB-5, 244

Charles T. Dillingham Company.........DLB-49

G. W. Dillingham Company............DLB-49

Edward and Charles Dilly
[publishing house].................DLB-154

Dilthey, Wilhelm 1833-1911 ....DLB-129

Dimitrova, Blaga 1922- ...DLB-181; CDWLB-4

Dimov, Dimitr 1909-1966 ....DLB-181

Dimsdale, Thomas J. 1831?-1866 ....DLB-186

Dinescu, Mircea 1950- DLB-232

Dinesen, Isak (see Blixen, Karen)

Ding Ling 1904-1986..................DLB-328

Dingelstedt, Franz von 1814-1881.......DLB-133

Dinis, Júlio (Joaquim Guilherme
Gomes Coelho) 1839-1871 ....DLB-287

Dintenfass, Mark 1941- Y-84

Diogenes, Jr. (see Brougham, John)

Diogenes Laertius circa 200........... DLB-176

DiPrima, Diane 1934- DLB-5, 16

Disch, Thomas M. 1940- DLB-8, 282

"Le Discours sur le style," Georges-Louis Leclerc
de Buffon........................DLB-314

Disgrace, 1999 Booker Prize winner,
J. M. Coetzee....................DLB-326

Diski, Jenny 1947- DLB-271

Disney, Walt 1901-1966................DLB-22

Disraeli, Benjamin 1804-1881 ....DLB-21, 55

D'Israeli, Isaac 1766-1848 ....DLB-107

DLB Award for Distinguished
Literary Criticism Y-02

Ditlevsen, Tove 1917-1976 ....DLB-214

Ditzen, Rudolf (see Fallada, Hans)

Divakaruni, Chitra Banerjee 1956- DLB-323

Dix, Dorothea Lynde 1802-1887......DLB-1, 235

Dix, Dorothy (see Gilmer, Elizabeth Meriwether)

Dix, Edwards and Company DLB-49

Dix, Gertrude circa 1874-? DLB-197

Dixie, Florence Douglas 1857-1905 ......DLB-174

Dixon, Ella Hepworth
1855 or 1857-1932.................DLB-197

Dixon, Paige (see Corcoran, Barbara)

Dixon, Richard Watson 1833-1900.......DLB-19

Dixon, Stephen 1936- DLB-130

DLB Award for Distinguished
Literary Criticism Y-02

Dmitriev, Andrei Viktorovich 1956- DLB-285

Dmitriev, Ivan Ivanovich 1760-1837 .....DLB-150

Dobell, Bertram 1842-1914 ....DLB-184

Dobell, Sydney 1824-1874 ....DLB-32

Dobie, J. Frank 1888-1964.............DLB-212

Dobles Yzaguirre, Julieta 1943- DLB-283

Döblin, Alfred 1878-1957.....DLB-66; CDWLB-2

Dobroliubov, Nikolai Aleksandrovich
1836-1861 ....DLB-277

Dobson, Austin 1840-1921 ....DLB-35, 144

Dobson, Rosemary 1920- DLB-260

Doctorow, E. L.
1931- DLB-2, 28, 173; Y-80; CDALB-6

Dodd, Susan M. 1946- DLB-244

Dodd, William E. 1869-1940............DLB-17

Anne Dodd [publishing house] DLB-154

Dodd, Mead and Company..............DLB-49

Doderer, Heimito von 1896-1966 ....DLB-85

B. W. Dodge and Company DLB-46

Dodge, Mary Abigail 1833-1896........DLB-221

Dodge, Mary Mapes
1831?-1905 ....DLB-42, 79; DS-13

Dodge Publishing Company DLB-49

Dodgson, Charles Lutwidge (see Carroll, Lewis)

Dodsley, Robert 1703-1764 ....DLB-95

R. Dodsley [publishing house]..........DLB-154

Dodson, Owen 1914-1983..............DLB-76

Dodwell, Christina 1951- DLB-204

Doesticks, Q. K. Philander, P. B.
(see Thomson, Mortimer)

Doheny, Carrie Estelle 1875-1958 ....DLB-140

Doherty, John 1798?-1854 ....DLB-190

Doig, Ivan 1939- DLB-206

Doinaş, Ştefan Augustin 1922- DLB-232

Dolet, Etienne 1509-1546 ....DLB-327

Domínguez, Sylvia Maida 1935- DLB-122

Donaghy, Michael 1954- DLB-282

Patrick Donahoe [publishing house] DLB-49

Donald, David H. 1920- DLB-17; Y-87

Donaldson, Scott 1928- DLB-111

La doncella Theodor late-thirteenth or fourteenth
century DLB-337

Doni, Rodolfo 1919- DLB-177

Donleavy, J. P. 1926- DLB-6, 173

Donnadieu, Marguerite (see Duras, Marguerite)

Donne, John
1572-1631 ....DLB-121, 151; CDBLB-1

Donnelly, Ignatius 1831-1901 ....DLB-12

R. R. Donnelley and Sons Company......DLB-49

Donoghue, Emma 1969- DLB-267

Donohue and Henneberry...............DLB-49

Donoso, José 1924-1996 .... DLB-113; CDWLB-3

M. Doolady [publishing house] DLB-49

Dooley, Ebon (see Ebon)

Doolittle, Hilda 1886-1961 .....DLB-4, 45; DS-15

Doplicher, Fabio 1938- DLB-128

Dor, Milo 1923- DLB-85

George H. Doran Company DLB-46

Dorat, Jean 1508-1588.................DLB-327

Dorcey, Mary 1950- DLB-319

Dorgelès, Roland 1886-1973 ....DLB-65

Dorn, Edward 1929-1999 ....DLB-5

Dorr, Rheta Childe 1866-1948 ....DLB-25

Cumulative Index

Dorris, Michael 1945-1997 . . . . .DLB-175

Dorset and Middlesex, Charles Sackville,
    Lord Buckhurst, Earl of 1643-1706 . . . .DLB-131

Dorsey, Candas Jane 1952- DLB-251

Dorst, Tankred 1925- DLB-75, 124

Dos Passos, John 1896-1970
    . . . . DLB-4, 9, 316; DS-1, 15; CDALB-5

    John Dos Passos: A Centennial
        Commemoration Y-96

    John Dos Passos: Artist Y-99

    John Dos Passos Newsletter Y-00

    U.S.A. (Documentary) DLB-274

Dostoevsky, Fyodor 1821-1881 . . . . DLB-238

Doubleday and Company DLB-49

Doubrovsky, Serge 1928- DLB-299

Dougall, Lily 1858-1923 . . . . DLB-92

Doughty, Charles M.
    1843-1926 . . . . DLB-19, 57, 174

Douglas, Lady Alfred (see Custance, Olive)

Douglas, Ellen (Josephine Ayres Haxton)
    1921- DLB-292

Douglas, Gavin 1476-1522 . . . . DLB-132

Douglas, Keith 1920-1944 . . . . DLB-27

Douglas, Norman 1868-1952 . . . . DLB-34, 195

Douglass, Frederick 1817-1895
    . . . . DLB-1, 43, 50, 79, 243; CDALB-2

    Frederick Douglass Creative Arts Center. Y-01

Douglass, William circa 1691-1752 . . . . DLB-24

Dourado, Autran 1926- DLB-145, 307

Dove, Arthur G. 1880-1946 . . . . DLB-188

Dove, Rita 1952- DLB-120; CDALB-7

Dover Publications DLB-46

Doves Press DLB-112

Dovlatov, Sergei Donatovich
    1941-1990 . . . . DLB-285

Dowden, Edward 1843-1913 . . . . DLB-35, 149

Dowell, Coleman 1925-1985 . . . . DLB-130

Dowland, John 1563-1626 . . . . .DLB-172

Downes, Gwladys 1915- DLB-88

Downing, J., Major (see Davis, Charles A.)

Downing, Major Jack (see Smith, Seba)

Dowriche, Anne
    before 1560-after 1613 . . . . .DLB-172

Dowson, Ernest 1867-1900 . . . . DLB-19, 135

William Doxey [publishing house] DLB-49

Doyle, Sir Arthur Conan
    1859-1930 . . .DLB-18, 70, 156, 178; CDBLB-5

    The Priory Scholars of New York Y-99

Doyle, Kirby 1932- DLB-16

Doyle, Roddy 1958- DLB-194, 326

Drabble, Margaret
    1939- DLB-14, 155, 231; CDBLB-8

    Tribute to Graham Greene. Y-91

Drach, Albert 1902-1995 . . . . DLB-85

Drachmann, Holger 1846-1908 . . . . DLB-300

Dracula (Documentary) DLB-304

Dragojević, Danijel 1934- DLB-181

Dragún, Osvaldo 1929-1999 . . . . DLB-305

Drake, Samuel Gardner 1798-1875 . . . . . . DLB-187

Drama (See Theater)

The Dramatic Publishing Company DLB-49

Dramatists Play Service DLB-46

Drant, Thomas
    early 1540s?-1578 . . . . DLB-167

Draper, John W. 1811-1882 . . . . DLB-30

Draper, Lyman C. 1815-1891 . . . . DLB-30

Drayton, Michael 1563-1631 . . . . DLB-121

Dreiser, Theodore 1871-1945
    . . . . DLB-9, 12, 102, 137; DS-1; CDALB-3

    The International Theodore Dreiser
        Society Y-01

    Notes from the Underground
        of *Sister Carrie* Y-01

Dresser, Davis 1904-1977 . . . . DLB-226

Drew, Elizabeth A.
    "A Note on Technique" [excerpt]
      (1926) DLB-36

Drewe, Robert 1943- DLB-325

Drewitz, Ingeborg 1923-1986 . . . . DLB-75

Drieu La Rochelle, Pierre 1893-1945 . . . . . DLB-72

Drinker, Elizabeth 1735-1807 . . . . DLB-200

Drinkwater, John 1882-1937 . . . . . .DLB-10, 19, 149

    The Friends of the Dymock Poets Y-00

Dropkin, Celia (Tsilye Dropkin)
    1887-1956 . . . . DLB-333

Droste-Hülshoff, Annette von
    1797-1848 . . . . DLB-133; CDWLB-2

The Drue Heinz Literature Prize
    Excerpt from "Excerpts from a Report
    of the Commission," in David
    Bosworth's *The Death of Descartes*
    An Interview with David Bosworth Y-82

Drummond, William, of Hawthornden
    1585-1649 . . . . DLB-121, 213

Drummond, William Henry 1854-1907 . . . DLB-92

Drummond de Andrade, Carlos
    1902-1987 . . . . DLB-307

Druzhinin, Aleksandr Vasil'evich
    1824-1864 . . . . DLB-238

Druzhnikov, Yuri 1933- DLB-317

Dryden, Charles 1860?-1931 . . . . .DLB-171

Dryden, John
    1631-1700 . . . . . . DLB-80, 101, 131; CDBLB-2

Držić, Marin
    circa 1508-1567 . . . . .DLB-147; CDWLB-4

Duane, William 1760-1835 . . . . DLB-43

Du Bartas, Guillaume 1544-1590 . . . . DLB-327

Dubé, Marcel 1930- DLB-53

Dubé, Rodolphe (see Hertel, François)

Du Bellay, Joachim 1522?-1560 . . . . DLB-327

Dubie, Norman 1945- DLB-120

Dubin, Al 1891-1945 . . . . DLB-265

Du Boccage, Anne-Marie 1710-1802 . . . . . DLB-313

Dubois, Silvia 1788 or 1789?-1889 . . . . . . DLB-239

Du Bois, W. E. B.
    1868-1963 . . . .DLB-47, 50, 91, 246; CDALB-3

Du Bois, William Pène 1916-1993 . . . . DLB-61

Dubrovina, Ekaterina Oskarovna
    1846-1913 . . . . DLB-238

Dubus, Andre 1936-1999 . . . . DLB-130

    Tribute to Michael M. Rea Y-97

Dubus, Andre, III 1959- DLB-292

Ducange, Victor 1783-1833 . . . . DLB-192

Du Chaillu, Paul Belloni 1831?-1903 . . . . DLB-189

Ducharme, Réjean 1941- DLB-60

Dučić, Jovan 1871-1943 . . . . . DLB-147; CDWLB-4

Duck, Stephen 1705?-1756 . . . . DLB-95

Gerald Duckworth and Company
    Limited DLB-112

Duclaux, Madame Mary (see Robinson, A. Mary F.)

Dudek, Louis 1918-2001 . . . . DLB-88

Dudintsev, Vladimir Dmitrievich
    1918-1998 . . . . DLB-302

Dudley-Smith, Trevor (see Hall, Adam)

Duell, Sloan and Pearce DLB-46

Duerer, Albrecht 1471-1528 . . . . .DLB-179

Duff Gordon, Lucie 1821-1869 . . . . DLB-166

Dufferin, Helen Lady, Countess of Gifford
    1807-1867 . . . . DLB-199

Duffield and Green DLB-46

Duffy, Maureen 1933- DLB-14, 310

Dufief, Nicholas Gouin 1776-1834 . . . . . . .DLB-187

Dufresne, John 1948- DLB-292

Dugan, Alan 1923-2003 . . . . DLB-5

Dugard, William 1606-1662 . . . . .DLB-170, 281

William Dugard [publishing house] DLB-170

Dugas, Marcel 1883-1947 . . . . DLB-92

William Dugdale [publishing house] DLB-106

Du Guillet, Pernette 1520?-1545 . . . . DLB-327

Duhamel, Georges 1884-1966 . . . . DLB-65

Dujardin, Edouard 1861-1949 . . . . DLB-123

Dukes, Ashley 1885-1959 . . . . DLB-10

Dumas, Alexandre *fils* 1824-1895 . . . . DLB-192

Dumas, Alexandre *père* 1802-1870 . . . . .DLB-119, 192

Dumas, Henry 1934-1968 . . . . DLB-41

du Maurier, Daphne 1907-1989 . . . . DLB-191

Du Maurier, George 1834-1896 . . . . .DLB-153, 178

Dummett, Michael 1925- DLB-262

Dunbar, Paul Laurence
    1872-1906 . . . . DLB-50, 54, 78; CDALB-3

    Introduction to *Lyrics of Lowly Life* (1896),
      by William Dean Howells DLB-50

Dunbar, William
    circa 1460-circa 1522 . . . . DLB-132, 146

Duncan, Dave 1933- DLB-251
Duncan, David James 1952- DLB-256
Duncan, Norman 1871-1916 ....DLB-92
Duncan, Quince 1940- DLB-145
Duncan, Robert 1919-1988 ....DLB-5, 16, 193
Duncan, Ronald 1914-1982...........DLB-13
Duncan, Sara Jeannette 1861-1922 ....DLB-92
Dunigan, Edward, and Brother DLB-49
Dunlap, John 1747-1812..............DLB-43
Dunlap, William 1766-1839....... DLB-30, 37, 59
Dunlop, William "Tiger" 1792-1848 ......DLB-99
Dunmore, Helen 1952- DLB-267
Dunn, Douglas 1942- DLB-40
Dunn, Harvey Thomas 1884-1952 ......DLB-188
Dunn, Stephen 1939- DLB-105
    "The Good, The Not So Good" DLB-105
Dunne, Dominick 1925- DLB-306
Dunne, Finley Peter 1867-1936 ....DLB-11, 23
Dunne, John Gregory 1932- Y-80
Dunne, Philip 1908-1992...............DLB-26
Dunning, Ralph Cheever 1878-1930 ....DLB-4
Dunning, William A. 1857-1922 ....DLB-17
Duns Scotus, John circa 1266-1308 ......DLB-115
Dunsany, Lord (Edward John Moreton
    Drax Plunkett, Baron Dunsany)
    1878-1957 .... DLB-10, 77, 153, 156, 255
Dunton, W. Herbert 1878-1936........DLB-188
John Dunton [publishing house] DLB-170
Dupin, Amantine-Aurore-Lucile (see Sand, George)
Du Pont de Nemours, Pierre Samuel
    1739-1817 ....DLB-313
Dupuy, Eliza Ann 1814-1880..........DLB-248
Durack, Mary 1913-1994.............DLB-260
Durand, Lucile (see Bersianik, Louky)
Duranti, Francesca 1935- DLB-196
Duranty, Walter 1884-1957 ....DLB-29
Duras, Marguerite (Marguerite Donnadieu)
    1914-1996 ....DLB-83, 321
Durfey, Thomas 1653-1723 ....DLB-80
Durova, Nadezhda Andreevna
    (Aleksandr Andreevich Aleksandrov)
    1783-1866 ....DLB-198
Durrell, Lawrence 1912-1990
    .... DLB-15, 27, 204; Y-90; CDBLB-7
William Durrell [publishing house] DLB-49
Dürrenmatt, Friedrich
    1921-1990 .... DLB-69, 124; CDWLB-2
Duston, Hannah 1657-1737 ....DLB-200
Dutt, Toru 1856-1877................DLB-240
E. P. Dutton and Company DLB-49
Duun, Olav 1876-1939...............DLB-297
Duvoisin, Roger 1904-1980...........DLB-61

Duyckinck, Evert Augustus
    1816-1878 ....DLB-3, 64, 250
Duyckinck, George L.
    1823-1863 ....DLB-3, 250
Duyckinck and Company DLB-49
Dwight, John Sullivan 1813-1893 .....DLB-1, 235
Dwight, Timothy 1752-1817 ....DLB-37
    America: or, A Poem on the Settlement
    of the British Colonies, by
    Timothy Dwight................DLB-37
Dybek, Stuart 1942- DLB-130
    Tribute to Michael M. Rea Y-97
Dyer, Charles 1928-................DLB-13
Dyer, Sir Edward 1543-1607 ....DLB-136
Dyer, George 1755-1841 ....DLB-93
Dyer, John 1699-1757................DLB-95
Dyk, Viktor 1877-1931...............DLB-215
Dylan, Bob 1941- DLB-16

E

Eager, Edward 1911-1964 ....DLB-22
Eagleton, Terry 1943- DLB-242
Eames, Wilberforce
    1855-1937 ....DLB-140
Earle, Alice Morse
    1853-1911 ....DLB-221
Earle, John 1600 or 1601-1665 ....DLB-151
James H. Earle and Company DLB-49
Early Medieval Spanish Theater DLB-337
East Europe
    Independence and Destruction,
    1918-1941....................DLB-220
    Social Theory and Ethnography:
    Language and Ethnicity in
    Western versus Eastern Man DLB-220
Eastlake, William 1917-1997 ....DLB-6, 206
Eastman, Carol ?- DLB-44
Eastman, Charles A. (Ohiyesa)
    1858-1939 .... DLB-175
Eastman, Max 1883-1969 ....DLB-91
Eaton, Daniel Isaac 1753-1814.........DLB-158
Eaton, Edith Maude 1865-1914.....DLB-221, 312
Eaton, Winnifred 1875-1954 ......DLB-221, 312
Eberhart, Richard
    1904-2005 ....DLB-48; CDALB-1
    Tribute to Robert Penn Warren Y-89
Ebner, Jeannie 1918-2004 ....DLB-85
Ebner-Eschenbach, Marie von
    1830-1916 ....DLB-81
Ebon 1942- DLB-41
E-Books' Second Act in Libraries............Y-02
Ecbasis Captivi circa 1045................DLB-148
Ecco Press DLB-46
Echard, Laurence 1670?-1730 ....DLB-336
Echegaray, José 1832-1916............DLB-329
Eckhart, Meister circa 1260-circa 1328 ...DLB-115

The Eclectic Review 1805-1868 ....DLB-110
Eco, Umberto 1932- DLB-196, 242
Eddison, E. R. 1882-1945 ....DLB-255
Edel, Leon 1907-1997................DLB-103
Edelfeldt, Inger 1956- DLB-257
J. M. Edelstein's Collection of Twentieth-
    Century American Poetry (A Century of Poetry,
    a Lifetime of Collecting) Y-02
Edes, Benjamin 1732-1803..............DLB-43
Edgar, David 1948- DLB-13, 233
    Viewpoint: Politics and
    Performance DLB-13
Edgerton, Clyde 1944- DLB-278
Edgeworth, Maria
    1768-1849 .... DLB-116, 159, 163
The Edinburgh Review 1802-1929..........DLB-110
Edinburgh University Press............DLB-112
Editing
    Conversations with Editors.............Y-95
    Editorial Statements DLB-137
    The Editorial Style of Fredson Bowers Y-91
    Editorial: The Extension of Copyright Y-02
    We See the Editor at Work Y-97
    Whose *Ulysses?* The Function of Editing...Y-97
The Editor Publishing Company.........DLB-49
Editorial Institute at Boston University.......Y-00
Edmonds, Helen Woods Ferguson
    (see Kavan, Anna)
Edmonds, Randolph 1900-1983 ....DLB-51
Edmonds, Walter D. 1903-1998 ....DLB-9
Edric, Robert (see Armitage, G. E.)
Edschmid, Kasimir 1890-1966..........DLB-56
Edson, Margaret 1961- DLB-266
Edson, Russell 1935- DLB-244
Edwards, Amelia Anne Blandford
    1831-1892 ....DLB-174
Edwards, Dic 1953- DLB-245
Edwards, Edward 1812-1886..........DLB-184
Edwards, Jonathan 1703-1758 ....DLB-24, 270
Edwards, Jonathan, Jr. 1745-1801 ....DLB-37
Edwards, Junius 1929- DLB-33
Edwards, Matilda Barbara Betham
    1836-1919 .... DLB-174
Edwards, Richard 1524-1566...........DLB-62
Edwards, Sarah Pierpont 1710-1758......DLB-200
James Edwards [publishing house].......DLB-154
Effinger, George Alec 1947- DLB-8
Egerton, George 1859-1945............DLB-135
Eggleston, Edward 1837-1902 ....DLB-12
Eggleston, Wilfred 1901-1986 ....DLB-92
Eglītis, Anšlavs 1906-1993.............DLB-220
Eguren, José María 1874-1942 ....DLB-290
Ehrenreich, Barbara 1941- DLB-246

Cumulative Index

Ehrenstein, Albert 1886-1950 . . . . DLB-81

Ehrhart, W. D. 1948- DS-9

Ehrlich, Gretel 1946- DLB-212, 275

Eich, Günter 1907-1972 . . . . DLB-69, 124

Eichendorff, Joseph Freiherr von
1788-1857 . . . . DLB-90

Eifukumon'in 1271-1342 . . . . DLB-203

Eigner, Larry 1926-1996 . . . . DLB-5, 193

Eikon Basilike 1649 . . . . DLB-151

Eilhart von Oberge
circa 1140-circa 1195 . . . . DLB-148

Einar Benediktsson 1864-1940 . . . . DLB-293

Einar Kárason 1955- DLB-293

Einar Már Guðmundsson 1954- DLB-293

Einhard circa 770-840 . . . . DLB-148

Eiseley, Loren 1907-1977 . . . . .DLB-275, DS-17

Eisenberg, Deborah 1945- DLB-244

Eisenreich, Herbert 1925-1986 . . . . DLB-85

Eisner, Kurt 1867-1919 . . . . DLB-66

Ekelöf, Gunnar 1907-1968 . . . . DLB-259

Eklund, Gordon 1945- Y-83

Ekman, Kerstin 1933- DLB-257

Ekwensi, Cyprian 1921- . . . DLB-117; CDWLB-3

Elaw, Zilpha circa 1790-? DLB-239

George Eld [publishing house] DLB-170

Elder, Lonne, III 1931- DLB-7, 38, 44

Paul Elder and Company DLB-49

Eldershaw, Flora (M. Barnard Eldershaw)
1897-1956 . . . . DLB-260

Eldershaw, M. Barnard (see Barnard, Marjorie and
Eldershaw, Flora)

The Elected Member, 1970 Booker Prize winner,
Bernice Rubens DLB-326

The Electronic Text Center and the Electronic
Archive of Early American Fiction at the
University of Virginia Library Y-98

Eliade, Mircea 1907-1986 . . . DLB-220; CDWLB-4

Elie, Robert 1915-1973 . . . . DLB-88

Elin Pelin 1877-1949 . . . . .DLB-147; CDWLB-4

Eliot, George
1819-1880 . . . . DLB-21, 35, 55; CDBLB-4

The George Eliot Fellowship Y-99

Eliot, John 1604-1690 . . . . DLB-24

Eliot, T. S. 1888-1965
. . . . . . DLB-7, 10, 45, 63, 245, 329; CDALB-5

T. S. Eliot Centennial: The Return
of the Old Possum Y-88

The T. S. Eliot Society: Celebration and
Scholarship, 1980-1999 . . . . Y-99

Eliot's Court Press DLB-170

Elizabeth I 1533-1603 . . . . DLB-136

Elizabeth von Nassau-Saarbrücken
after 1393-1456 . . . . .DLB-179

Elizondo, Salvador 1932- DLB-145

Elizondo, Sergio 1930- DLB-82

Elkin, Stanley
1930-1995 . . . . DLB-2, 28, 218, 278; Y-80

Elles, Dora Amy (see Wentworth, Patricia)

Ellet, Elizabeth F. 1818?-1877 . . . . DLB-30

Ellin, Stanley 1916-1986 . . . . DLB-306, 335

Elliot, Ebenezer 1781-1849 . . . . DLB-96, 190

Elliot, Frances Minto (Dickinson)
1820-1898 . . . . DLB-166

Elliott, Charlotte 1789-1871 . . . . DLB-199

Elliott, George 1923- DLB-68

Elliott, George P. 1918-1980 . . . . DLB-244

Elliott, Janice 1931-1995 . . . . DLB-14

Elliott, Sarah Barnwell 1848-1928 . . . . . . DLB-221

Elliott, Sumner Locke 1917-1991 . . . . DLB-289

Elliott, Thomes and Talbot DLB-49

Elliott, William, III 1788-1863 . . . . DLB-3, 248

Ellis, Alice Thomas (Anna Margaret Haycraft)
1932- DLB-194

Ellis, Bret Easton 1964- DLB-292

Ellis, Edward S. 1840-1916 . . . . DLB-42

Frederick Staridge Ellis
[publishing house] DLB-106

Ellis, George E.
"The New Controversy Concerning
Miracles DS-5

The George H. Ellis Company DLB-49

Ellis, Havelock 1859-1939 . . . . DLB-190

Ellison, Harlan 1934- DLB-8, 335

Tribute to Isaac Asimov Y-92

Ellison, Ralph
1914-1994 . . . DLB-2, 76, 227; Y-94; CDALB-1

Ellmann, Richard 1918-1987 . . . . . . DLB-103; Y-87

Ellroy, James 1948- DLB-226; Y-91

Tribute to John D. MacDonald Y-86

Tribute to Raymond Chandler Y-88

Eluard, Paul 1895-1952 . . . . DLB-258

Elyot, Thomas 1490?-1546 . . . . DLB-136

Elytis, Odysseus 1911-1996 . . . . DLB-329

Emanuel, James Andrew 1921- DLB-41

Emecheta, Buchi 1944- DLB-117; CDWLB-3

Emerson, Ralph Waldo
1803-1882 . . . . . DLB-1, 59, 73, 183, 223, 270;
DS-5; CDALB-2

Ralph Waldo Emerson in 1982 . . . . Y-82

The Ralph Waldo Emerson Society Y-99

Emerson, William 1769-1811 . . . . DLB-37

Emerson, William R. 1923-1997 . . . . Y-97

Emin, Fedor Aleksandrovich
circa 1735-1770 . . . . DLB-150

Emmanuel, Pierre 1916-1984 . . . . DLB-258

Empedocles fifth century B.C. DLB-176

Empson, William 1906-1984 . . . . DLB-20

Enchi Fumiko 1905-1986 . . . . DLB-182

"The Encyclopedia," Denis Diderot DLB-314

Ende, Michael 1929-1995 . . . . DLB-75

Endō Shūsaku 1923-1996 . . . . DLB-182

Engel, Marian 1933-1985 . . . . DLB-53

Engel'gardt, Sof'ia Vladimirovna
1828-1894 . . . . .DLB-277

Engels, Friedrich 1820-1895 . . . . DLB-129

Engle, Paul 1908-1991 . . . . DLB-48

Tribute to Robert Penn Warren Y-89

English, Thomas Dunn 1819-1902 . . . . . . DLB-202

The English Patient, 1992 Booker Prize winner,
Michael Ondaatje DLB-326

Ennius 239 B.C.-169 B.C. DLB-211

Enquist, Per Olov 1934- DLB-257

Enright, Anne 1962- DLB-267

Enright, D. J. 1920-2002 . . . . DLB-27

Enright, Elizabeth 1909-1968 . . . . . . DLB-22, 335

Enright, Nick 1950-2003 . . . . DLB-325

Epic, The Sixteenth-Century Spanish DLB-318

Epictetus circa 55-circa 125-130 . . . . .DLB-176

Epicurus 342/341 B.C.-271/270 B.C. DLB-176

d'Epinay, Louise (Louise-Florence-Pétronille Tardieu
d'Esclavelles, marquise d'Epinay)
1726-1783 . . . . DLB-313

Epps, Bernard 1936- DLB-53

Epshtein, Mikhail Naumovich 1950- . . DLB-285

Epstein, Julius 1909-2000 and
Epstein, Philip 1909-1952 . . . . DLB-26

Epstein, Leslie 1938- DLB-299

Editors, Conversations with Y-95

Equiano, Olaudah
circa 1745-1797 . . . . . . DLB-37, 50; CDWLB-3

Olaudah Equiano and Unfinished
Journeys: The Slave-Narrative
Tradition and Twentieth-Century
Continuities DLB-117

Eragny Press DLB-112

Erasmus, Desiderius 1467-1536 . . . . DLB-136

Erba, Luciano 1922- DLB-128

Erdman, Nikolai Robertovich
1900-1970 . . . . .DLB-272

Erdrich, Louise
1954- DLB-152, 175, 206; CDALB-7

Erenburg, Il'ia Grigor'evich 1891-1967 . . .DLB-272

Erichsen-Brown, Gwethalyn Graham
(see Graham, Gwethalyn)

Eriugena, John Scottus circa 810-877 . . . . DLB-115

Ernst, Paul 1866-1933 . . . . DLB-66, 118

Erofeev, Venedikt Vasil'evich
1938-1990 . . . . DLB-285

Erofeev, Viktor Vladimirovich
1947- DLB-285

Ershov, Petr Pavlovich 1815-1869 . . . . . . DLB-205

Erskine, Albert 1911-1993 . . . . Y-93

At Home with Albert Erskine Y-00

Erskine, John 1879-1951 . . . . DLB-9, 102

Erskine, Mrs. Steuart ?-1948 . . . . DLB-195

Ertel', Aleksandr Ivanovich 1855-1908 . . . . DLB-238	Everett, Edward 1794-1865 . . . . DLB-1, 59, 235	Farley, Harriet 1812-1907 . . . . DLB-239
Ervine, St. John Greer 1883-1971 . . . . DLB-10	Everson, R. G. 1903- DLB-88	Farley, Walter 1920-1989 . . . . DLB-22
Eschenburg, Johann Joachim 1743-1820 . . . . DLB-97	Everson, William 1912-1994 . . . . . DLB-5, 16, 212	Farmborough, Florence 1887-1978 . . . . DLB-204
	Evreinov, Nikolai 1879-1953 . . . . DLB-317	Farmer, Beverley 1941- DLB-325
Escofet, Cristina 1945- DLB-305	Ewald, Johannes 1743-1781 . . . . DLB-300	Farmer, Penelope 1939- DLB-161
Escoto, Julio 1944- DLB-145	Ewart, Gavin 1916-1995 . . . . DLB-40	Farmer, Philip José 1918- DLB-8
Esdaile, Arundell 1880-1956 . . . . DLB-201	Ewing, Juliana Horatia 1841-1885 . . . . DLB-21, 163	Farnaby, Thomas 1575?-1647 . . . . DLB-236
Esenin, Sergei Aleksandrovich 1895-1925 . . . . DLB-295	*The Examiner* 1808-1881 . . . . DLB-110	Farnese, Isabella (Suor Francesca di Gesù Maria) 1593-1651 . . . . DLB-339
Eshleman, Clayton 1935- DLB-5	Exley, Frederick 1929-1992 . . . . DLB-143; Y-81	Farningham, Marianne (see Hearn, Mary Anne)
Espaillat, Rhina P. 1932- DLB-282	Editorial: The Extension of Copyright Y-02	Farquhar, George circa 1677-1707 . . . . DLB-84
Espanca, Florbela 1894-1930 . . . . DLB-287	von Eyb, Albrecht 1420-1475 . . . . DLB-179	Farquharson, Martha (see Finley, Martha)
Espriu, Salvador 1913-1985 . . . . DLB-134	Eyre and Spottiswoode DLB-106	Farrar, Frederic William 1831-1903 . . . . . . DLB-163
Ess Ess Publishing Company DLB-49	Ezekiel, Nissim 1924-2004 . . . . DLB-323	Farrar, Straus and Giroux DLB-46
Essex House Press DLB-112	Ezera, Regīna 1930- DLB-232	Farrar and Rinehart DLB-46
Esson, Louis 1878-1943 . . . . DLB-260	Ezzo ?-after 1065 . . . . DLB-148	Farrell, J. G. 1935-1979 . . . . DLB-14, 271, 326
Essop, Ahmed 1931- DLB-225	**F**	Farrell, James T. 1904-1979 . . . . DLB-4, 9, 86; DS-2
Esterházy, Péter 1950- DLB-232; CDWLB-4		Fast, Howard 1914-2003 . . . . DLB-9
Estes, Eleanor 1906-1988 . . . . DLB-22	Faber, Frederick William 1814-1863 . . . . . . DLB-32	Faulkner, William 1897-1962 . . . . . . DLB-9, 11, 44, 102, 316, 330; DS-2; Y-86; CDALB-5
Estes and Lauriat DLB-49	Faber and Faber Limited DLB-112	
Estienne, Henri II (Henricus Stephanus) 1531-1597 . . . . DLB-327	Faccio, Rena (see Aleramo, Sibilla)	Faulkner and Yoknapatawpha Conference, Oxford, Mississippi Y-97
Estleman, Loren D. 1952- DLB-226	Facsimiles The Uses of Facsimile: A Symposium Y-90	Faulkner Centennial Addresses Y-97
Eszterhas, Joe 1944- DLB-185	Fadeev, Aleksandr Aleksandrovich 1901-1956 . . . . DLB-272	"Faulkner 100–Celebrating the Work," University of South Carolina, Columbia Y-97
Etherege, George 1636-circa 1692 . . . . DLB-80		
Ethridge, Mark, Sr. 1896-1981 . . . . DLB-127	Fagundo, Ana María 1938- DLB-134	
Ets, Marie Hall 1893-1984 . . . . DLB-22	Fainzil'berg, Il'ia Arnol'dovich (see Il'f, Il'ia and Petrov, Evgenii)	Impressions of William Faulkner Y-97
Etter, David 1928- DLB-105	Fair, Ronald L. 1932- DLB-33	William Faulkner and the People-to-People Program Y-86
Ettner, Johann Christoph 1654-1724 . . . . . DLB-168	Fairfax, Beatrice (see Manning, Marie)	William Faulkner Centenary Celebrations Y-97
Eucken, Rudolf 1846-1926 . . . . DLB-329	Fairlie, Gerard 1899-1983 . . . . DLB-77	
Eudora Welty Remembered in Two Exhibits Y-02	Faldbakken, Knut 1941- DLB-297	The William Faulkner Society Y-99
	Falkberget, Johan (Johan Petter Lillebakken) 1879-1967 . . . . DLB-297	George Faulkner [publishing house] DLB-154
Eugene Gant's Projected Works Y-01		Faulks, Sebastian 1953- DLB-207
Eupolemius fl. circa 1095 . . . . DLB-148	Fallada, Hans 1893-1947 . . . . DLB-56	Fauset, Jessie Redmon 1882-1961 . . . . DLB-51
Euripides circa 484 B.C.-407/406 B.C. DLB-176; CDWLB-1	*The Famished Road,* 1991 Booker Prize winner, Ben Okri DLB-326	Faust, Frederick Schiller (Max Brand) 1892-1944 . . . . DLB-256
Evans, Augusta Jane 1835-1909 . . . . DLB-239	Fancher, Betsy 1928- Y-83	Faust, Irvin 1924- DLB-2, 28, 218, 278; Y-80, 00
Evans, Caradoc 1878-1945 . . . . DLB-162	Fane, Violet 1843-1905 . . . . DLB-35	
Evans, Charles 1850-1935 . . . . DLB-187	Fanfrolico Press DLB-112	I Wake Up Screaming [Response to Ken Auletta] Y-97
Evans, Donald 1884-1921 . . . . DLB-54	Fanning, Katherine 1927- DLB-127	
Evans, George Henry 1805-1856 . . . . DLB-43	Fanon, Frantz 1925-1961 . . . . DLB-296	Tribute to Bernard Malamud Y-86
Evans, Hubert 1892-1986 . . . . DLB-92	Fanshawe, Sir Richard 1608-1666 . . . . DLB-126	Tribute to Isaac Bashevis Singer Y-91
Evans, Mari 1923- DLB-41	Fantasy Press Publishers DLB-46	Tribute to Meyer Levin Y-81
Evans, Mary Ann (see Eliot, George)	Fante, John 1909-1983 . . . . DLB-130; Y-83	Fawcett, Edgar 1847-1904 . . . . DLB-202
Evans, Nathaniel 1742-1767 . . . . DLB-31	Al-Farabi circa 870-950 . . . . DLB-115	Fawcett, Millicent Garrett 1847-1929 . . . . . DLB-190
Evans, Sebastian 1830-1909 . . . . DLB-35	Farabough, Laura 1949- DLB-228	Fawcett Books DLB-46
Evans, Ray 1915- DLB-265	Farah, Nuruddin 1945- DLB-125; CDWLB-3	Fay, Theodore Sedgwick 1807-1898 . . . . . . DLB-202
M. Evans and Company DLB-46	Farber, Norma 1909-1984 . . . . DLB-61	Fearing, Kenneth 1902-1961 . . . . DLB-9
Evaristi, Marcella 1953- DLB-233	*A Farewell to Arms* (Documentary) DLB-308	Federal Writers' Project DLB-46
Evenson, Brian 1966- DLB-335	Fargue, Léon-Paul 1876-1947 . . . . DLB-258	Federman, Raymond 1928- Y-80
Everett, Alexander Hill 1790-1847 . . . . DLB-59	Farigoule, Louis (see Romains, Jules)	Fedin, Konstantin Aleksandrovich 1892-1977 . . . . DLB-272
	Farjeon, Eleanor 1881-1965 . . . . DLB-160	Fedorov, Innokentii Vasil'evich (see Omulevsky, Innokentii Vasil'evich)

Cumulative Index

Fefer, Itzik (Itsik Fefer) 1900-1952....... DLB-333
Feiffer, Jules 1929- DLB-7, 44
Feinberg, Charles E. 1899-1988 ....DLB-187; Y-88
Feind, Barthold 1678-1721 .... DLB-168
Feinstein, Elaine 1930- DLB-14, 40
Feirstein, Frederick 1940- DLB-282
Feiss, Paul Louis 1875-1952 .... DLB-187
Feldman, Irving 1928- DLB-169
Felipe, Carlos 1911-1975............. DLB-305
Felipe, Léon 1884-1968............. DLB-108
Fell, Frederick, Publishers.............. DLB-46
Fellowship of Southern Writers............. Y-98
Felltham, Owen 1602?-1668....... DLB-126, 151
Felman, Shoshana 1942- DLB-246
Fels, Ludwig 1946- DLB-75
Felton, Cornelius Conway
 1807-1862................... DLB-1, 235
Fel'zen, Iurii (Nikolai Berngardovich Freidenshtein)
 1894?-1943................... DLB-317
Mothe-Fénelon, François de Salignac de la
 1651-1715 .... DLB-268
Fenn, Harry 1837-1911............... DLB-188
Fennario, David 1947- DLB-60
Fenner, Dudley 1558?-1587?.......... DLB-236
Fenno, Jenny 1765?-1803 .... DLB-200
Fenno, John 1751-1798 .... DLB-43
R. F. Fenno and Company DLB-49
Fenoglio, Beppe 1922-1963............DLB-177
Fenton, Geoffrey 1539?-1608 .... DLB-136
Fenton, James 1949- DLB-40
 The Hemingway/Fenton
  Correspondence Y-02
Ferber, Edna 1885-1968 ...... DLB-9, 28, 86, 266
Ferdinand, Vallery, III (see Salaam, Kalamu ya)
Ferguson, Adam 1723-1816 .... DLB-336
Ferguson, Sir Samuel 1810-1886........ DLB-32
Ferguson, William Scott 1875-1954....... DLB-47
Fergusson, Robert 1750-1774 .... DLB-109
Ferland, Albert 1872-1943.............. DLB-92
Ferlinghetti, Lawrence
 1919- DLB-5, 16; CDALB-1
 Tribute to Kenneth Rexroth............ Y-82
Fermor, Patrick Leigh 1915- DLB-204
Fern, Fanny (see Parton, Sara Payson Willis)
Fernández de Heredia, Juan
 circa 1310-1396 .... DLB-337
Ferrars, Elizabeth (Morna Doris Brown)
 1907-1995..................... DLB-87
Ferré, Rosario 1942- DLB-145
Ferreira, Vergílio 1916-1996 .... DLB-287
E. Ferret and Company DLB-49
Ferrier, Susan 1782-1854............. DLB-116
Ferril, Thomas Hornsby 1896-1988 ..... DLB-206

Ferrini, Vincent 1913- DLB-48
Ferron, Jacques 1921-1985 .... DLB-60
Ferron, Madeleine 1922- DLB-53
Ferrucci, Franco 1936- DLB-196
Fet, Afanasii Afanas'evich
 1820?-1892....................DLB-277
Fetridge and Company................ DLB-49
Feuchtersleben, Ernst Freiherr von
 1806-1849 .... DLB-133
Feuchtwanger, Lion 1884-1958.......... DLB-66
Feuerbach, Ludwig 1804-1872 .... DLB-133
Feuillet, Octave 1821-1890 .... DLB-192
Feydeau, Georges 1862-1921 .... DLB-192
Fibiger, Mathilde 1830-1872 .... DLB-300
Fichte, Johann Gottlieb 1762-1814 .... DLB-90
Ficke, Arthur Davison 1883-1945....... DLB-54
Fiction
 American Fiction and the 1930s....... DLB-9
 Fiction Best-Sellers, 1910-1945........ DLB-9
 Postmodern Holocaust Fiction....... DLB-299
 The Year in Fiction....... Y-84, 86, 89, 94–99
 The Year in Fiction: A Biased View Y-83
 The Year in U.S. Fiction............ Y-00, 01
 The Year's Work in Fiction: A Survey Y-82
Fiedler, Leslie A. 1917-2003 .... DLB-28, 67
 Tribute to Bernard Malamud........... Y-86
 Tribute to James Dickey............. Y-97
Field, Barron 1789-1846 .... DLB-230
Field, Edward 1924- DLB-105
Field, Eugene
 1850-1895 .... DLB-23, 42, 140; DS-13
Field, John 1545?-1588............... DLB-167
Field, Joseph M. 1810-1856 .... DLB-248
Field, Marshall, III 1893-1956 .... DLB-127
Field, Marshall, IV 1916-1965 .... DLB-127
Field, Marshall, V 1941- DLB-127
Field, Michael (Katherine Harris Bradley)
 1846-1914 .... DLB-240
 "The Poetry File"................. DLB-105
Field, Nathan 1587-1619 or 1620 .... DLB-58
Field, Rachel 1894-1942 .... DLB-9, 22
Fielding, Helen 1958- DLB-231
Fielding, Henry
 1707-1754 .... DLB-39, 84, 101; CDBLB-2
 "Defense of Amelia" (1752) DLB-39
 The History of the Adventures of Joseph Andrews
  [excerpt] (1742) DLB-39
 Letter to [Samuel] Richardson on Clarissa
  (1748)....................... DLB-39
 Preface to Joseph Andrews (1742) DLB-39
 Preface to Sarah Fielding's Familiar
  Letters (1747) [excerpt] DLB-39
 Preface to Sarah Fielding's The
  Adventures of David Simple (1744) ... DLB-39
 Review of Clarissa (1748) DLB-39

Tom Jones (1749) [excerpt] DLB-39
Fielding, Sarah 1710-1768 .... DLB-39
 Preface to The Cry (1754) DLB-39
Fields, Annie Adams 1834-1915........ DLB-221
Fields, Dorothy 1905-1974 .... DLB-265
Fields, James T. 1817-1881 .... DLB-1, 235
Fields, Julia 1938- DLB-41
Fields, Osgood and Company DLB-49
Fields, W. C. 1880-1946.............. DLB-44
Fierstein, Harvey 1954- DLB-266
Figes, Eva 1932- DLB-14, 271
Figuera, Angela 1902-1984............ DLB-108
Filicaia, Vincenzo de 1642-1707 .... DLB-339
Filmer, Sir Robert 1586-1653 .... DLB-151
Filson, John circa 1753-1788 .... DLB-37
Finch, Anne, Countess of Winchilsea
 1661-1720..................... DLB-95
Finch, Annie 1956- DLB-282
Finch, Robert 1900- DLB-88
Findley, Timothy 1930-2002........... DLB-53
Finlay, Ian Hamilton 1925- DLB-40
Finley, Martha 1828-1909............. DLB-42
Finn, Elizabeth Anne (McCaul)
 1825-1921 .... DLB-166
Finnegan, Seamus 1949- DLB-245
Finney, Jack 1911-1995................ DLB-8
Finney, Walter Braden (see Finney, Jack)
Fiorillo, Silvio 1560 or 1565?-1634?..... DLB-339
Firbank, Ronald 1886-1926 .... DLB-36
Firmin, Giles 1615-1697 .... DLB-24
First Edition Library/Collectors'
 Reprints, Inc...................... Y-91
Fischart, Johann
 1546 or 1547-1590 or 1591 ....DLB-179
Fischer, Karoline Auguste Fernandine
 1764-1842..................... DLB-94
Fischer, Tibor 1959- DLB-231
Fish, Stanley 1938- DLB-67
Fishacre, Richard 1205-1248 .... DLB-115
Fisher, Clay (see Allen, Henry W.)
Fisher, Dorothy Canfield
 1879-1958..................... DLB-9, 102
Fisher, Leonard Everett 1924- DLB-61
Fisher, Roy 1930- DLB-40
Fisher, Rudolph 1897-1934 .... DLB-51, 102
Fisher, Steve 1913-1980 .... DLB-226
Fisher, Sydney George 1856-1927....... DLB-47
Fisher, Vardis 1895-1968 .... DLB-9, 206
Fiske, John 1608-1677................ DLB-24
Fiske, John 1842-1901 ....DLB-47, 64
Fitch, Thomas circa 1700-1774 .... DLB-31
Fitch, William Clyde 1865-1909.......... DLB-7
FitzGerald, Edward 1809-1883.......... DLB-32
Fitzgerald, F. Scott 1896-1940
 .... DLB-4, 9, 86; Y-81, 92;
                 DS-1, 15, 16; CDALB-4
 F. Scott Fitzgerald: A Descriptive
  Bibliography, Supplement (2001) Y-01

F. Scott Fitzgerald Centenary Celebrations Y-96

F. Scott Fitzgerald Inducted into the American Poets' Corner at St. John the Divine; Ezra Pound Banned Y-99

"F. Scott Fitzgerald: St. Paul's Native Son and Distinguished American Writer": University of Minnesota Conference, 29-31 October 1982 .... Y-82

First International F. Scott Fitzgerald Conference Y-92

The Great Gatsby (Documentary) DLB-219

Tender Is the Night (Documentary) DLB-273

Fitzgerald, Penelope 1916-2000 .... DLB-14, 194, 326

Fitzgerald, Robert 1910-1985 .... Y-80

FitzGerald, Robert D. 1902-1987 .... DLB-260

Fitzgerald, Thomas 1819-1891 .... DLB-23

Fitzgerald, Zelda Sayre 1900-1948 .... Y-84

Fitzhugh, Louise 1928-1974 .... DLB-52

Fitzhugh, William circa 1651-1701 .... DLB-24

Flagg, James Montgomery 1877-1960 ..... DLB-188

Flanagan, Thomas 1923-2002 .... Y-80

Flanner, Hildegarde 1899-1987 .... DLB-48

Flanner, Janet 1892-1978 .... DLB-4; DS-15

Flannery, Peter 1951- DLB-233

Flaubert, Gustave 1821-1880 .... DLB-119, 301

Flavin, Martin 1883-1967 .... DLB-9

Fleck, Konrad (fl. circa 1220) DLB-138

Flecker, James Elroy 1884-1915 .... DLB-10, 19

Fleeson, Doris 1901-1970 .... DLB-29

Fleißer, Marieluise 1901-1974 .... DLB-56, 124

Fleischer, Nat 1887-1972 .... DLB-241

Fleming, Abraham 1552?-1607 .... DLB-236

Fleming, Ian 1908-1964 ... DLB-87, 201; CDBLB-7

Fleming, Joan 1908-1980 .... DLB-276

Fleming, May Agnes 1840-1880 .... DLB-99

Fleming, Paul 1609-1640 .... DLB-164

Fleming, Peter 1907-1971 .... DLB-195

Fletcher, Andrew 1653-1716 .... DLB-336

Fletcher, Giles, the Elder 1546-1611 ..... DLB-136

Fletcher, Giles, the Younger 1585 or 1586-1623 .... DLB-121

Fletcher, J. S. 1863-1935 .... DLB-70

Fletcher, John 1579-1625 .... DLB-58

Fletcher, John Gould 1886-1950 .... DLB-4, 45

Fletcher, Phineas 1582-1650 .... DLB-121

Flieg, Helmut (see Heym, Stefan)

Flint, F. S. 1885-1960 .... DLB-19

Flint, Timothy 1780-1840 .... DLB-73, 186

Fløgstad, Kjartan 1944- DLB-297

Florensky, Pavel Aleksandrovich 1882-1937 .... DLB-295

Flores, Juan de fl. 1470-1500 .... DLB-286

Flores y Blancaflor circa 1375-1400 .... DLB-337

Flores-Williams, Jason 1969- DLB-209

Florio, John 1553?-1625 .... DLB-172

Fludd, Robert 1574-1637 .... DLB-281

Flynn, Elizabeth Gurley 1890-1964 ...... DLB-303

Fo, Dario 1926- DLB-330; Y-97

Nobel Lecture 1997: Contra Jogulatores Obloquentes Y-97

Foden, Giles 1967- DLB-267

Fofanov, Konstantin Mikhailovich 1862-1911 .... DLB-277

Foix, J. V. 1893-1987 .... DLB-134

Foley, Martha 1897-1977 .... DLB-137

Folger, Henry Clay 1857-1930 .... DLB-140

Folio Society DLB-112

Follain, Jean 1903-1971 .... DLB-258

Follen, Charles 1796-1840 .... DLB-235

Follen, Eliza Lee (Cabot) 1787-1860 .... DLB-1, 235

Follett, Ken 1949- DLB-87; Y-81

Follett Publishing Company DLB-46

John West Folsom [publishing house] DLB-49

Folz, Hans between 1435 and 1440-1513 .... DLB-179

Fonseca, Manuel da 1911-1993 .... DLB-287

Fonseca, Rubem 1925- DLB-307

Fontane, Theodor 1819-1898 .... DLB-129; CDWLB-2

Fontenelle, Bernard Le Bovier de 1657-1757 .... DLB-268, 313

Fontes, Montserrat 1940- DLB-209

Fonvisin, Denis Ivanovich 1744 or 1745-1792 .... DLB-150

Foote, Horton 1916- DLB-26, 266

Foote, Mary Hallock 1847-1938 .... DLB-186, 188, 202, 221

Foote, Samuel 1721-1777 .... DLB-89

Foote, Shelby 1916-2005 .... DLB-2, 17

Forbes, Calvin 1945- DLB-41

Forbes, Ester 1891-1967 .... DLB-22

Forbes, John 1950-1998 .... DLB=325

Forbes, Rosita 1893?-1967 .... DLB-195

Forbes and Company DLB-49

Force, Peter 1790-1868 .... DLB-30

Forché, Carolyn 1950- DLB-5, 193

Ford, Charles Henri 1913-2002 .... DLB-4, 48

Ford, Corey 1902-1969 .... DLB-11

Ford, Ford Madox 1873-1939 .... DLB-34, 98, 162; CDBLB-6

Nathan Asch Remembers Ford Madox Ford, Sam Roth, and Hart Crane Y-02

J. B. Ford and Company DLB-49

Ford, Jesse Hill 1928-1996 .... DLB-6

Ford, John 1586-? DLB-58; CDBLB-1

Ford, R. A. D. 1915-1998 .... DLB-88

Ford, Richard 1944- DLB-227

Ford, Worthington C. 1858-1941 .... DLB-47

Fords, Howard, and Hulbert DLB-49

Foreman, Carl 1914-1984 .... DLB-26

Forester, C. S. 1899-1966 .... DLB-191

The C. S. Forester Society Y-00

Forester, Frank (see Herbert, Henry William)

Formalism, New

Anthologizing New Formalism DLB-282

The Little Magazines of the New Formalism DLB-282

The New Narrative Poetry DLB-282

Presses of the New Formalism and the New Narrative DLB-282

The Prosody of the New Formalism .. DLB-282

Younger Women Poets of the New Formalism DLB-282

Forman, Harry Buxton 1842-1917 .... DLB-184

Fornés, María Irene 1930- DLB-7

Forrest, Leon 1937-1997 .... DLB-33

Forsh, Ol'ga Dmitrievna 1873-1961 ...... DLB-272

Forster, E. M. 1879-1970 . DLB-34, 98, 162, 178, 195; DS-10; CDBLB-6
"Fantasy," from *Aspects of the Novel* (1927) DLB-178

Forster, Georg 1754-1794 .... DLB-94

Forster, John 1812-1876 .... DLB-144

Forster, Margaret 1938- DLB-155, 271

Forsyth, Frederick 1938- DLB-87

Forsyth, William "Literary Style" (1857) [excerpt] DLB-57

Forten, Charlotte L. 1837-1914 ...... DLB-50, 239

Pages from Her Diary DLB-50

Fortini, Franco 1917-1994 .... DLB-128

Fortune, Mary ca. 1833-ca. 1910 .... DLB-230

Fortune, T. Thomas 1856-1928 .... DLB-23

Fosdick, Charles Austin 1842-1915 .... DLB-42

Fosse, Jon 1959- DLB-297

Foster, David 1944- DLB-289

Foster, Genevieve 1893-1979 .... DLB-61

Foster, Hannah Webster 1758-1840 .... DLB-37, 200

Foster, John 1648-1681 .... DLB-24

Foster, Michael 1904-1956 .... DLB-9

Foster, Myles Birket 1825-1899 .... DLB-184

Foster, William Z. 1881-1961 .... DLB-303

Foucault, Michel 1926-1984 .... DLB-242

Robert and Andrew Foulis [publishing house] DLB-154

Fouqué, Caroline de la Motte 1774-1831 ... DLB-90

Fouqué, Friedrich de la Motte 1777-1843 .... DLB-90

Four Seas Company DLB-46

Four Winds Press DLB-46

Fournier, Henri Alban (see Alain-Fournier)

Fowler, Christopher 1953- DLB-267
Fowler, Connie May 1958- DLB-292
Fowler and Wells Company DLB-49
Fowles, John 1926- DLB-14, 139, 207; CDBLB-8
Fox, John 1939- DLB-245
Fox, John, Jr. 1862 or 1863-1919 ... DLB-9; DS-13
Fox, Paula 1923- DLB-52
Fox, Richard Kyle 1846-1922 .... DLB-79
Fox, William Price 1926- DLB-2; Y-81
   Remembering Joe Heller Y-99
Richard K. Fox [publishing house] DLB-49
Foxe, John 1517-1587 .... DLB-132
Fraenkel, Michael 1896-1957 .... DLB-4
Frame, Ronald 1953- DLB-319
France, Anatole 1844-1924 .... DLB-123, 330
France, Richard 1938- DLB-7
Francis, Convers 1795-1863 .... DLB-1, 235
Francis, Dick 1920- DLB-87; CDBLB-8
Francis, Sir Frank 1901-1988 .... DLB-201
Francis, H. E. 1924- DLB-335
Francis, Jeffrey, Lord 1773-1850 .... DLB-107
C. S. Francis [publishing house] DLB-49
Franck, Sebastian 1499-1542 ....DLB-179
Francke, Kuno 1855-1930 .... DLB-71
Françoise (Robertine Barry) 1863-1910 ... DLB-92
François, Louise von 1817-1893 .... DLB-129
Frank, Bruno 1887-1945 .... DLB-118
Frank, Leonhard 1882-1961 .... DLB-56, 118
Frank, Melvin 1913-1988 .... DLB-26
Frank, Waldo 1889-1967 .... DLB-9, 63
Franken, Rose 1895?-1988 ......DLB-228, Y-84
Franklin, Benjamin 1706-1790 .... DLB-24, 43, 73, 183; CDALB-2
Franklin, James 1697-1735 .... DLB-43
Franklin, John 1786-1847 .... DLB-99
Franklin, Miles 1879-1954 .... DLB-230
Franklin Library DLB-46
Frantz, Ralph Jules 1902-1979 .... DLB-4
Franzos, Karl Emil 1848-1904 .... DLB-129
Fraser, Antonia 1932- DLB-276
Fraser, G. S. 1915-1980 .... DLB-27
Fraser, Kathleen 1935- DLB-169
Frattini, Alberto 1922- DLB-128
Frau Ava ?-1127 .... DLB-148
Fraunce, Abraham 1558?-1592 or 1593 .. DLB-236
Frayn, Michael 1933- DLB-13, 14, 194, 245
Frazier, Charles 1950- DLB-292
Fréchette, Louis-Honoré 1839-1908 ...... DLB-99
Frederic, Harold 1856-1898 ... DLB-12, 23; DS-13
Freed, Arthur 1894-1973 .... DLB-265

Freeling, Nicolas 1927-2003 .... DLB-87
   Tribute to Georges Simenon Y-89
Freeman, Douglas Southall 1886-1953 ....DLB-17; DS-17
Freeman, Joseph 1897-1965 .... DLB-303
Freeman, Judith 1946- DLB-256
Freeman, Legh Richmond 1842-1915..... DLB-23
Freeman, Mary E. Wilkins 1852-1930 ....DLB-12, 78, 221
Freeman, R. Austin 1862-1943.......... DLB-70
Freidank circa 1170-circa 1233 .... DLB-138
Freiligrath, Ferdinand 1810-1876 .... DLB-133
Fremlin, Celia 1914- DLB-276
Frémont, Jessie Benton 1834-1902 ...... DLB-183
Frémont, John Charles 1813-1890 .... DLB-183, 186
French, Alice 1850-1934 .... DLB-74; DS-13
French, David 1939- DLB-53
French, Evangeline 1869-1960 .... DLB-195
French, Francesca 1871-1960 .... DLB-195
James French [publishing house]........... DLB-49
Samuel French [publishing house] DLB-49
Samuel French, Limited DLB-106
French Literature
   Georges-Louis Leclerc de Buffon, "Le Discours sur le style" DLB-314
   Marie-Jean-Antoine-Nicolas Caritat, marquis de Condorcet, "The Tenth Stage" .. DLB-314
   Sophie Cottin, *Claire d'Albe* DLB-314
   Declaration of the Rights of Man and of the Citizen DLB-314
   Denis Diderot, "The Encyclopedia".. DLB-314
   Epic and Beast Epic DLB-208
   French Arthurian Literature......... DLB-208
   Olympe de Gouges, *Declaration of the Rights of Woman* DLB-314
   Françoise d'Issembourg de Graffigny, *Letters from a Peruvian Woman* DLB-314
   Claude-Adrien Helvétius, *The Spirit of Laws* DLB-314
   Paul Henri Thiry, baron d'Holbach (writing as Jean-Baptiste de Mirabaud), *The System of Nature* DLB-314
   Pierre-Ambroise-François Choderlos de Laclos, *Dangerous Acquaintances* DLB-314
   Lyric Poetry DLB-268
   Louis-Sébastien Mercier, *Le Tableau de Paris* DLB-314
   Charles-Louis de Secondat, baron de Montesquieu, *The Spirit of Laws* .. DLB-314
   Other Poets DLB-217
   Poetry in Nineteenth-Century France: Cultural Background and Critical Commentary DLB-217
   Roman de la Rose: Guillaume de Lorris 1200 to 1205-circa 1230, Jean de Meun 1235/1240-circa 1305 .... DLB-208
   Jean-Jacques Rousseau, *The Social Contract* DLB-314

   Marquis de Sade, "Dialogue entre un prêtre et un moribond" DLB-314
   Saints' Lives DLB-208
   Troubadours, *Trobairitz,* and Trouvères DLB-208
   Anne-Robert-Jacques Turgot, baron de l'Aulne, "Memorandum on Local Government"................. DLB-314
   Voltaire, "An account of the death of the chevalier de La Barre" DLB-314
   Voltaire, *Candide* DLB-314
   Voltaire, *Philosophical Dictionary* DLB-314
French Theater
   Medieval French Drama DLB-208
   Parisian Theater, Fall 1984: Toward a New Baroque Y-85
Freneau, Philip 1752-1832............DLB-37, 43
   The Rising Glory of America DLB-37
Freni, Melo 1934- DLB-128
Fréron, Elie Catherine 1718-1776 .... DLB-313
Freshfield, Douglas W. 1845-1934 ....DLB-174
Freud, Sigmund 1856-1939............ DLB-296
Freytag, Gustav 1816-1895............. DLB-129
Frída Á. Sigurðardóttir 1940- DLB-293
Fridegård, Jan 1897-1968 .... DLB-259
Fried, Erich 1921-1988................ DLB-85
Friedan, Betty 1921-2006 .... DLB-246
Friedman, Bruce Jay 1930- DLB-2, 28, 244
Friedman, Carl 1952- DLB-299
Friedman, Kinky 1944- DLB-292
Friedrich von Hausen circa 1171-1190 ... DLB-138
Friel, Brian 1929- DLB-13, 319
Friend, Krebs 1895?-1967? DLB-4
Fries, Fritz Rudolf 1935- DLB-75
Frisch, Max 1911-1991...DLB-69, 124; CDWLB-2
Frischlin, Nicodemus 1547-1590.........DLB-179
Frischmuth, Barbara 1941- DLB-85
Fritz, Jean 1915- DLB-52
Froissart, Jean circa 1337-circa 1404 ..... DLB-208
Fromm, Erich 1900-1980 .... DLB-296
Fromentin, Eugene 1820-1876 .... DLB-123
Frontinus circa A.D. 35-A.D. 103/104..... DLB-211
Frost, A. B. 1851-1928 .... DLB-188; DS-13
Frost, Robert 1874-1963......... DLB-54; DS-7; CDALB-4
   The Friends of the Dymock Poets Y-00
Frostenson, Katarina 1953- DLB-257
Frothingham, Octavius Brooks 1822-1895 .... DLB-1, 243
Froude, James Anthony 1818-1894 ....DLB-18, 57, 144
Fruitlands 1843-1844 .... DLB-1, 223; DS-5
Fry, Christopher 1907-2005 .... DLB-13
   Tribute to John Betjeman............. Y-84
Fry, Roger 1866-1934................DS-10

Fry, Stephen 1957- DLB-207

Frye, Northrop 1912-1991 .... DLB-67, 68, 246

Fuchs, Daniel 1909-1993 ..... DLB-9, 26, 28; Y-93

   Tribute to Isaac Bashevis Singer Y-91

Fuentes, Carlos 1928- DLB-113; CDWLB-3

Fuertes, Gloria 1918-1998 ....DLB-108

Fugard, Athol 1932- DLB-225

The Fugitives and the Agrarians:
   The First Exhibition Y-85

Fujiwara no Shunzei 1114-1204 ....DLB-203

Fujiwara no Tameaki 1230s?-1290s? DLB-203

Fujiwara no Tameie 1198-1275 ....DLB-203

Fujiwara no Teika 1162-1241 ....DLB-203

Fuks, Ladislav 1923-1994 ....DLB-299

Fulbecke, William 1560-1603? DLB-172

Fuller, Charles 1939- DLB-38, 266

Fuller, Henry Blake 1857-1929 ....DLB-12

Fuller, John 1937- DLB-40

Fuller, Margaret (see Fuller, Sarah)

Fuller, Roy 1912-1991 ....DLB-15, 20

   Tribute to Christopher Isherwood........Y-86

Fuller, Samuel 1912-1997 ....DLB-26

Fuller, Sarah 1810-1850 .... DLB-1, 59, 73,
                  183, 223, 239; DS-5; CDALB-2

Fuller, Thomas 1608-1661 ....DLB-151

Fullerton, Hugh 1873-1945 ....DLB-171

Fullwood, William fl. 1568 ....DLB-236

Fulton, Alice 1952- DLB-193

Fulton, Len 1934- Y-86

Fulton, Robin 1937- DLB-40

Furbank, P. N. 1920- DLB-155

Furetière, Antoine 1619-1688 ....DLB-268

Furman, Laura 1945- Y-86

Furmanov, Dmitrii Andreevich
   1891-1926 ....DLB-272

Furness, Horace Howard 1833-1912 ......DLB-64

Furness, William Henry
   1802-1896 ....DLB-1, 235

Furnivall, Frederick James 1825-1910 ....DLB-184

Furphy, Joseph (Tom Collins)
   1843-1912 ....DLB-230

Furthman, Jules 1888-1966 ....DLB-26

   Shakespeare and Montaigne: A
   Symposium by Jules Furthman Y-02

Furui Yoshikichi 1937- DLB-182

Fushimi, Emperor 1265-1317 ....DLB-203

Futabatei Shimei (Hasegawa Tatsunosuke)
   1864-1909 ....DLB-180

Fyleman, Rose 1877-1957 ....DLB-160

G

G., 1972 Booker Prize winner,
   John Berger DLB-326

Gaarder, Jostein 1952- DLB-297

Gadallah, Leslie 1939- DLB-251

Gadamer, Hans-Georg 1900-2002 ....DLB-296

Gadda, Carlo Emilio 1893-1973 ....DLB-177

Gaddis, William 1922-1998 ....DLB-2, 278

   William Gaddis: A Tribute Y-99

Gág, Wanda 1893-1946 ....DLB-22

Gagarin, Ivan Sergeevich 1814-1882 .....DLB-198

Gagnon, Madeleine 1938- DLB-60

Gaiman, Neil 1960- DLB-261

Gaine, Hugh 1726-1807 ....DLB-43

Hugh Gaine [publishing house] DLB-49

Gaines, Ernest J.
   1933- DLB-2, 33, 152; Y-80; CDALB-6

Gaiser, Gerd 1908-1976 ....DLB-69

Gaitskill, Mary 1954- DLB-244

Galarza, Ernesto 1905-1984 ....DLB-122

Galaxy Science Fiction Novels DLB-46

Galbraith, Robert (or Caubraith)
   circa 1483-1544 ....DLB-281

Gale, Zona 1874-1938 .... DLB-9, 228, 78

Galen of Pergamon 129-after 210 ....DLB-176

Gales, Winifred Marshall 1761-1839 .....DLB-200

Galich, Aleksandr 1918-1977 ....DLB-317

Medieval Galician-Portuguese Poetry DLB-287

Gall, Louise von 1815-1855 ....DLB-133

Gallagher, Tess 1943- DLB-120, 212, 244

Gallagher, Wes 1911-1997 ....DLB-127

Gallagher, William Davis 1808-1894 ......DLB-73

Gallant, Mavis 1922- DLB-53

Gallegos, María Magdalena 1935- DLB-209

Gallico, Paul 1897-1976 ....DLB-9, 171

Gallop, Jane 1952- DLB-246

Galloway, Grace Growden 1727-1782 .....DLB-200

Galloway, Janice 1956- DLB-319

Gallup, Donald 1913-2000 ....DLB-187

Galsworthy, John 1867-1933
   .. DLB-10, 34, 98, 162, 330; DS-16; CDBLB-5

Galt, John 1779-1839 .... DLB-99, 116, 159

Galton, Sir Francis 1822-1911 ....DLB-166

Galvin, Brendan 1938- DLB-5

Gambaro, Griselda 1928- DLB-305

Gambit............................DLB-46

Gamboa, Reymundo 1948- DLB-122

Gammer Gurton's Needle DLB-62

Gan, Elena Andreevna (Zeneida R-va)
   1814-1842 ....DLB-198

Gandhi, Mohandas Karamchand
   1869-1948 ....DLB-323

Gandlevsky, Sergei Markovich
   1952- DLB-285

Gannett, Frank E. 1876-1957 ....DLB-29

Gant, Eugene: Projected Works...........Y-01

Gao Xingjian 1940- DLB-330; Y-00

   Nobel Lecture 2000: "The Case for
   Literature" Y-00

Gaos, Vicente 1919-1980...............DLB-134

García, Andrew 1854?-1943 ....DLB-209

García, Cristina 1958- DLB-292

García, Lionel G. 1935- DLB-82

García, Richard 1941- DLB-209

García, Santiago 1928- DLB-305

García Márquez, Gabriel
   1927- DLB-113, 330; Y-82; CDWLB-3

   The Magical World of Macondo.........Y-82

   Nobel Lecture 1982: The Solitude of
   Latin America......................Y-82

   A Tribute to Gabriel García Márquez.....Y-82

García Marruz, Fina 1923- DLB-283

García-Camarillo, Cecilio 1943- DLB-209

Garcilaso de la Vega circa 1503-1536.....DLB-318

Garcilaso de la Vega, Inca 1539-1616 ....DLB-318

Gardam, Jane 1928- DLB-14, 161, 231

Gardell, Jonas 1963- DLB-257

Garden, Alexander circa 1685-1756.......DLB-31

Gardiner, John Rolfe 1936- DLB-244

Gardiner, Margaret Power Farmer
   (see Blessington, Marguerite, Countess of)

Gardner, John
   1933-1982 .... DLB-2; Y-82; CDALB-7

Garfield, Leon 1921-1996 ....DLB-161

Garis, Howard R. 1873-1962............DLB-22

Garland, Hamlin 1860-1940 .. DLB-12, 71, 78, 186

   The Hamlin Garland Society Y-01

Garneau, François-Xavier 1809-1866 .....DLB-99

Garneau, Hector de Saint-Denys
   1912-1943 ....DLB-88

Garneau, Michel 1939- DLB-53

Garner, Alan 1934- DLB-161, 261

Garner, Helen 1942- DLB-325

Garner, Hugh 1913-1979 ....DLB-68

Garnett, David 1892-1981 ....DLB-34

Garnett, Eve 1900-1991................DLB-160

Garnett, Richard 1835-1906 ....DLB-184

Garnier, Robert 1545?-1590 ....DLB-327

Garrard, Lewis H. 1829-1887 ....DLB-186

Garraty, John A. 1920- DLB-17

Garrett, Almeida (João Baptista da Silva
   Leitão de Almeida Garrett)
   1799-1854 ....DLB-287

Garrett, George
   1929- DLB-2, 5, 130, 152; Y-83

   Literary Prizes......................Y-00

   My Summer Reading Orgy: Reading
   for Fun and Games: One Reader's
   Report on the Summer of 2001 ......Y-01

   A Summing Up at Century's End Y-99

Tribute to James Dickey................ Y-97

Tribute to Michael M. Rea............. Y-97

Tribute to Paxton Davis................ Y-94

Tribute to Peter Taylor................ Y-94

Tribute to William Goyen Y-83

A Writer Talking: A Collage Y-00

Garrett, John Work 1872-1942 .... DLB-187

Garrick, David 1717-1779 .... DLB-84, 213

Garrison, William Lloyd
1805-1879....... DLB-1, 43, 235; CDALB-2

Garro, Elena 1920-1998 .... DLB-145

Garshin, Vsevolod Mikhailovich
1855-1888 .... DLB-277

Garth, Samuel 1661-1719 .... DLB-95

Garve, Andrew 1908-2001 .... DLB-87

Gary, Romain 1914-1980 .... DLB-83, 299

Gascoigne, George 1539?-1577......... DLB-136

Gascoyne, David 1916-2001 .... DLB-20

Gash, Jonathan (John Grant) 1933- DLB-276

Gaskell, Elizabeth Cleghorn
1810-1865...... DLB-21, 144, 159; CDBLB-4

The Gaskell Society Y-98

Gaskell, Jane 1941- DLB-261

Gaspey, Thomas 1788-1871 .... DLB-116

Gass, William H. 1924- DLB-2, 227

Gates, Doris 1901-1987 .... DLB-22

Gates, Henry Louis, Jr. 1950- DLB-67

Gates, Lewis E. 1860-1924 .... DLB-71

Gatto, Alfonso 1909-1976 .... DLB-114

Gault, William Campbell 1910-1995 .... DLB-226

Tribute to Kenneth Millar Y-83

Gaunt, Mary 1861-1942............DLB-174, 230

Gautier, Théophile 1811-1872.......... DLB-119

Gautreaux, Tim 1947- DLB-292

Gauvreau, Claude 1925-1971 .... DLB-88

The Gawain-Poet
fl. circa 1350-1400 .... DLB-146

Gawsworth, John (Terence Ian Fytton
Armstrong) 1912-1970 .... DLB-255

Gay, Ebenezer 1696-1787 .... DLB-24

Gay, John 1685-1732................ DLB-84, 95

Gayarré, Charles E. A. 1805-1895 .... DLB-30

Charles Gaylord [publishing house] DLB-49

Gaylord, Edward King 1873-1974........ DLB-127

Gaylord, Edward Lewis 1919-2003 ..... DLB-127

Gazdanov, Gaito 1903-1971 .... DLB-317

Gébler, Carlo 1954- DLB-271

Geda, Sigitas 1943- DLB-232

Geddes, Gary 1940- DLB-60

Geddes, Virgil 1897-1989 .... DLB-4

Gedeon (Georgii Andreevich Krinovsky)
circa 1730-1763................ DLB-150

Gee, Maggie 1948- DLB-207

Gee, Shirley 1932- DLB-245

Geibel, Emanuel 1815-1884 .... DLB-129

Geiogamah, Hanay 1945- DLB-175

Geis, Bernard, Associates DLB-46

Geisel, Theodor Seuss 1904-1991.... DLB-61; Y-91

Gelb, Arthur 1924- DLB-103

Gelb, Barbara 1926- DLB-103

Gelber, Jack 1932- DLB-7, 228

Gélinas, Gratien 1909-1999 .... DLB-88

Gellert, Christian Fürchtegott
1715-1769 .... DLB-97

Gellhorn, Martha 1908-1998 .... Y-82, 98

Gems, Pam 1925- DLB-13

Genet, Jean 1910-1986 ....DLB-72, 321; Y-86

Genette, Gérard 1930- DLB-242

Genevoix, Maurice 1890-1980 .... DLB-65

Genis, Aleksandr Aleksandrovich
1953- DLB-285

Genlis, Stéphanie-Félicité Ducrest, comtesse de
1746-1830..................... DLB-313

Genovese, Eugene D. 1930- DLB-17

Gent, Peter 1942- Y-82

Geoffrey of Monmouth
circa 1100-1155 .... DLB-146

George, Elizabeth 1949- DLB-306

George, Henry 1839-1897 .... DLB-23

George, Jean Craighead 1919- DLB-52

George, W. L. 1882-1926 .... DLB-197

George III, King of Great Britain
and Ireland 1738-1820 .... DLB-213

Georgslied 896?.................... DLB-148

Gerber, Merrill Joan 1938- DLB-218

Gerhardie, William 1895-1977 .... DLB-36

Gerhardt, Paul 1607-1676 .... DLB-164

Gérin, Winifred 1901-1981............ DLB-155

Gérin-Lajoie, Antoine 1824-1882 .... DLB-99

German Literature
A Call to Letters and an Invitation
to the Electric Chair DLB-75

The Conversion of an Unpolitical
Man...................... DLB-66

The German Radio Play DLB-124

The German Transformation from the
Baroque to the Enlightenment.... DLB-97

Germanophilism DLB-66

A Letter from a New Germany Y-90

The Making of a People............ DLB-66

The Novel of Impressionism DLB-66

Pattern and Paradigm: History as
Design DLB-75

Premisses DLB-66

The 'Twenties and Berlin............ DLB-66

Wolfram von Eschenbach's Parzival:
Prologue and Book 3........... DLB-138

Writers and Politics: 1871-1918 ...... DLB-66

German Literature, Middle Ages
Abrogans circa 790-800 .... DLB-148

Annolied between 1077 and 1081..... DLB-148

The Arthurian Tradition and
Its European Context DLB-138

Cambridge Songs (Carmina Cantabrigensia)
circa 1050 .... DLB-148

Christus und die Samariterin circa 950 .. DLB-148

De Heinrico circa 980?............. DLB-148

Ecbasis Captivi circa 1045........... DLB-148

Georgslied 896? DLB-148

German Literature and Culture from
Charlemagne to the Early Courtly
Period DLB-148; CDWLB-2

The Germanic Epic and Old English
Heroic Poetry: Widsith, Waldere,
and The Fight at Finnsburg........ DLB-146

Graf Rudolf between circa
1170 and circa 1185........... DLB-148

Heliand circa 850................. DLB-148

Das Hildesbrandslied
circa 820 .... DLB-148; CDWLB-2

Kaiserchronik circa 1147 .... DLB-148

The Legends of the Saints and a
Medieval Christian
Worldview................... DLB-148

Ludus de Antichristo circa 1160 .... DLB-148

Ludwigslied 881 or 882 .... DLB-148

Muspilli circa 790-circa 850 .... DLB-148

Old German Genesis and Old German
Exodus circa 1050-circa 1130 .... DLB-148

Old High German Charms
and Blessings....... DLB-148; CDWLB-2

The Old High German Isidor
circa 790-800 .... DLB-148

Petruslied circa 854?............... DLB-148

Physiologus circa 1070-circa 1150 ..... DLB-148

Ruodlieb circa 1050-1075 .... DLB-148

"Spielmannsepen" (circa 1152
circa 1500).................... DLB-148

The Strasbourg Oaths 842......... DLB-148

Tatian circa 830................... DLB-148

Waltharius circa 825................ DLB-148

Wessobrunner Gebet circa 787-815 ..... DLB-148

German Theater
German Drama 800-1280 .... DLB-138

German Drama from Naturalism
to Fascism: 1889-1933......... DLB-118

Gernsback, Hugo 1884-1967 ....DLB-8, 137

Gerould, Katharine Fullerton
1879-1944..................... DLB-78

Samuel Gerrish [publishing house]....... DLB-49

Gerrold, David 1944- DLB-8

Gersão, Teolinda 1940- DLB-287

Gershon, Karen 1923-1993............ DLB-299

Gershwin, Ira 1896-1983 .... DLB-265

The Ira Gershwin Centenary........... Y-96

Gerson, Jean 1363-1429 .... DLB-208

Gersonides 1288-1344 .... DLB-115

Gerstäcker, Friedrich 1816-1872.........DLB-129

Gertsen, Aleksandr Ivanovich (see Herzen, Alexander)

Gerstenberg, Heinrich Wilhelm von 1737-1823.....................DLB-97

Gervinus, Georg Gottfried 1805-1871.....................DLB-133

Gery, John 1953- DLB-282

Geßner, Solomon 1730-1788 ....DLB-97

Geston, Mark S. 1946- DLB-8

Al-Ghazali 1058-1111..................DLB-115

Ghelderode, Michel de (Adolphe-Adhémar Martens) 1898-1962....................DLB-321

Ghose, Zulfikar 1935- DLB-323

Ghosh, Amitav 1956- DLB-323

The Ghost Road, 1995 Booker Prize winner, Pat Barker....................DLB-326

Gibbings, Robert 1889-1958 ....DLB-195

Gibbon, Edward 1737-1794 ....DLB-104, 336

Gibbon, John Murray 1875-1952........DLB-92

Gibbon, Lewis Grassic (see Mitchell, James Leslie)

Gibbons, Floyd 1887-1939 ....DLB-25

Gibbons, Kaye 1960- DLB-292

Gibbons, Reginald 1947- DLB-120

Gibbons, William eighteenth century DLB-73

Gibson, Charles Dana 1867-1944 ....DLB-188; DS-13

Gibson, Graeme 1934- DLB-53

Gibson, Margaret 1944- DLB-120

Gibson, Margaret Dunlop 1843-1920 ....DLB-174

Gibson, Wilfrid 1878-1962.............DLB-19

The Friends of the Dymock Poets........Y-00

Gibson, William 1914- DLB-7

Gibson, William 1948- DLB-251

Gide, André 1869-1951 ....DLB-65, 321, 330

Giguère, Diane 1937- DLB-53

Giguère, Roland 1929- DLB-60

Gil de Biedma, Jaime 1929-1990 ....DLB-108

Gil-Albert, Juan 1906-1994 ....DLB-134

Gilbert, Anthony 1899-1973 ....DLB-77

Gilbert, Elizabeth 1969- DLB-292

Gilbert, Sir Humphrey 1537-1583 ....DLB-136

Gilbert, Michael 1912- DLB-87

Gilbert, Sandra M. 1936- DLB-120, 246

Gilchrist, Alexander 1828-1861.........DLB-144

Gilchrist, Ellen 1935- DLB-130

Gilder, Jeannette L. 1849-1916.........DLB-79

Gilder, Richard Watson 1844-1909 ....DLB-64, 79

Gildersleeve, Basil 1831-1924 ....DLB-71

Giles, Henry 1809-1882................DLB-64

Giles of Rome circa 1243-1316 ....DLB-115

Gilfillan, George 1813-1878 ....DLB-144

Gill, Eric 1882-1940.................DLB-98

Gill, Sarah Prince 1728-1771 ....DLB-200

William F. Gill Company..............DLB-49

Gillespie, A. Lincoln, Jr. 1895-1950.......DLB-4

Gillespie, Haven 1883-1975 ....DLB-265

Gilliam, Florence fl. twentieth century......DLB-4

Gilliatt, Penelope 1932-1993 ....DLB-14

Gillott, Jacky 1939-1980 ....DLB-14

Gilman, Caroline H. 1794-1888........DLB-3, 73

Gilman, Charlotte Perkins 1860-1935 ....DLB-221

The Charlotte Perkins Gilman Society Y-99

W. and J. Gilman [publishing house]......DLB-49

Gilmer, Elizabeth Meriwether 1861-1951.....................DLB-29

Gilmer, Francis Walker 1790-1826........DLB-37

Gilmore, Mary 1865-1962.............DLB-260

Gilroy, Frank D. 1925- DLB-7

Gimferrer, Pere (Pedro) 1945- DLB-134

Ginger, Aleksandr S. 1897-1965.........DLB-317

Gingrich, Arnold 1903-1976 ....DLB-137

Prospectus From the Initial Issue of *Esquire* (Autumn 1933) DLB-137

"With the Editorial Ken," Prospectus From the Initial Issue of *Ken* (7 April 1938) DLB-137

Ginibi, Ruby Langford 1934- DLB-325

Ginsberg, Allen 1926-1997 ....DLB-5, 16, 169, 237; CDALB-1

Ginzburg, Evgeniia 1904-1977 ....DLB-302

Ginzburg, Lidiia Iakovlevna 1902-1990...DLB-302

Ginzburg, Natalia 1916-1991.........DLB-177

Ginzkey, Franz Karl 1871-1963 ....DLB-81

Gioia, Dana 1950- DLB-120, 282

Giono, Jean 1895-1970.............DLB-72, 321

Giotti, Virgilio 1885-1957 ....DLB-114

Giovanni, Nikki 1943- DLB-5, 41; CDALB-7

Giovannitti, Arturo 1884-1959..........DLB-303

Gipson, Lawrence Henry 1880-1971 ......DLB-17

Girard, Rodolphe 1879-1956 ....DLB-92

Giraudoux, Jean 1882-1944.........DLB-65, 321

Girondo, Oliverio 1891-1967...........DLB-283

Gissing, George 1857-1903 ......DLB-18, 135, 184

The Place of Realism in Fiction (1895)...DLB-18

Giudici, Giovanni 1924- DLB-128

Giuliani, Alfredo 1924- DLB-128

Gjellerup, Karl 1857-1919 ....DLB-300, 330

Glackens, William J. 1870-1938.........DLB-188

Gladilin, Anatolii Tikhonovich 1935- DLB-302

Gladkov, Fedor Vasil'evich 1883-1958....DLB-272

Gladstone, William Ewart 1809-1898...................DLB-57, 184

Glaeser, Ernst 1902-1963..............DLB-69

Glancy, Diane 1941- DLB-175

Glanvill, Joseph 1636-1680 ....DLB-252

Glanville, Brian 1931- DLB-15, 139

Glapthorne, Henry 1610-1643?..........DLB-58

Glasgow, Ellen 1873-1945 ....DLB-9, 12

The Ellen Glasgow Society Y-01

Glasier, Katharine Bruce 1867-1950......DLB-190

Glaspell, Susan 1876-1948 ......DLB-7, 9, 78, 228

Glass, Montague 1877-1934............DLB-11

Glassco, John 1909-1981 ....DLB-68

Glatstein, Jacob (Yankev Glatshteyn) 1896-1971 ....DLB-333

Glauser, Friedrich 1896-1938...........DLB-56

Glavin, Anthony 1946- DLB-319

F. Gleason's Publishing Hall DLB-49

Gleim, Johann Wilhelm Ludwig 1719-1803 ....DLB-97

Glendinning, Robin 1938- DLB-310

Glendinning, Victoria 1937- DLB-155

Glidden, Frederick Dilley (Luke Short) 1908-1975 ....DLB-256

Glinka, Fedor Nikolaevich 1786-1880 ....DLB-205

Glover, Keith 1966- DLB-249

Glover, Richard 1712-1785.............DLB-95

Glover, Sue 1943- DLB-310

Glück, Louise 1943- DLB-5

Glyn, Elinor 1864-1943 ....DLB-153

Gnedich, Nikolai Ivanovich 1784-1833 ...DLB-205

Gobineau, Joseph-Arthur de 1816-1882.....................DLB-123

The God of Small Things, 1997 Booker Prize winner, Arundhati Roy DLB-326

Godber, John 1956- DLB-233

Godbout, Jacques 1933- DLB-53

Goddard, Morrill 1865-1937 ....DLB-25

Goddard, William 1740-1817 ....DLB-43

Godden, Rumer 1907-1998 ....DLB-161

Godey, Louis A. 1804-1878 ....DLB-73

Godey and McMichael DLB-49

Godfrey, Dave 1938- DLB-60

Godfrey, Thomas 1736-1763 ....DLB-31

Godine, David R., Publisher DLB-46

Godkin, E. L. 1831-1902...............DLB-79

Godolphin, Sidney 1610-1643 ....DLB-126

Godwin, Gail 1937- DLB-6, 234

M. J. Godwin and Company............DLB-154

Godwin, Mary Jane Clairmont 1766-1841 ....DLB-163

Godwin, Parke 1816-1904........DLB-3, 64, 250

Godwin, William 1756-1836 .... DLB-39, 104, 142, 158, 163, 262, 336; CDBLB-3

Preface to *St. Leon* (1799) DLB-39

Goering, Reinhard 1887-1936 ....DLB-118

Cumulative Index

Goes, Albrecht 1908- DLB-69
Goethe, Johann Wolfgang von
    1749-1832............ DLB-94; CDWLB-2
Goetz, Curt 1888-1960............... DLB-124
Goffe, Thomas circa 1592-1629......... DLB-58
Goffstein, M. B. 1940- DLB-61
Gogarty, Oliver St. John 1878-1957 ... DLB-15, 19
Gogol, Nikolai Vasil'evich 1809-1852.... DLB-198
Goines, Donald 1937-1974 .... DLB-33
Gold, Herbert 1924- DLB-2; Y-81
    Tribute to William Saroyan Y-81
Gold, Michael 1893-1967 .... DLB-9, 28
Goldbarth, Albert 1948- DLB-120
Goldberg, Dick 1947- DLB-7
Golden Cockerel Press DLB-112
Goldfaden, Abraham (Avrom Goldfadn)
    1840-1908 .... DLB-333
Golding, Arthur 1536-1606 .... DLB-136
Golding, Louis 1895-1958 .... DLB-195
Golding, William
    1911-1993.......... DLB-15, 100, 255, 326,
                           330; Y-83; CDBLB-7
    Nobel Lecture 1993 .... Y-83
    The Stature of William Golding......... Y-83
Goldman, Emma 1869-1940........... DLB-221
Goldman, William 1931- DLB-44
Goldring, Douglas 1887-1960......... DLB-197
Goldschmidt, Meir Aron 1819-1887..... DLB-300
Goldsmith, Oliver 1730?-1774
    ... DLB-39, 89, 104, 109, 142, 336; CDBLB-2
Goldsmith, Oliver 1794-1861 .... DLB-99
Goldsmith Publishing Company......... DLB-46
Goldstein, Richard 1944- DLB-185
Goldsworthy, Peter 1951- DLB-325
Gollancz, Sir Israel 1864-1930 .... DLB-201
Victor Gollancz Limited DLB-112
Gomberville, Marin Le Roy, sieur de
    1600?-1674 .... DLB-268
Gombrowicz, Witold
    1904-1969 .... DLB-215; CDWLB-4
Gomez, Madeleine-Angélique Poisson de
    1684-1770..................... DLB-313
Gómez de Ciudad Real, Alvar (Alvar Gómez
    de Guadalajara) 1488-1538 .... DLB-318
Gómez-Quiñones, Juan 1942- DLB-122
Laurence James Gomme
    [publishing house] DLB-46
Gompers, Samuel 1850-1924 .... DLB-303
Gonçalves Dias, Antônio 1823-1864 .... DLB-307
Goncharov, Ivan Aleksandrovich
    1812-1891..................... DLB-238
Goncourt, Edmond de 1822-1896 ...... DLB-123
Goncourt, Jules de 1830-1870.......... DLB-123
Gonzales, Rodolfo "Corky" 1928- DLB-122

Gonzales-Berry, Erlinda 1942- DLB-209
    "Chicano Language" DLB-82
González, Angel 1925- DLB-108
Gonzalez, Genaro 1949- DLB-122
Gonzalez, N. V. M. 1915-1999 .... DLB-312
González, Otto-Raúl 1921- DLB-290
Gonzalez, Ray 1952- DLB-122
González de Mireles, Jovita
    1899-1983 .... DLB-122
González Martínez, Enrique
    1871-1952..................... DLB-290
González-T., César A. 1931- DLB-82
Gonzalo de Berceo
    circa 1195-circa 1264 .... DLB-337
Goodis, David 1917-1967 .... DLB-226
Goodison, Lorna 1947- DLB-157
Goodman, Allegra 1967- DLB-244
Goodman, Nelson 1906-1998.......... DLB-279
Goodman, Paul 1911-1972 .... DLB-130, 246
The Goodman Theatre DLB-7
Goodrich, Frances 1891-1984 and
    Hackett, Albert 1900-1995.......... DLB-26
Goodrich, Samuel Griswold
    1793-1860...............DLB-1, 42, 73, 243
S. G. Goodrich [publishing house] DLB-49
C. E. Goodspeed and Company......... DLB-49
Goodwin, Stephen 1943- Y-82
Googe, Barnabe 1540-1594 .... DLB-132
Gookin, Daniel 1612-1687 .... DLB-24
Gopegui, Belén 1963- DLB-322
Goran, Lester 1928- DLB-244
Gordimer, Nadine
    1923- DLB-225, 326, 330; Y-91
    Nobel Lecture 1991 .... Y-91
Gordin, Jacob (Yankev Gordin)
    1853-1909 .... DLB-333
Gordon, Adam Lindsay 1833-1870...... DLB-230
Gordon, Caroline
    1895-1981 .... DLB-4, 9, 102; DS-17; Y-81
Gordon, Charles F. (see OyamO)
Gordon, Charles William (see Connor, Ralph)
Gordon, Giles 1940- DLB-14, 139, 207
Gordon, Helen Cameron, Lady Russell
    1867-1949..................... DLB-195
Gordon, Lyndall 1941- DLB-155
Gordon, Mack 1904-1959 .... DLB-265
Gordon, Mary 1949- DLB-6; Y-81
Gordon, Thomas ca. 1692-1750 .... DLB-336
Gordone, Charles 1925-1995 .... DLB-7
Gore, Catherine 1800-1861 .... DLB-116
Gore-Booth, Eva 1870-1926 .... DLB-240
Gores, Joe 1931- DLB-226; Y-02
    Tribute to Kenneth Millar Y-83
    Tribute to Raymond Chandler.......... Y-88

Gorey, Edward 1925-2000 .... DLB-61
Gorgias of Leontini
    circa 485 B.C.-376 B.C. DLB-176
Gor'ky, Maksim 1868-1936 .... DLB-295
Gorodetsky, Sergei Mitrofanovich
    1884-1967 .... DLB-295
Gorostiza, José 1901-1979............ DLB-290
Görres, Joseph 1776-1848............. DLB-90
Gosse, Edmund 1849-1928 ..... DLB-57, 144, 184
Gosson, Stephen 1554-1624 ....DLB-172
    The Schoole of Abuse (1579) DLB-172
Gotanda, Philip Kan 1951- DLB-266
Gotlieb, Phyllis 1926- DLB-88, 251
Go-Toba 1180-1239 .... DLB-203
Gottfried von Straßburg
    died before 1230 ....DLB-138; CDWLB-2
Gotthelf, Jeremias 1797-1854........... DLB-133
Gottschalk circa 804/808-869 .... DLB-148
Gottsched, Johann Christoph
    1700-1766..................... DLB-97
Götz, Johann Nikolaus 1721-1781........ DLB-97
Goudge, Elizabeth 1900-1984.......... DLB-191
Gouges, Olympe de 1748-1793 .... DLB-313
    Declaration of the Rights of Woman...... DLB-314
Gough, John B. 1817-1886 .... DLB-243
Gough, Richard 1735-1809 .... DLB-336
Gould, Wallace 1882-1940 .... DLB-54
Gournay, Marie de 1565-1645 .... DLB-327
Govoni, Corrado 1884-1965 .... DLB-114
Govrin, Michal 1950- DLB-299
Gower, John circa 1330-1408 .... DLB-146
Goyen, William 1915-1983......DLB-2, 218; Y-83
Goytisolo, José Augustín 1928- DLB-134
Goytisolo, Juan 1931- DLB-322
Goytisolo, Luis 1935- DLB-322
Gozzano, Guido 1883-1916 .... DLB-114
Grabbe, Christian Dietrich 1801-1836 ... DLB-133
Gracq, Julien (Louis Poirier) 1910- DLB-83
Grade, Chaim (Khayim Grade)
    1910-1982 .... DLB-333
Grady, Henry W. 1850-1889 .... DLB-23
Graf, Oskar Maria 1894-1967 .... DLB-56
Graf Rudolf between circa 1170 and
    circa 1185..................... DLB-148
Graff, Gerald 1937- DLB-246
Graffigny, Françoise d'Issembourg de
    1695-1758..................... DLB-313
    Letters from a Peruvian Woman DLB-314
Richard Grafton [publishing house] DLB-170
Grafton, Sue 1940- DLB-226
Graham, Frank 1893-1965 .... DLB-241
Graham, George Rex 1813-1894 .... DLB-73

Graham, Gwethalyn (Gwethalyn Graham
    Erichsen-Brown) 1913-1965 ....DLB-88

Graham, Jorie 1951- DLB-120

Graham, Katharine 1917-2001 ....DLB-127

Graham, Lorenz 1902-1989..............DLB-76

Graham, Philip 1915-1963.............DLB-127

Graham, R. B. Cunninghame
    1852-1936 ....DLB-98, 135, 174

Graham, Shirley 1896-1977 ....DLB-76

Graham, Stephen 1884-1975 ....DLB-195

Graham, W. S. 1918-1986 ....DLB-20

William H. Graham [publishing house]....DLB-49

Graham, Winston 1910-2003............DLB-77

Grahame, Kenneth 1859-1932... DLB-34, 141, 178

Grainger, Martin Allerdale 1874-1941 .....DLB-92

Gramatky, Hardie 1907-1979 ....DLB-22

Gramcko, Ida 1924-1994 ....DLB-290

Gramsci, Antonio 1891-1937 ....DLB-296

La gran conquista de Ultramar
    thirteenth century ....DLB 337

Granada, Fray Luis de 1504-1588 ....DLB-318

Grand, Sarah 1854-1943 ....DLB-135, 197

Grandbois, Alain 1900-1975 ....DLB-92

Grandson, Oton de circa 1345-1397 .....DLB-208

Grange, John circa 1556-? DLB-136

Granger, Thomas 1578-1627 ....DLB-281

Granich, Irwin (see Gold, Michael)

Granin, Daniil 1918- DLB-302

Granovsky, Timofei Nikolaevich
    1813-1855 ....DLB-198

Grant, Anne MacVicar 1755-1838 ....DLB-200

Grant, Duncan 1885-1978 .... DS-10

Grant, George 1918-1988 ....DLB-88

Grant, George Monro 1835-1902 ....DLB-99

Grant, Harry J. 1881-1963..............DLB-29

Grant, James Edward 1905-1966 ....DLB-26

Grant, John (see Gash, Jonathan)

    War of the Words (and Pictures): The Creation
    of a Graphic Novel Y-02

Grass, Günter 1927- DLB-75, 124, 330; CDWLB-2

    Nobel Lecture 1999:
    "To Be Continued..." Y-99

    Tribute to Helen Wolff Y-94

Grasty, Charles H. 1863-1924 ....DLB-25

Grau, Shirley Ann 1929- DLB-2, 218

Graves, John 1920- Y-83

Graves, Richard 1715-1804 ....DLB-39

Graves, Robert 1895-1985
    ... DLB-20, 100, 191; DS-18; Y-85; CDBLB-6

    The St. John's College
    Robert Graves Trust Y-96

Gray, Alasdair 1934- DLB-194, 261, 319

Gray, Asa 1810-1888 ....DLB-1, 235

Gray, David 1838-1861 ....DLB-32

Gray, Simon 1936- DLB-13

Gray, Robert 1945- DLB-325

Gray, Thomas 1716-1771 .....DLB-109; CDBLB-2

Grayson, Richard 1951- DLB-234

Grayson, William J. 1788-1863 ....DLB-3, 64, 248

The Great Bibliographers Series Y-93

The Great Gatsby (Documentary).........DLB-219

"The Greatness of Southern Literature":
    League of the South Institute for the
    Study of Southern Culture and History
    ....Y-02

Grech, Nikolai Ivanovich 1787-1867......DLB-198

Greeley, Horace 1811-1872 ...DLB-3, 43, 189, 250

Green, Adolph 1915-2002 ....DLB-44, 265

Green, Anna Katharine
    1846-1935 ....DLB-202, 221

Green, Duff 1791-1875................DLB-43

Green, Elizabeth Shippen 1871-1954 .....DLB-188

Green, Gerald 1922- DLB-28

Green, Henry 1905-1973 ....DLB-15

Green, Jonas 1712-1767 ....DLB-31

Green, Joseph 1706-1780 ....DLB-31

Green, Julien 1900-1998 ....DLB-4, 72

Green, Paul 1894-1981 ...... DLB-7, 9, 249; Y-81

Green, T. H. 1836-1882............DLB-190, 262

Green, Terence M. 1947- DLB-251

T. and S. Green [publishing house] DLB-49

Green Tiger Press DLB-46

Timothy Green [publishing house] DLB-49

Greenaway, Kate 1846-1901 ....DLB-141

Greenberg, Joanne 1932- DLB-335

Greenberg: Publisher..................DLB-46

Greene, Asa 1789-1838 ....DLB-11

Greene, Belle da Costa 1883-1950.......DLB-187

Greene, Graham 1904-1991
    ....DLB-13, 15, 77, 100, 162, 201, 204;
    Y-85, 91; CDBLB-7

    Tribute to Christopher Isherwood Y-86

Greene, Robert 1558-1592..........DLB-62, 167

Greene, Robert Bernard (Bob), Jr.
    1947- DLB-185

Benjamin H Greene [publishing house]....DLB-49

Greenfield, George 1917 2000 ....Y 91, 00

    Derek Robinson's Review of George
    Greenfield's *Rich Dust* Y-02

Greenhow, Robert 1800-1854 ....DLB-30

Greenlee, William B. 1872-1953 ....DLB-187

Greenough, Horatio 1805-1852.......DLB-1, 235

Greenwell, Dora 1821-1882.........DLB-35, 199

Greenwillow Books DLB-46

Greenwood, Grace (see Lippincott, Sara Jane Clarke)

Greenwood, Walter 1903-1974 ......DLB-10, 191

Greer, Ben 1948- DLB-6

Greflinger, Georg 1620?-1677 ....DLB-164

Greg, W. R. 1809-1881 ....DLB-55

Greg, W. W. 1875-1959 ....DLB-201

Gregg, Josiah 1806-1850 ....DLB-183, 186

Gregg Press DLB-46

Gregory, Horace 1898-1982 ....DLB-48

Gregory, Isabella Augusta Persse, Lady
    1852-1932 ....DLB-10

Gregory of Rimini circa 1300-1358 ......DLB-115

Gregynog Press DLB-112

Greiff, León de 1895-1976 ....DLB-283

Greiffenberg, Catharina Regina von
    1633-1694 ....DLB-168

Greig, Noël 1944- DLB-245

Grekova, Irina (Elena Sergeevna Venttsel')
    1907-2002 ....DLB-302

Grenfell, Wilfred Thomason
    1865-1940 ....DLB-92

Grenville, Kate 1950- DLB-325

Gress, Elsa 1919-1988 ....DLB-214

Greve, Felix Paul (see Grove, Frederick Philip)

Greville, Fulke, First Lord Brooke
    1554-1628 ....DLB-62, 172

Grey, Sir George, K.C.B. 1812-1898 .....DLB-184

Grey, Lady Jane 1537-1554 ....DLB-132

Grey, Zane 1872-1939 ....DLB-9, 212

Zane Grey's West Society Y-00

Grey Owl (Archibald Stansfeld Belaney)
    1888-1938 ....DLB-92; DS-17

Grey Walls Press DLB-112

Griboedov, Aleksandr Sergeevich
    1795?-1829 ....DLB-205

Grice, Paul 1913-1988 ....DLB-279

Grier, Eldon 1917- DLB-88

Grieve, C. M. (see MacDiarmid, Hugh)

Griffin, Bartholomew fl. 1596 ....DLB-172

Griffin, Bryan

    "Panic Among the Philistines":
    A Postscript, An Interview
    with Bryan Griffin Y-81

Griffin, Gerald 1803-1840 ....DLB-159

The Griffin Poetry Prize Y-00

Griffith, Elizabeth 1727?-1793 ....DLB-39, 89

    Preface to *The Delicate Distress* (1769) ...DLB-39

Griffith, George 1857-1906 ....DLB-178

Ralph Griffiths [publishing house].......DLB-154

Griffiths, Trevor 1935- DLB-13, 245

S. C. Griggs and Company DLB-49

Griggs, Sutton Elbert 1872-1930 ....DLB-50

Grignon, Claude-Henri 1894-1976 ....DLB-68

Grigor'ev, Apollon Aleksandrovich
    1822-1864 ....DLB-277

Grigorovich, Dmitrii Vasil'evich 1822-1899 .... DLB-238

Grigson, Geoffrey 1905-1985 .... DLB-27

Grillparzer, Franz 1791-1872 .... DLB-133; CDWLB-2

Grimald, Nicholas circa 1519-circa 1562 .... DLB-136

Grimké, Angelina Weld 1880-1958 ... DLB-50, 54

Grimké, Sarah Moore 1792-1873 .... DLB-239

Grimm, Frédéric Melchior 1723-1807 .... DLB-313

Grimm, Hans 1875-1959 .... DLB-66

Grimm, Jacob 1785-1863 .... DLB-90

Grimm, Wilhelm 1786-1859 .... DLB-90; CDWLB-2

Grimmelshausen, Johann Jacob Christoffel von 1621 or 1622-1676 ..... DLB-168; CDWLB-2

Grimshaw, Beatrice Ethel 1871-1953 .....DLB-174

Grímur Thomsen 1820-1896 .... DLB-293

Grin, Aleksandr Stepanovich 1880-1932 .... DLB-272

Grindal, Edmund 1519 or 1520-1583.... DLB-132

Gripe, Maria (Kristina) 1923- DLB-257

Griswold, Rufus Wilmot 1815-1857................ DLB-3, 59, 250

Gronlund, Laurence 1846-1899 .... DLB-303

Grosart, Alexander Balloch 1827-1899 ... DLB-184

Grosholz, Emily 1950- DLB-282

Gross, Milt 1895-1953 .... DLB-11

Grosset and Dunlap DLB-49

Grosseteste, Robert circa 1160-1253..... DLB-115

Grossman, Allen 1932- DLB-193

Grossman, David 1954- DLB-299

Grossman, Vasilii Semenovich 1905-1964 .... DLB-272

Grossman Publishers DLB-46

Grosvenor, Gilbert H. 1875-1966 .... DLB-91

Groth, Klaus 1819-1899 .... DLB-129

Groulx, Lionel 1878-1967 .... DLB-68

Grove, Frederick Philip (Felix Paul Greve) 1879-1948...................... DLB-92

Grove Press......................... DLB-46

Groys, Boris Efimovich 1947- DLB-285

Grubb, Davis 1919-1980............... DLB-6

Gruelle, Johnny 1880-1938............. DLB-22

von Grumbach, Argula 1492-after 1563?...................DLB-179

Grundtvig, N. F. S. 1783-1872.......... DLB-300

Grymeston, Elizabeth before 1563-before 1604............ DLB-136

Grynberg, Henryk 1936- DLB-299

Gryphius, Andreas 1616-1664........... DLB-164; CDWLB-2

Gryphius, Christian 1649-1706 .... DLB-168

Guare, John 1938- DLB-7, 249

Guarini, Battista 1538-1612 .... DLB-339

Guarnieri, Gianfrancesco 1934- DLB-307

Guberman, Igor Mironovich 1936- DLB-285

Guðbergur Bergsson 1932- DLB-293

Guðmundur Böðvarsson 1904-1974..... DLB-293

Guðmundur Gíslason Hagalín 1898-1985 .... DLB-293

Guðmundur Magnússon (see Jón Trausti)

Guerra, Tonino 1920- DLB-128

Guest, Barbara 1920- DLB-5, 193

Guevara, Fray Antonio de 1480?-1545... DLB-318

Guèvremont, Germaine 1893-1968 ...... DLB-68

Guglielminetti, Amalia 1881-1941 ...... DLB-264

Guidacci, Margherita 1921-1992 .... DLB-128

Guillén, Jorge 1893-1984 .... DLB-108

Guillén, Nicolás 1902-1989............ DLB-283

Guilloux, Louis 1899-1980............. DLB-72

Guilpin, Everard circa 1572-after 1608?.............. DLB-136

Guiney, Louise Imogen 1861-1920....... DLB-54

Guiterman, Arthur 1871-1943 .... DLB-11

Gul', Roman 1896-1986 .... DLB-317

Gumilev, Nikolai Stepanovich 1886-1921 .... DLB-295

Günderrode, Caroline von 1780-1806..................... DLB-90

Gundulić, Ivan 1589-1638 ...DLB-147; CDWLB-4

Gunesekera, Romesh 1954- DLB-267, 323

Gunn, Bill 1934-1989 .... DLB-38

Gunn, James E. 1923- DLB-8

Gunn, Neil M. 1891-1973 .... DLB-15

Gunn, Thom 1929- DLB-27; CDBLB-8

Gunnar Gunnarsson 1889-1975 .... DLB-293

Gunnars, Kristjana 1948- DLB-60

Günther, Johann Christian 1695-1723 ... DLB-168

Gupta, Sunetra 1965- DLB-323

Gurik, Robert 1932- DLB-60

Gurney, A. R. 1930- DLB-266

Gurney, Ivor 1890-1937 .... Y-02

The Ivor Gurney Society Y-98

Guro, Elena Genrikhovna 1877-1913 .... DLB-295

Gustafson, Ralph 1909-1995 .... DLB-88

Gustafsson, Lars 1936- DLB-257

Gütersloh, Albert Paris 1887-1973 .... DLB-81

Guterson, David 1956- DLB-292

Guthrie, A. B., Jr. 1901-1991 .... DLB-6, 212

Guthrie, Ramon 1896-1973 .... DLB-4

Guthrie, Thomas Anstey (see Anstey, FC)

Guthrie, Woody 1912-1967 .... DLB-303

The Guthrie Theater DLB-7

Gutiérrez Nájera, Manuel 1859-1895 .... DLB-290

Guttormur J. Guttormsson 1878-1966 ... DLB-293

Gutzkow, Karl 1811-1878 .... DLB-133

Guy, Ray 1939- DLB-60

Guy, Rosa 1925- DLB-33

Guyot, Arnold 1807-1884................DS-13

Gwynn, R. S. 1948- DLB-282

Gwynne, Erskine 1898-1948 .... DLB-4

Gyles, John 1680-1755 .... DLB-99

Gyllembourg, Thomasine 1773-1856 .... DLB-300

Gyllensten, Lars 1921- DLB-257

Gyrðir Elíasson 1961- DLB-293

Gysin, Brion 1916-1986 .... DLB-16

H

H.D. (see Doolittle, Hilda)

Habermas, Jürgen 1929- DLB-242

Habington, William 1605-1654 .... DLB-126

Hacker, Marilyn 1942- DLB-120, 282

Hackett, Albert 1900-1995 .... DLB-26

Hacks, Peter 1928- DLB-124

Hadas, Rachel 1948- DLB-120, 282

Hadden, Briton 1898-1929............. DLB-91

Hagedorn, Friedrich von 1708-1754 ..... DLB-168

Hagedorn, Jessica Tarahata 1949- DLB-312

Hagelstange, Rudolf 1912-1984 .... DLB-69

Hagerup, Inger 1905-1985 .... DLB-297

Haggard, H. Rider 1856-1925 .... DLB-70, 156, 174, 178

Haggard, William (Richard Clayton) 1907-1993..................DLB-276; Y-93

Hagy, Alyson 1960- DLB-244

Hahn-Hahn, Ida Gräfin von 1805-1880 .. DLB-133

Haig-Brown, Roderick 1908-1976........ DLB-88

Haight, Gordon S. 1901-1985.......... DLB-103

Hailey, Arthur 1920-2004..........DLB-88; Y-82

Haines, John 1924- DLB-5, 212

Hake, Edward fl. 1566-1604............ DLB-136

Hake, Thomas Gordon 1809-1895....... DLB-32

Hakluyt, Richard 1552?-1616........... DLB-136

Halas, František 1901-1949 .... DLB-215

Halbe, Max 1865-1944................ DLB-118

Halberstam, David 1934-2007 .... DLB-241

Haldane, Charlotte 1894-1969 .... DLB-191

Haldane, J. B. S. 1892-1964 .... DLB-160

Haldeman, Joe 1943- DLB-8

Haldeman-Julius Company DLB-46

Hale, E. J., and Son DLB-49

Hale, Edward Everett 1822-1909 ....DLB-1, 42, 74, 235

Hale, Janet Campbell 1946- DLB-175

Hale, Kathleen 1898-2000 .... DLB-160

Hale, Leo Thomas (see Ebon)

Hale, Lucretia Peabody 1820-1900 . . . . DLB-42

Hale, Nancy
 1908-1988 . . . . DLB-86; DS-17; Y-80, 88

Hale, Sarah Josepha (Buell)
 1788-1879 . . . . DLB-1, 42, 73, 243

Hale, Susan 1833-1910 . . . . DLB-221

Hales, John 1584-1656 . . . . DLB-151

Halévy, Ludovic 1834-1908 . . . . DLB-192

Haley, Alex 1921-1992 . . . . DLB-38; CDALB-7

Haliburton, Thomas Chandler
 1796-1865 . . . . DLB-11, 99

Hall, Adam (Trevor Dudley-Smith)
 1920-1995 . . . . DLB-276

Hall, Anna Maria 1800-1881 . . . . DLB-159

Hall, Donald 1928- DLB-5

Hall, Edward 1497-1547 . . . . DLB-132

Hall, Halsey 1898-1977 . . . . DLB-241

Hall, James 1793-1868 . . . . DLB-73, 74

Hall, James B. 1918- DLB-335

Hall, Joseph 1574-1656 . . . . DLB-121, 151

Hall, Radclyffe 1880-1943 . . . . DLB-191

Hall, Rodney 1935- DLB-289

Hall, Sarah Ewing 1761-1830 . . . . DLB-200

Hall, Stuart 1932- DLB-242

Samuel Hall [publishing house] DLB-49

al-Hallaj 857-922 . . . . DLB-311

Hallam, Arthur Henry 1811-1833 . . . . DLB-32

On Some of the Characteristics of
 Modern Poetry and On the
 Lyrical Poems of Alfred
 Tennyson (1831) DLB-32

Halldór Laxness (Halldór Guðjónsson)
 1902-1998 . . . . DLB-293, 331

Halleck, Fitz-Greene 1790-1867 . . . . DLB-3, 250

Haller, Albrecht von 1708-1777 . . . . DLB-168

Halliday, Brett (see Dresser, Davis)

Halligan, Marion 1940- DLB-325

Halliwell-Phillipps, James Orchard
 1820-1889 . . . . DLB-184

Hallmann, Johann Christian
 1640-1704 or 1716? DLB-168

Hallmark Editions DLB-46

Halper, Albert 1904-1984 . . . . DLB-9

Halperin, John William 1941- DLB-111

Halpern, Moshe Leib (Moyshe Leyb Halpern)
 1886-1932 . . . . DLB-333

Halstead, Murat 1829-1908 . . . . DLB-23

Hamann, Johann Georg 1730-1788 . . . . . . DLB-97

Hamburger, Michael 1924- DLB-27

Hamilton, Alexander 1712-1756 . . . . DLB-31

Hamilton, Alexander 1755?-1804 . . . . DLB-37

Hamilton, Cicely 1872-1952 . . . . DLB-10, 197

Hamilton, Edmond 1904-1977 . . . . DLB-8

Hamilton, Elizabeth 1758-1816 . . . . . DLB-116, 158

Hamilton, Gail (see Corcoran, Barbara)

Hamilton, Gail (see Dodge, Mary Abigail)

Hamish Hamilton Limited DLB-112

Hamilton, Hugo 1953- DLB-267

Hamilton, Ian 1938-2001 . . . . DLB-40, 155

Hamilton, Janet 1795-1873 . . . . DLB-199

Hamilton, Mary Agnes 1884-1962 . . . . . . DLB-197

Hamilton, Patrick 1904-1962 . . . . DLB-10, 191

Hamilton, Virginia 1936-2002 . . . DLB-33, 52; Y-01

Hamilton, Sir William 1788-1856 . . . . DLB-262

Hamilton-Paterson, James 1941- DLB-267

Hammerstein, Oscar, 2nd 1895-1960 . . . DLB-265

Hammett, Dashiell
 1894-1961 . . . . DLB-226; DS-6; CDALB-5

 An Appeal in TAC Y-91

 The Glass Key and Other Dashiell
  Hammett Mysteries Y-96

 Knopf to Hammett: The Editoral
  Correspondence Y-00

 The Maltese Falcon (Documentary) DLB-280

Hammon, Jupiter 1711-died between
 1790 and 1806 . . . . DLB-31, 50

Hammond, John ?-1663 . . . . DLB-24

Hamner, Earl 1923- DLB-6

Hampson, John 1901-1955 . . . . DLB-191

Hampton, Christopher 1946- DLB-13

Hamsun, Knut 1859-1952 . . . . DLB-297, 330

Handel-Mazzetti, Enrica von 1871-1955 . . . DLB-81

Handke, Peter 1942- DLB-85, 124

Handlin, Oscar 1915- DLB-17

Hankin, St. John 1869-1909 . . . . DLB-10

Hanley, Clifford 1922- DLB-14

Hanley, James 1901-1985 . . . . DLB-191

Hannah, Barry 1942- DLB-6, 234

Hannay, James 1827-1873 . . . . DLB-21

Hannes Hafstein 1861-1922 . . . . DLB-293

Hano, Arnold 1922- DLB-241

Hanrahan, Barbara 1939-1991 . . . . DLB-289

Hansberry, Lorraine
 1930-1965 . . . . DLB-7, 38; CDALB-1

Hansen, Joseph 1923-2004 . . . . DLB-226

Hansen, Martin A. 1909-1955 . . . . DLB-214

Hansen, Thorkild 1927-1989 . . . . DLB-214

Hanson, Elizabeth 1684-1737 . . . . DLB-200

Hapgood, Norman 1868-1937 . . . . DLB-91

Happel, Eberhard Werner 1647-1690 . . . . DLB-168

Haq, Kaiser 1950- DLB-323

Harbach, Otto 1873-1963 . . . . DLB-265

The Harbinger 1845-1849 . . . . DLB-1, 223

Harburg, E. Y. "Yip" 1896-1981 . . . . DLB-265

Harcourt Brace Jovanovich DLB-46

Hardenberg, Friedrich von (see Novalis)

Harding, Walter 1917-1996 . . . . DLB-111

Hardwick, Elizabeth 1916- DLB-6

Hardy, Alexandre 1572?-1632 . . . . DLB-268

Hardy, Frank 1917-1994 . . . . DLB-260

Hardy, Thomas
 1840-1928 . . . . DLB-18, 19, 135; CDBLB-5

 "Candour in English Fiction" (1890) DLB-18

Hare, Cyril 1900-1958 . . . . DLB-77

Hare, David 1947- DLB-13, 310

Hare, R. M. 1919-2002 . . . . DLB-262

Hargrove, Marion 1919-2003 . . . . DLB-11

Häring, Georg Wilhelm Heinrich
 (see Alexis, Willibald)

Harington, Donald 1935- DLB-152

Harington, Sir John 1560-1612 . . . . DLB-136

Harjo, Joy 1951- DLB-120, 175

Harkness, Margaret (John Law)
 1854-1923 . . . . DLB-197

Harley, Edward, second Earl of Oxford
 1689-1741 . . . . DLB-213

Harley, Robert, first Earl of Oxford
 1661-1724 . . . . DLB-213

Harlow, Robert 1923- DLB-60

Harman, Thomas fl. 1566-1573 . . . . DLB-136

Harness, Charles L. 1915- DLB-8

Harnett, Cynthia 1893-1981 . . . . DLB-161

Harnick, Sheldon 1924- DLB-265

 Tribute to Ira Gershwin Y-96

 Tribute to Lorenz Hart Y-95

Harper, Edith Alice Mary (see Wickham, Anna)

Harper, Fletcher 1806-1877 . . . . DLB-79

Harper, Frances Ellen Watkins
 1825-1911 . . . . DLB-50, 221

Harper, Michael S. 1938- DLB-41

Harper and Brothers DLB-49

Harpur, Charles 1813-1868 . . . . DLB-230

Harraden, Beatrice 1864-1943 . . . . DLB-153

George G. Harrap and Company
 Limited DLB-112

Harriot, Thomas 1560-1621 . . . . DLB-136

Harris, Alexander 1805-1874 . . . . DLB-230

Harris, Benjamin ?-circa 1720 . . . . DLB-42, 43

Harris, Christie 1907-2002 . . . . DLB-88

Harris, Claire 1937- DLB-334

Harris, Errol E. 1908- DLB-279

Harris, Frank 1856-1931 . . . . DLB-156, 197

Harris, George Washington
 1814-1869 . . . . DLB-3, 11, 248

Harris, Joanne 1964- DLB-271

Harris, Joel Chandler
 1848-1908 . . . . DLB-11, 23, 42, 78, 91

 The Joel Chandler Harris Association Y-99

Harris, Mark 1922- DLB-2; Y-80

Tribute to Frederick A. Pottle........... Y-87

Harris, William 1720-1770 .... DLB-336

Harris, William Torrey 1835-1909 .... DLB-270

Harris, Wilson 1921- DLB-117; CDWLB-3

Harrison, Mrs. Burton
(see Harrison, Constance Cary)

Harrison, Charles Yale 1898-1954 .... DLB-68

Harrison, Constance Cary 1843-1920 ... DLB-221

Harrison, Frederic 1831-1923........ DLB-57, 190

"On Style in English Prose" (1898) ... DLB-57

Harrison, Harry 1925- DLB-8

James P. Harrison Company DLB-49

Harrison, Jim 1937- Y-82

Harrison, M. John 1945- DLB-261

Harrison, Mary St. Leger Kingsley
(see Malet, Lucas)

Harrison, Paul Carter 1936- DLB-38

Harrison, Susan Frances 1859-1935 ...... DLB-99

Harrison, Tony 1937- DLB-40, 245

Harrison, William 1535-1593.......... DLB-136

Harrison, William 1933- DLB-234

Harrisse, Henry 1829-1910............ DLB-47

Harry, J. S. 1939- DLB-325

The Harry Ransom Humanities Research Center
at the University of Texas at Austin Y-00

Harryman, Carla 1952- DLB-193

Harsdörffer, Georg Philipp 1607-1658 ... DLB-164

Harsent, David 1942- DLB-40

Hart, Albert Bushnell 1854-1943 .... DLB-17

Hart, Anne 1768-1834 .... DLB-200

Hart, Elizabeth 1771-1833............ DLB-200

Hart, Jonathan Locke 1956- DLB-334

Hart, Julia Catherine 1796-1867 .... DLB-99

Hart, Kevin 1954- DLB-325

Hart, Lorenz 1895-1943 .... DLB-265

Larry Hart: Still an Influence........... Y-95

Lorenz Hart: An American Lyricist...... Y-95

The Lorenz Hart Centenary Y-95

Hart, Moss 1904-1961 ....DLB-7, 266

Hart, Oliver 1723-1795................ DLB-31

Rupert Hart-Davis Limited............ DLB-112

Harte, Bret 1836-1902
........DLB-12, 64, 74, 79, 186; CDALB-3

Harte, Edward Holmead 1922- DLB-127

Harte, Houston Harriman 1927- DLB-127

Harte, Jack 1944- DLB-319

Hartlaub, Felix 1913-1945 .... DLB-56

Hartlebon, Otto Erich 1864-1905....... DLB-118

Hartley, David 1705-1757 .... DLB-252

Hartley, L. P. 1895-1972........... DLB-15, 139

Hartley, Marsden 1877-1943........... DLB-54

Hartling, Peter 1933- DLB-75

Hartman, Geoffrey H. 1929- DLB-67

Hartmann, Sadakichi 1867-1944........ DLB-54

Hartmann von Aue
circa 1160-circa 1205 ... DLB-138; CDWLB-2

Hartshorne, Charles 1897-2000 .... DLB-270

Haruf, Kent 1943- DLB-292

Harvey, Gabriel 1550?-1631.... DLB-167, 213, 281

Harvey, Jack (see Rankin, Ian)

Harvey, Jean-Charles 1891-1967 .... DLB-88

Harvill Press Limited DLB-112

Harwood, Gwen 1920-1995 .... DLB-289

Harwood, Lee 1939- DLB-40

Harwood, Ronald 1934- DLB-13

al-Hasan al-Basri 642-728 .... DLB-311

Hašek, Jaroslav 1883-1923 .. DLB-215; CDWLB-4

Haskins, Charles Homer 1870-1937...... DLB-47

Haslam, Gerald 1937- DLB-212

Hass, Robert 1941- DLB-105, 206

Hasselstrom, Linda M. 1943- DLB-256

Hastings, Michael 1938- DLB-233

Hatar, Győző 1914- DLB-215

The Hatch-Billops Collection DLB-76

Hathaway, William 1944- DLB-120

Hatherly, Ana 1929- DLB-287

Hauch, Carsten 1790-1872 .... DLB-300

Hauff, Wilhelm 1802-1827 .... DLB-90

Hauge, Olav H. 1908-1994............ DLB-297

Haugen, Paal-Helge 1945- DLB-297

Haugwitz, August Adolph von
1647-1706 .... DLB-168

Hauptmann, Carl 1858-1921 .... DLB-66, 118

Hauptmann, Gerhart
1862-1946 .....DLB-66, 118, 330; CDWLB-2

Hauser, Marianne 1910- Y-83

Havel, Václav 1936- DLB-232; CDWLB-4

Haven, Alice B. Neal 1827-1863 .... DLB-250

Havergal, Frances Ridley 1836-1879 .... DLB-199

Hawes, Stephen 1475?-before 1529...... DLB-132

Hawker, Robert Stephen 1803-1875 ..... DLB-32

Hawkes, John
1925-1998 ....DLB-2, 7, 227; Y-80, Y-98

John Hawkes: A Tribute Y-98

Tribute to Donald Barthelme Y-89

Hawkesworth, John 1720-1773 .... DLB-142

Hawkins, Sir Anthony Hope (see Hope, Anthony)

Hawkins, Sir John 1719-1789 ...DLB-104, 142, 336

Hawkins, Walter Everette 1883-? DLB-50

Hawthorne, Nathaniel 1804-1864
... DLB-1, 74, 183, 223, 269; DS-5; CDALB-2

The Nathaniel Hawthorne Society....... Y-00

The Old Manse DLB-223

Hawthorne, Sophia Peabody
1809-1871.................. DLB-183, 239

Hay, John 1835-1905 .... DLB-12, 47, 189

Hay, John 1915- DLB-275

Hayashi Fumiko 1903-1951 .... DLB-180

Haycox, Ernest 1899-1950 .... DLB-206

Haycraft, Anna Margaret (see Ellis, Alice Thomas)

Hayden, Robert 1913-1980 . DLB-5, 76; CDALB-1

Haydon, Benjamin Robert 1786-1846 ... DLB-110

Hayes, John Michael 1919- DLB-26

Hayley, William 1745-1820.......... DLB-93, 142

Haym, Rudolf 1821-1901............. DLB-129

Hayman, Robert 1575-1629 .... DLB-99

Hayman, Ronald 1932- DLB-155

Hayne, Paul Hamilton
1830-1886 ....DLB-3, 64, 79, 248

Hays, Mary 1760-1843 .... DLB-142, 158

Hayslip, Le Ly 1949- DLB-312

Hayward, John 1905-1965 .... DLB-201

Haywood, Eliza 1693?-1756 .... DLB-39

Dedication of Lasselia [excerpt]
(1723) DLB-39

Preface to The Disguis'd Prince
[excerpt] (1723) DLB-39

The Tea-Table [excerpt]............. DLB-39

Haywood, William D. 1869-1928....... DLB-303

Willis P. Hazard [publishing house] DLB-49

Hazlitt, William 1778-1830 .... DLB-110, 158

Hazzard, Shirley 1931- DLB-289; Y-82

Head, Bessie
1937-1986......... DLB-117, 225; CDWLB-3

Headley, Joel T. 1813-1897 ... DLB-30, 183; DS-13

Heaney, Seamus 1939- DLB-40, 330;
Y-95; CDBLB-8

Nobel Lecture 1994: Crediting Poetry Y-95

Heard, Nathan C. 1936- DLB-33

Hearn, Lafcadio 1850-1904 ...... DLB-12, 78, 189

Hearn, Mary Anne (Marianne Farningham,
Eva Hope) 1834-1909 .... DLB-240

Hearne, John 1926- DLB-117

Hearne, Samuel 1745-1792 .... DLB-99

Hearne, Thomas 1678?-1735 ...... DLB-213, 336

Hearst, William Randolph 1863-1951 .... CDALB-5

Hearst, William Randolph, Jr.
1908-1993 .... DLB-127

Heartman, Charles Frederick
1883-1953 .... DLB-187

Heat and Dust, 1975 Booker Prize winner,
Ruth Prawer Jhabvala DLB-326

Heath, Catherine 1924- DLB-14

Heath, James Ewell 1792-1862 .... DLB-248

Heath, Roy A. K. 1926- DLB-117

Heath-Stubbs, John 1918- DLB-27

Heavysege, Charles 1816-1876.......... DLB-99

Hebbel, Friedrich 1813-1863 .... DLB-129; CDWLB-2
Hebel, Johann Peter 1760-1826 .... DLB-90
Heber, Richard 1774-1833 .... DLB-184
Hébert, Anne 1916-2000 .... DLB-68
Hébert, Jacques 1923- DLB-53
Hebreo, León circa 1460-1520 .... DLB-318
Hecht, Anthony 1923- DLB-5, 169
Hecht, Ben 1894-1964 .... DLB-7, 9, 25, 26, 28, 86
Hecker, Isaac Thomas 1819-1888 ..... DLB-1, 243
Hedge, Frederic Henry 1805-1890 .... DLB-1, 59, 243; DS-5
Hefner, Hugh M. 1926- DLB-137
Hegel, Georg Wilhelm Friedrich 1770-1831 .... DLB-90
Heiberg, Johan Ludvig 1791-1860 .... DLB-300
Heiberg, Johanne Luise 1812-1890 ...... DLB-300
Heide, Robert 1939- DLB-249
Heidegger, Martin 1889-1976 .... DLB-296
Heidenstam, Verner von 1859-1940 ..... DLB-330
Heidish, Marcy 1947- Y-82
Heißenbüttel, Helmut 1921-1996 .... DLB-75
Heike monogatari DLB-203
Hein, Christoph 1944- DLB-124; CDWLB-2
Hein, Piet 1905-1996 .... DLB-214
Heine, Heinrich 1797-1856 .... DLB-90; CDWLB-2
Heinemann, Larry 1944- DS-9
William Heinemann Limited DLB-112
Heinesen, William 1900-1991 .... DLB-214
Heinlein, Robert A. 1907-1988 .... DLB-8
Heinrich, Willi 1920- DLB-75
Heinrich Julius of Brunswick| 1564-1613 .... DLB-164
Heinrich von dem Türlîn fl. circa 1230 .... DLB-138
Heinrich von Melk fl. after 1160 .... DLB-148
Heinrich von Veldeke circa 1145-circa 1190 .... DLB-138
Heinse, Wilhelm 1746-1803 .... DLB-94
Heinz, W. C. 1915- DLB-171
Heiskell, John 1872-1972 .... DLB-127
Hejinian, Lyn 1941- DLB-165
Helder, Herberto 1930- DLB-287
Heliand circa 850 .... DLB-148
Heller, Joseph 1923-1999 ...... DLB-2, 28, 227; Y-80, 99, 02
   Excerpts from Joseph Heller's USC Address, "The Literature of Despair" Y-96
   Remembering Joe Heller, by William Price Fox Y-99
   A Tribute to Joseph Heller Y-99
Heller, Michael 1937- DLB-165

Hellman, Lillian 1906-1984 ..... DLB-7, 228; Y-84
Hellwig, Johann 1609-1674 .... DLB-164
Helprin, Mark 1947- DLB-335; Y-85; CDALB-7
Helvétius, Claude-Adrien 1715-1771 ..... DLB-313
   The Spirit of Laws DLB-314
Helwig, David 1938- DLB-60
Hemans, Felicia 1793-1835 .... DLB-96
Hemenway, Abby Maria 1828-1890 ..... DLB-243
Hemingway, Ernest 1899-1961 ...... DLB-4, 9, 102, 210, 316, 330; Y-81, 87, 99; DS-1, 15, 16; CDALB-4
   A Centennial Celebration Y-99
   Come to Papa Y-99
   The Ernest Hemingway Collection at the John F. Kennedy Library Y-99
   Ernest Hemingway Declines to Introduce *War and Peace* Y-01
   Ernest Hemingway's Reaction to James Gould Cozzens Y-98
   Ernest Hemingway's Toronto Journalism Revisited: With Three Previously Unrecorded Stories Y-92
   Falsifying Hemingway Y-96
   A Farewell to Arms (Documentary) DLB-308
   Hemingway Centenary Celebration at the JFK Library Y-99
   The Hemingway/Fenton Correspondence Y-02
   Hemingway in the JFK Y-99
   The Hemingway Letters Project Finds an Editor Y-02
   Hemingway Salesmen's Dummies Y-00
   Hemingway: Twenty-Five Years Later Y-85
   A Literary Archaeologist Digs On: A Brief Interview with Michael Reynolds Y-99
   Not Immediately Discernible . . . but Eventually Quite Clear: The *First Light* and *Final Years* of Hemingway's Centenary Y-99
   Packaging Papa: *The Garden of Eden* Y-86
   Second International Hemingway Colloquium: Cuba Y-98
Hémon, Louis 1880-1913 .... DLB-92
Hempel, Amy 1951- DLB-218
Hempel, Carl G. 1905-1997 .... DLB-279
Hemphill, Paul 1936- Y-87
Hénault, Gilles 1920-1996 .... DLB-88
Henchman, Daniel 1689-1761 .... DLB-24
Henderson, Alice Corbin 1881-1949 ..... DLB-54
Henderson, Archibald 1877-1963 .... DLB-103
Henderson, David 1942- DLB-41
Henderson, George Wylie 1904-1965 ..... DLB-51
Henderson, Zenna 1917-1983 .... DLB-8
Henighan, Tom 1934- DLB-251
Henisch, Peter 1943- DLB-85
Henley, Beth 1952- Y-86
Henley, William Ernest 1849-1903 .... DLB-19

Henniker, Florence 1855-1923 .... DLB-135
Henning, Rachel 1826-1914 .... DLB-230
Henningsen, Agnes 1868-1962 .... DLB-214
Henry, Alexander 1739-1824 .... DLB-99
Henry, Buck 1930- DLB-26
Henry, Marguerite 1902-1997 .... DLB-22
Henry, O. (see Porter, William Sydney)
Henry, Robert Selph 1889-1970 .... DLB-17
Henry, Will (see Allen, Henry W.)
Henry VIII of England 1491-1547 ...... DLB-132
Henry of Ghent circa 1217-1229 - 1293 .... DLB-115
Henryson, Robert 1420s or 1430s-circa 1505 .... DLB-146
Henschke, Alfred (see Klabund)
Hensher, Philip 1965- DLB-267
Hensley, Sophie Almon 1866-1946 ...... DLB-99
Henson, Lance 1944- DLB-175
Henty, G. A. 1832-1902 .... DLB-18, 141
   The Henty Society Y-98
Hentz, Caroline Lee 1800-1856 .... DLB-3, 248
Heraclitus fl. circa 500 B.C. DLB-176
Herbert, Agnes circa 1880-1960 .... DLB-174
Herbert, Alan Patrick 1890-1971 ..... DLB-10, 191
Herbert, Edward, Lord, of Cherbury 1582-1648 .... DLB-121, 151, 252
Herbert, Frank 1920-1986 ...... DLB-8; CDALB-7
Herbert, George 1593-1633 ... DLB-126; CDBLB-1
Herbert, Henry William 1807-1858 ..... DLB-3, 73
Herbert, John 1926-2001 .... DLB-53
Herbert, Mary Sidney, Countess of Pembroke (see Sidney, Mary)
Herbert, Xavier 1901-1984 .... DLB-260
Herbert, Zbigniew 1924-1998 .... DLB-232; CDWLB-4
Herbst, Josephine 1892-1969 .... DLB-9
Herburger, Gunter 1932- DLB-75, 124
Herculano, Alexandre 1810-1877 .... DLB-287
Hercules, Frank E. M. 1917-1996 .... DLB-33
Herder, Johann Gottfried 1744-1803 ..... DLB-97
B. Herder Book Company DLB-49
Heredia, José-María de 1842-1905 ...... DLB-217
Herford, Charles Harold 1853-1931 ..... DLB-149
Hergesheimer, Joseph 1880-1954 ...... DLB-9, 102
Heritage Press DLB-46
Hermann the Lame 1013-1054 .... DLB-148
Hermes, Johann Timotheu 1738-1821 ..... DLB-97
Hermlin, Stephan 1915-1997 .... DLB-69
Hernández, Alfonso C. 1938- DLB-122
Hernández, Inés 1947- DLB-122
Hernández, Miguel 1910-1942 .... DLB-134
Hernton, Calvin C. 1932- DLB-38

Cumulative Index

Herodotus circa 484 B.C.-circa 420 B.C. DLB-176; CDWLB-1
Héroët, Antoine 1490?-1567? DLB-327
Heron, Robert 1764-1807 .... DLB-142
Herr, Michael 1940- DLB-185
Herrera, Darío 1870-1914 .... DLB-290
Herrera, Fernando de 1534?-1597 ...... DLB-318
Herrera, Juan Felipe 1948- DLB-122
E. R. Herrick and Company DLB-49
Herrick, Robert 1591-1674 .... DLB-126
Herrick, Robert 1868-1938 .... DLB-9, 12, 78
Herrick, William 1915-2004 .... Y-83
Herrmann, John 1900-1959 .... DLB-4
Hersey, John
  1914-1993 ... DLB-6, 185, 278, 299; CDALB-7
Hertel, François 1905-1985 .... DLB-68
Hervé-Bazin, Jean Pierre Marie (see Bazin, Hervé)
Hervey, John, Lord 1696-1743 .... DLB-101
Herwig, Georg 1817-1875 .... DLB-133
Herzen, Alexander (Aleksandr Ivanovich
  Gersten) 1812-1870 .... DLB-277
Herzog, Emile Salomon Wilhelm
  (see Maurois, André)
Hesiod eighth century B.C. DLB-176
Hesse, Hermann
  1877-1962 .... DLB-66, 330; CDWLB-2
Hessus, Eobanus 1488-1540 .... DLB-179
Heureka! (see Kertész, Imre and Nobel Prize
  in Literature: 2002) Y-02
Hewat, Alexander circa 1743-circa 1824 ... DLB-30
Hewett, Dorothy 1923-2002 .... DLB-289
Hewitt, John 1907-1987 .... DLB-27
Hewlett, Maurice 1861-1923 .... DLB-34, 156
Heyen, William 1940- DLB-5
Heyer, Georgette 1902-1974 .... DLB-77, 191
Heym, Stefan 1913-2001 .... DLB-69
Heyse, Paul 1830-1914 .... DLB-129, 330
Heytesbury, William
  circa 1310-1372 or 1373 .... DLB-115
Heyward, Dorothy 1890-1961 .... DLB-7, 249
Heyward, DuBose 1885-1940 .... DLB-7, 9, 45, 249
Heywood, John 1497?-1580? DLB-136
Heywood, Thomas 1573 or 1574-1641 .... DLB-62
Hiaasen, Carl 1953- DLB-292
Hibberd, Jack 1940- DLB-289
Hibbs, Ben 1901-1975 .... DLB-137
  "The Saturday Evening Post reaffirms
  a policy," Ben Hibb's Statement
  in *The Saturday Evening Post*
  (16 May 1942) DLB-137
Hichens, Robert S. 1864-1950 .... DLB-153
Hickey, Emily 1845-1924 .... DLB-199
Hickman, William Albert 1877-1957 ..... DLB-92
Hicks, Granville 1901-1982 .... DLB-246

Hidalgo, José Luis 1919-1947 .... DLB-108
Hiebert, Paul 1892-1987 .... DLB-68
Hieng, Andrej 1925- DLB-181
Hierro, José 1922-2002 .... DLB-108
Higgins, Aidan 1927- DLB-14
Higgins, Colin 1941-1988 .... DLB-26
Higgins, George V.
  1939-1999 .... DLB-2; Y-81, 98–99
  Afterword [in response to Cozzen's
    Mens Rea (or Something)] Y-97
  At End of Day: The Last George V.
    Higgins Novel Y-99
  The Books of George V. Higgins:
    A Checklist of Editions
    and Printings Y-00
  George V. Higgins in Class Y-02
  Tribute to Alfred A. Knopf Y-84
  Tributes to George V. Higgins Y-99
  "What You Lose on the Swings You Make
    Up on the Merry-Go-Round" Y-99
Higginson, Thomas Wentworth
  1823-1911 .... DLB-1, 64, 243
Highsmith, Patricia 1921-1995 .... DLB-306
Highwater, Jamake 1942?- DLB-52; Y-85
Highway, Tomson 1951- DLB-334
Hijuelos, Oscar 1951- DLB-145
Hildegard von Bingen 1098-1179 .... DLB-148
Das Hildesbrandslied
  circa 820 .... DLB-148; CDWLB-2
Hildesheimer, Wolfgang 1916-1991 .. DLB-69, 124
Hildreth, Richard 1807-1865 ... DLB-1, 30, 59, 235
Hill, Aaron 1685-1750 .... DLB-84
Hill, Geoffrey 1932- DLB-40; CDBLB-8
George M. Hill Company DLB-49
Hill, "Sir" John 1714?-1775 .... DLB-39
Lawrence Hill and Company,
  Publishers DLB-46
Hill, Joe 1879-1915 .... DLB-303
Hill, Leslie 1880-1960 .... DLB-51
Hill, Reginald 1936- DLB-276
Hill, Susan 1942- DLB-14, 139
Hill, Walter 1942- DLB-44
Hill and Wang DLB-46
Hillberry, Conrad 1928- DLB-120
Hillerman, Tony 1925- DLB-206, 306
Hilliard, Gray and Company DLB-49
Hills, Lee 1906-2000 .... DLB-127
Hillyer, Robert 1895-1961 .... DLB-54
Hilsenrath, Edgar 1926- DLB-299
Hilton, James 1900-1954 .... DLB-34, 77
Hilton, Walter died 1396 .... DLB-146
Hilton and Company DLB-49
Himes, Chester 1909-1984 .... DLB-2, 76, 143, 226
Joseph Hindmarsh [publishing house] ... DLB-170

Hine, Daryl 1936- DLB-60
Hingley, Ronald 1920- DLB-155
Hinojosa-Smith, Rolando 1929- DLB-82
Hinton, S. E. 1948- CDALB-7
Hippel, Theodor Gottlieb von
  1741-1796 .... DLB-97
Hippius, Zinaida Nikolaevna
  1869-1945 .... DLB-295
Hippocrates of Cos fl. circa
  425 B.C. DLB-176; CDWLB-1
Hirabayashi Taiko 1905-1972 .... DLB-180
Hirsch, E. D., Jr. 1928- DLB-67
Hirsch, Edward 1950- DLB-120
Hirschbein, Peretz (Perets Hirshbeyn)
  1880-1948 .... DLB-333
"Historical Novel," The Holocaust DLB-299
Hoagland, Edward 1932- DLB-6
Hoagland, Everett H., III 1942- DLB-41
Hoban, Russell 1925- DLB-52; Y-90
Hobbes, Thomas 1588-1679 ... DLB-151, 252, 281
Hobby, Oveta 1905-1995 .... DLB-127
Hobby, William 1878-1964 .... DLB-127
Hobsbaum, Philip 1932- DLB-40
Hobsbawm, Eric (Francis Newton)
  1917- DLB-296
Hobson, Laura Z. 1900-1986 .... DLB-28
Hobson, Sarah 1947- DLB-204
Hoby, Thomas 1530-1566 .... DLB-132
Hoccleve, Thomas
  circa 1368-circa 1437 .... DLB-146
Hoch, Edward D. 1930- DLB-306
Hochhuth, Rolf 1931- DLB-124
Hochman, Sandra 1936- DLB-5
Hocken, Thomas Morland 1836-1910 ... DLB-184
Hocking, William Ernest 1873-1966 .... DLB-270
Hodder and Stoughton, Limited DLB-106
Hodgins, Jack 1938- DLB-60
Hodgman, Helen 1945- DLB-14
Hodgskin, Thomas 1787-1869 .... DLB-158
Hodgson, Ralph 1871-1962 .... DLB-19
Hodgson, William Hope
  1877-1918 .... DLB-70, 153, 156, 178
Hoe, Robert, III 1839-1909 .... DLB-187
Hoeg, Peter 1957- DLB-214
Hoel, Sigurd 1890-1960 .... DLB-297
Hoem, Edvard 1949- DLB-297
Hoffenstein, Samuel 1890-1947 .... DLB-11
Hoffman, Alice 1952- DLB-292
Hoffman, Charles Fenno
  1806-1884 .... DLB-3, 250
Hoffman, Daniel 1923- DLB-5
  Tribute to Robert Graves Y-85

Hoffmann, E. T. A. 1776-1822 ....DLB-90; CDWLB-2

Hoffman, Frank B. 1888-1958..........DLB-188

Hoffman, William 1925- DLB-234

    Tribute to Paxton Davis Y-94

Hoffmanswaldau, Christian Hoffman von 1616-1679 ....DLB-168

Hofmann, Michael 1957- DLB-40

Hofmannsthal, Hugo von 1874-1929 ....DLB-81, 118; CDWLB-2

Hofmo, Gunvor 1921-1995 ....DLB-297

Hofstadter, Richard 1916-1970....... DLB-17, 246

Hofstein, David (Dovid Hofshteyn) 1889-1952 ....DLB-333

Hogan, Desmond 1950- DLB-14, 319

Hogan, Linda 1947- DLB-175

Hogan and Thompson DLB-49

Hogarth Press DLB-112; DS-10

Hogg, James 1770-1835 .... DLB-93, 116, 159

Hohberg, Wolfgang Helmhard Freiherr von 1612-1688 ....DLB-168

von Hohenheim, Philippus Aureolus Theophrastus Bombastus (see Paracelsus)

Hohl, Ludwig 1904-1980................DLB-56

Højholt, Per 1928- DLB-214

Holan, Vladimir 1905-1980............DLB-215

d'Holbach, Paul Henri Thiry, baron 1723-1789 ....DLB-313

    The System of Nature (as Jean-Baptiste de Mirabaud)....................DLB-314

Holberg, Ludvig 1684-1754............DLB-300

Holbrook, David 1923- DLB-14, 40

Holcroft, Thomas 1745-1809.....DLB-39, 89, 158

    Preface to *Alwyn* (1780) DLB-39

Holden, Jonathan 1941- DLB-105

    "Contemporary Verse Story-telling" ...DLB-105

Holden, Molly 1927-1981 ....DLB-40

Hölderlin, Friedrich 1770-1843 ....DLB-90; CDWLB-2

Holdstock, Robert 1948- DLB-261

Holiday, 1974 Booker Prize winner, Stanley Middleton................DLB-326

Holiday House.....................DLB-46

Holinshed, Raphael died 1580..........DLB-167

Holland, J. G. 1819-1881................ DS-13

Holland, Norman N. 1927- DLB-67

Hollander, John 1929- DLB-5

Holley, Marietta 1836-1926 ....DLB-11

Hollinghurst, Alan 1954- DLB-207, 326

Hollingshead, Greg 1947- DLB-334

Hollingsworth, Margaret 1940- DLB-60

Hollo, Anselm 1934- DLB-40

Holloway, Emory 1885-1977 ....DLB-103

Holloway, John 1920- DLB-27

Holloway House Publishing Company DLB-46

Holme, Constance 1880-1955 ....DLB-34

Holmes, Abraham S. 1821?-1908 ....DLB-99

Holmes, John Clellon 1926-1988.....DLB-16, 237

    "Four Essays on the Beat Generation" DLB-16

Holmes, Mary Jane 1825-1907 .....DLB-202, 221

Holmes, Oliver Wendell 1809-1894 ....DLB-1, 189, 235; CDALB-2

Holmes, Richard 1945- DLB-155

Holmes, Thomas James 1874-1959 ......DLB-187

The Holocaust "Historical Novel".......DLB-299

Holocaust Fiction, Postmodern DLB-299

Holocaust Novel, The "Second-Generation" DLB-299

Holroyd, Michael 1935- DLB-155; Y-99

Holst, Hermann E. von 1841-1904 ....DLB-47

Holt, John 1721-1784..................DLB-43

Henry Holt and Company DLB-49, 284

Holt, Rinehart and Winston DLB-46

Holtby, Winifred 1898-1935 ....DLB-191

Holthusen, Hans Egon 1913-1997........DLB-69

Hölty, Ludwig Christoph Heinrich 1748-1776.....................DLB-94

Holub, Miroslav 1923-1998 ....DLB-232; CDWLB-4

Holz, Arno 1863-1929 ....DLB-118

Home, Henry, Lord Kames (see Kames, Henry Home, Lord)

Home, John 1722-1808 ....DLB-84, 336

Home, William Douglas 1912-1992.......DLB-13

Home Publishing Company DLB-49

Homer circa eighth-seventh centuries B.C. DLB-176; CDWLB-1

Homer, Winslow 1836-1910 ....DLB-188

Homes, Geoffrey (see Mainwaring, Daniel)

Honan, Park 1928- DLB-111

Hone, William 1780-1842 .... DLB-110, 158

Hongo, Garrett Kaoru 1951- DLB-120, 312

Honig, Edwin 1919- DLB-5

Hood, Hugh 1928-2000.................DLB-53

Hood, Mary 1946- DLB-234

Hood, Thomas 1799-1845................DLB-96

Hook, Sidney 1902-1989 .... DLB-279

Hook, Theodore 1788-1841............DLB-116

Hooke, Nathaniel 1685?-1763 ....DLB-336

Hooker, Jeremy 1941- DLB-40

Hooker, Richard 1554-1600............DLB-132

Hooker, Thomas 1586-1647 ....DLB-24

hooks, bell 1952- DLB-246

Hooper, Johnson Jones 1815-1862 ....DLB-3, 11, 248

Hope, A. D. 1907-2000 ....DLB-289

Hope, Anthony 1863-1933 ....DLB-153, 156

Hope, Christopher 1944- DLB-225

Hope, Eva (see Hearn, Mary Anne)

Hope, Laurence (Adela Florence Cory Nicolson) 1865-1904 ....DLB-240

Hopkins, Ellice 1836-1904.............DLB-190

Hopkins, Gerard Manley 1844-1889 ....DLB-35, 57; CDBLB-5

Hopkins, John ?-1570..................DLB-132

Hopkins, John H., and Son DLB-46

Hopkins, Lemuel 1750-1801 ....DLB-37

Hopkins, Pauline Elizabeth 1859-1930 ....DLB-50

Hopkins, Samuel 1721-1803 ....DLB-31

Hopkinson, Francis 1737-1791 ....DLB-31

Hopkinson, Nalo 1960- DLB-251

Hopper, Nora (Mrs. Nora Chesson) 1871-1906 ....DLB-240

Hoppin, Augustus 1828-1896 ....DLB-188

Hora, Josef 1891-1945......DLB-215; CDWLB-4

Horace 65 B.C.-8 B.C........ DLB-211; CDWLB-1

Horgan, Paul 1903-1995 ..... DLB-102, 212; Y-85

    Tribute to Alfred A. Knopf Y-84

Horizon Press DLB-46

Horkheimer, Max 1895-1973..........DLB-296

Hornby, C. H. St. John 1867-1946.......DLB-201

Hornby, Nick 1957- DLB-207

Horne, Frank 1899-1974 ....DLB-51

Horne, Richard Henry (Hengist) 1802 or 1803-1884 ....DLB-32

Horne, Thomas 1608-1654 ....DLB-281

Horney, Karen 1885-1952 ....DLB-246

Hornung, E. W. 1866-1921 ....DLB-70

Horovitz, Israel 1939- DLB-7

Horta, Maria Teresa (see The Three Marias: A Landmark Case in Portuguese Literary History)

Horton, George Moses 1797?-1883? DLB-50

    George Moses Horton Society Y-99

Horváth, Ödön von 1901-1938......DLB-85, 124

Horwood, Harold 1923- DLB-60

E. and E. Hosford [publishing house] DLB-49

Hoskens, Jane Fenn 1693-1770?..........DLB-200

Hoskyns, John circa 1566-1638.....DLB-121, 281

Hosokawa Yūsai 1535-1610............DLB-203

Hospers, John 1918- DLB-279

Hospital, Janette Turner 1942- DLB-325

Hostovský, Egon 1908-1973 ....DLB-215

Hotchkiss and Company................DLB-49

Hotel du Lac, 1984 Booker Prize winner, Anita Brookner DLB-326

Hough, Emerson 1857-1923 .... DLB-9, 212

Houghton, Stanley 1881-1913 ....DLB-10

Houghton Mifflin Company DLB-49

Cumulative Index

Hours at Home........................DS-13

Household, Geoffrey 1900-1988.........DLB-87

Housman, A. E. 1859-1936...DLB-19; CDBLB-5

Housman, Laurence 1865-1959.........DLB-10

Houston, Pam 1962- DLB-244

Houwald, Ernst von 1778-1845.........DLB-90

Hovey, Richard 1864-1900............DLB-54

How Late It Was, How Late, 1994 Booker Prize winner, James Kelman...................DLB-326

Howard, Donald R. 1927-1987.........DLB-111

Howard, Maureen 1930- Y-83

Howard, Richard 1929- DLB-5

Howard, Roy W. 1883-1964............DLB-29

Howard, Sidney 1891-1939.......DLB-7, 26, 249

Howard, Thomas, second Earl of Arundel 1585-1646...................DLB-213

Howe, E. W. 1853-1937............DLB-12, 25

Howe, Henry 1816-1893..............DLB-30

Howe, Irving 1920-1993..............DLB-67

Howe, Joseph 1804-1873..............DLB-99

Howe, Julia Ward 1819-1910....DLB-1, 189, 235

Howe, Percival Presland 1886-1944.....DLB-149

Howe, Susan 1937- DLB-120

Howell, Clark, Sr. 1863-1936..........DLB-25

Howell, Evan P. 1839-1905............DLB-23

Howell, James 1594?-1666............DLB-151

Howell, Soskin and Company..........DLB-46

Howell, Warren Richardson 1912-1984....DLB-140

Howells, William Dean 1837-1920 ....DLB-12, 64, 74, 79, 189; CDALB-3

   Introduction to Paul Laurence Dunbar's *Lyrics of Lowly Life* (1896) DLB-50

   The William Dean Howells Society Y-01

Howitt, Mary 1799-1888..........DLB-110, 199

Howitt, William 1792-1879...........DLB-110

Hoyem, Andrew 1935- DLB-5

Hoyers, Anna Ovena 1584-1655.......DLB-164

Hoyle, Fred 1915-2001..............DLB-261

Hoyos, Angela de 1940- DLB-82

Henry Hoyt [publishing house]........DLB-49

Hoyt, Palmer 1897-1979..............DLB-127

Hrabal, Bohumil 1914-1997...........DLB-232

Hrabanus Maurus 776?-856...........DLB-148

Hronský, Josef Cíger 1896-1960........DLB-215

Hrotsvit of Gandersheim circa 935-circa 1000..............DLB-148

Hubbard, Elbert 1856-1915............DLB-91

Hubbard, Kin 1868-1930..............DLB-11

Hubbard, William circa 1621-1704......DLB-24

Huber, Therese 1764-1829............DLB-90

Huch, Friedrich 1873-1913............DLB-66

Huch, Ricarda 1864-1947.............DLB-66

Huddle, David 1942- DLB-130

Hudgins, Andrew 1951- DLB-120, 282

Hudson, Henry Norman 1814-1886.....DLB-64

Hudson, Stephen 1868?-1944..........DLB-197

Hudson, W. H. 1841-1922......DLB-98, 153, 174

Hudson and Goodwin................DLB-49

Huebsch, B. W., oral history...........Y-99

B. W. Huebsch [publishing house].......DLB-46

Hueffer, Oliver Madox 1876-1931......DLB-197

Huet, Pierre Daniel
   Preface to *The History of Romances* (1715).....................DLB-39

Hugh of St. Victor circa 1096-1141.....DLB-208

Hughes, David 1930- DLB-14

Hughes, Dusty 1947- DLB-233

Hughes, Hatcher 1881-1945..........DLB-249

Hughes, John 1677-1720..............DLB-84

Hughes, Langston 1902-1967......DLB-4, 7, 48, 51, 86, 228, 315; DS-15; CDALB-5

Hughes, Richard 1900-1976........DLB-15, 161

Hughes, Ted 1930-1998...........DLB-40, 161

Hughes, Thomas 1822-1896.......DLB-18, 163

Hugo, Richard 1923-1982..........DLB-5, 206

Hugo, Victor 1802-1885.......DLB-119, 192, 217

Hugo Awards and Nebula Awards........DLB-8

Huidobro, Vicente 1893-1948.........DLB-283

Hull, Richard 1896-1973..............DLB-77

Hulda (Unnur Benediktsdóttir Bjarklind) 1881-1946...................DLB-293

Hulme, Keri 1947- DLB-326

Hulme, T. E. 1883-1917..............DLB-19

Hulton, Anne ?-1779?...............DLB-200

Humanism, Sixteenth-Century Spanish.....................DLB-318

Humboldt, Alexander von 1769-1859....DLB-90

Humboldt, Wilhelm von 1767-1835.....DLB-90

Hume, David 1711-1776......DLB-104, 252, 336

Hume, Fergus 1859-1932..............DLB-70

Hume, Sophia 1702-1774............DLB-200

Hume-Rothery, Mary Catherine 1824-1885...................DLB-240

Humishuma (see Mourning Dove)

Hummer, T. R. 1950- DLB-120

Humor
   American Humor: A Historical Survey.....................DLB-11

   American Humor Studies Association....Y-99

   The Comic Tradition Continued [in the British Novel]...........DLB-15

   Humorous Book Illustration........DLB-11

   International Society for Humor Studies..Y-99

   Newspaper Syndication of American Humor......................DLB-11

   Selected Humorous Magazines (1820-1950)..................DLB-11

Bruce Humphries [publishing house]....DLB-46

Humphrey, Duke of Gloucester 1391-1447....................DLB-213

Humphrey, William 1924-1997............DLB-6, 212, 234, 278

Humphreys, David 1752-1818..........DLB-37

Humphreys, Emyr 1919- DLB-15

Humphreys, Josephine 1945- DLB-292

Hunayn ibn Ishaq 809-873 or 877......DLB-311

Huncke, Herbert 1915-1996............DLB-16

Huneker, James Gibbons 1857-1921...................DLB-71

Hunold, Christian Friedrich 1681-1721...................DLB-168

Hunt, Irene 1907- DLB-52

Hunt, Leigh 1784-1859.........DLB-96, 110, 144

Hunt, Violet 1862-1942...........DLB-162, 197

Hunt, William Gibbes 1791-1833........DLB-73

Hunter, Evan (Ed McBain) 1926-2005.................DLB-306; Y-82

   Tribute to John D. MacDonald.........Y-86

Hunter, Jim 1939- DLB-14

Hunter, Kristin 1931- DLB-33

   Tribute to Julian Mayfield.............Y-84

Hunter, Mollie 1922- DLB-161

Hunter, N. C. 1908-1971..............DLB-10

Hunter-Duvar, John 1821-1899.........DLB-99

Huntington, Henry E. 1850-1927......DLB-140

   The Henry E. Huntington Library......Y-92

Huntington, Susan Mansfield 1791-1823...................DLB-200

Hurd and Houghton.................DLB-49

Hurst, Fannie 1889-1968..............DLB-86

Hurst and Blackett..................DLB-106

Hurst and Company.................DLB-49

Hurston, Zora Neale 1901?-1960.........DLB-51, 86; CDALB-7

Husserl, Edmund 1859-1938..........DLB-296

Husson, Jules-François-Félix (see Champfleury)

Huston, John 1906-1987..............DLB-26

Hutcheson, Francis 1694-1746......DLB-31, 252

Hutchinson, Ron 1947- DLB-245

Hutchinson, R. C. 1907-1975..........DLB-191

Hutchinson, Thomas 1711-1780.....DLB-30, 31

Hutchinson and Company (Publishers) Limited..............DLB-112

Huth, Angela 1938- DLB-271

Hutton, Richard Holt 1826-1897........DLB-57

von Hutten, Ulrich 1488-1523.........DLB-179

Huxley, Aldous 1894-1963
   ......DLB-36, 100, 162, 195, 255; CDBLB-6

Huxley, Elspeth Josceline
  1907-1997 .... DLB-77, 204

Huxley, T. H. 1825-1895 .... DLB-57

Huyghue, Douglas Smith 1816-1891 ...... DLB-99

Huysmans, Joris-Karl 1848-1907 .... DLB-123

Hwang, David Henry
  1957- DLB-212, 228, 312

Hyde, Donald 1909-1966 .... DLB-187

Hyde, Mary 1912-2003 .... DLB-187

Hyman, Trina Schart 1939- DLB-61

I

Iavorsky, Stefan 1658-1722 .... DLB-150

Iazykov, Nikolai Mikhailovich
  1803-1846 .... DLB-205

Ibáñez, Armando P. 1949- DLB-209

Ibáñez, Sara de 1909-1971 .... DLB-290

Ibarbourou, Juana de 1892-1979 .... DLB-290

Ibn Abi Tahir Tayfur 820-893 .... DLB-311

Ibn Qutaybah 828-889 .... DLB-311

Ibn al-Rumi 836-896 .... DLB-311

Ibn Sa'd 784-845 .... DLB-311

Ibrahim al-Mawsili
  742 or 743-803 or 804 .... DLB-311

Ibn Bajja circa 1077-1138 .... DLB-115

Ibn Gabirol, Solomon
  circa 1021-circa 1058 .... DLB-115

Ibn al-Muqaffa' circa 723-759 .... DLB-311

Ibn al-Mu'tazz 861-908 .... DLB-311

Ibuse Masuji 1898-1993 .... DLB-180

Ichijō Kanera
  (see Ichijō Kaneyoshi)

Ichijō Kaneyoshi (Ichijō Kanera)
  1402-1481 .... DLB-203

Iffland, August Wilhelm
  1759-1814 .... DLB-94

Iggulden, John 1917- DLB-289

Ignatieff, Michael 1947- DLB-267

Ignatow, David 1914-1997 .... DLB-5

Ike, Chukwuemeka 1931- DLB-157

Ikkyū Sōjun 1394-1481 .... DLB-203

Iles, Francis
  (see Berkeley, Anthony)

Il'f, Il'ia (Il'ia Arnol'dovich Fainzil'berg)
  1897-1937 .... DLB-272

Illich, Ivan 1926-2002 .... DLB-242

Illustration
  Children's Book Illustration in the
    Twentieth Century DLB-61
  Children's Illustrators, 1800-1880 .... DLB-163
  Early American Book Illustration DLB-49
  The Iconography of Science-Fiction
    Art DLB-8
  The Illustration of Early German
    Literary Manuscripts, circa
    1150-circa 1300 .... DLB-148

Minor Illustrators, 1880-1914 .... DLB-141

Illyés, Gyula 1902-1983 ...... DLB-215; CDWLB-4

Imbs, Bravig 1904-1946 .... DLB-4; DS-15

Imbuga, Francis D. 1947- DLB-157

Immermann, Karl 1796-1840 .... DLB-133

Imru' al-Qays circa 526-circa 565 ..... DLB-311

In a Free State, 1971 Booker Prize winner,
  V. S. Naipaul DLB-326

Inchbald, Elizabeth 1753-1821 .... DLB-39, 89

Indiana University Press Y-02

Ingamells, Rex 1913-1955 .... DLB-260

Inge, William 1913-1973 ... DLB-7, 249; CDALB-1

Ingelow, Jean 1820-1897 .... DLB-35, 163

Ingemann, B. S. 1789-1862 .... DLB-300

Ingersoll, Ralph 1900-1985 .... DLB-127

The Ingersoll Prizes Y-84

Ingoldsby, Thomas (see Barham, Richard Harris)

Ingraham, Joseph Holt 1809-1860 ..... DLB-3, 248

Inman, John 1805-1850 .... DLB-73

Innerhofer, Franz 1944- DLB-85

Innes, Michael (J. I. M. Stewart)
  1906-1994 .... DLB-276

Innis, Harold Adams 1894-1952 .... DLB-88

Innis, Mary Quayle 1899-1972 .... DLB-88

Inō Sōgi 1421-1502 .... DLB-203

Inoue Yasushi 1907-1991 .... DLB-182

"The Greatness of Southern Literature":
  League of the South Institute for the
  Study of Southern Culture and History
  .... Y-02

International Publishers Company DLB-46

Internet (publishing and commerce)
  Author Websites Y-97
  The Book Trade and the Internet Y-00
  E-Books Turn the Corner Y-98
  The E-Researcher: Possibilities
    and Pitfalls Y-00
  Interviews on E-publishing Y-00
  John Updike on the Internet Y-97
  LitCheck Website Y-01
  Virtual Books and Enemies of Books Y-00

Interviews
  Adoff, Arnold Y-01
  Aldridge, John W. Y-91
  Anastas, Benjamin Y-98
  Baker, Nicholson Y-00
  Bank, Melissa Y-98
  Bass, T. J. Y-80
  Bernstein, Harriet Y-82
  Betts, Doris Y-82
  Bosworth, David Y-82
  Bottoms, David Y-83
  Bowers, Fredson Y-80
  Burnshaw, Stanley Y-97
  Carpenter, Humphrey Y-84, 99

Carr, Virginia Spencer Y-00
Carver, Raymond Y-83
Cherry, Kelly Y-83
Conroy, Jack Y-81
Coppel, Alfred Y-83
Cowley, Malcolm Y-81
Davis, Paxton Y-89
Devito, Carlo Y-94
De Vries, Peter Y-82
Dickey, James Y-82
Donald, David Herbert Y-87
Editors, Conversations with Y-95
Ellroy, James Y-91
Fancher, Betsy Y-83
Faust, Irvin Y-00
Fulton, Len Y-86
Furst, Alan Y-01
Garrett, George Y-83
Gelfman, Jane Y-93
Goldwater, Walter Y-93
Gores, Joe Y-02
Greenfield, George Y-91
Griffin, Bryan Y-81
Groom, Winston Y-01
Guilds, John Caldwell Y-92
Hamilton, Virginia Y-01
Hardin, James Y-92
Harris, Mark Y-80
Harrison, Jim Y-82
Hazzard, Shirley Y-82
Herrick, William Y-01
Higgins, George V. Y-98
Hoban, Russell Y-90
Holroyd, Michael Y-99
Horowitz, Glen Y-90
Iggulden, John Y-01
Jakes, John Y-83
Jenkinson, Edward B. Y-82
Jenks, Tom Y-86
Kaplan, Justin Y-86
King, Florence Y-85
Klopfer, Donald S. Y-97
Krug, Judith Y-82
Lamm, Donald Y-95
Laughlin, James Y-96
Lawrence, Starling Y-95
Lindsay, Jack Y-84
Mailer, Norman Y-97
Manchester, William Y-85
Max, D. T. Y-94
McCormack, Thomas Y-98
McNamara, Katherine Y-97
Mellen, Joan Y-94
Menaker, Daniel Y-97

Mooneyham, Lamarr	Y-82	
Murray, Les	Y-01	
Nosworth, David	Y-82	
O'Connor, Patrick	Y-84, 99	
Ozick, Cynthia	Y-83	
Penner, Jonathan	Y-83	
Pennington, Lee	Y-82	
Penzler, Otto	Y-96	
Plimpton, George	Y-99	
Potok, Chaim	Y-84	
Powell, Padgett	Y-01	
Prescott, Peter S.	Y-86	
Rabe, David	Y-91	
Rechy, John	Y-82	
Reid, B. L.	Y-83	
Reynolds, Michael	Y-95, 99	
Robinson, Derek	Y-02	
Rollyson, Carl	Y-97	
Rosset, Barney	Y-02	
Schlafly, Phyllis	Y-82	
Schroeder, Patricia	Y-99	
Schulberg, Budd	Y-81, 01	
Scribner, Charles, III	Y-94	
Sipper, Ralph	Y-94	
Smith, Cork	Y-95	
Staley, Thomas F.	Y-00	
Styron, William	Y-80	
Talese, Nan	Y-94	
Thornton, John	Y-94	
Toth, Susan Allen	Y-86	
Tyler, Anne	Y-82	
Vaughan, Samuel	Y-97	
Von Ogtrop, Kristin	Y-92	
Wallenstein, Barry	Y-92	
Weintraub, Stanley	Y-82	
Williams, J. Chamberlain	Y-84	

Into the Past: William Jovanovich's Reflections in Publishing Y-02

Ionesco, Eugène 1909-1994 .... DLB-321

Ireland, David 1927- DLB-289

The National Library of Ireland's New James Joyce Manuscripts Y-02

Irigaray, Luce 1930- DLB-296

Irving, John 1942- DLB-6, 278; Y-82

Irving, Washington 1783-1859
..... DLB-3, 11, 30, 59, 73, 74, 183, 186, 250; CDALB-2

Irwin, Grace 1907- DLB-68

Irwin, Will 1873-1948 .... DLB-25

Isaksson, Ulla 1916-2000 .... DLB-257

Iser, Wolfgang 1926- DLB-242

Isherwood, Christopher 1904-1986 .... DLB-15, 195; Y-86

The Christopher Isherwood Archive, The Huntington Library Y-99

Ishiguro, Kazuo 1954- DLB-194, 326

Ishikawa Jun 1899-1987 .... DLB-182

Iskander, Fazil' Abdulevich 1929- DLB-302

The Island Trees Case: A Symposium on School Library Censorship
An Interview with Judith Krug
An Interview with Phyllis Schlafly
An Interview with Edward B. Jenkinson
An Interview with Lamarr Mooneyham
An Interview with Harriet Bernstein Y-82

Islas, Arturo 1938-1991 .... DLB-122

Issit, Debbie 1966- DLB-233

Ivanišević, Drago 1907-1981 .... DLB-181

Ivanov, Georgii 1894-1954 .... DLB-317

Ivanov, Viacheslav Ivanovich 1866-1949 .... DLB-295

Ivanov, Vsevolod Viacheslavovich 1895-1963 .... DLB-272

Ivask, Yuri 1907-1986 .... DLB-317

Ivaska, Astrīde 1926- DLB-232

M. J. Ivers and Company DLB-49

Iwaniuk, Wacław 1915-2001 .... DLB-215

Iwano Hōmei 1873-1920 .... DLB-180

Iwaszkiewicz, Jarosław 1894-1980 .... DLB-215

Iyayi, Festus 1947- DLB-157

Izumi Kyōka 1873-1939 .... DLB-180

J

Jackmon, Marvin E. (see Marvin X)

Jacks, L. P. 1860-1955 .... DLB-135

Jackson, Angela 1951- DLB-41

Jackson, Charles 1903-1968 .... DLB-234

Jackson, Helen Hunt 1830-1885 .... DLB-42, 47, 186, 189

Jackson, Holbrook 1874-1948 .... DLB-98

Jackson, Laura Riding 1901-1991 .... DLB-48

Jackson, Shirley 1916-1965 .... DLB-6, 234; CDALB-1

Jacob, Max 1876-1944 .... DLB-258

Jacob, Naomi 1884?-1964 .... DLB-191

Jacob, Piers Anthony Dillingham (see Anthony, Piers)

Jacob, Violet 1863-1946 .... DLB-240

Jacobi, Friedrich Heinrich 1743-1819 .... DLB-94

Jacobi, Johann Georg 1740-1841 .... DLB-97

George W. Jacobs and Company DLB-49

Jacobs, Harriet 1813-1897 .... DLB-239

Jacobs, Joseph 1854-1916 .... DLB-141

Jacobs, W. W. 1863-1943 .... DLB-135

The W. W. Jacobs Appreciation Society .. Y-98

Jacobsen, J. P. 1847-1885 .... DLB-300

Jacobsen, Jørgen-Frantz 1900-1938 .... DLB-214

Jacobsen, Josephine 1908- DLB-244

Jacobsen, Rolf 1907-1994 .... DLB-297

Jacobson, Dan 1929- DLB-14, 207, 225, 319

Jacobson, Howard 1942- DLB-207

Jacques de Vitry circa 1160/1170-1240 .... DLB-208

Jæger, Frank 1926-1977 .... DLB-214

Ja'far al-Sadiq circa 702-765 .... DLB-311

William Jaggard [publishing house] DLB-170

Jahier, Piero 1884-1966 .... DLB-114, 264

al-Jahiz circa 776-868 or 869 .... DLB-311

Jahnn, Hans Henny 1894-1959 .... DLB-56, 124

Jaimes, Freyre, Ricardo 1866?-1933 .... DLB-283

Jakes, John 1932- DLB-278; Y-83
Tribute to John Gardner Y-82
Tribute to John D. MacDonald Y-86

Jakobína Johnson (Jakobína Sigurbjarnardóttir) 1883-1977 .... DLB-293

Jakobson, Roman 1896-1982 .... DLB-242

James, Alice 1848-1892 .... DLB-221

James, C. L. R. 1901-1989 .... DLB-125

James, Clive 1939- DLB-325

James, George P. R. 1801-1860 .... DLB-116

James, Henry 1843-1916
.... DLB-12, 71, 74, 189; DS-13; CDALB-3
"The Future of the Novel" (1899) DLB-18
"The Novel in [Robert Browning's] 'The Ring and the Book'" (1912) DLB-32

James, John circa 1633-1729 .... DLB-24

James, M. R. 1862-1936 .... DLB-156, 201

James, Naomi 1949- DLB-204

James, P. D. (Phyllis Dorothy James White) 1920- DLB-87, 276; DS-17; CDBLB-8
Tribute to Charles Scribner Jr. Y-95

James, Thomas 1572?-1629 .... DLB-213

U. P. James [publishing house] DLB-49

James, Will 1892-1942 .... DS-16

James, William 1842-1910 .... DLB-270

James VI of Scotland, I of England 1566-1625 .... DLB-151, 172
Ane Schort Treatise Conteining Some Revlis and Cautelis to Be Obseruit and Eschewit in Scottis Poesi (1584) DLB-172

Jameson, Anna 1794-1860 .... DLB-99, 166

Jameson, Fredric 1934- DLB-67

Jameson, J. Franklin 1859-1937 .... DLB-17

Jameson, Storm 1891-1986 .... DLB-36

Jančar, Drago 1948- DLB-181

Janés, Clara 1940- DLB-134

Janevski, Slavko 1920-2000 .... DLB-181; CDWLB-4

Janowitz, Tama 1957- DLB-292

Jansson, Tove 1914-2001 ....DLB-257

Janvier, Thomas 1849-1913 ....DLB-202

Japan
 "The Development of Meiji Japan"...DLB-180
 "Encounter with the West" DLB-180

Japanese Literature
 Letter from Japan Y-94, 98
 Medieval Travel Diaries DLB-203
 Surveys: 1987-1995 ....DLB-182

Jaramillo, Cleofas M. 1878-1956 ....DLB-122

Jaramillo Levi, Enrique 1944- DLB-290

Jarir after 650-circa 730 ....DLB-311

Jarman, Mark 1952- DLB-120, 282

Jarrell, Randall
 1914-1965 ....DLB-48, 52; CDALB-1

Jarrold and Sons..................DLB-106

Jarry, Alfred 1873-1907 ....DLB-192, 258

Jarves, James Jackson 1818-1888 ....DLB-189

Jasmin, Claude 1930- DLB-60

Jaunsudrabiņš, Jānis 1877-1962 ....DLB-220

Jay, John 1745-1829 ....DLB-31

Jean de Garlande (see John of Garland)

Jefferies, Richard 1848-1887.........DLB-98, 141
 The Richard Jefferies Society Y-98

Jeffers, Lance 1919-1985 ....DLB-41

Jeffers, Robinson
 1887-1962 ....DLB-45, 212; CDALB-4

Jefferson, Thomas
 1743-1826 ....DLB-31, 183; CDALB-2

Jégé 1866-1940.....................DLB-215

Jelinek, Elfriede 1946- DLB-85, 330

Jellicoe, Ann 1927- DLB-13, 233

Jemison, Mary circa 1742-1833 ....DLB-239

Jen, Gish 1955- DLB-312

Jenkins, Dan 1929- DLB-241

Jenkins, Elizabeth 1905- DLB-155

Jenkins, Robin 1912-2005 ....DLB-14, 271

Jenkins, William Fitzgerald (see Leinster, Murray)

Herbert Jenkins Limited DLB-112

Jennings, Elizabeth 1926- DLB-27

Jens, Walter 1923- DLB-69

Jensen, Axel 1932-2003 ....DLB-297

Jensen, Johannes V. 1873-1950......DLB-214, 330

Jensen, Merrill 1905-1980 ....DLB-17

Jensen, Thit 1876-1957.................DLB-214

Jephson, Robert 1736-1803 ....DLB-89

Jerome, Jerome K. 1859-1927.....DLB-10, 34, 135
 The Jerome K. Jerome Society Y-98

Jerome, Judson 1927-1991 ....DLB-105
 "Reflections: After a Tornado" DLB-105

Jerrold, Douglas 1803-1857 ....DLB-158, 159

Jersild, Per Christian 1935- DLB-257

Jesse, F. Tennyson 1888-1958 ....DLB-77

Jewel, John 1522-1571 ....DLB-236

John P. Jewett and Company............DLB-49

Jewett, Sarah Orne 1849-1909 ....DLB-12, 74, 221

Studies in American Jewish Literature........Y-02

Jewish Literature of Medieval Spain DLB-337

The Jewish Publication Society DLB-49

Jewsbury, Geraldine 1812-1880..........DLB-21

Jewsbury, Maria Jane 1800-1833 ....DLB-199

Jhabvala, Ruth Prawer
 1927- DLB-139, 194, 323, 326

Jiang Guangci 1901-1931...............DLB-328

Jiménez, Juan Ramón 1881-1958....DLB-134, 330

Jiménez de Rada, Rodrigo
 after 1170-1247 ....DLB-337

Jin, Ha 1956- DLB-244, 292

Joans, Ted 1928-2003................DLB-16, 41

Jodelle, Estienne 1532?-1573 ....DLB-327

Jōha 1525-1602 ....DLB-203

Jóhann Sigurjónsson 1880-1919.........DLB-293

Jóhannes úr Kötlum 1899-1972 ....DLB-293

Johannis de Garlandia (see John of Garland)

John, Errol 1924-1988 ....DLB-233

John, Eugenie (see Marlitt, E.)

John of Dumbleton
 circa 1310-circa 1349...............DLB-115

John of Garland (Jean de Garlande,
 Johannis de Garlandia)
 circa 1195-circa 1272 ....DLB-208

The John Reed Clubs DLB-303

Johns, Captain W. E. 1893-1968 ....DLB-160

Johnson, Mrs. A. E. ca. 1858-1922 ......DLB-221

Johnson, Amelia (see Johnson, Mrs. A. E.)

Johnson, B. S. 1933-1973 ....DLB-14, 40

Johnson, Charles 1679-1748...............DLB-84

Johnson, Charles 1948- DLB-33, 278

Johnson, Charles S. 1893-1956 ....DLB-51, 91

Johnson, Colin (Mudrooroo) 1938- DLB-289

Johnson, Denis 1949- DLB-120

Johnson, Diane 1934- Y-80

Johnson, Dorothy M. 1905–1984 ....DLB-206

Johnson, E. Pauline (Tekahionwake)
 1861-1913 ....DLB-175

Johnson, Edgar 1901-1995............DLB-103

Johnson, Edward 1598-1672 ....DLB-24

Johnson, Eyvind 1900-1976 ....DLB-259, 330

Johnson, Fenton 1888-1958 ....DLB-45, 50

Johnson, Georgia Douglas
 1877?-1966 ....DLB-51, 249

Johnson, Gerald W. 1890-1980 ....DLB-29

Johnson, Greg 1953- DLB-234

Johnson, Helene 1907-1995 ....DLB-51

Jacob Johnson and Company DLB-49

Johnson, James Weldon
 1871-1938 ....DLB-51; CDALB-4

Johnson, John H. 1918-2005 ....DLB-137
 "Backstage," Statement From the
 Initial Issue of *Ebony*
 (November 1945................DLB-137

Johnson, Joseph [publishing house] DLB-154

Johnson, Linton Kwesi 1952- DLB-157

Johnson, Lionel 1867-1902................DLB-19

Johnson, Nunnally 1897-1977 ....DLB-26

Johnson, Owen 1878-1952.................Y-87

Johnson, Pamela Hansford 1912-1981......DLB-15

Johnson, Pauline 1861-1913...............DLB-92

Johnson, Ronald 1935-1998...............DLB-169

Johnson, Samuel 1696-1772 ....DLB-24; CDBLB-2

Johnson, Samuel
 1709-1784 ....DLB-39, 95, 104, 142, 213
 Rambler, no. 4 (1750) [excerpt] DLB-39
 The BBC Four Samuel Johnson Prize
 for Non-fiction.....................Y-02

Johnson, Samuel 1822-1882..........DLB-1, 243

Johnson, Susanna 1730-1810 ....DLB-200

Johnson, Terry 1955- DLB-233

Johnson, Uwe 1934-1984......DLB-75; CDWLB-2

Benjamin Johnson [publishing house] DLB-49

Benjamin, Jacob, and Robert Johnson
 [publishing house] DLB-49

Johnston, Annie Fellows 1863-1931.......DLB-42

Johnston, Basil H. 1929- DLB-60

Johnston, David Claypole 1798?-1865....DLB-188

Johnston, Denis 1901-1984 ....DLB-10

Johnston, Ellen 1835-1873 ....DLB-199

Johnston, George 1912-1970 ....DLB-260

Johnston, George 1913-1970 ....DLB-88

Johnston, Sir Harry 1858-1927 ....DLB-174

Johnston, Jennifer 1930- DLB-14

Johnston, Mary 1870-1936................DLB-9

Johnston, Richard Malcolm 1822-1898 ....DLB-74

Johnston, Wayne 1958- DLB-334

Johnstone, Charles 1719?-1800? DLB-39

Johst, Hanns 1890-1978................DLB-124

Jokull Jakobsson 1933-1978 ....DLB 293

Jolas, Eugene 1894-1952 ....DLB-4, 45

Jolley, Elizabeth 1923- DLB-325

Jón Stefán Sveinsson or Svensson (see Nonni)

Jón Trausti (Guðmundur Magnússon)
 1873-1918 ....DLB-293

Jón úr Vör (Jón Jónsson) 1917-2000 .....DLB-293

Jónas Hallgrímsson 1807-1845 ....DLB-293

Jones, Alice C. 1853-1933 ....DLB-92

Jones, Charles C., Jr. 1831-1893 ....DLB-30

357

Jones, D. G. 1929- DLB-53	Into the Past: William Jovanovich's Reflections on Publishing Y-02	**K**
Jones, David 1895-1974 .. DLB-20, 100; CDBLB-7	[Response to Ken Auletta] Y-97	Kacew, Romain (see Gary, Romain)
Jones, Diana Wynne 1934- DLB-161	*The Temper of the West:* William Jovanovich.................... Y-02	Kafka, Franz 1883-1924 ..... DLB-81; CDWLB-2
Jones, Ebenezer 1820-1860............. DLB-32	Tribute to Charles Scribner Jr.......... Y-95	Kahn, Gus 1886-1941................. DLB-265
Jones, Ernest 1819-1868 .... DLB-32	Jovine, Francesco 1902-1950.......... DLB-264	Kahn, Roger 1927- DLB-171
Jones, Gayl 1949- DLB-33, 278	Jovine, Giuseppe 1922- DLB-128	Kaikō Takeshi 1939-1989............. DLB-182
Jones, George 1800-1870................ DLB-183	Joyaux, Philippe (see Sollers, Philippe)	Káinn (Kristján Níels Jónsson/Kristjan Niels Julius) 1860-1936 .... DLB-293
Jones, Glyn 1905-1995 .... DLB-15	Joyce, Adrien (see Eastman, Carol)	Kaiser, Georg 1878-1945......DLB-124; CDWLB-2
Jones, Gwyn 1907- DLB-15, 139	Joyce, James 1882-1941 ....DLB-10, 19, 36, 162, 247; CDBLB-6	*Kaiserchronik* circa 1147 .... DLB-148
Jones, Henry Arthur 1851-1929 .... DLB-10	Danis Rose and the Rendering of *Ulysses*....Y-97	Kaleb, Vjekoslav 1905- DLB-181
Jones, Hugh circa 1692-1760............ DLB-24	James Joyce Centenary: Dublin, 1982 .... Y-82	Kalechofsky, Roberta 1931- DLB-28
Jones, James 1921-1977........DLB-2, 143; DS-17	James Joyce Conference Y-85	Kaler, James Otis 1848-1912.......... DLB-12, 42
James Jones Papers in the Handy Writers' Colony Collection at the University of Illinois at Springfield..................... Y-98	A Joyce (Con)Text: Danis Rose and the Remaking of *Ulysses* Y-97	Kalmar, Bert 1884-1947 .... DLB-265
	The National Library of Ireland's New James Joyce Manuscripts....... Y-02	Kamensky, Vasilii Vasil'evich 1884-1961 .... DLB-295
The James Jones Society................ Y-92	The New *Ulysses*.................... Y-84	Kames, Henry Home, Lord 1696-1782 .... DLB-31, 104
Jones, Jenkin Lloyd 1911-2004 .... DLB-127	Public Domain and the Violation of Texts Y-97	Kamo no Chōmei (Kamo no Nagaakira) 1153 or 1155-1216 .... DLB-203
Jones, John Beauchamp 1810-1866...... DLB-202	The Quinn Draft of James Joyce's Circe Manuscript................. Y-00	Kamo no Nagaakira (see Kamo no Chōmei)
Jones, Joseph, Major (see Thompson, William Tappan)	Stephen Joyce's Letter to the Editor of *The Irish Times*................... Y-97	Kampmann, Christian 1939-1988 ...... DLB-214
Jones, LeRoi (see Baraka, Amiri)	*Ulysses,* Reader's Edition: First Reactions .. Y-97	Kandel, Lenore 1932- DLB-16
Jones, Lewis 1897-1939................. DLB-15	We See the Editor at Work............ Y-97	Kane, Sarah 1971-1999................. DLB-310
Jones, Madison 1925- DLB-152	Whose *Ulysses?* The Function of Editing .. Y-97	Kaneko, Lonny 1939- DLB-312
Jones, Marie 1951- DLB-233	Jozsef, Attila 1905-1937..... DLB-215; CDWLB-4	Kang, Younghill 1903-1972............. DLB-312
Jones, Preston 1936-1979 .... DLB-7	San Juan de la Cruz 1542-1591 .... DLB-318	Kanin, Garson 1912-1999.............. DLB-7
Jones, Rodney 1950- DLB-120	Juan Manuel 1282-1348 .... DLB-337	A Tribute (to Marc Connelly) Y-80
Jones, Thom 1945- DLB-244	Juarroz, Roberto 1925-1995 .... DLB-283	Kaniuk, Yoram 1930- DLB-299
Jones, Sir William 1746-1794........... DLB-109	Orange Judd Publishing Company....... DLB-49	Kant, Hermann 1926- DLB-75
Jones, William Alfred 1817-1900........ DLB-59	Judd, Sylvester 1813-1853........... DLB-1, 243	Kant, Immanuel 1724-1804 .... DLB-94
Jones's Publishing House DLB-49	*Judith* circa 930 .... DLB-146	Kantemir, Antiokh Dmitrievich 1708-1744 .... DLB-150
Jong, Erica 1942- DLB-2, 5, 28, 152	Juel-Hansen, Erna 1845-1922.......... DLB-300	Kantor, MacKinlay 1904-1977 .... DLB-9, 102
Jonke, Gert F. 1946- DLB-85	Julian of Norwich 1342-circa 1420 ..... DLB-1146	Kanze Kōjirō Nobumitsu 1435-1516 .... DLB-203
Jonson, Ben 1572?-1637 .... DLB-62, 121; CDBLB-1	Julius Caesar 100 B.C.-44 B.C. DLB-211; CDWLB-1	Kanze Motokiyo (see Zeimi)
Jonsson, Tor 1916-1951 .... DLB-297	June, Jennie (see Croly, Jane Cunningham)	Kaplan, Fred 1937- DLB-111
Jordan, June 1936- DLB-38	Jung, Carl Gustav 1875-1961 .... DLB-296	Kaplan, Johanna 1942- DLB-28
Jorgensen, Johannes 1866-1956 .... DLB-300	Jung, Franz 1888-1963 .... DLB-118	Kaplan, Justin 1925- DLB-111; Y-86
Jose, Nicholas 1952- DLB-325	Jünger, Ernst 1895-1998 ..... DLB-56; CDWLB-2	Kaplinski, Jaan 1941- DLB-232
Joseph, Jenny 1932- DLB-40	*Der jüngere Titurel* circa 1275.......... DLB-138	Kapnist, Vasilii Vasilevich 1758?-1823 ... DLB-150
Joseph and George Y-99	Jung-Stilling, Johann Heinrich 1740-1817 .... DLB-94	Karadžić, Vuk Stefanović 1787-1864 ....DLB-147; CDWLB-4
Michael Joseph Limited DLB-112	Junqueiro, Abílio Manuel Guerra 1850-1923 .... DLB-287	Karamzin, Nikolai Mikhailovich 1766-1826..................... DLB-150
Josephson, Matthew 1899-1978 .... DLB-4	Just, Ward (Ward S. Just) 1935- DLB-335	Karinthy, Frigyes 1887-1938 .... DLB-215
Josephus, Flavius 37-100 ....DLB-176	Justice, Donald 1925- Y-83	Karlfeldt, Erik Axel 1864-1931......... DLB-330
Josephy, Alvin M., Jr. Tribute to Alfred A. Knopf............. Y-84	Juvenal circa A.D. 60-circa A.D. 130 .... DLB-211; CDWLB-1	Karmel, Ilona 1925-2000 .... DLB-299
Josiah Allen's Wife (see Holley, Marietta)	The Juvenile Library (see M. J. Godwin and Company)	Karnad, Girish 1938- DLB-323
Josipovici, Gabriel 1940- DLB-14, 319		Karsch, Anna Louisa 1722-1791 .... DLB-97
Josselyn, John ?-1675 .... DLB-24		Kasack, Hermann 1896-1966 .... DLB-69
Joudry, Patricia 1921-2000 .... DLB-88		Kasai Zenzō 1887-1927 .... DLB-180
Jouve, Pierre Jean 1887-1976........... DLB-258		
Jovanovich, William 1920-2001 .... Y-01		

Kaschnitz, Marie Luise 1901-1974 . . . . DLB-69

Kassák, Lajos 1887-1967 . . . . DLB-215

Kaštelan, Jure 1919-1990 . . . . DLB-147

Kästner, Erich 1899-1974 . . . . DLB-56

Kataev, Evgenii Petrovich
(see Il'f, Il'ia and Petrov, Evgenii)

Kataev, Valentin Petrovich 1897-1986 . . . . DLB-272

Katenin, Pavel Aleksandrovich
1792-1853 . . . . DLB-205

Kattan, Naim 1928- DLB-53

Katz, Steve 1935- Y-83

Ka-Tzetnik 135633 (Yehiel Dinur)
1909-2001 . . . . DLB-299

Kauffman, Janet 1945- DLB-218; Y-86

Kauffmann, Samuel 1898-1971 . . . . DLB-127

Kaufman, Bob 1925-1986 . . . . DLB-16, 41

Kaufman, George S. 1889-1961 . . . . DLB-7

Kaufmann, Walter 1921-1980 . . . . DLB-279

Kavan, Anna (Helen Woods Ferguson
Edmonds) 1901-1968 . . . . DLB-255

Kavanagh, P. J. 1931- DLB-40

Kavanagh, Patrick 1904-1967 . . . . DLB-15, 20

Kaverin, Veniamin Aleksandrovich
(Veniamin Aleksandrovich Zil'ber)
1902-1989 . . . . DLB-272

Kawabata Yasunari 1899-1972 . . . . . . DLB-180, 330

Kay, Guy Gavriel 1954- DLB-251

Kaye-Smith, Sheila 1887-1956 . . . . DLB-36

Kazakov, Iurii Pavlovich 1927-1982 . . . . . DLB-302

Kazin, Alfred 1915-1998 . . . . DLB-67

Keane, John B. 1928-2002 . . . . DLB-13

Keary, Annie 1825-1879 . . . . DLB-163

Keary, Eliza 1827-1918 . . . . DLB-240

Keating, H. R. F. 1926- DLB-87

Keatley, Charlotte 1960- DLB-245

Keats, Ezra Jack 1916-1983 . . . . DLB-61

Keats, John 1795-1821 . . . . DLB-96, 110; CDBLB-3

Keble, John 1792-1866 . . . . DLB-32, 55

Keckley, Elizabeth 1818?-1907 . . . . DLB-239

Keeble, John 1944- Y-83

Keeffe, Barrie 1945- DLB-13, 245

Keeley, James 1867-1934 . . . . DLB-25

W. B. Keen, Cooke and Company DLB-49

The Mystery of Carolyn Keene Y-02

Kefala, Antigone 1935- DLB-289

Keillor, Garrison 1942- Y-87

Keith, Marian (Mary Esther MacGregor)
1874?-1961 . . . . DLB-92

Keller, Gary D. 1943- DLB-82

Keller, Gottfried 1819-1890 . . DLB-129; CDWLB-2

Keller, Helen 1880-1968 . . . . DLB-303

Kelley, Edith Summers 1884-1956 . . . . DLB-9

Kelley, Emma Dunham ?-? DLB-221

Kelley, Florence 1859-1932 . . . . DLB-303

Kelley, William Melvin 1937- DLB-33

Kellogg, Ansel Nash 1832-1886 . . . . DLB-23

Kellogg, Steven 1941- DLB-61

Kelly, George E. 1887-1974 . . . . DLB-7, 249

Kelly, Hugh 1739-1777 . . . . DLB-89

Kelly, Piet and Company DLB-49

Kelly, Robert 1935- DLB-5, 130, 165

Kelman, James 1946- DLB-194, 319, 326

Kelmscott Press DLB-112

Kelton, Elmer 1926- DLB-256

Kemble, E. W. 1861-1933 . . . . DLB-188

Kemble, Fanny 1809-1893 . . . . DLB-32

Kemelman, Harry 1908-1996 . . . . DLB-28

Kempe, Margery circa 1373-1438 . . . . . . DLB-146

Kempinski, Tom 1938- DLB-310

Kempner, Friederike 1836-1904 . . . . DLB-129

Kempowski, Walter 1929- DLB-75

Kenan, Randall 1963- DLB-292

Claude Kendall [publishing company] DLB-46

Kendall, Henry 1839-1882 . . . . DLB-230

Kendall, May 1861-1943 . . . . DLB-240

Kendell, George 1809-1867 . . . . DLB-43

Keneally, Thomas 1935- DLB-289, 299, 326

Kenedy, P. J., and Sons DLB-49

Kenkō circa 1283-circa 1352 . . . . DLB-203

Kenna, Peter 1930-1987 . . . . DLB-289

Kennan, George 1845-1924 . . . . DLB-189

Kennedy, A. L. 1965- DLB-271

Kennedy, Adrienne 1931- DLB-38

Kennedy, John Pendleton 1795-1870 . . . DLB-3, 248

Kennedy, Leo 1907-2000 . . . . DLB-88

Kennedy, Margaret 1896-1967 . . . . DLB-36

Kennedy, Patrick 1801-1873 . . . . DLB-159

Kennedy, Richard S. 1920- DLB-111; Y-02

Kennedy, William 1928- DLB-143; Y-85

Kennedy, X. J. 1929- DLB-5

Tribute to John Ciardi Y-86

Kennelly, Brendan 1936- DLB-40

Kenner, Hugh 1923-2003 . . . . DLB-67

Tribute to Cleanth Brooks Y-80

Mitchell Kennerley [publishing house] DLB-46

Kennett, White 1660-1728 . . . . DLB-336

Kenny, Maurice 1929- DLB-175

Kent, Frank R. 1877-1958 . . . . DLB-29

Kentfield, Calvin 1924-1975 . . . . DLB-335

Kenyon, Jane 1947-1995 . . . . DLB-120

Kenzheev, Bakhyt Shkurullaevich
1950- DLB-285

Keough, Hugh Edmund 1864-1912 . . . . . . DLB-171

Keppler and Schwartzmann DLB-49

Ker, John, third Duke of Roxburghe
1740-1804 . . . . DLB-213

Ker, N. R. 1908-1982 . . . . DLB-201

Keralio-Robert, Louise-Félicité de
1758-1822 . . . . DLB-313

Kerlan, Irvin 1912-1963 . . . . DLB-187

Kermode, Frank 1919- DLB-242

Kern, Jerome 1885-1945 . . . . DLB-187

Kernaghan, Eileen 1939- DLB-251

Kerner, Justinus 1786-1862 . . . . DLB-90

Kerouac, Jack
1922-1969 . . . DLB-2, 16, 237; DS-3; CDALB-1

Auction of Jack Kerouac's
On the Road Scroll Y-01

The Jack Kerouac Revival Y-95

"Re-meeting of Old Friends":
The Jack Kerouac Conference Y-82

Statement of Correction to "The Jack
Kerouac Revival" Y-96

Kerouac, Jan 1952-1996 . . . . DLB-16

Charles H. Kerr and Company DLB-49

Kerr, Orpheus C. (see Newell, Robert Henry)

Kersh, Gerald 1911-1968 . . . . DLB-255

Kertész, Imre DLB-299, 330; Y-02

Kesey, Ken 1935-2001 . . DLB-2, 16, 206; CDALB-6

Kessel, Joseph 1898-1979 . . . . DLB-72

Kessel, Martin 1901-1990 . . . . DLB-56

Kesten, Hermann 1900-1996 . . . . DLB-56

Keun, Irmgard 1905-1982 . . . . DLB-69

Key, Ellen 1849-1926 . . . . DLB-259

Key and Biddle DLB-49

Keynes, Sir Geoffrey 1887-1982 . . . . DLB-201

Keynes, John Maynard 1883-1946 . . . . DS-10

Keyserling, Eduard von 1855-1918 . . . . . DLB-66

al-Khalil ibn Ahmad circa 718-791 . . . . . . DLB-311

Khan, Adib 1949- DLB-323

Khan, Ismith 1925-2002 . . . . DLB-125

al-Khansa' fl. late sixth-mid
seventh centuries DLB-311

Kharik, Izi 1898-1937 . . . . DLB-333

Kharitonov, Evgenii Vladimirovich
1941-1981 . . . . DLB-285

Kharitonov, Mark Sergeevich 1937- DLB-285

Kharjas, The DLB-337

Khaytov, Nikolay 1919- DLB-181

Khemnitser, Ivan Ivanovich
1745-1784 . . . . DLB-150

Kheraskov, Mikhail Matveevich
1733-1807 . . . . DLB-150

Khlebnikov, Velimir 1885-1922 . . . . DLB-295

Khodasevich, Vladislav 1886-1939 . . . . . . DLB-317

Khomiakov, Aleksei Stepanovich
1804-1860 . . . . DLB-205

Khristov, Boris 1945- DLB-181

Khvoshchinskaia, Nadezhda Dmitrievna
1824-1889 .... DLB-238

Khvostov, Dmitrii Ivanovich
1757-1835 .... DLB-150

Kibirov, Timur Iur'evich (Timur
Iur'evich Zapoev) 1955- DLB-285

Kidd, Adam 1802?-1831 .... DLB-99

William Kidd [publishing house] DLB-106

Kidde, Harald 1878-1918 .... DLB-300

Kidder, Tracy 1945- DLB-185

Kiely, Benedict 1919- DLB-15, 319

Kieran, John 1892-1981 .... DLB-171

Kierkegaard, Søren 1813-1855 .... DLB-300

Kies, Marietta 1853-1899 .... DLB-270

Kiggins and Kellogg DLB-49

Kiley, Jed 1889-1962 .... DLB-4

Kilgore, Bernard 1908-1967 .... DLB-127

Kilian, Crawford 1941- DLB-251

Killens, John Oliver 1916-1987 .... DLB-33

Tribute to Julian Mayfield Y-84

Killigrew, Anne 1660-1685 .... DLB-131

Killigrew, Thomas 1612-1683 .... DLB-58

Kilmer, Joyce 1886-1918 .... DLB-45

Kilroy, Thomas 1934- DLB-233

Kilwardby, Robert circa 1215-1279 ..... DLB-115

Kilworth, Garry 1941- DLB-261

Kim, Anatolii Andreevich 1939- DLB-285

Kimball, Richard Burleigh 1816-1892 ... DLB-202

Kincaid, Jamaica 1949-
.... DLB-157, 227; CDALB-7; CDWLB-3

Kinck, Hans Ernst 1865-1926 .... DLB-297

King, Charles 1844-1933 .... DLB-186

King, Clarence 1842-1901 .... DLB-12

King, Florence 1936- Y-85

King, Francis 1923- DLB-15, 139

King, Grace 1852-1932 .... DLB-12, 78

King, Harriet Hamilton 1840-1920 ..... DLB-199

King, Henry 1592-1669 .... DLB-126

Solomon King [publishing house] DLB-49

King, Stephen 1947- DLB-143; Y-80

King, Susan Petigru 1824-1875 .... DLB-239

King, Thomas 1943- DLB-175, 334

King, Woodie, Jr. 1937- DLB-38

Kinglake, Alexander William
1809-1891 .... DLB-55, 166

Kingo, Thomas 1634-1703 .... DLB-300

Kingsbury, Donald 1929- DLB-251

Kingsley, Charles
1819-1875 ...... DLB-21, 32, 163, 178, 190

Kingsley, Henry 1830-1876 .... DLB-21, 230

Kingsley, Mary Henrietta 1862-1900 ..... DLB-174

Kingsley, Sidney 1906-1995 .... DLB-7

Kingsmill, Hugh 1889-1949 .... DLB-149

Kingsolver, Barbara
1955- DLB-206; CDALB-7

Kingston, Maxine Hong
1940- .. DLB-173, 212, 312; Y-80; CDALB-7

Kingston, William Henry Giles
1814-1880 .... DLB-163

Kinnan, Mary Lewis 1763-1848 .... DLB-200

Kinnell, Galway 1927- DLB-5; Y-87

Kinsella, John 1963- DLB-325

Kinsella, Thomas 1928- DLB-27

Kipling, Rudyard 1865-1936
.... DLB-19, 34, 141, 156, 330; CDBLB-5

Kipphardt, Heinar 1922-1982 .... DLB-124

Kirby, William 1817-1906 .... DLB-99

Kircher, Athanasius 1602-1680 .... DLB-164

Kireevsky, Ivan Vasil'evich 1806-1856 ... DLB-198

Kireevsky, Petr Vasil'evich 1808-1856 ... DLB-205

Kirk, Hans 1898-1962 .... DLB-214

Kirk, John Foster 1824-1904 .... DLB-79

Kirkconnell, Watson 1895-1977 .... DLB-68

Kirkland, Caroline M.
1801-1864 .... DLB-3, 73, 74, 250; DS-13

Kirkland, Joseph 1830-1893 .... DLB-12

Francis Kirkman [publishing house] DLB-170

Kirkpatrick, Clayton 1915-2004 .... DLB-127

Kirkup, James 1918- DLB-27

Kirouac, Conrad (see Marie-Victorin, Frère)

Kirsch, Sarah 1935- DLB-75

Kirst, Hans Hellmut 1914-1989 .... DLB-69

Kiš, Danilo 1935-1989 ..... DLB-181; CDWLB-4

Kita Morio 1927- DLB-182

Kitcat, Mabel Greenhow 1859-1922 ..... DLB-135

Kitchin, C. H. B. 1895-1967 .... DLB-77

Kittredge, William 1932- DLB-212, 244

Kiukhel'beker, Vil'gel'm Karlovich
1797-1846 .... DLB-205

Kizer, Carolyn 1925- DLB-5, 169

Kjaerstad, Jan 1953- DLB-297

Klabund 1890-1928 .... DLB-66

Klaj, Johann 1616-1656 .... DLB-164

Klappert, Peter 1942- DLB-5

Klass, Philip (see Tenn, William)

Klein, A. M. 1909-1972 .... DLB-68

Kleist, Ewald von 1715-1759 .... DLB-97

Kleist, Heinrich von
1777-1811 .... DLB-90; CDWLB-2

Klíma, Ivan 1931- DLB-232; CDWLB-4

Klimentev, Andrei Platonovic
(see Platonov, Andrei Platonovich)

Klinger, Friedrich Maximilian
1752-1831 .... DLB-94

Kliuev, Nikolai Alekseevich 1884-1937 .. DLB-295

Kliushnikov, Viktor Petrovich
1841-1892 .... DLB-238

Klopfer, Donald S.
Impressions of William Faulkner Y-97

Oral History Interview with Donald
S. Klopfer Y-97

Tribute to Alfred A. Knopf Y-84

Klopstock, Friedrich Gottlieb
1724-1803 .... DLB-97

Klopstock, Meta 1728-1758 .... DLB-97

Kluge, Alexander 1932- DLB-75

Kluge, P. F. 1942- Y-02

Knapp, Joseph Palmer 1864-1951 ...... DLB-91

Knapp, Samuel Lorenzo 1783-1838 ..... DLB-59

J. J. and P. Knapton [publishing house] .. DLB-154

Kniazhnin, Iakov Borisovich
1740-1791 .... DLB-150

Knickerbocker, Diedrich (see Irving, Washington)

Knigge, Adolph Franz Friedrich Ludwig,
Freiherr von 1752-1796 .... DLB-94

Charles Knight and Company DLB-106

Knight, Damon 1922-2002 .... DLB-8

Knight, Etheridge 1931-1992 .... DLB-41

Knight, John S. 1894-1981 .... DLB-29

Knight, Sarah Kemble 1666-1727 .... DLB-24, 200

Knight-Bruce, G. W. H. 1852-1896 ..... DLB-174

Knister, Raymond 1899-1932 .... DLB-68

Knoblock, Edward 1874-1945 .... DLB-10

Knopf, Alfred A. 1892-1984 .... Y-84

Knopf to Hammett: The Editoral
Correspondence Y-00

Alfred A. Knopf [publishing house] DLB-46

Knorr von Rosenroth, Christian
1636-1689 .... DLB-168

Knowles, John 1926-2001 .... DLB-6; CDALB-6

Knox, Frank 1874-1944 .... DLB-29

Knox, John circa 1514-1572 .... DLB-132

Knox, John Armoy 1850-1906 .... DLB-23

Knox, Lucy 1845-1884 .... DLB-240

Knox, Ronald Arbuthnott 1888-1957 .... DLB-77

Knox, Thomas Wallace 1835-1896 ..... DLB-189

Knudsen, Jakob 1858-1917 .... DLB-300

Knut, Dovid 1900-1955 .... DLB-317

Kobayashi Takiji 1903-1933 .... DLB-180

Kober, Arthur 1900-1975 .... DLB-11

Kobiakova, Aleksandra Petrovna
1823-1892 .... DLB-238

Kocbek, Edvard 1904-1981 .. DLB-147; CDWLB-4

Koch, C. J. 1932- DLB-289

Koch, Howard 1902-1995 .... DLB-26

Koch, Kenneth 1925-2002 .... DLB-5

Kōda Rohan 1867-1947 .... DLB-180

Koehler, Ted 1894-1973 .... DLB-265

Koenigsberg, Moses 1879-1945 . . . . .DLB-25	Kraf, Elaine 1946- Y-81	Kukučín, Martin 1860-1928 . . . . .DLB-215; CDWLB-4
Koeppen, Wolfgang 1906-1996 . . . . .DLB-69	Kramer, Jane 1938- DLB-185	Kulbak, Moyshe 1896-1937 . . . . .DLB-333
Koertge, Ronald 1940- DLB-105	Kramer, Larry 1935- DLB-249	Kumin, Maxine 1925- DLB-5
Koestler, Arthur 1905-1983 . . . . . . Y-83; CDBLB-7	Kramer, Mark 1944- DLB-185	Kuncewicz, Maria 1895-1989 . . . . .DLB-215
Kogawa, Joy 1935- DLB-334	Kranjčević, Silvije Strahimir 1865-1908 . . .DLB-147	Kundera, Milan 1929- DLB-232; CDWLB-4
Kohn, John S. Van E. 1906-1976 . . . . .DLB-187	Krasko, Ivan 1876-1958 . . . . .DLB-215	Kunene, Mazisi 1930- DLB-117
Kokhanovskaia (see Sokhanskaia, Nadezhda Stepanova)	Krasna, Norman 1909-1984. . . . . .DLB-26	Kunikida Doppo 1869-1908 . . . . .DLB-180
	Kraus, Hans Peter 1907-1988. . . . . .DLB-187	Kunitz, Stanley 1905-2006. . . . . .DLB-48
Kokoschka, Oskar 1886-1980 . . . . .DLB-124	Kraus, Karl 1874-1936 . . . . .DLB-118	Kunjufu, Johari M. (see Amini, Johari M.)
Kolatkar, Arun 1932-2004 . . . . .DLB-323	Krause, Herbert 1905-1976 . . . . .DLB-256	Kunnert, Gunter 1929- DLB-75
Kolb, Annette 1870-1967 . . . . .DLB-66	Krauss, Ruth 1911-1993 . . . . .DLB-52	Kunze, Reiner 1933- DLB-75
Kolbenheyer, Erwin Guido 1878-1962 .DLB-66, 124	Krauth, Nigel 1949- DLB-325	Kuo, Helena 1911-1999. . . . . .DLB-312
	Kreisel, Henry 1922-1991 . . . . .DLB-88	Kupferberg, Tuli 1923- DLB-16
Kolleritsch, Alfred 1931- DLB-85	Krestovsky V. (see Khvoshchinskaia, Nadezhda Dmitrievna)	Kuprin, Aleksandr Ivanovich 1870-1938 . . . . .DLB-295
Kolodny, Annette 1941- DLB-67		
Koltès, Bernard-Marie 1948-1989 . . . . . . .DLB-321	Krestovsky, Vsevolod Vladimirovich 1839-1895 . . . . .DLB-238	Kuraev, Mikhail Nikolaevich 1939- DLB-285
Kol'tsov, Aleksei Vasil'evich 1809-1842 . . . . .DLB-205		Kurahashi Yumiko 1935- DLB-182
	Kreuder, Ernst 1903-1972 . . . . .DLB-69	Kureishi, Hanif 1954- DLB-194, 245
Komarov, Matvei circa 1730-1812 . . . . . . .DLB-150	Krėvė-Mickevičius, Vincas 1882-1954. . . .DLB-220	Kürnberger, Ferdinand 1821-1879 . . . . . .DLB-129
Komroff, Manuel 1890-1974 . . . . .DLB-4	Kreymborg, Alfred 1883-1966. . . . . . . .DLB-4, 54	Kurz, Isolde 1853-1944 . . . . .DLB-66
Komunyakaa, Yusef 1947- DLB-120	Krieger, Murray 1923-2000 . . . . .DLB-67	Kusenberg, Kurt 1904-1983. . . . . .DLB-69
Kondoleon, Harry 1955-1994 . . . . .DLB-266	Krim, Seymour 1922-1989. . . . . .DLB-16	Kushchevsky, Ivan Afanas'evich 1847-1876. . . . . .DLB-238
Koneski, Blaže 1921-1993 . . . DLB-181; CDWLB-4	Kripke, Saul 1940- DLB-279	
Konigsburg, E. L. 1930- DLB-52	Kristensen, Tom 1893-1974 . . . . .DLB-214	Kushner, Tony 1956- DLB-228
Konparu Zenchiku 1405-1468? DLB-203	Kristeva, Julia 1941- DLB-242	Kuttner, Henry 1915-1958. . . . . .DLB-8
Konrád, György 1933- DLB-232; CDWLB-4	Kristján Níels Jónsson/Kristjan Niels Julius (see Káinn)	Kuzmin, Mikhail Alekseevich 1872-1936 . . . . .DLB-295
Konrad von Würzburg circa 1230-1287 . . . . .DLB-138		
	Kritzer, Hyman W. 1918-2002. . . . . .Y-02	Kuznetsov, Anatoli 1929-1979 . . . . . .DLB-299, 302
Konstantinov, Aleko 1863-1897 . . . . .DLB-147	Krivulin, Viktor Borisovich 1944-2001 . . .DLB-285	Kvitko, Leib (Leyb Kvitko) 1890-1952 . . . . .DLB-333
Konwicki, Tadeusz 1926- DLB-232	Krleža, Miroslav 1893-1981 . . . . DLB-147; CDWLB-4	
Koontz, Dean 1945- DLB-292		Kyd, Thomas 1558-1594 . . . . .DLB-62
Kooser, Ted 1939- DLB-105	Krock, Arthur 1886-1974. . . . . .DLB-29	Kyffin, Maurice circa 1560?-1598 . . . . . . .DLB-136
Kopit, Arthur 1937- DLB-7	Kroetsch, Robert 1927- DLB-53	Kyger, Joanne 1934- DLB-16
Kops, Bernard 1926?- DLB-13	Kropotkin, Petr Alekseevich 1842-1921. . .DLB-277	Kyne, Peter B. 1880-1957. . . . . .DLB-78
Korn, Rachel (Rokhl Korn) 1898-1982 . . . . .DLB-333	Kross, Jaan 1920- DLB-232	Kyōgoku Tamekane 1254-1332 . . . . .DLB-203
	Kruchenykh, Aleksei Eliseevich 1886-1968 . . . . .DLB-295	Kyrklund, Willy 1921- DLB-257
Kornbluth, C. M. 1923-1958 . . . . .DLB-8		
Körner, Theodor 1791-1813. . . . . .DLB-90	Krúdy, Gyula 1878-1933 . . . . .DLB-215	**L**
Kornfeld, Paul 1889-1942 . . . . .DLB-118	Krutch, Joseph Wood 1893-1970 . . . . DLB-63, 206, 275	
Korolenko, Vladimir Galaktionovich 1853-1921 . . . . .DLB-277		L. E. L. (see Landon, Letitia Elizabeth)
	Krylov, Ivan Andreevich 1769-1844. . . . . .DLB-150	Labé, Louise 1520?-1566 . . . . .DLB-327
Kosinski, Jerzy 1933-1991 . . . . . . DLB-2, 299; Y-82	Krymov, Iurii Solomonovich (Iurii Solomonovich Beklemishev) 1908-1941 . . . . .DLB-272	Laberge, Albert 1871-1960. . . . . .DLB-68
Kosmač, Ciril 1910-1980 . . . . .DLB-181		Laberge, Marie 1950- DLB-60
Kosovel, Srečko 1904-1926 . . . . .DLB-147		Labiche, Eugène 1815-1888. . . . . .DLB-192
Kostrov, Ermil Ivanovich 1755-1796. . . . . .DLB-150	Kubin, Alfred 1877-1959 . . . . .DLB-81	Labrunie, Gerard (see Nerval, Gerard de)
Kotzebue, August von 1761-1819. . . . . . . .DLB-94	Kubrick, Stanley 1928-1999. . . . . .DLB-26	La Bruyère, Jean de 1645-1696 . . . . .DLB-268
Kotzwinkle, William 1938- DLB-173	*Kudrun* circa 1230-1240 . . . . .DLB-138	La Calprenède 1609?-1663 . . . . .DLB-268
Kovačić, Ante 1854-1889 . . . . .DLB-147	Kuffstein, Hans Ludwig von 1582-1656 . .DLB-164	Lacan, Jacques 1901-1981 . . . . .DLB-296
Kovalevskaia, Sof'ia Vasil'evna 1850-1891 . . . . .DLB-277	Kuhlmann, Quirinus 1651-1689 . . . . .DLB-168	La Capria, Raffaele 1922- DLB-196
	Kuhn, Thomas S. 1922-1996 . . . . .DLB-279	La Ceppède, Jean de 1550?-1623. . . . . . . .DLB-327
Kovič, Kajetan 1931- DLB-181	Kuhnau, Johann 1660-1722 . . . . .DLB-168	La Chaussée, Pierre-Claude Nivelle de 1692-1754 . . . . .DLB-313
Kozlov, Ivan Ivanovich 1779-1840 . . . . . .DLB-205	Kukol'nik, Nestor Vasil'evich 1809-1868 . . . . .DLB-205	
Kracauer, Siegfried 1889-1966 . . . . .DLB-296		

Cumulative Index

Laclos, Pierre-Ambroise-François Choderlos de
   1741-1803 . . . . DLB-313

   Dangerous Acquaintances DLB-314

Lacombe, Patrice
   (see Trullier-Lacombe, Joseph Patrice)

Lacretelle, Jacques de 1888-1985 . . . . DLB-65

Lacy, Ed 1911-1968 . . . . DLB-226

Lacy, Sam 1903- DLB-171

Ladd, Joseph Brown 1764-1786 . . . . DLB-37

La Farge, Oliver 1901-1963 . . . . DLB-9

Lafayette, Marie-Madeleine, comtesse de
   1634-1693 . . . . DLB-268

Laferrière, Dany 1953- DLB-334

Laffan, Mrs. R. S. de Courcy
   (see Adams, Bertha Leith)

Lafferty, R. A. 1914-2002 . . . . DLB-8

La Flesche, Francis 1857-1932 . . . . DLB-175

La Fontaine, Jean de 1621-1695 . . . . DLB-268

Laforet, Carmen 1921-2004 . . . . DLB-322

Laforge, Jules 1860-1887 . . . . DLB-217

Lagerkvist, Pär 1891-1974 . . . . DLB-259, 331

Lagerlöf, Selma 1858-1940 . . . . DLB-259, 331

Lagorio, Gina 1922- DLB-196

La Guma, Alex
   1925-1985 . . . . DLB-117, 225; CDWLB-3

Lahaise, Guillaume (see Delahaye, Guy)

La Harpe, Jean-François de 1739-1803 . . . . . DLB-313

Lahiri, Jhumpa 1967- DLB-323

Lahontan, Louis-Armand de Lom d'Arce,
   Baron de 1666-1715? DLB-99

Lai He 1894-1943 . . . . DLB-328

Laing, Kojo 1946- DLB-157

Laird, Carobeth 1895-1983 . . . . Y-82

Laird and Lee DLB-49

Lake, Paul 1951- DLB-282

Lalić, Ivan V. 1931-1996 . . . . DLB-181

Lalić, Mihailo 1914-1992 . . . . DLB-181

Lalonde, Michèle 1937- DLB-60

Lamantia, Philip 1927- DLB-16

Lamartine, Alphonse de
   1790-1869 . . . . DLB-217

Lamb, Lady Caroline 1785-1828 . . . . DLB-116

Lamb, Charles
   1775-1834 . . . . . . DLB-93, 107, 163; CDBLB-3

Lamb, Mary 1764-1874 . . . . DLB-163

Lambert, Angela 1940- DLB-271

Lambert, Anne-Thérèse de (Anne-Thérèse de
   Marguenat de Courcelles, marquise de Lambert)
   1647-1733 . . . . DLB-313

Lambert, Betty 1933-1983 . . . . DLB-60

La Mettrie, Julien Offroy de
   1709-1751 . . . . DLB-313

Lamm, Donald
   Goodbye, Gutenberg? A Lecture at
   the New York Public Library,
   18 April 1995 . . . . Y-95

Lamming, George 1927- . . DLB-125; CDWLB-3

La Mothe Le Vayer, François de
   1588-1672 . . . . DLB-268

L'Amour, Louis 1908-1988 . . . . DLB-206; Y-80

Lampman, Archibald 1861-1899 . . . . DLB-92

Lamson, Wolffe and Company DLB-49

Lancer Books DLB-46

Lanchester, John 1962- DLB-267

Lander, Peter (see Cunningham, Peter)

Landesman, Jay 1919- and
   Landesman, Fran 1927- DLB-16

Landolfi, Tommaso 1908-1979 . . . . DLB-177

Landon, Letitia Elizabeth 1802-1838 . . . . . DLB-96

Landor, Walter Savage 1775-1864 . . . . . DLB-93, 107

Landry, Napoléon-P. 1884-1956 . . . . DLB-92

Landvik, Lorna 1954- DLB-292

Lane, Charles 1800-1870 . . . . . DLB-1, 223; DS-5

Lane, F. C. 1885-1984 . . . . DLB-241

Lane, Laurence W. 1890-1967 . . . . DLB-91

Lane, M. Travis 1934- DLB-60

Lane, Patrick 1939- DLB-53

Lane, Pinkie Gordon 1923- DLB-41

John Lane Company DLB-49

Laney, Al 1896-1988 . . . . DLB-4, 171

Lang, Andrew 1844-1912 . . . . . DLB-98, 141, 184

Langer, Susanne K. 1895-1985 . . . . DLB-270

Langevin, André 1927- DLB-60

Langford, David 1953- DLB-261

Langgässer, Elisabeth 1899-1950 . . . . DLB-69

Langhorne, John 1735-1779 . . . . DLB-109

Langland, William
   circa 1330-circa 1400 . . . . DLB-146

Langton, Anna 1804-1893 . . . . DLB-99

Lanham, Edwin 1904-1979 . . . . DLB-4

Lanier, Sidney 1842-1881 . . . . DLB-64; DS-13

Lanyer, Aemilia 1569-1645 . . . . DLB-121

Lao She 1899-1966 . . . . DLB-328

Lapointe, Gatien 1931-1983 . . . . DLB-88

Lapointe, Paul-Marie 1929- DLB-88

La Ramée, Pierre de (Petrus Ramus, Peter Ramus)
   1515-1572 . . . . DLB-327

Larcom, Lucy 1824-1893 . . . . DLB-221, 243

Lardner, John 1912-1960 . . . . DLB-171

Lardner, Ring 1885-1933
   . . . . . . DLB-11, 25, 86, 171; DS-16; CDALB-4

   Lardner 100: Ring Lardner
   Centennial Symposium Y-85

Lardner, Ring, Jr. 1915-2000 . . . . DLB-26, Y-00

Larivey, Pierre de 1541-1619 . . . . DLB-327

Larkin, Philip 1922-1985 . . . . . DLB-27; CDBLB-8

   The Philip Larkin Society Y-99

La Roche, Sophie von 1730-1807 . . . . DLB-94

La Rochefoucauld, François duc de
   1613-1680 . . . . DLB-268

La Rocque, Gilbert 1943-1984 . . . . DLB-60

Laroque de Roquebrune, Robert
   (see Roquebrune, Robert de)

Larrick, Nancy 1910-2004 . . . . DLB-61

Lars, Claudia 1899-1974 . . . . DLB-283

Larsen, Nella 1893-1964 . . . . DLB-51

Larsen, Thøger 1875-1928 . . . . DLB-300

Larson, Clinton F. 1919-1994 . . . . DLB-256

La Sale, Antoine de
   circa 1386-1460/1467 . . . . DLB-208

Las Casas, Fray Bartolomé de
   1474-1566 . . . . DLB-318

Lasch, Christopher 1932-1994 . . . . DLB-246

Lasdun, James 1958- DLB-319

Lasker-Schüler, Else 1869-1945 . . . . . DLB-66, 124

Lasnier, Rina 1915-1997 . . . . DLB-88

Lassalle, Ferdinand 1825-1864 . . . . DLB-129

Last Orders, 1996 Booker Prize winner,
   Graham Swift DLB-326

La Taille, Jean de 1534?-1611? DLB-327

Late-Medieval Castilian Theater DLB-286

Latham, Robert 1912-1995 . . . . DLB-201

Lathan, Emma (Mary Jane Latsis [1927-1997] and
   Martha Henissart [1929-]) DLB-306

Lathrop, Dorothy P. 1891-1980 . . . . DLB-22

Lathrop, George Parsons 1851-1898 . . . . . DLB-71

Lathrop, John, Jr. 1772-1820 . . . . DLB-37

Latimer, Hugh 1492?-1555 . . . . DLB-136

Latimore, Jewel Christine McLawler
   (see Amini, Johari M.)

Latin Histories and Chronicles of
   Medieval Spain DLB-337

Latin Literature, The Uniqueness of DLB-211

La Tour du Pin, Patrice de 1911-1975 . . . . DLB-258

Latymer, William 1498-1583 . . . . DLB-132

Laube, Heinrich 1806-1884 . . . . DLB-133

Laud, William 1573-1645 . . . . DLB-213

Laughlin, James 1914-1997 . . . . . . DLB-48; Y-96, 97

   A Tribute [to Henry Miller] Y-80

   Tribute to Albert Erskine Y-93

   Tribute to Kenneth Rexroth Y-82

   Tribute to Malcolm Cowley Y-89

Laumer, Keith 1925-1993 . . . . DLB-8

Lauremberg, Johann 1590-1658 . . . . DLB-164

Laurence, Margaret 1926-1987 . . . . DLB-53

Laurentius von Schnüffis 1633-1702 . . . . . DLB-168

Laurents, Arthur 1918- DLB-26

Laurie, Annie (see Black, Winifred)

Laut, Agnes Christiana 1871-1936 . . . . DLB-92

Lauterbach, Ann 1942- DLB-193

Lautréamont, Isidore Lucien Ducasse,
   Comte de 1846-1870 . . . . DLB-217

Lavater, Johann Kaspar 1741-1801 . . . . DLB-97

Lavin, Mary 1912-1996 . . . . DLB-15, 319

Law, John (see Harkness, Margaret)

Lawes, Henry 1596-1662 . . . . DLB-126

Lawler, Ray 1922- DLB-289

Lawless, Anthony (see MacDonald, Philip)

Lawless, Emily (The Hon. Emily Lawless)
1845-1913 . . . . DLB-240

Lawrence, D. H. 1885-1930
. . . . . DLB-10, 19, 36, 98, 162, 195; CDBLB-6

    The D. H. Lawrence Society of
    North America Y-00

Lawrence, David 1888-1973 . . . . DLB-29

Lawrence, Jerome 1915-2004 . . . . DLB-228

Lawrence, Seymour 1926-1994 . . . . Y-94

    Tribute to Richard Yates Y-92

Lawrence, T. E. 1888-1935 . . . . DLB-195

    The T. E. Lawrence Society Y-98

Lawson, George 1598-1678 . . . . DLB-213

Lawson, Henry 1867-1922 . . . . DLB-230

Lawson, John ?-1711 . . . . DLB-24

Lawson, John Howard 1894-1977 . . . . DLB-228

Lawson, Louisa Albury 1848-1920 . . . . DLB-230

Lawson, Robert 1892-1957 . . . . DLB-22

Lawson, Victor F. 1850-1925 . . . . DLB-25

Layard, Austen Henry 1817-1894 . . . . DLB-166

Layton, Irving 1912- DLB-88

LaZamon fl. circa 1200 . . . . DLB-146

Lazarević, Laza K. 1851-1890 . . . . DLB-147

Lazarus, George 1904-1997 . . . . DLB-201

Lazhechnikov, Ivan Ivanovich
1792-1869 . . . . DLB-198

Lea, Henry Charles 1825-1909 . . . . DLB-47

Lea, Sydney 1942- DLB-120, 282

Lea, Tom 1907-2001 . . . . DLB-6

Leacock, John 1729-1802 . . . . DLB-31

Leacock, Stephen 1869-1944 . . . . DLB-92

Lead, Jane Ward 1623-1704 . . . . DLB-131

Leadenhall Press DLB-106

"The Greatness of Southern Literature":
League of the South Institute for the
Study of Southern Culture and History
. . . . Y-02

Leakey, Caroline Woolmer 1827-1881 . . . . . DLB-230

Leapor, Mary 1722-1746 . . . . DLB-109

Lear, Edward 1812-1888 . . . . DLB-32, 163, 166

Leary, Timothy 1920-1996 . . . . DLB-16

W. A. Leary and Company DLB-49

Léautaud, Paul 1872-1956 . . . . DLB-65

Leavis, F. R. 1895-1978 . . . . DLB-242

Leavitt, David 1961- DLB-130

Leavitt and Allen DLB-49

Le Blond, Mrs. Aubrey 1861-1934 . . . . . . DLB-174

le Carré, John (David John Moore Cornwell)
1931- DLB-87; CDBLB-8

    Tribute to Graham Greene Y-91

    Tribute to George Greenfield Y-00

Lécavelé, Roland (see Dorgeles, Roland)

Lechlitner, Ruth 1901- DLB-48

Leclerc, Félix 1914-1988 . . . . DLB-60

Le Clézio, J. M. G. 1940- DLB-83

Leder, Rudolf (see Hermlin, Stephan)

Lederer, Charles 1910-1976 . . . . DLB-26

Ledwidge, Francis 1887-1917 . . . . DLB-20

Lee, Chang-rae 1965- DLB-312

Lee, Cherylene 1953- DLB-312

Lee, Dennis 1939- DLB-53

Lee, Don L. (see Madhubuti, Haki R.)

Lee, George W. 1894-1976 . . . . DLB-51

Lee, Gus 1946- DLB-312

Lee, Harper 1926- DLB-6; CDALB-1

Lee, Harriet 1757-1851 and
Lee, Sophia 1750-1824 . . . . DLB-39

Lee, Laurie 1914-1997 . . . . DLB-27

Lee, Leslie 1935- DLB-266

Lee, Li-Young 1957- DLB-165, 312

Lee, Manfred B. 1905-1971 . . . . DLB-137

Lee, Nathaniel circa 1645-1692 . . . . DLB-80

Lee, Robert E. 1918-1994 . . . . DLB-228

Lee, Sir Sidney 1859-1926 . . . . DLB-149, 184

    "Principles of Biography," in
    Elizabethan and Other Essays DLB-149

Lee, Tanith 1947- DLB-261

Lee, Vernon
1856-1935 . . . . DLB-57, 153, 156, 174, 178

Lee and Shepard DLB-49

Le Fanu, Joseph Sheridan
1814-1873 . . . . DLB-21, 70, 159, 178

Lefèvre d'Etaples, Jacques
1460?-1536 . . . . DLB-327

Leffland, Ella 1931- Y-84

le Fort, Gertrud von 1876-1971 . . . . DLB-66

Le Gallienne, Richard 1866-1947 . . . . DLB-4

Legaré, Hugh Swinton
1797-1843 . . . . DLB-3, 59, 73, 248

Legaré, James Mathewes 1823-1859 . . . . DLB-3, 248

Léger, Antoine-J. 1880-1950 . . . . DLB 88

Leggett, William 1801-1839 . . . . DLB-250

Le Guin, Ursula K.
1929- DLB-8, 52, 256, 275; CDALB-6

Lehman, Ernest 1920- DLB-44

Lehmann, John 1907-1989 . . . . DLB-27, 100

John Lehmann Limited DLB-112

Lehmann, Rosamond 1901-1990 . . . . DLB-15

Lehmann, Wilhelm 1882-1968 . . . . DLB-56

Leiber, Fritz 1910-1992 . . . . DLB-8

Leibniz, Gottfried Wilhelm 1646-1716 . . . . DLB-168

Leicester University Press DLB-112

Leigh, Carolyn 1926-1983 . . . . DLB-265

Leigh, W. R. 1866-1955 . . . . DLB-188

Leinster, Murray 1896-1975 . . . . DLB-8

Leiser, Bill 1898-1965 . . . . DLB-241

Leisewitz, Johann Anton 1752-1806 . . . . . . DLB-94

Leitch, Maurice 1933- DLB-14

Leithauser, Brad 1943- DLB-120, 282

Leivick, H[alper] (H. Leyvik)
1888-1962 . . . . DLB-333

Leland, Charles G. 1824-1903 . . . . DLB-11

Leland, John 1503?-1552 . . . . DLB-136

Leland, Thomas 1722-1785 . . . . DLB-336

Lemaire de Belges, Jean 1473-? DLB-327

Lemay, Pamphile 1837-1918 . . . . DLB 99

Lemelin, Roger 1919-1992 . . . . DLB-88

Lemercier, Louis-Jean-Népomucène
1771-1840 . . . . DLB-192

Le Moine, James MacPherson 1825-1912 . . DLB-99

Lemon, Mark 1809-1870 . . . . DLB-163

Le Moyne, Jean 1913-1996 . . . . DLB-88

Lemperly, Paul 1858-1939 . . . . DLB-187

Leñero, Vicente 1933- DLB-305

L'Engle, Madeleine 1918-2007 . . . . DLB-52

Lennart, Isobel 1915-1971 . . . . DLB-44

Lennox, Charlotte 1729 or 1730-1804 . . . . . DLB-39

Lenox, James 1800-1880 . . . . DLB-140

Lenski, Lois 1893-1974 . . . . DLB-22

Lentricchia, Frank 1940- DLB-246

Lenz, Hermann 1913-1998 . . . . DLB-69

Lenz, J. M. R. 1751-1792 . . . . DLB-94

Lenz, Siegfried 1926- DLB-75

León, Fray Luis de 1527-1591 . . . . DLB-318

Leonard, Elmore 1925- DLB-173, 226

Leonard, Hugh 1926- DLB-13

Leonard, William Ellery 1876-1944 . . . . . . DLB-54

Leong, Russell C. 1950- DLB-312

Leonov, Leonid Maksimovich
1899-1994 . . . . DLB-272

Leonowens, Anna 1834-1914 . . . . DLB-99, 166

Leont'ev, Konstantin Nikolaevich
1831-1891 . . . . DLB-277

Leopold, Aldo 1887-1948 . . . . DLB-275

LePan, Douglas 1914-1998 . . . . DLB-88

Lepik, Kalju 1920-1999 . . . . DLB-232

Leprohon, Rosanna Eleanor 1829-1879 . . . . DLB-99

Le Queux, William 1864-1927 . . . . DLB-70

Lermontov, Mikhail Iur'evich
1814-1841 . . . . DLB-205

Lerner, Alan Jay 1918-1986 . . . . DLB-265

Lerner, Max 1902-1992 . . . . DLB-29

Lernet-Holenia, Alexander 1897-1976..... DLB-85

Le Rossignol, James 1866-1969 .... DLB-92

Lesage, Alain-René 1668-1747 .... DLB-313

Lescarbot, Marc circa 1570-1642 .... DLB-99

LeSeur, William Dawson 1840-1917...... DLB-92

LeSieg, Theo. (see Geisel, Theodor Seuss)

Leskov, Nikolai Semenovich
1831-1895 .... DLB-238

Leslie, Doris before 1902-1982......... DLB-191

Leslie, Eliza 1787-1858 .... DLB-202

Leslie, Frank (Henry Carter)
1821-1880 .... DLB-43, 79

Frank Leslie [publishing house] DLB-49

Leśmian, Bolesław 1878-1937......... DLB-215

Lesperance, John 1835?-1891........... DLB-99

Lespinasse, Julie de 1732-1776.......... DLB-313

Lessing, Bruno 1870-1940............. DLB-28

Lessing, Doris
1919- DLB-15, 139; Y-85; CDBLB-8

Lessing, Gotthold Ephraim
1729-1781 .... DLB-97; CDWLB-2

The Lessing Society Y-00

L'Estoile, Pierre de 1546-1611.......... DLB-327

Le Sueur, Meridel 1900-1996 .... DLB-303

Lettau, Reinhard 1929-1996............ DLB-75

Letters from a Peruvian Woman, Françoise d'Issembourg
de Graffigny..................... DLB-314

The Hemingway Letters Project Finds
an Editor Y-02

Lever, Charles 1806-1872............... DLB-21

Lever, Ralph ca. 1527-1585............. DLB-236

Leverson, Ada 1862-1933.............. DLB-153

Levertov, Denise
1923-1997........... DLB-5, 165; CDALB-7

Levi, Peter 1931-2000................. DLB-40

Levi, Primo 1919-1987 .... DLB-177, 299

Levien, Sonya 1888-1960 .... DLB-44

Levin, Meyer 1905-1981......... DLB-9, 28; Y-81

Levin, Phillis 1954- DLB-282

Lévinas, Emmanuel 1906-1995 .... DLB-296

Levine, Norman 1923- DLB-88

Levine, Philip 1928- DLB-5

Levis, Larry 1946- DLB-120

Lévi-Strauss, Claude 1908- DLB-242

Levitov, Aleksandr Ivanovich
1835?-1877..................... DLB-277

Levy, Amy 1861-1889 .... DLB-156, 240

Levy, Benn Wolfe 1900-1973 .... DLB-13; Y-81

Levy, Deborah 1959- DLB-310

Lewald, Fanny 1811-1889............. DLB-129

Lewes, George Henry 1817-1878 .... DLB-55, 144

"Criticism in Relation to Novels"
(1863) DLB-21

The Principles of Success in Literature
(1865) [excerpt] DLB-57

Lewis, Agnes Smith 1843-1926..........DLB-174

Lewis, Alfred H. 1857-1914 .... DLB-25, 186

Lewis, Alun 1915-1944........... DLB-20, 162

Lewis, C. Day (see Day Lewis, C.)

Lewis, C. I. 1883-1964 ....DLB-270

Lewis, C. S. 1898-1963
.... DLB-15, 100, 160, 255; CDBLB-7

The New York C. S. Lewis Society Y-99

Lewis, Charles B. 1842-1924 .... DLB-11

Lewis, David 1941-2001...............DLB-279

Lewis, Henry Clay 1825-1850 .... DLB-3, 248

Lewis, Janet 1899-1999.................. Y-87

Tribute to Katherine Anne Porter Y-80

Lewis, Matthew Gregory
1775-1818...............DLB-39, 158, 178

Lewis, Meriwether 1774-1809...... DLB-183, 186

Lewis, Norman 1908-2003 .... DLB-204

Lewis, R. W. B. 1917-2002 .... DLB-111

Lewis, Richard circa 1700-1734......... DLB-24

Lewis, Saunders 1893-1985 .... DLB-310

Lewis, Sinclair 1885-1951
.... DLB-9, 102, 331; DS-1; CDALB-4

Sinclair Lewis Centennial Conference Y-85

The Sinclair Lewis Society............. Y-99

Lewis, Wilmarth Sheldon 1895-1979 .... DLB-140

Lewis, Wyndham 1882-1957 .... DLB-15

Time and Western Man
[excerpt] (1927) DLB-36

Lewisohn, Ludwig 1882-1955 ...DLB-4, 9, 28, 102

Leyendecker, J. C. 1874-1951 .... DLB-188

Leyner, Mark 1956- DLB-292

Lezama Lima, José 1910-1976...... DLB-113, 283

Lézardière, Marie-Charlotte-Pauline Robert de
1754-1835..................... DLB-313

L'Heureux, John 1934- DLB-244

Libbey, Laura Jean 1862-1924 .... DLB-221

Libedinsky, Iurii Nikolaevich
1898-1959 ....DLB-272

The Liberator DLB-303

Library History Group.................. Y-01

E-Books' Second Act in Libraries Y-02

The Library of America DLB-46

The Library of America: An Assessment
After Two Decades.................. Y-02

Libro de Alexandre
(early thirteenth century) DLB-337

Libro de Apolonio (late thirteenth century).. DLB-337

Libro del Caballero Zifar
(circa 1300-1325) DLB-337

Libro de miserio d'omne (circa 1300-1340) ... DLB-337

Licensing Act of 1737 .... DLB-84

Leonard Lichfield I [publishing house] DLB-170

Lichtenberg, Georg Christoph
1742-1799..................... DLB-94

The Liddle Collection Y-97

Lidman, Sara 1923-2004.............. DLB-257

Lieb, Fred 1888-1980 ....DLB-171

Liebling, A. J. 1904-1963 ....DLB-4, 171

Lieutenant Murray (see Ballou, Maturin Murray)

Life and Times of Michael K, 1983 Booker Prize winner,
J. M. Coetzee DLB-326

Life of Pi, 2002 Booker Prize winner,
Yann Martel..................... DLB-326

Lighthall, William Douw 1857-1954...... DLB-92

Lihn, Enrique 1929-1988 .... DLB-283

Lilar, Françoise (see Mallet-Joris, Françoise)

Lili'uokalani, Queen 1838-1917 .... DLB-221

Lillo, George 1691-1739 .... DLB-84

Lilly, J. K., Jr. 1893-1966.............. DLB-140

Lilly, Wait and Company DLB-49

Lily, William circa 1468-1522.......... DLB-132

Lim, Shirley Geok-lin 1944- DLB-312

Lima, Jorge de 1893-1953.............. DLB-307

Lima Barreto, Afonso Henriques de
1881-1922 .... DLB-307

Limited Editions Club DLB-46

Limón, Graciela 1938- DLB-209

Limonov, Eduard 1943- DLB-317

Lincoln and Edmands DLB-49

Lind, Jakov 1927- DLB-299

Linda Vilhjálmsdóttir 1958- DLB-293

Lindesay, Ethel Forence
(see Richardson, Henry Handel)

Lindgren, Astrid 1907-2002 ....DLB-257

Lindgren, Torgny 1938- DLB-257

Lindsay, Alexander William, Twenty-fifth
Earl of Crawford 1812-1880 .... DLB-184

Lindsay, Sir David circa 1485-1555 ..... DLB-132

Lindsay, David 1878-1945 .... DLB-255

Lindsay, Jack 1900-1990.................. Y-84

Lindsay, Lady (Caroline Blanche
Elizabeth Fitzroy Lindsay)
1844-1912 .... DLB-199

Lindsay, Norman 1879-1969........... DLB-260

Lindsay, Vachel
1879-1931............. DLB-54; CDALB-3

The Line of Beauty, 2004 Booker Prize winner,
Alan Hollinghurst DLB-326

Linebarger, Paul Myron Anthony
(see Smith, Cordwainer)

Ling Shuhua 1900-1990 .... DLB-328

Link, Arthur S. 1920-1998 ....DLB-17

Linn, Ed 1922-2000 .... DLB-241

Linn, John Blair 1777-1804 .... DLB-37

Lins, Osman 1924-1978 ....DLB-145, 307

Linton, Eliza Lynn 1822-1898 .... DLB-18

Linton, William James 1812-1897 . . . . .DLB-32	Guide to the Archives of Publishers, Journals, and Literary Agents in North American Libraries Y-93	The Ellen Glasgow Society Y-01
Barnaby Bernard Lintot [publishing house] DLB-170		Zane Grey's West Society Y-00
Lion Books. DLB-46	The Henry E. Huntington Library Y-92	The Ivor Gurney Society Y-98
Lionni, Leo 1910-1999. . . . . .DLB-61	The Humanities Research Center, University of Texas. Y-82	The Joel Chandler Harris Association Y-99
Lippard, George 1822-1854. . . . . .DLB-202	The John Carter Brown Library Y-85	The Nathaniel Hawthorne Society Y-00
Lippincott, Sara Jane Clarke 1823-1904 . . . . .DLB-43	Kent State Special Collections Y-86	The [George Alfred] Henty Society Y-98
	The Lilly Library .Y-84	George Moses Horton Society Y-99
J. B. Lippincott Company DLB-49	The Modern Literary Manuscripts Collection in the Special Collections of the Washington University Libraries Y-87	The William Dean Howells Society Y-01
Lippmann, Walter 1889-1974. . . . . .DLB-29		WW2 HMSO Paperbacks Society Y-98
Lipton, Lawrence 1898-1975 . . . . .DLB-16		American Humor Studies Association Y-99
Lisboa, Irene 1892-1958 . . . . .DLB-287		International Society for Humor Studies . . . Y-99
Liscow, Christian Ludwig 1701-1760. . . . . .DLB-97	A Publisher's Archives: G. P. Putnam Y-92	The W. W. Jacobs Appreciation Society . . .Y-98
	Special Collections at Boston University. .Y-99	The Richard Jefferies Society Y-98
Lish, Gordon 1934- DLB-130		The Jerome K. Jerome Society Y-98
Tribute to Donald Barthelme Y-89	The University of Virginia Libraries. Y-91	The D. H. Lawrence Society of North America Y-00
Tribute to James Dickey Y-97	The William Charvat American Fiction Collection at the Ohio State University Libraries Y-92	
Lisle, Charles-Marie-René Leconte de 1818-1894 . . . . .DLB-217		The T. E. Lawrence Society Y-98
		The [Gotthold] Lessing Society. Y-00
Lispector, Clarice 1925?-1977 . . . . . . .DLB-113, 307; CDWLB-3	Literary Societies Y-98–02	The New York C. S. Lewis Society Y-99
	The Margery Allingham Society Y-98	The Sinclair Lewis Society Y-99
LitCheck Website. .Y-01	The American Studies Association of Norway. .Y-00	The Jack London Research Center Y-00
Literary Awards and Honors. Y-81–02		The Jack London Society Y-99
Booker Prize Y-86, 96–98	The Arnold Bennett Society Y-98	The Cormac McCarthy Society Y-99
The Drue Heinz Literature Prize. Y-82	The Association for the Study of Literature and Environment (ASLE) Y-99	The Melville Society Y-01
The Elmer Holmes Bobst Awards in Arts and Letters Y-87		The Arthur Miller Society. Y-01
		The Milton Society of America. Y-00
The Griffin Poetry Prize Y-00	Belgian Luxembourg American Studies Association Y-01	International Marianne Moore Society Y-98
Literary Prizes [British] DLB-15, 207		International Nabokov Society Y-99
National Book Critics Circle Awards Y-00–01	The E. F. Benson Society Y-98	The Vladimir Nabokov Society Y-01
	The Elizabeth Bishop Society Y-01	The Flannery O'Connor Society. Y-99
The National Jewish Book Awards Y-85	The [Edgar Rice] Burroughs Bibliophiles. .Y-98	The Wilfred Owen Association. Y-98
		Penguin Collectors' Society. Y-98
Nobel Prize Y-80–02	The Byron Society of America Y-00	The [E. A.] Poe Studies Association Y-99
Winning an Edgar. Y-98	The Lewis Carroll Society of North America Y-00	The Katherine Anne Porter Society Y-01
The Literary Chronicle and Weekly Review 1819-1828. . . . . .DLB-110		The Beatrix Potter Society Y-98
	The Willa Cather Pioneer Memorial and Education Foundation Y-00	The Ezra Pound Society Y-01
Literary Periodicals:		The Powys Society Y-98
Callaloo. Y-87	New Chaucer Society Y-00	Proust Society of America. Y-00
Expatriates in Paris DS-15	The Wilkie Collins Society Y-98	The Dorothy L. Sayers Society Y-98
New Literary Periodicals: A Report for 1987. . . . . .Y-87	The James Fenimore Cooper Society Y-01	The Bernard Shaw Society Y-99
	The Stephen Crane Society. Y-98, 01	The Society for the Study of Southern Literature Y-00
A Report for 1988. . . . . .Y-88	The E. E. Cummings Society Y-01	
A Report for 1989. . . . . .Y-89	The James Dickey Society. Y-99	The Wallace Stevens Society. Y-99
A Report for 1990. . . . . .Y-90	John Dos Passos Newsletter Y-00	The Harriet Beecher Stowe Center Y-00
A Report for 1991. . . . . .Y-91	The Priory Scholars [Sir Arthur Conan Doyle] of New York Y-99	The R. S. Surtees Society Y-98
A Report for 1992. . . . . .Y-92		The Thoreau Society Y-99
A Report for 1993. . . . . .Y-93	The International Theodore Dreiser Society Y-01	The Tilling [E. F. Benson] Society. Y-98
Literary Research Archives		The Trollope Societies. Y-00
The Anthony Burgess Archive at the Harry Ransom Humanities Research Center Y-98	The Friends of the Dymock Poets. Y-00	H. G. Wells Society Y-98
	The George Eliot Fellowship. Y-99	The Western Literature Association Y-99
	The T. S. Eliot Society: Celebration and Scholarship, 1980-1999. . . . . .Y-99	The William Carlos Williams Society. Y-99
Archives of Charles Scribner's Sons DS-17		The Henry Williamson Society. Y-98
Berg Collection of English and American Literature of the New York Public Library Y-83	The Ralph Waldo Emerson Society Y-99	The [Nero] Wolfe Pack Y-99
	The William Faulkner Society. Y-99	The Thomas Wolfe Society. Y-99
	The C. S. Forester Society. Y-00	Worldwide Wodehouse Societies. Y-98
The Bobbs-Merrill Archive at the Lilly Library, Indiana University Y-90	The Hamlin Garland Society Y-01	
	The [Elizabeth] Gaskell Society. Y-98	
Die Fürstliche Bibliothek Corvey Y-96	The Charlotte Perkins Gilman Society Y-99	

Cumulative Index

The W. B. Yeats Society of N.Y. Y-99

The Charlotte M. Yonge Fellowship. Y-98

Literary Theory
The Year in Literary Theory Y-92–Y-93

Literature at Nurse, or Circulating Morals (1885),
by George Moore. DLB-18

Litt, Toby 1968- DLB-267, 319

Littell, Eliakim 1797-1870 . . . . DLB-79

Littell, Robert S. 1831-1896 . . . . DLB-79

Little, Brown and Company DLB-49

Little Magazines and Newspapers DS-15

Selected English-Language Little
Magazines and Newspapers
[France, 1920-1939] DLB-4

The Little Magazines of the
New Formalism DLB-282

The Little Review 1914-1929 . . . . DS-15

Littlewood, Joan 1914-2002 . . . . DLB-13

Liu, Aimee E. 1953- DLB-312

Liu E 1857-1909 . . . . DLB-328

Lively, Penelope 1933- . . . DLB-14, 161, 207, 326

Liverpool University Press DLB-112

The Lives of the Poets (1753) DLB-142

Livesay, Dorothy 1909-1996 . . . . DLB-68

Livesay, Florence Randal 1874-1953 . . . . . . DLB-92

Livings, Henry 1929-1998 . . . . DLB-13

Livingston, Anne Home 1763-1841 . . . DLB-37, 200

Livingston, Jay 1915-2001 . . . . DLB-265

Livingston, Myra Cohn 1926-1996 . . . . . . DLB-61

Livingston, William 1723-1790 . . . . DLB-31

Livingstone, David 1813-1873 . . . . DLB-166

Livingstone, Douglas 1932-1996 . . . . DLB-225

Livshits, Benedikt Konstantinovich
1886-1938 or 1939 . . . . DLB-295

Livy 59 B.C.-A.D. 17 . . . . DLB-211; CDWLB-1

Liyong, Taban lo (see Taban lo Liyong)

Lizárraga, Sylvia S. 1925- DLB-82

Llamazares, Julio 1955- DLB-322

Llewellyn, Kate 1936- DLB-325

Llewellyn, Richard 1906-1983 . . . . DLB-15

Lloréns Torres, Luis 1876-1944 . . . . DLB-290

Edward Lloyd [publishing house] DLB-106

Llull, Ramon (1232?-1316?) DLB-337

Lobato, José Bento Monteiro
1882-1948 . . . . DLB-307

Lobel, Arnold 1933- DLB-61

Lochhead, Liz 1947- DLB-310

Lochridge, Betsy Hopkins (see Fancher, Betsy)

Locke, Alain 1886-1954 . . . . DLB-51

Locke, David Ross 1833-1888 . . . . DLB-11, 23

Locke, John 1632-1704 . . . . . DLB-31, 101, 213, 252

Locke, Richard Adams 1800-1871 . . . . DLB-43

Locker-Lampson, Frederick
1821-1895 . . . . DLB-35, 184

Lockhart, John Gibson
1794-1854. . . . . DLB-110, 116 144

Locklin, Gerald 1941- DLB-335

Lockridge, Francis 1896-1963. . . . . DLB-306

Lockridge, Richard 1898-1982 . . . . DLB-306

Lockridge, Ross, Jr. 1914-1948 . . . . . DLB-143; Y-80

Locrine and Selimus DLB-62

Lodge, David 1935- DLB-14, 194

Lodge, George Cabot 1873-1909 . . . . DLB-54

Lodge, Henry Cabot 1850-1924. . . . . DLB-47

Lodge, Thomas 1558-1625. . . . . DLB-172

Defence of Poetry (1579) [excerpt]. DLB-172

Loeb, Harold 1891-1974 . . . . DLB-4; DS-15

Loeb, William 1905-1981 . . . . DLB-127

Loesser, Frank 1910-1969. . . . . DLB-265

Lofting, Hugh 1886-1947 . . . . DLB-160

Logan, Deborah Norris 1761-1839. . . . . . DLB-200

Logan, James 1674-1751 . . . . DLB-24, 140

Logan, John 1923-1987. . . . . DLB-5

Logan, Martha Daniell 1704?-1779 . . . . . . DLB-200

Logan, William 1950- DLB-120

Logau, Friedrich von 1605-1655 . . . . DLB-164

Logue, Christopher 1926- DLB-27

Lohenstein, Daniel Casper von
1635-1683 . . . . DLB-168

Lohrey, Amanda 1947- DLB-325

Lo-Johansson, Ivar 1901-1990 . . . . DLB-259

Lokert, George (or Lockhart)
circa 1485-1547 . . . . DLB-281

Lomonosov, Mikhail Vasil'evich
1711-1765 . . . . DLB-150

London, Jack
1876-1916. . . . . DLB-8, 12, 78, 212; CDALB-3

The Jack London Research Center Y-00

The Jack London Society. Y-99

The London Magazine 1820-1829. . . . . DLB-110

Long, David 1948- DLB-244

Long, H., and Brother DLB-49

Long, Haniel 1888-1956. . . . . DLB-45

Long, Ray 1878-1935 . . . . DLB-137

Longfellow, Henry Wadsworth
1807-1882. . . . . . . DLB-1, 59, 235; CDALB-2

Longfellow, Samuel 1819-1892. . . . . DLB-1

Longford, Elizabeth 1906-2002 . . . . DLB-155

Tribute to Alfred A. Knopf. Y-84

Longinus circa first century DLB-176

Longley, Michael 1939- DLB-40

T. Longman [publishing house] DLB-154

Longmans, Green and Company DLB-49

Longmore, George 1793?-1867. . . . . DLB-99

Longstreet, Augustus Baldwin
1790-1870 . . . . DLB-3, 11, 74, 248

D. Longworth [publishing house] DLB-49

Lønn, Øystein 1936- DLB-297

Lonsdale, Frederick 1881-1954. . . . . DLB-10

Loos, Anita 1893-1981 . . . . . DLB-11, 26, 228; Y-81

Lopate, Phillip 1943- Y-80

Lope de Rueda 1510?-1565? DLB-318

Lopes, Fernão 1380/1390?-1460?. DLB-287

Lopez, Barry 1945- DLB-256, 275, 335

López, Diana (see Isabella, Ríos)

López, Josefina 1969- DLB-209

López de Ayala, Pero (1332-1407) DLB-337

López de Córdoba, Leonor (1362 or
1363-1412?/1430? DLB-337

López de Mendoza, Íñigo
(see Santillana, Marqués de)

López Velarde, Ramón 1888-1921 . . . . . . DLB-290

Loranger, Jean-Aubert 1896-1942. . . . . . . DLB-92

Lorca, Federico García 1898-1936 . . . . . . DLB-108

Lord, John Keast 1818-1872 . . . . DLB-99

Lorde, Audre 1934-1992 . . . . DLB-41

Lorimer, George Horace 1867-1937 . . . . . DLB-91

A. K. Loring [publishing house] DLB-49

Loring and Mussey. DLB-46

Lorris, Guillaume de (see *Roman de la Rose*)

Lossing, Benson J. 1813-1891. . . . . DLB-30

Lothar, Ernst 1890-1974 . . . . DLB-81

D. Lothrop and Company DLB-49

Lothrop, Harriet M. 1844-1924 . . . . DLB-42

Loti, Pierre 1850-1923 . . . . DLB-123

Lotichius Secundus, Petrus 1528-1560 . . . . DLB-179

Lott, Emmeline fl. nineteenth century . . . DLB-166

Louisiana State University Press. Y-97

Lounsbury, Thomas R. 1838-1915. . . . . . . DLB-71

Louÿs, Pierre 1870-1925 . . . . DLB-123

Løveid, Cecile 1951- DLB-297

Lovejoy, Arthur O. 1873-1962 . . . . DLB-270

Lovelace, Earl 1935- DLB-125; CDWLB-3

Lovelace, Richard 1618-1657 . . . . DLB-131

John W. Lovell Company. DLB-49

Lovell, Coryell and Company DLB-49

Lover, Samuel 1797-1868 . . . . DLB-159, 190

Lovesey, Peter 1936- DLB-87

Tribute to Georges Simenon Y-89

Lovinescu, Eugen
1881-1943 . . . . DLB-220; CDWLB-4

Lovingood, Sut
(see Harris, George Washington)

Low, Samuel 1765-? DLB-37

Lowell, Amy 1874-1925 . . . . DLB-54, 140

Lowell, James Russell 1819-1891 ...... DLB-1, 11, 64, 79, 189, 235; CDALB-2

Lowell, Robert 1917-1977 .... DLB-5, 169; CDALB-7

Lowenfels, Walter 1897-1976 .... DLB-4

Lowndes, Marie Belloc 1868-1947 .... DLB-70

Lowndes, William Thomas 1798-1843 .... DLB-184

Humphrey Lownes [publishing house] ... DLB-170

Lowry, Lois 1937- DLB-52

Lowry, Malcolm 1909-1957 ... DLB-15; CDBLB-7

Lowry, Robert 1919-1994 .... DLB-335

Lowther, Pat 1935-1975 .... DLB-53

Loy, Mina 1882-1966 .... DLB-4, 54

Loynaz, Dulce María 1902-1997 .... DLB-283

Lozeau, Albert 1878-1924 .... DLB-92

Lu Ling 1923-1994 .... DLB-328

Lu Xun 1881-1936 .... DLB-328

Lu Yin 1898?-1934 .... DLB-328

Lubbock, Percy 1879-1965 .... DLB-149

Lubrano, Giacomo 1619-1692 or 1693 .... DLB-339

Lucan A.D. 39-A.D. 65 .... DLB-211

Lucas, E. V. 1868-1938 .... DLB-98, 149, 153

Fielding Lucas Jr. [publishing house] DLB-49

Luce, Clare Booth 1903-1987 .... DLB-228

Luce, Henry R. 1898-1967 .... DLB-91

John W. Luce and Company DLB-46

Lucena, Juan de ca. 1430-1501 .... DLB-286

Lucian circa 120-180 .... DLB-176

Lucie-Smith, Edward 1933- DLB-40

Lucilius circa 180 B.C.-102/101 B.C. DLB-211

Lucini, Gian Pietro 1867-1914 .... DLB-114

Luco Cruchaga, Germán 1894-1936 ..... DLB-305

Lucretius circa 94 B.C.-circa 49 B.C. DLB-211; CDWLB-1

Luder, Peter circa 1415-1472 .... DLB-179

Ludlam, Charles 1943-1987 .... DLB-266

Ludlum, Robert 1927-2001 .... Y-82

Ludus de Antichristo circa 1160 .... DLB-148

Ludvigson, Susan 1942- DLB-120

Ludwig, Jack 1922- DLB-60

Ludwig, Otto 1813-1865 .... DLB-129

Ludwigslied 881 or 882 .... DLB-148

Luera, Yolanda 1953- DLB-122

Luft, Lya 1938- DLB-145

Lugansky, Kazak Vladimir (see Dal', Vladimir Ivanovich)

Lugn, Kristina 1948- DLB-257

Lugones, Leopoldo 1874-1938 .... DLB-283

Luhan, Mabel Dodge 1879-1962 .... DLB-303

Lukács, Georg (see Lukács, György)

Lukács, György 1885-1971 .... DLB-215, 242; CDWLB-4

Luke, Peter 1919-1995 .... DLB-13

Lummis, Charles F. 1859-1928 .... DLB-186

Lundkvist, Artur 1906-1991 .... DLB-259

Lunts, Lev Natanovich 1901-1924 .... DLB-272

F. M. Lupton Company DLB-49

Lupus of Ferrières circa 805-circa 862 .... DLB-148

Lurie, Alison 1926- DLB-2

Lussu, Emilio 1890-1975 .... DLB-264

Lustig, Arnošt 1926- DLB-232, 299

Luther, Martin 1483-1546 .... DLB-179; CDWLB-2

Luzi, Mario 1914-2005 .... DLB-128

L'vov, Nikolai Aleksandrovich 1751-1803 .... DLB-150

Lyall, Gavin 1932-2003 .... DLB-87

Lydgate, John circa 1370-1450 .... DLB-146

Lyly, John circa 1554-1606 .... DLB-62, 167

Lynch, Martin 1950- DLB-310

Lynch, Patricia 1898-1972 .... DLB-160

Lynch, Richard fl. 1596-1601 .... DLB-172

Lynd, Robert 1879-1949 .... DLB-98

Lynds, Dennis (Michael Collins) 1924- DLB-306

Tribute to John D. MacDonald Y-86

Tribute to Kenneth Millar Y-83

Why I Write Mysteries: Night and Day ... Y-85

Lynes, Jeanette 1956- DLB-334

Lyon, Matthew 1749-1822 .... DLB-43

Lyotard, Jean-François 1924-1998 .... DLB-242

Lyricists
Additional Lyricists: 1920-1960 ..... DLB-265

Lysias circa 459 B.C.-circa 380 B.C. DLB-176

Lytle, Andrew 1902-1995 .... DLB-6; Y-95

Tribute to Caroline Gordon Y-81

Tribute to Katherine Anne Porter Y-80

Lytton, Edward (see Bulwer-Lytton, Edward)

Lytton, Edward Robert Bulwer 1831-1891 .... DLB-32

M

Maass, Joachim 1901-1972 .... DLB-69

Mabie, Hamilton Wright 1845-1916 ...... DLB-71

Mac A'Ghobhainn, Iain (see Smith, Iain Crichton)

MacArthur, Charles 1895-1956 ..... DLB-7, 25, 44

Macaulay, Catherine 1731-1791 ..... DLB-104, 336

Macaulay, David 1945- DLB-61

Macaulay, Rose 1881-1958 .... DLB-36

Macaulay, Thomas Babington 1800-1859 .... DLB-32, 55; CDBLB-4

Macaulay Company DLB-46

MacBeth, George 1932-1992 .... DLB-40

Macbeth, Madge 1880-1965 .... DLB-92

MacCaig, Norman 1910-1996 .... DLB-27

MacDiarmid, Hugh 1892-1978 .... DLB-20; CDBLB-7

MacDonald, Ann-Marie 1958- DLB-334

MacDonald, Cynthia 1928- DLB-105

MacDonald, George 1824-1905 .... DLB-18, 163, 178

MacDonald, John D. 1916-1986 .... DLB-8, 306; Y-86

MacDonald, Philip 1899?-1980 .... DLB-77

Macdonald, Ross (see Millar, Kenneth)

Macdonald, Sharman 1951- DLB-245

MacDonald, Wilson 1880-1967 .... DLB-92

Macdonald and Company (Publishers) ... DLB-112

MacEwen, Gwendolyn 1941-1987 .... DLB-53, 251

Macfadden, Bernarr 1868-1955 .... DLB-25, 91

MacGregor, John 1825-1892 .... DLB-166

MacGregor, Mary Esther (see Keith, Marian)

Macherey, Pierre 1938- DLB-296

Machado, Antonio 1875-1939 .... DLB-108

Machado, Manuel 1874-1947 .... DLB-108

Machado de Assis, Joaquim Maria 1839-1908 .... DLB-307

Machar, Agnes Maule 1837-1927 .... DLB-92

Machaut, Guillaume de circa 1300-1377 .... DLB-208

Machen, Arthur Llewelyn Jones 1863-1947 .... DLB-36, 156, 178

MacIlmaine, Roland fl. 1574 .... DLB-281

MacInnes, Colin 1914-1976 .... DLB-14

MacInnes, Helen 1907-1985 .... DLB-87

Mac Intyre, Tom 1931- DLB-245

Mačiulis, Jonas (see Maironis, Jonas)

MacIvor, Daniel 1962- DLB-334

Mack, Maynard 1909-2001 .... DLB-111

Mackall, Leonard L. 1879-1937 .... DLB-140

MacKay, Isabel Ecclestone 1875-1928 ..... DLB-92

Mackay, Shena 1944- DLB-231, 319

MacKaye, Percy 1875-1956 .... DLB-54

Macken, Walter 1915-1967 .... DLB-13

MacKenna, John 1952- DLB-319

Mackenzie, Alexander 1763-1820 ...... DLB-99

Mackenzie, Alexander Slidell 1803-1848 .... DLB-183

Mackenzie, Compton 1883-1972 ..... DLB-34, 100

Mackenzie, Henry 1745-1831 .... DLB-39

The Lounger, no. 20 (1785) DLB-39

Mackenzie, Kenneth (Seaforth Mackenzie) 1913-1955 .... DLB-260

Mackenzie, William 1758-1828 .... DLB-187

Mackey, Nathaniel 1947- DLB-169

Cumulative Index

Mackey, William Wellington 1937- DLB-38

Mackintosh, Elizabeth (see Tey, Josephine)

Mackintosh, Sir James 1765-1832 .... DLB-158

Macklin, Charles 1699-1797 .... DLB-89

Maclaren, Ian (see Watson, John)

Maclaren-Ross, Julian 1912-1964 .... DLB-319

MacLaverty, Bernard 1942- DLB-267

MacLean, Alistair 1922-1987 .... DLB-276

MacLean, Katherine Anne 1925- DLB-8

Maclean, Norman 1902-1990 .... DLB-206

MacLeish, Archibald 1892-1982
.... DLB-4, 7, 45; Y-82; DS-15; CDALB-7

MacLennan, Hugh 1907-1990 .... DLB-68

MacLeod, Alistair 1936- DLB-60

Macleod, Fiona (see Sharp, William)

Macleod, Norman 1906-1985 .... DLB-4

Mac Low, Jackson 1922-2004 .... DLB-193

MacMahon, Bryan 1909-1998 .... DLB-319

Macmillan and Company DLB-106

The Macmillan Company DLB-49

Macmillan's English Men of Letters,
    First Series (1878-1892) DLB-144

MacNamara, Brinsley 1890-1963 .... DLB-10

MacNeice, Louis 1907-1963 .... DLB-10, 20

Macphail, Andrew 1864-1938........... DLB-92

Macpherson, James 1736-1796 ..... DLB-109, 336

Macpherson, Jay 1931- DLB-53

Macpherson, Jeanie 1884-1946......... DLB-44

Macrae Smith Company DLB-46

MacRaye, Lucy Betty (see Webling, Lucy)

John Macrone [publishing house] DLB-106

MacShane, Frank 1927-1999........... DLB-111

Macy-Masius DLB-46

Madden, David 1933- DLB-6

Madden, Sir Frederic 1801-1873....... DLB-184

Maddow, Ben 1909-1992 .... DLB-44

Maddux, Rachel 1912-1983 .... DLB-234; Y-93

Madgett, Naomi Long 1923- DLB-76

Madhubuti, Haki R. 1942- DLB-5, 41; DS-8

Madison, James 1751-1836............ DLB-37

Madsen, Svend Åge 1939- DLB-214

Madrigal, Alfonso Fernández de (El Tostado)
    ca. 1405-1455.................. DLB-286

Maeterlinck, Maurice 1862-1949 ... DLB-192, 331

The Little Magazines of the
    New Formalism DLB-282

Magee, David 1905-1977 .... DLB-187

Maginn, William 1794-1842 .... DLB-110, 159

Maggi, Carlo Maria 1630-1699 ...... DLB-339

Magoffin, Susan Shelby 1827-1855 ..... DLB-239

Mahan, Alfred Thayer 1840-1914 .... DLB-47

Mahapatra, Jayanta 1928- DLB-323

Maheux-Forcier, Louise 1929- DLB-60

Mahfūz, Najīb (Naguib Mahfouz)
    1911-2006 .... DLB-331; Y-88

    Nobel Lecture 1988 .... Y-88

Mahin, John Lee 1902-1984 .... DLB-44

Mahon, Derek 1941- DLB-40

Maiakovsky, Vladimir Vladimirovich
    1893-1930 .... DLB-295

Maikov, Apollon Nikolaevich
    1821-1897..................... DLB-277

Maikov, Vasilii Ivanovich 1728-1778..... DLB-150

Mailer, Norman 1923-2007
    .... DLB-2, 16, 28, 185, 278; Y-80, 83, 97;
                                    DS-3; CDALB-6

    Tribute to Isaac Bashevis Singer......... Y-91

    Tribute to Meyer Levin Y-81

Maillart, Ella 1903-1997 .... DLB-195

Maillet, Adrienne 1885-1963 .... DLB-68

Maillet, Antonine 1929- DLB-60

Maillu, David G. 1939- DLB-157

Maimonides, Moses 1138-1204 .... DLB-115

Main Selections of the Book-of-the-Month
    Club, 1926-1945 .... DLB-9

Mainwaring, Daniel 1902-1977.......... DLB-44

Mair, Charles 1838-1927 .... DLB-99

Mair, John circa 1467-1550 .... DLB-281

Maironis, Jonas 1862-1932 .. DLB-220; CDWLB-4

Mais, Roger 1905-1955 .... DLB-125; CDWLB-3

Maitland, Sara 1950- DLB-271

Major, Andre 1942- DLB-60

Major, Charles 1856-1913 .... DLB-202

Major, Clarence 1936- DLB-33

Major, Kevin 1949- DLB-60

Major Books....................... DLB-46

Makanin, Vladimir Semenovich
    1937- DLB-285

Makarenko, Anton Semenovich
    1888-1939 ....DLB-272

Makemie, Francis circa 1658-1708 .... DLB-24

The Making of Americans Contract............ Y-98

Makovsky, Sergei 1877-1962.......... DLB-317

Maksimov, Vladimir Emel'ianovich
    1930-1995 .... DLB-302

Maksimović, Desanka
    1898-1993 ....DLB-147; CDWLB-4

Malamud, Bernard 1914-1986
    .... DLB-2, 28, 152; Y-80, 86; CDALB-1

    Bernard Malamud Archive at the
        Harry Ransom Humanities
        Research Center Y-00

Mălăncioiu, Ileana 1940- DLB-232

Malaparte, Curzio
    (Kurt Erich Suckert) 1898-1957 ..... DLB-264

Malerba, Luigi 1927- DLB-196

Malet, Lucas 1852-1931.............. DLB-153

Malherbe, François de 1555-1628 ...... DLB-327

Mallarmé, Stéphane 1842-1898 ....DLB-217

Malleson, Lucy Beatrice (see Gilbert, Anthony)

Mallet-Joris, Françoise (Françoise Lilar)
    1930- DLB-83

Mallock, W. H. 1849-1923...........DLB-18, 57

"Every Man His Own Poet; or,
    The Inspired Singer's Recipe
    Book" (1877) DLB-35

"Le Style c'est l'homme" (1892)...... DLB-57

Memoirs of Life and Literature (1920),
    [excerpt]................. DLB-57

Malone, Dumas 1892-1986 ....DLB-17

Malone, Edmond 1741-1812........... DLB-142

Malory, Sir Thomas
    circa 1400-1410 - 1471 ... DLB-146; CDBLB-1

Malouf, David 1934- DLB-289

Malpede, Karen 1945- DLB-249

Malraux, André 1901-1976............ DLB-72

The Maltese Falcon (Documentary) DLB-280

Malthus, Thomas Robert
    1766-1834................... DLB-107, 158

Maltz, Albert 1908-1985............. DLB-102

Malzberg, Barry N. 1939- DLB-8

Mamet, David 1947- DLB-7

Mamin, Dmitrii Narkisovich
    1852-1912 .... DLB-238

Manaka, Matsemela 1956- DLB-157

Mañas, José Ángel 1971- DLB-322

Manchester University Press DLB-112

Mandel, Eli 1922-1992................ DLB-53

Mandel'shtam, Nadezhda Iakovlevna
    1899-1980 .... DLB-302

Mandel'shtam, Osip Emil'evich
    1891-1938 .... DLB-295

Mandeville, Bernard 1670-1733 .... DLB-101

Mandeville, Sir John
    mid fourteenth century DLB-146

Mandiargues, André Pieyre de
    1909-1991 .... DLB-83

Manea, Norman 1936- DLB-232

Manfred, Frederick 1912-1994 ....DLB-6, 212, 227

Manfredi, Gianfranco 1948- DLB-196

Mangan, Sherry 1904-1961 .... DLB-4

Manganelli, Giorgio 1922-1990 .... DLB-196

Manger, Itzik (Itsik Manger)
    1901-1969 .... DLB-333

Mani Leib (Mani Leyb Brahinsky)
    1883-1953 .... DLB-333

Manilius fl. first century A.D. DLB-211

Mankiewicz, Herman 1897-1953 .... DLB-26

Mankiewicz, Joseph L. 1909-1993 .... DLB-44

Mankowitz, Wolf 1924-1998 .... DLB-15

Manley, Delarivière 1672?-1724 ...... DLB-39, 80

Preface to *The Secret History, of Queen Zarah, and the Zarazians* (1705) DLB-39	Margolin, Anna (Rosa Lebensbaum [Roza Lebensboym]) 1887-1952]) DLB-333	Marsh, George Perkins 1801-1882..................DLB-1, 64, 243
Mann, Abby 1927- DLB-44	Margoshes, Dave 1941- DLB-334	Marsh, James 1794-1842 ....DLB-1, 59
Mann, Charles 1929-1998...............Y-98	Marguerite de Navarre 1492-1549......DLB-327	Marsh, Narcissus 1638-1713 ....DLB-213
Mann, Emily 1952- DLB-266	Margulies, Donald 1954- DLB-228	Marsh, Ngaio 1899-1982...............DLB-77
Mann, Heinrich 1871-1950 ....DLB-66, 118	Mariana, Juan de 1535 or 1536-1624 ....DLB-318	Marshall, Alan 1902-1984..............DLB-260
Mann, Horace 1796-1859..........DLB-1, 235	Mariani, Paul 1940- DLB-111	Marshall, Edison 1894-1967 ....DLB-102
Mann, Klaus 1906-1949................DLB-56	Marías, Javier 1951- DLB-322	Marshall, Edward 1932- DLB-16
Mann, Mary Peabody 1806-1887 ....DLB-239	Marie de France fl. 1160-1178 ....DLB-208	Marshall, Emma 1828-1899.............DLB-163
Mann, Thomas 1875-1955 ....DLB-66, 331; CDWLB-2	Marie-Victorin, Frère (Conrad Kirouac) 1885-1944......................DLB-92	Marshall, James 1942-1992 ....DLB-61
Mann, William D'Alton 1839-1920 ......DLB-137	Marin, Biagio 1891-1985..............DLB-128	Marshall, Joyce 1913- DLB-88
Mannin, Ethel 1900-1984 ....DLB-191, 195	Marinella, Lucrezia 1571?-1653 ....DLB-339	Marshall, Paule 1929- DLB-33, 157, 227
Manning, Emily (see Australie)	Marinetti, Filippo Tommaso 1876-1944 ....DLB-114, 264	Marshall, Tom 1938-1993 ....DLB-60
Manning, Frederic 1882-1935 ....DLB-260	Marinina, Aleksandra (Marina Anatol'evna Alekseeva) 1957- DLB-285	Marsilius of Padua circa 1275-circa 1342 ....DLB-115
Manning, Laurence 1899-1972..........DLB-251	Marinković, Ranko 1913-2001 ....DLB-147; CDWLB-4	Mars-Jones, Adam 1954- DLB-207, 319
Manning, Marie 1873?-1945 ....DLB-29	Marino, Giambattista 1569-1625........DLB-339	Marson, Una 1905-1965 ....DLB-157
Manning and Loring DLB-49	Marion, Frances 1886-1973 ....DLB-44	Marston, John 1576-1634............DLB-58, 172
Mannyng, Robert fl. 1303-1338 ....DLB-146	Marius, Richard C. 1933-1999 ....Y-85	Marston, Philip Bourke 1850-1887 ....DLB-35
Mano, D. Keith 1942- DLB-6	Marivaux, Pierre Carlet de Chamblain de 1688-1763 ....DLB-314	Martel, Yann 1963- DLB-326, 334
Manor Books.....................DLB-46	Markandaya, Kamala 1924-2004........DLB-323	Martens, Kurt 1870-1945...............DLB-66
Manrique, Gómez 1412?-1490..........DLB-286	Markevich, Boleslav Mikhailovich 1822-1884 ....DLB-238	Martí, José 1853-1895 ....DLB-290
Manrique, Jorge ca. 1440-1479. ....DLB-286	Markfield, Wallace 1926-2002..........DLB-2, 28	Martial circa A.D. 40-circa A.D. 103 ....DLB-211; CDWLB-1
Mansfield, Katherine 1888-1923 ....DLB-162	Markham, E. A. 1939- DLB-319	William S. Martien [publishing house].....DLB-49
Mantel, Hilary 1952- DLB-271	Markham, Edwin 1852-1940 ....DLB-54, 186	Martin, Abe (see Hubbard, Kin)
Manuel, Niklaus circa 1484-1530. ....DLB-179	Markish, David 1938- DLB-317	Martin, Catherine ca. 1847-1937 ....DLB-230
Manzini, Gianna 1896-1974...........DLB-177	Markish, Peretz (Perets Markish) 1895-1952 ....DLB-333	Martin, Charles 1942- DLB-120, 282
Mao Dun 1896-1981 ....DLB-328	Markle, Fletcher 1921-1991 .... DLB-68; Y-91	Martin, Claire 1914- DLB-60
Mapanje, Jack 1944- DLB-157	Marlatt, Daphne 1942- DLB-60	Martin, David 1915-1997...............DLB-260
Maraini, Dacia 1936- DLB-196	Marlitt, E. 1825-1887................DLB-129	Martin, Jay 1935- DLB-111
Maraise, Marie-Catherine-Renée Darcel de 1737-1822......................DLB-314	Marlowe, Christopher 1564-1593 .... DLB-62; CDBLB-1	Martin, Johann (see Laurentius von Schnüffis)
Maramzin, Vladimir Rafailovich 1934- DLB-302	Marlyn, John 1912-1985 ....DLB-88	Martin, Thomas 1696-1771 ....DLB-213
March, William (William Edward Campbell) 1893-1954 ....DLB-9, 86, 316	Marmion, Shakerley 1603-1639..........DLB-58	Martin, Violet Florence (see Ross, Martin)
Marchand, Leslie A. 1900-1999.........DLB-103	Marmontel, Jean-François 1723-1799 .....DLB-314	Martin du Gard, Roger 1881-1958 ...DLB-65, 331
Marchant, Bessie 1862-1941 ....DLB-160	Der Marner before 1230-circa 1287......DLB-138	Martineau, Harriet 1802-1876 .... DLB-21, 55, 159, 163, 166, 190
Marchant, Tony 1959- DLB-245	Marnham, Patrick 1943- DLB-204	Martínez, Demetria 1960- DLB-209
Marchenko, Anastasiia Iakovlevna 1830-1880 ....DLB-238	Marot, Clément 1496-1544 ....DLB-327	Martínez de Toledo, Alfonso 1398?-1468 ....DLB-286
Marchessault, Jovette 1938- DLB-60	The *Marprelate Tracts* 1588-1589.........DLB-132	Martínez, Eliud 1935- DLB-122
Marcinkevičius, Justinas 1930- DLB-232	Marquand, John P. 1893-1960........DLB-9, 102	Martínez, Max 1943- DLB-82
Marcos, Plínio (Plínio Marcos de Barros) 1935-1999 ....DLB-307	Marques, Helena 1935- DLB-287	Martínez, Rubén 1962- DLB-209
Marcus, Frank 1928- DLB-13	Marqués, René 1919-1979 ....DLB-113, 305	Martín Gaite, Carmen 1925-2000 ....DLB-322
Marcuse, Herbert 1898-1979 ....DLB-242	Marquis, Don 1878-1937 ....DLB-11, 25	Martín-Santos, Luis 1924-1964 ....DLB-322
Marden, Orison Swett 1850-1924 ....DLB-137	Marriott, Anne 1913-1997 ....DLB-68	Martinson, Harry 1904-1978.......DLB-259, 331
Marechera, Dambudzo 1952-1987.......DLB-157	Marryat, Frederick 1792-1848 ....DLB-21, 163	Martinson, Moa 1890-1964............DLB-259
Marek, Richard, Books DLB-46	Marsé, Juan 1933- DLB-322	Martone, Michael 1955- DLB-218
Mares, E. A. 1938- DLB-122	Marsh, Capen, Lyon and Webb DLB-49	Martyn, Edward 1859-1923.............DLB-10
		Marvell, Andrew 1621-1678 ....DLB-131; CDBLB-2
		Marvin X 1944- DLB-38

Marx, Karl 1818-1883 .... DLB-129

Marzials, Theo 1850-1920 .... DLB-35

Masefield, John 1878-1967
.... DLB-10, 19, 153, 160; CDBLB-5

Masham, Damaris Cudworth, Lady
1659-1708..................... DLB-252

Masino, Paola 1908-1989 .... DLB-264

Mason, A. E. W. 1865-1948 .... DLB-70

Mason, Bobbie Ann
1940- DLB-173; Y-87; CDALB-7

Mason, F. van Wyck (Geoffrey Coffin, Frank W. Mason, Ward Weaver) 1901-1978..... DLB-306

Mason, William 1725-1797 .... DLB-142

Mason Brothers DLB-49

The Massachusetts Quarterly Review
1847-1850...................... DLB-1

The Masses DLB-303

Massey, Gerald 1828-1907 .... DLB-32

Massey, Linton R. 1900-1974 .... DLB-187

Massie, Allan 1938- DLB-271

Massinger, Philip 1583-1640 .... DLB-58

Masson, David 1822-1907 .... DLB-144

Masters, Edgar Lee
1868-1950 .... DLB-54; CDALB-3

Masters, Hilary 1928- DLB-244

Masters, Olga 1919-1986 .... DLB-325

Mastronardi, Lucio 1930-1979 .... DLB-177

Mat' Maria (Elizaveta Kuz'mina-Karavdeva Skobtsova, née Pilenko) 1891-1945 .... DLB-317

Matevski, Mateja 1929- ... DLB-181; CDWLB-4

Mather, Cotton
1663-1728....... DLB-24, 30, 140; CDALB-2

Mather, Increase 1639-1723 .... DLB-24

Mather, Richard 1596-1669 .... DLB-24

Matheson, Annie 1853-1924........... DLB-240

Matheson, Richard 1926- DLB-8, 44

Matheus, John F. 1887-1986 .... DLB-51

Mathews, Aidan 1956- DLB-319

Mathews, Cornelius 1817?-1889... DLB-3, 64, 250

Elkin Mathews [publishing house] DLB-112

Mathews, John Joseph 1894-1979 .... DLB-175

Mathias, Roland 1915- DLB-27

Mathis, June 1892-1927 .... DLB-44

Mathis, Sharon Bell 1937- DLB-33

Matković, Marijan 1915-1985.......... DLB-181

Matoš, Antun Gustav 1873-1914 .... DLB-147

Matos Paoli, Francisco 1915-2000 ...... DLB-290

Matsumoto Seichō 1909-1992 .... DLB-182

The Matter of England 1240-1400 ...... DLB-146

The Matter of Rome early twelfth to late
fifteenth century................ DLB-146

Matthew of Vendôme
circa 1130-circa 1200 .... DLB-208

Matthews, Brander
1852-1929 .... DLB-71, 78; DS-13

Matthews, Brian 1936- DLB-325

Matthews, Jack 1925- DLB-6

Matthews, Victoria Earle 1861-1907..... DLB-221

Matthews, William 1942-1997 .... DLB-5

Matthías Jochumsson 1835-1920 .... DLB-293

Matthías Johannessen 1930- DLB-293

Matthiessen, F. O. 1902-1950 .... DLB-63

Matthiessen, Peter 1927- DLB-6, 173, 275

Maturin, Charles Robert 1780-1824...... DLB-178

Matute, Ana María 1926- DLB-322

Maugham, W. Somerset 1874-1965
..... DLB-10, 36, 77, 100, 162, 195; CDBLB-6

Maupassant, Guy de 1850-1893......... DLB-123

Maupertuis, Pierre-Louis Moreau de
1698-1759..................... DLB-314

Maupin, Armistead 1944- DLB-278

Mauriac, Claude 1914-1996 .... DLB-83

Mauriac, François 1885-1970 .... DLB-65, 331

Maurice, Frederick Denison 1805-1872 ... DLB-55

Maurois, André 1885-1967............ DLB-65

Maury, James 1718-1769............... DLB-31

Mavor, Elizabeth 1927- DLB-14

Mavor, Osborne Henry (see Bridie, James)

Maxwell, Gavin 1914-1969............ DLB-204

Maxwell, William
1908-2000 .... DLB-218, 278; Y-80

Tribute to Nancy Hale Y-88

H. Maxwell [publishing house] DLB-49

John Maxwell [publishing house] DLB-106

May, Elaine 1932- DLB-44

May, Karl 1842-1912 .... DLB-129

May, Thomas 1595/1596-1650.......... DLB-58

Mayer, Bernadette 1945- DLB-165

Mayer, Mercer 1943- DLB-61

Mayer, O. B. 1818-1891 .... DLB-3, 248

Mayes, Herbert R. 1900-1987 .... DLB-137

Mayes, Wendell 1919-1992............ DLB-26

Mayfield, Julian 1928-1984............ DLB-33; Y-84

Mayhew, Henry 1812-1887 ..... DLB-18, 55, 190

Mayhew, Jonathan 1720-1766.......... DLB-31

Mayne, Ethel Colburn 1865-1941 ...... DLB-197

Mayne, Jasper 1604-1672 .... DLB-126

Mayne, Seymour 1944- DLB-60

Mayor, Flora Macdonald 1872-1932..... DLB-36

Mayröcker, Friederike 1924- DLB-85

Mayr, Suzette 1967- DLB-334

Mazrui, Ali A. 1933- DLB-125

Mažuranić, Ivan 1814-1890 .... DLB-147

Mazursky, Paul 1930- DLB-44

McAlmon, Robert 1896-1956... DLB-4, 45; DS-15

"A Night at Bricktop's" Y-01

McArthur, Peter 1866-1924 .... DLB-92

McAuley, James 1917-1976 .... DLB-260

Robert M. McBride and Company DLB-46

McCabe, Patrick 1955- DLB-194

McCafferty, Owen 1961- DLB-310

McCaffrey, Anne 1926- DLB-8

McCaffrey, Steve 1947- DLB-334

McCann, Colum 1965- DLB-267

McCarthy, Cormac 1933- DLB-6, 143, 256

The Cormac McCarthy Society......... Y-99

McCarthy, Mary 1912-1989......... DLB-2; Y-81

McCarthy, Shaun Lloyd (see Cory, Desmond)

McCay, Winsor 1871-1934............ DLB-22

McClane, Albert Jules 1922-1991........DLB-171

McClatchy, C. K. 1858-1936 .... DLB-25

McClellan, George Marion 1860-1934.... DLB-50

"The Negro as a Writer" DLB-50

McCloskey, Robert 1914-2003 .... DLB-22

McCloy, Helen 1904-1992 .... DLB-306

McClung, Nellie Letitia 1873-1951 ...... DLB-92

McClure, James 1939-2006 ....DLB-276

McClure, Joanna 1930- DLB-16

McClure, Michael 1932- DLB-16

McClure, Phillips and Company DLB-46

McClure, S. S. 1857-1949 .... DLB-91

A. C. McClurg and Company DLB-49

McCluskey, John A., Jr. 1944- DLB-33

McCollum, Michael A. 1946- Y-87

McConnell, William C. 1917- DLB-88

McCord, David 1897-1997 .... DLB-61

McCord, Louisa S. 1810-1879 .... DLB-248

McCorkle, Jill 1958- DLB-234; Y-87

McCorkle, Samuel Eusebius 1746-1811 ... DLB-37

McCormick, Anne O'Hare 1880-1954.... DLB-29

McCormick, Kenneth Dale 1906-1997....... Y-97

McCormick, Robert R. 1880-1955 ...... DLB-29

McCourt, Edward 1907-1972 .... DLB-88

McCoy, Horace 1897-1955............. DLB-9

McCrae, Hugh 1876-1958 .... DLB-260

McCrae, John 1872-1918 .... DLB-92

McCrumb, Sharyn 1948- DLB-306

McCullagh, Joseph B. 1842-1896........ DLB-23

McCullers, Carson
1917-1967...... DLB-2, 7, 173, 228; CDALB-1

McCulloch, Thomas 1776-1843 .... DLB-99

McCunn, Ruthanne Lum 1946- DLB-312

McDermott, Alice 1953- DLB-292

McDonald, Forrest 1927- DLB-17

McDonald, Walter 1934- DLB-105, DS-9
   "Getting Started: Accepting the Regions You Own—or Which Own You"...................DLB-105
   Tribute to James Dickey Y-97
McDougall, Colin 1917-1984............DLB-68
McDowell, Katharine Sherwood Bonner 1849-1883...................DLB-202, 239
Obolensky McDowell [publishing house]................DLB-46
McEwan, Ian 1948- DLB-14, 194, 319, 326
McFadden, David 1940- DLB-60
McFall, Frances Elizabeth Clarke (see Grand, Sarah)
McFarland, Ron 1942- DLB-256
McFarlane, Leslie 1902-1977 ....DLB-88
McFee, William 1881-1966 ....DLB-153
McGahan, Andrew 1966-................DLB-325
McGahern, John 1934- DLB-14, 231, 319
McGee, Thomas D'Arcy 1825-1868 ......DLB-99
McGeehan, W. O. 1879-1933........DLB-25, 171
McGill, Ralph 1898-1969................DLB-29
McGinley, Phyllis 1905-1978 ....DLB-11, 48
McGinniss, Joe 1942- DLB-185
McGirt, James E. 1874-1930 ....DLB-50
McGlashan and Gill...................DLB-106
McGough, Roger 1937- DLB-40
McGrath, John 1935- DLB-233
McGrath, Patrick 1950- DLB-231
McGraw, Erin 1957- DLB-335
McGraw-Hill DLB-46
McGuane, Thomas 1939- DLB-2, 212; Y-80
   Tribute to Seymour Lawrence...........Y-94
McGuckian, Medbh 1950- DLB-40
McGuffey, William Holmes 1800-1873 ....DLB-42
McGuinness, Frank 1953- DLB-245
McHenry, James 1785-1845.............DLB-202
McIlvanney, William 1936- DLB-14, 207
McIlwraith, Jean Newton 1859-1938......DLB-92
McInerney, Jay 1955- DLB-292
McInerny, Ralph 1929- DLB-306
McIntosh, Maria Jane 1803-1878....DLB-239, 248
McIntyre, James 1827-1906..............DLB-99
McIntyre, O. O. 1884-1938..............DLB-25
McKay, Claude 1889-1948.....DLB-4, 45, 51, 117
The David McKay Company DLB-49
McKay, Don 1942- DLB-334
McKean, William V. 1820-1903..........DLB-23
McKenna, Stephen 1888-1967..........DLB-197
The McKenzie Trust Y-96
McKerrow, R. B. 1872-1940............DLB-201
McKinley, Robin 1952- DLB-52

McKnight, Reginald 1956- DLB-234
McLachlan, Alexander 1818-1896........DLB-99
McLaren, Floris Clark 1904-1978 ....DLB-68
McLaverty, Michael 1907-1992 ....DLB-15
McLean, Duncan 1964- DLB-267
McLean, John R. 1848-1916 ....DLB-23
McLean, William L. 1852-1931..........DLB-25
McLennan, William 1856-1904..........DLB-92
McLoughlin Brothers..................DLB-49
McLuhan, Marshall 1911-1980 ....DLB-88
McMaster, John Bach 1852-1932........DLB-47
McMillan, Terry 1951- DLB-292
McMurtry, Larry 1936- DLB-2, 143, 256; Y-80, 87; CDALB-6
McNally, Terrence 1939- DLB-7, 249
McNeil, Florence 1937- DLB-60
McNeile, Herman Cyril 1888-1937.......DLB-77
McNickle, D'Arcy 1904-1977........DLB-175, 212
McPhee, John 1931- DLB-185, 275
McPherson, James Alan 1943- DLB-38, 244
McPherson, Sandra 1943- Y-86
McTaggart, J. M. E. 1866-1925 ....DLB-262
McWhirter, George 1939- DLB-60
McWilliam, Candia 1955- DLB-267
McWilliams, Carey 1905-1980 ....DLB-137
   "*The Nation's* Future," Carey McWilliams's Editorial Policy in *Nation* DLB-137
Mda, Zakes 1948- DLB-225
Mead, George Herbert 1863-1931.......DLB-270
Mead, L. T. 1844-1914 ....DLB-141
Mead, Matthew 1924- DLB-40
Mead, Taylor circa 1931- DLB-16
Meany, Tom 1903-1964...............DLB-171
Mears, Gillian 1964- DLB-325
Mechthild von Magdeburg circa 1207-circa 1282...............DLB-138
Medieval Galician-Portuguese Poetry DLB-287
Medieval Spanish Debate Literature.....DLB-337
Medieval Spanish Epics DLB-337
Medieval Spanish Exempla Literature....DLB-337
Medieval Spanish Spiritual Literature DLB-337
Medill, Joseph 1823-1899 ....DLB-43
Medoff, Mark 1940- DLB-7
Meek, Alexander Beaufort 1814-1865....................DLB-3, 248
Meeke, Mary ?-1816 ....DLB-116
Mehta, Ved 1934- DLB-323
Mei, Lev Aleksandrovich 1822-1862.....DLB-277
Meinke, Peter 1932- DLB-5
Meireles, Cecília 1901-1964............DLB-307
Mejía, Pedro 1497-1551 ....DLB-318

Mejia Vallejo, Manuel 1923- DLB-113
Melanchthon, Philipp 1497-1560 ....DLB-179
Melançon, Robert 1947- DLB-60
Mell, Max 1882-1971.............DLB-81, 124
Mellow, James R. 1926-1997 ....DLB-111
Mel'nikov, Pavel Ivanovich 1818-1883.....................DLB-238
Meltzer, David 1937- DLB-16
Meltzer, Milton 1915- DLB-61
Melville, Elizabeth, Lady Culross circa 1585-1640..................DLB-172
Melville, Herman 1819-1891........DLB-3, 74, 250; CDALB-2
   The Melville Society Y-01
Melville, James (Roy Peter Martin) 1931- DLB-276
"Memorandum on Local Government," Anne-Robert-Jacques Turgot, bacon de l'Aulne.....................DLB-314
Mena, Juan de 1411-1456 ....DLB-286
Mena, María Cristina 1893-1965....DLB-209, 221
Menaker, Daniel 1941- DLB-335
Menander 342-341 B.C.-circa 292-291 B.C. DLB-176; CDWLB-1
Menantes (see Hunold, Christian Friedrich)
Mencke, Johann Burckhard 1674-1732 ...DLB-168
Mencken, H. L. 1880-1956 ....DLB-11, 29, 63, 137, 222; CDALB-4
   "Berlin, February, 1917" Y-00
   From the Initial Issue of *American Mercury* (January 1924)................DLB-137
   Mencken and Nietzsche: An Unpublished Excerpt from H. L. Mencken's *My Life as Author and Editor*.......................Y-93
Mendele Moykher Sforim (Solomon Jacob Abramowitz [Sholem Yankev Abramovitsch]) 1836-1917 ....DLB-333
Mendelssohn, Moses 1729-1786.........DLB-97
Mendes, Catulle 1841-1909............DLB-217
Méndez M., Miguel 1930- DLB-82
Mendoza, Diego Hurtado de 1504-1575....................DLB-318
Mendoza, Eduardo 1943- DLB-322
Menzini, Benedetto 1646-1704..........DLB-339
The Mercantile Library of New York Y-96
Mercer, Cecil William (see Yates, Dornford)
Mercer, David 1928-1980 ....DLB-13, 310
Mercer, John 1704-1768 ....DLB-31
Mercer, Johnny 1909-1976 ....DLB-265
Mercier, Louis-Sébastien 1740-1814......DLB-314
   Le Tableau de Paris.................DLB-314
Meredith, George 1828-1909 ....DLB-18, 35, 57, 159; CDBLB-4
Meredith, Louisa Anne 1812-1895 ..DLB-166, 230
Meredith, Owen (see Lytton, Edward Robert Bulwer)

Cumulative Index

Meredith, William 1919- DLB-5
Meres, Francis
  Palladis Tamia, Wits Treasurie (1598)
  [excerpt] DLB-172
Merezhkovsky, Dmitrii Sergeevich
  1865-1941 .... DLB-295
Mergerle, Johann Ulrich
  (see Abraham ä Sancta Clara)
Mérimée, Prosper 1803-1870 ...... DLB-119, 192
Merino, José María 1941- DLB-322
Merivale, John Herman 1779-1844 ...... DLB-96
Meriwether, Louise 1923- DLB-33
Merleau-Ponty, Maurice 1908-1961 ..... DLB-296
Merlin Press DLB-112
Merriam, Eve 1916-1992 .... DLB-61
The Merriam Company DLB-49
Merril, Judith 1923-1997 .... DLB-251
  Tribute to Theodore Sturgeon Y-85
Merrill, James 1926-1995 .... DLB-5, 165; Y-85
Merrill and Baker DLB-49
The Mershon Company DLB-49
Merton, Thomas 1915-1968 .... DLB-48; Y-81
Merwin, W. S. 1927- DLB-5, 169
Julian Messner [publishing house] DLB-46
Mészöly, Miklós 1921- DLB-232
J. Metcalf [publishing house] DLB-49
Metcalf, John 1938- DLB-60
The Methodist Book Concern DLB-49
Methuen and Company DLB-112
Meun, Jean de (see *Roman de la Rose*)
Mew, Charlotte 1869-1928 .... DLB-19, 135
Mewshaw, Michael 1943- Y-80
  Tribute to Albert Erskine Y-93
Meyer, Conrad Ferdinand 1825-1898 .... DLB-129
Meyer, E. Y. 1946- DLB-75
Meyer, Eugene 1875-1959 .... DLB-29
Meyer, Michael 1921-2000 .... DLB-155
Meyers, Jeffrey 1939- DLB-111
Meynell, Alice 1847-1922 .... DLB-19, 98
Meynell, Viola 1885-1956 .... DLB-153
Meyrink, Gustav 1868-1932 .... DLB-81
Mézières, Philipe de circa 1327-1405 .... DLB-208
Michael, Ib 1945- DLB-214
Michael, Livi 1960- DLB-267
Michaëlis, Karen 1872-1950 .... DLB-214
Michaels, Anne 1958- DLB-299
Michaels, Leonard 1933-2003 .... DLB-130
Michaux, Henri 1899-1984 .... DLB-258
Micheaux, Oscar 1884-1951 .... DLB-50
Michel of Northgate, Dan
  circa 1265-circa 1340 .... DLB-146
Micheline, Jack 1929-1998 .... DLB-16

Michener, James A. 1907?-1997 .... DLB-6
Micklejohn, George circa 1717-1818 ...... DLB-31
Middle Hill Press DLB-106
Middleton, Christopher 1926- DLB-40
Middleton, Conyers 1683-1750 .... DLB-336
Middleton, Richard 1882-1911 .... DLB-156
Middleton, Stanley 1919- DLB-14, 326
Middleton, Thomas 1580-1627 .... DLB-58
Midnight's Children, 1981 Booker Prize winner,
  Salman Rushdie DLB-326
Miegel, Agnes 1879-1964 .... DLB-56
Mieželaitis, Eduardas 1919-1997 .... DLB-220
Miguéis, José Rodrigues 1901-1980 ..... DLB-287
Mihailović, Dragoslav 1930- DLB-181
Mihalić, Slavko 1928- DLB-181
Mikhailov, A.
  (see Sheller, Aleksandr Konstantinovich)
Mikhailov, Mikhail Larionovich
  1829-1865 .... DLB-238
Mikhailovsky, Nikolai Konstantinovich
  1842-1904 .... DLB-277
Miles, Josephine 1911-1985 .... DLB-48
Miles, Susan (Ursula Wyllie Roberts)
  1888-1975 .... DLB-240
Miliković, Branko 1934-1961 .... DLB-181
Milius, John 1944- DLB-44
Mill, James 1773-1836 .... DLB-107, 158, 262
Mill, John Stuart
  1806-1873 ...... DLB-55, 190, 262; CDBLB-4
  Thoughts on Poetry and Its Varieties
    (1833) DLB-32
Andrew Millar [publishing house] DLB-154
Millar, John 1735-1801 .... DLB-336
Millar, Kenneth
  1915-1983 .... DLB-2, 226; Y-83; DS-6
Millás, Juan José 1946- DLB-322
Millay, Edna St. Vincent
  1892-1950 .... DLB-45, 249; CDALB-4
Millen, Sarah Gertrude 1888-1968 ...... DLB-225
Miller, Andrew 1960- DLB-267
Miller, Arthur 1915-2005 .. DLB-7, 266; CDALB-1
  The Arthur Miller Society Y-01
Miller, Caroline 1903-1992 .... DLB-9
Miller, Eugene Ethelbert 1950- DLB-41
  Tribute to Julian Mayfield Y-84
Miller, Heather Ross 1939- DLB-120
Miller, Henry
  1891-1980 .... DLB-4, 9; Y-80; CDALB-5
Miller, Hugh 1802-1856 .... DLB-190
Miller, J. Hillis 1928- DLB-67
Miller, Jason 1939- DLB-7
Miller, Joaquin 1839-1913 .... DLB-186
Miller, May 1899-1995 .... DLB-41
Miller, Paul 1906-1991 .... DLB-127

Miller, Perry 1905-1963 .... DLB-17, 63
Miller, Sue 1943- DLB-143
Miller, Vassar 1924-1998 .... DLB-105
Miller, Walter M., Jr. 1923-1996 .... DLB-8
Miller, Webb 1892-1940 .... DLB-29
James Miller [publishing house] DLB-49
Millett, Kate 1934- DLB-246
Millhauser, Steven 1943- DLB-2
Millican, Arthenia J. Bates 1920- DLB-38
Milligan, Alice 1866-1953 .... DLB-240
Mills, Magnus 1954- DLB-267
Mills and Boon DLB-112
Milman, Henry Hart 1796-1868 .... DLB-96
Milne, A. A. 1882-1956 ..... DLB-10, 77, 100, 160
Milner, Ron 1938- DLB-38
William Milner [publishing house] DLB-106
Milnes, Richard Monckton (Lord Houghton)
  1809-1885 .... DLB-32, 184
Milton, John
  1608-1674 ..... DLB-131, 151, 281; CDBLB-2
  The Milton Society of America Y-00
Miłosz, Czesław
  1911-2004 .... DLB-215, 331; CDWLB-4
Minakami Tsutomu 1919- DLB-182
Minamoto no Sanetomo 1192-1219 ..... DLB-203
Minco, Marga 1920- DLB-299
The Minerva Press DLB-154
Minnesang circa 1150-1280 .... DLB-138
  The Music of *Minnesang* DLB-138
Minns, Susan 1839-1938 .... DLB-140
Minsky, Nikolai 1855-1937 .... DLB-317
Minton, Balch and Company DLB-46
Minyana, Philippe 1946- DLB-321
Mirbeau, Octave 1848-1917 .... DLB-123, 192
Mirikitani, Janice 1941- DLB-312
Mirk, John died after 1414? DLB-146
Miró, Gabriel 1879-1930 .... DLB-322
Miró, Ricardo 1883-1940 .... DLB-290
Miron, Gaston 1928-1996 .... DLB-60
A Mirror for Magistrates DLB-167
Mirsky, D. S. 1890-1939 .... DLB-317
Mishima Yukio 1925-1970 .... DLB-182
Mistral, Frédéric 1830-1914 .... DLB-331
Mistral, Gabriela 1889-1957 .... DLB-283, 331
Mistry, Rohinton 1952- DLB-334
Mitchel, Jonathan 1624-1668 .... DLB-24
Mitchell, Adrian 1932- DLB-40
Mitchell, Donald Grant
  1822-1908 .... DLB-1, 243; DS-13
Mitchell, Gladys 1901-1983 .... DLB-77
Mitchell, James Leslie 1901-1935 .... DLB-15

Mitchell, John (see Slater, Patrick)

Mitchell, John Ames 1845-1918..........DLB-79

Mitchell, Joseph 1908-1996.......DLB-185; Y-96

Mitchell, Julian 1935- DLB-14

Mitchell, Ken 1940- DLB-60

Mitchell, Langdon 1862-1935.............DLB-7

Mitchell, Loften 1919-2001..............DLB-38

Mitchell, Margaret 1900-1949...DLB-9; CDALB-7

Mitchell, S. Weir 1829-1914.............DLB-202

Mitchell, W. J. T. 1942- DLB-246

Mitchell, W. O. 1914-1998..............DLB-88

Mitchison, Naomi Margaret (Haldane)
 1897-1999 ....DLB-160, 191, 255, 319

Mitford, Mary Russell 1787-1855....DLB-110, 116

Mitford, Nancy 1904-1973.............DLB-191

Mitford, William 1744-1827............DLB-336

Mittelholzer, Edgar
 1909-1965 ....DLB-117; CDWLB-3

Mitterer, Erika 1906-2001 ....DLB-85

Mitterer, Felix 1948- DLB-124

Mitternacht, Johann Sebastian
 1613-1679 ....DLB-168

Miyamoto Yuriko 1899-1951...........DLB-180

Mizener, Arthur 1907-1988 ....DLB-103

Mo, Timothy 1950- DLB-194

Moberg, Vilhelm 1898-1973 ....DLB-259

Las Mocedades de Rodrigo (circa 1300)......DLB-337

Modern Age Books DLB-46

Modern Language Association of America
 The Modern Language Association of
 America Celebrates Its Centennial ...Y-84

The Modern Library DLB-46

Modiano, Patrick 1945- DLB-83, 299

Modjeska, Drusilla 1946- DLB-325

Moffat, Yard and Company.............DLB-46

Moffet, Thomas 1553-1604..............DLB-136

Mofolo, Thomas 1876-1948............DLB-225

Mohr, Nicholasa 1938- DLB-145

Moix, Ana María 1947- DLB-134

Molesworth, Louisa 1839-1921 ....DLB-135

Molière (Jean-Baptiste Poquelin)
 1622-1673 ....DLB-268

Møller, Poul Martin 1794-1838..........DLB-300

Möllhausen, Balduin 1825-1905 ....DLB-129

Molnár, Ferenc 1878-1952...DLB-215; CDWLB-4

Molnár, Miklós (see Mészöly, Miklós)

Molodowsky, Kadya (Kadye Molodovski)
 1894-1975 ....DLB-333

Momaday, N. Scott
 1934- DLB-143, 175, 256; CDALB-7

Mommsen, Theodor 1817-1903.........DLB-331

Monkhouse, Allan 1858-1936 ....DLB-10

Monro, Harold 1879-1932..............DLB-19

Monroe, Harriet 1860-1936..........DLB-54, 91

Monsarrat, Nicholas 1910-1979.........DLB-15

Montagu, Lady Mary Wortley
 1689-1762 ....DLB-95, 101

Montague, C. E. 1867-1928............DLB-197

Montague, John 1929- DLB-40

Montaigne, Michel de 1533-1592.......DLB-327

Montale, Eugenio 1896-1981.......DLB-114, 331

Montalvo, Garci Rodríguez de
 ca. 1450?-before 1505 ....DLB-286

Montalvo, José 1946-1994.............DLB-209

Montemayor, Jorge de 1521?-1561?......DLB-318

Montero, Rosa 1951- DLB-322

Monterroso, Augusto 1921-2003.......DLB-145

Montesquieu, Charles-Louis de Secondat, baron de
 1689-1755 ....DLB-314

 The Spirit of Laws DLB-314

Montesquiou, Robert de 1855-1921 .....DLB-217

Montgomerie, Alexander
 circa 1550?-1598 ....DLB-167

Montgomery, James 1771-1854 .....DLB-93, 158

Montgomery, John 1919- DLB-16

Montgomery, Lucy Maud
 1874-1942 ....DLB-92; DS-14

Montgomery, Marion 1925- DLB-6

Montgomery, Robert Bruce (see Crispin, Edmund)

Montherlant, Henry de 1896-1972...DLB-72, 321

The Monthly Review 1749-1844...........DLB-110

Monti, Ricardo 1944- DLB-305

Montigny, Louvigny de 1876-1955 ....DLB-92

Montoya, José 1932- DLB-122

Moodie, John Wedderburn Dunbar
 1797-1869......................DLB-99

Moodie, Susanna 1803-1885 ....DLB-99

Moody, Joshua circa 1633-1697.........DLB-24

Moody, William Vaughn 1869-1910 ...DLB-7, 54

Moon Tiger, 1987 Booker Prize winner,
 Penelope Lively DLB-326

Moorcock, Michael 1939- DLB-14, 231, 261, 319

Moore, Alan 1953- DLB-261

Moore, Brian 1921-1999 ....DLB-251

Moore, Catherine L. 1911-1987..........DLB-8

Moore, Clement Clarke 1779-1863.......DLB-42

Moore, Dora Mavor 1888-1979.........DLB-92

Moore, G. E. 1873-1958...............DLB-262

Moore, George 1852-1933....DLB-10, 18, 57, 135

 Literature at Nurse, or Circulating Morals
  (1885) DLB-18

Moore, Lorrie 1957- DLB-234

Moore, Marianne
 1887-1972.........DLB-45; DS-7; CDALB-5

 International Marianne Moore Society....Y-98

Moore, Mavor 1919- DLB-88

Moore, Richard 1927- DLB-105

"The No Self, the Little Self, and
 the Poets" DLB-105

Moore, T. Sturge 1870-1944 ....DLB-19

Moore, Thomas 1779-1852 ....DLB-96, 144

Moore, Ward 1903-1978 ....DLB-8

Moore, Wilstach, Keys and Company.....DLB-49

Moorehead, Alan 1901-1983............DLB-204

Moorhouse, Frank 1938- DLB-289

Moorhouse, Geoffrey 1931- DLB-204

Moorish Novel of the Sixteenth
 Century, The....................DLB-318

The Moorland-Spingarn Research
 Center DLB-76

Moorman, Mary C. 1905-1994.........DLB-155

Mora, Pat 1942- DLB-209

Moraes, Dom 1938-2004...............DLB-323

Moraes, Vinicius de 1913-1980.........DLB-307

Moraga, Cherríe 1952- DLB-82, 249

Morales, Alejandro 1944- DLB-82

Morales, Mario Roberto 1947- DLB-145

Morales, Rafael 1919- DLB-108

Morality Plays: Mankind circa 1450-1500
 and Everyman circa 1500 ....DLB-146

Morand, Paul 1888-1976 ....DLB-65

Morante, Elsa 1912-1985...............DLB-177

Morata, Olympia Fulvia 1526-1555.......DLB-179

Moravia, Alberto 1907-1990 ....DLB-177

Mordaunt, Elinor 1872-1942 ....DLB-174

Mordovtsev, Daniil Lukich 1830-1905...DLB-238

More, Hannah
 1745-1833 ....DLB-107, 109, 116, 158

More, Henry 1614-1687 ....DLB-126, 252

More, Sir Thomas
 1477/1478-1535 ....DLB-136, 281

Morejón, Nancy 1944- DLB-283

Morellet, André 1727-1819.............DLB-314

Morency, Pierre 1942- DLB-60

Moreno, Dorinda 1939- DLB-122

Moretti, Marino 1885-1979 ....DLB-114, 264

Morgan, Berry 1919-2002................DLB-6

Morgan, Charles 1894-1958 ....DLB-34, 100

Morgan, Edmund S. 1916- DLB-17

Morgan, Edwin 1920- DLB-27

Morgan, John Pierpont 1837-1913.......DLB-140

Morgan, John Pierpont, Jr. 1867-1943....DLB-140

Morgan, Robert 1944- DLB-120, 292

Morgan, Sally 1951- DLB-325

Morgan, Sydney Owenson, Lady
 1776?-1859 ....DLB-116, 158

Morgner, Irmtraud 1933-1990...........DLB-75

Morhof, Daniel Georg 1639-1691.......DLB-164

Mori, Kyoko 1957- DLB-312

Mori Ōgai 1862-1922 ....DLB-180

Cumulative Index

Mori, Toshio 1910-1980 . . . . DLB-312

Móricz, Zsigmond 1879-1942 . . . . DLB-215

Morier, James Justinian
    1782 or 1783?-1849 . . . . DLB-116

Mörike, Eduard 1804-1875 . . . . DLB-133

Morin, Paul 1889-1963 . . . . DLB-92

Morison, Richard 1514?-1556 . . . . DLB-136

Morison, Samuel Eliot 1887-1976 . . . . DLB-17

Morison, Stanley 1889-1967 . . . . DLB-201

Moritz, Karl Philipp 1756-1793 . . . . DLB-94

Moriz von Craûn circa 1220-1230 . . . . DLB-138

Morley, Christopher 1890-1957 . . . . DLB-9

Morley, John 1838-1923 . . . . DLB-57, 144, 190

Moro, César 1903-1956 . . . . DLB-290

Morris, George Pope 1802-1864 . . . . DLB-73

Morris, James Humphrey (see Morris, Jan)

Morris, Jan 1926- DLB-204

Morris, Lewis 1833-1907 . . . . DLB-35

Morris, Margaret 1737-1816 . . . . DLB-200

Morris, Mary McGarry 1943- DLB-292

Morris, Richard B. 1904-1989 . . . . DLB-17

Morris, William 1834-1896
    . . . . . DLB-18, 35, 57, 156, 178, 184; CDBLB-4

Morris, Willie 1934-1999 . . . . Y-80

    Tribute to Irwin Shaw Y-84

    Tribute to James Dickey Y-97

Morris, Wright
    1910-1998 . . . . DLB-2, 206, 218; Y-81

Morrison, Arthur 1863-1945 . . . . DLB-70, 135, 197

Morrison, Charles Clayton 1874-1966 . . . . DLB-91

Morrison, John 1904-1998 . . . . DLB-260

Morrison, Toni 1931-
    . . . . . DLB-6, 33, 143, 331; Y-81, 93; CDALB-6

    Nobel Lecture 1993 . . . . Y-93

Morrissy, Mary 1957- DLB-267

William Morrow and Company DLB-46

Morse, James Herbert 1841-1923 . . . . DLB-71

Morse, Jedidiah 1761-1826 . . . . DLB-37

Morse, John T., Jr. 1840-1937 . . . . DLB-47

Morselli, Guido 1912-1973 . . . . DLB-177

Morte Arthure, the *Alliterative* and the
    Stanzaic circa 1350-1400 . . . . DLB-146

Mortimer, Favell Lee 1802-1878 . . . . DLB-163

Mortimer, John
    1923- DLB-13, 245, 271; CDBLB-8

Morton, Carlos 1942- DLB-122

Morton, H. V. 1892-1979 . . . . DLB-195

John P. Morton and Company DLB-49

Morton, Nathaniel 1613-1685 . . . . DLB-24

Morton, Sarah Wentworth 1759-1846 . . . . DLB-37

Morton, Thomas circa 1579-circa 1647 . . . . DLB-24

Moscherosch, Johann Michael
    1601-1669 . . . . DLB-164

Humphrey Moseley
    [publishing house] DLB-170

Möser, Justus 1720-1794 . . . . DLB-97

Moses, Daniel David 1952- DLB-334

Mosley, Nicholas 1923- DLB-14, 207

Mosley, Walter 1952- DLB-306

Moss, Arthur 1889-1969 . . . . DLB-4

Moss, Howard 1922-1987 . . . . DLB-5

Moss, Thylias 1954- DLB-120

Motion, Andrew 1952- DLB-40

Motley, John Lothrop
    1814-1877 . . . . DLB-1, 30, 59, 235

Motley, Willard 1909-1965 . . . . DLB-76, 143

Mott, Lucretia 1793-1880 . . . . DLB-239

Benjamin Motte Jr.
    [publishing house] DLB-154

Motteux, Peter Anthony 1663-1718 . . . . . . DLB-80

Mottram, R. H. 1883-1971 . . . . DLB-36

Mount, Ferdinand 1939- DLB-231

Mouré, Erin 1955- DLB-60

Mourning Dove (Humishuma) between
    1882 and 1888?-1936 . . . . DLB-175, 221

Movies
    Fiction into Film, 1928-1975: A List
      of Movies Based on the Works
      of Authors in British Novelists,
      1930-1959 . . . . DLB-15

    Movies from Books, 1920-1974 . . . . DLB-9

Mowat, Farley 1921- DLB-68

A. R. Mowbray and Company,
    Limited DLB-106

Mowrer, Edgar Ansel 1892-1977 . . . . DLB-29

Mowrer, Paul Scott 1887-1971 . . . . DLB-29

Edward Moxon [publishing house] DLB-106

Joseph Moxon [publishing house] DLB-170

Moyes, Patricia 1923-2000 . . . . DLB-276

Mphahlele, Es'kia (Ezekiel)
    1919- DLB-125, 225; CDWLB-3

Mrożek, Sławomir 1930- . . . DLB-232; CDWLB-4

Mtshali, Oswald Mbuyiseni
    1940- DLB-125, 225

Mu Shiying 1912-1940 . . . . DLB-328

al-Mubarrad 826-898 or 899 . . . . DLB-311

Mucedorus DLB-62

Mudford, William 1782-1848 . . . . DLB-159

Mudrooroo (see Johnson, Colin)

Mueller, Lisel 1924- DLB-105

Muhajir, El (see Marvin X)

Muhajir, Nazzam Al Fitnah (see Marvin X)

Muhammad the Prophet circa 570-632 . . . DLB-311

Mühlbach, Luise 1814-1873 . . . . DLB-133

Muir, Edwin 1887-1959 . . . . DLB-20, 100, 191

Muir, Helen 1937- DLB-14

Muir, John 1838-1914 . . . . DLB-186, 275

Muir, Percy 1894-1979 . . . . DLB-201

Mujū Ichien 1226-1312 . . . . DLB-203

Mukherjee, Bharati 1940- DLB-60, 218, 323

Mulcaster, Richard 1531 or 1532-1611 . . . DLB-167

Muldoon, Paul 1951- DLB-40

Mulisch, Harry 1927- DLB-299

Mulkerns, Val 1925- DLB-319

Müller, Friedrich (see Müller, Maler)

Müller, Heiner 1929-1995 . . . . DLB-124

Müller, Maler 1749-1825 . . . . DLB-94

Muller, Marcia 1944- DLB-226

Müller, Wilhelm 1794-1827 . . . . DLB-90

Mumford, Lewis 1895-1990 . . . . DLB-63

Munby, A. N. L. 1913-1974 . . . . DLB-201

Munby, Arthur Joseph 1828-1910 . . . . DLB-35

Munday, Anthony 1560-1633 . . . . DLB-62, 172

Mundt, Clara (see Mühlbach, Luise)

Mundt, Theodore 1808-1861 . . . . DLB-133

Munford, Robert circa 1737-1783 . . . . DLB-31

Mungoshi, Charles 1947- DLB-157

Munk, Kaj 1898-1944 . . . . DLB-214

Munonye, John 1929- DLB-117

Muñoz Molina, Antonio 1956- DLB-322

Munro, Alice 1931- DLB-53

George Munro [publishing house] DLB-49

Munro, H. H.
    1870-1916 . . . . DLB-34, 162; CDBLB-5

Munro, Neil 1864-1930 . . . . DLB-156

Norman L. Munro [publishing house] DLB-49

Munroe, Kirk 1850-1930 . . . . DLB-42

Munroe and Francis DLB-49

James Munroe and Company DLB-49

Joel Munsell [publishing house] DLB-49

Munsey, Frank A. 1854-1925 . . . . DLB-25, 91

Frank A. Munsey and Company DLB-49

Mura, David 1952- DLB-312

Murakami Haruki 1949- DLB-182

Muratov, Pavel 1881-1950 . . . . DLB-317

Murayama, Milton 1923- DLB-312

Murav'ev, Mikhail Nikitich 1757-1807 . . . DLB-150

Murdoch, Iris 1919-1999
    . . . . DLB-14, 194, 233, 326; CDBLB-8

Murdock, James
    From *Sketches of Modern Philosophy* DS-5

Murdoch, Rupert 1931- DLB-127

Murfree, Mary N. 1850-1922 . . . . DLB-12, 74

Murger, Henry 1822-1861 . . . . DLB-119

Murger, Louis-Henri (see Murger, Henry)

Murnane, Gerald 1939- DLB-289

Murner, Thomas 1475-1537 . . . . DLB-179

Muro, Amado 1915-1971 . . . . DLB-82

Murphy, Arthur 1727-1805..........DLB-89, 142
Murphy, Beatrice M. 1908-1992.........DLB-76
Murphy, Dervla 1931- DLB-204
Murphy, Emily 1868-1933..............DLB-99
Murphy, Jack 1923-1980 ....DLB-241
John Murphy and Company DLB-49
Murphy, John H., III 1916- DLB-127
Murphy, Richard 1927-1993 ....DLB-40
Murphy, Tom 1935- DLB-310
Murray, Albert L. 1916- DLB-38
Murray, Gilbert 1866-1957 ....DLB-10
Murray, Jim 1919-1998 ....DLB-241
John Murray [publishing house] DLB-154
Murray, Judith Sargent
  1751-1820 ....DLB-37, 200
Murray, Les 1938- DLB-289
Murray, Pauli 1910-1985 ....DLB-41
Murry, John Middleton 1889-1957 ......DLB-149
  "The Break-Up of the Novel"
    (1922).....................DLB-36
Murry, John Middleton, Jr. (see Cowper, Richard)
Musäus, Johann Karl August
  1735-1787....................DLB-97
Muschg, Adolf 1934- DLB-75
Musil, Robert
  1880-1942........DLB-81, 124; CDWLB-2
Muspilli circa 790-circa 850 ....DLB-148
Musset, Alfred de 1810-1857 ....DLB-192, 217
Benjamin B. Mussey
  and Company DLB-49
Muste, A. J. 1885-1967.................DLB-303
Mutafchieva, Vera 1929- DLB-181
Mutis, Alvaro 1923- DLB-283
Mwangi, Meja 1948- DLB-125
Myers, Frederic W. H.
  1843-1901 ....DLB-190
Myers, Gustavus 1872-1942 ....DLB-47
Myers, L. H. 1881-1944................DLB-15
Myers, Walter Dean 1937- DLB-33
Myerson, Julie 1960- DLB-267
Mykle, Agnar 1915-1994 ....DLB-297
Mykolaitis-Putinas,
  Vincas 1893-1967 ....DLB-220
Myles, Eileen 1949- DLB-193
Myrdal, Jan 1927- DLB-257
Mystery
  1985: The Year of the Mystery:
    A Symposium..................Y-85
  Comments from Other Writers.........Y-85
  The Second Annual New York Festival
    of Mystery Y-00
  Why I Read Mysteries Y-85
  Why I Write Mysteries: Night and Day,
    by Michael Collins Y-85

N

Na Prous Boneta circa 1296-1328 ....DLB-208
Nabl, Franz 1883-1974................DLB-81
Nabokov, Véra 1902-1991 ....Y-91
Nabokov, Vladimir 1899-1977 ...... DLB-2, 244,
  278, 317; Y-80, 91; DS-3; CDALB-1
  International Nabokov Society Y-99
  An Interview [On Nabokov], by
    Fredson Bowers Y-80
  Nabokov Festival at Cornell Y-83
  The Vladimir Nabokov Archive in the
    Berg Collection of the New York
    Public Library: An Overview........Y-91
  The Vladimir Nabokov Society Y-01
Nádaši, Ladislav (see Jégé)
Naden, Constance 1858-1889 ....DLB-199
Nadezhdin, Nikolai Ivanovich
  1804-1856 ....DLB-198
Nadir, Moshe (Moyshe Nadir; Isaac Reis [Yitskhok
  Reyz]) 1885-1943 ....DLB-333
Nadson, Semen Iakovlevich 1862-1887 ...DLB-277
Naevius circa 265 B.C.-201 B.C..........DLB-211
Nafis and Cornish DLB-49
Nagai Kafū 1879-1959 ....DLB-180
Nagel, Ernest 1901-1985 ....DLB-279
Nagibin, Iurii Markovich 1920-1994.....DLB-302
Nagrodskaia, Evdokiia Apollonovna
  1866-1930 ....DLB-295
Nahman of Bratslav (Nakhmen Bratslaver)
  1772-1810 ....DLB-333
Naidus, Leib (Leyb Naydus)
  1890-1918 ....DLB-333
Naipaul, Shiva 1945-1985 .... DLB-157; Y-85
Naipaul, V. S. 1932-
  ....DLB-125, 204, 207, 326, 331;
       Y-85, 01; CDBLB-8; CDWLB-3
  Nobel Lecture 2001: "Two Worlds" Y-01
Nakagami Kenji 1946-1992 ....DLB-182
Nakano-in Masatada no Musume (see Nijō, Lady)
Nałkowska, Zofia 1884-1954...........DLB-215
Namora, Fernando 1919-1989..........DLB-287
Joseph Nancrede [publishing house] DLB-49
Naranjo, Carmen 1930- DLB-145
Narayan, R. K. 1906-2001 ....DLB-323
Narbikova, Valeriia Spartakovna
  1958- DLB-285
Narezhny, Vasilii Trofimovich
  1780-1825 ....DLB-198
Narrache, Jean (Emile Coderre)
  1893-1970 ....DLB-92
Nasby, Petroleum Vesuvius (see Locke, David Ross)
Eveleigh Nash [publishing house] DLB-112
Nash, Ogden 1902-1971................DLB-11
Nashe, Thomas 1567-1601?...........DLB-167
Nason, Jerry 1910-1986 ....DLB-241
Nasr, Seyyed Hossein 1933- DLB-279

Nast, Condé 1873-1942 ....DLB-91
Nast, Thomas 1840-1902..............DLB-188
Nastasijević, Momčilo 1894-1938 ....DLB-147
Nathan, George Jean 1882-1958 ....DLB-137
Nathan, Robert 1894-1985 ....DLB-9
Nation, Carry A. 1846-1911 ....DLB-303
National Book Critics Circle Awards......Y-00–01
The National Jewish Book Awards Y-85
Natsume Sōseki 1867-1916 ....DLB-180
Naughton, Bill 1910-1992 ....DLB-13
Nava, Michael 1954- DLB-306
Navarro, Joe 1953- DLB-209
Naylor, Gloria 1950- DLB-173
Nazor, Vladimir 1876-1949 ....DLB-147
Ndebele, Njabulo 1948- DLB-157, 225
Neagoe, Peter 1881-1960.................DLB-4
Neal, John 1793-1876..........DLB-1, 59, 243
Neal, Joseph C. 1807-1847 ....DLB-11
Neal, Larry 1937-1981 ....DLB-38
The Neale Publishing Company DLB-49
Nearing, Scott 1883-1983...............DLB-303
Nebel, Frederick 1903-1967.............DLB-226
Nebrija, Antonio de 1442 or 1444-1522 ..DLB-286
Nedreaas, Torborg 1906-1987 ....DLB-297
F. Tennyson Neely [publishing house]......DLB-49
Negoițescu, Ion 1921-1993 ....DLB-220
Negri, Ada 1870-1945 ....DLB-114
Nehru, Pandit Jawaharlal 1889-1964.....DLB-323
Neihardt, John G. 1881-1973.......DLB-9, 54, 256
Neidhart von Reuental
  circa 1185-circa 1240 ....DLB-138
Neilson, John Shaw 1872-1942 ....DLB-230
Nekrasov, Nikolai Alekseevich
  1821-1877 ....DLB-277
Nekrasov, Viktor Platonovich
  1911-1987 ....DLB-302
Neledinsky-Meletsky, Iurii Aleksandrovich
  1752-1828 ....DLB-150
Nelligan, Emile 1879-1941..............DLB-92
Nelson, Alice Moore Dunbar 1875-1935 ...DLB-50
Nelson, Antonya 1961- DLB-244
Nelson, Kent 1943- DLB-234
Nelson, Richard K. 1941- DLB-275
Nelson, Thomas, and Sons [U.K.].......DLB-106
Nelson, Thomas, and Sons [U.S.]........DLB-49
Nelson, William 1908-1978 ....DLB-103
Nelson, William Rockhill 1841-1915......DLB-23
Nemerov, Howard 1920-1991 ..... DLB-5, 6; Y-83
Németh, László 1901-1975 ....DLB-215
Nepos circa 100 B.C.-post 27 B.C...........DLB-211
Nėris, Salomėja 1904-1945 ..DLB-220; CDWLB-4

Cumulative Index

Neruda, Pablo 1904-1973 .... DLB-283, 331

Nerval, Gérard de 1808-1855.......... DLB-217

Nervo, Amado 1870-1919............. DLB-290

Nesbit, E. 1858-1924 ....DLB-141, 153, 178

Ness, Evaline 1911-1986............... DLB-61

Nestroy, Johann 1801-1862............ DLB-133

Nettleship, R. L. 1846-1892............ DLB-262

Neugeboren, Jay 1938- DLB-28, 335

Neukirch, Benjamin 1655-1729......... DLB-168

Neumann, Alfred 1895-1952 .... DLB-56

Neumann, Ferenc (see Molnár, Ferenc)

Neumark, Georg 1621-1681............ DLB-164

Neumeister, Erdmann 1671-1756....... DLB-168

Nevins, Allan 1890-1971..........DLB-17; DS-17

Nevinson, Henry Woodd 1856-1941 .... DLB-135

The New American Library............ DLB-46

New Directions Publishing Corporation... DLB-46

The New Monthly Magazine 1814-1884..... DLB-110

New York Times Book Review Y-82

John Newbery [publishing house]....... DLB-154

Newbolt, Henry 1862-1938 .... DLB-19

Newbound, Bernard Slade (see Slade, Bernard)

Newby, Eric 1919- DLB-204

Newby, P. H. 1918-1997 .... DLB-15, 326

Thomas Cautley Newby
  [publishing house] DLB-106

Newcomb, Charles King 1820-1894... DLB-1, 223

Newell, Peter 1862-1924............... DLB-42

Newell, Robert Henry 1836-1901........ DLB-11

Newhouse, Edward 1911-2002......... DLB-335

Newhouse, Samuel I. 1895-1979......... DLB-127

Newman, Cecil Earl 1903-1976 .... DLB-127

Newman, David 1937- DLB-44

Newman, Frances 1883-1928 .... Y-80

Newman, Francis William 1805-1897.... DLB-190

Newman, G. F. 1946- DLB-310

Newman, John Henry
  1801-1890 .... DLB-18, 32, 55

Mark Newman [publishing house] DLB-49

Newmarch, Rosa Harriet 1857-1940..... DLB-240

George Newnes Limited................ DLB-112

Newsome, Effie Lee 1885-1979.......... DLB-76

Newton, A. Edward 1864-1940 .... DLB-140

Newton, Sir Isaac 1642-1727........... DLB-252

Nexø, Martin Andersen 1869-1954 ..... DLB-214

Nezval, Vítěslav
  1900-1958............ DLB-215; CDWLB-4

Ngugi wa Thiong'o
  1938- DLB-125; CDWLB-3

Niatum, Duane 1938- DLB-175

The *Nibelungenlied* and the *Klage*
  circa 1200..................... DLB-138

Nichol, B. P. 1944-1988 .... DLB-53

Nicholas of Cusa 1401-1464.......... DLB-115

Nichols, Ann 1891?-1966 .... DLB-249

Nichols, Beverly 1898-1983 .... DLB-191

Nichols, Dudley 1895-1960 .... DLB-26

Nichols, Grace 1950- DLB-157

Nichols, John 1940- Y-82

Nichols, Mary Sargeant (Neal) Gove
  1810-1884 .... DLB-1, 243

Nichols, Peter 1927- DLB-13, 245

Nichols, Roy F. 1896-1973 .... DLB-17

Nichols, Ruth 1948- DLB-60

Nicholson, Edward Williams Byron
  1849-1912 .... DLB-184

Nicholson, Geoff 1953- DLB-271

Nicholson, Norman 1914-1987......... DLB-27

Nicholson, William 1872-1949 .... DLB-141

Ní Chuilleanáin, Eiléan 1942- DLB-40

Nicol, Eric 1919- DLB-68

Nicolai, Friedrich 1733-1811........... DLB-97

Nicolas de Clamanges circa 1363-1437... DLB-208

Nicolay, John G. 1832-1901 and
  Hay, John 1838-1905 .... DLB-47

Nicole, Pierre 1625-1695 .... DLB-268

Nicolson, Adela Florence Cory (see Hope, Laurence)

Nicolson, Harold 1886-1968........DLB-100, 149

"The Practice of Biography," in
  *The English Sense of Humour and
  Other Essays*................... DLB-149

Nicolson, Nigel 1917-2004 .... DLB-155

Ní Dhuibhne, Éilís 1954- DLB-319

Niebuhr, Reinhold 1892-1971......DLB-17; DS-17

Niedecker, Lorine 1903-1970 .... DLB-48

Nieman, Lucius W. 1857-1935 .... DLB-25

Nietzsche, Friedrich
  1844-1900 .... DLB-129; CDWLB-2

Mencken and Nietzsche: An Unpublished
  Excerpt from H. L. Mencken's *My Life
  as Author and Editor*................ Y-93

Nievo, Stanislao 1928- DLB-196

Niggli, Josefina 1910-1983 .... Y-80

Nightingale, Florence 1820-1910 .... DLB-166

Nijō, Lady (Nakano-in Masatada no Musume)
  1258-after 1306 .... DLB-203

Nijō Yoshimoto 1320-1388 .... DLB-203

Nikitin, Ivan Savvich 1824-1861........DLB-277

Nikitin, Nikolai Nikolaevich 1895-1963...DLB-272

Nikolev, Nikolai Petrovich 1758-1815.... DLB-150

Niles, Hezekiah 1777-1839 .... DLB-43

Nims, John Frederick 1913-1999 .... DLB-5

  Tribute to Nancy Hale Y-88

Nin, Anaïs 1903-1977 .... DLB-2, 4, 152

Nína Björk Árnadóttir 1941-2000...... DLB-293

Niño, Raúl 1961- DLB-209

Nissenson, Hugh 1933- DLB-28, 335

Der Nister (Pinchas Kahanovitch [Pinkhes
  Kahanovitsh]) 1884-1950.......... DLB-333

Niven, Frederick John 1878-1944 .... DLB-92

Niven, Larry 1938- DLB-8

Nixon, Howard M. 1909-1983......... DLB-201

Nizan, Paul 1905-1940 .... DLB-72

Njegoš, Petar II Petrović
  1813-1851 ....DLB-147; CDWLB-4

Nkosi, Lewis 1936- DLB-157, 225

Noah, Mordecai M. 1785-1851......... DLB-250

Noailles, Anna de 1876-1933 .... DLB-258

Nobel Peace Prize
  The Nobel Prize and Literary Politics Y-88
  Elie Wiesel........................ Y-86

Nobel Prize in Literature
  Shmuel Yosef Agnon DLB-329
  Vicente Aleixandre............ DLB-108, 329
  Ivo Andrić DLB-147, 329; CDWLB-4
  Miguel Ángel Asturias DLB-113, 290,
      329; CDWLB-3
  Samuel Beckett........ DLB-13, 15, 233, 319,
      321, 329; Y-90; CDBLB-7
  Saul Bellow DLB-2, 28, 299, 329;
      Y-82; DS-3; CDALB-1
  Jacinto Benavente................ DLB-329
  Henri Bergson DLB-329
  Bjørnstjerne Bjørnson............ DLB-329
  Heinrich Böll ...DLB-69, 329; Y-85; CDWLB-2
  Joseph Brodsky DLB-285, 329; Y-87
  Pearl S. Buck DLB-9, 102, 329; CDALB-7
  Ivan Bunin DLB-317, 329
  Albert Camus............DLB-72, 321, 329
  Elias Canetti....DLB-85, 124, 329; CDWLB-2
  Giosuè Carducci DLB-329
  Camilo José Cela DLB-322, 329; Y-89
  Sir Winston Churchill DLB-100, 329;
      DS-16; CDBLB-5
  J. M. Coetzee DLB-225, 326, 329
  Grazia Deledda DLB-264, 329
  Jose Echegaray DLB-329
  T. S. Eliot....... DLB-7, 10, 45, 63, 245, 329;
      Y-88, 99; CDALB-5
  Odysseus Elytis DLB-329
  Rudolf Eucken................... DLB-329
  William Faulkner DLB-9, 11, 44, 102, 316,
      330; DS-2; Y-86; CDALB-5
  Dario Fo..................DLB-330; Y-97
  Anatole France DLB-123, 330
  John Galsworthy DLB-10, 34, 98, 162,
      330; DS-16; CDBLB-5
  Gao Xingjian DLB-330; Y-00
  Gabriel García Márquez............DLB-13,
      330; Y-82; CDWLB-3
  André Gide DLB-65, 321, 330
  Karl Gjellerup DLB-300, 330
  William Golding DLB-15, 100, 255,

326, 330; Y-83; CDBLB-7
Nadine Gordimer DLB-225, 326, 330; Y-91
Günter Grass....... DLB-75, 124, 330; Y-99
Halldór Laxness DLB-293, 331
Knut Hamsun DLB-297, 330
Gerhart Hauptmann DLB-66, 118, 330; CDWLB-2
Seamus Heaney..........DLB-40, 330; Y-95; CDBLB-8
Verner von Heidenstam DLB-330
Ernest Hemingway DLB-4, 9, 102, 210, 316, 330; Y-81, 87, 99; DS-1, 15, 16; CDALB-4
Hermann Hesse.....DLB-66, 330; CDWLB-2
Paul Heyse DLB-129, 330
Elfriede Jelinek DLB-85, 330
Johannes V. Jensen DLB-214, 330
Juan Ramón Jiménez..........DLB-134, 330
Eyvind Johnson..............DLB-259, 330
Erik Axel Karlfeldt DLB-330
Yasunari Kawabata DLB-180, 330
Imre Kertész DLB-299, 330; Y-02
Rudyard Kipling DLB-19, 34, 141, 156, 330; CDBLB-5
Pär Lagerkvist................DLB-259, 331
Selma Lagerlöf................DLB-259, 331
Sinclair Lewis
....DLB-9, 102, 331; DS-1; CDALB-4
Maurice Maeterlinck..........DLB-192, 331
Najīb Mahfūz Y-88, 331; Y-88
Thomas Mann DLB-66, 331; CDWLB-2
Roger Martin du Gard DLB-65, 331
Harry Martinson DLB-259, 331
François Mauriac..........DLB-65, 331
Czesław Miłosz DLB-215, 331; CDWLB-4
Frédéric Mistral.......... DLB-215, 331; D
Gabriela Mistral DLB-283, 331
Theodor Mommsen DLB-331
Eugenio Montale..........DLB-114, 331
Toni Morrison
..DLB-6, 33, 143, 331; Y-81, 93; CDALB-6
V. S. Naipaul
.... DLB-125, 204, 207, 326, 331; Y-85, 01; CDBLB-8; CDWLB-3
Pablo Neruda DLB-283, 331
Kenzaburō Ōe.......... DLB-182, 331; Y-94
Eugene O'Neill DLB-7, 331; CDALB-5
Boris Pasternak DLB-302, 331
Octavio Paz DLB-290, 331; Y-90, 98
Saint-John Perse..............DLB-258, 331
Harold Pinter ...DLB-13, 310, 331; CDBLB-8
Luigi Pirandello..............DLB-264, 331
Henrik Pontoppidan DLB-300, 331
Salvatore Quasimodo DLB-114, 332
Władysław Stanisław Reymont DLB-332
Romain Rolland DLB-65, 332

Bertrand Russell DLB-100, 262, 332
Nelly Sachs DLB-332
José Saramago DLB-287, 332; Y-98
Jean-Paul Sartre DLB-72, 296, 321, 332
George Seferis DLB-332
Jaroslav Seifert
.... DLB-215, 332; Y-84; CDBLB-4
George Bernard Shaw
.... DLB-10, 57, 190, 332; CDBLB-6
Mikhail Aleksandrovich Sholokov
.... DLB-272, 332
Henryk Sienkiewicz..............DLB-332
Frans Eemil Sillanpää DLB-332
Claude Simon DLB-83, 332; Y-85
Isaac Bashevis Singer
...DLB-6, 28, 52, 278, 332; Y-91; CDALB-1
Aleksandr Solzhenitsyn........DLB-302, 332
Wole Soyinka
..... DLB-125, 332; Y-86, 87; CDWLB-3
Carl Spitteler DLB-129, 332
John Steinbeck
...... DLB-7, 9, 212, 275, 309, 332; DS-2; CDALB-5
Sully Prudhomme DLB-332
Wisława Szymborska DLB-232, 332; Y-96; CDWLB-4
Rabindranath Tagore DLB-323, 332
Sigrid Undset DLB-297, 332
Derek Walcott
......DLB-117, 332; Y-81, 92; CDWLB-3
Patrick White DLB-260, 332
William Butler Yeats
..... DLB-10, 19, 98, 156, 332; CDBLB-5
Nobre, António 1867-1900.............DLB-287
Nodier, Charles 1780-1844............DLB-119
Noël, Marie (Marie Mélanie Rouget) 1883-1967 ....DLB-258
Noel, Roden 1834-1894................DLB-35
Nogami Yaeko 1885-1985 ....DLB-180
Nogo, Rajko Petrov 1945- DLB-181
Nolan, William F. 1928- DLB-8
Tribute to Raymond Chandler Y-88
Noland, C. F. M. 1810?-1858 ....DLB-11
Noma Hiroshi 1915-1991 ....DLB-182
Nonesuch Press DLB-112
Creative Nonfiction Y-02
Nonni (Jón Stefán Sveinsson or Svensson) 1857-1944 ....DLB-293
Noon, Jeff 1957- DLB-267
Noonan, Robert Phillipe (see Tressell, Robert)
Noonday Press....................DLB-46
Noone, John 1936- DLB-14
Nora, Eugenio de 1923- DLB-134
Nordan, Lewis 1939- DLB-234
Nordbrandt, Henrik 1945- DLB-214
Nordhoff, Charles 1887-1947 ....DLB-9

Norén, Lars 1944- DLB-257
Norfolk, Lawrence 1963- DLB-267
Norman, Charles 1904-1996...........DLB-111
Norman, Marsha 1947- DLB-266; Y-84
Norris, Charles G. 1881-1945 ....DLB-9
Norris, Frank
1870-1902 ....DLB-12, 71, 186; CDALB-3
Norris, Helen 1916- DLB-292
Norris, John 1657-1712................DLB-252
Norris, Leslie 1921- DLB-27, 256
Norse, Harold 1916- DLB-16
Norte, Marisela 1955- DLB-209
North, Marianne 1830-1890 ....DLB-174
North, Roger 1651-1734...............DLB-336
North Point Press....................DLB-46
Nortje, Arthur 1942-1970..........DLB-125, 225
Norton, Alice Mary (see Norton, Andre)
Norton, Andre 1912-2005 ....DLB-8, 52
Norton, Andrews 1786-1853 ....DLB-1, 235; DS-5
Norton, Caroline
1808-1877 ....DLB-21, 159, 199
Norton, Charles Eliot
1827-1908 ....DLB-1, 64, 235
Norton, John 1606-1663 ....DLB-24
Norton, Mary 1903-1992...............DLB-160
Norton, Thomas 1532-1584 ....DLB-62
W. W. Norton and Company DLB-46
Norwood, Robert 1874-1932 ....DLB-92
Nosaka Akiyuki 1930- DLB-182
Nossack, Hans Erich 1901-1977 ....DLB-69
Notker Balbulus circa 840-912..........DLB-148
Notker III of Saint Gall
circa 950-1022 ....DLB-148
Notker von Zweifalten ?-1095 ....DLB-148
Nourse, Alan E. 1928-1992 ....DLB-8
Novak, Slobodan 1924- DLB-181
Novak, Vjenceslav 1859-1905 ....DLB-147
Novakovich, Josip 1956- DLB-244
Novalis 1772-1801 .... DLB-90; CDWLB-2
Novaro, Mario 1868-1944...............DLB-114
Novás Calvo, Lino 1903-1983..........DLB-145
Novelists
Library Journal Statements and
Questionnaires from First Novelists Y-87
Novels
The Columbia History of the American Novel
A Symposium on Y-92
The Great Modern Library Scam........Y-98
Novels for Grown-Ups Y-97
The Proletarian Novel................DLB-9
Novel, The "Second-Generation" Holocaust
..............................DLB-299
The Year in the Novel...... Y-87–88, Y-90–93
Novels, British

Cumulative Index

"The Break-Up of the Novel" (1922),
by John Middleton Murry....... DLB-36

The Consolidation of Opinion: Critical
Responses to the Modernists..... DLB-36

"Criticism in Relation to Novels"
(1863), by G. H. Lewes......... DLB-21

"Experiment in the Novel" (1929)
[excerpt], by John D. Beresford... DLB-36

"The Future of the Novel" (1899), by
Henry James................. DLB-18

The Gay Science (1866), by E. S. Dallas
[excerpt]..................... DLB-21

A Haughty and Proud Generation
(1922), by Ford Madox Hueffer.. DLB-36

Literary Effects of World War II..... DLB-15

"Modern Novelists –Great and Small"
(1855), by Margaret Oliphant.... DLB-21

The Modernists (1932),
by Joseph Warren Beach........ DLB-36

A Note on Technique (1926), by
Elizabeth A. Drew [excerpts]..... DLB-36

Novel-Reading: *The Works of Charles
Dickens; The Works of W. Makepeace
Thackeray* (1879),
by Anthony Trollope........... DLB-21

Novels with a Purpose (1864), by
Justin M'Carthy............... DLB-21

"On Art in Fiction" (1838),
by Edward Bulwer............. DLB-21

The Present State of the English Novel
(1892), by George Saintsbury.... DLB-18

Representative Men and Women:
A Historical Perspective on
the British Novel, 1930-1960..... DLB-15

"The Revolt" (1937), by Mary Colum
[excerpts].................... DLB-36

"Sensation Novels" (1863), by
H. L. Manse DLB-21

Sex, Class, Politics, and Religion [in
the British Novel, 1930-1959].... DLB-15

Time and Western Man (1927),
by Wyndham Lewis [excerpts]... DLB-36

Noventa, Giacomo
1898-1960 .... DLB-114

Novikov, Nikolai Ivanovich
1744-1818..................... DLB-150

Novomeský, Laco 1904-1976......... DLB-215

Nowlan, Alden 1933-1983 .... DLB-53

Nowra, Louis 1950- DLB-325

Noyes, Alfred 1880-1958 .... DLB-20

Noyes, Crosby S. 1825-1908........... DLB-23

Noyes, Nicholas 1647-1717 .... DLB-24

Noyes, Theodore W. 1858-1946........ DLB-29

Nozick, Robert 1938-2002 ....DLB-279

N-Town Plays circa 1468 to early
sixteenth century................ DLB-146

Nugent, Frank 1908-1965............ DLB-44

Nunez, Sigrid 1951- DLB-312

Nušić, Branislav
1864-1938 ....DLB-147; CDWLB-4

David Nutt [publishing house]........ DLB-106

Nwapa, Flora
1931-1993 .... DLB-125; CDWLB-3

Nye, Edgar Wilson (Bill)
1850-1896 .... DLB-11, 23, 186

Nye, Naomi Shihab 1952- DLB-120

Nye, Robert 1939- DLB-14, 271

Nyka-Niliūnas, Alfonsas 1919- DLB-220

O

Oakes, Urian circa 1631-1681 .... DLB-24

Oakes Smith, Elizabeth
1806-1893 .... DLB-1, 239, 243

Oakley, Violet 1874-1961 .... DLB-188

Oates, Joyce Carol 1938-
............DLB-2, 5, 130; Y-81; CDALB-6

Tribute to Michael M. Rea............ Y-97

Ōba Minako 1930- DLB-182

Ober, Frederick Albion 1849-1913 ...... DLB-189

Ober, William 1920-1993................ Y-93

Oberholtzer, Ellis Paxson 1868-1936 ..... DLB-47

The Obituary as Literary Form Y-02

Obradović, Dositej 1740?-1811......... DLB-147

O'Brien, Charlotte Grace 1845-1909 .... DLB-240

O'Brien, Edna
1932- DLB-14, 231, 319; CDBLB-8

O'Brien, Fitz-James 1828-1862 .... DLB-74

O'Brien, Flann (see O'Nolan, Brian)

O'Brien, Kate 1897-1974................ DLB-15

O'Brien, Tim
1946- DLB-152; Y-80; DS-9; CDALB-7

Ó Cadhain, Máirtín 1905-1970......... DLB-319

O'Casey, Sean 1880-1964..... DLB-10; CDBLB-6

Occom, Samson 1723-1792............DLB-175

Occomy, Marita Bonner 1899-1971 ...... DLB-51

Ochs, Adolph S. 1858-1935 .... DLB-25

Ochs-Oakes, George Washington
1861-1931 .... DLB-137

Ockley, Simon 1678-1720 .... DLB-336

O'Connor, Flannery 1925-1964
........DLB-2, 152; Y-80; DS-12; CDALB-1

The Flannery O'Connor Society Y-99

O'Connor, Frank 1903-1966 .... DLB-162

O'Connor, Joseph 1963- DLB-267

O'Conor, Charles, of Belanagare
1709/1710-1791................. DLB-336

Octopus Publishing Group........... DLB-112

Oda Sakunosuke 1913-1947 .... DLB-182

Odell, Jonathan 1737-1818 .... DLB-31, 99

O'Dell, Scott 1903-1989 .... DLB-52

Odets, Clifford 1906-1963 ....DLB-7, 26

Odhams Press Limited DLB-112

Odio, Eunice 1922-1974 .... DLB-283

Odoevsky, Aleksandr Ivanovich
1802-1839 .... DLB-205

Odoevsky, Vladimir Fedorovich
1804 or 1803-1869............... DLB-198

Odoevtseva, Irina 1895-1990 ....DLB-317

O'Donnell, Peter 1920- DLB-87

O'Donovan, Michael (see O'Connor, Frank)

O'Dowd, Bernard 1866-1953 .... DLB-230

Ōe, Kenzaburō 1935- DLB-182, 331; Y-94

Nobel Lecture 1994: Japan, the
Ambiguous, and Myself Y-94

Oehlenschläger, Adam 1779-1850...... DLB-300

O'Faolain, Julia 1932- DLB-14, 231, 319

O'Faolain, Sean 1900-1991........ DLB-15, 162

Off-Loop Theatres DLB-7

Offord, Carl Ruthven 1910-1990 .... DLB-76

Offshore, 1979 Booker Prize winner,
Penelope Fitzgerald DLB-326

Offutt, Chris 1958- DLB-335

O'Flaherty, Liam 1896-1984.... DLB-36, 162; Y-84

Ogarev, Nikolai Platonovich 1813-1877 ...DLB-277

J. S. Ogilvie and Company........... DLB-49

Ogilvy, Eliza 1822-1912 .... DLB-199

Ogot, Grace 1930- DLB-125

O'Grady, Desmond 1935- DLB-40

Ogunyemi, Wale 1939- DLB-157

O'Hagan, Howard 1902-1982 .... DLB-68

O'Halloran, Sylvester 1728-1807 .... DLB-336

O'Hara, Frank 1926-1966 ....DLB-5, 16, 193

O'Hara, John
1905-1970... DLB-9, 86, 324; DS-2; CDALB-5

John O'Hara's Pottsville Journalism...... Y-88

O'Hare, Kate Richards 1876-1948 ...... DLB-303

O'Hegarty, P. S. 1879-1955........... DLB-201

Ohio State University
The William Charvat American Fiction
Collection at the Ohio State
University Libraries Y-92

Okada, John 1923-1971 .... DLB-312

Okara, Gabriel 1921- DLB-125; CDWLB-3

O'Keeffe, John 1747-1833 .... DLB-89

Nicholas Okes [publishing house].......DLB-170

Okigbo, Christopher
1930-1967 ....DLB-125; CDWLB-3

Okot p'Bitek 1931-1982 .....DLB-125; CDWLB-3

Okpewho, Isidore 1941- DLB-157

Okri, Ben 1959- DLB-157, 231, 319, 326

Ólafur Jóhann Sigurðsson 1918-1988.... DLB-293

The Old Devils, 1986 Booker Prize winner,
Kingsley Amis DLB-326

Old Dogs / New Tricks? New Technologies,
the Canon, and the Structure of
the Profession.................... Y-02

Old Franklin Publishing House DLB-49

Old German Genesis and *Old German Exodus*
circa 1050-circa 1130 .... DLB-148

The *Old High German Isidor*
  circa 790-800 .... DLB-148

Older, Fremont 1856-1935 .... DLB-25

Oldham, John 1653-1683 .... DLB-131

Oldman, C. B. 1894-1969 .... DLB-201

Oldmixon, John 1673?-1742 .... DLB-336

Olds, Sharon 1942- DLB-120

Olearius, Adam 1599-1671 .... DLB-164

O'Leary, Ellen 1831-1889 .... DLB-240

O'Leary, Juan E. 1879-1969 .... DLB-290

Olesha, Iurii Karlovich 1899-1960 ... DLB-272

Oliphant, Laurence 1829?-1888 .... DLB-18, 166

Oliphant, Margaret 1828-1897 .... DLB-18, 159, 190

  "Modern Novelists–Great and Small"
  (1855) DLB-21

Oliveira, Carlos de 1921-1981 .... DLB-287

Oliver, Chad 1928-1993 .... DLB-8

Oliver, Mary 1935- DLB-5, 193

Ollier, Claude 1922- DLB-83

Olsen, Tillie 1912/1913-2007
  .... DLB-28, 206; Y-80; CDALB-7

Olson, Charles 1910-1970 .... DLB-5, 16, 193

Olson, Elder 1909-1992 .... DLB-48, 63

Olson, Sigurd F. 1899-1982 .... DLB-275

The Omega Workshops DS-10

Omotoso, Kole 1943- DLB-125

Omulevsky, Innokentii Vasil'evich
  1836 [or 1837]-1883 .... DLB-238

Ondaatje, Michael 1943- DLB-60, 323, 326

O'Neill, Eugene
  1888-1953 .... DLB-7, 331; CDALB-5

  Eugene O'Neill Memorial Theater
  Center DLB-7

  Eugene O'Neill's Letters: A Review ... Y-88

Onetti, Juan Carlos
  1909-1994 .... DLB-113; CDWLB-3

Onions, George Oliver 1872-1961 ..... DLB-153

Onofri, Arturo 1885-1928 .... DLB-114

O'Nolan, Brian 1911-1966 .... DLB-231

Oodgeroo of the Tribe Noonuccal
  (Kath Walker) 1920-1993 .... DLB-289

Opie, Amelia 1769-1853 .... DLB-116, 159

Opitz, Martin 1597-1639 .... DLB-164

Oppen, George 1908-1984 .... DLB-5, 165

Oppenheim, E. Phillips 1866-1946 .... DLB-70

Oppenheim, James 1882-1932 .... DLB-28

Oppenheimer, Joel 1930-1988 .... DLB-5, 193

Optic, Oliver (see Adams, William Taylor)

Orczy, Emma, Baroness 1865-1947 ..... DLB-70

Oregon Shakespeare Festival Y-00

Origo, Iris 1902-1988 .... DLB-155

O'Riordan, Kate 1960- DLB-267

Orlovitz, Gil 1918-1973 .... DLB-2, 5

Orlovsky, Peter 1933- DLB-16

Ormond, John 1923- DLB-27

Ornitz, Samuel 1890-1957 .... DLB-28, 44

O'Rourke, P. J. 1947- DLB-185

Orozco, Olga 1920-1999 .... DLB-283

Orten, Jiří 1919-1941 .... DLB-215

Ortese, Anna Maria 1914- DLB-177

Ortiz, Lourdes 1943- DLB-322

Ortiz, Simon J. 1941- DLB-120, 175, 256

Ortnit and *Wolfdietrich* circa 1225-1250 ..... DLB-138

Orton, Joe 1933-1967 .... DLB-13, 310; CDBLB-8

Orwell, George (Eric Arthur Blair)
  1903-1950 .... DLB-15, 98, 195, 255; CDBLB-7

  The Orwell Year Y-84

  (Re-)Publishing Orwell Y-86

Ory, Carlos Edmundo de 1923- DLB-134

Osbey, Brenda Marie 1957- DLB-120

Osbon, B. S. 1827-1912 .... DLB-43

Osborn, Sarah 1714-1796 .... DLB-200

Osborne, John 1929-1994 .... DLB-13; CDBLB-7

Oscar and Lucinda, 1988 Booker Prize winner,
  Peter Carey DLB-326

Osgood, Frances Sargent 1811-1850 ... DLB-250

Osgood, Herbert L. 1855-1918 .... DLB-47

James R. Osgood and Company DLB-49

Osgood, McIlvaine and Company DLB-112

O'Shaughnessy, Arthur 1844-1881 ..... DLB-35

Patrick O'Shea [publishing house] ... DLB-49

Osipov, Nikolai Petrovich
  1751-1799 .... DLB-150

Oskison, John Milton 1879-1947 ...... DLB-175

Osler, Sir William 1849-1919 .... DLB-184

Osofisan, Femi 1946- DLB-125; CDWLB-3

Ostenso, Martha 1900-1963 .... DLB-92

Ostrauskas, Kostas 1926- DLB-232

Ostriker, Alicia 1937- DLB-120

Ostrovsky, Aleksandr Nikolaevich
  1823-1886 .... DLB-277

Ostrovsky, Nikolai Alekseevich
  1904-1936 .... DLB-272

Osundare, Niyi 1947- DLB-157; CDWLB-3

Oswald, Eleazer 1755-1795 .... DLB-43

Oswald von Wolkenstein
  1376 or 1377-1445 .... DLB-179

Otero, Blas de 1916-1979 .... DLB-134

Otero, Miguel Antonio 1859-1944 ..... DLB-82

Otero, Nina 1881-1965 .... DLB-209

Otero Silva, Miguel 1908-1985 .... DLB-145

Otfried von Weißenburg
  circa 800-circa 875? DLB-148

Otis, Broaders and Company DLB-49

Otis, James (see Kaler, James Otis)

Otis, James, Jr. 1725-1783 .... DLB-31

Otsup, Nikolai 1894-1958 .... DLB-317

Ottaway, James 1911-2000 .... DLB-127

Ottendorfer, Oswald 1826-1900 .... DLB-23

Ottieri, Ottiero 1924-2002 .... DLB-177

Otto-Peters, Louise 1819-1895 .... DLB-129

Otway, Thomas 1652-1685 .... DLB-80

Ouellette, Fernand 1930- DLB-60

Ouida 1839-1908 .... DLB-18, 156

Outing Publishing Company DLB-46

Overbury, Sir Thomas
  circa 1581-1613 .... DLB-151

The Overlook Press DLB-46

Ovid 43 B.C.-A.D. 17 .... DLB-211; CDWLB-1

Oviedo, Gonzalo Fernández de
  1478-1557 .... DLB-318

Owen, Guy 1925-1981 .... DLB-5

Owen, John 1564-1622 .... DLB-121

John Owen [publishing house] DLB-49

Peter Owen Limited DLB-112

Owen, Robert 1771-1858 .... DLB-107, 158

Owen, Wilfred
  1893-1918 .... DLB-20; DS-18; CDBLB-6

  A Centenary Celebration Y-93

  The Wilfred Owen Association Y-98

The Owl and the Nightingale
  circa 1189-1199 .... DLB-146

Owsley, Frank L. 1890-1956 .... DLB-17

Oxford, Seventeenth Earl of, Edward
  de Vere 1550-1604 .... DLB-172

OyamO (Charles F. Gordon)
  1943- DLB-266

Ozerov, Vladislav Aleksandrovich
  1769-1816 .... DLB-150

Ozick, Cynthia
  1928- DLB-28, 152, 299; Y-82

  First Strauss "Livings" Awarded
  to Cynthia Ozick and
  Raymond Carver
  An Interview with Cynthia Ozick ... Y-83

  Tribute to Michael M. Rea Y-97

P

Pace, Richard 1482?-1536 .... DLB-167

Pacey, Desmond 1917-1975 .... DLB-88

Pacheco, José Emilio 1939- DLB-290

Pack, Robert 1929- DLB-5

Paddy Clarke Ha Ha Ha, 1993 Booker Prize winner,
  Roddy Doyle DLB-326

Padell Publishing Company DLB-46

Padgett, Ron 1942- DLB-5

Padilla, Ernesto Chávez 1944- DLB-122

L. C. Page and Company DLB-49

Page, Louise 1955- DLB-233

Page, P. K. 1916- DLB-68

Page, Thomas Nelson 1853-1922 ....DLB-12, 78; DS-13

Page, Walter Hines 1855-1918 .... DLB-71, 91

Paget, Francis Edward 1806-1882....... DLB-163

Paget, Violet (see Lee, Vernon)

Pagliarani, Elio 1927- DLB-128

Pagnol, Marcel 1895-1974............. DLB-321

Pain, Barry 1864-1928 ....DLB-135, 197

Pain, Philip ?-circa 1666 .... DLB-24

Paine, Robert Treat, Jr. 1773-1811 .... DLB-37

Paine, Thomas 1737-1809 .... DLB-31, 43, 73, 158; CDALB-2

Painter, George D. 1914- DLB-155

Painter, William 1540?-1594.......... DLB-136

Palazzeschi, Aldo 1885-1974....... DLB-114, 264

Palei, Marina Anatol'evna 1955- DLB-285

Palencia, Alfonso de 1424-1492 .... DLB-286

Palés Matos, Luis 1898-1959 .... DLB-290

Paley, Grace 1922- DLB-28, 218

Paley, William 1743-1805 .... DLB-252

Palfrey, John Gorham 1796-1881................. DLB-1, 30, 235

Palgrave, Francis Turner 1824-1897 ...... DLB-35

Palissy, Bernard 1510?-1590? DLB-327

Palmer, Joe H. 1904-1952.............DLB-171

Palmer, Michael 1943- DLB-169

Palmer, Nettie 1885-1964 .... DLB-260

Palmer, Vance 1885-1959 .... DLB-260

Paltock, Robert 1697-1767............. DLB-39

Paludan, Jacob 1896-1975 .... DLB-214

Paludin-Müller, Frederik 1809-1876 ..... DLB-300

Pan Books Limited DLB-112

Panaev, Ivan Ivanovich 1812-1862 ...... DLB-198

Panaeva, Avdot'ia Iakovlevna 1820-1893 .... DLB-238

Panama, Norman 1914-2003 and Frank, Melvin 1913-1988........... DLB-26

Pancake, Breece D'J 1952-1979......... DLB-130

Panduro, Leif 1923-1977............... DLB-214

Panero, Leopoldo 1909-1962 .... DLB-108

Pangborn, Edgar 1909-1976 .... DLB-8

Panizzi, Sir Anthony 1797-1879......... DLB-184

Panneton, Philippe (see Ringuet)

Panova, Vera Fedorovna 1905-1973 ..... DLB-302

Panshin, Alexei 1940- DLB-8

Pansy (see Alden, Isabella)

Pantheon Books DLB-46

Papadat-Bengescu, Hortensia 1876-1955...................... DLB-220

Papantonio, Michael 1907-1976......... DLB-187

Paperback Library DLB-46

Paperback Science Fiction............. DLB-8

Papini, Giovanni 1881-1956 .... DLB-264

Paquet, Alfons 1881-1944............. DLB-66

Paracelsus 1493-1541 ....DLB-179

Paradis, Suzanne 1936- DLB-53

Páral, Vladimír, 1932- DLB-232

Pardoe, Julia 1804-1862 .... DLB-166

Paré, Ambroise 1510 or 1517?-1590..... DLB-327

Paredes, Américo 1915-1999 .... DLB-209

Pareja Diezcanseco, Alfredo 1908-1993 .. DLB-145

Parents' Magazine Press DLB-46

Paretsky, Sara 1947- DLB-306

Parfit, Derek 1942- DLB-262

Parise, Goffredo 1929-1986 ....DLB-177

Parish, Mitchell 1900-1993 .... DLB-265

Parizeau, Alice 1930-1990............. DLB-60

Park, Ruth 1923?- DLB-260

Parke, John 1754-1789 .... DLB-31

Parker, Dan 1893-1967................ DLB-241

Parker, Dorothy 1893-1967 ...... DLB-11, 45, 86

Parker, Gilbert 1860-1932.............. DLB-99

Parker, James 1714-1770 .... DLB-43

Parker, John [publishing house] DLB-106

Parker, Matthew 1504-1575 .... DLB-213

Parker, Robert B. 1932- DLB-306

Parker, Stewart 1941-1988 .... DLB-245

Parker, Theodore 1810-1860 ... DLB-1, 235; DS-5

Parker, William Riley 1906-1968 .... DLB-103

J. H. Parker [publishing house]......... DLB-106

Parkes, Bessie Rayner (Madame Belloc) 1829-1925 .... DLB-240

Parkman, Francis 1823-1893 ....DLB-1, 30, 183, 186, 235

Parks, Gordon 1912- DLB-33

Parks, Tim 1954- DLB-231

Parks, William 1698-1750............. DLB-43

William Parks [publishing house]........ DLB-49

Parley, Peter (see Goodrich, Samuel Griswold)

Parmenides late sixth-fifth century B.C. DLB-176

Parnell, Thomas 1679-1718.............. DLB-95

Parnicki, Teodor 1908-1988 .... DLB-215

Parnok, Sofiia Iakovlevna (Parnokh) 1885-1933 .... DLB-295

Parr, Catherine 1513?-1548 .... DLB-136

Parra, Nicanor 1914- DLB-283

Parrington, Vernon L. 1871-1929 .....DLB-17, 63

Parrish, Maxfield 1870-1966........... DLB-188

Parronchi, Alessandro 1914- DLB-128

Parshchikov, Aleksei Maksimovich (Raiderman) 1954- DLB-285

Partisan Review..................... DLB-303

Parton, James 1822-1891 .... DLB-30

Parton, Sara Payson Willis 1811-1872................DLB-43, 74, 239

S. W. Partridge and Company DLB-106

Parun, Vesna 1922- DLB-181; CDWLB-4

Pascal, Blaise 1623-1662................DLB-268

Pasinetti, Pier Maria 1913- DLB-177

Tribute to Albert Erskine............. Y-93

Pasolini, Pier Paolo 1922-1975 ......DLB-128, 177

Pastan, Linda 1932- DLB-5

Pasternak, Boris 1890-1960 .... DLB-302, 331

Paston, George (Emily Morse Symonds) 1860-1936 ....DLB-149, 197

The Paston Letters 1422-1509............ DLB-146

Pastoral Novel of the Sixteenth Century, The DLB-318

Pastorius, Francis Daniel 1651-circa 1720 .... DLB-24

Patchen, Kenneth 1911-1972 .... DLB-16, 48

Pater, Walter 1839-1894 ...DLB-57, 156; CDBLB-4

Aesthetic Poetry (1873) DLB-35

"Style" (1888) [excerpt] DLB-57

Paterson, A. B. "Banjo" 1864-1941...... DLB-230

Paterson, Katherine 1932- DLB-52

Patmore, Coventry 1823-1896 .... DLB-35, 98

Paton, Alan 1903-1988...........DLB-225; DS-17

Paton, Joseph Noel 1821-1901 .... DLB-35

Paton Walsh, Jill 1937- DLB-161

Patrick, Edwin Hill ("Ted") 1901-1964....DLB-137

Patrick, John 1906-1995 .... DLB-7

Pattee, Fred Lewis 1863-1950........... DLB-71

Patterson, Alicia 1906-1963 ....DLB-127

Patterson, Eleanor Medill 1881-1948 ..... DLB-29

Patterson, Eugene 1923- DLB-127

Patterson, Joseph Medill 1879-1946 ...... DLB-29

Pattillo, Henry 1726-1801.............. DLB-37

Paul, Elliot 1891-1958 .... DLB-4; DS-15

Paul, Jean (see Richter, Johann Paul Friedrich)

Paul, Kegan, Trench, Trubner and Company Limited DLB-106

Peter Paul Book Company DLB-49

Stanley Paul and Company Limited..... DLB-112

Paulding, James Kirke 1778-1860................DLB-3, 59, 74, 250

Paulin, Tom 1949- DLB-40

Pauper, Peter, Press................... DLB-46

Paustovsky, Konstantin Georgievich 1892-1968 ....DLB-272

Pavese, Cesare 1908-1950 ....DLB-128, 177

Pavić, Milorad 1929- DLB-181; CDWLB-4

Pavlov, Konstantin 1933- DLB-181

Pavlov, Nikolai Filippovich 1803-1864 .... DLB-198

Pavlova, Karolina Karlovna 1807-1893 .... DLB-205

Pavlović, Miodrag 1928- DLB-181; CDWLB-4	Pelletier, Aimé (see Vac, Bertrand)	Perry, Matthew 1794-1858.............DLB-183
Pavlovsky, Eduardo 1933- DLB-305	Pelletier, Francine 1959- DLB-251	Perry, Sampson 1747-1823.............DLB-158
Paxton, John 1911-1985................DLB-44	Pellicer, Carlos 1897?-1977.............DLB-290	Pers, Ciro di 1599-1663................DLB-339
Payn, James 1830-1898 ....DLB-18	Pemberton, Sir Max 1863-1950..........DLB-70	Perse, Saint-John 1887-1975 ....DLB-258, 331
Payne, John 1842-1916 ....DLB-35	de la Peña, Terri 1947- DLB-209	Persius A.D. 34-A.D. 62.................DLB-211
Payne, John Howard 1791-1852.........DLB-37	Penfield, Edward 1866-1925 ....DLB-188	Perutz, Leo 1882-1957................DLB-81
Payson and Clarke.....................DLB-46	Penguin Books [U.K.] DLB-112	Pesetsky, Bette 1932- DLB-130
Paz, Octavio 1914-1998 ... DLB-290, 331; Y-90, 98	Fifty Penguin Years Y-85	Pessanha, Camilo 1867-1926............DLB-287
Nobel Lecture 1990....................Y-90	Penguin Collectors' Society............Y-98	Pessoa, Fernando 1888-1935 ....DLB-287
Pazzi, Roberto 1946- DLB-196	Penguin Books [U.S.]..................DLB-46	Pestalozzi, Johann Heinrich 1746-1827.....DLB-94
Pea, Enrico 1881-1958................DLB-264	Penn, William 1644-1718................DLB-24	Peter, Laurence J. 1919-1990 ....DLB-53
Peabody, Elizabeth Palmer 1804-1894.....................DLB-1, 223	Penn Publishing Company..............DLB-49	Peter of Spain circa 1205-1277 ....DLB-115
	Penna, Sandro 1906-1977..............DLB-114	Peterkin, Julia 1880-1961.................DLB-9
Preface to *Record of a School: Exemplifying the General Principles of Spiritual Culture*.................. DS-5	Pennell, Joseph 1857-1926 ....DLB-188	Peters, Ellis (Edith Pargeter) 1913-1995......................DLB-276
	Penner, Jonathan 1940- Y-83	
Elizabeth Palmer Peabody [publishing house] DLB-49	Pennington, Lee 1939- Y-82	Peters, Lenrie 1932- DLB-117
	Penton, Brian 1904-1951 ....DLB-260	Peters, Robert 1924- DLB-105
Peabody, Josephine Preston 1874-1922 ...DLB-249	Pepper, Stephen C. 1891-1972 ....DLB-270	"Foreword to *Ludwig of Bavaria*"......DLB-105
Peabody, Oliver William Bourn 1799-1848 ....DLB-59	Pepys, Samuel 1633-1703 ....DLB-101, 213; CDBLB-2	Petersham, Maud 1889-1971 and Petersham, Miska 1888-1960 ....DLB-22
Peace, Roger 1899-1968.................DLB-127	Percy, Thomas 1729-1811 ....DLB-104	Peterson, Charles Jacobs 1819-1887......DLB-79
Peacham, Henry 1578-1644?............DLB-151	Percy, Walker 1916-1990 .... DLB-2; Y-80, 90	Peterson, Len 1917- DLB-88
Peacham, Henry, the Elder 1547-1634 ....DLB-172, 236	Tribute to Caroline Gordon Y-81	Peterson, Levi S. 1933- DLB-206
	Percy, William 1575-1648...............DLB-172	Peterson, Louis 1922-1998...............DLB-76
Peachtree Publishers, Limited DLB-46	Perec, Georges 1936-1982 ....DLB-83, 299	Peterson, T. B., and Brothers............DLB-49
Peacock, Molly 1947- DLB-120	Perelman, Bob 1947- DLB-193	Petitclair, Pierre 1813-1860................DLB-99
Peacock, Thomas Love 1785-1866.....DLB-96, 116	Perelman, S. J. 1904-1979...........DLB-11, 44	Petrescu, Camil 1894-1957.............DLB-220
Pead, Deuel ?-1727.....................DLB-24	Peretz, Isaac Leib (Yitskhok Leybush Perets) 1852-1915 ....DLB-333	Petronius circa A.D. 20-A.D. 66 ....DLB-211; CDWLB-1
Peake, Mervyn 1911-1968......DLB-15, 160, 255		
Peale, Rembrandt 1778-1860 ....DLB-183	Perez, Raymundo "Tigre" 1946- DLB-122	Petrov, Aleksandar 1938- DLB-181
Pear Tree Press.....................DLB-112	Pérez de Ayala, Ramón 1880-1962 ......DLB-322	Petrov, Evgenii (Evgenii Petrovich Kataev) 1903-1942 ....DLB-272
Pearce, Philippa 1920- DLB-161	Pérez de Guzmán, Fernán ca. 1377-ca. 1460 ....DLB-286	
H. B. Pearson [publishing house]........DLB-49		Petrov, Gavriil 1730-1801...............DLB-150
Pearson, Hesketh 1887-1964 ....DLB-149	Pérez-Reverte, Arturo 1951- DLB-322	Petrov, Valeri 1920- DLB-181
Peattie, Donald Culross 1898-1964 .....DLB-275	Peri Rossi, Cristina 1941- DLB-145, 290	Petrov, Vasilii Petrovich 1736-1799.......DLB-150
Pechersky, Andrei (see Mel'nikov, Pavel Ivanovich)	Perkins, Eugene 1932- DLB-41	Petrović, Rastko 1898-1949............. DLB-147; CDWLB-4
Peck, George W. 1840-1916..........DLB-23, 42	Perkins, Maxwell The Claims of Business and Literature: An Undergraduate Essay Y-01	
H. C. Peck and Theo. Bliss [publishing house] DLB-49		Petrus Alfonsi (Pedro Alfonso, Pierre Alphonse) fl. 1106-circa 1125 ....DLB-337
	Perkins, William 1558-1602............DLB-281	
Peck, Harry Thurston 1856-1914 .....DLB-71, 91	Perkoff, Stuart Z. 1930-1974 ....DLB-16	Petrushevskaia, Liudmila Stefanovna 1938- DLB-285
Peden, William 1913-1999..............DLB-234	Perley, Moses Henry 1804-1862 ....DLB-99	
Tribute to William Goyen..............Y-83	Permabooks........................DLB-46	*Petruslied* circa 854?..................DLB-148
Peele, George 1556-1596 ....DLB-62, 167	Perovsky, Aleksei Alekseevich (Antonii Pogorel'sky) 1787-1836 .....DLB-198	Petry, Ann 1908-1997 ....DLB-76
Pegler, Westbrook 1894-1969............DLB-171		Pettie, George circa 1548-1589...........DLB-136
Péguy, Charles 1873-1914 ....DLB-258	Perrault, Charles 1628-1703 ....DLB-268	Pétur Gunnarsson 1947- DLB-293
Peirce, Charles Sanders 1839-1914 ......DLB-270	Perri, Henry 1561-1617 ....DLB-236	Peyton, K. M. 1929- DLB-161
Pekić, Borislav 1930-1992 ...DLB-181; CDWLB-4	Perrin, Alice 1867-1934 ....DLB-156	Pfaffe Konrad fl. circa 1172 ....DLB-148
Pelecanos, George P. 1957- DLB-306	Perruchi, Andrea 1651-1704. ....DLB-339	Pfaffe Lamprecht fl. circa 1150 ....DLB-148
Peletier du Mans, Jacques 1517-1582 .....DLB-327	Perry, Anne 1938- DLB-276	Pfeiffer, Emily 1827-1890...............DLB-199
Pelevin, Viktor Olegovich 1962- DLB-285	Perry, Bliss 1860-1954 ....DLB-71	Pforzheimer, Carl H. 1879-1957........DLB-140
Pellegrini and Cudahy DLB-46	Perry, Eleanor 1915-1981................DLB-44	Phaedrus circa 18 B.C.-circa A.D. 50......DLB-211
	Perry, Henry (see Perri, Henry)	Phaer, Thomas 1510?-1560 ....DLB-167
		Phaidon Press Limited DLB-112

Pharr, Robert Deane 1916-1992 . . . . DLB-33

Phelps, Elizabeth Stuart 1815-1852. . . . . . DLB-202

Phelps, Elizabeth Stuart 1844-1911. . . DLB-74, 221

Philander von der Linde
(see Mencke, Johann Burckhard)

Philby, H. St. John B. 1885-1960 . . . . DLB-195

Philip, Marlene Nourbese 1947- . . .DLB-157, 334

Philippe, Charles-Louis 1874-1909 . . . . DLB-65

Philips, John 1676-1708. . . . . DLB-95

Philips, Katherine 1632-1664 . . . . DLB-131

Phillipps, Sir Thomas 1792-1872. . . . . DLB-184

Phillips, Caryl 1958- DLB-157

Phillips, David Graham
1867-1911. . . . . DLB-9, 12, 303

Phillips, Jayne Anne 1952- DLB-292; Y-80

    Tribute to Seymour Lawrence Y-94

Phillips, Robert 1938- DLB-105

    "Finding, Losing, Reclaiming: A Note
on My Poems". DLB-105

    Tribute to William Goyen Y-83

Phillips, Stephen 1864-1915 . . . . DLB-10

Phillips, Ulrich B. 1877-1934. . . . . DLB-17

Phillips, Wendell 1811-1884 . . . . DLB-235

Phillips, Willard 1784-1873 . . . . DLB-59

Phillips, William 1907-2002 . . . . DLB-137

Phillips, Sampson and Company DLB-49

Phillpotts, Adelaide Eden (Adelaide Ross)
1896-1993 . . . . DLB-191

Phillpotts, Eden 1862-1960. . .DLB-10, 70, 135, 153

Philo circa 20-15 B.C.-circa A.D. 50 . . . . . . .DLB-176

Philosophical Dictionary, Voltaire DLB-314

Philosophical Library DLB-46

Philosophy
    Eighteenth-Century Philosophical
Background DLB-31

    Philosophic Thought in Boston DLB-235

    Translators of the Twelfth Century:
Literary Issues Raised and
Impact Created DLB-115

Elihu Phinney [publishing house] DLB-49

Phoenix, John (see Derby, George Horatio)

PHYLON (Fourth Quarter, 1950),
The Negro in Literature:
The Current Scene. DLB-76

Physiologus circa 1070-circa 1150. . . . . DLB-148

II.O. (Pi O, Peter Oustabasides)
1951- DLB-325

Piccolo, Lucio 1903-1969 . . . . DLB-114

Pichette, Henri 1924-2000 . . . . DLB-321

Pickard, Tom 1946- DLB-40

William Pickering [publishing house] DLB-106

Pickthall, Marjorie 1883-1922. . . . . DLB-92

Picoult, Jodi 1966- DLB-292

Pictorial Printing Company DLB-49

Piel, Gerard 1915-2004. . . . . DLB-137

"An Announcement to Our Readers,"
Gerard Piel's Statement in *Scientific
American* (April 1948) DLB-137

Pielmeier, John 1949- DLB-266

Piercy, Marge 1936- DLB-120, 227

Pierre, DBC 1961- DLB-326

Pierro, Albino 1916-1995 . . . . DLB-128

Pignotti, Lamberto 1926- DLB-128

Pike, Albert 1809-1891. . . . . DLB-74

Pike, Zebulon Montgomery 1779-1813. . . DLB-183

Pillat, Ion 1891-1945. . . . . DLB-220

Pil'niak, Boris Andreevich (Boris Andreevich
Vogau) 1894-1938 . . . . .DLB-272

Pilon, Jean-Guy 1930- DLB-60

Pinar, Florencia fl. ca. late
fifteenth century DLB-286

Pinckney, Eliza Lucas 1722-1793. . . . . DLB-200

Pinckney, Josephine 1895-1957. . . . . DLB-6

Pindar circa 518 B.C.-circa 438 B.C.
. . . . DLB-176; CDWLB-1

Pindar, Peter (see Wolcot, John)

Pineda, Cecile 1942- DLB-209

Pinero, Arthur Wing 1855-1934. . . . . DLB-10

Piñero, Miguel 1946-1988. . . . . DLB-266

Pinget, Robert 1919-1997 . . . . DLB-83

Pinkerton, John 1758-1825 . . . . DLB-336

Pinkney, Edward Coote
1802-1828 . . . . DLB-248

Pinnacle Books DLB-46

Piñon, Nélida 1935- DLB-145, 307

Pinski, David (Dovid Pinski)
1872-1959. . . . . DLB-333

Pinsky, Robert 1940- Y-82

    Reappointed Poet Laureate Y-98

Pinter, Harold 1930-
    . . . . DLB-13, 310, 331; CDBLB-8

    Writing for the Theatre DLB-13

Pinto, Fernão Mendes 1509/1511?-1583. . DLB-287

Piontek, Heinz 1925- DLB-75

Piozzi, Hester Lynch [Thrale]
1741-1821. . . . . .DLB-104, 142

Piper, H. Beam 1904-1964 . . . . DLB-8

Piper, Watty DLB-22

Pirandello, Luigi 1867-1936 . . . . DLB-264, 331

Pirckheimer, Caritas 1467-1532 . . . . .DLB-179

Pirckheimer, Willibald 1470-1530. . . . . . .DLB-179

Pires, José Cardoso 1925-1998 . . . . DLB-287

Pisar, Samuel 1929- Y-83

Pisarev, Dmitrii Ivanovich 1840-1868. . . . .DLB-277

Pisemsky, Aleksei Feofilaktovich
1821-1881 . . . . DLB-238

Pitkin, Timothy 1766-1847 . . . . DLB-30

Pitter, Ruth 1897-1992 . . . . DLB-20

Pix, Mary 1666-1709 . . . . DLB-80

Pixerécourt, René Charles Guilbert de
1773-1844. . . . . DLB-192

Pizarnik, Alejandra 1936-1972 . . . . DLB-283

Plá, Josefina 1909-1999. . . . . DLB-290

Plaatje, Sol T. 1876-1932. . . . . DLB-125, 225

Planchon, Roger 1931- DLB-321

Plante, David 1940- Y-83

Plantinga, Alvin 1932- DLB-279

Platen, August von 1796-1835 . . . . DLB-90

Plath, Sylvia
1932-1963 . . . . DLB-5, 6, 152; CDALB-1

Plato circa 428 B.C.-348-347 B.C.
. . . . DLB-176; CDWLB-1

Plato, Ann 1824-?. DLB-239

Platon 1737-1812. . . . . DLB-150

Platonov, Andrei Platonovich (Andrei
Platonovich Klimentev)
1899-1951 .DLB-272

Platt, Charles 1945- DLB-261

Platt and Munk Company DLB-46

Plautus circa 254 B.C.-184 B.C.
. . . . DLB-211; CDWLB-1

Playboy Press DLB-46

John Playford [publishing house] DLB-170

Der Pleier fl. circa 1250 . . . . DLB-138

Pleijel, Agneta 1940- DLB-257

Plenzdorf, Ulrich 1934- DLB-75

Pleshcheev, Aleksei Nikolaevich
1825?-1893. . . . . .DLB-277

Plessen, Elizabeth 1944- DLB-75

Pliekšāne, Elza Rozenberga (see Aspazija)

Pliekšāns, Jānis (see Rainis, Jānis)

Plievier, Theodor 1892-1955 . . . . DLB-69

Plimpton, George 1927-2003 . .DLB-185, 241; Y-99

Pliny the Elder A.D. 23/24-A.D. 79 . . . . . . DLB-211

Pliny the Younger
circa A.D. 61-A.D. 112. . . . . DLB-211

Plomer, William
1903-1973. . . . . .DLB-20, 162, 191, 225

Plotinus 204-270 . . . . .DLB-176; CDWLB-1

Plowright, Teresa 1952- DLB-251

Plume, Thomas 1630-1704 . . . . DLB-213

Plumly, Stanley 1939- DLB-5, 193

Plumpp, Sterling D. 1940- DLB-41

Plunkett, James 1920-2003 . . . . DLB-14

Plutarch
circa 46-circa 120 . . . . . . .DLB-176; CDWLB-1

Plymell, Charles 1935- DLB-16

Pocket Books DLB-46

Podestá, José J. 1858-1937 . . . . DLB-305

Poe, Edgar Allan 1809-1849
. . . . .DLB-3, 59, 73, 74, 248; CDALB-2

The Poe Studies Association Y-99

Poe, James 1921-1980 . . . . DLB-44

Poema de Alfonso XI (1348). DLB-337

Poema de Fernán González
(between 1251 and 1258) DLB-337

The Poet Laureate of the United States Y-86

Statements from Former Consultants
in Poetry Y-86

Poetry
Aesthetic Poetry (1873) DLB-35

A Century of Poetry, a Lifetime of
Collecting: J. M. Edelstein's
Collection of Twentieth-
Century American Poetry. Y-02

"Certain Gifts," by Betty Adcock DLB-105

Concrete Poetry. DLB-307

Contempo Caravan: Kites in a
Windstorm Y-85

"Contemporary Verse Story-telling,"
by Jonathan Holden DLB-105

"A Detail in a Poem," by Fred
Chappell DLB-105

"The English Renaissance of Art"
(1908), by Oscar Wilde. DLB-35

"Every Man His Own Poet; or,
The Inspired Singer's Recipe
Book" (1877), by
H. W. Mallock DLB-35

"Eyes Across Centuries: Contemporary
Poetry and 'That Vision Thing,'"
by Philip Dacey. DLB-105

A Field Guide to Recent Schools
of American Poetry. Y-86

"Finding, Losing, Reclaiming:
A Note on My Poems,
by Robert Phillips" DLB-105

"The Fleshly School of Poetry and Other
Phenomena of the Day" (1872). . . . DLB-35

"The Fleshly School of Poetry:
Mr. D. G. Rossetti" (1871) DLB-35

The G. Ross Roy Scottish Poetry Collection
at the University of South Carolina . . . Y-89

"Getting Started: Accepting the Regions
You Own—or Which Own You,"
by Walter McDonald DLB-105

"The Good, The Not So Good," by
Stephen Dunn. DLB-105

The Griffin Poetry Prize Y-00

The Hero as Poet. Dante; Shakspeare
(1841), by Thomas Carlyle. DLB-32

"Images and 'Images,'" by Charles
Simic. DLB-105

"Into the Mirror," by Peter Cooley . . . DLB-105

"Knots into Webs: Some Autobiographical
Sources," by Dabney Stuart DLB-105

"L'Envoi" (1882), by Oscar Wilde. DLB-35

"Living in Ruin," by Gerald Stern. . . . DLB-105

Looking for the Golden Mountain:
Poetry Reviewing Y-89

Lyric Poetry (French) DLB-268

Medieval Galician-Portuguese
Poetry DLB-287

"The No Self, the Little Self, and the
Poets," by Richard Moore DLB-105

On Some of the Characteristics of Modern
Poetry and On the Lyrical Poems of
Alfred Tennyson (1831) DLB-32

The Pitt Poetry Series: Poetry Publishing
Today Y-85

"The Poetry File," by Edward
Field DLB-105

Poetry in Nineteenth-Century France:
Cultural Background and Critical
Commentary DLB-217

The Poetry of Jorge Luis Borges Y-86

"The Poet's Kaleidoscope: The Element
of Surprise in the Making of the
Poem" by Madeline DeFrees. DLB-105

The Pre-Raphaelite Controversy. DLB-35

Protest Poetry in Castile DLB-286

"Reflections: After a Tornado,"
by Judson Jerome DLB-105

Statements from Former Consultants
in Poetry Y-86

Statements on the Art of Poetry DLB-54

The Study of Poetry (1880), by
Matthew Arnold DLB-35

A Survey of Poetry Anthologies,
1879-1960 . . . . DLB-54

Thoughts on Poetry and Its Varieties
(1833), by John Stuart Mill DLB-32

Under the Microscope (1872), by
A. C. Swinburne DLB-35

The Unterberg Poetry Center of the
92nd Street Y Y-98

Victorian Poetry: Five Critical Views . . DLBV-35

Year in Poetry Y-83–92, 94–01

Year's Work in American Poetry Y-82

Poets
The Lives of the Poets (1753) DLB-142

Minor Poets of the Earlier
Seventeenth Century DLB-121

Other British Poets Who Fell
in the Great War. DLB-216

Other Poets [French] DLB-217

Second-Generation Minor Poets of
the Seventeenth Century DLB-126

Third-Generation Minor Poets of
the Seventeenth Century DLB-131

Pogodin, Mikhail Petrovich 1800-1875. . . . DLB-198

Pogorel'sky, Antonii
(see Perovsky, Aleksei Alekseevich)

Pohl, Frederik 1919- DLB-8

Tribute to Isaac Asimov Y-92

Tribute to Theodore Sturgeon Y-85

Poirier, Louis (see Gracq, Julien)

Poláček, Karel 1892-1945 . . . DLB-215; CDWLB-4

Polanyi, Michael 1891-1976 . . . . DLB-100

Pole, Reginald 1500-1558 . . . . DLB-132

Polevoi, Nikolai Alekseevich 1796-1846. . . DLB-198

Polezhaev, Aleksandr Ivanovich
1804-1838 . . . . DLB-205

Poliakoff, Stephen 1952- DLB-13

Polidori, John William 1795-1821 . . . . . . DLB-116

Polite, Carlene Hatcher 1932- DLB-33

Pollard, Alfred W. 1859-1944 . . . . DLB-201

Pollard, Edward A. 1832-1872 . . . . DLB-30

Pollard, Graham 1903-1976 . . . . DLB-201

Pollard, Percival 1869-1911 . . . . DLB-71

Pollard and Moss. DLB-49

Pollock, Sharon 1936- DLB-60

Polonsky, Abraham 1910-1999 . . . . DLB-26

Polonsky, Iakov Petrovich 1819-1898 . . . . DLB-277

Polotsky, Simeon 1629-1680 . . . . DLB-150

Polybius circa 200 B.C.-118 B.C. DLB-176

Pomialovsky, Nikolai Gerasimovich
1835-1863 . . . . DLB-238

Pomilio, Mario 1921-1990 . . . . DLB-177

Pompéia, Raul (Raul d'Avila Pompéia)
1863-1895 . . . . DLB-307

Ponce, Mary Helen 1938- DLB-122

Ponce-Montoya, Juanita 1949- DLB-122

Ponet, John 1516?-1556 . . . . DLB-132

Ponge, Francis 1899-1988 . . . . . . DLB-258; Y-02

Poniatowska, Elena
1933- DLB-113; CDWLB-3

Ponsard, François 1814-1867 . . . . DLB-192

William Ponsonby [publishing house] DLB-170

Pontiggia, Giuseppe 1934- DLB-196

Pontoppidan, Henrik 1857-1943 . . . . DLB-300, 331

Pony Stories, Omnibus Essay on DLB-160

Poole, Ernest 1880-1950 . . . . DLB-9

Poole, Sophia 1804-1891 . . . . DLB-166

Poore, Benjamin Perley 1820-1887 . . . . . . DLB-23

Popa, Vasko 1922-1991 . . . . . DLB-181; CDWLB-4

Pope, Abbie Hanscom 1858-1894 . . . . . . DLB-140

Pope, Alexander
1688-1744 . . . . . . DLB-95, 101, 213; CDBLB-2

Poplavsky, Boris 1903-1935. . . . . DLB-317

Popov, Aleksandr Serafimovich
(see Serafimovich, Aleksandr Serafimovich)

Popov, Evgenii Anatol'evich 1946- DLB-285

Popov, Mikhail Ivanovich
1742-circa 1790 . . . . DLB-150

Popović, Aleksandar 1929-1996. . . . . DLB-181

Popper, Karl 1902-1994 . . . . DLB-262

Popular Culture Association/
American Culture Association. Y-99

Popular Library DLB-46

Poquelin, Jean-Baptiste (see Molière)

Porete, Marguerite ?-1310 . . . . DLB-208

Porlock, Martin (see MacDonald, Philip)

Porpoise Press DLB-112

Porta, Antonio 1935-1989 . . . . DLB-128

Porter, Anna Maria 1780-1832 . . . . . DLB-116, 159

Porter, Cole 1891-1964 . . . . DLB-265

Porter, David 1780-1843 . . . . DLB-183

Porter, Dorothy 1954- DLB-325

Porter, Eleanor H. 1868-1920 .... DLB-9

Porter, Gene Stratton (see Stratton-Porter, Gene)

Porter, Hal 1911-1984 .... DLB-260

Porter, Henry circa sixteenth century DLB-62

Porter, Jane 1776-1850 .... DLB-116, 159

Porter, Katherine Anne 1890-1980
.......DLB-4, 9, 102; Y-80; DS-12; CDALB-7

    The Katherine Anne Porter Society Y-01

Porter, Peter 1929- DLB-40, 289

Porter, William Sydney (O. Henry)
1862-1910. .... DLB-12, 78, 79; CDALB-3

Porter, William T. 1809-1858 ..... DLB-3, 43, 250

Porter and Coates DLB-49

Portillo Trambley, Estela 1927-1998 ..... DLB-209

Portis, Charles 1933- DLB-6

Medieval Galician-Portuguese Poetry DLB-287

Posey, Alexander 1873-1908 .... DLB-175

Possession, 1990 Booker Prize winner,
A. S. Byatt DLB-326

Postans, Marianne circa 1810-1865 ...... DLB-166

Postgate, Raymond 1896-1971 .... DLB-276

Postl, Carl (see Sealsfield, Carl)

Postmodern Holocaust Fiction DLB-299

Poston, Ted 1906-1974 .... DLB-51

Potekhin, Aleksei Antipovich
1829-1908 .... DLB-238

Potok, Chaim 1929-2002 .... DLB-28, 152

    A Conversation with Chaim Potok Y-84

    Tribute to Bernard Malamud Y-86

Potter, Beatrix 1866-1943 .... DLB-141

    The Beatrix Potter Society Y-98

Potter, David M. 1910-1971 .... DLB-17

Potter, Dennis 1935-1994 .... DLB-233

John E. Potter and Company DLB-49

Pottle, Frederick A. 1897-1987 .... DLB-103; Y-87

Poulin, Jacques 1937- DLB-60

Pound, Ezra 1885-1972
.... DLB-4, 45, 63; DS-15; CDALB-4

    The Cost of the *Cantos:* William Bird
to Ezra Pound Y-01

    The Ezra Pound Society Y-01

Poverman, C. E. 1944- DLB-234

Povey, Meic 1950- DLB-310

Povich, Shirley 1905-1998 .... DLB-171

Powell, Anthony 1905-2000 ... DLB-15; CDBLB-7

    The Anthony Powell Society: Powell and
the First Biennial Conference Y-01

Powell, Dawn 1897-1965
    Dawn Powell, Where Have You Been
All Our Lives? Y-97

Powell, John Wesley 1834-1902 .... DLB-186

Powell, Padgett 1952- DLB-234

Powers, J. F. 1917-1999 .... DLB-130

Powers, Jimmy 1903-1995 .... DLB-241

Pownall, David 1938- DLB-14

Powys, John Cowper 1872-1963 ..... DLB-15, 255

Powys, Llewelyn 1884-1939 .... DLB-98

Powys, T. F. 1875-1953 .... DLB-36, 162

    The Powys Society Y-98

Poynter, Nelson 1903-1978 .... DLB-127

Prada, Juan Manuel de 1970- DLB-322

Prado, Adélia 1935- DLB-307

Prado, Pedro 1886-1952 .... DLB-283

Prados, Emilio 1899-1962 .... DLB-134

Praed, Mrs. Caroline (see Praed, Rosa)

Praed, Rosa (Mrs. Caroline Praed)
1851-1935 .... DLB-230

Praed, Winthrop Mackworth 1802-1839 .. DLB-96

Praeger Publishers DLB-46

Praetorius, Johannes 1630-1680 .... DLB-168

Pratolini, Vasco 1913-1991 .... DLB-177

Pratt, E. J. 1882-1964 .... DLB-92

Pratt, Samuel Jackson 1749-1814 .... DLB-39

Preciado Martin, Patricia 1939- DLB-209

Préfontaine, Yves 1937- DLB-53

Prelutsky, Jack 1940- DLB-61

Prentice, George D. 1802-1870 .... DLB-43

Prentice-Hall DLB-46

Prescott, Orville 1906-1996 .... Y-96

Prescott, William Hickling
1796-1859 .... DLB-1, 30, 59, 235

Prešeren, France
1800-1849 .... DLB-147; CDWLB-4

Presses (*See also* Publishing)
    Small Presses in Great Britain and
Ireland, 1960-1985 .... DLB-40

    Small Presses I: Jargon Society Y-84

    Small Presses II: The Spirit That Moves
Us Press Y-85

    Small Presses III: Pushcart Press Y-87

Preston, Margaret Junkin
1820-1897 .... DLB-239, 248

Preston, May Wilson 1873-1949 .... DLB-188

Preston, Thomas 1537-1598 .... DLB-62

Preti, Girolamo 1582-1626 .... DLB-339

Prévert, Jacques 1900-1977 .... DLB-258

Prévost d'Exiles, Antoine François
1697-1763 .... DLB-314

Price, Anthony 1928- DLB-276

Price, Reynolds 1933- DLB-2, 218, 278

Price, Richard 1723-1791 .... DLB-158

Price, Richard 1949- Y-81

Prichard, Katharine Susannah
1883-1969 .... DLB-260

Prideaux, John 1578-1650 .... DLB-236

Priest, Christopher 1943- DLB-14, 207, 261

Priestley, J. B. 1894-1984
.... DLB-10, 34, 77, 100, 139; Y-84; CDBLB-6

Priestley, Joseph 1733-1804 .... DLB-252, 336

Prigov, Dmitrii Aleksandrovich 1940- .. DLB-285

Prime, Benjamin Young 1733-1791 .... DLB-31

Primrose, Diana floruit circa 1630 ...... DLB-126

Prince, F. T. 1912-2003 .... DLB-20

Prince, Nancy Gardner
1799-circa 1856 .... DLB-239

Prince, Thomas 1687-1758 .... DLB-24, 140

Pringle, Thomas 1789-1834 .... DLB-225

Printz, Wolfgang Casper 1641-1717 ..... DLB-168

Prior, Matthew 1664-1721 .... DLB-95

Prisco, Michele 1920-2003 .... DLB-177

Prishvin, Mikhail Mikhailovich
1873-1954 .... DLB-272

Pritchard, William H. 1932- DLB-111

Pritchett, V. S. 1900-1997 .... DLB-15, 139

Probyn, May 1856 or 1857-1909 .... DLB-199

Procter, Adelaide Anne 1825-1864 ... DLB-32, 199

Procter, Bryan Waller 1787-1874 ..... DLB-96, 144

Proctor, Robert 1868-1903 .... DLB-184

Prokopovich, Feofan 1681?-1736 .... DLB-150

Prokosch, Frederic 1906-1989 .... DLB-48

Pronzini, Bill 1943- DLB-226

Propertius circa 50 B.C.-post 16 B.C.
.... DLB-211; CDWLB-1

Propper, Dan 1937- DLB-16

Prose, Francine 1947- DLB-234

Protagoras circa 490 B.C.-420 B.C. DLB-176

Protest Poetry in Castile
ca. 1445-ca. 1506 .... DLB-286

Proud, Robert 1728-1813 .... DLB-30

Proulx, Annie 1935- DLB-335

Proust, Marcel 1871-1922 .... DLB-65

    Marcel Proust at 129 and the Proust
Society of America Y-00

    Marcel Proust's *Remembrance of Things Past:*
The Rediscovered Galley Proofs Y-00

Prutkov, Koz'ma Petrovich
1803-1863 .... DLB-277

Prynne, J. H. 1936- DLB-40

Przybyszewski, Stanislaw 1868-1927 ...... DLB-66

Pseudo-Dionysius the Areopagite floruit
circa 500 .... DLB-115

Public Lending Right in America
    PLR and the Meaning of Literary
Property Y-83

    Statement by Sen. Charles
McC. Mathias, Jr. PLR Y-83

    Statements on PLR by American Writers. ... Y-83

Public Lending Right in the United Kingdom
    The First Year in the United Kingdom. ... Y-83

Publishers [listed by individual names]
    Publishers, Conversations with:
        An Interview with Charles Scribner III. .. Y-94

An Interview with Donald Lamm Y-95
An Interview with James Laughlin Y-96
An Interview with Patrick O'Connor Y-84
Publishing
    The Art and Mystery of Publishing:
        Interviews Y-97
    Book Publishing Accounting: Some Basic
        Concepts Y-98
    1873 Publishers' Catalogues DLB-49
    The Literary Scene 2002: Publishing, Book
        Reviewing, and Literary Journalism . . . Y-02
    Main Trends in Twentieth-Century
        Book Clubs DLB-46
    Overview of U.S. Book Publishing,
        1910-1945 . . . . DLB-9
    The Pitt Poetry Series: Poetry Publishing
        Today Y-85
    Publishing Fiction at LSU Press Y-87
    The Publishing Industry in 1998:
        Sturm-und-drang.com Y-98
    The Publishing Industry in 1999 . . . . Y-99
    Publishers and Agents: The Columbia
        Connection Y-87
    Responses to Ken Auletta Y-97
    Southern Writers Between the Wars DLB-9
    The State of Publishing Y-97
    Trends in Twentieth-Century
        Mass Market Publishing DLB-46
    The Year in Book Publishing Y-86
Pückler-Muskau, Hermann von
    1785-1871 . . . . DLB-133
Puértolas, Soledad 1947- DLB-322
Pufendorf, Samuel von 1632-1694 . . . . DLB-168
Pugh, Edwin William 1874-1930 . . . . DLB-135
Pugin, A. Welby 1812-1852 . . . . DLB-55
Puig, Manuel 1932-1990 . . . . DLB-113; CDWLB-3
Puisieux, Madeleine d'Arsant de
    1720-1798 . . . . DLB-314
Pulgar, Hernando del (Fernando del Pulgar)
    ca. 1436-ca. 1492 . . . . DLB-286
Pulitzer, Joseph 1847-1911 . . . . DLB-23
Pulitzer, Joseph, Jr. 1885-1955 . . . . DLB-29
Pulitzer Prizes for the Novel, 1917-1945 . . . . DLB-9
Pulliam, Eugene 1889-1975 . . . . DLB-127
Purcell, Deirdre 1945- DLB-267
Purchas, Samuel 1577?-1626 . . . . DLB-151
Purdy, Al 1918-2000 . . . . DLB-88
Purdy, James 1923- DLB-2, 218
Purdy, Ken W. 1913-1972 . . . . DLB-137
Pusey, Edward Bouverie 1800-1882 . . . . . . DLB-55
Pushkin, Aleksandr Sergeevich
    1799-1837 . . . . DLB-205
Pushkin, Vasilii L'vovich
    1766-1830 . . . . DLB-205
Putnam, George Palmer
    1814-1872 . . . . DLB-3, 79, 250, 254
G. P. Putnam [publishing house] DLB-254

G. P. Putnam's Sons [U.K.] DLB-106
G. P. Putnam's Sons [U.S.] DLB-49
    A Publisher's Archives: G. P. Putnam Y-92
Putnam, Hilary 1926- DLB-279
Putnam, Samuel 1892-1950 . . . . DLB-4; DS-15
Puttenham, George 1529?-1590 . . . . DLB-281
Puzo, Mario 1920-1999 . . . . DLB-6
Pyle, Ernie 1900-1945 . . . . DLB-29
Pyle, Howard
    1853-1911 . . . . DLB-42, 188; DS-13
Pyle, Robert Michael 1947- DLB-275
Pym, Barbara 1913-1980 . . . . . . DLB-14, 207; Y-87
Pynchon, Thomas 1937- DLB-2, 173
Pyramid Books DLB-46
Pyrnelle, Louise-Clarke 1850-1907 . . . . DLB-42
Pythagoras circa 570 B.C.-? DLB-176

Q

Qays ibn al-Mulawwah circa 680-710 . . . . DLB-311
Qian Zhongshu 1910-1998 . . . . DLB-328
Quad, M. (see Lewis, Charles B.)
Quaritch, Bernard 1819-1899 . . . . DLB-184
Quarles, Francis 1592-1644 . . . . DLB-126
The Quarterly Review 1809-1967 . . . . DLB-110
Quasimodo, Salvatore 1901-1968 . . . DLB-114, 332
Queen, Ellery (see Dannay, Frederic, and
    Manfred B. Lee)
Queen, Frank 1822-1882 . . . . DLB-241
The Queen City Publishing House DLB-49
Queirós, Eça de 1845-1900 . . . . DLB-287
Queneau, Raymond 1903-1976 . . . . . . DLB-72, 258
Quennell, Peter 1905-1993 . . . . DLB-155, 195
Quental, Antero de
    1842-1891 . . . . DLB-287
Quesada, José Luis 1948- DLB-290
Quesnel, Joseph 1746-1809 . . . . DLB-99
Quiller-Couch, Sir Arthur Thomas
    1863-1944 . . . . DLB-135, 153, 190
Quin, Ann 1936-1973 . . . . DLB-14, 231
Quinault, Philippe 1635-1688 . . . . DLB-268
Quincy, Samuel, of Georgia
    fl. eighteenth century DLB-31
Quincy, Samuel, of Massachusetts
    1734-1789 . . . . DLB-31
Quindlen, Anna 1952- DLB-292
Quine, W. V. 1908-2000 . . . . DLB-279
Quinn, Anthony 1915-2001 . . . . DLB-122
Quinn, John 1870-1924 . . . . DLB-187
Quiñónez, Naomi 1951- DLB-209
Quintana, Leroy V. 1944- DLB-82
Quintana, Miguel de 1671-1748
    A Forerunner of Chicano
        Literature DLB-122

Quintilian circa A.D. 40-circa A.D. 96 . . . . . DLB-211
Quintus Curtius Rufus
    fl. A.D. 35 . . . . DLB-211
Harlin Quist Books DLB-46
Quoirez, Françoise (see Sagan, Françoise)

R

Raabe, Wilhelm 1831-1910 . . . . DLB-129
Raban, Jonathan 1942- DLB-204
Rabe, David 1940- DLB-7, 228; Y-91
Rabelais, François 1494?-1593 . . . . DLB-327
Rabi'ah al-'Adawiyyah circa 720-801 . . . . . DLB-311
Raboni, Giovanni 1932- DLB-128
Rachilde 1860-1953 . . . . DLB-123, 192
Racin, Kočo 1908-1943 . . . . DLB-147
Racine, Jean 1639-1699 . . . . DLB-268
Rackham, Arthur 1867-1939 . . . . DLB-141
Raczymow, Henri 1948- DLB-299
Radauskas, Henrikas
    1910-1970 . . . . DLB-220; CDWLB-4
Radcliffe, Ann 1764-1823 . . . . DLB-39, 178
Raddall, Thomas 1903-1994 . . . . DLB-68
Radford, Dollie 1858-1920 . . . . DLB-240
Radichkov, Yordan 1929-2004 . . . . DLB-181
Radiguet, Raymond 1903-1923 . . . . DLB-65
Radishchev, Aleksandr Nikolaevich
    1749-1802 . . . . DLB-150
Radnóti, Miklós 1909-1944 . . DLB-215; CDWLB-4
Radrigán, Juan 1937- DLB-305
Radványi, Netty Reiling (see Seghers, Anna)
Rafat, Taufiq 1927-1998 . . . . DLB-323
Rahv, Philip 1908-1973 . . . . DLB-137
Raich, Semen Egorovich 1792-1855 . . . . . DLB-205
Raičković, Stevan 1928- DLB-181
Raiderman (see Parshchikov, Aleksei Maksimovich)
Raimund, Ferdinand Jakob 1790-1836 . . . . . DLB-90
Raine, Craig 1944- DLB-40
Raine, Kathleen 1908-2003 . . . . DLB-20
Rainis, Jānis 1865-1929 . . . . . DLB-220; CDWLB-4
Rainolde, Richard
    circa 1530-1606 . . . . DLB-136, 236
Rainolds, John 1549-1607 . . . . DLB-281
Rakić, Milan 1876-1938 . . . . . DLB-147; CDWLB-4
Rakosi, Carl 1903-2004 . . . . DLB-193
Ralegh, Sir Walter
    1554?-1618 . . . . DLB-172; CDBLB-1
Raleigh, Walter
    Style (1897) [excerpt] DLB-57
Ralin, Radoy 1923-2004 . . . . DLB-181
Ralph, Julian 1853-1903 . . . . DLB-23
Ramanujan, A. K. 1929-1993 . . . . DLB-323
Ramat, Silvio 1939- DLB-128

Cumulative Index

Ramée, Marie Louise de la (see Ouida)

Ramírez, Sergío 1942- DLB-145

Ramke, Bin 1947- DLB-120

Ramler, Karl Wilhelm 1725-1798 .... DLB-97

Ramon Ribeyro, Julio 1929-1994 .... DLB-145

Ramos, Graciliano 1892-1953 .... DLB-307

Ramos, Manuel 1948- DLB-209

Ramos Sucre, José Antonio 1890-1930 ... DLB-290

Ramous, Mario 1924- DLB-128

Rampersad, Arnold 1941- DLB-111

Ramsay, Allan 1684 or 1685-1758 .... DLB-95

Ramsay, David 1749-1815 .... DLB-30

Ramsay, Martha Laurens 1759-1811 ..... DLB-200

Ramsey, Frank P. 1903-1930 .... DLB-262

Ranch, Hieronimus Justesen
  1539-1607 .... DLB-300

Ranck, Katherine Quintana 1942- DLB-122

Rand, Avery and Company DLB-49

Rand, Ayn 1905-1982 .... DLB-227, 279; CDALB-7

Rand McNally and Company DLB-49

Randall, David Anton 1905-1975 ...... DLB-140

Randall, Dudley 1914-2000 .... DLB-41

Randall, Henry S. 1811-1876 .... DLB-30

Randall, James G. 1881-1953 .... DLB-17

The Randall Jarrell Symposium: A Small
  Collection of Randall Jarrells Y-86

Excerpts From Papers Delivered at the
  Randall Jarrel Symposium Y-86

Randall, John Herman, Jr. 1899-1980 .... DLB-279

Randolph, A. Philip 1889-1979 .... DLB-91

Anson D. F. Randolph
  [publishing house] DLB-49

Randolph, Thomas 1605-1635 ...... DLB-58, 126

Random House DLB-46

Rankin, Ian (Jack Harvey) 1960- DLB-267

Henry Ranlet [publishing house] DLB-49

Ransom, Harry 1908-1976 .... DLB-187

Ransom, John Crowe
  1888-1974 .... DLB-45, 63; CDALB-7

Ransome, Arthur 1884-1967 .... DLB-160

Rao, Raja 1908- DLB-323

Raphael, Frederic 1931- DLB-14, 319

Raphaelson, Samson 1896-1983 .... DLB-44

Rare Book Dealers
  Bertram Rota and His Bookshop Y-91
  An Interview with Glenn Horowitz Y-90
  An Interview with Otto Penzler Y-96
  An Interview with Ralph Sipper Y-94
  New York City Bookshops in the
    1930s and 1940s: The Recollections
    of Walter Goldwater Y-93

Rare Books
  Research in the American Antiquarian
    Book Trade Y-97

Two Hundred Years of Rare Books and
  Literary Collections at the
  University of South Carolina Y-00

Rascón Banda, Víctor Hugo 1948- DLB-305

Rashi circa 1040-1105 .... DLB-208

Raskin, Ellen 1928-1984 .... DLB-52

Rasputin, Valentin Grigor'evich
  1937- DLB-302

Rastell, John 1475?-1536 .... DLB-136, 170

Rattigan, Terence
  1911-1977 .... DLB-13; CDBLB-7

Raven, Simon 1927-2001 .... DLB-271

Ravenhill, Mark 1966- DLB-310

Ravnkilde, Adda 1862-1883 .... DLB-300

Rawicz, Piotr 1919-1982 .... DLB-299

Rawlings, Marjorie Kinnan 1896-1953
  .... DLB-9, 22, 102; DS-17; CDALB-7

Rawlinson, Richard 1690-1755 .... DLB-213

Rawlinson, Thomas 1681-1725 .... DLB-213

Rawls, John 1921-2002 .... DLB-279

Raworth, Tom 1938- DLB-40

Ray, David 1932- DLB-5

Ray, Gordon Norton 1915-1986 ... DLB-103, 140

Ray, Henrietta Cordelia 1849-1916 ...... DLB-50

Raymond, Ernest 1888-1974 .... DLB-191

Raymond, Henry J. 1820-1869 ...... DLB-43, 79

Raymond, René (see Chase, James Hadley)

Razaf, Andy 1895-1973 .... DLB-265

al-Razi 865?-925? DLB-311

Razón de amor con los denuestos del agua y el vino
  (1230-1250) DLB-337

Rea, Michael 1927-1996 .... Y-97

Michael M. Rea and the Rea Award for
  the Short Story Y-97

Reach, Angus 1821-1856 .... DLB-70

Read, Herbert 1893-1968 .... DLB-20, 149

Read, Martha Meredith
  fl. nineteenth century DLB-200

Read, Opie 1852-1939 .... DLB-23

Read, Piers Paul 1941- DLB-14

Reade, Charles 1814-1884 .... DLB-21

Reader's Digest Condensed Books DLB-46

Readers Ulysses Symposium Y-97

Reading, Peter 1946- DLB-40

Reading Series in New York City Y-96

Reaney, James 1926- DLB-68

Rebhun, Paul 1500?-1546 .... DLB-179

Rèbora, Clemente 1885-1957 .... DLB-114

Rebreanu, Liviu 1885-1944 .... DLB-220

Rechy, John 1934- DLB-122, 278; Y-82

Redding, J. Saunders 1906-1988 ...... DLB-63, 76

J. S. Redfield [publishing house] DLB-49

Redgrove, Peter 1932-2003 .... DLB-40

Redmon, Anne 1943- Y-86

Redmond, Eugene B. 1937- DLB-41

Redol, Alves 1911-1969 .... DLB-287

James Redpath [publishing house] DLB-49

Reed, Henry 1808-1854 .... DLB-59

Reed, Henry 1914-1986 .... DLB-27

Reed, Ishmael
  1938- DLB-2, 5, 33, 169, 227; DS-8

Reed, Rex 1938- DLB-185

Reed, Sampson 1800-1880 .... DLB-1, 235

Reed, Talbot Baines 1852-1893 .... DLB-141

Reedy, William Marion 1862-1920 ..... DLB-91

Reese, Lizette Woodworth 1856-1935 .... DLB-54

Reese, Thomas 1742-1796 .... DLB-37

Reeve, Clara 1729-1807 .... DLB-39

  Preface to The Old English Baron
    (1778) DLB-39

  The Progress of Romance (1785)
    [excerpt] DLB-39

Reeves, James 1909-1978 .... DLB-161

Reeves, John 1926- DLB-88

Reeves-Stevens, Garfield 1953- DLB-251

Régio, José (José Maria dos Reis Pereira)
  1901-1969 .... DLB-287

Henry Regnery Company DLB-46

Rêgo, José Lins do 1901-1957 .... DLB-307

Rehberg, Hans 1901-1963 .... DLB-124

Rehfisch, Hans José 1891-1960 .... DLB-124

Reich, Ebbe Kløvedal 1940- DLB-214

Reid, Alastair 1926- DLB-27

Reid, B. L. 1918-1990 .... DLB-111

Reid, Christopher 1949- DLB-40

Reid, Forrest 1875-1947 .... DLB-153

Reid, Helen Rogers 1882-1970 .... DLB-29

Reid, James fl. eighteenth century DLB-31

Reid, Mayne 1818-1883 .... DLB-21, 163

Reid, Thomas 1710-1796 .... DLB-31, 252

Reid, V. S. (Vic) 1913-1987 .... DLB-125

Reid, Whitelaw 1837-1912 .... DLB-23

Reilly and Lee Publishing Company DLB-46

Reimann, Brigitte 1933-1973 .... DLB-75

Reinmar der Alte circa 1165-circa 1205 .. DLB-138

Reinmar von Zweter
  circa 1200-circa 1250 .... DLB-138

Reisch, Walter 1903-1983 .... DLB-44

Reizei Family DLB-203

Religion
  A Crisis of Culture: The Changing
    Role of Religion in the
    New Republic DLB-37

The Remains of the Day, 1989 Booker Prize winner,
    Kazuo Ishiguro DLB-326

Remarque, Erich Maria
    1898-1970 . . . . DLB-56; CDWLB-2

Remington, Frederic
    1861-1909 . . . . DLB-12, 186, 188

Remizov, Aleksei Mikhailovich
    1877-1957 . . . . .DLB-295

Renaud, Jacques 1943- DLB-60

Renault, Mary 1905-1983 . . . . .Y-83

Rendell, Ruth (Barbara Vine)
    1930- DLB-87, 276

Rensselaer, Maria van Cortlandt van
    1645-1689 . . . . .DLB-200

Repplier, Agnes 1855-1950 . . . . .DLB-221

Reshetnikov, Fedor Mikhailovich
    1841-1871 . . . . .DLB-238

Restif (Rétif) de La Bretonne, Nicolas-Edme
    1734-1806 . . . . .DLB-314

Rettenbacher, Simon 1634-1706. . . . . .DLB-168

Retz, Jean-François-Paul de Gondi,
    cardinal de 1613-1679 . . . . .DLB-268

Reuchlin, Johannes 1455-1522. . . . . .DLB-179

Reuter, Christian 1665-after 1712 . . . . . . .DLB-168

Fleming H. Revell Company DLB-49

Reverdy, Pierre 1889-1960. . . . . .DLB-258

Reuter, Fritz 1810-1874 . . . . .DLB-129

Reuter, Gabriele 1859-1941 . . . . .DLB-66

Reventlow, Franziska Gräfin zu
    1871-1918 . . . . .DLB-66

Review of Reviews Office DLB-112

Rexroth, Kenneth 1905-1982
    . . . . . . DLB-16, 48, 165, 212; Y-82; CDALB-1

    The Commercialization of the Image
        of Revolt. .DLB-16

Rey, H. A. 1898-1977. . . . . .DLB-22

Reyes, Carlos José 1941- DLB-305

Reymont, Władysław Stanisław
    1867-1925 . . . . .DLB-332

Reynal and Hitchcock DLB-46

Reynolds, G. W. M. 1814-1879 . . . . .DLB-21

Reynolds, John Hamilton
    1794-1852 . . . . .DLB-96

Reynolds, Sir Joshua 1723-1792 . . . . .DLB-104

Reynolds, Mack 1917-1983 . . . . .DLB-8

Reza, Yazmina 1959- DLB-321

Reznikoff, Charles 1894-1976 . . . . . . .DLB-28, 45

Rhetoric
    Continental European Rhetoricians,
        1400-1600, and Their Influence
        in Reaissance England DLB-236

    A Finding Guide to Key Works on
        Microfilm .DLB-236

    Glossary of Terms and Definitions of
        Rhetoic and Logic DLB-236

Rhett, Robert Barnwell 1800-1876. . . . . . . .DLB-43

Rhode, John 1884-1964 . . . . .DLB-77

Rhodes, Eugene Manlove 1869-1934 . . . .DLB-256

Rhodes, James Ford 1848-1927 . . . . .DLB-47

Rhodes, Richard 1937- DLB-185

Rhys, Jean 1890-1979
    . . . . DLB-36, 117, 162; CDBLB-7; CDWLB-3

Ribeiro, Bernadim
    fl. ca. 1475/1482-1526/1544 . . . . .DLB-287

Ricardo, David 1772-1823 . . . . .DLB-107, 158

Ricardou, Jean 1932- DLB-83

Riccoboni, Marie-Jeanne (Marie-Jeanne de
    Heurles Laboras de Mézières Riccoboni)
    1713-1792 . . . . .DLB-314

Rice, Anne (A. N. Roquelare, Anne Rampling)
    1941- DLB-292

Rice, Christopher 1978- DLB-292

Rice, Elmer 1892-1967 . . . . .DLB-4, 7

Rice, Grantland 1880-1954 . . . . DLB-29, 171

Rich, Adrienne 1929- DLB-5, 67; CDALB-7

Richard, Mark 1955- DLB-234

Richard de Fournival
    1201-1259 or 1260 . . . . .DLB-208

Richards, David Adams 1950- DLB-53

Richards, George circa 1760-1814 . . . . . . .DLB-37

Richards, I. A. 1893-1979. . . . . .DLB-27

Richards, Laura E. 1850-1943 . . . . .DLB-42

Richards, William Carey 1818-1892 . . . . . .DLB-73

Grant Richards [publishing house]. DLB-112

Richards, Charles F. 1851-1913. . . . . .DLB-71

Richardson, Dorothy M. 1873-1957. . . . . . .DLB-36

    The Novels of Dorothy Richardson
        (1918), by May Sinclair. DLB-36

Richardson, Henry Handel
    (Ethel Florence Lindesay Robertson)
    1870-1946 . . . . DLB-197, 230

Richardson, Jack 1935- DLB-7

Richardson, John 1796-1852 . . . . .DLB-99

Richardson, Samuel
    1689-1761 . . . . .DLB-39, 154; CDBLB-2

    Introductory Letters from the Second
        Edition of *Pamela* (1741) DLB-39

    Postscript to [the Third Edition of]
        Clarissa (1751) DLB-39

    Preface to the First Edition of
        Pamela (1740) DLB-39

    Preface to the Third Edition of
        Clarissa (1751) [excerpt] DLB-39

    Preface to Volume 1 of *Clarissa*
        (1747) DLB-39

    Preface to Volume 3 of *Clarissa*
        (1748) DLB-39

Richardson, Willis 1889-1977. . . . . .DLB-51

Riche, Barnabe 1542-1617 . . . . .DLB-136

Richepin, Jean 1849-1926 . . . . .DLB-192

Richler, Mordecai 1931-2001 . . . . .DLB-53

Richter, Conrad 1890-1968 . . . . .DLB-9, 212

Richter, Hans Werner 1908-1993. . . . . .DLB-69

Richter, Johann Paul Friedrich
    1763-1825 . . . . DLB-94; CDWLB-2

Joseph Rickerby [publishing house] DLB-106

Rickword, Edgell 1898-1982 . . . . .DLB-20

Riddell, Charlotte 1832-1906. . . . . .DLB-156

Riddell, John (see Ford, Corey)

Ridge, John Rollin 1827-1867 . . . . .DLB-175

Ridge, Lola 1873-1941. . . . . .DLB-54

Ridge, William Pett 1859-1930 . . . . .DLB-135

Riding, Laura (see Jackson, Laura Riding)

Ridler, Anne 1912-2001 . . . . .DLB-27

Ridruego, Dionisio 1912-1975 . . . . .DLB-108

Riel, Louis 1844-1885 . . . . .DLB-99

Riemer, Johannes 1648-1714 . . . . .DLB-168

Riera, Carme 1948- DLB-322

Rifbjerg, Klaus 1931- DLB-214

Riffaterre, Michael 1924- DLB-67

A Conversation between William Riggan
    and Janette Turner Hospital Y-02

Riggs, Lynn 1899-1954 . . . . .DLB-175

Riis, Jacob 1849-1914 . . . . .DLB-23

John C. Riker [publishing house] DLB-49

Riley, James 1777-1840 . . . . .DLB-183

Riley, John 1938-1978 . . . . .DLB-40

Rilke, Rainer Maria
    1875-1926 . . . . DLB-81; CDWLB-2

Rimanelli, Giose 1926- DLB-177

Rimbaud, Jean-Nicolas-Arthur
    1854-1891 . . . . .DLB-217

Rinehart and Company DLB-46

Ringuet 1895-1960. . . . . .DLB-68

Ringwood, Gwen Pharis 1910-1984. . . . . . .DLB-88

Rinser, Luise 1911-2002 . . . . .DLB-69

Rinuccini, Ottavio 1562-1621 . . . . .DLB-339

Ríos, Alberto 1952- DLB-122

Ríos, Isabella 1948- DLB-82

Ripley, Arthur 1895-1961 . . . . .DLB-44

Ripley, George 1802-1880 . . . . . DLB-1, 64, 73, 235

The Rising Glory of America:
    Three Poems .DLB-37

The Rising Glory of America: Written in 1771
    (1786), by Hugh Henry Brackenridge
    and Philip Freneau DLB-37

Riskin, Robert 1897-1955 . . . . .DLB-26

Risse, Heinz 1898-1989. . . . . .DLB-69

Rist, Johann 1607-1667 . . . . .DLB-164

Ristikivi, Karl 1912-1977 . . . . .DLB-220

Ritchie, Anna Mowatt 1819-1870 . . . . .DLB-3, 250

Ritchie, Anne Thackeray 1837-1919 . . . . . .DLB-18

Ritchie, Thomas 1778-1854 . . . . .DLB-43

Rites of Passage, 1980 Booker Prize winner,
    William Golding DLB-326

The Ritz Paris Hemingway Award Y-85

Mario Varga Llosa's Acceptance Speech . . Y-85	Roblès, Emmanuel 1914-1995 . . . . DLB-83	Ronsard, Pierre de 1524-1585 . . . . DLB-327
Rivard, Adjutor 1868-1945. . . . . DLB-92	Roccatagliata Ceccardi, Ceccardo 1871-1919. . . . . DLB-114	Rook, Clarence 1863-1915. . . . . DLB-135
Rive, Richard 1931-1989 . . . . DLB-125, 225	Rocha, Adolfo Correira da (see Torga, Miguel)	Roosevelt, Theodore 1858-1919 . . . . DLB-47, 186, 275
Rivera, José 1955- DLB-249	Roche, Billy 1949- DLB-233	Root, Waverley 1903-1982. . . . . DLB-4
Rivera, Marina 1942- DLB-122	Rochester, John Wilmot, Earl of 1647-1680. . . . . DLB-131	Root, William Pitt 1941- DLB-120
Rivera, Tomás 1935-1984. . . . . DLB-82	Rochon, Esther 1948- DLB-251	Roquebrune, Robert de 1889-1978. . . . . . DLB-68
Rivers, Conrad Kent 1933-1968. . . . . DLB-41	Rock, Howard 1911-1976. . . . . DLB-127	Rorty, Richard 1931- DLB-246, 279
Riverside Press DLB-49	Rockwell, Norman Perceval 1894-1978 . . DLB-188	Rosa, João Guimarães 1908-1967 . . . DLB-113, 307
Rivington, James circa 1724-1802. . . . . . . DLB-43	Rodgers, Carolyn M. 1945- DLB-41	Rosales, Luis 1910-1992. . . . . DLB-134
Charles Rivington [publishing house]. . . . DLB-154	Rodgers, W. R. 1909-1969 . . . . DLB-20	Roscoe, William 1753-1831 . . . . DLB-163
Rivkin, Allen 1903-1990. . . . . DLB-26	Rodney, Lester 1911- DLB-241	Rose, Dilys 1954- DLB-319
Roa Bastos, Augusto 1917-2005 . . . . DLB-113	Rodoreda, Mercé 1908-1983 . . . . DLB-322	Rose, Reginald 1920-2002 . . . . DLB-26
Robbe-Grillet, Alain 1922- DLB-83	Rodrigues, Nelson 1912-1980. . . . . DLB-307	Rose, Wendy 1948- DLB-175
Robbins, Tom 1936- Y-80	Rodríguez, Claudio 1934-1999. . . . . DLB-134	Rosegger, Peter 1843-1918 . . . . DLB-129
Roberts, Charles G. D. 1860-1943 . . . . . . DLB-92	Rodríguez, Joe D. 1943- DLB-209	Rosei, Peter 1946- DLB-85
Roberts, Dorothy 1906-1993 . . . . DLB-88	Rodriguez, Judith 1936- DLB-325	Rosen, Norma 1925- DLB-28
Roberts, Elizabeth Madox 1881-1941 . . . . DLB-9, 54, 102	Rodríguez, Luis J. 1954- DLB-209	Rosenbach, A. S. W. 1876-1952 . . . . DLB-140
Roberts, John (see Swynnerton, Thomas)	Rodriguez, Richard 1944- DLB-82, 256	Rosenbaum, Ron 1946- DLB-185
Roberts, Kate 1891-1985 . . . . DLB-319	Rodríguez Julia, Edgardo 1946- DLB-145	Rosenbaum, Thane 1960- DLB-299
Roberts, Keith 1935-2000. . . . . DLB-261	Roe, E. P. 1838-1888 . . . . DLB-202	Rosenberg, Isaac 1890-1918. . . . . DLB-20, 216
Roberts, Kenneth 1885-1957 . . . . DLB-9	Roethke, Theodore 1908-1963 . . . . DLB-5, 206; CDALB-1	Rosenfarb, Chava (Khave Roznfarb) 1923- DLB-333
Roberts, Michèle 1949- DLB-231	Rogers, Jane 1952- DLB-194	Rosenfeld, Isaac 1918-1956 . . . . DLB-28
Roberts, Theodore Goodridge 1877-1953. . . . . DLB-92	Rogers, Pattiann 1940- DLB-105	Rosenfeld, Morris (Moris Roznfeld) 1862-1923 . . . . DLB-333
Roberts, Ursula Wyllie (see Miles, Susan)	Rogers, Samuel 1763-1855 . . . . DLB-93	Rosenthal, Harold 1914-1999. . . . . DLB-241
Roberts, William 1767-1849 . . . . DLB-142	Rogers, Will 1879-1935 . . . . DLB-11	Jimmy, Red, and Others: Harold Rosenthal Remembers the Stars of the Press Box. Y-01
James Roberts [publishing house]. DLB-154	Rohmer, Sax 1883-1959 . . . . DLB-70	
Roberts Brothers. DLB-49	Roig, Montserrat 1946-1991. . . . . DLB-322	Rosenthal, M. L. 1917-1996 . . . . DLB-5
A. M. Robertson and Company DLB-49	Roiphe, Anne 1935- Y-80	Rosenwald, Lessing J. 1891-1979 . . . . . . .DLB-187
Robertson, Ethel Florence Lindesay (see Richardson, Henry Handel)	Rojas, Arnold R. 1896-1988. . . . . DLB-82	Rospigliosi, Giulio (Pope Clement IX) 1600-1669 . . . . DLB-339
Robertson, William 1721-1793 . . . . . DLB-104, 336	Rojas, Fernando de ca. 1475-1541 . . . . . . DLB-286	Ross, Alexander 1591-1654 . . . . DLB-151
Robin, Leo 1895-1984 . . . . DLB-265	Roland de la Platière, Marie-Jeanne (Madame Roland) 1754-1793 . . . . DLB-314	Ross, Harold 1892-1951. . . . . .DLB-137
Robins, Elizabeth 1862-1952 . . . . DLB-197	Rolfe, Edwin (Solomon Fishman) 1909-1954 . . . . DLB-303	Ross, Jerry 1926-1955 . . . . DLB-265
Robinson, A. Mary F. (Madame James Darmesteter, Madame Mary Duclaux) 1857-1944 . . . . DLB-240	Rolfe, Frederick William 1860-1913 . . . . DLB-34, 156	Ross, Leonard Q. (see Rosten, Leo)
		Ross, Lillian 1927- DLB-185
Robinson, Casey 1903-1979 . . . . DLB-44	Rolland, Romain 1866-1944. . . . . DLB-65, 332	Ross, Martin 1862-1915 . . . . DLB-135
Robinson, Derek 1932- Y-02	Rolle, Richard circa 1290-1300 - 1349 . . . DLB-146	Ross, Sinclair 1908-1996. . . . . DLB-88
Robinson, Edwin Arlington 1869-1935 . . . . DLB-54; CDALB-3	Rölvaag, O. E. 1876-1931. . . . . DLB-9, 212	Ross, W. W. E. 1894-1966 . . . . DLB-88
Review by Derek Robinson of George Greenfield's Rich Dust. Y-02	Romains, Jules 1885-1972 . . . . DLB-65, 321	Rosselli, Amelia 1930-1996 . . . . DLB-128
	A. Roman and Company DLB-49	Rossen, Robert 1908-1966 . . . . DLB-26
Robinson, Henry Crabb 1775-1867 . . . . . DLB-107	Roman de la Rose: Guillaume de Lorris 1200/1205-circa 1230, Jean de Meun 1235-1240-circa 1305. . . . . DLB-208	Rosset, Barney 1922- Y-02
Robinson, James Harvey 1863-1936. . . . . DLB-47		Rossetti, Christina 1830-1894. . . DLB-35, 163, 240
Robinson, Lennox 1886-1958. . . . . DLB-10	Romano, Lalla 1906-2001 . . . . .DLB-177	Rossetti, Dante Gabriel 1828-1882 . . . . DLB-35; CDBLB-4
Robinson, Mabel Louise 1874-1962 . . . . . DLB-22	Romano, Octavio 1923- DLB-122	
Robinson, Marilynne 1943- DLB-206	Rome, Harold 1908-1993 . . . . DLB-265	The Stealthy School of Criticism (1871). DLB-35
Robinson, Mary 1758-1800 . . . . DLB-158	Romero, Leo 1950- DLB-122	
Robinson, Richard circa 1545-1607 . . . . . DLB-167	Romero, Lin 1947- DLB-122	Rossner, Judith 1935- DLB-6
Robinson, Therese 1797-1870 . . . . . . DLB-59, 133	Romero, Orlando 1945- DLB-82	Rostand, Edmond 1868-1918. . . . . DLB-192
Robison, Mary 1949- DLB-130		Rosten, Leo 1908-1997. . . . . DLB-11

Rostenberg, Leona 1908-2005..........DLB-140

Rostopchina, Evdokiia Petrovna
 1811-1858.....................DLB-205

Rostovsky, Dimitrii 1651-1709..........DLB-150

Rota, Bertram 1903-1966.............DLB-201

 Bertram Rota and His Bookshop........Y-91

Roth, Gerhard 1942-...........DLB-85, 124

Roth, Henry 1906?-1995..............DLB-28

Roth, Joseph 1894-1939..............DLB-85

Roth, Philip
 1933-......DLB-2, 28, 173; Y-82; CDALB-6

Rothenberg, Jerome 1931-..........DLB-5, 193

Rothschild Family...................DLB-184

Rotimi, Ola 1938-..................DLB-125

Rotrou, Jean 1609-1650..............DLB-268

Rousseau, Jean-Jacques 1712-1778........DLB-314

 The Social Contract................DLB-314

Routhier, Adolphe-Basile 1839-1920......DLB-99

Routier, Simone 1901-1987............DLB-88

George Routledge and Sons...........DLB-106

Roversi, Roberto 1923-...............DLB-128

Rowe, Elizabeth Singer 1674-1737.....DLB-39, 95

Rowe, Nicholas 1674-1718.............DLB-84

Rowlands, Ian 1964-..................DLB-310

Rowlands, Samuel circa 1570-1630......DLB-121

Rowlandson, Mary
 circa 1637-circa 1711...........DLB-24, 200

Rowley, William circa 1585-1626........DLB-58

Rowling, J. K.
 The Harry Potter Phenomenon.........Y-99

Rowse, A. L. 1903-1997...............DLB-155

Rowson, Susanna Haswell
 circa 1762-1824................DLB-37, 200

Roy, Arundhati 1961-............DLB-323, 326

Roy, Camille 1870-1943................DLB-92

The G. Ross Roy Scottish Poetry Collection
 at the University of South Carolina......Y-89

Roy, Gabrielle 1909-1983..............DLB-68

Roy, Jules 1907-2000..................DLB-83

The Royal Court Theatre and the English
 Stage Company....................DLB-13

The Royal Court Theatre and the New
 Drama..........................DLB-10

The Royal Shakespeare Company
 at the Swan.......................Y-88

Royall, Anne Newport 1769-1854....DLB-43, 248

Royce, Josiah 1855-1916...............DLB-270

The Roycroft Printing Shop............DLB-49

Royde-Smith, Naomi 1875-1964.........DLB-191

Royster, Vermont 1914-1996............DLB-127

Richard Royston [publishing house].....DLB-170

Rozanov, Vasilii Vasil'evich
 1856-1919......................DLB-295

Różewicz, Tadeusz 1921-..............DLB-232

Ruark, Gibbons 1941-.................DLB-120

Ruban, Vasilii Grigorevich 1742-1795....DLB-150

Rubens, Bernice 1928-2004.....DLB-14, 207, 326

Rubião, Murilo 1916-1991.............DLB-307

Rubina, Dina Il'inichna 1953-........DLB-285

Rubinshtein, Lev Semenovich 1947-...DLB-285

Rudd and Carleton...................DLB-49

Rudd, Steele (Arthur Hoey Davis).......DLB-230

Rudkin, David 1936-..................DLB-13

Rudnick, Paul 1957-..................DLB-266

Rudnicki, Adolf 1909-1990............DLB-299

Rudolf von Ems circa 1200-circa 1254....DLB-138

Ruffhead, Owen 1723-1769.............DLB-336

Ruffin, Josephine St. Pierre 1842-1924.....DLB-79

Rufo, Juan Gutiérrez 1547?-1620?.......DLB-318

Ruganda, John 1941-..................DLB-157

Ruggles, Henry Joseph 1813-1906........DLB-64

Ruiz, Juan, Arcipreste de Hita
 1330-1343.......................DLB-337

Ruiz de Burton, María Amparo
 1832-1895..................DLB-209, 221

Rukeyser, Muriel 1913-1980............DLB-48

Rule, Jane 1931-......................DLB-60

Rulfo, Juan 1918-1986......DLB-113; CDWLB-3

Rumaker, Michael 1932-...........DLB-16, 335

Rumens, Carol 1944-..................DLB-40

Rummo, Paul-Eerik 1942-.............DLB-232

Runyon, Damon 1880-1946.....DLB-11, 86, 171

Ruodlieb circa 1050-1075.............DLB-148

Rush, Benjamin 1746-1813.............DLB-37

Rush, Rebecca 1779-?.................DLB-200

Rushdie, Salman 1947-......DLB-194, 323, 326

Rusk, Ralph L. 1888-1962.............DLB-103

Ruskin, John
 1819-1900......DLB-55, 163, 190; CDBLB-4

Russ, Joanna 1937-.....................DLB-8

Russell, Benjamin 1761-1845...........DLB-43

Russell, Bertrand 1872-1970....DLB-100, 262, 332

Russell, Charles Edward 1860-1941......DLB-25

Russell, Charles M. 1864-1926.........DLB-188

Russell, Eric Frank 1905-1978..........DLB-255

Russell, Fred 1906-2003...............DLB-241

Russell, George William (see AE)

Russell, Countess Mary Annette Beauchamp
 (see Arnim, Elizabeth von)

Russell, Willy 1947-..................DLB-233

B. B. Russell and Company.............DLB-49

R. H. Russell and Son.................DLB-49

Rutebeuf fl.1249-1277.................DLB-208

Rutherford, Mark 1831-1913............DLB-18

Ruxton, George Frederick
 1821-1848.......................DLB-186

R-va, Zeneida (see Gan, Elena Andreevna)

Ryan, Gig 1956-......................DLB-325

Ryan, James 1952-....................DLB-267

Ryan, Michael 1946-....................Y-82

Ryan, Oscar 1904-....................DLB-68

Rybakov, Anatolii Naumovich
 1911-1994......................DLB-302

Ryder, Jack 1871-1936................DLB-241

Ryga, George 1932-1987...............DLB-60

Rylands, Enriqueta Augustina Tennant
 1843-1908......................DLB-184

Rylands, John 1801-1888..............DLB-184

Ryle, Gilbert 1900-1976...............DLB-262

Ryleev, Kondratii Fedorovich
 1795-1826......................DLB-205

Rymer, Thomas 1643?-1713.......DLB-101, 336

Ryskind, Morrie 1895-1985.............DLB-26

Rzhevsky, Aleksei Andreevich
 1737-1804......................DLB-150

S

The Saalfield Publishing Company.......DLB-46

Saba, Umberto 1883-1957..............DLB-114

Sábato, Ernesto 1911-......DLB-145; CDWLB-3

Saberhagen, Fred 1930-.................DLB-8

Sabin, Joseph 1821-1881...............DLB-187

Sabino, Fernando (Fernando Tavares Sabino)
 1923-2004......................DLB-307

Sacer, Gottfried Wilhelm 1635-1699.....DLB-168

Sachs, Hans 1494-1576......DLB-179; CDWLB-2

Sachs, Nelly 1891-1970................DLB-332

Sá-Carneiro, Mário de 1890-1916........DLB-287

Sack, John 1930-2004..................DLB-185

Sackler, Howard 1929-1982..............DLB-7

Sackville, Lady Margaret 1881-1963....DLB-240

Sackville, Thomas 1536-1608 and
 Norton, Thomas 1532-1584........DLB-62

Sackville, Thomas 1536-1608..........DLB-132

Sackville-West, Edward 1901-1965......DLB-191

Sackville-West, Vita 1892-1962......DLB-34, 195

Sacred Hunger, 1992 Booker Prize winner,
 Barry Unsworth..................DLB-326

Sá de Miranda, Francisco de
 1481-1588?.....................DLB-287

Sade, Marquis de (Donatien-Alphonse-François,
 comte de Sade) 1740-1814..........DLB-314

 "Dialogue entre un prêtre et un
 moribond"......................DLB-314

Sadlier, Mary Anne 1820-1903..........DLB-99

D. and J. Sadlier and Company..........DLB-49

Sadoff, Ira 1945-.....................DLB-120

Sadoveanu, Mihail 1880-1961..........DLB-220

Sadur, Nina Nikolaevna 1950-.........DLB-285

Sáenz, Benjamin Alire 1954-..........DLB-209

Cumulative Index

Saenz, Jaime 1921-1986 .... DLB-145, 283
Saffin, John circa 1626-1710 .... DLB-24
Sagan, Françoise 1935- DLB-83
Sage, Robert 1899-1962 .... DLB-4
Sagel, Jim 1947- DLB-82
Sagendorph, Robb Hansell 1900-1970 ... DLB-137
Sahagún, Carlos 1938- DLB-108
Sahgal, Nayantara 1927- DLB-323
Sahkomaapii, Piitai (see Highwater, Jamake)
Sahl, Hans 1902-1993 .... DLB-69
Said, Edward W. 1935- DLB-67
Saigyō 1118-1190 .... DLB-203
Saijo, Albert 1926- DLB-312
Saiko, George 1892-1962 .... DLB-85
Sainte-Beuve, Charles-Augustin
  1804-1869 .... DLB-217
Saint-Exupéry, Antoine de 1900-1944 ..... DLB-72
Saint-Gelais, Mellin de 1490?-1558 ...... DLB-327
St. John, J. Allen 1872-1957 .... DLB-188
St John, Madeleine 1942- DLB-267
St. Johns, Adela Rogers 1894-1988 ...... DLB-29
St. Omer, Garth 1931- DLB-117
Saint Pierre, Michel de 1916-1987 ...... DLB-83
Saintsbury, George 1845-1933 .... DLB-57, 149
  "Modern English Prose" (1876) DLB-57
  The Present State of the English
    Novel (1892), ... DLB-18
Saint-Simon, Louis de Rouvroy, duc de
  1675-1755 .... DLB-314
St. Dominic's Press DLB-112
The St. John's College Robert Graves Trust ... Y-96
St. Martin's Press DLB-46
St. Nicholas 1873-1881 .... DS-13
Saiokuken Sōchō 1448-1532 .... DLB-203
Saki (see Munro, H. H.)
Salaam, Kalamu ya 1947- DLB-38
Salacrou, Armand 1899-1989 .... DLB-321
Šalamun, Tomaž 1941- ... DLB-181; CDWLB-4
Salas, Floyd 1931- DLB-82
Sálaz-Marquez, Rubén 1935- DLB-122
Salcedo, Hugo 1964- DLB-305
Salemson, Harold J. 1910-1988 .... DLB-4
Salesbury, William 1520?-1584? DLB-281
Salinas, Luis Omar 1937- DLB-82
Salinas, Pedro 1891-1951 .... DLB-134
Salinger, J. D.
  1919- DLB-2, 102, 173; CDALB-1
Salkey, Andrew 1928-1995 .... DLB-125
Sallust circa 86 B.C.-35 B.C.
  .... DLB-211; CDWLB-1
Salt, Waldo 1914-1987 .... DLB-44
Salter, James 1925- DLB-130

Salter, Mary Jo 1954- DLB-120
Saltus, Edgar 1855-1921 .... DLB-202
Saltykov, Mikhail Evgrafovich
  1826-1889 .... DLB-238
Salustri, Carlo Alberto (see Trilussa)
Salverson, Laura Goodman 1890-1970 .... DLB-92
Samain, Albert 1858-1900 .... DLB-217
Sampson, Richard Henry (see Hull, Richard)
Samuels, Ernest 1903-1996 .... DLB-111
Sanborn, Franklin Benjamin
  1831-1917 .... DLB-1, 223
Sánchez, Florencio 1875-1910 .... DLB-305
Sánchez, Luis Rafael 1936- DLB-145, 305
Sánchez, Philomeno "Phil" 1917- DLB-122
Sánchez, Ricardo 1941-1995 .... DLB-82
Sánchez, Saúl 1943- DLB-209
Sanchez, Sonia 1934- DLB-41; DS-8
Sánchez de Arévalo, Rodrigo
  1404-1470 .... DLB-286
Sánchez de Badajoz, Diego ?-1552? DLB-318
Sánchez Ferlosio, Rafael 1927- DLB-322
Sand, George 1804-1876 .... DLB-119, 192
Sandburg, Carl
  1878-1967 .... DLB-17, 54; CDALB-3
Sandel, Cora (Sara Fabricius)
  1880-1974 .... DLB-297
Sandemose, Aksel 1899-1965 .... DLB-297
Sanders, Edward 1939- DLB-16, 244
Sanderson, Robert 1587-1663 .... DLB-281
Sandoz, Mari 1896-1966 .... DLB-9, 212
Sandwell, B. K. 1876-1954 .... DLB-92
Sandy, Stephen 1934- DLB-165
Sandys, George 1578-1644 .... DLB-24, 121
Sangster, Charles 1822-1893 .... DLB-99
Sanguineti, Edoardo 1930- DLB-128
Sanjōnishi Sanetaka 1455-1537 .... DLB-203
San Pedro, Diego de fl. ca. 1492 .... DLB-286
Sansay, Leonora ?-after 1823 .... DLB-200
Sansom, William 1912-1976 .... DLB-139
Santa Maria Egipçiaca thirteenth-fourteenth
  centuries DLB-337
Sant'Anna, Affonso Romano de
  1937- DLB-307
Santayana, George
  1863-1952 ...... DLB-54, 71, 246, 270; DS-13
Santiago, Danny 1911-1988 .... DLB-122
Santillana, Marqués de (Íñigo López de Mendoza)
  1398-1458 .... DLB-286
Santmyer, Helen Hooven 1895-1986 .... Y-84
Santos, Bienvenido 1911-1996 .... DLB-312
Sanvitale, Francesca 1928- DLB-196
Sapidus, Joannes 1490-1561 .... DLB-179
Sapir, Edward 1884-1939 .... DLB-92

Sapper (see McNeile, Herman Cyril)
Sappho circa 620 B.C.-circa 550 B.C.
  .... DLB-176; CDWLB-1
Saramago, José 1922- DLB-287, 332; Y-98
  Nobel Lecture 1998: How Characters
    Became the Masters and the Author
    Their Apprentice Y-98
Sarban (John W. Wall) 1910-1989 ...... DLB-255
Sardou, Victorien 1831-1908 .... DLB-192
Sarduy, Severo 1937-1993 .... DLB-113
Sargent, Pamela 1948- DLB-8
Saro-Wiwa, Ken 1941- DLB-157
Saroyan, Aram
  Rites of Passage [on William Saroyan] ... Y-83
Saroyan, William
  1908-1981 ..... DLB-7, 9, 86; Y-81; CDALB-7
Sarraute, Nathalie 1900-1999 .... DLB-83, 321
Sarrazin, Albertine 1937-1967 .... DLB-83
Sarris, Greg 1952- DLB-175
Sarrocchi, Margherita 1560-1617 .... DLB-339
Sarton, May 1912-1995 .... DLB-48; Y-81
Sartre, Jean-Paul
  1905-1980 .... DLB-72, 296, 321, 332
Sassoon, Siegfried
  1886-1967 .... DLB-20, 191; DS-18
  A Centenary Essay Y-86
  Tributes from Vivien F. Clarke and
    Michael Thorpe Y-86
Sata Ineko 1904-1998 .... DLB-180
Saturday Review Press DLB-46
Saunders, George W. 1958- DLB-335
Saunders, James 1925-2004 .... DLB-13
Saunders, John Monk 1897-1940 .... DLB-26
Saunders, Margaret Marshall
  1861-1947 .... DLB-92
Saunders and Otley DLB-106
Saussure, Ferdinand de 1857-1913 ...... DLB-242
Savage, James 1784-1873 .... DLB-30
Savage, Marmion W. 1803?-1872 .... DLB-21
Savage, Richard 1697?-1743 .... DLB-95
Savard, Félix-Antoine 1896-1982 .... DLB-68
Savery, Henry 1791-1842 .... DLB-230
Saville, (Leonard) Malcolm 1901-1982 ... DLB-160
Saville, 1976 Booker Prize winner,
  David Storey DLB-326
Savinio, Alberto 1891-1952 .... DLB-264
Sawyer, Robert J. 1960- DLB-251
Sawyer, Ruth 1880-1970 .... DLB-22
Sayer, Mandy 1963- DLB-325
Sayers, Dorothy L.
  1893-1957 ..... DLB-10, 36, 77, 100; CDBLB-6
  The Dorothy L. Sayers Society Y-98
Sayle, Charles Edward 1864-1924 ...... DLB-184
Sayles, John Thomas 1950- DLB-44

Sbarbaro, Camillo 1888-1967 .... DLB-114

Scala, Flaminio (Flavio) 1552-1624 ...... DLB-339

Scalapino, Leslie 1947- DLB-193

Scannell, Vernon 1922- DLB-27

Scarry, Richard 1919-1994 .... DLB-61

Scève, Maurice circa 1502-circa 1564 ..... DLB-327

Schack, Hans Egede 1820-1859 .... DLB-300

Schaefer, Jack 1907-1991 .... DLB-212

Schaeffer, Albrecht 1885-1950 .... DLB-66

Schaeffer, Susan Fromberg 1941- ...DLB-28, 299

Schaff, Philip 1819-1893 .... DS-13

Schaper, Edzard 1908-1984 .... DLB-69

Scharf, J. Thomas 1843-1898 .... DLB-47

Schede, Paul Melissus 1539-1602 .... DLB-179

Scheffel, Joseph Viktor von 1826-1886 ...DLB-129

Scheffler, Johann 1624-1677 .... DLB-164

Schéhadé, Georges 1905-1999 .... DLB-321

Schelling, Friedrich Wilhelm Joseph von
    1775-1854 .... DLB-90

Scherer, Wilhelm 1841-1886 .... DLB-129

Scherfig, Hans 1905-1979 .... DLB-214

Schickele, René 1883-1940 .... DLB-66

Schiff, Dorothy 1903-1989 .... DLB-127

Schiller, Friedrich
    1759-1805 .... DLB-94; CDWLB-2

Schindler's Ark, 1982 Booker Prize winner,
    Thomas Keneally DLB-326

Schirmer, David 1623-1687 .... DLB-164

Schlaf, Johannes 1862-1941 .... DLB-118

Schlegel, August Wilhelm 1767-1845 ...... DLB-94

Schlegel, Dorothea 1763-1839 .... DLB-90

Schlegel, Friedrich 1772-1829 .... DLB-90

Schleiermacher, Friedrich 1768-1834 ..... DLB-90

Schlesinger, Arthur M., Jr. 1917- DLB-17

Schlumberger, Jean 1877-1968 .... DLB-65

Schmid, Eduard Hermann Wilhelm
    (see Edschmid, Kasimir)

Schmidt, Arno 1914-1979 .... DLB-69

Schmidt, Johann Kaspar (see Stirner, Max)

Schmidt, Michael 1947- DLB-40

Schmidtbonn, Wilhelm August
    1876-1952 .... DLB-118

Schmitz, Aron Hector (see Svevo, Italo)

Schmitz, James H. 1911-1981 .... DLB-8

Schnabel, Johann Gottfried 1692-1760 ....DLB-168

Schnackenberg, Gjertrud 1953- DLB-120

Schnitzler, Arthur
    1862-1931 .... DLB-81, 118; CDWLB-2

Schnurre, Wolfdietrich 1920-1989 .... DLB-69

Schocken Books DLB-46

Scholartis Press DLB-112

Scholderer, Victor 1880-1971 .... DLB-201

The Schomburg Center for Research
    in Black Culture DLB-76

Schönbeck, Virgilio (see Giotti, Virgilio)

Schönherr, Karl 1867-1943 .... DLB-118

Schoolcraft, Jane Johnston 1800-1841 .... DLB-175

School Stories, 1914-1960 .... DLB-160

Schopenhauer, Arthur 1788-1860 .... DLB-90

Schopenhauer, Johanna 1766-1838 .... DLB-90

Schorer, Mark 1908-1977 .... DLB-103

Schottelius, Justus Georg 1612-1676 ..... DLB-164

Schouler, James 1839-1920 .... DLB-47

Schoultz, Solveig von 1907-1996 .... DLB-259

Schrader, Paul 1946- DLB-44

Schreiner, Olive
    1855-1920 .... DLB-18, 156, 190, 225

Schroeder, Andreas 1946- DLB-53

Schubart, Christian Friedrich Daniel
    1739-1791 .... DLB-97

Schubert, Gotthilf Heinrich 1780-1860 .... DLB-90

Schücking, Levin 1814-1883 .... DLB-133

Schulberg, Budd 1914- DLB-6, 26, 28; Y-81

    Excerpts from USC Presentation
    [on F. Scott Fitzgerald] Y-96

F. J. Schulte and Company DLB-49

Schulz, Bruno 1892-1942 .... DLB-215; CDWLB-4

Schulze, Hans (see Praetorius, Johannes)

Schupp, Johann Balthasar 1610-1661 ..... DLB-164

Schurz, Carl 1829-1906 .... DLB-23

Schuyler, George S. 1895-1977 .... DLB-29, 51

Schuyler, James 1923-1991 .... DLB-5, 169

Schwartz, Delmore 1913-1966 .... DLB-28, 48

Schwartz, Jonathan 1938- Y-82

Schwartz, Lynne Sharon 1939- DLB-218

Schwarz, Sibylle 1621-1638 .... DLB-164

Schwarz-Bart, Andre 1928- DLB-299

Schwerner, Armand 1927-1999 .... DLB-165

Schwob, Marcel 1867-1905 .... DLB-123

Sciascia, Leonardo 1921-1989 .... DLB-177

Science Fiction and Fantasy
    Documents in British Fantasy and
    Science Fiction DLB-178
    Hugo Awards and Nebula Awards DLB-8
    The Iconography of Science-Fiction
    Art DLB-8
    The New Wave DLB-8
    Paperback Science Fiction DLB-8
    Science Fantasy DLB-8
    Science-Fiction Fandom and
    Conventions DLB-8
    Science-Fiction Fanzines: The Time
    Binders DLB-8
    Science-Fiction Films DLB-8
    Science Fiction Writers of America
    and the Nebula Award DLB-8

Selected Science-Fiction Magazines and
    Anthologies DLB-8

A World Chronology of Important Science
    Fiction Works (1818-1979) DLB-8

The Year in Science Fiction
    and Fantasy Y-00, 01

Scot, Reginald circa 1538-1599 .... DLB-136

Scotellaro, Rocco 1923-1953 .... DLB-128

Scott, Alicia Anne (Lady John Scott)
    1810-1900 .... DLB-240

Scott, Catharine Amy Dawson
    1865-1934 .... DLB-240

Scott, Dennis 1939-1991 .... DLB-125

Scott, Dixon 1881-1915 .... DLB-98

Scott, Duncan Campbell 1862-1947 ...... DLB-92

Scott, Evelyn 1893-1963 .... DLB-9, 48

Scott, F. R. 1899-1985 .... DLB-88

Scott, Frederick George 1861-1944 ...... DLB-92

Scott, Geoffrey 1884-1929 .... DLB-149

Scott, Harvey W. 1838-1910 .... DLB-23

Scott, John 1948- DLB-325

Scott, Lady Jane (see Scott, Alicia Anne)

Scott, Paul 1920-1978 .... DLB-14, 207, 326

Scott, Sarah 1723-1795 .... DLB-39

Scott, Tom 1918-1995 .... DLB-27

Scott, Sir Walter 1771-1832
    ...... DLB-93, 107, 116, 144, 159; CDBLB-3

Scott, William Bell 1811-1890 .... DLB-32

Walter Scott Publishing Company
    Limited DLB-112

William R. Scott [publishing house] DLB-46

Scott-Heron, Gil 1949- DLB-41

Scribe, Eugène 1791-1861 .... DLB-192

Scribner, Arthur Hawley 1859-1932 .... DS-13, 16

Scribner, Charles 1854-1930 .... DS-13, 16

Scribner, Charles, Jr. 1921-1995 .... Y-95

    Reminiscences DS-17

Charles Scribner's Sons DLB-49; DS-13, 16, 17

    Archives of Charles Scribner's Sons DS-17

Scribner's Magazine DS-13

Scribner's Monthly DS-13

Scripps, E. W. 1854-1926 .... DLB-25

Scudder, Horace Elisha 1838-1902 .... DLB-42, 71

Scudder, Vida Dutton 1861-1954 .... DLB-71

Scudéry, Madeleine de 1607-1701 .... DLB-268

Scupham, Peter 1933- DLB-40

The Sea, 2005 Booker Prize winner,
    John Banville DLB-326

The Sea, The Sea, 1978 Booker Prize winner,
    Iris Murdoch DLB-326

Seabrook, William 1886-1945 .... DLB-4

Seabury, Samuel 1729-1796 .... DLB-31

Seacole, Mary Jane Grant 1805-1881 .... DLB-166

The Seafarer circa 970 .... DLB-146

Cumulative Index

Sealsfield, Charles (Carl Postl) 1793-1864.................DLB-133, 186

Searle, John R. 1932- DLB-279

Sears, Edward I. 1819?-1876........... DLB-79

Sears Publishing Company............ DLB-46

Seaton, George 1911-1979 .... DLB-44

Seaton, William Winston 1785-1866...... DLB-43

Sebillet, Thomas 1512-1589........... DLB-327

Martin Secker [publishing house]....... DLB-112

Martin Secker, and Warburg Limited.... DLB-112

The "Second Generation" Holocaust Novel...................... DLB-299

Sedgwick, Arthur George 1844-1915..... DLB-64

Sedgwick, Catharine Maria 1789-1867..........DLB-1, 74, 183, 239, 243

Sedgwick, Ellery 1872-1960 .... DLB-91

Sedgwick, Eve Kosofsky 1950- DLB-246

Sedley, Sir Charles 1639-1701.......... DLB-131

Seeberg, Peter 1925-1999 .... DLB-214

Seeger, Alan 1888-1916................ DLB-45

Seers, Eugene (see Dantin, Louis)

Seferis, George 1900-1971............. DLB-332

Segal, Erich 1937- Y-86

Segal, Lore 1928- DLB-299

Šegedin, Petar 1909-1998 .... DLB-181

Seghers, Anna 1900-1983.... DLB-69; CDWLB-2

Seid, Ruth (see Sinclair, Jo)

Seidel, Frederick Lewis 1936- Y-84

Seidel, Ina 1885-1974 .... DLB-56

Seifert, Jaroslav 1901-1986 ...DLB-215, 332; Y-84; CDWLB-4

Jaroslav Seifert Through the Eyes of the English-Speaking Reader........ Y-84

Three Poems by Jaroslav Seifert........ Y-84

Seifullina, Lidiia Nikolaevna 1889-1954.. DLB-272

Seigenthaler, John 1927- DLB-127

Seizin Press....................... DLB-112

Séjour, Victor 1817-1874 .... DLB-50

Séjour Marcou et Ferrand, Juan Victor (see Séjour, Victor)

Sekowski, Józef-Julian, Baron Brambeus (see Senkovsky, Osip Ivanovich)

Selby, Bettina 1934- DLB-204

Selby, Hubert Jr. 1928-2004 .... DLB-2, 227

Selden, George 1929-1989 .... DLB-52

Selden, John 1584-1654 .... DLB-213

Selenić, Slobodan 1933-1995 .... DLB-181

Self, Edwin F. 1920- DLB-137

Self, Will 1961- DLB-207

Seligman, Edwin R. A. 1861-1939 ...... DLB-47

Selimović, Meša 1910-1982........... DLB-181; CDWLB-4

Sellars, Wilfrid 1912-1989 ....DLB-279

Sellings, Arthur (Arthur Gordon Ley) 1911-1968 .... DLB-261

Selous, Frederick Courteney 1851-1917...DLB-174

Seltzer, Chester E. (see Muro, Amado)

Thomas Seltzer [publishing house]....... DLB-46

Selvadurai, Shyam 1965- DLB-323

Selvon, Sam 1923-1994..... DLB-125; CDWLB-3

Semel, Nava 1954- DLB-299

Semmes, Raphael 1809-1877 .... DLB-189

Senancour, Etienne de 1770-1846....... DLB-119

Sena, Jorge de 1919-1978 .... DLB-287

Sendak, Maurice 1928- DLB-61

Sender, Ramón J. 1901-1982 .... DLB-322

Seneca the Elder circa 54 B.C.-circa A.D. 40.......... DLB-211

Seneca the Younger circa 1 B.C.-A.D. 65..... DLB-211; CDWLB-1

Senécal, Eva 1905-1988 .... DLB-92

Sengstacke, John 1912-1997 .... DLB-127

Senior, Olive 1941- DLB-157

Senkovsky, Osip Ivanovich (Józef-Julian Sekowski, Baron Brambeus) 1800-1858 ....DLB-198

Šenoa, August 1838-1881....DLB-147; CDWLB-4

Sentimental Fiction of the Sixteenth Century DLB-318

Sepamla, Sipho 1932- DLB-157, 225

Serafimovich, Aleksandr Serafimovich (Aleksandr Serafimovich Popov) 1863-1949 ....DLB-272

Serao, Matilde 1856-1927............. DLB-264

Seredy, Kate 1899-1975............... DLB-22

Sereni, Vittorio 1913-1983 .... DLB-128

William Seres [publishing house]........DLB-170

Sergeev-Tsensky, Sergei Nikolaevich (Sergei Nikolaevich Sergeev) 1875-1958 .....DLB-272

Serling, Rod 1924-1975................ DLB-26

Sernine, Daniel 1955- DLB-251

Serote, Mongane Wally 1944- DLB-125, 225

Serraillier, Ian 1912-1994 .... DLB-161

Serrano, Nina 1934- DLB-122

Service, Robert 1874-1958 .... DLB-92

Sessler, Charles 1854-1935 .... DLB-187

Seth, Vikram 1952- DLB-120, 271, 323

Seton, Elizabeth Ann 1774-1821........ DLB-200

Seton, Ernest Thompson 1860-1942 ....DLB-92; DS-13

Seton, John circa 1509-1567 .... DLB-281

Setouchi Harumi 1922- DLB-182

Settle, Mary Lee 1918- DLB-6

Seume, Johann Gottfried 1763-1810...... DLB-94

Seuse, Heinrich 1295?-1366 ....DLB-179

Seuss, Dr. (see Geisel, Theodor Seuss)

Severianin, Igor' 1887-1941........... DLB-295

Severin, Timothy 1940- DLB-204

Sévigné, Marie de Rabutin Chantal, Madame de 1626-1696 ....DLB-268

Sewall, Joseph 1688-1769 .... DLB-24

Sewall, Richard B. 1908-2003......... DLB-111

Sewall, Samuel 1652-1730............. DLB-24

Sewell, Anna 1820-1878 .... DLB-163

Sewell, Stephen 1953- DLB-325

Sexton, Anne 1928-1974... DLB-5, 169; CDALB-1

Seymour-Smith, Martin 1928-1998 ..... DLB-155

Sgorlon, Carlo 1930- DLB-196

Shaara, Michael 1929-1988 .... Y-83

Shabel'skaia, Aleksandra Stanislavovna 1845-1921 .... DLB-238

Shadwell, Thomas 1641?-1692.......... DLB-80

Shaffer, Anthony 1926-2001........... DLB-13

Shaffer, Peter 1926- DLB-13, 233; CDBLB-8

Muhammad ibn Idris al-Shafi'i 767-820.. DLB-311

Shaftesbury, Anthony Ashley Cooper, Third Earl of 1671-1713........ DLB-101, 336

Shaginian, Marietta Sergeevna 1888-1982 ....DLB-272

Shairp, Mordaunt 1887-1939 .... DLB-10

Shakespeare, Nicholas 1957- DLB-231

Shakespeare, William 1564-1616..... DLB-62, 172, 263; CDBLB-1

The New Variorum Shakespeare........ Y-85

Shakespeare and Montaigne: A Symposium by Jules Furthman................ Y-02

$6,166,000 for a *Book!* Observations on *The Shakespeare First Folio: The History of the Book*...................... Y-01

Taylor-Made Shakespeare? Or Is "Shall I Die?" the Long-Lost Text of Bottom's Dream?............. Y-85

The Shakespeare Globe Trust Y-93

Shakespeare Head Press.............. DLB-112

Shakhova, Elisaveta Nikitichna 1822-1899 ....DLB-277

Shakhovskoi, Aleksandr Aleksandrovich 1777-1846..................... DLB-150

Shalamov, Varlam Tikhonovich 1907-1982..................... DLB-302

al-Shanfara fl. sixth century DLB-311

Shange, Ntozake 1948- DLB-38, 249

Shapcott, Thomas W. 1935- DLB-289

Shapir, Ol'ga Andreevna 1850-1916..... DLB-295

Shapiro, Gerald 1950- DLB-335

Shapiro, Karl 1913-2000.............. DLB-48

Sharon Publications DLB-46

Sharov, Vladimir Aleksandrovich 1952- DLB-285

Sharp, Margery 1905-1991............ DLB-161

Sharp, William 1855-1905 .... DLB-156

Sharpe, Tom 1928- DLB-14, 231

Shaw, Albert 1857-1947................ DLB-91

Shaw, George Bernard
1856-1950 ... DLB-10, 57, 190, 332; CDBLB-6

    The Bernard Shaw Society Y-99

    "Stage Censorship: The Rejected
    Statement" (1911) [excerpts] DLB-10

Shaw, Henry Wheeler 1818-1885 ....DLB-11

Shaw, Irwin
1913-1984 ...... DLB-6, 102; Y-84; CDALB-1

Shaw, Joseph T. 1874-1952.............DLB-137

    "As I Was Saying," Joseph T. Shaw's
    Editorial Rationale in *Black Mask*
    (January 1927)...............DLB-137

Shaw, Mary 1854-1929 ....DLB-228

Shaw, Robert 1927-1978............DLB-13, 14

Shaw, Robert B. 1947- DLB-120

Shawn, Wallace 1943- DLB-266

Shawn, William 1907-1992............DLB-137

Frank Shay [publishing house]...........DLB-46

Shchedrin, N. (see Saltykov, Mikhail Evgrafovich)

Shcherbakova, Galina Nikolaevna
1932- DLB-285

Shcherbina, Nikolai Fedorovich
1821-1869 ....DLB-277

Shea, John Gilmary 1824-1892 ....DLB-30

Sheaffer, Louis 1912-1993 ....DLB-103

Sheahan, Henry Beston (see Beston, Henry)

Shearing, Joseph 1886-1952 ....DLB-70

Shebbeare, John 1709-1788..............DLB-39

Sheckley, Robert 1928- DLB-8

Shedd, William G. T. 1820-1894 ....DLB-64

Sheed, Wilfrid 1930- DLB-6

Sheed and Ward [U.S.] DLB-46

Sheed and Ward Limited [U.K.] DLB-112

Sheldon, Alice B. (see Tiptree, James, Jr.)

Sheldon, Edward 1886-1946 ....DLB-7

Sheldon and Company DLB-49

Sheller, Aleksandr Konstantinovich
1838-1900.......................DLB-238

Shelley, Mary Wollstonecraft 1797-1851
.... DLB-110, 116, 159, 178; CDBLB-3

    Preface to *Frankenstein; or, The
    Modern Prometheus* (1818) DLB-178

Shelley, Percy Bysshe
1792-1822 ...... DLB-96, 110, 158; CDBLB-3

Shelnutt, Eve 1941- DLB-130

Shem Tov de Carrión (Isaac Ibn Ardutiel)
fl. circa 1350-1360................DLB-337

Shen Congwen 1902-1988.............DLB-328

Shenshin (see Fet, Afanasii Afanas'evich)

Shenstone, William 1714-1763............DLB-95

Shepard, Clark and Brown DLB-49

Shepard, Ernest Howard 1879-1976......DLB-160

Shepard, Sam 1943- DLB-7, 212

Shepard, Thomas, I, 1604 or 1605-1649 ...DLB-24

Shepard, Thomas, II, 1635-1677 ....DLB-24

Shepherd, Luke fl. 1547-1554...........DLB-136

Sherburne, Edward 1616-1702..........DLB-131

Sheridan, Frances 1724-1766 ....DLB-39, 84

Sheridan, Richard Brinsley
1751-1816 .... DLB-89; CDBLB-2

Sherman, Francis 1871-1926 ....DLB-92

Sherman, Martin 1938- DLB-228

Sherriff, R. C. 1896-1975........ DLB-10, 191, 233

Sherrod, Blackie 1919- DLB-241

Sherry, Norman 1935- DLB-155

    Tribute to Graham Greene Y-91

Sherry, Richard 1506-1551 or 1555......DLB-236

Sherwood, Mary Martha 1775-1851 .....DLB-163

Sherwood, Robert E. 1896-1955 ... DLB-7, 26, 249

Shevyrev, Stepan Petrovich
1806-1864 ....DLB-205

Shi Tuo (Lu Fen) 1910-1988 ....DLB-328

Shiel, M. P. 1865-1947.................DLB-153

Shields, Carol 1935-2003 ....DLB-334

Shiels, George 1886-1949 ....DLB-10

Shiga Naoya 1883-1971 ....DLB-180

Shiina Rinzō 1911-1973 ....DLB-182

Shikishi Naishinnō 1153?-1201 ....DLB-203

Shillaber, Benjamin Penhallow
1814-1890 ....DLB-1, 11, 235

Shimao Toshio 1917-1986 ....DLB-182

Shimazaki Tōson 1872-1943 ....DLB-180

Shimose, Pedro 1940- DLB-283

Shine, Ted 1931- DLB-38

Shinkei 1406-1475 ....DLB-203

Ship, Reuben 1915-1975 ....DLB-88

Shirer, William L. 1904-1993 ....DLB-4

Shirinsky-Shikhmatov, Sergii Aleksandrovich
1783-1837 ....DLB-150

Shirley, James 1596-1666 ....DLB-58

Shishkov, Aleksandr Semenovich
1753-1841 ....DLB-150

Shmelev, I. S. 1873-1950 ....DLB-317

Shockley, Ann Allen 1927- DLB-33

Sholem Aleichem (Sholem Aleykhem; Sholem Yakov
Rabinowitz [Sholem Yankev Rabinovitsch])
1859-1916 ....DLB-333

Sholokhov, Mikhail Aleksandrovich
1905-1984 ....DLB-272, 332

Shōno Junzō 1921- DLB-182

Shore, Arabella 1820?-1901.............DLB-199

Shore, Louisa 1824-1895 ....DLB-199

Short, Luke (see Glidden, Frederick Dilley)

Peter Short [publishing house] DLB-170

Shorter, Dora Sigerson 1866-1918 ....DLB-240

Shorthouse, Joseph Henry 1834-1903 .....DLB-18

Short Stories
    Michael M. Rea and the Rea Award
    for the Short Story Y-97

    The Year in Short Stories Y-87

    The Year in the Short Story.......Y-88, 90–93

Shōtetsu 1381-1459 ....DLB-203

Showalter, Elaine 1941- DLB-67

Shreve, Anita 1946- DLB-292

Shteiger, Anatolii 1907-1944............DLB-317

Shukshin, Vasilii Makarovich
1929-1974 ....DLB-302

Shulevitz, Uri 1935- DLB-61

Shulman, Max 1919-1988 ....DLB-11

Shute, Henry A. 1856-1943 ....DLB-9

Shute, Nevil (Nevil Shute Norway)
1899-1960 ....DLB-255

Shuttle, Penelope 1947- DLB-14, 40

Shvarts, Evgenii L'vovich 1896-1958.....DLB-272

Sibawayhi circa 750-circa 795...........DLB-311

Sibbes, Richard 1577-1635 ....DLB-151

Sibiriak, D. (see Mamin, Dmitrii Narkisovich)

Siddal, Elizabeth Eleanor 1829-1862 .....DLB-199

Sidgwick, Ethel 1877-1970 ....DLB-197

Sidgwick, Henry 1838-1900.............DLB-262

Sidgwick and Jackson Limited..........DLB-112

Sidhwa, Bapsi 1939- DLB-323

Sidney, Margaret (see Lothrop, Harriet M.)

Sidney, Mary 1561-1621 ....DLB-167

Sidney, Sir Philip
1554-1586.............DLB-167; CDBLB-1

    An Apologie for Poetrie (the Olney edition,
    1595, of *Defence of Poesie*) DLB-167

Sidney's Press.........................DLB-49

The Siege of Krishnapur, 1973 Booker Prize winner,
    J. G. Farrell DLB-326

Sienkiewicz, Henryk 1846-1916.........DLB-332

Sierra, Rubén 1946- DLB-122

Sierra Club Books DLB-49

Siger of Brabant circa 1240-circa 1284....DLB-115

Sigourney, Lydia Huntley
1791-1865 ...... DLB-1, 42, 73, 183, 239, 243

Silkin, Jon 1930-1997..................DLB-27

Silko, Leslie Marmon
1948- DLB-143, 175, 256, 275

Sillanpää, Frans Eemil 1888-1964 ....DLB-332

Silliman, Benjamin 1779-1864 ....DLB-183

Silliman, Ron 1946- ....DLB 169

Silliphant, Stirling 1918-1996...........DLB-26

Sillitoe, Alan 1928- DLB-14, 139; CDBLB-8

    Tribute to J. B. Priestly Y-84

Silman, Roberta 1934- DLB-28

Silone, Ignazio (Secondino Tranquilli)
1900-1978 ....DLB-264

Silva, Beverly 1930- DLB-122

Silva, Clara 1905-1976 ....DLB-290

Silva, José Asunció 1865-1896 ....DLB-283

Cumulative Index

Silverberg, Robert 1935- DLB-8	Singer, Mark 1950- DLB-185	Small, Maynard and Company DLB-49
Silverman, Kaja 1947- DLB-246	Singh, Khushwant 1915- DLB-323	Smart, Christopher 1722-1771 .... DLB-109
Silverman, Kenneth 1936- DLB-111	Singmaster, Elsie 1879-1958 .... DLB-9	Smart, David A. 1892-1957 .... DLB-137
Simak, Clifford D. 1904-1988 .... DLB-8	Siniavsky, Andrei (Abram Tertz) 1925-1997 .... DLB-302	Smart, Elizabeth 1913-1986 .... DLB-88
Simcoe, Elizabeth 1762-1850 .... DLB-99	Sinisgalli, Leonardo 1908-1981 .... DLB-114	Smart, J. J. C. 1920- DLB-262
Simcox, Edith Jemima 1844-1901 .... DLB-190	Siodmak, Curt 1902-2000 .... DLB-44	Smedley, Menella Bute 1820?-1877 ..... DLB-199
Simcox, George Augustus 1841-1905 ..... DLB-35	Sîrbu, Ion D. 1919-1989 .... DLB-232	William Smellie [publishing house] DLB-154
Sime, Jessie Georgina 1868-1958 .... DLB-92	Siringo, Charles A. 1855-1928 .... DLB-186	Smiles, Samuel 1812-1904 .... DLB-55
Simenon, Georges 1903-1989 .... DLB-72; Y-89	Sissman, L. E. 1928-1976 .... DLB-5	Smiley, Jane 1949- DLB-227, 234
Simic, Charles 1938- DLB-105	Sisson, C. H. 1914-2003 .... DLB-27	Smith, A. J. M. 1902-1980 .... DLB-88
"Images and 'Images'" DLB-105	Sitwell, Edith 1887-1964 .... DLB-20; CDBLB-7	Smith, Adam 1723-1790 ...... DLB-104, 252, 336
Simionescu, Mircea Horia 1928- DLB-232	Sitwell, Osbert 1892-1969 .... DLB-100, 195	Smith, Adam (George Jerome Waldo Goodman) 1930- DLB-185
Simmel, Georg 1858-1918 .... DLB-296	Sivanandan, Ambalavaner 1923- DLB-323	Smith, Alexander 1829-1867 .... DLB-32, 55
Simmel, Johannes Mario 1924- DLB-69	Sixteenth-Century Spanish Epic, The DLB-318	"On the Writing of Essays" (1862) ... DLB-57
Valentine Simmes [publishing house] DLB-170	Skácel, Jan 1922-1989 .... DLB-232	Smith, Amanda 1837-1915 .... DLB-221
Simmons, Ernest J. 1903-1972 .... DLB-103	Skalbe, Kārlis 1879-1945 .... DLB-220	Smith, Betty 1896-1972 .... Y-82
Simmons, Herbert Alfred 1930- DLB-33	Skármeta, Antonio 1940- DLB-145; CDWLB-3	Smith, Carol Sturm 1938- Y-81
Simmons, James 1933- DLB-40	Skavronsky, A. (see Danilevsky, Grigorii Petrovich)	Smith, Charles Henry 1826-1903 .... DLB-11
Simms, William Gilmore 1806-1870 .... DLB-3, 30, 59, 73, 248	Skeat, Walter W. 1835-1912 .... DLB-184	Smith, Charlotte 1749-1806 .... DLB-39, 109
Simms and M'Intyre DLB-106	William Skeffington [publishing house] .. DLB-106	Smith, Chet 1899-1973 .... DLB-171
Simon, Claude 1913-2005 ..... DLB-83, 332; Y-85	Skelton, John 1463-1529 .... DLB-136	Smith, Cordwainer 1913-1966 .... DLB-8
Nobel Lecture Y-85	Skelton, Robin 1925-1997 .... DLB-27, 53	Smith, Dave 1942- DLB-5
Simon, Neil 1927- DLB-7, 266	Škėma, Antanas 1910-1961 .... DLB-220	Tribute to James Dickey Y-97
Simon and Schuster DLB-46	Skinner, Constance Lindsay 1877-1939 .... DLB-92	Tribute to John Gardner Y-82
Simonov, Konstantin Mikhailovich 1915-1979 .... DLB-302	Skinner, John Stuart 1788-1851 .... DLB-73	Smith, Dodie 1896-1990 .... DLB-10
Simons, Katherine Drayton Mayrant 1890-1969 .... Y-83	Skipsey, Joseph 1832-1903 .... DLB-35	Smith, Doris Buchanan 1934-2002 .... DLB-52
Simović, Ljubomir 1935- DLB-181	Skou-Hansen, Tage 1925- DLB-214	Smith, E. E. 1890-1965 .... DLB-8
Simpkin and Marshall [publishing house] DLB-154	Skrzynecki, Peter 1945- DLB-289	Smith, Elihu Hubbard 1771-1798 .... DLB-37
Simpson, Helen 1897-1940 .... DLB-77	Škvorecký, Josef 1924- DLB-232; CDWLB-4	Smith, Elizabeth Oakes (Prince) (see Oakes Smith, Elizabeth)
Simpson, Louis 1923- DLB-5	Slade, Bernard 1930- DLB-53	Smith, Eunice 1757-1823 .... DLB-200
Simpson, N. F. 1919- DLB-13	Slamnig, Ivan 1930- DLB-181	Smith, F. Hopkinson 1838-1915 .... DS-13
Sims, George 1923-1999 .... DLB-87; Y-99	Slančeková, Božena (see Timrava)	Smith, George D. 1870-1920 .... DLB-140
Sims, George Robert 1847-1922 ... DLB-35, 70, 135	Slataper, Scipio 1888-1915 .... DLB-264	Smith, George O. 1911-1981 .... DLB-8
Sinán, Rogelio 1902-1994 .... DLB-145, 290	Slater, Patrick 1880-1951 .... DLB-68	Smith, Goldwin 1823-1910 .... DLB-99
Sinclair, Andrew 1935- DLB-14	Slaveykov, Pencho 1866-1912 .... DLB-147	Smith, H. Allen 1907-1976 .... DLB-11, 29
Sinclair, Bertrand William 1881-1972 .... DLB-92	Slaviček, Milivoj 1929- DLB-181	Smith, Harry B. 1860-1936 .... DLB-187
Sinclair, Catherine 1800-1864 .... DLB-163	Slavitt, David 1935- DLB-5, 6	Smith, Hazel Brannon 1914-1994 .... DLB-127
Sinclair, Clive 1948- DLB-319	Sleigh, Burrows Willcocks Arthur 1821-1869 .... DLB-99	Smith, Henry circa 1560-circa 1591 ..... DLB-136
Sinclair, Jo 1913-1995 .... DLB-28	Sleptsov, Vasilii Alekseevich 1836-1878 ... DLB-277	Smith, Horatio (Horace) 1779-1849 .... DLB-96, 116
Sinclair, Lister 1921- DLB-88	Slesinger, Tess 1905-1945 .... DLB-102	Smith, Iain Crichton (Iain Mac A'Ghobhainn) 1928-1998 .... DLB-40, 139, 319
Sinclair, May 1863-1946 .... DLB-36, 135	Slessor, Kenneth 1901-1971 .... DLB-260	Smith, J. Allen 1860-1924 .... DLB-47
The Novels of Dorothy Richardson (1918) DLB-36	Slick, Sam (see Haliburton, Thomas Chandler)	Smith, James 1775-1839 .... DLB-96
Sinclair, Upton 1878-1968 ...... DLB-9; CDALB-5	Sloan, John 1871-1951 .... DLB-188	Smith, Jessie Willcox 1863-1935 .... DLB-188
Upton Sinclair [publishing house] DLB-46	Sloane, William, Associates DLB-46	Smith, John 1580-1631 .... DLB-24, 30
Singer, Isaac Bashevis 1904-1991 ...DLB-6, 28, 52, 278, 332, 333; Y-91; CDALB-1	Slonimsky, Mikhail Leonidovich 1897-1972 .... DLB-272	Smith, John 1618-1652 .... DLB-252
Singer, Israel Joshua (Yisroel-Yehoyshue Zinger) 1893-1944 .... DLB-333	Sluchevsky, Konstantin Konstantinovich 1837-1904 .... DLB-277	Smith, Josiah 1704-1781 .... DLB-24
		Smith, Ken 1938- DLB-40
		Smith, Lee 1944- DLB-143; Y-83

Smith, Logan Pearsall 1865-1946........DLB-98	The Society for Textual Scholarship and *TEXT* Y-87	Sorokin, Vladimir Georgievich 1955- DLB-285
Smith, Margaret Bayard 1778-1844......DLB-248	The Society for the History of Authorship, Reading and Publishing Y-92	Sorrentino, Gilbert 1929- DLB-5, 173; Y-80
Smith, Mark 1935- Y-82	Söderberg, Hjalmar 1869-1941 ....DLB-259	Sosa, Roberto 1930- DLB-290
Smith, Michael 1698-circa 1771 ....DLB-31	Södergran, Edith 1892-1923 ....DLB-259	Sotheby, James 1682-1742 ....DLB-213
Smith, Pauline 1882-1959 ....DLB-225	Soffici, Ardengo 1879-1964 ....DLB-114, 264	Sotheby, John 1740-1807 ....DLB-213
Smith, Red 1905-1982 ....DLB-29, 171	Sofola, 'Zulu 1938- DLB-157	Sotheby, Samuel 1771-1842 ....DLB-213
Smith, Roswell 1829-1892 ....DLB-79	Sokhanskaia, Nadezhda Stepanovna (Kokhanovskaia) 1823?-1884 ....DLB-277	Sotheby, Samuel Leigh 1805-1861.......DLB-213
Smith, Samuel Harrison 1772-1845 ....DLB-43	Sokolov, Sasha (Aleksandr Vsevolodovich Sokolov) 1943- DLB-285	Sotheby, William 1757-1833.........DLB-93, 213
Smith, Samuel Stanhope 1751-1819.......DLB-37	Solano, Solita 1888-1975 ....DLB-4	Soto, Gary 1952- DLB-82
Smith, Sarah (see Stretton, Hesba)	Soldati, Mario 1906-1999.............. DLB-177	Soueif, Ahdaf 1950- DLB-267
Smith, Sarah Pogson 1774-1870 ....DLB-200	Soledad (see Zamudio, Adela)	Souster, Raymond 1921- DLB-88
Smith, Seba 1792-1868..........DLB-1, 11, 243	Šoljan, Antun 1932-1993 ....DLB-181	The *South English Legendary* circa thirteenth-fifteenth centuries DLB-146
Smith, Stevie 1902-1971 ....DLB-20	Sollers, Philippe (Philippe Joyaux) 1936- DLB-83	Southerland, Ellease 1943- DLB-33
Smith, Sydney 1771-1845...............DLB-107	Sollogub, Vladimir Aleksandrovich 1813-1882....................DLB-198	Southern, Terry 1924-1995 ....DLB-2
Smith, Sydney Goodsir 1915-1975........DLB-27	Sollors, Werner 1943- DBL-246	Southern Illinois University Press Y-95
Smith, Sir Thomas 1513-1577 ....DLB-132	Solmi, Sergio 1899-1981 ....DLB-114	Southern Literature Fellowship of Southern Writers..........Y-98
Smith, Vivian 1933- DLB-325	Sologub, Fedor 1863-1927 ....DLB-295	The Fugitives and the Agrarians: The First Exhibition Y-85
Smith, W. Gordon 1928-1996 ....DLB-310	Solomon, Carl 1928- DLB-16	"The Greatness of Southern Literature": League of the South Institute for the Study of Southern Culture and History......................Y-02
Smith, Wendell 1914-1972 ....DLB-171	Solórzano, Carlos 1922- DLB-305
Smith, William fl. 1595-1597 ....DLB-136	Soloukhin, Vladimir Alekseevich 1924-1997 ....DLB-302
Smith, William 1727-1803 ....DLB-31	Solov'ev, Sergei Mikhailovich 1885-1942 ....DLB-295	The Society for the Study of Southern Literature Y-00
A General Idea of the College of Mirania (1753) [excerpts] DLB-31	Solov'ev, Vladimir Sergeevich 1853-1900 ....DLB-295	Southern Writers Between the Wars....DLB-9
Smith, William 1728-1793 ....DLB-30	Solstad, Dag 1941- DLB-297	Southerne, Thomas 1659-1746 ....DLB-80
Smith, William Gardner 1927-1974 ....DLB-76	Solway, David 1941- DLB-53	Southey, Caroline Anne Bowles 1786-1854 ....DLB-116
Smith, William Henry 1808-1872 ....DLB-159	Solzhenitsyn, Aleksandr 1918- ....DLB-302, 332 Solzhenitsyn and America..............Y-85	Southey, Robert 1774-1843 .....DLB-93, 107, 142
Smith, William Jay 1918- DLB-5	Southwell, Robert 1561?-1595..........DLB-167
Smith, Elder and Company DLB-154	Some Basic Notes on Three Modern Genres: Interview, Blurb, and Obituary..........Y-02	Southworth, E. D. E. N. 1819-1899......DLB-239
Harrison Smith and Robert Haas [publishing house] DLB-46	Sowande, Bode 1948- DLB-157
J. Stilman Smith and Company DLB-49	Somerville, Edith Œnone 1858-1949.....DLB-135	Tace Sowle [publishing house]..........DLB-170
W. B. Smith and Company DLB-49	*Something to Answer For,* 1969 Booker Prize winner, P. H. Newby DLB-326	Soyfer, Jura 1912-1939................DLB-124
W. H. Smith and Son.................DLB-106	Soyinka, Wole 1934- ....DLB-125, 332; Y-86, 87; CDWLB-3 Nobel Lecture 1986: This Past Must Address Its Present Y-86
Leonard Smithers [publishing house].....DLB-112	Somov, Orest Mikhailovich 1793-1833 ...DLB-198
Smollett, Tobias 1721-1771.........DLB-39, 104; CDBLB-2	Sønderby, Knud 1909-1966 ....DLB-214
Dedication to *Ferdinand Count Fathom* (1753) DLB-39	Sone, Monica 1919- DLB-312	Spacks, Barry 1931- DLB-105
Song, Cathy 1955- DLB-169, 312	Spalding, Frances 1950- DLB-155
Preface to *Ferdinand Count Fathom* (1753) DLB-39	Sonnevi, Göran 1939- DLB-257	Spanish Byzantine Novel, The..........DLB-318
Sono Ayako 1931- DLB-182	Spanish Travel Writers of the Late Middle Ages DLB-286
Preface to *Roderick Random* (1748) DLB-39	Sontag, Susan 1933-2004.............DLB-2, 67
Smythe, Francis Sydney 1900-1949 ......DLB-195	Sophocles 497/496 B.C.-406/405 B.C. DLB-176; CDWLB-1	Spark, Muriel 1918- DLB-15, 139; CDBLB-7
Snelling, William Joseph 1804-1848......DLB-202	Michael Sparke [publishing house] DLB-170
Snellings, Rolland (see Touré, Askia Muhammad)	Šopov, Aco 1923-1982 ....DLB-181	Sparks, Jared 1789-1866..........DLB-1, 30, 235
Snodgrass, W. D. 1926- DLB-5	Sorel, Charles ca.1600-1674 ....DLB-268	Sparshott, Francis 1926- DLB-60
Snorri Hjartarson 1906-1986 ....DLB-293	Sørensen, Villy 1929- DLB-214	Späth, Gerold 1939- DLB-75
Snow, C. P. 1905-1980 .....DLB-15, 77; DS-17; CDBLB-7	Sorensen, Virginia 1912-1991 ....DLB-206	Spatola, Adriano 1941-1988 ....DLB-128
Snyder, Gary 1930- DLB-5, 16, 165, 212, 237, 275	Sorge, Reinhard Johannes 1892-1916 ....DLB-118	Spaziani, Maria Luisa 1924- DLB-128
Sobiloff, Hy 1912-1970.................DLB-48		*Specimens of Foreign Standard Literature* 1838-1842 ....DLB-1
The Social Contract, Jean-Jacques Rousseau....................DLB-314		

Cumulative Index

The Spectator 1828- DLB-110

Spedding, James 1808-1881 . . . . DLB-144

Spee von Langenfeld, Friedrich
1591-1635 . . . . DLB-164

Speght, Rachel 1597-after 1630 . . . . DLB-126

Speke, John Hanning 1827-1864 . . . . DLB-166

Spellman, A. B. 1935- DLB-41

Spence, Catherine Helen 1825-1910 . . . . . DLB-230

Spence, Thomas 1750-1814 . . . . DLB-158

Spencer, Anne 1882-1975 . . . . DLB-51, 54

Spencer, Charles, third Earl of Sunderland
1674-1722 . . . . DLB-213

Spencer, Elizabeth 1921- DLB-6, 218

Spencer, George John, Second Earl Spencer
1758-1834 . . . . DLB-184

Spencer, Herbert 1820-1903 . . . . DLB-57, 262

"The Philosophy of Style" (1852) DLB-57

Spencer, Scott 1945- Y-86

Spender, J. A. 1862-1942 . . . . DLB-98

Spender, Stephen 1909-1995 . . . DLB-20; CDBLB-7

Spener, Philipp Jakob 1635-1705 . . . . DLB-164

Spenser, Edmund
circa 1552-1599 . . . . DLB-167; CDBLB-1

Envoy from *The Shepheardes Calender*. . . . DLB-167

"The Generall Argument of the
Whole Booke," from
The Shepheardes Calender DLB-167

"A Letter of the Authors Expounding
His Whole Intention in the Course
of this Worke: Which for that It
Giueth Great Light to the Reader,
for the Better Vnderstanding
Is Hereunto Annexed,"
from *The Faerie Queene* (1590) DLB-167

"To His Booke," from
The Shepheardes Calender (1579) . . . DLB-167

"To the Most Excellent and Learned
Both Orator and Poete, Mayster
Gabriell Haruey, His Verie Special
and Singular Good Frend E. K.
Commendeth the Good Lyking of
This His Labour, and the Patronage
of the New Poete," from
The Shepheardes Calender DLB-167

Sperr, Martin 1944- DLB-124

Spewack, Bella Cowen 1899-1990 . . . . . . DLB-266

Spewack, Samuel 1899-1971 . . . . DLB-266

Spicer, Jack 1925-1965 . . . . DLB-5, 16, 193

Spiegelman, Art 1948- DLB-299

Spielberg, Peter 1929- Y-81

Spielhagen, Friedrich 1829-1911 . . . . DLB-129

"*Spielmannsepen*" (circa 1152-circa 1500) . . . DLB-148

Spier, Peter 1927- DLB-61

Spillane, Mickey 1918-2006 . . . . DLB-226

Spink, J. G. Taylor 1888-1962 . . . . DLB-241

Spinrad, Norman 1940- DLB-8

Tribute to Isaac Asimov Y-92

Spires, Elizabeth 1952- DLB-120

The Spirit of Laws, Claude-Adrien
Helvétius DLB-314

The Spirit of Laws, Charles-Louis de Secondat, baron
de Montesquieu DLB-314

Spitteler, Carl 1845-1924 . . . . DLB-129, 332

Spivak, Lawrence E. 1900-1994 . . . . DLB-137

Spofford, Harriet Prescott
1835-1921 . . . . DLB-74, 221

Sponde, Jean de 1557-1595 . . . . DLB-327

Sports
Jimmy, Red, and Others: Harold
Rosenthal Remembers the Stars
of the Press Box Y-01

The Literature of Boxing in England
through Arthur Conan Doyle Y-01

Notable Twentieth-Century Books
about Sports DLB-241

Sprigge, Timothy L. S. 1932- DLB-262

Spring, Howard 1889-1965 . . . . DLB-191

Springs, Elliott White 1896-1959 . . . . DLB-316

Sproxton, Birk 1943-2007 . . . . DLB-334

Squibob (see Derby, George Horatio)

Squier, E. G. 1821-1888 . . . . DLB-189

Staal-Delaunay, Marguerite-Jeanne Cordier de
1684-1750 . . . . DLB-314

Stableford, Brian 1948- DLB-261

Stacpoole, H. de Vere 1863-1951 . . . . DLB-153

Staël, Germaine de 1766-1817 . . . . . . DLB-119, 192

Staël-Holstein, Anne-Louise Germaine de
(see Staël, Germaine de)

Staffeldt, Schack 1769-1826 . . . . DLB-300

Stafford, Jean 1915-1979 . . . . DLB-2, 173

Stafford, William 1914-1993 . . . . DLB-5, 206

Stallings, Laurence 1894-1968 . . . . . DLB-7, 44, 316

Stallworthy, Jon 1935- DLB-40

Stampp, Kenneth M. 1912- DLB-17

Stănescu, Nichita 1933-1983 . . . . DLB-232

Stanev, Emiliyan 1907-1979 . . . . DLB-181

Stanford, Ann 1916-1987 . . . . DLB-5

Stangerup, Henrik 1937-1998 . . . . DLB-214

Stanihurst, Richard 1547-1618 . . . . DLB-281

Stanitsky, N. (see Panaeva, Avdot'ia Iakovlevna)

Stankevich, Nikolai Vladimirovich
1813-1840 . . . . DLB-198

Stanković, Borisav ("Bora")
1876-1927 . . . . DLB-147; CDWLB-4

Stanley, Henry M. 1841-1904 . . . . DLB-189; DS-13

Stanley, Thomas 1625-1678 . . . . DLB-131

Stannard, Martin 1947- DLB-155

William Stansby [publishing house] DLB-170

Stanton, Elizabeth Cady 1815-1902 . . . . . . DLB-79

Stanton, Frank L. 1857-1927 . . . . DLB-25

Stanton, Maura 1946- DLB-120

Stapledon, Olaf 1886-1950 . . . . DLB-15, 255

Star Spangled Banner Office DLB-49

Stark, Freya 1893-1993 . . . . DLB-195

Starkey, Thomas circa 1499-1538 . . . . DLB-132

Starkie, Walter 1894-1976 . . . . DLB-195

Starkweather, David 1935- DLB-7

Starrett, Vincent 1886-1974 . . . . DLB-187

Stationers' Company of London, The DLB-170

Statius circa A.D. 45-A.D. 96 . . . . DLB-211

Staying On, 1977 Booker Prize winner,
Paul Scott DLB-326

Stead, Christina 1902-1983 . . . . DLB-260

Stead, Robert J. C. 1880-1959 . . . . DLB-92

Steadman, Mark 1930- DLB-6

Stearns, Harold E. 1891-1943 . . . . . . DLB-4; DS-15

Stebnitsky, M. (see Leskov, Nikolai Semenovich)

Stedman, Edmund Clarence 1833-1908 . . . DLB-64

Steegmuller, Francis 1906-1994 . . . . DLB-111

Steel, Flora Annie 1847-1929 . . . . . . DLB-153, 156

Steele, Max 1922-2005 . . . . Y-80

Steele, Richard
1672-1729 . . . . DLB-84, 101; CDBLB-2

Steele, Timothy 1948- DLB-120

Steele, Wilbur Daniel 1886-1970 . . . . DLB-86

Wallace Markfield's "Steeplechase" Y-02

Steere, Richard circa 1643-1721 . . . . DLB-24

Stefán frá Hvítadal (Stefán Sigurðsson)
1887-1933 . . . . DLB-293

Stefán Guðmundsson (see Stephan G. Stephansson)

Stefán Hörður Grímsson
1919 or 1920-2002 . . . . DLB-293

Steffens, Lincoln 1866-1936 . . . . DLB-303

Stefanovski, Goran 1952- DLB-181

Stegner, Wallace
1909-1993 . . . . DLB-9, 206, 275; Y-93

Stehr, Hermann 1864-1940 . . . . DLB-66

Steig, William 1907-2003 . . . . DLB-61

Stein, Gertrude 1874-1946
. . . . DLB-4, 54, 86, 228; DS-15; CDALB-4

Stein, Leo 1872-1947 . . . . DLB-4

Stein and Day Publishers DLB-46

Steinbarg, Eliezer (Eliezer Shtaynbarg)
1880-1932 . . . . DLB-333

Steinbeck, John 1902-1968 . . . .
DLB-7, 9, 212, 275, 309, 332; DS-2; CDALB-5

John Steinbeck Research Center,
San Jose State University Y-85

The Steinbeck Centennial Y-02

Steinem, Gloria 1934- DLB-246

Steiner, George 1929- DLB-67, 299

Steinhoewel, Heinrich 1411/1412-1479 . . . . DLB-179

Steinn Steinarr (Aðalsteinn Kristmundsson)
1908-1958 . . . . DLB-293

Steinunn Sigurðardóttir 1950- DLB-293

Steloff, Ida Frances 1887-1989 . . . . DLB-187

Stendhal 1783-1842 . . . . DLB-119

Stephan G. Stephansson (Stefán Guðmundsson) 1853-1927 ....DLB-293

Stephen, Leslie 1832-1904 ...... DLB-57, 144, 190

Stephen Family (Bloomsbury Group) DS-10

Stephens, A. G. 1865-1933...............DLB-230

Stephens, Alexander H. 1812-1883 ....DLB-47

Stephens, Alice Barber 1858-1932.......DLB-188

Stephens, Ann 1810-1886 ....DLB-3, 73, 250

Stephens, Charles Asbury 1844?-1931.....DLB-42

Stephens, James 1882?-1950 ....DLB-19, 153, 162

Stephens, John Lloyd 1805-1852 ....DLB-183, 250

Stephens, Michael 1946- DLB-234

Stephensen, P. R. 1901-1965 ....DLB-260

Sterling, George 1869-1926 ....DLB-54

Sterling, James 1701-1763................DLB-24

Sterling, John 1806-1844 ....DLB-116

Stern, Gerald 1925- DLB-105

"Living in Ruin" DLB-105

Stern, Gladys B. 1890-1973 ....DLB-197

Stern, Madeleine B. 1912- DLB-111, 140

Stern, Richard 1928- DLB-218; Y-87

Stern, Stewart 1922- DLB-26

Sterne, Laurence 1713-1768 ... DLB-39; CDBLB-2

Sternheim, Carl 1878-1942............DLB-56, 118

Sternhold, Thomas ?-1549.................DLB-132

Steuart, David 1747-1824 ....DLB-213

Stevens, Henry 1819-1886................DLB-140

Stevens, Wallace 1879-1955 ....DLB-54; CDALB-5

The Wallace Stevens Society............Y-99

Stevenson, Anne 1933- DLB-40

Stevenson, D. E. 1892-1973 ....DLB-191

Stevenson, Lionel 1902-1973 ....DLB-155

Stevenson, Robert Louis 1850-1894 ....DLB-18, 57, 141, 156, 174; DS-13; CDBLB-5

"On Style in Literature: Its Technical Elements" (1885)....DLB-57

Stewart, Donald Ogden 1894-1980 ....DLB-4, 11, 26; DS-15

Stewart, Douglas 1913-1985 ....DLB-260

Stewart, Dugald 1753-1828 ....DLB-31

Stewart, George, Jr. 1848-1906 ....DLB-99

Stewart, George R. 1895-1980 ....DLB-8

Stewart, Harold 1916-1995 ....DLB-260

Stewart, J. I. M. (see Innes, Michael)

Stewart, Maria W. 1803?-1879............DLB-239

Stewart, Randall 1896-1964................DLB-103

Stewart, Sean 1965- DLB-251

Stewart and Kidd Company DLB-46

Sthen, Hans Christensen 1544-1610 ......DLB-300

Stickney, Trumbull 1874-1904 ....DLB-54

Stieler, Caspar 1632-1707..................DLB-164

Stifter, Adalbert 1805-1868 ..DLB-133; CDWLB-2

Stiles, Ezra 1727-1795 ....DLB-31

Still, James 1906-2001 .... DLB-9; Y-01

Stirling, S. M. 1953- DLB-251

Stirner, Max 1806-1856 ....DLB-129

Stith, William 1707-1755..................DLB-31

Stivens, Dal 1911-1997..................DLB-260

Elliot Stock [publishing house]..........DLB-106

Stockton, Annis Boudinot 1736-1801.....DLB-200

Stockton, Frank R. 1834-1902 ..DLB-42, 74; DS-13

Stockton, J. Roy 1892-1972 ....DLB-241

Ashbel Stoddard [publishing house].......DLB-49

Stoddard, Charles Warren 1843-1909 ....DLB-186

Stoddard, Elizabeth 1823-1902 ....DLB-202

Stoddard, Richard Henry 1825-1903 ....DLB-3, 64, 250; DS-13

Stoddard, Solomon 1643-1729...........DLB-24

Stoker, Bram 1847-1912 .... DLB-36, 70, 178; CDBLB-5

On Writing Dracula, from the Introduction to Dracula (1897) ...DLB-178

Dracula (Documentary) DLB-304

Frederick A. Stokes Company DLB-49

Stokes, Thomas L. 1898-1958 ....DLB-29

Stokesbury, Leon 1945- DLB-120

Stolberg, Christian Graf zu 1748-1821.....DLB-94

Stolberg, Friedrich Leopold Graf zu 1750-1819 ....DLB-94

Stone, Lucy 1818-1893 ....DLB-79, 239

Stone, Melville 1848-1929 ....DLB-25

Stone, Robert 1937- DLB-152

Stone, Ruth 1915- DLB-105

Stone, Samuel 1602-1663................DLB-24

Stone, William Leete 1792-1844..........DLB-202

Herbert S. Stone and Company..........DLB-49

Stone and Kimball DLB-49

Stoppard, Tom 1937- DLB-13, 233; Y-85; CDBLB-8

Playwrights and Professors DLB-13

Storey, Anthony 1928- DLB-14

Storey, David 1933- ... DLB-13, 14, 207, 245, 326

Storm, Theodor 1817-1888 ....DLB-129; CDWLB-2

Storni, Alfonsina 1892-1938 ....DLB-283

Story, Thomas circa 1670-1742 ....DLB-31

Story, William Wetmore 1819-1895....DLB-1, 235

Storytelling: A Contemporary Renaissance....Y-84

Stoughton, William 1631-1701..........DLB-24

Stout, Rex 1886-1975.................DLB-306

Stow, John 1525-1605 ....DLB-132

Stow, Randolph 1935- DLB-260

Stowe, Harriet Beecher 1811-1896......DLB-1,12, 42, 74, 189, 239, 243; CDALB-3

The Harriet Beecher Stowe Center.......Y-00

Stowe, Leland 1899-1994................DLB-29

Stoyanov, Dimitr Ivanov (see Elin Pelin)

Strabo 64/63 B.C.-circa A.D. 25..........DLB-176

Strachey, Lytton 1880-1932......DLB-149; DS-10

Preface to Eminent Victorians DLB-149

William Strahan [publishing house]......DLB-154

Strahan and Company.................DLB-106

Strand, Mark 1934- DLB-5

The Strasbourg Oaths 842 ....DLB-148

Stratemeyer, Edward 1862-1930 ....DLB-42

Strati, Saverio 1924- DLB-177

Stratton and Barnard..................DLB-49

Stratton-Porter, Gene 1863-1924 ..DLB-221; DS-14

Straub, Peter 1943- Y-84

Strauß, Botho 1944- DLB-124

Strauß, David Friedrich 1808-1874 ......DLB-133

Strauss, Jennifer 1933- DLB-325

The Strawberry Hill Press DLB-154

Strawson, P. F. 1919- DLB-262

Streatfeild, Noel 1895-1986 ....DLB-160

Street, Cecil John Charles (see Rhode, John)

Street, G. S. 1867-1936.................DLB-135

Street and Smith.....................DLB-49

Streeter, Edward 1891-1976.............DLB-11

Streeter, Thomas Winthrop 1883-1965 ...DLB-140

Stretton, Hesba 1832-1911.........DLB-163, 190

Stribling, T. S. 1881-1965 ....DLB-9

Der Stricker circa 1190-circa 1250.......DLB-138

Strickland, Samuel 1804-1867 ....DLB-99

Strindberg, August 1849-1912 ....DLB-259

Stringer, Arthur 1874-1950 ....DLB-92

Stringer and Townsend DLB-49

Strittmatter, Erwin 1912-1994 ....DLB-69

Strniša, Gregor 1930-1987 ....DLB-181

Strode, William 1630-1645 ....DLB-126

Strong, L. A. G. 1896-1958 ....DLB-191

Strother, David Hunter (Porte Crayon) 1816-1888 ....DLB-3, 248

Strouse, Jean 1945- DLB-111

Strugatsky, Arkadii Natanovich 1925- DLB-302

Strugatsky, Boris Natanovich 1933- DLB-302

Strype, John 1643-1737................DLB-336

Stuart, Dabney 1937- DLB-105

"Knots into Webs: Some Autobiographical Sources".......DLB-105

Stuart, Gilbert 1743-1786...............DLB-336

Stuart, Jesse 1906-1984 ..... DLB-9, 48, 102; Y-84

Lyle Stuart [publishing house] DLB-46

Stuart, Ruth McEnery 1849?-1917 ......DLB-202

Cumulative Index

Stub, Ambrosius 1705-1758............DLB-300

Stubbs, Harry Clement (see Clement, Hal)

Stubenberg, Johann Wilhelm von
    1619-1663......................DLB-164

Stuckenberg, Viggo 1763-1905.........DLB-300

Studebaker, William V. 1947-........DLB-256

Studies in American Jewish Literature.......Y-02

Studio........................DLB-112

Stukeley, William 1687-1765..........DLB-336

Stump, Al 1916-1995................DLB-241

Sturgeon, Theodore 1918-1985......DLB-8; Y-85

Sturges, Preston 1898-1959............DLB-26

Styron, William 1925-2006
    ....DLB-2, 143, 299; Y-80; CDALB-6

    Tribute to James Dickey...............Y-97

Suard, Jean-Baptiste-Antoine
    1732-1817......................DLB-314

Suárez, Clementina 1902-1991.........DLB-290

Suárez, Mario 1925-.................DLB-82

Suassuna, Ariano 1927-..............DLB-307

Such, Peter 1939-...................DLB-60

Suckling, Sir John 1609-1641?......DLB-58, 126

Suckow, Ruth 1892-1960............DLB-9, 102

Sudermann, Hermann 1857-1928.......DLB-118

Sue, Eugène 1804-1857................DLB-119

Sue, Marie-Joseph (see Sue, Eugène)

Suetonius circa A.D. 69-post A.D. 122....DLB-211

Suggs, Simon (see Hooper, Johnson Jones)

Sui Sin Far (see Eaton, Edith Maude)

Suits, Gustav 1883-1956....DLB-220; CDWLB-4

Sukenick, Ronald 1932-2004......DLB-173; Y-81

    An Author's Response................Y-82

Sukhovo-Kobylin, Aleksandr Vasil'evich
    1817-1903......................DLB-277

Suknaski, Andrew 1942-..............DLB-53

Sullam, Sara Copio circa 1592-1641.....DLB-339

Sullivan, Alan 1868-1947..............DLB-92

Sullivan, C. Gardner 1886-1965........DLB-26

Sullivan, Frank 1892-1976.............DLB-11

Sully Prudhomme (René François-Armand
    Prudhomme) 1839-1907...........DLB-332

Sulte, Benjamin 1841-1923............DLB-99

Sulzberger, Arthur Hays 1891-1968.....DLB-127

Sulzberger, Arthur Ochs 1926-........DLB-127

Sulzer, Johann Georg 1720-1779........DLB-97

Sumarokov, Aleksandr Petrovich
    1717-1777......................DLB-150

Summers, Hollis 1916-1987.............DLB-6

Sumner, Charles 1811-1874............DLB-235

Sumner, William Graham 1840-1910....DLB-270

Henry A. Sumner
    [publishing house]................DLB-49

Sundman, Per Olof 1922-1992........DLB-257

Supervielle, Jules 1884-1960..........DLB-258

Surtees, Robert Smith 1803-1864........DLB-21

    The R. S. Surtees Society.............Y-98

Sutcliffe, Matthew 1550?-1629........DLB-281

Sutcliffe, William 1971-..............DLB-271

Sutherland, Efua Theodora 1924-1996...DLB-117

Sutherland, John 1919-1956............DLB-68

Sutro, Alfred 1863-1933...............DLB-10

Sutzkever, Abraham (Avrom Sutzkever)
    1913-..........................DLB-333

Svava Jakobsdóttir 1930-.............DLB-293

Svendsen, Hanne Marie 1933-........DLB-214

Svevo, Italo (Ettore Schmitz)
    1861-1928......................DLB-264

Swados, Harvey 1920-1972.........DLB-2, 335

Swain, Charles 1801-1874..............DLB-32

Swallow Press......................DLB-46

Swan Sonnenschein Limited..........DLB-106

Swanberg, W. A. 1907-1992...........DLB-103

Swedish Literature
    The Literature of the Modern
      Breakthrough................DLB-259

Swenson, May 1919-1989..............DLB-5

Swerling, Jo 1897-1964................DLB-44

Swift, Graham 1949-............DLB-194, 326

Swift, Jonathan
    1667-1745......DLB-39, 95, 101; CDBLB-2

Swinburne, A. C.
    1837-1909..........DLB-35, 57; CDBLB-4

    Under the Microscope (1872).........DLB-35

Swineshead, Richard floruit circa 1350...DLB-115

Swinnerton, Frank 1884-1982...........DLB-34

Swisshelm, Jane Grey 1815-1884........DLB-43

Swope, Herbert Bayard 1882-1958.......DLB-25

Swords, James ?-1844................DLB-73

Swords, Thomas 1763-1843............DLB-73

T. and J. Swords and Company.........DLB-49

Swynnerton, Thomas (John Roberts)
    circa 1500-1554.................DLB-281

Sykes, Ella C. ?-1939................DLB-174

Sylvester, Josuah 1562 or 1563-1618....DLB-121

Symonds, Emily Morse (see Paston, George)

Symonds, John Addington
    1840-1893....................DLB-57, 144

    "Personal Style" (1890)............DLB-57

Symons, A. J. A. 1900-1941..........DLB-149

Symons, Arthur 1865-1945......DLB-19, 57, 149

Symons, Julian 1912-1994.....DLB-87, 155; Y-92

    Julian Symons at Eighty..............Y-92

Symons, Scott 1933-.................DLB-53

Synge, John Millington
    1871-1909..........DLB-10, 19; CDBLB-5

Synge Summer School: J. M. Synge
    and the Irish Theater, Rathdrum,
    County Wiclow, Ireland...........Y-93

Syrett, Netta 1865-1943..........DLB-135, 197

The System of Nature, Paul Henri Thiry,
    baron d'Holbach (as Jean-Baptiste
    de Mirabaud)...................DLB-314

Szabó, Lőrinc 1900-1957.............DLB-215

Szabó, Magda 1917-.................DLB-215

Szymborska, Wisława
    1923-........DLB-232, 332; Y-96; CDWLB-4

    Nobel Lecture 1996:
      The Poet and the World...........Y-96

T

Taban lo Liyong 1939?-..............DLB-125

al-Tabari 839-923...................DLB-311

Tablada, José Juan 1871-1945.........DLB-290

Le Tableau de Paris, Louis-Sébastien
    Mercier........................DLB-314

Tabori, George 1914-................DLB-245

Tabucchi, Antonio 1943-.............DLB-196

Taché, Joseph-Charles 1820-1894........DLB-99

Tachihara Masaaki 1926-1980.........DLB-182

Tacitus circa A.D. 55-circa A.D. 117
    ....DLB-211; CDWLB-1

Tadijanović, Dragutin 1905-..........DLB-181

Tafdrup, Pia 1952-..................DLB-214

Tafolla, Carmen 1951-................DLB-82

Taggard, Genevieve 1894-1948.........DLB-45

Taggart, John 1942-.................DLB-193

Tagger, Theodor (see Bruckner, Ferdinand)

Tagore, Rabindranath 1861-1941...DLB-323, 332

Taiheiki late fourteenth century.........DLB-203

Tait, J. Selwin, and Sons..............DLB-49

Tait's Edinburgh Magazine 1832-1861......DLB-110

The Takarazaka Revue Company..........Y-91

Talander (see Bohse, August)

Talese, Gay 1932-..................DLB-185

    Tribute to Irwin Shaw................Y-84

Talev, Dimitr 1898-1966.............DLB-181

Taliaferro, H. E. 1811-1875..........DLB-202

Tallent, Elizabeth 1954-.............DLB-130

TallMountain, Mary 1918-1994........DLB-193

Talvj 1797-1870.................DLB-59, 133

Tamási, Áron 1897-1966..............DLB-215

Tammsaare, A. H.
    1878-1940..............DLB-220; CDWLB-4

Tan, Amy 1952-.........DLB-173, 312; CDALB-7

Tandori, Dezső 1938-................DLB-232

Tanner, Thomas 1673/1674-1735.......DLB-213

Tanizaki Jun'ichirō 1886-1965.........DLB-180

Tapahonso, Luci 1953-...............DLB-175

The Mark Taper Forum................DLB-7

Taradash, Daniel 1913-2003 . . . . .DLB-44

Tarasov-Rodionov, Aleksandr Ignat'evich
  1885-1938 . . . . .DLB-272

Tarbell, Ida M. 1857-1944 . . . . .DLB-47

Tardieu, Jean 1903-1995 . . . . .DLB-321

Tardivel, Jules-Paul 1851-1905. . . . . .DLB-99

Targan, Barry 1932- DLB-130

  Tribute to John Gardner Y-82

Tarkington, Booth 1869-1946 . . . . .DLB-9, 102

Tashlin, Frank 1913-1972. . . . . .DLB-44

Tasma (Jessie Couvreur) 1848-1897 . . . . .DLB-230

Tassoni, Alessandro 1565-1635 . . . . .DLB-339

Tate, Allen 1899-1979 . . . . . . DLB-4, 45, 63; DS-17

Tate, James 1943- DLB-5, 169

Tate, Nahum circa 1652-1715. . . . . .DLB-80

Tatian circa 830. .DLB-148

Taufer, Veno 1933- DLB-181

Tauler, Johannes circa 1300-1361. . . . . . . .DLB-179

Tavares, Salette 1922-1994. . . . . .DLB-287

Tavčar, Ivan 1851-1923 . . . . .DLB-147

Taverner, Richard ca. 1505-1575 . . . . .DLB-236

Taylor, Ann 1782-1866. . . . . .DLB-163

Taylor, Bayard 1825-1878 . . . . . . .DLB-3, 189, 250

Taylor, Bert Leston 1866-1921. . . . . .DLB-25

Taylor, Charles H. 1846-1921 . . . . .DLB-25

Taylor, Edward circa 1642-1729. . . . . .DLB-24

Taylor, Elizabeth 1912-1975 . . . . .DLB-139

Taylor, Sir Henry 1800-1886 . . . . .DLB-32

Taylor, Henry 1942- DLB-5

  Who Owns American Literature. Y-94

Taylor, Jane 1783-1824. . . . . .DLB-163

Taylor, Jeremy circa 1613-1667 . . . . .DLB-151

Taylor, John 1577 or 1578 - 1653 . . . . .DLB-121

Taylor, Mildred D. 1943- DLB-52

Taylor, Peter 1917-1994 . . . DLB-218, 278; Y-81, 94

Taylor, Susie King 1848-1912 . . . . .DLB-221

Taylor, William Howland 1901-1966. . . . . .DLB-241

William Taylor and Company DLB-49

Teale, Edwin Way 1899-1980 . . . . .DLB-275

Teasdale, Sara 1884-1933. . . . . .DLB-45

Teffi, Nadezhda 1872-1952. . . . . .DLB-317

Teillier, Jorge 1935-1996. . . . . .DLB-283

Telles, Lygia Fagundes 1924- DLB-113, 307

The Temper of the West: William Jovanovich Y-02

Temple, Sir William 1555?-1627 . . . . .DLB-281

Temple, Sir William 1628-1699 . . . . .DLB-101

Temple, William F. 1914-1989 . . . . .DLB-255

Temrizov, A. (see Marchenko, Anastasia Iakovlevna)

Tench, Watkin ca. 1758-1833. . . . . .DLB-230

Tencin, Alexandrine-Claude Guérin de
  1682-1749 . . . . .DLB-314

Tender Is the Night (Documentary) DLB-273

Tendriakov, Vladimir Fedorovich
  1923-1984 . . . . .DLB-302

Tenn, William 1919- DLB-8

Tennant, Emma 1937- DLB-14

Tenney, Tabitha Gilman 1762-1837 . . . DLB-37, 200

Tennyson, Alfred 1809-1892 . . DLB-32; CDBLB-4

  On Some of the Characteristics of
    Modern Poetry and On the Lyrical
    Poems of Alfred Tennyson
    (1831) DLB-32

Tennyson, Frederick 1807-1898 . . . . .DLB-32

Tenorio, Arthur 1924- DLB-209

"The Tenth Stage," Marie-Jean-Antoine-Nicolas
  Caritat, marquis de Condorcet DLB-314

Tepl, Johannes von
  circa 1350-1414/1415 . . . . .DLB-179

Tepliakov, Viktor Grigor'evich
  1804-1842 . . . . .DLB-205

Terence circa 184 B.C.-159 B.C. or after
  . . . . DLB-211; CDWLB-1

St. Teresa of Ávila 1515-1582 . . . . .DLB-318

Terhune, Albert Payson 1872-1942 . . . . .DLB-9

Terhune, Mary Virginia 1830-1922 . . . . DS-13

Terpigorev, Sergei Nikolaevich (S. Atava)
  1841-1895 . . . . .DLB-277

Terry, Megan 1932- DLB-7, 249

Terson, Peter 1932- DLB-13

Tesich, Steve 1943-1996. . . . . .Y-83

Tessa, Delio 1886-1939 . . . . .DLB-114

Testi, Fulvio 1593-1646 . . . . .DLB-339

Testori, Giovanni 1923-1993
  . . . . DLB-128, 177

Texas
  The Year in Texas Literature Y-98

Tey, Josephine 1896?-1952. . . . . .DLB-77

Thacher, James 1754-1844 . . . . .DLB-37

Thacher, John Boyd 1847-1909 . . . . .DLB-187

Thackeray, William Makepeace
  1811-1863 . . . DLB-21, 55, 159, 163; CDBLB-4

Thames and Hudson Limited DLB-112

Thanet, Octave (see French, Alice)

Thaxter, Celia Laighton
  1835-1894 . . . . .DLB-239

Thayer, Caroline Matilda Warren
  1785-1844 . . . . .DLB-200

Thayer, Douglas H. 1929- DLB-256

Theater
  Black Theatre: A Forum [excerpts] DLB-38

  Community and Commentators:
    Black Theatre and Its Critics DLB-38

  German Drama from Naturalism
    to Fascism: 1889-1933 . . . . .DLB-118

  A Look at the Contemporary Black
    Theatre Movement DLB-38

  The Lord Chamberlain's Office and
    Stage Censorship in England DLB-10

  New Forces at Work in the American
    Theatre: 1915-1925 . . . . .DLB-7

  Off Broadway and Off-Off Broadway. . .DLB-7

  Oregon Shakespeare Festival. Y-00

  Plays, Playwrights, and Playgoers DLB-84

  Playwrights on the Theater DLB-80

  Playwrights and Professors DLB-13

  Producing *Dear Bunny, Dear Volodya*:
    The Friendship and the Feud Y-97

  Viewpoint: Politics and Performance,
    by David Edgar DLB-13

  Writing for the Theatre,
    by Harold Pinter. DLB-13

  The Year in Drama Y-82–85, 87–98

  The Year in U.S. Drama Y-00

Theater, English and Irish
  Anti-Theatrical Tracts DLB-263

  The Chester Plays circa 1505-1532;
    revisions until 1575. . . . . .DLB-146

  Dangerous Years: London Theater,
    1939-1945. . . . . .DLB-10

  A Defense of Actors DLB-263

  The Development of Lighting in the
    Staging of Drama, 1900-1945 . . . .DLB-10

  Education DLB-263

  The End of English Stage Censorship,
    1945-1968. . . . . .DLB-13

  Epigrams and Satires. DLB-263

  Eyewitnesses and Historians DLB-263

  Fringe and Alternative Theater in
    Great Britain. DLB-13

  The Great War and the Theater,
    1914-1918 [Great Britain] DLB-10

  Licensing Act of 1737 . . . . .DLB-84

  Morality Plays: *Mankind* circa 1450-1500
    and *Everyman* circa 1500 . . . . .DLB-146

  The New Variorum Shakespeare Y-85

  N-Town Plays circa 1468 to early
    sixteenth century. DLB-146

  Politics and the Theater. DLB-263

  Practical Matters DLB-263

  Prologues, Epilogues, Epistles to Readers,
    and Excerpts from Plays. DLB-263

  The Publication of English
    Renaissance Plays DLB-62

  Regulations for the Theater DLB-263

  Sources for the Study of Tudor and
    Stuart Drama DLB-62

  Stage Censorship: "The Rejected Statement"
    (1911), by Bernard Shaw
    [excerpts] .DLB-10

  Synge Summer School: J. M. Synge and
    the Irish Theater, Rathdrum,
    County Wiclow, Ireland Y-93

  The Theater in Shakespeare's Time . . .DLB-62

  The Theatre Guild DLB-7

  The Townely Plays fifteenth and
    sixteenth centuries DLB-146

  The Year in British Drama Y-99–01

  The Year in Drama: London. Y-90

  The Year in London Theatre Y-92

A Yorkshire Tragedy DLB-58

Theaters
- The Abbey Theatre and Irish Drama, 1900-1945 .... DLB-10
- Actors Theatre of Louisville DLB-7
- American Conservatory Theatre DLB-7
- Arena Stage DLB-7
- Black Theaters and Theater Organizations in America, 1961-1982: A Research List DLB-38
- The Dallas Theater Center DLB-7
- Eugene O'Neill Memorial Theater Center DLB-7
- The Goodman Theatre DLB-7
- The Guthrie Theater DLB-7
- The Mark Taper Forum DLB-7
- The National Theatre and the Royal Shakespeare Company: The National Companies DLB-13
- Off-Loop Theatres DLB-7
- The Royal Court Theatre and the English Stage Company DLB-13
- The Royal Court Theatre and the New Drama DLB-10
- The Takarazaka Revue Company Y-91

Thegan and the Astronomer fl. circa 850 .... DLB-148

Thelwall, John 1764-1834 .... DLB-93, 158

Theocritus circa 300 B.C.-260 B.C. DLB-176

Theodorescu, Ion N. (see Arghezi, Tudor)

Theodulf circa 760-circa 821 .... DLB-148

Theophrastus circa 371 B.C.-287 B.C. DLB-176

Thériault, Yves 1915-1983 .... DLB-88

Thério, Adrien 1925- DLB-53

Theroux, Paul 1941- DLB-2, 218; CDALB-7

Thesiger, Wilfred 1910-2003 .... DLB-204

They All Came to Paris DS-15

Thibaudeau, Colleen 1925- DLB-88

Thiele, Colin 1920- DLB-289

Thielen, Benedict 1903-1965 .... DLB-102

Thiong'o Ngugi wa (see Ngugi wa Thiong'o)

Thiroux d'Arconville, Marie-Geneviève 1720-1805 .... DLB-314

This Quarter 1925-1927, 1929-1932 .... DS-15

Thoma, Ludwig 1867-1921 .... DLB-66

Thoma, Richard 1902-1974 .... DLB-4

Thomas, Audrey 1935- DLB-60

Thomas, D. M.
1935- ... DLB-40, 207, 299; Y-82; CDBLB-8
- The Plagiarism Controversy Y-82

Thomas, Dylan
1914-1953 .... DLB-13, 20, 139; CDBLB-7
- The Dylan Thomas Celebration Y-99

Thomas, Ed 1961- DLB-310

Thomas, Edward 1878-1917 .... DLB-19, 98, 156, 216
- The Friends of the Dymock Poets Y-00

Thomas, Frederick William 1806-1866 .. DLB-202

Thomas, Gwyn 1913-1981 .... DLB-15, 245

Thomas, Isaiah 1750-1831 .... DLB-43, 73, 187

Thomas, Johann 1624-1679 .... DLB-168

Thomas, John 1900-1932 .... DLB-4

Thomas, Joyce Carol 1938- DLB-33

Thomas, Lewis 1913-1993 .... DLB-275

Thomas, Lorenzo 1944- DLB-41

Thomas, Norman 1884-1968 .... DLB-303

Thomas, R. S. 1915-2000 ..... DLB-27; CDBLB-8

Isaiah Thomas [publishing house] DLB-49

Thomasîn von Zerclære circa 1186-circa 1259 .... DLB-138

Thomason, George 1602?-1666 .... DLB-213

Thomasius, Christian 1655-1728 .... DLB-168

Thompson, Daniel Pierce 1795-1868 .... DLB-202

Thompson, David 1770-1857 .... DLB-99

Thompson, Dorothy 1893-1961 .... DLB-29

Thompson, E. P. 1924-1993 .... DLB-242

Thompson, Flora 1876-1947 .... DLB-240

Thompson, Francis 1859-1907 .... DLB-19; CDBLB-5

Thompson, George Selden (see Selden, George)

Thompson, Henry Yates 1838-1928 ..... DLB-184

Thompson, Hunter S. 1939-2005 .... DLB-185

Thompson, Jim 1906-1977 .... DLB-226

Thompson, John 1938-1976 .... DLB-60

Thompson, John R. 1823-1873 .... DLB-3, 73, 248

Thompson, Judith 1954- DLB-334

Thompson, Lawrance 1906-1973 .... DLB-103

Thompson, Maurice 1844-1901 .... DLB-71, 74

Thompson, Ruth Plumly 1891-1976 ..... DLB-22

Thompson, Thomas Phillips 1843-1933 ... DLB-99

Thompson, William 1775-1833 .... DLB-158

Thompson, William Tappan 1812-1882 .... DLB-3, 11, 248

Thomson, Cockburn "Modern Style" (1857) [excerpt] DLB-57

Thomson, Edward William 1849-1924 ... DLB-92

Thomson, James 1700-1748 .... DLB-95

Thomson, James 1834-1882 .... DLB-35

Thomson, Joseph 1858-1895 .... DLB-174

Thomson, Mortimer 1831-1875 .... DLB-11

Thomson, Rupert 1955- DLB-267

Thon, Melanie Rae 1957- DLB-244

Thor Vilhjálmsson 1925- DLB-293

Þórarinn Eldjárn 1949- DLB-293

Þórbergur Þórðarson 1888-1974 .... DLB-293

Thoreau, Henry David 1817-1862 .... DLB-1, 183, 223, 270, 298; DS-5; CDALB-2

The Thoreau Society Y-99

The Thoreauvian Pilgrimage: The Structure of an American Cult .. DLB-223

Thorne, William 1568?-1630 .... DLB-281

Thornton, John F. [Response to Ken Auletta] Y-97

Thorpe, Adam 1956- DLB-231

Thorpe, Thomas Bangs 1815-1878 .... DLB-3, 11, 248

Thorup, Kirsten 1942- DLB-214

Thott, Birgitte 1610-1662 .... DLB-300

Thrale, Hester Lynch (see Piozzi, Hester Lynch [Thrale])

The Three Marias: A Landmark Case in Portuguese Literary History (Maria Isabel Barreno, 1939- ; Maria Teresa Horta, 1937- ; Maria Velho da Costa, 1938-) DLB-287

Thubron, Colin 1939- DLB-204, 231

Thucydides circa 455 B.C.-circa 395 B.C. DLB-176

Thulstrup, Thure de 1848-1930 .... DLB-188

Thümmel, Moritz August von 1738-1817 .... DLB-97

Thurber, James 1894-1961 .... DLB-4, 11, 22, 102; CDALB-5

Thurman, Wallace 1902-1934 .... DLB-51
- "Negro Poets and Their Poetry" DLB-50

Thwaite, Anthony 1930- DLB-40
- The Booker Prize, Address Y-86

Thwaites, Reuben Gold 1853-1913 ...... DLB-47

Tibullus circa 54 B.C.-circa 19 B.C. DLB-211

Ticknor, George 1791-1871 .... DLB-1, 59, 140, 235

Ticknor and Fields DLB-49

Ticknor and Fields (revived) DLB-46

Tieck, Ludwig 1773-1853 .... DLB-90; CDWLB-2

Tietjens, Eunice 1884-1944 .... DLB-54

Tikkanen, Märta 1935- DLB-257

Tilghman, Christopher circa 1948 ...... DLB-244

Tilney, Edmund circa 1536-1610 .... DLB-136

Charles Tilt [publishing house] DLB-106

J. E. Tilton and Company DLB-49

Time-Life Books DLB-46

Times Books DLB-46

Timothy, Peter circa 1725-1782 .... DLB-43

Timrava 1867-1951 .... DLB-215

Timrod, Henry 1828-1867 .... DLB-3, 248

Tindal, Henrietta 1818?-1879 .... DLB-199

Tindal, Nicholas 1688-1774 .... DLB-336

Tinker, Chauncey Brewster 1876-1963 .... DLB-140

Tinsley Brothers DLB-106

Tiptree, James, Jr. 1915-1987 .... DLB-8

Tišma, Aleksandar 1924-2003 .... DLB-181

Titus, Edward William 1870-1952 .... DLB-4; DS-15

Tiutchev, Fedor Ivanovich 1803-1873 .... DLB-205

Tlali, Miriam 1933- DLB-157, 225

Todd, Barbara Euphan 1890-1976 ...... DLB-160

Todorov, Tzvetan 1939- DLB-242

Tofte, Robert
  1561 or 1562-1619 or 1620 .... DLB-172

Tóibín, Colm 1955- DLB-271

Toklas, Alice B. 1877-1967 .... DLB-4; DS-15

Tokuda Shūsei 1872-1943 .... DLB-180

Toland, John 1670-1722 .... DLB-252, 336

Tolkien, J. R. R.
  1892-1973 ...... DLB-15, 160, 255; CDBLB-6

Toller, Ernst 1893-1939 .... DLB-124

Tollet, Elizabeth 1694-1754 .... DLB-95

Tolson, Melvin B. 1898-1966 .... DLB-48, 76

Tolstaya, Tatyana 1951- DLB-285

Tolstoy, Aleksei Konstantinovich
  1817-1875 .... DLB-238

Tolstoy, Aleksei Nikolaevich 1883-1945 ... DLB-272

Tolstoy, Leo 1828-1910 .... DLB-238

Tomalin, Claire 1933- DLB-155

Tómas Guðmundsson 1901-1983 .... DLB-293

Tomasi di Lampedusa, Giuseppe
  1896-1957 .... DLB-177

Tomlinson, Charles 1927- DLB-40

Tomlinson, H. M. 1873-1958 .... DLB-36, 100, 195

Abel Tompkins [publishing house] DLB-49

Tompson, Benjamin 1642-1714 .... DLB-24

Tomson, Graham R.
  (see Watson, Rosamund Marriott)

Ton'a 1289-1372 .... DLB-203

Tondelli, Pier Vittorio 1955-1991 .... DLB-196

Tonks, Rosemary 1932- DLB-14, 207

Tonna, Charlotte Elizabeth 1790-1846 .... DLB-163

Jacob Tonson the Elder
  [publishing house] DLB-170

Toole, John Kennedy 1937-1969 .... Y-81

Toomer, Jean 1894-1967 .... DLB-45, 51; CDALB-4

Topsoe, Vilhelm 1840-1881 .... DLB-300

Tor Books DLB-46

Torberg, Friedrich 1908-1979 .... DLB-85

Torga, Miguel (Adolfo Correia da Rocha)
  1907-1995 .... DLB-287

Torre, Francisco de la ?-? DLB-318

Torrence, Ridgely 1874-1950 .... DLB 54, 249

Torrente Ballester, Gonzalo
  1910-1999 .... DLB-322

Torres-Metzger, Joseph V. 1933- DLB-122

Torres Naharro, Bartolomé de
  1485?-1523? DLB-318

El Tostado (see Madrigal, Alfonso Fernández de)

Toth, Susan Allen 1940- Y-86

Richard Tottell [publishing house] DLB-170

"The Printer to the Reader,"
  (1557) DLB-167

Tough-Guy Literature DLB-9

Touré, Askia Muhammad 1938- DLB-41

Tourgée, Albion W. 1838-1905 .... DLB-79

Tournemir, Elizaveta Sailhas de (see Tur, Evgeniia)

Tourneur, Cyril circa 1580-1626 .... DLB-58

Tournier, Michel 1924- DLB-83

Frank Tousey [publishing house] DLB-49

Tower Publications DLB-46

Towers, Joseph 1737-1799 .... DLB-336

Towne, Benjamin circa 1740-1793 .... DLB-43

Towne, Robert 1936- DLB-44

The Townely Plays fifteenth and sixteenth
  centuries DLB-146

Townsend, Sue 1946- DLB-271

Townshend, Aurelian
  by 1583-circa 1651 .... DLB-121

Toy, Barbara 1908-2001 .... DLB-204

Tozzi, Federigo 1883-1920 .... DLB-264

Tracy, Honor 1913-1989 .... DLB-15

Traherne, Thomas 1637?-1674 .... DLB-131

Traill, Catharine Parr 1802-1899 .... DLB-99

Train, Arthur 1875-1945 .... DLB-86; DS-16

Tranquilli, Secondino (see Silone, Ignazio)

The Transatlantic Publishing Company ... DLB-49

The Transatlantic Review 1924-1925 .... DS-15

The Transcendental Club
  1836-1840 .... DLB-1; DLB-223

Transcendentalism DLB-1; DLB-223; DS-5

  "A Response from America," by
    John A. Heraud DS-5

  Publications and Social Movements DLB-1

  The Rise of Transcendentalism,
    1815-1860 .... DS-5

  Transcendentalists, American DS-5

  "What Is Transcendentalism? By a
    Thinking Man," by James
    Kinnard Jr. DS-5

transition 1927-1938 .... DS-15

Translations (Vernacular) in the Crowns of
  Castile and Aragon 1352-1515 ...... DLB-286

Tranströmer, Tomas 1931- DLB-257

Tranter, John 1943- DLB-289

Travel Writing
  American Travel Writing, 1776-1864
    (checklist) DLB-183

  British Travel Writing, 1940-1997
    (checklist) DLB-204

  Travel Writers of the Late
    Middle Ages DLB-286

  (1876-1909) DLB-174

  (1837-1875) DLB-166

  (1910-1939) DLB-195

Traven, B. 1882?/1890?-1969? DLB-9, 56

Travers, Ben 1886-1980 .... DLB-10, 233

Travers, P. L. (Pamela Lyndon)
  1899-1996 .... DLB-160

Trediakovsky, Vasilii Kirillovich
  1703-1769 .... DLB-150

Treece, Henry 1911-1966 .... DLB-160

Treitel, Jonathan 1959- DLB-267

Trejo, Ernesto 1950-1991 .... DLB-122

Trelawny, Edward John
  1792-1881 .... DLB-110, 116, 144

Tremain, Rose 1943- DLB-14, 271

Tremblay, Michel 1942- DLB-60

Trenchard, John 1662-1723 .... DLB-336

Trent, William P. 1862-1939 .... DLB-47, 71

Trescot, William Henry 1822-1898 .... DLB-30

Tressell, Robert (Robert Phillipe Noonan)
  1870-1911 .... DLB-197

Trevelyan, Sir George Otto
  1838-1928 .... DLB-144

Trevisa, John circa 1342-circa 1402 ...... DLB-146

Trevisan, Dalton 1925- DLB-307

Trevor, William 1928- DLB-14, 139

Triana, José 1931- DLB-305

Trierer Floyris circa 1170-1180 .... DLB-138

Trifonov, Iurii Valentinovich
  1925-1981 .... DLB-302

Trillin, Calvin 1935- DLB-185

Trilling, Lionel 1905-1975 .... DLB-28, 63

Trilussa 1871-1950 .... DLB-114

Trimmer, Sarah 1741-1810 .... DLB-158

Triolet, Elsa 1896-1970 .... DLB-72

Tripp, John 1927- DLB-40

Trocchi, Alexander 1925-1984 .... DLB-15

Troisi, Dante 1920-1989 .... DLB-196

Trollope, Anthony
  1815-1882 .... DLB-21, 57, 159; CDBLB-4

  Novel-Reading: *The Works of Charles
    Dickens; The Works of W. Makepeace
    Thackeray* (1879) DLB-21

  The Trollope Societies Y-00

Trollope, Frances 1779-1863 .... DLB-21, 166

Trollope, Joanna 1943- DLB-207

Troop, Elizabeth 1931- DLB-14

Tropicália DLB-307

Trotter, Catharine 1679-1749 .... DLB-84, 252

Trotti, Lamar 1898-1952 .... DLB-44

Trottier, Pierre 1925- DLB-60

Trotzig, Birgitta 1929- DLB-257

Troupe, Quincy Thomas, Jr. 1943- DLB-41

John F. Trow and Company DLB-49

Trowbridge, John Townsend 1827-1916 ... DLB-202

Trudel, Jean-Louis 1967- DLB-251

True History of the Kelly Gang, 2001 Booker Prize winner,
  Peter Carey DLB-326

Truillier-Lacombe, Joseph-Patrice
  1807-1863 .... DLB-99

Trumbo, Dalton 1905-1976 .... DLB-26

Trumbull, Benjamin 1735-1820 .... DLB-30
Trumbull, John 1750-1831 .... DLB-31
Trumbull, John 1756-1843 .... DLB-183
Trunk, Yehiel Teshaia (Yekhiel Yeshayda Trunk) 1888-1961 .... DLB-333
Truth, Sojourner 1797?-1883 .... DLB-239
Tscherning, Andreas 1611-1659 .... DLB-164
Tsubouchi Shōyō 1859-1935 .... DLB-180
Tsvetaeva, Marina Ivanovna 1892-1941 .... DLB-295
Tuchman, Barbara W. Tribute to Alfred A. Knopf Y-84
Tucholsky, Kurt 1890-1935 .... DLB-56
Tucker, Charlotte Maria 1821-1893 .... DLB-163, 190
Tucker, George 1775-1861 .... DLB-3, 30, 248
Tucker, James 1808?-1866?............ DLB-230
Tucker, Nathaniel Beverley 1784-1851................ DLB-3, 248
Tucker, St. George 1752-1827 .... DLB-37
Tuckerman, Frederick Goddard 1821-1873.................. DLB-243
Tuckerman, Henry Theodore 1813-1871 .... DLB-64
Tumas, Juozas (see Vaizgantas)
Tunis, John R. 1889-1975 .... .DLB-22, 171
Tunstall, Cuthbert 1474-1559 .... DLB-132
Tunström, Göran 1937-2000.......... DLB-257
Tuohy, Frank 1925- DLB-14, 139
Tupper, Martin F. 1810-1889 .... DLB-32
Tur, Evgeniia 1815-1892............... DLB-238
Turbyfill, Mark 1896-1991 .... DLB-45
Turco, Lewis 1934- Y-84
Tribute to John Ciardi Y-86
Turgenev, Aleksandr Ivanovich 1784-1845................. DLB-198
Turgenev, Ivan Sergeevich 1818-1883................. DLB-238
Turgot, baron de l'Aulne, Anne-Robert-Jacques 1727-1781 .... DLB-314
"Memorandum on Local Government"................ DLB-314
Turini Bufalini, Francesca 1553-1641 .... DLB-339
Turnbull, Alexander H. 1868-1918...... DLB-184
Turnbull, Andrew 1921-1970 .... DLB-103
Turnbull, Gael 1928- DLB-40
Turnèbe, Odet de 1552-1581 .... DLB-327
Turner, Arlin 1909-1980............... DLB-103
Turner, Charles (Tennyson) 1808-1879.................. DLB-32
Turner, Ethel 1872-1958............... DLB-230
Turner, Frederick 1943- DLB-40
Turner, Frederick Jackson 1861-1932 ....DLB-17, 186
A Conversation between William Riggan and Janette Turner Hospital............ Y-02

Turner, Joseph Addison 1826-1868 ...... DLB-79
Turpin, Waters Edward 1910-1968....... DLB-51
Turrini, Peter 1944- DLB-124
Tusquets, Esther 1936- DLB-322
Tutuola, Amos 1920-1997... DLB-125; CDWLB-3
Twain, Mark (see Clemens, Samuel Langhorne)
Tweedie, Ethel Brilliana circa 1860-1940 ....DLB-174
A Century of Poetry, a Lifetime of Collecting: J. M. Edelstein's Collection of Twentieth-Century American Poetry YB-02
Twombly, Wells 1935-1977............. DLB-241
Twysden, Sir Roger 1597-1672 .... DLB-213
Tyard, Pontus de 1521?-1605 .... DLB-327
Ty-Casper, Linda 1931- DLB-312
Tyler, Anne 1941- DLB-6, 143; Y-82; CDALB-7
Tyler, Mary Palmer 1775-1866 .... DLB-200
Tyler, Moses Coit 1835-1900 ....DLB-47, 64
Tyler, Royall 1757-1826................ DLB-37
Tylor, Edward Burnett 1832-1917 .... DLB-57
Tynan, Katharine 1861-1931 ...... DLB-153, 240
Tyndale, William circa 1494-1536 ...... DLB-132
Tynes, Maxine 1949- DLB-334
Tyree, Omar 1969- DLB-292

U

Uchida, Yoshiko 1921-1992 .. DLB-312; CDALB-7
Udall, Nicholas 1504-1556............. DLB-62
Ugrešić, Dubravka 1949- DLB-181
Uhland, Ludwig 1787-1862............ DLB-90
Uhse, Bodo 1904-1963................ DLB-69
Ujević, Augustin "Tin" 1891-1955 .... DLB-147
Ulenhart, Niclas fl. circa 1600 .... DLB-164
Ulfeldt, Leonora Christina 1621-1698 ... DLB-300
Ulibarrí, Sabine R. 1919-2003 .... DLB-82
Ulica, Jorge 1870-1926 .... DLB-82
Ulitskaya, Liudmila Evgen'evna 1943- DLB-285
Ulivi, Ferruccio 1912- DLB-196
Ulizio, B. George 1889-1969 .... DLB-140
Ulrich von Liechtenstein circa 1200-circa 1275 .... DLB-138
Ulrich von Zatzikhoven before 1194-after 1214 .... DLB-138
'Umar ibn Abi Rabi'ah 644-712 or 721 .. DLB-311
Unaipon, David 1872-1967............ DLB-230
Unamuno, Miguel de 1864-1936 ... DLB-108, 322
Under, Marie 1883-1980 ... DLB-220; CDWLB-4
Underhill, Evelyn 1875-1941 .... DLB-240
Undset, Sigrid 1882-1949.............DLB-297, 332
Ungaretti, Giuseppe 1888-1970 .... DLB-114

Unger, Friederike Helene 1741-1813..................... DLB-94
United States Book Company DLB-49
Universal Publishing and Distributing Corporation.................... DLB-46
University of Colorado Special Collections at the University of Colorado at Boulder Y-98
Indiana University Press................. Y-02
The University of Iowa Writers' Workshop Golden Jubilee Y-86
University of Missouri Press............... Y-01
University of South Carolina The G. Ross Roy Scottish Poetry Collection Y-89
Two Hundred Years of Rare Books and Literary Collections at the University of South Carolina Y-00
The University of South Carolina Press...... Y-94
University of Virginia The Book Arts Press at the University of Virginia Y-96
The Electronic Text Center and the Electronic Archive of Early American Fiction at the University of Virginia Library Y-98
University of Virginia Libraries......... Y-91
University of Wales Press............. DLB-112
University Press of Florida Y-00
University Press of Kansas Y-98
University Press of Mississippi............. Y-99
Unnur Benediktsdóttir Bjarklind (see Hulda)
Uno Chiyo 1897-1996 .... DLB-180
Unruh, Fritz von 1885-1970 .... DLB-56, 118
Unsworth, Barry 1930- DLB-194. 326
Unt, Mati 1944- DLB-232
The Unterberg Poetry Center of the 92nd Street Y Y-98
Untermeyer, Louis 1885-1977 .... DLB-303
T. Fisher Unwin [publishing house] DLB-106
Upchurch, Boyd B. (see Boyd, John)
Updike, John 1932- DLB-2, 5, 143, 218, 227; Y-80, 82; DS-3; CDALB-6
John Updike on the Internet Y-97
Tribute to Alfred A. Knopf Y-84
Tribute to John Ciardi Y-86
Upīts, Andrejs 1877-1970 .... DLB-220
Uppdal, Kristofer 1878-1961 .... DLB-297
Upton, Bertha 1849-1912............. DLB-141
Upton, Charles 1948- DLB-16
Upton, Florence K. 1873-1922 .... DLB-141
Upward, Allen 1863-1926 .... DLB-36
Urban, Milo 1904-1982 .... DLB-215
Ureña de Henríquez, Salomé 1850-1897 . DLB-283
Urfé, Honoré d' 1567-1625 ....DLB-268
Urista, Alberto Baltazar (see Alurista)
Urquhart, Fred 1912-1995 .... DLB-139

Urquhart, Jane 1949- DLB-334
Urrea, Luis Alberto 1955- DLB-209
Urzidil, Johannes 1896-1970 ....DLB-85
U.S.A. (Documentary) DLB-274
Usigli, Rodolfo 1905-1979 ....DLB-305
Usk, Thomas died 1388 ....DLB-146
Uslar Pietri, Arturo 1906-2001 ......DLB-113
Uspensky, Gleb Ivanovich
    1843-1902 ....DLB-277
Ussher, James 1581-1656................DLB-213
Ustinov, Peter 1921-2004..............DLB-13
Uttley, Alison 1884-1976 ....DLB-160
Uz, Johann Peter 1720-1796 ....DLB-97

V

Vadianus, Joachim 1484-1551 ....DLB-179
Vac, Bertrand (Aimé Pelletier) 1914- DLB-88
Vācietis, Ojārs 1933-1983 ....DLB-232
Vaculík, Ludvík 1926- DLB-232
Vaičiulaitis, Antanas 1906-1992........DLB-220
Vaičiūnaite, Judita 1937- DLB-232
Vail, Laurence 1891-1968 ....DLB-4
Vail, Petr L'vovich 1949- DLB-285
Vailland, Roger 1907-1965 ....DLB-83
Vaižgantas 1869-1933 ....DLB-220
Vajda, Ernest 1887-1954.................DLB-44
Valdés, Alfonso de circa 1490?-1532 .....DLB-318
Valdés, Gina 1943- DLB-122
Valdes, Juan de 1508-1541 ....DLB-318
Valdez, Luis Miguel 1940- DLB-122
Valduga, Patrizia 1953- DLB-128
Vale Press.............................DLB-112
Valente, José Angel 1929-2000.........DLB-108
Valenzuela, Luisa 1938- ...DLB-113; CDWLB-3
Valera, Diego de 1412-1488............DLB-286
Valeri, Diego 1887-1976 ....DLB-128
Valerius Flaccus fl. circa A.D. 92........DLB-211
Valerius Maximus fl. circa A.D. 31......DLB-211
Valéry, Paul 1871-1945................DLB-258
Valesio, Paolo 1939- DLB-196
Valgardson, W. D. 1939-................DLB-60
Valle, Luz 1899-1971 ....DLB-290
Valle, Víctor Manuel 1950- DLB-122
Valle-Inclán, Ramón del
    1866-1936 ....DLB-134, 322
Vallejo, Armando 1949- DLB-122
Vallejo, César Abraham 1892-1938 ......DLB-290
Vallès, Jules 1832-1885.................DLB-123
Vallette, Marguerite Eymery (see Rachilde)
Valverde, José María 1926-1996 ....DLB-108

Vampilov, Aleksandr Valentinovich (A. Sanin)
    1937-1972.....................DLB-302
Van Allsburg, Chris 1949- DLB-61
Van Anda, Carr 1864-1945 ....DLB-25
Vanbrugh, Sir John 1664-1726............DLB-80
Vance, Jack 1916?- DLB-8
Vančura, Vladislav
    1891-1942............DLB-215; CDWLB-4
Vanderhaege, Guy 1951- DLB-334
van der Post, Laurens 1906-1996........DLB-204
Van Dine, S. S. (see Wright, Willard Huntington)
Van Doren, Mark 1894-1972........DLB-45, 335
van Druten, John 1901-1957 ....DLB-10
Van Duyn, Mona 1921-2004 ....DLB-5
    Tribute to James Dickey Y-97
Van Dyke, Henry 1852-1933......DLB-71; DS-13
Van Dyke, Henry 1928- DLB-33
Van Dyke, John C. 1856-1932.........DLB-186
Vane, Sutton 1888-1963................DLB-10
Van Gieson, Judith 1941- DLB-306
Vanguard Press DLB-46
van Gulik, Robert Hans 1910-1967........DS-17
van Herk, Aritha 1954- DLB-334
van Itallie, Jean-Claude 1936- DLB-7
Van Loan, Charles E. 1876-1919 ......DLB-171
Vann, Robert L. 1879-1940 ....DLB-29
Van Rensselaer, Mariana Griswold
    1851-1934 ....DLB-47
Van Rensselaer, Mrs. Schuyler
    (see Van Rensselaer, Mariana Griswold)
Van Vechten, Carl 1880-1964 ....DLB-4, 9, 51
van Vogt, A. E. 1912-2000.........DLB-8, 251
Varela, Blanca 1926- DLB-290
Vargas Llosa, Mario
    1936- DLB-145; CDWLB-3
    Acceptance Speech for the Ritz Paris
    Hemingway Award................Y-85
Varley, John 1947- Y-81
Varnhagen von Ense, Karl August
    1785-1858 ....DLB-90
Varnhagen von Ense, Rahel
    1771-1833 ....DLB-90
Varro 116 B.C.-27 B.C. DLB-211
Vasilenko, Svetlana Vladimirovna
    1956- DLB-285
Vasiliu, George (see Bacovia, George)
Vásquez, Richard 1928- DLB-209
Vassa, Gustavus (see Equiano, Olaudah)
Vassalli, Sebastiano 1941- DLB-128, 196
Vassanji, M. G. 1950- DLB-334
Vaugelas, Claude Favre de 1585-1650 ....DLB-268
Vaughan, Henry 1621-1695..............DLB-131
Vaughan, Thomas 1621-1666 ....DLB-131

Vaughn, Robert 1592?-1667 ....DLB-213
Vaux, Thomas, Lord 1509-1556 ....DLB-132
Vazov, Ivan 1850-1921......DLB-147; CDWLB-4
Vázquez Montalbán, Manuel
    1939- DLB-134, 322
Véa, Alfredo, Jr. 1950- DLB-209
Veblen, Thorstein 1857-1929...........DLB-246
Vedel, Anders Sørensen 1542-1616 ......DLB-300
Vega, Janine Pommy 1942- DLB-16
Veiller, Anthony 1903-1965............DLB-44
Velásquez-Trevino, Gloria 1949- DLB-122
Veley, Margaret 1843-1887 ....DLB-199
Velleius Paterculus
    circa 20 B.C.-circa A.D. 30 ....DLB-211
Veloz Maggiolo, Marcio 1936- DLB-145
Vel'tman, Aleksandr Fomich
    1800-1870 ....DLB-198
Venegas, Daniel ?-? DLB-82
Venevitinov, Dmitrii Vladimirovich
    1805-1827 ....DLB-205
Verbitskaia, Anastasiia Alekseevna
    1861-1928 ....DLB-295
Verde, Cesário 1855-1886 ....DLB-287
Vergil, Polydore circa 1470-1555 ....DLB-132
Veríssimo, Erico 1905-1975 ....DLB-145, 307
Verlaine, Paul 1844-1896..............DLB-217
Vernacular Translations in the Crowns of
    Castile and Aragon 1352-1515 ......DLB-286
Verne, Jules 1828-1905 ....DLB-123
Vernon God Little, 2003 Booker Prize winner,
    DBC Pierre DLB-326
Verplanck, Gulian C. 1786-1870 ....DLB-59
Vertinsky, Aleksandr 1889-1957 ....DLB-317
Very, Jones 1813-1880 ....DLB-1, 243; DS-5
Vesaas, Halldis Moren 1907-1995 ....DLB-297
Vesaas, Tarjei 1897-1970................DLB-297
Vian, Boris 1920-1959............DLB-72, 321
Viazemsky, Petr Andreevich
    1792-1878 ....DLB-205
Vicars, Thomas 1591-1638 ....DLB-236
Vicente, Gil 1465-1536/1540?......DLB-287, 318
Vickers, Roy 1888?-1965................DLB-77
Vickery, Sukey 1779-1821 ....DLB-200
Victoria 1819-1901 ....DLB-55
Victoria Press..........................DLB-106
La vida de Lazarillo de Tormes DLB-318
Vidal, Gore 1925- DLB-6, 152; CDALB-7
Vidal, Mary Theresa 1815-1873 ....DLB-230
Vidmer, Richards 1898-1978 ....DLB-241
Viebig, Clara 1860-1952 ....DLB-66
Vieira, António, S. J. (Antonio Vieyra)
    1608-1697 ....DLB-307
Viereck, George Sylvester 1884-1962 .....DLB-54

Viereck, Peter 1916- DLB-5

Vietnam War (ended 1975)
Resources for the Study of Vietnam War
Literature..................... DLB-9

Viets, Roger 1738-1811................. DLB-99

Vigil-Piñon, Evangelina 1949- DLB-122

Vigneault, Gilles 1928- DLB-60

Vigny, Alfred de 1797-1863.....DLB-119, 192, 217

Vigolo, Giorgio 1894-1983............ DLB-114

Vik, Bjorg 1935- DLB-297

The Viking Press DLB-46

Vila-Matas, Enrique 1948- DLB-322

Vilde, Eduard 1865-1933............. DLB-220

Vilinskaia, Mariia Aleksandrovna
(see Vovchok, Marko)

Villa, José García 1908-1997........... DLB-312

Villanueva, Alma Luz 1944- DLB-122

Villanueva, Tino 1941- DLB-82

Villard, Henry 1835-1900.............. DLB-23

Villard, Oswald Garrison 1872-1949 .. DLB-25, 91

Villarreal, Edit 1944- DLB-209

Villarreal, José Antonio 1924- DLB-82

Villaseñor, Victor 1940- DLB-209

Villedieu, Madame de (Marie-Catherine
Desjardins) 1640?-1683.............. DLB-268

Villegas, Antonio de ?-? DLB-318

Villegas de Magnón, Leonor
1876-1955..................... DLB-122

Villehardouin, Geoffroi de
circa 1150-1215 .... DLB-208

Villemaire, Yolande 1949- DLB-60

Villena, Enrique de
ca. 1382/84-1432 .... DLB-286

Villena, Luis Antonio de 1951- DLB-134

Villiers, George, Second Duke
of Buckingham 1628-1687 .... DLB-80

Villiers de l'Isle-Adam, Jean-Marie
Mathias Philippe-Auguste,
Comte de 1838-1889 .... DLB-123, 192

Villon, François 1431-circa 1463?....... DLB-208

Vinaver, Michel (Michel Grinberg)
1927- DLB-321

Vine Press..................... DLB-112

Viorst, Judith 1931- DLB-52

Vipont, Elfrida (Elfrida Vipont Foulds,
Charles Vipont) 1902-1992 .... DLB-160

Viramontes, Helena María 1954- DLB-122

Virgil 70 B.C.-19 B.C.....DLB-211; CDWLB-1

Vischer, Friedrich Theodor 1807-1887 ... DLB-133

Vitier, Cintio 1921- DLB-283

Vitrac, Roger 1899-1952............ DLB-321

Vitruvius circa 85 B.C.-circa 15 B.C. DLB-211

Vitry, Philippe de 1291-1361 .... DLB-208

Vittorini, Elio 1908-1966 .... DLB-264

Vivanco, Luis Felipe 1907-1975......... DLB-108

Vives, Juan Luis 1493-1540 .... DLB-318

Vivian, E. Charles (Charles Henry Cannell,
Charles Henry Vivian, Jack Mann,
Barry Lynd) 1882-1947 .... DLB-255

Viviani, Cesare 1947- DLB-128

Vivien, Renée 1877-1909 .... DLB-217

Vizenor, Gerald 1934- DLB-175, 227

Vizetelly and Company DLB-106

Vladimov, Georgii
1931-2003 .... DLB-302

Voaden, Herman 1903-1991........... DLB-88

Voß, Johann Heinrich 1751-1826 .... DLB-90

Vogau, Boris Andreevich
(see Pil'niak, Boris Andreevich)

Voigt, Ellen Bryant 1943- DLB-120

Voinovich, Vladimir Nikolaevich
1932- DLB-302

Vojnović, Ivo 1857-1929 .....DLB-147; CDWLB-4

Vold, Jan Erik 1939- DLB-297

Volkoff, Vladimir 1932- DLB-83

P. F. Volland Company............... DLB-46

Vollbehr, Otto H. F.
1872?-1945 or 1946 .... DLB-187

Vologdin (see Zasodimsky, Pavel Vladimirovich)

Voloshin, Maksimilian Aleksandrovich
1877-1932..................... DLB-295

Volponi, Paolo 1924-1994............DLB-177

Voltaire (François-Marie Arouet)
1694-1778..................... DLB-314

"An account of the death of the chevalier de
La Barre"................... DLB-314

Candide DLB-314

Philosophical Dictionary............. DLB-314

Vonarburg, Élisabeth 1947- DLB-251

von der Grün, Max 1926- DLB-75

Vonnegut, Kurt 1922-2007 ....DLB-2, 8, 152;
Y-80; DS-3; CDALB-6

Tribute to Isaac Asimov............... Y-92

Tribute to Richard Brautigan........... Y-84

Voranc, Prežihov 1893-1950......... DLB-147

Voronsky, Aleksandr Konstantinovich
1884-1937.....................DLB-272

Vorse, Mary Heaton 1874-1966 .... DLB-303

Vovchok, Marko 1833-1907 .... DLB-238

Voynich, E. L. 1864-1960............ DLB-197

Vroman, Mary Elizabeth
circa 1924-1967 .... DLB-33

W

Wace, Robert ("Maistre")
circa 1100-circa 1175 .... DLB-146

Wackenroder, Wilhelm Heinrich
1773-1798..................... DLB-90

Wackernagel, Wilhelm 1806-1869 ...... DLB-133

Waddell, Helen 1889-1965........... DLB-240

Waddington, Miriam 1917-2004........ DLB-68

Wade, Henry 1887-1969............... DLB-77

Wagenknecht, Edward 1900-2004 ...... DLB-103

Wägner, Elin 1882-1949.............. DLB-259

Wagner, Heinrich Leopold 1747-1779..... DLB-94

Wagner, Henry R. 1862-1957.......... DLB-140

Wagner, Richard 1813-1883........... DLB-129

Wagoner, David 1926- DLB-5, 256

Wah, Fred 1939- DLB-60

Waiblinger, Wilhelm 1804-1830......... DLB-90

Wain, John
1925-1994 ...DLB-15, 27, 139, 155; CDBLB-8
Tribute to J. B. Priestly................ Y-84

Wainwright, Jeffrey 1944- DLB-40

Waite, Peirce and Company DLB-49

Wakeman, Stephen H. 1859-1924 ....DLB-187

Wakoski, Diane 1937- DLB-5

Walahfrid Strabo circa 808-849 .... DLB-148

Henry Z. Walck [publishing house] DLB-46

Walcott, Derek
1930- .. DLB-117, 332; Y-81, 92; CDWLB-3

Nobel Lecture 1992: The Antilles:
Fragments of Epic Memory.......... Y-92

Robert Waldegrave [publishing house]....DLB-170

Waldis, Burkhard circa 1490-1556?......DLB-178

Waldman, Anne 1945- DLB-16

Waldrop, Rosmarie 1935- DLB-169

Walker, Alice 1900-1982.............. DLB-201

Walker, Alice
1944- DLB-6, 33, 143; CDALB-6

Walker, Annie Louisa (Mrs. Harry Coghill)
circa 1836-1907 .... DLB-240

Walker, George F. 1947- DLB-60

Walker, John Brisben 1847-1931......... DLB-79

Walker, Joseph A. 1935- DLB-38

Walker, Kath (see Oodgeroo of the Tribe Noonuccal)

Walker, Margaret 1915-1998 ....DLB-76, 152

Walker, Obadiah 1616-1699 .... DLB-281

Walker, Ted 1934- DLB-40

Walker, Evans and Cogswell Company ... DLB-49

Wall, John F. (see Sarban)

Wallace, Alfred Russel 1823-1913 ...... DLB-190

Wallace, Dewitt 1889-1981.............DLB-137

Wallace, Edgar 1875-1932 .... DLB-70

Wallace, Lew 1827-1905............. DLB-202

Wallace, Lila Acheson 1889-1984........DLB-137

"A Word of Thanks," From the Initial
Issue of Reader's Digest
(February 1922)...............DLB-137

Wallace, Naomi 1960- DLB-249

Wallace Markfield's "Steeplechase" Y-02

Wallace-Crabbe, Chris 1934- DLB-289

Wallant, Edward Lewis
1926-1962 ....DLB-2, 28, 143, 299

Waller, Edmund 1606-1687 .... DLB-126

Walpole, Horace 1717-1797 . . . . . DLB-39, 104, 213

    Preface to the First Edition of
        The Castle of Otranto (1764) DLB-39, 178

    Preface to the Second Edition of
        The Castle of Otranto (1765) DLB-39, 178

Walpole, Hugh 1884-1941 . . . . DLB-34
Walrond, Eric 1898-1966 . . . . DLB-51
Walser, Martin 1927- DLB-75, 124
Walser, Robert 1878-1956 . . . . DLB-66
Walsh, Ernest 1895-1926 . . . . DLB-4, 45
Walsh, Robert 1784-1859 . . . . DLB-59
Walters, Henry 1848-1931 . . . . DLB-140
Waltharius circa 825 . . . . DLB-148
Walther von der Vogelweide
    circa 1170-circa 1230 . . . . DLB-138
Walton, Izaak
    1593-1683 . . . . DLB-151, 213; CDBLB-1
Walwicz, Ania 1951- DLB-325
Wambaugh, Joseph 1937- DLB-6; Y-83
Wand, Alfred Rudolph 1828-1891 . . . . DLB-188
Wandor, Michelene 1940- DLB-310
Waniek, Marilyn Nelson 1946- DLB-120
Wanley, Humphrey 1672-1726 . . . . DLB-213
War of the Words (and Pictures):
    The Creation of a Graphic Novel Y-02
Warburton, William 1698-1779 . . . . DLB-104
Ward, Aileen 1919- DLB-111
Ward, Artemus (see Browne, Charles Farrar)
Ward, Arthur Henry Sarsfield (see Rohmer, Sax)
Ward, Douglas Turner 1930- DLB-7, 38
Ward, Mrs. Humphry 1851-1920 . . . . DLB-18
Ward, James 1843-1925 . . . . DLB-262
Ward, Lynd 1905-1985 . . . . DLB-22
Ward, Lock and Company DLB-106
Ward, Nathaniel circa 1578-1652 . . . . DLB-24
Ward, Theodore 1902-1983 . . . . DLB-76
Wardle, Ralph 1909-1988 . . . . DLB-103
Ware, Henry, Jr. 1794-1843 . . . . DLB-235
Ware, William 1797-1852 . . . . DLB-1, 235
Warfield, Catherine Ann 1816-1877 . . . . . . DLB-248
Waring, Anna Letitia 1823-1910 . . . . DLB-240
Frederick Warne and Company [U.K.] DLB-106
Frederick Warne and Company [U.S.] DLB-49
Warner, Anne 1869-1913 . . . . DLB-202
Warner, Charles Dudley 1829-1900 . . . . . . DLB-64
Warner, Marina 1946- DLB-194
Warner, Rex 1905-1986 . . . . DLB-15
Warner, Susan 1819-1885 . . . . DLB-3, 42, 239, 250
Warner, Sylvia Townsend
    1893-1978 . . . . DLB-34, 139
Warner, William 1558-1609 . . . . DLB-172
Warner Books DLB-46

Warr, Bertram 1917-1943 . . . . DLB-88
Warren, John Byrne Leicester
    (see De Tabley, Lord)
Warren, Lella 1899-1982 . . . . Y-83
Warren, Mercy Otis 1728-1814 . . . . . . DLB-31, 200
Warren, Robert Penn 1905-1989 . . . . . DLB-2, 48,
        152, 320; Y-80, 89; CDALB-6
    Tribute to Katherine Anne Porter Y-80
Warren, Samuel 1807-1877 . . . . DLB-190
Warszawski, Oser (Oyzer Varshavski)
    1898-1944 . . . . DLB-333
Die Wartburgkrieg circa 1230-circa 1280 . . . . DLB-138
Warton, Joseph 1722-1800 . . . . DLB-104, 109
Warton the Younger, Thomas
    1728-1790 . . . . DLB-104, 109, 336
Warung, Price (William Astley)
    1855-1911 . . . . DLB-230
Washington, George 1732-1799 . . . . DLB-31
Washington, Ned 1901-1976 . . . . DLB-265
Wassermann, Jakob 1873-1934 . . . . DLB-66
Wasserstein, Wendy 1950-2006 . . . . DLB-228
Wassmo, Herbjorg 1942- DLB-297
Wasson, David Atwood 1823-1887 . . . . DLB-1, 223
Watanna, Onoto (see Eaton, Winnifred)
Waten, Judah 1911?-1985 . . . . DLB-289
Waterhouse, Keith 1929- DLB-13, 15
Waterman, Andrew 1940- DLB-40
Waters, Frank 1902-1995 . . . . DLB-212; Y-86
Waters, Michael 1949- DLB-120
Watkins, Tobias 1780-1855 . . . . DLB-73
Watkins, Vernon 1906-1967 . . . . DLB-20
Watmough, David 1926- DLB-53
Watson, Colin 1920-1983 . . . . DLB-276
Watson, Ian 1943- DLB-261
Watson, James Wreford (see Wreford, James)
Watson, John 1850-1907 . . . . DLB-156
Watson, Rosamund Marriott
    (Graham R. Tomson) 1860-1911 . . . . DLB-240
Watson, Sheila 1909-1998 . . . . DLB-60
Watson, Thomas 1545?-1592 . . . . DLB-132
Watson, Wilfred 1911-1998 . . . . DLB-60
W. J. Watt and Company DLB-46
Watten, Barrett 1948- DLB-193
Watterson, Henry 1840-1921 . . . . DLB-25
Watts, Alan 1915-1973 . . . . DLB-16
Watts, Isaac 1674-1748 . . . . DLB-95
Franklin Watts [publishing house] DLB-46
Waugh, Alec 1898-1981 . . . . DLB-191
Waugh, Auberon 1939-2000 . . . DLB-14, 194; Y-00
Waugh, Evelyn 1903-1966
    . . . . DLB-15, 162, 195; CDBLB-6
Way and Williams DLB-49
Wayman, Tom 1945- DLB-53

Wearne, Alan 1948- DLB-325
Weatherly, Tom 1942- DLB-41
Weaver, Gordon 1937- DLB-130
Weaver, Robert 1921- DLB-88
Webb, Beatrice 1858-1943 . . . . DLB-190
Webb, Francis 1925-1973 . . . . DLB-260
Webb, Frank J. fl. 1857 . . . . DLB-50
Webb, James Watson 1802-1884 . . . . DLB-43
Webb, Mary 1881-1927 . . . . DLB-34
Webb, Phyllis 1927- DLB-53
Webb, Sidney 1859-1947 . . . . DLB-190
Webb, Walter Prescott 1888-1963 . . . . DLB-17
Webbe, William ?-1591 . . . . DLB-132
Webber, Charles Wilkins
    1819-1856? DLB-202
Weber, Max 1864-1920 . . . . DLB-296
Webling, Lucy (Lucy Betty MacRaye)
    1877-1952 . . . . DLB-240
Webling, Peggy (Arthur Weston)
    1871-1949 . . . . DLB-240
Webster, Augusta 1837-1894 . . . . DLB-35, 240
Webster, John
    1579 or 1580-1634? DLB-58; CDBLB-1
    The Melbourne Manuscript Y-86
Webster, Noah
    1758-1843 . . . . DLB-1, 37, 42, 43, 73, 243
Webster, Paul Francis 1907-1984 . . . . DLB-265
Charles L. Webster and Company DLB-49
Weckherlin, Georg Rodolf 1584-1653 . . . . DLB-164
Wedekind, Frank
    1864-1918 . . . . DLB-118; CDWLB-2
Weeks, Edward Augustus, Jr.
    1898-1989 . . . . DLB-137
Weeks, Stephen B. 1865-1918 . . . . DLB-187
Weems, Mason Locke 1759-1825 . . DLB-30, 37, 42
Weerth, Georg 1822-1856 . . . . DLB-129
Weidenfeld and Nicolson DLB-112
Weidman, Jerome 1913-1998 . . . . DLB-28
Weigl, Bruce 1949- DLB-120
Weil, Jiří 1900-1959 . . . . DLB-299
Weinbaum, Stanley Grauman
    1902-1935 . . . . DLB-8
Weiner, Andrew 1949- DLB-251
Weintraub, Stanley 1929- DLB-111; Y82
Weise, Christian 1642-1708 . . . . DLB-168
Weisenborn, Gunther 1902-1969 . . . . . DLB-69, 124
Weiss, John 1818-1879 . . . . DLB-1, 243
Weiss, Paul 1901-2002 . . . . DLB-279
Weiss, Peter 1916-1982 . . . . DLB-69, 124
Weiss, Theodore 1916-2003 . . . . DLB-5
Weissenberg, Isaac Meir (Yitskhok-Meyer Vaysenberg)
    1878-1938 . . . . DLB-333
Weiß, Ernst 1882-1940 . . . . DLB-81

Cumulative Index

Weiße, Christian Felix 1726-1804 . . . . DLB-97
Weitling, Wilhelm 1808-1871 . . . . DLB-129
Welch, Denton 1915-1948 . . . . DLB-319
Welch, James 1940- DLB-175, 256
Welch, Lew 1926-1971? DLB-16
Weldon, Fay 1931- DLB-14, 194, 319; CDBLB-8
Wellek, René 1903-1995 . . . . DLB-63
Weller, Archie 1957- DLB-325
Wells, Carolyn 1862-1942 . . . . DLB-11
Wells, Charles Jeremiah
   circa 1800-1879 . . . . DLB-32
Wells, Gabriel 1862-1946 . . . . DLB-140
Wells, H. G. 1866-1946
   . . . . DLB-34, 70, 156, 178; CDBLB-6
   H. G. Wells Society Y-98
   Preface to *The Scientific Romances of
   H. G. Wells* (1933) DLB-178
Wells, Helena 1758?-1824 . . . . DLB-200
Wells, Rebecca 1952- DLB-292
Wells, Robert 1947- DLB-40
Wells-Barnett, Ida B. 1862-1931 . . . . . DLB-23, 221
Welsh, Irvine 1958- DLB-271
Welty, Eudora 1909-2001 . . . . . . DLB-2, 102, 143;
                        Y-87, 01; DS-12; CDALB-1
   Eudora Welty: Eye of the Storyteller Y-87
   Eudora Welty Newsletter Y-99
   Eudora Welty's Funeral Y-01
   Eudora Welty's Ninetieth Birthday Y-99
   Eudora Welty Remembered in
   Two Exhibits Y-02
Wendell, Barrett 1855-1921 . . . . DLB-71
Wentworth, Patricia 1878-1961 . . . . DLB-77
Wentworth, William Charles
   1790-1872 . . . . DLB-230
Wenzel, Jean-Paul 1947- DLB-321
Werder, Diederich von dem 1584-1657 . . DLB-164
Werfel, Franz 1890-1945 . . . . DLB-81, 124
Werner, Zacharias 1768-1823 . . . . DLB-94
The Werner Company DLB-49
Wersba, Barbara 1932- DLB-52
Wescott, Glenway
   1901-1987 . . . . DLB-4, 9, 102; DS-15
Wesker, Arnold
   1932- DLB-13, 310, 319; CDBLB-8
Wesley, Charles 1707-1788 . . . . DLB-95
Wesley, John 1703-1791 . . . . DLB-104
Wesley, Mary 1912-2002 . . . . DLB-231
Wesley, Richard 1945- DLB-38
Wessel, Johan Herman 1742-1785 . . . . . . DLB-300
A. Wessels and Company DLB-46
Wessobrunner Gebet circa 787-815 . . . . DLB-148
West, Anthony 1914-1988 . . . . DLB-15
   Tribute to Liam O'Flaherty Y-84
West, Cheryl L. 1957- DLB-266

West, Cornel 1953- DLB-246
West, Dorothy 1907-1998 . . . . DLB-76
West, Jessamyn 1902-1984 . . . . DLB-6; Y-84
West, Mae 1892-1980 . . . . DLB-44
West, Michael Lee 1953- DLB-292
West, Michelle Sagara 1963- DLB-251
West, Morris 1916-1999 . . . . DLB-289
West, Nathanael
   1903-1940 . . . . DLB-4, 9, 28; CDALB-5
West, Paul 1930- DLB-14
West, Rebecca 1892-1983 . . . . DLB-36; Y-83
West, Richard 1941- DLB-185
West and Johnson DLB-49
Westcott, Edward Noyes 1846-1898 . . . . . DLB-202
The Western Literature Association Y-99
The Western Messenger
   1835-1841 . . . . DLB-1; DLB-223
Western Publishing Company DLB-46
Western Writers of America Y-99
The Westminster Review 1824-1914 . . . . DLB-110
Weston, Arthur (see Webling, Peggy)
Weston, Elizabeth Jane circa 1582-1612 . . DLB-172
Wetherald, Agnes Ethelwyn 1857-1940 . . . DLB-99
Wetherell, Elizabeth (see Warner, Susan)
Wetherell, W. D. 1948- DLB-234
Wetzel, Friedrich Gottlob 1779-1819 . . . . . DLB-90
Weyman, Stanley J. 1855-1928 . . . . . DLB-141, 156
Wezel, Johann Karl 1747-1819 . . . . DLB-94
Whalen, Philip 1923-2002 . . . . DLB-16
Whalley, George 1915-1983 . . . . DLB-88
Wharton, Edith 1862-1937 . . . . DLB-4, 9, 12,
                     78, 189; DS-13; CDALB-3
Wharton, William 1925- Y-80
Whately, Mary Louisa 1824-1889 . . . . . . DLB-166
Whately, Richard 1787-1863 . . . . DLB-190
   Elements of Rhetoric (1828;
   revised, 1846) [excerpt] DLB-57
Wheatley, Dennis 1897-1977 . . . . DLB-77, 255
Wheatley, Phillis
   circa 1754-1784 . . . . . . DLB-31, 50; CDALB-2
Wheeler, Anna Doyle 1785-1848? DLB-158
Wheeler, Charles Stearns 1816-1843 . . DLB-1, 223
Wheeler, Monroe 1900-1988 . . . . DLB-4
Wheelock, John Hall 1886-1978 . . . . DLB-45
   From John Hall Wheelock's
   Oral Memoir Y-01
Wheelwright, J. B. 1897-1940 . . . . DLB-45
Wheelwright, John circa 1592-1679 . . . . . . DLB-24
Whetstone, George 1550-1587 . . . . DLB-136
Whetstone, Colonel Pete (see Noland, C. F. M.)
Whewell, William 1794-1866 . . . . DLB-262
Whichcote, Benjamin 1609?-1683 . . . . . . DLB-252

Whicher, Stephen E. 1915-1961 . . . . DLB-111
Whipple, Edwin Percy 1819-1886 . . . . . DLB-1, 64
Whitaker, Alexander 1585-1617 . . . . DLB-24
Whitaker, Daniel K. 1801-1881 . . . . DLB-73
Whitcher, Frances Miriam
   1812-1852 . . . . DLB-11, 202
White, Andrew 1579-1656 . . . . DLB-24
White, Andrew Dickson 1832-1918 . . . . . . DLB-47
White, E. B. 1899-1985 . . . DLB-11, 22; CDALB-7
White, Edgar B. 1947- DLB-38
White, Edmund 1940- DLB-227
White, Ethel Lina 1887-1944 . . . . DLB-77
White, Hayden V. 1928- DLB-246
White, Henry Kirke 1785-1806 . . . . DLB-96
White, Horace 1834-1916 . . . . DLB-23
White, James 1928-1999 . . . . DLB-261
White, Patrick 1912-1990 . . . . DLB-260, 332
White, Phyllis Dorothy James (see James, P. D.)
White, Richard Grant 1821-1885 . . . . DLB-64
White, T. H. 1906-1964 . . . . DLB-160, 255
White, Walter 1893-1955 . . . . DLB-51
Wilcox, James 1949- DLB-292
William White and Company DLB-49
White, William Allen 1868-1944 . . . . . . DLB-9, 25
White, William Anthony Parker
   (see Boucher, Anthony)
White, William Hale (see Rutherford, Mark)
Whitchurch, Victor L. 1868-1933 . . . . DLB-70
Whitehead, Alfred North
   1861-1947 . . . . DLB-100, 262
Whitehead, E. A. (Ted Whitehead)
   1933- DLB-310
Whitehead, James 1936- Y-81
Whitehead, William 1715-1785 . . . . . . DLB-84, 109
Whitfield, James Monroe 1822-1871 . . . . . DLB-50
Whitfield, Raoul 1898-1945 . . . . DLB-226
Whitgift, John circa 1533-1604 . . . . DLB-132
Whiting, John 1917-1963 . . . . DLB-13
Whiting, Samuel 1597-1679 . . . . DLB-24
Whitlock, Brand 1869-1934 . . . . DLB-12
Whitman, Albery Allson 1851-1901 . . . . . . DLB-50
Whitman, Alden 1913-1990 . . . . Y-91
Whitman, Sarah Helen (Power)
   1803-1878 . . . . DLB-1, 243
Whitman, Walt
   1819-1892 . . . DLB-3, 64, 224, 250; CDALB-2
Albert Whitman and Company DLB-46
Whitman Publishing Company DLB-46
Whitney, Geoffrey
   1548 or 1552?-1601 . . . . DLB-136
Whitney, Isabella fl. 1566-1573 . . . . DLB-136
Whitney, John Hay 1904-1982 . . . . DLB-127
Whittemore, Reed 1919-1995 . . . . DLB-5

Whittier, John Greenleaf 1807-1892 ....DLB-1, 243; CDALB-2
Whittlesey House DLB-46
Whyte, John 1941-1992................DLB-334
Wickham, Anna (Edith Alice Mary Harper) 1884-1947 ....DLB-240
Wickram, Georg circa 1505-circa 1561 ...DLB-179
Wicomb, Zoë 1948- DLB-225
Wideman, John Edgar 1941- DLB-33, 143
Widener, Harry Elkins 1885-1912.......DLB-140
Wiebe, Rudy 1934- DLB-60
Wiechert, Ernst 1887-1950...............DLB-56
Wied, Gustav 1858-1914 ....DLB-300
Wied, Martina 1882-1957 ....DLB-85
Wiehe, Evelyn May Clowes (see Mordaunt, Elinor)
Wieland, Christoph Martin 1733-1813 ....DLB-97
Wienbarg, Ludolf 1802-1872............DLB-133
Wieners, John 1934- DLB-16
Wier, Ester 1910-2000 ....DLB-52
Wiesel, Elie 1928- DLB-83, 299; Y-86, 87; CDALB-7
  Nobel Lecture 1986: Hope, Despair and Memory Y-86
Wiggin, Kate Douglas 1856-1923 ....DLB-42
Wiggins, Marianne 1947- DLB-335
Wigglesworth, Michael 1631-1705........DLB-24
Wilberforce, William 1759-1833 ....DLB-158
Wilbrandt, Adolf 1837-1911.............DLB-129
Wilbur, Richard 1921- ...DLB-5, 169; CDALB-7
  Tribute to Robert Penn Warren Y-89
Wilcox, James 1949- DLB-292
Wild, Peter 1940- DLB-5
Wilde, Lady Jane Francesca Elgee 1821?-1896 ....DLB-199
Wilde, Oscar 1854-1900 . DLB-10, 19, 34, 57, 141, 156, 190; CDBLB-5
  "The Critic as Artist" (1891).........DLB-57
  "The Decay of Lying" (1889) DLB-18
  "The English Renaissance of Art" (1908) DLB-35
  "L'Envoi" (1882) DLB-35
  Oscar Wilde Conference at Hofstra University....................Y-00
Wilde, Richard Henry 1789-1847 ....DLB-3, 59
W. A. Wilde Company DLB-49
Wilder, Billy 1906-2002................DLB-26
Wilder, Laura Ingalls 1867-1957 ....DLB-22, 256
Wilder, Thornton 1897-1975........DLB-4, 7, 9, 228; CDALB-7
  Thornton Wilder Centenary at Yale Y-97
Wildgans, Anton 1881-1932 ....DLB-118
Wilding, Michael 1942- DLB-325
Wiley, Bell Irvin 1906-1980 ....DLB-17
John Wiley and Sons DLB-49
Wilhelm, Kate 1928- DLB-8
Wilkes, Charles 1798-1877.............DLB-183

Wilkes, George 1817-1885 ....DLB-79
Wilkins, John 1614-1672 ....DLB-236
Wilkinson, Anne 1910-1961 ....DLB-88
Wilkinson, Christopher 1941- DLB-310
Wilkinson, Eliza Yonge 1757-circa 1813 ...DLB-200
Wilkinson, Sylvia 1940- Y-86
Wilkinson, William Cleaver 1833-1920....DLB-71
Willard, Barbara 1909-1994............DLB-161
Willard, Emma 1787-1870 ....DLB-239
Willard, Frances E. 1839-1898.........DLB-221
Willard, Nancy 1936- DLB-5, 52
Willard, Samuel 1640-1707 ....DLB-24
L. Willard [publishing house].............DLB-49
Willeford, Charles 1919-1988 ....DLB-226
William of Auvergne 1190-1249 ....DLB-115
William of Conches circa 1090-circa 1154................DLB-115
William of Ockham circa 1285-1347 .....DLB-115
William of Sherwood 1200/1205-1266/1271 ....DLB-115
The William Charvat American Fiction Collection at the Ohio State University Libraries Y-92
Williams, Ben Ames 1889-1953.........DLB-102
Williams, C. K. 1936- DLB-5
Williams, Chancellor 1905-1992 ....DLB-76
Williams, Charles 1886-1945...DLB-100, 153, 255
Williams, Denis 1923-1998 ....DLB-117
Williams, Emlyn 1905-1987..........DLB-10, 77
Williams, Garth 1912-1996 ....DLB-22
Williams, George Washington 1849-1891..DLB-47
Williams, Heathcote 1941- DLB-13
Williams, Helen Maria 1761-1827 .....DLB-158
Williams, Hugo 1942- DLB-40
Williams, Isaac 1802-1865 ....DLB-32
Williams, Joan 1928- DLB-6
Williams, Joe 1889-1972...............DLB-241
Williams, John A. 1925- DLB-2, 33
Williams, John E. 1922-1994 ....DLB-6
Williams, Jonathan 1929- DLB-5
Williams, Joy 1944- DLB-335
Williams, Miller 1930- DLB-105
Williams, Nigel 1948- DLB-231
Williams, Raymond 1921-1988 ..DLB-14, 231, 242
Williams, Roger circa 1603-1683.........DLB-24
Williams, Rowland 1817-1870 ....DLB-184
Williams, Samm-Art 1946- DLB-38
Williams, Sherley Anne 1944-1999 ....DLB-41
Williams, T. Harry 1909-1979 ....DLB-17
Williams, Tennessee 1911-1983 .....DLB-7; Y-83; DS-4; CDALB-1
Williams, Terry Tempest 1955- ...DLB-206, 275
Williams, Ursula Moray 1911- DLB-160
Williams, Valentine 1883-1946 ....DLB-77

Williams, William Appleman 1921-1990...DLB-17
Williams, William Carlos 1883-1963......DLB-4, 16, 54, 86; CDALB-4
  The William Carlos Williams Society......Y-99
Williams, Wirt 1921-1986...............DLB-6
A. Williams and Company DLB-49
Williams Brothers DLB-49
Williamson, David 1942- DLB-289
Williamson, Henry 1895-1977..........DLB-191
  The Henry Williamson Society..........Y-98
Williamson, Jack 1908- DLB-8
Willingham, Calder Baynard, Jr. 1922-1995 ....DLB-2, 44
Williram of Ebersberg circa 1020-1085 ...DLB-148
Willis, Browne 1682-1760 ....DLB-336
Willis, John circa 1572-1625.............DLB-281
Willis, Nathaniel Parker 1806-1867 ....DLB-3, 59, 73, 74, 183, 250; DS-13
Willis, Ted 1918-1992 ....DLB-310
Willkomm, Ernst 1810-1886 ....DLB-133
Wills, Garry 1934- DLB-246
  Tribute to Kenneth Dale McCormick Y-97
Willson, Meredith 1902-1984 ....DLB-265
Willumsen, Dorrit 1940- DLB-214
Wilmer, Clive 1945- DLB-40
Wilson, A. N. 1950- DLB-14, 155, 194
Wilson, Angus 1913-1991 ......DLB-15, 139, 155
Wilson, Arthur 1595-1652..............DLB-58
Wilson, August 1945-2005 ....DLB-228
Wilson, Augusta Jane Evans 1835-1909 ...DLB-42
Wilson, Colin 1931- DLB-14, 194
  Tribute to J. B. Priestly Y-84
Wilson, Edmund 1895-1972 ....DLB-63
Wilson, Ethel 1888-1980 ....DLB-68
Wilson, F. P. 1889-1963................DLB-201
Wilson, Harriet E. 1827/1828?-1863? DLB-50, 239, 243
Wilson, Harry Leon 1867-1939 ....DLB-9
Wilson, John 1588-1667 ....DLB-24
Wilson, John 1785-1854................DLB-110
Wilson, John Anthony Burgess (see Burgess, Anthony)
Wilson, John Dover 1881-1969 ....DLB-201
Wilson, Lanford 1937- DLB-7
Wilson, Margaret 1882-1973 ....DLB-9
Wilson, Michael 1914-1978 ....DLB-44
Wilson, Mona 1872-1954...............DLB-149
Wilson, Robert Charles 1953- DLB-251
Wilson, Robert McLiam 1964- DLB-267
Wilson, Robley 1930- DLB-218
Wilson, Romer 1891-1930.............DLB-191
Wilson, Thomas 1524-1581 ....DLB-132, 236
Wilson, Woodrow 1856-1924 ....DLB-47

Cumulative Index

Effingham Wilson [publishing house] DLB-154

Wimpfeling, Jakob 1450-1528 .... DLB-179

Wimsatt, William K., Jr. 1907-1975 .... DLB-63

Winchell, Walter 1897-1972 .... DLB-29

J. Winchester [publishing house] DLB-49

Winckelmann, Johann Joachim
1717-1768 .... DLB-97

Winckler, Paul 1630-1686 .... DLB-164

Wind, Herbert Warren 1916-2005 .... DLB-171

John Windet [publishing house] DLB-170

Windham, Donald 1920- DLB-6

Windsor, Gerard 1944- DLB-325

Wing, Donald Goddard 1904-1972 ..... DLB-187

Wing, John M. 1844-1917 .... DLB-187

Allan Wingate [publishing house] DLB-112

Winnemucca, Sarah 1844-1921 .... DLB-175

Winnifrith, Tom 1938- DLB-155

Winsloe, Christa 1888-1944 .... DLB-124

Winslow, Anna Green 1759-1780 .... DLB-200

Winsor, Justin 1831-1897 .... DLB-47

John C. Winston Company DLB-49

Winters, Yvor 1900-1968 .... DLB-48

Winterson, Jeanette 1959- DLB-207, 261

Winther, Christian 1796-1876 .... DLB-300

Winthrop, John 1588-1649 .... DLB-24, 30

Winthrop, John, Jr. 1606-1676 .... DLB-24

Winthrop, Margaret Tyndal
1591-1647 .... DLB-200

Winthrop, Theodore 1828-1861 .... DLB-202

Winton, Tim 1960- DLB-325

Wirt, William 1772-1834 .... DLB-37

Wise, Francis 1695-1767 .... DLB-336

Wise, John 1652-1725 .... DLB-24

Wise, Thomas James 1859-1937 .... DLB-184

Wiseman, Adele 1928-1992 .... DLB-88

Wishart and Company DLB-112

Wisner, George 1812-1849 .... DLB-43

Wister, Owen 1860-1938 .... DLB-9, 78, 186

Wister, Sarah 1761-1804 .... DLB-200

Wither, George 1588-1667 .... DLB-121

Witherspoon, John 1723-1794 .... DLB-31

The Works of the Rev. John Witherspoon
(1800-1801) [excerpts] DLB-31

Withrow, William Henry 1839-1908 ..... DLB-99

Witkacy (see Witkiewicz, Stanisław Ignacy)

Witkiewicz, Stanisław Ignacy
1885-1939 .... DLB-215; CDWLB-4

Wittenwiler, Heinrich before 1387-
circa 1414? DLB-179

Wittgenstein, Ludwig 1889-1951 .... DLB-262

Wittig, Monique 1935- DLB-83

Witting, Amy (Joan Austral Levick, née Fraser)
1918-2001 .... DLB-325

Wodehouse, P. G.
1881-1975 .... DLB-34, 162; CDBLB-6

Worldwide Wodehouse Societies Y-98

Wodrow, Robert 1679-1734 .... DLB-336

Wohmann, Gabriele 1932- DLB-75

Woiwode, Larry 1941- DLB-6

Tribute to John Gardner Y-82

Wolcot, John 1738-1819 .... DLB-109

Wolcott, Roger 1679-1767 .... DLB-24

Wolf, Christa 1929- DLB-75; CDWLB-2

Wolf, Friedrich 1888-1953 .... DLB-124

Wolfe, Gene 1931- DLB-8

Wolfe, Thomas 1900-1938 ....
DLB-9, 102, 229; Y-85; DS-2, DS-16; CDALB-5

"All the Faults of Youth and Inexperience":
A Reader's Report on
Thomas Wolfe's *O Lost* Y-01

Emendations for *Look Homeward, Angel* Y-00

Eugene Gant's Projected Works Y-01

Fire at the Old Kentucky Home
[Thomas Wolfe Memorial] Y-98

Thomas Wolfe Centennial
Celebration in Asheville Y-00

The Thomas Wolfe Collection at
the University of North Carolina
at Chapel Hill Y-97

The Thomas Wolfe Society Y-97, 99

Wolfe, Tom 1931- DLB-152, 185

John Wolfe [publishing house] DLB-170

Reyner (Reginald) Wolfe
[publishing house] DLB-170

Wolfenstein, Martha 1869-1906 .... DLB-221

Wolff, David (see Maddow, Ben)

Wolff, Egon 1926- DLB-305

Wolff, Helen 1906-1994 .... Y-94

Wolff, Tobias 1945- DLB-130

Tribute to Michael M. Rea Y-97

Tribute to Raymond Carver Y-88

Wolfram von Eschenbach
circa 1170-after 1220 ... DLB-138; CDWLB-2

Wolfram von Eschenbach's *Parzival*:
Prologue and Book 3 .... DLB-138

Wolker, Jiří 1900-1924 .... DLB-215

Wollstonecraft, Mary 1759-1797
.... DLB-39, 104, 158, 252; CDBLB-3

Women

Women's Work, Women's Sphere:
Selected Comments from Women
Writers DLB-200

Women Writers in Sixteenth-Century
Spain DLB-318

Wondratschek, Wolf 1943- DLB-75

Wong, Elizabeth 1958- DLB-266

Wong, Nellie 1934- DLB-312

Wong, Shawn 1949- DLB-312

Wongar, B. (Sreten Bozic) 1932- DLB-325

Wood, Anthony à 1632-1695 .... DLB-213

Wood, Benjamin 1820-1900 .... DLB-23

Wood, Charles 1932-1980 .... DLB-13

The Charles Wood Affair:
A Playwright Revived Y-83

Wood, Mrs. Henry 1814-1887 .... DLB-18

Wood, Joanna E. 1867-1927 .... DLB-92

Wood, Sally Sayward Barrell Keating
1759-1855 .... DLB-200

Wood, William fl. seventeenth century DLB-24

Samuel Wood [publishing house] DLB-49

Woodberry, George Edward
1855-1930 .... DLB-71, 103

Woodbridge, Benjamin 1622-1684 .... DLB-24

Woodbridge, Frederick J. E. 1867-1940 ... DLB-270

Woodcock, George 1912-1995 .... DLB-88

Woodhull, Victoria C. 1838-1927 .... DLB-79

Woodmason, Charles circa 1720-? DLB-31

Woodress, James Leslie, Jr. 1916- DLB-111

Woods, Margaret L. 1855-1945 .... DLB-240

Woodson, Carter G. 1875-1950 .... DLB-17

Woodward, C. Vann 1908-1999 .... DLB-17

Woodward, Stanley 1895-1965 .... DLB-171

Woodworth, Samuel 1785-1842 .... DLB-250

Wooler, Thomas 1785 or 1786-1853 ..... DLB-158

Woolf, David (see Maddow, Ben)

Woolf, Douglas 1922-1992 .... DLB-244

Woolf, Leonard 1880-1969 .... DLB-100; DS-10

Woolf, Virginia 1882-1941
.... DLB-36, 100, 162; DS-10; CDBLB-6

"The New Biography," *New York Herald
Tribune*, 30 October 1927 .... DLB-149

Woollcott, Alexander 1887-1943 .... DLB-29

Woolman, John 1720-1772 .... DLB-31

Woolner, Thomas 1825-1892 .... DLB-35

Woolrich, Cornell 1903-1968 .... DLB-226

Woolsey, Sarah Chauncy 1835-1905 ..... DLB-42

Woolson, Constance Fenimore
1840-1894 .... DLB-12, 74, 189, 221

Worcester, Joseph Emerson
1784-1865 .... DLB-1, 235

Wynkyn de Worde [publishing house] DLB-170

Wordsworth, Christopher 1807-1885.....DLB-166

Wordsworth, Dorothy 1771-1855........DLB-107

Wordsworth, Elizabeth 1840-1932.......DLB-98

Wordsworth, William
   1770-1850..........DLB-93, 107; CDBLB-3

Workman, Fanny Bullock
   1859-1925.....................DLB-189

World Literature Today: A Journal for the
   New Millennium....................Y-01

World Publishing Company............DLB-46

World War I (1914-1918)................DS-18

   The Great War Exhibit and Symposium
      at the University of South Carolina...Y-97

   The Liddle Collection and First World
      War Research....................Y-97

   Other British Poets Who Fell
      in the Great War................DLB-216

   The Seventy-Fifth Anniversary of
      the Armistice: The Wilfred Owen
      Centenary and the Great War Exhibit
      at the University of Virginia.........Y-93

World War II (1939–1945)

   Literary Effects of World War II......DLB-15

   World War II Writers Symposium
      at the University of South Carolina,
      12–14 April 1995.................Y-95

   WW2 HMSO Paperbacks Society.......Y-98

R. Worthington and Company..........DLB-49

Wotton, Sir Henry 1568-1639..........DLB-121

Wouk, Herman 1915-........Y-82; CDALB-7

   Tribute to James Dickey...............Y-97

Wreford, James 1915-1990..............DLB-88

Wren, Sir Christopher 1632-1723.......DLB-213

Wren, Percival Christopher 1885-1941...DLB-153

Wrenn, John Henry 1841-1911.........DLB-140

Wright, C. D. 1949-.................DLB-120

Wright, Charles 1935-........DLB-165; Y-82

Wright, Charles Stevenson 1932-.......DLB-33

Wright, Chauncey 1830-1875..........DLB-270

Wright, Frances 1795-1852.............DLB-73

Wright, Harold Bell 1872-1944..........DLB-9

Wright, James 1927-1980
   ....DLB-5, 169; CDALB-7

Wright, Jay 1935-....................DLB-41

Wright, Judith 1915-2000.............DLB-260

Wright, Louis B. 1899-1984............DLB-17

Wright, Richard 1908-1960
   ....DLB-76, 102; DS-2; CDALB-5

Wright, Richard B. 1937-.............DLB-53

Wright, S. Fowler 1874-1965..........DLB-255

Wright, Sarah Elizabeth 1928-.........DLB-33

Wright, T. H. "Style" (1877) [excerpt].....DLB-57

Wright, Willard Huntington (S. S. Van Dine)
   1887-1939................DLB-306; DS-16

Wrightson, Patricia 1921-............DLB-289

Wrigley, Robert 1951-...............DLB-256

Writers' Forum.........................Y-85

Writing

   A Writing Life......................Y-02

   On Learning to Write...............Y-88

   The Profession of Authorship:
      Scribblers for Bread................Y-89

   A Writer Talking: A Collage............Y-00

Wroth, Lawrence C. 1884-1970.........DLB-187

Wroth, Lady Mary 1587-1653..........DLB-121

Wu Jianren (Wo Foshanren)
   1866-1910......................DLB-328

Wu Zuxiang 1908-1994...............DLB-328

Wumingshi (Bu Baonan) 1917-2002.....DLB-328

Wurlitzer, Rudolph 1937-............DLB-173

Wyatt, Sir Thomas circa 1503-1542......DLB-132

Wycherley, William
   1641-1715............DLB-80; CDBLB-2

Wyclif, John circa 1335-1384..........DLB-146

Wyeth, N. C. 1882-1945........DLB-188; DS-16

Wyle, Niklas von circa 1415-1479.......DLB-179

Wylie, Elinor 1885-1928.............DLB-9, 45

Wylie, Philip 1902-1971................DLB-9

Wyllie, John Cook 1908-1968..........DLB-140

Wyman, Lillie Buffum Chace
   1847-1929......................DLB-202

Wymark, Olwen 1934-...............DLB-233

Wynd, Oswald Morris (see Black, Gavin)

Wyndham, John (John Wyndham Parkes
   Lucas Beynon Harris) 1903-1969....DLB-255

Wynne-Tyson, Esmé 1898-1972........DLB-191

X

Xenophon circa 430 B.C.-circa 356 B.C......DLB-176

Xiang Kairan (Pingjiang Buxiaoshengj
   Buxiaosheng) 1890-1957...........DLB-328

Xiao Hong 1911-1942................DLB-328

Xu Dishan (Luo Huasheng)
   1893-1941......................DLB-328

Xu Zhenya 1889-1937................DLB-328

Y

Yahp, Beth 1964-....................DLB-325

Yamamoto, Hisaye 1921-.............DLB-312

Yamanaka, Lois-Ann 1961-...........DLB-312

Yamashita, Karen Tei 1951-...........DLB-312

Yamauchi, Wakako 1924-............DLB-312

Yang Kui 1905-1985.................DLB-328

Yasuoka Shōtarō 1920-..............DLB-182

Yates, Dornford 1885-1960.........DLB-77, 153

Yates, J. Michael 1938-...............DLB-60

Yates, Richard 1926-1992...DLB-2, 234; Y-81, 92

Yau, John 1950-...............DLB-234, 312

Yavorov, Peyo 1878-1914.............DLB-147

Ye Shaojun (Ye Shengtao) 1894-1988.....DLB-328

Yearsley, Ann 1753-1806..............DLB-109

Yeats, William Butler 1865-1939
   ....DLB-10, 19, 98, 156, 332; CDBLB-5

Yehoash (Yehoyesh; Solomon Bloomgarden
   [Shloyme Blumgarten]) 1872-1927....DLB-333

   The W. B. Yeats Society of N.Y..........Y-99

Yellen, Jack 1892-1991................DLB-265

Yep, Laurence 1948-.............DLB-52, 312

Yerby, Frank 1916-1991...............DLB-76

Yezierska, Anzia 1880-1970.........DLB-28, 221

Yolen, Jane 1939-....................DLB-52

Yonge, Charlotte Mary 1823-1901....DLB-18, 163

   The Charlotte M. Yonge Fellowship......Y-98

The York Cycle circa 1376-circa 1569....DLB-146

A Yorkshire Tragedy...................DLB-58

Thomas Yoseloff [publishing house]......DLB-46

Youd, Sam (see Christopher, John)

Young, A. S. "Doc" 1919-1996.........DLB-241

Young, Al 1939-.....................DLB-33

Young, Arthur 1741-1820.............DLB-158

Young, Dick 1917 or 1918-1987.........DLB-171

Young, Edward 1683-1765.............DLB-95

Young, Frank A. "Fay" 1884-1957.......DLB-241

Young, Francis Brett 1884-1954.........DLB-191

Young, Gavin 1928-.................DLB-204

Young, Stark 1881-1963.......DLB-9, 102; DS-16

Young, Waldeman 1880-1938..........DLB-26

William Young [publishing house]........DLB-49

Young Bear, Ray A. 1950-............DLB-175

Yourcenar, Marguerite 1903-1987...DLB-72; Y-88

Yovkov, Yordan 1880-1937....DLB-147; CDWLB-4

Yu Dafu 1896-1945..................DLB-328

Yushkevich, Semen 1868-1927..........DLB-317

Yver, Jacques 1520?-1570?.............DLB-327

Z

Zachariä, Friedrich Wilhelm 1726-1777....DLB-97

Zagajewski, Adam 1945-.............DLB-232

409

Cumulative Index

Zagoskin, Mikhail Nikolaevich 1789-1852................DLB-198

Zaitsev, Boris 1881-1972.............DLB-317

Zajc, Dane 1929- DLB-181

Zālīte, Māra 1952- DLB-232

Zalygin, Sergei Pavlovich 1913-2000....DLB-302

Zamiatin, Evgenii Ivanovich 1884-1937..DLB-272

Zamora, Bernice 1938- DLB-82

Zamudio, Adela (Soledad) 1854-1928...DLB-283

Zand, Herbert 1923-1970.............DLB-85

Zangwill, Israel 1864-1926......DLB-10, 135, 197

Zanzotto, Andrea 1921- DLB-128

Zapata Olivella, Manuel 1920-........DLB-113

Zapoev, Timur Iur'evich (see Kibirov, Timur Iur'evich)

Zasodimsky, Pavel Vladimirovich 1843-1912....................DLB-238

Zebra Books......................DLB-46

Zebrowski, George 1945- DLB-8

Zech, Paul 1881-1946................DLB-56

Zeidner, Lisa 1955- DLB-120

Zeidonis, Imants 1933- DLB-232

Zeimi (Kanze Motokiyo) 1363-1443.....DLB-203

Zelazny, Roger 1937-1995...............DLB-8

Zeng Pu 1872-1935...................DLB-328

Zenger, John Peter 1697-1746.......DLB-24, 43

Zepheria.........................DLB-172

Zernova, Ruf' 1919-2004............DLB-317

Zesen, Philipp von 1619-1689..........DLB-164

Zhadovskaia, Iuliia Valerianovna 1824-1883....................DLB-277

Zhang Ailing (Eileen Chang) 1920-1995....................DLB-328

Zhang Henshui 1895-1967............DLB-328

Zhang Tianyi 1906-1985 ....DLB-328

Zhao Shuli 1906-1970................DLB-328

Zhukova, Mar'ia Semenovna 1805-1855....................DLB-277

Zhukovsky, Vasilii Andreevich 1783-1852....................DLB-205

Zhvanetsky, Mikhail Mikhailovich 1934- DLB-285

G. B. Zieber and Company DLB-49

Ziedonis, Imants 1933- CDWLB-4

Zieroth, Dale 1946- DLB-60

Zigler und Kliphausen, Heinrich Anshelm von 1663-1697 ....DLB-168

Zil'ber, Veniamin Aleksandrovich (see Kaverin, Veniamin Aleksandrovich)

Zimmer, Paul 1934- DLB-5

Zinberg, Len (see Lacy, Ed)

Zincgref, Julius Wilhelm 1591-1635.....DLB-164

Zindel, Paul 1936- DLB-7, 52; CDALB-7

Zinnes, Harriet 1919- DLB-193

Zinov'ev, Aleksandr Aleksandrovich 1922- DLB-302

Zinov'eva-Annibal, Lidiia Dmitrievna 1865 or 1866-1907.............DLB-295

Zinzendorf, Nikolaus Ludwig von 1700-1760....................DLB-168

Zitkala-Ša 1876-1938................DLB-175

Zīverts, Mārtiņš 1903-1990...........DLB-220

Zlatovratsky, Nikolai Nikolaevich 1845-1911....................DLB-238

Zola, Emile 1840-1902...............DLB-123

Zolla, Elémire 1926- DLB-196

Zolotow, Charlotte 1915- DLB-52

Zoshchenko, Mikhail Mikhailovich 1895-1958....................DLB-272

Zschokke, Heinrich 1771-1848.........DLB-94

Zubly, John Joachim 1724-1781........DLB-31

Zu-Bolton, Ahmos, II 1936- DLB-41

Zuckmayer, Carl 1896-1977........DLB-56, 124

Zukofsky, Louis 1904-1978..........DLB-5, 165

Zupan, Vitomil 1914-1987............DLB-181

Župančič, Oton 1878-1949...DLB-147; CDWLB-4

zur Mühlen, Hermynia 1883-1951.......DLB-56

Zweig, Arnold 1887-1968.............DLB-66

Zweig, Stefan 1881-1942..........DLB-81, 118

Zwicky, Fay 1933- DLB-325

Zwicky, Jan 1955- DLB-334

Zwinger, Ann 1925- DLB-275

Zwingli, Huldrych 1484-1531..........DLB-179

Ø

Øverland, Arnulf 1889-1968 ....DLB-297

PQ
4082
.S484

2008